September 5-9, 2011
Szeged, Hungary

AF764905

Association for
Computing Machinery

Advancing Computing as a Science & Profession

SIGSOFT/FSE'11

Proceedings of the 19th ACM SIGSOFT Symposium on
Foundations of Software Engineering

Sponsored by:

SIGSOFT

Association for
Computing Machinery

Advancing Computing as a Science & Profession

The Association for Computing Machinery
2 Penn Plaza, Suite 701
New York, New York 10121-0701

Copyright © 2011 by the Association for Computing Machinery, Inc. (ACM). Permission to make digital or hard copies of portions of this work for personal or classroom use is granted without fee provided that copies are not made or distributed for profit or commercial advantage and that copies bear this notice and the full citation on the first page. Copyright for components of this work owned by others than ACM must be honored. Abstracting with credit is permitted. To copy otherwise, to republish, to post on servers or to redistribute to lists, requires prior specific permission and/or a fee. Request permission to republish from: Publications Dept., ACM, Inc. Fax +1 (212) 869-0481 or <permissions@acm.org>.

For other copying of articles that carry a code at the bottom of the first or last page, copying is permitted provided that the per-copy fee indicated in the code is paid through the Copyright Clearance Center, 222 Rosewood Drive, Danvers, MA 01923 (USA).

Notice to Past Authors of ACM-Published Articles
ACM intends to create a complete electronic archive of all articles and/or other material previously published by ACM. If you have written a work that has been previously published by ACM in any journal or conference proceedings prior to 1978, or any SIG Newsletter at any time, and you do NOT want this work to appear in the ACM Digital Library, please inform permissions@acm.org, stating the title of the work, the author(s), and where and when published.

ISBN: 978-1-4503-0443-6

Additional copies may be ordered prepaid from:

ACM Order Department
PO Box 30777
New York, NY 10087-0777, USA

Phone: 1-800-342-6626 (USA and Canada)
+1-212-626-0500 (Global)
Fax: +1-212-944-1318
E-mail: acmhelp@acm.org
Hours of Operation: 8:30 am – 4:30 pm ET

ACM Order Number 594114

Printed in the USA

Foreword

On behalf of the entire Organizing Committee it is our great pleasure to welcome you to the *8th joint meeting of the European Software Engineering Conference and the ACM SIGSOFT Symposium on the Foundations of Software Engineering,* an internationally renowned forum for researchers, practitioners, and educators to present and discuss the most recent innovations, trends, experiences, and challenges in the field of software engineering.

Every second year FSE is jointly organized with ESEC on the Old Continent of Europe. This year's host city is Szeged in the South of Hungary. Szeged, which has always been referred to as the city of sunshine, is simply beautiful and has an atmosphere that no other city has in Hungary. Its sights, like the Votive church, the Synagogue, the Hero's Arch, and the University of Szeged all give a distinct character to the town. From September until late June, the local cafés, restaurants, shops, and streets are all noisy from the lively bustle of university students and the whole town is turned into a nest of youthful spirit. Let us invite you to be part of this unique atmosphere and enjoy your stay during the ESEC/FSE 2011 Conference.

This year's program promises to be very exciting. The research track call for papers attracted 203 papers from all continents. After extensive virtual and physical discussions, the Program Committee accepted 34 papers covering a large veriety of software engineering topics – ranging from mining software archives and empirical studies over program analysis and testing to collaboration, models, and requirements. Three papers received an ACM SIGSOFT Distinguished Paper Award; they are marked in the table of contents.

With this ESEC/FSE, we especially wanted to encourage authors to provide *artifacts* – tools or data sets that would help others to build on earlier work. A third of the authors of accepted papers submitted artifacts, judged and assessed by an Artifact Evaluation Board. Authors were enthusiastic about participating and eager to improve their packages, further motivated by a 1,000 US$ Best Artifact Award from Microsoft Research. Overall, seven artifacts were found to meet or exceed expectations, and thus are especially recommended by the Board as a base for future research; you will find them marked in the table of contents.

The whole-day *industrial track* is another newly added element of the ESEC/FSE program with the purpose to facilitate an open exchange of ideas between academic researchers and practitioners in industry. ESEC/FSE 2011 will also feature *Technical Briefings*, an all-day event for communicating the state of topics related to software engineering. This year's conference also offers a comprehensive student program, including the Doctoral Symposium, the Technical Briefings and the *PhD Working Groups* (PWGs). PWGs are offered for PhD students and other young (pre-doc) researchers with the aim of providing them with the opportunity to meet prominent senior researchers in certain software engineering fields and work with them throughout the conference week.

Organizing such a complex event as ESEC/FSE 2011 has been a team effort. First, we would like to thank the authors for providing the content of the program. We deeply appreciate the hard work of the program committees of several tracks when reviewing papers and providing feedback for authors. We would also like to express my gratitude to the University of Szeged for hosting the conference, our sponsors ACM and SIGSOFT, and our generous corporate supporters: Microsoft Research, Ericsson, DEAK Zrt., IBM Research, and FrontEndART Software. Last but not least, let us thank the organizing committee for their effort and dedicated work in putting together ESEC/FSE 2011.

Tibor Gyimóthy
ESEC/FSE 2011 General Chair
University of Szeged, Hungary

Andreas Zeller
ESEC/FSE 2011 Program Chair
Saarland University, Saarbrücken, Germany

Message from the Doctoral Symposium Chairs

The future strength and vitality of any research community depend crucially on doctoral students; they are literally and unequivocally the future of the discipline. This conference places great importance on creating a supportive and responsive environment for its future lifeblood.

The *ESEC/FSE Doctoral Symposium 2011* continues a trend of interactive meetings held to encourage and nurture the next generation of Software Engineering researchers by providing a specific and dedicated forum for doctorial students. The symposium allows doctoral students to present their plans and to discuss their current work with other doctoral students and with more senior colleagues in the Software Engineering research community.

The Doctoral Symposium called for the submission of four-page abstracts, authored by the PhD student, describing the problem addressed by their research with reference to the state of the art in the field. In response to this call, the 2011 Doctorial Symposium received 12 submissions, of which we were able to select 10 excellent abstracts for inclusion in the symposium.

We would like to express our thanks to the distinguished scientists and scholars who form the 2011 Doctorial Symposium review panel. These are: Myra Cohen, Prem Devanbu, Max Di Penta, Mary Jean Harrold, Phil McMinn and Laurie Williams. The panel will provide students with feedback on their dissertations, as well as guidance on future research directions. Moreover, we would like to thank Laurie and Prem who will enrich the symposium program talking to students about how to write excellent Software Engineering papers and how to perform reliable Software Engineering empirical studies.

This year, ESEC/FSE also features a PhD Working Groups (PWGs) activity in which doctoral students will work in groups to review and document an aspect of Software Engineering. There will also be a related programme of presentations and social activities designed to welcome doctoral students and to allow them to become fully engaged with the international research community in Software Engineering. The PWGs were organized and supported by Árpád Beszédes to whom we extend our sincere thanks, both for managing the PWGs and also for supporting our work in managing the Doctoral Symposium. The organization of the event proceeded smoothly thanks to the support of the ESEC organizing committee. Our work would have been impossible without the support of Tibor Gyimóthy, the general chair and Andreas Zeller, the program chair.

We would also like to thank Wes Weimer, the Graduate Student track chair for the co-located event SSBSE 2011: the 3rd International Symposium on Search Based Software Engineering, who obtained significant funding for the National Science Foundation of the USA and others, which we were able to deploy to support attendance of doctorial students at both ESEC/FSE 2011 and SSBSE 2011.

We hope you enjoy the 2011 Doctoral Symposium!

Antonia Bertolino
ISTI-CNR, Pisa, Italy

Mark Harman
University College London, UK

ESEC/FSE 2011 New Ideas Track

This year, the ESEC/FSE program includes, for the first time, a New Ideas track. The goal of the New Ideas track was to provide researchers with a forum to promote new and original research projects, to seek feedback on novel directions in a research program, and to discover opportunities for new research collaborations. Prospective participants in the New Ideas track were invited to submit a short paper describing a single and well-defined idea at an early stage of investigation.

The call for papers attracted 43 submissions from 20 different countries of Europe, North and South America, Asia, and Australia. Each submission was reviewed by at least three members of the 25-person program committee. The evaluation criteria included the demonstrated or argued novelty and originality of the idea, the clarity of the idea's description, and the relevance of the idea to the themes of ESEC/FSE. The program committee accepted 11 papers. The authors of accepted papers were invited to present a short talk on their idea during a parallel session and a poster during the conference's poster session.

The success of ESEC/FSE's first New Ideas track is due to the efforts of many: authors, reviewers, and conference organizers. In particular we acknowledge the hard and timely work of the members of the program committee:

Andrew Begel *(Microsoft Research, USA)*
Eric Bodden *(Darmstadt University of Technology, Germany)*
Paulo Borba *(Federal University of Pernambuco, Brazil)*
Travis Breaux *(Carnegie Mellon University, USA)*
Cristian Cadar *(Imperial College London, UK)*
Antonio Carzaniga *(University of Lugano, Switzerland)*
Li-Te Cheng *(IBM Watson Research Center, USA)*
S.C. Cheung *(Hong Kong University of Science and Technology, China)*
James Clause *(University of Delaware, USA)*
Irina Coman *(Free University of Bolzano, Italy)*
Ivica Crnkovic *(Mälardalen University, Sweden)*
Krzysztof Czarnecki *(University of Waterloo, Canada)*
Laurence Duchien *(INRIA - University of Lille, France)*
Sebastian Elbaum *(University on Nebraska, Lincoln, USA)*
Paul Gruenbacher *(Johannes Kepler University Linz, Austria)*
John Grundy *(Swinburne University of Technology, Australia)*
Reid Holmes *(University of Waterloo, Canada)*
Paola Inverardi *(University dell'Aquila, Italy)*
Christine Julien *(University of Texas at Austin, USA)*
Natalia Juristo *(Universidad Politécnica de Madrid, Spain)*
Walid Maalej *(Munich University of Technology, Germany)*
Tim Menzies *(West Virginia University, USA)*
Narayan Ramasubbu *(Singapore Management University, Singapore)*
Wilhelm Schäfer *(University of Paderborn, Germany)*
Willem Visser *(Stellenbosch University, South Africa)*

We hope that you enjoy the New Ideas track. Perhaps it contains the seed of your next research idea.

Martin Robillard
Chair, ESEC/FSE New Ideas Track
McGill University, Canada

ESEC/FSE 2011 Tool Demonstrations Track

The ESEC/FSE 2011 Tool Demonstrations Track provides an opportunity for researchers and practitioners to present and discuss the most recent advances, experiences, and challenges in the field of software engineering with the goal of allowing live presentation of new research tools. The research tool demonstrations are intended to highlight underlying scientific contributions. Whereas a regular research paper aims to point out the scientific contribution of a new software engineering approach, a tool demonstration paper provides a good opportunity to show how the scientific approach has been transferred into a working tool.

ESEC/FSE 2011 attracted 30 tool demonstration papers, submitted from 18 different countries of Europe, North America, Asia, and Australia. Each submission was rigorously reviewed by at least three members of the program committee. The evaluation criteria included, among others, the originality, the relevance to the ESEC/FSE audience, the technical soundness, the presentation quality, and the appropriate consideration of relevant literature. The program committee accepted 14 tool demonstration papers. The authors of accepted papers were invited to give a formal presentation and a live demonstration of their tool during dedicated sessions of the conference.

We would like to warmly thank all the authors for their high-quality submissions. We are also grateful to all the program committee members, Bram Adams, Goetz Botterweck, Marco D'Ambros, Serge Demeyer, Danny Dig, Bernd Fischer, Tudor Girba, Abram Hindle, Holger Kienle, Mircea Lungu, Rocco Oliveto, Denys Poshyvanyk, Romain Robbes, Jurgen Vinju and Thomas Zimmermann, and to the additional reviewers Malcom Gethers, Collin Mcmillan, Stas Negara, Cosmin Radoi, and Vadim Zaytsev, for their invaluable contribution and help to produce this exciting tool demonstrations program. Last but not least, we would like to sincerely thank all the members of the ESEC/FSE 2011 organizing committee, with whom it has been great pleasure and privilege to work.

We hope you will all enjoy ESEC/FSE 2011, and in particular its Tool Demonstrations Track!

Michele Lanza
REVEAL @ Faculty of Informatics
University of Lugano, Switzerland

Anthony Cleve
Faculty of Computer Science
University of Namur, Belgium

Message from the ESEC/FSE 2011 Workshops Chairs

ESEC/FSE 2011 workshops, held before the main conference, aimed to provide opportunities for exchanging views, advancing ideas and discussing preliminary results in various areas of software engineering research and applications.

We have received 9 workshop proposals on a broad selection of topics. Each was reviewed by at least three members of the workshop selection committee consisting of Emmanual Letier, Nenad Medvidovic, Luciano Baresi and Cristina Gacek. The selection process was based on the following criteria:

- Relevance, timeliness and expected interest in the workshop topics
- Expected level of participant involvement and discussion
- The organizers' experience and ability to lead a successful workshop.

We also tried to minimize redundancy and maximize synergy with other ESEC/FSE events. The workshop selection process was handled using Easychair.

We selected 6 workshops and encouraged two of them to merge to form one event. In addition, the workshop program included PASTE 2011, which is an established workshop that was chosen to be co-located with ESEC/FSE'11.

Two of the workshops did not receive a sufficient number of high-quality submissions and decided not to run this year. The remaining six workshops are listed below and linked from http://2011.esec-fse.org/workshops:

- IWPSE-EVOL 2011 - 12th International Workshop on Principles on Software Evolution and 7th ERCIM Workshop on Software Evolution
- PASTE 2011 - 10th ACM SIGPLAN-SIGSOFT Workshop on Program Analysis for Software Tools and Engineering
- SSE 2011 - 4th International Workshop on Social Software Engineering
- WoSQ 2011 - International Workshop on Software Quality
- ASAS 2011 - Workshop on Assurances for Self-Adaptive Systems
- WebQUeST 2011 - Web Quality, Security, and Testing

We thank the workshop organizers, the authors of contributed papers, the workshop keynote speakers, our workshop selection committee, and of course the excellent ESEC/FSE'11 organizing team (especially the General Chair Tibor Gyimóthy, the Web master László Vidács, and the Publications Chair Gordon Fraser) for helping us put together an excellent workshop program. We hope you enjoy it!

Marsha Chechik
University of Toronto

Henry Muccini
University of L'Aquila, Italy

ESEC/FSE 2011 PhD Working Groups

ESEC/FSE 2011 features PhD Working Groups (PWG), a special program for PhD students and other young researchers providing them with a unique opportunity to actively participate in the conference and contribute to a richer conference program. PWG is a part of the Student Package together with the main conference, Technical Briefings, and the Doctoral Symposium.

The aim of the working groups is to conduct small surveys on given Software Engineering topics by interviewing conference participants and researching the field. The groups are led by fellow young researchers with PhD degrees knowledgeable in the selected fields, and supervised by senior researchers (mentors), who are top rated experts in the given fields. This way, valuable contacts may be established with other researchers in the area. The working groups will present their findings on the last day of the conference, before the closing session.

Furthermore, the University of Szeged supports talented young researchers, especially from – though not limited to – the surrounding developing countries, who have limited financial resources to participate in such a premier conference. The support grant is offered in the form of a significantly reduced registration fee and by providing help in finding affordable transportation and accommodation.

The PhD Working Groups program has been organized in close cooperation with the organizers of the other tracks offered to students. Specifically, we would like to express our most sincere thanks to the Doctoral Symposium Chairs Antonia Bertolino and Mark Harman, and to the members of the Doctoral Symposium Panel for their most valuable help in making this a successful event.

We would also like to thank the mentors and the group leaders for guiding the group members in their work throughout the conference week. Without their enthusiastic work the PhD Working Groups program would have been impossible.

We hope that you will enjoy the PhD Working Groups program either as a group member or as a conference participant. We sincerely believe that many new relationships will be established among the doctoral students and other researchers.

Árpád Beszédes
PhD Working Groups Chair
University of Szeged, Hungary

Table of Contents

Empirical Studies

Analysis I

Debugging

Collaboration

Testing

Configurations

Analysis II

Defects

Analysis III

Mining

Doctoral Symposium — Development Documentation

New Ideas I

New Ideas II

Workshop Summaries

ESEC/FSE 2011 Conference Organization

General Chair: Tibor Gyimóthy *(University of Szeged, Hungary)*

Program Chair: Andreas Zeller *(Saarland University, Germany)*

Workshop Chairs: Henry Muccini *(University of L'Aquila, Italy)*
Marsha Chechik *(University of Toronto, Canada)*

Doctoral Symposium Chairs: Mark Harman *(University College London, UK)*
Antonia Bertolino *(ISTI-CNR, Italy)*

PhD Working Groups Chair: Árpád Beszédes *(University of Szeged, Hungary)*

Industrial Track Chairs: Frank Tip *(IBM Research, USA)*
Volker Gruhn *(University of Duisburg-Essen, Germany)*

New Ideas Track Chair: Martin Robillard *(McGill University, Canada)*

Tool Demonstrations Track Chairs: Michele Lanza *(University of Lugano, Switzerland)*
Anthony Cleve *(University of Namur & Université Libre de Bruxelles, Belgium)*

Technical Briefings Track Chair: Lionel Briand *(Simula Research Laboratory, Norway)*

Artifact Evaluation Chairs: Shriram Krishnamurthi *(Brown University, USA)*
Carlo Ghezzi *(Politecnico di Milano, Italy)*

Publicity Chair: Andrian Marcus *(Wayne State University, USA)*

Local Organization Chairs: Árpád Beszédes *(University of Szeged, Hungary)*
László Vidács *(University of Szeged, Hungary)*

Publications Chair: Gordon Fraser *(Saarland University, Germany)*

Web Chair: László Vidács *(University of Szeged, Hungary)*

Conference Arrangements: Patricia Frittman *(University of Szeged, Hungary)*

Program Committee: Víctor Braberman *(Universidad de Buenos Aires, Argentina)*
Lionel Briand *(Simula Research Laboratory, Norway)*
Tevfik Bultan *(University of California, Santa Barbara, USA)*
Licia Capra *(University College London, UK)*
Antonio Carzaniga *(University of Lugano, Switzerland)*
Rudolf Ferenc *(University of Szeged, Hungary)*
Carlo Ghezzi *(Politecnico di Milano, Italy)*
Holger Giese *(HPI Potsdam, Germany)*
Martin Glinz *(University of Zürich, Switzerland)*
Mark Harman *(University College London, UK)*
Valerie Issarny *(INRIA, France)*
Sunghun Kim *(Hong Kong UST, China)*
Andy Ko *(University of Washington, USA)*
Shriram Krishnamurthi *(Brown University, USA)*
Mira Mezini *(TU Darmstadt, Germany)*
Henry Muccini *(University of L'Aquila, Italy)*
Nachiappan Nagappan *(Microsoft Research, USA)*
Aditya Nori *(Microsoft Research, India)*
Corina Pasareanu *(NASA, USA)*
Mauro Pezze *(University of Lugano, Switzerland, and University of Milano, Italy)*
Klaus Pohl *(University of Essen-Duisburg, Germany)*
Martin Robillard *(McGill University, Canada)*
Wilhelm Schaefer *(University of Paderborn, Germany)*
Yannis Smaragdakis *(University of Athens, Greece, and University of Massachusetts, USA)*
Margaret-Anne Storey *(University of Victoria, Canada)*
Zhendong Su *(University of California, Davis, USA)*
Mandana Vaziri *(IBM Research, USA)*

ESEC/FSE 2011 Additional Reviewers

Muath Alkhalaf
Jorge Aranda
Andrea Arcuri
Fernando Asteasuain
Tibor Bakota
Moritz Balz
Earl Barr
Basil Becker
Steffen Becker
Eya Ben Charrada
Nebil Ben Mabrouk
Domenico Bianculli
Eric Bodden
Gargi Bougie
Pietro Braione
Christian Brenner
Christopher Brink
Ning Chen
Ruzanna Chitchyan
Hernan Czemerinski
Barthélémy Dagenais
Giovanni Denaro
Stefan Dziwok
Nicolas D´ippolito
Davide Falessi
Jens Frieben
Lajos Jeno Fulop
Mark Gabel
Gregor Gabrysiak
Diego Garbervetsky
Tamas Gergely
Joe Gibbs Politz
Nils Göde
Michael Goedicke
Lars Grammel
Joel Greenyer
Arjun Guha
Regina Hebig
Christian Heinzemann
Peter Hegedus
Stephan Hildebrandt
Nicolas Hoby
Cédric Jeanneret
Yue Jia
Lingxiao Jiang
Gabriella Kakuja-Toth
David Kawrykow
Johannes Kinder
Peter Kortvelyesi
Christian Krause
Jens Krinke
Akash Lal
Leen Lambers
Kim Lauenroth
Vu Le
Ondrej Lhotak
Soo Ling Lim
Ivano Malavolta
Leonardo Mariani
Hernan Melgratti
Andreas Metzger
Matthias Meyer
Andrea Mocci
Martin Monperrus
Del Myers
Csaba Nagy
Shiva Nejati
Stefan Neumann
Jaideep Nijjar
Esteban Pavese
Uwe Pohlmann
Claudia Priesterjahn
Sriram Rajamani
Tristan Ratchford
Christoph Reichenbach
Jan Rieke
Peter Rigby
Erik Rogstad
Kristin Rozier
Neha Rungta
Mehrdad Sabetzadeh
Lajos Schrettner
Andreas Seibel
Norbert Seyff
German Sibay
Istvan Siket
Jamie Starke
Reinhard Stoiber
Oliver Sudmann
Fangqi Sun
Yida Tao
Bastian Tenbergen
Matthias Tichy
Massimo Tivoli
Oksana Tkachuk
Dietrich Travkin
Christoph Treude
Gias Uddin
Kapil Vaswani
Martin Vechev
Thomas Vogel
Markus von Detten
Sebastian Wätzoldt
Chao Wang
Dustin Wüest
Liang Xu
Annie Ying
Apostolos Zarras
Thomas Zimmermann

ESEC/FSE 2011 Sponsor & Supporters

Sponsor: SIGSOFT — Special Interest Group on Software Engineering

Institutional Supporter: Universitas Scientiarum Szegediensis · Szegedi Tudományegyetem

Gold Supporters: Microsoft Research, D·E·A·K, Ericsson, FrontendART

Silver Supporter: IBM Research

Building Advanced Mechatronic Systems

Wilhelm Schäfer
University of Paderborn
Germany
wilhelm@upb.de

Mechatronics is the engineering discipline concerned with the construction of systems incorporating mechanical, electronical and information technology components. Typical examples of mechatronic systems are automotive applications, e.g. advanced braking systems, fly/steer-by-wire or active suspension techniques, but also DVD-players or washing machines. Mechatronic systems are characterised by a combination of basic mechanical devices with a processing unit monitoring and controlling it via a number of actuators and sensors. This leads to massive improvements in product performance and flexibility. The introduction of mechatronics as a tight integration of mechanical, electronically and information-driven units allowed for turning conventionally designed mechanical components into smart devices.

Today we see the first steps in the emergence of the next generation of mechatronic systems. While "intelligence" in the behavior has so far always been achieved by gathering information (and reacting to it) from the one single machine, the usage and retrieval of information in the future will be characterized by an exchange of information between different machines. This can for instance already be seen in the automotive and rail domain.

Intelligent lighting systems combine information about their environment obtained from their own sensors with those collected by other cars. In the Paderborn rail system shuttles autonomously form convoys as to reduce air resistance and optimize energy consumption.

In the talk we survey current state of the art in the development of mechatronic systems from a software engineering point of view. Based on identified weaknesses of existing approaches we present our own approach called Mechatronic UML. Mechatronic UML supports model-driven development of mechatronic systems addressing complex coordination between system components under hard real-time constraints and reconfiguration of control algorithms at runtime to adjust the system behavior to changing system goals as well as target platform specific code generation. Modeling is based on a syntactically and semantically rigorously defined and partially refined subset of UML. It uses a slightly refined version of component diagrams, coordination patterns, and a refined version of state charts including the notion of time which are called Real time state charts. Verification of safety properties is based on a special kind of compositional model checking to make it scalable. Model checking exploits an underlying unifying semantics which is formally defined using graph transformation systems. The last part of the talk is devoted to pointing out future developments and research challenges which we believe characterize advanced mechatronic systems of the future.

Categories and Subject Descriptors: D.2.4 [Software Engineering]: Software/Program Verification - *Model checking*

General Terms:
Design

Keywords:
Mechatronic UML, Graph Transformations, Real Time

Copyright is held by the author/owner(s).
ESEC/FSE'11, September 5–9, 2011, Szeged, Hungary.
ACM 978-1-4503-0443-6/11/09.

Keynote Talk

Software Architecture: Reflections on an Evolving Discipline

David Garlan and Mary Shaw
Carnegie Mellon University
Pittsburgh, PA, USA
garlan@cs.cmu.edu and mary.shaw@cs.cmu.edu

Abstract

Software Architecture emerged in the 1990's as an important sub-field of software engineering. While good architectural design had long been recognized as critical to the success of any complex software system, before then the practice of architecting had relied largely on ad hoc, uncodified, and idiosyncratic techniques and knowledge. By the 2000's the field had matured to the point where there were widely-recognized taxonomies of architectural patterns, techniques for formally representing and analyzing architectures, methods for reviewing an architectural design, widespread adoption of architectural product lines and composition frameworks, and techniques for ensuring conformance between an architecture and an implementation of it. In this talk we reflect on the key enablers of a discipline of software architecture that led to these advances, the central ideas that form its core, and its enduring principles that continue to shape the field of software engineering. We consider both the important concepts on which it builds, as well as those that have built on top of it. Finally, we examine some of the important new trends and challenges that are likely to have an impact on how software architecture will evolve in the future.

Categories & Subject Descriptors: D.2.11 Software Architectures.

General Terms: Design.

Bios

David Garlan is a Professor of Computer Science and Director of Software Engineering Professional Programs in the School of Computer Science at Carnegie Mellon University. He received his Ph.D. from Carnegie Mellon in 1987 and worked as a software architect in industry between 1987 and 1990. His interests include software architecture, self-adaptive systems, formal methods, and cyber-physical systems. He is considered to be one of the founders of the field of software architecture, and, in particular, formal representation and analysis of architectural designs. He is a co-author of two books on software architecture: "Software Architecture: Perspectives on an Emerging Discipline", and "Documenting Software Architecture: Views and Beyond." In 2005 he received a Stevens Award Citation for "fundamental contributions to the development and understanding of software architecture as a discipline in software engineering."

Mary Shaw is the Alan J. Perlis Professor of Computer Science, Co-Director of the Sloan Software Industry Center, and member of the Institute for Software Research International and the Human Computer Interaction Institute at Carnegie Mellon University. She has been a member of this faculty since completing the Ph.D. degree at Carnegie-Mellon in 1972. Her research interests lie primarily in the areas of programming systems and software engineering, particularly value-driven software design, software architecture, programming languages, specifications, and abstraction techniques. Dr. Shaw is an author or editor of seven books and more than one hundred forty papers and technical reports. In 1993 she received the Warnier prize for contributions to software engineering. She is a Fellow of the Association for Computing Machinery (ACM), the Institute for Electrical and Electronics Engineers (IEEE) and the American Association for the Advancement of Science (AAAS). She is also a member of the Society of the Sigma Xi, the New York Academy of Sciences, and a member emeritus of Working Group 2.4 (System Implementation Languages) of the International Federation of Information Processing Societies. In addition, she has served on a number of advisory and review panels, conference program committees, and editorial boards.

Copyright is held by the author/owner(s).
ESEC/FSE'11, September 5–9, 2011, Szeged, Hungary.
ACM 978-1-4503-0443-6/11/09.

ELI-ALPS – The Ultrafast Challenges in Hungary

Gábor Szabó
Department of Optics and Quantum Electronics
University of Szeged, Hungary
gszabo@physx.u-szeged.hu

ABSTRACT

The ELI – Extreme Light Infrastructure – or as it is commonly referred to: the SUPERLASER will be one of the large research facilities of the European Union. ELI will be built with a joint international effort to form an integrated infrastructure comprised of three branches. The ELI Beamline Facility (Prague, Czech Republic) will mainly focus on particle acceleration and X-ray generation, while the ELI Nuclear Physics Facility (Magurele, Romania) will be dealing with laser-based nuclear physics as well as high field physics. In the talk we introduce the ELI Attosecond Light Pulse Source (ELI-ALPS) to be built in Szeged, Hungary.

The primary mission of the ELI-ALPS Research Infrastructure is to provide the international scientific community with a broad range of ultrafast light sources, especially with coherent XUV and X-ray radiation, including single attosecond pulses. Thanks to this combination of parameters never achieved before, energetic attosecond X-ray pulses of ELI-ALPS will enable recording freeze-frame images of the dynamical electronic-structural behaviour of complex atomic, molecular and condensed matter systems, with attosecond-picometer resolution. The secondary purpose is to contribute to the scientific and technological development towards generating 200 PW pulses, being the ultimate goal of the ELI project. ELI-ALPS will be operated also as a user facility and hence serve basic and applied research in physical, chemical, material and biomedical sciences as well as industrial applications.

The Facility will be built by the end of 2015 from a budget exceeding 240M EUR. The building and the IT infrastructure, from high speed internal networking, remote controlled system alignment, targetry and data aquisition through laser and radiation safety tools until security systems, will challenge the state of the art of similar research facilities.

Categories and Subject Descriptors

J.2 [**Physical sciences and engineering**]: Physics

General Terms

Experimentation, Measurement, Performance

Keywords

ELI, attosecond light pulse

Biography

Gábor Szabó received his MS and PhD degrees in physics from JATE University, Szeged, Hungary, in 1978 and 1981, respectively. From 1978 to the present he has been working at University of Szeged where he has been a full professor in the Department of Optics and Quantum Electronics since 1994. Since 2010 he has been the rector of the University of Szeged. He has also visited scientists at both Max Planck Institute, Göttingen, Germany, and Rice University, Houston, Texas. Dr. Szabó is a member of the Hungarian Physical Society, he is the chairman of the Hungarian Association for Innovation, and has been a member of Hungarian Academy of Sciences since 2010. His research activities include photoacoustic spectroscopy, ultrafast laser spectroscopy, generation of femtosecond pulses, nonlinear optics, optimum control of quantum systems, medical applications of lasers.

Copyright is held by the author/owner(s).
ESEC/FSE'11, September 5–9, 2011, Szeged, Hungary.
ACM 978-1-4503-0443-6/11/09.

Don't Touch My Code! Examining the Effects of Ownership on Software Quality

Christian Bird
Microsoft Research
cbird@microsoft.com

Nachiappan Nagappan
Microsoft Research
nachin@microsoft.com

Brendan Murphy
Microsoft Research
bmurphy@microsoft.com

Harald Gall
University of Zurich
gall@ifi.uzh.ch

Premkumar Devanbu
University of California, Davis
ptdevanbu@ucdavis.edu

ABSTRACT

Ownership is a key aspect of large-scale software development. We examine the relationship between different ownership measures and software failures in two large software projects: Windows Vista and Windows 7. We find that in all cases, measures of ownership such as the number of low-expertise developers, and the proportion of ownership for the top owner have a relationship with both pre-release faults and post-release failures. We also empirically identify reasons that low-expertise developers make changes to components and show that the removal of low-expertise contributions dramatically decreases the performance of contribution based defect prediction. Finally we provide recommendations for source code change policies and utilization of resources such as code inspections based on our results.

Categories and Subject Descriptors

D.2.8 [**Software Engineering**]: Metrics—*Process metrics*

General Terms

Measurement, Management, Human Factors

Keywords

Empirical Software Engineering, Ownership, Expertise, Quality

1. INTRODUCTION

Many recent studies [6, 9, 26, 29] have shown that human factors play a significant role in the quality of software components. *Ownership* is a general term used to describe whether one person has responsibility for a software component, or if there is no one clearly responsible developer. There is a relationship between the number of people working on a binary and failures [5, 26]. However, to our knowledge, the effect of ownership has not been studied in depth in commercial contexts. Based on our observations and discussions with project managers, we suspect that when there is no clear point of contact and the contributions to a software component are spread across many developers, there is an increased chance of communication breakdowns, misaligned goals, inconsistent interfaces and semantics, all leading to lower quality.

Interestingly, unlike some aspects of software which are known to be related to defects such as dependency complexity, or size, ownership is something that can be deliberately changed by modifying processes and policies. Thus, the answer to the question: *"How much does ownership affect quality?"* is important as it is *actionable*. Managers and team leads can make better decisions about how to govern a project by knowing the answer. If ownership has a big effect, then policies to enforce strong code ownership can be put into place; managers can also watch out for code which is contributed by developers who have inadequate relevant prior experience. If ownership has little effect, then the normal bottlenecks associated with having one person in charge of each component can be removed, and available talent reassigned at will.

We have observed that many industrial projects encourage high levels of code ownership. In this paper, we examine ownership and software quality. We make the following contributions in this paper:

1. We define and validate measures of ownership that are related to software quality.
2. We present an in depth quantitative study of the effect of these measures of ownership on pre-release and post-release defects for multiple large software projects.
3. We identify reasons that components have many low-expertise developers contributing to them.
4. We propose recommendations for dealing with the effects of low ownership.

2. THEORY & RELATED WORK

A number of prior studies have examined the effect of developer contribution behavior on software quality.

Rahman & Devanbu [30] examined the effects of ownership & experience on quality in several open-source projects, using a fine-grained approach based on fix-inducing fragments of code, and report findings similar to those of our paper. However, they operationalize ownership differently,

Permission to make digital or hard copies of all or part of this work for personal or classroom use is granted without fee provided that copies are not made or distributed for profit or commercial advantage and that copies bear this notice and the full citation on the first page. To copy otherwise, to republish, to post on servers or to redistribute to lists, requires prior specific permission and/or a fee.
ESEC/FSE'11, September 5–9, 2011, Szeged, Hungary.
Copyright 2011 ACM 978-1-4503-0443-6/11/09 ...$10.00.

and ownership policies and practices in OSS and commercial software are quite different. Thus the similarity of effect is striking. Furthermore, Rahman & Devanbu do not study the relationship of minor contribution on software dependencies; nor do they consider social network measures.

Weyuker *et al.* [35], examined the effect of including team size in prediction models. They use a count of the developers that worked on each component, but do not examine the proportion of work, which we account for. They found a negligible increase in failure prediction accuracy when adding team size to their models. We differ in that we examine the *proportion* of contributions made by each developer to a component. Further, we are not interested in prediction, but rather determining if there is a statistically significant *relationship* between ownership and failures.

Similarly, Meneely and Williams examined the relationship of the number of developers working on parts of the Linux kernel with security vulnerabilities [19]. They found that when more than nine developers contribute to a source file, it is sixteen times more likely to include a security vulnerability.

New methods such as Extreme Programming (XP) [4] profess collective code ownership but there has been little empirical evidence or backing of this data on reasonably mature/complex or large systems. Our study is the first to empirically quantify the effect code owners (and low-expertise contributors) have on the overall code quality.

Domain, application, and even component-specific knowledge are important aids for helping developers to maintin high quality software. Boh *et al.* found that project specific expertise has a much larger impact on the time required to perform development tasks than high levels of diverse experience in unrelated projects [7]. In a qualitative study of 17 commercial software projects, Curtis *et al.* [10] found that "the thin spread of application domain knowledge" was one of the top three salient problems. They also found that one common trait among engineers categorized as "exceptional" was that they had deep domain knowledge, and understood how the system design would generate the system behavior customers expected, even under exceptional circumstances. Such knowledge is not easily obtained. One systems engineer explained, "Someone had to spend a hundred million to put that knowledge in my head. It didn't come free."

The question naturally arises, how can we determine who has such domain knowledge? Fortunately, there is a wealth of literature that uses the prior development activity on a component as a proxy for expertise and knowledge with respect to the component. As examples Expertise Browser from Mockus *et al.* [22] and Expertise Recommender from McDonald and Ackerman [18] both use measures of the amount of work that a developer has performed on a software component to recommend component experts. Fritz *et al.* found that the ability of a developer to answer questions about a piece of code in a system was strongly determined by whether the developer had authored some of the code, and how much time was spent authoring it [15].

Mockus and Weiss used properties of an individual change to predict the probability of that change causing a failure [23]. They found that changes made by developers that were more experienced with a piece of code were less likely to induce failure. Three of their fourteen measures capture the experience of a developer history (by counting prior changes) and they were significant in prediction.

In a study of offshoring and succession in software development [21], Mockus evaluated a number of succession measures with the goal of being able to automatically identify mentors for developers working on a per-component basis. A succession measure based on ownership was able to accurately pinpoint the most likely method and was used in a large scale study evaluating the factors affecting productivity in project succession and offshoring.

Research in other domains, such as manufacturing, has found that when a worker performs a task repeatedly, the labor requirements to complete subsequent work in the same task decreases and the quality increases [11]. Software development differs from these domains in that workers do not perform the exact same task repeatedly. Rather, software development represents a form of constant problem solving in which tasks are rarely exactly the same, but may be similar. Nonetheless, developers gain project and component specific knowledge as they repeatedly perform tasks on the same systems [32]. Banker *et al.* found that increased experience increases a developer's knowledge of the architectural domain of the system [1]. Repeatedly using a particular API, or working on a particular system creates *episodic knowledge*. Robillard indicates that the lack of such knowledge negatively affects the quality of software [31]. Indeed, Basili and Caldiera present an approach for improving quality in software development through learning and experience by establishing "experience factories" [2]. They claim that by reusing knowledge, products, and experience, companies can maintain high quality levels because developers do not need to constantly acquire new knowledge and expertise as they work on different projects. Drawing on these ideas, we develop ownership measures which consider the number of times that a developer works on a particular component, with the idea that each exposure is a learning experience and increases the developer's knowledge and abilities.

there is a knowledge-sharing factor at play as well. The set of developers that contribute to a component implicitly form a team that has shared knowledge regarding the semantics and design of the component. Coordination is a known problem in software development [16]. In fact, another of the top three problems identified in Curtis' study [10] was "communication and coordination breakdowns." Working in such a group always creates a need for sharing and integrating knowledge across all members [8]. Cataldo *et al.* showed that communication breakdowns delay tasks [9]. If a member of this team devotes little attention to the team and/or the component, they may not acquire the knowledge required to make changes to the component without error. We attempt to operationalize these team members in this paper and examine their effect on quality.

If ownership of a particular component in a system (whether it be a file, class, module, plugin, or subsystem) is a valid proxy for expertise, then what is the effect of having most changes made by those with little expertise? Is it better to have one clear owner of a software component? We operationalize ownership in two key ways here and formally define our measures in section 3. One measure of ownership is how much of the development activity for a component comes from one developer. If one developer makes 80% of the changes to a component, then we say that the component has high ownership. The other way that we measure ownership is by determining how many low-expertise developers are working on a component. If many developers

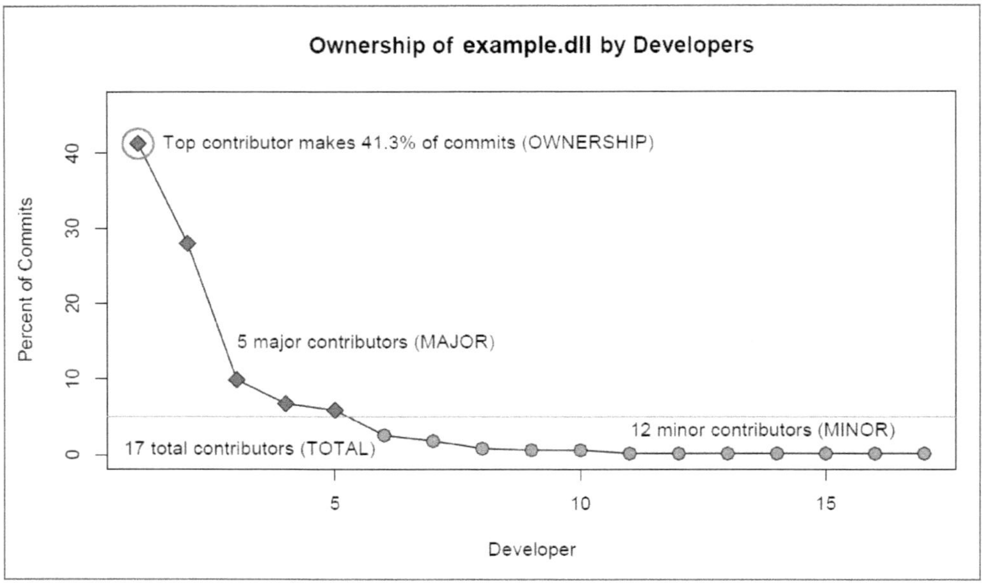

Figure 1: Graph of the proportion of commits to `example.dll` by developers during the Vista development cycle, showing the four measures of ownership used in this paper.

are all making few changes to a component, then there are many non-experts working on the component and we label the component as having low ownership.

We expect that having one clear "owner" for a component will lead to fewer failures and that when many non-experts are making changes, indicating that ownership is spread across many contributors, the component will have more failures.

3. TERMINOLOGY AND METRICS

We adopt Basili's goal question metric approach [3] to frame our study of ownership. Our goal is to understand the relationship between ownership and software quality. We also hope to gain an understanding of how this relationship varies with the development process in use. Achievement of this goal can lead to more informed development decisions or possibly process policy changes resulting in software with fewer defects.

In order to reach this goal, we ask a number of specific questions:

1. Are higher levels of ownership associated with less defects?

2. Is there a negative effect when a software entity is developed by many people with low ownership?

3. Are these effects related to the development process used?

In order to answer these questions, we propose a number of ownership metrics and use them to evaluate our hypotheses of ownership. We begin by defining some important terms and metrics used throughout the rest of this paper:

- **Software Component** – This is a unit of development that has some core functionality. Defects can be traced back to a specific component and software changes from developers can also be traced to a component. In Windows, a component is a compiled binary.

- **Contributor** – A contributor to a software component is someone who has made commits/software changes to the component.

- **Proportion of Ownership** – The proportion of ownership (or simply ownership) of a contributor for a particular component is the ratio of number of commits that the contributor has made relative to the total number of commits for that component. Thus, if Cindy has made 20 commits to `ie9.dll` and there are a total of 100 commits to `ie9.dll` then Cindy has an ownership of 20%.

- **Minor Contributor** – A developer who has made changes to a component, but whose ownership is below 5% is considered a minor contributor to that component. This threshold was chosen based on examination of distributions of ownership[1]. We refer to a commit from a minor contributor as a minor contribution.

- **Major Contributor** – A developer who has made changes to a component and whose ownership is at or above 5% is a major contributor to the component and a commit from such a developer is a major contribution.

Note that we examine the number of *changes* to a component made by a developer rather than the actual number of lines modified. Within Windows, each change corresponds to one fix or enhancement and individual changes are quite small, usually on the order of tens of lines. We use number of changes because each change represents an "exposure" of the developer to the code and because the previous measure of experience used by Mockus and Weiss also used the number of changes. However, prior literature [14] has shown high

[1] A sensitivity analysis with threshold values ranging from 2% to 10% yielded similar results.

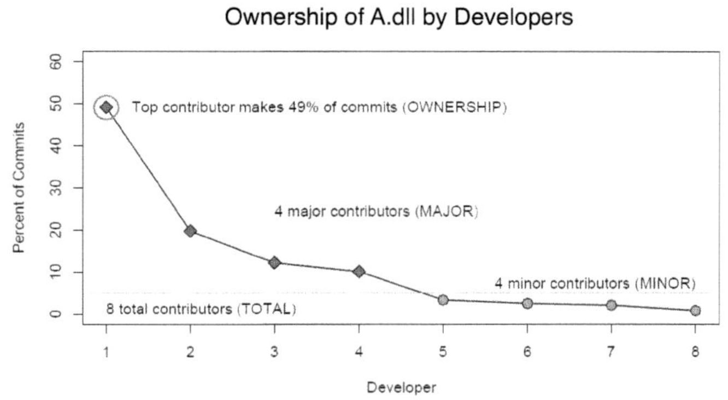

(a) A.dll

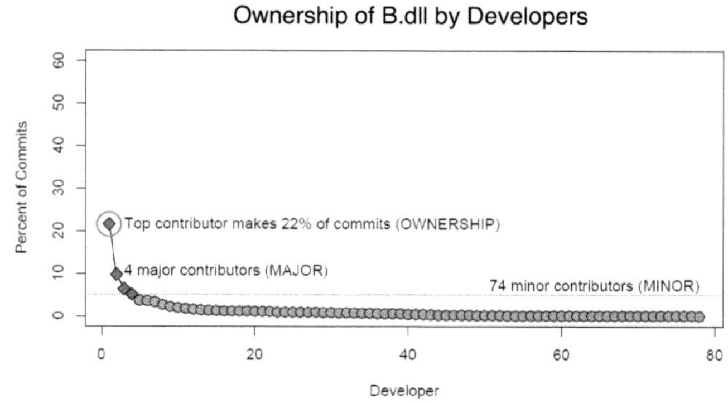

(b) B.dll

Figure 2: Ownership graphs for two binaries in Windows

correlation (above 0.9) between number of changes and number of lines contributed and we have found similar results in Windows, indicating that our results would not change significantly. With these terms defined, we now introduce our metrics.

- MINOR – number of minor contributors
- MAJOR – number of major contributors
- TOTAL – total number of contributors
- OWNERSHIP – proportion of ownership for the contributor with the highest proportion of ownership

Figure 1 shows the proportion of commits for each of the developers that contributed to `example.dll` in Windows, in decreasing order. This library had a total of 918 commits made during the development cycle. The top contributing engineer made 379 commits, roughly 41%. Five engineers made at least 5% of the commits (at least 46 commits). Twelve engineers made less than 5% of the commits (less than 46 commits). Finally, there were a total of seventeen engineers that made commits to the binary. Thus, our metrics for `example.dll` are:

Metric	Value
MINOR	12
MAJOR	5
TOTAL	17
OWNERSHIP	0.41

4. HYPOTHESES

We begin with the observation that a developer with lower expertise is more likely to introduce bugs into the code. A developer who has made a small proportion of the commits to a binary likely has less expertise and is more likely to make an error. We expect that as the number of developers working on a component increases, the component may become "fragmented" and the difficulty of vetting and coordinating all these minor contributions becomes an obstacle to good quality. Thus if MINOR is high, quality suffers.

Hypothesis 1 - Software components with many minor contributors will have more failures than software components that have fewer.

We also look at the proportion of ownership for the highest contributing developer for each component (OWNERSHIP). If OWNERSHIP is high, that indicates that there is one developer who "owns" the component and has a high level of expertise. This person can also act as a single point of contact for others who need to use the component, need changes to it, or just have questions about it. We theorize that when such a person exists, the software quality is higher resulting in fewer failures.

Hypothesis 2 - Software components with a high level of ownership will have fewer failures than components with lower top ownership levels.

If the number of minor contributors negatively affects software quality, the next question to ask is, "Why do some binaries have so many minor contributors?" We have observed both at Microsoft and also within OSS projects such as Python and Postgres, that during the process of maintenance, feature addition, or bug fixing, owners of one component often need to modify other components that the first relies on or is relied upon by. As a simple example, a developer tasked with fixing media playback in Internet Explorer may need to make changes to the media playback interface library even though the developer is not the designated owner and has limited experience with this component. This leads to our hypothesis.

Hypothesis 3 - Minor contributors to components will be Major contributors to other components that are related through dependency relationships

Finally, if low-expertise contributions do have a large impact on software quality, then we expect that defect prediction techniques will be affected by their inclusion or removal. We therefore replicate prior defect prediction techniques and compare results when using all data, data derived only from changes by minor contributors and, and data derived only from changes to major contributors. We expect that when data from minor contributors is removed, the quality of the defect prediction will suffer.

Hypothesis 4 - Removal of minor contribution information from defect prediction techniques will decrease performance dramatically.

Category	Metric	Windows Vista Pre-release Failures	Windows Vista Post-release Failures	Windows 7 Pre-release Failures	Windows 7 Post-release Failures
Ownership Metrics	TOTAL	0.84	0.70	0.92	0.24
	MINOR	0.86	0.70	0.93	0.25
	MAJOR	0.26	0.29	-0.40	-0.14
	OWNERSHIP	-0.49	-0.49	-0.29	-0.02
"Classic" Metrics	Size	0.75	0.69	0.70	0.26
	Churn	0.72	0.69	0.71	0.26
	Complexity	0.70	0.53	0.56	0.37

Table 1: Bivariate Spearman correlation of ownership and code metrics with pre- and post-release failures in Windows Vista and Windows 7. All correlations are statistically significant except for that of OWNERSHIP and post-release failures in Windows 7.

5. DATA COLLECTION AND ANALYSIS

This data presents an opportunity to investigate hypotheses regarding code ownership. In this study, we examine Windows Vista and Windows 7.

Windows Vista and Windows 7 is developed entirely by Microsoft, who have processes and policies that favor strong code ownership. Windows Vista and 7 were developed by a few thousand software developers and is composed of thousands of individual executable files (`.exe`), shared libraries (`.dll`), and drivers (`.sys`), which we collectively refer to as *binaries*. We track the development history from the release of Windows Server 2003 to the release of Windows 7 and include pre-release defects as well as post-release failures in Vista and 7 as software quality indicators.

We require several types of data. The most important data are the commit histories and software failures. Software repositories record the contents of every change made to a piece of software, along with the change author, the time of change, and an associated log message that may be indicative of the type of change (e.g. introducing a feature, or fixing a bug). We collected the number of changes made by each developer to each source file and used a mapping of source files to binaries in order to determine the number of changes made by each developer to each binary. Although the source code management system uses branches heavily, we only recorded changes from developers that were edits to the source code. Branching operations (e.g. branching and merging) were not counted as changes.

We also gathered both pre-release and post-release software failures for all three projects. We gathered the failures recorded prior to release and in the first six months after release. Because of the information contained in the failures, we can automatically trace them back to the binaries that caused them, but cannot reliably trace them to the source files that caused the failures. We only count failures that the development team deemed important enough to fix.

Finally, we gathered source code metrics including various size, complexity, and churn metrics. This information is gathered from both the source code repositories and the build process.

5.1 Analysis Techniques

We use a number of methods to examine the relationship between ownership and software quality.

We began with a correlation analysis of both pre- and post-release failures with each of the ownership metrics as well as a number of other metrics such as test coverage, complexity, size, dependencies, and churn (shown in Table 1). The results indicated that pre- and post-release defects in had strong relationships with MINOR, TOTAL, and OWNERSHIP. Windows 7 binaries have few post-release failures. Thus the correlation values between metrics and and post-release failures are noticeably lower than the other failure categories (although all except the correlation with OWNERSHIP are still statistically significant).

However, we also observed some relationship between code attributes and ownership metrics. For example, Figure 2 shows data for two anonymized binaries in Windows with vastly different ownership profiles. The binary depicted in Figure 2-b (`B.dll`) has more failures than the binary in Figure 2-a (`A.dll`), eight times as many pre-release failures and twice as many post-release failures. However, `B.dll` is also a larger binary and experienced far more churn during the development cycle. Thus it is not clear whether the increase in failures is attributable to more minor contributors or other measures such as size, complexity, and churn, which are known to be related to defects [25, 28] and are likely related to the number of minor contributors. Prior research has shown that when characteristics such as size are not considered, they may affect the validity of other software metrics [13].

To overcome this problem, we used *multiple linear regression*. Linear regression, is primarily used in two different ways. First, it can be used to make predictions about an outcome based on prior data (for instance predicting how many failures a software component may have based on characteristics of the components). We stress that while our regression analysis does use failures as the dependent variable in our models, the purpose of this paper is **not** to predict failures.

Second, linear regression enables us to examine the effect of one or more variables on an outcome when controlling for other variables. We use it for this purpose in an effort to examine the *relationship* of our ownership measures *when controlling for source code characteristics such as size, complexity, and churn.*

A linear regression model for failures indicates which variables have an effect on failures, how large the effect is, in what direction (i.e. if failures go up when a metric goes up or when it goes down), and how much of the variance

Model	Windows Vista		Windows 7	
	Pre-release Failures	Post-release Failures	Pre-release Failures	Post-release Failures
Base (code metrics)	26%	29%	24%	18%
Base + TOTAL	40%*(+14%)	35%*(+6%)	68%* (+35%)	21%* (+3%)
Base + MINOR	46%*(+20%)	41%*(+12%)	70%* (+46%)	21%* (+3%)
Base + MINOR + MAJOR	48%*(+2%)	43%*(+2%)	71%* (+1%)	22% (+1%)
Base + MINOR + MAJOR + OWNERSHIP	50%*(+2%)	44%*(+1%)	72%* (+1%)	22% (+0%)

Table 2: Variance in failures for the base model which includes standard metrics of complexity, size, and churn, as well as the models with MINOR and OWNERSHIP added. An asterisk* denotes that a model showed statistically significant improvement when the additional variable was added.

in the number of failures is explained by the metrics. We compare the amount of variance in failures explained by a model that includes the ownership metrics to a model that does not include them. There are many measures of churn, complexity, and size. However, to avoid multi-collinearity and over-fitting, we include only one of each measure in the model; We choose the measure which results in the best base model. This gives an indication of how much ownership actually affects software failures. We examined the improvement in amount of variance in failures explained by the metrics (commonly referred to as the adjusted R^2) and examine improved goodness of fit using F-tests to determine if the addition of an ownership metric improves the model by a statistically significant degree [12].

Linear regression models can be reliably interpreted if certain assumptions hold. Two key assumptions are that the residuals are normally distributed, and not correlated with any of the independent variables. In our analysis, we found that the distribution of failures was almost always heavily right skewed, which led to a similar skew in the residuals. When we transformed the dependent variable to be the `log` of the number of failures, the skew diminished, and the residuals fit the normality assumption. This data transformation was applied to all dependent variables except for post-release failures in Vista, where linear regression assumptions were met by the raw data.

6. RESULTS

We now present the results of our analysis of Windows Vista and Windows 7. Table 2 illustrates the results of our analysis. We denote with an asterisk*, cases where a goodness-of-fit F-test indicated that the addition of a variable improved the model by a statistically significant degree. The value in parentheses indicates the percent increase in variance explained over the model without the added variable. For example, in Table 2 the Base+MINOR +MAJOR model in Vista explains 48% of the variance in pre-release failures which is 2% more than the Base+MINOR model which explains 46%. the Base+MINOR model explains 20% more of the variance in pre-release failures than the Base model. Adding an independent variable to a model can never decrease the variance explained, so we use the adjusted R^2 measure which penalizes models that have additional variables.

We built five statistical models of failures for pre- and post-release defects in Windows Vista and Windows 7 (summarized in Table 2). The first model contains only the classical source code metrics: size, complexity, and churn. We refer to this as the base model. This model showed that churn, size, and complexity all have a statistically significant effect on both pre and post-release failures. In addition, these metrics are able to explain 26% of the variance in pre-release failures and 29% of the variance in post-release failures in Vista and 24% and 28% in Windows 7.

In the second model, we added TOTAL to the classic variables. This examines the effect of team size on defects and does not include any measures of the proportion of contributions made by individual members. All models exhibitted a statistically significant improvement in variance explained.

Next, we added MINOR to the set of predictor variables in the base model. This was done to determine if the total number of developers has a different effect on quality than the number of minor contributors. The statistics showed that MINOR is positively related to both pre and post-release failures to a statistically significant degree. The addition of MINOR increased the proportion of variance in pre-release failures to 46% and post-release failures to 41%. The gains shown by MINOR were stronger than those shown by TOTAL for both types of failures to a statistically significant degree, in all cases except for post-release failures in Windows 7, indicating that MINOR has a larger effect on failures.

The addition of MAJOR and OWNERSHIP showed smaller gains, but were often still statistically significant. We found similar results regardless of the order that these variables were added to the models. OWNERSHIP was found to have a negative relationship with failures to a statistically significant degree and MAJOR had a positive relationship, but was much smaller than MINOR. MINOR still showed more of an effect than OWNERSHIP and MAJOR even when it was added last (not shown). The final models account for up to 72% of variance in failures. In all cases, ownership had a stronger relationship with pre-release failures than post-release failures and the models in general were less explanatory. This may indicate that there are already measures being taken (e.g. increased testing, more stringent quality controls, etc.) between implementation completion and release to counteract the effects of poor ownership.

For all metrics that measure ownership levels there is a clear trend of having a statistically significant relationship to failures in Windows. In all cases, MAJOR and OWNERSHIP show less of an effect than MINOR or TOTAL, indicating that the number of higher-expertise contributors has marginal effect on quality, although the results are still statistically significant.

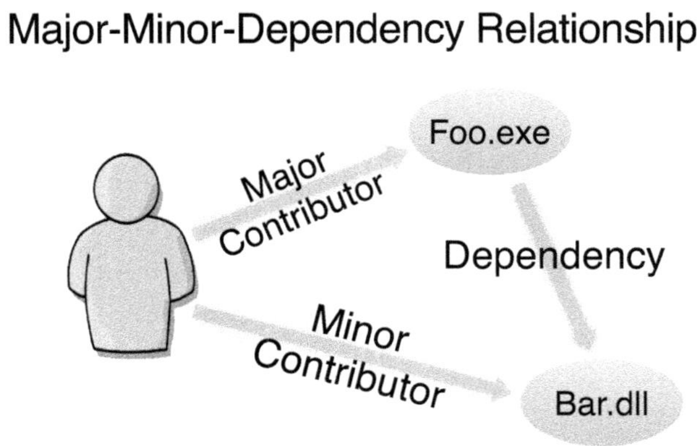

Figure 3: Illustration of the major-minor-dependency relationship commonly observed in Vista

The results of our analysis of ownership in both releases of Windows can be interpreted as follows:

1. *The number of minor contributors has a strong positive relationship with both pre- and post-release failures even when controlling for metrics such as size, churn, and complexity.*
2. *Higher levels of ownership for the top contributor to a component results in fewer failures when controlling for the same metrics, but the effect is smaller than the number of minor contributors.*
3. *Ownership has a stronger relationship with pre-release failures than post-release failures.*
4. *Measures of ownership and standard code measures show a much smaller relationship to post-release failures in Windows 7.*

7. EFFECTS OF MINOR CONTRIBUTORS

One of the key findings in our analysis was that the number of minor contributors has a strong relationship with failures in both releases of Windows. Since Microsoft has the capability to make changes to practices based on these findings, we were eager to gain a deeper understanding of this phenomenon. To this end, we performed two more detailed analyses in order to examine the minor contributors further.

First, we observed that almost all developers were major contributors to some binaries and minor contributors to others; very few developers never played a major contributor role. This led us to investigate the obvious question: *Given a particular developer, is there a relationship between a component to which she is a major contributor, and one to which she is a minor contributor?*

Second, we adapted a fault prediction study carried out by Pinzger *et al.* [29] and examined the effect of modifying the study in ways related to ownership.

7.1 Dependency Analysis

The majority of developers that contributed to Windows acted as major contributors to some binaries and minor contributors to others. There were very few developers who are only minor contributors. This fact is an indication of strong code ownership, as it shows that nearly everyone has a main responsibility for at least one binary.

Discussions with engineers at Microsoft indicated that often an engineer who was the owner of one binary would make changes to another binary whose services he or she used, often in the process of addressing reported bugs. In our context this would show up as one engineer who was a major contributor to some binary, A, and a minor contributor to some binary, B, with a dependency relationship between A and B. We call this a *Major-Minor-Dependency* relationship, which is illustrated in Figure 3.

Cataldo *et al.* found that making changes to a depending component without coordinating with the other stakeholders (in our case, the owner) of the component increases the likelihood of faults [9]. We have no record of the communication between developers of Windows. However, the fact that a minor contributor has, by definition, made few if any prior contributions to a component suggests that their participation in the component's implicit team is likely minimal, increasing the risk of a introducing a bug.

But does this actually happen? Is a developer D, working on binary *Foo.exe*, statistically more likely to be a minor contributor to a binary *Bar.dll*, just because *Foo.exe* depends on *Bar.dll*? If so, how many of the minor contributors to components can this phenomenon account for? If the majority of minor contributors are a result of component owners making changes do depending or dependent components to accomplish their own tasks such as resolving failures, then deliberate steps could be taken to avoid this type of risky behavior.

To investigate this further, we employed a static analysis tool, MaX [33], to detect dependency relationships between binaries. MaX uses debugging information files that are generated during compilation to identify these relationships, which include method calls, read and writes to the registry, IPC, COM calls, and use of types. We were unable to obtain the required debugging information files for Windows 7 and thus limit our analysis here to Vista. Using this tool, we constructed a dependency graph that includes all of the binaries in Windows Vista.

The next step is to determine whether the major-minor-dependency phenomenon occurs statistically more often than would be expected by chance. But what exactly does "by chance" mean? We model "chance" by generating a large, plausible, random sample of contributions; we can then compare the *observed* frequency of major-minor-dependency with the frequency in the *generated* sample. Our plausible random model is that each developer chooses their contributions at random, while preserving their rate of minor and major contributions. In other words, a developer is just as hardworking, but her choice of where to contribute is not influenced by dependencies in the code. Using this model, we generate a large sample of simulated contribution graphs. This gives us a basis for comparison to evaluate observed, real-world contribution behavior is influenced by dependencies between modules.

This "bootstrapping" approach comes from the statistical theory of random graphs [20, 24, 27]. A phenomenon is judged statistically significant if the actual, observed phenomenon occurs rarely in the generated sample graphs. Following previous techniques [24, 27], we use a *graph-rewiring* method to bootstrap our random ensemble, based on the ob-

	Windows Vista				Windows 7			
	Pre-release		Post-release		Pre-release		Post-release	
SNA Metric	Minor	Major	Minor	Major	Minor	Major	Minor	Major
Degree Centrality	0.861	0.909	0.668	0.599	0.931	0.797	0.269	0.319
Closeness Centrality	0.624	-0.098	0.602	0.107	0.737	0.167	0.130	0.013
Reachability	0.647	-0.091	0.618	0.119	0.747	0.176	0.135	0.018
Betweenness Centrality	0.703	0.146	0.601	0.132	0.748	0.285	0.289	0.154
Hierarchy	0.420	-0.273	0.176	-0.244	0.298	-0.302	0.136	-0.055
Effective Size	0.775	0.311	0.649	0.286	0.884	0.391	0.223	0.196

Table 3: Correlation of Social Network Analysis metrics on the contribution network with pre- and post-release failures. Columns labeled "Minor" are correlations of failures with metrics computed on networks composed only of minor contribution edges. Columns labeled "Major" are from networks made up of major contribution edges. For the majaority of metrics, removing the minor edges drops the correlations considerably. For some metrics, the direction of correlation actually changes for "Major".

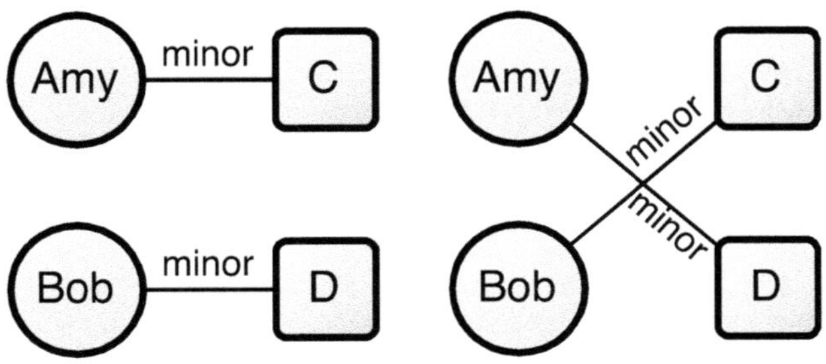

(a) before (b) after

Figure 4: An illustration of graph rewiring. Rewiring preserves the number of minor and major edges per developer and per binary, but randomizes the organization of the contribution network.

served frequency of commits from individuals. In each generated random sample, each developer makes the same number of major and minor contributions as in the observed real sample, but the contributions are chosen at random from the given set of components. We check to see how often a "majorly contributed component" for a developer has an actual dependency on a "minorly contributed component" for the same developer in these generated random samples. If the frequency of major-minor-dependency relationships that occur in the ensemble of simulated samples differs significantly from that of the observed real sample, then we can conclude that the phenomenon most likely represents some real, intended behavior, and not simply a chance occurrence.

Graph rewiring is performed as follows in our context. For the sake of convenience we refer to an edge connecting a binary to one of its major contributors as a *major edge* and an edge connecting a binary to one if its minor contributors as a *minor edge*. Two edges that are either both major edges or both minor edges are selected at random and endpoints of both are switched as shown in Figure 4. Thus, after the switch, the number of major and major contributions for each developer node and each component node remains the same.

After performing E^2 rewirings where E is the number of contribution edges in the graph, a sufficiently random graph is obtained. We created 10,000 such random contribution graphs and compared the frequency of major-minor-dependency relationships to the frequency in the observed, actual contribution graph. We found that in the observed Vista contribution graph, 52% of the binaries had minor contributors who were major contributors to other binaries that the original had a dependency with. In contrast, this relationship only existed for an average of 24% of the binaries in the random networks with the same minor and major contribution degree distributions. The maximum value for the normally distributed frequency of this phenomenon out of all 10,000 graphs was 32% of the time, indicating that 52% is definitely a statistically significant difference, and the phenomenon that we are observing does not occur by chance.

In Vista, one common reason that a developer is a minor contributor to a binary is that he/she is a major contributor to a depending binary. This allows for processes to be put into place to recognize and either minimize or aid minor contributions.

7.2 Effects on Network Metrics

In 2007, Pinzger *et al.* reported a method to find fault prone binaries in Windows Vista based on contribution networks [29]. A contribution network is composed of binaries and the developers that contributed to those binaries. Thus, a node representing a developer is connected to all binaries the developer has contributed to and a node representing a binary is connected to all developers that contributed to it. Figure 5 shows an example of a contribution network with boxes representing binaries and circles representing developers. Major contribution edges are solid and minor contribution edges are dashed.

The field of social network analysis has developed a number of metrics that measure various attributes of nodes in a network. For instance, the degree of a node is the number of direct connections that it has and can be indicative of how important the node is within the local network. Other metrics measure how much information can flow through a node, the average distance from a node to all other nodes, how much "power" a node exerts over its neighbors, etc. An in-depth discussion of these metrics can be found in Wasserman and Faust [34]. Pinzger *et al.* found that these measures had a strong relationship with post-release failures in Windows Vista and in a prior study [6] we found that these measures were able to predict failures in ECLIPSE accurately as well.

Specifically, Pinzger *et al.* built a predictor for fault prone binaries using this method, it identified 90% of the fault prone binaries in Vista (recall) and 85% of the binaries that it classified as fault prone actually were (precision). This was a dramatic increase over the predictive power of prior methods that used source code metrics.

We adapted that study, and examined the effect of removing minor and major contributor edges. In Figure 5, such minor edges are indicated by the dashed lines. The topological effect of removing minor edges, as shown in Figure 5, is that many pairs of binaries that had short connecting paths through minor contributors are disconnected. Our findings focused on two key aspects of the results. First, we examined the correlation between social network measures and post-release failures in the complete network and the network with minor edges removed. Second, we measured the change in the ability of a predictor to identify fault prone binaries when removing major or minor contribution edges.

Table 3 shows the strength of relationship of six network measures with pre- and post-release failures. These particular metrics are chosen because they had the highest correlation with failures among those collected. Columns labelled with Minor shows the correlations of SNA metrics calculated on networks that contain only minor contribution edges and those labelled with Major shows correlations from networks of major contribution edges. For all metrics except for node degree, the networks that consider major contributions have dramatically lower correlations. In fact, for the case of Hierarchy, the sign of the correlation is negative, indicating that higher value of hierarchy in the major contribution networks were associated with fewer failures. These findings clearly indicate that the edges from minor contributors embody much of the important structure of the contributions graph. So much so that their removal results in a decrease in the discriminatory power of these metrics.

We also built a predictor from these measures for identifying fault prone binaries in Windows Vista and Windows 7 using the same approach as Pinzger *et al.* [29]. They trained a logistic regression model on a randomly chosen two thirds of the binaries in the contribution network and then evaluated the model based on its results when classifying the remaining third.

This process was repeated fifty times, each with a different random split of the data and the measures of performance, precision, recall, and F-score — standard measures of information retrieval [17] — were averaged across all runs.

Their original model based on the complete network identified 90% of the fault prone binaries and 85% of its fault prone predictions were correct (their evaluation was based on a prior Windows release). When the predictor was trained using the same methods on the network with minor contributors removed, it identified only 58% of the fault prone binaries and around 44% of its fault prone predictions were correct. In Pinzger's formulation of the prediction approach, random guessing would result in 50% for both measures. Thus a predictor based on network measures for a network containing major contributor only does marginally better than one that chose binaries purely at random. Table 4 shows the performance when a predictor is trained on the complete network as well as the networks with minor contributions removed and major contributions removed.

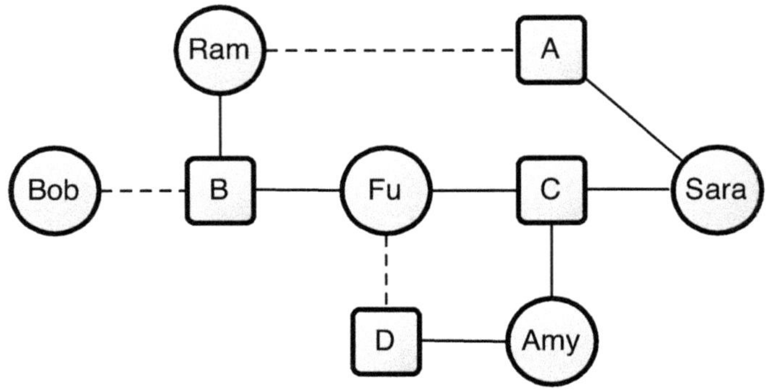

Figure 5: An example contribution network. Boxes represent binaries and circles represent developers who contributed to them. A dashed line between a binary and developer indicates a minor contributor relationship.

We also show results for pre-release failures in Vista as well as pre- and post-release failures for Windows 7. In all cases, models built on minor contributions performed better than those based on major contributions to a statistically significant degree. In the case of Vista post-release failures, minor contribution prediciton models perform better than models based on the entire network, and models based on the entire network were never statistically better than those based on minor contributions

We therefore conclude the minor contribution edges provide the "signal" used by defect predictors that are based on the contribution network. Without them, the ability to predict failure prone components is greatly diminished, further supporting our hypothesis that they are strongly related to software quality.

8. DISCUSSION

Our findings are valuable in a number of ways. We have shown that for both versions of Windows, ownership does indeed have a relationship with code quality. This observation is an actionable result, as this is an aspect of software development that can be controlled and monitored to some degree by management decisions on development process and policies. In all projects, the addition of MINOR improved the regression models for both pre- and post-release failures to a statistically significant degree. After controlling for known software quality factors, binaries with more minor contributors had more pre- and post-release failures in both versions of Windows. Thus *hypothesis 1 is empirically supported in both projects.*

The analysis of OWNERSHIP is a little bit different. In this case, we saw a small, but still statistically significant effect in pre- and post-release failures for Vista and pre-release failures for Windows 7. Part of this may be attributable to a moderate relationship between the MINOR and OWNERSHIP, but although OWNERSHIP was significant in all models when removing MINOR, the effect was smaller. Nonetheless, in all cases, higher values for OWNERSHIP was associated with lower numbers of failures. We therefore conclude that *hypothesis 2 is supported in the case of Windows Vista and in pre-release data for Windows 7.*

The results of empirical software engineering studies do

	Windows Vista						Windows 7					
	Pre-release			Post-release			Pre-release			Post-release		
SNA Metric	All	Minor	Major	All	Minor	Major	All	Minor	Major	All	Minor	Major
Precision	90%	87%	83%	75%	84%	44%	89%	88%	80%	12%	11%	8%
Recall	91%	93%	91%	82%	88%	58%	92%	93%	87%	66%	75%	61%
F-Score	91%	89%	87%	78%	86%	50%	90%	90%	84%	21%	20%	14%

Table 4: Performance of network based failure predictors for pre- and post-release failures for Vista and Windows 7

not always generalize to settings where a different process is used. The process that is used may dictate the effect of other factors on software quality as well. Therefore, when determining the applicability of a research result to a software project, the context of the study must be taken in account. Microsoft employs strong ownership practices and our results are much more likely to hold in other industrial settings where similar policies are in place. Examining the effect of ownership in contexts where ownership is not stressed as highly, such as in many open source software (OSS) projects, is an area of continued study as we attempt to understand the interaction between ownership, quality, and varying software processes.

For contexts in which strong ownership *is* practiced or where empirical studies are consistent with our own findings, we make the following recommendations regarding the development process based on our findings:

1. *Changes made by minor contributors should be reviewed with more scrutiny.* Changes made by minor contributors should be exposed to greater scrutiny than changes made by developers who are experienced with the source for a particular binary. When possible, major contributors should perform these code inspections. If a major contributor cannot perform all inspections, he or she should focus on inspecting changes by minor contributors.

2. *Potential minor contributors should communicate desired changes to developers experienced with the respective binary.* Often minor contributors to one binary are major contributors to a depending binary. Rather than making a desired change directly, these developers should contact a major contributor and communicate the desired change so that it can be made by someone who has higher levels of expertise.

3. *Components with low ownership should be given priority by QA resources.* Metrics such as MINOR and OWNERSHIP should be used in conjunction with source code based metrics to identify those binaries with a high potential for having many post-release failures. When faced with limited resources for quality-control efforts, these binaries should have priority.

It may not always be possible to follow these recommendations (for instance, in cases where too many potential contributors need changes to a component for one developer to handle), however they should be followed as much as possible within reason. These recommendations are currently being evaluated at Microsoft. We plan to investigate the relationship of the ownership measures used in this paper with software quality in other projects at Microsoft that differ in size and process domain (e.g. projects utilizing agile). Further, we plan to observe the results of projects that follow these recommendations.

9. CONCLUSION

We have examined the relationship between ownership and software quality in two large software development projects. We found that high levels of ownership, specifically operationalized as high values of OWNERSHIP and MAJOR, and low values of MINOR, are associated with less defects.

An investigation into the effects of minor and major contributions on network based defect prediction found that removing minor contribution edges severely impaired predictive power. We also found that when a component has a minor contributor, the same developer is a major contributor to a dependent component approximately half of the time, uncovering at least one significant reason for high levels of minor contributions. Changes to policies regarding tasks that would lead to this behavior, such as defect resolution and feature implementation, should be implemented and evaluated.

For organizations where ownership has a strong relationship with defects, we have presented recommendations which are currently being evaluated at Microsoft. As our measures of ownership are cheap and lightweight, we encourage other researchers and practitioners to perform and report their findings of similar analyses so that we can build a body of knowledge regarding ownership and quality in various domains and contexts.

10. REFERENCES

[1] R. Banker, G. Davis, and S. Slaughter. Software development practices, software complexity, and software maintenance performance: A field study. *Management Science*, 44(4):433–450, 1998.

[2] V. Basili and G. Caldiera. Improve Soft-ware Quality by Reusing Knowledge and Experience. *Sloan Management Review*, 37:55–55, 1995.

[3] V. Basili, G. Caldiera, and H. Rombach. The Goal Question Metric Approach. *Encyclopedia of Software Engineering*, 1:528–532, 1994.

[4] K. Beck and C. Andres. *Extreme Programming Explained: Embrace Change.* Addison-Wesley Reading, MA, 2005.

[5] C. Bird, N. Nagappan, P. Devanbu, H. Gall, and B. Murphy. Does distributed development affect software quality? an empirical case study of windows vista. In *Proc. of the International Conference on Software Engineering*, 2009.

[6] C. Bird, N. Nagappan, P. Devanbu, H. Gall, and B. Murphy. Putting it All Together: Using

Socio-Technical Networks to Predict Failures. In *Proceedings of the 17th International Symposium on Software Reliability Engineering*. IEEE Computer Society, 2009.

[7] W. Boh, S. Slaughter, and J. Espinosa. Learning from experience in software development: A multilevel analysis. *Management Science*, 53(8):1315–1331, 2007.

[8] F. Brooks. *The Mythical Man-Month: Essays on Software Engineering, 20th Anniversary Edition*. Addison-Wesley, 1995.

[9] M. Cataldo, P. Wagstrom, J. Herbsleb, and K. Carley. Identification of coordination requirements: implications for the Design of collaboration and awareness tools. *Proceedings of the 2006 20th anniversary conference on Computer supported cooperative work*, pages 353–362, 2006.

[10] B. Curtis, H. Krasner, and N. Iscoe. A field study of the software design process for large systems. *Communication of the ACM*, 31(11):1268–1287, 1988.

[11] E. Darr, L. Argote, and D. Epple. The acquisition, transfer, and depreciation of knowledge in service organizations: Productivity in franchises. *Management Science*, 41(11):1750–1762, 1995.

[12] S. Dowdy, S. Wearden, and D. Chilko. *Statistics for research*. John Wiley & Sons, third edition, 2004.

[13] K. El Emam, S. Benlarbi, N. Goel, and S. N. Rai. The confounding effect of class size on the validity of object-oriented metrics. *IEEE Transactions of Software Engineering*, 27(7):630–650, 2001.

[14] S. Elbaum and J. Munson. Code churn: A measure for estimating the impact of code change. In *Proceedings of the International Conference on Software Maintenance*, 1998.

[15] T. Fritz, G. Murphy, and E. Hill. Does a programmer's activity indicate knowledge of code? In *Proc. of the ACM SIGSOFT symposium on The foundations of software engineering*, page 350. ACM, 2007.

[16] R. Kraut and L. Streeter. Coordination in software development. *Communications of the ACM*, 38(3):69–81, 1995.

[17] F. W. Lancaster. *Information Retrieval Systems: Characteristics, Testing, and Evaluation*. Wiley, 2nd edition, 1979.

[18] D. W. McDonald and M. S. Ackerman. Expertise recommender: a flexible recommendation system and architecture. In *Proc. of the ACM conference on Computer supported cooperative work*, 2000.

[19] A. Meneely and L. A. Williams. Secure open source collaboration: an empirical study of linus' law. In *Proceedings of the ACM Conference on Computer and Communications Security*, 2009.

[20] R. Milo, N. Kashtan, S. Itzkovitz, M. E. J. Newman, and U. Alon. On the uniform generation of random graphs with prescribed degree sequences. *Arxiv preprint cond-mat/0312028*, 2003.

[21] A. Mockus. Succession: Measuring transfer of code and developer productivity. In *Proceedings of the 31st International Conference on Software Engineering*, 2009.

[22] A. Mockus and J. D. Herbsleb. Expertise browser: a quantitative approach to identifying expertise. In *Proc. of the 24th International Conference on Software Engineering*, 2002.

[23] A. Mockus and D. Weiss. Predicting risk of software changes. *Bell Labs Technical Journal*, 5(2):169–180, 2000.

[24] M. Molloy and B. Reed. A critical point for random graphs with a given degree sequence. *Random Struct. Algorithms*, 6(2-3):161–179, 1995.

[25] N. Nagappan and T. Ball. Use of relative code churn measures to predict system defect density. *Proceedings of the 27th International Conference on Software Engineering*, pages 284–292, May 2005.

[26] N. Nagappan, B. Murphy, and V. Basili. The influence of organizational structure on software quality: an empirical case study. In *Proc. of the 30th international conference on Software engineering*, 2008.

[27] M. E. J. Newman, S. H. Strogatz, and D. J. Watts. Random graphs with arbitrary degree distributions and their applications. *Phys. Rev. E*, 64(2):026118, Jul 2001.

[28] T. Ostrand, E. Weyuker, and R. Bell. Where the bugs are. In *Proceedings of the ACM SIGSOFT international symposium on Software testing and analysis*, 2004.

[29] M. Pinzger, N. Nagappan, and B. Murphy. Can developer-module networks predict failures? In *Proceedings of the 16th ACM SIGSOFT International Symposium on Foundations of software engineering*, 2008.

[30] F. Rahman and P. Devanbu. Ownership, Experience and Defects: a fine-grained study of Authorship. In *Proceedings ICSE 2011, To appear*, 2011.

[31] P. Robillard. The role of knowledge in software development. *Communications of the ACM*, 42(1):92, 1999.

[32] M. Sacks. *On-the-Job Learning in the Software Industry. Corporate Culture and the Acquisition of Knowledge*. Quorum Books, 88 Post Road West, Westport, CT 06881., 1994.

[33] A. Srivastava, J. Thiagarajan, and C. Schertz. Efficient Integration Testing using Dependency Analysis. Technical Report MSR-TR-2005-94, Microsoft Research, 2005.

[34] S. Wasserman and K. Faust. *Social network analysis: Methods and applications*. Cambridge University Press, 1994.

[35] E. J. Weyuker, T. J. Ostrand, and R. M. Bell. Do too many cooks spoil the broth? using the number of developers to enhance defect prediction models. *Empirical Softw. Engg.*, 13(5):539–559, 2008.

ReLink: Recovering Links between Bugs and Changes

Rongxin Wu†, Hongyu Zhang†, Sunghun Kim§ and S.C. Cheung§

†School of Software, Tsinghua University
Beijing 100084, China
wrx09@mails.tsinghua.edu.cn, hongyu@tsinghua.edu.cn

§Department of Computer Science and Engineering
The Hong Kong University of Science and Technology, Hong Kong, China
{hunkim, scc}@cse.ust.hk

ABSTRACT

Software defect information, including links between bugs and committed changes, plays an important role in software maintenance such as measuring quality and predicting defects. Usually, the links are automatically mined from change logs and bug reports using heuristics such as searching for specific keywords and bug IDs in change logs. However, the accuracy of these heuristics depends on the quality of change logs. Bird et al. found that there are many missing links due to the absence of bug references in change logs. They also found that the missing links lead to biased defect information, and it affects defect prediction performance.

We manually inspected the explicit links, which have explicit bug IDs in change logs and observed that the links exhibit certain features. Based on our observation, we developed an automatic link recovery algorithm, ReLink, which automatically learns criteria of features from explicit links to recover missing links. We applied ReLink to three open source projects. ReLink reliably identified links with 89% precision and 78% recall on average, while the traditional heuristics alone achieve 91% precision and 64% recall. We also evaluated the impact of recovered links on software maintainability measurement and defect prediction, and found the results of ReLink yields significantly better accuracy than those of traditional heuristics.

Categories and Subject Descriptors

D.2.7 [**Software Engineering**]: Distribution, Maintenance, and Enhancement–*Restructuring, reverse engineering, and reengineering,* D.2.8 [**Software Engineering**]: Metrics – *Product metrics*

General Terms

Bias, Measurement, Experimentation

Keywords

Mining software repository, missing links, data quality, bugs, changes.

Permission to make digital or hard copies of all or part of this work for personal or classroom use is granted without fee provided that copies are not made or distributed for profit or commercial advantage and that copies bear this notice and the full citation on the first page. To copy otherwise, or republish, to post on servers or to redistribute to lists, requires prior specific permission and/or a fee.
ESEC/FSE'11, September 5–9, 2011, Szeged, Hungary.
Copyright 2011 ACM 978-1-4503-0443-6/11/09...$10.00.

1. INTRODUCTION

Software defect information, including links between bug reports in bug tracking system and committed changes in source code repository, is the key information for software maintenance such as measuring software quality and predicting defects. It is possible to understand software maintenance efforts based on quality metrics derived from the links between bugs and changes, such as the percentage of buggy files [22, 33]. Defect information is also used to train models for defect prediction [17, 18, 33, 35, 36].

To collect links between bugs and changes automatically, many researchers mine bug reports in bug tracking systems and change logs in version archives. Heuristics traditionally used include searching for keywords (such as "Fixed" or "Bug") and bug IDs (such as "#42233") [5, 21, 27, 28, 33, 34] in change logs.

Recent studies revealed that these heuristics likely yield biased defect data, since they primarily rely on the comments in change logs [6, 7, 25]. Developers often maintain high quality change logs, but it is possible that they omit bug references in change logs. For example, when a developer fixes a bug in a revision, she may not document the fixed bug ID in the change log. Then, traditional heuristics miss the links between the bug and the change. As a result, defect information collected by traditional heuristics includes bias, especially lots of false negatives – missing links. Bird and Bachmann et al. confirmed this problem and reported that 54% of fixed bugs in the bug database are not linked to change logs [6, 7].

Unfortunately, these biased defect data affect software quality measurement and defect prediction performance. Bird et al. found that the BugCache algorithm [17] is sensitive to the biased data [7]. Kim et al. found that the change classification algorithm [16] is also sensitive to the biased data [18] when the number of instances is small. It is desirable to collect more accurate defect information by recovering the missing links.

To explore possibilities of recovering the missing links automatically, we conducted a qualitative study to identify characteristics of explicit links based on the bug IDs in change logs. We found that the links between bugs and changes exhibit certain features. For example, the bug-fixing time is close to the change-commit time, the change logs and the bug reports share textual similarity, and the developers responsible for a bug are typically the committers of the bug-fixing change.

Based on these findings, we propose an automatic link recovery algorithm, ReLink. Relink automatically learns satisfaction criteria of features from explicit links, and by applying the learned criteria it checks if the features of an unknown link satisfy the criteria. If the unknown link satisfies all the feature criteria, it is considered a valid link.

We have applied ReLink to three open source projects (ZXing, OpenIntents, and Apache) and two simulation studies (on Apache and Eclipse MAT). We have evaluated the recovered links by comparing them to the ground truth links, which are manually recovered and verified links. Our experimental results are promising: on average, for the three open source projects, ReLink recovered links with 78% recall and 89% precision, while the traditional heuristics can only identify links with 64% recall and 91% precision.

We have also evaluated the practical impact of defect information obtained by ReLink. We measured the effects of ReLink on several software maintainability metrics. We also built defect prediction models using defect information with/without ReLink. Our experimental results indicate ReLink has nontrivial positive impacts on the maintenance studies.

In summary, our paper makes the following contributions:

- We propose ReLink, an automatic link recovery algorithm. We also report our experimental evaluation of ReLink.
- We report an empirical study on measuring the impact of recovered links on maintenance studies, especially on software defect prediction.

The remainder of this paper is organized as follows. In Section 2, we describe the traditional heuristics for mining links and their main challenges. In Section 3, we present ReLink, the proposed approach to mining links. We evaluate the performance of ReLink in Section 4 and its practical effects on software maintenance studies in Section 5. Sections 6 and 7 discuss the threats to validity and the related work respectively. We conclude the paper in Section 8.

2. MINING LINKS: TRADITIONAL HEURISTICS

This section reviews the use of traditional heuristics to mine the links between bugs and changes. In addition, we evaluate the quality of links mined with traditional heuristics, and discuss the involved challenges.

2.1 Traditional Heuristics

During software maintenance, it is common that changes and bugs are recorded in version control systems (such as CVS and SVN) and bug tracking systems (such as BugZilla), respectively. Developers often maintain change logs describing what they have changed and what bugs they have dealt with.

Traditional heuristics to identify bug-fixing changes rely on the premise that *developers leave hints or links about bug fixes in the change logs*. They look for specific keywords such as 'fixed', 'bug', and for information linking to bugs such as bug ID references in change logs. These traditional heuristics are widely used to mark bug fixes, identify bug-introducing changes, and build defect prediction models [5, 14, 16, 21, 27, 28, 33, 34].

However, the results of traditional heuristics largely rely on the change log quality. Recently, Bird et al. [7] noticed that, only a fraction of bug fixes are labeled in change logs explicitly, and this causes systematic biases in finding the links. The biases can significantly reduce the effectiveness of the follow-up studies. To overcome this challenge, Bird et al. [8] developed a manual link recovery tool, LINKSTER. The manually recovered links might be much more accurate. However, the practice does not scale because it requires significant manual effort.

2.2 Evaluation of Traditional Heuristics

To evaluate traditional heuristics and measure the number of missing links, we performed a replication study of Bird et al.'s [7] on two Android open source projects. In this study, we adopted the traditional heuristics proposed by Bachmann and Bernstein [5]:

1) Scan through the change logs for bug IDs in a given format (e.g. "issue 681", "bug 239" and so on).
2) Exclude all false-positive bug numbers (e.g. "r420", "2009-05-07 10:47:39 -0400" and so on).
3) Check if there are other potential bug number formats or false positive number formats, add the new formats and scan the logs iteratively.
4) Check if potential bug numbers exist in the bug-tracking database with their status marked as fixed.

Based on these heuristics we mined the links between change logs and bug reports. Then, we measured the number of fixed bugs successfully linked to change logs, as well as the number of links identified.

The two projects, ZXing[1] and OpenIntents[2], which we studied are highly active Android projects. ZXing is a barcode image-processing library for Android-based phones, and OpenIntents is an open intents library. Table 1 shows the results of the replication study. For ZXing, only 40.7% (55 out of 135) of the fixed bugs were found linked to change logs and 48.2% of the links were identified. Similarly, only 54 out of 101 bugs were linked to change logs for OpenIntents and 67.4% links were identified. Our results are consistent with Bird et al.'s results for Apache project [6]. They showed that 256 out of 559 (46%) bugs were linked and there were many missing links. In the next section, we briefly discuss the reasons of having missing links and the challenges of using traditional heuristics.

Table 1: Linking results of the traditional heuristics

Project	Revi-sions	# Fixed Bugs	% Linked Bugs	# Links	% Links Identified
ZXing	1-1694	135	40.7%	143	48.2%
OpenIntents	1-2890	101	53.5%	129	67.4%

2.3 Challenges

As shown in Table 1, there is a large number of bugs that cannot be linked to the committed changes by traditional heuristics. However, the results do not necessarily mean these bugs are not associated with any committed changes. We manually investigated the unlinked bugs and identified the following reasons that cause missing links:

Missing bug reference in change logs

Since leaving explicit bug reference in change logs is optional to developers, it is possible that developers do not write related bug IDs after they have fixed bugs. In this case, traditional heuristics fail to identify links between change logs and bugs. For example,

[1] http://code.google.com/p/zxing/

[2] http://www.openintents.org/

consider the change log[3] and the bug report[4] in Figure 1, which are taken from the ZXing project. There are no bug ID references in the change log therefore traditional heuristics cannot identify which bug the revision 148 has fixed.

However, our manual examination found that this change log can be actually linked to a bug report: we searched through all bug reports and found that the bug report #18 contained similar problem descriptions as the change log. Also, we noticed that there was a bug-fixing comment made for bug #18 on Jan 22, 2008, by the developer "srowen@gmail.com". The revision #148 was also committed on Jan 22, 2008 by the author "srowen". Therefore, it is likely that the revision #148 is linked to bug #18 (we also checked the source code and confirmed this link). The commonalities give an indicator of the link between the bug and the change. They provide clues to recover the missing link.

Change Log (Revision: 148; Author: srowen; Date: Jan 22, 2008)
Name of midlet is "ZXingMIDlet", not "ZXingMidlet"!

Bug Report (Issue 18; Status: Fixed)**:**
Reported by herf...@yahoo.com, Jan 11, 2008
Issue 18: does not work on nokia 5300

Comment 1 by project member srowen@gmail.com, Jan 11, 2008
Which version, regular or basic? ...
...
Comment 3 by herf...@yahoo.com, Jan 12, 2008
I tested both of them (regular and basic) but in both case it just make an exception...
...
Comment 5 by project member srowen@gmail.com, Jan 22, 2008
...The class is called "ZXingMIDlet" but the exception mentions "ZXingMidlet" (note different capitalization). It looks like the manifest file I wrote gets this wrong. ...

Comment 6 by project member srowen@gmail.com, Jan 22, 2008
I think I have fixed this particular problem by correcting...
Can you try the most recent version from...

Figure 1: An example of missing links

Irregular bug reference formats

The traditional heuristics, such as Bachmann and Bernstein's approach [5], search for patterns in change logs using regular expressions (e.g. "issue 681", "bug 239" and so on). However, our manual examination found that developers used many different ways to give bug references in change logs, such as "solve problem 681", "Fixed for #239", "see #149", "for ~~Issue 143~~" ("Issue 143" is strikethrough and marked-up in HTML), etc. Developers may also occasionally make typos such as "fic 239" [23]. The format may even vary across change logs within the same project, as different open source contributors may have their own preferences. It is not easy to develop a single, generic tool to support all possible bug reference formats.

The above analysis motivates us to develop a new link recovery algorithm. In our approach, we identify features of links between bugs and changes, and apply them to recover the missing links.

[3] http://code.google.com/p/zxing/source/detail?r=148

[4] http://code.google.com/p/zxing/issues/detail?id=18

3. RELINK: RECOVERING LINKS BETWEEN BUGS AND CHANGES

In this section, we present ReLink, a new approach to recovering the links between bugs and changes.

3.1 Features of Links

Our approach is based on the identification of features of the links between bugs and changes. First, we identify explicit links, which are links that can be discovered by traditional heuristics. We then analyze the features of these links. Through this analysis, we have identified the following features, which can be later used to recover the missing links:

Time Interval: This is the interval between the time (t_f) when a bug was fixed as given by its bug report and the time (t_c) when the corresponding bug fix was committed at the code repository. The interval ($t_f - t_c$) is a useful feature because it leverages the knowledge that a bug should be fixed after its creation and before its closure. After developers have committed the code change for a bug fix (at time t_c), they are obliged to update the bug report (at time t_f) that the bug has been fixed. Therefore, t_f should be greater than but close to t_c for a linked bug and its committed code change.

Bug Owner and Change Committer: For linked bugs and changes, there exists a mapping between the bug owner and the change committer. Ideally, the committer who makes the bug-fixing changes should be the person who is responsible for fixing the bug. It is also possible that the change committer and the bug owner are different persons, but the mapping between them could be identified by mining the software repositories (which will be discussed in Section 3.2.2).

Text Similarity: This is the textual similarity between bug reports and change logs. For linked bugs and changes, the natural language descriptions in the bug report are often similar to those in the change logs, as they may refer to the same issue and share similar keywords.

3.2 Mining Features of Links

3.2.1 The Interval between the Bug-fixing time and the Change-Commit Time

Although the interval between bug-fixing time and the commit time is a useful feature for mining links, determining the length of such an interval is a nontrivial task. We observed from our empirical studies that developers do not always change the status of bugs to "Fixed" in the bug tracking system immediately after they have committed the bug-fixing changes. For example, we investigated the explicit links of the ZXing project mined by traditional heuristics, and observed when developers change the bugs' status to "Fixed" after the bug-fixing change is committed. We found that for 20% of explicit links, their bug-fixing time and change-commit time differ by more than one day. The bug-fixing time and the change-commit time could be far apart. Our first research challenge is therefore to determine the actual bug-fixing time from each bug report.

With further investigations, we found that most bug comments are related to bug-fixing activities, as developers often post comments to the bug tracking system to report a bug fix and notify the bug reporter. Therefore, we could determine the bug-fixing time according to the time of comments in bug reports. For example, consider the change log and the bug report in Figure 1. The revision #148 was committed on Jan 22, 2008. There was also a bug-fixing comment made for bug #18 on Jan 22, 2008, by the change committer ("srowen").

We also empirically verified the time interval feature using the explicit links. For ZXing and OpenIntents, on average, each bug received 2-3 comments. For more than 93% of the links, the intervals between bug-comment time and the change-commit time were less than 24 hours. For more than 96% of the links, the intervals were less than one week. The results indicate that in most cases, the change-commit time is close to a bug-comment time.

3.2.2 *Mapping between Bug Owners and Change Committers*

When bugs are assigned to a certain developer to fix, the developer information P_b is recorded by bug tracking systems. When bug-fixing changes are committed, the committer information P_c is recorded by version control systems. In our empirical studies, we compared the change committers and the bug report owners for linked bugs and changes. We found that they may not have the same names. This is because developers may use different login names in different scenarios. It is also possible that there is an appointed person in the team to confirm bug fixes and change bug status. Table 2 gives some examples for the identified mappings between committers and bug owners.

Table 2: Examples of the mapping between bug owners and change committers

Bug Owner P_b	Change Committer P_c	Project
dswitkin@gmail.com	dswitkin	ZXing
dswitkin@google.com	dswitkin@google.com	ZXing
srowen@gmail.com	srowen	ZXing
peli0101@googlemail.com	peli0101	Openintents
Will Rowe	wrowe	Apache
Erik Abele	erikabele	Apache

To identify the mappings between bug owners and change committers, we again examined the comments in bug reports. Our empirical studies found that developers often actively discuss bug-related issues and announce bug fixes via the bug tracking system. Therefore, it is likely that one of the commenters is the bug owner who is responsible for bug fixing. For example, in the ZXing project, for 99% of links that are found by traditional heuristics, the developers who committed bug-fixing changes posted bug comments in the bug tracking system. In the OpenIntents project, all developers who fixed bugs posted comments in the bug reports.

3.2.3 *The Similarity between Bug Reports and Change Logs*

Information Retrieval (IR) technology is commonly used to process textual documents in natural languages. In this project, we treat bug reports and change logs as texts and compare their similarities.

It is expected that for linked bugs and changes, bug reports and change logs exhibit certain similarity. To compute the similarity between bug reports and change logs, we first extract text features. Our approach adopts the Vector Space Model (VSM), a widely used model in IR technology [9]. In VSM, a document is represented as an n dimension vector $<w_1, w_2, w_3, \ldots w_n>$, where n is the number of distinct terms and w_i ($1 \leq w_i \leq n$) represents the weight of a unique term.

One of the most important issues in text processing is to select appropriate terms to represent the entire documents. In our case, the number of terms in bug reports and change logs could be large. To select the representative terms, we use the following steps to help reduce dimensions:

1) Remove stop words. Stop words are the words that have no strong meaning, such as "a", "an", "the" and so on.
2) Use one term to represent all other terms that have the same stemmer. For example, the tokens "fixing", "fixes", and "fixed" all share the same root "fix", thus we use "fix" to represent the others.
3) Use one term to represent all synonymous words. We apply the tool WordNet [12] to facilitate the selection of the synonymous words. For example, according to the definitions in the WordNet dictionary, the words "additional" and "extra" are synonymous words, therefore we can replace "additional" with "extra".

After selecting the terms in bug reports and change logs, we then calculate the weight for each term. In our approach, we use Term Frequency-Inverse Document Frequency (TFIDF) metric [9] to calculate the weight. The basic idea of TFIDF is that the weight w_i of a term in a document increases with its occurrence frequency in the specific document and decreases with its occurrence frequency in other documents. Formally:

$$w_i = tf_i \times idf_i \qquad (1)$$

where tf_i represents the occurrence frequency of the term t_i in the specific document, and idf_i represents the inverse document frequency, defined as:

$$idf_i = \log \frac{|D|}{|\{d : t_i \in d\}|} \qquad (2)$$

where $|D|$ represents the number of documents and $|\{d: t_i \in d\}|$ represents the number of documents that contain the i-th index term. We use the above formulas to extract features from all bug reports and change logs, and to compute the n dimension vector.

After obtaining the vector space model using TFIDF, we measure the similarity between a bug report and a change log using the Cosine similarity measure [9]:

$$Sim = \frac{\sum_{i=1}^{n} w_{1i} w_{2i}}{\sqrt{\sum_{i=1}^{n} w_{1i}^2 \times \sum_{i=1}^{n} w_{2i}^2}} \qquad (3)$$

It is expected that the linked bug reports and change logs share certain text similarity, thus the larger the Cosine similarity measure, the more a link is likely to be valid.

3.3 Learning Criteria of Features

In this section, we describe how we determine the thresholds of features so that these features can characterize most of the real links. Such thresholds can be treated as criteria for determining links – if the features of an unknown link satisfy the criteria, the link is likely to be valid. Otherwise it is irrelevant and should be removed.

Determining the criteria of features is nontrivial. For example, a lower threshold enables us to relate more fixed bugs and committed changes, but the links identified contain more false positives. On the other hand, a higher threshold can reduce false positives, but less missing-links could be identified.

To determine the criteria of features, we learn from the explicit links that can be identified through traditional heuristics (*Le*). For the time interval feature and the text similarity feature, their values vary independently. When these two features are applied to *Le*, different values can result in selecting different sets of links and lead to different F-measures. We propose a search-based algorithm, which exhaustively searches for the optimal combination of these two values so that the maximum F-measure can be achieved. Figure 2 shows our algorithm for determining the threshold values of these two features.

```
DetermineThresholds (Le: links between bugs and changes identified by the traditional heuristics)
1  Assign the time interval T with a small initial value T0
2  Assign the text similarity threshold S with a small initial
     value S0
3  Select links in Le that satisfy T and S, and compute
       F-measure
4  Increase S by a small step s1
5  Repeat steps 3-4 until the maximum threshold Sm is reached
6  Increase T by a small step s2
7  Repeat steps 3-6 until T reaches the maximum threshold Tm
8  Choose the threshold values Tt and St that achieve the best
     F-measure (if ties exist, choose the first occurrence of
     Tt and St)
9  Return Tt and St
```

Figure 2: Determining the thresholds of features

In our experimentation, we specify T_0=1, $s2$=1, and T_m = 30, which means that we try the time interval from 1 day to 30 days. We specify S_0=0, $s1$=0.01, and S_m = 1, which means that we try from text similarity 0 to 1, with steps of 0.01. In total, our algorithm executes at most 30*100 times, in which we search for the combination of *S* and *T* that maximizes F-measure. Based on the identified optimal values T_t and S_t, a criterion is formed: *a link is considered irrelevant if its time interval and text similarity values are above the thresholds.*

```
DetermineMappings (Le: links between bugs and changes identified by the traditional heuristics)
1  Initialize the set of mappings M=Φ
2  For each link l in Le
3          For each mapping m between l's change committer
             and bug commenter
4                  If (m is not in M)
5                          Add m to M
6                  EndIf
7          EndFor
8  EndFor
9  Return M
```

Figure 3: Determining the mappings between bug owners and change committer

We also learn the mappings between bug owners and change committers from the explicit links identified by the traditional heuristics. We extract all relationships between a bug commenter and a change committer and form the mapping set. The algorithm is described in Figure 3. The criterion for this feature is: *a link is considered irrelevant if none of its bug commenters is mapped to its change committer.*

3.4 Recovering the Missing Links

A large and evolving project tends to contain a lot of fixed bugs and committed changes. This results in a large number of potential links between bugs and changes. Furthermore, there are also many types of relationships between bugs and changes (as illustrated in Figure 4):

- one to one: one bug could be fixed by one change;
- many to many: one bug could be fixed by multiple changes, and one change could fix multiple bugs
- no relationship: a change could be a non-bug fixing change, thus it does not link to any bug.

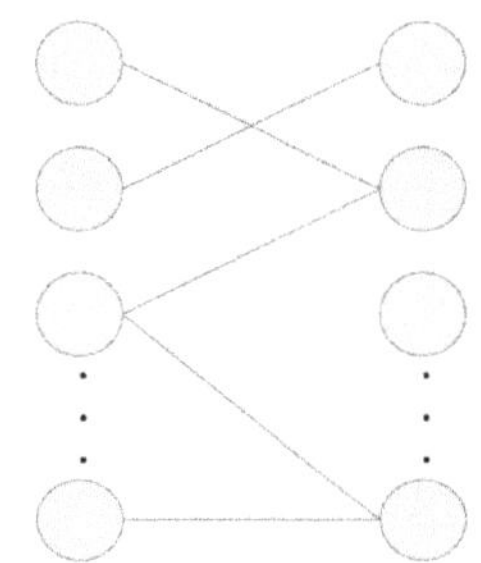

Figure 4: The relationships between bugs and changes

```
1   Store all possible links between bugs and links in L
2   Initialize the set Lr =Φ
3   Mine links Le between bugs and changes using
      the traditional heuristics
4   DetermineThresholds (Le)
5   DetermineMappings(Le)
6   For each link l in (L – Le)
7       If there is mapping between l's bug commenter and l's
          change committer
8           If any of l's bug comment time is within the time
              interval threshold Tt
9               If the text similarity between l's bug report and
                  change log is within threshold St
10                  add l to Lr
11              EndIf
12          EndIf
13      EndIf
14  EndFor
15  Return Lr + Le
```

Figure 5: The ReLink algorithm

To automatically identify the links between bugs and changes, we propose a link recovery approach, ReLink. ReLink is based on the identified features. The algorithm of ReLink is described in Figure

5: we first determine the satisfaction criteria of features by applying the algorithms described in Figures 2 and 3 (lines 3-5). The criteria include the time interval between the bug-fixing time and the change-commit time, the text similarity threshold, and the mappings between the bug owners and the change committers. ReLink automatically learns the criteria from the explicit links that can be identified by traditional heuristics. For each unknown link that cannot be identified by traditional heuristics (line 6), ReLink checks if the link satisfies all criteria (lines 7-9). If it satisfies, we consider it a valid link (line 10). After checking all the unknown links, ReLink returns the recovered set of links between bugs and changes (line 15). The overall process of ReLink is also illustrated in Figure 6.

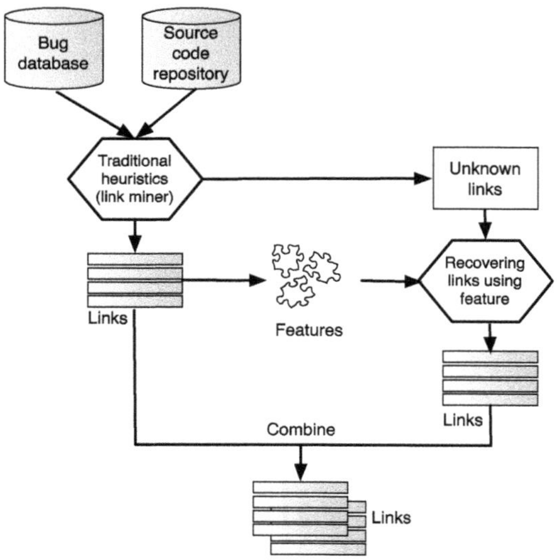

Figure 6: The overall process of ReLink

4. EVALUATION

This section presents evaluation results of ReLink.

4.1 Subject Projects and Experimental Setup

We investigated two projects as shown in Table 1. These two projects (ZXing and OpenIntents) are highly active Android projects hosted by Google Code. We collected their change logs from the SVN repository and bug reports from the Google Code issue tracking system. To obtain the ground truth (the "golden set") of the links, we manually read change logs, bug reports, and the corresponding code changes to establish links between changes and bug reports. The manual annotation was performed by two people: one identifying the links and the other verifying the results.

We also experimented with the Apache dataset that was provided by Bachmann and Bird et al. [6]. In the Apache dataset, the links between defects and bugs were manually annotated by an Apache core developer (Justin Erenkrantz) using the LINKSTER tool [6]. We treated this dataset as a "golden set" and used it to evaluate the performance of ReLink.

To further evaluate the performance of ReLink when the bug IDs are absent from change logs, we conducted a simulation study as follows: we first collect a high quality dataset with most of the links identified, and then intentionally remove bug IDs in 50% of the change logs. Traditional heuristics fail to identify the links associated with these changes due to the absence of the bug IDs. We evaluate the performance of ReLink on recovering these missing links. We choose the Apache project and the Eclipse Memory Analyzer (MAT)[5] project in this simulation experiment as they have a high percentage of linked bugs. To overcome the randomness introduced by the 50% sampling, we perform the simulation experiment 10 times and compute the average results.

To facilitate the experiments, we have developed a tool for ReLink. The tool automatically collects information from source code repository and bug tracking system, builds the links between bugs and changes, and outputs the identified links. It is developed in Java, and runs on Windows and Linux. It consists of more than 10K lines of code.

4.2 Evaluation Metrics

Our experiments can lead to four kinds of results: a link we identify is a true link (*TP*), a link we identify is not a true link (*FP*), a link we miss is a true link (*FN*), and a link we miss is not a true link (*TN*). We use Recall, Precision, and F-measure as evaluation metrics. The definitions of these metrics are as follows:

- Precision = $\frac{TP}{TP+FP}$

This metric indicates how accurate the experiment result is.

- Recall = $\frac{TP}{TP+FN}$

This metric indicates the coverage of the experiment result.

- F-measure = $\frac{2 \times Precision \times Recall}{Precision + Recall}$

This metric takes the precision and the recall into consideration. It is a combined metric. In this study, we adopt the F1 metric, which weights precision and recall equally [32].

4.3 Evaluation Results

4.3.1 Comparisons to the Golden Set

Table 3 shows the experimental results for the three projects we investigated.

The ZXing project contains 135 fixed bugs. For the traditional approach, we adopted the heuristics proposed by Bachmann and Bernstein [5] and identified links for 57 (42.2%) fixed bugs without any false positives. Our approach, ReLink, identified links for 95 (70.4%) fixed bugs with 10% false positives. In ZXing, there are 143 links between bugs and changes. ReLink can successfully identify 107 links among them, leading to a Recall of 74.8%, which is much higher than that achieved by the traditional heuristics. The precision of ReLink is 0.9, which is marginally lower than that of the traditional approach. In terms of the F-measure, ReLink also outperforms the traditional approach (0.820 vs. 0.651).

For OpenIntents project, the percentage of linked bugs found by ReLink is 4% more than that of the traditional heuristics. There are 129 links between bugs and changes in the project. ReLink successfully recovered 95 of them. Compared to the traditional heuristics, the Recall is improved by almost 10%. Both approaches can achieve high precisions, with ReLink resulting in a better overall F-measure.

---

[5] http://www.eclipse.org/mat/

Table 3: Evaluation results

Project	Period	Revisions	#Fixed Bugs	Approach	% Linked Bugs	Recovery Links		
						Precision	Recall	F-measure
ZXing	11/2007-12/2010	1-1694	135	Traditional	42.2%	1.0 (69/69)	0.482 (69/143)	0.651
				ReLink	70.4%	0.90 (107/118)	0.748 (107/143)	0.820
OpenIntents	12/2007-12/2010	1-2890	101	Traditional	69.3%	1.0 (87/87)	0.674 (87/129)	0.805
				ReLink	73.3%	1.0 (95/95)	0.731 (95/129)	0.847
Apache	11/2004-4/2008	76294-899841	686	Traditional	77.1%	0.746 (791/1060)	0.764 (791/1035)	0.755
				ReLink	89.8%	0.747 (904/1210)	0.873 (904/1035)	0.805
Apache Simulation	11/2004-4/2008	76294-899841	686	Traditional	38.2%	0.741	0.375	0.498
				ReLink	53.0%	0.682	0.523	0.592
Eclipse MAT Simulation	4/2008-2/2011	10-1070	108	Traditional	49.1%	1	0.418	0.582
				ReLink	96.3%	0.858	0.623	0.718

For Apache project, the golden set identified by the Apache developer contains 1035 links between bugs and changes. ReLink successfully recovered 904 links, while the traditional heuristics recovered only 791 links. ReLink improves the Precision as well, leading to a better F-measure (0.805).

The experimental results confirm that ReLink can achieve better overall performance than the traditional heuristics.

4.3.2 Simulation Study

For the Apache simulation study, traditional heuristics lead to an average recall of 0.375 due to the removal of bug IDs from 50% of change logs. ReLink can achieve a much higher recall of 0.523. This is because ReLink uses feature criteria to identify links. Overall, the traditional heuristics lead to F-measure 0.498, while ReLink achieves F-measure 0.592.

For the Eclipse MAT simulation study, traditional heuristics lead to a low recall of 0.418 due to the removal of bug IDs from 50% of change logs. ReLink can achieve a much higher recall of 0.623. Overall, the traditional heuristics lead to F-measure 0.582, while ReLink achieves F-measure 0.718, a significant improvement.

For the simulation studies, Table 3 only shows the average results of 10 simulations. We also performed the paired-sample t-test to check if the F-measures with ReLink were statistically significantly better than the traditional heuristics. The t-test results confirmed that ReLink can lead to better F-measures than the traditional heuristics, at significance level 0.01. All simulation results confirm that ReLink can recover links with reasonable accuracy.

4.4 Discussion

Traditional heuristics identify links for a certain percentage of bugs, but they fail to identify links for the bugs that have no bug ID references in committed changes. As our experimental results show, ReLink is more effective to recover the links between bugs and changes than the traditional heuristics. ReLink can significantly reduce false negatives (missing links) – Table 3 shows that the recall values of ReLink are 6%-26% higher than those of traditional heuristics. The higher recall values are achieved because ReLink can identify links even the bug IDs are missing from the change logs, or the bug reference formats are irregular. Unlike traditional heuristics, ReLink does not use regular expressions to search for links. Instead, it identifies features of links and checks the satisfiability of unknown links. The performance of ReLink (measured in terms of F-measure) is better than that of traditional methods for all studied projects.

Still ReLink may introduce false negatives. For example, Table 3 shows that ReLink missed 25.2% of links in ZXing and 26.9% links in OpenIntents. We found two major reasons for false negatives. One reason is that there are no similar keywords between bug reports and change logs for some links, causing very low text similarity. Thus ReLink discards these links as irrelevant. The other reason is that some bugs have long intervals between the change-commit time and the bug-fixing time. As a result, these bugs fail to satisfy the time interval threshold. Figure 7 shows such an example in OpenIntents. The change for fixing the bug 217 was committed on Aug 22, 2009. The status of the bug 217 was not updated to "Fixed" until Sep 22, 2009. Note that, all these missing links are not identifiable by traditional heuristics either.

Change Log (Revision: 2293; Author: rmceoin; Date: Aug 22, 2009)
OI Safe: large patch, added Search activty, completely redid autolock, added preference 'Lock on screen lock' with default of true....

Bug Report (Issue 217; Status: fixed)**:**
What steps will reproduce the problem?
1: Unlock OI Safe...
2: Leave screen on PassEdit
...
After step 6, screen should auto-lock.

Comment 1 by project member rmceoin@gmail.com,Mar 10,2009
...Also fails with PassView.

Comment 2 by project member rmceoin@gmail.com,Sep 22,2009
...Status: Fixed

Figure 7: An example of false negative cases

Change Log (Revision: 99398; Author: trawick; Date: Apr 17, 2003)
merge this fix into 2.0.46-dev:\n\n ... PR 18649 [Justin Erenkrantz, Jeff Trawick]
Bug Report (bug 18649; Status: closed):
...enable-layout broken in 2.0.45. In 2.0.45, --enable-layout no longer works...

Figure 8: An example of false positive cases

Bachmann et al. [6] also discovered that, some bugs in Apache projects are actually "bugs incognito", i.e., these bugs were only discussed in developer mailing list and were not stored/tracked using bug track systems. Like traditional heuristics, ReLink cannot discover links for this type of bugs either. Mining mailing lists and recovering more links remain as future work.

ReLink may also introduce false positives. We manually examined these false positives in Table 3. We found that the false positives of ReLink in the Apache project overlapped largely with those identified by traditional heuristics. These links were incorrectly identified due to reasons such as merge of changes. Figure 8 shows an example of false positive case in Apache introduced by the merge of changes. Revision 99398 was actually a merge of the bug fix (PR 18649) found in version 2.0.45 into a new version (2.0.46).

There are ways to reduce ReLink's number of false positives. For example, we can modify the ReLink algorithm (before line 15 in Figure 5) to let it double-check the links *Le* mined by the traditional heuristics - if a link *l* in *Le* does not satisfy the feature criteria, ReLink considers *l* an irrelevant link and removes it. We have compared the performance of the revised ReLink (called ReLink-), ReLink and traditional heuristics for the Apache project. The results are shown in Figure 9. ReLink- can achieve better precision than the other two methods. However, the recall of ReLink- is lower because of the tradeoff between recall and precision. Overall, ReLink-'s F-measure is better than that of the traditional heuristics, but slightly worse than ReLink. Investigating techniques that can further reduce the number of false positives and at the same time improve the recall value will be our important future work.

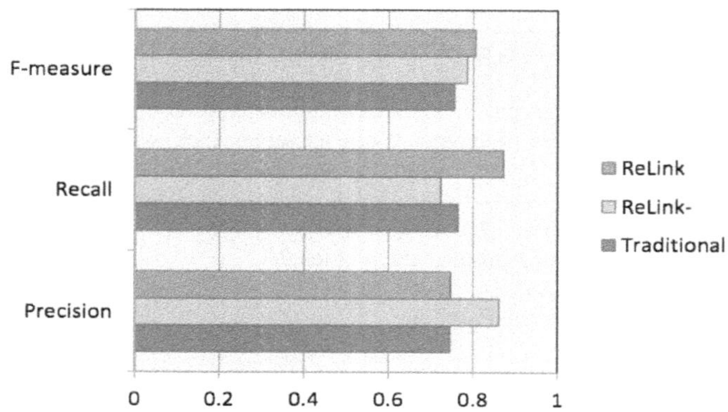

Figure 9: The performance of ReLink-

5. Practical Effects of ReLink

We have shown that ReLink can identify the links between bugs and changes more accurately than the traditional heuristics. The immediate next question would be the practical effects of the results. In this section, we show the implications of our results on software maintenance studies, especially on maintainability measurement and defect prediction.

5.1 Implications of Results on Maintainability Measurement

Many maintenance metrics have been proposed to understand maintenance activities and measure software maintainability. For example:

- The percentage of bug-fixing changes [15, 16, 21]: changes can be classified into many categories such as corrective changes (for bug fixing), adaptive changes (e.g., for accommodating new features), and perfective changes (e.g., for refactoring). Knowing the percentage of bug-fixing changes can help understand maintenance efforts spent on bug-fixing activities.
- The percentage of buggy files [33]: this is the percentage of defective files (files containing at least one bug). It can help measure software quality.
- Mean Time to Fix [22]: this is to measure the average time a team spends on fixing a bug. It can help measure a maintenance team's bug-fixing ability. The time spent for fixing a bug is calculated as the interval between bug report open time and bug-fixing change commit time.

Table 4. The comparisons of measurement data

Project	Linking approaches	%Bug-fixing changes	%Buggy files	Mean Time to Fix(days)
ZXing	Golden	8.1% (138/1694)	29.6% (118/399)	7.5
	Traditional	4.0% (67/1694)	14.8% (59/399)	10.2
	ReLink	6.3% (107/1694)	20.8% (83/399)	7.3
OpenIntents	Golden	4.2% 121/2890	4.9% (36/742)	25.1
	Traditional	2.9% (83/2890)	2.6% (19/742)	21.2
	ReLink	3.3% (94/2890)	4.0% (30/742)	25.1
Apache	Golden	2.3% (976/43167)	50.5% (98/194)	159.7
	Traditional	1.7% (753/43167)	47.9% (93/194)	178.9
	ReLink	2.0% (866/43167)	52.1% (101/194)	153.9

These metrics can be derived from the links between bugs and changes. After identifying the links, we know which bugs/changes are linked and which are not. Therefore we can collect the corresponding data and compute the metrics. As the quality of links collected by ReLink is higher than that collected by the traditional heuristics, we can obtain better measurement data for the above-mentioned metrics. Table 4 shows the measurement data we collected for the studied projects using the traditional heuristics and ReLink. We can see that the measures derived from links obtained by ReLink are closer to the actual ones, while the measures obtained by traditional heuristics contain larger discrepancies. For example, for ZXing, the actual percentage of bug-fixing changes is 8.1%. The measures derived from ReLink and traditional heuristics are 6.3% and 4.0% respectively. The ZXing team's actual mean time to fix value is 7.5 days per bug. The measures derived from ReLink and traditional heuristics are 7.3 and 10.2 respectively. Clearly ReLink leads to more accurate measurement, thus it helps project teams better understand and plan their maintenance activities.

5.2 Defect Prediction with Relink

To measure the impact of ReLink on software defect prediction, we built commonly-used file level defect prediction models using defect data collected from traditional heuristics and ReLink, and measured the performance of the models to predict ground truth defects.

5.2.1 Data Collection

We collected metric data and defect data for the studied projects, and built a classification model to predict the defect-proneness of the files. The metric data includes file-level static code complexity measures collected by the *Understand for Java/Understand for C++* tool[6], such as lines of code, cyclomatic complexity, average lines of comments, etc. The defect data contains buggy instances (files) collected through analyzing the identified links between bugs and changes.

The *buggy* and *clean* labels are assigned based on links between change logs and bugs. If a commit is linked to a bug, we assume the files in the commit are buggy. To label files, we use the links obtained from three different approaches: traditional heuristics, ReLink, and the ground truth. Table 5 summarizes the datasets used in this experiment. The datasets contain different percentages of buggy files. For example, the ZXing project contains 399 files, among which 29.6% of the files are buggy in the "Golden" (ground truth) dataset, 14.8% files are buggy in the "Traditional" dataset, and 20.8% files are buggy in the "ReLink" dataset.

Table 5. Defect Prediction Dataset

Subject	Version	# of files	# of metrics	Linking approaches	% of buggy
ZXing	1.6	399	41	Traditional	14.8%
				ReLink	20.8%
				Golden	29.6%
Open-Intents	Revision 1088~2073	56	41	Traditional	10.7%
				ReLink	28.6%
				Golden	39.3%
Apache	2.0	194	60	Traditional	57.2%
				ReLink	46.9%
				Golden	50.5%

5.2.2 Prediction and Evaluation Models

After collecting the metric data and buggy labels, we built a classification model using a popular machine-learning algorithm, Decision Tree (J48 in the Weka implementation [31, 32]).

We adopted the 10-fold cross validation technique to train and evaluate the model. When the 9-fold is used as a training set, we used the labels from three datasets: Traditional, ReLink, and Golden. However, for the 1-fold (test set), we used the labels obtained from the Golden set, which are manually recovered ground truth links (Figure 10). Note that the ultimate goal of defect prediction is to identify ground truth (actual) defects.

Since the performance may vary based on instances in each fold, we ran this 10-fold cross validation model 100 times (100 10-fold), and computed the average performance. To measure the prediction model's performance, we used the standard measures such as Precision, Recall, and F-measure [32].

5.2.3 Results

Table 6 presents the prediction results using three different approaches. The prediction performance of using ReLink is much better than that of using traditional heuristics. For example, the F-measure with Traditional is 0.257 for OpenIntents, while the F-measure with ReLink is 0.706, a significant improvement. Similarly, for ZXing, the F-measure with ReLink is 0.325, while F-measure with Traditional is only 0.171. For Apache, ReLink also improved the prediction accuracy.

We have also performed the paired-sample t-test to check if the improvements in F-measures are statistically significant. The t-test results confirmed that they are statistically significant, at the 99% confidence level (p-value < 0.01).

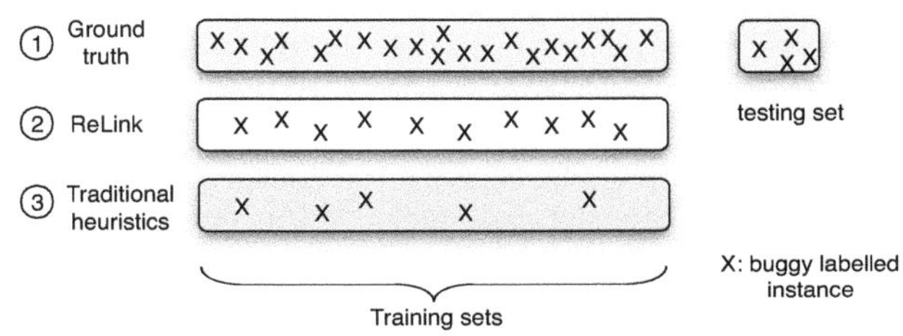

Figure 10: An example of false positive cases

Table 6. Prediction Results (Decision Tree)

Subject	Linking approaches	Precision	Recall	F-measure
ZXing	Traditional	0.346	0.114	0.171
	ReLink	0.432	0.261	0.325
	Golden	0.476	0.435	0.454
Open-Intents	Traditional	0.405	0.188	0.257
	ReLink	0.779	0.645	0.706
	Golden	0.742	0.683	0.711
Apache	Traditional	0.672	0.727	0.698
	ReLink	0.716	0.748	0.731
	Golden	0.709	0.713	0.711

These results clearly indicate that the defect information collected by ReLink improves the defect prediction performance. However, we noticed that the improvement varies across projects. For example, ReLink significantly improved the prediction accuracy of ZXing, while the improvement of Apache seems marginal. There are a few possible explanations for these results. First, as we showed in Table 3, the quality of Apache change logs is decent. As a result, traditional heuristics can mine links with reasonable accuracy. Basically, the quality of Apache defect information derived by traditional heuristics and that by ReLink do not have huge differences. Note that ReLink is still able to improve the prediction accuracy because of the more accurate defect information derived.

ReLink significantly improved the prediction performance of OpenIntents. As we showed in Table 3, ReLink is able to recover

[6] http://www.scitools.com/

many links missed by traditional heuristics. In addition, the number of instances of OpenIntents is small. As we also found in a recent study [18], prediction models for a subject with a small number of instances are more sensitive to noise. Since ReLink provides much accurate defect information, the prediction performance of OpenIntents is significantly improved.

6. THREATS TO VALIDITY

There are potential threats to the validity of our work:

- For the two Android projects, the golden sets of links were collected by us manually. To assure their quality, two people were involved: one annotating the links and the other verifying them. However, it is difficult to guarantee that the golden sets do not contain any false negatives or false positives. Even for the Apache dataset, which was manually examined by an Apache core developer, its quality is not completely assured because the developer may not recall all bug-fixing activities happened several months or years ago.
- Our approach is based on the assumption that the descriptions of bugs and committed changes are similar. In our investigation, we found that many open source projects hosted by Google Code follow the features we described. However, for projects that do not satisfy the assumption, our approach would be under threat.
- All datasets used in our experiments were collected from open source projects. We need to evaluate the performance of ReLink on commercial projects. This remains as future work.

7. RELATED WORK

Real-world data are often noisy, which may affect interpretations and models derived from the data. The data quality problem has also been observed by some software engineering researchers. For example, Mockus [20] noted that in many realistic scenarios the data quality is low (e.g., some change data could be missing), which could affect the outcome of an empirical study. Myrtveit et al. [24] and Strike et al. [29] also noticed the problem of missing and incomplete data in software effort estimation. In [1, 10, 11], authors analyzed the quality of bug reports and change logs. Liebchen and Sheppard [19] investigated the data quality issue and found that among hundreds of software engineering papers only four suggested that the data quality issue may affect their analysis results. In this paper, we focus on software process data and propose methods to improve data quality.

To improve the correctness of identified links between defects and changes, Fisher et al. [13, 14] discussed the confidence of links. They took file names specified in the bug tracking databases and change logs into account. If the files exist in both of them, the confidence of the links will be higher. Śliwerski et al. [28] proposed to verify the links by semantic analysis. A link is valid if it satisfies one of the conditions such as whether the bug has been resolved as Fixed at least once, whether the short description of the bug report is contained in the committed change log, etc. Bachmann et al. [5] improved Fischer's approach by excluding all false-positive numbers that have a defined format. They validated the linked bug report by checking the relationship between the bug-fixing date and the change commit date.

Although many researchers proposed various kinds of approaches to verify the links, the quality of the software process data is still not good enough. Bachmann and Bird et al. [6, 7] showed strong evidence that, only a fraction of bug fixes are explicitly labeled in the source code repository, and there exist systematic biases in finding the links. The bias could affect the effectiveness of the studies based on the process data such as software defect prediction. Nguyen et al. [25] also found that biases existed in a commercial project (IBM Jazz) that enforced strict development guidelines. In order to find the missing links, Bird et al. [8] developed the tool "LINKSTER" to facilitate identification of links manually. However, their tool requires manual effort, and thus is difficult to scale up.

Our work is also related to the traceability analysis among software artifacts. Many researchers have proposed information retrieval (IR) based techniques to recover traceability links between source code and text documents (such as development journals, error logs, and emails) [2, 3, 4]. Runeson et al. [26] and Wang et al. [30] applied IR techniques to compare text similarity between two bug reports, thereby identifying potentially duplicate bug reports. In our work, we apply IR techniques to compare text similarity between bug reports and change logs, thereby recovering traceability links between bugs and changes.

8. CONCLUSIONS AND FUTURE WORK

To automatically collect links between bugs and changes, traditional heuristics look for explicit links to bugs in change logs. Recent studies have shown that traditional heuristics could be biased, since developers may not leave explicit links in change logs. In this paper, we have proposed ReLink, an automatic link recovery algorithm. ReLink is based on automatically learned feature criteria from explicit links. Our experimental results have shown that ReLink is able to recover links reliably. We have also shown that the more accurate defect information collected by ReLink has positive impacts on the follow-up software maintenance studies, including defect prediction models.

Our experimental results confirm that defect information collected using traditional heuristics should be used with caution. It is desirable to use link recovery algorithms and to perform careful inspection of the collected defect information. ReLink is the first step toward this direction.

In future more research on recovering links is needed in order to obtain more accurate defect data. We will also apply our approach to industrial projects to evaluate its usefulness.

Our tool and the experimental data used in this paper are available at:

http://www.cse.ust.hk/~scc/ReLink.htm

ACKNOWLEDGEMENTS

This research is supported by the Hong Kong RGC/GRF grant 612108, the NSFC grant 61073006, and the Tsinghua University research project 2010THZ0. We thank Christian Bird for providing us with the annotated Apache dataset, and Lichao Liu for validating the golden set data for Android projects.

REFERENCES

[1] J. Aranda and G. Venolia. The secret life of bugs: Going past the errors and omissions in software repositories. In *ICSE'09*, pages 298–308, May 2009.

[2] G. Antoniol, G. Canfora, G. Casazza, A. De Lucia, and E. Merlo. 2002. Recovering Traceability Links between Code and Documentation, *IEEE Trans. Softw. Eng. 28*, 10 October 2002, 970-983.

[3] A. Bacchelli, M. D'Ambros, M. Lanza, R. Robbes, Benchmarking Lightweight Techniques to Link E-Mails and Source Code. In *WCRE'09*, Lille, France, pp. 205-214, Oct 2009.

[4] A. Bacchelli, M. Lanza, and R. Robbes, Linking e-mails and source code artifacts. In *ICSE '10*, Vol. 1. ACM, New York, NY, USA, 375-384.

[5] A. Bachmann and A. Bernstein. Software process data quality and characteristics - a historical view on open and closed source projects. In *IWPSE-Evol'09*, pages 119-128, Amsterdam, The Netherlands, August 2009.

[6] A. Bachmann, C. Bird, F. Rahman, P. Devanbu, and A. Bernstein, The Missing Links: Bugs and Bug-fix Commits. In *FSE'10*, 97-106, Santa Fe, New Mexico, USA, Nov 2010.

[7] C. Bird, A. Bachmann, E.Aune, J. Duffy, A. Bernstein, V.Filkov, and P. Devanbu, Fair and balanced?: bias in bug-fixing datasets. In *ESEC/FSE'09*, Aug. 2009, 121-130.

[8] C. Bird, A. Bachmann, F. Rahman, and A. Bernstein, LINKSTER: enabling efficient manual inspection and annotation of mined data. In *FSE'10*, 369-370, Santa Fe, New Mexico, USA, Nov 2010.

[9] R. Baeza-Yates and B. Ribeiro-Neto, *Modern Information Retrieval*, Addison Wesley, 1999.

[10] N. Bettenburg, R. Premraj, T. Zimmermann, and S. Kim. Duplicate bug reports considered harmful... really? In *ICSM'08*, pages 337–345, October 2008.

[11] K. Chen, S. R. Schach, L. Yu, J. Offutt, and G. Z. Heller. Open-source change logs. *Emp. Softw. Eng.*, 9(3):197–210, 2004.

[12] C. Fellbaum, *WordNet: An Electronic Lexical Database*, Cambridge, MA: MIT Press, 1998.

[13] M. Fischer, M. Pinzger, and H. Gall. Analyzing and relating bug report data for feature tracking. In *WCRE'03*, pages 90-99, Victoria, Canada, November 2003.

[14] M. Fischer, M. Pinzger, and H. C. Gall. Populating a release history database from version control and bug tracking systems. In *ICSM'03*, pages 23-32, Amsterdam, Netherlands, September 2003.

[15] A. Hindle, D. M. German, R. C. Holt: What do large commits tell us?: a taxonomical study of large commits. In *MSR 2008*, pp. 99-108, May 2008.

[16] S. Kim, T. Zimmermann, K. Pan and E. Whitehead Jr., Automatic Identification of Bug-Introducing Changes. In *ASE'06*, Tokyo, Japan, September 2006.

[17] S. Kim, T. Zimmermann, E. J. Whitehead Jr., and A. Zeller. Predicting faults from cached history. In *ICSE'07*, pages 489–498, Washington, DC, USA, 2007.

[18] S. Kim, H. Zhang, R. Wu and L. Gong, Dealing with Noise in Defect Prediction. In *ICSE'11*, Honolulu, Hawaii, USA, May 2011.

[19] G. Liebchen and M. Shepperd. Data sets and data quality in software engineering. In *PROMISE'08*, 39–44, May 2008.

[20] A. Mockus, Missing Data in Software Engineering, *Empirical Methods in Software Engineering*. The MIT Press, 2000.

[21] A. Mockus and L. G. Votta, Identifying Reasons for Software Changes Using Historic Databases. In *ICSM 2000*, San Jose, CA, USA, 2000, pp. 120-130.

[22] A. Mockus, R. T. Fielding, and J. D. Herbsleb. Two case studies of open source software development: Apache and mozilla. *ACM Trans. Softw. Eng. Methodol.*, 11(3):309–346, 2002.

[23] A. Murgia, G. Concas, M. Marchesi, R. Tonelli, A machine learning approach for text categorization of fixing-issue commits on CVS. In *ESEM 2010*, Bolzano-Bozen, Italy, Sep 2010.

[24] I. Myrtveit, E. Stensrud, and U. H. Olsson. Analyzing Data Sets with Missing Data: An Empirical Evaluation of Imputation Methods and Likelihood-Based Methods. *IEEE Trans. on Software Engineering,* 27(11), pp.999-1013, 2001.

[25] T. H. D. Nguyen, B. Adams, A. E. Hassan, A Case Study of Bias in Bug-Fix Datasets. In *WCRE'10*, pp. 259-268.

[26] P. Runeson, M. Alexanderson, O. Nyholm, Detection of Duplicate Defect Reports Using Natural Language Processing. In *ICSE'07,* 499-510, May 2007.

[27] A. Schroter, T. Zimmermann, R. Premraj, and A. Zeller. If your bug database could talk... In *ICSE'06*, pages 18–20, Rio de Janeiro, Brazil, September 2006.

[28] J. Sliwerski, T. Zimmermann, and A. Zeller. When do changes induce fixes? In *MSR'05*, pages 24-28, Saint Louis, Missouri, USA, May 2005. ACM.

[29] K. Strike, K. E. Emam, and N. Madhavji. Software Cost Estimation with Incomplete Data. *IEEE Trans. on Software Engineering*, 27(10), pp.890-908, 2001.

[30] X. Wang, L. Zhang, T. Xie, J. Anvik, and J. Sun, An approach to detecting duplicate bug reports using natural language and execution information. In *ICSE'08*, pages 461-470, Leipzig, Germany, 2008

[31] WEKA: http://www.cs.waikato.ac.nz/ml/weka/

[32] I.H. Witten and E. Frank, *Data Mining: Practical Machine Learning Tools and Techniques with Java Implementation*, second ed., Morgan Kaufmann, 2005.

[33] T. Zimmermann, R. Premraj, and A. Zeller. Predicting defects for eclipse. In *PROMISE'07*, pages 1-9, Minneapolis, Minnesota, USA, May 2007.

[34] T. Zimmermann and P. Weissgerber. Preprocessing cvs data for Fine-grained analysis. In *MSR'04*, pages 2-6, Edinburgh, Scotland, UK, May 2004.

[35] H. Zhang and R. Wu, Sampling Program Quality, *Proc. ICSM 2010*, Timisoara, Romania, Sep 2010, pp. 1-10.

[36] H. Zhang, An Investigation of the Relationships between Lines of Code and Defects. In *ICSM'09*, Edmonton, Canada, September 2009, pp. 274-28.

How Do Fixes Become Bugs?

A Comprehensive Characteristic Study on Incorrect Fixes in Commercial and Open Source Operating Systems

Zuoning Yin‡, Ding Yuan‡, Yuanyuan Zhou†, Shankar Pasupathy*, Lakshmi Bairavasundaram*
‡Department of Computer Science, Univ. of Illinois at Urbana-Champaign, Urbana, IL 61801, USA
{zyin2, dyuan3}@cs.uiuc.edu
†Department of Computer Science and Engineering, Univ. of California, San Diego, La Jolla , CA 92093, USA
yyzhou@cs.ucsd.edu
*NetApp Inc., Sunnyvale, CA 94089, USA
{pshankar, lakshmib}@netapp.com

ABSTRACT

Software bugs affect system reliability. When a bug is exposed in the field, developers need to fix them. Unfortunately, the bug-fixing process can also introduce errors, which leads to buggy patches that further aggravate the damage to end users and erode software vendors' reputation.

This paper presents a comprehensive characteristic study on incorrect bug-fixes from large operating system code bases including Linux, OpenSolaris, FreeBSD and also a mature *commercial* OS developed and evolved over the last *12* years, investigating not only the mistake patterns during bug-fixing but also the possible *human reasons* in the development process when these incorrect bug-fixes were introduced. Our major findings include: (1) at least 14.8%~24.4% of sampled fixes for post-release bugs [1] in these large OSes are incorrect and have made impacts to end users. (2) Among several common bug types, concurrency bugs are the most difficult to fix correctly: 39% of concurrency bug fixes are incorrect. (3) Developers and reviewers for incorrect fixes usually do not have enough knowledge about the involved code. For example, 27% of the incorrect fixes are made by developers who have never touched the source code files associated with the fix. Our results provide useful guidelines to design new tools and also to improve the development process. Based on our findings, the commercial software vendor whose OS code we evaluated is building a tool to improve the bug fixing and code reviewing process.

Categories and Subject Descriptors: D.2.0 [Software Engineering]: General

General Terms: Reliability

[1]These only include those fixes for bugs discovered after software releases.

Permission to make digital or hard copies of all or part of this work for personal or classroom use is granted without fee provided that copies are not made or distributed for profit or commercial advantage and that copies bear this notice and the full citation on the first page. To copy otherwise, to republish, to post on servers or to redistribute to lists, requires prior specific permission and/or a fee.
ESEC/FSE'11, September 5–9, 2011, Szeged, Hungary.
Copyright 2011 ACM 978-1-4503-0443-6/11/09 ...$10.00.

Keywords: Incorrect fixes, software bugs, bug fixing, human factor, testing

1. INTRODUCTION

1.1 Motivation

As a man-made artifact, software suffers from various errors, referred to as software bugs, which cause crashes, hangs or incorrect results and significantly threaten not only the reliability but also the security of computer systems. Bugs are detected either during testing before release or in the field by customers post-release. Once a bug is discovered, developers usually need to fix it. In particular, for bugs that have direct, severe impact on customers, vendors usually make releasing timely patches the highest priority in order to minimize the amount of system down time.

Unfortunately, fixes to bugs are not bullet proof since they are also written by human. Some fixes either do not fix the problem completely or even introduce new problems. For example, in April 2010, McAfee released a patch which incorrectly identified a critical Windows system file as a virus [8]. As a result, after applying this patch, thousands of systems refused to boot properly, had lost their network connections, or both. In 2005, Trend Micro also released a buggy patch which introduced severe performance degradation [22]. The company received over 370,000 calls from customers about this issue and eventually spent more than $8 million to compensate customers. The above two incidents are not the only cases in recent history. As a matter of fact, there were many other similar events [2, 15, 4] in the past which put the names of big companies such as Microsoft, Apple and Intel under spotlight.

We had also conducted a study on *every* security patch released by Microsoft in its security bulletin [1] since January 2000 to April 2010. Surprisingly, out of the total 720 released security patches, 72 of them were buggy when they were first released. These patches were expected to fix some severe problems. Once released, they were usually applied to millions of users automatically. Therefore, they would have enormous impacts and damages to end users as well as software vendors' reputation.

Mistakes in bug fixes may be caused by many possible reasons. First, bug fixing is usually under very tight time schedule, typically with deadlines in days or even hours,

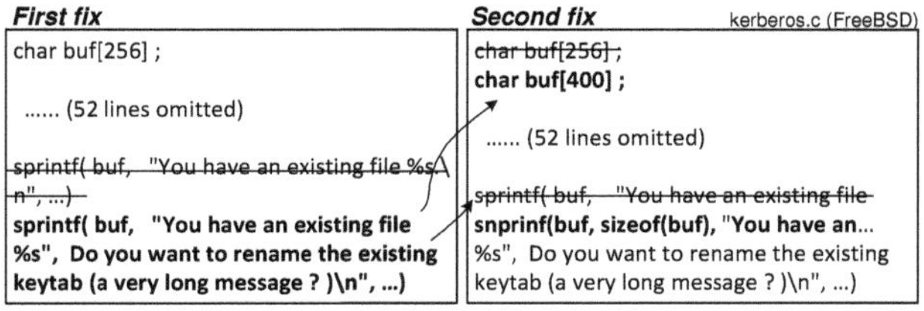

Figure 1: An incorrect fix example from FreeBSD. A part of the first fix appended a console message with some additional information, unfortunately introducing a buffer overflow (The added lines are in bold while the deleted lines are crossed out).

definitely not weeks. Such time pressure can cause *fixers* [2] to have much less time to think cautiously, especially about the potential side-effects and the interaction with the rest of the system. Similarly, such time pressure prevents testers from conducting thorough regression tests before releasing the fix. Figure 1 shows a real world example from FreeBSD, the original bug fix appended a log message with additional information. Unfortunately, the fixer did not pay attention to the buffer length defined 52 lines upwards in the same file and introduced a buffer overflow.

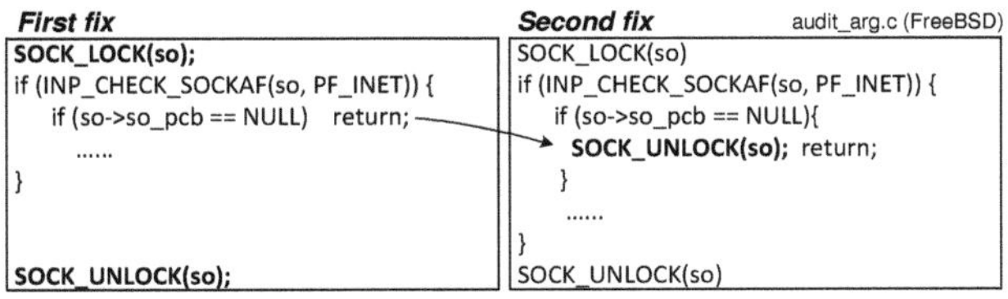

Figure 2: An incorrect fix example from FreeBSD. The first fix tried to fix a data race bug by adding locks, which then introduced a deadlock as it forgot to release the lock via *SOCK_UNLOCK* before *return*.

Second, bug fixing usually has a narrow focus (e.g., removing the bug) comparing to general development. As such, the fixer regards fixing the target bug as the sole objective and accomplishment to be evaluated by his/her manager. Therefore, he/she would pay much more attention to the bug itself than the correctness of the rest of the system. Similarly, such narrowly focused mindset may also be true for the testers: Tester may just focus on if the bug symptom observed previously is gone, but forget to test some other aspects, in particular how the fix interacts with other parts and whether it introduces new problems. As shown in Figure 2, the fixer just focused on removing the data race bug by adding locks. While the data race bug was removed, the fix unfortunately introduced a new bug: a deadlock. This deadlock was obviously not discovered during regression testing.

Third, the two factors above can be further magnified if fixers or reviewers are not familiar with the related code. While an ideal fixer could be someone with the most knowledge about the related code, in reality it may not always be the case. Sometimes, it may be difficult to know who is the best person to do the fix. Even if such person is known, he/she may be busy with other tasks or has moved to other projects, and is therefore unavailable to perform the fix. Sometimes, it is due to the development and maintenance process. Some software projects have separate teams for developing and maintaining software. All these real world situations can lead to the case that the fixer does not have enough knowledge about the code he/she is fixing, and consequently increases the chance of an incorrect fix. This might help explaining the incorrect fix shown in Figure 3 from the commercial OS we evaluated. When we measure the fixer's knowledge based on how many lines he had contributed to the file involved in the patch, we found that he had never touched this file in the past, indicating that he may not have sufficient relevant knowledge to fix the bug correctly.

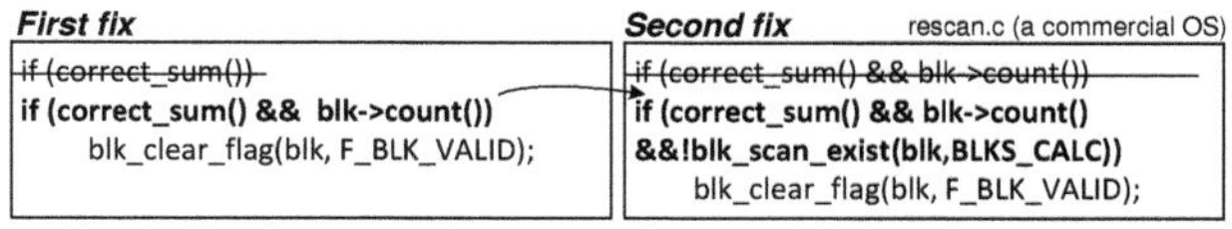

Figure 3: An incorrect fix that hadn't fixed the problem completely. *This example is from the large commercial OS we evaluated.* The first fix tried to address a semantic bug by modifying the *if* condition. Unfortunately, the revised condition was still not restrictive enough.

Regardless what is the reason for introducing these errors during bug fixing and why they were not caught before release, their common existences and severe impacts on users and vendors have raised some serious concerns about the bug fixing process. In order to come up with better process and more effective tools to address this problem, we need to first thoroughly understand the characteristics of incorrect fixes, including:

- *How significant is the problem of incorrect fixes?* More specifically, what percentages of bug fixes are incorrect? How severe are the problems caused by incorrect fixes?
- *What types of bugs are difficult to fix correctly?* Are some types of bugs just more difficult to fix correctly so that fixers, testers and code reviewers for these types of bug fixes should pay more attention and effort to avoid mistakes?
- *What are the common mistakes made in bug fixes?* Are there any patterns among incorrect bug fixes? If there are some common patterns, such knowledge would help alerting developers to pay special attention to certain aspects during bug fixing. Additionally, it may also inspire new tools to catch certain incorrect fixes automatically.
- *What aspects in the development process are correlated to the correctness of bug fixing?* For example, does fixers and reviewers' relevant knowledge have a high correlation to incorrect fixes?

A few recent studies had been conducted on certain aspects of incorrect fixes [6, 36, 33, 13]. For example, Śliwerski *et al.* [36] proposed an effective way to automatically locate fix-inducing changes and studied the incorrect fix ratios in Eclipse and Mozilla. They found developers are easier to make mistakes during bug fixing on Friday. Purushothaman *et al.* [33] studied the incorrect fix ratio in a switching system from Lucent, but their focus was on the impact of one-line changes. Gu *et al.* [13] studied the incorrect fix ratio in three Apache projects, but they focused on providing a new patch validation tool.

While these studies have revealed some interesting findings, most of them focused more on incorrect fix ratios and studied only open source code bases, providing one of the first steps toward understanding incorrect bug fixes. This

[2]we will refer the developer who fixes the bug as the "fixer" in the rest of the paper.

Importance of Incorrect Fixes	Implications
(1) At least 14.8%~24.4% of examined fixes for post-release bugs are incorrect. 43% of the examined incorrect fixes can cause crashes, hangs, data corruptions or security problems.	Although the ratio of incorrect fixes is not very high, the impact of the incorrect fixes indicate that the problem of incorrect fixes is significant and worth special attention.
(2) Among common types of bugs and based on our samples, fixes on concurrency bugs (39% of them) are most error-prone, followed by semantic bugs (17%) and then memory bugs (14%).	Developers and testers should be more cautious when fixing concurrency bugs.
Incorrect fixes to Concurrency bugs	**Implications**
(3) Fixes on data race bugs can easily introduce new deadlock bugs or do not completely fix the problem.	The synchronization code added for fixing data races need to be examined in more detail to avoid new deadlock. Knowing all the access locations to the shared objects is the key to fix data race completely.
(4) Fixes to deadlock bugs might reveal bugs which were hidden by the previous deadlock.	Fixers need to further examine the path after deadlock in case there are some bugs hidden due to the existence of the deadlock.
Incorrect fixes to Memory bugs	**Implications**
(5) Fixing buffer overflows by statically increasing the buffer size is still vulnerable to future overflows. Fixing buffer overflows by dynamically allocating memory could introduce null pointer dereference bugs if the allocated memory is used without check.	It is better to use safe string functions (e.g., *snprintf*) or bound checking to fix buffer overflow. Fixers need to be aware of the potential memory leaks and the failure of allocation when fixing buffer overflows by dynamically allocating memory.
(6) Fixing memory leaks can introduce dangling pointer bugs when freeing the memory without nullifying the pointer, and memory corruption when freeing something that should not be freed, or do not solve the problem completely when forgetting to free the members of a structure.	It is good to nullify the pointer after freeing the memory. It is also important to clearly understand what and when should be freed to avoid overreaction. Fixers should remember to free the structure members when freeing a complex structure to avoid an incomplete fix.
Human reasons to incorrect fixes	**Implications**
(7) Comparing to correct fixes, the developers who introduced incorrect fixes have less knowledge (or familiarity) with the relevant code. *27%* of the incorrect fixes are even made by fixers who previously had never touched the files involved in the fix.	Code knowledge has influence on the correctness of bug fixes. It is dangerous to let developers who are not familiar with the relevant code to make the fix.
(8) Interestingly, in most of the cases, the developers who are most familiar (5~6 times of the actual fixers) with the relevant code of these incorrect fixes are still working on the project, but unfortunately were not selected to do the fixes.	Having a right software maintenance process and selecting the right person to fix a bug is important.
(9) The code reviewers for incorrect fixes also have very poor relevant knowledge.	It is also important to select a developer who is familiar with the relevant code as the code-reviewer.

Table 1: Our major findings of real world incorrect bug fix characteristics and their implications. Please take our methodology and potential threats to validity into consideration when you interpret and draw any conclusions.

paper goes much beyond prior work, studying both commercial and open source, large operating system projects, and investigating not only incorrect fix percentages, but also other characteristics such as mistake patterns during bug fixing, types of bugs that are difficult to fix correctly, as well as the potential reasons in the development process for introducing incorrect bug fixes.

1.2 Our Contribution

To the best of our knowledge, this paper presents one of the most comprehensive characteristic studies on incorrect fixes from large OSes including a mature *commercial* OS developed and evolved over the last 12 years and three open-source OSes (FreeBSD, OpenSolaris and Linux), exploring not only the mistake patterns but also the possible *human reasons* in the development process when these incorrect fixes were introduced. More specifically, from these four OS code bases, we carefully examined each of the 970 randomly selected fixes for post-release bugs and identified the incorrect fixes. To gain a deeper understanding of what types of bugs are more difficult to fix correctly as well as the common mistakes made during fixing those bugs, we further sampled another set of 320 fixes on certain important types of bugs. The details of our methodology and potential threats to validity are described in Section 2.

Our major findings are summarized in Table 1. These findings provide useful guidelines for patch testing and validations as well as bug triage process. For example, *motivated from our findings, the large software vendor whose OS code was evaluated in our study is building a tool to improve its bug fixing and code review process.*

While we believe that the systems and fixes we examined well represent the characteristics in large operating systems, we do not intend to draw any general conclusions about all the applications. In particular, we should note that all of the characteristics and findings in this study are associated with the types of the systems and the programming languages they use. Therefore, our results should be taken with the specific system types and our methodology in mind.

Paper outline: In Section 2, we discuss the methodology used in our study and threats to validity. Section 2. After that we present our detailed results on the incorrect fix ratio in Section 3. Then we further study which types of bugs are more difficult to fix and what common mistakes could be made in Section 4. After that we study the human factors which could lead to incorrect fixes in Section 5. Section 6 is the related work and we conclude in Section 7.

2. METHODOLOGY

In this section, we first discuss the software projects used in our study (Section 2.1), the techniques to find incorrect fixes (Section 2.2), how we select bug samples (Section 2.3) and how we study the influence of human factors on bug fixing(Section 2.4). At the end, we talk about the threats to the validity of our study (Section 2.5).

2.1 Software projects under study

App	LoC	Open src?
The commercial OS	confidential	N
FreeBSD	9.97M	Y
Linux	10.94M	Y
OpenSolaris	12.99M	Y

Table 2: The four OSes that our study uses.

Table 2 lists the four code bases we studied, including a commercial, closed-source OS from a large software vendor [3] and three open-source OSes (FreeBSD, Linux and OpenSolaris). We chose to study OS code because they are large, complex and their reliability is critically important. Additionally, as OS code is developed by many programmers, contains lots of components, uses a variety of data structures and algorithms, it could provide us a broad base to understand incorrect fix examples.

The four OSes have different architectures. The commercial OS is especially designed for high-reliability systems with many enterprise customers like big financial companies and government agencies. It has evolved for almost 12 years. The other three open-source OSes have different origins. FreeBSD originates from academia (Berkeley Unix). OpenSolaris originates from a commercial OS (Solaris). Linux completely originates from the open-source community. We think the variety in data sources would help us find general software laws or interesting specificities.

These OSes usually have multiple branches (series) in their OS families. We focus on those branches which are both stable and widely deployed. For the commercial OS, we chose the branch which is most widely deployed. For FreeBSD, we chose FreeBSD 7 series. For Linux, we chose Linux 2.6 series. For Opensolaris, it has a different release model so we just studied the releases since its 2008.5 version.

In order to further preserve the privacy and reputation for the software vendor, we anonymized the results in Section 3, 4 and 5. The four code bases will be just referred as A, B, C and D with the mapping information hidden. We know that such anonymization may prevent us from making some interesting comparison between open source and commercial code bases, but fortunately we can still make many other findings like the ones summarized in Introduction.

2.2 Finding incorrect fixes

The definition of incorrect fix: A bug fix f_x is defined as an incorrect fix if there is another following bug fix f_y that fixes either a new problem introduced by f_x, or the original problem that was not completely fixed by f_x.

Note that we consider only fixes to bugs, not any general or non-essential changes [16] (e.g., feature addition or renaming). This is identified by checking whether a fix is associated with a bug report. This screening criteria is important to the fidelity of our study since bug reports often contain rich information which is important for us to understand the fix. It is hard to obtain a complete picture from the bug fix itself alone.

Unfortunately, the link between fixes and bug reports is not always systematically maintained [5]. For the commercial OS and OpenSolaris, the SCM (software configuration management) systems record the link between every bug report and every change. However, for FreeBSD and Linux, such links are only documented voluntarily by developers in an unstructured way. To identify such links, we use a method similar to the methods used in [11, 36, 40]. The main idea is to leverage the verbal information in the bug reports or change logs to reconstruct the links. For example, developers may write "*the bug is fixed by change 0a134fad*" in a bug report. Then we can link the bug to the change 0a134fad.

[3]Due to confidentiality agreement, we can neither mention the company's name nor the LoC of its OS.

After the above process, we will have a set of bug fixes linked with bug reports. We then randomly select a target number of bug fixes and then semi-automatically check whether each one is an incorrect fix or not. We call the process semi-automatic because we use a two-step process: first step automatically selects potential incorrect fix candidates, while the second step manually verifies each candidate.

Two techniques are used in the first step to automatically identify potential incorrect fix candidates. First, we look at the *source code overlap* between changes. This technique is similar to the methods used in [36, 33]. If there is source code overlap between two changes, then the latter change may be made to correct the previous change. More specifically, if a latter change f_y overwrites or deletes the code written in the previous change f_x or f_y just adds code in the proximity (+/-25 lines) of f_x, we regard f_x as an incorrect fix candidate for manual examination. The second technique is to search for specific keywords in the bug report and change log of each fix that may suggest an incorrect fix. For example, if we find "*this patch fixed a regression introduced by the fix in Bug 12476*" in the bug report linked with f_y, we regard the fix in "Bug 12476" as an incorrect fix candidate. In general, we find the first technique to be more comprehensive.

Please note that the first step is only identifying candidates. We still need to manually examine each candidate, which is the unique challenge in our study. We examined all the relevant code related to each fix. We also examined the bug reports and change logs to get proof from developer's explanation. For some fixes, we even discussed with developers of these systems to ensure the correct understanding on them. Then based on all the evidences we got, we finally decide whether a fix is incorrect or not.

Also note that the first step may prune a few incorrect fixes out, especially those incorrect fixes whose next fixes in a completely different location without any overlap at all (i.e. beyond the +/-25 lines proximity). But we expect such incorrect fixes are very rare as two subsequent fixes to the same problem usually has good locality in terms of code changes. And we did try to relax the proximity requirement to be "within" the same file but did not find more incorrect fixes.

2.3 The target bugs to study

In this study we used two sets of bug fixes with different focuses.

Sample set 1: To get this sample set, we first randomly sampled a total of 2,000 bug fixes (500 from each OS) that are associated with bug reports. From these 2,000 bug fixes, we further select only those fixes to *post-release* bugs (970 in total). Selecting such post-release bug fixes allows us to focus on fixes to bugs that made high impacts to both customers and vendors. Post-release bugs are selected after the random sampling instead of before the sampling because the manual effort in verifying all bug fixes would be too huge. We then use the process described in the previous subsection to identify and study incorrect fixes.

Sample set 2: This sample set is used to further zoom in certain bug types observed in *sample set 1* whose fixes are most error-prone. Specifically, we chose to study the fixes to memory leak, buffer overflow, data race and deadlock bugs. However, it is difficult to reuse the bugs in *sample set 1*, since there are not statistically sufficient number of bug fixes for these types of bugs. Therefore, we deliberately sampled more bug fixes focusing on these four types. Specifically, we used all the related keywords to search for the bug fixes of a specific type. Keyword search is enough to get these bug fixes since there are only limited ways to name them. Then we randomly selected 20 from each type for each code base. In total, we sampled 320 fixes which provide us a richer base-set to study the incorrect fixed patterns. This set is only used in Section 4.

2.4 Measuring code knowledge

To understand why a programmer cannot fix a bug correctly, we also dive deeper into his/her knowledge about the relevant code. In this study, we measure code knowledge by checking the cumulative "authorship" of each line of code at a particular version, which can be systematically measured. From SCM, we obtain the authorship of each line for a file at a given version by using commands such as "svn annotate". Assume a developer d, a file F, a function f and a version v, we calculate code knowledge at two levels of granularity:

$$K\_File_{d,F,v} = \frac{\text{The LoC written by } d \text{ for } F \text{ at } v}{\text{The total LoC in } F \text{ at } v}$$

$$K\_Func_{d,f,F,v} = \frac{\text{The LoC written by } d \text{ for } f \text{ in } F \text{ at } v}{\text{The total LoC in the } f \text{ at } v}$$

We use percentage as the unit of K_File and K_Func. For example, "$K\_File_{d,F,v}$=75%" means 75% of code lines in F at version v are written by d. d may write these code lines in any version that is not later than v. Both fixers' and reviewers' knowledge are measured in our study in this way.

2.5 Threats to validity

Real world empirical studies are all subject to validity problems, so is our study. Potential threats to the validity of our study are the representativeness of the selected software projects, the representativeness of the incorrect fix samples, our classification process and evaluation methodology.

Representativeness of software: Both commercial and open-source software are covered in this study, so we believe that we have a good coverage for at least OS code. We do not intend to draw any general conclusions in all software, but some of the findings such as fixers and reviewers' knowledge would also apply to other applications.

Representativeness of bug fix samples: We studied only those bug fixes that could be linked to a bug report. The set of fixes that cannot be linked were not covered, and some of our findings might not hold in them [5]. Fortunately, the results from the commercial OS and OpenSolaris are immune to this threat since every bug fix is linked to a bug report. Since the results from FreeBSD and Linux show a similar trend as the commercial OS and OpenSolaris, which may ease the concern on this threat for this problem.

As discussed earlier, there is also a potential problem in our automatic filtering process, i.e., we can potentially filter out an incorrect fix if its subsequent fix does not have any proximity in code location. Fortunately our exercises of relaxing the proximity constraint did not discover any more incorrect fixes, which indicates that the amount of missed incorrect fixes should be very low.

Threats of manual classification: Our study involves manual classification on bug reports and fixes which cannot be replaced by automatic techniques. Therefore, subjectivity is inevitable. However, we tried our best to minimize such subjectivity by using double verification. Also the authors have previous experience in studying bugs and familiar with OSes [19, 42, 38, 21]. For every incorrect fix candidate, we examined all the information sources we could have, including source code, bug reports, change logs, etc. Besides, for some fixes we also discussed with developers of these systems to ensure the correct understanding on them. Since we manually examined each incorrect fix candidate and classify it as incorrect only if we have concrete evidence, we are confident that the number of false positives should be very low.

Limitation in measuring the knowledge: The way we measure code knowledge is relatively simple since we only want to check the fixers and reviewers' knowledge in a coarse-grain, qualitative way. A more sophisticated knowledge model might provide us more accurate results in Section 5, which remains as our future study.

3. IS INCORRECT FIX REALLY A SIGNIFICANT PROBLEM?

The ratio of incorrect fixes among all bug fixes and the impact of bugs introduced by incorrect fixes are important for us to accurately understand whether incorrect bug fix is a significant problem. As described in Section 2, we first randomly sampled 2,000 bug fixes from the four OSes (500 from each OS), among them 970 are fixes to post-release bugs.

App	# of post-release bug fixes	# of incorrect fixes	Ratio
A	189	39	20.6%±3.0%
B	309	46	14.8%±2.9%
C	267	41	15.3%±2.6%
D	205	50	24.4%±3.7%

Table 3: The ratio of incorrect fixes on sampled post-release bugs in the four OSes. A 95% confidence interval is used.

Table 3 shows the ratio of incorrect fixes based on our samples is 14.8%~24.4% among the four OSes. As discussed in Section 2.5, this is only a lower-bound estimation. Considering that the fixes on post-release bugs would be applied by a lot of customers and users, even this ratio can still have significant impact. Since regression testing had already been applied before releasing the fixes, it also indicates general testing techniques may need to be tailored to be more effective in capturing the errors in patches.

We further studied the impact of the bugs introduced by the examined incorrect fixes. We judge the impact based on the symptoms described in the bug reports. We found 14.0% of them introduced crash, 8.4% caused system to hang, 15.4% led to data corruption or data loss, 5.6% caused security problem, 7.0% degraded the performance, and 45.1% introduced incorrect functionality. Some bugs introduced are actually more severe than the original bugs. Moreover, for some bugs, they could even be incorrectly fixed for several times.

Finding: At least 14.8%~24.4% of the sampled bug fixes are incorrect. Moreover, 43% of the incorrect fixes resulted in severe bugs that caused crash, hang, data corruption or security problems.

Implication: Incorrect fix is indeed a significant problem that requires special attentions from software vendors.

4. INCORRECT FIX PATTERNS

Though bug fix patterns had already been studied in [17, 31], few had studied the patterns of incorrect fixes before. In this section, we first study which types of bugs are more likely to introduce incorrect fixes. Then we probe deeper into each of these bug types and try to understand their incorrect fix patterns via case studies. Finally, we discuss how we can leverage those patterns to detect incorrect fixes in the testing process.

4.1 Which types of bugs are more difficult to fix correctly?

We classified all the 970 sampled fixes into three categories based on the bugs they fix: memory bug, concurrency bug or semantic bug. Semantic bugs are those bugs that cannot be classified as memory or concurrency bug and are usually application specific problems. This classification is adopted from previous literature [19].

App	Concurrency	Memory	Semantic
A	4/13 (31%)	3/17 (18%)	32/159 (20%)
B	9/21 (43%)	5/44 (13%)	32/244 (13%)
C	7/19 (37%)	6/43 (14%)	28/205 (14%)
D	10/23 (44%)	5/30 (17%)	35/152 (23%)
Overall	30/76 (39%)	19/134 (14%)	127/760 (17%)

Table 4: The number of incorrect fixes among all the sampled fixes and the incorrect fix ratio for the three categories of bugs in the four OSes.

Table 4 shows the ratio of incorrect fixes to each type of bug. Based on our samples, concurrency bugs have the largest incorrect fix ratio (39% overall), indicating concurrency bugs are the hardest to fix. Semantic bugs and memory bugs have similar ratio, 17% and 14%, respectively.

We focus on studying concurrency bugs and memory bugs, while only providing some high level discussion on semantic bugs (Section 4.2.5). This is because semantic bugs have very diverse root causes so that it is difficult to observe general patterns from their fixes and the mistakes in the fixes.

Bug types and their percentages			
data race	33%	deadlock	29%
buffer overflow	8%	memory leak	6%
uninitialized read	4%	null pointer deref	4%

Table 5: The most observed bug types among all the concurrency bugs and memory bugs being fixed incorrectly. Only top six are shown.

To select the important types of bugs for a detailed study, we further dive into all the concurrency bugs and memory bugs being fixed incorrectly to see which sub-types are most observed. The result is shown in Table 5. Among all the bug types, data race (33%), deadlock (29%), buffer overflow (8%) and memory leak (6%) are the top four types of the most observed concurrency bugs and memory bugs which were fixed incorrectly. Therefore, we just focused on the characteristics of bug fixes to these four types of bugs.

App	Bug types			
	race	deadlock	buf overflow	mem leak
A	9/20 (45%)	5/20 (25%)	2/20 (10%)	1/20 (5%)
B	11/20 (55%)	6/20 (30%)	1/20 (5%)	3/20(15%)
C	11/20 (55%)	8/20 (40%)	3/20 (15%)	0/20 (0%)
D	8/20 (40%)	9/20 (45%)	1/20 (5%)	4/20 (20%)
All	39/80 (49%)	28/80 (35%)	7/80 (9%)	8/80 (10%)

Table 6: The number of incorrect fixes among the all the fixes and the incorrect fix ratio for the four important types of bugs from *sample set 2*.

Table 6 further shows the ratio of incorrect fixes for these four types of bugs. The result is from 320 fixes only to these bug types (*sample set 2* mentioned in Section 2.3), where for each type we randomly sampled 20 fixes from each code base. We use this data set instead of the one used above because among the original 970 fixes (*sample set 1* mentioned in Section 2.3), there are not statistically sufficient number of bug fixes for these four types of bugs. *sample set 2* provides us a richer base-set of incorrect fixes to conduct our case studies in Section 4.2. As indicated in Table 6, fixes to data race and deadlock are most error-prone, with an incorrect fix ratio of 49% and 35% respectively, which is generally 4x~6x of buffer overflow and memory leak.

Finding: Based on our samples, concurrency bugs are the most difficult (39%) to fix right. Among concurrency and memory bugs which were fixed incorrectly, the four most observed bug types are: data race, deadlock, buffer overflow and memory leak.

Implication: Developers and testers should be more cautious when fixing concurrency bugs. The allocation of fixing and testing resources could consider the types of bugs to be fixed.

4.2 Mistakes in bug fixing

After understanding which types of bugs are more difficult to fix right, it would be interesting to understand the common mistakes (patterns) when fixing a particular type of bugs and the consequence introduced by those incorrect fixes. In this Section, we use the incorrect fix examples got from *sample set 2*. Generally, we find there are two types of incorrect fixes: *incomplete fixes* and *introducing new problems*, while each type of bug also has its own incorrect fix patterns. We also discuss techniques to detect or reveal these mistakes: either extending current techniques or suggesting new approaches.

4.2.1 Fixing data races

The most common practice for fixing data race is to add synchronization primitives (e.g., locks) to create mutual exclusion on shared resources. However, delivering a correct fix requires deep reasoning on all the side-effects of the newly added synchronization, which is often error-prone.

Specifically, adding locks might introduce deadlock. This incorrect fix pattern is observed in all the four code bases we evaluated and in 16.4% (6 out of 39) of the incorrect fixes to data race bugs. Figure 4 shows one of the examples. In the first fix, a lock *sc* was added to avoid a race. However, the function *bus_teardown_intr* is not supposed

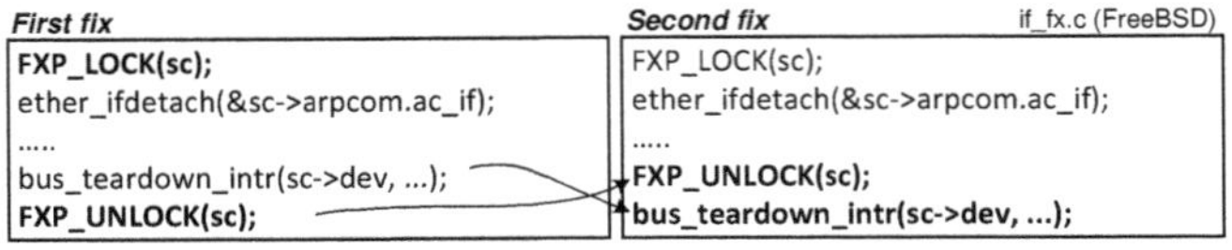

Figure 4: Incorrect fix to a data race introduced a deadlock. The function *bus_teardown_intr* cannot be called with lock held, otherwise deadlock will be introduced.

to be called inside the critical section, otherwise it can lead to deadlock. Unfortunately, developers were not aware of this rule and made the incorrect fix. To fix this deadlock, *bus_teardown_intr* was moved out of the critical section. Figure 2 (in Section 1) is another example of this pattern that fixing data race introduces deadlock. The fixer forgot to release the lock via *SOCK_UNLOCK* before a *return* statement therefore a deadlock happened.

Implications: When adding synchronization primitives, fixers need to make sure the newly added primitives (e.g., lock) will not introduce deadlocks with the existing synchronization code. This can be checked by extending deadlock detectors to only focus on the synchronization primitives newly added. Besides, lock and unlocks should be added in pairs along all the execution paths in the newly formed atomic region. This can be checked automatically by extending some existing path-sensitive bug detection tools such as RacerX [9] or PR-Miner [20] to only scan the code regions touched by the fix.

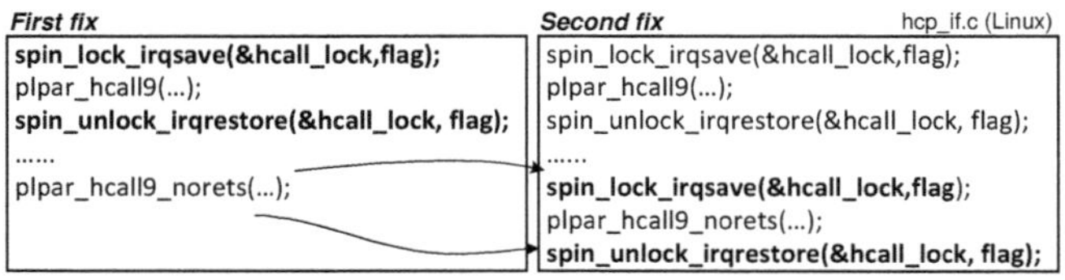

Figure 5: Fix to a data race was not complete. The first fix only added locks to protect function *plpar_hcall9*, while forgot to protect *plpar_hcall9_noret* (which contains the access to the same shared objects in *plpar_hcall9*).

Fixing data races could be incomplete such that not all the data races are fixed. This incorrect fix pattern is observed in three of the code bases we evaluated and in 10.2% (4 out of 39) of the incorrect fixes to data race bugs. For example, as shown in Figure 5, when adding locks, the developer forgets to lock all the places she should lock.

Implications: For a complete fix to data race, it is important to know all the accesses to the shared objects which could race with each others. We can design checkers to detect where the same shared objects are protected by lock in some paths but unprotected in some others [10], and make these checkers focus only on checking the patched code.

4.2.2 Fixing deadlocks

To fix a deadlock, developers may either reverse the order of locks, or even drop some locks. However, these means need to be applied with caution.

Specifically, fixing deadlocks could still lead to deadlock bugs. This incorrect fix pattern is observed in three of the code bases we evaluated and in 14.3% (4 out of 28) of the incorrect fixes to deadlocks. Figure 6 shows such an example. The root cause of this incorrect fix is similar to the one

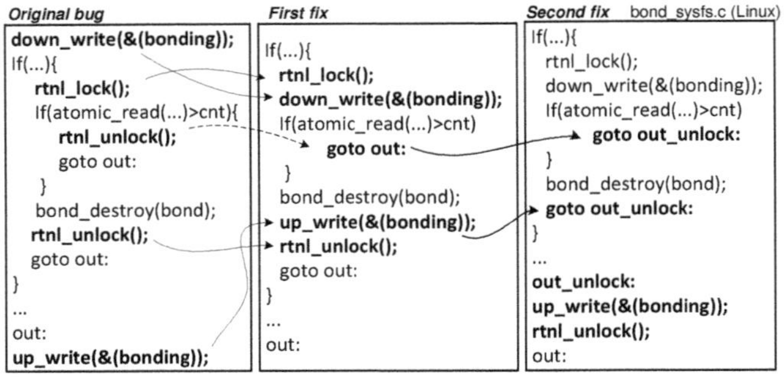

Figure 6: Incorrect fix to a deadlock introduced a new deadlock. The first fix reversed the order of locks to prevent deadlock, but forgot to release locks before taking a *goto* path.

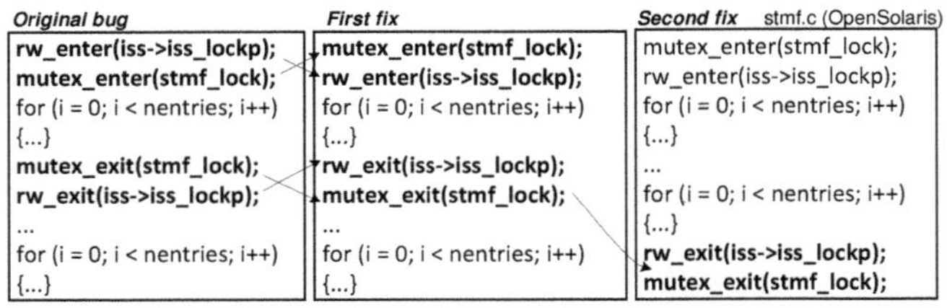

Figure 7: A fix to a deadlock exposed a hidden data race bug.

in Figure 2. Therefore we can again extend some current path-sensitive bug detection tools to spot the deadlock.

Additionally, fixing deadlock may reveal some other bugs that were originally hidden by the deadlock, especially data race bugs. This incorrect fix pattern is observed in two of the code bases we evaluated and in 7.1% (2 out of 28) of the incorrect fixes to deadlocks. Though we only spotted 2 such cases, we think this is still an interesting pattern. Figure 7 shows one of the examples. There are two bugs in the original code: a deadlock caused by the wrong order of the two locks, and a data race caused by an unprotected shared variable in the second *for* loop. However, the data race is hidden by the existence of the deadlock since the execution would not even reach the second *for* loop due to the deadlock. The first fix resolved the deadlock. However, it also enables the execution to proceed so that the data race is much easier to manifest.

Implications: The hang introduced by deadlock bugs might prevent some execution paths from being exercised thoroughly, which could make some bugs hidden in those paths difficult to manifest. After removing deadlock bugs, fixers should further test those execution paths.

4.2.3 Fixing buffer overflow

We also found some interesting incorrect fixes examples for memory bugs. However, since the total numbers of incorrect fixes to buffer overflows and memory leaks in *sample set2* is not statistically large enough (7 and 8 respectively), we do not claim those examples are frequently observed incorrect fix patterns. However, we assume these examples could be common for the incorrect fixes to buffer overflows and memory leaks (shown in Section 4.2.4) if we can further enlarge our sample set.

Common techniques to fix buffer overflow include: a) restrict the length of the data which will be stored into buffer by using safe string functions (e.g., *snprintf*) or do bound checking b) increase the buffer size statically from stack c) allocate larger buffer dynamically from heap to replace a stack buffer.

Based on our observation, technique a) is usually safe and seldom introduces any further incorrect fixes since it eradicates the chance of a buffer overflow in the future.

Implications: The good practice to fix buffer overflow is to use safe string functions or do bound check when possible.

First fix

```
~~vm_offset_t avail[10];~~
vm_offset_t avail[20];
for (indx = 0; avail[indx + 1] != 0; indx += 2)
    size1 = avail[indx + 1] - avail[indx];
```

Second fix machdep.c (FreeBSD)

```
~~vm_offset_t avail[20];~~
vm_offset_t avail[100];
for (indx = 0; avail[indx + 1] != 0; indx += 2)
    size1 = avail[indx + 1] - avail[indx];
```

Figure 8: Incorrect fix to a buffer overflow by increasing static buffer size. The first fix enlarged the buffer size to 20, but the size was still not big enough. Under certain input, *avail* was still overflown.

Technique b) is potentially problematic if the developer cannot anticipate the input size accurately. The buffer size after increasing may still be not enough for an untested input in the future. As shown in Figure 8, the first fix was incomplete. After it increased the size of *avail* to 20, *avail* was still overflown later. Actually even the second fix might still be flawed. Since the developer does not add a bound check, a future input beyond the size 100 could still overflow *avail*.

Implications: Increasing the static buffer size can be dangerous if the input size cannot be accurately estimated.

First fix

```
~~char tempMail[24];~~
char *tempMail;
len = strlen(tmpdir);
tempMail = (char *) malloc (len+...);
strcpy(tempMail, tmpdir);
```

Second fix temp.c (FreeBSD)

```
char *tempMail;
len = strlen(tmpdir);
if((tempMail = malloc(len + ...)) == NULL)
        panic("Out of memory");
strcpy(tempMail, tmpdir);
```

Figure 9: Incorrect fix to a buffer overflow by allocating heap memory. The first fix allocated heap memory to replace stack buffer, but the return value of malloc was unchecked.

For technique c), developers need to be aware of the rules to use memory allocation functions. The memory allocated needs to be freed after use, otherwise it may introduce a memory leak. Besides, developers need to consider to do error handling if memory allocation fails. As shown in Figure 9, the fixer did fix the buffer overflow, but introduced a potential invalid memory access.

Implications: When allocating memory dynamically to fix buffer overflow, developers also need to follow the safety rules of using memory allocation functions.

4.2.4 Fixing memory leak

Once a memory leak is detected, writing fixes may be straightforward, but mistakes can still be made.

Specifically, fixing memory leak can introduce dangling pointer or null pointer dereference if the pointer would still be accessed after the free. Figure 10 shows an example where a dangling pointer bug was introduced.

Implications: It is a good practice to nullify the pointer after freeing it, which can avoid dangling pointer bugs.

Developer may also not be aware of the condition to free an object. They should only free an object when it is no longer used. If they overreact, they could mistakenly free an object still in use under certain conditions. Figure 11 shows such an example which led to data corruption.

First fix

```
void blk_online_work(online_t *p) {
  ......
  kmem_free(p);
  return;
}

void blk_scan(){
  blk_online_work(info);
  find_blk_by_id(info, WIT_FS)
}
```

Second fix toc.c (a commercial OS)

```
void blk_online_work(online_t *p) {
  ......
  kmem_free(p);
  p = null
  return;
}
void blk_scan(){
  blk_online_work(info);
  find_blk_by_id(info, WIT_FS)
}
```

Figure 10: Incorrect fix to memory leak introduced a dangling pointer. The pointer *p* was later used in function *find_blk_by_id* with null pointer check. However, the first fix simply freed *p* without nullifying it.

First fix

```
......
acm_free(M_USM,case_username);
```

Second fix auth.c (a commercial OS)

```
if (IS_DEFAULT(get_choices())) {
    acm_free(M_USM,case_username);
}
```

Figure 11: Incorrect fix to a memory leak introduced data corruption. The first fix freed the data indexed by *case_username* unconditionally. However, the data should be freed only under certain conditions.

Implications: Before fixing memory leak, developers should make sure when and what should be freed.

First fix

```
if (lseek(cat->fd, nextSet, 0) == -1) {
    ......
    free(cat->set);
}
```

Second fix msgcat.c (FreeBSD)

```
if (lseek(cat->fd, nextSet, 0) == -1) {
    ......
    if (!cat->set->tag)  free(cat->set->data);
    free(cat->set);
}
```

Figure 12: Incomplete fix to a memory leak. The first fix only freed *cat->set* but forgot to free its member *data*.

Besides, fixing memory leak can be incomplete. For some complex data structures, fixers may forget to free all their members. Figure 12 shows such an example.

Implications: For complex data structures, fixers should remember to free all their members.

4.2.5 Fixing semantic bugs

Semantic bugs have very diverse root causes, so the ways to fix them are also diversified. However, we still observed one common incorrect fix pattern for semantic bugs: conditions (e.g., *if* condition) are difficult to fix correctly. As shown in Figure 3 in Section 1, the first fix to the *if* condition was still not restrictive enough. Though this pattern is frequently observed, it is not easy to leverage current techniques to detect them. We think fixing semantic bugs correctly may require more application specific knowledge from fixers.

4.2.6 General approaches to detect incorrect fixes

Understanding the impact of the change: A fundamental reason for developers to make mistakes during bug fixing is that they do not know all the potential impacts of the newly fixed code. For example, in Figure 4, the fixer was not aware that the newly added lock *sc* would deadlock with the function *bus_teardown_intr*. If all such potential "influenced code" (either through control- or data-dependency) is clearly presented to developers, they may have better chances to detect the errors. We envision compiler techniques such as program slicing [41, 12, 14, 43] can be extended to analyze such information, using the dependencies to the patch as the slicing criterion.

App	Actual fixer for incorrect fixes		Actual fixer for correct fixes		Potential optimal fixer	
	K_File	K_Func	K_File	K_Func	K_File	K_Func
A	13.2% (*0.022*)	18.1% (*0.046*)	18.3% (*0.019*)	20.5% (*0.012*)	65.0% (*0.043*)	75.1% (*0.031*)
B	9.5% (*0.013*)	11.5% (*0.023*)	15.4% (*0.016*)	27.9% (*0.031*)	39.7% (*0.024*)	51.4% (*0.022*)
C	12.8% (*0.024*)	16.1% (*0.037*)	17.2% (*0.021*)	18.4% (*0.023*)	69.8% (*0.031*)	78.1% (*0.026*)
D	7.9% (*0.017*)	12.5% (*0.035*)	15.5% (*0.024*)	16.4% (*0.021*)	78.0% (*0.023*)	78.4% (*0.039*)
AVG	10.9%	14.6%	16.6%	20.8%	63.1%	70.8%

Table 7: The fixers' average code knowledge on the buggy files/functions. The *variance* of the code knowledge is shown in the parentheses. Code knowledge is shown in the form of percentage (e.g., 13.2% means a knowledge value of 0.132). "Potential optimal fixer" is the developer with the most knowledge on the buggy files/functions but might not be always assigned the bug fixing task.

Apply checkers incrementally As discussed before, it is possible for some existing bug detection tools (checkers) [20, 9, 10] to detect some types of incorrect fixes. However, applying these tools directly on the full code base after the fix is not practical: it may take a very long time for them to scan the entire code base, which may be redundant with the original testing steps, or not always necessary. Also it may produce too many false positives. Instead, developers may want to check the code influenced by the patch first. One observation is that sometimes, just checking within the function boundary is enough to detect problems in the patch. For example, in Figure 2 (Section 1), a path-sensitive checker that simply checks the rule "lock is always paired with an unlock" can easily detect the missed *SOCK_UNLOCK* by only scanning the function that the patch modified.

Dealing with incomplete fixes Some incomplete fixes are introduced by the fact that fixers may forget to fix all the buggy regions with the same root cause. This types of incomplete fixes can be mitigated by using technique [30, 28] which searches for other places that have the same patterns or usage scenarios in entire code. For example, in Figure 5, the first fix that suggested certain shared objects need to be protected. Then developers can try to find the other places where those objects are accessed without protection. However, this technique is less effective when a consistent pattern is difficult to learn. Moreover, those incomplete fixes related to conditions (Figure 3 in Section 1) cannot be solved by this technique.

5. LACK OF KNOWLEDGE

Multiple factors can influence developers to make an incorrect fix. In this section, we focus on programmers' code knowledge. Intuitively, if a file or a function is mostly written by a developer, the developer may have higher chance to give a correct fix to a bug rooted in that file or function.

We first measured the *K_File* and *K_Func* (defined in Section 2.4) for the fixers who made the incorrect fixes. The incorrect fixes are from *sample set 1*. The results are shown in Table 7. We found that in general these fixers who made the incorrect fixes were not knowledgeable about the buggy files/functions. Specifically, they had only contributed on average 10.9% to the files and 14.6% to the functions involved in the patch before they made the incorrect fix. In comparison, Table 7 also shows the fixers' knowledge in *correct* fixes. The correct fixes are from the complement of the incorrect fix set (Table 3). We found those fixers who made the correct fixes had contributed on average 16.6% to the files and 20.8% to the functions. In other words, the knowledge of the fixers who made the correct fixes is 1.5 times of that of the fixers who made the incorrect fix based on our code knowledge metrics, indicating source code knowledge could be a factor to incorrect fixes.

But can we really find a developer who is *more knowledgeable* than the actual fixer of the incorrect fix? Table 7 also answered this question: surprisingly, by selecting the most knowledgeable developer who is still active in the development when the bugs need to be fixed as the fixer, the *K_File* and *K_Func* can reach as high as 63.1% and 70.8% respectively, which is 5~6 times of the knowledge of the actual fixers in incorrect fixes. Additionally, by selecting the two of the most knowledgeable developers as reviewers (two is the average number of reviewers in the OSes we studied), the *K_File* and *K_Func* can reach 68.2% and 78.8% respectively, which is 6~7 times of the knowledge of the actual reviewers on each incorrect fix. Note that these "potential optimal fixers" are still reachable when the bugs were opened, which suggests that the current bug fixing and reviewing process is not always assigning the problem to the developers who could be most "knowledgeable" with the bug.

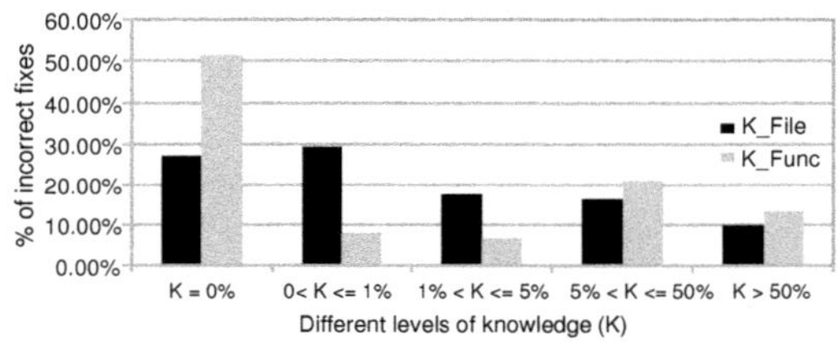

Figure 13: The distribution of incorrect fixes in different knowledge scales.

Figure 13 further studies why the *K_File* and *K_Func* in incorrect fixes are low by probing deeper into the distribution of incorrect fixes in different knowledge scales. We found the low *K_File* and *K_Func* are caused by a large portion of incorrect fixes that were made by fixers with *zero* prior knowledge to the buggy files/functions. As shown in Figure 13, *27.2% of the fixers had not contributed any lines to the file (K_File = 0%) they were about to fix*. It is even worse at the function level. 51.4% of fixers had not contributed any lines of code to the function they were about to fix. These "*first touches*" could be dangerous since the developer could have little knowledge about the particular part of code when they are doing the fix.

Besides studying the effect of code knowledge in terms of *K_File* and *K_Func*, we further study the code knowledge in terms of whether the fixer actually fixed the lines of code previously written by him. The intuition behind this is that even though a fixer had written small amount of code (i.e., small *K_File*/*K_func*), as long as the fixer was modifying the code regions that he had written, he might be still considered as the knowledgeable person for the fix. Specifically, for each fix, if any code line modified by the fix was also previously written by the same fixer, we count this fixer is fixing his own code. The result is shown in Table 8.

App	for incorrect fixes	for correct fixes
A	7.7%	26.2%
B	16.4%	44.8%
C	18.2%	25.9%
D	8.0%	24.1%
AVG	12.6%	30.3%

Table 8: The percentage of fixes that fixer is fixing his own code. For example, the number 7.7% in the first cell means: among all the incorrect fixes from OS A, 7.7% of them were actually fixed by developers who were fixing their own code.

Table 8 shows large difference between correct fixes and incorrect fixes. The ratio of the fixers who fixed their own code for correct fixes is 2.5 times of the ratio for incorrect fixes (30.3% v.s. 12.6%). This suggests fewer fixers (in term of ratio) are fixing their own code for incorrect fixes than for correct fixes, which further suggests that fixing code written by others might be prone to incorrect fixes.

Based on our study in code knowledge, a software vendor is building a tool to find knowledgeable fixers and reviewers. Sometimes when the bug report just arrives it may be unclear which files/functions contain the bug. In these cases the knowledge is more useful to assign *reviewers* who are knowledgeable to the files/functions involved in the fix after the fix is made. This knowledge can also be used in prioritizing patch testing efforts to pay more attentions to the patches fixed by less-knowledgeable fixers.

Finding: The fixers' knowledge on the buggy files/functions in correct fixes is 1.5 times of the fixers' knowledge in incorrect fixes. Fewer fixers (in term of ratio) are fixing their own code for incorrect fixes than for correct fixes. Moreover, nearly 27% of the incorrect fixes are made by developers who have not contributed a single line to the entire file they are about to fix. The potential "Optimal" developer who is most familiar with the buggy code has 5~6 times knowledge of that of the actual fixer in incorrect fixes.

Implication: It might be beneficial to assign the bugs to developers with more knowledge during the bug-triage process. The knowledge can also be considered as a factor in prioritizing the testing efforts on patches.

6. RELATED WORK

Studying incorrect fixes As briefly discussed in Introduction, several previous studies [6, 36, 33, 13] had also studied incorrect fixes. Our work is complementary in several ways: (1) we focus on large OS code, while previous studies focused on certain types of applications. (2)We study both commercial and open source code bases, while previous work studied only either open source or commericial. (3) Previous studies more focused on measuring incorrect fix ratios, while we went much beyond and also studied what types of bug fixes are more error-prone, the common mistake patterns, as well as the possible human reason in the development process for introducing incorrect fixes.

Śliwerski *et al.* [36] proposed an effective way to automatically locate fix-inducing changes by linking a version archive to a bug database. They studied the incorrect fix ratio in Eclipse and Mozilla and also found developers are easier to make incorrect changes on Friday. Purushothaman *et al.* [33] studied the incorrect fix ratio in a switching system from Lucent, but their focus was the impact of one-line changes. Gu *et al.* [13] studied the incorrect fix ratio in three Apache projects, but they focused on providing a tool to validate the patch. Baker *et al.* [6] visualized the incorrect fix ratio for a switch system in AT&T.

Human factors The influence of code knowledge on general code changes had been explored in [34, 26]. Mockus *et al.* [26] found that changes made by more experienced developers were less likely to induce failures. Rahman *et al.* [34] found file owner with higher knowledge is less associated with fix-inducing code. Our study focused on *bug fixes* and measured the knowledge of the fixers who made the incorrect fixes in commercial and widely used open source OSes. We found 27% of the incorrect fixes are made by fixers with *zero* knowledge, suggesting there might be some flaws in the overall bug assignment process. Some work [3, 24] also studied human factors for designing recommendation systems. Anvik *et al.* [3] suggested to assign fixer based on bug history. McDonald *et al.* [24] suggested to find the person who last modified the code. We proposed to assign fixer/reviewer based on code knowledge defined at line level. Besides, other aspects of human factors had also been studied. Meneely *et al.* [25] found that independent developer groups were more likely to introduce a vulnerability. Bird *et al.* [7] found that a binary might be more buggy if more developers are working on it. Nagappan *et al.* [27] studied the organizational structure and used it to build model to predict the failure proneness in Windows Vista.

Taming incorrect fixes There are different ways to solve the problem of incorrect fixes including predicting or isolating buggy changes [37, 18, 23, 44], patch validation [13, 39], automatic patching [32] and regression testing [35, 29]. Śliwerski *et al.* built a plug-in for Eclipse which shows the risk of changing a particular code location based on previous revision information. Kim *et al.* [18] also leveraged the historical source repository data to train models for predicting the correctness of a future change. McCamant *et al.* [23] compared operational abstractions generated from the old component and the new component to predict the safety of a component upgrade. Zeller *et al.* [44] proposed automated delta debugging to locate the bug introducing changes. ClearView [32] automatically generates patches without human intervention, which can reduce the chance of incorrect fixes. Besides, regression testing [35, 29] is also a common practise to ensure patches don't break the previously working functionalities. Our study discovered some incorrect fix patterns which are helpful for detecting/exposing/avoiding incorrect fixes. We studied what mistakes programmers should be aware of during bug fixing, which are also useful to design new detection tools to detect errors in fixes. Besides, we also proposed a bug assignment process based on code knowledge, which is being implemented by a large software vendor.

7. CONCLUSION AND FUTURE WORK

This paper presents one of the most comprehensive characteristic studies on incorrect bug-fixes from large operating system code bases, including a commercial OS project. We first studied the ratio and impact of incorrect fixes, and found incorrect fix is a significant problem that requires special attention. We also studied the common patterns of mistakes made in incorrect fixes that can be used to alert the programmers as well as to design detection tools to catch incorrect fixes. We finally studied the code knowledge of developers and found 27% of incorrect fixes are made by developers who have not contributed a single line to the entire file they are about to fix. A tool based on our findings to assign the most-knowledgeable developer to fix/review the bug is being built into the bug assignment process of a large software vendor.

Though we had already done some preliminary study on the the fixes to semantics bugs, there are still some interesting questions waiting to be answered considering their diversity. Therefore, we plan to have a more comprehensive study on the fixes to semantics bugs in the future. Besides, we also plan to extend the characteristic study to non-OS applications, such as server applications and client applications. Another possible direction we want to proceed is to build some checkers to detect incorrect fixes based on the patterns we learned.

8. REFERENCES

[1] Microsoft security bulletin. `http://www.microsoft.com/technet/security/current.aspx`.

[2] After buggy patch, criminals exploit Windows flaw. `http://www.infoworld.com/d/security-central/after-buggy-patch-criminals-exploit-windows-flaw-848`.

[3] J. Anvik, L. Hiew, and G. C. Murphy. Who should fix this bug? In *ICSE'06*.

[4] Apple updates leopard again. `http://voices.washingtonpost.com/fasterforward/2008/02/apple_updates_leopardagain.html`.

[5] A. Bachmann, C. Bird, F. Rahman, P. Devanbu, and A. Bernstein. The missing links: Bugs and bug-fix commits. In *FSE'10*.

[6] M. J. Baker and S. G. Eick. Visualizing software systems. In *ICSE'94*.

[7] C. Bird, N. Nagappan, P. Devanbu, H. Gall, and B. Murphy. Does distributed development affect software quality? An empirical case study of Windows Vista. In *ICSE'09*.

[8] Buggy McAfee update whacks Windows XP PCs. `http://news.cnet.com/8301-1009_3-20003074-83.html`.

[9] D. Engler and K. Ashcraft. RacerX: effective, static detection of race conditions and deadlocks. In *SOSP'03*.

[10] D. Engler, D. Y. Chen, S. Hallem, A. Chou, and B. Chelf. Bugs as deviant behavior: a general approach to inferring errors in systems code. In *SOSP'01*.

[11] M. Fischer, M. Pinzger, and H. Gall. Populating a release history database from version control and bug tracking systems. In *ICSM'03*.

[12] K. B. Gallagher and J. R. Lyle. Using program slicing in software maintenance. *IEEE Transactions on Software Engineering*, 17(8):751–761, 1991.

[13] Z. Gu, E. T.Barr, D. J.Hamilton, and Z. Su. Has the bug really been fixed? In *ICSE'10*.

[14] M. Harman, D. Binkley, and S. Danicic. Amorphous program slicing. *Journal of Systems and Software*, 68(1):45–64, October 2003.

[15] Intel reissues buggy patch. `http://www.pcworld.com/businesscenter/article/126918/rss.html`.

[16] D. Kawrykow and M. P. Robillard. Non-essential changes in version histories. In *ICSE'11*, May 2011.

[17] S. Kim, K. Pan, and J. E. James Whitehead. Memories of bug fixes. In *FSE'06*, November 2006.

[18] S. Kim, E. J. Whitehead, Jr., and Y. Zhang. Classifying Software Changes: Clean or Buggy? *IEEE Trans. Software Engineering*, 34(2):181–196, March 2008.

[19] Z. Li, L. Tan, X. Wang, S. Lu, Y. Zhou, and C. Zhai. Have things changed now? An empirical study of bug characteristics in modern open source software. In *ASID'06*.

[20] Z. Li and Y. Zhou. PR-Miner: Automatically extracting implicit programming rules and detecting violations in large software code. In *FSE'05*.

[21] S. Lu, S. Park, E. Seo, and Y. Zhou. Learning from mistakes – a comprehensive study on real world concurrency bug characteristics. In *ASPLOS*, March 2008.

[22] McAfee to reimburse customers for bad patch. `http://www.computerworlduk.com/technology/security-products/prevention/news/index.cfm?newsId=20005`.

[23] S. McCamant and M. D. Ernst. Predicting problems caused by component upgrades. In *FSE'03*.

[24] D. W. McDonald and M. S. Ackerman. Expertise recommender: a flexible recommendation system and architecture. In *CSCW'00*.

[25] A. Meneely and L. Williams. Secure open source collaboration: An empirical study of linus's law. In *CCS'09*.

[26] A. Mockus and D. M. Weiss. Predicting risk of software changes. *Bell Labs Technical Journal*, 5:169–180, 2000.

[27] N. Nagappan, B. Murphy, and V. R. Basili. The influence of organizational structure on software quality. In *ICSE'08*.

[28] T. T. Nguyen, H. A. Nguyen, N. H. Pham, J. Al-Kofahi, and T. N. Nguyen. Recurring bug fixes in object-oriented programs. In *ICSE'10*, May 2010.

[29] A. Orso, N. Shi, and M. J. Harrold. Scaling regression testing to large software systems. In *FSE'04*.

[30] Y. Padioleau, J. Lawall, R. R. Hansen, and G. Muller. Documenting and automating collateral evolutions in linux device drivers. In *Eurosys'08*.

[31] K. Pan, S. Kim, and J. E. James Whitehead. Toward an understanding of bug fix patterns. *Empirical Software Engineering*, 14(3):286–315, November 2009.

[32] J. H. Perkins, S. Kim, S. Larseng, S. Amarasinghe, J. Bachrach, M. Carbin, C. Pachecod, F. Sherwood, S. Sidiroglou, G. Sullivan, W.-F. Wong, Y. Zibin, M. D. Ernst, and M. Rinard. Automatically patching errors in deployed software. In *SOSP'09*, October 2009.

[33] R. Purushothaman and D. E. Perry. Towards understanding the rhetoric of small changes. In *MSR'04*.

[34] F. Rahman and P. Devanbu. Ownership and experience in fix-inducing code. In *UC Davis Department of Computer Science, Technical Report CSE-2010-4*, 2010.

[35] G. Rothermel, R. H. Untch, C. Chu, and M. J. Harrold. Prioritizing test cases for regression testing. *IEEE Transactions on Software Engineering*, 27:929–948, 2001.

[36] J. Śliwerski, T. Zimmermann, and A. Zeller. When do changes induce fixes? In *MSR'05*.

[37] J. Śliwerski, T. Zimmermann, and A. Zeller. Hatari: Raising risk awareness (research demonstration). In *FSE'05*, September 2005.

[38] L. Tan, D. Yuan, and Y. Zhou. /* icomment: Bugs or bad comments? */. In *SOSP*, October 2007.

[39] J. Tucek, W. Xiong, and Y. Zhou. Efficient online validationwith delta execution. In *ASPLOS'09*.

[40] D. Čubranić and G. C. Murphy. Hipikat: Recommending pertinent software development artifacts. In *ICSE'03*.

[41] M. Weiser. Program slicing. In *ICSE'83*.

[42] Z. Yin, M. Caesar, and Y. Zhou. Towards understanding bugs in open source router software. *ACM SIGCOMM Computer Communication Review*, 40(3):34–40, July 2010.

[43] D. Yuan, H. Mai, W. Xiong, L. Tan, Y. Zhou, and S. Pasupathy. Sherlog: error diagnosis by connecting clues from run-time logs. In *ASPLOS'10*.

[44] A. Zeller. Yesterday, my program worked. today, it does not. why? In *FSE'99*.

CSSL: A Logic for Specifying Conditional Scenarios

Shoham Ben-David
University of Toronto
Toronto, Canada
shoham@cs.toronto.edu

Marsha Chechik
University of Toronto
Toronto, Canada
chechik@cs.toronto.edu

Arie Gurfinkel
SEI/CMU
Pittsburgh, USA
arie@cmu.edu

Sebastian Uchitel
University of Buenos Aires, Argentina
Imperial College London, UK
suchitel@dc.uba.ar

ABSTRACT

Scenarios and use cases are popular means of describing the intended system behaviour. They support a variety of features and, notably, allow for two different interpretations: existential and universal. These modalities allow a progressive shift from examples to general rules about the expected system behaviour. The combination of modalities in a scenario-based specification poses technical challenges when automated reasoning is to be provided. In particular, the use of conditional existential scenarios, of which use cases with preconditions are a common example, require reasoning in branching time. Yet, formally grounded approaches to requirements engineering and industrial verification approaches shy away from branching-time logics due to their relatively unintuitive semantics.

In this paper, we define an extension of an (industry standard) linear-time logic with sufficient branching expressiveness to allow capturing conditional existential statements. The resulting logic, called CSSL (Conditional Scenario Specification Language), has an efficient model-checking procedure. It supports reasoning about heterogeneous requirements specifications that include universal and existential statements in the form of use cases and conditional existential scenarios, and other sequence chart variants, in addition to general (linear) liveness and safety properties. We report on two industrial case studies in which the logic was used to specify and verify scenarios and properties.

Categories and Subject Descriptors

D.2.4 [**Software Engineering**]: Software/Program Verification—*Model checking*

General Terms

Design, Verification

1. INTRODUCTION

Scenarios, use case and user stories are popular means of describing intended system behaviour [20, 31, 17, 1, 26]. They provide an intuitive framework for describing *examples* of how the system-to-be, its environment and users are expected to interact.

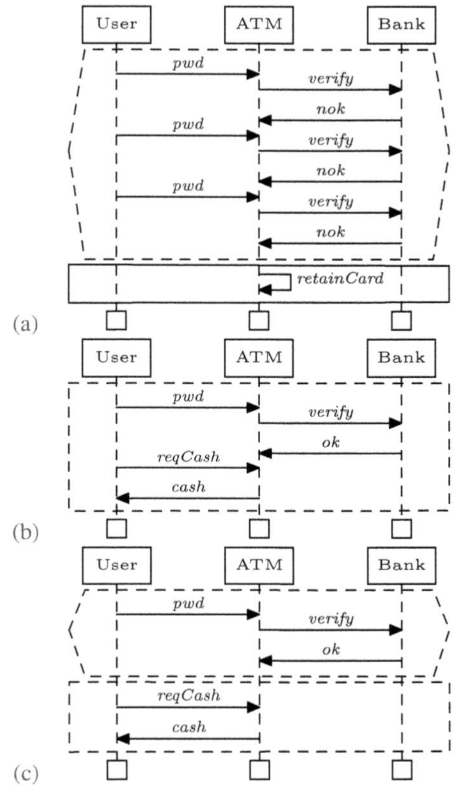

Figure 1: Several ATM scenarios: (a) P_2: a universal conditional scenario; (b) P_3: an existential scenario; (c) P_4: an existential conditional scenario.

Languages for formally describing scenario-based specifications have extended preliminary and widespread notations such as the ITU 1992 standard Message Sequence Charts (MSCs) [16] to allow for a variety of features. One important extension, embodied in Live Sequence Charts (LSCs) [9], is the possibility of distinguishing between existential and universal scenarios to allow a progressive shift from examples to general rules about the expected system behaviour [12], within one specification framework.

The combination of modalities in a scenario-based specification poses technical challenges when automated reasoning is to be provided. In particular, the use of conditional existential scenarios, of which use cases [17], when used with preconditions, are a notable example, require reasoning in branching time. Yet, formally grounded approaches to requirements engineering [30, 33] (and

Permission to make digital or hard copies of all or part of this work for personal or classroom use is granted without fee provided that copies are not made or distributed for profit or commercial advantage and that copies bear this notice and the full citation on the first page. To copy otherwise, to republish, to post on servers or to redistribute to lists, requires prior specific permission and/or a fee.
ESEC/FSE'11, September 5–9, 2011, Szeged, Hungary.
Copyright 2011 ACM 978-1-4503-0443-6/11/09 ...$10.00.

Name (Type)	Description	Logical Expression	Exp. Res.
P_1 (U)	A non-authenticated user may never withdraw cash	LTL: $G(\text{logout} \rightarrow (\neg\text{cash}\ U\ (\text{verify} \wedge X(\text{ok}))))$	T
		PSL, CSSL: $G(\text{logout} \rightarrow (\neg\text{cash}\ U\ \text{verify} \cdot \text{ok}))$	T
P_2 (UC)	Three consecutive unsuccessful login attempts must lead to retaining the user's card	LTL: $G(\text{pwd} \rightarrow X(\text{verify} \rightarrow X(\text{nok} \rightarrow X(\text{pwd} \rightarrow \ldots \rightarrow X(\text{nok} \rightarrow X\text{retainCard}))))$	T
		PSL, CSSL: $G((\text{pwd} \cdot \text{verify} \cdot \text{nok})^3 \mapsto \text{nok} \cdot \text{retainCard})$	T
P_3 (E)	It is possible for the user to be authenticated, and then request and obtain cash	LTL: $G(\text{pwd} \rightarrow X(\text{verify} \rightarrow X(\text{ok} \rightarrow X(\text{reqCash} \rightarrow G(\neg\text{cash})))))$	F
		PSL: $G((\text{pwd} \cdot \text{verify} \cdot \text{ok} \cdot \text{reqCash}) \mapsto G(\neg\text{cash}))$	F
		CSSL: *true* $\mid\!\leadsto$ $(\text{pwd} \cdot \text{verify} \cdot \text{ok} \cdot \text{reqCash} \cdot \text{cash})$	T
P_4 (EC)	Whenever a user successfully logs into an ATM, it should be possible for her to request and obtain cash	LTL, PSL : N/A	N/A
		CSSL: $G((\text{pwd} \cdot \text{verify} \cdot \text{ok}) \mid\!\leadsto X(\text{reqCash} \cdot \text{cash}))$	T
P_5 (EC)	After login, it should be possible to withdraw money before changing the pin	LTL, PSL : N/A	N/A
		CSSL: $G((\text{pwd} \cdot \text{verify} \cdot \text{ok}) \mid\!\leadsto (\neg\text{changePin}\ U\ (\text{reqCash} \cdot \text{cash})))$	T
P_6 (EC)	After login, it should be possible to change the pin before withdrawing money	LTL, PSL : N/A	N/A
		CSSL: $G((\text{pwd} \cdot \text{verify} \cdot \text{ok}) \mid\!\leadsto (\neg(\text{reqCash} \cdot \text{cash})\ U\ \text{changePin}))$	T
P_7 (EC)	A legitimate user should not be limited in the number of operations she is allowed	LTL, PSL : N/A	N/A
		CSSL: $G((\text{pwd} \cdot \text{verify} \cdot \text{ok}) \mid\!\leadsto (G\ \neg\text{logout}) \wedge (GF(\text{reqCash} \vee \ldots \vee \text{changePin})))$	T

Table 1: Several properties of the ATM system. The column "Type" lists the scenario type: universal conditional (UC), existential conditional (EC), existential (E) or universal(U).

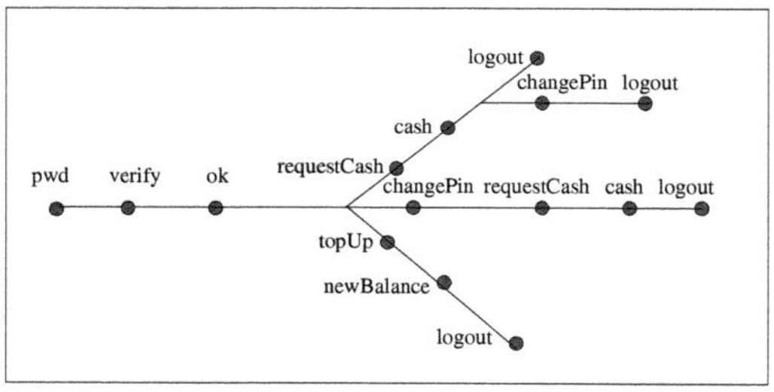

Figure 2: A collection of behaviors of an ATM system.

industrial verification researchers [35]) shy away from branching-time logics due to their relatively unintuitive semantics.

In this paper, we define an extension of a linear-time logic with sufficient branching expressiveness to allow expressing conditional existential statements. The resulting logic, called CSSL (Conditional Scenario Specification Language), has an efficient model-checking procedure and therefore supports reasoning about heterogeneous requirements specifications that include universal and existential statements in the form of use cases and conditional existential scenarios, LSCs, MSCs, and other sequence chart variants, in addition to general (linear) liveness and safety properties.

Conditional Existential and Universal Scenarios. An existential scenario specifies behavior that the system is expected to exhibit, among others which are yet to be specified or are specified elsewhere. For example, an existential scenario P_3 of the ATM system is depicted in Figure 1(b) using a notation in the style of MSCs. The interpretation of the scenario is: "it is possible for the user to be authenticated, and then request and obtain cash". We denote that the scenario is to be interpreted existentially using a dashed line around the sequence chart.

Conditional scenarios are, loosely, statements of the form "if x then y", where x and y are scenarios. For instance, a conditional universal scenario P_2 is depicted using an LSC notation in Figure 1(a). The top part, enclosed in a dashed bracket, is a conditional, called a *prefix* (or, in the LSC terminology, a *pre-chart*). The bottom part, enclosed in a solid rectangle, is the *suffix* (or, in the LSC terminology, a *main chart*).

Conditional universal scenarios are interpreted as follows: whenever the prefix holds, then the suffix *must follow*. Hence, the scenario of Figure 1(a) states that when three consecutive authentication failures occur, the ATM must retain the user's card.

Conditional existential scenarios, although syntactically very similar to their universal counterparts, are interpreted differently. In Figure 1(c), we depict an conditional existential scenario P_4 in the notation style of eTS [29]. The suffix is enclosed in a dashed rectangle to distinguish it from universal conditional scenarios. The interpretation of conditional existential scenarios is that when the prefix occurs, then the suffix should be *possible*. Thus, the conditional existential scenario of Figure 1(c) states that whenever a user successfully logs into an ATM, it *should be possible* for her to request and obtain cash.

Unlike conditional *universal* statements, conditional existential statements do not forbid behaviour. That is, there can be an execution of the system where the prefix is true but the suffix is not. For example, it is possible to have an execution of the ATM system where a user successfully logs in and then tops up her mobile phone rather than withdrawing cash. However, conditional existential statements require that every time the prefix holds, *some* continuation where the suffix holds must exist. This semantics, albeit with a different syntax, is frequently found in the form of use cases with a preconditions: [17] When the precondition holds, it is expected (but not mandatory) that the user be able to "execute" the use case.

Thus, conditional existential statements refer to the possibilities or branches of behaviour that are available. When the current state of the system is that the user has logged in, a number of possibilities may exist, but obtaining cash must be one of them (see Figure 2). Table 1 shows three other existential conditional scenarios, P_5, P_6 and P_7, capturing possible interactions between the user and the ATM system, once she logs in. Several other examples of existential conditional scenarios are described in the TV controller case study in Section 5.1.

Reasoning about System Behaviour. Automated reasoning about specifications is an important software engineering task that can help identify problems early and thus result in cheaper fixes. Reasoning requires representing statements about system behaviour in some formal language – a logic. Temporal logics have been used to reason about software system behaviour extensively. Specifically, *linear* temporal logics such as LTL [23] and its more recent extension, Property Specification Language (PSL) [14, 10], which adds regular expressions, are strongly favoured for describing requirements [30, 33] as they have a relatively intuitive semantics.

For example, properties P_1-P_3 are expressed in LTL as shown in Table 1: P_1 is a (non-conditional) universal statement , P_2 a conditional universal statement and P_3 is a non-conditional existential statement. Note that to verify that a system satisfies P_3 described as a scenario in Figure 1(b), it is necessary to check that the LTL formalization of P_3 does not hold. A *counterexample* to the property acts as a witness of the existential statement. We indicate this by putting "F" as the expected result (Exp. Res.) in Table 1. In addition, note that for P_2 (and other properties), we assumed that events occur consecutively. Relaxing this assumption would result in a more complex LTL formula (with lots of "until"s).

Table 1 also lists properties $P_1 - P_3$ in PSL. These show that PSL can be more compact and more convenient for capturing sequences of events, commonly found in scenarios. The properties use a familiar regular expression syntax, with "$\cdot$" expressing concatenation and "x^n" or "x^*" – finite repetition of string x. For example, in the PSL expression of property P_2 in Table 1, the entire string of `pwd`, `verify` and `nok` repeats three times. The PSL formalization of P_3 uses the *suffix implication operator* ($\mapsto$) which captures the intended semantics of conditional universal scenarios: when the left hand side holds, the right hand side must follow.

Conditional existential scenarios, on the other hand, cannot be expressed using linear logics, since their combination of universal and existential fragments requires branching (and has, in fact, been formalized using CTL and CTL* [28]).

CSSL: Conditional Scenario Specification Language. In this paper, we define and study an extension of PSL with sufficient branching expressiveness to allow us to capture conditional existential statements by enriching PSL with a top-level branching operator called "branching suffix implication", and denoted by a symbol $\mapsto\!\!\!\rightsquigarrow$. The resulting logic, called CSSL, allows us to compose "true" linear fragments specifying prefix and suffix. For example, the prefix of the existential conditional scenario P_4 in Table 1 is expressed as (pwd$\cdot$verify$\cdot$ok), i.e., a regular expression consisting of concatenation of three individual events. Its suffix is X(reqCash $\cdot$ cash), describing that in the next state, `reqCash` should happen, followed by `cash`. Thus, the entire scenario is required "globally" and is expressed in CSSL as $P_4 = G((\text{pwd} \cdot \text{verify} \cdot \text{ok}) \mapsto\!\!\!\rightsquigarrow X(\text{reqCash} \cdot \text{cash}))$. CSSL expressions for scenarios P_5, P_6, and P_7 are shown in Table 1 as well. Moreover, while only the negation of the existential property P_3 can be expressed in PSL or LTL, the property can be easily expressed in CSSL, with the prefix *true* (see Table 1).

The resulting logic is strictly more expressive than PSL and is in fact a fragment of CTL* extended with regular expressions. Yet, unlike the full CTL*, this language has an efficient model-checking procedure. CSSL is not the only tractable fragment of CTL*. Linear tractable fragments include LTL and PSL (which, as we said earlier, are not expressive enough for conditional existential statements). A branching logic CTL is also tractable; yet it is not an option because it does not extend PSL (specifically, its regular expressions) and does not support expressing sequences of events commonly present in scenarios. Our approach contributes a tractable linear logic with regular expressions and limited branching.

Contributions. This paper makes the following contributions:

- We introduce a new operator, called *branching suffix implication*, extending PSL, and show that this operator is useful for expressing existential conditional scenarios. Therefore, heterogeneous specifications that include use cases, sequence chart variants and general (linear) safety and liveness properties can now be expressed in the same "linear with a bit of branching" language CSSL.
- We show that CSSL is not more computationally complex than PSL. We then develop a model-checking algorithm for CSSL, implemented on top of NuSMV [7].
- We report on our experience using CSSL to specify and verify properties of two industrial examples.

The rest of the paper is organized as follows: In Section 2, we give the technical background; introduce the new logic CSSL in Section 3 and, in Section 4, describe how to model-check this logic, including our implementation on top of NuSMV. We report on two case studies in Section 5. After comparing our approach to related work in Section 6, we conclude in Section 7 with a summary and an outline of future research directions.

2. BACKGROUND

In this section, we present the necessary definitions and notation.

Models and Properties.

DEFINITION 1 (KRIPKE STRUCTURE). *Let AP be a finite set of atomic propositions. A* Kripke structure *K over AP is a tuple $K = (S, I, R, L)$, where S is a finite set of states, $I \subseteq S$ is the set of initial states, $R \subseteq S \times S$ is a* total *transition relation, that is, for every state $s \in S$ there is a state $s' \in S$ such that $R(s, s')$, and L is a labeling function $L : S \to 2^{AP}$ that labels each state with the set of variables true in that state.*

We say that $\pi = s_0, s_1, \ldots$ is a *path* in K iff $s_0 \in I$ and $\forall i$, $(s_i, s_{i+1}) \in R$. We denote by π^k the suffix of π starting at s_k.

DEFINITION 2 (LINEAR TEMPORAL LOGIC (LTL) [23]). *Given a finite set AP of atomic propositions, formulas of LTL are recursively defined as follows:*

- *Every atomic proposition is an LTL formula.*
- *If φ and ψ are LTL formulas, then so are $\neg\varphi$, $\varphi \wedge \psi$, $X\varphi$ and $[\varphi U \psi]$,*

where X and U stand for the "next" and the "until" operators, respectively.

Additional operators "future" and "globally" are defined as syntactic sugar using the ones above:

$$F\varphi = [\mathit{true}\ U \varphi] \qquad G\varphi = \neg F \neg\varphi$$

The formal semantics of an LTL formula is defined with respect to an infinite path $\pi = s_0, s_1, \ldots$ of a given Kripke structure $K = (S, I, R, L)$, where $s_0 \in I$:

$$\begin{array}{lll} \pi^i \models p & \text{iff} & p \in L(s_i) \\ \pi^i \models \neg\varphi & \text{iff} & \pi^i \not\models \varphi \\ \pi^i \models \varphi \wedge \psi & \text{iff} & (\pi^i \models \varphi) \wedge (\pi^i \models \psi) \\ \pi^i \models X\varphi & \text{iff} & \pi^{i+1} \models \varphi \\ \pi^i \models [\varphi U \psi] & \text{iff} & \exists k \geq i \text{ s.t. } (\pi^k \models \psi) \wedge \\ & & (\forall i \leq j < k \,.\, \pi^j \models \varphi) \end{array}$$

A formula φ holds in a Kripke structure K, denoted $K \models \varphi$, iff it holds in every path of K.

DEFINITION 3 (COMPUTATION TREE LOGIC (CTL) [8]). *Given a finite set AP of atomic propositions, CTL formulas are recursively defined as follows:*

- *Every atomic proposition is a CTL formula.*

- *If φ and ψ are CTL formulas then so are $\neg\varphi$, $\varphi \wedge \psi$, $AX\varphi$, $EX\varphi$, $A[\varphi U \psi]$ and $E[\varphi U \psi]$,*

where AX and EX are "forall next" and "exist next" operators, and AU and EU are "forall until" and "exists until" operators, respectively.

Additional operators, "forall/exists future" and "forall/exists globally", are defined as syntactic sugar over the ones above:

$$AF\varphi = A[\text{true } U\varphi] \qquad EF\varphi = E[\text{true } U\varphi]$$
$$AG\varphi = \neg E[\text{true } U\neg\varphi] \qquad EG\varphi = \neg A[\text{true } U\neg\varphi]$$

The formal semantics of a CTL formula is defined with respect a Kripke structure $K = (S, I, R, L)$.The notation $K, s \models \varphi$ means that the formula φ is true in state s of the Kripke structure K.

$$
\begin{array}{lll}
K, s \models p & \text{iff} & p \in L(s) \\
K, s \models \neg\varphi & \text{iff} & K, s \not\models \varphi \\
K, s \models \varphi \wedge \psi & \text{iff} & (K, s \models \varphi) \wedge (K, s \models \psi) \\
K, s_0 \models AXp & \text{iff} & \text{for all paths } (s_0, s_1, \ldots) \,.\, K, s_1 \models p \\
K, s_0 \models EXp & \text{iff} & \text{for some path } (s_0, s_1, \ldots) \,.\, K, s_1 \models p \\
K, s_0 \models A[\varphi U \psi] & \text{iff} & \text{for all paths } (s_0, s_1, \ldots). \\
 & & (\exists i \geq 0 \,.\, K, s_i \models \psi) \wedge \\
 & & (\forall 0 \leq j < i \,.\, K, s_j \models \varphi) \\
K, s_0 \models E[\varphi U \psi] & \text{iff} & \text{for some path } (s_0, s_1, \ldots). \\
 & & (\exists i \geq 0 \,.\, K, s_i \models \psi) \wedge \\
 & & (\exists 0 \leq j < i \,.\, K, s_j \models \varphi)
\end{array}
$$

We say that a CTL formula φ holds in a Kripke structure $K = (S, I, R, L)$ iff $\forall s_i \in I \,.\, K, s_i \models \varphi$.

Definition 4 (Fair Computation). *Let b be Boolean expression over AP and K be a Kripke structure. We say that a computation path π of K is* fair *with respect to the fairness constraint b iff the LTL formula $GF(b)$ holds on π.*

We write $K, s \models_{fair} \varphi$ for fair *satisfaction of φ by K and s that is defined as $\models$ above with all "paths" replaced by "fair paths".*

Automata and Computations.

Definition 5 (Automaton). *An* automaton *A is a tuple $(Q, \Sigma, \delta, Q_0, F)$ where: Q is a finite set of states, Σ is a finite set of symbols (the* alphabet*), $\delta \subseteq Q \times \Sigma \times Q$ is a* total *transition relation , $Q_0 \subseteq Q$ is the set of initial states and $F \subseteq Q$ is the set of final (accepting) states.*

A *run* r of an automaton on an input word $w = a_0, a_1, \ldots$ is a (finite or infinite) sequence of states $q_0, q_1, \ldots$, where $\forall i, q_i \in Q$ such that $q_0 \in Q_0$, $(q_i, a_i, q_{i+1}) \in \delta$.

We use two kinds of automata: non-deterministic finite automata (NFA) and non-deterministic Büchi automata (NBA). If A is an NFA, runs over it are finite. We say that a run $r = q_0, q_1, \ldots, q_n$ is *accepting* iff $q_n \in F$. Thus, an NFA accepts finite words over Σ. The universe of finite words is denoted by Σ^*.

Runs of an NBA A are infinite. For a run r, we define *Inf*(r) to be the set of states that occur infinitely often in r. We say that r is *accepting* iff *Inf*$(r) \cap F \neq \emptyset$. Thus, NBA automata accept infinite words over Σ. The universe of infinite words is denoted by Σ^ω.

A word $w \in \Sigma^* \cup \Sigma^\omega$ is *accepted* by A iff there exists as accepting run for it. The language of A, denoted $\mathcal{L}(\mathcal{A})$, is the set of all words accepted by A.

Definition 6 (Fusion Automaton [10]). *Let $A = (Q_A, \Sigma_A, \delta_A, Q_A^0, F_A)$ be an NFA and $B = (Q_B, \Sigma_B, \delta_B, Q_B^0, F_B)$ be an NFA or an NBA. The fusion automaton of A and B is an automaton $A \circ B = (Q_A \cup Q_B, \Sigma_A \cup \Sigma_B, \delta_{A \circ B}, Q_A^0, F_B)$, such that*

$$\delta_{A \circ B} = \delta_A \cup \delta_B \cup \{(q, a, q') \mid \exists f \in F_A \,.\, (q, a, f) \in \delta_A \wedge \exists i \in Q_B^0 \,.\, (i, a, q') \in \delta_B\}\,.$$

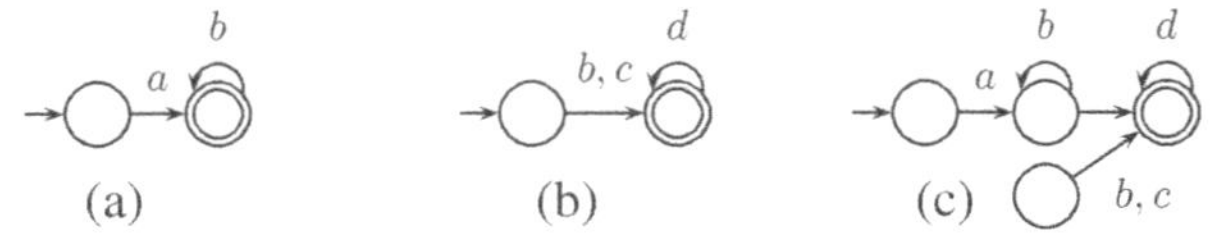

Figure 3: Automata for: (a) $a \cdot b^*$, (b) $(b + c) \cdot d^*$, and (c) the fusion $(a \cdot b^*) \circ ((b + c) \cdot d^*)$.

The fusion automaton $A \circ B$ has the initial states of A, and the final states of B. The transitions to a final state of A are fused with the transitions from an initial state of B. Note that while A is an NFA, B can be either an NFA or an NBA, and the resulting fusion automaton $A \circ B$ is of the same type as B. An example of a fusion automaton over NFAs in Figure 3(a) and Figure 3(b) is shown in Figure 3(c).

3. CONDITIONAL SCENARIO SPECIFICATION LANGUAGE (CSSL)

In this section, we define the syntax and semantics of Conditional Scenario Specification Language (CSSL). CSSL extends PSL with a *branching suffix implication* (BSI). We first review PSL and then describe syntax and semantics of the new branching operator, illustrating it on properties of our running example.

3.1 Property Specification Language (PSL)

PSL adds regular expressions to LTL via the operator $\mapsto$, known as the *suffix implication operator*. The formula $r \mapsto \varphi$ (read r "suffix-implies" φ) requires that *if* there exists a non-empty prefix of the path satisfying r *then* the suffix starting at the last letter of the prefix should satisfy φ.

Definition 7 (SEREs). *Sequentially Extended Regular Expressions (SEREs) of PSL are built from a set AP of atomic propositions, defined recursively as follows:*

- *Every Boolean expression over AP is a SERE.*
- *If r and s are SEREs, then so are r^*, $r \cdot s$, $r \circ s$, $r \cup s$, and $r \cap s$,*

where r^* is the Kleene star operator, $r \cdot s$ is the concatenation of two SEREs, $r \circ s$ is fusion – the concatenation of two SEREs with an overlap of one state, $r \cup s$ is the union and $r \cap s$ is the intersection of two SEREs, respectively.

We omit SERE operators that can be defined from the ones above.

Let $K = (S, I, R, L)$ be a Kripke structure. The *language* of SERE over K is a set of finite paths, defined inductively as follows:

$$
\begin{array}{lll}
\mathcal{L}(b) & = & \{s \mid s \in S \wedge b \in L(s)\} \\
\mathcal{L}(r^*) & = & \{\varepsilon\} \cup \{\pi \mid \exists n \geq 1 \,.\, \pi = \pi_1 \cdot \pi_2 \cdot \ldots \cdot \pi_n \wedge \\
 & & \forall 1 \leq i \leq n \,.\, \pi_i \in \mathcal{L}(r)\} \\
\mathcal{L}(r \cdot s) & = & \{\pi_1 \cdot \pi_2 \mid \pi_1 \in \mathcal{L}(r) \wedge \pi_2 \in \mathcal{L}(s)\} \\
\mathcal{L}(r \circ s) & = & \{\pi_1 \cdot s \cdot \pi_2 \mid \pi_1 \cdot s \in \mathcal{L}(r) \wedge s \cdot \pi_2 \in \mathcal{L}(s)\} \\
\mathcal{L}(r \cup s) & = & \mathcal{L}(r) \cup \mathcal{L}(s) \\
\mathcal{L}(r \cap s) & = & \mathcal{L}(r) \cap \mathcal{L}(s)
\end{array}
$$

Definition 8 (PSL). *PSL formulas are defined inductively:*

- *Every Boolean expression over AP is a PSL formula.*

- *If φ and ψ are PSL formulas and r a SERE, then the following are PSL formulas: $\neg\varphi$, $\varphi \wedge \psi$, $\varphi U \psi$, $X\varphi$, $r \mapsto \varphi$, and $r \diamond\!\!\rightarrow \varphi$.*

The *suffix implication operator* $r \mapsto \varphi$ states that whenever a prefix of the path matches a SERE r, then the suffix of the path (with one state overlapping) must satisfy φ.

The *suffix conjunction operator* $r \diamond\!\!\rightarrow \varphi$ holds iff there exists some prefix of the path that matches r and the (overlapping) suffix satisfies φ. Note that the suffix conjunction operator is dual to the suffix implication: $\neg(r \mapsto \varphi) = r \diamond\!\!\rightarrow \neg\varphi$.

The semantics of PSL formulas is defined with respect to infinite paths in a Kripke structure $K = (S, I, R, L)$. The semantics of a Boolean expression b and the formulas $\neg\varphi$, $\varphi \wedge \psi$, $\varphi\ U\ \psi$ and $X\varphi$ are the same as those for LTL. Let $\pi = s_0, s_1, ...$ be a path in K. We define semantics of the two suffix operators below:

$$\pi^i \models r \mapsto \varphi \quad \text{iff} \quad \forall j\,.\,(s_i \cdot \dots \cdot s_j \in \mathcal{L}(r) \Rightarrow \pi^j \models \varphi)$$
$$\pi^i \models r \diamond\!\!\rightarrow \varphi \quad \text{iff} \quad \exists j\,.\,(s_i \cdot \dots \cdot s_j \in \mathcal{L}(r) \wedge \pi^j \models \varphi)$$

Several PSL properties are shown in Table 1. Note that in some formulas $r \leadsto \psi$, we use a regular expression r' as ψ. This should be read as an abbreviation for $r' \diamond\!\!\rightarrow$ *true*. For property P_1, neither the suffix implication nor the suffix conjunction operator is being used, and so the expression of the property is the same as LTL. Properties P_2 and P_3 use the suffix implication operator.

3.2 Branching Suffix Implication (BSI)

We now enrich PSL with a branching construct $\leadsto$, called "branching suffix implication" (BSI). Intuitively, $p \leadsto \psi$, where p is a regular expression and ψ a PSL formula, is satisfied by a Kripke structure K iff every finite path in K that satisfies p can be extended with a suffix (in K) that satisfies ψ.

DEFINITION 9 (BSI SATISFACTION). *Let r be a regular expression, ψ be a PSL formula, and $K = (S, I, R, L)$ be a Kripke structure. Then, $K, s \models (r \leadsto \psi)$ iff for all paths $\pi = (s_0, \dots, s_n)$ in K s.t. $\pi \models r$, there exists a suffix $\pi' = (s'_0, \dots, s'_k)$ s.t. $\pi \cdot \pi'$ is a path in K and $\pi' \models \psi$.*

We say $K \models r \leadsto \psi$ iff $\forall s_0 \in I\,.\,K, s_0 \models (r \leadsto \psi)$.

Additional operators "next" and "globally" are defined as syntactic sugar using the BSI operator:

$$X(r \leadsto \psi) = \mathit{true} \cdot r \leadsto \psi \qquad G(r \leadsto \psi) = \mathit{true}^* \cdot r \leadsto \psi$$

The resulting language, which includes PSL together with BSI, is called CSSL.

Table 1 lists several properties that use the new BSI operator (corresponding to $P_3 - P_7$). Note that most of these use the operator "globally" introduced above.

Consider the CSSL expression of property P_3. With prefix *true*, it easily allows us to specify the existential scenario as a property which is intended to hold in the system. Properties $P_3 - P_7$ illustrate that the suffix for a BSI operator can be an arbitrary LTL formula. Moreover, this suffix is finite for properties $P_3 - P_6$ and infinite for property P_7.

Since CSSL subsumes PSL, all scenarios in Table 1, corresponding to all four scenario types, are expressible in this new language.

4. MODEL-CHECKING CSSL

In this section, we discuss how to model-check CSSL properties. Specifically, we show how to reduce model-checking of a CSSL property with a BSI operator, of the form $\varphi = r \leadsto \psi$, to the CTL model checking, via the construction of an auxiliary automaton.

We give the construction and prove its correctness in Section 4.1 and analyze its complexity in Section 4.2. In Section 4.3, we discuss the implementation of our method in NuSMV [7], and illustrate it on the ATM example. In the rest of this section, when we say a CSSL formula, we always mean a formula like φ above.

4.1 From CSSL to CTL

Let $K = (S, I, R, L)$ be a Kripke structure and $\varphi = r \leadsto \psi$ be a CSSL specification. Without loss of generality, we assume that $\epsilon \notin \mathcal{L}(r)$, where ϵ is the empty string. Otherwise, we simply extend K with a dummy initial state and modify both r and ψ to skip that state.

In order to model check whether φ holds in K ($K \models \varphi$), we build an automaton A_φ and a CTL formula P_φ such that

$$K \models \varphi \iff K \times A_\varphi \models P_\varphi.$$

In order to reduce a CSSL formula $\varphi = r \leadsto \psi$ to CTL, we first build the automaton A_φ (see below) and then use it to derive the CTL formula P_φ. Depending on ψ, the reduction is either *finite* or *infinite*, If ψ holds after a finite number of steps, i.e., its satisfaction is detected by an NFA, we call it a *finite* formula. For example, as in the CSSL expression of property P_5. Otherwise, it needs an NBA, which makes it an *infinite* formula, e.g., as in the CSSL expression of property P_7, ¬login should hold forever.

Note that our *finite* and *infinite* classification is based on the witnesses, and is dual to the standard notions of *safety* and *liveness* that are based on counterexamples. A safety formula, e.g., Gp, is one for which a counterexample is finite. A liveness formula, e.g., Fp, is one for which the counterexample is infinite. On the other hand, we say that Gp is *infinite* because its witness is infinite, and, similarly, Fp is *finite*.

4.1.1 Finite Suffix

Given a formula $\varphi = r \leadsto \psi$, where ψ is finite, our goal is to build an automaton A_φ and a CTL formula $P_{\varphi_{\text{fin}}}$.

We first build two NFAs: A_r that accepts $\mathcal{L}(r)$, and A_ψ that accepts ψ. Both automata are built using standard methods [13, 36]. We then build A_φ – a *fusion* automaton (see Definition 6) of A_r and A_ψ.

For $P_{\varphi_{\text{fin}}}$, we introduce three new atomic propositions.

- *in_A*$_\psi$ is true exactly when A_φ is in one of the states that originated from A_ψ;
- *at_F*$_r$ is true exactly when A_φ is in a final state of A_r;
- *at_F*$_\psi$ is true exactly when A_φ is in a final state of A_ψ.

The CTL formula $P_{\varphi_{\text{fin}}}$ is defined as follows:

$$P_{\varphi_{\text{fin}}} = AG((EX\ \mathit{at\_F}_\varphi) \Rightarrow EX(\mathit{in\_A}_\psi \wedge EF\ \mathit{at\_F}_\psi)) \quad (1)$$

The prefix of the formula, $EX\ \mathit{at\_F}_\varphi$, identifies those states s on the execution paths that have a one-step (EX) continuation to an accepting state of A_r. Recall that in the fusion automaton A_φ, we added transitions from one state before final in A_r to one state after initial in A_ψ. We thus require that s has a one-step continuation that 'lands' in a state of A_ψ. We further require that one of the branches that land in A_ψ have a continuation leading to the final state of A_ψ (denoted *at_F*$_\psi$), which is where ψ is accepted.

The above construction allows us to perform model-checking of CSSL formulas using standard CTL model-checking tools.

Correctness. To show correctness of the above construction, we need to show that $K \models \varphi \iff K \times A_\varphi \models P_{\varphi_{\text{fin}}}$.

Proof: Let $\varphi = r \mapsto \psi$ be a CSSL formula and let A_r and A_ψ be the automata for the prefix r and the (finite) suffix ψ, respectively. Let A_φ be the fusion automaton of A_r and A_ψ, and let P be as defined by (1).

Assume $K \times A_\varphi \not\models P$. We show that $K \not\models r \mapsto \psi$. From the assumption, let $(s_0, a_0) \cdots (s_n, a_n)$ be the counterexample to the AG part of P. Then, the path $\pi = s_0, \ldots, s_n$ satisfies r since A_r has an accepting run $a_0, \ldots, a_{n+1}$ on π. Note that the run has one more state than letters in the input. Assume that $s_n \not\models EX in\_A_\psi$. Then, by construction of the fusion automaton, the path $s_0, \ldots, s_n$ cannot be continued to satisfy the CSSL formula. Assume $s_n \models EX in\_A_\psi$ and $s_n \not\models EX(in\_A_\psi \wedge EF at\_F_\psi)$. Then, there is no continuation of the path $s_0, \ldots, s_n$ that satisfies the suffix. This completes the proof.

For the other direction, assume $K \not\models r \mapsto \psi$. Then there exists a path $s_0, \ldots, s_n$ in K that satisfies r and cannot be continued to satisfy ψ (i.e., a counterexample to $r \mapsto \psi$). Thus, there exists an execution $(s_0, a_0), \ldots, (s_n, a_n), (s_{n+1}, a_{n+1})$ of $K \times A_\varphi$ such that a_{n+1} is an accepting state of A_r. Assume by contradiction that there exists a continuation $(s_n, b_1), \ldots, (s_{n+m}, b_m)$ such that b_m is an accepting state of A_ψ. Then the path $s_0, \ldots, s_n, \ldots, s_{n+m-1}$ satisfies $r \mapsto \psi$; hence, $s_0 \ldots, s_n$ is not a counterexample. This contradicts our assumption that $K \not\models r \mapsto \psi$. □

4.1.2 *Infinite Suffix*

Let $\varphi = p \mapsto \psi$, where ψ is infinite. A_ψ is now an NBA and so is the fusion automaton A_φ. That is, for a computation path to be accepted, a final state of A_φ should be visited infinitely often. We reduce the infinite case to *fair* CTL. The acceptance condition of A_φ is translated into a fairness constraint. Note that using at_F_ψ as a fairness constraint is too strong: it would mean that only paths where at_F_ψ appears infinitely often are checked; a bug, if it exists, would be masked. Instead, we introduce another atomic proposition, in_A_r, which is true exactly when A_φ is in one of the states that originated from A_r, and define $in\_A_r \vee at\_F_\psi$ to be the fairness constraint.

The (fair) CTL formula for this case is given below:

$$P_{\varphi_{\text{inf}}} = AG((EX\ at\_F_\varphi) \Rightarrow EX(in\_A_\psi \wedge EG\ \top)) \quad (2)$$

As in the finite case, we first identify the states s on the execution paths that have a one-step (EX) continuation to an accepting state of A_r. We then require that each s has a one-step continuation that 'lands' in a state of A_ψ. At this point, we only require that one of the branches that continue to A_ψ has an infinite continuation. This is sufficient, since the fairness constraint ensures that infinite paths left in the model (that can no longer visit states from A_r) are those on which a final state of A_ψ is visited infinitely often. Thus, ψ holds on those paths.

Correctness. To show correctness of the above construction, we need to show that $K \models \varphi \iff K \times A_\varphi \models_{\text{fair}} P_{\varphi_{\text{inf}}}$.

Proof: Assume $K \times A_\varphi \not\models P_{\varphi_{\text{inf}}}$. Then there exists a path $(s_0, a_0) \cdots (s_n, a_n)$ in $K \times A_\varphi$ (under the fairness constraint) such that $(s_n, a_n) \models (EX\ at\_F_\varphi)$ but $(s_n, a_n) \not\models EX(in\_A_\psi \wedge EG\ \top)$. The path $\pi = s_0, \ldots, s_n$ in K satisfies r since A_r has an accepting run $a_0, \ldots, a_{n+1}$ on π. We have to show that s_n has no continuation satisfying ψ. Assume by contradiction that a continuation $\pi^n = s_n, s_{n+1}, \ldots$ such that $\pi^n \models \psi$ does exist in K. By the construction of the fusion automaton, there exists a path $(s_n, a_n), (s_{n+1}, a_{n+1}), \ldots$ in $K \times A_\varphi$ such that $a_n, a_{n+1}, \ldots$ is a run of A_ψ that accepts ψ. This means that $a_n, a_{n+1}, \ldots$ visits a final state of A_ψ infinitely often, and thus it is a *fair* computation. We have found a fair path, starting at (s_n, a_n) on which $EX(in\_A_\psi \wedge EG\ \top)$ holds, contradicting our assumption.

For the other direction, assume $K \not\models r \mapsto \psi$. Then there exists a path $s_0, \ldots, s_n$ in K that satisfies r and cannot be continued to satisfy ψ. Thus, there exists an execution path $\pi = (s_0, a_0), \ldots, (s_n, a_n), (s_{n+1}, a_{n+1})$ of $K \times A_\varphi$ such that a_{n+1} is an accepting state of A_r. Note that π can be continued with $(s_{n+2}, a_{n+2}), (s_{n+3}, a_{n+3}), \ldots$, where $a_{n+2}, a_{n+3}, \ldots$ are states of A_r (because of the totality of the transition relation). Note further that this path is *fair* (it stays in states from A_r forever). Thus, state (s_n, a_n) exists in a fair path of $K \times A_\varphi$. We know that $(s_n, a_n) \models (EX\ \ at\_F_\varphi)$ (along π). We have to show that $(s_n, a_n) \not\models EX(in\_A_\psi \wedge EG\ \ \top)$. Assume by contradiction that it does. Then from (s_n, a_n) there is a continuation $\pi' = (s'_{n+1}, a'_{n+1}), (s'_{n+2}, a'_{n+2}), (s'_{n+3}, a'_{n+3}), \ldots$ that enters the automaton A_ψ, and is infinite. By the fairness constraint, π' must be *fair*, and since it is out of A_r, it must visit an accepting state of A_ψ infinitely often. Thus, $s_n, s'_{n+1}, , s'_{n+2}, s'_{n+3} \ldots$ is a path in K that satisfies ψ, which contradicts our assumption that such a path does not exist. □

4.2 Complexity

The complexity of CTL model checking is linear in the size of the model and the formula [8]. Model-checking complexity of a CSSL formula $\varphi = r \mapsto \psi$ on a Kripke structure K is $O(|K| \times |A_\varphi| \times |P_\varphi|)$. Note that the size of P_φ is constant and does not depend of φ. The size of A_φ is $O(|A_r| + |A_\psi|)$, where $|A_r| = O(|r|)$. The size of A_ψ depends on ψ. In the general case, we need to build a Büchi automaton for the LTL formula ψ, which is of size $2^{|\psi|}$. The complexity of model checking of CSSL is thus $O(|K| \times |r| \times 2^{|\psi|})$, which is the model-checking complexity of the original PSL.

Yet, for some PSL formulas, the size of the automaton A_ψ can be of size $|\psi|$. For such cases, model-checking complexity of CSSL is $O(|K| \times |r| \times |\psi|)$, i.e., if model-checking of ψ is efficient, then so is model-checking of the resulting CSSL (and PSL) formula.

Thus, we are able to enrich PSL with a branching operator without incurring an additional model-checking cost.

4.3 Implementation and Illustration

We have implemented the translation of a CSSL formula $\varphi = r \mapsto \psi$ on top of the model checker NuSMV.

Let SM_r be the state machine for the prefix r and SM_ψ – the state machine for the suffix. We illustrate the construction using two properties specified in Table 1: P_5, for the finite suffix case, and P_7 for the infinite suffix.

We start with property P_5, where

$$\begin{aligned} r &= \textit{true}^* \cdot \text{pwd} \cdot \text{verify} \cdot \text{ok} \\ \psi &= (\neg\text{changePin}\ U\ (\text{reqCash} \wedge X(\text{cash}))) \end{aligned}$$

The code for SM_r in the language of NuSMV, is shown in Figure 4, lines 3-11. It describes a simple non-deterministic state machine, with its initial state set by the `init` statement, and transitions determined by a `case` statement. `case`*s* are evaluated top to bottom. When the first condition becomes *true*, its corresponding assignment is executed, determining the `next` state. The language allows specification of non-deterministic transitions, captured in a set. These mean that the machine may non-deterministically

```
1: VAR SMr : {1,2,3,4,accept,sink};
2: ASSIGN
3:   init(SMr) := {1,2};
4:   next(SMr) :=
5:     case
6:       SMr = 1                 : {1,2};
7:       SMr = 2 & pwd           : 3;
8:       SMr = 3 & verify        : 4;
9:       SMr = 4 & ok            : accept;
10:      TRUE                    : sink;
11:    esac;
12:
13: DEFINE SMrCanAccept := (SMr = 4 & ok);
14:
15: VAR SMpsi : {wait,1,2,3,accept,sink};
16: ASSIGN
17:   init(SMpsi) := wait;
18:   next(SMpsi) :=
19:   case
20:     SMpsi = wait & !SMrCanAccept : wait;
21:     SMpsi = wait & reqCash       :{wait,3};
22:     SMpsi = wait & !changePin    :{wait,1,2};
23:     SMpsi = 1 & !changePin       :{1,2};
24:     SMpsi = 2 &  reqCash         : 3;
25:     SMpsi = 3 &  cash            : accept;
26:     TRUE                         : sink;
27:   esac;
28:
29: DEFINE In_SMpsi := !(SMpsi in {wait,sink});
30:
31: SPEC AG(EX(SMr=accept) ->
32:       EX (In_SMpsi & EF (SMpsi = accept)))
```

Figure 4: NuSMV code for checking property P_5.

choose an element of the set as its next-state value and its initial value.

The main challenge in the implementation is the *fusion* of SM_r and SM_ψ, since SM_ψ starts working in the initial state of the system while we need it to start operating only when SM_r has reached an accepting state. To solve this problem, we add a `wait` state to SM_ψ, in which it starts and stays until SM_r has (almost) reached an accepting state. At that point, SM_ψ is triggered and starts its intended work.

On line 13, we `DEFINE SMrCanAccept` as a "going to accept" signal, used to trigger the suffix automaton SM_ψ. We then implement SM_ψ in lines 15-27. While SM_ψ can leave the `wait` state in lines 21 and 22, we allow it to stay in `wait` as one of the non-deterministic options. This is done to accommodate cases where SM_r reaches the accepting state more than once on a given path, and thus SM_ψ should be triggered more than once as well.

Using SM_r and SM_ψ, and the intermediate definition of the signal `In_SMpsi`, we specify the property to be checked as shown on lines 31-32 in Figure 4. This model is verifiable by NuSMV.

We now consider the property P_7 in Table 1, where

$$r = true^* \cdot \text{pwd} \cdot \text{verify} \cdot \text{ok}$$
$$\psi = (G\, \neg\text{logout}) \wedge (GF(\text{reqCash} \vee \ldots \vee \text{changePin}))$$

Here, the suffix is infinite. In order to encode an NBA automaton to represent it, we need to use NuSMV's fairness mechanism.

The state machine for the prefix r is the same as in Figure 4. The state machine for the suffix ψ is given in Figure 5, lines 1-13. We then make additional definition in line 15 and add a fairness constraint (line 17). This ensures that no legal path is omitted for the wrong reason. We can now define the specification as shown in lines 19-20, and the resulting code is again verifiable by NuSMV.

```
1: DEFINE Operation: (reqCash | ... | changePin);
2: VAR SMpsiInf : {wait,1,2,accept,sink};
3: ASSIGN
4:   init(SMpsiInf) := wait;
5:   next(SMpsiInf) :=
6:   case
7:     SMpsiInf = wait & !SMrCanAccept     : wait;
8:     SMpsiInf = wait &  SMrCanAccept     :{wait,1};
9:     SMpsiInf = 1 & !logout              :{1,2};
10:    SMpsiInf = 2 & Operation & !logout  :accept;
11:    SMpsiInf = accept & !logout         : 1;
12:    TRUE                                :sink;
13:  esac;
14:
15: DEFINE In_SMpsiInf := !(SMpsiInf in {wait,sink});
16:
17: FAIRNESS (SMpsiInf in {wait,accept})
18:
19: SPEC AG (EX(SMr=accept)
20:          -> EX (In_SMpsiInf & EG True))
```

Figure 5: NuSMV code for checking property P_7.

(a) (b)

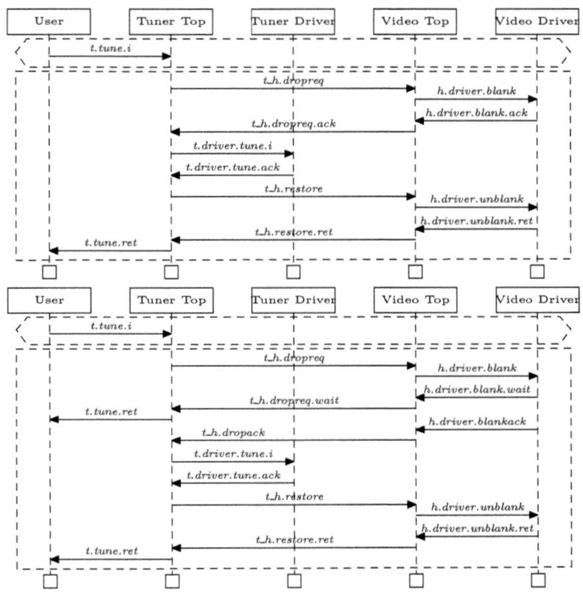

Figure 6: Two scenarios of the TV system.

5. CASE STUDIES

In this section, we present our experience specifying and verifying CSSL properties for two realistic examples. These examples and the underlying tool support have been successfully evaluated by the ESEC/FSE artifact evaluation committee.

5.1 Philips TV Controller Protocol

We describe the application of CSSL to the specification and verification of an industrial protocol for a product family of Philips television sets [34]. The product family supports sets with multiple tuners and video output devices that can be configured by the television user to display several signals in different configurations. The protocol is concerned with controlling the signal path in a TV to avoid visual artefacts. To do so, it coordinates between four main component types: video and tuner tops which perform horizontal communication to route the signal path, and video and tuner drivers that perform vertical communication between their corresponding top and physical device.

The key property that the protocol must ensure is that the signal

Name	Expression	Result
TV_1	G(t_h.restore.ret $\Rightarrow$ ($\bigwedge_{i \in Freq}$ $\neg$t.driver.tune.i U (t_h.dropreq.ack $\vee$ t_h.dropack)))	Yes
TV_2	*true** $\cdot$ t.tune.i $\leadsto$ (t_h.dropreq $\cdot$ h.driver.blank $\cdot$ h.driver.blank.ack $\cdot$ t_h.dropreq.ack $\cdot$ t.driver.tune.i $\cdot$ t.driver.tune.ack $\cdot$ t_h.restore $\cdot$ h.driver.unblank $\cdot$ h.driver.unblank.ret $\cdot$ t_h.restore.ret $\cdot$ t.tune.ret)	No
TV_3	*true** $\cdot$ t.tune.i $\leadsto$ (t_h.dropreq $\cdot$ h.driver.blank $\cdot$ h.driver.blank.wait $\cdot$ t_h.dropreq.wait $\cdot$ (t.tune.ret $\cdot$ h.driver.blankack $\mid$ h.driver.blankack $\cdot$ t.tune.ret) $\cdot$ t_h.dropack $\cdot$ t.driver.tune.i $\cdot$ t.driver.tune.ack $\cdot$ t_h.restore $\cdot$ h.driver.unblank $\cdot$ h.driver.unblank.ret $\cdot$ t_h.restore.ret $\cdot$ t_h.dropack.ret $\cdot$ h.driver.blankack.ret)	No
TV_4	*true** $\cdot$ t.tune.i $\leadsto$ (t_h.dropreq $\cdot$ h.driver.blank $\cdot$ h.driver.blank.ack $\cdot$ t_h.dropreq.ack $\cdot$ t.driver.tune.i $\cdot$ t.driver.tune.wait $\cdot$ (t.tune.ret $\cdot$ t.driver.tuneack $\mid$ t.driver.tuneack $\cdot$ t.tune.ret) $\cdot$ t_h.restore $\cdot$ h.driver.unblank $\cdot$ h.driver.unblank.ret $\cdot$ t_h.restore.ret $\cdot$ t.driver.tuneack.ret)	No
TV_2'	*See Section 5.1*	Yes
TV_3'	*See Section 5.1*	Yes
TV_4'	*See Section 5.1*	Yes
TV_5	(*true** $\cdot$ t_h.dropreq.wait $\cdot$ $\neg$(t_h.dropack $\vee$ t.tune.ret $\vee$ t.tune.i)*) $\leadsto$ (t.tune.ret $\cdot$ t.tune.i)	Yes
TV_6	(*true** $\cdot$ t.driver.tune.wait $\cdot$ $\neg$(t.driver.tuneack $\vee$ t.tune.ret $\vee$ t.tune.i)*) $\leadsto$ ($\neg$t.driver.tuneack U t.tune.i)	Yes
TV_7	G(t_h.dropreq.ack $\Rightarrow$ X(t_h.dropack $\Rightarrow$ ($\neg$t_h.dropreq U t_h.restore.ret)))	Yes
TV_8	(*true** $\cdot$ t_h.dropreq.wait $\cdot$ $\neg$(t_h.dropack $\vee$ t.tune.ret $\vee$ t.tune.i)* $\cdot$ t.tune.i) $\leadsto$ (*true* $\cdot$ t.tune.ret $\cdot$ t.driver.tune.i $\cdot$ t.driver.tuneack $\cdot$ t_h.restore $\cdot$ t_h.restore.ret $\cdot$ t_h.dropack.ret)	Yes
TV_9	(*true** $\cdot$ t.tune.i) $\leadsto$ (($\neg$t.tune.j $\wedge$ $\neg$t.driver.tune.j)* $\cdot$ t.driver.tune.i)	Yes

Table 2: Properties of the TV Controller Protocol.

frequency on the wire connected to a video device is only changed by the tuner driver when the video device has been blanked. We formalize it as a CSSL property TV_1 later in this section. First, we look at some simple scenarios involving this protocol.

The simplest scenario, which consists of a TV set with one tuner and one video device, is when the user changes the channel on which the tuner top receives a `t.tune.i` request, where i is the frequency of the channel to be displayed. Then the tuner top requests the video top to blank the screen (`t_h.dropreq`). The video top requests the video driver to blank the video device (`h.driver.blank`), receives an acknowledgment (`h.driver.blank.ack`) and then acknowledges the tuner top's request (`t_h.dropreq.ack`). The tuner top then requests the tuner driver to change its signal to frequency i (`t.driver.tune.i`) and once it receives the acknowledgment (`t.driver.tune.ack`), requests the video top, which, in turn, requests the video driver to unblank the screen and display the image being sent over the wire (`t_h.restore`, `h.driver.unblank`, `h.driver.unblank.ret`, `t_h.restore.ret`). This behaviour is specified as an existential triggered scenario shown in Figure 6(a) and formalized in CSSL as property TV_2. This and other properties of the TV system are shown in Table 2.

Part of the complexity of the protocol is that requests from tops to drivers may not be acknowledged immediately. For instance, the video driver may respond to a blanking request from a video top with a `h.driver.blank.wait` event rather than with `h.driver.blank.ack`. In this case, the protocol returns and waits for an upcall, `h.driver.blankack` from the video driver to the video top, informing it that the video has finally been blanked. The upcall is sent to the tuner top (`t_h.dropack`) which proceeds as in the previous scenario to change the wire frequency and then acknowledges the upcall (`t_h.dropack.ret`) to the video top which, in turn, acknowledges it to the video driver (`h.driver.blankack.ret`). This behavior is specified in Figure 6(b) and formalized as a CSSL property TV_3. Events `t.tune.ret` and `h.driver.blankack` can occur in any order.

The tuner driver may not acknowledge straight away, responding with `t.driver.tune.wait` rather than `t.driver.tune.ack` to a request of changing the signal's frequency. In this case, the protocol returns and awaits an upcall from the tuner driver (`t.driver.tuneack`). When the upcall occurs, the video is unblanked and the upcall acknowledged (`t.driver.tuneack.ret`). Events `t.tune.ret` and `t.driver.tuneack` can occur in this scenario in any order, as captured in property TV_4 (see Table 2).

A key aspect of this protocol, which can be traced to a responsiveness requirement, is that the protocol must process user tuning requests while the TV set is in intermediate states (i.e., those where it is waiting for an upcall from the tuner device or video device). Such properties can be expressed as existential triggered scenarios and formalized in CSSL as TV_5 and TV_6, respectively.

Another important aspect of the protocol, which can be traced to efficiency constraints, is that it must not request blanking the screen if it is already blanked. This is a safety property, formalized in CSSL as TV_7. TV_7 together with TV_5 and TV_6 are inconsistent with the first three existential scenarios, $TV_2 - TV_4$. The latter require that if users request tuning the TV set, then the protocol must be able to do so in three different ways (depending on whether devices acknowledge or upcall). Each of these scenarios requests that it be possible to blank the video device. TV_5 requires user tune requests to be processed while the video screen is blanked; hence, in conjunction with any of $TV_2 - TV_4$, the protocol must able to process the user's request by (among other things) blanking the screen. However, this would violate property TV_7.

Scenarios $TV_2 - TV_4$ are too strong, since the trigger part of the scenario (or the prefix of the CSSL formula) does not account for the possible states in which the TV set may be in when receiving a `t.tune.i` command. They require the behaviour (the main chart of the scenario or the suffix of the CSSL formula) that should only be required when the protocol is idle (i.e., when the frequency being displayed on the video device is that of the last `t.tune` command). This can be formalized by changing the prefix in $TV_2 - TV_4$ to be

$$true^* \cdot \text{t.tune.i} \cdot (\bigwedge_{j \in Freq} \neg\text{t.tune.j})^* \cdot \text{t.driver.tune.i} \cdot (\bigwedge_{j \in Freq} \neg\text{t.tune.j})^* \cdot (\text{t.driver.tune.ack} \vee \text{t.driver.tuneack}) \cdot (\bigwedge_{j \in Freq} \neg\text{t.tune.j})^* \cdot \text{t.tune.i}$$

resulting in new properties, $TV_2' - TV_4'$, respectively.

There are many properties that are relevant to the protocol in this case study. Due to space restrictions, we mention two final conditional existential statements related to the responsiveness of requests to tune the TV set. The first one, called TV_8, strengthens TV_6 by exemplifying one way in which `t.tune` must be processed when it is received while waiting for the screen to be blanked. The other, called TV_9, states that whenever the tuner is requested to tune on frequency i (`t.tune.i`), then it must be possible for the next frequency change on the wire to be to frequency i.

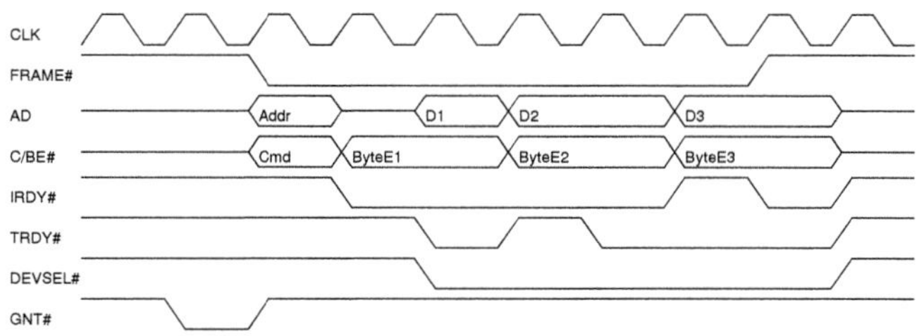

Figure 7: An example of a PCI transaction.

Finally, we now formalize the main safety property TV_1, discussed in the beginning of this section. `t_h.dropreq.ack` and `t_h.dropack` are sent from the video top to the tuner top as are the events that indicate that the video device has been blanked, and `t_h.restore.ret` (sent from the video top to the tuner top) is the only event that indicates that the video device has been unblanked.

In order to verify properties $TV_1 - TV_9$ and $TV_2' - TV_4'$, we took a sample model of the TV-tuner, expressed in FSP [21] and originally written by Magee and van Ommering [34] (the latter is one of the original protocol developers). Using a simple LTSA-to-SMV converter, we converted it into the format of NuSMV. Then each of the properties has been encoded in CTL using the process described in Section 4. Table 2 shows the result of verifying all of the properties formalized above against the NuSMV model of the protocol. The table shows that properties $TV_2 - TV_4$ fail, whereas others hold. All properties took under a second to verify, so we do not list the exact running times. While the protocol model is relatively complex, it is quite small by NuSMV's standards, and thus the analysis took a very short time.

We chose to start our presentation with properties that do not hold in the model. While it is commonplace to present, as use cases or scenarios, examples of behaviours that a system is expected to exhibit, often the preconditions or triggers of such scenarios are too weak. When this happens, the suffix behaviour is exhibited in cases when, in fact, it should not. Conditions for existential statements can be complicated to get right, as we have experienced during this case study, and we certainly welcomed having mechanized model-checking support to help us debug our specs. In fact, they underwent several iterations before they took their current, correct, form. Furthermore, our current model-checking approach converts the CSSL property to (fair) CTL, which means that counterexamples that NuSMV produced were very incomplete (see a discussion in Section 7).

5.2 PCI

Our second case study demonstrates the usefulness of the branching-suffix implication operator and thus the resulting CSSL logic in a different setting, that of hardware verification.

The *Peripheral Component Interconnect* (PCI) [27] is a local bus protocol commonly used for the communication between hardware devices (such as network cards, modems and USB ports) inside a computer. While multiple devices may be connected to a single PCI bus, we describe here a typical transaction between one initiator (or "master") and one target device. All signals of the PCI protocol are 'active low', that is, are asserted when dropped from 1 to 0.

A transaction on a PCI bus starts with the initiator asserting its FRAME#, and at the same time driving the address of the target device on the address/data (A/D) bus, as well as the command (the type of transaction) on the C/BE bus. The cycle in which FRAME# is asserted is called the *address-phase*. The selected device, once recognizing its address, asserts the DEVSEL# signal. In a write transaction, the initiator, when ready, drives the data to be transferred on the A/D bus and asserts its IRDY# signal. This is the beginning of a *data-phase*. When the target is ready to read the data, it asserts its TRDY# signal; until then, the IRDY# must remain active. Whenever both TRDY# and IRDY# are asserted together, the data held in the A/D bus is assumed to be transferred, and this is the end of a data-phase. In a read transaction, the target device is the one responsible to drive the data on the A/D bus, asserting TRDY# when the data is ready for transfer. A transaction may have multiple data-phases, and each one may last one cycle (if IRDY# and TRDY# are active together in consecutive cycles) or more if one or more of IRDY#, TRDY# are inactive for some cycles. The last data-phase is indicated by the initiator with FRAME# de-asserting when IRDY# is being asserted. One cycle after the last data-phase ends, IRDY#, DEVSEL# and TRDY# must all be de-asserted. Figure 7 demonstrates a simple PCI transaction with 3 data phases. Another target-driven signal (which does not appear in Figure 7) is the STOP# signal. It is used by the target to indicate that it cannot complete the transaction. If STOP# is asserted, with or without the assertion of TRDY#, it means that the target requests the initiator to end the current transaction and "retry" it later.

In order to verify a PCI target device, we model the behavior of the *initiator device*, mainly that of FRAME#, IRDY# and the C/BE bus, that control the command of the transactions. For simplicity, we model only bit 0 (C/BE[0]) of this bus, which determines whether the transaction is a read (0) or a write (1). For the verification to be thorough, our model of the initiator allows all legal behaviors to occur.

We concentrate on checking the dependency between the assertion of TRDY# and IRDY#. The PCI specification indicates that each of the initiator and target is free to assert its corresponding RDY# signal when ready. In read transactions, however, the initiator is allowed to wait until the target asserts TRDY# before asserting its IRDY# (so it can have more than one cycle to process the data). If both the initiator and the target condition the assertion of their RDY# signals on the assertion of the other's, this results in a deadlock. The above case was a real problem found in verification of the PCI component performed by an industrial partner.

Such a problem can be identified by checking the following CSSL property: "If when FRAME# is asserted (address-phase) C/BE[0]=0 (it is a read transaction), then at the beginning of every data-phase that is not retried, there exists at least one continuation where TRDY# is asserted before IRDY#." It is formalized as follows (F stands for FRAME#, D for DEVSEL#, S for STOP#, I and T for IRDY and TRDY, respectively):

$$(true^* \cdot \mathsf{F} \cdot (\neg \mathsf{F} \wedge (\mathsf{C/BE[0]=0})) \cdot (\neg \mathsf{F})^* \cdot (\neg \mathsf{F} \wedge \neg \mathsf{D} \wedge \mathsf{S} \wedge ((\mathsf{T} \wedge \mathsf{I}) \vee (\neg \mathsf{T} \wedge \neg \mathsf{I}))) \mapsto X((\mathsf{I} \wedge \mathsf{S})\ U\ \neg \mathsf{T}).$$

Such a property failed when checked on the original model, exposing an error identified after the built PCI bus was used in the field.

It is common knowledge that verification engineers naturally think about universal properties, which is one of the reasons why industrial standards are based on linear temporal logics. This case study demonstrates that universal properties are not sufficient, since there are bugs that require some branching to be detected. CSSL adds just the right amount of branching needed.

6. RELATED WORK

Scenarios. Our work is concerned with reasoning about the system behaviour in the presence of universal and existential statements, and, in particular, of conditional existential statements which are commonplace in scenario and use-case specifications. Hence, our work is related to a large body of work in the area of scenario-based specifications which were originally conceived as existential, i.e., example based, specifications.

The ITU Message Sequence Chart standard [16] and, subsequently, the UML Sequence Diagrams are widespread notations for documenting scenarios which in their original formulations do not provide mechanisms for distinguishing between existential and universal statements and, in practice, have been interpreted existentially. Many variants of these languages have been proposed. The first to support multiple modalities is LSC [9]. However, LSCs do not support conditional existential scenarios. Although the original formulation of existential LSCs included a prechart (a prefix) P and a main chart (a suffix) M, their semantics is equivalent to a non-conditional existential scenario that concatenates both charts (i.e., $P \cdot M$). Later versions of LSCs, e.g., [3], drop the existential prechart. Indeed, formalization of LSC semantics can be given in linear temporal logic. CSSL is capable of supporting a more expressive language than LSCs, one that includes proper conditional existential scenarios.

Sibay et al. [28] present a language with conditional existential and conditional universal scenarios. The language semantics is provided in terms of CTL, and verification is done through construction of Modal Transition Systems (MTS) [19], model merging, and MTS weak alphabet refinement [5]. The language is restricted to two temporal patterns: a triggered existential statement of the form $AG(\mathit{trigger} \Rightarrow \bigwedge_w EXw)$, where w ranges over the language of the main chart, and a triggered universal statement of the form $AG(\mathit{trigger} \Rightarrow \bigwedge_w EXw \wedge AX \bigvee_w w)$, where w ranges of the language of the main chart. The languages of the trigger and main chart are defined by a finite partial orderings of events. CSSL can express properties not expressible by the scenario language of [28].

Arguably the most widespread form of conditional existential statements are use cases [17], when they are used with preconditions, as advocated in popular software engineering practitioners' literature [25]. The importance of documenting and reasoning about such kinds of statements can be inferred from popular development methods such as RIP [18], and has been argued for from multiple perspectives such as supporting "what-if" elaboration of requirements specifications [22] and the progressive shift from existential statements, in the form of examples and use-cases, to universal statements in the form of declarative properties [12]. This motivates the need for a logic with the expressiveness of CSSL.

Branching properties. It is often assumed that linear properties are easy to express and, thus, linear logics are widely used to specify requirements [30, 33]. On the other hand, branching is seen as confusing and often avoided, and, thus, there are very few approaches which use branching logics. Yet some forms of branching are essential. For example, an industrial case study [24] showed that properties that are natural in the early design phases (especially when some information is uncertain) are branching. The authors of the study informally proposed the same branching pattern that underlies CSSL. We are unaware of other approaches to extend existing logics with "limited" branching.

Logic and model-checking. The early 2000's saw an activity, led by the IEEE Accellera committee, to define an industrial temporal logic language. In addition to PSL [14], it yielded the Standard for SystemVerilog Assertions (SVA) [15]. Both PSL and SVA are linear languages with regular expressions. They are supported by major CAD vendors (see [4]). The use of regular expressions improves both the expressive power and usability of these languages.

However, neither of these languages can express widespread branching properties like existential conditional statements. While PSL's standard defines an "optional branching extension", it is essentially CTL, which does not allow the use of linear temporal operators or regular expressions.

CTL* is a very expressive language which allows combination of linear and branching temporal operators (but not regular expressions) and is more than adequate for capturing scenarios. However, not only is specifying properties in CTL* highly non-intuitive, we are not aware of any model-checkers for it.

The model-checking method introduced in this paper combines auxiliary automata with temporal logic specifications, where the propositions used in the specification are derived from the automata states. This was inspired by the work described in [2], where automata are embedded into regular expression-based specifications. In [2], this approach was used to gain reusability as well as to reduce the overall size of the automata built. In this paper, it gives us a clean way to implement a fusion automaton, and thus to add branching capabilities to an otherwise linear language.

7. CONCLUSION AND FUTURE WORK

Software engineers use a variety of languages to specify the intended behaviour of a software system. These include scenarios, use cases, declarative global properties, as well as local operational properties such as preconditions for actions. This heterogeneity is due to the different contexts in which such languages are used (initial elicitation and elaboration stages, communication with stakeholders, final complete specification, communication with designers, etc.); however, it poses technical challenges when such specifications need to be analyzed automatically. In particular, the use of conditional existential scenarios (or use cases) require reasoning in branching time while grounded approaches to behaviour specification and verification shy away from branching-time logics due to their relatively unintuitive semantics.

In this paper, we introduced an extension to PSL which gives "just enough branching" to be able to capture existential conditional scenarios without an increase in the model-checking complexity. The resulting language, called CSSL, can be used for formalizing and reasoning about heterogeneous specification that include use-cases, variants of sequence chart notations and general (linear) safety and liveness properties. We showed how to do model-checking of CSSL properties using NuSMV and illustrated the usefulness of CSSL on two real-life examples.

Like all branching properties, CSSL has a fundamental problem with counterexamples produced when a property fails. Since a CSSL formula $r \leadsto \psi$ consists of a universal and an existential part, when it fails, the counterexample is provided only for the universal part, demonstrating a path on which r holds. To demonstrate failure of ψ, we would have to produce the entire set of continuations of this path. This makes debugging difficult, especially if ψ is a long formula. In the future, we are interested in creating an automated support for debugging failed CSSL properties.

Our work on formal reasoning of scenario languages is not limited to verification, when the model of the system is already given. Scenarios are often used as a specification language for software, as a prototyping mechanism, and as a way to synthesize an operational model [32]. In this context, efficient algorithms for *satisfiability*, *synthesis* and *vacuity detection* are a must [5]. Satisfiability allows us to determine whether a set of CSSL properties is consistent, i.e., whether it is possible to build a model in which all of these properties hold. Vacuity [11] enables us to check whether a formula holds "for the wrong reason", i.e., vacuously. This can happen when a universal prefix of conditional scenarios is false, and thus the property is always true. It would also be interesting not only to tell that a property is vacuous but also to determine the cause of this vacuity [11]. Finally, given a (consistent) set of CSSL properties, it would be very desirable to synthesize a preliminary operational model which is guaranteed to satisfy them.

Synthesis, satisfiability and vacuity checking algorithms exist for CTL*, so we have a clear upper bound on the complexity of the corresponding CSSL procedures. However, we are yet to determine whether algorithms with better lower bounds for CSSL exist.

Finally, PSL allows us to specify safety properties of the system-to-be, thus providing an *over-approximation* of its behaviour. Our new operator, BSI, allows us to express existential and conditional existential scenarios, describing *under-approximations* of the behaviour of the system-to-be. We are interested in studying whether CSSL can effectively replace μ-calculus as the language characterizing properties of partial behavioural models, synthesized from properties and scenarios [6, 32].

Acknowledgements. We thank the anonymous ESEC/FSE referees for their suggestions for improving the paper and Winnie Lam for her help with the tool support. The work was partially funded by ERC PBM-FIMBSE, CONICET, UBACyT X021, PIP112-200801-00955KA4, PICT-PAE 37279, NSERC and Ontario Postgraduate Fellowship.

8. REFERENCES

[1] I. F. Alexander and N. Maiden, editors. *Scenarios, Stories, Use Cases: Through the Systems Development Life-Cycle.* Wiley, 2004.

[2] S. Ben-David, D. Fisman, and S. Ruah. "Embedding Finite Automata within Regular Expressions". *Theor. Comput. Sci.*, 404(3):202–218, 2008.

[3] Y. Bontemps, P. Heymans, and P.-Y. Schobbens. "From Live Sequence Charts to State Machines and Back: A Guided Tour". *IEEE TSE*, 31(12):999–1014, 2005.

[4] D. Borionne, M. Liu, P. Ostier, and L. Fesquet. "PSL-based Online Monitoring of Digital Systems". In *Proc. of FDL'05*, pages 465–479, 2005.

[5] G. Brunet, M. Chechik, D. Fischbein, N. D'Ippolito, and S. Uchitel. "Weak Alphabet Merging of Partial Behaviour Models". *ACM TOSEM*, 2011. To appear.

[6] M. Chechik, A. Gurfinkel, S. Uchitel, and S. Ben-David. "Raising Level of Abstraction with Partial Models: A Vision". In *Proc. of NSF/MSR Wrksp. on Usable Verification*, 2010.

[7] A. Cimatti, E. Clarke, E. Giunchiglia, F. Giunchiglia, M. Pistore, M. Roveri, R. Sebastiani, and O. Tacchella. "NuSMV 2: An Opensource Tool for Symbolic Model Checking". In *Proceedings of CAV'02*, pages 359–364. Springer, 2002.

[8] E.M. Clarke and E.A. Emerson. "Design and synthesis of synchronization skeletons using Branching Time Temporal Logic". In *Proc. Workshop on Logics of Programs*, volume 131 of *LNCS*, pages 52–71. Springer-Verlag, 1981.

[9] W. Damm and D. Harel. "LSCs: Breathing Life into Message Sequence Charts". *FMSD*, 19:45–80, 2001.

[10] C. Eisner and D. Fisman. *A Practical Introduction to PSL.* Springer, 2006.

[11] A. Gurfinkel and M. Chechik. "How Vacuous Is Vacuous?". In *Proc. of TACAS'04*, volume 2988 of *LNCS*, pages 451–466, March 2004.

[12] D. Harel and R. Marelly. *Come, Let's Play: Scenario-Based Programming Using LSC's and the Play-Engine.* Springer-Verlag New York, Inc., 2003.

[13] J.E. Hopcroft and J.D. Ullman. *Introduction to Automata Theory, Languages, and Computation.* Addison-Wesley, 1979.

[14] IEEE Standard for Property Specification Language (PSL), Annex B. IEEE Std 1850™-2010.

[15] IEEE Standard for SystemVerilog, Annex F. IEEE Std 1800™-2009.

[16] ITU-TS. ITU-TS Recommendation Z.120: Message Sequence Chart (MSC). Geneva, 1992.

[17] I. Jacobson. *Object-Oriented Software Engineering: a Use Case driven Approach.* Addison–Wesley, 1995.

[18] I. Jacobson, G. Booch, and J. Rumbaugh. *The Unified Development Process.* Addison-Wesley, 1999.

[19] K. G. Larsen and B. Thomsen. "A Modal Process Logic". In *Proc. of LICS*, pages 203–210, July 1988.

[20] S. Leue and T. Systä, editors. *Scenarios: Models, Transformations and Tools*, volume 3466 of *LNCS*. Springer, 2005.

[21] J. Magee and J. Kramer. *"Concurrency - State Models and Java Programs"*. John Wiley, 1999.

[22] N. Maiden and S. Robertson. "Developing Use Cases and Scenarios in the Requirements Process". In *Proc. of ICSE'05*, pages 561–570, 2005.

[23] A. Pnueli. "The Temporal Logic of Programs". In *Proc. of IEEE Symp. on Foundation of Comp. Sci.*, pages 46–57, 1977.

[24] A. Post, I. Menzel, and A. Podelski. "Applying Restricted English Grammar on Automotive Requirements – Does it Work? A Case Study". In *Proc. of REFSQ'11*, volume 6606 of *LNCS*, pages 166–180. Springer, 2011.

[25] R.S. Pressman. *Software Engineering: A Practitioner's Approach.* McGraw-Hill, 7th edition, 2010.

[26] K. Schwaber. *Agile Project Management With Scrum.* Microsoft Press, 2004.

[27] T. Shanley and D. Anderson. *PCI System Architecture.* Mindshare, Inc., 4th edition, 1999.

[28] G. Sibay, V. Braberman, S. Uchitel, and J. Kramer. "Synthesizing Modal Transition Systems from Triggered Scenarios", March 2010. submitted for journal publication.

[29] G. Sibay, S. Uchitel, and V. Braberman. "Existential Live Sequence Charts Revisited". In *Proceedings of ICSE'08*, pages 41–50, 2008.

[30] R. Smith, G. Avrunin, L. Clarke, and L. Osterweil. "PROPEL: An Approach Supporting Property Elucidation". In *Proceedings of ICSE'02*, pages 11–21, 2002.

[31] A. G. Sutcliffe, N.A.M. Maiden, S. Minocha, and D. Manuel. "Supporting Scenario-Based Requirements Engineering". *IEEE TSE*, 24:1072–1088, 1998.

[32] S. Uchitel, G. Brunet, and M. Chechik. "Behavioural Model Synthesis from Properties and Scenarios". *IEEE TSE*, 3(35):384–406, 2009.

[33] Axel van Lamsweerde. *Requirements Engineering: From System Goals to UML Models to Software Specifications.* Wiley, 2009.

[34] R. van Ommering, F. van der Linden, J. Kramer, and J. Magee. "The KOALA Component Model for Consumer Electronics Software". *IEEE Computer*, 33(3):78–85, 2000.

[35] M.Y. Vardi. "Branching vs. Linear Time: Final Showdown". In *Proc. of TACAS'01*, pages 1–22, 2001.

[36] M.Y. Vardi and P. Wolper. "An Automata-Theoretic Approach to Automatic Program Verification (Preliminary Report)". In *Proc. of LICS'86*, pages 332–344, 1986.

Using an SMT Solver for Interactive Requirements Prioritization

Francis Palma, Angelo Susi, Paolo Tonella
Fondazione Bruno Kessler, Software Engineering Research Unit
Trento, Italy
fpalma, susi, tonella@fbk.eu

ABSTRACT

The prioritization of requirements is a crucial activity in the early phases of the software development process. It consists of finding an order relation among requirements, considering several requirements characteristics, such as stakeholder preferences, technical constraints, implementation costs and user perceived value.

We propose an interactive approach to the problem of prioritization based on Satisfiability Modulo Theory (SMT) techniques and pairwise comparisons. Our approach resorts to interactive knowledge acquisition whenever the relative priority among requirements cannot be determined based on the available information. Synthesis of the final ranking is obtained via SMT constraint solving.

The approach has been evaluated on a set of requirements from a real healthcare project. Results show that it overcomes other interactive state-of-the-art prioritization approaches in terms of effectiveness, efficiency and robustness to decision maker errors.

Categories and Subject Descriptors

D.2.1 [**Software Engineering**]: Requirements/Specifications

General Terms

Management

Keywords

Requirements prioritization, constraint solving

1. INTRODUCTION

Requirements prioritization is the process of specifying a total or partial order relation on a set of requirements under analysis. This process is of paramount importance in the first phases of the software development process when the scheduling of the software releases is planned and requirements are assigned to the releases, considering the stakeholder expectations, implementation costs, time and technical constraints.

Several approaches to requirements prioritization have been proposed in the last few years [5, 6, 7, 8, 9, 10, 13, 15]. Some approaches [8, 9, 15] rely on the definition of models that weight the attributes of the requirements (e.g., development costs, value for users, implementation effort) *a priori*, without any reference to the instances of requirements under analysis. Other approaches [5, 6, 7, 10, 13] allow the decision maker to formulate the ordering *ex-post*, on the basis of the characteristics of the specific set of requirements that is considered, without relying on predefined schemes.

Among the prioritization techniques used in the latter category, the Analytical Hierarchy Process (AHP) [12] is widely referenced. It exploits pairwise comparisons to extract the user[1] knowledge with respect to the ranking of the requirements. The AHP method suffers scalability problems, since it defines the prioritization through user assessment of all the possible pairs of requirements. Hence, the number of pairwise comparisons asked to the user is quadratic with the number of requirements.

In order to address the scalability problem of AHP, some techniques have been proposed [2, 4, 14]. They sub-sample the exhaustive set of pairwise comparisons, while trying to achieve comparable performance as AHP. IAHP (Incomplete Analytic Hierarchy Process) [4] and IGA (Interactive Genetic Algorithm) [14] are two of the most successful attempts made in this direction.

In this paper we propose an *ex-post* approach based on the use of Satisfiability Modulo Theory (SMT) techniques for the synthesis of a ranking from the constraints. We rely on pairwise preference elicitation, to extract relevant knowledge from the user, only when the available knowledge does not allow the disambiguation of the relative priority of a set of requirements. We use an SMT solver to compose the elicited preferences with the relevant ordering criteria induced by the attributes describing the requirements and encoded as constraints. The final objective is that of minimizing the user decision-making effort, increasing as much as possible the accuracy of the final requirements ranking.

Specifically, pairs elicited from the user and initial constraints on the relative ordering of requirements define the set of constraints to be satisfied. Elicitation of stakeholders' preferences and optimization are conducted at the same

Permission to make digital or hard copies of all or part of this work for personal or classroom use is granted without fee provided that copies are not made or distributed for profit or commercial advantage and that copies bear this notice and the full citation on the first page. To copy otherwise, to republish, to post on servers or to redistribute to lists, requires prior specific permission and/or a fee.
ESEC/FSE'11, September 5–9, 2011, Szeged, Hungary.
Copyright 2011 ACM 978-1-4503-0443-6/11/09 ...$10.00.

[1]The user of the prioritized requirements is the development team (system architect, requirements analysts, etc.) and should not be confused with the final user of the system under development.

time and influence each other. In fact, the set of stakeholder constraints is specified incrementally, based on the unresolved priorities under the available constraints. Elicited constraints are iteratively composed with the constraints coming from other sources.

We evaluated our SMT approach comparing it with other state-of-the-art interactive prioritization techniques (IAHP and IGA in particular). Results indicate that SMT substantially outperforms them, while keeping the user effort (in terms of number of elicited pairs) acceptable. Moreover, we compared interactive and non-interactive prioritization, observing an increased performance when interaction with the decision maker takes place. We also evaluated the robustness of our method with respect to decision maker's errors.

This paper is structured as follows: in Section 2 we describe the background for our work, Section 3 presents the proposed approach and algorithm. In Section 4 we comment a set of experimental evaluations on effectiveness, robustness and efficiency of the approach. The empirical assessment was conducted on a set of requirements from a real healthcare project. Relevant related works are discussed in Section 5. Conclusions and future work are presented in Section 6.

2. BACKGROUND

Here we briefly introduce two quite successful, state-of-the-art methods for interactive prioritization of requirements: Interactive Genetic Algorithm (IGA) [14] and Incomplete Analytic Hierarchy Process (IAHP) [4]. Both methods have the objective of synthesizing an approximation of the ranking of a set of N requirements, minimizing the effort associated with the interactive input required from the decision maker (consisting of pairwise comparisons).

2.1 Interactive GA

In [14] we presented an Interactive Genetic Algorithm (IGA) to achieve the minimization of the disagreement between a total order of prioritized requirements and the various constraints coming from the domain knowledge, that are either encoded with the requirements or expressed iteratively by the user during the prioritization process.

In the approach we exploit the interactive input from the user whenever the fitness function cannot be computed precisely based on the information available. Specifically, each individual in the population being evolved by the genetic algorithm represents an alternative prioritization Pr_i of the N requirements. Two examples of such individuals are: $Pr_1 = \langle R_1, R_5, R_4, R_3, R_2 \rangle$, or $Pr_2 = \langle R_1, R_4, R_5, R_3, R_2 \rangle$. When individuals having a high fitness (i.e., a low disagreement with the constraints) cannot be distinguished, since their fitness function evaluates to a plateau, user input is requested interactively, in the form of preferences between pairs of requirements, so specifying if R_i is before or after R_j in the user ideal ranking, so as to make the fitness function landscape better suited for further minimization. In this way, knowledge about the constraints in the domain can help the method to minimize the amount of knowledge elicited from the decision maker, so decreasing her/his effort. The prioritization process terminates when a low disagreement is reached, a time out is reached or the allocated elicitation budget is over.

2.2 Incomplete AHP

IAHP [4] is a variant of the Analytic Hierarchy Process (AHP) [12] that can deal with incomplete information (pairwise comparisons) from the user. It was designed to support scalability of AHP to requirements whose size make AHP prohibitively expensive (the number of pairs that must be elicited to apply AHP is quadratic with the number of requirements).

In particular, AHP implements a pairwise comparison iterative process in which the decision maker is required to specify a preference as an integer value $p_{ij} \in [1 \dots 9]$, between two requirements R_i and R_j. The value can be mapped to a qualitative measure of the preference relation, as summarized in Table 1. After assigning a preference value to one of the two requirements (say, R_i) compared to the other one (R_j), the preference value for the least preferred requirement (R_j) is the reciprocal of p_{ij}, so, $p_{ji} = 1/p_{ij}$. When all the pairs have been elicited, a ranking is synthesized through the computation of the principal eigenvector of the matrix p_{ij}, the components of which determine the rank of each requirement.

Preference p_{ij}	Definition
1	R_i Equally important to R_j
3	R_i Moderately more important than R_j
5	R_i Strongly more important than R_j
7	R_i Very strongly more important than R_j
9	R_i Extremely more important than R_j
2, 4, 6, 8	For compromise between the above values

Table 1: A possible fundamental scale in the interval $[1 \dots 9]$ used with AHP

IAHP overcomes the AHP scalability problem by minimizing the number of pairs elicited from the decision maker, while maintaining a good trade-off between the precision of the final solution and the effort of the decision maker. This is done by calculating, at each iteration of the elicitation process, a prediction of the next most promising pair to be asked to the decision maker in order to find a stable and good approximation of the target ranking, early before eliciting all the $N(N-1)/2$ pairs for the set of N requirements.

The high level steps of the IAHP process are: *(i)* the decision maker provides $N-1$ judgments which form a connected graph; *(ii)* using the available pairwise comparisons, the missing comparisons are estimated by taking the geometric mean of the intensities over a spanning tree (this results in a weight matrix); *(iii)* the derivatives of the weight matrix with respect to the missing matrix elements are computed and the next pairwise comparison to ask is determined based on such derivatives; *(iv)* if the stopping criteria are met (e.g., maximum number of elicitations or convergence metrics below threshold), then the computation stops and a rank is produced by calculating the principal eigenvector of the estimated matrix; otherwise the selected comparison is elicited and the algorithm iterates.

Differently from IGA, that can also exploit the initial knowledge from the domain, IAHP relies only on the knowledge acquired interactively from the user.

3. APPROACH

The prioritization approach we propose aims at minimizing the disagreement between a total order of prioritized requirements and the various constraints that are either encoded with the requirements or that are expressed iteratively by the user during the prioritization process. We use SMT solvers to achieve such a minimization, taking advantage of interactive input from the requirement engineer whenever the solver produces more than one prioritized list of requirements having the same disagreement with the available constraints. The prioritization process terminates when a unique solution at minimum disagreement is found or the maximum allowed number of pairwise comparisons is reached.

Req	Prio	Deps
R_1	High	R_2, R_3
R_2	Low	R_3
R_3	Low	
R_4	Medium	R_2
R_5	Medium	

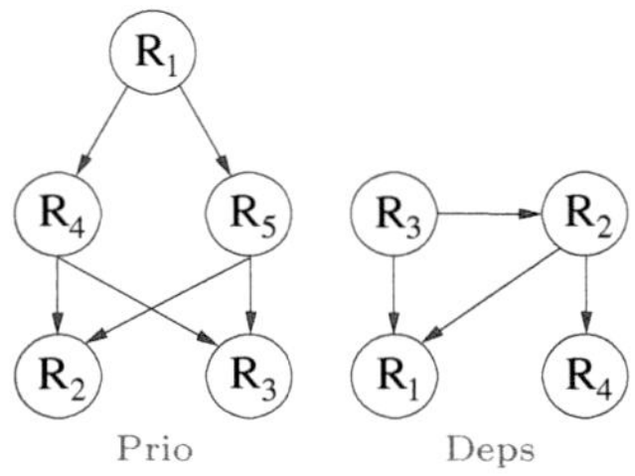

Table 2: Requirements with priority and dependencies

Let us consider the five requirements listed in Table 2. For each requirement we consider the priority expressed by the requirement engineer who collected them and the dependencies the requirement may have with other requirements. For conciseness, in Table 2 we omit other important elements of a requirement (e.g., the textual description). Constraints upon requirements can be represented by means of a *constraint* graph. In a constraint graph, an edge between two requirements indicates that, according to the related dependency or priority, the requirement associated with the source of the edge should be implemented before the target requirement. Edges may be weighted, to actually quantify the strength or importance of each constraint. When encoded in the input language of the SMT solver, such constraints will be retractable constraints which are given the weight labeling the edge (or 1 if no weight is given). An infinite weight is used for constraints that must necessarily hold in the final ordering of the requirements. These will be non-retractable constraints for the SMT solver.

At the right of Table 2, we show the constraint graph induced by the *priority* (Prio) property of the requirements and the constraint graph induced by the *dependencies* (Deps) between requirements. Requirements with *High* priority should precede those with *Medium* priority. Hence the edges (R_1, R_4) and (R_1, R_5) in the graph Prio. Similarly, the precedence between *Medium* and *Low* priority requirements induces the four edges at the bottom of the constraint graph Prio. Requirement R_1 depends on R_2, R_3, hence the implementation of R_2, R_3 should precede that of R_1, which gives raise to the edges (R_2, R_1) and (R_3, R_1) in Deps.

It is possible to encode the requirements prioritization problem as a MAX-SAT[2] problem. An SMT solver will find an integer assignment which maximizes the weight of the retractable constraints that are satisfied by the solution (minimum cost of unsatisfied constraints). The encoding is described formally in the next section. Intuitively, it consists of an assignment of positions (integers between 1 and N, for N requirements) to the components of an integer array x of size N. The assignment must define a permutation of the positions, hence there should be no repetition of positions. This is easily encoded as a set of inequalities between pairs of positions ($x[i] \neq x[j] \quad \forall\, i \neq j$). The other constraints (from the constraint graphs) are encoded as inequalities (e.g., $x[1] < x[4]$ and $x[1] < x[5]$ for the two edges at the top of the constraint graph Prio). The solutions to the MAX-SAT problem produced by the SMT solver are all requirement orderings that violate the minimum number of retractable constraints (e.g., Deps and Prio), or have minimum cost of violation, in case different weights are given to different constraints. The encoding of the requirement prioritization problem in Table 2 for the SMT solver Yices[3] is shown in Figure 1.

[2]Technically we are exploiting a MAX-SMT solver.

```
(set-evidence! true)
(define x::(-> nat nat))
(define N::nat 5)

;; Only permutations of positions are allowed
(assert (forall (i::(subrange 1 N)) (and (>= (x i) 1) (<= (x i) N))))
(assert (forall (i::(subrange 1 (- N 1)))
          (forall (j::(subrange (+ i 1) N)) (/= (x i) (x j)))))

;; Prio
(assert+ (< (x 1) (x 4)) 1)
(assert+ (< (x 1) (x 5)) 1)
(assert+ (< (x 1) (x 2)) 1)
(assert+ (< (x 1) (x 3)) 1)
(assert+ (< (x 4) (x 2)) 1)
(assert+ (< (x 4) (x 3)) 1)
(assert+ (< (x 5) (x 2)) 1)
(assert+ (< (x 5) (x 3)) 1)

;;Deps
(assert+ (< (x 3) (x 2)) 1)
(assert+ (< (x 3) (x 1)) 1)
(assert+ (< (x 3) (x 4)) 1)
(assert+ (< (x 2) (x 1)) 1)
(assert+ (< (x 2) (x 4)) 1)

(max-sat)
```

Figure 1: Encoding of the constraints in Table 2 for the SMT solver Yices

Id	Reqs	Disagree
Pr_1	$< R_1, R_5, R_4, R_3, R_2 >$	4
Pr_2	$< R_1, R_4, R_5, R_3, R_2 >$	4
Pr_3	$< R_1, R_5, R_3, R_4, R_2 >$	4
Pr_4	$< R_1, R_5, R_3, R_2, R_4 >$	4

Table 3: Prioritized requirements and related minimum disagreement

After encoding the constraint graphs in Table 2 as retractable assertions (`assert+` in Figure 1) and running an SMT solver (e.g., Yices) on them, we obtain the four prioritized lists of requirements shown in Table 3 (the solver must be run four times to obtain the complete set of prioritizations, each time negating the previously found solutions). These are all prioritized lists having the same, minimum cost of retracted assertions (i.e., 4). Such a cost is called *disagreement* and it represents the number of constraints that are not respected by the resulting requirement positions. The first two prioritizations Pr_1 and Pr_2 are in complete

[3]http://yices.csl.sri.com/

agreement with the constraint graph Prio, while they violate some of the edges of Dep (namely, (R_3, R_1), (R_3, R_2), (R_2, R_4) and the transitive constraint (R_3, R_4)). Pr_3 violates (R_4, R_3) from Prio and (R_2, R_4), (R_2, R_1), (R_3, R_1) from Dep. Pr_4 violates (R_4, R_2), (R_4, R_3) from Prio and (R_3, R_1), (R_2, R_1) from Dep.

Prios	Disagreement pairs
(Pr_1, Pr_2)	(R_4, R_5)
(Pr_1, Pr_3)	(R_3, R_4)
(Pr_1, Pr_4)	(R_3, R_4), (R_2, R_4)
(Pr_2, Pr_3)	(R_4, R_5), (R_3, R_4)
(Pr_2, Pr_4)	(R_4, R_5), (R_3, R_4) , (R_2, R_4)
(Pr_3, Pr_4)	(R_2, R_4)

Table 4: Pairwise comparisons to resolve ties

In order to choose among the alternative prioritizations at minimum disagreement, we compare them and determine the pairs of requirements that are ordered differently in different prioritized lists. For example, if we compare Pr_1 and Pr_2 from Table 3, we can notice that they differ on the relative ordering of R_4 and R_5. We say that these two prioritizations are in disagreement with respect to the requirement pair (R_4, R_5). Table 4 shows the disagreement pairs for each comparison of prioritizations at minimum cost (taken from Table 3). For example, Pr_2 and Pr_3 differ on the relative ordering of two requirement pairs: (R_4, R_5) and (R_3, R_4). If we take the union of the requirement pairs on which the four minimum cost prioritizations differ, we get three pairs: (R_2, R_4), (R_3, R_4), (R_4, R_5) (see Table 4). These are the causes of the ties between the four prioritizations determined by the SMT solver. We can discriminate among such four prioritizations if we can decide on the precedence holding for the disagreement pairs. Hence, the information to be elicited from the user consists of pairwise comparisons between requirements that are ordered differently in equally scored prioritizations.

The user is requested to express a precedence relationship between each pair in the disagreement computed for prioritizations in a tie. Given a disagreement pair of requirements (e.g., R_4, R_5), the elicited ranking may state that one requirement should have precedence over the other one (e.g., $R_4 \rightarrow R_5$; or, $R_5 \rightarrow R_4$) or the user may answer *don't know*. In the first case an edge is introduced in the elicited constraint graph Eli, a third constraint graph that adds to Prio and Dep and is obtained by gathering interactive user input. In the second case no edge is introduced. In our running example, the user would be requested to compare (R_2, R_4), (R_3, R_4) and (R_4, R_5). Indeed, the first two cases represent a situation where the available precedence information is contradictory. In fact, the precedence graph Prio gives precedence to R_4, while Deps gives precedence to R_2, R_3. Hence, it is entirely justified to request additional user input, to resolve an inconsistency which is already present in the requirement documents, when considering different properties or constraints. The third comparison requested to the user, (R_4, R_5), is a case where no precedence information is available in the requirement documents. As a consequence, it is impossible for the SMT solver to distinguish, e.g., between Pr_1 and Pr_2, whose only difference consist of the ordering of R_4 w.r.t. R_5. Again, asking for additional user input makes perfect sense.

After collecting user input in terms of pairwise comparisons, the existing elicited constraint graph Eli (initially empty) is augmented with the new edges. The appearance of cycles in the elicited graph indicates the existence of contradictory information. This is managed automatically by the SMT solver, which will satisfy some constraints in the cycle and will retract some others.

When the new elicited constraint graph is available, the SMT solutions at minimum cost are recomputed. Such solutions are expected to be much more discriminative than the previous ones, thanks to the additional information gathered through interaction. Only pairs that actually make a difference in the optimal orderings are submitted to the user for assessment. After a number of iterations, the algorithm is expected to have successfully discriminated all prioritizations at minimum cost, thanks to the input elicited from the user, leading to the final selection of the prioritization with lowest disagreement w.r.t. all precedence graphs (including the elicited one).

3.1 Algorithm

In this section, we describe the interactive algorithm that implements the approach presented in the previous section. Before introducing the algorithm, we provide a formal definition of the intuitive notion of disagreement and we formalize the SMT problem to be solved. We define disagreement in the general case where two partial orders are compared. A special case, quite relevant to the proposed method, is when one or both orders are total ones.

$$dis(ord_1, ord_2) = \{(p, q) \in ord_1^* \mid (q, p) \in ord_2^*\} \qquad (1)$$

The disagreement between two (partial or total) orders ord_1, ord_2, defined upon the same set of elements R, is the set of pairs in the transitive closure of the first order, ord_1^*, that appear reversed in the second order closure ord_2^*. A measure of disagreement is given by the size of the set $dis(ord_1, ord_2)$.

The requirement prioritization problem can be formulated as the problem of assigning the integer values taken from the set of requirement positions $P = \{1, \ldots, N\}$, where N is the number of requirements, to the components of an integer array x, such that no two different array components hold the same value (i.e., the assignment defines a permutation of P):

$$\forall i \in P, j \in P : x_i \in P, x_j \in P, i \neq j \Rightarrow x_i \neq x_j \qquad (2)$$

Among all permutations defined by equation (2), we want to determine those that minimize the number of unsatisfied constraints. This is achieved by encoding the constraint graphs as retractable inequality constraints: $x_i < x_j$ whenever there is a path between R_i and R_j in the constraint graphs. The minimum number of such constraints that are retracted in the MAX-SAT solution found by the SMT solver gives the disagreement between the found solution and the constraint graphs. The SMT solver can be iterated so as to enumerate all solutions at minimum disagreement (i.e., at minimum constraint violation cost).

Algorithm 1 contains the pseudocode of the interactive algorithm used to prioritize a set of requirements R. The other input of the algorithm is a set of one or more partial orders $(ord_1, ..., ord_k)$, derived from the requirement documents (e.g., priority, dependencies, etc.). Step 3 sets an important parameter of the algorithm. Namely, the maximum number of pairwise comparisons that can be reasonably requested to the user. The default value for it is 100.

Algorithm 1 Compute prioritized requirements

Input R: set of requirements
Input $ord_1, ..., ord_k$: partial orders defining constraints upon R ($ord_i \subseteq R \times R$)
Output $\langle R_1, ..., R_n \rangle$: ordered list of requirements
1: *Solutions* := $\emptyset$
2: *elicitedPairs* := 0
3: *maxElicitedPairs* := *MAX_ELI_PAIRS* (default = 100)
4: *eliOrd* := $\emptyset$
5: **while** $|Solutions| \neq 1 \wedge elicitedPairs < maxElicitedPairs$ **do**
6: *Solutions* := MAX_SAT($ord_1, ..., ord_k, eliOrd$)
7: **if** $|Solutions| \neq 1$ **then**
8: *eliOrd* := *eliOrd* $\cup$ elicit pairwise comparisons from user for disagreement pairs up to *maxElicitedPairs*
9: increment *elicitedPairs* by the number of elicited pairwise comparisons
10: **end if**
11: **end while**
12: return Pr_{min}, a requirement list from *Solutions* with minimum *disagreement*

The algorithm iterates until a unique solution to the prioritization problem is found or the maximum number of pairwise comparisons has been requested (see condition of *while* loop at step 5). In the body of the loop, the SMT solver is invoked at step 6. The solver receives in input a set of retractable assertions, associated with the constraints graphs (including the elicited constraint graph). Such graphs are turned into inequality assertions as explained above. In addition to such retractable assertions, the SMT solver adds always the constraints expressed in equation (2) as non retractable assertions. The solver is repeatedly executed, so as to enumerate all solutions having the same minimum cost. Technically, this is achieved by adding an assertion that negates the previously found solution and asking for another solution to the new formulation of the problem. MAX_SAT return the set of all such minimum cost solutions.

If more than one solution is produced by the solver, the disagreement pairs for them is determined and the user is requested input to disambiguate them (steps 7-10). The user input is encoded as an additional constraint graph, *eliOrd*, which introduces new retractable assertions in the next iteration of the algorithm.

If the algorithm terminates because the size of *Solutions* is one, then the unique solution found is returned as Pr_{min}. If the algorithm terminates because the maximum number of elicitations has been reached, but no unique solution has been found, any randomly selected solution from the set *Solutions* is returned.

The most distinguishing property of this algorithm is that it resorts to user input only when the available information is insufficient and at the same time availability of more information allows for a better requirement ordering. Hence, the requests made to the user are limited and the information provided by the user is expected to be most beneficial to finding a good prioritization.

4. EXPERIMENTAL RESULTS

We applied the IGA algorithm to prioritize the requirements of a real software system, as part of the project ACube (Ambient Aware Assistance) [1]. ACube is a large research project funded by the local government of the Autonomous Province of Trento, in Italy, aiming at designing a complex system to be deployed in nursing homes to support medical and assistance staff. In such context, an important activity has been the analysis of the system requirements, to obtain the best trade-off between costs and quality improvement of services in specialized centers for people with severe motor or cognitive impairments. From the technical point of view, the project envisages a network of sensors distributed in the environment or embedded in users' clothes. This technology monitors the nursing home guests and operators without influencing their usual daily life activities. Through advanced automatic reasoning algorithms, the data acquired through the sensor network are used to promptly recognize emergency situations and to prevent possible threats for the guests themselves.

The user requirements analysis phase produced 60 user requirements, 49 technical requirements[4] and four macro-scenarios. Specifically, the macro scenarios are: (i) "localization and tracking to detect falls of patients", (ii) "localization and tracking to detect patients escaping from the nursing home", (iii) "identification of dangerous behaviors of patients"; plus (iv) a comprehensive scenario that involves the simultaneous presence of the previous three scenarios.

Out of these macro-scenarios, detailed scenarios have been analyzed together with the 49 technical requirements. Examples of such technical requirements are: *"TR7: The system identifies the presence of a person in a given area"* or *"TR9: The system identifies the identity of the persons in the scene"*.

Id	Macro-scenario	Number of requirements
FALL	Monitoring falls	26
ESC	Monitoring escapes	23
MON	Monitoring dangerous behavior	21
ALL	The three scenarios	49

Table 5: The four macro-scenarios and the number of technical requirements associated with them.

Table 5 summarizes the number of technical requirements for each macro-scenario. Together with the set of technical requirements, two sets of technical constraints have been collected during requirements elicitation: *Priority* and *Dependency*, representing respectively the priorities among requirements and their dependencies. Specifically, the *Priority* constraint has been built on the basis of the users' needs and it is defined as a function that associates each technical requirement to a number (in the range 1–500), indicating the priority of the technical requirement with respect to the priority of the user requirements it is intended to address. The *Dependency* feature is defined on the basis of the technical dependencies between requirements and is a function that links a requirement to the set of other requirements it depends on.

Finally, the ACube software architect specified the *Gold Standard* (GS) prioritization for each of the four macro-scenarios. The GS prioritization is the ordering given by the software architect to the requirements when planning

[4]We consider here only functional requirements.

their implementation during the ACube project. We take advantage of the availability of GS in the experimental evaluation of the proposed algorithm, in that we are able to compare the final ordering produced by the algorithm with the one defined by the software architect (that we consider the ideal one).

4.1 Research questions

The experiments we conducted aim at answering the following research questions.

RQ1 (Comparison) *Does the SMT-based method produce improved prioritizations compared to IAHP and IGA?*

We compare SMT-based interactive prioritization with the state of the art interactive requirement prioritization technique IAHP [4] and with our previous work IGA [14]. The output of SMT-based prioritization is compared with the output of the IAHP and IGA algorithms, at equal number of pairs elicited from the user. We vary such number from low to high values, in order to investigate the regions where one approach is superior to the other (i.e., the degree of information incompleteness each approach can accommodate).

To assess the performance of IGA and IAHP we use two main metrics: disagreement with GS and average distance from the position of each requirement in the GS. The latter metrics is highly correlated with the former, but it has the advantage of being more easily interpretable than disagreement. In fact, disagreement involves a quadratic number of comparisons (each pair of requirements w.r.t. GS order), hence its absolute value is not straightforward to understand and compare. On the contrary, the distance between the position of each requirement in the prioritization produced by our algorithm and the position of the same requirement in the GS gives a direct clue on the number of requirements that are incorrectly positioned before or after the requirement being considered.

RQ2 (Role of interaction) *Does SMT-based interactive prioritization produce improved prioritizations compared to non-interactive SMT-based prioritization?*

Our research hypothesis is that user knowledge plays an important role in requirement prioritization. RQ2 is designed to test such hypothesis. To assess the importance of the information elicited from the user, we compare the output of SMT before any pair is elicited from the user with the output of the same method after completing the elicitation of pairwise comparisons from the user to resolve ties.

RQ3 (Robustness) *Is the SMT-based method more robust than IAHP and IGA with respect to errors committed by the user during the elicitation of pairwise comparisons?*

In order to test the robustness of SMT in comparison with IAHP and IGA at increasing user error rates, we simulate such errors by means of a simple stochastic model. We fix a probability of committing an elicitation error, say p_e. Then, during the execution of the SMT, IAHP and IGA algorithms, whenever a pairwise comparison is elicited from the user, we generate a response in agreement with the GS with probability $1 - p_e$ and we generate an error (i.e., a response in disagreement with the GS) with probability p_e. We varied the probability of user error p_e from 5% to 20%.

RQ4 (Performance) *How execution time of SMT grows at increasing number of elicited pairs during the prioritization process compared to the execution time growth of IGA and IAHP?*

This research question deals with the time performance of the three methods being compared: SMT, IAHP and IGA. Low execution time and low increasing of time (for a growing number of elicited pairs) of the constraint solving/optimization step is fundamental to allow online usage of the proposed method. In fact, the time between an elicitation and the next one is determined by the execution time of the algorithm that performs the required constraint solving/optimization steps and then determines which pairwise comparisons are to be elicited next. Such time should be acceptable from the point of view of the decision maker who answers the pairwise comparison questions.

4.2 Results

We implemented the algorithm described in Section 3 in C++, using the C SMT solver library provided with the SMT tool Yices. IAHP and IGA have been implemented in Java. As a consequence, absolute execution times are not directly comparable, but we are more interested in their growth over elicited pairs. The software and the experimental data are available online at `http://selab.fbk.eu/smt-req-prio`. For space reasons, we hereby report only a subset of the experimental results. The interested reader can find the complete set of results in a technical report available online at `http://se.fbk.eu/en/techreps`.

Since the algorithms used in the experiments involve some degree of randomness at various steps (e.g., IGA selects between mutation and crossover operators randomly, according to a predefined probability), whenever not stated differently, results are based on 20 replications of each experiment. We report the average and the distribution of the data values (using boxplots). Statistical significance of the differences observed among the evaluated techniques was assessed by means of the ANOVA statistical test. When the algorithm involves the user interactively, we simulate the user response by means of an artificial user which replies automatically. In the default setting, the artificial user makes no elicitation error, i.e., it always replies to a pairwise comparison with a relative ordering of the two requirements being compared which is consistent with the GS. When p_e, the probability of user error, is set to a value greater than zero, the artificial user occasionally makes errors: with error probability p_e, it replies to a pairwise comparison with a relative ordering of the two requirements which is the opposite of that found in the GS.

Table 6 shows a summary of the main results obtained in the experiments. Details by research question are reported below. The results reported in Table 6 have been obtained for the ALL macro scenario with a different number of elicited pairs and variations in user error rate, p_e. We obtained similar tables for the other macro scenarios (i.e. MON, FALL, ESC). The first column represents the number of elicited pairs that was used as user knowledge. In the first two cases (i.e. maximum 25 & 50 pairwise comparisons) SMT made use of the maximum allowed number of elicited pairs. In the third case (i.e. maximum 100 pairwise

		SMT		SMT ($p_e = 5\%$)			SMT ($p_e = 10\%$)			SMT ($p_e = 20\%$)			IGA		IAHP	
Eli.pairs	Actual	Dis	AD	Err	Dis	AD	Err	Dis	AD	Err	Dis	AD	Dis	AD	Dis	AD
25	25	92	3.18	1	102	3.43	3	102	3.42	5	101	3.39	124	4.06	478	13.60
50	50	90	3.14	3	92	3.16	5	95	3.22	10	98	3.31	120	3.82	208	6.30
100	84	73	2.78	4	75	2.86	8	79	2.94	17	85	3.10	114	3.69	187	5.75

Table 6: Comparison table of disagreement and average distance among SMT, IGA & IAHP at different user error rates for ALL scenario

comparisons) SMT elicited only 84 pairs and reached the minimized prioritization before consuming all allowed comparisons. Columns 3 and 4 shows the disagreement (Dis) and average distance (AD) with GS for each setting. Columns 5 to 7, 8 to 10 and 11 to 13 show the different outcomes for user error rate 5%, 10% and 20%, where for each case, the first column (Err) represents the number of pairs that were answered by the user wrongly. Columns 14-15 & 16-17 represent average Dis and AD for IGA and IAHP respectively. With 100 elicited pairs, SMT has a disagreement of 73 (with user error probability p_e equal to 0), 75 (p_e equal to 5%), 79 (p_e equal to 10%) and 85 (p_e equal to 20%), all of which are better than IGA (114) and IAHP (187) with no user error (p_e equal to 0%).

RQ1 *(Comparison).*

Figure 2 (top) shows the performance of the SMT-based approach, compared to IGA and IAHP, by considering the difference between the prioritization produced by the algorithm and the GS for the ALL macro scenario after eliciting 25 pairs. Similar plots have been obtained for the other scenarios (MON, FALL and ESC). We can observe that SMT outperforms both IGA and IAHP. After eliciting only 25 pairs from the user, SMT produced a prioritization with an average disagreement of 92, with a small variability due to the random choice of a solution from the set of *Solutions* (in the case more than one is available at the end of the prioritization algorithm), whereas IGA and IAHP have an average disagreement of 124 and 478 respectively. Even though IGA is more consistent than IAHP and produces much improvement with little user knowledge, the SMT-based approach produces an even better prioritization. In this case, the performance of IAHP is definitely worse than IGA, but SMT still shows improvements over IGA, even when little knowledge from the user is available.

Figure 2 (middle) shows the results obtained for the ALL macro scenario after eliciting 50 pairwise comparisons. SMT produced a prioritization with an average disagreement of 90, whereas IGA and IAHP have an average disagreement of 120 and 208 respectively. IGA outperformed IAHP, but the SMT-based approach further improves the prioritization produced by IGA. At this stage we are assuming the user is error-free, thus making no mistake in answering the pairwise comparisons.

Figure 2 (bottom) shows the results obtained with a maximum of 100 pairwise comparisons. SMT produced the best prioritization, with an average disagreement of 73, whereas IGA and IAHP have an average disagreement of 114 and 187 respectively. The degree of improvement of IGA with respect to IAHP and that of SMT with respect to IGA is almost equal and significantly large. Actually, as indicated in Table 6, the SMT-based interactive approach converged to the optimal solution after just 84 pairwise comparisons (out of the 100 available in this setting), hence reducing the elicitation effort with respect to the maximum allowed.

Statistical significance of the observed differences among the three methods was tested using ANOVA; the results are summarized in Table 7. In particular, we report the p-values for the Disagreement and Avarage Distance (see Table 6 for a summary of the values for Avarage Distance) for the comparison of the three methods for each of the three numbers of elicited pairs (25, 50, 100).

Methods	Disagreement p-value	Aver. Distance p-value
SMT25, IGA25, IAHP25	$<$2.2e-16	$<$2.2e-16
SMT50, IGA50, IAHP50	$<$2.2e-16	$<$2.2e-16
SMT100, IGA100, IAHP100	9.8e-05	10.31e-05

Table 7: Analysis of variance (ANOVA) comparing SMT, IGA and IAHP (while 0% error)

RQ2 *(Role of interaction).*

Figure 3 shows the comparison between the performance of interactive and non-interactive SMT-based prioritization, by considering the difference between the prioritization produced by the algorithm and the GS. In RQ2, we experimented with the same settings as RQ1, by assigning the value of *MAX_ELI_PAIRS* to 0, 25, 50, 100. In Figure 3 (top), non_iSMT represents the disagreement for non-interactive SMT, while iSMT_25, iSMT_50 and iSMT_100 represent the disagreement for interactive SMT while eliciting 25, 50 and 100 pairs from the user respectively. From Figure 3 it is clearly visible that while we are eliciting more pairs form the user, the fitness is getting better in terms of disagreement with GS. The non-interactive SMT-based approach produces a prioritization having disagreement 115. After eliciting 25, 50 and 100 pairs form the user, the SMT-based interactive approach produces prioritizations having a disagreement of 92, 90 and 73 respectively. The improvement of interactive SMT, compared to non interactive SMT, after eliciting 100 pairs is almost 50%.

Figure 3 (bottom) shows the comparison on average distance between interactive and non-interactive SMT, by considering the positional difference between the prioritization produced by the algorithm and the GS. While eliciting more pairs form the user, the fitness is getting better in terms of average distance. Non-interactive SMT produces a prioritization with average distance of 3.84. After eliciting 25, 50 and 100 pairs form the user, interactive SMT produces a prioritization with average distance of 3.18, 3.14 and 2.78 respectively. The improvement of iSMT_100 over non_iSMT is around 50% also in terms of average distance.

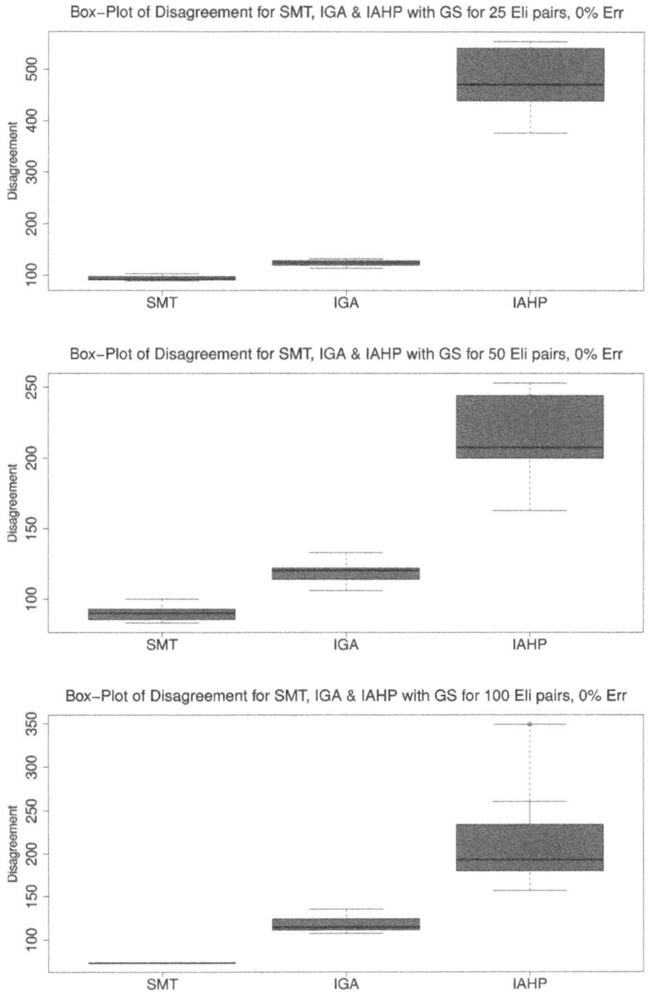

Figure 2: Disagreement with GS after eliciting at most 25 (top), 50 (middle) and 100 (bottom) pairs from the user in the ALL scenario

RQ3 *(Robustness).*

In Figure 4, we show that even if the performance of the SMT-based interactive approach degrades at increasing user error rates, it always produces an improved prioritization compared to IGA and IAHP with a user who does not make any mistake. We show this for 50 elicited pairs, but similar results are available for a different number of elicited pairs. With no error SMT produces a prioritization with a disagreement of 90. At 5%, 10% and 20% error rate, the disagreement becomes 92, 95 and 98 respectively. On the other hand, even if the user makes no error (i.e. error-free user), the disagreement of the prioritizations produced by IGA and IAHP is 120 and 208. We obtained similar plots for the other three macro scenarios (MON, FALL, ESC).

In Figure 5 we compare the robustness of SMT with the two other approaches considered in this work, IGA and IAHP. Here we show the results obtained for ALL. Similar results have been obtained for the other macro scenarios. The SMT-based interactive approach is substantially more robust than the others. At increasing user error rates, the performance of IGA and IAHP is degrading to a higher degree. SMT

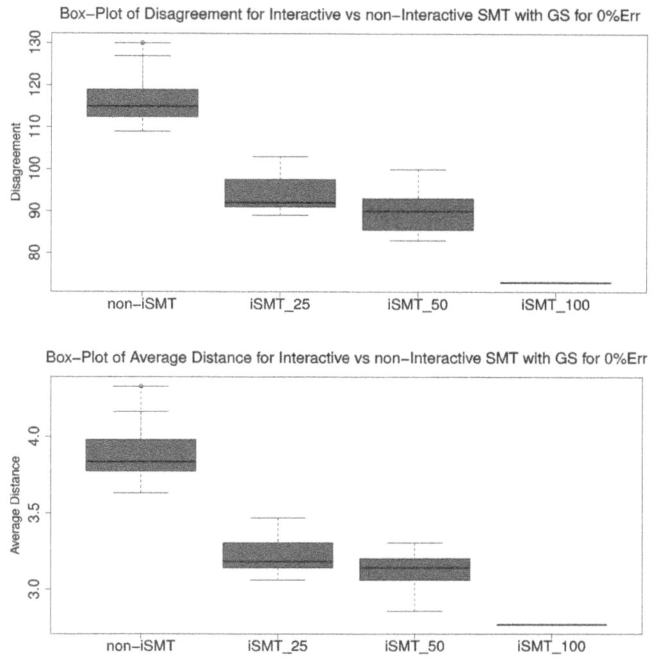

Figure 3: Disagreement (top) and average distance (bottom) with GS for interactive and non-interactive SMT after eliciting 25, 50, 100 pairs from the user in the ALL scenario

has also a degrading performance at increased error rates, but it outperforms IGA and IAHP to a large extent. For an error rate of 5% SMT, IGA and IAHP have a disagreement of 92, 120 and 236 respectively. For a 10% error rate, these are 95, 119 and 277. For an error rate of 20%, the disagreements with GS become 98, 123 and 331 respectively. So, clearly the SMT-based interactive approach is more robust then IGA and IAHP.

RQ4 *(Performance).*

Table 8 shows the comparison among execution times of SMT, IGA and IAHP. All execution times in the table are obtained from the system time of each execution and are measured in seconds, with a very small observable variabil-

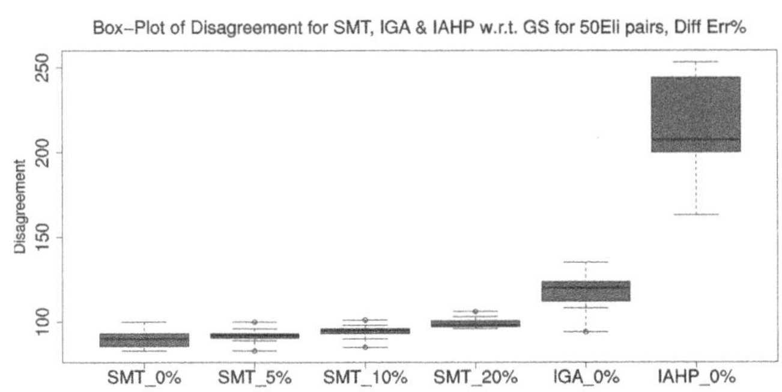

Figure 4: Robustness of SMT: Disagreement for SMT at different user error rates; IGA and IAHP with error-free user, after eliciting 50 pairs in the ALL scenario

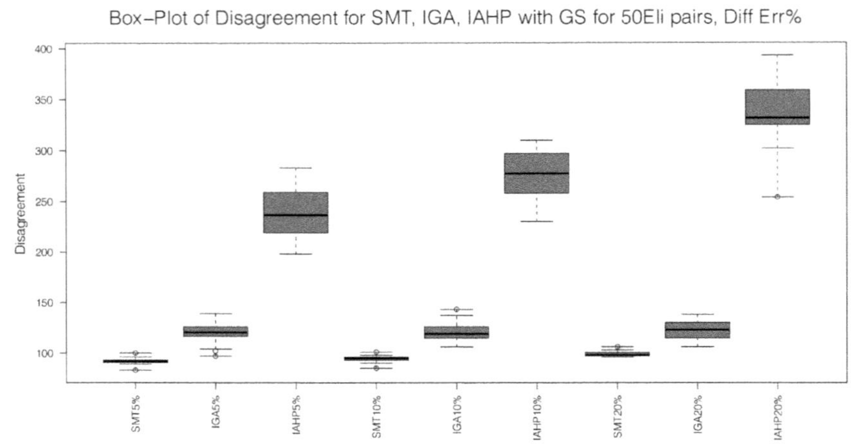

Figure 5: Robustness of SMT: Disagreement for SMT, IGA and IAHP after eliciting 50 pairs at different user error rates in the ALL scenario

Pairs	SMT	IGA	IAHP
25	46s	640s	4s
50	51s	840s	6s
100	50s	1080s	128s

Table 8: Prioritization time (system time) required by SMT, IGA and IAHP for the ALL scenario

ity between different runs. The experiments were performed on an Intel Core2 Duo 2.10GHz machine with 3GB of memory, running the 32bit Windows Vista OS. The overall prioritization process time is much lower when using SMT as compared to IGA. IAHP is more efficient than SMT at 25 and 50 elicited pairs, but its performance seems to suffer a non-linear degradation when the number of elicitations increases. In fact, at 100 elicited pairs, the execution time of IAHP jumps from 4s to 128s. On the contrary, SMT seems to have little dependence on the number of elicitations. At 100 elicited pairs it remains almost constant and it is substantially inferior than IAHP.

If we approximate the time distance between two consecutive pairwise comparisons with the execution time per elicited pair, we observed that SMT leaves the user waiting for the next comparison for a time between 0.5s and 2s approximately. IGA introduces longer intervals between elicitations (between 10s and 15s), while IAHP has very short intervals (around 0.15s) when at most 25 or 50 pairs are elicited. This interval increases to 1.2s for 100 elicited pairs. We can conclude that the execution times of SMT and IAHP are compatible with an interactive, online usage of the algorithm, while IGA introduces longer waiting times, which may be annoying for the user. Moreover, IAHP seems to have a non linear time behavior with respect to the maximum number of elicited pairs.

4.3 Discussion

Based on the data collected from our experiments (due to space limitations, we showed only a portion of them in this paper), we can answer positively to all our research questions. When comparing the prioritizations produced by the considered algorithms with GS, both in terms of disagreement and of position distance, interactive SMT outperforms substantially IGA and IAHP (RQ1). Moreover, interactive SMT outperforms non-interactive SMT (RQ2), hence showing that user input plays a key role in producing a prioritization of requirements which gets close to the reference, gold standard one. The behavior of the algorithm is robust with respect to the presence of elicitation errors committed by the user (RQ3). Up to 20% user error rate, SMT outperforms IGA and IAHP, even when these are run at 0% user error rate. Finally, our proposed SMT-based interactive approach consumes much less system-time compared to IGA. This is true in comparison to IAHP only at a high number of elicited pairs (e.g., 100). The estimated time between consecutive pairwise elicitations (0.001s–0.95s) is compatible with online usage of the tool.

If we look at the average distance of each requirement from the position it has in the GS, we can see that such a distance is quite low (2–3 positions). This indicates that the approximate solution produced by our method is close enough to the ideal solution to be usable in practice. Of course, further studies are needed to evaluate the acceptability of the approximate solution by the users.

In several cases, even though we set the maximum number of pair elicitations to 50 or 100, the SMT based approach used a lower number of pairs (i.e., 31 for MON, 34 for ESC, 42 for FALL and 84 for ALL), converging to a final requirement ordering which at the same time improves IGA and IAHP, and requires less user effort (pairwise comparisons). Hence, we think the cost/benefit trade off offered by the SMT-based interactive approach as compared to IGA and IAHP, as well as AHP, which requires exhaustive pairwise comparisons, is extremely advantageous. With an elicitation effort reduced to less than 10% of the one required by AHP (in the ALL scenario, $49 \times 48 / 2 = 1{,}176$ pairwise comparisons), SMT produces an approximate ordering which has a quite low average distance from the requirement positions in the GS, substantially lower than IGA and IAHP. More empirical investigation is necessary to assess the actual, practical viability and acceptability of the trade off offered by SMT, as compared to AHP, IGA and IAHP. We plan to conduct such empirical studies, involving real (vs. artificial) users, as part of our future work.

4.4 Threats to validity

The main threat to the validity of our case study concerns the *external validity*, i.e., the possibility to generalize our findings to requirements collected for other systems and having different features. Since we conducted one case study, the natural way to corroborate our findings and make them applicable to other systems is by replicating this study on other, different cases. Although considering just one case, we did our best to exploit it as much as possible. Specifically, we considered three macro scenarios in addition to the complete one, which enlarges a bit the scope of generalizability of the results.

Other threats to validity concern the *construct validity*, i.e., the observations we made to test our research hypotheses. Specifically, we used disagreement and requirement position distance as the metrics that determine the algorithm's performance. For the time performance, we measured system time. Other metrics may be more meaningful or more appropriate. On the other hand, disagreement is widely used in the related literature and position distance is a better interpretable alternative. Another construct validity threat might be related to the simple user error model we used to simulate a user who occasionally makes errors. We will experiment with more sophisticated models in the future. To minimize the *conclusion validity* threats (concerning the possibility to reject the null hypothesis), whenever we report a difference to exist between two datasets, we checked our claim using statistical tests.

5. RELATED WORKS

Several techniques are currently exploited in prioritization approaches. Many of them consist of assigning a rank to each requirement in a set according to a specific decision making criterion. The rank of a requirement can be expressed as its relative position with respect to the other requirements in the set, as in *Bubble sort* or *Binary search* procedures, or as an absolute measure of the evaluation criterion for the requirement, as in *Cumulative voting* [9]. Other techniques consist of assigning each requirement to one specific class among a set of predefined priority classes, as for instance in *Numerical Assignment* [9, 15] and in *Top-ten requirements* [8].

Some approaches share a prioritization process that consists of a selection of one or more prioritization criteria including business goals and technical features, the acquisition of requirements priorities on the basis of the criteria, eliciting such priorities from the stakeholders, and the integration of the acquired orderings into the final one [6, 13, 5, 10, 11].

Among them, CBRank [2] adopts a preference elicitation process that combines sets of preferences elicited from human decision makers with sets of constraints which are automatically computed through machine learning techniques; it also exploits knowledge about (partial) rankings of the requirements that may be encoded in the description of the requirements themselves as requirement attributes (e.g., priorities or preferences). Differently from our method, CBRank has no way to encode constraints such as dependencies, which play a key role in requirements prioritization.

The Analytical Hierarchy Process (AHP) [12] can be considered the reference method for prioritizing alternatives. It adopts a pairwise comparison strategy, allowing to define the prioritization criteria through a priority assessment of all the possible pairs of requirements. As highlighted above, this method becomes impractical as soon as the number of requirements increases. Harker [4] proposed the method incomplete AHP (IAHP), to minimize the number of pairs elicited from the decision maker maintaining a good trade-off between the precision of the final solution and the effort of the decision maker.

Among the methods exploiting search based techniques, in particular genetic algorithms, the EVOLVE method [3] supports continuous planning for incremental software development. This approach is based on an iterative optimization method supported by a genetic algorithm. Zhang et al. [16] focus on the specific Multi-Objective Next Release Problem (MONRP) and present the results of an empirical study on the suitability of weighted and Pareto optimal genetic algorithms (NSGA-II in particular), providing evidence to support the claim that NSGA-II is well suited to the MONRP. These two works overcome the problems of scalability of methods such as AHP, but they do not produce a total ordering of requirements. Rather, they group requirements for the planning of the next release.

In our previous work [14], we proposed an approach based on Interactive Genetic Algorithm (IGA) to minimize the amount of knowledge, in terms of pairwise evaluations, that has to be elicited from the user. The present work represents a substantial advancement of IGA in terms of faster convergence, improved final solution, increased robustness and diminished user effort, as apparent from the experimental results.

6. CONCLUSIONS AND FUTURE WORK

In this paper we proposed an approach to the requirements prioritization problem relying on Satisfiability Modulo Theory techniques. The approach is interactive and is based on a pairwise preference elicitation process to extract relevant knowledge from the decision makers that is encoded as constraints. This knowledge is then combined with the knowledge related to the ordering criteria induced by requirements characteristics, such as implementation costs, values for the users, implementation dependencies, that are also encoded as constraints.

The aim is that of minimizing the user decision-making effort, in terms of number of pairwise comparison to be specified, increasing as much as possible the accuracy of the final requirements ranking.

To validate the approach we conducted experiments on a set of requirements from a real healthcare project. Results show that our approach overcomes other state-of-the-art interactive approaches such as IAHP and IGA, both in terms of disagreement between the ideal solution and the solution obtained via the methods and in terms of execution time. Moreover, we verified the importance of the interaction with the decision maker, which increases substantially the performance of the SMT approach with respect to a non interactive version of the same algorithm. The method is also robust with respect to user errors, maintaining good performance even when the percentage of errors is around 20%.

In our future work we plan to conduct empirical studies involving human subjects (requirement analysts) to assess the usability of the method and the acceptability of the approximate solution produced at the end of the pairwise elicitation.

7. REFERENCES

[1] R. Andrich, F. Botto, V. Gower, C. Leonardi, O. Mayora, L. Pigini, V. Revolti, L. Sabatucci, A. Susi, and M. Zancanaro. ACube: User-Centred and Goal-Oriented techniques. Technical report, Fondazione Bruno Kessler - IRST, 2010.

[2] P. Avesani, C. Bazzanella, A. Perini, and A. Susi. Facing scalability issues in requirements prioritization with machine learning techniques. In *RE 2005*, pages 297–306, 2005.

[3] D. Greer and G. Ruhe. Software release planning: an evolutionary and iterative approach. *Information and Software Technology*, 46(4):243–253, 2004.

[4] P. T. Harker. Incomplete Pairwise Comparisons in the Analytic Hierarchy Process. *Math. Modelling*, 9(11):837 – 848, 1987.

[5] H. P. In, D. Olson, and T. Rodgers. Multi-criteria preference analysis for systematic requirements negotiation. In *COMPSAC 2002*, pages 887–892, 2002.

[6] J. Karlsson. Software Requirements Prioritizing. In *Proceedings of 2nd International Conference on Requirements Engineering (ICRE '96)* , pages 110–116, April 1996.

[7] J. Karlsson and K. Ryan. A cost-value approach for prioritizing requirements. *IEEE Software*, 14(5):67–74, 1997.

[8] S. Lauesen. *Software requirements: styles and techniques*. Addison Wesley, 2002.

[9] D. Leffingwell and D. Widrig. *Managing Software Requirements: A Unified Approach*. Addison-Wesley Longman Inc., 2000.

[10] F. Moisiadis. Prioritising software requirements. In *SERP 2002*, June 2002.

[11] A. Ngo-The and G. Ruhe. Requirements negotiation under incompleteness and uncertainty. In *Proceedings of the Fifteenth International Conference on Software Engineering & Knowledge Engineering, SEKE*, pages 586–593, San Francisco Bay, CA, USA, July 2003.

[12] T. L. Saaty and L. G. Vargas. *Models, Methods, Concepts & Applications of the Analytic Hierarchy Process*. Kluwer Academic, 2000.

[13] S. Sivzittian and B. Nuseibeh. Linking the Selection of Requirements to Market Value: A Portfolio - Based Approach. In *REFSQ 2001*, 2001.

[14] P. Tonella, A. Susi, and F. Palma. Using Interactive GA for Requirements Prioritization. In *2nd International Symposium on Search Based Software Engineering*, pages 57–66. IEEE, 2010.

[15] K. E. Wiegers. *Software Requirements. Best Practices*. Microsoft Press, 1999.

[16] Y. Zhang, M. Harman, and S. A. Mansouri. The multi-objective next release problem. In *GECCO '07*, pages 1129–1137. ACM, 2007.

Modeling the HTML DOM and Browser API in Static Analysis of JavaScript Web Applications

Simon Holm Jensen*
Aarhus University
simonhj@cs.au.dk

Magnus Madsen*
Aarhus University
magnusm@cs.au.dk

Anders Møller*
Aarhus University
amoeller@cs.au.dk

ABSTRACT

Developers of JavaScript web applications have little tool support for catching errors early in development. In comparison, an abundance of tools exist for statically typed languages, including sophisticated integrated development environments and specialized static analyses. Transferring such technologies to the domain of JavaScript web applications is challenging. In this paper, we discuss the challenges, which include the dynamic aspects of JavaScript and the complex interactions between JavaScript, HTML, and the browser. From this, we present the first static analysis that is capable of reasoning about the flow of control and data in modern JavaScript applications that interact with the HTML DOM and browser API.

One application of such a static analysis is to detect type-related and dataflow-related programming errors. We report on experiments with a range of modern web applications, including Chrome Experiments and IE Test Drive applications, to measure the precision and performance of the technique. The experiments indicate that the analysis is able to show absence of errors related to missing object properties and to identify dead and unreachable code. By measuring the precision of the types inferred for object properties, the analysis is precise enough to show that most expressions have unique types. By also producing precise call graphs, the analysis additionally shows that most invocations in the programs are monomorphic. We furthermore study the usefulness of the analysis to detect spelling errors in the code. Despite the encouraging results, not all problems are solved and some of the experiments indicate a potential for improvement, which allows us to identify central remaining challenges and outline directions for future work.

Categories and Subject Descriptors

D.2.5 [**Software Engineering**]: Testing and Debugging

General Terms

Languages, Algorithms, Verification

*Supported by The Danish Research Council for Technology and Production, grant no. 09-064210.

Permission to make digital or hard copies of all or part of this work for personal or classroom use is granted without fee provided that copies are not made or distributed for profit or commercial advantage and that copies bear this notice and the full citation on the first page. To copy otherwise, to republish, to post on servers or to redistribute to lists, requires prior specific permission and/or a fee.
ESEC/FSE'11, September 5–9, 2011, Szeged, Hungary.
Copyright 2011 ACM 978-1-4503-0443-6/11/09 ...$10.00.

1. INTRODUCTION

A JavaScript web application is in essence an HTML page with JavaScript code and other resources, such as CSS stylesheets and image files. Program execution is driven by events in the user's browser: the page is initially loaded, the user interacts with the mouse and keyboard, timeouts occur, AJAX response messages are received from the server, etc. The event handler code reacts by modifying the program state and the HTML page via its DOM (Document Object Model) and by interacting with the browser API, for example to register new event handlers. Compared to other software platforms, the state of the art in development of such web applications is rather primitive, which makes it difficult to write and maintain robust applications. Statically typed languages, such as Java and C#, have long benefited from advanced IDEs and static analysis techniques with rich capabilities of locating likely programming errors during development. Examples of such tools include Eclipse, Visual Studio, FindBugs, and Klocwork. In contrast, existing tool support for JavaScript web application development is mostly limited to syntax highlighting and primitive code completion in IDEs, such as Eclipse, NetBeans, and Visual Studio, often combined with record/play testing frameworks, such as Selenium, Watir, and Sahi.

The goal of our research is to develop static program analysis techniques that can detect—or show absence of—potential programming errors in JavaScript web applications. We focus on general errors that can be detected without the use of application-specific code annotations. Examples of such errors are (1) dead or unreachable code, which often indicates unintended behavior, (2) calls to built-in functions with a wrong number of arguments or with arguments of unexpected types, and (3) uses of the special JavaScript value `undefined` (which appears when attempting to read a missing object property) at dereferences or at function calls. The existence of the `undefined` value and implicit type coercions in the language means that even minor spelling errors, for example in a property name, often has surprising consequences at runtime. With statically typed languages, the type systems provide a strong foundation for detecting such errors. In contrast, because of the dynamic nature of JavaScript web application code, our analysis must be capable of reasoning about the flow of control and data throughout the applications.

We strive to make the analysis *sound*, meaning that all control flow and dataflow that is possible in the program being analyzed is captured by the analysis such that guarantees can be made about absence of errors. Also, it must be sufficiently *precise* and *fast* such that the user is not overwhelmed with spurious warnings and that the analysis can be integrated into the development cycle.

As an example, Figure 1 shows excerpts from a modern JavaScript web application. If one wants to detect or show absence of errors of the kinds discussed above, a static analysis must reason about the subtle flow of control and data between the JavaScript code, the HTML code, and the browser event system, as explained in the figure text.

TAJS is a program analysis tool for JavaScript [11,12]. To this point, TAJS has been developed to faithfully model the JavaScript language and the core library as specified in the ECMAScript standard [4]. Most real JavaScript programs, however, exist in the context of an HTML page and operate in browsers where they access the HTML DOM and the browser API, which causes considerable challenges to the analysis of the flow of control and data [18]. We now take the step of extending TAJS to also model these aspects of JavaScript web applications.

In summary, the contributions of this paper are the following:

- We discuss the key challenges (Section 2) and suggest an approach toward modeling the JavaScript web application platform in static analysis (Section 4). In particular, this involves considerations about modeling the HTML pages and the event system.
- We show how the TAJS analysis (Section 2.2) can be extended to accommodate for the HTML DOM and the browser API. As result, we obtain the first static analysis tool that is capable of reasoning about the flow of control and data in JavaScript web applications.
- Through experimental evaluation we demonstrate that our model is sufficient to show absence of errors and to detect dead and unreachable code. In addition, we evaluate the precision of the types and call graphs inferred by the analysis (Section 5). We identify strengths and weaknesses of the approaches we have taken and suggest directions for future work (Section 7).

Several program analysis tools and techniques for JavaScript have been developed [1,3,5–11,15,19], however, none of them provide a detailed model of the HTML DOM and the browser API, although all JavaScript web applications utilize those mechanisms. We describe connections to related work in Section 6.

2. CHALLENGES

We begin with a brief tour of the technologies involved and explain the central challenges that exist when developing static analyses for JavaScript web applications. Experienced JavaScript programmers who are used to reasoning "manually" about the behavior of their programs will recognize the issues brought forth here.

2.1 The JavaScript Language

The first obstacle we face is the JavaScript language itself. JavaScript has higher-order functions and closures, exceptions, extensive type coercion rules, and a flexible object model where methods and fields can be added or change types and inheritance relations can be modified during execution. As shown by Richards et al. [18], commonly made assumptions in the research literature about JavaScript programs are often violated by the code actually being written by programmers, and JavaScript is described as "a harsh terrain for static analysis".

Implementations largely follow the ECMAScript standard [4], however, there are subtle deviations. One such example is that many browsers for performance reasons do not implement the specified behavior of deleting properties of the `arguments` object (as in `delete arguments[0]`). Another example is that many browsers for security reasons do not correctly invoke the currently defined `Object` function when constructing objects from literals (as in `x={}`). Other peculiar JavaScript features and incompatibility issues are discussed in the paper on JavaScript semantics by Maffeis et al. [16]. One choice we must make is whether to model the standard or one or more of the existing implementations. We return to this issue in Section 3.

On top of the language, ECMAScript contains a standard library consisting of 161 functions and other objects that all need to be modeled somehow by any tool that analyzes JavaScript web applications. Of particular interest is the `eval` function and its variant `Function` that allow dynamic construction of program code from text strings. Reasoning statically about the behavior of such code obviously requires knowledge about which strings may appear. Even so, studies of how these constructs are used in practice indicate that many cases are amenable to static analysis [14,17,18].

For now, we focus on the 3rd edition of ECMAScript (ECMA-262), which is currently the most widely used version. Supporting the more recent 5th edition requires the analysis to also reason about getters and setters, sealed and frozen objects, stronger reflection capabilities, and the so-called strict mode semantics, in addition to a range of new standard library functions.

2.2 The HTML DOM and Browser API

The browser environment gives rise to additional challenges. The JavaScript representation of HTML documents, CSS properties, and the event system is specified by the W3C DOM standards[2]. The HTML5 specification is currently being developed by the WHATWG group[3]. Together, these specifications contribute additional hundreds of functions and other objects to the program state. It is well known to all web application programmers that browsers do not adhere to these standards. Browsers provide non-standard functionality, and many standard features are not supported[4]. In particular the event systems differ between browsers. Another problem is that no standard exists for the `window` object that acts as the global JavaScript object. Incompatibilities in the underlying JavaScript interpreters mostly involve subtle corner cases in the language, as discussed above, and often go unnoticed by the programmers. In contrast, incompatibilities in the browser environments are a major concern. When developing a program analysis, we need to choose which of these variations to model.

A typical workaround is seen in the following function `addEvent` from the Google Chrome Experiment *Tetris*[5].

[1] `http://www.chromeexperiments.com/detail/js-touch/`

[2] `http://www.w3.org/DOM/`

[3] `http://www.whatwg.org/`

[4] `http://www.quirksmode.org/`

[5] `http://www.chromeexperiments.com/detail/domtris/`

```
1  <html>
2  <head>
3  <script type=''text/javascript''>
4  window.P3D = {
5    texture: null,
6    g: null
7  };
8
9  P3D.clear = function(f, w, h) {
10   var g = this.g;
11   g.beginPath();
12   g.fillStyle = f;
13   g.fillRect(0, 0, w, h);
14 }
15
16 function TouchApp() {
17   var _this = this;
18
19   this.canvas = document.getElementById("cv");
20   P3D.g = this.canvas.getContext("2d");
21   //...
22
23   this.mViewport = {};
24   this.mViewport.w = 480;
25   this.mViewport.h = 300;
26   //...
27
28   var tex = new Image();
29   this.ipod.texture = tex;
30   tex.onload = function(){ _this.start(); };
31   tex.src = "20090319144649.png";
32   //...
33 }
34
35 TouchApp.prototype = {
36   start: function() {
37     //...
38     this.onInterval();
39   },
40
41   onInterval: function() {
42     //...
43     P3D.clear("#000",
44               this.mViewport.w,
45               this.mViewport.h);
46     //...
47     setTimeout(function(){
48       _this.onInterval();
49     }, 20);
50   }
51   //...
52 }
53 //...
54 </script>
55 </head>
56   <body onload="void( new TouchApp() );">
57     <canvas id="cv" width="480" height="300"/>
58     //...
59   </body>
60 </html>
```

The code at the left is an excerpt from the Google Chrome Experiment *js touch* (where `//...` indicates omitted code). It displays a 3D model of an iPhone and allows the user to interact with it by moving the mouse. The application is written in pure JavaScript and uses the new HTML5 `canvas` object.

Obviously, many things could go wrong when programming such an application. Three examples of correctness properties that the programmer may consider are: (1) Is the parameter `g` on line 11 always an object with a `beginPath` function? If not, a runtime error will occur when that line is executed. (2) In the call to the function `fillRect` on line 13, are the arguments always numeric? If not, the function call will not have the desired effect. (3) Is the function `P3D.clear` on line 9 reachable in some execution? If not, presumably there is an error in the control flow.

To catch such errors – or to show their absence, a static analysis must know about the flow of control and data in the program. In brief, the browser first loads the HTML page and executes the top-level JavaScript code and `load` event handlers. It then executes other event handlers for user input, timeouts, and other events that occur.

In this example application, the code on line 56 in the `onload` attribute of the `body` element creates a new `TouchApp` object and invokes its constructor function defined on line 16. This function looks up the JavaScript DOM object representing the canvas element on line 19 and then stores a reference to its associated `CanvasRenderingContext2D` in the `g` property of the `P3D` object on line 20. Note that `P3D` is a globally available object. Next, on line 28, the constructor function creates a new `Image` object, sets its `load` event handler to the `start` function and finally sets its `src` property. The browser loads the requested image and fires the `load` handler. The `start` function, defined on line 36, does some work and then invokes the `onInterval` function. This function, defined on line 41, calls `P3D.clear` with appropriate arguments taken from the `this.mViewport` object. Finally, using a call to `setTimeout`, it registers itself to be invoked by the browser 20ms later.

By automating this kind of reasoning, a static analysis can detect likely errors in the application code. Analyzing a complex JavaScript program, such as this one, requires a precise model of the JavaScript language, the HTML DOM, and the browser API. For this application, our analysis tool is capable of showing in 9 seconds among many other properties that (1) the variable `g` does always hold an object with a `beginPath` function, (2) the `fillRect` function is always called with numeric arguments, and (3) the function `P3D.clear` is likely to be reachable. In addition, the analysis reports that 98.9% of all property access operations are guaranteed free from `TypeError` exceptions caused by dereferencing `undefined` or `null` and that all calls to browser API functions are given arguments of meaningful types. More statistics for the unabridged experiment is in Section 5.

Figure 1: Excerpts from the Google Chrome Experiment *JS Touch*[1].

```
function addEvent(el, event, handler) {
  if (el.addEventListener)
    el.addEventListener(event, handler, false);
  else if (el.attachEvent)
    el.attachEvent("on" + event, handler);
}
```

Reasoning statically about the behavior of such code requires not only modeling of different browsers but also flow sensitivity (i.e. taking statement order into account) and even path sensitivity (i.e. considering the branch conditions) to see that the calls to `addEventListener` and `attachEvent` do not cause `TypeError` exceptions.

Since all execution is driven by events, the analysis must also model the event system, which includes the dynamic registration and removal of different kinds of event handlers, as in the `addEvent` function above, the event bubbling and capturing mechanism, and the event object properties that depend on the specific kind of event. The event handlers work as callbacks, which often leads to fragmented code with unclear flow of control that the static analysis must resolve. A small example is seen in the Chrome Experiment *Aquarium*[6] (abbreviated for presentation):

[6] `http://www.chromeexperiments.com/detail/aquarium/`

```
function mmouse(event) {
  mousex=event.pageX;
  mousey=event.pageY;
}
function work() {
  var dx=mousex-pesti[x].x;
  var dy=mousey-pesti[x].y;
  //...
}
setInterval(work,10);
```

The function `mmouse`, which is elsewhere registered as an event handler, stores information about the event in two global variables, `mousex` and `mousey`, that are read in another event handler, `work`. Unless these two variables are properly initialized, `dx` and `dy` will get the special value `NaN` if the `work` function happens to be triggered before `mmouse`, which will likely result in an error later in the execution.

For event handlers defined as HTML attributes, the HTML document structure interferes with the execution scope chains that are used when resolving variables. If an event handler defined literally as an attribute in an HTML element is triggered, the scope chain includes all the DOM objects that make up the path from the HTML element to the root of the document. This means that dataflow in the JavaScript code in general cannot be analyzed separately from the HTML code. The following example illustrates this mechanism:

```
<script type=''text/javascript''>
  var src = "foo.png";
</script>
<img src="bar.png" onclick="alert(src)"/>
```

The value of `src` inside the `onclick` event handler is that of the `src` attribute of the `img` element, not `foo.png` as one might have expected.

Many properties in the ECMAScript native objects have special attributes, such as *ReadOnly*, which also must be accounted for unless sacrificing either soundness or precision. Likewise, many DOM objects behave differently from ordinary objects. As an example, a new `form` element is created with `document.createElement('form')`, not with `new HTMLFormElement` although all `form` elements inherit from `HTMLFormElement.prototype`.

Besides the extent and the variations of browser environments, other concerns when developing a static analysis tool relate to the prevalence of nontrivial built-in setters, that is, assignment operations that involve complex conversions or other side-effects. For example, writing to the `onclick` property of an HTML element object causes a string to be treated as event handler code. Another example is the use of *value correspondence* where HTML element attributes are represented in multiple JavaScript objects. For instance, the `src` attribute value of an `img` element appears both directly as a property of the `img` element object and indirectly as a property of an object that can be reached via the `attributes` property of the `img` element object. These are essentially aliases (although the former is always an absolute URL even when the latter is a relative URL), and modifications to one also affect the other, much like the connection between ordinary JavaScript function parameters and the `arguments` object. Consider also the `window.location` property, which holds a `Location` object. Assigning a new URL string to this property causes the browser to go to that URL after the current event handler and various unload handlers have been executed. As yet another example, writing a string to the (also nonstandard but widely used) `innerHTML` property of an element object causes the string to be parsed as HTML and converted to a DOM object structure, which then replaces the element contents.

A related issue is the *element lookup* mechanism, which provides support for `getElementById` and related functions. If an element with an `id` attribute is inserted into the HTML document, it is automatically added to the browser's element ID table for quick lookup. Similarly, `documents.images` automatically contains references to all images in the current HTML document.

2.3 Application Development Practice

Further complications are introduced by common application development practice. Although JavaScript is an interpreted language (perhaps with JIT compilation, transparently to the programmer) in practice it makes sense to distinguish between "source code" and "executable code". The reason is that JavaScript web application code is often subjected to *minification* (and sometimes also *obfuscation*) to reduce the code size and thereby make the applications load faster. A related trick is *lazy loading* where the applications are divided into parts that are loaded incrementally using AJAX or dynamically constructed `script` elements.

An example of lazy loading using a dynamically created `script` tag occurs in the Google Analytics[7] tool for collecting visitor statistics:

```
<script type="text/javascript">
  (function() {
    var ga = document.createElement('script');
    ga.type = 'text/javascript';
    ga.async = true;
    ga.src =
      ('https:' == document.location.protocol ?
       'https://ssl' :
       'http://www') + '.google-analytics.com/ga.js';
    var s = document.getElementsByTagName('script')[0];
    s.parentNode.insertBefore(ga, s);
  })();
</script>
```

Since our aim is to develop an analysis tool that can help the programmers catch errors during development, we choose to focus on the source code stage, as the programmers see the application before these techniques are applied. This means that we in many cases sidestep the issue of analyzing dynamically generated code. It also means, however, that the analysis tool we develop is not designed to be used for all the JavaScript web application code that is immediately available on public web sites, such as Gmail or Office Web Apps.

Many applications build on libraries that alleviate browser incompatibility problems, provide class-like abstractions and advanced GUI widgets and effects, and simplify common tasks, such as navigation in the HTML DOM structures and AJAX communication. This includes general libraries, for example jQuery, MooTools, and Prototype, but also a myriad of more specialized libraries, such as plugins for jQuery. From a static analysis point of view, libraries such as these in many cases make it difficult to track flow of control and data. By providing their own abstractions on top of event handling and DOM objects, a high degree of context sensitivity and detailed modeling of heap structures may be required by the analysis. An example of a challenging library construct is the `$` function in jQuery, which has very different behavior depending on whether it is passed a function, an HTML string, a CSS string, or a DOM element.

[7]`http://www.google.com/analytics/`

3. THE TAJS ANALYZER

We base the current work on the TAJS analysis tool that is described in previous publications [11,12]. TAJS is a whole-program flow analysis that supports the full JavaScript language as defined in the ECMA-262 specification [4], including the entire standard library except `eval`. The analysis is designed to be sound (although working with a real-world language and having no standardized formal semantics of the language nor of the HTML DOM and browser API, soundness is not formally proven). To this point, we do not consider the deviations from the ECMAScript standard that are discussed in Section 2.1, the reason being that these deviations are mostly corner cases that are irrelevant to most applications we have studied. If the need should arise, for all the deviations we are aware of, it is only a matter of making minor adjustments to the analysis tool.

TAJS is based on the classic monotone framework [13] using a highly specialized analysis lattice structure. The lattice is based on constant propagation for all the possible primitive types of JavaScript values. In addition, the lattice includes call graph information, allowing on-the-fly construction of the call graph to handle higher-order functions. It also contains a model of the heap based on allocation site abstraction extended with recency abstraction [2].

The analysis is object sensitive, meaning that it distinguishes between calling contexts with different values of `this`. It is also flow sensitive, meaning that it distinguishes between different program points (maintaining separate abstract states for different program points), and it has a simple form of path sensitivity to distinguish between different branches of conditionals.

On top of this, lazy propagation is used to ensure that only relevant parts of the abstract states are propagated, which improves both performance and precision [12].

Altogether, this foundation largely addresses the challenges that are directly related to the ECMAScript language specification.

4. MODELING THE HTML DOM AND BROWSER API

We now present our approach to extending the analysis to accommodate for the HTML DOM and the browser API.

Regarding the multitude of APIs supported by different browsers that exist, we choose to model the parts that we believe is most widely used: the DOM Core, DOM HTML, and DOM Events modules of the W3C recommendations (Level 2, plus selected parts of Level 3), the essential parts of `window`[8] and related nonstandard objects, and the `canvas` and related objects from WHATWG's HTML5 (as of January 2011). The latter allows us to test the analysis on web applications that exploit cutting edge functionality supported by the newest browsers.

In total, the extensions comprise around 250 abstract objects with 500 properties and 200 transfer functions. To give an impression of the complexity, Figure 2 shows a small part of the object hierarchy of the initial abstract state. Each node represents an abstract object with its associated properties and functions, and the edges represent internal prototype links. The symbols @ and * in the names indicate whether the abstract objects represent single or multiple concrete objects.

[8] `https://developer.mozilla.org/en/DOM/window`

4.1 HTML Objects

The HTML page and resources linked to from the page define not only the program code but also the initial state for the execution, including the HTML document object structure, element lookup tables, and event handlers.

At runtime, each HTML element gives rise to a range of JavaScript objects, and new HTML elements can be created dynamically. We need a bounded representation to ensure that the program analysis terminates (technically, the analysis lattice must have finite height), thus abstraction is necessary. A simple approach is to represent all HTML objects as one abstract object. This is essentially what is done in other program analyses [7,8] that perform a less detailed analysis than what we aim for. To preserve the inheritance relationships between the DOM objects, we choose an abstraction where all constructor objects and prototype objects are kept separate and that distinguishes between HTML elements of different kinds but where multiple elements of the same kind are merged. As an example, the **`HTMLInputElement`** abstract object (see Figure 2) models all HTML `input` elements. It has properties such as `accessKey` and `checked`, which in the analysis have types `String` and `Boolean`, respectively. The abstract object inherits from **`HTMLInputElement.prototype`**. This object contains common functionality, such as the `focus` function, shared by all **`HTMLInputElement`** objects. Looking further up the prototype chain we find **`HTMLElement.prototype`**, `Element.prototype` and finally `Node.prototype`, which define shared functionality of increasingly general character. Other types of HTML elements, such as `form` or `canvas` elements are similarly modeled by separate abstract objects. This approach respects the inheritance relationships and it smoothly handles programs that dynamically modify the central DOM objects, for example by adding new methods to the prototype objects.

To model the element lookup mechanism (see Section 2.2), we extend TAJS's notion of abstract states with appropriate maps, e.g. from element IDs to sets of abstract objects. The initial abstract state is populated with the IDs that occur in the HTML page. If the HTML page contains an `input` element with an attribute `id="foo"` then the ID map in the abstract state maps `foo` to the **`HTMLInputElement`** abstract object. These maps are updated during the dataflow analysis if new `id` attributes are inserted into the page. As result, `getElementById` and related functions are modeled soundly and with reasonable precision.

4.2 Events

As discussed in Section 2.2, the analysis must be extended to model dynamic registration, triggering, and removal of event handlers. This can be done with various levels of precision. We describe our choices in the following and evaluate the resulting system in Section 5.

First, we extend TAJS's abstract states again, this time with a collection of set of references to abstract objects that model the event handler function objects. To distinguish between different kinds of events and event objects, we maintain one such set for each of the following categories of events: *load*, *mouse*, *keyboard*, *timeout*, *ajax*, and *other*. Object references are added to these sets either statically, due to presence of event attributes (`onload`, `onclick`, etc.) in the HTML page, or dynamically when encountering calls to `addEventListener` or assignments to event attributes during

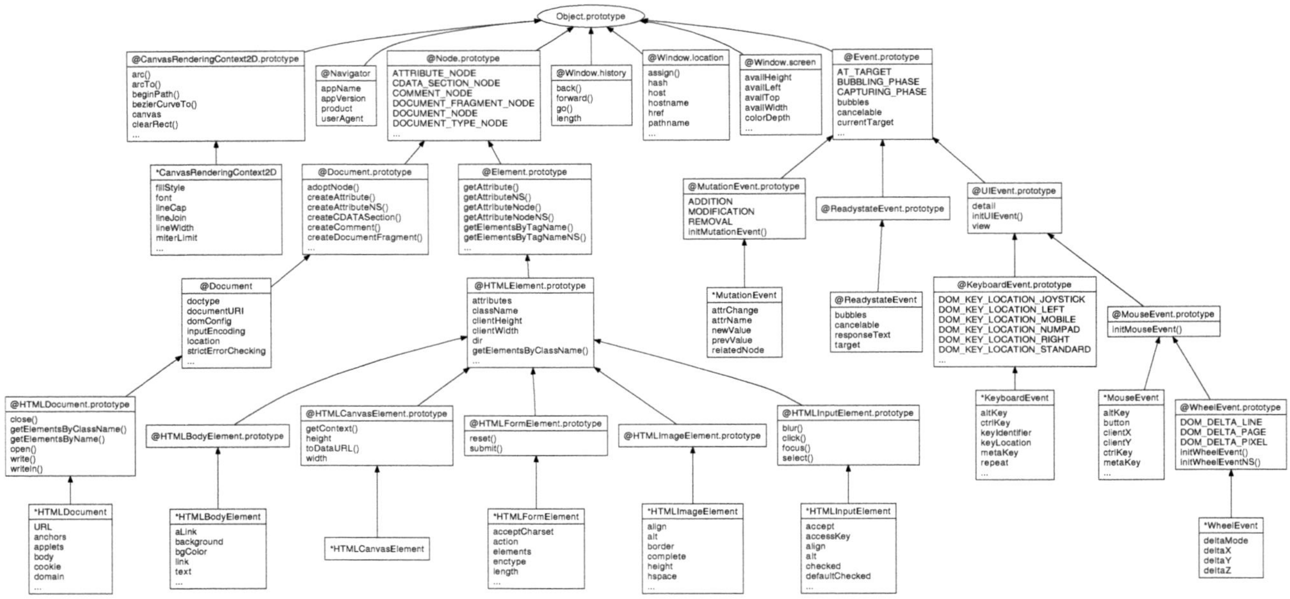

Figure 2: An excerpt from the HTML object hierarchy.

the analysis. This means that the abstract states always contain an upper approximation of which event handlers exist. Note that we choose to abstract away the information about where in the HTML DOM tree the event handlers are registered (i.e. the `currentTarget` of the events). This allows us to ignore event bubbling and capturing. Similarly, we ignore removal of event handlers (`removeEventListener`). These choices may of course affect precision, but analysis soundness is preserved.

Next, we need to model how events are triggered. A JavaScript web application is executed by first running the top-level code and then, until the page is unloaded, running event handlers as reaction to events. Each event handler is executed until completion, without being interrupted when new events occur.

In TAJS, JavaScript program code is represented by flow graphs, which are graphs where nodes correspond to primitive instructions and edges correspond to control flow (see [11]). We have considered different approaches to incorporating the event handler execution loop after the top-level code in the flow graph:

- As a single loop where all event handlers in the current abstract state are executed non-deterministically. This is a simple and sound approach, but it does not maintain the order of execution of the individual event handlers.
- Using a state machine to model the currently registered event handlers. This is a considerably more complex approach, but it can in principle more precisely keep track of the possible order of execution of the event handlers.

Through preliminary experiments we have found for the correctness properties that we focus on, the execution order of event handlers is often not crucial for the analysis precision. However, we found that it is important to model the fact that *load* handlers are executed before the other kinds of event handlers. For this reason, we model the execution of

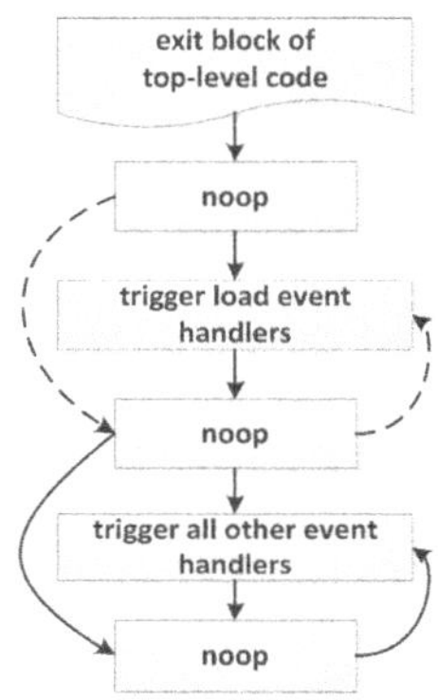

Figure 3: Modeling events in the flow graphs.

event handlers as shown in Figure 3. (To simplify the illustration we here ignore flow of runtime exceptions.) The flow graph for the top-level JavaScript is extended to include two non-deterministic event loops, first one for the *load* event handlers and then one for the other kinds.

If only a single *load* handler is registered (and it is not subsequently removed) then we know that it is definitely executed once, and thus we can effectively remove the dashed edges. This increases precision because otherwise all state initialized by *load* handlers would be modeled as maybe absent.

When triggering event handlers, we exploit the fact that the abstract states distinguish between the different event categories listed above. This allows us to model the event objects appropriately, for example using the abstract object `KeyboardEvent` (see Figure 2) to model keyboard event objects. Moreover, the analysis abstraction used in TAJS already has a fine-grained model of scope chains, so it is relatively easy to incorporate the HTML element objects to take the issues regarding scope chains (see Section 2.2) into account.

4.3 Special Object Properties

As discussed in Section 2.2, writes to certain object properties, such as `onclick`, `src`, and `innerHTML`, have special side-effects. The TAJS analysis infrastructure conveniently supports specialized transfer functions for such operations. This allows us to trigger the necessary modifications of the abstract state when property write operations occur for certain combinations of abstract objects and property names. With this, we can easily handle code such as the following that dynamically constructs an `img` element and sets the `id` and `onclick` properties, which affects not only the `img` object itself but also the element ID lookup map and the event handler set:

```
var i = document.createElement("img");
f.id = "myImage";
f.onclick = function {...}
```

With this approach, the abstractions made elsewhere in the analysis can in principle lead to a cascade of spurious warnings. If the analysis detects a property write operation that involves one of the relevant objects but where the property name is unknown due to abstraction, a fully sound analysis would be required to trigger all the possible specialized transfer functions, which could cause a considerable loss of analysis precision. Instead, if this situation occurs, we choose to sacrifice soundness such that the analysis simply emits a general warning and skips the modeling of the special side-effects for that particular property write operation. In our experiments (see Section 5), this occurs 0 times, indicating that the analysis is generally precise enough to avoid the problem.

4.4 Dynamically Generated Code

We extend TAJS to support certain common cases involving `eval` and the related functions `Function`, `setTimeout`, and `setInterval`. Programmers who are not familiar with higher-order functions often simulate them by using strings instead, such as in this example from the program *Fractal Landscape*[9]:

```
animInterval = setInterval("animatedDraw()", 100);
```

This code works because the function `setInterval` supports being called with a string that will get evaluated in the global scope at the specified intervals. To accommodate for this, TAJS recognizes the syntax of a string consisting of a simple function call. The analysis transfer function for `setInterval` collects not only function objects but also such strings that represent event handler functions. When modeling the triggering of event handlers, the latter functions are then looked up in the global scope.

An often used application of `eval` is to parse JSON data received using AJAX. JSON data describes simple JavaScript object structures that cannot contain functions. TAJS can be configured to assume that string values that are read from AJAX connections contain only JSON data. We model this with the special dataflow value `JSONString`. If this abstract value is passed to `eval`, the analysis knows that no side-effects can happen, so the result can be modeled using an abstract value consisting of a generic abstract object and unknown primitive values.

[9] `http://10k.aneventapart.com/Entry/60`

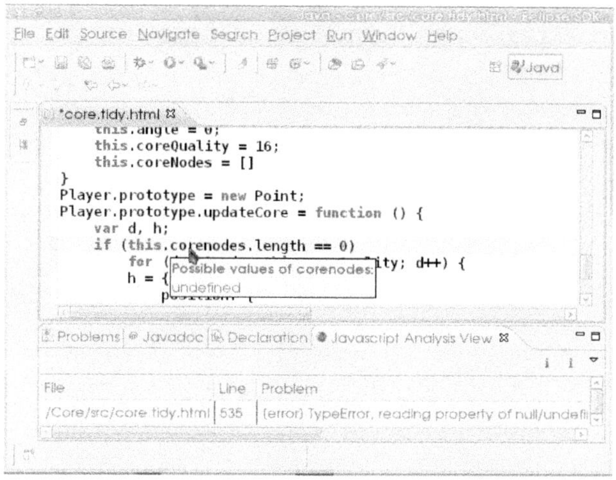

Figure 4: The TAJS analysis plug-in for Eclipse, reporting a programming error and highlighting the type inferred for the selected expression.

5. EVALUATION

We have extended the pre-existing TAJS analysis tool according to Section 4. The tool is implemented in Java and uses the JavaScript parser from the Mozilla Rhino project[10]. The new extensions amount to 7,500 lines of code on top of the existing 21,000 lines (excluding Rhino). Separately, the analysis is integrated into the Eclipse IDE as a plug-in that allows the programmer to view various aspects of the analysis results, as demonstrated in Figure 4.

5.1 Research Questions

With the implementation, we consider the following research questions regarding the quality of the analysis:

Q1 We wish to study the ability of the tool to detect programming errors of the kinds discussed in Section 1. Given that we do not expect many errors in the benchmark programs that presumable are thoroughly tested already, one way to study the analysis precision is to ask: To what extent can the analysis show the absence of errors in real programs? Since the analysis is designed to be sound (however see Section 4.3), absence of a warning from the tool can be interpreted as absence of an error in the program being analyzed.

Q2 For programs with errors (again, of the kinds discussed in Section 1), can the analysis help the programmer find the errors? Specifically, are the warning messages produced by the tool useful toward leading the programmer to the source of the errors?

Q3 Having a good approximation of the call graph of a program is a foundation for other potential applications, such as program comprehension or optimization. This leads to the question: How precise is the call graph inferred by the analysis?

Q4 Similarly to the previous question, how precise are the inferred types?

Q5 Does the analysis succeed in identifying dead or unreachable code? In some situations, dead or unreach-

[10] `http://www.mozilla.org/rhino`

able code is unintended by the programmer and hence indicates errors. The ability of the analysis tool to detect such code can in principle also be used to reduce application code size before deployment.

5.2 Benchmark Programs

Our benchmark programs are drawn from three different sources: *Chrome Experiments*[11], *Internet Explorer 9 Test Drive*[12] and the *10K Apart Challenge*[13]. Chrome Experiments consist of JavaScript web applications that demonstrate the JavaScript features of the Chrome browser. Despite the name, the majority of these applications can be executed in any modern browser. Most of the applications use the new HTML5 `canvas` element to create graphics in various ways including games and simulations. Internet Explorer 9 Test Drive is a collection of applications written to test and demonstrate features of the newest version of the Internet Explorer browser. We exclude applications that contain no or very little JavaScript code or rely on Flash or other browser plug-ins. The 10K Apart Challenge collection consists of JavaScript web applications that are less than 10KB in size including code and markup.

The programmers of some of the 10K Apart Challenge applications have applied `eval` creatively to reduce the code size in ways that we believe are not representative of ordinary JavaScript web applications. For this reason, we disregard applications that syntactically use `eval` in other ways than those covered in Section 4.4. Moreover, analyzing applications that involve large libraries, such as jQuery, MooTools, and Prototype, is particularly challenging for the reasons discussed in Section 2.3. At present, we limit our level of ambition to applications that do not depend on such libraries. The applications we thereby exclude can form an interesting basis for future work on static analysis in relation to `eval` or libraries.

The resulting collection of 53 JavaScript web applications is listed in Table 1 and available at `http://www.brics.dk/TAJS/dom-benchmarks`. In the table, the columns LOC, BB, and Time show the number of lines of code (pretty-printed and including HTML), the number of basic blocks of JavaScript code, and the analysis time (running on a 2.53Ghz Mac OS X computer with 4GB of memory). Dynamically generated code of the kind discussed in Section 4.4 appears in 17% of the applications. All the applications involve HTML and the event system, so none of them could be analyzed with TAJS before the new extensions described in this paper.

5.3 Experiments and Results

We address each research question, Q1–Q5, in turn with experiments and evaluation.

For Q1, we focus on the following kinds of likely errors:

- Invoking a non-function value as a function.
- Accessing a property of the special values `undefined` or `null`.
- Reading an absent object property using the fixed-property notation (we here ignore operations that use the notation for dynamically computed property names).

The first two cause `TypeError` exceptions; the third yields the value `undefined`. Technically, these situations are not necessarily errors, but they are rarely intended by the programmer. One exception is that absent properties may appear in browser feature detection code, in which case the analysis can help ensuring that the code works for the browser being modeled.

For each error category we measure the percentage of flow graph nodes for which TAJS decides not to issue a warning of the particular kind. The results are shown in the three columns labelled CF, PA and FPU in Table 1, corresponding to the three kinds of likely errors. We see that TAJS is able to show absence of these particular kinds of errors for most of the program code, in many cases more than 90% of the places in the code where the errors could potentially occur. There are a few outliers that get lower results: Both *Tetris* and *Minesweeper* rely on multi-dimensional arrays for most of their state, which leads to imprecision in property reads. Complex object models, such as in the *Raytracer* benchmark, are also the cause of some imprecision.

As we do not expect our benchmarks to contain any of the error conditions listed above, we answer Q2 by introducing errors into the benchmark programs at random. We simulate spelling errors made by the programmer by picking a random read or write property operation that uses the fixed-property notation (i.e. the `.` operator) and replacing the property name with a different one. For each benchmark, we run the analysis repeatedly and manually inspect whether each spelling error results in a warning by the analysis tool and how "useful" this warning is. We measure usefulness by two criteria: the source location of the warning that is issued should be close to where the error is inserted, and the warning should be prominent, i.e. appear near the top in the list of analysis messages.

This process has been carried out for a random subset of our benchmark programs. All show a common pattern: Spelling errors at read operations are reliably detected with a warning that appears at the top of the list of analysis messages. Not surprisingly, spelling errors introduced at write operations have more diverse consequences, as any warning will only occur when the program later attempts to read the property that was affected. Furthermore, errors introduced in connection to side-effects that are not modeled by TAJS, such as the DOM property `style`, are often not detected.

We present the results for the *Mr. Potato Gun* benchmark as a representative example. We analyzed it 50 times with a different spelling error introduced each time. In 84% of the cases the error resulted in one or more warnings. Of the errors introduced, 7 were in write operations and 43 in read operations. Only one of the write operation errors was detected, resulting in the warning `ReferenceError, reading absent property: (computed name)`, which is a high-priority warning that is issued for the location where the program tries to read the property that was misspelled. For the read operations, each error was reported as a warning such as `ReferenceError, reading absent property: AQ` issued for the exact source location of the error.

These experiments indicate that the information obtained by the analysis can be useful for detecting spelling errors in the program code, but a more thorough investigation is necessary to give a solid answer to Q2.

For Q3 we wish to evaluate the precision of the computed call graph. This is measured by calculating the ratio of call

[11] `http://www.chromeexperiments.com/`
[12] `http://ie.microsoft.com/testdrive/`
[13] `http://10k.aneventapart.com/`

	LOC	BB	CF	PA	FPU	UF	DC	MC	ATS	Time
3D Demo	1205	1770	99.2	97.9	98.9	125/58	7	100.0%	1.1	8.0s
Another World	1477	1437	100.0	99.3	98.3	45/0	0	100.0%	1.3	20.7s
Apophis	1140	1319	100.0	80.4	80.4	58/0	0	100.0%	1.1	16.3s
Aquarium	166	151	93.7	87.6	72.8	9/0	0	100.0%	1.3	3.2s
Bing-Bong	1148	1176	100.0	87.9	92.5	66/0	2	100.0%	1.1	17.9s
Blob	596	748	100.0	95.6	97.4	37/2	19	100.0%	1.0	6.4s
Bomomo	2905	3885	80.6	96.3	61.2	170/8	10	100.0%	1.3	57.1s
Breathing Galaxies	101	101	94.7	100.0	91.3	5/0	0	100.0%	1.0	1.3s
Browser Ball	434	771	99.0	97.7	98.1	32/11	0	100.0%	1.0	4.2s
Burn Canvas	180	207	100.0	97.7	100.0	12/0	0	100.0%	1.1	0.9s
Catch It	207	200	97.2	86.0	98.6	11/0	0	100.0%	1.1	3.3s
Core	566	611	100.0	98.7	98.4	23/1	10	100.0%	1.0	5.6s
JS Touch	1452	762	100.0	98.9	98.1	48/8	9	100.0%	1.1	5.8s
Kaleidoscope	249	334	98.9	88.6	82.1	14/1	3	100.0%	1.1	6.1s
Keylight	731	791	99.4	96.1	98.7	37/0	24	100.0%	1.0	7.4s
Liquid Particles	253	205	100.0	98.5	100.0	11/4	2	100.0%	1.0	1.8s
Magnetic	415	339	100.0	95.5	100.0	19/0	1	100.0%	1.0	4.1s
Orange Tunnel	102	133	100.0	80.3	100.0	7/1	0	100.0%	1.1	2.6s
Plane Deformations	552	514	100.0	100.0	95.1	17/0	5	100.0%	1.5	1.5s
Plasma	204	228	100.0	100.0	100.0	9/0	2	100.0%	1.1	1.6s
Raytracer	1380	1515	87.2	93.7	55.5	78/24	33	90.1%	1.3	20.6s
Starfield	231	393	98.7	79.0	87.6	21/6	2	100.0%	1.2	2.9s
Tetris	827	803	95.1	79.6	58.8	39/4	2	100.0%	1.8	9.7s
Trail	212	166	100.0	98.0	98.2	10/0	0	100.0%	1.0	12s
Voronoi	525	1066	100.0	78.8	99.7	70/7	10	99.5%	1.1	10.5s
Water Type	309	266	100.0	95.0	97.2	14/0	0	100.0%	1.1	1.9s
Asteroid Belt	319	707	100.0	94.6	97.0	27/5	30	100.0%	1.1	3.1s
Browser Flip	507	324	100.0	88.5	97.6	10/0	1	100.0%	1.1	3.2s
FishIE	336	717	99.4	96.0	95.5	19/2	30	100.0%	1.0	3.3s
Flying Images	589	497	100.0	97.5	91.8	33/0	0	100.0%	1.0	3.9s
Mr. Potato Gun	817	1015	98.7	97.6	95.0	31/1	12	100.0%	1.1	7.8s
10k World	439	930	100.0	86.9	91.4	47/2	3	100.0%	1.1	15.1s
3D Maker	427	773	100.0	67.3	70.5	29/3	0	100.0%	1.2	10.3s
Attractor	445	696	97.0	92.3	91.2	34/0	1	100.0%	1.3	5.8s
Defend Yourself	517	601	94.7	78.6	90.1	31/0	0	100.0%	1.1	7.9s
Earth Night Lights	129	245	100.0	100.0	100.0	14/0	0	100.0%	1.0	1.1s
Filterrific	697	995	96.5	86.7	72.3	55/0	4	99.0%	1.2	29.8s
Flatwar	444	685	99.2	97.4	93.6	19/1	0	100.0%	1.1	6.9s
Floating Bubbles	381	693	100.0	89.9	99.7	39/6	23	100.0%	1.1	6.4s
Fractal Landscape	171	162	100.0	100.0	97.7	7/0	0	100.0%	1.0	0.8s
Gravity	231	258	98.7	87.3	90.9	9/0	0	100.0%	1.0	5.2s
Heatmap	255	350	95.1	93.6	87.3	30/1	2	97.3%	1.1	3.1s
Last Man Standing	300	570	100.0	95.9	100.0	33/1	2	100.0%	1.1	4.2s
Lines	459	931	97.3	88.5	93.9	22/6	2	100.0%	1.2	4.7s
Minesweeper	175	358	100.0	81.4	68.5	15/0	3	100.0%	1.3	4.7s
NBody	479	450	99.1	68.7	43.6	15/0	0	100.0%	1.6	50.8s
RGB Color Wheel	455	700	97.7	82.7	85.0	38/0	2	100.0%	1.1	5.6s
Sinuous	349	488	100.0	96.3	98.5	23/0	10	100.0%	1.0	5.5s
Snowpar	338	519	100.0	88.6	88.6	31/0	0	100.0%	1.2	3.2s
Stairs to Heaven	210	422	100.0	94.5	100.0	25/8	1	100.0%	1.0	2.5s
Sudoku	316	612	96.2	81.0	60.4	33/0	0	100.0%	1.3	12.1s
TicTacToe	304	590	100.0	74.0	100.0	19/0	0	100.0%	1.2	7.4s
Zmeyko	344	601	100.0	96.7	96.3	33/1	0	100.0%	1.0	7.0s

Table 1: Benchmark results for Chrome Experiments, IE Test Drive and 10K Apart Challenge applications. The columns from left to right are: lines of code (LOC), number of basic blocks (BB), percentage of call site operations shown to invoke a function value (CF), property read operations where the base object is shown to be non-`null` and non-`undefined` (PA), fixed-property read operations not resulting in `undefined` (FPU), number of functions in total / number of functions shown to be definitely unreachable (UF), number of dead code operations (DC), percentage of call sites that are shown to be monomorphic (MC), average type size for all property read operations (ATS), and analysis time (Time).

sites with a single invocation target compared to the total number of call sites in the program. If this ratio is one then every call site is monomorphic, i.e. it has a single invocation target. If a call site has a non-function value as a potential invocation target this is not included in the number of targets, since such a value would always result in a runtime error. This measure can be seen in the MC column. In Table 1 we see that despite the fact that JavaScript supports both the prototype lookup mechanism and higher-order functions, the analysis is able to show for 49 of the 53 of the benchmark programs that all call sites have a single invocation target, which gives testimony to the high precision of the analysis.

For Q4 we wish to measure the precision of the computed types. The analysis tracks values of the following types: *boolean*, *number*, *string*, *object* (including null and function values) and the special type *undefined*. This means that an object property could potentially hold values of up to five different types. We measure this aspect of the accuracy of the analysis by calculating the average number of different types for all property read operations in the given program (excluding operations that the analysis finds to be unreachable). If this number is 1 then every read operation results in values of a unique type on all possible executions. The ATS column in Table 1 shows the resulting numbers. Despite the fact that the types of object properties may change dynamically in JavaScript, we note that the analysis is precise enough to show that the average number of different types for each property read operation in these benchmarks is quite close to 1. Of the 26,870 property read operations that appear in the benchmarks, the analysis finds that at most 4,019 can have multiple types.

For the last research question, Q5, we measure both unreachable code and dead code. Unreachable code consists of operations (i.e. flow graph nodes) that are never executed, and dead code is defined to be reachable assignments to properties that are never read. Write operations to special DOM properties, such as `onload`, may have side-effects, so even if there are no corresponding read operations in the program we do not count them as dead code.

The column labelled UF in Table 1 contains the total number of function in the program and how many of them are determined by TAJS to be unreachable. Some of the benchmarks use third-party libraries that are inlined directly in the source code, which explains the large number of unreachable functions in some benchmarks, such as *3D Demo* and *Raytracer*. All code that is found to be unreachable can safely be removed (unless the analysis detects the special situation discussed in Section 4.3), which would significantly reduce code size in some cases. Most current minifiers either unsoundly remove all functions not referenced syntactically in the code or simply do not remove any functions at all. With static analysis, guaranteed behavior preserving minification becomes possible.

The column labelled DC lists the number of dead code operations in each program. We see that the analysis is capable of locating many instances of dead code. Most of the dead code being detected appears to be code left from earlier revisions of the programs. For example, in the *Keylight* benchmark, a flag named `mouseIsDown` is set in all event handlers but it is never read.

The main threat to validity of our conclusions is that our benchmarks may not be representative for typical JavaScript web applications. For the reasons described in Section 5.2 we have excluded applications that rely on large libraries or on complex dynamically generated code. We will focus our attention on these two remaining challenges in future work. Nevertheless, the benchmarks we consider are written by many different programmers, they exhibit a large variety of the functionality supported by the HTML DOM and the browser API, and our experiments show that the program analysis is able to infer many nontrivial properties about their behavior.

6. RELATED WORK

Previous work on static analysis of JavaScript code has focused on the language itself, and often for restricted subsets of the language. To the best of our knowledge, the work reported on in this paper is the first that also models the nontrivial connections between the HTML page and the program code in JavaScript web applications.

One of the first attempts at developing static analysis for JavaScript was done by Anderson et al. who developed a type system and inference algorithm for modeling definite presence and potential absence of object properties in a small subset of JavaScript [1]. The abstract domain used in TAJS subsumes such information. Other early work includes Thiemann's type system [19]. It has a soundness proof but no implementation. Although not tied to JavaScript in particular, Thiemann has also designed a type system for catching errors related to manipulation of DOM structures, in particular to ensure that no loops occur [20].

More recently, Jang and Choe have presented a points-to analysis for a restricted subset of JavaScript based on set constraints [10]. The points-to results are used for optimizations that inline property accesses. In comparison, our analysis yields points-to information as part of the result and supports more features of the language.

The Gatekeeper project by Guarnieri and Livshits includes an Andersen-style points-to analysis for JavaScript [6, 7]. The results of the analysis are used for verifying custom security policies expressed in datalog. The analysis uses a mock-up of the DOM API written in JavaScript and essentially ignores the HTML constituents.

Perhaps most closely related to our work is that of Guha et al. who use a k-CFA analysis to extract a model of the client behavior in an AJAX application as seen from the server [8]. Their paper briefly discusses some of the challenges that relate to events, dynamically generated code, and libraries, but the focus of the paper is on the application for building intrusion-preventing proxies. In comparison, our analysis has a more precise treatment of dataflow and event handlers in connection to the DOM.

Recent work by Guha et al. considers a combination of a type system and a flow analysis to reason about uses of the `typeof` operator in JavaScript code with type annotations [9]. The `typeof` operator appears in 11 of our 53 benchmarks, and TAJS models it with a special transfer function.

Chugh et al. use staged information flow analysis to protect against dynamic loading of malicious code [3]. The analysis identifies fields that can flow into dynamically loaded code and creates runtime monitors to ensure that they are not accessed from untrusted code. The analysis uses a coarse abstraction of the HTML page and the browser API, without considering the challenges we describe in Section 2.

Logozzo and Venter's RATA analysis uses light-weight abstract interpretation to specialize the general JavaScript number type to integer and floating point types for optimization purposes [15]. Making this distinction in the abstract domain used in TAJS would be a straightforward task.

One way to guide the design of an analysis is to survey the practical use of the language. In one such survey by Richards et al., it is shown that many of the dynamic features of JavaScript are not widely used in practice [18]. The study shows that the majority of method invocations in JavaScript are monomorphic. Our experimental results confirm this observation, but using practically sound static analysis instead of runtime measurements. In later work, the use of `eval` is studied [17]. The authors show that the categories of `eval` that are now supported by TAJS, i.e. JSON data and simple function calls, are often used. It is also shown that `eval` is used for lazy loading and as artifacts of generated code, which, as discussed in Section 2.3, is outside the scope of TAJS.

7. CONCLUSION

We have presented the first static analysis that is capable of reasoning precisely about the control flow and dataflow in JavaScript applications that run in a browser environment. The analysis has been implemented as an extension of the TAJS tool and models both the DOM model of the HTML page and browser API. This includes the HTML element object hierarchy and the event-driven execution model. In the process we have identified the key areas where modeling the browser is important for precision and challenging for static analysis.

Our experimental evaluation of the performance of the analysis indicates that (1) the analysis is able to show absence of common programming errors in the benchmark programs, (2) the analysis can help detecting potential errors, such as misspelled property names, (3) the computed call graphs are precise as most call sites are shown to be monomorphic, (4) the computed types are precise as many expressions are shown to have unique types, and (5) the analysis is able to identify dead code and unreachable functions. Such information can give a foundation for providing better tool support for JavaScript web application developers.

Interesting challenges remain. First, more work is required for investigating the more complicated uses of dynamically generated code. Second, better techniques are needed to handle commonly used libraries. Third, the techniques presented here can be adapted to model other JavaScript environments, such as desktop widgets or browser extensions.

8. REFERENCES

[1] C. Anderson, P. Giannini, and S. Drossopoulou. Towards type inference for JavaScript. In *Proc. 19th European Conference on Object-Oriented Programming, ECOOP '05*, volume 3586 of *LNCS*. Springer-Verlag, July 2005.

[2] G. Balakrishnan and T. W. Reps. Recency-abstraction for heap-allocated storage. In *Proc. 13th International Static Analysis Symposium, SAS '06*, volume 4134 of *LNCS*. Springer-Verlag, August 2006.

[3] R. Chugh, J. A. Meister, R. Jhala, and S. Lerner. Staged information flow for JavaScript. In *Proc. ACM SIGPLAN Conference on Programming Language Design and Implementation, PLDI '09*, June 2009.

[4] ECMA. ECMAScript Language Specification, 3rd edition. ECMA-262.

[5] S. Fink and J. Dolby. WALA – The T.J. Watson Libraries for Analysis. `http://wala.sourceforge.net/`.

[6] S. Guarnieri and B. Livshits. Gulfstream: Staged static analysis for streaming JavaScript applications. In *Proc. USENIX Conference on Web Application Development, WebApps '10*, June 2010.

[7] S. Guarnieri and V. B. Livshits. Gatekeeper: Mostly static enforcement of security and reliability policies for JavaScript code. In *Proc. 18th USENIX Security Symposium, Security '09*, August 2009.

[8] A. Guha, S. Krishnamurthi, and T. Jim. Using static analysis for Ajax intrusion detection. In *Proc. 18th International Conference on World Wide Web, WWW '09*, May 2009.

[9] A. Guha, C. Saftoiu, and S. Krishnamurthi. Typing local control and state using flow analysis. In *Proc. Programming Languages and Systems, 20th European Symposium on Programming, ESOP '11*, LNCS. Springer-Verlag, March/April 2011.

[10] D. Jang and K.-M. Choe. Points-to analysis for JavaScript. In *Proc. 24th Annual ACM Symposium on Applied Computing, SAC '09, Programming Language Track*, March 2009.

[11] S. H. Jensen, A. Møller, and P. Thiemann. Type analysis for JavaScript. In *Proc. 16th International Static Analysis Symposium, SAS '09*, volume 5673 of *LNCS*, pages 238–255. Springer-Verlag, August 2009.

[12] S. H. Jensen, A. Møller, and P. Thiemann. Interprocedural analysis with lazy propagation. In *Proc. 17th International Static Analysis Symposium, SAS '10*, volume 6337 of *LNCS*, pages 238–256. Springer-Verlag, September 2010.

[13] J. B. Kam and J. D. Ullman. Monotone data flow analysis frameworks. *Acta Informatica*, 7:305–317, 1977. Springer-Verlag.

[14] R. Kromann-Larsen and R. Simonsen. Statisk analyse af JavaScript: Indledende arbejde. Master's thesis, Department of Computer Science, Aarhus University, 2007. (In Danish).

[15] F. Logozzo and H. Venter. RATA: Rapid atomic type analysis by abstract interpretation - application to JavaScript optimization. In *Proc. 19th International Conference on Compiler Construction, CC '10*, volume 6011 of *LNCS*. Springer-Verlag, March 2010.

[16] S. Maffeis, J. C. Mitchell, and A. Taly. An operational semantics for JavaScript. In *Proc. 6th Asian Symposium on Programming Languages and Systems, APLAS '08*, volume 5356 of *LNCS*. Springer-Verlag, December 2008.

[17] G. Richards, C. Hammer, B. Burg, and J. Vitek. The eval that men do – a large-scale study of the use of eval in JavaScript applications. In *Proc. 25th European Conference on Object-Oriented Programming, ECOOP '11*, LNCS. Springer-Verlag, July 2011.

[18] G. Richards, S. Lebresne, B. Burg, and J. Vitek. An analysis of the dynamic behavior of Javascript programs. In *Proc. ACM SIGPLAN Conference on Programming Language Design and Implementation, PLDI '10*, June 2010.

[19] P. Thiemann. Towards a type system for analyzing JavaScript programs. In *Proc. Programming Languages and Systems, 14th European Symposium on Programming, ESOP '05*, April 2005.

[20] P. Thiemann. A type safe DOM API. In *Proc. 10th International Workshop on Database Programming Languages, DBPL '05*, volume 3774 of *LNCS*. Springer-Verlag, 2005.

The Onion Patch: Migration in Open Source Ecosystems

Corey Jergensen, Anita Sarma
Computer Science and Engineering Department
University of Nebraska, Lincoln
Lincoln, NE, USA 98588
{cjergens, asarma}@cse.unl.edu

Patrick Wagstrom
IBM TJ Watson Research Center
19 Skyline Drive, Hawthorne
NY, USA 10532
pwagstro@us.ibm.com

ABSTRACT
Past research established that individuals joining an Open Source community typically follow a socialization process called "the onion model": newcomers join a project by first contributing at the periphery through mailing list discussions and bug trackers and as they develop skill and reputation within the community they advance to central roles of contributing code and making design decisions. However, the modern Open Source landscape has fewer projects that operate independently and many projects under the umbrella of software ecosystems that bring together projects with common underlying components, technology, and social norms. Participants in such an ecosystems may be able to utilize a significant amount of transferrable knowledge when moving between projects in the ecosystem and, thereby, skip steps in the onion model. In this paper, we examine whether the onion model of joining and progressing in a standalone Open Source project still holds true in large project ecosystems and how the model might change in such settings.

Categories and Subject Descriptors
D.2.9 [**Software Engineering**]: Management: *programming teams*: D.2.8 [**Software Engineering**]: Metrics: *process metrics*

General Terms
Human Factors, Management, and Measurement.

Keywords
Open Source software, project ecosystem, contribution model.

1. INTRODUCTION
Open Source projects have been widely studied by researchers in the fields of software engineering, computer supported cooperative-work, and management [7, 28]. Research has included studies of motivational factors that drive volunteers to contribute time and code towards the common public good [18, 22, 31], the socialization process through which newcomers become active community members [10, 29], the sustainability of Open Source projects given their high rates of turnover and barriers to contribution [27], and the underlying social organizations in Open Source projects [2-3, 24].

One of the overarching attributes of Open Source is that it draws expertise and contributions from a pool of volunteers. Because these volunteers often exhibit high turnover rates, there is a need to understand how projects continue to recruit, educate, and socialize volunteers to maintain vibrancy [27, 31]. The past characterization of the development (or socialization) process maintains that new comers start at the periphery with low technical skill requirements, for example by posting to project mailing lists or participating in project chat rooms. As the skills and experience of the user evolves they may choose to report bugs, which requires a small amount of technical skill. Through their contributions users continue to build their reputation in the community and some may migrate toward more technical and central roles such as code contribution and moderation. This model, called the onion model, depicts roles as concentric layers with high skill, high reputation roles at the center and low technical skill and reputation at the periphery [6, 19, 32]. Variations on the model have been qualitatively and empirically validated in a number of projects (e.g., Apache [25], Freenet [29], Netscape [19], Mozilla [26], Python [10], and others [28]).

These studies form the foundation of our understanding of Open Source software. The existing characterization of Open Source projects is based on studies of large individual projects. However, these characterizations may be somewhat outdated in light of recent changes. Many modern Open Source projects strongly resemble large enterprise products that comprise numerous smaller, related projects, engage individuals as wells as corporations, and involve contributions from volunteers as well as paid members [4]. This new genre of Open Source, termed OSS 2.0 by Fitzgerald [12], is significantly different from its standalone individual antecedents. Earlier lessons and insights about Open Source projects might not hold true in this new collaborative landscape populated by complex software ecosystems and further studies to characterize this emergent OSS 2.0 phenomenon are required [4, 12]. For example, the Eclipse Foundation, which has its roots in the Eclipse Integrated Development Environment (IDE), which was released as Open Source by IBM, has expanded to encompass a wide variety of end user tools based on a common set of technologies beyond just the IDE experience, and include tools for developing complex web applications on the client and server, version control tools, and identity management. The foundation has numerous and significant contributions from some of the largest players in technology including IBM, Intel, and Oracle, in addition to substantial participation from volunteers and university students [9, 30]. Open Source ecosystems may have a variety of different focuses, such as GNOME and KDEs efforts to create desktop environments [23], developer tools and web infrastructure from Apache [22, 26], and support for Open Source programming languages [4], among others.

While past studies provided insight into how Open Source communities function, most do not address the interconnected nature of modern OSS 2.0 style ecosystems. Since projects in an ecosystem share underlying technical infrastructure and often follow similar social norms, members can participate in multiple projects or move across projects in an ecosystem with relative ease. The socialization process of the onion model may not hold true if developers can easily move from one project to another and utilize

Permission to make digital or hard copies of all or part of this work for personal or classroom use is granted without fee provided that copies are not made or distributed for profit or commercial advantage and that copies bear this notice and the full citation on the first page. To copy otherwise, or republish, to post on servers or to redistribute to lists, requires prior specific permission and/or a fee.
ESEC/FSE'11, September 5-9, 2011, Szeged, Hungary.
Copyright 2011 ACM 978-1-4503-0443-6/11/09...$10.00.

much of their knowledge and reputation from elsewhere in the ecosystem. This leads to our first research question:

RQ1: To what extent do members migrate across projects in software project ecosystems?

When a developer joins a project from elsewhere in the ecosystem, rather than starting the socialization and technical knowledge acquisition process from scratch, it is likely that some of their reputation and technical skill will allow the developer to bypass portions of the basic socialization process. The manifestation of this knowledge transfer process, however, is unknown. Does existing knowledge allow a developer to bypass the socializations process, or merely compress the duration? This gives rise to our second research question:

RQ2: When members migrate across projects can they use knowledge common across projects to jumpstart their contribution to a new project?

Finally, previous research has suggested that experience and tenure in an individual project is a driving force in moving developers toward the center or core of a project [3, 26]. This is predicated on developers taking time to learn the code and build up reputation in the community. However, developers in an OSS 2.0 ecosystem are not only able to transfer general process information and reputation from one project to another, but may be able to reuse their technical expertise in shared code components or social expertise in enhancing a particular area. This can improve their ability to directly contribute to the core of a project. In such an environment, where developers can fluidly move from one project to another related project it is not known whether experience and tenure within a project are the primary factors affecting the centrality of contributions or if other factors overshadow these. This brings us to our third research question:

RQ3: In an interconnected software ecosystem, what factors affect the contribution type and quality?

We answer these questions through a longitudinal analysis of a selection of projects in the GNOME ecosystem. These are stable and mature Open Source projects that have attracted significant contributions from volunteer and commercial developers. These projects provide a rich data source because they all have between six to ten years of project archival history. The projects also have a significant overlap of developers, that is, there are many developers who have contributed to multiple projects in the period of our study. For each of these projects, we analyzed mail messages from project mailing lists, comments and actions from the project bug trackers, and code contributions made through the project version control systems. We further refined contributions through the version control system into source code contributions and other types of contributions, such as translation, documentation, and media. This allows a further differentiation of project members and a more robust analysis of developer progression paths and the centrality of developer contributions.

We find that within our sample there is a significant population that is active on multiple projects within the ecosystem. Based on an analysis of patterns that developers follow in joining individual projects and when participating in the entire ecosystem, we find that there is little evidence of individuals following the pure onion model. Rather, we identify multiple patterns that are contradictory to the model or otherwise compress the model. For example, a large majority of developers only made technical contributions to the project. In the subset of the six projects that we analyzed we found 81.65% of members participating in only technical medium, of which 64.67% were active only in source code repositories.

We also note, that in most cases prior experience in a project ecosystem does not have an effect on the centrality of contribution when controlling for tenure within a project. In fact, the longer a developer is associated with a project, the lower the centrality of their contributions. After further generalization of this behavior we find that new developers and those who have been active for between 2 and 5 releases both have about the same level of centrality for contributions to project source code, while very experienced developers tend to move away from direct code creation tasks, leading to lower centrality of contributions.

Finally, we attempt to uncover broader trends that may lead to a higher centrality of contribution. We find that there are certain very specific domains, specifically translation and internationalization, where there appears to be transferrable knowledge across projects in the ecosystem that allows a developer to quickly make high centrality contributions to project source code.

The rest of the paper is organized as follows: In Section 2, we discuss some of the background on the socialization process in Open Source projects and build our hypotheses. Sections 3 and 4 describe our data and present our analysis. In Section 5, we discuss our findings. Sections 6 and 7 close out the paper with a discussion of possible threats to research validity and our conclusions.

2. SOCIALIZATION PROCESS IN OSS

Prior studies have identified a variety of barriers that newcomers face in the course of immigrating to a new Open Source project [11, 18]. Open Source projects typically do not provide formal mentoring and training for newcomers and it is the responsibility of the newcomer to identify the appropriate technical tasks and start contributing [10, 29]. Most projects have a public list of open bugs and issues and newcomers are encouraged to start their investigations there or by addressing a concern the individual developer has identified. It is rare that newcomers are specifically directed to technical tasks. For example in an analysis of the Freenet project, von Krogh et al. found that only 1 in 6 newcomers were given specific technical tasks to work on [29]. Instead, a majority of newcomers were given general encouragement after expressing an interest in joining the community through the mailing list. Further, many projects lack an explicit architecture or system design, making it difficult for newcomers to understand the system before they can start contributing [10]. Finally, irrespective of the depth of technical knowledge that a user may possess, making significant technical contributions to a community requires social standing and identity in the community. In most projects, commit access is only given after a newcomer has proved their worth and potential to the active community members; a process that limits the overall potential contributions of newcomers to the project [10, 29].

The process through which newcomers gain access rights and become code contributors have been studied by many researchers [1, 6, 19]. The most common Open Source development model is called the onion model. This model postulates that members in an Open Source community have different roles ranging from peripheral users to core contributors and these roles are arranged as concentric layers – forming layers in the onion. More specifically, the following roles have been suggested (progressing from most central and most technical layer to outer layers that are the least technical): project leader, core developer, active developer, bug fixer, bug reporter, documenters, users (active in mail messages), and peripheral user.

von Krogh et al. conducted a qualitative study of the transition of roles in Open Source and proposed the concept of a "joining script" for new developers joining a community [29]. They categorized members into three broad groups: *joiners* are members who are active only in mailing lists, *newcomers* are members who have just gained commit access, and *developers* are active members with commit access who have shown strength of contributions and a technical ability. Potential developers (*joiners*) start by joining project mailing lists that allow them to converse about the project and learn some of the social norms and technical capabilities of the project. As they participate for extended periods of time potential developers learn how to properly participate in the community by submitting bugs, triaging bugs, and eventually working to track down the technical details of bugs by submitting small patches. After a *joiner* has shown competence with managing bugs they may be offered the ability to become a committer (*newcomer*) to a project, which allows them to directly modify the project source code without the need of an intermediary. After an intermediary trial period *newcomers* are considered to have transitioned to *developer*, if no major concerns were raised.

In a complimentary study, Duchenaut identified trajectories for individuals based on successful stories of Open Source developers [10]. One such trajectory has the following stages: (1) peripheral monitoring of activity, (2) bug reporting and patch suggestions, (3) commit rights and bug fixing, (4) module level leadership, (5) becoming vested in the community, and (6) gaining approval of core members for far reaching (architectural) changes. His study suggests that to succeed in becoming a part of the community there are social "rites of passage" at each stage in which peripheral members must gain the acceptance of core members and that political maneuverings are often needed to create an identify for oneself and gain acceptance from the community leaders.

While no consistent naming scheme has arisen for roles in Open Source projects (e.g., maintainers instead of core member, patchers instead of bug fixers [10, 32]), a consistent finding is that members near the center of the model exert more influence over the technical decisions of the project as well as other factors affecting the community [3, 10, 22]. For example, in Linux, the project leader, Linus Torvalds, has the final say regarding technical directions. In Apache, the board of directors forms the core layer and is responsible for making final decisions regarding project plans and features. The onion model of role progression is considered meritocratic and as members gain experience and make larger contributions to the project they migrate to more central roles in the community [32]. This general model of immigration and participation in Open Source projects as a process of moving from non-technical to technical processes provides a foundation to our first hypothesis:

Hypothesis 1: New comers to project communities will begin by participating in the least technically challenging medium, before moving to more technical mediums.

Other studies have also shown the importance of social factors for the success in Open Source projects. Oh and Jeon [27] found that the social network and the strength of the ties in the community was a good indicator for retention of members in the community in the face of external factors such as other projects, monetary incentives, etc. Bird et al. found that in the Open Source communities that they studied (Apache, Postgres), attaining developer status was dependent on the tenure of that individual in the project and that the social status of an individual was a stronger criterion for success [2]. They identified the inherent social structures in the community based on mail messages and found that successful members were also social hubs. In their seminal study von Krogh et al. found that developers who had generational knowledge (active across multiple releases) made more far-reaching changes, whereas new developers largely made localized changes [29]. This leads to our second hypothesis:

Hypothesis 2: As developers gain more experience in a project they will contribute more to the core of the project source code.

The central premise of the onion model is that the progression from a passive user to an active developer entails a learning process, both from a social and technical perspective. However, when projects are interrelated the time needed to learn the social culture or technology might be lower. Project ecosystems often constitute projects that are heavily interrelated. For example, Eclipse hosts a multitude of projects that all are built on a common technology and utilize a common development infrastructure [9]. Similarly, Apache contains numerous common libraries that are shared amongst projects written in both Java and C. It also has a formal process for development and participation, the Apache Way, which describes how developers are to communicate and manage projects [13, 22]. GNOME, a successful desktop environment for Linux and Unix systems, likewise has a consistent infrastructure across projects that contain common libraries and widgets that allow developers to leverage knowledge gained in related projects [16]. Such common infrastructure, therefore, should reduce the amount of new technical and social knowledge that must be acquired when moving between projects. This is the premise of our third hypothesis:

Hypothesis 3: Developers who have been active on related projects in the same ecosystem will be able to transfer knowledge and reputation to short-circuit the onion model of participation and contribute to the core of a project sooner than those who have not.

In summary, the immigration process in Open Source projects has a strong social component. However, the majority of these studies have been performed on individual projects. To the best of our knowledge we are the first to study the development process model in an Open Source ecosystem. Prior work by Dagenais et al. [8] investigates how newcomers get on board new projects within a corporate environment by studying how they learn about the technical landscape and the social culture of individual projects. Findings from the study recommend mentoring guidance, frequent feedback, and creating a project landscape with (technology) markers to make it easier for newcomer to understand the system. Although, this study is for a commercial project, it relates to our work since it investigates migration across projects in a community. However, its findings are not fully applicable to Open Source ecosystems, which have very different characteristics with much less hands-on training and feedback provided to newcomers.

3. DATA COLLECTION

For our analysis, we examined the ecosystem around the GNOME project, an effort to create a robust and usable desktop environment for Linux and other Open Source operating systems. Founded in 1997, GNOME has a fairly open policy of accepting new projects into the ecosystem, which gives the project the ability to use GNOME servers for infrastructure needs. Throughout the history of GNOME there have been more than 1,200 different projects -- many of which are smaller projects that never made it into the official distribution of GNOME.

3.1 Background of GNOME

GNOME is built on a set of common technologies and libraries that include, among others, a common graphical user interface toolkit with associated user interface guidelines; components for common tasks such as displaying images, libraries for managing program configuration and processing XML files, and mechanisms for translation across the ecosystem. These shared technologies do not, however, enforce a required programming language or set of programming paradigms. The project uses a number of different programming languages for key components including C, C++, Python, C#, and in some older cases, scheme [15-16].

In addition to common technical interfaces, the ecosystem also has a shared environment for managing the technical and social parts of a project. It provides a common hosting framework for project source code (originally CVS, later Subversion, and now git [17]), defect and request management (Bugzilla), and discussion and decision making (mailing lists and real-time chat). The project has an overall foundation board that manages the major directions and business aspects of the ecosystem, but individual projects are given significant amounts of autonomy. Individuals within the community are elected or appointed to major roles in the ecosystem that cross project boundaries, such as release manager [16, 21].

To make our analysis tractable and test our hypotheses, we had to filter the community down to a subset of projects that have multiple releases as part of the official GNOME desktop and have a significant number of developers, bug reporters, and people active on project mailing lists. Further, to understand immigration across projects we needed to select those projects that have a significant overlap in project membership.

3.2 Data Collected

We collected data for the GNOME project from 1997 to 2007, including data from mailing list archives, bug tracking system, and source code repository. In total, more than 1,000 developers made nearly 2.5 million changes to files grouped into approximately 480,000 commits. We worked with the project administrators to obtain a copy of the complete bug database for the project, which contained 790,000 comments on 250,000 bugs, reported by 26,000 different people. This data was loaded into a large database with a single schema that integrates all of these data streams.

As is common with many long-running Open Source projects, the different data streams were not seamlessly integrated with one another, with individuals using different account names for project mailing lists, bug trackers, and source code repository. One of the authors worked with members of the community, and utilized information from norms and practices, such as referencing bug numbers in source code commit messages, to link together all the elements. The most difficult part of cross-linking the GNOME data was in normalizing user names across databases. While, a large part of the normalization process was automated (matching performed by comparing email addresses and provided user names across data sources), it was necessary to consult with individuals in the community to correctly identify and validate the names and identities for about 10% of the participants.

The openness of the community also means that it is easy for anyone to sign up for project mailing lists and report bugs, yielding thousands of individuals with only peripheral interest in the community. As we are concerned with the immigration process through which a member becomes a committer, we examine only those individuals who eventually obtained direct commit access to the project source code. Furthermore, as the community keeps almost all file-based artifacts in project code repositories, including translations and other non-code related files, we had the opportunity to investigate whether members whose contributions are non source code (e.g., translators, documenters, and artists) follow a different path to become a committer. We, therefore separately analyze contributions made to the project source code repository according to the type of artifact contributed. That is, we differentiate between source code, project documentation, project build scripts, translations, and other artifacts. For the purpose of our study, we are most interested in the two largest categories of artifacts, actual project source code (e.g. C, C++, python, etc) and project translations and documentation.

For our analysis, we selected a subset of six projects. These projects were selected on the basis of their extensive history, availability of archival artifacts, prominence in the ecosystem and the overlap of developers between these projects. Three projects are end user applications and three are utility or library packages:

- Project 134: An end user application for viewing and lightweight graphics manipulation.
- Project 135: A web browser that is customized to integrate into the desktop environment.
- Project 190: A library and several tools for applications to manage settings in a standard and unified method. Most end user applications in the ecosystem rely on this library as a critical piece of infrastructure. All projects in the subset we examine utilize this library as a key component.
- Project 377: A collection of utilities for developers and end-users alike to make the most out of their desktop experience.
- Project 378: A system level library for the transparent manipulation of files and other file-like resources on the local machine and across network connections. The use of this library is not required by all end user applications; however, all applications in this subset utilize this library.
- Project 405: An extensible end user spreadsheet application.

4. ANALYSIS

To understand the effect of ecosystems and interconnectedness of projects on the "joining script" of members, we began by analyzing the overlap of individuals who committed code to multiple projects in the ecosystem. In the matrix shown in Table 1, the diagonal shows the total number of unique individuals who were identified as contributing source code (as opposed to translations, documentation, and media) to the project source code repository during the period of study and other cells show the number of developers in common between the two projects.

Table 1: Overlap of Source Code Committers Between Projects in Study

	134	135	190	377	378	405
134	102	32	70	54	73	45
135		85	41	37	44	22
190			148	73	97	54
377				163	74	63
378					175	58
405						124

Despite the broad spectrum of projects in our study, we see that there is a significant overlap of individuals contributing source code to the projects. In fact we see 97 developers who are common across projects numbered 378 and 190. When we expand our observations to include all those who made contributions to the project source code repository (including documentation and translations), we see that, indeed, there is a much greater overlap between projects as seen in Table 2.

Table 2: Overlap of All Committers Between Projects in Study

	134	135	190	377	378	405
134	210	120	162	163	164	107
135		154	122	123	121	69
190			225	169	181	109
377				281	166	133
378					261	112
405						187

Going beyond project source code repositories and including other major project archival mediums (mailing lists and bug tracker), we see that each of these projects attracted significant numbers of contributors and engaged users, many of whom were also active in other projects within the ecosystem as shown in Table 3.

Table 3: Overlap of Participants in Mailing Lists, Bug Tracker, and Source Code Repository Between Projects

	134	135	190	377	378	405
134	369	216	244	264	273	175
135		716	222	226	285	162
190			541	263	311	189
377				475	290	203
378					690	211
405						1,085

Having established that each of these projects within the GNOME ecosystem have a significant number of contributors and that there is significant overlap between individuals working on each project, in the remainder of this section we analyze our research questions: first by examining the pattern of interaction that leads a new contributor to become a developer in section 4.1, followed by an analysis of how project tenure affects the centrality of developer contributions in section 4.2, an evaluation of ecosystem tenure in section 4.3, and a principle component analysis to identify different factors that effects centrality of developer contribution in section 4.4.

4.1 Introductory Interaction Patterns

We begin by analyzing the progression paths of members across the project archives. We performed two different levels of analysis to examine the evolution of developers. At the first level, we examine how developers join individual projects and at the next level we take the pool of developer contributions as a whole across the entire set of six projects that we are examining. For each level, we build a pattern of the developer's contributions by identifying the first appearance of a developer's contributions in each of the three archival mediums: mails, bug tracking, and source code. The release of the first contribution in each medium is recorded and a progression path is established.

We grouped the progression paths into five major categories based on their relationship to the socialization process in the software ecosystem. In the most literal sense, we consider that a developer followed the onion model if they first contributed to project mailing lists, then in a subsequent release contributed to the project bug tracker, and in a yet later release contributed to project source code. We note that many developers may not spread these actions over three or more six-month release cycles, so we identify a similar accelerated progression. Table 4 provides a breakdown of the number of individuals in each progression path.

Table 4. Progression Across Social and Technical Mediums.

	Individual projects		Ecosystem subset	
Category	Members	Percent	Members	Percent
Social-tech	24	1.82%	25	5.45%
Accelerated	100	7.58%	82	17.86%
Tech-social	118	8.95%	103	22.44%
Technical	224	16.98%	74	16.12%
Source only	853	64.67%	175	38.13%

Social-technical path: This includes members who start in social medium (mail) and then progress to technical mediums in subsequent releases. We expanded this category from the original onion model where members progress from mailing lists to bug tracker activities and then to code commits, to also include members who started in mailing lists but then received commit access and then were found to participate in the project bug tracker. We did so, because it might be possible that members contributed to technical discussions of patches through the mailing list as opposed to relying on the project bug tracker. A key criterion for this category is that members are active in only one medium during a release period.

Accelerated path: This category includes members who start in mailing list (social medium) and then participate in either technical medium (e.g., bug tracker or code), but have multiple kinds of contribution during the same release. For example, we found individuals who appear in both mailing lists and bug tracker in the same release. We also found individuals who participated in all three mediums in the initial release. We combined all paths that involved members who first started with a social process and then moved to technical contributions into one group, since it is possible that our analysis at the release stage might miss members who follow the traditional model, but where each stage lasts for weeks.

Technical-social path: This path is contrary to what has been proposed in the onion model. We found members who started by participating in bug tracker or project source code repositories and then moving to mailing list participation. While in total this path contributes a relatively small percentage, the interesting fact is that these members participated in the social medium only after at least one release of participating in the technical medium.

Technical only path: This category includes members who have participated only in technical medium. Table 4 further subdivides this category into members who had only contributed to project source code repositories and members who had contributed source code and participated in the bug tracker in any order (code contribution followed by bug tracker activity, or vice versa). This directly contradicts the onion model and shows that members in a project ecosystem can start by directly contributing to code without prior socialization.

Our analysis shows that very few project members follow the socialization process as predicted by the onion model, even when we combine the "social" and "accelerated" categories (9.44% when we combine the "Social-Tech" and the "Accelerated" patterns). We only found a small percentage of users (8.95%) participating in social medium after making technical contributions. Our largest group consisted of users who directly contributed to technical medium (81.65% when we combine the "Technical" and the "Source only" patterns). We therefore conclude that there is little support for our first hypothesis that newcomers to project communities begin by participating in the least technically challenging medium, before moving to more technical mediums.

Next, we wanted to test whether a reason for the high percentage of users directly contributing to a project could arise because these members have experienced the socialization process in another project within the ecosystem. We tracked user contributions and their progression across all the six projects (see Table 4). By doing so, we see a near tripling of people who follow some portion of the onion model (individual projects: 1.82+7.58=9.4), which increased to 23.3 (5.45+17.86), an increase by 2.47; while the number of developers contributing only to the technical mediums has fallen to 54.25% (combining the "Technical" and "Source only" paths). This shows that within the broader ecosystem developers tend to follow a socialization process more similar to those proposed in hypothesis 1, but still only a quarter of developers follow a variation of the pattern. Therefore, at the ecosystem level we also reject hypothesis 1.

4.2 Project Tenure and Code Centrality

After identifying the overlap of developers in projects and general paths that developers take after joining a project, we evaluated the effect tenure has on participation in a project, specifically with respect to code centrality. That is, we investigate whether the number of releases during which a participant is active in a project affects whether they make core contributions. von Krogh et al. found that members with generational knowledge (active across multiple releases) made changes that spanned multiple files, whereas new developers typically made changes that involved a smaller set of localized files [29]. Similarly, Duchenaut claimed that developers need certain social status before they can implement high impact changes [10].

To evaluate the centrality of a developer's contributions, we needed a method to score the centrality of each commit made to the project source code repository. Source code can be thought of as forming a network of different files that are related to each other. There are a variety of ways to construct such a network, for example one can use call graphs or package imports in languages such as Java, or use the concept of logical commits [14]. We chose to use the latter since it is not dependent on a particular programming language and works for projects that use multiple programming languages. Briefly, this method infers connections between two different files in the source code repository when they are committed together. For example, if a developer commits files A, B, and C to the repository at the same time and as part of the same commit, we infer that there is some common thread between files A, B, and C and create a triad in the network between those files. The more times that files are committed together, the higher the weight that is placed on the edges. As a project evolves, this slowly creates a more complete network-based view of the project history and source code.

Once a network of source code is created, it is possible to use various social network analysis metrics to generate a numeric centrality score for each file in the network at each time period, thus identifying the files that are considered to be most central to the project. Although there are a variety of different candidate metrics, many are not applicable on disconnected networks or make assumptions about the structure of disconnected networks that are not appropriate for our analysis. One metric that is robust and avoids issues with network structure while maintaining a consistent implementation is eigenvector centrality [5, 20]. Mathematically, eigenvector centrality is the first eigenvector of the adjacency matrix formulation of the network. In general terms the interpretation of eigenvector centrality is such that nodes with high eigenvector centrality tend to be connected to many other nodes with high eigenvector centrality, while nodes with low eigenvector centrality tend to have few connections that are primarily to other low scoring nodes. When we refer to the centrality of a file at a particular release we refer to the eigenvector centrality of that file based on the network of logical commits generated from all commits up to and including that release cycle. In this way we preserve relationships from the past while building the network for future changes. For the purposes of this work, we consider only source code files contained in the project source code repository and exclude other files such as those that support translation and documentation.

Since we are interested in the centrality of a developer's contribution, the file level centralities need to be translated into developer centrality. This requires attributing the centrality score of the file to the developer who committed it. However, note that commits made by developers often touch multiple files and developers typically make numerous commits during each community release cycle. Therefore, for an individual developer's commit we define the centrality as the mean of the eigenvector centrality of each of the files that comprises the commit. From this we generate an overall source code centrality score for each developer, which is the sum of the centralities for each of the commits. In our calculations, a developer can become prominent in a project either through making many commits to files with low or medium centralities, or by making many fewer commits to files with high centrality scores, both of which are valuable measures about the importance of developers' contributions.

In addition to the centrality of files and developers, we collect other pieces of information for each developer in the community to assist us in understanding how a developer progresses within the community. Unless otherwise specified, these metrics are collected for each developer on each project on which they worked during each time period in which they were active.

- Source Code Commits: Total number of commits containing source code, documentation, and translation.
- Mail Count: Number of messages posted to project mailing lists and the number of responses obtained from those messages.
- Tracker Activity: Number of comments created in project bug tracker and total number of actions in the bug tracker. These discussions are often technical in nature and focus on a specific defect or feature.
- Project Experience: Number of releases since the developer's first activity on the project.
- Project Active Experience: Total number of releases in which the developer was active on the project. This is Project Experience minus the number of releases for which the developer made no contributions to the project.

In the process of building a regression model it is necessary to evaluate predictor variables for independence from one another, and also whether or not there is an undue reliance on the dependent variable. We examined the correlation of the various variables to the outcome metric, Source Code Centrality, and the other collected variables. We found three variables that had sufficient independence for use as control variables in a regression model:

Mail Count, Tracker Activity and Project Experience. We could not use Source Code Commits in the regression because the dependent variable, Source Code Centrality, is a construct that relies on a multiplicative transform of Source Code Commits and therefore had a very high correlation. Project active experience could not be used because it had a very high correlation, approximately 0.96, with Project Experience. We selected Project Experience as our variable of choice as it is the best depiction of the fact that tenure accrues over the entire time a member is involved in a project.

Instead of performing a simple regression with a single intercept, we acknowledge that there is significant variance between the projects in the ecosystem and instead create a regression model with multiple intercepts, one for each project. The output of this regression model can be seen in Table 5.

Table 5: Base Regression Model Illustrating Relationship Between Project Experience and Source Code Centrality

Variable	Estimate	Significance
Mail Count	0.0675	< .0001
Tracker Activity	0.0100	<.0001
Project Experience	-0.0522	0.0253
Adj R-squared: 0.4777, F: 311.4 on 9 and 3046 DF, p < .0001		

In this basic model, we find that as expected social activities such as posting messages to project mailing lists and combination of social and technical activities such as being active on a project bug tracker increase the Source Code centrality for a developer, as shown by the positive sign on the estimates from the regression model. This indicates a relationship between general project activity and Source Code centrality, but we also find that the number of releases that a developer has been active on the project, which has a negative sign on the regression estimate, decreases the overall Source Code centrality for the developer. In essence, while controlling for other social and socio-technical activities, the longer a developer remains active on a project, the lower the expected level of Source Code centrality. This may appear in contrast to other findings that show that tenure increases importance in a project [1, 3], but we note that we are examining Source Code centrality, and not an overall metric for importance in the project. A developer with significant experience on a project may have shifted to a different role that involves more leadership and less actual development.

Our analysis shows that our second hypothesis: *"as developers gain more technical experience in a project they will contribute more to the core of project source code"* is not supported.

To gain further insight into the lack of effect of a developer's tenure in a project we performed additional analyses. Additional explorations utilizing mathematical manipulations of Project Experience provided little insight, however, a simple binning algorithm that grouped developers into three categories, New (first release), Normal (second through fifth release), and Experienced (sixth or more release), provided additional insight when used in a regression model as shown in Table 6.

We once again find that the centrality of commits to the project source code repository decreases the longer a developer has been contributing to a project (as seen by the low estimate and non-significance in results for Experienced Developers). However, there is only a slight difference between new developers and developers who have been active for between 2-5 total releases (estimates of 0.5917 and 0.5489 with significant values). This suggests that centrality for developers slightly increase for Normal Developers and then reduces for Experienced Developers.

Table 6: Enhanced Model Illustrating Relationship Between Project Experience and Source Code Centrality

Variable	Estimate	Significance
Mail Count	0.0653	< .0001
Activity Count	0.0099	<.0001
New Developer	0.5917	<.0001
Normal Developer	0.5489	<.0001
Experienced Developer	0.2327	0.2315
Adj R-squared: 0.4773, F: 279.9 on 10 and 3045 DF, p < .0001		

It is unclear what happens to the fate of experienced developers. A random examination of six developers who were active for six or more releases on a single project showed that three of the developers remained central to the project in core leadership roles, two of the developers made many fewer contributions to project source code because they had adopted broader leadership roles in the community (e.g. release manager and member of the foundation board), and the sixth developer stopped contributing to developer source code entirely, instead focusing on bugs and shepherding the process of evaluating new feature requests for the project.

Additional explorations with different combinations and numbers of bins for developer experience yielded no additional insight. These results suggest that experienced developers can follow several different paths, some remain active code contributors while others may transition into more managerial or leadership roles focusing instead on managing the community. Because of this dispersion of roles we do not see a net effect of tenure in a project on developers' code centrality and, therefore, reject hypothesis 2.

4.3 Ecosystem Tenure and Code Centrality

In the next part of our work, we evaluated whether overall tenure in the ecosystem had an impact on developers' code centrality. If it is true that there is substantial transferrable knowledge between different projects in the ecosystem then developers with experience on other projects in the ecosystem should achieve higher levels of Source Code centrality at an accelerated rate.

To assist in this model, in addition to the metrics collected in the previous section we also collect the following metrics:

- Prior Experience: Number of releases the developer was active on other projects before their first contribution to the project in question (calculated once per developer per project).
- Total Experience: Number of releases since the developer was first active in the ecosystem.
- Total Active Experience: Number of previous releases for which the developer made contributions in the ecosystem. Functionally, this is the Total Experience minus the number of releases for which the developer made no contributions to projects in the ecosystem.

For a developer who is completely new to the entire ecosystem, their prior experience will be '0' and their total experience and total active experience will be the same as in the previous section.

In most cases, we found that developers were active without any major breaks in participation. The correlation between Total Experience and Total Active Experience was 0.97, preventing their mutual use in a single regression model. The correlation between Total Experience and Project Experience was 0.78, indicating that in most cases it is inappropriate to use both variables in a regression model. We select Prior Experience as the more relevant additional metric for depicting experience in the ecosystem.

Thus, building on the models in the previous section we add the additional variable of Prior Experience to evaluate to what degree a developer's experience on projects in the ecosystem prior to joining this project affects the centrality of their contributions. The results of this regression are shown in Table 7 and indicate that a developer's Prior Experience in the ecosystem does not play a role in the centrality of source code commits as evidenced by the negative estimate and non-significance of the result. Therefore, we reject hypothesis 3.

Table 7: Regression Model Relating Project Experience, Ecosystem Experience, and Source Code Centrality

Variable	Estimate	Significance
Mail Count	0.0675	< .0001
Activity Count	0.0100	<.0001
Project Experience	-0.0533	0.0232
Prior Experience	-0.0138	0.6809
Adj R-squared: 0.4775, F: 280.2 on 10 and 3045 DF, p < .0001		

4.4 Broad Factors that Affect Code Centrality

As we found that prior experience was not indicative of code centrality, we examined the data to find other factors that may be related to increased developer centrality. Further, a major problem that we faced in the analysis of this community is the fact that many of the variables related to developer participation that can be collected from the archives were highly correlated, making their use inappropriate in a regression model. However, it is possible to gain additional insight into which variables have the greatest effect on our dependent variable by performing a principal component analysis and using those components as predictors for Source Code Centrality. This also allows for broader generalization of attributes that lead to an increase in Source Code centrality. Table 8 (column 1) lists the variables that we collected from the archives: C, C#, Java code commits, documentation related commits, translation commits, total number of mail messages, number of messages started by a developer, number responses to the original message by a developer, bug tracker activity (e.g. bugs opened, closed, statuses changed), comments left in the bug tracker, and the five experience variables previously discussed.

There were four components that had a standard deviation of greater than one and ten factors with a standard deviation of less than one. In keeping with convention, we selected the four components with greatest explanatory power for further analysis. The interpretations of the factors, as presented in Table 8 are as follows:

Table 8: Major Component Loadings from Principal Component Analysis

Component	1	2	3	4
Std Dev	2.3286	1.8840	1.1644	1.0550
Source Commits	-0.371			0.254
Doc Commits	-0.386			0.275
Trans Commits	-0.145		-0.215	0.492
Message Count	-0.388			-0.159
Message Started	-0.343		0.194	-0.442
Message Responses	-0.341		0.187	-0.445
Bug Tracker Activity	-0.367			0.232
Bug Tracker Comments	-0.388			
Prior Experience		-0.146	0.773	0.311
Total Experience		-0.502	0.229	
Total Active Experience		-0.476	-0.300	-0.138
Project Experience		-0.509	0.147	
Project Active Experience		-0.467	-0.310	-0.126

Component 1: The inverse of artifacts created by the developer, which translates to the inverse of total participation. Developers who score very low on this component have created numerous artifacts in any of the archival mediums.

Component 2: The inverse of the time that a developer has spent on the project. New developers will score higher on this component than developers who have been active in the community or project for a significant amount of time.

Component 3: Broad social experience. Developers who score high on this component have been active on mailing lists and have been in the ecosystem for a long time. In contrast, developers who score lower are newer to the ecosystem and project. Note that translators can fall in the latter group since translation is often a more solitary role within the community and translators frequently pop in and out of projects.

Component 4: Technical medium expertise. Developers scoring high in the component have been active in both the bug tracker and Source Code repositories, but less active on project mailing lists. They typically have significant amounts of experience in the ecosystem, but may be new to a project. An expert translator who enters a project to improve its support for internationalization would score high on this component.

As before, we create a regression model to evaluate the relationship between these generated components and Source Code Centrality. We again allow the intercept for each project to vary to account for differences in code structure in the ecosystem. The results can be seen in Table 9.

Table 9: Regression Model Illustrating Relationship Between Generated Components and Source Code Centrality

Variable	Estimate	Significance
Component 1	-1.0341	< .0001
Component 2	0.1848	<.0001
Component 3	-0.1230	0.0001
Component 4	0.6600	<.0001
Adj R-squared: 0.6268, F: 514.1 on 10 and 3045 DF, p < .0001		

Unsurprisingly we find that developers who create the most artifacts, as shown by a low score in Component 1, typically have the highest Source Code Centrality (negative regression estimate and highly significant). This is to be expected from our definition of Source Code centrality.

We also find that individuals with more experience in the project, as shown by a lower score in component 2 will have lower overall Source Code centrality (on account of the component loadings being the inverse of overall experience and the positive sign on the estimate in the regression model). This reinforces our findings from earlier in section 4.2 and 4.3 that experience in the community leads to a lower level of Source Code Centrality.

Component 3 shows that individuals with broad social experience typically have lower amounts of Source Code Centrality. Remember, developers with high social experience rate high in the component loading and the component has a negative estimate in our regression, which leads to the above conclusion. This could be as a result of a distribution of work within the projects (e.g. some people write code, some people manage aspects of the project on the mailing lists). The reverse interpretation is that developers with little experience in the ecosystem and few social contributions on mail messages may be more likely to contribute centralized source code.

Component 4 indicates that developers with expertise in the technical mediums, particularly those involved in translation and internationalization, and those who also have prior experience in the ecosystem but may be new to the project have the ability to achieve high levels of Source Code centrality. In this narrow context, we see some of the only evidence that prior experience in the project ecosystem may allow an individual to sidestep some of the standard learning processes and begin to commit directly to core elements of the project.

Therefore, we see that while hypothesis 3 can generally be rejected across the ecosystem, there are some small niches where it may hold true. In particular, this appears to hold true for the specialized case of translators migrating across projects in the ecosystem, as evidenced by component 4.

5. DISCUSSION

From our analysis of developers in the selected projects we found significant overlap in the population of developers between projects. This held true not only for developers who wrote the code for the projects, but also individuals who documented, translated, created other media, and even the engaged users who were only active on project mailing lists. This established the strong possibility that developers would have a shared body of transferrable knowledge that they can take from one project to another and answers research question 1 by showing that developers do move between and participate in multiple projects in an ecosystem, often times in significant numbers.

Surprisingly, however, when we analyzed the progression paths of individual developers, both within individual projects and across the projects in the ecosystem, we found many individuals who eschewed social communication mediums and focused only on the technical mediums, in strong contrast to what was predicted by the onion model of Open Source participation. At the individual project level fewer than 1 in 10 developers follows the onion model predicted pattern of moving from social to socio-technical to technical mediums. When we broadened our analysis to include the entire ecosystem we found slightly stronger signs of the onion model as 23.31% of the members followed the onion model suggested progression from social to technical mediums.

In contrast to the onion model, a majority of participants were found to have participated only in technical medium (81.65% per project and 54.25% when looking at all six projects). This is contrary to most current studies that have analyzed the development process in Open Source projects, albeit these were conducted on single, standalone projects. One explanation for these results could be that developers who jump right in with code contributions might have undergone a socialization process in another project in the ecosystem that helped them jumpstart their contribution; or there might be other social communication medium such as direct person-person email or real-time chat (IRC) that were used by these technical contributors for which we do not have archival data. The lack of support for the onion model and for our first hypothesis suggests that the joining script for developers, especially in the new category of OSS 2.0 projects, is still a fertile field of research. Particularly, the interaction of additional communication mediums, such as blogs, Twitter, real team chat, social software development sites such as GitHub[1] and BitBucket[2], and social networking sites in combination with the increased participation of commercial firms means that Open Source has evolved significantly in the last ten years and that previous models of social participation may need to be updated for the current state of the art in Open Source software development.

The next step was to analyze whether prior experience, either on a single project or in the broader ecosystem had any effect on the contribution of developers. As opposed to simply summing up the number of commits that an individual made, we calculated the centrality of each developer's contribution as a proxy for the importance or depth of contribution. In this way, an individual who changes files that are considered to be central to the project will score higher than a developer who is highly active but focuses all of their work on a peripheral component such as a plugin.

In contrast to our expectations and hypothesis 2 and 3, we found that experience in communities, both in individual projects and the ecosystem as a whole, play little role in the centrality of contributions to project source code. In fact, new developers were slightly more likely to have central contributions than experienced developers and those developers with extensive experience were found to have widely varying levels of centrality. There are many possible reasons for this phenomenon. First, it is possible that experienced developers, such as those who have been active for six or more releases, are venturing into project management and leadership roles, which require more time focusing on management or architecture than actual development. While it is likely that these developers have a deep and robust understanding of the project source code and architecture, it may be that their skills and experience are better utilized in managing and shepherding other users; a finding that was partially echoed by a random examination of experienced developers.

A possible cause for the lack of effect of prior experience across projects in the ecosystem could be as a result of the structure of the projects themselves. The bulk of the code for most of the projects was written in C, a language that isn't always as amenable to modular code structures as managed languages such as Java and Python. If developers migrate across projects in the ecosystem and bring with them a feature gift to the new project [29], it is possible that the architecture of the new project requires substantial modifications to core elements of the project, therefore increasing the centrality of the new developer's contributions by virtue of the number of modifications made and the location of those modifications.

When we attempted to identify additional factors that played a role in source code centrality as per research question 3, we found one group of developers who appeared to benefit from learning in the ecosystem: translators. A major influencing factor of this is likely the very standard method for internationalization across all projects. A translator can introduce internationalization features to a project with modifications to only a handful of header files and by modifying references to strings in the project in a fairly mechanical manner, something that is easily reproducible across projects. The actions of translators and other individuals who do not write code are ripe for future research.

In summary, the major implications of our study relate to the process of managing a software development team. For individual projects, we found little evidence for the commonly discussed "onion" model of participation that involves individuals migrating from the edges of a project to the core through a gradual socializa-

[1] https://github.com/

2 https://bitbucket.org/

tion process, although there was slightly more support in connected ecosystems. This suggests that open source projects should re-evaluate the process used for socializing new developers and eventually awarding committer status. For software engineering researchers, this study provides a foundation for understanding participation in complex systems using a multi-modal approach, for example, using source code, email, bug trackers, and other social media to understand participation.

Finally, our study provides an impetus for re-evaluating the commonly accepted onion model, which may be overly limiting. Complex ecosystems involve developers moving across multiple projects. A well-designed architecture can facilitate this flow of individuals and knowledge. Further, because of this migration and a subsequent lack of generational knowledge, further investigations into technology and methods that help in externalizing the semantic knowledge of experienced developers is needed.

6. THREATS TO VALIDITY

As our findings are in contrast to many previous studies of individual Open Source projects, we must be conscientious of the limits of our research and the possible threats to the internal, construct, and external validity of our work.

Internal validity: Our analysis is based on data extracted from public project archives – mailing lists, bug trackers, and source code repositories. We have largely assumed that social interactions and decision making are conducted via mailing lists and we could have missed communication that occurred through personal email, IRC channels or face-to-face meetings during conferences and developer meetings. However, research literature suggests that Open Source socialization processes largely occur through project mailing lists, so in this respect we are in line with previous literature but we realize that this might not be sufficient to understand the communication in modern open source projects [3, 24]. Further Open Source norms and traditions encourage project discussions and communications to take place in the developer mailing lists [13]. Next, our treatment of comments in the bug tracker as a technical activity may be problematic. While most discussions are about a particular issue or defect, there are situations where users post non-technical information to the bug tracker, such as feature requests, however these requests rarely come from experienced project developers who have commit access and are a minority of discussions.

Construct validity: There are three major construct validity threats to our study. First, the use of a release as a unit of analysis for our regressions and analysis of interaction patterns, which was done to provide a consistent way of comparing across projects as all projects followed the same 6 month cycle, may be problematic if developers move through the onion model phases in shorter time periods than the 6-month release cycles in GNOME. We accommodated this concern where feasible, for example, when calculating the progression paths in section 5.1 we optimistically considered individuals to have followed a "social-technical" path even when their first contributions to social and technical mediums were in the same release. The second threat to construct validity lies in the creation and use of Source Code Centrality as a proxy for core contributions. Past research has often used the raw amount of contribution (e.g., number of commits or lines of code changed) as a measure of developer activity [26, 29] or mailing list communications as a measure of centrality in a project network [2, 16]. In our study, we needed a finer grained measure to characterize both the volume and importance of contributions, which allowed us to identify whether prior experience enabled developers to start making complicated, central changes earlier. Logical commits were used to create the network as they provide a language agnostic method to associate source code files and eigenvector centrality was used because of its general robustness in the face of various network topologies. Third, our analysis centers on code contributions in a project and, therefore, ignores contributions of other stakeholders in a project (e.g., architects, testers) and their socialization processes. However, note that past literature that has demonstrated the existence of the onion model investigated the socialization process of developers based on their code contributions and is similar to our study.

External validity: Finally, there is a chance that GNOME may not be a suitable sample of an Open Source ecosystem, limiting the degree to which we can generalize our findings to other Open Source ecosystems. Further, our study considered a subset of six projects with significant history and participation as representative of the greater GNOME ecosystem. The fact that these six projects are well adopted within the community, have long histories, and significant participation may make them outliers in the broader context of the GNOME ecosystem. It is possible that other projects might demonstrate different socialization processes.

7. CONCLUSIONS

Within a modern OSS 2.0 project ecosystem our results are substantially in contrast to earlier research conducted on individual projects when the state of Open Source software development had not yet evolved to its current state. In particular, this work is novel because to the best of the authors' knowledge it is the first study to consider these contributions in the context of an ecosystem. We found little support for the traditional onion model within a single project, although it was supported slightly more often when contributions across multiple projects in the ecosystem were considered. Our results show that prior experience in the project or the ecosystem does not seem to have a high effect on the overall centrality of a developer's contribution. Further, we found that tenure in a project or even the ecosystem did not have a high impact on the centrality of one's code contributions when measured using our metric that takes into account both number of contributions and the eigenvector centrality. Our findings provide interesting insights and contradict existing assumptions of the onion model; these findings merit further explorations into project ecosystems.

In future work, we intend to further investigate these relationships in modern OSS 2.0 communities. In particular the adoption of decentralized version control systems such as git and collaborative development sites like GitHub and BitBucket has fundamentally rewritten the socialization process by allowing anyone to fork project code and begin working on a project without the need for formal designation as a committer. The degree to which these sites support code annotation and discussion may both decrease the number of people following the onion model and also assist new developers in understanding complex technical aspects of project source code. While this makes the development process more accessible, it also has the potential to make contributions more difficult by requiring developers to request that their code be pulled into the main branch for each set of patches, rather than receiving committer status once for all time.

Open Source has changed significantly over the past decade. What we know about the socialization process in Open Source projects may not be true in the ecosystems of Open Source 2.0. The evolution of tools, project ecosystems, and the increasing ability of developers to easily move between different projects create a variety of social and technical effects that require more study.

8. ACKNOWLEDGMENTS

This research is supported by grants NSF IIS-0414698, NSF CCF-1016134, AFSOR FA9550-09-1-0129, and an NSF Graduate Research Fellowship to the third author. The authors also thank James Herbsleb for his assistance in structuring the original research questions.

9. REFERENCES

[1] C. Bird, A. Gourley, P. Devanbu, M. Gertz, and A. Swaminathan. Mining email social Networks. In *Third International Workshop on Mining Software Repositories*, pages 137-143. IEEE, 2006.

[2] C. Bird, A. Gourley, P. Devanbu, A. Swaminathan, and G. Hsu. Open borders? Immigration in open source projects. In *Fourth International Workshop on Mining Software Repositories*. IEEE, 2007.

[3] C. Bird, D. Pattison, R. D'Souza, V. Filkov, and P. Devanbu. Latent social structure in open source projects. In *16th ACM SIGSOFT International Symposium on Foundations of Software Engineering*, pages 24-35. ACM, 2008.

[4] C. Boldyreff, K. Crowston, B. Lundell, and A. Wasserman. Open source ecosystems: diverse communities interacting. In *5th International Conference on Open Source Systems*. Springer, 2009.

[5] P. Bonacich. Power and centrality: a family of measures. *American Journal of Sociology*, 92:1170-1182. March 1987.

[6] K. Crowston and J. Howison. The social structure of open source software development teams. *First Monday*, 10(2), February 2005.

[7] K. Crowston, K. Wei, J. Howison, and A. Wiggins. Free/libre open source software development: what we know and what we do not know. *ACM Computing Surveys*, 44(2), 2012 (Forthcoming).

[8] B. Dagenais, H. Ossher, R. Bellamy, M. Robillard, and J. de Vries. Moving into a new software project landscape. In *32nd ACM/IEEE International Conference on Software Engineering - Volume 1*, pages 275-284, ACM, May 2010.

[9] J. Des Rivieres and J. Wiegand. Eclipse: A platform for integrating development tools. *IBM Systems Journal*, 43(2):371-383, 2004.

[10] N. Ducheneaut. Socialization in an open source software community: a socio-technical analysis. *Computer Supported Cooperative Work*, 14(4):323-368, 2005.

[11] R. Farzan, L. Dabbish, R. Kraut, and T. Postmes. Increasing commitment to online communities via building social attachment. In *ACM 2011 Conference on Computer Supported Cooperative Work*, 321-330, ACM, March 2011.

[12] B. Fitzgerald. The transformation of open source software. *MIS Quarterly*, 30(3):587-598, September 2006.

[13] K.Fogel. *Producing open source software: how to run a successful free software project*, O'Reilly Media, Sebastapol, California, 2005.

[14] H. Gall, K. Hajek, and M. Jazayeri. Detection of logical coupling based on product release history. In *14th IEEE International Conference on Software Maintenance*, pages 190-198, IEEE Press, March 1998.

[15] D. German. The evolution of the GNOME project. In *2nd International Workshop on Open Source Software*, 2002.

[16] D. German. The GNOME project: a case study of open source, global software development. *Software Process: Improvement and Practice*, 8(4):201-215, 2003.

[17] git. the fast version control system: http://git-scm.com/

[18] G. Hertel, S. Niedner, S. Hermann. Motivation of software developers in open source projects: an internet-based survey of contributors to the Linux kernel. *Research Policy*, 23(7):1159-1177, July 2003.

[19] C. Jensen and W. Scacchi. Role migration and advancement processes in OSSD projects: a comparative case study. In *International Conference on Software Engineering*, pages 364-374. IEEE, 2007.

[20] L. Katz, A new status index derived from sociometric analysis. *Psychometrika*, 18(1):39-43, March 1953.

[21] S. Koch and G. Schneider. Effort, cooperation and coordination in an open source software project: GNOME. *Information Systems Journal*, 12(1):27-42, January 2002.

[22] K. Lakhani and E. Von Hippel. How open source software works: "free" user-to-user assistance. *Research Policy*, 32(6):923-943, June 2003.

[23] J. Lerner and J. Tirole. Some simple economics of open source. *Journal of Industrial Economics*, 50(2):197-234, June 2002.

[24] A. Meneely, L. Wililams, W. Snipes, and J. Osborne. Predicting failures with developer networks and social network analysis. In *16th ACM SIGSOFT International Symposium on the Foundations of Software Engineering*, pages 12-23. ACM, 2008.

[25] A. Mockus, R. Fielding, and J. Herbsleb. A case study of open source software development: the Apache server. In *22nd International Conference on Software Engineering*, pages 263-272. ACM, 2000.

[26] A. Mockus, R. Fielding, and J. Herbsleb. Two case studies of open source software development: Apache and Mozilla. *ACM Transactions Software Engineering Methodology*, 11(3):309-346, July 2002.

[27] W. Oh and S. Jeon. Membership Herding and Network Stability in the Open Source Community: The Ising Perspective. *Management Science*, 53(7):1068-1101, July 2007.

[28] W. Scacchi. Free/open source software development: recent research results and emerging opportunities. In *6th Joint Meeting on European Software Engineering Conference and the ACM SIGSOFT Symposium on the Foundations of Software Engineering*, pages 459-468. ACM, September 2007.

[29] G. von Krogh, S. Spaeth, and K. Lakhani. Community, joining, and specialization in open source software innovation: a case study. *Research Policy*, 32(7):1217-1241, July 2003.

[30] A. Wolfe. Eclipse: A platform becomes an open-source woodstock. *ACM Queue*,1(8):14-16, 2003.

[31] B. Xu and D. R. Jones. Volunteers' participation in open source software development: a study from the social-relational perspective. *ACM SIGMIS Database*, 41(3):69-84, August, 2010.

[32] Y. Ye and K. Kishida. Toward an understanding of the motivation of open source software developers. In *25th International Conference on Software Engineering*, pages 419- 429, IEEE Computer Society, May 2003.

Does Adding Manpower Also Affect Quality? An Empirical, Longitudinal Analysis

Andrew Meneely
North Carolina State University
890 Oval Drive, EB2 Box 8206
Raleigh, North Carolina, USA 27695
apmeneel@ncsu.edu

Pete Rotella
Cisco Systems, Inc.
7025 Kit Creek Rd. Bldg. 10
Research Triangle Park, NC 27709
protella@cisco.com

Laurie Williams
North Carolina State University
890 Oval Drive, EB2 Box 8206
Raleigh, North Carolina, USA 27695
lawilli3@ncsu.edu

ABSTRACT

With each new developer to a software development team comes a greater challenge to manage the communication, coordination, and knowledge transfer amongst teammates. Fred Brooks discusses this challenge in *The Mythical Man-Month* by arguing that rapid team expansion can lead to a complex team organization structure. While Brooks focuses on productivity loss as the negative outcome, poor product quality is also a substantial concern. But if team expansion is unavoidable, can any quality impacts be mitigated? Our objective is to guide software engineering managers by empirically analyzing the effects of team size, expansion, and structure on product quality. We performed an empirical, longitudinal case study of a large Cisco networking product over a five year history. Over that time, the team underwent periods of no expansion, steady expansion, and accelerated expansion. Using team-level metrics, we quantified characteristics of team expansion, including team size, expansion rate, expansion acceleration, and modularity with respect to department designations. We examined statistical correlations between our monthly team-level metrics and monthly product-level metrics. Our results indicate that increased team size and linear growth are correlated with later periods of better product quality. However, periods of accelerated team expansion are correlated with later periods of reduced software quality. Furthermore, our linear regression prediction model based on team metrics was able to predict the product's post-release failure rate within a 95% prediction interval for 38 out of 40 months. Our analysis provides insight for project managers into how the expansion of development teams can impact product quality.

Categories and Subject Descriptors

D.2.8 [**Software Engineering**]: Metrics – *process metrics, product metrics.*

General Terms

Measurement, Human Factors

Keywords

Longitudinal analysis, team expansion metric, modularity, Brooks' Law, developer, linear regression

Permission to make digital or hard copies of all or part of this work for personal or classroom use is granted without fee provided that copies are not made or distributed for profit or commercial advantage and that copies bear this notice and the full citation on the first page. To copy otherwise, or republish, to post on servers or to redistribute to lists, requires prior specific permission and/or a fee.

ESEC/FSE'11, September 5-9, 2011, Szeged, Hungary.

Copyright 2011 ACM 978-1-4503-0443-6/11/09...$10.00.

1. INTRODUCTION

With each new developer to a software development team comes a greater challenge to manage the communication, coordination, and knowledge transfer amongst teammates. Lack of team cohesion, miscommunications, and misguided effort can all lead to problems in the software product.

Following a similar line of reasoning, Fred Brooks discusses the challenge of team expansion directly in his widely-known book, *The Mythical Man-Month* [4]:

> "...training cannot be partitioned, so this part of the added effort varies linearly with the number of workers. [...] The added effort of communicating may fully counteract the division of the original [development] task."
>
> "Adding manpower to a late project makes it later."

The latter quote is known as "Brooks' Law." While Brooks was specifically discussing effort estimation and productivity, one could apply a similar argument to software quality. Too many new developers in a short period of time can potentially lead to problems, such as inconsistent implementation or poor system integration.

But is team expansion an unavoidably high risk? Or can successful development teams undergo healthy growth as the product progresses? Risk management practices often account for new teammates [18], so teams can plan ahead for some developer turnover and handle it gracefully.

Furthermore, the structure of the team as it expands can also affect software quality. Brooks describes software development as "an exercise in complex interrelationships" [4], and describes the development team as a socio-technical network of communication and coordination (a structure since defined as a developer network [2], [7], [9], [10], [13], [19]). When the team organization becomes too complex, collaboration suffers. For instance, developers may choose to only collaborate on code within their own department and avoid developing across departments, despite the advantage of having the added perspective from other departments.

Therefore, if team expansion is a high risk, what are the elements of team expansion that can be mitigated? An analysis of software quality inspired by Brooks' Law must take into account team size, how fast the team expands, and team structure over time. Our research objective is *to guide software engineering managers during periods of team expansion by empirically analyzing the effects of team size, expansion, and structure on product quality.*

We examined statistical correlations between periods of team expansion and the observed effects on product quality in a large

Cisco networking product over a five year period. We measured team size, expansion rate, expansion acceleration, and modularity of the team with respect to departments. Our data came from the version control logs, the defect tracking system, historical records from the Human Resources department, and the failure tracking database.

The contributions of this paper are:

- Statistically significant associations that help researchers and practitioners better understand the risks of expanding a team; and
- A predictive model that can help the practitioners of our case study to accurately predict upcoming product quality measurements.

The rest of this paper is organized as follows. Sections 2 and 3 cover background and related work on analyzing large software development teams and software quality. Section 4 describes our study design and the metrics we used to analyze team expansion and structure. Sections 5, 6, and 7 present the case study and the results of the empirical analysis and its limitations. Section 8 discusses how our study applies to Brooks' Law and product quality. Lastly, sections 9 and 10 discuss future work and a summary of the study.

2. BACKGROUND

In this section, we define various terms relating to software quality and network analysis.

2.1 Quality and Metric Terminology

In software reliability, a **failure** is "the inability of a software system or component to perform its required functions within specified performance requirements" [6]. A **fault** is "an incorrect step, process, or data definition in a computer program. Note: a fault, if encountered, may cause a failure" [6].

We use the term **team-level** metric to indicate that the metric is collected as one measurement for the entire team for a given period of time. Also, we use the term **product-level** metric to indicate that the metric is collected as one measurement of the product's overall quality for a given period of time.

2.2 Network Analysis

Our analysis involves quantifying measures of networks. In this section, we provide background with regard to network analysis.

Network analysis is the study of characterizing and quantifying network structures, represented by graphs [3]. In network analysis, vertices of a graph are called **nodes**, and **edges** are the names for connections between exactly two nodes. The **degree** of a node is defined as the number of neighboring nodes that a node has.

To analyze the structure of a team in terms of company organization, we use the **modularity** metric [3]. Modularity is a measure of how the network is spread with respect to organization. Modularity requires a method of logically grouping nodes together, called "partitioning". By definition, each node is placed in exactly one partition. The modularity value is computed based on edges where both nodes are in the same partition and the number of edges that cross partitions. Modularity is computed using the following pseudo code in Figure 1.

```
Input
Graph G with nodes in set V and with e edges
Partitions P1, P2,…,PN contain nodes in V
Algorithm
modularity = 0.0
for each partition Pi
 for each node v1, v2 in Pi where v1!=v2
   if an edge between v1 and v2 exists
    modularity += 1 - degree(v1)*degree(v2)/(2*e)
   else
    modularity -= degree(v1)*degree(v2)/(2*e)
  endif
 endfor
endfor
modularity = modularity/(2*e)
```

Figure 1. Pseudo code for computing modularity.

The terms involving the nodes' degrees are designed to account for a random re-wiring of network as a way to mitigate potentially missing or mistaken edges in the network [3]. The output of the modularity measure is a decimal value between -1.0 and 1.0. A value near 1.0 (highly modular) indicates that most of the edges are within the partitions; a value near -1.0 (anti-modular) indicates that most of the edges cross boundaries and are not within partitions; a value near zero (not modular) indicates that edges are crossing partitions as often as staying within partitions.

3. RELATED WORK

The topic of measuring the structure of development teams have been examined in several recent empirical studies. All of the studies, however, examine file-level metrics that reflect the overall team. None of the studies use team-level metrics nor examined the relationship between team-level metrics and product-level metrics. Many of the studies make use of the developer network, which we formally define in Section 4.3.

The closest study to ours was a file-level analysis on an AT&T product performed by Weyuker, et al. [17]. The researchers began their project with a predictive model that could identify 75% of the system's faults in 20% of the source code files. Using the version control logs, the researchers counted the number of committers to a source code file. In their case study, adding the "number of developers" metric to their predictive model only provided a modest improvement over previous predictive results, finding 81, 94, and 76% of the faults on average. However, they found that files changed by additional developers were more likely to have faults. They concluded that "too many cooks can spoil the broth", although, which is consistent with the argument Brooks presents.

Meneely et al. [10] examined the relationship between developer activity metrics and reliability. The empirical case study examined three major releases of a large, proprietary networking product. The authors used developer centrality metrics from a developer network to examine whether source code files are more likely to have failures if they were changed by developers who are peripheral to the network. The authors formed a model that included metrics of developer centrality, recent code churn (the degree to which a file was changed recently), and lines of code to predict failures from one release to the next. Their model's prioritization found 58% of the system's test failures in 20% of the files, where a perfect prioritization would have found 61%. Since their analysis used only file-level metrics, they did not examine team expansion or organization.

Bird et al. [1] examined social structures in open source projects. Discussing connections and contradictions between some of Brooks' ideas [4] and the bazaar-like development of open source projects, the authors empirically examine how open source developers self-organize. The authors use similar network structures as our developer network to find the presence of sub-communities within open source projects. In addition to examining version control change logs, the authors mined email logs and other artifacts of several open source projects to find a community structure. The authors conclude that sub-communities do exist in open source projects, as evidenced by the project artifacts exhibiting a social network structure that resembles collaboration networks in other disciplines. The authors did not examine team expansion or structure in terms of modularity.

Shin et al. [14] evaluated the statistical connection between vulnerabilities and metrics of complexity, code churn, and developer activity. The study denotes two case studies of large, open source projects: multiple releases of Mozilla Firefox and the RHEL4 kernel. Among the findings include a statistically significant correlation between metrics of all three categories and security vulnerabilities. Also, in the Mozilla project, a model containing all three types of metrics was able to find 70.8% of the known vulnerabilities by selecting only 10.9% of the project's files.

Pinzger et al. [12] proposed a variation on the developer network, called a contribution network. The contribution network is designed to use version control data to quantify the direct and indirect contribution of developers on specific resources of the project. The researchers were able to predict reliability failures in binaries of Microsoft Windows Vista by applying centrality metrics to the contribution network. Files that were contributed to by many developers, especially by developers who were making many different contributions themselves, were found to be more failure-prone than files developed in relative isolation. The authors did not examine team expansion or organization.

Nagappan et al. [11] created a logistic regression model for failures in the Windows Vista operating system. The model was based on what they called "Overall Organizational Ownership" (OOW). The metrics for OOW included concepts like organizational cohesiveness and diverse contributions. Among the findings is that more edits made by many, non-cohesive developers leads to more problems post-release. The OOW model was able to predict with 87% average precision and 84% average recall. The OOW model bears a resemblance to the contribution network in that both models attempt to differentiate healthy changes in software from the problematic changes.

In addition to the prediction and validity studies, other studies have provided additional insight into team development using social network analysis in general. Sarma et al. have developed a tool that visualizes many different aspects of development artifacts, including the developer network [13]. Also, Begel et al. have developed a tool at Microsoft that utilizes development artifacts to aid in finding people with specific expertise in a project [1].

Treude and Storey [15] approached the problem of awareness in large development teams by examining current tools. They performed a qualitative and quantitative case study of IBM's Jazz development platform to examine how developers use highly configurable features like dashboards and feeds. According to the researchers, some developers reported that dashboards provide an increased peripheral awareness and overview of the project's status. Feeds were reported to help developers track the lower level tasks of the project, such as updates to fault reports or upcoming deadlines. The results indicate that an integrated development platform like Jazz can provide valuable team-level and task-level awareness to software developers.

4. METHODOLOGY

In this section, we describe how we conducted our longitudinal case study, including the metrics we used.

4.1 Study Design

Our empirical analysis is a statistical correlation study between team metrics and product quality. We set up this study as a longitudinal analysis of a single development team at Cisco that underwent expansion over time. To incorporate time into our analysis, we used a shifting *time window* for the team metrics. The time window is the period of time in which we collected the team metrics, representing a data point in our analysis.

The quality of the product as experienced by the customer, however, does not change at the same time as the team changes. A lag exists between changes in the team and changes in the experienced product quality. During this lag period, developers can be stabilizing the product, testers are performing their final system tests, and the product is delivered to customers' production environments. Thus, in our study, we take this delay into account between the team changing in the time window under study and a snapshot of the product's overall quality. Figure 2 depicts how the time window fits on the production/development timeline.

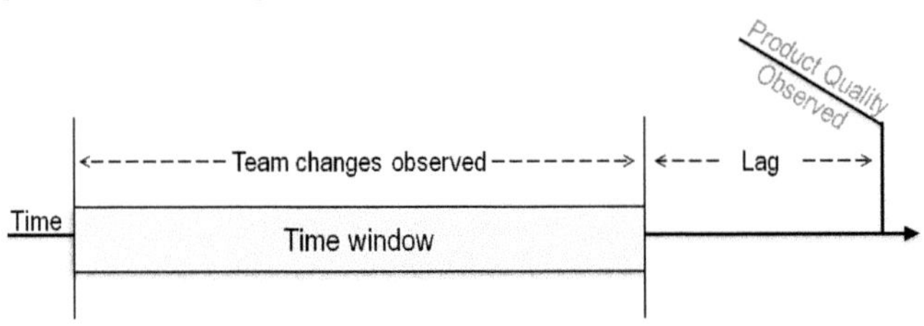

Figure 2. Study timeline

In regard to how to set up the time lag, we must answer the following question:

Time Lag: *What is the time lag between changes in the team and corresponding changes in product quality?*

The results of the time lag analysis can be found in Section 6.1.

Next, we focus our analysis on three main research questions. The first question is related to association, which answers for us specific questions about the relationship between our team metrics and product quality on the individual level.

Association: *Are team expansion and organization metrics statistically associated with software quality? Specifically with respect to Q_{size}, Q_{rate}, $Q_{acceleration}$, and $Q_{modularity}$.*

- Q_{size}. *Does an expanded team result in reduced product quality?*
- Q_{rate}. *Does a team with a high expansion rate result in reduced product quality?*
- $Q_{acceleration}$. *Does a team with an accelerated expansion rate result in reduced product quality?*
- $Q_{modularity}$. *Does a team that does not collaborate across departments result in reduced product quality?*

For each of the four sub-questions, we formulate a metric in this study. The metrics for the first three questions are defined in Section 4.2, the metric for the fourth question is defined in Section 4.3, and the metric for product quality is defined in Section 4.4. The results of this analysis can be found in Section 6.2.

Next, we use predictability to estimate the strength of the correlation between all of the team metrics and the product quality metric. Practically speaking, prediction also has a direct use to the managers in our case study project because each month team leads set an expected quality goal (i.e., an expected failures-per-hour goal) for the product. Cisco upper management uses the failures-per-hour metric and its goal as a guide for process improvement. Managers at Cisco can use the predictive model we used in this analysis to better inform the goal-setting process.

Predictability: *Can we use team metrics to predict months where product quality will be reduced?*

The results of the predictability analysis can be found in Section 6.3.

Lastly, our prediction results could be sensitive to slight variations in the time lag parameters. Thus, we examine what our prediction results would have been if with differing time lag parameters.

Sensitivity: *Would using different time lag parameters yield different prediction results?*

The results of the sensitivity analysis can be found in Section 6.4.

4.2 Team Size and Expansion Metrics

To estimate the size of the development team for a given time period, we counted the number of distinct developers who made version control changes to source code files on the product. We call this metric *NumCommitters*. Since the NumCommitters metric is based on version control logs, it only includes teammates who made changes to the code and does not include counts of management and other non-coding employees.

To measure how quickly the team expands, we use two measures: *NumNewCommitters* and *ExpansionAcceleration*. We define NumNewCommitters as the number of committers who had never previously made a commit to the product in its history. We define ExpansionAcceleration as the slope of the change in the number of monthly new committers over a given period of time. The two metrics represent velocity of the team size and acceleration of the team size, respectively.

For example, suppose we examine the version control logs for a three-month period of time, and we find that 300 committers made changes to the code. During that three-month period, suppose that the team had ten new developers for the first month, then 15 developers the next month, then 20 developers in the third month. In total, the team had 45 new developers in this three-month period. Furthermore, the team's growth increased by five developers per month. Thus, in this example, NumCommitters is 300, NumNewCommitters is 45, and ExpansionAcceleration is 5.

4.3 Team Structure Metric

To measure the overall structure of the team, we first need to define how we quantify "structure". We used a *developer network* to examine the structure of our development team. Developer networks have been used for analyzing teams [2], predicting failures [10], and predicting vulnerabilities [7], [8], [14]. The purpose of a developer network is to represent the complex system of socio-technical[1] relationships between developers in a software development project.

We define our developer network as a graph where the nodes represent a developer on the team. Edges exist where two developers made a version control commit to the same source code file on the same version control branch within the time window under study. Edges represent places where two developers were likely working on the same code, which in most cases means the developers are collaborating with each other [9]. Following results in a previous study, we do not apply numeric weights to the edges [9].

While the version control logs provide records of which developers are working on the different parts of the code, the logs and resulting developer network do not provide any information on the formal organization of the team. Teammates could be collaborating on code only within departments, or not working with other developers within the same department.

To measure how much code is being changed by developers of the same department, we used a modularity metric called *DepartmentModularity*. Using historical data from the Human Resources Department at Cisco, we obtained the department identifiers for all the developers. We then applied the modularity metric (defined in Section 2) to the developer network using departments as partitions.

We chose departments as our partitioning boundary in this case study because each department has its own budget. As a result, developers in a given department are focused on producing departmental components while simultaneously focusing on integrating departmental components with other departments' components.

A highly modular team (modularity near 1.0) indicates that the code changed by two developers on the same version control branch was mostly within departments. Likewise, a team can also be highly anti-modular (modularity near -1.0) or not modular at all (modularity near 0.0).

For example, suppose the version control logs and human resources data contained the following records in Table 1. The resulting developer network, with department partitions, can be found in Figure 3. From a visual inspection of the network, most of the edges are within department boundaries, making the team modular. For this example, the modularity metric value is 0.47, indicating that the team is highly modular with respect to departments.

---

[1] We use "socio-technical" to describe the connection between two people in the context of work-related collaboration [5], [16].

Table 1. DepartmentModularity example data

Developer	Department	Files Changed
Andy	DeptA	File1, File2
Laurie	DeptA	File2, File3, File4
Pete	DeptA	File1, File3, File7
Aaron	DeptB	File4, File5
Mei	DeptB	File5, File6
John	DeptC	File7, File8
Jerrod	DeptC	File6, File9
Ben	DeptC	File9
Raza	DeptC	File8, File9

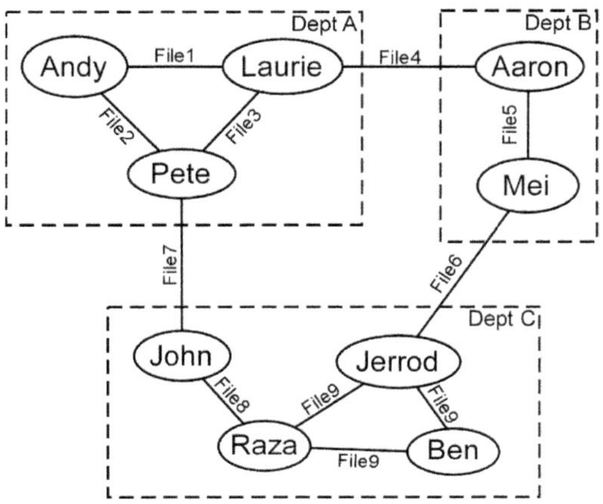

Figure 3. Example developer network with department partitions

4.4 Product Quality Metric

We used *failures-per-hour* as our product quality metric. We define failures-per-hour as the number of customer-reported software failures that were eventually traced to a software fault per hour of usage of the product.

The failures-per-hour metric is intended to evaluate product quality from the point of view of the customer. Since failures-per-hour is based on failures, not faults, the metric is sensitive to situations when multiple customers encountered the same fault, making the failure-per-hour metric more representative of the customer experience. However, using failures as a quality metric alone would also be dependent on the number of customers and the amount of product usage in addition to the quality of the product. If the product's usage remained constant, then failures would be an adequate product quality metric alone. However, to be safe, we use an "hours of usage" term to normalize failures against the possibility of expanding or contracting market for the product.

5. CASE STUDY

We performed our analysis on a large Cisco networking product that uses this goal-setting process. The product has over 54,000 source code files and is being changed by hundreds of developers at any given time.

At Cisco, managers track the progress of a project using a goal-setting practice. Managers dialog with team leads and decide on goals for various metrics, including software quality metrics like failures-per-hour. Thus, the failures-per-hour metric is a standard, vetted quality metric used on hundreds of Cisco products and is followed closely by the managers of our case study.

As a part of the goal-setting dialog, managers and team leads discuss upcoming quality concerns based on the team's progress. From collective experience at Cisco, using the time window (as shown in Figure 1 of Section 4) to guide scoping of the goal-setting discussions has shown to be an accurate way of viewing the team's status. Specifically, Cisco managers have found that using a time window for goal-setting is more advantageous than tracking failures by individual features and branches because a time window accounts for the entire team's activity (e.g. feature enhancement, maintenance) and is more accurate in practice.

To observe the activity of the development team, we analyzed the version control logs and the failure tracking system. Nearly every change to the source code required a defect or feature recorded. In this project, both developers and testers commit changes to the code, so the NumCommitters metric includes some testers in addition to developers.

For modularity, we also investigated several ways of partitioning developers other than departments, but did not find the measures to be truly representative of logical partitions in this particular case study (i.e. they are not internally valid). We examined "same supervisor" as a way to partition developers, but some departments were more formally hierarchical than others, confounding the partitions. We also examined "same business unit," but found that the partition boundaries were too coarse to truly represent how the team is organized.

Figure 4 is a graph of the failures-per-hour metric over time, with the y-axis units hidden to protect proprietary information. Generally speaking, the failures-per-hour for this project has decreased over time, indicating that the overall quality of the product has generally improved. The largest spikes in reduced quality correspond to new major feature releases of the product.

Figure 4. Failures per hour over time

Lastly, we only considered changes to source code files, which for this project are files who names have the following extensions: .java, .jsp, .jspf, .tld, .js, .script, .sql, .c, .h, .cpp, .hpp, .py, .sh, .bat, .pl, .bas, .asp, .xsl, and .wsdl.

6. ANALYSIS RESULTS

In this section, we examine the answers to our research questions in Section 4.1. We used the R statistics package[2] v2.11.1 for our statistical analysis.

6.1 Time Lag

Research Question: *What is the time lag between changes in the team and corresponding changes in product quality?*

In our case study, when the team introduced problems to the code, the customer did not experience the drop in quality immediately. Our team would release a new version of the product every three to six months, often maintaining multiple releases at a time and porting fixes across different releases. All changes to the system underwent system testing prior to release, as well. If a customer were experiencing poor product quality today, then the development that caused or missed the problem would have happened several months ago, which we will refer to as the *time lag*.

We are looking to find appropriate values of two time lag parameters: *minimum time lag* and *maximum time lag* to define the time window. The minimum time lag represents the minimum amount of time between changing code and the customer being exposed to that change. The maximum time lag represents the furthest amount of time prior to release such that changes are still in the same release that the customer experiences. For example, the minimum and maximum time lags for an average one-year release cycle with a stabilization period of two months would be 2 and 14 months, respectively.

To determine an appropriate time lag, we used the average window of time between introducing new, later-to-be-found faulty files and the customer finding a bug. In those specific cases, the new source code would have gone through the normal testing and stabilization as part of the team's development process, and was (wrongly) deemed to be correct before release. Any faults found in these source code files after release had to be injected into that new source code file during our time window. Note that we are not assuming that the faults in the new code were *caused* by team expansion, rather, we are using the injection-to-customer time as an indicator of the typical time lag between development and customer experience.

We performed a manual investigation of the defect tracking system and version control logs to find new, later-to-be-found faulty source code files. We looked for examples of source code files that were both introduced as part of new development and later had to be fixed for a fault found by a customer after the product's release. To ensure that the example files were representative, we directed our search to find source code files in various components of the system, committed and tested by different groups of developers, and introduced at different times over the project history.

In the course of manual investigation, we were specifically identifying source code that represented new development. For example, code was considered new development if its initial introduction was explicitly recorded as a new feature. Sometimes new code would be introduced as a result of a defect report that required major re-implementation (and thus, new source code files). We discarded any examples where the new source code was reported to be imported from another system, a refactoring, or the result of any other minor improvement activity that did not represent new development.

Such source code files were rare, yet highly informative. Our search surfaced 23 source code files in 17 different components. No two source code files were involved in the same external defect.

The minimum amount of time between the new code being introduced and the first customer-found defect was 4 months. We used 4 months for our minimum time lag. To determine the maximum time lag, we had some large outliers that could be the result of the customer not finding the defects. We used the upper bound of the 95% confidence interval of the time lag, which was 12.0 months (mean was 9.2 months). Thus, for a given failure-per-hour measurement, we examine what happened in the team in the prior 4-12 months.

To examine the sensitivity of these parameters on our prediction results, we report our prediction results based on varying time lag parameters in Section 6.4.

Figure 5 depicts the timeline with our time lag parameters. Since the failures-per-hour metric is captured monthly, we shift our time window monthly. Therefore, each team metric data point in our analysis comes from a different time window.

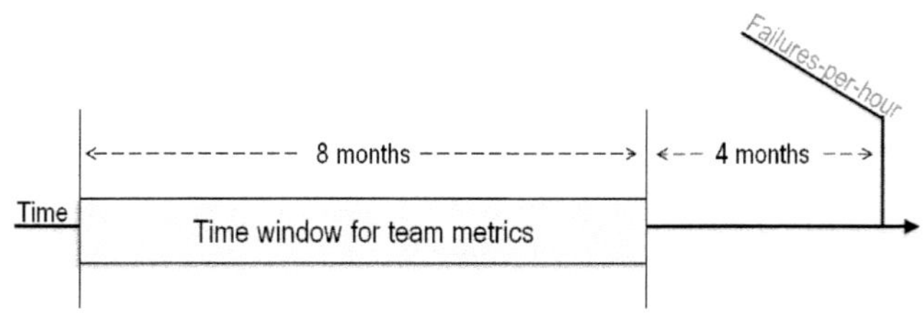

Figure 5. Time window with lag parameters determined in Section 6.1

A summary of the team metrics based on our time lag parameters for this project can be found in Table 2.

Table 2. Summary of the case study project

Metric	Minimum	Maximum
NumCommitters	244	390
NumNewCommitters	49	118
ExpansionAcceleration	-3.6 committers per $(month)^2$	6.3 committers per $(month)^2$
DepartmentModularity	0.26	0.44

As Table 2 shows, the size of the team in committers changed from 244 to 390 (over 60%) from its smallest size to its largest size during that five-year period. Every 8-month window had at least 49 new committers to the project, meaning that the team was consistently under some form of expansion over a long period of time. Some windows had as much as 118 new committers, which was 34% of all the committers at that time. While the team was consistently under growth, the acceleration of growth sometimes increased and decreased per month. Lastly, the team's modularity was always positive, meaning that the team was always modular with respect to departments.

[2] http://www.r-project.org

6.2 Association: Are Team Metrics Associated With Product Quality Metrics?

To test for association, we used simple linear regression. Simple linear regression measures the linear relationship between an independent variable and a dependent variable. Our independent variables were our team metrics and our dependent variable was the failures-per-hour metric.

The outcome of the analysis is a p-value (comparing to 0.05) that indicates whether or not the team metric is associated with software quality. The Pearson R^2 measure describes the percentage of the variance explained by the metric alone, giving evidence of the strength of the correlation. Lastly, we indicate whether the metric was positively or inversely correlated with a high failure rate (i.e. reduced software quality). The results can be found in Table 3.

Table 3. Team metrics association with reduced quality

Metric	p-value<0.05?	R^2	Correlation w/ Reduced Quality
NumCommitters	Yes	0.38	Inverse
NumNewCommitters	Yes	0.26	Inverse
ExpansionAcceleratio n	Yes	0.19	Positive
DepartmentModularity	Yes	0.23	Positive

With regard to NumCommitters, the inverse correlation indicates that when the team was large, the product quality was better. This result does not surprise us given that we already knew that the team generally expanded over time and the product generally improved over time, as shown in Figure 3. With NumNewCommitters, times of having many new developers were also inversely correlated with reduced quality. That is, when new developers were on the team, the team later had better product quality. However, ExpansionAcceleration was positively correlated with failures-per-hour. This positive correlation indicates that periods of accelerating expansion are correlated with periods of relatively poor software quality.

Therefore, periods of large team size and linear team growth are correlated with better quality, but periods of *accelerated growth* are correlated with periods of relatively poor quality.

For modularity, we see that periods of high team modularity are correlated with periods of relatively poor product quality. However, we do not conclude that having a modular team is universally a bad characteristic. As shown in Table 2 of Section 6.1, the team's modularity was never negative, so the potential "sweet spot" of modularity may still be a positive number, but should not be exceedingly high (i.e. close to 1.0).

We examined potential correlations (i.e. collinearity) amongst our team metrics to see if the team metrics are similar to each other. We tested our metrics again by performing multiple regression analysis against the failure-per-hour metric with combinations of two and three variables at a time, and tested if all of the variables were still statistically significant. We found that all of the variables were still statistically significant in this analysis, with one exception. When we combined NumCommitters, NumNewCommitters, and ExpansionAcceleration into one model, the NumCommitters metric became statistically insignificant at a $p<0.05$ level. That is, the variation in the failures-per-hour metric can be explained by the team's rate of growth without the need for accounting for its actual size. This evidence suggests that the velocity and acceleration of growth of a development team has more to do with quality than its overall size.

We also provide the Pearson correlation coefficients between each of the variables in Table 4. The one metric that was strongly correlated with the other variables was NumCommitters. That is, when the team was large, the team also had many new developers and was more modular. Interestingly, times of having many new developers were not found to be statistically correlated with having high expansion acceleration, most likely stemming from the fact that, in many of the time periods, the team underwent a linear, non-accelerated growth.

Therefore, with respect to Q_{size}, we conclude that an expanded team does not necessarily result in reduced quality because the rate and acceleration of expansion statistically explain the large team size and its observed effects on reduced quality. For Q_{rate}, our results indicate that linear growth in the team was not associated with reduced product quality. However, for $Q_{acceleration}$, we conclude that accelerated team expansion is associated with reduced product quality. Lastly, for $Q_{modularity}$, we conclude that when collaboration between departments is low, the product quality also reduces.

6.3 Predictability: How Often Are We Right?

Our first step in predictability was to create a model. We selected our variables based upon our association results (described in Section 6.2) and internal correlation analysis (Table 4) where we found that combining our metrics together rendered the NumCommitters variable statistically insignificant. Therefore, the multiple linear regression model uses the following three metrics: NumNewCommitters, ExpansionAcceleration, and DepartmentModularity.

A key element of prediction is the *supervised model*. A supervised model is a method of combining multiple metrics into a regression equation that predicts values of the failures-per-hour metric. In our study, we use multiple linear regression analysis as our

Table 4. Pearson correlation coefficients between the team metrics.

	NumCommitters	NumNewCommitters	ExpansionAcceleration	DepartmentModularity
NumCommittters	1.00	0.49	0.0*	0.51
NumNewCommitters		1.00	0.0*	0.53
ExpansionAcceleration			1.00	0.0*
DeptartmentModularity				1.00

*Coefficient not statistically different from 0 at a $p<0.05$ level

predictive model. Supervised models require a *training set* and a *validation set* of data, which are taken from the method validation.

We used a time-based validation technique to provide a simulation of how the model could have performed at specific times in history. Instead of randomly partitioning the data points into folds (as is widely used in cross-validation), we iterated over each month in history and trained our model on only data available prior to the month in question, then tested against the current month.

For the prediction analysis, we analyzed a 58 month history, with a 12 month delay from the beginning of the time window to the failures-per-hour metric. For training a multiple regression model, we required at least 6 months of training data to properly train the model. Therefore, our time validation prediction results are from 40 months in total.

To evaluate our model, we report the adjusted Pearson R^2 value for the model on the training set and examine how often the model was able to predict within a 95% prediction interval in our validation phase. Our prediction model on its own training set had an R^2 of 0.66 and was able to predict 38 out of 40 time periods over time. Figure 6 show the 95% prediction intervals and the actual failures-per-hour rate (the y-axis have no unit labels are hidden to protect proprietary information).

Our predictions results indicate that three metrics, based solely upon team growth and structure, have a linear relationship that explains 66% of the variation in the product's quality.

6.4 Prediction Sensitivity

While we performed our analysis with a time lag of 4 to 12 months, we also are interested in how sensitive our results are to adjusting those time lag parameters. We present our prediction results with several different time lag parameters in Table 5, with highlighted top row being our best estimation for time lag according to the analysis in Section 6.1. We did not choose our time lag parameters based on this analysis; we performed this investigation after choosing our 4-12 month time lag parameters.

Table 5. Prediction sensitivity to varying time lag parameters

Min. Time Lag	Max. Time Lag	Months in 95% Prediction interval	Adj. R^2
4 months	12 months	38/40 (95%)	0.66
1 month	9 months	31/38 (82%)	0.53
6 months	14 months	32/40 (80%)	0.34
1 month	15 months	33/37 (89%)	0.21

The sensitivity analysis shows that the predictions are, in fact, somewhat sensitive to varying time windows. The prediction intervals, however, do still provide strong prediction results, meaning that even if our choice of time lag parameters is slightly off, the prediction results would have been strong. Interestingly, the parameters we chose based on our own manual investigations of source code yielded the strongest prediction results.

7. LIMITATIONS

The results of this study are in the form of statistical correlations, which means that our study does not unequivocally prove that accelerated team expansion affects quality. Furthermore, our study has only been applied to one case study, and further studies can reveal if these results are consistent across teams.

The longitudinal structure of the analysis assumes that the time lag from changes in the team to changes in the product quality is a constant factor over time. In reality, the actual lag may vary as a result of many different factors. Sometimes a product is rushed to customers, or possibly delayed for more testing. Our sensitivity analysis in Section 6.4 mitigates this limitation by showing that our predictions are somewhat sensitive to the time lag, but not sensitive to the point that strong prediction is not possible with parameters that are off by a few months. As we apply our models to Cisco's goal-setting process, we will examine the validity of our 4-12 month time lag parameters according our case study and adjust them as necessary.

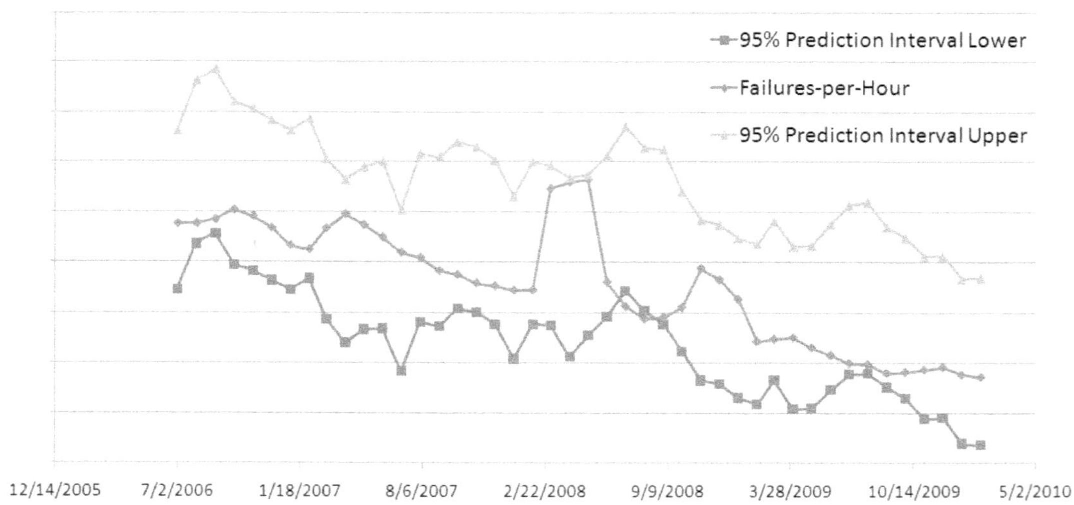

Figure 6. 95% prediction intervals for time-based prediction

8. BROOKS' LAW & PRODUCT QUALITY

The results of this study show that expanding a team does not have a high risk of reduced quality, but that accelerating the expansion of a team can be high risk to product quality. We do not believe that this result contradicts the spirit of Brooks' Law at all. Rather, we submit that these results serve as a clarification of what Brooks was discussing regarding his law.

Adding developers to a team requires significant overhead, such as training, increased communication, and increased coordination. Even in situations where the new teammates are veteran developers, software projects are filled with project-specific and domain-specific knowledge that new teammates would need to be briefed on [4]. Teams can plan for new developer overhead, but when the project is already late, as Brooks' Law states, the team may not have the time to adequately plan ahead.

Like project lateness, accelerating the expansion of a team can also undermine the development team's planning. For example, if a team is used to adding three new developers per month, they will have likely have experience in allocating time with coworkers to train in the new developers. As time passes, planning for the training effort required of three developers per month becomes easier with experience as long as that rate remains constant. Planning for *accelerated* expansion, however, means the team will have to plan for more new developers each month. The acceleration introduces an increase in the time and the number of coworkers allocated to train people in. Each month would have worse and worse training overhead than the month before, which is difficult to plan for and introduces the risk of negative outcomes like lateness or poor quality.

Fortunately, expansion acceleration can be mitigated. For example, suppose a manager decides to expand the team by 12 new developers over the course of three months. An option involving acceleration would be to add two new developers in the first month, then four the second month, then six in the third month. Instead, the same expansion of adding 12 developers in three months can be accomplished without acceleration with a steady rate of four new developers per month. Based upon the findings of this case study, we would recommend the steady growth option over the accelerated option.

9. FUTURE WORK

We will be applying our metrics and study methodology to other case studies within Cisco. The data sources we used for this case study are available for many other different projects with different domains and varying team sizes. We plan to investigate if our results replicate across teams, particularly in situations where teams remained a constant size or reduced in size. One additional case study has a team size of over a thousand committers, which could provide added insight for teams that are an order of magnitude larger than the case study of this paper.

Beyond cross-project analysis, we will be continuing to investigate other ways of using metrics to aid the goal-setting practice at Cisco. One metric to examine is turnover, or losing developers while also gaining new developers. The case study in this paper had minimal turnover, so we did not include it in this study. Additionally, we are considering ways of quantifying developer expertise and experience so that we can separate out situations where the new committers are inexperienced or not. Lastly, we are also examining other team-level network analysis measures that quantify the structure of a team in different ways. Developer centrality is one file-level measure used in other studies that could be aggregated on a team level.

10. SUMMARY

Our research objective is to guide software engineering managers during periods of team expansion by empirically analyzing the effects of team size, growth, and structure on product quality. We performed an empirical, longitudinal case study on a large networking product that grew from 249 to 390 committers. We presented several team-level metrics that can be used to assess and track the growth and modularity of software development teams. In our case study, we found that the team expanded in size over time and was also able to improve quality over time. However, periods of accelerated expansion and highly modular team organization were correlated with relatively poor software quality from the point of view of the customer. In fact, rate and acceleration of team expansion together are enough to explain the team size association with product quality. Our results (a) help researchers and practitioners better understand how team expansion can be a high risk; and (b) help practitioners, including the subjects of our case study, predict upcoming failures-per-hour measurements by monitoring team expansion and organization metrics. We believe that the results of this case study warrant further investigation into the specific ways that adding manpower to a team can help or hurt the products quality.

11. ACKNOWLEDGMENTS

We thank the Realsearch group at North Carolina State University for their valuable feedback. This work was supported by Cisco Systems, Inc. and by the Army Research Office managed by the NCSU Secure Open Systems Initiative.

12. REFERENCES

[1] A. Begel, Y. P. Khoo, and T. Zimmermann, "Codebook: discovering and exploiting relationships in software repositories," in *32nd ACM/IEEE International Conference on Software Engineering*, pp. 125-134, 2010.

[2] C. Bird, D. Pattison, R. D'Souza, V. Filkov, and P. Devanbu, "Latent Social Structure in Open Source Projects," in *16th ACM SIGSOFT International Symposium on Foundations of Software Engineering (FSE)*, pp. 24-35, 2008.

[3] U. Brandes and T. Erlebach, *Network Analysis: Methodological Foundations*, 1st ed. Springer, 2005.

[4] F. P. Brooks, *The Mythical Man-Month: Essays on Software Engineering, Anniversary Edition*, Anniversary. Addison-Wesley Professional, 1995.

[5] T. G. Cummings, "Self-Regulating Work Groups: A Socio-Technical Synthesis," *The Academy of Management Review*, vol. 3, no. 3, pp. 625-634, Jul. 1978.

[6] ISO/IEC 24765, "Software and Systems Engineering Vocabulary." 2006.

[7] A. Meneely and L. Williams, "Secure Open Source Collaboration: an Empirical Study of Linus' Law," in *Int'l Conference on Computer and Communications Security (CCS)*, pp. 453-462, 2009.

[8] A. Meneely and L. Williams, "Strengthening the Empirical Analysis of the Relationship Between Linus' Law and Software Security," in *Proceedings of the 2010*

ACM-IEEE International Symposium on Empirical Software Engineering and Measurement, pp. 1-10, 2010.

[9] A. Meneely and L. Williams, "Socio-Technical Developer Networks: Should We Trust Our Measurements?," in *International Conference on Software Engineering (ICSE)*, 2011.

[10] A. Meneely, L. Williams, W. Snipes, and J. Osborne, "Predicting Failures with Developer Networks and Social Network Analysis," in *Proceedings of the 16th ACM SIGSOFT International Symposium on Foundations of software engineering*, pp. 13-23, 2008.

[11] N. Nagappan, B. Murphy, and V. Basili, "The Influence of Organizational Structure on Software Quality: An Empirical Case Study," in *30th International Conference on Software Engineering (ICSE)*, pp. 521-530, 2008.

[12] M. Pinzger, N. Nagappan, and B. Murphy, "Can Developer-Module Networks Predict Failures?," in *16th ACM SIGSOFT International Symposium on Foundations of Software Engineering (FSE)*, pp. 2-12, 2008.

[13] A. Sarma, L. Maccherone, P. Wagstrom, and J. Herbsleb, "Tesseract: Interactive Visual Exploration of Socio-Technical Relationships in Software Development," in *31st International Conference on Software Engineering (ICSE)*, pp. 23-33, 2009.

[14] Y. Shin, A. Meneely, L. Williams, and J. Osborne, "Evaluating Complexity, Code Churn, and Developer Activity Metrics as Indicators of Software Vulnerabilities," *IEEE Transactions on Software Engineering (TSE)*, vol. to appear, 2011.

[15] C. Treude and M.-A. Storey, "Awareness 2.0: staying aware of projects, developers and tasks using dashboards and feeds," in *Proceedings of the 32nd ACM/IEEE International Conference on Software Engineering - Volume 1*, pp. 365–374, 2010.

[16] E. L. Trist and K. W. Bamforth, "Some social and psychological consequences of the longwall method of coal-getting," *Technology, Organizations and Innovation: The early debates*, p. 79, 2000.

[17] E. J. Weyuker, T. J. Ostrand, and R. M. Bell, "Do Too Many Cooks Spoil the Broth? Using the Number of Developers to Enhance Defect Prediction Models," *Empirical Softw. Engg.*, vol. 13, no. 5, pp. 539-559, 2008.

[18] R. C. Williams, J. A. Walker, and A. J. Dorofee, "Putting risk management into practice," *Software, IEEE*, vol. 14, no. 3, pp. 75-82, 1997.

[19] T. Wolf, A. Schroter, D. Damian, and T. Nguyen, "Predicting Build Failures Using Social Network Analysis on Developer Communication," in *31st International Conference on Software Engineering (ICSE)*, pp. 1-11, 2009.

Effective Communication of Software Development Knowledge Through Community Portals

Christoph Treude, Margaret-Anne Storey
Dept. of Computer Science, University of Victoria
ctreude@uvic.ca, mstorey@uvic.ca

ABSTRACT

Knowledge management plays an important role in many software organizations. Knowledge can be captured and distributed using a variety of media, including traditional help files and manuals, videos, technical articles, wikis, and blogs. In recent years, web-based community portals have emerged as an important mechanism for combining various communication channels. However, there is little advice on how they can be effectively deployed in a software project.

In this paper, we present a first study of a community portal used by a closed source software project. Using grounded theory, we develop a model that characterizes documentation artifacts along several dimensions, such as content type, intended audience, feedback options, and review mechanisms. Our findings lead to actionable advice for industry by articulating the benefits and possible shortcomings of the various communication channels in a knowledge-sharing portal. We conclude by suggesting future research on the increasing adoption of community portals in software engineering projects.

Categories and Subject Descriptors

D.2.9 [**Software Engineering**]: Management

General Terms

Documentation, Human Factors

Keywords

Community Portal, Knowledge, Documentation

1. INTRODUCTION AND MOTIVATION

Software development is knowledge-intensive [25], and the effective management and exchange of knowledge is key in every software organization. Knowledge is distributed through various artifacts and media forms, from formal documentation and technical articles, to blogs and wikis. However, many organizations struggle with the effective exchange and dissemination of knowledge across the community [15, 28].

Although various forms of documentation exist, software projects encounter many knowledge management challenges [9, 24]: How should knowledge be distributed? How should knowledge be kept up to date? How should feedback be solicited? How should knowledge be organized for easy access? There is no roadmap for what kind of information is best presented in a given artifact, and new forms of documentation, such as wikis and blogs, have evolved [20]. Unlike more formal mechanisms, wikis and blogs are easy to create and maintain. However, they do not offer the same authoritativeness that comes with traditional documentation, and they can become outdated and less concise over time [5]. While the informality of a wiki page or blog is sometimes enough, users often expect reviewed technical articles.

One mechanism that has emerged recently and brings various communication channels together is the use of web or community portals. Such portals are not just used in software communities, but are essential to companies, such as Amazon.com, eBay or TripAdvisor, where they enable the development of communities around products. Similarly, many of today's software projects wish to solicit feedback and input from a broader community of users, beta-testers, and stakeholders. While several projects use community portals, such as Microsoft's MSDN[1] or IBM's Jazz[2], the use of portals for software development projects has not been studied yet. It is unclear how portals can play an effective role in software development, and how different communication channels and artifacts should be utilized.

This paper presents a first study of a successful software project – IBM's Rational Team Concert – and its use of a community portal. Our methodology follows a grounded theory approach, using data from 13 semi-structured interviews with developers, ethnographic field notes gathered during observations on-site, and quantitative data on the content of the community portal. Based on our findings, we develop a model of artifacts in a community portal that characterizes the artifacts along different dimensions, such as intended audience, content type, feedback options, and review mechanisms. We provide actionable advice on how a community portal can provide benefits to a software project, and we discuss how the different channels and artifacts available in a portal can be used effectively. We also identify the shortcomings of different artifacts, and suggest improve-

Permission to make digital or hard copies of all or part of this work for personal or classroom use is granted without fee provided that copies are not made or distributed for profit or commercial advantage and that copies bear this notice and the full citation on the first page. To copy otherwise, to republish, to post on servers or to redistribute to lists, requires prior specific permission and/or a fee.
ESEC/FSE'11, September 5–9, 2011, Szeged, Hungary.
Copyright 2011 ACM 978-1-4503-0443-6/11/09 ...$10.00.

[1]http://msdn.microsoft.com/en-us/
[2]https://jazz.net/pub/index.jsp

ments to current tools and processes. With this research, we aim to assist managers and developers in their decisions about using community portals.

The remainder of this paper is structured as follows. Related work is summarized in Section 2. In Section 3, we describe the community portal case study, and in Section 4, we introduce our methodology. In Section 5, we report our findings and describe a knowledge artifact model. We discuss our findings in Section 6, and we report limitations of our work in Section 7. Section 8 concludes the paper and outlines future work.

2. BACKGROUND AND RELATED WORK

We discuss three areas that are key to our research: knowledge management, documentation in software development, and the use of community portals to share information.

2.1 Knowledge in Software Development

Knowledge management has long been recognized as essential to software development [14]. Rowley [26] defines knowledge management as *"concerned with the exploitation and development of the knowledge assets of an organization with a view to furthering the organization's objectives. The knowledge to be managed includes both explicit, documented knowledge, and tacit, subjective knowledge."* How knowledge is managed in an organization depends on the particular style of software development. Plan-based or traditional methods usually rely on the management of explicit knowledge, while Agile methods rely on the management of tacit knowledge [22].

The number of studies on knowledge management in software development projects is limited. An overview of knowledge management in software engineering was conducted by Rus *et al.* [27]. The focus of their review is on motivations for knowledge management, different approaches to knowledge management, and factors that are important when implementing knowledge management strategies in companies.

Dingsøyr and Conradi [8] report on a literature survey of the lessons learned on the actions taken by companies, the effects and benefits of these actions, and descriptions of the strategies for knowledge management. Bjørnson and Dingsøyr [2] also identified the following main finding across several papers: there is a need not to focus exclusively on explicit knowledge but also on tacit knowledge.

Within knowledge management, the transfer of knowledge is particularly challenging. As described by Komi-Sirviö *et al.* [17], sharing knowledge is difficult in the light of short-term goals and companies often fall back to needs-based approaches for knowledge transfer. Knowledge transfer is essential when integrating new developers into a team. In a recent study using grounded theory, Dagenais *et al.* [4] identify early experimentation, internalization of structures and cultures, and progress validation as the main factors for the integration of newcomers. They also found that documentation was often not helpful and outdated.

Our research focuses on the knowledge captured in a community portal and on how to present it effectively.

2.2 Documentation in Software Development

Documentation has long been prominent in the list of recommended software engineering practices [6]. In 1986, Parnas and Clements [23] described a design process in which documentation plays a major role. They argue that many developers regard documentation as a necessary evil, written only as an afterthought to adhere to bureaucratic regulations. Therefore, documentation ends up being incomplete and inaccurate. Parnas and Clements identified four organizational issues that lead to those problems: poor organization of the documents which makes it harder to maintain them, boring prose that leads to inattentive reading, confusing and inconsistent terminology, and myopia caused by authors who know the documented system too well to take a comprehensive point of view.

In a survey of software professionals, Forward and Lethbridge [10] found that content, up-to-dateness, availability, and the use of examples are the most important document attributes. In a related study, Lethbridge *et al.* [19] explored how software engineers use and maintain documentation. They found that most software engineers do not update documentation in a timely manner, with the exception being highly-structured, easily-maintained forms of documentation, such as test cases and in-line comments.

Kajko-Mattsson [15] reports on a study in which she found poor documentation practices, even though her interviewees understood the necessity of documentation. Her participants identified the lack of a detailed documentation model as the main problem. Similar results were found in a study by Visconti and Cook [28]. They discovered a maturity gap between policies and the adherence to those policies.

Dagenais and Robillard [5] conducted a study to understand how documentation in open source projects is created and maintained. Among other findings, they report that the use of wikis for documentation has several shortcomings, such as a lack of authoritativeness, and that the use of a separate documentation team results in naming inconsistencies and out-of-date documentation.

Recent trends, such as agile documentation [1], suggest that executable products should be preferred over static documentation. From the agile point-of-view, documentation should be just good enough and it should only be updated *"when it hurts"* [1]. The rationale behind this is that the fundamental issue is communication, not documentation, and that comprehensive documentation does not ensure project success. While the developers in our study did not use agile documentation, only some of the documentation was formally organized, whereas other parts of the community portal evolved without strict rules.

2.3 Research on Community Portals

Community portals have become a platform used by online communities for the dissemination of information on the Web [13]. Members of a community can find relevant information on portals and can often contribute their own content. These community portals attract a disproportionately large amount of web traffic and engage visitors with free content [7]. Kondatova and Goldfarb [18] identify three objectives of such portals and the communities surrounding them: to supply content to users, to encourage members to contribute, and to facilitate communication and interaction. Portals aim to meet these objectives by offering various forums, wikis, mailing lists, and other communication mechanisms [18]. As Millen [21] points out, the archive of conversation in an online community is often a valuable information resource.

To date, research on community portals has focused on areas such as education and e-Government. Katz [16] examines how the use of portals allows educational institutions to integrate information and services used by their communities, and aims to guide institutions in their decisions about using portals. Gant and Gant [12] found the responsibilities of simultaneously providing breadth and depth in online content to be a challenge for governments using portals.

As mentioned earlier, the use of community portals by software development projects has not been studied yet. Several open source projects, such as Eclipse[3], PHP[4] or the Apache HTTP Server[5], offer portals that bring together a variety of artifacts, such as bug trackers, mailing lists, forums, wikis, and events. More recently, commercial products, such as Microsoft's Visual Studio or IBM's Jazz, have started using community portals. For example, the MSDN portal[6] features a library with API references, code samples and tutorials, a learning section, forums, and a blog. Next, we describe the IBM Jazz community portal in more detail.

3. THE COMMUNITY PORTAL

IBM's Jazz is a technology platform for collaborative software delivery and the development of products on top of the platform is made transparent through the community portal jazz.net. The first product developed on the Jazz platform is Rational Team Concert (RTC), a software development team collaboration tool that was first released in 2008. Recent additions to the Jazz platform include products such as Rational Insight and Rational Build Forge. In our study, we focus on RTC as it is the most mature of the Jazz products.

Jazz.net hosts the entire development process including work items, developer mailing lists, the development wiki, forums, the team blog, and a library. The library features technical articles, podcasts, presentations, videos, and official product documentation, with tags organizing all artifacts in the library. All artifacts on jazz.net contain information that indicates their associated product, with some artifacts belonging to more than one product. Figure 1 shows a screenshot of one of the portal pages. All content is accessible to users after a free registration.

Figure 1: The IBM Jazz community portal

Technical articles are written by developers and product experts, and explore tasks, use cases, solutions, and concepts in depth. Podcasts stem from various sources, including news and updates about Jazz products, and often feature Jazz developers and managers. The presentations have been given by developers and product managers at conferences, or they are simply informational. Videos are produced by Jazz developers or experts, and typically demonstrate the use of Jazz products or introduce enhancements. The official product documentation consists of HTML content that is part of the product releases. The content is produced by a separate documentation team and is also accessible through the product help menus. Table 1 shows the different RTC-related artifacts that were available on jazz.net at the time of our study. Developers started to contribute to the community portal in the summer of 2007.

[3]http://www.eclipse.org/
[4]http://www.php.net/
[5]http://httpd.apache.org/
[6]http://msdn.microsoft.com/en-us/

Table 1: RTC-related artifacts on jazz.net

type	amount
forum	8,413 threads
wiki	3,334 pages
mailing list	3,292 messages
blog	77 posts
official product documentation	4 manuals
library	93 articles
	58 videos
	30 presentations
	7 podcasts

4. RESEARCH METHODOLOGY

Here, we outline the research methodology used to understand how software developer knowledge is communicated through the Jazz portal. We cover the setting of our study, as well as the data collection and analysis methods used.

4.1 Research Setting

Our study took place with the development team of Rational Team Concert at IBM in the summer of 2010. The team consists of approximately 150 contributors in about 30 functional teams, with some teams acting as sub-teams of larger teams, and with many contributors assigned to multiple teams. The team members are located at approximately 15 locations, primarily in North America and Europe. The development follows the *"Eclipse Way"* development process [11]. Created by the Eclipse Development team, this process is an agile, iteration-based process with a focus on consistent, on-time delivery of software through continuous integration, testing, and incremental planning.

4.2 Data Collection

Our methodology followed a mixed methods approach, collecting both quantitative and qualitative data to allow for triangulation. To gather quantitative data on jazz.net, we used web scraping to download the artifacts shown in Table 1, along with their tags. At the time of our data extraction, the RTC team was working on milestones towards the 3.0 release. The quantitative data was collected to gain initial insights into the kinds of artifacts available on the community portal. These insights were used to guide our qualitative data collection that was done through a series of 13 semi-structured interviews. Seven interviews were conducted in person at an IBM location, and the remaining six interviews were conducted by phone. We interviewed five developers, four component leads, the RTC development manager, the RTC project administrator, and two client developers that work on Jazz-related projects inside IBM. For the remainder of this paper, we use D1 to D5 to refer to the developers, L1 to L4 to refer to the component leads, M1 and M2 to refer to the individuals with project-wide tasks, and C1 and C2 to refer to the client developers.

The initial interview script contained about 40 questions on participants' use of jazz.net[7]. As expected with grounded theory, new questions emerged which led us to refine the interview questions used during the course of the study. We asked our interviewees how they learn about Jazz functionalities, what kind of questions they ask using jazz.net, and how they use the published artifacts. We also investigated whether they had ever contributed content, and if so, who or what had triggered that contribution. We asked if there were perceived gaps in the documentation, and about potential tool and process enhancements. We used follow-up questions for clarifications and additional details, trying to understand the scenarios that had led to the creation and use of different artifacts. In addition, one of our researchers spent three months on-site, frequently engaging in informal discussions with developers regarding their use of jazz.net, and facilitating the member checking of our findings. These observations were recorded using ethnographic field notes and allowed for insights into the internal processes that were not revealed in interviews, in particular the processes that would ultimately lead to the creation of new artifacts.

4.3 Data Analysis

Our data analysis followed the grounded theory approach as described by Corbin and Strauss [3]. Grounded theory implies that data collection and analysis are interrelated processes, and that concepts are the basic units of analysis. These concepts are obtained using *"open coding"* in which the collected data is conceptualized line by line and concepts are only created when they are present repeatedly. We applied open coding to the transcripts of our interviews, to the data downloaded from jazz.net, and to the field notes collected on site. Based on the concepts, more abstract categories are developed and related. Each category is developed in terms of its properties, dimensions, conditions, and consequences. In the next step, called *"axial coding"*, data is put together in new ways, thus making explicit connections between categories and sub-categories. Sampling in grounded theory is done on theoretical grounds where incidents and events are sampled rather than subjects or data sources. In the final step of *"selective coding"*, the core category is identified and systematically related to other categories. Since all findings in a grounded theory study are linked to specific evidence, we are able to attribute all the findings we reported to interview quotes, field notes, or specific content on jazz.net. We considered all quantitative and qualitative data collected in our study during the analysis.

5. MODEL OF KNOWLEDGE ARTIFACTS

The *"core category"* identified in our grounded theory study is a set of key characteristics of different artifacts in a community portal. We can distinguish the artifacts along eight different dimensions that emerged from the axial and selective coding as part of our data analysis. The dimensions underline the particular role of each artifact.

[7]The set of questions used in the interviews is available online at http://tinyurl.com/jazz-net.

Content: the type of content typically presented in the artifact.
Audience: the audience for which the artifact is intended.
Trigger: the motivation that triggers the creation of a new artifact.
Collaboration: the extent of collaboration during the creation of a new artifact.
Review: the extent to which new artifacts are reviewed before publication.
Feedback: the extent to which readers can give feedback.
Fanfare: the amount of fanfare with which a new artifact is released.
Time Sensitivity: the time sensitivity of information in the artifact.

For the official product documentation, technical articles, blog posts, and the developer wiki, we analyzed these dimensions in detail. Figures 2 and 3 summarize the findings and show an example for each kind of artifact. We focus on these particular kinds of artifacts because they are also common in other community portals and in software development in general. The findings can be traced back to quotes from the interviews we conducted, and the interviewees are noted in the figures and text using subscript. Where relevant, we also discuss the artifacts and the ethnographic field notes that we analyzed related to the dimensions. The following sections report on each of the dimensions in detail. In addition, Section 5.9 highlights several explicit and implicit connections between the artifacts.

5.1 What content is communicated?

Content is the first dimension along which the different artifacts of the community portal can be distinguished. The official product documentation is based on **features** and does not cover scenarios: *"I would try to cover all the corner cases, and I found those were often omitted in the help doc because the effort to get into those corner cases were lengthy things. You would have to have a whole section of how to put yourself into a corner, and then a whole other section of how to get yourself out of this corner."*$_{D5}$ However, documenting scenarios is important: *"It's always good to document a widget, but it's more important in many cases to document a process and being able to follow the process of how you do an upgrade or how you do a plan and all the widgets that you touch during that. [...] It's the context of how you use the widget that's much more important."*$_{C2}$

This need is addressed by technical articles that feature **scenarios** and offer more depth than the official documentation. D4 described the reason to write an article: *"Because I wanted to put in a lot of screenshots, and also explain what's happening. [...] You had to write some text around it. Why you're doing something and why is that needed."* Technical articles also differ in their style of writing: *"Articles spice it up a little. There's more pictures and more personal I guess. People have their own style."*$_{D1}$

Tags also shed light on the content of different kinds of artifacts. The tags are assigned by a single person$_{L3}$. Table 2 shows the most-used tags per type. Videos are typically used for high-level overviews or demos$_{L3,D2}$, whereas presentations are related to conferences.

Blogs add a **personal** note to the artifacts on the community portal: *"a personal view on something and not really documentation. [...] You want to make people aware of something or tell them about something, but more like a*

Official Product Documentation

*What **content** is communicated?*
- feature descriptions $_{D5, C2}$
- no scenarios $_{D5, C2}$

*Which **audience** is reached?*
- buying customers $_{M1}$

*What **triggers** the production of new artifacts?*
- a new product release

*To what extent is content produced **collaboratively**?*
- content is produced by a separate documentation team $_{M1, M2, D3}$

*To what extent is content **reviewed** before publication?*
- content undergoes rigorous reviews $_{M1}$

*To what extent can readers give **feedback**?*
- no option to give feedback

*With how much **fanfare** are new artifacts released?*
- same fanfare as product releases $_{D5}$

*How **time sensitive** is the information?*
- information is outdated quickly $_{M2, D5}$
- content is never updated

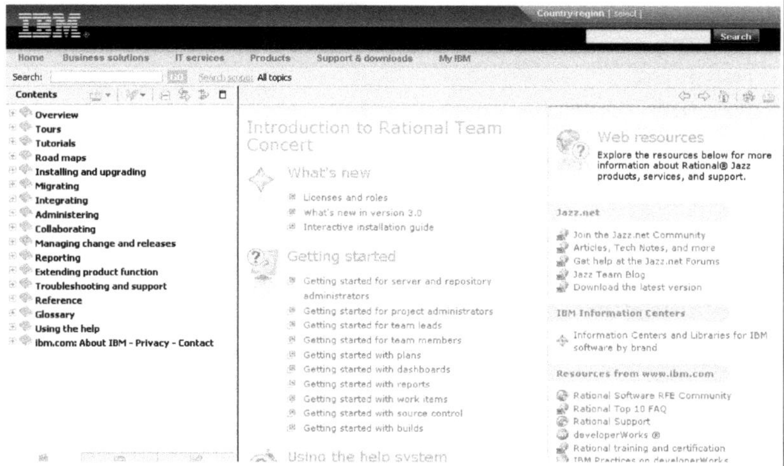

Technical Articles

*What **content** is communicated?*
- scenarios, how-to $_{D4, D5}$
- typically more depth than the official product documentation $_{M1, M2, D5}$

*Which **audience** is reached?*
- individuals outside the development team $_{L1, L2, D2, D4, D5}$

*What **triggers** the production of new artifacts?*
- user questions $_{M1, M2, L1, L2, D3, D5}$
- organized documentation efforts $_{M2, L1, L3, D1, D3, D4, D5}$
- feature promotion $_{L1, D1, D3}$

*To what extent is content produced **collaboratively**?*
- content is mostly produced through solo efforts $_{M1, L1, D1, D4}$

*To what extent is content **reviewed** before publication?*
- content is reviewed before publication $_{L2, D1, D3, D5}$
- content is less formal than the official product documentation $_{M1, D1}$

*To what extent can readers give **feedback**?*
- new feedback section recently implemented $_{L3}$

*With how much **fanfare** are new artifacts released?*
- new content is released without much fanfare $_{M1, L2, L4}$
- some individuals learn about new content through twitter etc $_{D1, C1}$

*How **time sensitive** is the information?*
- information is not outdated quickly $_{L1}$
- most information is related to one particular release $_{L2, L3, D5}$
- content is rarely updated $_{M2, L1, D1, D3, D4}$
- producing new content takes time $_{D3, D5}$

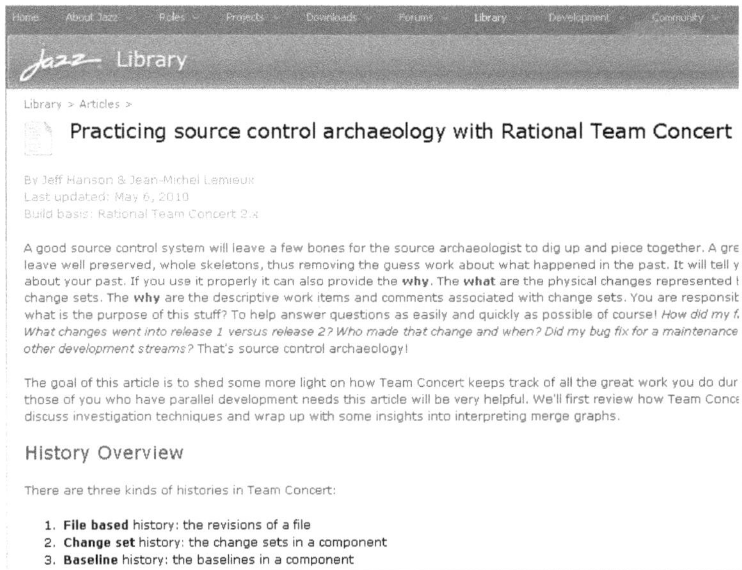

Figure 2: Model of Artifacts in a Community Portal—Findings for Product Documentation and Articles

Table 2: Most-used tags in jazz.net library by type

type	top two tags
article	agile (15), getting started (15)
video	how-to (12), introduction (7)
presentation	RSC 2009 (9), agile (5)
podcast	agile (3), scrum (2)
official doc	help (4)

teaser, you can go somewhere else to find the actual documentation. It's more like you write about something new and cool and what you think about it." $_{L1}$ Therefore, the blog also plays a role in **marketing** $_{L4,D3,C1}$. The most commonly-used tags on blog posts are *rational-team-concert* (26 posts), *video* (13 posts), *self-hosting* (12 posts), and *conference* (11 posts). Most blog posts are related to RTC and provide a conference report or give a view on the Jazz team's self-hosting experience.

The developer wiki plays many roles in the internal development processes, ranging from **planning** to descriptions of **scenarios**, detailed **instructions** or lists of **references** to other resources. Occasionally, wiki content goes beyond supporting development processes: *"He's written some really good wiki topics. The material there is really going beyond what we typically have in the wiki and really should be as help or as articles."* $_{L2}$

5.2 Which audience is reached?

A community portal caters to a diverse audience: *"A good percentage of our community are internal IBMers, business partners, students, academics as well as customers."* $_{L3}$ From a documentation point of view, the distinction of **end users**

Blog Posts

What ***content*** *is communicated?*
- case studies $_{C1}$
- personal views $_{L1, L3, C1}$
- marketing $_{L4, D3, C1}$

Which ***audience*** *is reached?*
- the community surrounding the project $_{L3, L4}$

What ***triggers*** *the production of new artifacts?*
- user questions $_{M1, M2, L1, L2, D3, D5}$
- feature promotion $_{L1, D1, D3}$

To what extent is content produced ***collaboratively****?*
- content is mostly produced through solo efforts $_{L4}$

To what extent is content ***reviewed*** *before publication?*
- content is reviewed before publication $_{L4}$

To what extent can readers give ***feedback****?*
- comment section exists

With how much ***fanfare*** *are new artifacts released?*
- more fanfare than new articles $_{L4}$

How ***time sensitive*** *is the information?*
- information is time sensitive $_{M2}$
- content is rarely updated $_{M2}$
- producing new content takes time $_{L4}$

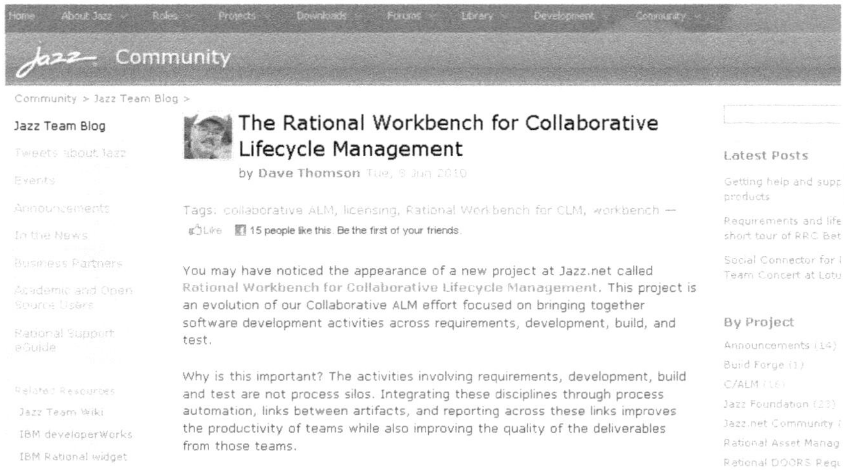

Developer Wiki

What ***content*** *is communicated?*
- plans $_{D3, D5}$, scenarios $_{M1, L1}$, instructions $_{D5, C1}$, references $_{L2, D5}$

Which ***audience*** *is reached?*
- individuals inside the development team $_{L1, L2, L3, L4, D4, C2}$
- sometimes individuals outside the development team $_{M1, M2, L1, L2, D1, D3, D5}$

What ***triggers*** *the production of new artifacts?*
- need to support development work $_{M1, L4, D1, D5}$

To what extent is content produced ***collaboratively****?*
- content is mostly produced through solo efforts $_{M1, M2, L2}$
- some content is produced collaboratively $_{L1, L4, D3}$

To what extent is content ***reviewed*** *before publication?*
- content is rarely reviewed $_{M1, L2}$
- content is not formal $_{M1, D2, D3}$

To what extent can readers give ***feedback****?*
- no option to give feedback

With how much ***fanfare*** *are new artifacts released?*
- no fanfare for new content $_{D2}$

How ***time sensitive*** *is the information?*
- content is changed often $_{M2, L2, D2, D5}$
- content can be stale $_{M1, M2, L1, L2, D1, D2, D3}$
- content is easy to add to $_{L2, D1, D3}$

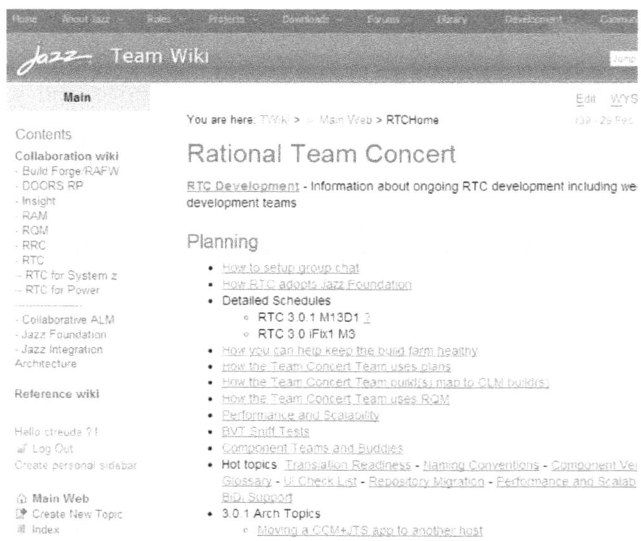

Figure 3: Model of Artifacts in a Community Portal—Findings for Blog Posts and Developer Wiki

and **client developers** is particularly interesting: *"There's two kinds of customers. We have customers who are using the product and trying to do something, and then we have third party developers. And third party developers are – for them to see the wiki makes sense, because we have instructions on how to make stuff."* $_{D3}$ In addition, some communication with customers is done outside of the community portal for confidentiality reasons $_{L2}$.

The intended audience of the official product documentation, technical articles, and the blog is **outside** of the development team. The intended audience for wiki pages is more difficult to determine, and some of the developers have contradicting views on the role of the wiki: *"For the wiki it's developers [...] that I actually have on my [chat] list or where I can put a name to a face."* $_{D5}$ However, customers are occasionally pointed to wiki pages: *"We also point customers to wiki pages. But wiki pages are typically [more] interesting for development teams. It's not as polished usually as articles and probably also not as maintained."* $_{L1}$ For customers, it is important to distinguish between official and informal wiki content: *"I'm not sure if customers should be taking that [wiki page] and making plans, planning their day on that."* $_{D5}$ However, outdated wiki content is of concern: *"Once or twice I've had customers say I'm trying to do stuff from the design document. And it's structured as instructions which is dangerous because they're not correct."* $_{D3}$

5.3 What triggers the production of new artifacts?

There are no formal conventions as to what knowledge should be externalized in technical articles, blog posts, or wiki pages: *"We haven't gotten to the point where we've had to dictate how often certain articles are developed. The content has flown fairly actively, especially with videos. People* *are getting in the habit of delivering release videos at each release with demos and how-to articles. So so far it's been able to happen organically."*$_{L3}$ Articles are not written systematically but *ad hoc*$_{D3,D4}$, and without a formal process to trigger articles on certain topics, choosing the right things to document is subjective: *"The features we choose to work on, they're chosen in an ad hoc manner and we do the same thing with our documentation."*$_{D3}$ Initially, contributions to the blog were organized: *"When we first started doing it, a [...] bunch of us were pulled together and were asked to contribute."*$_{L4}$ However, blog posts now occur in an *ad hoc* manner as well, and over the last three years, there have been 43 different blog authors.

In the following paragraphs, we discuss common motivations for producing content that emerged from our study: user questions, organized efforts, self-promotion, and support of development work.

Knowledge is externalized in the form of articles and blog posts when users repeatedly ask the same **question**$_{M1,M2,L1,L2,D3,D5}$, or when developers expect many questions on a subject: *"Because we have a feeling that there will be so many users that have the same questions that it will be more beneficial to sit down, write the article once."*$_{D5}$ Questions arise from the forum$_{M2}$, they are reported back from customer representatives$_{L3}$, they come from feedback to other parts of the documentation$_{D4}$, or they come by email: *"I try and take every email conversation that I end up having and put it into an article."*$_{M2}$ The motivation for creating wiki pages is similar: *"I wanted not to be the sole source of this information. I wanted them to have a place that they could go and look and refer back to."*$_{D2}$

Some of the articles are the result of **organized efforts** among developers: *"There are efforts internally where groups of people get together and say, what's missing? [...] What are the customers asking for? We need this article or that article. [...] Some of the articles come up that way, and then other articles just happen organically as the team decides [...] they want to write an article on a particular topic."*$_{L3}$ Several of our interviewees reported that they had prompted articles from other individuals$_{M2,L3}$ or that articles had been delegated to them$_{L1,D1,D3,D4,D5}$.

Technical articles and blog posts are also written by developers who want to **promote** a feature they authored$_{L1,D3}$ or who want to promote themselves: *"Part of my thought is also, when I put my name on something, if and when I ever want to be interviewed for something, I want it to be on my resume."*$_{D3}$ D1 had a similar motivation for his article: *"'Cause I wrote it I want to get exposure."*

The externalization of knowledge to the wiki mainly happens to **support development work**, either for an initial *"brain dump"*$_{D5}$, as a central entity for resources$_{D1}$, to facilitate a discussion$_{M1,D5}$, or to *"stage something that needs to be formalized"*$_{D5}$. L4 explains: *"It becomes kind of an open email if you will, to evolve an idea."*

5.4 To what extent is content produced collaboratively?

Artifacts on a community portal also differ in the amount of collaboration that happens around them. The official product documentation is written by a separate **documentation team**, a process which involves a certain amount of interaction with the core developers$_{D5}$. Authoring technical articles, blog posts, and wiki pages is usually a **solo** effort, and only involves other individuals for reviews. For selected wiki pages such as descriptions of parts of the system architecture, the amount of **collaboration** can be higher: *"There's one wiki page that we have on how to set up the development environment [...] and this is something where anybody can add information, and actually also does."*$_{L1}$

The author information on articles is another indicator of collaborative content. Out of 93 technical articles, 35 have 1 author associated with them, 9 articles have 2 authors, 2 articles have 3 authors, and 1 article has 5 authors. An additional 34 articles have at least 1 team name as author, and 12 articles do not have any author information.

5.5 To what extent is content reviewed before publication?

Since the official product documentation is part of the product release, it has to undergo a **formal** review process in which content is reviewed by technical writers as well as by the product teams of the documented components. *"They go through a pretty rigorous process of producing that content working with the various teams that provide the features. [...] So the quality of it is very good."*$_{M1}$ The official product documentation has commitment from the developers and it is also the only artifact that is translated into other languages. Such a process is not transferable to all kinds of artifacts as it requires a lot of resources and therefore only happens once for every major release.

Technical articles are **less formal**. While there are internal reviews before content is posted online, the style is more personal: *"The articles tend to be an easy read, they're more down to earth and personal and not like you learn at school how they have to be formal and very professional and impersonal."*$_{D1}$ Blog posts have to undergo a similar internal review process where one individual on the team proof-reads content before it is posted online. Initially, there was some guidance on blogging: *"When we first started writing blogs for jazz.net, someone who had been a blogger [...] before that, he basically gave us guidance in the Jazz sphere. He said read these guidelines before you write blogs."*$_{L4}$

Wikis are the **least formal** of the artifacts and are rarely reviewed. However, contributors are aware that the wiki is open to the public and some of the wiki content, such as details of new features, has to be coordinated with management$_{M1}$. The lack of review often leads to inconsistencies on the wiki: *"There's pages that I think they're just sitting there, there's just certain people who know about that – they're just often in their own little world."*$_{D2}$

5.6 To what extent can readers give feedback?

Feedback is another dimension that distinguishes the different kinds of artifacts on a community portal. While the official documentation does not allow for feedback, and the developer wiki is read-only for everybody outside the core developer team, a feedback section has recently been implemented for technical articles, podcasts, and other items in the library. 40 of the 58 videos on jazz.net are hosted on YouTube, which provides view counts (considered as implicit feedback) and allows comments. At the time of our study, the videos had a median of 1,074 views, ranging from 188 to 17,157[8]. Only 7 videos had comments, with a maximum of 2 comments per video.

[8]An introductory video for RTC, available online at http://www.youtube.com/watch?v=ILvsGQQqAF0.

Blog posts invite interaction with a **commenting** feature. At the time of our study, there was a total of 183 comments on 77 blog posts. 28 blog posts had no comments, 15 blog posts had 1 comment, and 7 posts had 2 comments. 27 posts had 3 comments or more, with a maximum of 12 comments per post. Blog posts with a lot of comments are typically product announcements or discussions of new functionality.

Community members can also **vote** on blog posts. At the time of our study, 446 votes had been cast. The most voted-for post had 22 votes, and only 4 out of the 77 posts had not received any votes. On average, articles received 4.6 stars out of 5, and only 6 articles received less than 4 stars. A recent addition is the option to *"like"* posts using Facebook Connect, and 4 out of the 10 newest posts had already received more than 10 likes at the time of our study. While the web traffic[9] for artifacts, such as technical articles in the library, is monitored as well, pure numbers do not allow conclusions about the usefulness of the content$_{L3}$.

Feedback is often generic: *"I got a thumbs up, like good thing to do, but not any specific critique on my writing. More like, that's a good thing to do, keep doing that."*$_{D2}$ Some developers even go out of their way to search for feedback: *"There's no feedback and I don't really know what's happened, I don't know if people read [the article]. [...] Then by searching just to see how exposed it was, I found a few forum discussions on jazz.net [about the article]."*$_{D1}$

While the forum and the article comment feature were designed for users to give feedback$_{L3,D4}$, feedback comes through different channels$_{L1,L4,D3}$. Questions about content on jazz.net are mostly asked through direct communication channels, such as chat$_{L1,D5}$ or email$_{M2,L2}$. The customers often work within IBM and therefore have access to the internal instant messaging system$_{L1,C1}$.

Developers are aware that putting their name on artifacts can lead to many questions$_{D3}$ or spam$_{D4}$. *"Usually once you have documented something that people are using, then they come back to you directly with questions."*$_{L1}$ During our ethnographic observations, we also encountered an instance of a developer deciding not to write an article because they anticipated a high workload due to questions and feedback.

5.7 With how much fanfare are new artifacts released?

Artifacts also differ in the fanfare with which they are released and in the number of people that are aware of a new artifact after its creation. While the official product documentation is released alongside the products once a year, blog posts have a higher impact than articles. *"Articles are a little bit quieter."*$_{L4}$ This is confirmed by developers who are not aware of new articles$_{M1}$ or only read articles when prompted$_{L2}$. Other developers follow the JazzDotNet twitter account to learn about new articles$_{C1}$, or they check the feed on the front page of the portal$_{D1}$. New or changed wiki pages have the lowest amount of fanfare as the wiki implementation used by this group does not offer notifications.

5.8 How time sensitive is the information?

Some artifacts are more time sensitive than others. The official product documentation gets **outdated** quickly, mainly because it is only updated once a year (see Table 1). Technical articles are less time sensitive due to the nature of the topics: *"I think the topics are usually chosen so that they stay valid for a longer time. [...] An article that describes for example customization of a work item, these are longer lived features that we do not break as easily."*$_{L1}$ For articles, knowing which release they belong to is important: *"We try to mark every article as relevant to a particular release."*$_{L3}$

For articles and blog posts, the **writing process** takes a few days$_{L4,D3,D5}$, and there is more flexibility on when they are published: *"Sometimes we write articles after the fact. So we didn't get time, we delivered the feature late or something, or we didn't get to document it in time for the release, so then we say OK, we're going to write an article."*$_{M1}$ Developers also choose to write articles after the code freeze point at the end of a release cycle$_{D3}$. However, the review process can lead to publishing delays: *"I've had experiences in the past where I want to get something out in timely way but because of the review it doesn't necessarily get there."*$_{L4}$

Technical articles, blog posts, and wiki pages contain tools to **update** content, but most authors in our study have never updated their articles$_{L1,D1,D3}$. Since the website is hosted by a specific team, developers were unsure what the article change process would be after the initial publication$_{D1}$. In other cases, developers passed on the ownership of an article before they switched teams to make sure updates would happen: *"For the second release of the product, one of my team members here updated the article. [...] He took ownership."*$_{D4}$ Blog posts are more time sensitive than articles, but only one of the developers in our study had made updates to a blog post$_{M2}$. This is because blogs express personal views and usually do not feature technical details$_{L1,L3,C1}$.

In contrast, wiki pages are quick and easy to create and modify: *"I think the wiki is good 'cause it can be sort of fast and loose for getting content out there and the articles tend to be more reviewed, and they're also harder to change after the fact."*$_{L2}$ There is no formal process outlining when wiki pages should change, and some developers only update their wiki pages if they are reminded by somebody else$_{M2,D3}$ or if they happen to see that something is wrong$_{D1}$. Updates are usually done to describe new features$_{M2}$, to answer questions$_{L2}$, or to reorganize a few pages$_{L2}$. Wiki pages aimed at customers are kept current$_{L2}$ and the index is also kept up to date$_{M2}$.

Readers cannot expect all wiki pages to be up to date: *"If it's incorrect I would say, it's a wiki, you can't expect that to be correct."*$_{D5}$ A wiki page implicitly conveys the **uncertainty** of its content: *"It helps us to communicate to customers that it's actually not done yet."*$_{M1}$ As observed by many of our interviewees, wiki pages can have stale content: *"We write a topic on something and then we walk away from it, we just ignore it."*$_{D3}$

5.9 Artifact Connections

Artifacts on a community portal, with all their characteristics as shown in Figures 2 and 3, cannot be treated separately. There are several explicit and implicit connections between them. For example, content or structure can be reused from different artifacts. The structure for an article can come from a wiki page$_{D5}$, a blog post can be distilled from wiki pages$_{L4}$, wiki pages can draw content from forum posts$_{L2}$, and forum posts can be referenced in work items$_{D1}$.

Several wiki pages have the potential to be turned into technical articles or blog posts, but that does not happen often: *"If we had something that we were formulating on*

[9]Data on web traffic was not made available to us.

the wiki and we're getting feedback and so forth and we're altering it over time – once we have decided that it's final, we could basically copy and paste all the stuff and put it in a better looking web page. An article possibly, depending on what it is, or some official document. I can't actually think of specific cases where it has [happened]. [...] We tend to leave a lot of the stuff [on the wiki]."$_{M1}$ Another example is an article created by L4: *"[I added] an article that basically has no content just a description and a link to our wiki [...] using all the keywords that make sense to find it. And that way when somebody goes in looking for this information, [...] we point them into the wiki, which isn't ideal but it does surface the content."*

Relationships between artifacts also exist from a client developer's perspective. C2 describes using the wiki and technical articles as his first place to go for questions, and posting to the forum if he cannot locate an answer: *"That's the fallback. And if I don't get a response in the forum I actually will post a defect or an enhancement."*

6. DISCUSSION

One of the goals of our research is to provide advice to managers and developers on how to effectively use a community portal. In this section, we present advice on the findings from our case study of a successful software project that leverages a community portal.

Make content available, but clearly distinguish different media forms.

One major advantage of a community portal is the accessibility of all artifacts: *"Because it's actually just as likely that an answer for a question is going to be in a forum or in a mailing list as is it going to be in a wiki."*$_{C2}$ Even though not all content is produced with the intent to contribute to documentation, it can help developers inside and outside of the team to understand a system.

However, wiki pages that are created to support development work and that are often not as well structured as other documentation sources on the community portal should be flagged as draft material. This distinction is currently not always clear: *"So people do have confusion about what's real and what's – what's been approved versus just draft."*$_{M2}$ Individuals from outside the core development team find it difficult to navigate the wiki$_{C2}$ and they encounter stale content$_{C1}$. The lack of structure is also a concern for developers on the team$_{D2,D3}$.

Clearly distinguishing different media forms is also a challenge for search interfaces: *"If you do a search, you're confronted with a blend of all the media and different types of it."*$_{C1}$ Jazz.net offers a main search interface that searches the entire content of the community portal, as well as specific searches for the wiki, the library, and the forum. Most of our interviewees found the current search to be insufficient$_{L1,L2,L3,D2,D3,D4,C1,C2}$. As an alternative to search, the wiki index page is kept up to date$_{L2}$ and tags are used on artifacts in the library.

Make it easier to move content into more formal media formats.

Different media forms in community portals are often disconnected. Content is rarely transferred from informal wiki pages into more formal articles or into the official product documentation. Instead, developers create workarounds, such as articles, that point to a wiki page$_{L4}$. Often, good content is never published beyond wiki pages because developers lack the time to push for a new article or blog post$_{L2}$. Resources are wasted by replicating information that already exists in other parts of the community portal. Part of the problem is the use of a separate documentation team for producing the official product documentation. With the plethora of information on a community portal, the first step when writing a new piece of documentation should be to check if related content already exists.

Be aware of the implications of different media artifacts and channels.

As we have shown with the model of knowledge artifacts in a community portal, different media artifacts and channels have different implications (see Figures 2 and 3). To ensure the effective exchange and dissemination of knowledge, developers and managers need to be aware of these implications:

- Content in **wiki** pages is often **stale**. Therefore, readers will not look at the wiki for reliable information, but rather use it as a backup option if information is not available elsewhere. To communicate important information to the community, articles and blog posts are better suited.
- The **official product documentation** is **reviewed** rigorously. With that in mind, it can serve as the most reliable way to communicate knowledge in a community portal.
- When content is produced by a separate documentation team, **updates** may not be feasible. In such a case, information may become outdated quickly and can only be fixed with a new product release. Consequently, an update process for articles may be needed.
- In this project, new **blog** posts created more "buzz" or **fanfare** than articles or wiki pages. Thus, if there is a need to make a project's community aware of something, a blog post may be the best-suited medium.
- Writing can be **time consuming**, in particular for technical articles and blog posts. In addition, those media forms may need to undergo a review process. To get content out **quickly**, the **wiki** may be the best solution. However, readers may only find wiki pages if they are pointed to them explicitly.
- To solicit **feedback** from readers, articles and blog posts typically offer more **comment** functionality than the official product documentation or the wiki.

Offer developers a medium with a low entry barrier for fast externalization of knowledge.

Developers often prefer to externalize their knowledge in the form of wiki pages because wikis are easy to add to$_{L2,D1,D3}$. To encourage documentation, it is important that developers have such a medium at hand where they can externalize knowledge without having to worry about the correctness of content or whether customers will understand the entire context. While it makes sense to have official documentation artifacts, such as articles or blog posts, undergo a review cycle, developers also need a platform for producing content with a lower entry barrier.

Involve the community in a project's documentation.
Unlike other forms of documentation, community portals allow for community involvement. While the number of documentation contributors outside the development team is still limited$_{M1,D1}$, there have been successful instances: *"I got someone [...] who had been asking me a lot of questions and I said, well, you write an article. I had a draft ready, but that was still a skeleton and I said, here's a draft, go write your own style to it. It took a while, [...] but he ended up taking all the screenshots, taking my text and doing stuff and I just reviewed it."*$_{M2}$ In particular, articles on topics such as best practices could be written by client developers and end users$_{M1}$. Such contributions could even be encouraged with incentives as they provide considerable value to the community portal$_{M1}$. Review processes would have to be in place to ensure quality. However, giving write access to community members is not realistic for all content, and in particular, not for the wiki. Other ways to increase community involvement could involve more options for marking up and commenting on content. In general, the entry barrier for community members to contribute to the documentation could be lowered$_{D3}$ by making the process more obvious and by offering easily-accessed web forms for contributions. Recent additions to jazz.net, such as commenting and voting features for library content, are steps in the right direction$_{L3}$, but more could be done to increase community involvement.

Provide readers with an option to give feedback.
Feedback on documentation often comes through direct communication channels. Readers try to contact the content author via email or chat rather than ask questions on the forum. While this was not intended, it underlines the importance of the social aspect of documentation. Readers want to know who authored certain content and they want to be able to contact those individuals. However, with different systems for blog, technical articles, official product documentation, and the wiki, it is difficult to locate all contributions of a single individual.

Our study has also shown that readers take advantage of lightweight ways to give feedback, such as rating of content or *"liking"* artifacts using Facebook Connect. These mechanisms have the potential to involve more readers and gather feedback on the quality and usefulness of content. In addition, implicit feedback, such as view counts, should be attended to.

7. LIMITATIONS

As with any research methodology, there are limitations with our choice of research methods. The first limitation of our study lies in the number of interviewees. However, we triangulated data from the interviews with artifact data from the community portal and with ethnographic field notes gathered during the three months spent on site with RTC developers. Also, the interviewees had different backgrounds, from managers to relatively new team members. We focused on the authors instead of the readers in this study to understand their use of the portal. Investigating the reader's perspective will be future work.

While the documentation landscape for RTC was fairly stable at the time of our study, new projects, such as Rational Insight, had been added to jazz.net shortly before our study. We focused our study on RTC as the mature part of jazz.net, but we cannot rule out that other projects might have influenced our findings.

Our conclusions are limited to the jazz.net portal community. However, Jazz is one of the first platforms that opened up its development process to the community without being open source, and therefore provides a unique case between open source and traditional closed source projects. Also, we focus on blogs, wikis, official product documentation, and technical articles in our study. All of these artifacts are widely used in different contexts to document software. Other community portals should be studied to gain further insights into their role in software development.

8. CONCLUSIONS AND FUTURE WORK

Community portals for software projects facilitate the exchange and dissemination of knowledge through many different kinds of artifacts. In this first case study of a software project community portal, we found that RTC developers need different channels, such as blog posts, wiki pages, technical articles and the official product documentation, to externalize different kinds of knowledge. Each of these artifacts play a role in capturing knowledge that can help users, client developers, and team members understand a system. Developers often externalize knowledge without being prompted by formal processes. They respond to questions, promote their part of the system or themselves, support development processes, or contribute through organized efforts.

Unlike traditional forms of documentation, community portals have the potential to involve a community composed of client developers and end users in the process of externalizing developer knowledge. Our study of jazz.net has shown first evidence of such involvement, and it has also highlighted areas where tools and processes could be improved to encourage more participation.

Recent feature additions, such as mechanisms to *"like"* articles, to vote on blog posts and articles, and to comment on parts of the documentation, are further steps towards involving external individuals in the process of documenting software. Further studies will have to be conducted to understand the effects of such mechanisms. In addition, we need to consider the customer's perspective on the role of community portals, and we need to examine other community portals to fully understand how the burden of documentation can be lessened by sharing it among a larger group of contributors with different roles and responsibilities.

We expect the role of community portals to increase in both open source and closed source projects. The findings from our study and from future studies will help improve how they are used to support communication and collaboration in software engineering projects.

Acknowledgments

We wish to thank the team that granted us access to their repositories and conducted interviews with us. This research is supported by a fellowship from IBM. We also appreciate suggestions from Gargi Bougie and Nancy Songtaweesin as well as the logistical support and editing by Cassandra Petrachenko.

9. REFERENCES

[1] S. W. Ambler. Agile/lean documentation: Strategies for agile software development. http://www.agilemodeling.com/essays/agileDocumentation.htm, accessed in March 2011.

[2] F. Bjørnson and T. Dingsøyr. Knowledge management in software engineering: A systematic review of studied concepts, findings and research methods used. *Information and Software Technology*, 50(11):1055–1068, 2008.

[3] J. M. Corbin and A. Strauss. Grounded theory research: Procedures, canons, and evaluative criteria. *Qualitative Sociology*, 13(1):3–21, 1998.

[4] B. Dagenais, H. Ossher, R. K. E. Bellamy, M. P. Robillard, and J. P. de Vries. Moving into a new software project landscape. In *ICSE '10: Proc. of the 32nd Intl. Conf. on Software Engineering*, pages 275–284, New York, NY, USA, 2010. ACM.

[5] B. Dagenais and M. P. Robillard. Creating and evolving developer documentation: understanding the decisions of open source contributors. In *FSE '10: Proc. of the 18th Intl. Symp. on Foundations of software engineering*, pages 127–136, New York, NY, USA, 2010. ACM.

[6] S. C. B. de Souza, N. Anquetil, and K. M. de Oliveira. A study of the documentation essential to software maintenance. In *SIGDOC '05: Proc. of the 23rd Intl. Conf. on Design of communication*, pages 68–75, New York, NY, USA, 2005. ACM.

[7] R. M. Dewan, M. L. Freimer, A. Seidmann, and J. Zhang. Web portals: Evidence and analysis of media concentration. *J. Manage. Inf. Syst.*, 21:181–199, October 2004.

[8] T. Dingsøyr and R. Conradi. A survey of case studies of the use of knowledge management in software engineering. *Intl. Journal of Software Engineering and Knowledge Engineering*, 12(4):391–414, 2002.

[9] B. Fluri, M. Würsch, E. Giger, and H. C. Gall. Analyzing the co-evolution of comments and source code. *Software Quality Control*, 17(4):367–394, 2009.

[10] A. Forward and T. C. Lethbridge. The relevance of software documentation, tools and technologies: a survey. In *DocEng '02: Proc. of the Symp. on Document engineering*, pages 26–33, New York, NY, USA, 2002. ACM.

[11] R. Frost. Jazz and the eclipse way of collaboration. *IEEE Softw.*, 24(6):114–117, 2007.

[12] J. Gant and D. Gant. Web portal functionality and state government e-service. In *Proc. of the 35th Annual Hawaii Intl. Conf. on System Sciences*, pages 1627–1636, 2002.

[13] S. Grzonkowski, A. Gzella, S. R. Kruk, J. G. Breslin, T. Woroniecki, and J. Dobrzanski. Sharing information across community portals with foafrealm. *Int. J. Web Based Communities*, 5:351–370, 2009.

[14] J. D. Herbsleb and D. Moitra. Guest editors' introduction: Global software development. *IEEE Softw.*, 18(2):16–20, 2001.

[15] M. Kajko-Mattsson. A survey of documentation practice within corrective maintenance. *Empirical Softw. Eng.*, 10(1):31–55, 2005.

[16] R. N. Katz. *Promise and Peril of Portal Technologies in Higher Education*. John Wiley & Sons, Inc., New York, NY, USA, 2002.

[17] S. Komi-Sirviö, A. Mäntyniemi, and V. Seppänen. Toward a practical solution for capturing knowledge for software projects. *IEEE Softw.*, 19(3):60–62, 2002.

[18] I. Kondratova and I. Goldfarb. Design concepts for virtual research and collaborative environments. In *Proc. of the 10th ISPE Intl. Conf. on Concurrent Engineering*, pages 797–803, The Netherlands, 2003. A. A. Balkema Publishers.

[19] T. C. Lethbridge, J. Singer, and A. Forward. How software engineers use documentation: The state of the practice. *IEEE Softw.*, 20(6):35–39, 2003.

[20] B. Leuf and W. Cunningham. *The Wiki way: quick collaboration on the Web*. Addison-Wesley Longman Publishing Co., Inc., Boston, MA, USA, 2001.

[21] D. R. Millen. Community portals and collective goods: Conversation archives as an information resource. In *Proc. of the 33rd Hawaii Intl. Conf. on System Sciences - Volume 3*, page 3030, Washington, DC, USA, 2000. IEEE.

[22] S. Nerur and V. Balijepally. Theoretical reflections on agile development methodologies. *Commun. ACM*, 50(3):79–83, 2007.

[23] D. L. Parnas and P. C. Clements. A rational design process: How and why to fake it. *IEEE Trans. Softw. Eng.*, 12(2):251–257, 1986.

[24] A. L. Powell, J. C. French, and J. C. Knight. A systematic approach to creating and maintaining software documentation. In *SAC '96: Proc. of the Symp. on Applied Computing*, pages 201–208, New York, NY, USA, 1996. ACM.

[25] P. N. Robillard. The role of knowledge in software development. *Commun. ACM*, 42(1):87–92, 1999.

[26] J. Rowley. What is knowledge management. *Library Management*, 20(8):416–419, 1999.

[27] I. Rus and M. Lindvall. Guest editors' introduction: Knowledge management in software engineering. *IEEE Softw.*, 19(3):26–38, 2002.

[28] M. Visconti and C. R. Cook. An overview of industrial software documentation practice. In *SCCC '02: Proc. of the XII Intl. Conf. of the Chilean Computer Science Society*, page 179, Washington, DC, USA, 2002. IEEE.

Proving Programs Robust *

Swarat Chaudhuri
Rice University
swarat@rice.edu

Sumit Gulwani
Microsoft Research
sumitg@microsoft.com

Roberto Lublinerman
Pennsylvania State University
rluble@psu.edu

Sara Navidpour
Pennsylvania State University
ssn123@psu.edu

ABSTRACT

We present a program analysis for verifying *quantitative robustness properties* of programs, stated generally as: "If the inputs of a program are perturbed by an arbitrary amount ϵ, then its outputs change at most by $K\epsilon$, where K can depend on the size of the input but not its value." Robustness properties generalize the analytic notion of continuity—e.g., while the function e^x is continuous, it is not robust. Our problem is to verify the robustness of a function P that is coded as an imperative program, and can use diverse data types and features such as branches and loops.

Our approach to the problem soundly decomposes it into two subproblems: (a) verifying that the *smallest possible* perturbations to the inputs of P do not change the corresponding outputs significantly, even if control now flows along a different control path; and (b) verifying the robustness of the computation along each control-flow path of P. To solve the former subproblem, we build on an existing method for verifying that a program encodes a *continuous function* [5]. The latter is solved using a static analysis that bounds the magnitude of the slope of any function computed by a control flow path of P. The outcome is a sound program analysis for robustness that uses proof obligations which do not refer to ϵ-changes and can often be fully automated using off-the-shelf SMT-solvers.

We identify three application domains for our analysis. First, our analysis can be used to guarantee the predictable execution of embedded control software, whose inputs come from physical sources and can suffer from error and uncertainty. A guarantee of robustness ensures that the system does not react disproportionately to such uncertainty. Second, our analysis is directly applicable to *approximate computation*, and can be used to provide foundations for a recently-proposed program approximation scheme called *loop perforation*. A third application is in database privacy: proofs of robustness of queries are essential to *differential privacy*, the most popular notion of privacy for statistical databases.

*This research was supported by NSF CAREER Award #0953507 ("Robustness Analysis of Uncertain Programs: Theory, Algorithms, and Tools").

Permission to make digital or hard copies of all or part of this work for personal or classroom use is granted without fee provided that copies are not made or distributed for profit or commercial advantage and that copies bear this notice and the full citation on the first page. To copy otherwise, to republish, to post on servers or to redistribute to lists, requires prior specific permission and/or a fee.
ESEC/FSE'11, September 5–9, 2011, Szeged, Hungary.
Copyright 2011 ACM 978-1-4503-0443-6/11/09 ...$10.00.

Categories and Subject Descriptors

F.3.2 [**Logics and Meanings of Programs**]: Semantics of programming languages—*Program analysis*.; F.3.1 [**Logics and Meanings of Programs**]: Specifying and Verifying and Reasoning about Programs—*Mechanical verification*; G.1.0 [**Numerical Analysis**]: General—*Error analysis*

General Terms

Theory, Verification

Keywords

Lipschitz, Continuity, Quantitative Program Analysis, Sensitivity, Robustness, Uncertainty, Perturbations, Program Approximation.

1. INTRODUCTION

Uncertainty in computation [12] has long been a topic of interest to computer science. Depending on the context, uncertainty in the operation of programs can be a curse or a blessing. On one hand, uncertain operating environments may cause system failures—consider, for example, an aircraft controller that reacts unpredictably to noisy sensor data and causes a crash. On the other hand, randomized and approximate algorithms deliberately inject uncertainty into their data to trade off quality of results for better performance. Uncertainty of both forms is rife in a world where cyber-physical systems are ubiquitous [15] and applications suited to approximation and randomization are ascendant. Love or hate uncertainty, you increasingly cannot ignore it.

Robustness is a system property critical to reasoning about program behavior under uncertainty. A program is robust (in the sense of this paper) if a perturbation to its inputs can only lead to proportional changes in its outputs. This means that a robust avionic controller reacts predictably to noise in the measurements made by the plane's sensors. Also, if a program P is robust, then the output $P(x)$ of P on an input x can be approximated "safely" by $P(x')$, where x' is a value close to x—as x and x' are close, so must be $P(x)$ and $P(x')$. If uncertainty is our enemy, a proof of robustness shows that our program is relatively safe from it; if we want to introduce uncertainty in our computation for performance gains, robustness ensures that it is safe to do so.

```
DIJK(G : graph, src : node)
for each node v in G
    d[v] :=⊥;   prev[v] := UNDEF ;
d[src] := 0;   WL := set of all nodes in G;
while WL ≠ ∅
    choose node w ∈ WL such that d[w] is minimal;
    remove w from WL;
    for each neighbor v of w
        z := d[w] + G[w, v];
        if z < d[v]
            then   d[v] := z;   prev[v] := w
```

Figure 1: Dijkstra's shortest-path algorithm

A system to formally verify the robustness of everyday programs would then seem to be of considerable practical importance. A step to this end was taken by Chaudhuri et al [5], who presented a program analysis to verify that a program encodes a *continuous function*. A function is continuous if *infinitesimal*—or arbitrarily small—changes to its inputs can only cause infinitesimal changes to its outputs. This makes such a function robust in a sense. Such a formulation of robustness is particularly valuable in the setting of programs, where violation of robustness is often due to discontinuities introduced by control constructs like branches and loops. A provably continuous program is free from violations of this sort. At the same time, continuity is too weak a robustness property for many settings, as a small but non-infinitesimal change to the inputs of a continuous function can create disproportionately large changes to its outputs. For example, while the function e^x is continuous, there is no bound on the change in its output on a small finite change to its input x.

In this paper, we investigate a stronger, quantitative formulation of robustness of programs that does not suffer from this limitation. We believe that this formulation, based on the analytic notion of *Lipschitz continuity*, is a canonical notion of robustness for programs. By this definition, a program is robust if a change of $\pm\epsilon$ to its inputs, for any ϵ, results in a change of $\pm K\epsilon$ to its outputs, where K does not depend on the values of the input variables. The multiplier K—known as the *robustness parameter*—quantifies the extent of this robustness.

For example, consider the implementation *Dijk* of Dijkstra's shortest-paths algorithm in Fig. 1—here G is a graph with real-valued edge-weights and N edges, and *src* is the source node. The output of the program is the table d of shortest-path distances in G. We note that *Dijk* is robust with a robustness parameter N (from now on, N*-robust*): if each edge-weight in G changes by $\pm\epsilon$, then each output $d[i]$ changes at most by $\pm N\epsilon$. But how do we verify the above robustness property from the text of programs like *Dijk*, which use features like branches, loops, and arrays?

One way is to first prove that *Dijk* computes shortest paths, and then to establish that the costs of these paths change proportionally on changes to the edge-weights of G. Such a proof, however, would be highly specialized and impossible to automate. Our goal, instead, is to develop a proof system that reasons about robustness without having to prove full functional correctness, is applicable to a wide range of algorithms, and is mostly automated.

To see how we achieve this goal, consider programs like *Dijk* whose inputs and outputs are from dense domains. Key to our analysis of robustness for such programs P is the following metatheorem: P is K-robust if, first, P encodes a continuous function, and, second, each control flow path of P computes a function that is linear in the values (but not the size) of the input, and the magnitude of the slope of this line is bounded by K. The first property accounts for the possibility of different control flow on the perturbed and unperturbed input, and can be verified using an existing analysis [5]. As for the latter property, we offer a new static analysis for it. The final outcome is a program analysis that can verify the robustness of programs over continuous data types, can be automated using off-the-shelf SMT-solvers (we provide an implementation on top of the Z3 solver), and can verify the robustness of many everyday programs. For example, we establish the property for the program *Dijk* by showing that: (1) The effect of each loop iteration on the array d can be written as $d[v_1] := c_1 \cdot d[v_2] + c_2 \cdot a + c_3$, where a is the weight of some edge of G, $d[v_1]$ and $d[v_2]$ are elements of d, and c_1, c_2, c_3 are constants with $|c_1| \leq 1$ and $|c_2| \leq 1$; and (2) Each edge-weight of the input graph G is used *only once* as an operand during an addition.

We identify three application domains for our analysis. First, our analysis can be used to guarantee the predictable execution of embedded control programs, whose inputs come from physical sources and can therefore be noisy or uncertain. Second, we investigate the application of our system in approximate computations that trade off accuracy of results for resource savings. In particular, we demonstrate that a robustness analysis can be used to provide foundations for a recently-proposed program approximation heuristic called *loop perforation* [20]. Third, our analysis can be used in the synthesis of information release mechanisms that satisfy *differential privacy* [10], perhaps the most popular definition of privacy for statistical databases.

Summary of contributions and organization

Now we summarize this paper's contributions:

- We give a canonical, quantitative definition of robustness of programs (Sec. 2).
- We present a sound program analysis that can be used to verify the robustness of a given program (Sec. 3). (Sec. 5).
- We present a prototype implementation of our proof system, built on top of the Z3 SMT-solver (Sec. 5).
- We identify three application domains for our analysis. (Sec. 4)

2. ROBUSTNESS OF PROGRAMS

Now we formalize our notion of robustness of programs. We begin by fixing a language IMP of imperative arithmetic programs. For simplicity, we allow IMP only two data types: reals (`real`) and arrays of reals (`realarr`). Other popular types such as records, tuples, and functional lists/trees can be added without changing the analysis significantly. Our robustness analysis can be extended to programs with discrete typed inputs such as integers. We intend to present this extension in a future work. Also, we assume that reals in IMP are infinite-precision rather than floating-point, and treat arithmetic and comparison operations on them as unit-time oracles. Thus, our programs are equivalent to Blum-Shub-Smale Turing machines [2]. While this idealized semantics rules out reasoning about floating-point rounding errors, we can use it to prove the absence of robustness bugs due to flawed logic (arguably, it is this semantics that forms the mental model of programmers as they design numerical algorithms). We intend to pursue a floating-point modeling of continuous data in future work.

As for perturbations, they can change the *value* of a datum but not its type or size, the latter being 1 if the datum is a real, and N if it is an array of length N. We assume, for each type τ and size N, a *metric*[1] $d_{\tau,N}$. An ϵ-change to a value x of type τ and size N is assumed to result in a value y, of type τ and size N, such that $d_{\tau,N}(x,y) = \epsilon$. In particular, the type `real` is associated with the Euclidean metric, defined as $d_{\mathtt{real},1}(x,y) = |x-y|$. We let an ϵ-change to an array consist of ϵ-changes to any number of its elements. Formally, the metric over arrays of length N whose elements are of type τ is the L_∞-*norm*:

$$d_{\text{array of } \tau, N}(A,B) = \max_i \{d_\tau(A[i], B[i])\}.$$

Now we offer the syntax of arithmetic expressions e, boolean expressions b, and programs P in Imp:

$$\begin{array}{lcl} e & ::= & x \mid c \mid e_1 + e_2 \mid e_1 \cdot e_2 \mid A[i] \\ b & ::= & e > 0 \mid e = 0 \mid b_1 \wedge b_2 \mid \neg b \\ P & ::= & \textbf{skip} \mid x := e \mid A[i] := e \mid \textbf{if } b \textbf{ then } P_1 \textbf{ else } P_2 \\ & & \mid \textbf{while } b \textbf{ do } P_1 \mid P_1; P_2 \end{array}$$

Here x is a variable, c is a constant, A is an array variable, i an integer variable or constant, and the arithmetic and boolean operators are as usual. We let each statement be annotated with a distinct *label*.

As for semantics, let us only consider programs P that *terminate on all inputs*. The semantics of P is the standard denotational semantics [27] for imperative programs (except as mentioned earlier, we assume unit-time operations on reals). Formally, let us associate with each variable x a set $Cloc(x)$ of *concrete memory locations*. A *state* of P is a map σ that assigns a value in Val_τ to each program variable x of type τ. We denote the set of all states of P by $\Sigma(P)$. Each state induces, in the usual way, an assignment of *contents* to each location $y \in Cloc(x)$, for each variable x. We use the notation $\sigma(y)$ to denote the content of location y at state σ. The semantics of the program P, and an expression e of type τ appearing in it, are now defined by two functions $[\![P]\!] : \Sigma(P) \to \Sigma(P)$ and $[\![e]\!] : \Sigma(P) \to Val_\tau$, where Val_τ is the set of values of type τ. Intuitively, $[\![e]\!](\sigma)$ is the value of e at state σ, and $[\![P]\!](\sigma)$ is the state at which P terminates after starting execution from σ. In addition, we assume definitions of *control flow paths* (sequences of labels) and *executions* (sequences of states) of P. These definitions are all standard, and hence omitted.

Robustness of programs. Our definition of robustness of programs is based on the analytic notion of *Lipschitz continuity* [1]. Intuitively, a program P is K-robust if any additive ϵ-change to the input of P can only change the output of P by $\pm K\epsilon$. Note that ϵ is arbitrary, so that the output of a K-robust program changes proportionally on *any* change to the inputs, and not just small ones.

As a program can have multiple inputs and outputs, we define robustness with respect to an *input variable* x_{in} and an *output variable* x_{out}. If P is robust with respect to x_{in} and x_{out}, a change to the initial value of any x_{in}, while keeping the remaining variables fixed, must only cause a proportional change to the final value of x_{out}. Variables other than x_{out} can change arbitrarily.

Also, we allow robustness parameters that are not just constants, but depend on the *size of the input*. For example, suppose the size of x_{in} is N, and an ϵ-change to it changes the output by $N\epsilon$. Then P is N-*robust* with respect to x_{in}. We model this by letting a robustness parameter K be a function of type $\mathbb{N} \to \mathbb{R}$, rather than just a real.

Finally, our definition allows a program to be robust only within a certain subset Σ' of the input space, without assertions about the effect of perturbations on states outside Σ' (capturing the fact that many realistic programs are robust only within certain regions of their input space).

Formally, for a variable x (say of type τ) and a state σ, let $Size(x,\sigma)$ be the size of the value of x at σ. Now let $\epsilon \in \mathbb{R}^+$; also let $\sigma' \in \Sigma(P)$ such that $\sigma(x,\sigma) = Size(x,\sigma') = N$. The state σ' is an (ϵ,x)-*perturbation* of σ, and is denoted by $Pert_{\epsilon,x}(\sigma,\sigma')$, if $d_{\tau,N}(\sigma(x),\sigma'(x)) < \epsilon$, and for all other variables y, we have $\sigma(y) = \sigma'(y)$. The states σ and σ' are (ϵ,x)-*close* (written as $\sigma \approx_{\epsilon,x} \sigma'$) if $d_{\tau,m}(\sigma(x),\sigma'(x)) < \epsilon$. Now we define:

Definition 1 (Robustness of programs). *Consider a function $K : \mathbb{N} \to \mathbb{R}$ and a set of states $\Sigma' \subseteq \Sigma$. The program P is* K-robust *within Σ' with respect to the input x_{in} and the output x_{out} if for all $\sigma, \sigma' \in \Sigma'$ and $\epsilon \in \mathbb{R}^+$, we have*

$$Pert_{\epsilon,x_{in}}(\sigma,\sigma') \Longrightarrow [\![P]\!](\sigma) \approx_{m,x_{out}} [\![P]\!](\sigma')$$

where $m = K(Size(x_{in},\sigma)) \cdot \epsilon$. □

Definition 2 (Continuity of programs [5]). *The program P is continuous within $\Sigma' \subseteq \Sigma$ with respect to the input x_{in} and the output x_{out} if for all $\epsilon \in \mathbb{R}^+, \sigma \in \Sigma'$, there exists a $\delta \in \mathbb{R}^+$ such that for all $\sigma' \in \Sigma'$,*

$$Pert_{\delta,x_{in}}(\sigma,\sigma') \Longrightarrow [\![P]\!](\sigma) \approx_{\epsilon,x_{out}} [\![P]\!](\sigma'). \quad \square$$

If P is continuous by the above, then *infinitesimal* perturbations to x_{in} (that keep the state within the set Σ') can only cause infinitesimal changes to x_{out}. Not all continuous programs are robust. For example, a program computing x^2, given arbitrary $x \in \mathbb{R}$, is continuous but non-robust. Now we consider a few everyday programs that are robust or continuous by the above definitions:

Example 1 (Sorting). *Consider a correct implementation P of a sorting algorithm that takes in an array A_{in} of reals, and returns a sorted array A_{out}. The program is 1-robust, with respect to input A_{in} and output A_{out}, within $\Sigma(P)$: for any $\epsilon > 0$, if each element of A_{in} is perturbed at most by $\pm\epsilon$, then the maximum change to an element of the output A_{out} is $\pm\epsilon$ as well. Note that this observation is not at all obvious, as we are speaking of* arbitrary *changes to A_{in} here, and as even the minutest change to A_{in} can alter the position of a given item in A_{out} arbitrarily.*

Example 2 (Shortest paths, MSTs). *Let SP be a correct implementation of a shortest-path algorithm (e.g., Dijk; Fig. 1). We view the graph G on which SP operates as a perturbable array of reals such that $G[i]$ is the weight of the i-th edge. An ϵ-change to G thus amounts to a maximum*

[1] Recall that a *metric* over a set S is a function $d : S \times S \to \mathbb{R} \cup \{\infty\}$ such that for all x, y, z, we have: (1) $d(x,y) \geq 0$, with $d(x,y) = 0$ iff $x = y$; (2) $d(x,y) = d(y,x)$; and (3) $d(x,y) + d(y,z) \geq d(x,z)$.

```
KRUSKAL(G : graph)
for each node v in G do  C[v] := {v};
WL := set of all edges in G; cost := 0; T := ∅;
while WL ≠ ∅
    choose edge (v, w) ∈ WL
            such that G(v, w) is minimal;
    remove (v, w) from WL;
    if C[v] ≠ C[w] then
            add edge (v, w) to T;
            cost := cost + G(v, w);
            C[v] := C[w] := C[v] ∪ C[w];
```

Figure 2: Kruskal's algorithm

change of $\pm\epsilon$ to any edge-weight of G, while keeping the node and edge structure intact.

One output of SP is the array d of shortest-path distances in G—i.e., $d[i]$ is the length of the shortest path from the source node src to the i-th node u_i of G. A second output is the array π whose i-th element is a sequence of nodes forming a minimal-weight path between src and u_i. Let the distance between two elements of π be 0 if they are identical, and ∞ otherwise.

As it happens, SP is N-robust everywhere within $\Sigma(P)$ with respect to the output d—if each edge weight in G changes by an amount ϵ, a shortest path weight can change at most by $(N\epsilon)$. However, an ϵ-change to G may add or subtract elements from π—i.e., perturb π by the amount ∞. Therefore, SP is not K-robust with respect to the output π for any K.

Similar arguments apply to a program MST computing minimum spanning trees in a graph G (Kruskal's algorithm; Fig. 2). Suppose the program has two outputs: a sequence T of edges forming a minimum spanning tree, and the cost of this tree. MST is N-robust within $\Sigma(MST)$ if the output is cost, but not robust if the output is T.

3. VERIFYING ROBUSTNESS

In this section, we present our program analysis for robustness. The inputs of the analysis are a program P, symbolic encodings of a set Σ' of $\Sigma(P)$ and a function $K : \mathbb{N} \to \mathbb{R}$, an input variable x_{in}, and an output variable x_{out}. Our goal is to soundly judge P K-robust within Σ' with respect to x_{in} and x_{out}.

3.1 Piecewise K-robustness and K-linearity

Consider, first, the simple scenario where P has a single real-valued variable x. Note that each control flow path of P computes a differentiable function over the inputs. Now suppose we can show that each control flow path of P represents a robust computation (in this case, P is said to be *piecewise K-robust*). Piecewise robustness does not entail robustness: a perturbation to the initial value of x can cause P to execute along a different control flow path, leading to a completely different final state. However, if P is *continuous* as well as piecewise K-robust, then P is K-robust as well, e.g. the function $abs(x) = |x|$, where $x \in \mathbb{R}$, is continuous as well as piecewise 1-robust—hence 1-robust. On the other hand, the continuous function "**if**$(x > 0)$**then**x^2**else**x" is nonrobust because x^2 is not piecewise robust within $x \in \mathbb{R}$.

The above observation can be generalized to settings where P has multiple variables of different types. Our analysis exploits it to decompose the problem of robustness analysis into two independent subproblems: that of verifying continuity and piecewise K-robustness of P.

For any program P and any set of states Σ' of P, let $\Sigma'_{(i)}$ denote the set of states $\sigma \in \Sigma'$ such that starting from σ, P executes along its i-th control flow path (we assume a global order on control flow paths). Let us now define:

DEFINITION 3 (PIECEWISE K-ROBUSTNESS). *Let P be a program, $\Sigma' \subseteq \Sigma(P)$ a set of states, K a function of type $\mathbb{N} \to \mathbb{R}$, and $x_{in}, x_{out} \in Var(P)$. P is* piecewise K-robust *within $\Sigma' \subseteq \Sigma(P)$ with respect to input x_{in} and output x_{out} if for all i, P is K-robust within $\Sigma_{(i)}$ with respect to x_{in} and x_{out}.*

We establish piecewise robustness using the weaker property of *piecewise K-linearity*, which says that the function computed by each control flow path of P is a linear function, and that the absolute value of its slope is bounded by K:

DEFINITION 4 (PIECEWISE K-LINEARITY). *Let P be a program, $\Sigma' \subseteq \Sigma(P)$ a set of states, K a function of type $\mathbb{N} \to \mathbb{R}$, and $x_{in}, x_{out} \in Var(P)$. P is* K-linear *within Σ' w.r.t. input x_{in} and output x_{out} if for each $z \in Cloc(x_{in})$, $y \in Cloc(x_{out})$, $\sigma \in \Sigma'$, we have the relationship*

$$([\![P]\!](\sigma))(y) \quad = \quad \left(\sum_{z \in Cloc(x_{in})} c_{z,y} \cdot z \right) + \tau,$$

where τ is an expression whose free variables range over the set $\bigcup_{x' \neq x_{in}} Cloc(x')$, and $\sum_z |c_{z,y}| \leq K(Size(x_{in}, \sigma))$. P is piecewise K-linear *within $\Sigma' \subseteq \Sigma(P)$ with respect to input x_{in} and output x_{out} if for all i, P is K-linear within $\Sigma_{(i)}$ with respect to x_{in} and x_{out}.*

It is not hard to see that:

THEOREM 1. *If P is piecewise K-linear, then P is piecewise K-robust.*

EXAMPLE 3 (DIJKSTRA'S ALGORITHM). *Consider, once again, the procedure Dijk in Fig. 1. While the dependence between G and d is complex, Dijk is piecewise N-robust in G and d. To see why, consider any control flow path π of Dijk and view it as a straight-line program. Suppose the addition operation in Line 8 of Dijk is executed M times in this program. As we only remove elements from the worklist WL, a specific edge $G[w, v]$ is used at most once as an operand of this addition. Consequently, we have $M \leq N$, where N is the size of G. Let M' be the number of times Line 10 assigns the result of this addition to an element of d. We have $M' \leq M \leq N$. It is easy to see that this means that π is N-linear with respect to input G and output d. As the set of control flow paths in Dijk is countable and each path is N-linear with respect to G and d, Dijk is piecewise N-robust within $\Sigma(Dijk)$ with respect to G and d.*

3.2 Robustness

Now we apply the notion of piecewise robustness and piecewise linearity in the analysis of robustness.

THEOREM 2. *Let P be a program, $\Sigma' \subseteq \Sigma(P)$, and x_{in} and x_{out} be variables of dense types. P is K-robust within*

```
INSERTION-SORT(A : realarr)
for i := 1 to (|A| − 1)
    z := A[i]; j := i − 1;
    while j ≥ 0 and A[j] > z
        A[j + 1] := A[j]; j := j − 1;
    A[j + 1] := z;
```

Figure 3: Insertion sort

Σ' with respect to input x_{in} and output x_{out} if and only if: (1) P is continuous within Σ' w.r.t. input x_{in} and output x_{out}; and (2) P is piecewise K-robust within Σ' with respect to input x_{in} and output x_{out}.

By Theorem 2, the problem of robustness analysis can be decomposed soundly and completely into the problems of verifying continuity and piecewise robustness. We establish these conditions independently. The first criterion is proved using a sound program analysis due to Chaudhuri et al [5] (from now on, we call this system CONT). To prove the second property, we prove P to be piecewise K-linear, and use Theorem 1. However, for reasons outlined later, no existing sound abstraction that we know of is suited to precise and efficient analysis of piecewise linearity—a new solution is needed.

Piecewise linearity using arithmetic-freedom

It is sometimes possible to establish piecewise linearity using traditional dataflow analysis. Let a program Q be free of arithmetic operations—i.e., if $x := e$ is an assignment in the program, then the evaluation of e does not require arithmetic. In this case, each control flow path in Q encodes a 1-linear function, which means that Q is piecewise 1-linear. Generalizing, let a program P be *arithmetic-free* with respect to input x_{in} and outputs x_{out} if all data flows from x_{in} to x_{out} are free of arithmetic operations. A program can be shown arithmetic-free in this sense using standard slicing techniques. We can use a program like Q above as an abstraction of P. Application in the verification of piecewise robustness stems from the fact that:

THEOREM 3. *If a program P is arithmetic-free within $\Sigma' \subseteq \Sigma(P)$ with respect to input x_{in} and output x_{out}, then P is piecewise 1-linear within Σ' with respect to input x_{in} and output x_{out}.*

EXAMPLE 4 (SORTING). *The seemingly trivial abstraction of arithmetic-freedom can in fact be used to prove the robustness of several challenging, array-manipulating algorithms. Consider Insertion Sort (Fig. 3), where the array A is the input as well as the output. A lightweight analysis can prove this algorithm arithmetic-free, at all input states, with respect to the input A and output A. While arithmetic does occur in the program, it only updates the index i, whose value does not depend on the original contents of A. Other algorithms like Mergesort and Bubblesort can be proved arithmetic-free in the same way. Separately, we prove these algorithms continuous using* CONT, *which gives us a proof of 1-robustness.*

Piecewise linearity with robustness matrices

In most realistic programs, however, arithmetic-freedom will not suffice, and some form of quantitative reasoning will be

$$\text{(Skip)}\ \frac{}{\textbf{skip} \vdash \mathbf{I}}$$

$$\text{(Assign)}\ \frac{}{x_i := e \vdash \nabla} \quad \text{where}$$

$$\forall j,k : \nabla_{jk} = \begin{cases} \left|\frac{\partial e}{\partial x_k}\right| & \text{if } j = i \text{ and } \frac{\partial e}{\partial x_k} \text{ is constant} \\ \infty & \text{if } j = i \text{ and } \frac{\partial e}{\partial x_k} \text{ depends on the } x_m\text{-s} \\ 1 & \text{if } j = k \neq i \\ 0 & \text{otherwise} \end{cases}$$

$$\text{(Weaken)}\ \frac{P' \vdash \nabla \qquad \forall i,j : \nabla_{ij} \leq \nabla'_{ij}}{P' \vdash \nabla'}$$

$$\text{(Sequence)}\ \frac{P_1 \vdash \nabla_1 \qquad P_2 \vdash \nabla_2}{P_1; P_2 \vdash \nabla_2 \cdot \nabla_1}$$

$$\text{(Ite)}\ \frac{P_1 \vdash \nabla_1 \qquad P_2 \vdash \nabla_2}{\textbf{if } b \textbf{ then } P_1 \textbf{ else } P_2 \vdash \max(\nabla_1, \nabla_2)}$$

$$\text{(While)}\ \frac{P' = \textbf{while } b \textbf{ do } P'' \qquad P'' \vdash \nabla'' \qquad Bound(P', M)}{P' \vdash (\nabla'')^M}$$

Figure 4: System ROBMAT **for propagating robustness matrices**

necessary. A natural first question is: can we use a traditional numerical abstract domain—such as polyhedra [9]—for such reasoning? The answer, unfortunately, seems to be no. Consider the program

$$\textbf{if } (x + y > 0) \textbf{ then } z := x + y \textbf{ else } z := -x - y$$

Our goal is to prove this program piecewise 1-linear with respect to input x and output y. Unfortunately, the best invariant that we can establish at the end of the branch using the polyhedra domain is $(z \geq x + y) \wedge (z \geq -x - y)$. These constraints permit z to be a linear function of x with slope equal to ∞—hence the best we can say is that the program is ∞-robust! The key issue here is that we need a form of *disjunctive* reasoning to track quantities (absolute values of slopes) computed along different paths. While there is a plethora of abstract domains for disjunctive reasoning about programs [6, 7], none of them, so far as we know, is suitable for this purpose. Now we present a simple static analysis that fulfils our needs.

Here, an abstract state—known as a *robustness matrix*—tracks, for each pair of memory locations x and y, a bound on the slope of the expression relating the current value of x to the initial value of y. This information is propagated through the program using an abstract interpretation.

For brevity, we make a few simplifying assumptions in this presentation. First, we assume that all variables of P are real valued. The analysis that we have actually implemented can handle arrays by abstracting each unbounded array using a finite number of abstract memory locations. As this array abstraction is standard but adds significantly to the notation, we omit its details. Also, we only show how to derive piecewise linearity judgments holding over the entire space $\Sigma(P)$. A generalization to judgments conditioned by $\Sigma' \subseteq \Sigma(P)$ is, however, easy to construct. Finally, we view a program state not as a map but as a vector $\langle r_1, \ldots, r_n \rangle$, where r_i is the value of the i-th variable x_i. The denotational semantics of any program Q is thus a function $[\![Q]\!] : \mathbb{R}^n \to \mathbb{R}^n$. Now we define a *robustness matrix* ∇ for P to be an $n \times n$ matrix whose elements ∇_{ij} are non-negative reals.

To understand the interpretation of this matrix, we recall the classic definition of a *Jacobian* from vector calcu-

```
x := a {∇_{x,a} = 1}
y := b {∇_{x,a} = 1, ∇_{y,b} = 1}
if (x ≤ y)
    then   z := −2x + y
  {∇_{x,a} = 1, ∇_{y,b} = 1, ∇_{z,x} = 2, ∇_{z,y} = 1, ∇_{z,a} = 2, ∇_{z,b} = 1}
    else   z := 3y + x; {∇_{x,a} = 1, ∇_{y,b} = 1, ∇_{z,x} = 1,
                         ∇_{z,y} = 3, ∇_{z,a} = 1, ∇_{z,b} = 3}
{∇_{x,a} = 1, ∇_{y,b} = 1, ∇_{z,x} = 2, ∇_{z,y} = 3, ∇_{z,a} = 2, ∇_{z,b} = 3}
```

Figure 5: Piecewise robustness using robustness matrices

lus. The Jacobian of a function $f : \mathbb{R}^n \to \mathbb{R}^n$ with inputs $x_1^{in}, \ldots, x_n^{in} \in \mathbb{R}$ and outputs $x_1, \ldots, x_n \in \mathbb{R}$ is the matrix

$$J_f = \begin{pmatrix} \frac{\partial x_1}{\partial x_1^{in}} & \cdots & \frac{\partial x_1}{\partial x_n^{in}} \\ \cdots & & \cdots \\ \frac{\partial x_n}{\partial x_1^{in}} & \cdots & \frac{\partial x_n}{\partial x_n^{in}} \end{pmatrix}$$

If f is a differentiable function, then for each x_i and x_j^{in}, it is K-robust with respect to input x_j and output x_i, where K is any upper bound on $|\frac{\partial x_i}{\partial x_j^{in}}|$. In our setting, the expression relating the inputs and outputs of a single control flow path is differentiable; consequently, we can verify the robustness of this expression by propagating a Jacobian along it (strictly, entries in the actual matrix that we carry are constant upper bounds on the absolute values of the terms $\partial x_i / \partial x_j^{in}$). It is possible to carry out this propagation using the chain rule of differentiation. Of course, due to branches, a program P need not be differentiable. This is where abstract interpretation comes handy—we *merge* multiple Jacobians propagated along different paths into a *robustness matrix* that overestimates the robustness parameter of P. Such a merge demands an abstract join operator $\sqcup$: for robustness matrices ∇ and ∇', we define $(\nabla \sqcup \nabla')$ to be the matrix M such that for all i, j, we have $M_{ij} = \max(\nabla_{ij}, \nabla'_{ij})$.

Note that with the above strategy, we will infer robustness matrices even for discontinuous programs. This is, of course, acceptable, as the present analysis only verifies piecewise robustness—continuity is judged separately by CONT.

The goal of our analysis—call it ROBMAT—is to syntactically derive facts of the form $P' \vdash \nabla$, read as: "∇ is the robustness matrix for the subprogram P'." The structural rules for the analysis are shown in Fig. 4. Here, $\mathbf{I}$ is the identity matrix. The assertion $Bound(P', M)$ states that the while-loop P' terminates in M or less steps—this condition can be established either via an auxiliary checker or by manual annotation (here M is a constant; in settings involving arrays, M can be a function of the size of the input). We observe that the robustness matrix for $P_1; P_2$ obtained by multiplying the matrices for P_1 and P_2—this rule follows from the chain rule of calculus. This rule is generalized into the rule for while-loops. We have:

THEOREM 4. *If the system* ROBMAT *derives the judgment* $P \vdash \nabla$, *then for all* i, j, P *is piecewise* ∇_{ij}*-linear within* $\Sigma(P)$ *with respect to the input* x_j *and the output* x_i.

EXAMPLE 5. *Fig. 5 shows the result of applying a dataflow analysis based on* ROBMAT *to a simple program. The annotations depict the robustness matrices* ∇ *propagated to the various program points—we use the more readable notation* $\nabla_{y,z}$ *to refer to the matrix entry* ∇_{ij} *if* y *and* z *are respectively the* i*-th and* j*-th variables. Observe, in particular, how the robustness matrices from the two branches of the program are merged.*

$$P \;::=\; \langle\text{all syntactic forms in } \textsc{Imp}\rangle \mid \langle\text{the form } Q \text{ below}\rangle$$

```
l: while b
     θ := nondeterministically chosen u ∈ U;
     R(U, θ, x_in[θ], x_out)
```

Figure 6: The language LIMP (P represents programs).

$$(\text{LinLoop})\;\frac{UseOnce(\theta, U, Q) \qquad PLin(R, k, x_{in}[\theta], x_{out}) \qquad PLin(R, 1, x_{out}, x_{out})}{PLin(Q, k.N, x_{in}, x_{out})}$$

Figure 7: Proof rule LINLOOP (Q is an abstract loop)

Piecewise linearity with linear loops

A problem with the robustness matrix abstraction is that it does not satisfactorily handle loops iterating over unbounded data structures. For example, let us try to use it to prove Dijkstra's algorithm (Fig. 1) piecewise linear w.r.t. input G and output d. Here, each iteration makes multiple assignments to d and is consequently piecewise K-linear for $K \geq 2$. As the main loop iterates N times, the complete algorithm is then piecewise $O(2^N)$-robust. However, by the reasoning in Ex. 3, Dijkstra's algorithm is piecewise N-linear. Now we present an abstraction that can establish this and similar facts. A key insight here is to treat the locations of the input variable x_{in} as *resources*, and to establish an assertion of the form "Each location of x_{in} is used at most once during the execution of the loop."

To express our conservative abstractions, we extend the language IMP with a syntactic form for loops with restricted nondeterministic choice. We call this extended language LIMP. Its syntax is as in Figure 6. Here:

- U is a set—the *iteration space* for the loop in the syntactic form Q. Its elements are called *choices*.
- x_{in} is an unbounded data structure (e.g. an array).
- θ is a special variable, called the *current choice variable*. Every iteration starts by picking an element of U and storing it in θ.
- x_{out} is the output variable.
- $R(U, \theta, x_{in}[\theta], x_{out})$ (henceforth R) is an IMP program that does not write to θ, or use elements of x_{in} other than $x_{in}[\theta]$, but can read θ and read or update the iteration space U, element $x_{in}[\theta]$, and the output x_{out}.

We call a program of form Q an *abstract loop*—henceforth, Q denotes an arbitrary, fixed abstract loop. For simplicity, we only consider the analysis of abstract loops—an extension to all LIMP programs involves a combination of the present abstraction with the previous abstractions. As before, we restrict ourselves to programs that terminate on all inputs.

The main loops in Figs. 1 and 2 are abstract loops. For example, the workset WL, the graph G, the node u, and the array d in Figure 1 respectively correspond to the iteration space U, the input variable x_{in}, the choice variable θ, and the output variable x_{out}.

Now we present a rule (Fig. 7) for proving piecewise N-linearity of LIMP programs. As before, for brevity, we only derive robustness judgments that hold over the entire $\Sigma(P)$. We denote by $PLin(P, k.N, x_{in}, x_{out})$ the judgment "P is piecewise $k.N$-linear within $\Sigma(P)$ with respect to x_{in} and x_{out}."

A key premise for the rule is the assertion $UseOnce(\theta, U, Q)$, which states that the *values of* θ *chosen during a complete execution of* Q *are all distinct.* As the variable θ is used to index the data array x_{in}, we can also see this assertion to mean that each memory location in x_{in} is used at most once during a run of Q. We establish the property $UseOnce(\theta, U, Q)$ using a few syntactic sufficient conditions that apply to several common classes of programs. For example, if Q is a for-loop over the indices of x_{in}, and θ is the (monotonically increasing or decreasing) index variable, then we have $UseOnce(\theta, U, Q)$. For another example, consider Dijkstra's algorithm (Fig. 1), where an element w is removed from the workset WL in each iteration, never to be re-inserted again. In this case, letting Q_{Dijk} be the main loop (Lines 4-10) of the program, we have $UseOnce(w, WL, Q_{Dijk})$. Another example in this class is Kruskal's algorithm (Fig. 2), where we iterate over a workset that initially contains all edges of the input graph. Because edges are removed from but never added to this set, we have a use-once invariant similar to that in *Dijk*. Lastly, observe the premises $PLin(R, k, x_{in}[\theta], x_{out})$ and $PLin(R, 1, x_{out}, x_{out})$. These are typically derived using one of our other abstractions—e.g., robustness matrices.

To see the intuition behind the rule LinLoop, consider the simple case where x_{out} is a `real`. By the premises, the effect of each iteration on x_{out} can be summarized by assignments

$$x_{out} := c_1 \cdot x_{out} + c_2 \cdot x_{in}[\theta] + c_3$$

where c_1, c_2, and c_3 are constants with $|c_1| \leq 1$ and $|c_2| \leq k$. As each location in x_{in} is used only once and our norm over arrays is L_∞, this means the complete loop is piecewise $k.N$-linear with respect to output x_{out}.[2] We can show that:

Theorem 5 (Soundness). *If the rule* LinLoop *infers the judgment* $PLin(Q, N, x_{in}, x_{out})$, *then the abstract loop* Q *is piecewise* N*-linear within* $\Sigma(Q)$ *with respect to input* x_{in} *and output* x_{out}.

Example 6 (Kruskal's algorithm). *For an application of the rule* LinLoop, *consider Kruskal's algorithm (2), whose main loop can be abstracted using an abstract loop. To analyze this loop, we establish the use-once property as discussed earlier. All that is left is to show that the loop body (Line 5-9) is piecewise 1-linear. This is easy to do using the robustness matrix abstraction. A similar strategy applies to several other examples, such as Dijkstra's or Bellman-Ford's shortest-path algorithms.*

4. APPLICATIONS

In this section, we identify three motivating application domains for our analysis. As this paper is primarily a foundational contribution, our discussions here use small, illustrative code fragments. The challenges of scaling to large real-world benchmarks is left for future work.

[2]Interestingly, if the metric for arrays were the L_1-norm rather than the L_∞-norm, then the rule LinLoop would be sound even if we changed its conclusion to $PLin(Q, k, x_{in}, x_{out})$.

```
CALC_TRANS_SLOW_TORQUES(angle : real, speed : real)
limit := 29; pressure1 := 0; pressure2 := 0;
if (angle ≥ 27∧ angle < 35) then limit :=41;
elseif (angle ≥ 35∧ angle < 50) then limit :=63;
elseif (angle ≥ 50∧ angle < 65) then limit :=109;
elseif (angle ≥ 65) then limit := 127;
if (3 * speed ≤ limit)
   then   gear := 3; pressure1 := 1000;
   else   gear := 4; pressure1 := 1000;
if (gear ≥ 3) then pressure2 := 1000
```

Figure 8: Code from a car transmission controller

4.1 Robustness of embedded control software

Robustness is a critical system property for many embedded control systems. The sensor data that drives these systems is often prone to noise and errors, and unpredictable changes to system behavior due to this sort of uncertainty can have catastrophic consequences. A proof that the system reacts predictably to perturbations in its inputs is therefore of crucial practical importance. Unsurprisingly, control theorists have studied the problem of robust controller design thoroughly [28]. However, approaches to the problem in control theory are concerned with deriving abstractly defined laws for robust control, rather than proving the robustness of the software that ultimately implements them. This is a gap that a program analysis of robustness a la our paper can fill.

As an example of how to apply our analysis to this space, we consider the code fragment in Fig. 8, derived from a software implementation of a transmission shift control system [3]. Robustness of this fragment, under a different definition of robustness, was previously studied by Majumdar and Saha [16]. Given the car speed and the throttle angle, the operator `calc_trans_slow_torques` computes a pair of pressure values `pressure1` and `presure2`, which are applied to actuators related to the car transmission system. A careful analysis reveals that the output `pressure1` is constant, which means the function is 1-robust in that output. On the other hand, it is not continuous in the second output `pressure2`, hence is not K-robust for any K. Sec. 5 reports on the results of our implementation on this example.

4.2 Robustness in approximate computation

Another application for our analysis is in *approximate computation*, where the goal is to trade off the accuracy of a computation for resource savings. Rather than approximate solutions for specific problems, language-based program approximation [20] involves program transformations that are just like traditional compiler optimizations but, when applied to a program, lead to an *approximately* equivalent program. Such approaches are especially applicable to domains like image and signal processing, where programs compute continuous values with negotiable accuracy.

While such approximation schemes have been much discussed of late, very little is understood at this time about their theoretical foundations. Now we show that a robustness analysis such as ours can provide foundations for one such scheme, called *loop perforation* [20, 19]. The loop perforation optimization is applicable to expensive computational loops over large datasets; what it does is simply skip every alternate iteration in certain long-running loops. The empirical observation in many cases, this bizarre and obvi-

```
while (...)
  if (y ↦ P(y)), where y ∈ [x[i] − ε, x[i] + ε], is in table
      then    z := F(z, P(y))
      else    z := F(z, P(x[i])); tabulate (x[i] ↦ P(x[i]))
  G(...);
```

Figure 9: Approximate memoization for loops

ously unsound optimization does not significantly affect the accuracy of the final output. In [20], a profiling compiler is proposed that exploits this fact and identifies loop iterations that can be skipped.

As for the theoretical foundations of loop perforation, a recent paper [19] shows that if the loop under consideration follows certain computational patterns and the dataset on which the loop operates follows certain probability distributions, then loop perforation is "probabilistically sound"—i.e., the output of loop perforation is guaranteed to be within reasonable bounds with high probability. Now we show that such a guarantee is available for *any* loop that satisfies certain robustness requirements of the sort studied in this paper. This means that our analysis can be used to identify loops that can be correctly perforated, and can serve as a static guidance mechanism for a perforating compiler.

Approximate memoization. Before we show how robustness relates to loop perforation, let us offer a more general approximation scheme. Consider a loop Q of form

$$\textbf{while}\ (\ldots)\ \{\ z := F(z, P(x[i])); G(\ldots)\}.$$

Here x is a large, read-only array that is the "input variable" for the loop (for simplicity, we let elements of x to be reals). The variable z is the "output variable;" P and F are side-effect-free computations, and $G(\ldots)$ is a procedure that cannot write to z but can have other effects (in particular, it can update i). The function P is expensive, and we would like to eliminate calls to it.

Our first approximation of Q consists of a sort of *approximate memoization* of P. Suppose that, in a loop iteration, prior to making a call to $P(x[i])$, we find that P was previously evaluated on some $x[j]$ such that $x[j] \approx x[i]$. Then rather than evaluating $P(x[i])$, we simply use the (cached) value $P(x[j])$. The pseudocode for the optimized loop is given in Fig. 9. Note that the memoization only applies to P and not to the effectful routine G.

Robustness of Q is needed for this approximation to be "sound." Denote by $Q(x)$ the final value of z on input x; also, suppose Q is K-robust with respect to the input x and output z. In that case, the scheme in Fig. 9 is equivalent to a transformation that replaces Q by a program Q' that, on any input x: (1) perturbs x by an amount $\delta \leq \epsilon$, resulting in an array x'; and (2) returns $Q(x')$. Importantly, Q' evaluates G not on the perturbed array x' but the original array x—this means that the side-effects of Q' (i.e., updates to variables aside from z) are the same as that of Q.

By the robustness of Q, the outputs $Q(x)$ and $Q(x')$ on x and x' differ at most by $K \cdot \epsilon$. If this value is suitably small (and we can make it be, by selecting ϵ suitably), the optimization approximately preserves the semantics of Q. But if Q is non-robust, these two outputs may be very different.

Loop perforation. One obvious objection to the above scheme is that the complexity of table lookup will make it impractical. However, we now demonstrate that under some extra assumptions, this scheme reduces to a scheme that is, almost exactly, loop perforation. First, let us restrict ourselves to for-loops iterating over an array x—i.e., we assume Q to have the form

$$\textbf{for}\ 0 \leq i < N\ \textbf{do}\ z := F(z, P(x[i])); G(\ldots)$$

where $N = |x|$, and the imperative procedure G does not modify either z or the induction variable i of the loop.

Second, let us assume that the input dataset x exhibits *locality*—i.e., any two successive elements in x are approximately equal with high probability. Note that this property holds in most multimedia datasets—for example, in most images neighboring pixels, for the most part, have similar colors. We formalize the above using a model defined in Misailovic et al [19] that views x as a random variable that is generated by a random walk with independent increments. In more detail, the variable $x[0]$ is a fixed constant, and $z_i = x[i+1] - x[i]$ follows a normal distribution $\mathcal{N}$ with mean μ and variance σ^2.

As successive elements in x are likely to be close in value, we can use $x[i]$ for an approximate proxy of the value $x[i+1]$. In that case we can replace Q by a program $\widehat{Q}$ that, rather than computing an entire sequence of values $P(x[i+1]), \ldots, P(x[i+m])$ (for a suitable m), simply uses the cached value $P(x[i])$ as a proxy for each of these. Observe that we have now arrived at an approximation scheme that is quite like loop perforation!

There is, however, an important distinction between this scheme and the version of loop perforation presented in prior work [20, 19]. As the latter scheme skips loop iterations entirely, it is not applicable when the loop body performs discrete computations, pointer updates, etc., in addition to calling P (these computations are encapsulated within the routine G). Perforating these loops may lead not only to inaccurate results but to system crashes. Our approach, on the other hand, does not skip any iterations, but only the call to P inside the iterations.

As for the analysis of error produced by the loop perforation transformation, let us define the *output error* for the transformation to be $Err_Q(x) = d(Q(x), \widehat{Q}(x))$. Now observe that $\widehat{Q}(x) = Q(x')$ where for all i, $(x[i] - x'[i]) \sim \mathcal{N}(\mu, \sigma^2)$. Because we use the L_∞ norm as the distance measure over arrays, we have, for every $a > 0$, the property

$$\begin{aligned} \mathbb{P}[d(x,x') > a] &= \mathbb{P}[\exists i : |x[i] - x'[i]| > a] \\ &\leq N \cdot \mathbb{P}[|x[i] - x'[i]| > a] \\ &\leq N \cdot (1 - (\Phi_{\mathcal{N}}(a) - \Phi_{\mathcal{N}}(-a))) \end{aligned}$$

where $\Phi_{\mathcal{N}}$ is the cumulative distribution function of the distribution $\mathcal{N}$.

Let $\chi = 1 - (\Phi_{\mathcal{N}}(a) - \Phi_{\mathcal{N}}(-a))$. Note that for χ decreases as a increases, and is approximately 0.03 for $a = 3 \cdot \sigma$. By the K-robustness of Q, we have:

$$\mathbb{P}[Err_Q(x) > K \cdot a] \leq N \cdot \chi.$$

The above can be seen as a "probabilistic" soundness result for loop perforation: if the loop Q is robust with a low robustness parameter, then the probability of loop perforation introducing a significant error is low. Indeed, one can give an intuitive interpretation to perforation here: it amounts to sampling the dataset x at a lower frequency, which is acceptable if the process is robust. What all of this means is that

```
INSIDEERROR(FGmap: BinaryImage)
1  samples :=0; error := 0;
2  for cam:= 1 to nCams
3     for cylndr := 0 to nParts
4           s1,s2 := vectors on sides of body part;
5           m := vector connecting midpoints of s1 and s2;
6           n1 := |m| / vStep; n2 := |m| / hStep;
7           for i := 1 to n1
8              δ1 = i/n1;
9              p1 := cylndr[0] + (s1.x * δ1, s1.y * δ1);
10             p2 := cylndr[3] + (s2.x * δ1, s2.y * δ1);
11             m := p2 - p1;
12             for j := 1 to n2
13                   δ2 := j/n2;
14                   p3 := p1 + (m.x * δ2, m.y * δ2);
15                   error := error + (1-FGmap(p3));
16                   samples++;
17 return error/samples;
```

Figure 10: Bodytrack's `InsideError` function

one can use a robustness analysis such as ours to determine whether a given loop is suitable for perforation.

For a concrete example, consider the code fragment in Fig. 10, from the computer vision application called *Bodytrack* in the PARSEC benchmarks [21]. (Perforation of this application was studied in [20].) The goal of this application is to track the major body components of a moving subject; the code in Fig. 10 performs a sampling computation inside a cylinder (a projected body part). In this code, the loops at lines 2, 3, 7, and 12 can be perforated with good results [20]. However, we observe that the reason behind this is that the sampling process performed between lines 4 to 17 is robust. This robustness property can be proved by our analysis.

4.3 Differential privacy

Robustness analysis can also be helpful in guaranteeing privacy in statistical databases, where a trusted party wants to disseminate aggregate data about a population while preserving the privacy of individual members of the population. The dominant notion of privacy in this setting is *differential privacy* [10], which asserts that the result of a statistical query should not be affected substantially by the presence or absence of a single individual. A known strategy to "privatize" statistical queries is to add some noise to the result; the amount of noise needed is related to how sensitive is the query to individual changes of the data set. Our notion of K-robustness can be used to establish the sensitivity of the query. Suppose we have a query `over_six_feet` (Fig. 11) which returns the number of individuals that are over six feet tall in a population. Let us represent the set of rows in the database as two arrays of the same size: `heights`, an array of reals and `rows`, an array of reals whose element values will range over [0,1] representing its presence or absence in the populations. The first array, `heights`, contains the height of the individual while the second, `rows` specifies whether a certain row is present or not in the set. The row is present in the database if its corresponding array element (in the first array representing the rows) is 1 and absent if it is 0; note that we allow all real values between 0 and 1.

To compute the amount of noise to be used for ϵ-differential privacy, one first needs to determine the robustness parameter of the query with respect to a suitable metric. In differential privacy, we are only interested in determining the robustness of `over_six_feet` with respect to the first parameter, `rows`. Note that for this case we will need to use the L_1-norm on the type `realarray`. With this norm we can prove that `over_six_feet` is 1-robust, as removing or adding an element to the set will imply a change to only one of the elements of the `rows` array by 1, making the L_1 norm of the difference to be 1. The rules needed for this proof can be obtained by a simple modification of the rules that we have presented (which assume the L_∞ norm). According to [10] random noise with variance $1/\epsilon$ will be needed so that the query `over_six_feet` is ϵ-differentially private. Thus, our analysis can guide the amount of noise that needs to be added to ensure the differential privacy guarantee.

```
OVER_SIX_FEET(rows : realarray, heights : realarray)
result := 0;
for i := 0 to n
    if (heights[i] > 6)
         then    result := result + row[i];
```

Figure 11: A 1-robust query

5. EXPERIMENTS

We implemented our robustness analysis on top of the Z3 SMT-solver, and used the tool to verify the robustness of several classic algorithms from an undergraduate computer science textbook, as well as the code fragments in Section 4. Now we report on some experiments using this tool.

Sorting Algorithms. Our tool was able to verify the robustness of several classic sorting algorithms that take an array A_{in} and return the sorted array A_{out}. In particular, we considered *InsertionSort, BubbleSort, SelectionSort* and *MergeSort*. In [5] those four algorithms where proved continuous with respect to A_{in} and A_{out} using proof system CONT. This time we proved that the computation of A_{out} is arithmetic free, hence 1-robust due to continuity.

Shortest Path Algorithms. We verified the robustness of several shortest path algorithms. Recall that single source shortest path is N-robust with respect to the input array of edge weights. The proof for the particular shortest path algorithms such as *Dijk* and *Bellman-Ford*, consists of the following. In [5] we have proved these algorithms continuous on the input array. To prove piecewise N-robustness of the loop we prove that the loop body is piecewise 1-robust with respect to the array variable, and with respect to output variable. This is done using the rule ROBMAT on an abstraction of loop body. It follows from our method that after executing the loop, the output variable d is N-linear with respect to the array of edge waits. Given that it is piecewise N-linear and continuous we can conclude that it is N-robust. It must be noted that the nested loop structure in *Dijk* can be abstracted as one single loop in LIMP. Our proof system is unable to prove N-robustness for some shortest path algorithms such as *Floyd-Warshall.*

Minimum Spanning Tree Algorithms. The minimun spanning tree problem is N-robust, as explained in Example 2. The proofs for the particular spanning tree algorithms,

Kruskall and *Prim*, are similar to that of the shortest path algorithms. Continuity is proved using the CONT proof system of [5]. Piecewise N-linearity follows by expressing the loop in LIMP and proving piecewise 1-robustness of the loop body. Now we conclude that the aforementioned algorithms are N-robust. Again our proof system can not prove N-robustness for some spanning tree algorithms like *Boruvka's*.

Knapsack Algorithms. The integer-knapsack algorithm takes as input a weight array c and a value array v, and a knapsack capacity *Budget* and returns the set of items with maximum combined value tot_v such that their combined weight is less than the knapsack capacity. Clearly value of tot_v is N-robust in v. To prove N-robustness of our recursive *Knapsack* implementation we first prove the algorithm continuous using CONT [5]. The prover uses a fixpoint procedure to prove piecewise K-robustness assuming K-robustness for the recursive function calls, while probing for different values of K (0,1 and n). In order to prove piecewise N-linearity, the function was manually rewritten to make it explicit the array partitioning operation at each recursive call, where the input arrays are partitioned in two, one containing only the first element, and the other containing the rest. The tool keeps track of this partitioning to prove N-linearity for the addition operation in line 5. At each fixpoint iteration linearity of the function body is established using proof system ROBMAT.

Car Transmission Controller Example (Fig. 8). The algorithm produces two outputs in two variables, pressure1 and pressure2. The tool determines 1-robustness on pressure1, and non robust on pressure2. To arrive to that conclusion the tool uses the proof system ROBMAT in conjunction to the SMT solver to discharge proof obligations for each discontinuity. These proof obligations arise due to the proof rule ITE-CON presented in continuity analysis [5].

Loop perforation examples. Our proof rules are able to establish robustness proofs for several other code segments from the Parsec Benchmark Suite [21] where loop perforation is empirically successful [20].

In particular, our rules can prove the robustness of the loops for the ImageMeasurement class in the Bodytrack application (including the one shown in Fig. 10), where loop perforation is reported to work. A second example comes from `x264`, a media application that performs H.264 encoding on a video stream. Two outermost loops in function `pixel_satd_wxh` are claimed to be amenable to perforation with good results by [20]. We looked at the code snippet inside the body of the nested loops: similar to the example in bodytrack, perforating these loops will result in sampling less points in a coarser way, and the computation inside the body of the loop is a robust computation.

However, not all loops that are empirically amenable to loop perforation are provably robust by our analysis. Examples include the loop in the `pFL()` routine in the StreamCluster application, and a loop in the `ParticleFilter::Update` method in Bodytrack. We leave for future work a proof principle that can explain why these (and similar) loops can be successfully perforated.

Implementation and Experimental Setup. Our tool is implemented in C#, relying on the Z3 SMT solver to discharge proof obligations and the Phoenix Compiler Framework to process the input program. The bulk of the new analysis computes facts about linear dependences between variables and parameters and is implemented as a fixpoint computation that finds the solution of dataflow equations derived from the proof rules. Some proof obligations are discharged in the process by the SMT-solver. In the future we plan to use an optimization toolbox to have better guesses for the minimum bound. Some proofs involving arrays, e.g. *MergeSort*, requires to keep track of the accesses to the array, with purpose to ensure disjoint access to elements of the array. Finally, as mentioned earlier, we manually rewrote some of the programs to fit the abstraction language LIMP. The performance results reported in table 1 were obtained on a Core2 Duo 2.53 Ghz with 4GB of RAM.

Example	Time	# SMT proofs	Proof method
BubbleSort	0.250	1	continuity + arithmetic freedom
InsertionSort	0.098	1	continuity + arithmetic freedom
SelectionSort	0.293	3	continuity + arithmetic freedom
MergeSort	0.560	3	continuity + arithmetic freedom + array partitioning
Dijkstra	0.454	3	continuity + robustness matrix + linear loops
Bellman-Ford	0.316	1	continuity + robustness matrix + linear loops
Kruskal	1.198	1	continuity + robustness matrix + linear loops
Prim	0.547	3	continuity + robustness matrix + linear loops
Knapsack	1.480	3	continuity + robustness matrix + array partitioning
Controller	8.770	60	continuity + robustness matrix

Table 1: Benchmark Examples

6. RELATED WORK

Robustness is a standard correctness property in control theory [22, 23], and there is an entire subfield of control theory studying the design and analysis of robust (control) systems. However, the systems studied by this literature methods are abstractly defined using differential equations and hybrid automata, rather than programs. As far as we know, the only effort to generally define and study the robustness of embedded control *software* can be found in [16, 17] on test generation for robustness. There, robustness is formulated as: "If the input of the program P changes by an amount less than ϵ, where ϵ is a *fixed* constant, then the output changes by only slightly." In contrast, we verify the stronger property that *any* perturbation to the inputs will change the output proportionally. Many applications (e.g., differential privacy) demand this stronger formulation.

In addition, there are many efforts in the abstract interpretation literature that, while not verifying robustness explicitly, reason about the uncertainty in a program's behavior due to floating-point rounding and sensor errors [11, 18, 8, 6, 7]. Several of these approaches have been successfully applied to large embedded code bases. However, none of them reason systematically about divergent control flow caused due to uncertainty, which we can thanks to our continuity analysis. Also, none of the abstractions developed in this space seem suitable for an analysis of piecewise robustness that is needed to verify robustness.

So far as we know, Hamlet [13] was the first to argue for a testing methodology for Lipschitz-continuity of software. However, he failed to offer new program analysis techniques. Reed and Pierce [25] have since given a type system that can verify the Lipschitz-continuity of functional programs, as a component of a new language for differential privacy [24]. While the system can seamlessly handle functional data structures such as lists and maps, it does not, unlike our analysis, handle control flow, and would deem any program containing a conditional branch to be nonrobust. Also, this work does not consider any application other than differential privacy.

Robustness and stability of numerical algorithms are also well-studied topics in the numerical analysis literature [14]. However, the proofs studied there are manual, and specialized to specific numerical algorithms. Other related literatures include that on automatic differentiation (AD) [4], where the goal is to transform a program P into a program that returns the derivative of P where it exists. But AD does not attempt verification—no attempt is made to certify a program as differentiable or Lipschitz.

Finally, language-based approaches to program approximation are still very new [20, 19, 26]. In particular, there is only one existing paper [19] studying the theory of language-based program approximation.

7. CONCLUSION

We have presented a program analysis to quantify the *robustness* of a program to uncertainty in its inputs. Our analysis is sound, and decomposes the verification of robustness into the independent subproblems of verifying continuity and piecewise robustness.

In future work, we intend to extend our robustness analysis to programs that manipulate discrete data types like integers and boolean arrays in addition to continuous ones (like the ones studied here). This extension is especially important as discrete types are often used in real-world applications, in particular embedded control code. Another interesting question is the generation of test inputs that trigger robustness bugs—i.e. pairs of inputs that are close in value, but on which the program behaves very differently. A third interesting direction is a notion of robustness for *reactive programs*, where we must consider perturbations not only in the program inputs, but also in the environment with which the program interacts.

8. REFERENCES

[1] L. Ambrosio and P. Tilli. *Topics on analysis in metric spaces.* Oxford University Press, 2004.

[2] L. Blum, M. Shub, and S. Smale. On a theory of computation over the real numbers; np completeness, recursive functions and universal machines (extended abstract). In *FOCS*, 1988.

[3] D. Bostic, W. P. Milam, Y. Wang, and J. A. Cook. Smart vehicle baseline report. http://vehicle.berkeley.edu/mobies, 2001.

[4] M. Bucker, G. Corliss, P. Hovland, U. Naumann, and B. Norris. *Automatic differentiation: applications, theory and implementations.* Birkhauser, 2006.

[5] S. Chaudhuri, S. Gulwani, and R. Lublinerman. Continuity analysis of programs. In *POPL*, pages 57–70, 2010.

[6] L. Chen, A. Miné, J. Wang, and P. Cousot. Interval polyhedra: An abstract domain to infer interval linear relationships. In *SAS*, pages 309–325, 2009.

[7] L. Chen, A. Miné, J. Wang, and P. Cousot. An abstract domain to discover interval linear equalities. In *VMCAI*, pages 112–128, 2010.

[8] P. Cousot, R. Cousot, J. Feret, L. Mauborgne, A. Miné, D. Monniaux, and X. Rival. The ASTREÉ analyzer. In *ESOP*, pages 21–30, 2005.

[9] P. Cousot and N. Halbwachs. Automatic discovery of linear restraints among variables of a program. In *POPL*, pages 84–96, 1978.

[10] C. Dwork. Differential privacy. In *ICALP*, 2006.

[11] E. Goubault. Static analyses of the precision of floating-point operations. In *SAS*, pages 234–259, 2001.

[12] J. Halpern. *Reasoning about uncertainty.* The MIT Press, 2003.

[13] D. Hamlet. Continuity in sofware systems. In *ISSTA*, 2002.

[14] F. Iavernaro, F. Mazzia, and D. Trigiante. Stability and conditioning in numerical analysis. *Journal of Num. Analysis, Industrial and Applied Math.*, 1(1):91–112, 2006.

[15] E. Lee. Cyber physical systems: Design challenges. In *ISORC*, pages 363–369, 2008.

[16] R. Majumdar and I. Saha. Symbolic robustness analysis. *Real-Time Systems Symposium, IEEE International*, 0:355–363, 2009.

[17] R. Majumdar, I. Saha, and Zilong Wang. Systematic testing for control applications. In *Formal Methods and Models for Codesign (MEMOCODE), 2010 8th IEEE/ACM International Conference on*, pages 1 –10, 2010.

[18] A. Miné. Relational abstract domains for the detection of floating-point run-time errors. In *ESOP*, pages 3–17, 2004.

[19] S. Misailovic, D. M. Roy, and M. Rinard. Probabilistically accurate program transformations. In *SAS*, 2011.

[20] S. Misailovic, S. Sidiroglou, H. Hoffman, and M. Rinard. Quality of service profiling. In *ICSE*, 2010.

[21] The Parsec benchmark suite. http://parsec.cs.princeton.edu, 2009.

[22] S. Pettersson and B. Lennartson. Stability and robustness for hybrid systems. In *Decision and Control*, pages 1202–1207, Dec 1996.

[23] Andreas Podelski and Silke Wagner. Model checking of hybrid systems: From reachability towards stability. In *HSCC*, pages 507–521, 2006.

[24] J. Reed, A. Aviv, D. Wagner, A. Haeberlen, B. Pierce, and J. Smith. Differential privacy for collaborative security. In *Eurosec*, 2010.

[25] J. Reed and B. Pierce. Distance makes the types grow stronger: A calculus for differential privacy. In *ICFP*, 2010.

[26] S. Sidiroglou, S. Misailovic, H. Hoffman, and M. Rinard. Managing performance vs. accuracy trade-offs with loop perforation. In *FSE*, 2011.

[27] G. Winskel. *The formal semantics of programming languages.* The MIT Press, 1993.

[28] G. Zames. Input-output feedback stability and robustness, 1959-85. *IEEE Control Systems*, 16(3), 1996.

Checking Conformance of a Producer and a Consumer*

Evan Driscoll, Amanda Burton, and Thomas Reps
Computer Sciences Department, University of Wisconsin – Madison
{driscoll,burtona,reps}@wisc.edu

ABSTRACT

This paper addresses the problem of identifying incompatibilities between two programs that operate in a producer/consumer relationship. It describes the techniques that are incorporated in a tool called PCCA (**P**roducer-**C**onsumer **C**onformance **A**nalyzer), which attempts to (i) determine whether the consumer is prepared to accept all messages that the producer can emit, or (ii) find a counter-example: a message that the producer can emit and the consumer considers ill-formed.

Categories and Subject Descriptors

D.2.12 [**Software Engineering**]: Interoperability

General Terms

Algorithms, Reliability

Keywords

producer-consumer compatibility, language containment, visibly pushdown automata

1. INTRODUCTION

Complex systems today are made up of many communicating components. For instance, a modern fuel-injected engine has a number of sensors that send their current measurements to the engine-control unit, which decides what the optimum fuel-air mixture should be. It emits messages to other components, such as the fuel pumps and fuel injectors, to carry out its decisions.

*Supported by NSF under grants CCF-0540955, CCF-0810053, CCF-0904371, and CCF-0701957; by ONR under grants N00014-{09-1-0510, 10-M-0251}, by ARL under grant W911NF-09-1-0413; and by AFRL under grants FA9550-09-1-0279 and FA8650-10-C-7088. Any opinions, findings, and conclusions or recommendations expressed in this material are those of the author(s) and do not necessarily reflect the views of the sponsoring agencies.

Permission to make digital or hard copies of all or part of this work for personal or classroom use is granted without fee provided that copies are not made or distributed for prof t or commercial advantage and that copies bear this notice and the full citation on the f rst page. To copy otherwise, to republish, to post on servers or to redistribute to lists, requires prior specif c permission and/or a fee.
ESEC/FSE'11, September 5–9, 2011, Szeged, Hungary.
Copyright 2011 ACM 978-1-4503-0443-6/11/09 ...$10.00.

In such systems, it is vitally important to ensure that the messages that one component sends to another are understood by the receiving component, otherwise runtime errors will occur. Send/receive incompatibilities can drive up the cost of developing a system because different components of a system are often developed by different development teams or different subcontractors, and thus compatibility problems may not be detected until integration time. (The cost of fixing errors found late in the development process is usually much higher than that of errors found earlier.)

Consider an example system made up of the producer and consumer shown in Figs. 1 and 2, respectively. The producer is a program that monitors a sensor, and periodically sends a "packet" of data to the consumer.[1] The system uses an abbreviated protocol: if the sensor data has not changed since the last message, then only the Boolean literal `false` is sent. Line 2 in Fig. 1 makes this decision.

As presented, these components are correct: both "speak" the same protocol. However, consider a buggy version of the consumer that does not account for the possibility that the producer sends an abbreviated message, and always expects the full packet. This code is shown in Fig. 3.

To find this bug, can we reason about the languages over which each component operates? In the consumer, we know that the `updateReading` function always reads a `double` and then a `bool`. Furthermore, each time through the loop in the buggy version of `main`, the consumer reads a `bool` then the `double`–`bool` sequence from `updateReading`. Thus we can determine that the input language of the buggy consumer, expressed as a regular expression over types that the consumer reads, is `(bool double bool)+`. Similarly, we can determine that the output language of the producer, expressed as a regular expression, is `(bool | bool double bool)+`.

From these two language descriptions we can see that one of the components is buggy: the string `bool bool`, is in the producer's language but not in the consumer's. This disparity suggests that some execution of the producer could output two Boolean values, but *no* execution of the consumer would expect to read that message.

A similar analysis suggests that Fig. 2's consumer is correct. The language it expects is `(bool (double bool)?)+`, which is equivalent to what we inferred for the producer.

We describe a technique for determining whether two components are compatible, which proceeds along lines similar to this example: we infer a model of the output language of the producer, infer a model of the input language of the

[1]We use *packet* to refer to the data that the components communicate each time through their "loop".

```
sendReading(Sensor* device, int prev)
    if device→setting == prev then
        writeBool(false);
    else
        writeBool(true);
        writeDouble(device→setting);
        writeBool(device→valid);
loop(Sensor* device, int prev)
    ... // update device with new readings
    sendReading(device, prev);
    if ... then
        loop(device, device→setting);
main()
    Sensor device;
    loop(&device, -1);
```

Figure 1: Example producer

```
updateReading(int* setting, bool* valid)
    *setting = readDouble();
    *valid = readBool();
main()
    int setting;
    bool valid;
    while ... do
        if readBool() then
            updateReading (&setting, &valid);
        ... // do something with current readings
```

Figure 2: Example consumer

consumer, and determine whether the two descriptions are compatible. However, we also investigate using a richer family of languages than just regular languages for the format descriptions, and thus the check of whether the models are compatible is more than straight language-containment.

This paper addresses the following problem: *Given two programs that operate in a producer/consumer relationship, (i) determine whether the consumer is prepared to accept all messages that the producer can emit, or (ii) find a counter-example: a message that the producer can emit but the consumer considers ill-formed.*

We have implemented our technique in a tool called PCCA (for **P**roducer-**C**onsumer **C**onformance **A**nalyzer). Given the two source programs, along with information about which functions perform I/O (see §4.1), PCCA infers a description of the language that the producer generates and a description of the language that the consumer expects, and (roughly speaking) determines whether the former is a subset of the latter.

PCCA starts out by creating an automaton P that models the producer, which accepts an over-approximation of the language that the producer emits. We have two versions of PCCA: one creates a pushdown automaton (PDA) and the other creates a standard finite automaton (FA). Similarly, PCCA produces an automaton C for the consumer, which accepts an over-approximation of the language that the consumer expects. Our goal becomes determining whether $L(P) \subseteq L(C)$. For the FA version, we do this directly. For the PDA version, this question is undecidable with a direct

```
main()
    while ... do
        readBool();
        updateReading (&setting, &valid);
        ... // do something with current readings
```

Figure 3: Example buggy consumer. (updateReading is the same as in Fig. 2.)

approach; thus we actually use a restricted form of PDAs called *visibly pushdown automata* [3, 2] (VPAs) to model the components' behaviors. While less powerful than full PDAs, VPAs provide enough power to recognize important classes of non-regular languages, such as balanced parentheses.

Unlike PDAs, the restrictions on VPAs allow them to retain closure under complementation and intersection, and thus language containment is decidable. However, when using VPAs we must make internal calls and returns explicit in the words of the languages that PCCA infers from the components. If PCCA were to check containment of these languages directly, we would be requiring that the two components have the same internal call/return structure, which is undesirable. To compensate, PCCA "enriches" the consumer's VPA C—and hence its language $L(C)$—so that differences in the call/return structures of the producer and the consumer do not preclude answering the language-containment question. (This step is explained in more detail in §3.2.)

To test language containment, PCCA performs a set-difference operation to compute $L(P) \setminus L(C)$ (for the FA version) or $L(P) \setminus L(\text{Enrich}(C))$ (for the VPA version) by complementing the righthand automaton intersecting the result with P. Finally, it tests whether the language of the VPA produced by the intersection is empty. If so, then the subset holds, and PCCA reports the components are compatible; if not, then there is a counter-example in the difference and PCCA reports the components are incompatible.

The techniques used in PCCA are "transport-agnostic" as long as the producer and the consumer use a stream-like interface to communicate. That is, PCCA can analyze a pair of programs—or even the *same* program playing the roles of both producer and consumer—that share files, send information over sockets, or use standard I/O.

Because it is necessary to approximate each component's language, the technique we have developed has some limitations. Both approximations are over-approximations: i.e., the producer's model may say that the producer can emit a string that can never actually be emitted by the producer, and similarly for the consumer. Consequently, the compatibility-checking technique can have both false positives and false negatives, which puts PCCA among other bug-hunting approaches, such as work developed by Engler et al. [16, 22] as well as many other authors.

Our contributions can be summarized as follows:

- We describe our approach to format inference, inspired by Lim et al. [23], and its application to component compatibility.
- The model of the program can be described using a context-free language, but testing language containment for CFLs is not decidable. We describe how to side-step this problem by using VPAs, making the internal calls and returns of the components explicit, and performing our Enrich operation.

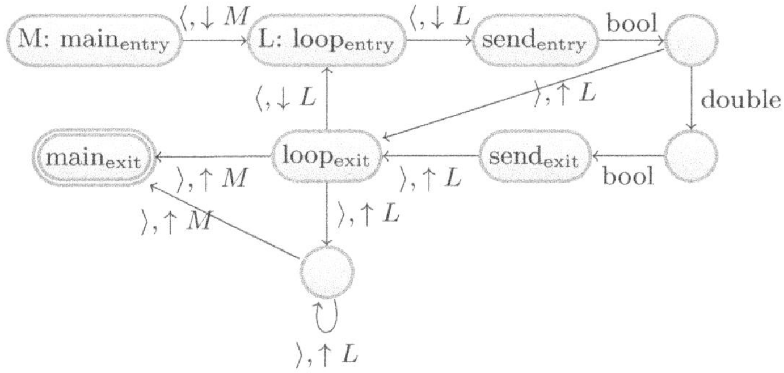

Figure 4: The producer's VPA. To reduce clutter, all transitions to the implicit "stuck state" are omitted and sendReading is abbreviated as send.

- We compare the results of a VPA-based model to those obtained by using ordinary finite automata.
- We describe a new algorithm for determining the emptyness of a VPA, which builds on existing work related to pushdown systems.
- We implemented our techniques in a tool called PCCA, and demonstrate its utility on several examples.

Organization. The remainder of the paper is organized as follows: §2 discusses our goals and the methods we use to achieve them. §3 discusses the indiv steps that that make up our technique when PCCA is operating using VPAs. §4 describes the prototype implementation. §5 presents experimental results. §6 discusses related work. §7 has a brief discussion of future work.

2. OVERVIEW

We now give a description of our technique, framed around how it operates on the example considered in the Introduction. We first consider the producer and the correct version of the consumer, as presented in Figs. 1 and 2, respectively. (Ex. 2.3 covers the buggy version of the consumer.)

From the standpoint of checking that the producer and consumer are compatible, even this simplified example has a number of challenging features. In particular,

1. The producer's `loop` procedure uses recursion instead of iteration. In contrast, the consumer is more straightforward: it reads values in a loop.
2. The calls to the write functions in the producer and the read functions in the consumer are organized differently. The producer calls all the `write_*` functions from the same procedure, while the consumer reads the second two fields (`double bool`) in a different procedure from the one in which it reads the first (`bool`).

PCCA is provided the information that the `read_*` and `write_*` functions are "special" (in that they perform I/O); in §4.1, we discuss how this information can be supplied.

As mentioned earlier, PCCA is able to use two different formalisms to model the components: visibly pushdown automata (VPA) and standard finite automata (FA).

2.1 Visibly Pushdown Automata

From each component we infer a visibly pushdown automaton when operating in that mode. VPAs [3] are a restriction of ordinary pushdown automata, and can be used in program analysis to capture the matched call and return structure of execution traces through multi-procedure programs. In essense, each alphabet symbol describes whether a VPA is allowed to push or pop a symbol from its stack. We formally define VPAs in §3.1, but for purposes of this section it suffices to know that, even though they share some power with general PDAs, determining language containment of two VPAs remains decidable, in contrast to PDAs.

In our application, the alphabet consists of the types that are emitted by the producer and read by the consumer, as well as distinguished call and return symbols $\langle$ and $\rangle$.

For expository purposes, we talk about the producer automaton "emitting" strings. Neither FAs nor VPAs actually emit anything (except a yes/no answer); what we mean is that a given string is accepted by the producer's automaton. However, if a string is accepted by the producer's automaton, that means it could be emitted by the producer program, and it is often convenient to think of the automata as being the components themselves, rather than models.

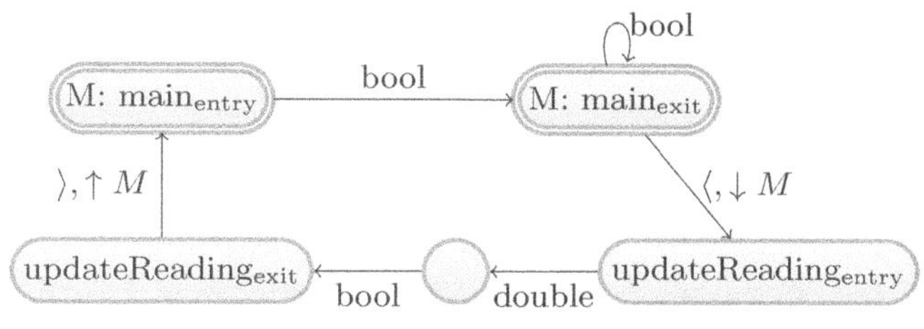

Figure 5: The consumer's VPA.

2.2 Inferring The I/O Format

The first step in the process is to infer an automaton that approximates the language of each component. In the case of the producer, we wish to infer the language of all possible outputs; in the case of the consumer, we wish to infer the language of all expected inputs.

The idea behind our technique is to create automata that mimic the control-flow behavior of the source programs. Each automaton that PCCA generates has the same language as one created by transliterating the program's interprocedural control-flow graph (ICFG) in the following manner:

1. There is one state $\tilde{c}$ for each ICFG node c.
2. If a call site c can call an I/O function that outputs or expects a value of type τ, we add a transition on τ from $\tilde{c}$ to its corresponding return node. In the VPA model, this transition does not modify the stack.
3. If a call site c can call a non-I/O function f with entry node f_e and exit node f_x, we add one transition from $\tilde{c}$ to $\tilde{f}_e$ and a second transition from $\tilde{f}_x$ to the corresponding return site. In the FA model, both transitions are ε transitions. In the VPA model, the first transition is on the symbol $\langle$ and pushes $\tilde{c}$ onto the VPA's stack, and the second transition is on the symbol $\rangle$ under the condition that $\tilde{c}$ is at the top of the stack (which is then popped).
4. All other transitions in the ICFG become ε-transitions. In the VPA version, these do not modify the stack.
5. The entry node of main becomes the start state, and the exit node becomes the sole accepting state.

However, if we used this naive translation, the resulting automata would be extremely large, which would cause problems during the determinization phase of PCCA.[2]

Instead of treating the ICFG as a whole, PCCA proceeds procedure-by-procedure through the program. For each procedure, it looks at the *intra*procedural CFG and carries out the above translation, except that step 3 is replaced by the following:

- If a call site c can call a non-I/O function f, we add an *internal* transition from $\tilde{c}$ to the corresponding return, labeled with a generated symbol `call_f`.

(Also, the VPA's starting and accepting states are the entry and exit nodes of that procedure.)

Even in the VPA version, because each procedure's automation has no transitions that modify the stack (stack operations only happen on a call or return), it can be interpreted as a standard finite-state machine. We do this, and use the standard algorithms to determinize and minimize each procedure's machine. (PCCA's implementation uses the OpenFST library for this purpose [1].) The efficiency upshot is that this technique turns what would be a multiplicative factor into an additive one, thus dramatically reducing the time spent in determinization.

Once we have the collection of minimized automata, we combine all the automata into one and "restore" the call and return transitions. We replace each transition that moves from state c to r when reading a symbol `call_f` with a pair of transitions that match those in the original step 3:

- We add a transition from c to f's entry point. In the FA version, this is an ε transition; in the VPA version, it is on the symbol $\langle$ and pushes c onto the stack.
- We add a transition from the exit point of f to r. In the FA version, this is an ε transition; in the VPA version, it is on the symbol $\rangle$ and requires that c appears at the top of the stack (which is then popped).

Finally, we have to perform one more determinization step in case connecting the procedures adds nondeterminism.

This translation essentially abstracts the program to its control flow only: data is not considered. One could envision a higher-fidelity translation that weaves selected data elements (or abstractions of data elements) into the automata we infer, but of course there is a trade-off between precision and automaton size.

Figs. 4 and 5 show the VPAs that are inferred from the code in Figs. 1 and 2, respectively. (To reduce clutter, Figs. 4 and 5 have ε-transitions collapsed, which removes 7 states and a comparable number of transitions in each automaton.) Call-transitions have labels of the form "$\langle, \downarrow X$", where X is the state at the source of the transition, and $\downarrow X$ means that X is pushed onto the call stack. Return-transitions have labels of the form "$\rangle, \uparrow X$", which means that the machine can make the transition only if state X is on the top of the stack; in so doing, it pops X. The FA version is similar, except that all call and return transitions are replaced with ε transitions.

Knowledge about I/O functions. PCCA needs information about what function calls can perform I/O. There are a number of ways the user can provide such information (see §4.1).

One important point is that there needs to be agreement between the producer and consumer regarding what types are used. The first, and easiest, issue related to this point is that the names of the types must agree.

The second issue is that the granularity of the I/O function specifications must agree. Consider our example. As written, both the producer and consumer have I/O operations expressed in terms of their constituent C types. It would also be possible to have the producer and consumer store values in a two-element structure `SensorData`, and do a "bulk read/write" with `fread()/fwrite()` to operate on the struct as a whole. In such a case, it would be reasonable to say that the type of that I/O operation was `SensorData`. However, the two approaches cannot be mixed: the consumer and producer need to agree on the granularity.

Remark. The need for agreement between the producer and consumer on the granularity of types is not a fundamental limitation: it would be possible to have the user specify that `SensorData` is a {`double`, `bool`} struct at either the format-inference stage or after the VPAs are constructed, and it should even be possible to extract this information from struct definitions in the code. We have not investigated these avenues at this point; however, with the current implementation the user has the ability to specify, for example, that a particular call to `fread/fwrite` operates on a `double` and then a `bool`. □

2.3 Enriching the Consumer's VPA

This section applies to the VPA version of PCCA only; §3.2 describes the operation formally.

It would be too restrictive to demand that the producer and consumer perform calls and returns at corresponding moments during their executions. The VPAs that we infer from the producer and consumer follow the same call/return behavior as the original programs; thus the strings in the languages of the producer and consumer models contain internal call and return symbols that are not actually present in the messages between components. Checking containment of the languages of the inferred models would require that the components agree in this respect.

Our running example illustrates the issue. Each "packet" consists of a Boolean, optionally followed by a double and a Boolean. The producer sends the entire packet within one function (`sendReading`), but the consumer reads the first Boolean, and then calls another function (`updateReading`) to read the remaining values of the packet.

The consequence of the producer and consumer having different calling structure is that the substrings that correspond to the same packet are different in the producer's language and the consumer's language.

EXAMPLE 2.1 Consider the string `bool double bool`, emitted by Fig. 1's code when the producer performs just one iteration—hence the string contains just a single packet. For the producer's VPA (Fig. 4), the string would be $\langle$ $\langle$ `bool double bool` $\rangle$ $\rangle$, while for the consumer's VPA (Fig. 5), the corresponding string would be `bool` $\langle$ `double bool` $\rangle$. These strings have $\langle$ and $\rangle$ in different locations. □

To accommodate the different nesting structures, we "enrich" the consumer's VPA so that it can use nondeterminism to guess when the producer makes an internal call or return and insert the corresponding symbol into its own strings.

EXAMPLE 2.2 For the example discussed in Ex. 2.1, the language of the consumer's enriched VPA contains not just `bool`

[2] As shown in §5, determinization dominates execution time.

⟨ `double bool` ⟩ but also ⟨ ⟨ `bool double bool` ⟩ ⟩. The latter string is in the languages of both the producer's VPA and the consumer's enriched VPA. □

After enrichment, a counterexample to the language containment (and an indication of incompatibility) is a string that the producer's NWA can emit where it is impossible to add and/or remove balanced parentheses and arrive at a string that the consumer's NWA accepts.

EXAMPLE 2.3 For the buggy consumer in Fig. 3, the original language contains strings such as `bool` ⟨ `double bool` ⟩, but not, for instance `bool bool` (which is in the producer's VPA's language). Denote by C_e the VPA inferred for the buggy consumer. No matter how you add parentheses to `bool bool`, you will not arrive at a string in the language of Enrich(C_e); this will be a counterexample to language containment. □

If an analyst knows that both components use the same call/return structure, he can omit the enrichment step to obtain a more precise comparison of the two languages. Without the approximation caused by Enrich, a "compatible" result is more credible; however, if there is uncertainty in the call/return assumption, an "incompatible" result is less credible.

2.4 Language Containment

Once we have the producer automaton P and the consumer automaton C' (for the VPA version, C' is the enriched consumer automaton), determining the set difference, and thus containment, of their languages is straightforward: $L(P) \setminus L(C') = \emptyset$ iff $L(P) \cap \overline{L(C')} = \emptyset$. Both FAs and VPAs are closed under all of these operations, so all that is necessary is to take C', complement it, intersect it with P, and test the resulting VPA for emptiness. §3 discusses this step in greater detail for VPAs.

2.5 Helping PCCA Improve its Results

We now return to the running example to illustrate how the programmer could improve the results of the analysis. We start by describing a bug that PCCA would not be able to find, and then explain how to modify the code—but without changing the actual protocol—so that the bug *is* found.

Suppose that the specification of the protocol changed during development: the final `bool` field was not originally needed, but was added later. Suppose that the implementation of the producer *was* changed to emit this field, but the consumer was not updated. (In other words, line 7 in Fig. 1 was added at the time the specification changed. The consumer *should* have been changed to add line 3 in Fig. 2, but that line was erroneously omitted.)

This situation would almost certainly signify a bug, but it would *not* be detected by our tool. The reason is that there is no association between the function call on lines 3 and 5 in the producer, which writes the first `bool` in each packet, and line 8 in the consumer, which reads it. Instead, the consumer could "use" the call on `readBool` on line 8 to consume the final field of the *previous* packet, then not call `updateReading` during that iteration.

We can modify the source code of the producer and consumer to make it possible for our technique to detect the previous bug. The problem that our technique has with detecting this bug is that what the producer and consumer thought were packets got out of sync. By inserting a "phony" I/O call at the start or end of each loop (e.g., in the ellipsis on line 9 of the producer and between lines 8 and 9 in the consumer), we can make the packet divisions visible to PCCA, allowing it to check that the producer's and consumer's packets cannot get out of sync.

The phony calls would have a type that does not appear in the packet itself; in our experiments we have called it `SEP`. The key point to realize is that this "type" does not have to have any material presence in any of the communications, and in fact the function that performs the phony I/O can be completely empty.

This idea can be generalized to "hijack" the compatibility algorithm to ensure that *events* that should occur during the execution of the producer and consumer occur in the proper order. From this point of view, a write operation is essentially an event, during which the fact that the program communicates is only incidental.

3. FORMALIZATION OF VPA-BASED CONTAINMENT CHECKING

This section discusses the details of how PCCA determines whether the producer's language is a subset of the (enriched) consumer's when using visibly pushdown automata (VPAs). Using VPAs provides a potential benefit over FAs (see §3.3) but introduces a number of complications to the process that are not present with standard finite automata.

3.1 Visibly Pushdown Automata

DEFINITION 3.1 ([3]) A VPA is a pushdown automaton (PDA) that operates on a tagged alphabet and whose stack accesses are restricted by the current symbol. A **tagged alphabet** $\tilde{\Sigma}$ is a partition of a normal alphabet into disjoint subsets Σ, Σ_c, and Σ_r. In our application, $\Sigma_c = \{\langle\}$, $\Sigma_r = \{\rangle\}$, and Σ is the set of types on which the program being analyzed operates. (In program analysis, pairs of symbols in Σ_c and Σ_r are often used to model program calls and returns; they can also be used to represent other matched entities such as opening and closing XML tags.)

A **visibly pushdown automaton** V is a 6-tuple $(Q, \tilde{\Sigma}, \Gamma_\perp, \delta, q_0, F)$ where Q is the set of states, $\tilde{\Sigma}$ is a tagged alphabet, $\Gamma_\perp$ is the stack alphabet (with $\perp$, a special bottom-of-stack symbol, and $\Gamma = \Gamma_\perp \setminus \{\perp\}$), $q_0 \in Q$ is the initial state, and $F \subseteq Q$ is the set of final states. The transition relation, δ, is the union of three components:

- $\delta_i \subseteq (Q \times \Sigma) \times Q$
- $\delta_c \subseteq (Q \times \Sigma_c) \times (Q \times \Gamma)$
- $\delta_r \subseteq (Q \times \Sigma_r \times \Gamma_\perp) \times Q$

A VPA M reads its input and makes transitions on each symbol as follows. If the current symbol is σ, the current state is q, and γ is at the top of the stack, then:

- If $\sigma \in \Sigma$, then M selects a transition $((q, \sigma), q')$ from δ_i and changes its control state to q'.
- If $\sigma \in \Sigma_c$, M selects a transition $((q, \sigma), (q', \gamma'))$ from δ_c, pushes γ' onto its stack, and changes to state q'.
- If $\sigma \in \Sigma_r$, M selects a transition $((q, \sigma, \gamma), q')$ from δ_r, pops γ from its stack, and changes to state q'.

The VPA accepts its input if there is a run that ends in a final state $f \in F$.

The behavior above can be expressed as limiting the operation of a standard PDA in the following way: when reading $\sigma \in \Sigma$, the VPA cannot access the stack; when reading

$\sigma_c \in \Sigma_c$, the VPA must push exactly one symbol; and when reading $\sigma_r \in \Sigma_r$, the VPA must pop exactly one symbol. In this way, the VPA's stack accesses are visible in each input.

We refer to the $\sigma \in \Sigma$ as **internal** symbols, the $\sigma_c \in \Sigma_c$ (and the positions in a string at which they appear) as **calls**, and $\sigma_r \in \Sigma_r$ (and their positions) as **returns**. □

We take $\Gamma = Q$ and construct VPAs that, when in state q with a call as the current symbol, push q onto the stack.[3] We also allow internal ε-transitions in the natural way.

3.2 Enrichment

As discussed at a high level in §2.3, it is unreasonable to demand that the producer and consumer have the same call/return structure, so we introduce an "enriching" operation, denoted by Enrich, that when applied to the consumer's VPA will relax the requirement. Enrich creates new transitions in the consumer's VPA that allow it to make arbitrary calls and returns. In essence, this allows the consumer's VPA to emulate the call/return structure of the producer's VPA. Enrich is defined as follows:

Definition 3.2 Given VPA $A = (Q, \Sigma, q_0, \delta, F)$, augment δ with the following transitions:

1. For every state p, introduce a call transition $\delta_c(p, \langle, p)$.
2. For every pair of states (p, q), introduce a return transition $\delta_r(p, q, \rangle, p)$.
3. For every call transition $\delta_c(p, \langle, q)$ in the original VPA, introduce a ε-transition $\delta_i(p, \varepsilon, q)$.
4. For every return transition $\delta_r(p, p', \rangle, q)$ in the original VPA, introduce a ε-transition $\delta_i(p, \varepsilon, q)$. □

Items 1 and 2 allow the consumer's enriched VPA to perform extra call or return moves to emulate the producer VPA, while items 3 and 4 allow the consumer's enriched VPA to omit calls or returns, in case the producer has fewer.

Example 3.3 The example discussed in Exs. 2.1 and 2.2 requires all four steps: to match the producer, the consumer needs to add two calls to the beginning of the input string, add two matching returns to the end of the input string, and remove the "extra" call between the first "bool" and "double" and its corresponding return. □

While in theory it is possible either to enrich the consumer to match the producer or enrich the producer to match the consumer, in practice only the former is reasonable. The goal of the containment check is to determine the emptiness $L(P) \setminus L(C)$. Enriching a VPA enlarges its language, so this operation adds some error E to one of the operands, resulting in either $(L(P) \cup E) \setminus L(C)$ or $L(P) \setminus (L(C) \cup E)$. Unfortunately, the error introduced by enriching the producer's VPA invariably leads to false positives: for the consumer to accept everything that the enriched producer emits, the consumer would have to accept every possible call structure of every string the producer emits.

3.3 Benefits of Using VPAs

There are several kinds of automata that we could have chosen. For instance, the FA version of PCCA models each program as a single finite automaton. This approach removes the need for the enrich operation because calls and returns are not represented explicitly in the languages.

```
outputInt()
    writeInt();
producerMain()
    if ... then
        outputInt();
    else
        writeChar(); outputInt(); writeChar();
inputInt1()
    readInt();
inputInt2()
    readInt();
consumerMain()
    if ... then
        inputInt1();
    else
        readChar(); inputInt2(); readChar();
```

Figure 6: Components that illustrate the benefits of VPAs

The trade-offs between VPAS and FAs mirror trade-offs that one can make in traditional interprocedural dataflow analysis. The simplest way of performing such analysis is to build the ICFG and run the analysis as if call and return edges were just normal intraprocedural control-flow edges. However, that approach loses precision because of suprious data flows from one call site c_1, into the called function f, and then out the return edge to a different call site c_2. A similar kind of imprecision can affect the FA version of PCCA.

For instance, Fig. 6 shows a producer and consumer for which FAs and VPAs produce different results. Due to space constraints we omit diagrams of the inferred automata. The FA version of PCCA infers `int | char int char` for the language of the consumer, but `int | char int | int char | char int char` for the producer. The producer's language contains two words that are not in the language of the consumer, thus the FA version of PCCA reports that the components are incompatible.

One way of getting around this problem is to perform function inlining: each call site c gets its own copy of the procedure f, which is only called from c and only returns to c. This eliminates the suprious control flows, but at the cost of a potentially exponentially larger model. It would be possible to do exactly the same thing in our domain: create a single FSM, but inline procedures.

A more sophisticated mechanism for eliminating these spurious flows uses context-free-language reachability techniques [31]. This marks each call/return edge pair with a distinct set of matched parentheses; possible executions of the program correspond only to strings with matched parentheses. The dataflow problem can be formulated so that only flows along such well-matched paths are considered. Our use of VPAs closely mirrors this approach for the producer.[4]

[3]Following [3], this restriction is called a "weakly-hierarchical VPA", and does not reduce the expressiveness.

[4]CFL-reachability distinguishes acceptable return edges from unacceptable ones by whether the brackets match; our VPAs distinguish them by whether the corresponding call site is on the VPA's stack.

The code in Fig. 6 benefits from this increase in precision. The VPA's constraints on the return transitions from the exit node of `outputInt` to each of the two return sites restricts the data flow, thus the producer's language is inferred to be ⟨ `int` ⟩ | `char` ⟨ `int` ⟩ `char`. The VPA version of PCCA reports that the two components are compatible.

Unfortunately, this benefit only applies to the producer's model: the enrich operation we do to the consumer essentially makes a regular approximation out of the original. We have not investigated applying the ideas of inlining to obtain increased precision, although we think it would be possible.

In other words, using VPAs to model the components provides a way to obtain a context-sensitive analysis in one of the components without the exponential blowup of inlining.

3.4 Complement and Intersection

As mentioned in §2.4, determining the set difference of the producer VPA and the enriched consumer VPA, is straightforward: $L(P) \setminus L(\text{Enrich}(C)) = \emptyset$ iff $L(P) \cap \overline{L(\text{Enrich}(C))} = \emptyset$, and VPAs support all of the required operations.

3.5 Checking Emptiness

Although other algorithms are known even for general PDAs, for completeness we describe a new algorithm that we devised, which harnesses previously known operations for answering reachability queries on pushdown systems (PDSs). Our approach is purely automata-theoretic, and does not translate the VPA language to a context-free grammar. We can use the *witness tracing* [32] feature supported by the PDS reachability operation (*post**) to trace non-emptiness answers back to a string that is in the producer's VPA's language but not in the consumer's; such a string suggests a potential bug in one of the components.

To describe the algorithm, it is necessary to review some known results about PDSs [5, 14].

DEFINITION 3.4 A **pushdown system** (PDS) is a three-tuple $\mathcal{P} = (P, \Gamma, \Delta)$, where P is a finite set of **control locations**, Γ is a finite set of **stack symbols**, and $\Delta \subseteq P \times \Gamma \times P \times \Gamma^*$ is a finite set of **rules**. A **configuration** of $\mathcal{P}$ is a pair $\langle p, u \rangle$ where $p \in P$ and $u \in \Gamma^*$. A rule $r \in \Delta$ is written as $\langle p, \gamma \rangle \hookrightarrow \langle p', u \rangle$, where $p, p' \in P$, $\gamma \in \Gamma$, and $u \in \Gamma^*$. The rules define a **transition relations** $\Rightarrow$ on configurations of $\mathcal{P}$ as follows: If $r = \langle p, \gamma \rangle \hookrightarrow \langle p', u' \rangle$, then $\langle p, \gamma u \rangle \Rightarrow \langle p', u' u \rangle$ for all $u \in \Gamma^*$. □

Because the number of configurations of a PDS is unbounded, it is useful to use finite automata to describe certain infinite sets of configurations.

DEFINITION 3.5 A **configuration automaton** that defines a language of configurations of PDS $\mathcal{P} = (P, \Gamma, \Delta)$ is a finite-state automaton $\mathcal{C} = (S, \Gamma, \rightarrow, P, F)$, where S is a finite set of states, $\mathcal{C}$ uses $\mathcal{P}$'s set of stack symbols Γ as its alphabet, $\rightarrow \subseteq S \times \Gamma \times S$ is the transition relation, the set of initial states consists of $\mathcal{P}$'s set of control locations P (which must be a subset of S), and $F \subseteq S$ is the set of final states. We say that a configuration $\langle p, u \rangle$ is **accepted** by configuration automaton $\mathcal{C}$ if $\mathcal{C}$ can accept u (in the ordinary sense from the theory of finite-state automata) when it is started in the state p; that is, $p \xrightarrow{u}{}^* s$, where $s \in F$. A set of configurations is said to be **regular** if some configuration automaton accepts it. □

Let $\Rightarrow^*$ denote the reflexive transitive closure of $\Rightarrow$. For a set of configurations C, $pre^*_{\mathcal{P}}(C) \stackrel{\text{def}}{=} \{c' \mid \exists c \in C : c' \Rightarrow^* c\}$ and $post^*_{\mathcal{P}}(C) \stackrel{\text{def}}{=} \{c' \mid \exists c \in C : c \Rightarrow^* c'\}$—i.e., backward and forward reachability, respectively, with respect to transition relation $\Rightarrow$. When C is a regular language of configurations, automata for the configuration languages $pre^*_{\mathcal{P}}(C)$ and $post^*_{\mathcal{P}}(C)$ can be constructed by algorithms that run in time polynomial in the size of $\mathcal{P}$ [5, 14].

Given a VPA A, the first step of checking whether $L(A) = \emptyset$ is to convert A to a PDS $\mathcal{P}_A$.

DEFINITION 3.6 Given VPA $A = (Q, \tilde{\Sigma}, Q, \delta, q_0, F)$, we define PDS $\mathcal{P}_A = (\{s\}, Q, \Delta)$, where each transition of A is converted to one or two rules in Δ, as follows:

- For each transition $((q, \sigma), q') \in \delta$, Δ has a rule $\langle s, q \rangle \hookrightarrow \langle s, q' \rangle$.
- For each transition $((q, \sigma_c), (q', \gamma)) \in \delta$, Δ has a rule $\langle s, q \rangle \hookrightarrow \langle s, q'\, q \rangle$. (This pushes q' onto the stack, the top of which is currently q.)
- For each transition $((q, \gamma, \sigma_r), q') \in \delta$, Δ has two rules, $\langle s, q \rangle \hookrightarrow \langle s_x, \varepsilon \rangle$ and $\langle s_x, \gamma \rangle \hookrightarrow \langle s, q' \rangle$. (Conceptually this can be thought of as a single transition $\langle s, q\, \gamma \rangle \hookrightarrow \langle s, q' \rangle$ of a prefix rewriting system [8].)

One can interpret this conversion as simply moving the information in the VPA's finite control into the top symbol of the stack. □

In our application, the initial state of the producer's VPA is $\texttt{main}_{\texttt{entry}}$, and the only final state is $\texttt{main}_{\texttt{exit}}$. Assuming that `main` is never invoked recursively, we only consider perfectly-matched strings (those with balanced calls and returns) and whether the set of perfectly-matched strings is empty. To test this condition, we create trivial configuration automata for the languages of initial-state and final-state configurations (where the machine has an empty stack)

$$\begin{aligned} L(\text{InitialConfigurations}) &= \{\langle s, q_0 \rangle\} \\ &= \{\langle s, \texttt{main}_{\texttt{entry}} \rangle\} \\ L(\text{FinalConfigurations}) &= \{\langle s, f \rangle \mid f \in F\} \\ &= \{\langle s, \texttt{main}_{\texttt{exit}} \rangle\} \end{aligned}$$

We can check whether the set of perfectly-matched strings is empty by answering the question of whether there is a path in the transition relation $\Rightarrow$ from a configuration in $L(\text{InitialConfigurations})$ to a configuration in $L(\text{FinalConfigurations})$. One way to answer this question is to check whether the language of the finite-state automaton constructed as follows is empty:

$$\text{FinalConfigurations} \cap post^*_{\mathcal{P}_A}(\text{InitialConfigurations}). \quad (1)$$

(This reduces the question of VPA emptiness to emptiness of the language of an ordinary FA.)

Remark. The more general question of VPA emptiness when non-perfectly-matched strings are of interest can also be addressed using Eqn. (1): one merely has to use more elaborate languages of initial and final configurations. □

4. IMPLEMENTATION

This section describes a prototype implementation of the ideas presented in §2 and §3 in a tool called PCCA (**P**roducer-**C**onsumer **C**onformance **A**nalyzer).

PCCA has two phases: inference and compatibility. During the inference phase, PCCA uses CodeSurfer/C [10] to perform pointer analysis and build an interprocedural control-flow graph (ICFG) and call graph for each component. It traverses the ICFG to create a list of all call sites that (directly) call an I/O function (see §4.1), then traverses the call graph to determine which procedures to prune (see §4.2). It then traverses the ICFG again to create the automaton for each procedure as described in §2.2, minimizes each of them, and combines them into our model of the program.

During the compatibility phase, PCCA reads the automaton produced for each component and proceeds with the compatibility check according to PCCA's mode. For the VPA-mode, PCCA actually uses a formalism called Nested-Word Automata (NWAs) instead of VPAs, but each is essentially an alternative expression of the other [3]. We use an extension to the WALi library that implements NWAs [6].

4.1 Seeding the System with I/O Functions

PCCA requires information about (i) what function calls of the producer can perform output, and (ii) what function calls of the consumer can perform input. There are a number of ways such information can be supplied to PCCA:

1. The user can provide a list of I/O functions (e.g. `readBoolean`, `writeInt`, as in the example) and their associated types. For calls to standard functions such as `puts`, PCCA is already equipped with such mappings.
2. For calls to `printf`- or `scanf`-style procedures, if the format string is a constant in the code, PCCA will parse the string to determine the types being operated on.

   The implementation is flexible enough so that the producer or consumer can contain user-defined procedures with `printf`/`scanf`-like format-strings, provided that the format-string syntax is either the same as what is used by `printf` or what is used by `scanf`. PCCA just needs to know the name of the procedure and which formal parameter holds the format string.
3. If all else fails, the user can supply comments that annotate procedure-call sites to specify that a particular call site performs either input or output. The annotation includes the type that is operated on. This method also allows the user to selectively choose only some call sites to a particular procedure.
4. Finally, the list of procedure-call sites that the tool should consider to be I/O functions is explicitly materialized in a text file, so the user can add, remove, or change call sites in that list, or even generate it by different means. (In fact, in the current version of PCCA, the techniques described in items 1 and 2 are implemented by one program, and the technique described in item 3 is implemented by a second program.)

4.2 Removing Irrelevant Procedures

To reduce the size of the inferred VPA, PCCA prunes procedures that cannot possibly participate in I/O operations. If there is no path from the entry of procedure P to the exit of procedure P along which an I/O procedure is invoked, P can be discounted entirely. One of the first steps of PCCA is to traverse the call graph generated by CodeSurfer, determine which procedures can transitively call an I/O function, and ignore all others. As illustrated in columns 3 and 4 of Fig. 7 (see §5), the effect of pruning is substantial, reducing the number of procedures by as much as 90%.

5. EXPERIMENTS

To test the capabilities of PCCA, we ran it on a small corpus of examples (whose characteristics are listed in columns 2 and 3 of Fig. 7). The experiments were run on a system with dual quad-core, 2.27GHz Xeon E5520s processors; however, PCCA is entirely single-threaded. The system has 12 GB of memory, and runs Red Hat Enterprise Linux 5.

The experiments were designed to test whether PCCA would detect bugs in producer-consumer pairs that were buggy, correctly identify (presumably) correct code as having the language-containment property, and scale to realistic programs. We also compared the results between the FA and VPA-based modes of operation to determine whether the potential benefits discussed in §3.3 arose.

Each example consisted of a pair of programs—a producer and a consumer. In several cases, we used the program as both the producer and the consumer, which makes sense for programs that read and write the same format.

The examples are as follows:[5]

- *ex-prod/ex-cons* make up our running example (stubs for the I/O functions are included in the count),
- *ex-prod/ex-cons-fig3* uses the buggy version of the consumer presented in Fig. 3,
- *ex-prod-§2.5/ex-cons-§2.5* are buggy versions of the running example, modified as described at the end of §2.5 with the separator to mark the packets,
- *gzip* and *bzip2* are the common Unix compression/decompression utilities,
- *gzip-fixed* uses a modified version of *gzip* (discussed below) to eliminate an erroneous report,
- *png2ico* is an image-conversion program, which we compare to a hand-written specification.

Reported times are the median of 5 runs. The numbers for the FA version use NWAs with no call or return transitions. This gives an apples-to-apples comparison with NWAs, but is slower than an alternative implementation that converts each NWA to an OpenFST acceptor, determinizes with OpenFST, and converts back. All times are less than 1 sec. with the latter approach. There *is* an intrinsic cost to using an NWA representation, but we feel that most of the difference between our FA numbers and OpenFST's indicates room for improving the WALi implementation. (That would improve the NWA version as well.)

We also performed an informal experiment using the VPA version without Enrich (as mentioned at the end of §2.3). We tested programs that read and write trees in infix and prefix notation. Both the standard VPA version of PCCA and the no-Enrich version reported that the infix components are compatible with each other, that the prefix components are compatible with each other, and that each is incompatible with the other. As discussed in §2.3, the compatibility results are more credible for the no-Enrich version; the incompatibility results are more credible for the standard VPA version.

Omitting the Enrich step also dramatically decreased determinization time; even the *gzip-fix-cons* could be determinized in less than one second. Thus, it might be beneficial to try to combine enrichment and determinization.

Two of the tests, *gzip* and *png2ico*, required relatively minor modifications. *gzip* uses input and output operations

[5]Our experiments can be found at `http://www.cs.wisc.edu/wpis/examples/pcca/`

Test	LOC	#Funcs Orig.	Pruned	$\|Q\|$	#I/O	Infer aut.	VPA version (sec.) ¬C	Total	OK?	FA version (sec.) ¬C	Total	OK?
ex-prod	43	11	3	9	4	2.12	0.35	4.90	Y	0.10	4.76	Y
ex-cons	26	7	2	5	3	2.24						
ex-prod	43	11	3	9	4	2.12	0.16	4.49	N	0.10	4.61	N
ex-cons-fig3	25	7	2	5	3	2.09						
ex-prod-§2.5	43	11	3	10	5	2.29	0.70	4.87	N	0.10	5.09	N
ex-cons-§2.5	25	7	2	5	3	2.40						
gzip-prod	4396	100	17	51	25	26.3	123	177	N*	101	157	N*
gzip-cons	4396	100	24	71	50	27.8						
gzip-prod	4396	100	17	51	25	26.3	583	646	Y	102	156	Y
gzip-fix-cons	4389	100	24	73	51	27.8						
bzip2-prod	5772	121	15	32	8	26.3	47.7	102	Y	47.1	101	Y
bzip2-cons	5772	121	13	29	10	27.4						
png2ico-prod	806	39	1	22	29	9.48	14.4	33.1	Y	0.16	10.1	Y
ico-spec-cons	n/a	n/a	n/a	26	28	n/a						

Figure 7: The experiments. "LOC" is lines of code, "orig." is the number of functions in the program, "pruned" is that number after pruning. $|Q|$ is the number of states in the inferred automaton (equal between the two variants). "# I/O" is the (static) number of calls to I/O functions. "Infer aut." is the time (sec.) to produce the automata for every procedure in the program. (The output of this step is used for both the VPA and FA versions.) For both the VPA and FA version, ¬C is the time (sec.) to determinize and complement the automaton. (Determinizing each procedure's FA is not included in this time, but takes a negligible amount of time in all experiments.) "Total" is the end-to-end time for analysis, including the inference step. "OK?" reports the output of PCCA.

much like those in our running example, except implemented as macros. Because PCCA uses the control-flow graph generated by CodeSurfer/C, these macros are not visible, so we replaced the macro definitions with functions. In addition, *gzip* calls the function that actually performs the compression or decompression through a function pointer. CodeSurfer/C performs points-to analysis, but PCCA does not yet take such indirect calls into account; thus we modified the source to call the function directly. (This is not a fundamental limitation of our technique, though imprecise pointer analysis could lead to further imprecision.) A final modification that applies in a similar manner to both *gzip* and *png2ico* will be described in their respective sections.

As shown in Fig. 7, PCCA reports that some commonly-used programs operate in a correct manner with regard to their I/O behavior, regardless of the automaton model used. PCCA also detects synthetic programming errors in small examples, as shown by the second pair of examples.

As can be seen in the results, the potential VPA benefits did not appear to affect the results of the analysis. (PCCA does report different results for the example in §3.3, but we do not include that experiment in Fig. 7.) This result surprised us, and in the future we plan to look at additional examples to see whether any of them benefit from VPAs.

gzip. The analysis of *gzip* reported a erroneous bug in the distributed version; we examine the issues more closely here. For *gzip*, the actual compressed data appears as just a sequence of bytes, so the compatibility check essentially is testing the compatibility of the code that reads and writes the header and footer. Fig. 8 describes the header format of a *gzip* file. The code that writes this header (in `zip.c`) corresponds very closely to the header format:

```
put_byte(GZIP_MAGIC[0]); /* magic header */
put_byte(GZIP_MAGIC[1]);
put_byte(DEFLATED);      /* compression method */
...
put_byte(flags);         /* general flags */
put_long(time_stamp);
...
put_byte((uch)deflate_flags); /* extra flags */
put_byte(OS_CODE);
```

For this code, PCCA infers the format specified in Fig. 8.

However, the code that *reads* the header is reported to be incompatible; this is a false positive. Unlike the output functions, input is always done one byte at a time:

```
stamp  = (ulg)get_byte();
stamp |= ((ulg)get_byte()) << 8;
stamp |= ((ulg)get_byte()) << 16;
stamp |= ((ulg)get_byte()) << 24;
```

Because the consumer reads the `time_stamp` field as four `bytes` instead of one `long`, it appears incompatible. This is similar to the issue of granularity of types discussed in §2.2.

To address this, we replaced this code (and similar code that reads `long` fields in the footer) with a new `get_long` function. This function can be implemented in terms of four bytewise reads; as long as PCCA is told that `get_long` performs I/O, PCCA will recognize the call as reading a `long`. (In addition to helping PCCA, we feel that the modified code is cleaner: by having the code for reading and writing a `long` in one place, it is easier for the programmer to see that those functions agree, for instance by reading and writing the bytes in the same order. It should even be possible to use our techniques to perform this check as well, by giving different types to each byte in the `long`.)

After making this change, PCCA reports that the programs are compatible. It is unclear why there is such a dramatic difference between the time it takes to determinize each version of the consumer in the VPA version. The input VPAs are of almost identical size and makeup, but it appears that the extra `long` alphabet symbol in the revised version causes

ID1	ID2	CM	FLG	MTIME	XFL	OS	···

ID1, ID2	Fixed constants; *gzip*'s "magic number"
CM	Compression algorithm
FLG	Flags, as a bitmap
MTIME	The modification time of the original file
XFL	Compression-method-specific flags
OS	ID of the OS where the file was compressed

Figure 8: The specification of *gzip*'s header format. Each field is 1 byte except for MTIME, which is 4.

the determinized VPA to be much bigger (176 states vs. 27). (Note that neither of these automata are minimal; it could be that the extra size in the revised version could be reduced to be more in line with the original version.) The sizes of the two automata in the FA version are much closer.

png2ico. For *png2ico*, we demonstrate a slightly different application of our techniques. Instead of comparing a producer to a consumer, we compare a producer to a manually-crafted specification acting as the consumer. This checks that the producer emits only messages that are allowed by the specification. In the case of *png2ico*, we see that the program indeed appears to conform to the specification.

We manually crafted an automaton that describes the format of an icon file [18] and used that as the consumer. For the ICO format, this was reasonably straightforward and took less than two hours. The automaton allows PCCA to check header information, similar to *gzip* but with a much richer format. An icon file can hold several different images. In addition to a global header (that mainly says how many images there are), there is a directory that gives the offset and other information about each image and a header for the image data itself. We can check all of this, leaving only the raw image data itself appearing as a "meaningless" byte stream. (We cannot check that the image headers actually appear at the correct offsets, however.)

While most of the output from *png2ico* is done through the functions `WriteByte`, `WriteWord`, and `WriteDWord`, there are three places where a raw write is done using `fwrite`. Two of these locations write a sequence of raw bytes of an image to the file. We could reasonably infer just `byte*` for those calls (similar to how the actual compressed data comes across in *gzip*), however we decided to put in a bit of extra effort to obtain higher confidence in the result. The two `fwrite` calls correspond to the "xor mask" and "and mask" of the bitmap. We manually specified that the first `fwrite` call outputs "xor mask" bytes and the second call outputs "and mask" bytes, and required that each bitmap in the icon file contains a sequence of "xor mask" bytes followed by a sequence of "and mask" bytes. However, there is one call to `WriteByte` amongst those writing the "xor mask", so we had to manually change the type of that call to match that of the preceding `fwrite`. (We repeated the experiment but just used `byte*`, and PCCA still reported compatibility.)

The third call to `fwrite` is used instead of a sequence of four `WriteByte` calls; the reason the author choose this is not clear. We replaced this `fwrite` with the four individual `WriteByte` calls. In the future we hope to implement the ability to automatically break apart a write such as this, to make such manual intervention unnecessary.

We only report the results for the version with specific types. The other variants we tried did not have much effect.

6. RELATED WORK

Inferring Input or Output Formats of Programs. PCCA's format-inference techniques, as well as the problem in general, was inspired by the File Format Extractor tool (FFE) by Lim et al. [23]. FFE infers output models of x86 executables using a weighted pushdown system. We skip the WPDS step, performing the procedure discussed in §2.2 instead. The minimization we perform on each procedure's model gets us the benefits intended by FFE's use of WPDSs, and produces far smaller automata.

Inferring input formats of executables has received much attention lately, particularly in the context of protocol reverse engineering for network security [7, 12, 34, 24, 25]. However, most of this work involves the use of dynamic-analysis techniques.

Komondoor and Ramalingam developed methods to recover an object-oriented data model from a program written in weakly-typed languages, such as Cobol [21]. It is capable of recovering information about the record structure of entities that occur in a file, as well as information about subtyping relationships between such entities.

Checking Compatibility/Conformance. Rajamani and Rehof [30] developed a way to check that an implementation model I extracted from a message-passing program conforms to a specification S. Their goal was to support modular reasoning; they established that if I conforms to S and P is any environment in which P and S cannot starve waiting to send or receive messages, then P and I also cannot starve.

A related question is checking conformance of software components as software evolves and components are replaced or upgraded. Clarke et al. [9] survey several approaches that have been devised to answer the question, including interface automata, behavioral subtyping [26], input/output-based compatibility of upgrades [27], and model checking.

There have also been many papers on session types, starting with [17, 15, 29]. In some sense, this body of work has the same goal that we have—helping to ensure that different components communicate properly—but their approach is far different. Session types, at a high level, convey much the same information as our inferred languages. (For instance, in the syntax of [17], "`↑int; (↑char & ↑double)`" is the type of a component that emits an `int` followed by either a `char` or `double`.) Some recent work, e.g. [19], is integrating session types into common programming languages.

In most of this literature, session types need to be incorporated into the language being used to write the components, which means they cannot be applied to legacy software without rewriting it. In contrast to these papers, our work analyzes existing C/C++ code for compatibility by inferring the format. In return for this re-engineering, session types support richer interactions than we currently do; most notably, it can specify bidirectional communications.

Recently there have been advances in inferring session types, which is much closer to our goal. Mezzina [28] and

Collingbourne and Kelly [11] each developed such an algorithm. Collingbourne's is particularly related, as they implemented their technique in a source-to-source translator for C++. However, neither paper really gives enough information on how it performs in practice to compare to PCCA.

In a similar vein – and actually of equivalent power – are channel contracts from the Singularity OS [13]. Channel contracts specify a protocol between two endpoints as a state machine, where each state specifies messages that each endpoint can send or receive. Fähndrich et al. describe an analysis that verifies certain memory-safety properties in programs that use channel contracts. More recent work has analyzed channel contracts with respect to deadlocks [33] and developed formal type theories for channels [4].

7. FUTURE WORK

We have a number of extensions to the basic idea described in this paper in mind; we describe two of them here. The discussion in this paper is framed from the point of view that the VPA alphabet consists of the actual programming language types used by the programs. However, our approach is more flexible. It is possible to have even finer-granularity types. To do this, we would use types that do not correspond to those in C. For instance, it would be possible to have an `int_ascii` symbol for an integer expressed in ASCII digits (e.g., the three-byte sequence "255") and `int_bin` for an integer in binary (e.g., the four bytes 0x000000FF). (§2.5 described how a particular way of using a phony I/O call to help PCCA detect bugs; this idea expands that technique.) It should also be possible to extend our work to include information about the *values* that are read or written—for instance, to specify that `write_int` outputs a "4" or that `write_int` outputs a value in the range "[4,7]" (and similarly for the input operations of the consumer). This would require a change to the compatibility portion as well.

Second, there are some engineering tasks that should make it easier to get more helpful results. For example, we can implement the technique mentioned in the remark at the end of §2.2, where we make it possible to break apart automatically a structure or array type into its component fields. This would allow the producer and consumer to use data structures that are organized differently from one another but have the same semantic meaning, and would avoid the most invasive changes we had to make in our experiments.

8. REFERENCES

[1] C. Allauzen, M. Riley, J. Schalkwyk, W. Skut, and M. Mohri. OpenFst: A general and efficient weighted finite-state transducer library. In *CIAA*, 2007.

[2] R. Alur and P. Madhusudan. Visibly pushdown languages. In *STOC*, 2004.

[3] R. Alur and P. Madhusudan. Adding nesting structure to words. *J. ACM*, 56(3), 2009.

[4] V. Bono, C. Messa, and L. Padovani. Typing copyless message passing. In *ESOP*, 2011.

[5] A. Bouajjani, J. Esparza, and O. Maler. Reachability analysis of pushdown automata: Application to model checking. In *CONCUR*, 1997.

[6] A. Burton, A. Thakur, E. Driscoll, , and T. Reps. WALi: Nested-word automata. TR-1675, Comp. Sci. Dept., Univ. of Wisconsin, Madison, WI, July 2010.

[7] J. Caballero and D. Song. Polyglot: Automatic extraction of protocol format using dynamic binary analysis. In *CCS*, 2007.

[8] D. Caucal. On the regular structure of prefix rewriting. In *CAAP*, 1990.

[9] E. Clarke, N. Sharygina, and N. Sinha. Program compatibility approaches. In *FMCO*, 2005.

[10] CodeSurfer system. www.grammatech.com/products/codesurfer.

[11] P. Collingbourne and P. Kelly. Inference of session types from control flow. *ENTCS*, 238(6), 2010.

[12] W. Cui, M. Peinado, K. Chen, H. Wang, and L. Irun-Briz. Tupni: Automatic reverse engineering of input formats. In *CCS*, 2008.

[13] M. Fähndrich, M. Aiken, C. Hawblitzel, O. Hodson, G. Hunt, J. R. Larus, and S. Levi. Language support for fast and reliable message-based communication in Singularity OS. In *EuroSys*. 2006.

[14] A. Finkel, B.Willems, and P. Wolper. A direct symbolic approach to model checking pushdown systems. *ENTCS*, 9, 1997.

[15] S. Gay, V. Vasconcelos, and A. Ravara. Session types for inter-process communication. TR-2003-133, Dept. of Computing Sci., Univ. of Glasgow, March 2003.

[16] S. Hallem, B. Chelf, Y. Xie, and D. Engler. A system and language for building system-specific, static analyses. In *PLDI*, 2002.

[17] K. Honda. Types for dyadic interaction. In *CONCUR*. 1993.

[18] J. Hornick. Icons. `http://msdn.microsoft.com/en-us/library/ms997538.aspx`.

[19] R. Hu, D. Kouzapas, O. Pernet, N. Yoshida, and K. Honda. Type-safe eventful sessions in java. In *ECOOP*. 2010.

[20] N. Kidd, A. Lal, and T. Reps. WALi: The Weighted Automaton Library, 2007. www.cs.wisc.edu/wpis/wpds/download.php.

[21] R. Komondoor and G. Ramalingam. Recovering data models via guarded dependences. In *WCRE*, 2007.

[22] T. Kremenek, P. Twohey, G. Back, A. Ng, and D. Engler. From uncertainty to belief: inferring the specification within. In *OSDI*, 2006.

[23] J. Lim, T. Reps, and B. Liblit. Extracting output formats from executables. In *WCRE*, 2006.

[24] Z. Lin, X. Jiang, D. Xu, and X. Zhang. Automatic protocol format reverse engineering through context-aware monitored execution. In *NDSS*, 2008.

[25] Z. Lin and X. Zhang. Deriving input syntactic structure from execution. In *FSE*, 2008.

[26] B. Liskov and J. Wing. Behavioral subtyping using invariants and constraints. In H. Bowman and J. Derrick, editors, *Formal Methods for Distributed Processing: An Object Oriented Approach*. Cambridge Univ. Press, 2001.

[27] S. McCamant and M. Ernst. Early identification of incompatibilities in multicomponent upgrades. In *ECOOP*, 2004.

[28] L. Mezzina. How to infer finite session types in a calculus of services and sessions. In D. Lea and G. Zavattaro, editors, *Coordination Models and Languages*. 2008.

[29] O. Nierstrasz and M. Papathomas. Viewing object as patterns of communicating agents. In *OOPSLA*, 1990.

[30] S. Rajamani and J. Rehof. Conformance checking for models of asynchronous message passing software. In *CAV*, 2002.

[31] T. Reps, S. Horwitz, and M. Sagiv. Precise interprocedural dataflow analysis via graph reachability. In *POPL*, 1995.

[32] S. Schwoon. *Model-Checking Pushdown Systems*. PhD thesis, TUM, Munich, Germany, July 2002.

[33] Z. Stengel and T. Bultan. Analyzing Singluarity channel contracts. In *ISSTA*. 2009.

[34] G. Wondracek, P. Comparetti, C. Kruegel, and E. Kirda. Automatic network protocol analysis. In *NDSS*, 2008.

Managing Performance vs. Accuracy Trade-offs With Loop Perforation

Stelios Sidiroglou   Sasa Misailovic   Henry Hoffmann
Martin Rinard
Computer Science and Artificial Intelligence Laboratory
Massachusetts Institute of Technology
{stelios,misailo,hank,rinard}@csail.mit.edu

ABSTRACT

Many modern computations (such as video and audio encoders, Monte Carlo simulations, and machine learning algorithms) are designed to trade off accuracy in return for increased performance. To date, such computations typically use ad-hoc, domain-specific techniques developed specifically for the computation at hand.

Loop perforation provides a general technique to trade accuracy for performance by transforming loops to execute a subset of their iterations. A criticality testing phase filters out *critical loops* (whose perforation produces unacceptable behavior) to identify *tunable loops* (whose perforation produces more efficient and still acceptably accurate computations). A perforation space exploration algorithm perforates combinations of tunable loops to find Pareto-optimal perforation policies. Our results indicate that, for a range of applications, this approach typically delivers performance increases of over a factor of two (and up to a factor of seven) while changing the result that the application produces by less than 10%.

Categories and Subject Descriptors

C.4 [**Performance of Systems**]: Reliability, availability, and serviceability

General Terms

Performance, Reliability, Experimentation

Keywords

Profiling, Loop Perforation, Quality of Service

1. INTRODUCTION

Many computations are designed to produce approximate results. Lossy video encoders, for example, are designed to give up perfect fidelity in return for faster encoding and smaller encoded videos [38]. Machine learning algorithms are designed to produce probabilistic models that capture some, but not all, aspects of phenomena that are difficult (if not impossible) to model with complete accuracy [15]. Monte-Carlo computations use random simulation to deliver inherently approximate solutions to complex systems of equations that are, in many cases, computationally infeasible to solve exactly [18].

Permission to make digital or hard copies of all or part of this work for personal or classroom use is granted without fee provided that copies are not made or distributed for profit or commercial advantage and that copies bear this notice and the full citation on the first page. To copy otherwise, to republish, to post on servers or to redistribute to lists, requires prior specific permission and/or a fee.
ESEC/FSE'11, September 5–9, 2011, Szeged, Hungary.
Copyright 2011 ACM 978-1-4503-0443-6/11/09 ...$10.00.

This paper presents and evaluates a technique, *loop perforation*, for generating new variants of computations that produce approximate results. These variants occupy different points in the underlying performance vs. accuracy tradeoff space. Our results show that perforating appropriately selected loops can produce significant performance gains (up to a factor of seven reduction in overall execution time) in return for small (less than 10%) accuracy losses. Our results also show that the generated variants occupy a broad region of points within the tradeoff space, giving users and systems significant flexibility in choosing a variant that best satisfies their needs in the current usage context.

1.1 Loop Perforation

Loop perforation transforms loops to execute a subset of their iterations. The goal is to reduce the amount of computational work (and therefore the amount of time and/or other resources such as power) that the computation requires to produce its result. Of course, perforation may (and in our experience, almost always does) cause the computation to produce a different result. But approximate computations can often tolerate such changes as long as they do not unacceptably reduce the accuracy. Our implemented system uses the following techniques to find effective perforations:

- **Criticality Testing:** It perforates each loop in turn, executing the perforated computation on representative inputs to filter out *critical* loops whose perforation causes the computation to produce unacceptable results, crash, increase its execution time, or execute with a memory error. Filtering out such critical loops enables the subsequent perforation space exploration algorithm to focus on the remaining *tunable* loops that respond well to loop perforation.
- **Perforation Space Exploration:** It explores the space of variants generated by perforating combinations of tunable loops together. Our implemented system supports both exhaustive and greedy search algorithms. The result of the exploration is a set of Pareto-optimal variants, each of which maximizes performance for a specific accuracy loss bound when run on representative inputs.

1.2 Experimental Results

We evaluate our implemented system on applications from the PARSEC benchmark suite [6]. Our results show that the perforation space exploration algorithm can find perforations that deliver significant performance increases for five of the seven applications. Specifically, our performance measurements show that the perforated applications can run as much as seven times faster than the original applications while producing outputs that differ by less than 10% from the corresponding outputs of the original applications. Our results also show that the perforation space exploration algorithm finds effective perforations — our evaluation of the source code of the applications indicates that the final perforations are appropriate for a wide range of inputs (and not just the training and production inputs used in the experimental evaluation).

1.3 Scope

Applications that interact well with loop perforation have some flexibility to change the result that they produce (subject, of course, to accuracy requirements). They also contain some underlying source of redundancy that enables them to produce an acceptable result even after discarding parts of their computation. Applications that process sensory data such as video, audio, and images often have both the redundancy and the flexibility required for loop perforation to work well. Other classes of applications include Monte Carlo simulations, information retrieval and machine learning computations, and the wide variety of scientific and economics computations for which the important consideration is producing an output within an acceptable precision range. Our results show that loop perforation can often improve the performance of all of these kinds of applications while preserving acceptable accuracy.

We acknowledge that many computations (for example, compilers, databases, and operating systems) may have hard logical correctness requirements that leave them with little or none of this kind of flexibility. We therefore do not claim that loop perforation is a universally applicable technique. Our experimental results show, however, that when the computation is amenable to loop perforation (and many of our benchmark applications are), loop perforation can be surprisingly effective at improving the performance while maintaining acceptable accuracy.

1.4 Why Loop Perforation Works

We have identified local computational patterns that interact well with loop perforation [24, 32, 25]. Examples include the Sum pattern (which computes the sum of a set of numbers) and the Argmin pattern (which computes the index and value of a minimum array element). An analysis of these patterns delivers a probabilistic guarantee that (under appropriate assumptions) the perforated computation is highly likely to produce a result that is close to the result that the original computation would have produced [24, 25].

While many of the perforated loops in our benchmark applications are instances of these patterns, they are also embedded as components within a larger application. Because the probabilistic analysis does not address how the effect of the perforation propagates through the application as a whole (which may either amplify or dampen it), it provides, at best, only a partial explanation for why it is acceptable to perforate these loops.

In this paper we identify *global computational patterns* that interact well with loop perforation. Analyzing the interaction between these patterns and the local perforated computations, we can understand why loop perforation works well for the application as a whole (and not just for the local computations embedded within the application). We identify the following global patterns (see Section 7 for more details):

- **Search Space Enumeration:** The application iterates over a search space of items. The perforated computation skips some of the items, returning one of the items from the remaining part of the search space.
- **Search Metric:** The application uses a *search metric* to drive a search for the most desirable item from a set of items:
  - **Selection:** A *selection* metric quantifies the desirability of each item encountered during the search.
  - **Filtering:** A *filtering* metric determines if the search should remove the item from a set of active items.
  - **Termination:** A *termination* metric determines if the search should terminate, either because an acceptable item has been found or because the likelihood of finding a more desirable item appears to be small.

  Perforating a search metric computation produces a new, less accurate but more efficiently computable metric. The effect is that the perforated search may return a less desirable but still acceptable item.

  We note that some applications use the same metric for more than one purpose. In this case the metric is a combined selection, filtering, and/or termination metric.
- **Monte-Carlo Simulation:** The application performs a Monte-Carlo simulation. The perforated computation evaluates fewer samples to produce a (potentially) less accurate result more efficiently.
- **Iterative Improvement:** The application repeatedly improves an approximate result to obtain a more accurate result. The perforated computation performs fewer improvement steps to produce a (potentially) less accurate result more efficiently.
- **Data Structure Update:** The application traverses a data structure, updating elements of the data structure with computed values. The perforated computation skips some of the elements, leaving the previous values in the skipped elements.

Successful perforations exploit computations that are partially redundant at both the local (loop) and global (application) level. This redundancy often appears when computations process multiple items to obtain a single result. For example, a computation that searches a set to find the most desirable item is partially redundant when the set contains similar items — searching only a subset of the items is likely to produce an item that is close to the most desirable item in the set.

We note that many of our applications perform inherently approximate computations, for example because they work with approximate models of reality or because exact solutions are too expensive to compute. In such cases perforation may make an already approximate computation even more approximate.

1.5 Uses of Loop Perforation

Potential uses of loop perforation include:

- **Performance Enhancement:** Guided by the parameters of the tradeoff space, a user can select a desired level of performance that provides acceptable accuracy. Or the user can select a desired accuracy, then use loop perforation to maximize the delivered performance.
- **Energy Savings:** Because loop perforation can reduce the computation required to produce an acceptable result, and computation translates directly into energy consumption, loop perforation can reduce the energy required to produce the result. Moreover, for real-time computations, loop perforation may free up the time required to enable additional synergistic energy-saving optimizations such as voltage scaling [28].
- **New Platforms or Contexts:** Applications often come tuned for use in a specific context or computational platform (for example, desktop machines). Loop perforation can support effective redeployment onto a new platform (for example, mobile devices) or into a new context with different performance or accuracy requirements.
- **Dynamic Adaptation:** Our implemented compiler can generate code that can dynamically move between different variants as the computation executes [16]. This capability enables the construction of control systems that use loop perfo-

ration to dynamically adapt application behavior to satisfy real-time deadlines in the face of changes (such as clock speed changes, load variations, or processor loss) in the underlying computational platform [16].
- **Developer Insight:** A developer can examine the perforation to gain insight into where it is possible to trade accuracy for increased performance [26]. The developer may then choose to accept the perforated computation as is, use the perforated computation as a starting point for further optimization, or use the perforation to identify computations that are suitable targets for manual optimization.

1.6 Contributions

This paper makes the following contributions:

- **Loop Perforation**: It presents and evaluates loop perforation as an automatic technique for generating multiple variants of approximate computations, with the different variants occupying different points in the underlying performance vs. accuracy tradeoff space.
- **Criticality Testing:** It presents a criticality testing algorithm that identifies tunable loops that respond well to perforation.
- **Perforation Space Exploration:** It presents and evaluates exhaustive and greedy algorithms for exploring the perforation space to find a set of Pareto-optimal perforations.
- **Experimental Results**: It presents experimental results for applications from the PARSEC benchmark suite. These results show that loop perforation can deliver significant performance improvements (the perforated applications run up to seven times faster than the original applications) while maintaining accurate execution (the results from the perforated applications differ by at most 10% from the original results).
- **Global Patterns:** It identifies and analyzes global computational patterns (for example, loops that combine multiple partially redundant values and searches driven by perforatable metrics) that interact well with loop perforation. These patterns explain why loop perforation works well for our benchmark applications and can serve as a foundation for the broader application of loop perforation across a large range of applications.

We have previously proposed the use of loop perforation for *quality of service profiling* to help developers find suitable manual optimization targets [26]. This paper presents a new criticality testing methodology for identifying perforatable loops, a new methodology for exploring a perforation space with multiple loop perforation rates, experimental results that characterize the induced performance vs. accuracy tradeoff space for a broad range of perforation rates and inputs (including results that characterize how well results from training input generalize to previously unseen production inputs), and an identification of specific global computational patterns that work well with loop perforation, including an explanation of why loop perforation is applicable to these patterns. Together, these results support the use of loop perforation as an optimization in its own right rather than simply as a profiling technique.

2. PERFORATION TRANSFORMATION

We implement loop perforation within the LLVM compiler framework [20]. The perforator works with any loop that the existing LLVM loop canonicalization pass, *loop-simplify*, can convert into the following form:

```
for (i = 0; i < b; i++) { ... }
```

In this form, the loop has an unique induction variable (in the code above, `i`) initialized to `0` and incremented by `1` on every iteration, with the loop terminating when the induction variable `i` exceeds the bound (in the code above, `b`). The class of loops that LLVM can convert into this form includes, for example, `for` loops that initialize an induction variable to an arbitrary initial value, increment the induction variable by an arbitrary constant value on each iteration, and terminate when the induction variable exceeds an arbitrary bound.

The loop perforation transformation takes as a parameter a loop perforation rate r, which represents the expected percentage of loop iterations to skip. Interleaving perforation transforms the loop to perform every `n`-th iteration (here the perforation rate is r = `1-1/n`). Conceptually, the perforated computation looks like (see [16] for a more detailed treatment):

```
for (i = 0; i < b; i += n) { ... }
```

All of the experimental results in this paper use interleaving perforation. Our implemented perforator can also apply truncation perforation (which skips a contiguous sequence of iterations at either the beginning or the end of the loop) or random perforation (which randomly skips loop iterations) [16].

3. ACCURACY METRIC

The accuracy metric measures the difference between an output from the original program and a corresponding output from the perforated program run on the same input. We decompose the metric into two parts: an *output abstraction*, which maps an output to a number or set of numbers, and an *accuracy calculation*, which measures the difference between the output abstractions from the original and perforated executions. The output abstraction typically selects relevant numbers from an output file or files or computes a measure (such as peak signal to noise ratio) of the quality of the output. Many approximate computations come with such quality measures already defined and available (see Section 5).

The accuracy calculation computes the metric *acc* as a weighted mean scaled difference between the output abstraction components $o_1, \ldots, o_m$ from the original program and the output abstraction components $\hat{o}_1, \ldots, \hat{o}_m$ from the perforated program [31]:

$$acc = \frac{1}{m} \sum_{i=1}^{m} w_i \left| \frac{o_i - \hat{o}_i}{o_i} \right| \quad (1)$$

Here each weight w_i captures the relative importance of the ith component of the output abstraction. Note that the closer the accuracy metric *acc* is to zero, the more accurate the perforated program. We often report accuracy metrics as percentages.

4. PERFORATION EXPLORATION

The loop perforation space exploration algorithm takes as input an application, an accuracy metric for that application, a set of training inputs, an accuracy bound b (a maximum acceptable accuracy metric for the application), and a set of perforation rates (in our experiments, 0.25, 0.50, 0.75, and 1 iteration). The algorithm produces a set S of loops to perforate at specified perforation rates.

4.1 Criticality Testing

The criticalility testing algorithm (Algorithm 1) starts with a set of candidate loops L and perforation rates R. L consists of the loops (identified by profiling) that account for at least 1% of the executed instructions (with a cutoff after the top 25 loops). In general, perforating a candidate loop may cause the program to crash, generate unacceptable output, produce an infinite loop, or decrease its

Algorithm 1 (Criticality Testing) Find the set of tunable loops P in A given training inputs T and accuracy bound b

Inputs:
A - an application
T - a set of representative inputs
b - an accuracy bound
L - a set of candidate loops for perforation
R - a set of perforation rates
Outputs: P - a set of tunable loops and perforation rates for A given b and T

```
P = ∅
for ⟨l, r⟩ ∈ L × R do
  Let A⟨l,r⟩ be A with l perforated at rate r
  for t ∈ T do
    Run A⟨l,r⟩ on t, record speedup sp_t and accuracy acc_t
    sp‾ = (Σ_{t∈T} sp_t)/||T|| ; acc‾ = (Σ_{t∈T} acc_t)/||T||
  if acc‾ < b ∧ sp‾ > 1 then
    for t ∈ T do
      Run A⟨l,r⟩ using Valgrind to find Err_t (memory errors)
    if ∪_{t∈T} E_t = ∅ then
      P = P ∪ {⟨l, r⟩}
return P
```

Algorithm 2 (Greedy Exploration) Find a set S of loops to perforate in A given training inputs T and accuracy bound b

Inputs:
A - an application
T - a set of representative inputs
b - an accuracy bound
P - a set of tunable loops generated by Algorithm 1
Outputs: S - a set of loops to perforate in A given b

```
P′ = { ⟨l, r⟩ | ⟨l, r⟩ ∈ P ∧ ∀p, score⟨l,r⟩ ≤ score⟨l,p⟩ }
S = ∅
for ⟨l, r⟩ ∈ P′ in sorted order according to score⟨l,p⟩ do
  C = S ∪ {⟨l, r⟩}
  Let A_C be A with all loops in C perforated
  for t ∈ T do
    Run A_C on t, record speedup sp_t and accuracy acc_t
    sp‾ = (Σ_{t∈T} sp_t)/||T||; acc‾ = (Σ_{t∈T} acc_t)/||T||
  if acc‾ < b ∧ sp‾ > 1 then
    for t ∈ T do
      Run A_C using Valgrind to find Err_t (memory errors)
    if ∪_{t∈T} E_t = ∅ then
      S = C
return S
```

performance. Algorithm 1 is designed to find and remove such *critical* loops from the set of candidate loops. The algorithm perforates each loop in turn at each of the specified perforation rates, then runs the perforated program on the training inputs. It filters out a loop if its perforation 1) fails to improve the performance (as measured by the speedup sp, which is the execution time of the perforated application divided by the execution time of the original unperforated program running on the same input), 2) causes the application to exceed the accuracy bound b or, 3) introduces memory errors (such as out of bounds reads or writes, reads to uninitialized memory, memory leaks, double frees, etc.). If the memory error causes the execution to crash on some input t, its accuracy loss acc_t is ∞. The result of criticality testing is the set of tunable loops $P = \{\langle l_0, r_0\rangle, \ldots, \langle l_n, r_n\rangle\}$, where $\langle l_i, r_i\rangle$ specifies the perforation of loop l_i at rate r_i.

4.2 Perforation Space Exploration Algorithms

We next present two algorithms (exhaustive and greedy) for exploring the performance vs. accuracy tradeoff space of perforated programs.

Exhaustive Exploration Algorithm. The exhaustive perforation space exploration algorithm starts with the set of tunable loops, then exhaustively explores all combinations of tunable loops l at their specified perforation rates r. The algorithm executes all combinations on all training inputs and records the resulting speedup and accuracy. It also runs each combination under Valgrind [27], discarding the combination if Valgrind detects a memory error. We use the results to compute the set of Pareto-optimal perforations in the induced performance vs. accuracy tradeoff space. A perforation is Pareto-optimal if there is no other perforation that provides both better performance and better accuracy.

This approach is feasible for applications (such as those in our set of benchmarks) that spend most of their time in relatively few loops. If exhaustive exploration is infeasible, it is possible to either use the greedy algorithm or drop enough of the least time-consuming tunable loops to make exhaustive exploration feasible. Hybrid approaches are also possible.

Greedy Exploration Algorithm. Algorithm 2 uses a greedy strategy to search the loop perforation space to produce, for a given accuracy bound b, a set of loops and corresponding perforation rates $S = \{\langle l_0, r_0\rangle, \ldots, \langle l_n, r_n\rangle\}$ that maximize performance subject to b. The algorithm uses a heuristic scoring metric to prioritize loop/perforation rate pairs. The scoring metric for a pair $\langle l, r\rangle$ is based on the harmonic mean of terms that estimate the performance increase and accuracy loss of the perforated program:

$$score_{\langle l,r\rangle} = \frac{2}{\dfrac{1}{\overline{sp}_{\langle l,r\rangle} - 1} + \dfrac{1}{1 - \dfrac{\overline{acc}_{\langle l,r\rangle}}{b}}} \tag{2}$$

where $\overline{sp}_{\langle l,r\rangle}$ and $\overline{acc}_{\langle l,r\rangle}$ are the mean speedup and accuracy metric (respectively) for the $\langle l, r\rangle$ perforation over all training inputs and b is the accuracy bound. In comparison to other heuristic functions based on arithmetic mean or geometric mean, this harmonic mean based metric requires a much higher performance increase to select the loop that causes a small increase in accuracy loss.

The algorithm first computes a set of pairs P'. For each tunable loop l, P' contains the pair $\langle l, r\rangle$, where r maximizes $score_{\langle l,r\rangle}$. It then sorts the pairs in P' by $score_{\langle l,r\rangle}$. The algorithm maintains a set S of $\langle l, r\rangle$ pairs that can be perforated together without violating the accuracy bound b. At each step, the algorithm produces a new version of the application with the loops in $S \cup \langle l, r\rangle$ perforated. If the additional perforation of $\langle l, r\rangle$ keeps the overall accuracy within b, the algorithm adds the pair $\langle l, r\rangle$ into S. Note that for each loop l, this algorithm considers only its best perforation rate r (according to $score_{\langle l,r\rangle}$).

5. BENCHMARKS AND INPUTS

We evaluate loop perforation using a set of benchmark applications from the PARSEC 1.0 benchmark suite [6]. These applications were chosen to be representative of modern and emerging workloads for the next generation of processor architectures. We collect all results using a cluster of Intel x86 servers with dual 3.16 GHz Xeon X5460 quad-core processors.

We use the following applications: x264, bodytrack, swaptions, ferret, canneal, blackscholes, and streamcluster. Together these benchmarks represent a broad range of application domains including financial analysis, media processing, computer vision, engineering, data mining, and similarity search. For each benchmark we acquire a set of evaluation inputs, then pseudorandomly par-

Benchmark	Training Inputs	Production Inputs	Source
x264	4 HD videos of 200+ frames	12 HD videos of 200+ frames	PARSEC & xiph.org [1]
bodytrack	sequence of 100 frames	sequence of 261 frames	PARSEC & additional input provided by benchmark authors
swaptions	64 swaptions	512 swaptions	PARSEC & randomly generated swaptions
ferret	256 image queries	3500 image queries	PARSEC
canneal	4 netlists of 2M+ elements	16 netlists of 2M+ elements	PARSEC & additional inputs provided by benchmark authors
blackscholes	64K options	10M options	PARSEC
streamcluster	4 streams of 19K-100K data points	10 streams of 100K data points	UCI Machine Learning Repository [2]

1: Summary of Training and Production Inputs

tition the inputs into training and production inputs. We use the training inputs to drive the loop perforation space exploration algorithm (Section 4) and the production inputs to evaluate how well the resulting perforations generalize to unseen inputs.

Table 1 summarizes the sources of the evaluation inputs. For each application, the PARSEC benchmark suite contains "native" inputs designed to represent the inputs that the application is likely to encounter in practical use. With the exception of streamcluster, we always include these inputs in the set of evaluation inputs. For many of the benchmarks we also include other representative inputs, typically to increase the coverage range of the evaluation set, to promote an effective partition into reasonably-sized training and production sets, or to compensate for deficiencies in the native PARSEC inputs.

The PARSEC benchmark suite also contains the following benchmarks: facesim, dedup, fluidanimate, freqmine, and vips. We do not include freqmine and vips because these benchmarks do not successfully compile with the LLVM compiler. We do not include dedup and fluidanimate because these applications produce complex binary output files. Not having deciphered the meaning of these files, we were unable to develop meaningful accuracy metrics. We do not include facesim because it does not produce any output at all (except timing information).

x264. This media application performs H.264 encoding on raw video data. It outputs a file containing the raw (uncompressed) input video encoded according to the H.264 standard. The output abstraction for the accuracy metric extracts the peak-signal-to-noise ratio (PSNR) (which measures the quality of the encoded video) and the bitrate (which measures the compression achieved by the encoder). The accuracy calculation (see Section 3) weights each component equally (with a weight of one). If the reference decoder fails to parse the encoded video during training, we record an accuracy metric of 100% and reject the perforation. This accuracy metric captures the two most important attributes of a video encoder: the quality of the encoded video and the compression achieved through the encoding. The native PARSEC input contains only a single video. We therefore augment the evaluation input set with additional inputs from xiph.org [1].

Bodytrack. This computer vision application uses an annealed particle filter to track the movement of a human body [12]. It produces two output files: a text file containing a series of vectors representing the positions of the body over time and a series of images graphically depicting the information in the vectors overlaid on the video frames from the cameras. The output abstraction extracts the vectors that represent the position of the body. In the accuracy calculation, the weight of each vector is proportional to its magnitude. Vectors which represent larger body parts (such as the torso) therefore have a larger influence on the accuracy metric than vectors that represent smaller body parts (such as forearms).

The application requires data collected from carefully calibrated cameras. The native PARSEC input contains a single sequence of 261 frames. We augment the evaluation input set with another sequence of 100 frames. We obtained this sequence from the maintainers of the PARSEC benchmark suite.

Swaptions. This financial analysis application uses a Monte Carlo simulation to solve a partial differential equation that prices a portfolio of swaptions. The output abstraction simply extracts the swaption prices. The distortion calculation weights the corrected swaption prices equally (with a weight of one). The resulting accuracy metric directly captures the ability of the perforated application to produce accurate swaption prices.

Each input to this application contains a set of parameters for each swaption. The native PARSEC input simply repeats the same parameters multiple times, causing the application to repeatedly calculate the same swaption price. We therefore augment the evaluation input set with additional randomly generated parameters so that the application computes prices for a range of swaptions.

Ferret. This application performs a content-based similarity search of an image database. For each input query image, ferret outputs a list of similar images found in its database. The accuracy metric computes the intersection of the sets of images returned by the perforated and original versions, divides the size of this set by the size of the set of images returned by the original version, then subtracts this number from one. So if both versions return 10 images, 9 of which are the same, the accuracy is 0.1. We use the 3500 image queries from the PARSEC benchmark suite.

Canneal. This engineering application uses simulated annealing to minimize the routing cost of a microchip design. Canneal prints a number representing the total routing cost of a netlist representing the chip design; we use this cost as the output abstraction. The resulting accuracy metric directly captures the application's ability to reduce routing costs. The PARSEC benchmark contains only one large netlist. We obtained additional input netlists from the maintainers of the PARSEC benchmark suite.

Blackscholes. This financial analysis application solves a partial differential equation to compute the price of a portfolio of European options. The PARSEC application produces no output. We therefore modified the application to print the option prices to a file. The output abstraction extracts these option prices. The distortion calculation weights these prices equally (with a weight of one). The resulting accuracy metric directly captures the ability of the perforated application to compute accurate option prices. The native input from the PARSEC benchmark suite contains 10 million different option parameters. We do not augment this input set with additional inputs.

Streamcluster. This data mining application solves the online clustering problem. The program outputs a file containing the cluster centers found for the input data set. The output abstraction extracts the quality of the clustering as measured by the BCubed metric [3]. The resulting accuracy metric directly captures the ability of the application to solve the clustering problem. The native PARSEC input consists of a randomly generated set of points drawn from a uniform distribution. For this input all clusterings have equal quality and all clustering algorithms (even the trivial algorithm that outputs no clustering at all) have identical accuracy. We therefore use the evaluation input set with more realistic inputs from the UCI Machine Learning Repository [2].

6. EXPERIMENTAL RESULTS

We next present experimental results for the loop perforation space exploration algorithms (Section 4) for our benchmark applications (Section 5). We use the training inputs to drive the exploration; the result is a set of Pareto-optimal perforations in the loop perforation space. We then run selected Pareto-optimal perforations on the production inputs to evaluate how well the training results generalize to previously unseen inputs.

6.1 Criticality Testing Results

Table 2 presents timing results for the criticality testing runs (Algorithm 1). The table contains a row for each application. The second column (Accuracy) presents timing results for executions that measure the speedup and accuracy of different perforations. The third column (Valgrind) presents timing results for executions that use Valgrind to find memory errors. Each entry of the form $X(Y)$ indicates that algorithm considered X different combinations of perforated loops and that the executions took a total of Y minutes to complete. The total execution times range from 6 minutes for blackscholes to approximately 64 hours for streamcluster, with other applications requiring significantly less time. It is, of course, possible to execute different criticality testing runs in parallel on different machines. We performed all of our runs on eight dual quad Intel Xenon 3.1 GHz machines (so the wall clock times required to perform the runs are approximately a factor of eight less than the total execution times reported in Table 2).

Application	Algorithm 1		Total
	Accuracy	Valgrind	Time
x264	500 (108m)	110 (840m)	949m
bodytrack	100 (35m)	47 (1316m)	1351m
swaptions	100 (7m)	16 (108m)	115m
ferret	100 (17m)	40 (53m)	71m
canneal	256 (405m)	60 (540m)	945m
blackscholes	24 (0.5m)	12 (5m)	5.5m
streamcluster	500 (3083m)	17 (782m)	3865m

2: Criticality Testing Statistics for Benchmark Applications

Table 3 summarizes, for each application, the fate of each loop in the criticality testing algorithm from Section 4.1. Each column presents results for a given perforation rate (0.25, 0.5, 0.75 and 1 iteration) for an accuracy bound of 10% . The first row (Candidate) presents the starting number of candidate loops. This number is always 25 unless the application has fewer than 25 loops that account for 1% of the executed instructions (see Section 4).

The second row (Crash) presents the number of loops that Algorithm 1 filters out because perforating the loop caused the application to terminate with an error. The third row (Accuracy) presents the number of loops filtered by the algorithm because perforating the loop caused the application to violate the corresponding accuracy bound. The fourth row (Speed) presents the number of remaining loops that Algorithm 1 filters out because perforating the loop does not improve the overall performance (this typically happens for tight loops at a 0.25 perforation rate). The fifth row (Valgrind) presents the number of remaining loops that Algorithm 1 filters out because their perforation introduces a latent memory error detected by the Valgrind memcheck tool [27].

6.2 Perforation Space Exploration Results

Figures 1 through 6 present the results of the exhaustive loop perforation space exploration algorithm. The graphs plot a single point for each explored perforation. The y coordinate of the point is the mean speedup of the perforation (over all training inputs).

x264				
Filter	0.25%	0.50%	0.75%	1 iter
Candidate	25	25	25	25
Crash	1	1	1	1
Accuracy	6	7	7	6
Speed	16	12	10	11
Valgrind	0	0	1	1
Remaining	2	6	6	6
bodytrack				
Filter	0.25%	0.50%	0.75%	1 iter
Candidate	25	25	25	25
Crash	2	5	7	1
Accuracy	1	1	2	2
Speed	12	10	1	1
Valgrind	3	1	6	8
Remaining	7	8	9	13
swaptions				
Filter	0.25%	0.50%	0.75%	1 iter
Candidate	25	25	25	25
Crash	3	6	8	0
Accuracy	13	12	13	16
Speed	5	4	2	2
Valgrind	2	2	1	5
Remaining	2	1	1	2
ferret				
Filter	0.25%	0.50%	0.75%	1 iter
Candidate	25	25	25	25
Crash	8	12	12	6
Accuracy	13	11	11	17
Speed	0	0	0	0
Valgrind	0	0	0	0
Remaining	4	2	2	2
canneal				
Filter	0.25%	0.50%	0.75%	1 iter
Candidate	16	16	16	16
Crash	7	10	10	6
Accuracy	1	1	1	4
Speed	7	4	4	5
Valgrind	0	0	0	0
Remaining	1	1	1	1
blackscholes				
Filter	0.25%	0.50%	0.75%	1 iter
Candidate	6	6	6	6
Accuracy	4	4	4	4
Speed	1	1	1	1
Valgrind	0	0	0	0
Remaining	1	1	1	1
streamcluster				
Filter	0.25%	0.50%	0.75%	1 iter
Candidate	15	15	15	15
Crash	1	1	2	4
Accuracy	0	0	0	0
Speed	13	11	8	7
Valgrind	0	0	0	0
Remaining	1	3	5	4

3: Criticality Testing Results for Individual Loops

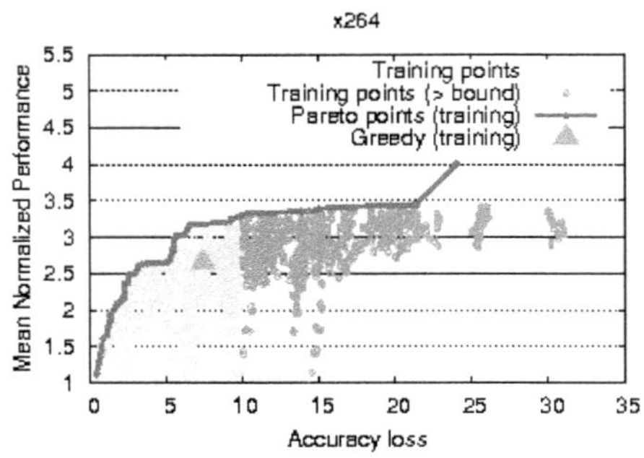

1: x264 (exhaustive)

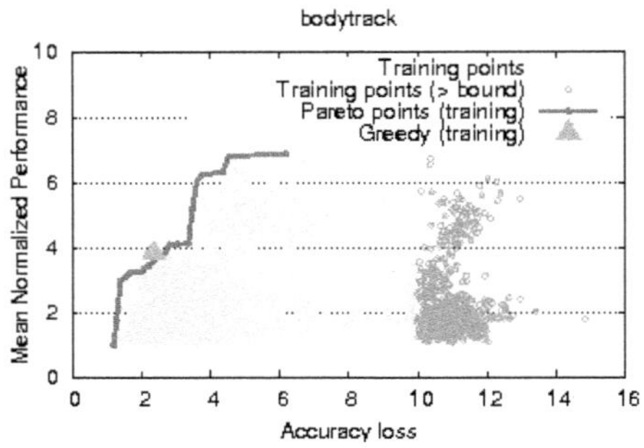

2: Bodytrack (exhaustive)

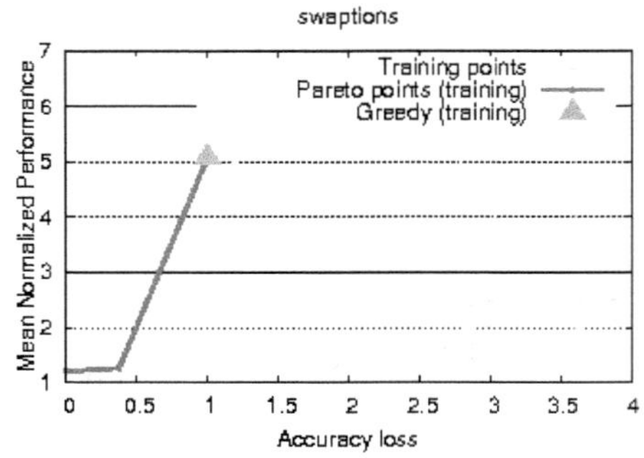

3: Swaptions (exhaustive)

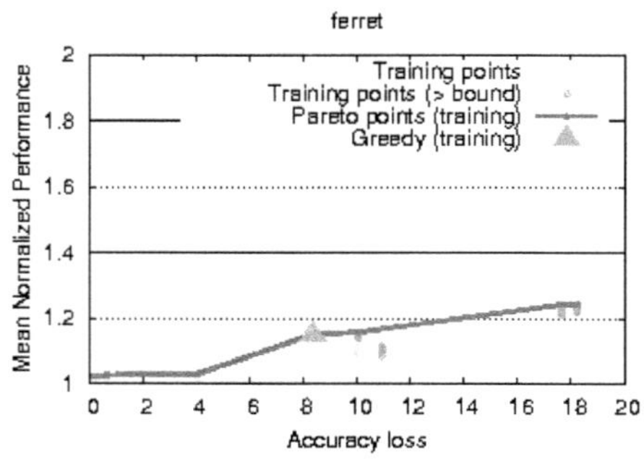

4: Ferret (exhaustive)

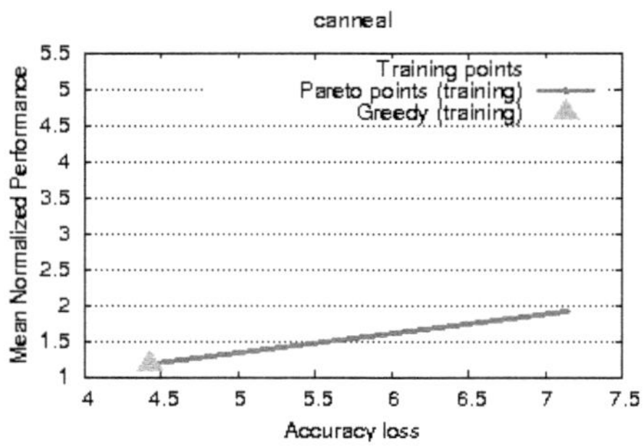

5: Canneal (exhaustive)

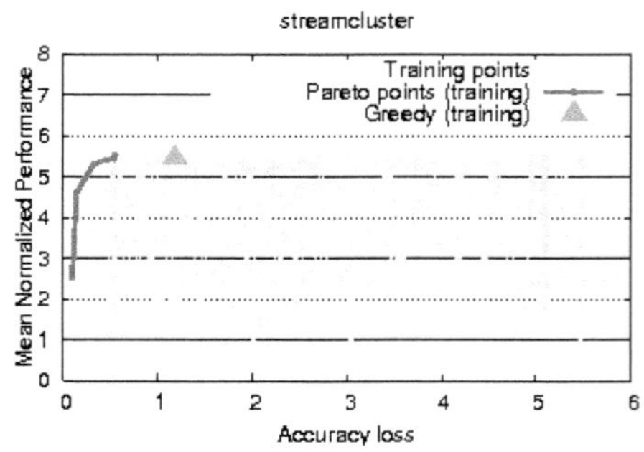

6: Streamcluster (exhaustive)

The x coordinate is the corresponding percentage accuracy loss of the perforation. Green points have accuracy losses below 10%; red points have accuracy losses above 10%. The blue line in each graph connects the points from Pareto-optimal perforations (a perforation is Pareto-optimal if there is no other perforation that provides both better performance and better accuracy). The pink triangle identifies the perforation that the greedy algorithm produces.

The graphs show that, for these applications, loop perforation is usually able to increase performance on the training inputs by at least a factor of two (up to a factor of seven for bodytrack) while reducing the accuracy by less than 10% (ferret is the exception). The graphs also illustrate the broad range of points in the performance vs. accuracy tradeoff space that the loop perforation space exploration algorithm is able to find.

The graphs show that the greedy algorithm is able to find points with good combinations of performance and accuracy, but that these points are sometimes less than optimal. We attribute this lack of optimality, in part, to the fact that the greedy algorithm explores only one perforation rate for each loop, specifically the highest priority rate as identified by Equation 2. In some cases this equation conservatively ranks perforations with low speedup and high accuracy over perforations with higher speedup but lower accuracy (even though the lower accuracy is still within the accuracy bound). This is the reason, for example, that the greedy algorithm does not find a better point for canneal (Figure 5).

Table 4 presents the time required to run the exhaustive and greedy exploration algorithms. There is a row for each application and a column for the exhaustive and greedy algorithms. Each entry of the form $X(Y)$ indicates that algorithm considered X different perforated versions of the application and that the runs took a total of Y minutes to complete. As before, the reported times represent the total computation time for execution on a dual quad Intel Xeon running at 3.1 GHz. The exhaustive search times range from 1 minute (for blackscholes) to about 65 hours (for streamcluster). The second column presents the time required to complete the

Application	Exhaustive	Greedy
x264	3071 (665m)	6 (9m)
bodytrack	5624 (1968m)	14 (33m)
swaptions	32 (9m)	4 (7m)
ferret	255 (43m)	6 (2m)
canneal	2 (12m)	1 (11m)
blackscholes	19 (1m)	3 (0.5m)
streamcluster	639 (3941m)	5 (31m)

4: Exhaustive and Greedy Search Times

greedy exploration algorithm (Algorithm 2). Note that these times do not include the time required to complete the criticality testing algorithm (Algorithm 1) — Table 2 presents the time required to complete this criticality testing algorithm. The greedy algorithm explores substantially fewer points than and executes in a fraction of the time of the exhaustive algorithm.

6.3 Training and Production Results

Table 5 presents accuracy and speedup results for selected Pareto-optimal perforations in the loop perforation space. There is a row for each application and a group of columns for the training and production inputs. Each group of columns presents results for the Pareto-optimal perforation for four accuracy bounds b: 2.5%, 5%, 7.5%, and 10%. Each entry of the form $X(Y\%)$ presents the corresponding mean speedup X and mean accuracy Y for that combination of application, bound, and input set. With the exception of ferret, all applications show a reasonable correlation between training and production results, indicating that the results from the training inputs generalize well to other inputs.

7. PERFORATION EVALUATION

We next discuss, for each application, our source-code based evaluation of the tunable loops in Pareto-optimal perforations. Table 6 presents data for every loop which is perforated in at least

Application	Training				Production			
	2.5%	5%	7.5%	10%	2.5%	5%	7.5%	10%
x264	2.38 (2.5%)	2.66 (5%)	3.17 (6.53%)	3.25 (9.31%)	2.34 (5.15%)	2.53 (6.08%)	3.12 (8.72%)	3.19 (10.3%)
bodytrack	3.44 (2.23%)	6.32 (4.36%)	6.89 (6.19%)	6.89 (6.19%)	2.70 (4.00%)	4.93 (6.12%)	4.811 (6.58%)	4.811 (6.58%)
swaptions	5.08 (1%)	5.08 (1%)	5.08 (1%)	5.08 (1%)	5.05 (0.2%)	5.05 (0.2%)	5.05 (0.2%)	5.05 (0.2%)
ferret	1.02 (0.2%)	1.03 (4%)	1.03 (4%)	1.16 (10%)	1.002 (0.15%)	1.02 (0.23%)	1.02 (0.23%)	1.07 (7.90%)
canneal	1.14 (4.38%)	1.18 (4.43%)	1.913 (7.14%)	1.913 (7.14%)	1.14 (4.38%)	1.14 (4.38%)	1.46 (7.88%)	1.46 (7.88%)
blackscholes	33 (0.0%)	33 (0.0%)	33 (0.0%)	33 (0.0%)	28.9 (0.0%)	28.9 (0.0%)	28.9 (0.0%)	28.9 (0.0%)
streamcluster	5.51 (0.54%)	5.51 (0.54%)	5.51 (0.54%)	5.51 (0.54%)	4.87 (1.71%)	4.87 (1.71%)	4.87 (1.71%)	4.87 (1.71%)

5: Training and Production Results for Pareto-optimal Perforations for Varying Accuracy Bounds

x264		
Function	Time	Type
x264_mb_analyse_inter_p16x16	64.20%	SSE / Argmin
x264_pixel_sad_16x16, outer	55.80%	SMS+T / Sum
x264_pixel_sad_16x16, inner	54.60%	SMS+T / Sum
x264_me_search_ref	25.00%	SSE / Argmin
pixel_satd_wxh, outer	18.50%	SMS+T / Sum
pixel_satd_wxh, inner	18.30%	SMS+T / Sum
bodytrack		
Function	Time	Type
Update	77.00%	II
ImageErrorInside, inner	37.00%	SME / Ratio
ImageErrorEdge, inner	29.10%	SME / Ratio
InsideError, outer	28.90%	SME / Sum
IntersectingCylinders	1.16%	SMF+SSE
swaptions		
Function	Time	Type
HJM_Swaption_Blocking, outer	100.00%	MC / Mean
HJM_SimPath_Forward_Blocking, outer	45.80%	DSU
HJM_SimPath_Forward_Blocking, inner	31.00%	DSU
Discount_Factors_Blocking	1.97%	DSU
ferret		
Function	Time	Type
emd	37.60%	SMS+II
LSH_query_bootstrap, outer	27.10%	SSE
LSH_query_bootstrap, middle	26.70%	SSE
LSH_query_bootstrap, inner	2.70%	SSE
canneal		
Function	Time	Type
reload	2.38%	DSU
blackscholes		
Function	Time	Type
bs_thread	98.70%	–
streamcluster		
Function	Time	Type
pFL, inner	98.50%	II
pgain	84.00%	SME+T+DSU
dist	69.30%	SME+T / Sum
pgain	5.01%	SME+T

6: Patterns in Pareto-optimal Perforations

one Pareto-optimal variant with an accuracy loss under 10%. The first column presents the function in which the loop appears and (when the loop appears in a loop nest) whether the loop is an inner loop or outer loop of a loop nest. The second column presents the percentage of time spent in each loop (before perforation). The third column presents both the global (as discussed in Section 1) and local (as presented in [25]) computation patterns for the loop. For example, the entry for the first loop in x264 is SSE/Argmin, which indicates that the global pattern for the loop is the Search Space Enumeration pattern, while the local pattern is the Argmin pattern. Some loops are not an instance of any of the identified local patterns. In this case we present the global pattern only.

x264. The x264 encoder divides each frame into *blocks*, then performs the encoding at the granularity of blocks. *Motion estimation* attempts to find a block from a previously encoded frame that is similar to the block that x264 is currently attempting to encode. If it finds such a block, x264 encodes the delta over this previously encoded block. Motion estimation consumes the vast majority of the computation time in x264.

All of the tunable loops in x264 appear in the motion estimation computation. Two of these loops (`x264_mb_analyze_inter_p16x16` and `x264_search_ref`) are instances of the Search Space Enumeration global pattern and the Argmin local pattern (which computes the index and value of the minimum element in an array of elements [25]). The first (`x264_mb_analyze_inter_p16x16`) searches previously encoded reference frames to find a block that is a good match for the block that x264 is currently encoding. Perforating this loop causes x264 to search fewer reference frames. The second (`x264_search_ref`) is given a single reference frame and searches within that frame to find a good match. Perforating this loop causes x264 to consider fewer blocks within the frame.

All of the remaining loops are instances of the Search Metric for both Selection and Termination global pattern and the Sum local pattern (which computes the sum of a set of numbers [25]). These loops all compute a metric that measures how well the current block matches a previously encoded block. Perforating these loops causes x264 to skip pixels when it computes the metric, producing a new, less accurate, but more efficiently computable metric. In addition to using this metric to select the previously encoded block that is the best match, x264 also uses the metric to decide when it should terminate the search (within a frame, x264 terminates the search when it fails to find a new desirable block after a given number of probes). Because the perforated metric makes fewer distinctions between blocks, perforation will typically cause the search to terminate with fewer probes.

All of these perforations may cause x264 to choose a less desirable previously encoded block as a starting point for encoding the current block. But because there is significant redundancy in the set of previously encoded blocks (typically, many previously encoded blocks are a reasonably good match for the current block), the results show that x264 is still usually able to find a good block even after perforation.

Bodytrack. Bodytrack uses an annealed particle filter to track the movement of specific parts of a human body (head, torso, arms, and legs) as a person moves through a scene [12]. At each input video frame bodytrack starts with a probabilistic model of the position of the body from the previous frame. This model consists of a weighted set of *particles*. Each particle consists of a set of angles between body parts that together specify a body pose. Each particle is assigned a weight (a likelihood that it accurately represents the current body pose). The goal of the computation is to compute a new model of the body in the current frame as a weighted average of the particles. Bodytrack starts with the model from the previous frame, then refines the model by iterating through multiple annealing layers. At each annealing layer it processes each particle to create a representation of the body position and location as a set of cylinders, each of which represents a specific body part.

It then compares this representation to image processing data from the current frame, then uses the comparison to update the weight of the corresponding particle.

The `Update` loop performs the annealing steps. Because these steps are designed to improve the accuracy of the model, we identify this loop as an instance of the Iterative Improvement global pattern (even though it is possible for an individual step to produce a slightly less accurate model). Perforating this loop causes bodytrack to perform fewer annealing steps and produce a potentially less accurate model more efficiently.

The `ImageErrorInside`, `ImageErrorEdge`, and `InsideError` loops compute a metric that characterizes how closely the body pose for a given particle matches the observed image data. These loops select a number of sample points along the edges and interiors of the cylinders that represent the body position. We identify these loops as instances of the Search Metric for Selection pattern — they compute values that measure how closely the particle matches the image data. Two of these loops are instances of the Ratio local pattern (which computes the ratio of two sums [25]). The third is an instance of the Sum local pattern. Perforating these loops causes bodytrack to consider only a subset of the sample points when it computes the metric. The result is a more efficiently computable but potentially less accurate metric.

The `IntersectingCylinders` loop iterates over all pairs of cylinders in a given particle to compute if any of the pairs intersect. If so, bodytrack removes the particle from the model (and may potentially replace it with a new particle). We identify this loop as an instance of the Search Metric for Filtering pattern because it computes a simple metric (either the particle is valid or invalid). We also identify this loop as an instance of the Search Space Enumeration pattern because it enumerates all pairs of cylinders. Perforating this loop causes bodytrack to consider only a subset of the pairs of cylinders. The result is that bodytrack may consider a particle to be valid even though it represents an unrealistic body pose. Bodytrack will therefore keep the particle in the model instead of filtering it out. Because these particles represent unrealistic positions, they will typically be given little or no weight in the model and will therefore have little or no effect on the accuracy. Note that this effect may actually decrease the performance (although we observed little or no impact on the performance or accuracy in practice).

Swaptions. Swaptions uses Monte Carlo simulation to price a portfolio of swaptions. Each iteration of the `HJM_Swaption_Blocking` loop computes a single Monte-Carlo sample. Each complete execution of this loop computes the price of a single swaption. Perforating this loop causes swaptions to compute each swaption price with fewer Monte-Carlo samples. Because of the way the computation is coded, the perforation produces prices that are predictably biased by the perforation rate. The system therefore uses extrapolation (as described in [31]) to correct the bias.

The `HJM_SimPath_Forward_Blocking` loop updates the matrix representing the path of the forward interest rate. This matrix is later used to calculate the swaption price. Perforating the computation leaves the skipped matrix elements at their initial value of 0. The `Discount_Factors_Blocking` loop updates a data structure containing discount factors used to compute the price of the swaptions. Perforating the computation leaves the skipped elements at their initial value of 1. Our results show that both of these perforations have minimal impact on the accuracy of the computation.

Ferret. Given a query image, ferret performs a content-based similarity search to return the N images in its image database most similar to the query image. Ferret first decomposes the query image into a set of segments, extracts a feature vector from each segment, indexes its image database to find candidate similar images, ranks the candidate images by measuring the distance between the query image and the candidate images, then returns the highest ranked images. The computation has two main phases. The first phase uses an efficient hash-based technique to retrieve a fixed-length (double the number of requested images) list of likely candidate images from the database. The second phase performs a more accurate comparison between the retrieved images and the query image.

The `LSH_query_bootstrap` loops execute as part of the first phase. The first two loops iterate over lists of images indexed in selected hash buckets to extract the set of candidate images from the database. Perforating these loops causes ferret to skip some of these images so that they are not considered during the subsequent search (these images will therefore not appear in the search result). We identify these loops as instances of the Search Space Enumeration pattern because they iterate over (part of) the search space.

The remaining `LSH_query_bootstrap` loop finds where to insert the current candidate image in the fixed-length sorted list of search results. Perforating this loop may cause the candidate image to appear in the list out of order. Because the second phase further processes the images in this list, the final set of retrieved images is presented to the user in sorted order.

The `emd` loop executes as part of the second phase. This loop computes the *earth mover* distance metric between the query image and the current candidate image from the image database. Because ferret uses this metric to select the most desirable images to return, we identify the loop as an instance of the Search Metric for Selection pattern. This metric is also used for the final sorting of the images according to desirability. Interestingly enough, this search metric is implemented as an instance of the Iterative Improvement pattern – it improves the distance estimate until it obtains an optimal distance measure or exceeds a maximum number of iterations. Perforating this loop creates a new, more efficient, but less accurate metric. As a result, the program may return a different set and/or ordering of images to the user.

Canneal. Canneal uses simulated annealing to place and route an input netlist with the goal of minimizing the total wire length. The reload loop traverses the state vector for the Mersenne twister random number generator to reinitialize the vector. For our set of inputs, the resulting change in the generated sequence of random numbers causes canneal to execute marginally more efficiently.

Blackscholes. The experimental results show that it is possible to perforate the outer loop in `bs_thread` without changing the output at all. Further investigation reveals that this loop simply repeats the same computation multiple times and was apparently added to the benchmark to increase the workload.

Streamcluster. Streamcluster partitions sets of points into clusters, with each cluster centered around one of the points. Each clustering consists of a set of points representing the cluster centers. The goal is to find a set of cluster centers that minimizes the inter- and intra-cluster distances. Streamcluster uses a version of the *facility location* algorithm to find an approximately optimal clustering. The algorithm contains a while loop that executes a sequence of clustering rounds, each of which attempts to improve the clustering from the previous round. The while loop terminates if a round fails to generate a clustering with significantly improved cost.

The `pFL` loop executes once per round. Each iteration of this loop generates (by adding a randomly chosen new candidate cluster center to the current set of cluster centers) and evaluates a new candidate clustering. If this candidate clustering improves on the current clustering, the loop body updates the current clustering (optionally merging some of the clusters). We identify this loop as an instance of both the Search Space Enumeration pattern (because it iterates over a part of the search space of candidate clusterings) and the Iterative Improvement pattern (because it uses the current clustering to generate improved clusterings). Perforating the pFL loop therefore causes streamcluster to consider fewer candidate clusterings per round. The result is that streamcluster performs fewer attempts to improve the clustering before the next round termination check, which may in turn cause streamcluster to produce a less desirable clustering more efficiently.

We note that the following comment appears in the source code above the definition of the constant (ITER) that controls the number of iterations of the pFL loop:

```
/* higher ITER --> more likely to get correct number of centers */
/* higher ITER also scales the running time almost linearly */
```

This comment reflects the fact that the number of iterations of the pFL loop controls a performance vs. accuracy tradeoff (which is not exposed to the user of the application). In effect, the perforation space exploration algorithm rediscovers this tradeoff.

The first pgain loop calculates the partial cost of a candidate clustering by computing sums of distances between data points and the new cluster center. It also marks the data points that would be assigned to the new cluster center. The second pgain loop uses the computed partial sums to compute the total cost of the candidate clustering. We identify these loops as instances of the Search Metrics for Selection (because the computed costs are used to select desirable clusterings) and Termination (because the facility location algorithm uses this cost as a measure of progress, and stops if the progress is too small) pattern. Perforating these loops produces a less accurate but more efficiently computable cluster cost metric. We also identify the first pgain loop as an instance of the Data Structure Update pattern. Perforating this loop may leave some of the data points assigned to an old cluster, even though these points should be assigned to the newly opened cluster.

The dist loop computes the distance between two points. We identify this loop as an instance of the Search Metric for Selection and Termination pattern because it is used to compute candidate clustering costs. It is also an instance of the Sum local pattern. Perforating this loop causes streamcluster to compute the distance between points using a subset of the coordinates of the points. The result is a more efficiently computable but less accurate distance metric.

8. RELATED WORK

Trading accuracy for other benefits is a well-known technique. It has been shown that one can trade accuracy for performance [31, 30, 13, 21, 17], robustness [31, 8], energy consumption [13, 9, 34, 31, 17], fault tolerance [9, 34, 31], and efficient parallel execution [23, 22]. We note that developers have, for years, manually developed algorithms (most prominently, lossy compression algorithms [36, 7]) that are designed to operate at a variety of points in a performance vs. accuracy tradeoff space. In this section we focus on more general techniques that are designed for relatively broad classes of applications.

Loop Perforation and Task Skipping. As we have earlier discussed [25], loop perforation [16, 26] can be seen as a special case of task skipping [31, 30]. The first publication on task skipping used linear regression to obtain empirical statistical models of the time and accuracy effects of skipping tasks and identified the use of these models in purposefully skipping tasks to reduce the amount of resources required to perform the computation while preserving acceptable accuracy [31].

The first publication on loop perforation presented a purely empirical justification of loop perforation with no formal statistical, probabilistic, or discrete logical reasoning used to justify the transformation [16]. The first statistical justification of loop perforation used Monte Carlo simulation to evaluate the effect of perforating local computational patterns [32]. The first probabilistic justification for loop perforation used static analysis of local computational patterns and also presented the use of profiling runs on representative inputs and developer specifications to obtain the required probability distribution information [24, 25].

Chaudhuri et al. present a program analysis for automatically determining whether a function is continuous [10]. The reasoning is deterministic and worst-case. An extension of this research introduces a notion of function robustness, and, under an input locality condition, presents an approximate memoization approach similar to loop perforation [11]. For a special case when the inputs form a Gaussian random walk and the loop body is a robust function, the paper derives a probabilistic bound to provide a justification for applying loop perforation.

These previous analyses (with the exception of the empirical task skipping analysis [31, 30]) all focus on local computations and do not address the effect of loop perforation on global end-to-end application performance and accuracy. The present paper, in contrast, provides empirical results that characterize the global performance and accuracy effects of loop perforation for our set of benchmarks. It also identifies a set of global computational patterns and explains why these patterns interact well with loop perforation. We anticipate that others may be able to identify these or similar patterns in other applications and use these patterns to justify the application of loop perforation to these applications.

Multiple Implementations. Researchers have developed several systems that allow programmers to provide multiple implementations for a given piece of functionality, with different implementations potentially occupying different points in the performance vs. accuracy tradeoff space. Such systems include Petabricks [4], Green [5], Eon [33], and PowerDial [17]. Petabricks is a parallel language and compiler that developers can use to provide alternate implementations of a given piece of functionality. Green also provides constructs that developers can use to specify alternate implementations. The alternatives typically exhibit different performance and accuracy characteristics. Petabricks and Green both contain algorithms that explore the tradeoff space to find points with desirable performance and accuracy characteristics.

Eon [33] is a coordination language for power-aware computing that enables developers to adapt their algorithms to different energy contexts. In a similar vein, energy-aware adaptation for mobile applications [13], adapts to changing system demands by dynamically adjusting application input quality. For example, to save energy the system may switch to a lower quality video input to reduce the computation of the video decoder.

PowerDial exploits multiple implementations without requiring the developer to explicitly modify the application [17]. Instead, PowerDial converts existing command-line parameters into data structures that a control system can manipulate to dynamically adapt to changes (such as load and clock rate) in the underlying computing platform.

In contrast to systems such as Petabricks, Green, Eon, and PowerDial, loop perforation can find accuracy vs. performance tradeoffs even when none are directly exposed in the application. Instead of requiring the developer to provide multiple implementations of the same functionality or find and annotate potential optimization opportunities, our system generates and explores a performance vs. accuracy tradeoff space to find multiple potentially desirable points in the tradeoff space. Other systems have provided mechanisms that are designed to allow developers to identify loops that perform iterative refinement [5, 4]. Loop perforation, in contrast, can automatically discover instances of a range of computational patterns that include, but are not limited to, iterative refinement.

Autotuners. Autotuners explore a range of equally accurate implementation alternatives to find the alternative or combination of alternatives that deliver the best performance on the current computational platform [37, 39, 14]. Researchers have also developed APIs that an application can use to expose variables for external control (by, for example, the operating system) [29, 19, 35]. Loop perforation, in contrast, operates on applications written in standard languages to find perforations which improve performance while maintaining acceptable, but not necessarily identical, accuracy.

9. CONCLUSION

Standard approaches for obtaining applications that can trade accuracy in return for enhanced performance have focused on the manual development of new algorithms for specific applications. Our results show that loop perforation can effectively augment a range of applications with the ability to operate at various attractive points in the tradeoff space, with perforated applications often able to deliver significant performance improvements (typically around a factor of two reduction in running time) at the cost of a small (typically 5% or less) decrease in the accuracy.

We acknowledge that loop perforation is not appropriate for all applications. But within its target class of applications, results from our implemented loop perforation system show that it can dramatically increase the ability of applications to trade off accuracy in return for other benefits such as increased performance and decreased energy consumption.

10. REFERENCES

[1] Xiph.org.

[2] D. N. A. Asuncion. UCI machine learning repository, 2007.

[3] E. Amigo, J. Gonzalo, and J. Artiles. A comparison of extrinsic clustering evaluation metrics based on formal constraints. In *Information Retrieval Journal*. Springer Netherlands, July 2008.

[4] J. Ansel, C. Chan, Y. L. Wong, M. Olszewski, Q. Zhao, A. Edelman, and S. Amarasinghe. Petabricks: A language and compiler for algorithmic choice. In *PLDI '09*, Jun 2009.

[5] W. Baek and T. Chilimbi. Green: a framework for supporting energy-conscious programming using controlled approximation. In *PLDI '10*, 2010.

[6] C. Bienia, S. Kumar, J. P. Singh, and K. Li. The PARSEC benchmark suite: Characterization and architectural implications. In *PACT '08*, Oct 2008.

[7] K. Brandenburg. MP3 and AAC explained. In *AES 17th International Conference on High-Quality Audio Coding*, 1999.

[8] S. Chakradhar, A. Raghunathan, and J. Meng. Best-Effort Parallel Execution Framework for Recognition and Mining Applications. In *IPDPS*, 2009.

[9] L. Chakrapani, K. Muntimadugu, A. Lingamneni, J. George, and K. Palem. Highly energy and performance efficient embedded computing through approximately correct arithmetic: A mathematical foundation and preliminary experimental validation. In *International conference on Compilers, architectures and synthesis for embedded systems*, 2008.

[10] S. Chaudhuri, S. Gulwani, and R. Lublinerman. Continuity analysis of programs. In *POPL '10*.

[11] S. Chaudhuri, S. Gulwani, R. Lublinerman, and S. Navidpour. Proving Programs Robust. In *FSE '11*, 2011.

[12] J. Deutscher and I. Reid. Articulated body motion capture by stochastic search. *International Journal of Computer Vision*, 2005.

[13] J. Flinn and M. Satyanarayanan. Energy-aware adaptation for mobile applications. In *SOSP '99*.

[14] M. Frigo and S. G. Johnson. FFTW: An adaptive software architecture for the FFT. In *Proc. 1998 IEEE Intl. Conf. Acoustics Speech and Signal Processing*, pages 1381–1384.

[15] J. Hartigan and M. Wong. A k-means clustering algorithm. *Journal of the Royal Statistical Society C*, 28:100–108, 1979.

[16] H. Hoffmann, S. Misailovic, S. Sidiroglou, A. Agarwal, and M. Rinard. Using Code Perforation to Improve Performance, Reduce Energy Consumption, and Respond to Failures . Technical Report MIT-CSAIL-TR-2009-042, MIT, Sept. 2009.

[17] H. Hoffmann, S. Sidiroglou, M. Carbin, S. Misailovic, A. Agarwal, and M. Rinard. Dynamic Knobs for Responsive Power-Aware Computing. In *ASPLOS '11*, March 2011.

[18] M. Kalos and P. Whitlock. *Monte Carlo Methods*. Wiley-VCH, 2008.

[19] P. Keleher, J. Hollingsworth, and D. Perkovic. Exposing application alternatives. In *ICDCS '99*.

[20] C. Lattner and V. Adve. LLVM: A Compilation Framework for Lifelong Program Analysis & Transformation. In *CGO '04*.

[21] J. Meng, A. A. Raghunathan, and S. B. Chakradhar. Exploiting the Forgiving Nature of Applications for Scalable Parallel Execution. In *IPDPS*, 2010.

[22] S. Misailovic, D. Kim, and M. Rinard. Automatic Parallelization with Statistical Accuracy Bounds. Technical Report MIT-CSAIL-TR-2010-007, MIT, 2010.

[23] S. Misailovic, D. Kim, and M. Rinard. Parallelizing Sequential Programs With Statistical Accuracy Test. Technical Report MIT-CSAIL-TR-2010-038, 2010.

[24] S. Misailovic, D. Roy, and M. Rinard. Probabilistic and Statistical Analysis of Perforated Patterns. Technical Report MIT-CSAIL-TR-2011-003, MIT, 2011.

[25] S. Misailovic, D. Roy, and M. Rinard. Probabilistically Accurate Program Transformations. In *SAS '11*, 2011.

[26] S. Misailovic, S. Sidiroglou, H. Hoffmann, and M. Rinard. Quality of Service Profiling. In *ICSE*, 2010.

[27] N. Nethercote and J. Seward. Valgrind A Program Supervision Framework. *Electronic Notes in Theoretical Computer Science*, 2003.

[28] P. Pillai and K. Shin. Real-time dynamic voltage scaling for low-power embedded operating systems. In *SOSP '01*, page 102, 2001.

[29] R. Ribler, J. Vetter, H. Simitci, and D. Reed. Autopilot: adaptive control of distributed applications. In *High Performance Distributed Computing*, July 1998.

[30] M. Rinard. Using early phase termination to eliminate load imbalances at barrier synchronization points. In *OOPSLA '07*.

[31] M. Rinard. Probabilistic accuracy bounds for fault-tolerant computations that discard tasks. In *Proceedings of the 20th annual international conference on Supercomputing*, 2006.

[32] M. Rinard, H. Hoffmann, S. Misailovic, and S. Sidiroglou. Patterns and statistical analysis for understanding reduced resource computing. In *Onward! '10*.

[33] J. Sorber, A. Kostadinov, M. Garber, M. Brennan, M. D. Corner, and E. D. Berger. Eon: a language and runtime system for perpetual systems. In *SenSys '07*.

[34] P. Stanley-Marbell and D. Marculescu. Deviation-Tolerant Computation in Concurrent Failure-Prone Hardware. Technical Report ESR-2008-01, Eindhoven University of Technology, January 2008.

[35] C. Tapus, I. Chung, and J. Hollingsworth. Active harmony: Towards automated performance tuning. In *Supercomputing, ACM/IEEE 2002 Conference*, 2002.

[36] G. Wallace. The JPEG still picture compression standard. *IEEE Transactions on Consumer Electronics*, 1991.

[37] R. Whaley and J. Dongarra. Automatically tuned linear algebra software. In *ACM/IEEE conference on Supercomputing (CDROM)*.

[38] x264. http://www.videolan.org/x264.html.

[39] J. Xiong, J. Johnson, R. W. Johnson, and D. Padua. SPL: A language and compiler for DSP algorithms. In *PLDI '01*.

Partial Replay of Long-Running Applications

Alvin Cheung, Armando Solar-Lezama, and Samuel Madden
MIT CSAIL
{akcheung, asolar, madden}@csail.mit.edu

ABSTRACT

Bugs in deployed software can be extremely difficult to track down. Invasive logging techniques, such as logging all nondeterministic inputs, can incur substantial runtime overheads. This paper shows how symbolic analysis can be used to re-create path equivalent executions for very long running programs such as databases and web servers. The goal is to help developers debug such long-running programs by allowing them to walk through an execution of the last few requests or transactions leading up to an error. The challenge is to provide this functionality without the high runtime overheads associated with traditional replay techniques based on input logging or memory snapshots. Our approach achieves this by recording a small amount of information about program execution, such as the direction of branches taken, and then using symbolic analysis to reconstruct the execution of the last few inputs processed by the application, as well as the state of memory before these inputs were executed.

We implemented our technique in a new tool called *bbr*. In this paper, we show that it can be used to replay bugs in long-running single-threaded programs starting from the middle of an execution. We show that bbr incurs low recording overhead (avg. of 10%) during program execution, which is much less than existing replay schemes. We also show that it can reproduce real bugs from web servers, database systems, and other common utilities.

Categories and Subject Descriptors
D.2.5 [Software Engineering] – Testing and Debugging
General Terms Reliability, Performance

1. INTRODUCTION

A large amount of research effort has been devoted to the problem of identifying bugs and helping programmers pinpoint their root causes. However, not all bugs are equal. Most development organizations already have more bug reports than resources to fix them. As such, a bug from an important customer is much more critical than a bug discovered by an automated test generator. Unfortunately, pinpointing and fixing such critical bugs in the field can be very challenging. Stack traces and core dumps can be helpful when dealing with some errors, and statistical bug isolation can be used when a bug affects large numbers of users. However, for bugs only manifest as a result of a specific input, these techniques are not useful.

The gold standard for pinpointing such bugs is program replay. If users could provide a log of the entire execution of their system or all of its inputs, then identifying and fixing such bugs would be simple: when the bug is observed, you would have a complete trace of the execution that could be used to reproduce and fix the bug. In fact, replay tools exist that able to reconstruct an execution by either taking periodic snapshots of the system state [33], or by logging all non-deterministic inputs to the target program, such as the return values from non-deterministic functions (e.g., `random`), system calls, and user inputs [17]. The problem with these tools, however, is that while they can reproduce the exact scenario that leads to the buggy behavior (modulo hardware failures), they can significantly slow down the normal execution of the program and produce very large data logs that may grow without bound as long as the program keeps executing. This makes them impractical for debugging systems like databases and web servers that may run for months at a time.

To mitigate this runtime overhead problem, there has been work done on performing software replay using symbolic execution [31, 15, 19]. The idea is to capture a subset of the program state during runtime, thus incurring less overhead, and then use symbolic execution to reconstruct the missing information. Even though the reconstructed state might not be exactly the same as the one that the user experienced, it is nonetheless useful for debugging purposes, since it is usually the case that the same bug can be triggered by multiple execution traces. Thus, as long as the reconstructed trace can still trigger the bug then it is good enough. Unfortunately, all the previous work focuses on replaying programs from the beginning of the execution, and today's symbolic execution engines (which rely on SMT solvers) are not able to replay programs that have been running for days or months.

In this paper, we explore the idea of using symbolic execution to perform *partial* replay from the middle of executions, rather than replaying long-running programs from the very beginning. By doing this, we avoid having to store and transmit very large logs (as required by deterministic replayers) and mitigate the very long replay times that can result from symbolic execution. Our tool, called *bbr*, is the first

Permission to make digital or hard copies of all or part of this work for personal or classroom use is granted without fee provided that copies are not made or distributed for profit or commercial advantage and that copies bear this notice and the full citation on the first page. To copy otherwise, to republish, to post on servers or to redistribute to lists, requires prior specific permission and/or a fee.
ESEC/FSE'11, September 5–9, 2011, Szeged, Hungary.
Copyright 2011 ACM 978-1-4503-0443-6/11/09 ...$10.00.

such partial symbolic replay tool. To use bbr, the developer annotates the code with checkpoints, for instance at places in the program that mark the transition from processing one request or phase to the next, such as at each invocation of the query parser in a database server. bbr collects a log during program execution and, when a checkpoint is reached, discards all logged data that was previously collected, limiting the size of the logs that need to be maintained. When the program terminates, the developer gives the (partial) log to bbr to replay starting from the last checkpoint. bbr symbolically executes the program, generating constraints when the program uses values that were not recorded. At the end of the symbolic execution, the constraints are solved to find the program state at the beginning of the replay. The solved state might not be exactly the same as the one in the original execution, but it is one guaranteed to take the same control flow path when executed with the logged data. We refer to this as a *branch-deterministic* replay, and we show that such a replay is as useful as a fully deterministic replay in debugging a number of real-world bugs, while avoiding the expensive cost of the data-logging approaches.

Unlike the data-logging based schemes, bbr works by recording control flow (one bit per branch) and accessed array indices into a log during program execution, as well the current stack and file offset information for the currently opened files. when a checkpoint is taken. This amounts to much less data than in the data-log based approaches (which can accumulate large logs even in partial replay scenarios).

In summary, this paper makes the following contributions:

- We introduce the idea of partial symbolic replay at an arbitrary program point in the target application, which lets users replay long-running programs without the burden of maintaining large logs. Furthermore, we develop an algorithm to handle pointer aliases that arise during partial replay without using the theory of bit-vector arrays, which, as our results show, gives poor performance.
- We propose the concept of branch-deterministic replay by recording control flow and non-constant array indices, and demonstrate its applicability to data-intensive applications, showing low runtime overhead and small log sizes as compared to other existing replayers.
- We identify several techniques that enable replaying of real-world applications in our bbr prototype, including a new memory model, separating constraints into independent subgroups during solving, and building a parallel solver implementation.
- We show that our technique can scale to replay real programs, including sqlite running on a 10 GB TPC-C database and two different web servers. Our runtime overheads range from 1% to 33%, with reasonable replay and solving times. We also show that we can reproduce several real bugs in these systems.

The rest of this paper is organized as follows. In Section 2, we overview the architecture of bbr and provide a sample usage scenario. In Section 3, we discuss in detail the design of the different components of bbr. Section 4 describes our experimental evaluation of bbr on a number of different real-world applications. Finally, Section 5 surveys related work, followed by conclusions in Section 6.

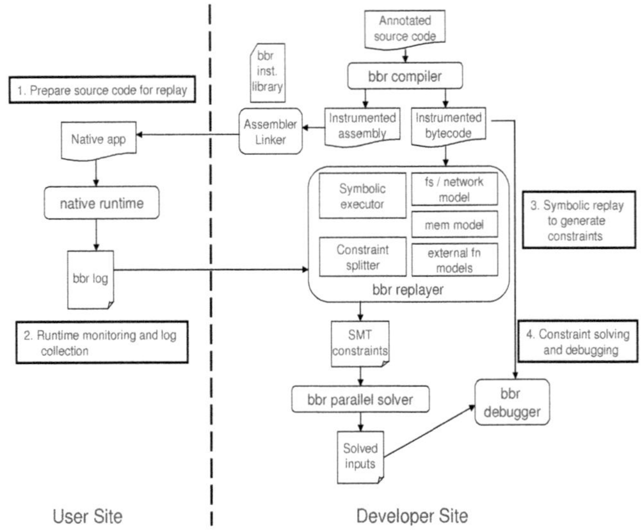

Figure 1: bbr system overview, highlighting steps in the replay process

2. OVERVIEW

bbr consists of five components: a bytecode compiler, a library for the instrumentation routines, a bytecode replayer, a parallel solver, and a debugger. Fig. 1 shows the steps involved in using bbr for replay.

We illustrate the operation of these components through a real-world bug in memcached. In version 1.2.6, a bug was found in decrementing an existing value in the cache [1]. The (slightly abridged) code is as follows:

```
     char *do_add_delta (item *it, const int64_t delta) {
2622 int64_t value = ITEM_data(it);
     ...
2631 if (incr) {
       ...
2634 } else {
2635   value -= delta;
2636   if(value < 0) {
         value = 0;
       }
       MEMCACHED_COMMAND_DECR(ITEM_key(it), value);
```

The function first obtains the existing value for a key from the cache at line 2622 before performing the decrement. Then, if the resulting value is negative, the code simply sets the new value to be 0. This is a bug since `value` is treated as a signed entity, contrary to memcached's specifications. If the existing value is a large number with the most significant bit set, then decrementing it will result in 0. In the following, we describe how a developer can use bbr to replay and debug this problem.

2.1 Preparing for Replay

To use bbr, the developer first prepares the source code by inserting the bbr checkpoint annotations. The annotation can be inserted in two ways: at a program point for which the developer would like to start replay from (e.g., at the point that processes each incoming requests), or configured as a timing parameter (e.g., take a checkpoint every five minutes). In our example, the developer can put the annotation at the program point that calls different functions (e.g., `do_add_delta`) based on the incoming request type.

The developer then uses the *bbr compiler* to compile the code into LLVM bytecode. The bbr compiler links the user code with a modified version of the uClibc [2] library (which we use because it can be easily compiled into LLVM bytecode). During compilation, the compiler inserts instrumentation routines to record two types of data. First, bbr records the values of conditional branches, in the example the branch conditions at lines 2631 and 2636. Next, bbr records the values of non-constant indices into arrays (none in this case). The instrumented code is then compiled to native assembly and linked with the *bbr instrumentation library* to produce the final native memcached distribution.

2.2 Runtime Monitoring

The user starts using the instrumented memcached server in her application. As the application issues operations against the memcached server, the bbr library embedded in the server intercepts the branch outcomes and array indices from the running program and stores them in an in-memory buffer, which is periodically flushed to disk when it becomes full. When the checkpoint annotation is hit, the library takes a lightweight snapshot of the running program. It also discards any logs that are previously written to disk. In our example, the user has been running her application normally until one day she observes that memcached returns 0 for a decrement and causes her application to return an incorrect result. Believing that it is a problem in the server, she files a report to the memcached developer along with the log generated by bbr.

2.3 Symbolic Replay

The developer would like to find out why 0 was returned in the decrement operation, which is not obvious by just looking at the code. With the collected log and the instrumented bytecode, the developer uses the *bbr replayer* to replay. The replayer symbolically executes the bytecode from the last checkpoint. In our example, at line 2622, `ITEM_data` loads the data from the heap pointed to by `it`, whose contents are unknown since it was stored prior to the checkpoint. When that happens, the replayer creates a fresh symbolic variable v to represent the contents at the memory pointed to by `it` and assign that to `value`. At the branch point in line 2631, the replayer reads the branch log and finds that the branch was not taken, and jumps to line 2634. At line 2635, `value` is assigned to be $v - d$, where the symbolic variable d represents the value of the program variable `delta`. Finally, at line 2636, from the branch log the replayer learns that the branch was taken, and because the branching condition involves symbolic variables, it generates the constraint $v - d < 0$ and continues execution.

2.4 Solving and Debugging

The replayer saves the generated constraints to a file at the end of the replay, which are then given to the *bbr parallel solver* to solve. In our example, the solver solves for possible values of v and d in order to produce a branch-deterministic execution from the last checkpoint. Suppose the solver returns $2^{63} + 1$ for v, and 1 for d. To map these results back to the program, bbr comes with a *debugger*. The debugger allows the developer to specify the values to be printed when an instruction is reached during symbolic execution. A sample session is as follows (italic text represents user inputs):

```
bbr-db> print delta at 2622; print value at 2622;
bbr-db> run
at 2622:  delta = 1
at 2622:  value = 9223372036854775809 // 2^63 + 1
```

With the output above and by following the program logic, the developer realizes the cause of the bug, and fixes her code accordingly. Even though the solved values might not be exactly the same as those that the user originally saw (in fact, the insertion of the key into the cache could have happened a long time ago with a different value in the original execution), the developer is still able to use bbr to diagnose the problem by finding an execution that leads to the behavior observed by the user.

The debugger also allows the developer to request a new feasible variable assignment if she isn't satisfied with a given assignment by appending extra constraints. In the example above, perhaps the developer knows that the value of `delta` was not 1, and thus the solution does not represent a feasible program state. In that case, she can tell the debugger that `delta` does not equal to 1, and ask the debugger to generate another set of values for `delta` and `value`.

In contrast, in order to use existing tools to replay the bug, the developer would either have to rely on the user to provide a detailed use case that illustrates the bug, or to collect data logs that have recorded the values of all non-deterministic data since memcached started (which could have been a long time ago), or to write assertions and rely on test generators to hit upon the bug, all of which are costly and error-prone.

In the next section, we discuss the details of the design of the bbr replayer.

3. BBR DESIGN

We begin by explaining the implementation of the recording mechanism, followed by that of the replayer and parallel constraint solver.

3.1 Instrumentation for Recording

As discussed in Section 2, calls to the instrumentation functions are added to the user code during compilation with the bbr compiler to collect the necessary data for replay. These functions are implemented in a separate library that is linked with the instrumented assembly when producing the native executable. Each conditional branch generates 1 bit of data, and other types of data (such as array indices) are 4 bytes each. To reduce disk overhead, we use a double-buffering mechanism where we log data in one buffer in memory. When the buffer fills (or the program terminates), we flush it to disk in the background and start recording into the other buffer. Section 4.1 reports the overhead of data collection. When a checkpoint annotation is reached, bbr records the current stack and the state of open files (see Section 3.2.4 for details) so that replay can start at the appropriate program point. The contents of registers and heap memory are not saved, making the operation very fast.

3.2 Replayer Design

Once data logs are collected, the developer feeds them to the replayer, which uses them to generate the constraints used to solve for inputs and program state consistent with the log. Using the branch log, the stream of bytecode instructions (Fig. 2) in the original execution is reconstructed,

$$\begin{aligned}
\mathsf{PExpr}\ (e_p) &::= n \mid r \mid \mathsf{unop}\ e_p \mid e_{p1}\ \mathsf{binop}\ e_{p2} \mid b\ ?\ e_{p1} : e_{p2} \\
\mathsf{CExpr}\ (e_c) &::= e_p \mid \mathsf{BitVector} \mid (l, n) \\
\mathsf{Cond}\ (b) &::= \mathsf{True} \mid \mathsf{False} \mid \neg b \mid e_{p1}\ \mathsf{comp}\ e_{p2} \mid b_1 \wedge b_2 \mid b_1 \vee b_2 \\
\mathsf{Stmt}\ (s) &::= r = \mathsf{malloc}(n) \mid r = e_p \mid *r = e_p \mid r = *e_p \mid \mathsf{assert}\ b \\
\mathsf{Program}\ (p) &::= s; p
\end{aligned}$$

$$n \in \mathbf{N},\ r \in \{\text{program variables}\}$$
$$(l, n) \in \{\text{memory locations}\},\ \mathsf{unop} \in \{-, !\}$$
$$\mathsf{binop} \in \{+, -, *, /, \mathsf{mod}, \mathsf{band}, \mathsf{bor}, \mathsf{xor}, \mathsf{shl}, \mathsf{lshr}, \mathsf{ashr}\}$$
$$\mathsf{comp} \in \{=, >, <, \geq, \leq, \neq\}$$

We denote a memory location as (l, n), where l represents an allocation, and n is the offset from the base of allocation.

Figure 2: Language of bytecode instructions

and instructions are emulated to generate constraints. The constraint generation process mirrors the symbolic execution done in concolic analysis (e.g., [18]); the main difference is that instead of getting our concrete data from the execution itself, we get it from the log. This subtle difference requires tradeoffs in terms of how much we can rely on symbolic vs. concrete reasoning, and has implications for the design of the symbolic state and constraint generation.

3.2.1 Modeling State

The most interesting aspect of the state maintained by the replayer is memory representation. Traditionally, the easiest way to model memory has been by using the theory of arrays, modeling memory as a giant array that gets updated with every write operation. This approach is very general, but puts too much strain on the SMT solver [35]. At the other extreme, if we know the concrete address of every load and store, we can model the heap as a map that gets modified by read and write operations [32, 18, 23, 34]. This is very efficient because the solver doesn't have to reason about aliasing, but it also requires a lot of concrete knowledge about the execution. In our system, we know the addresses for all memory accesses except those involving memory allocated before the start of replay, and the key to our approach is to leverage the concrete information we have rather than relying on the theory of arrays to discover it.

The first important element of our representation is that it models the heap as a collection of independent buffers produced by malloc rather than as a flat array. In this view, a pointer is a pair (l, n), where l is the base address of a buffer assigned by malloc, and n is an offset into the buffer. The benefit of this is that during runtime we only need to record n and only when it is statically unknown in LLVM array element access instructions.[1] The main downside of this approach is that we assume pointer arithmetic to be able to change only n but not l, which prevents the system from reproducing errors caused by unsafe memory operations. In exchange for this, we are able to scale to large, long-running programs and to reproduce real bugs that are often much harder to discover than memory errors (see Section 4.2).

In addition to the heap $h : (l, n) \rightarrow e_c$, the replayer maintains an environment $\sigma : r \rightarrow e_c$ that maps variables to the symbolic values currently assigned to them, as well as an alias map $a : l \rightarrow \{l_0, \ldots, l_k\}$ that stores may-alias locations for a given allocation l. Finally, b represents the set of constraints accumulated so far in the execution. Together, the four entities (σ, h, b, a) make up the state of the replayer.

[1] Field in records are accessed in the same way, however n is always statically known in such cases.

$$[\![r = \mathsf{malloc}(n)]\!](\sigma, h, b, a) = (\sigma[r \rightarrow (l, 0)], h, b, a[l \rightarrow \{\}])$$
$$\text{where } l \text{ is a fresh memory location}$$
$$[\![r = e_p]\!](\sigma, h, b, a) = (\sigma[r \rightarrow [\![e_p]\!]], h, b, a)$$
$$[\![\mathsf{assert}\ b_1]\!](\sigma, h, b, a) = (\sigma, h, b \wedge b_1, a)$$

Figure 3: Semantics for non-memory instructions

3.2.2 Symbolic Execution of Memory Operations

Our treatment of non-memory operations is similar to standard symbolic execution [32], as illustrated by Fig. 3. However, memory operations present new challenges. First of all, a read or a write to an address (l, n) is easy to handle if we know the concrete values of l and n, since we can just read or update the corresponding entry in our model of the heap. The challenge comes when we lack information about an address as a consequence of partial replay. The reason partial replay makes this difficult is because when we read a location that was written to before the start of the log, we know nothing about its contents, and if it contains an address, we have no information about either l or n, or about its aliasing relationship with other addresses.

Because of this, our system does not know the invariants the non-replayed execution enforced on memory contents. For the replayed portion of the program, bbr ensures that for every location (l, n), and all its potentially aliased locations (l_i, n), the following invariant is maintained:

$$\mathsf{SolverValue}(l, n) = \mathsf{SolverValue}(l_i, n) \Rightarrow$$
$$\mathsf{SolverValue}(h[(l, c)]) = \mathsf{SolverValue}(h[(l_i, c)])$$

In other words, if the solver decides that l_i is actually aliased to l, then the symbolic expression in $h[(l, c)]$ should evaluate to the same value as the symbolic expression in $h[(l_i, c)]$.

In the following, we show this invariant is preserved in memory operations, and describe how we handle memory locations initialized before the start of partial replay.

Address Initialization: Consider reading from or writing to memory whose address is stored in variable variable r. If $\sigma[r]$ maps to some location (l, n), then the operation proceeds as described below. Otherwise, r holds a value that was written before the start of partial replay (i.e., $\sigma[r] = \perp$). When this happens, the system assigns a fresh symbolic variable bv to represent r. Furthermore, it assigns bv a brand new base address l_r that is different from all the l's currently in use by the program, updates $\sigma[r \rightarrow (l_r, 0)]$, and generates the constraint $bv = (l_r, 0)$. To account for the possibility of aliases, the system updates the alias map a to keep track of all the other l's that may be aliased with l_r. Our current implementation assumes that two memory locations can be aliased to each other only if the program variables for which they were originally allocated for have the same static type, and that a memory location cannot be aliased to some offset within another location (e.g., array variables a and b can be aliased to each other, but a cannot be aliased to the addresses of $b[1]$, $b[2]$, etc, and vice versa). Notice that this is just one possible mechanism for computing alias information, which we chose as it proved sufficient for replaying a variety of programs. Users can supply more precise alias information obtained elsewhere, e.g., from the output of an alias algorithm, or by logging all memory addresses in load and store instructions.

Memory Writes: Memory writes are processed according to the following rule:

$$\frac{\begin{array}{c} h' = h[\ ((l_j, c) \to (l_i) = (l_j)\ ?\ e_c : h[(l_j, c)]) \wedge \\ ((l_i, c) \to b_i\ ?\ e_c : h[(l_i, c)])\ ] \\ \{(l_j)\} = a[(l_i)] \qquad \{(l_i, c, b_i)\} = \mathsf{GetLoc}(\sigma[r]) \end{array}}{\langle *r = e_c, (\sigma, h, b, a)\rangle \to (\sigma, h', b, a)}$$

This rule conditionally updates every address that is potentially aliased with the address stored in r. The rule uses the function GetLoc to account for the fact that the address in r might itself have been the result of some conditional updates, so instead of a single address, GetLoc returns a guarded list of the possible addresses stored in $\sigma[r]$. If $\sigma[r]$ is a simple address (l_r, c), $\mathsf{GetLoc}(\sigma[r])$ returns (l_r, c, True), but in general, $\sigma[r]$ can be a complicated expression evaluating to different (l_i, c_i) under different conditions b_i. However, since we logged the value of the offsets, the rule can assume that those are fixed for all choices. For each memory location (l_i, c) that is returned by GetLoc, we store a conditional expression that evaluates to e_c only if $*r$ does indeed evaluate to (l_i, c); i.e., if b_i is true. For each memory location l_j that is aliased with each l_i, we update $h[(l_j, c)]$ to a conditional that reduces to e_c if l_j is indeed aliased to l_i.

An important assumption in the rule above is that since we always know the offsets for memory accesses, we only have to track aliases among the base addresses. In the special case that an address is allocated with a call to malloc after the start of replay, there is no ambiguity as to what address is contained in a memory location, GetLoc simply returns one possible location for $*r$, and that location has no aliases, so the rule simply reduces to standard heap update:

$$\frac{\{(l_i, c_i, \mathsf{True})\} = \mathsf{GetLoc}(\sigma[r]) \qquad h' = h[(l_i, c_i) \to e_c]}{\langle *r = e_c, (\sigma, h, b, a)\rangle \to (\sigma, h', b, a)}$$

Memory Reads: Loading from memory presents similar complications and is processed using the following rule:

$$\frac{\begin{array}{c} \{(l_i, c_i, b_i)\} = \mathsf{GetLoc}(e_c) \qquad h[(l_i, c_i)] \neq \bot \\ \sigma' = \sigma[r \to \forall_i b_i \Rightarrow h[(l_i, c_i)]] \end{array}}{\langle r = *e_c, (\sigma, h, b, a)\rangle \to (\sigma', h, b, a)}$$

The notation $\forall_i b_i \Rightarrow e_i$ above should be read as a switch statement that produces e_i if b_i is true. Note that we do not load from any of the may-alias locations of $*e_c$ since the store rule above ensures that their values will be equivalent if the alias turns out to be real.

In summary, in the case where we have the log from the start of execution, our strategy for memory operations reduces to the very efficient modeling of memory as a map. Conversely, when we have no information about aliasing and all our locations are unknown, our strategy is just an inefficient implementation of the theory of arrays. For our purposes, however, this is ideal because it exploits all the concrete information available with the system, and allows us to deal with aliasing uncertainty while still exploiting any aliasing information that we can provide.

3.2.3 External Function Calls

A common issue in the symbolic execution of real-world programs is handling external functions such as libc and system calls. The typical solution, and the one we follow, is to provide a model of those functions. bbr follows the approach used in Klee [18] by linking a modified version of the uClibc library with the target program, which greatly reduces the number of libc functions that we need to model. We model a subset of system calls using bit vector values. For instance, we use a 4 byte bit vector to model the user ID of the calling process. Thus calls to `getuid` will return that bit vector. We currently model over 100 Linux system calls but do not model the state of devices or the kernel.

3.2.4 File Descriptors and Network Sockets

bbr implements a simple symbolic file system where each file is modeled as follows:

- An array of symbolic expressions, where each entry in the array represents one byte in the file.
- A 4 byte integer for the current file offset.
- A 4 byte integer representing the file flags (read / write / both, and append / overwrite mode).
- A 4 byte integer representing the file permissions.
- A 4 byte integer representing the file size.

The file descriptor itself is modeled as a 4 byte bit vector variable, and the file system is a map from the file descriptors to the structure listed above. bbr currently supports typical file system calls, and network sockets are modeled similarly, except that they are append-only and do not support seek.

Because the file metadata are modeled as real integers (rather than bit vectors), bbr records values from file system operations (as mentioned in Section2) in order to maintain each file's internal state during symbolic execution. For instance, the return values from `read` calls are recorded so that the current file offset can be correctly updated.

We experimented with using bit vectors and the theory of arrays to represent the file contents, but this did not scale, while the approach above did. This is because the programs we experimented with operate on large files, but do not necessarily process each byte within those files (e.g., databases may only read a few tuples from a loaded page). Modeling these files with the theory of arrays caused a large number of bit vector variables to be created for indices that are not referenced. Our approach, which records additional information during runtime (4 bytes per each invocation of `read`, `write`, `lseek`, etc), allows us to implement our own file model that generates less complicated constraints, which saves a substantial amount of constraint solving time while adding relatively little additional recording state.

3.3 Soundness and Completeness

For partial replay, we define soundness as the fact that all program executions (i.e., the starting heap state and execution path) solved by the replayer are indeed feasible traces of the target program although not necessarily the same as the original execution, and completeness as the ability to solve for program executions given the input logs, provided that the inputs were from an actual execution.

bbr is unsound since the initial state of the heap generated at the beginning of the partial trace might not correspond to a feasible heap from the original program. This is because the system might miss some of the invariants that the non-recorded portion of the program enforces on the heap, so it might generate a heap that violates these unstated invariants. On the other hand, bbr is incomplete since we might not be able to replay executions that violate our assumptions, namely the independent allocation and non-overlapping assumption, the memory alias assumptions, and the fact that we do not model the hardware or the kernel state. In practice, that means we cannot determine the memory locations that are overwritten in a buffer overflow attack (although we can still detect writing out of allocated boundaries errors), or replay an execution that is caused by malfunctioning hardware.

3.4 Parallel Constraint Solver

Symbolic execution produces a set of constraints. The bit vector variables in the constraints correspond to heap contents before the start of replay, the non-deterministic inputs that were read, as well as return values any external function invocations during the execution. The constraints need to be solved in order to re-create the values that would cause the execution to take the same control flow path as in the original run. A straight-forward implementation would send all the generated constraints to a constraint solver to solve in one bundle. We found, however, that this is quite slow as the constraint sets can be very large.

Instead, we subdivide the constraints into independent portions that can be solved separately. Specifically, we found that although there are a large number of symbolic variables, it is frequently the case that each variable is only related to a handful of other variables. For instance, in replaying a web server, each byte that is read from the incoming socket is modeled as a bit vector variable as mentioned in Section 3.2.4. While it is likely that there will be constraints that bind the variables generated from reading the same socket (e.g., a constraint that the first three bytes read from the socket must be the characters 'GET'), it is unlikely that there will be constraints that bind variables from one socket read to those from reads from different sockets, where each socket corresponds to a unique HTTP request.

Thus, bbr includes a constraints analyzer that separates the constraints into independent groups. Formally, the constraints form a graph $G(V, E)$, where each vertex $v \in V$ represents a bit vector variable, and each edge $e \in E$ between two vertices v_1 and v_2 represents a constraint binding the variables represented by v_1 and v_2. Given G, the constraint analyzer processes E and splits G into its independent components. At the end of the analysis, each of the independent components are written to a file. The parallel solver in bbr then solves the components individually. Because most solvers are single-threaded, this also allows us to parallelize solving by running each component in a separate instance of the solver with a separate thread.

In addition to reducing solving time, splitting constraints into independent components can help identify components that may not need to be solved. For example, the constraints generated from replaying the thttpd web server (see Section 4) separate nicely into independent components as expected, with each component corresponding to an HTTP request. Most components take a relatively short time to solve, but one component takes substantially longer. Examining constraints involved in that component reveals that they involve not the bytes that are read from the request sockets, but instead bind the return values from multiple invocations of `gettimeofday` together. Looking at the code for the server, we found that it implements a number of timers for house-keeping tasks such as clearing lingering connections. The timer structure maintains a field `time` that stores the next time that the timer should be fired. After processing each incoming connection, the server iterates through all timers to check if any of them should be run by passing in the current time (by calling `gettimeofday`). The check routine then compares the current time with the `time` field in the timers and either fires the timer or reschedules, creating dependencies between each invocation of the check (and thereby `gettimeofday`) routine. This routine runs many times per minute, and the solver is quite slow at solving it.

In this case, however, these constraints represent a small portion of the program which is unlikely to contain bugs, and not solving them reduces solving time substantially. In general, it is possible to use the outputs of any subset of the constraints to attempt to reconstruct a bug, thanks to our parallel solver. If one portion of the constraints is taking a long time to solve, the programmer can run the program on the values from the constraints that have been solved so far with the debugger to see if the bug is reproduced. In the case of the `gettimeofday` constraints described above, they don't impact the results of interest (namely the contents of the incoming HTTP requests), so we do not need to wait for the solver to finish solving them.

3.5 Using the output of the solver

The output of the solver is an assignment to each variable involved in the constraints. bbr provides a debugger that takes in the instrumented bytecode and the solved outputs. Similar to the replayer, the debugger performs symbolic execution from the replay starting point. When an instruction that generates symbolic data is encountered, instead of creating symbolic variables, the debugger substitutes values from the solved outputs. Like gdb, the user can specify a list of values to be printed on the screen when they are executed.

For files and sockets that were used during execution, bbr further provides a utility that assembles the contents that were read from the solved output. bbr is able to do that due to the naming conventions of symbolic variables when they are created. Thus, if the developer is interested in viewing what values were read from a specific socket, she can first use the bbr debugger to identify the file descriptor number that the socket was assigned during replay, and then use the utility to assemble all the contents that were read from that descriptor number, rather than printing out the values of the descriptor number and the contents of the read buffer after each `recv` call.

As discussed in Section 2, if the user is not satisfied with the solved outputs, say because she has extra information about the original program state, she can provide that to the debugger in terms of extra constraints (e.g., some variable must have a certain value). The debugger then appends those constraints with the existing ones, and solves for another plausible program state if one exists.

4. EXPERIMENTS

In this section, we describe our evaluation of the three central claims of this paper:

- First, we compare the runtime overhead of bbr to other replay schemes. We measure both the overhead in terms of slowdown to the running program and the size of the logs generated.

sqlite	We ran 20k TPC-C [4] transactions on top of a 10G database representing 10 warehouses and measured the time to complete all transactions. Checkpoints are taken every 5 transactions.
memcached	We inserted or updated 10k keys into the cache, with values of size 800k each, and measured the time to complete all operations. Checkpoints are taken every 10 operations on the server.
tcpdump	We asked tcpdump to print the details from a packet dump of 1G in size, and measured the time to process all the packets. Checkpoints are taken every 5 packets that are processed.
betaftpd	We fetched 50 files from the server, each of size 1G, and measured the time to complete all operations. Checkpoints are taken every 5 fetches.
thttpd	(same as betaftpd)
ghttpd	(same as betaftpd)

Figure 4: Description of benchmarks

- Next, we chose different types of bugs from real-world applications and examine bbr's ability to replay them.
- Finally, we measure the effectiveness of the alias-aware memory model and constraint partitioning in bbr in replaying programs.

bbr is implemented with 11k LOC of C++ using LLVM version 2.6. We experimented with several different SMT solver implementations, but we only report numbers from those using Z3 [3] as that was the solver that we found to scale the best. For these experiments, replay was run on a 32-bit Ubuntu machine with 2GB of RAM, while the constraint solving was done on a 64-bit 4-core machine running Z3 version 2.14 on Windows Server 2003 with 24GB of RAM.

4.1 Overhead Experiments

In the first experiment, we measured the time and space overhead that different programs incur while collecting logs with periodic checkpoints. The programs we replayed are listed in Fig. 4. Fig. 5 shows the results of the time overhead experiment, in terms of slowdown relative to an uninstrumented binary, while Fig. 6 and Fig. 7 show the log sizes that were generated by the different recording schemes.[2] All data collections were done using the bbr instrumentation library. We report the results from running five different versions of each application, namely:

- [**Native**]: Native uninstrumented version.
- [**bbr**]: bbr instrumented version with periodic checkpoints at frequencies shown in Fig. 4.
- [**non-det**]: Instrumented version that collects all non-deterministic data from the beginning of program execution. This models the overhead of a whole-program, fully deterministic replayer.
- [**snapshot**]: Same as non-det, except that every time a checkpoint annotation is reached, we fork a process to create a core dump, and all previously collected data are deleted. This models the overhead of a partial replayer that takes periodic snapshots of memory and logs non-deterministic inputs that were received between snapshots.
- [**loads**]: Instrumented version that records the values of all memory loads. To reduce the amount of logging, we use the technique from iDNA [17] where we only record loads whose values are not predictable at runtime (i.e., the store to a location was not an explicit instruction in the application but rather a side-effect of a system call, such as storing to the buffer in `read`).

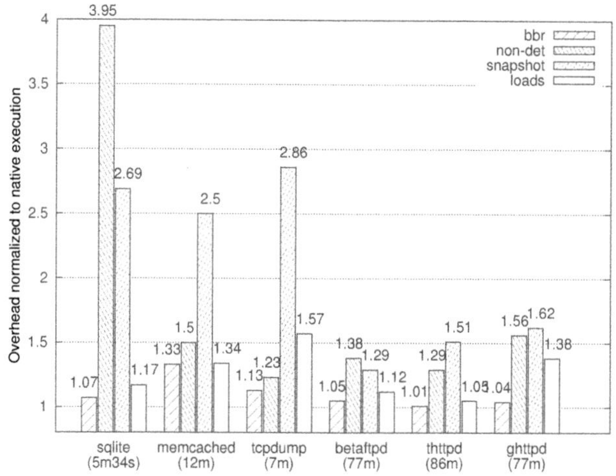

Figure 5: Normalized execution time (relative to uninstrumented binary=1) for different applications, with uninstrumented times shown at bottom.

Benchmark	bbr	non-det	snapshot	loads
sqlite	7k	20G	1G	250M
memcached	16k	8G	600M	569M
tcpdump	3k	2.6G	150M	200M
betaftpd	72M	50G	5.1G	550M
thttpd	100M	50G	5.1G	300M
ghttpd	99M	50G	5.2G	2.2G

Figure 6: Log size experiment results

The timing overhead experiment shows that bbr incurs the least overhead as compared to the other replay modes, varying from 1% for thttpd to 33% for memcached, with an overall average of 10%, which is significantly faster than the other schemes. This is due to the smaller amount of data that bbr needs to write as compared to the data-logging schemes. The more computationally intensive applications (e.g., sqlite) incur more overhead since they are more likely to hit branch instructions during their executions.

In terms of log sizes, bbr outperforms the other schemes by a significant amount. This is expected because for applications such as betaftpd, the majority of non-deterministic data comes from the contents of the files that are read and sent back to the user. So in the case of non-det, the size of the log is roughly equal to the size of files that were read. The core dump snapshots help somewhat, since all previously recorded non-deterministic data are discarded when a snapshot is taken. As the size of the core dump is directly proportional to the amount of memory that is currently being used by the program, for a computationally-intensive application such as sqlite, the log in the snapshot case is dominated by the size of the core dump, whereas in data-intensive applications such as web servers, the log size is dominated by the non-deterministic data log. Finally, loads reduces log sizes by only recording the load values that are affected by system calls and subsequently read by the application. However, the log sizes are still larger than those

[2]The checkpoints were placed at sensible program points, such as where the web server starts to process a new HTTP request. We tried placing the annotation at different but semantically similar locations and did not notice much difference in replay and solving times.

Benchmark	bbr	non-det	snapshot	loads
sqlite	1.4k/op	1M/op	0.2G/op	12.5k/op
memcached	1.6k/op	0.8M/op	60M/op	56.9k/op
tcpdump	0.6k/op	0.3M/op	30M/op	20k/op
betaftpd	14.4M/op	1G/op	1G/op	55M/op
thttpd	20M/op	1G/op	1G/op	6M/op
ghttpd	19.8M/op	1G/op	1G/op	44M/op

Figure 7: Log growth rates in overhead experiment

# Requests	bbr	non-det	snapshot	loads
10	46M	10G	5.1G	47M
30	46M	30G	5.3G	150M
50	46M	50G	5.6G	300M

Figure 8: Log sizes with varying # of requests

from bbr, since for some applications (such as sqlite and tcpdump), most of the values that are affected by system calls are indeed loaded by the application afterwards, for instance the read buffers in **read** and **recv** calls.

Since the number of operations stored in the various logs are not the same (e.g., bbr takes periodic checkpoints to reduce log sizes whereas non-det keeps the entire log from the beginning of execution), Fig. 7 presents the same results by showing the log growth rates instead. The results show that the bbr logs grow much slower as compared to others. Thus, even if the user decides to keep around all the bbr log files rather than having the system truncate them at each checkpoint (perhaps due to uncertainty as to which checkpoint the replay should start), bbr will still have the smallest log file sizes as compared to other schemes.

Next, we reran the experiment for betaftpd, varying the number of requests issued in order to characterize the size of the data logs as the running time of the application increases (the results show that the execution overhead is relatively insensitive to the number of requests). The results are shown in Fig. 8. Observe that the log sizes for the non-det and loads schemes grow proportionally with execution time due to the lack of log truncation. And while the log sizes are roughly the same for bbr and snapshot, bbr incurs much less runtime overhead because it writes less data to disk, as shown in Fig. 5.

To understand how these numbers compare to other replay tools, we compared our time overheads to those reported for other replay tools on similar data-intensive programs. PRES [31] reports an overhead of 43% when recording all basic blocks while running MySQL, and 1977% when recording PBZip2. R2 [24] reports an overhead of 200% when logging all data from win32 system calls while running MySQL. iTarget [37] reports a slowdown of 58% when performing whole program replay on BerkeleyDB. ODR [15] reports a slowdown of nearly 400% on MySQL. Other tools designed to collect data during normal execution on different benchmarks report similar or larger overheads. For example, program shepherding [28] reports up to 760% and iDNA [17] reports an average of 1189%. In summary, the overheads of bbr are generally low enough (with an average of 10%) to be deployed as an online tool during normal program execution.

4.2 Reproducing Bugs

In our next experiment, we used bbr to replay different types of bugs from real-world programs. Fig. 9 shows the list of bugs that we tried to replay. We describe a few representative bugs in detail in Section 4.2.1 below.

We set up the applications in a similar way as in the overhead experiment, except that we input a request that would expose or trigger the bug. We then terminated the application (if it had not already terminated due to errors), and collected the logs. Given the log, we asked bbr to reproduce a plausible execution of the program from the last checkpoint. Fig. 10 shows some statistics about the bbr executions, specifically:

- [**LOC**]: Number of LLVM instructions emulated.
- [**# br**]: Number of conditional branch values recorded.
- [**Replay**]: Time taken for bbr's symbolic execution.
- [**Split**]: Time taken to split the generated constraints into independent components.
- [**# constr**]: Total number of SMT constraints generated. Note that constraints that reduce to True are not included, thus the number of constraints can be smaller than number of conditional branches.
- [**# groups**]: Number of independent groups created.
- [**# vars**]: # of bit vector variables in the constraints.
- [**Solve**]: Time taken for parallel solving.
- [**Debug?**]: Whether the solved inputs can be used to identify the original bug.

These experiments show that bbr is able to symbolically execute a wide-range of real-world data-intensive applications and generate constraints that can be solved within a reasonable amount of time. Most of the replay time was spent in symbolic execution. Note that the number of conditional branch values recorded is typically much fewer than the number of constraints generated. That is because of peephole optimizations on the constraint expressions that bbr performs to eliminate constraints that reduces to True, and also because some of the conditional branches are not based on non-deterministic values in the program, so no constraints were generated.

4.2.1 *Bug Walkthrough*

Here we discuss a few bugs in detail. As discussed in Section 2, the decrement bug in memcached was caused by the incorrect treatment of the stored values as signed entities. Using bbr, we were able to solve for inputs and state of the value store that would trigger the problem. Notice that even though bbr did not record the contents of the request from the user, it was nonetheless able to reconstruct it given the branching decisions recorded during parsing of the request.

For the sqlite bugs, rather than a complete database file, the output of the solver is a combination of heap values and a partial database file that was read while processing the transactions since the last checkpoint. As described in Section 3.5, these outputs cannot be used directly to run sqlite and reproduce the bug, since the solved input file is incomplete. However, these solved values can still help developers debug. For instance, the collation bug was caused by an error in the implementation of the comparison operator between two expression trees, causing it to return the wrong cached value rather than performing the actual comparison. Using the solved values from the partial replay and the branch log, we were able to observe the error by tracking the solved values that were used as inputs to the comparison function, thanks to the bbr debugger. When invoked with those values, the function returns the incorrect value that triggers the bug.

For the bugs in tcpdump, bbr solved for the contents of the incoming packets that cause the infinite loops. While the contents were not exactly identical to the original ones, we have verified that they cause the same problems when fed into tcpdump.

sqlite cast	Error in the processing of queries with multiple selection predicates when one of the predicates involves a cast. The code mistakenly reuses the results from the predicate without the cast for those with the cast [5].
sqlite join	Error in processing natural self-joins. Mistake in identifying the table to join leads to returning extra rows [6].
sqlite collate	In the processing of aggregates, the code mistakenly treats aggregates with collation and without collation as equivalent. As a result, instead of executing each aggregate the cached results are returned [7].
memcached decr	Error in treating unsigned entities as signed leads to the wrong value being returned as a result of decrement [1].
memcache CAS	When a part of an existing value is updated, the code forgets to updates its CAS (a unique identifier for the value), leading to the same CAS being returned both before and after the update, violating the specification [8].
tcpdump BGP	The code for displaying BGP packets contains an error in the checking of the loop condition that always returns true. As a result, the loop never terminates [9].
tcpdump ISIS	In printing ISIS packets, the code does not update how many bytes have been processed. Because of that, the printing code goes into an infinite loop. This is a different bug than the one above [10].
tcpdump RSVP	The code for displaying RSVP packets does not check if the end of packet has been reached. As a result, the printing code goes into an infinite loop. This is a different bug than those above [11].
betaftpd char	Betaftpd does not properly handle non-Latin characters (such as 'á'). As a result, it returns not found when a user requests a file with such characters as filename, even though the file exists.
thttpd defang	When returning an error message to a http request, the code expands '>' and '<' characters into their HTML equivalents. However, it forgets to check if it has already reached the end of the buffer allocated to hold the escaped error message, thus leading to a write out of bounds error [12].
ghttpd CGI	When generating the pathname for a CGI, the code simply concats the names of the CGI directory and the CGI executable together, without checking whether the length of the result exceeds the preallocated buffer [13].
ghttpd log	The request logging code in ghttpd does not check the length of the filename in the GET request. As a result, it can write into memory that is beyond the size of the buffer preallocated to hold the log message [14].

Figure 9: Description of bugs replayed

Bug	LOC	# br	Replay	Split	# constr	# groups	# vars	Solve	Debug?
sqlite cast	2420548	83883	1225s	2s	86245	2140	11320	5hr	Y
sqlite join	1705078	149762	1011s	4s	71596	2891	11127	4hr	Y
sqlite collate	2546778	132084	820s	2s	67890	1272	9750	3hr	Y
memcached decr	8708	1744	286s	0.67s	811	158	1342	13s	Y
memcached CAS	24837	2249	1955s	3.74s	1705	265	2483	158s	Y
tcpdump BGP	2947998	247161	31s	0.08s	13476	147	362	1s	Y
tcpdump ISIS	61769562	4634390	370s	0.65s	235081	86	228	5s	Y
tcpdump RSVP	1108294	83341	93.8s	0.03s	11541	233	233	1s	Y
betaftpd char	122036	9869	7s	0.01s	950	106	358	1s	N
thttpd defang	514879	55521	542s	1.06s	21003	2153	6105	2s	Y
ghttpd CGI	352710	31297	40s	0.01s	8553	728	784	2s	Y
ghttpd log	344662	45054	40s	0.01s	8570	698	753	1s	Y

Figure 10: Replay experiment results

In general, for all of the bugs that bbr was able to replay, even though the solved instances of the database contents / network packets / http requests / etc are not necessarily the exact same one as in the original input, they still exhibit the errors. This illustrates the power of our approach – recording branches and a few extra pieces of data is enough for developers to debug the problem in hand. Also, observe that without using bbr's partial replay ability, in order to replay these bugs it would be necessary to record all non-deterministic data from the beginning, or take periodic snapshots of the heap, which would be very costly as demonstrated. In both cases, there is a a huge overhead in both time and data log sizes. Furthermore, as our experiment shows, the longer the program runs, the worse the problem becomes.

bbr failed to replay the betaftpd non-Latin character bug. This is because the bug was caused by the lack of checking the characters that are read from the incoming socket before passing them to `open`. The constraints generated from symbolic execution simply bound the length of the file requested (since the code checks for '\0'), but not the contents that were read (this is precisely the reason why the bug exists). As a result, the solver returned a random filename that does not trigger the bug when re-executed. While the developer can use the bbr debugger to request another plausible value for the filename, it is unlikely that she will be able to hit upon one that causes the problem within a reasonable amount of time given the unconstrained nature of the bug. This illustrates a limitation of bbr – the ability to construct a trace that leads to the problem relies on the fact that the buggy execution is sufficiently bound by the bbr logs. Otherwise, the solver might return a trace that does not trigger the error, even though it is branch-deterministic.

Finally, we note that for a few of these bugs (e.g., those from ghttpd), it is possible to replay them by just recording the incoming requests after the last checkpoint, since they do not involve the internal state of the program. However, it would be very difficult for a developer to know a priori whether the bugs that her program exhibits will involve the internal state of the application or not, unless the application keeps no internal state whatsoever, which is highly unlikely. For instance, the sqlite and memcached bugs are related to the internal state of the program (in particular, the cached values in memory). Thus, it would not be possible to replay such bugs simply by recording incoming requests.

4.3 Constraint Splitting

Next, we look at the effectiveness of splitting constraints into independent groups, using ghttpd and betaftpd as examples. We replayed different number of requests coming into the two servers and measured the solving time. We chose these two applications since they have relatively simple internal states, and each incoming request should be independent from each other in terms of the constraints that are generated. We compared the time taken to solve the generated constraints all at once from a single file (Single), and the total time needed to solve the split constraints, using 1000 threads for the parallel solver on a 4 core machine (Split).

# reqs	# const.	# vars	# groups	single	split
ghttpd web server					
5	8547	750	698	8s	1s
10	20383	1923	823	20s	5s
50	60384	5330	2314	32m	6m
betaftpd ftp server					
5	960	358	106	2s	1s
10	1534	533	210	40s	10s
50	13223	1903	530	40m	13m

Figure 11: Constraint splitting experiment results

The results are of the experiment are shown in Fig. 11.

The results show a huge difference between parallel and single-threaded solving. We believe that one possible reason for the substantial slowdown in the single-threaded case is because of cache misses when the input problem size becomes large. We have also noticed that the solver frequently suffers from memory thrashing in the single-threaded case (on a machine with 24GB of physical RAM), which further contributes to the slowdown. While one might argue that this is a relatively obvious way to speed up solving, we have compared our results with different solver implementations (Z3, yices, stp), and none of them seem to have this feature in place, possibly because constraint solvers are traditionally targeted to solving instances where most variables are related, but not instances with a large number of independent components. Given that the time needed to do constraint splitting is relatively small as compared to the replay time (as shown in Fig. 10), it appears worthwhile to use parallel solving for replay.

4.4 Memory Model Implementation

Lastly, we looked at the performance differences between different memory models in our replay engine. As discussed in Section 3.2, bbr models memory as a conceptual mapping from program variables to constraint expressions. Internally, this is implemented using two maps, one that maps program variables to memory locations, and one that maps memory locations to contents in memory. There are different ways to implement the second map. We experimented with several different implementations for a 32-bit memory (i.e., addresses are 32-bit each) and compared the time it took to symbolically execute three different small programs:

1. [**wc**]: word count on an empty file (37k LLVM LOC).
2. [**db connect**]: a simple application that connects to a sqlite database (66k LLVM LOC).
3. [**db query**]: application that connects and issues a select query to a sqlite database (341k LLVM LOC).

Debug printouts were turned on so they took longer to run. The different memory model implementations include:

1. A single Z3 bit vector array [Z3 bit vector(8) $\rightarrow$ Z3 bit vector(8)]. This is the most general representation based on the theory of arrays.
2. For an allocation site of n bytes, create a Z3 bit vector of length $8n$, with the entire memory modeled as a `std::map` [`uint` $\rightarrow$ Z3 bit vector($8n$)].
3. A single `std::map` [`uint` $\rightarrow$ Z3 bit vector(8)].
4. A Z3 bit vector array for each allocation site, with the entire memory modeled as a single `std::map` [`uint` $\rightarrow$ Z3 bit vector array].
5. For an allocation site of n bytes, create a `std::vector` of size n, with each entry being an 8-bit Z3 bit vector to model a byte, and the entire memory is modeled as a single `std::map` [`uint` $\rightarrow$ `std::vector` of Z3 bit vector(8)].

Impl. #	wc	db connect	db query
1	13m	52m	>1hr
2	>1hr	crashed	crashed
3	8m	15m	>1hr
4	15m	35m	>1hr
5	47s	1.9m	17m
6	10s	42s	2m

Figure 12: Memory modeling experiment results

6. We built our own data structure to represent a bit vector and implemented a number of peephole optimizations. A single `std::map` [custom bit vector(8) $\rightarrow$ custom bit vector(8)] is then used to model memory. This is the implementation we used for the operations described in Section 3.2.2.

Fig. 12 reports different memory model implementations and their replay times. "crashed" means the experiment exhausted the address space on a 32-bit machine and crashed. As the experiment shows, using the Z3 theory of arrays incurs a substantial replay overhead in real programs, since each read / write to the array potentially creates a new array data structure. Using Z3 bit vectors still incurs some overhead in the solver, possibly due to housekeeping routines such as structural hashing. Note that the programs above were replayed from the entry point and no memory aliases were involved. We anticipate that the performance of the first 5 implementations to perform much worse in partial replay with memory aliases, and thus built our own representation of expressions at the end.

5. RELATED WORK

A number of bug replay tools based on symbolic execution have been proposed recently. However, to our knowledge, no tools support partial symbolic replay for long running programs, which fundamentally distinguishes our approach. In [19], the authors proposed to record input traces during execution, and perform symbolic execution to generate bug cases for the developer. However, they used a trace logger with high overhead [17], and it is not clear if their approach is scalable to long-running programs. ESD [40] uses a path searching approach similar to model checking to reproduce bugs. It has no runtime overhead, but requires a coredump, makes no guarantee regarding how long it would take to regenerate the bug, and is tricky to use for replaying non-crash or hang bugs. ODR [15] targets multicore bugs and collects data traces during normal execution. They report a substantial runtime overhead because of data collection and also a long solving time. PRES [31] is similar to ODR but reproduces bugs iteratively with significant slowdowns.

Replaying executions deterministically from data logs has been a topic in systems research for many years, with the emphasis on using different mechanisms to reduce the runtime overhead and log sizes [30, 33, 22, 17, 25] and recording at the operating systems level rather than application level [27]. Recent tools such as R2 [24] and iTarget [37] allow users to decide what data to be logged in order to reduce recording overhead, but at the expense of not being able to reproduce all executions. These tools generally have higher runtime overheads for data-intensive programs than bbr.

At the other end are techniques that automatically find bugs without any inputs. These range from static analysis tools [16, 21, 29] to dynamic tools such as model checkers [36, 38]. Advances in SMT solvers and symbolic execution have enabled new test generation tools such as concolic testing [32, 34] and other test generators based on symbolic execution [23, 18]. These tools focus on finding all sorts of bugs, rather than reproducing a specific bug in hand.

Our memory model is inspired by the work done in test generation for languages that include pointer operations. In [35], the authors proposed a memory model that maintains heaps for different types of objects and introduces constraints to enforce the disjointness among the different object heaps. bbr imposes similar assumptions on object types and their alias properties. In [20], the authors proposed a region-based approach, with each address represented by a memory location object similar to that in bbr, and each location can point to different concrete addresses depending on alias resolution. In [39], a hybrid memory model was proposed with a concrete store and a symbolic store implemented using theory of arrays, which led to our initial memory model implementation. There is similar work in languages without explicit pointer constructs such as [26].

6. CONCLUSIONS

We presented bbr, a *branch-deterministic* replayer that performs low-overhead replay by logging only a small amount of data at runtime. We also proposed the notion of *partial replay*, which allows users to replay long running data-intensive programs with bounded log sizes. To make our approach scale, we introduced several new techniques, including a new memory model for handling aliased addresses, and a partitioning approach for parallel solving. We showed that these techniques allow bbr to efficiently replay a number of data-intensive programs, and can reproduce real bugs in long-running programs, including sqlite and several web servers.

7. ACKNOWLEDGEMENTS

We thank the anonymous reviewers for their valuable feedback. We also thank Lidong Zhou, Vijay Ganesh, and Nikolaj Bjørner for their helpful discussions.

References

[1] http://code.google.com/p/memcached/issues/detail?id=21.
[2] http://www.uclibc.org.
[3] http://research.microsoft.com/en-us/um/redmond/projects/z3/.
[4] http://www.tpcc.org.
[5] http://www.sqlite.org/src/info/eb5548a849.
[6] http://www.sqlite.org/src/info/b73fb0bd64.
[7] http://www.sqlite.org/src/info/360c6073e197.
[8] http://code.google.com/p/memcached/issues/detail?id=15.
[9] CVE-2005-1279.
[10] CVE-2005-1278.
[11] CVE-2005-1280.
[12] CVE-2003-0899.
[13] CVE-2001-0820.
[14] CVE-2002-1904.
[15] G. Altekar and I. Stoica. Odr: output-deterministic replay for multicore debugging. In *SOSP*, pages 193–206, 2009.
[16] T. Ball, R. Majumdar, T. D. Millstein, and S. K. Rajamani. Automatic predicate abstraction of c programs. In *PLDI*, pages 203–213, 2001.
[17] S. Bhansali, W.-K. Chen, S. de Jong, A. Edwards, R. Murray, M. Drinić, D. Mihočka, and J. Chau. Framework for instruction-level tracing and analysis of program executions. In *Proceedings of the 2nd international conference on Virtual execution environments*, VEE '06, pages 154–163, 2006.
[18] C. Cadar, D. Dunbar, and D. R. Engler. Klee: Unassisted and automatic generation of high-coverage tests for complex systems programs. In *OSDI*, pages 209–224, 2008.
[19] M. Castro, M. Costa, and J.-P. Martin. Better bug reporting with better privacy. In *ASPLOS*, pages 319–328, 2008.
[20] B. Elkarablieh, P. Godefroid, and M. Y. Levin. Precise pointer reasoning for dynamic test generation. In *ISSTA*, pages 129–140, 2009.
[21] D. R. Engler and K. Ashcraft. Racerx: effective, static detection of race conditions and deadlocks. In *SOSP*, pages 237–252, 2003.
[22] D. Geels, G. Altekar, S. Shenker, and I. Stoica. Replay debugging for distributed applications. In *USENIX Annual Technical Conference*, pages 289–300, 2006.
[23] P. Godefroid, M. Y. Levin, and D. A. Molnar. Automated whitebox fuzz testing. In *NDSS*, 2008.
[24] Z. Guo, X. Wang, J. Tang, X. Liu, Z. Xu, M. Wu, M. F. Kaashoek, and Z. Zhang. R2: An application-level kernel for record and replay. In *OSDI*, pages 193–208, 2008.
[25] J. Huang, P. Liu, and C. Zhang. Leap: lightweight deterministic multi-processor replay of concurrent java programs. In *SIGSOFT FSE*, pages 207–216, 2010.
[26] S. Khurshid, C. S. Pasareanu, and W. Visser. Generalized symbolic execution for model checking and testing. In *TACAS*, pages 553–568, 2003.
[27] S. T. King, G. W. Dunlap, and P. M. Chen. Debugging operating systems with time-traveling virtual machines. In *USENIX Annual Technical Conference*, pages 1–15, 2005.
[28] V. Kiriansky, D. Bruening, and S. P. Amarasinghe. Secure execution via program shepherding. In *USENIX Security Symposium*, pages 191–206, 2002.
[29] R. Manevich, M. Sridharan, S. Adams, M. Das, and Z. Yang. Pse: explaining program failures via postmortem static analysis. In *SIGSOFT FSE*, pages 63–72, 2004.
[30] R. H. B. Netzer and M. H. Weaver. Optimal tracing and incremental reexecution for debugging long-running programs. In *PLDI*, pages 313–325, 1994.
[31] S. Park, Y. Zhou, W. Xiong, Z. Yin, R. Kaushik, K. H. Lee, and S. Lu. Pres: probabilistic replay with execution sketching on multiprocessors. In *SOSP*, pages 177–192, 2009.
[32] K. Sen, D. Marinov, and G. Agha. Cute: a concolic unit testing engine for c. In *ESEC/SIGSOFT FSE*, pages 263–272, 2005.
[33] S. M. Srinivasan, S. Kandula, C. R. Andrews, and Y. Zhou. Flashback: A lightweight extension for rollback and deterministic replay for software debugging. In *USENIX Annual Technical Conference*, pages 29–44, 2004.
[34] N. Tillmann and J. de Halleux. Pex-white box test generation for .net. In *TAP*, pages 134–153, 2008.
[35] D. Vanoverberghe, N. Tillmann, and F. Piessens. Test input generation for programs with pointers. In *TACAS*, pages 277–291, 2009.
[36] W. Visser, C. S. Pasareanu, and S. Khurshid. Test input generation with java pathfinder. In *ISSTA*, pages 97–107, 2004.
[37] M. Wu, F. Long, X. Wang, Z. Xu, H. Lin, X. Liu, Z. Guo, H. Guo, L. Zhou, and Z. Zhang. Language-based replay via data flow cut. In *FSE-18*, 2010.
[38] J. Yang, T. Chen, M. Wu, Z. Xu, X. Liu, H. Lin, M. Yang, F. Long, L. Zhang, and L. Zhou. Modist: Transparent model checking of unmodified distributed systems. In *NSDI*, pages 213–228, 2009.
[39] J. Yang, C. Sar, P. Twohey, C. Cadar, and D. R. Engler. Automatically generating malicious disks using symbolic execution. In *IEEE Symposium on Security and Privacy*, pages 243–257, 2006.
[40] C. Zamfir and G. Candea. Execution synthesis: a technique for automated software debugging. In *EuroSys*, pages 321–334, 2010.

Mitigating the Confounding Effects of Program Dependences for Effective Fault Localization

George K. Baah
Georgia Institute of Technology
Atlanta, GA 30332
baah@cc.gatech.edu

Andy Podgurski
Case Western Reserve University
Cleveland, OH 44106
podgurski@case.edu

Mary Jean Harrold
Georgia Institute of Technology
Atlanta, GA 30332
harrold@cc.gatech.edu

ABSTRACT

Dynamic program dependences are recognized as important factors in software debugging because they contribute to triggering the effects of faults and propagating the effects to a program's output. The effects of dynamic dependences also produce significant confounding bias when statistically estimating the causal effect of a statement on the occurrence of program failures, which leads to poor fault-localization results. This paper presents a novel causal-inference technique for fault localization that accounts for the effects of dynamic data and control dependences and thus, significantly reduces confounding bias during fault localization. The technique employs a new dependence-based causal model together with matching of test executions based on their dynamic dependences. The paper also presents empirical results indicating that the new technique performs significantly better than existing statistical fault-localization techniques as well as our previous fault localization technique based on causal-inference methodology.

Categories and Subject Descriptors: D.2.5 [Software Engineering]: Testing and Debugging—*Debugging aids, Diagnostics*

General Terms: Algorithms, Experimentation

Keywords: causal inference, potential outcome model, matching, fault localization, program analysis, debugging

1. INTRODUCTION

The pervasive impact of software systems and applications on society requires software developers to ensure that their products are of high quality. However, software development is a human process, and developers unintentionally introduce faults into software that cause it to fail under certain conditions. When software failures are observed, developers engage in *debugging* to find and fix the fault(s). *Fault localization* is the part of debugging that involves locating faults in a program. Because of the size and complexity of many software products, fault localization is often a difficult and time-consuming task, which contributes significantly to the cost of software development and maintenance.

To reduce the cost of fault localization, researchers have proposed automated statistical fault-localization techniques (e.g., [1, 4, 13, 15, 16, 17]). These techniques compute statistical measures of association between the execution of individual program statements (or other entities) and the occurrence of program failures, using execution data from passing and failing executions (e.g., coverage information). The measures are called *suspiciousness scores*. The techniques rank program statements in decreasing order of their suspiciousness scores for examination by developers. The intuition underlying this approach is that the program statements most strongly associated with failures are the most likely to be faulty. However, statistical association does not necessarily indicate causation [12]. Thus, statements with high suspiciousness scores may not be faulty, and faulty statements may have low suspiciousness scores. Consequently, existing statistical fault-localization techniques can perform poorly with certain programs and faults.

In recent work [5], we showed that statistical fault-localization techniques based on measures of association between the occurrence of certain runtime events (e.g., coverage of a given statement) and the occurrence of program failures are subject to *confounding bias*, because of influences between statements in a program. For example, with a number of coverage-based statistical fault-localization techniques, a correct statement s_c and a faulty statement s_f that happen to be covered by the same subset of test cases will necessarily receive the same suspiciousness score. More generally, any other statement that influences s_c and s_f and also influences the occurrence of failures will confound the suspiciousness scores of s_c and s_f. To accurately assess the distinct effects of covering s_c and s_f on the occurrence of failures, it is necessary to adjust for such confounding factors.

To address the confounding influence of some program statements on the suspiciousness scores of other statements, we presented a preliminary *causal inference model* for software fault localization [5] (see Section 2). We used this model to estimate the *causal effect* of covering a statement s on the occurrence of program failures. To "control" or "adjust" for confounding by other statements, the model incorporates a coverage-indicator variable for the forward control dependence predecessor of s (in addition to a coverage indicator for s itself). The model is grounded in the extensive body of research on making causal inferences from observational data, which spans such diverse fields as econometrics, the social sciences, epidemiology, statistics, and computer

Permission to make digital or hard copies of all or part of this work for personal or classroom use is granted without fee provided that copies are not made or distributed for profit or commercial advantage and that copies bear this notice and the full citation on the first page. To copy otherwise, to republish, to post on servers or to redistribute to lists, requires prior specific permission and/or a fee.

ESEC/FSE'11, September 5–9, 2011, Szeged, Hungary.

Copyright 2011 ACM 978-1-4503-0443-6/11/09 ...$10.00.

science [18, 21]. We contrasted the model analytically with several existing fault-localization metrics that do not address confounding, and presented empirical results indicating that the model (1) is significantly more effective than some of those techniques and (2) can be incorporated into other techniques to improve their performance. These results suggest that existing methodology for making causal inferences from observational data is very relevant to statistical fault localization.

However, it is easy to see that our previous model does not address all possible sources of confounding in fault localization, such as runtime patterns of data dependences (data flows), the values taken on by inputs and program variables, and non-determinism because of concurrency [5]. Making the best use of causal-inference methodology in software fault localization will require determining the relative importance of such factors and devising effective and reasonably efficient ways of controlling for them.

In this paper, we present a new technique that controls for local patterns of both dynamic data dependences and dynamic control dependences that can confound the estimated causal effect of covering a statement s on the occurrence of program failures, which for brevity we call the *failure-causing effect* of s. Static and dynamic data and control dependences have long been recognized as important factors in software testing and debugging, because they contribute both to triggering the effects of faults and to propagating those effects to a program's output [22, 24, 26]. Our technique uses information about dynamic data and control dependences to reduce confounding bias—more than is possible with our previous model—and to thereby rank statements more effectively for fault localization.

When estimating the failure-causing effect of a statement s, confounding bias due to dynamic data and control dependences affecting s can be reduced by considering two groups of executions: those that cover s (referred to as the *treatment group*) and those that do not cover s (referred to as the *control group*). The executions that cover s should have the same pattern of dynamic data and control dependences as the executions that do not cover s, in which case the groups are said to be *balanced*. In practice, the set of test cases or operational executions used in statistical fault localization is usually given, and the subset of them that cover and do not cover a particular statement s cannot be assumed to be balanced.

To achieve relative balance between the treatment and control groups and thus reduce confounding bias, our technique employs a classical causal-inference technique called *matching*. For each program statement s, the executions in the two groups are reorganized so that they are similar with respect to dynamic data and control dependences that directly affect s. Each execution e that covers s is matched with the execution not covering s that is most similar to e, as measured by applying the Mahalanobis-distance metric [18] to dynamic dependence information collected from the executions. After matching, the failure-causing effect of s is estimated based on the outcomes of the matched executions.

In this paper, we also present empirical results indicating that our new technique yields fault-localization rankings that are more effective than those obtained with our previous causal model [5] and with several well-known statistical fault-localization techniques. For example, our new technique performs better than our old technique on 61.4% of 272 faulty program versions, with an average fault-localization improvement of 8.57%. Our new technique also performs better than Tarantula [13] on 72.06% of the versions, with an average fault-localization improvement of 11.44%.

The main benefit of our work is that it provides a practical way to use both data and control dependence information to reduce confounding bias and thereby improve the effectiveness of statistical fault localization. Another benefit is that basing our technique on accepted causal-inference methodology will help to put statistical fault localization on a sounder footing and stimulate further improvements.

The contributions of the paper are

- A new statistical fault-localization technique that uses a new causal model, based on dynamic data and control dependences, together with covariate matching to more accurately estimate the causal effect of covering a particular program statement on program failures.
- Empirical results indicating that our new technique is more effective than our previous causal technique and other statistical fault-localization techniques.

2. BACKGROUND

In this section, we first present background on the potential-outcome model for causal inference and the dynamic program-dependence graph. We then describe our previous causal-inference model for statistical fault localization [5], which is based on the potential outcome model [18], on Pearl's Structural Causal Model [21], and on dynamic program-dependence analysis [10].

2.1 Potential Outcome Model

The *potential-outcome model* [18] provides a theoretical basis for estimating causal effects using data from either observational studies or randomized experiments. Suppose that a researcher wants to estimate the effect of a new or existing treatment, and suppose further that a set of units or subjects are available to the researcher. Let T be a binary variable that takes on the value $t_i = 1$ for a unit u_i if u_i receives the treatment and that takes on the value $t_i = 0$ if u_i does not receive the treatment. Let Y represent the outcome for an arbitrary unit. The potential outcome model associates with Y two *potential-outcome random variables*: Y^1 and Y^0. Variable Y^1 represents the potential outcome for a *treated* unit, and variable Y^0 represents the potential outcome for an *untreated* (control) unit. The *individual-level causal effect* of treatment for a unit u_i is defined as $y_i^1 - y_i^0$, where y_i^1 and y_i^0 are the realizations of Y^1 and Y^0 for unit i. We assume that for any given unit, only one of Y^1 and Y^0 can be observed; the other variable's value is *counterfactual* (counter to the facts) for that unit. This implies it is impossible to estimate $y_i^1 - y_i^0$ directly.[1]

Because individual-level treatment effects cannot be estimated, *average treatment effects* are estimated instead. For the scenario above, the average treatment effect τ is defined to be the difference between the expected outcomes of the two groups:

$$\tau = E[Y^1] - E[Y^0] \tag{1}$$

where E[·] is the expectation operator. Suppose that a *randomized experiment* is conducted in which a researcher ran-

[1]This problem has been called the *fundamental problem of causal inference* [12].

domly assigns units to either the treatment group or the control group, and suppose an outcome y_i is observed for each unit u_i. Then the difference $\bar{y}_1 - \bar{y}_0$ between the sample means for the treatment group and the control group, respectively, is an unbiased estimator of τ. The estimate is unbiased because random treatment assignment tends to ensure that the treatment group and the control group are balanced with respect to the distributions of confounding variables, whether or not the variables are observed. Consequently, the treatment variable T is independent of the potential outcomes Y^1 and Y^0,

$$(Y^1, Y^0) \perp\!\!\!\perp T \tag{2}$$

and so knowing whether a unit is assigned to treatment does not provide any information about Y^1 and Y^0.

It is typically assumed that execution data to be used for statistical fault localization is generated from a set of existing test cases or is collected in the field from operational executions. In both cases, statistical fault localization is a kind of observational study rather than a randomized experiment, because the executions were not randomly assigned to either the treatment group (e.g., executions covering a statement s) or the control group (e.g., executions not covering s). Note that creating test cases specifically to achieve coverage of every conditional branch does not ensure that the test cases that cover a statement s are otherwise similar to the test cases that do not cover s.

To estimate average treatment effects based on observational data, statistical techniques that "control for" or "condition on" the observed values of potential confounding variables [18] are used. An unbiased estimate of the average treatment effects of treatment variable T on outcome variable Y can be obtained by conditioning on a set X of covariates that render T *conditionally independent* of the potential outcome variables Y^1 and Y^0,

$$(Y^1, Y^0) \perp\!\!\!\perp T \mid X \tag{3}$$

In this case, the average treatment effect τ is given by the equation

$$\tau = E[E[Y \mid T = 1, X] - E[Y \mid T = 0, X]] \tag{4}$$

where $E[\cdot \mid \cdot]$ is the conditional expectation operator. (The outer, unconditional expectation is evaluated with respect to the probability distribution of X.)

One way of controlling for observed confounders when estimating an average treatment effect is to include them as predictors in a *statistical regression model* [18], such as the linear model

$$Y = \alpha + \tau T + \beta X + \varepsilon \tag{5}$$

In this model, Y is the outcome variable, T is the treatment variable, X is a vector of covariates that includes the observed confounders, and ε is a random error term that (ideally) does not depend on the values of T and X. Equation 5 implies that $E[Y \mid T, X] = \alpha + \tau T + \beta X$. The fitted value $\hat{\tau}$ of the coefficient τ is an unbiased average-treatment-effect estimate, assuming the model is correctly specified.

2.2 Dynamic Program Dependences

Informally, in a program P, statement s_2 is *control dependent* [10] on a statement s_1 if, as indicated by the control-flow graph (CFG) for P,[2] s_1 determines whether s_2 is executed. Statement s_1 *dominates* statement s_2 in the CFG if all paths from P's entry to s_2 contains s_1. The *control dependence graph* (CDG) of P is a directed graph where nodes represent statements in P and edges represent control dependences. Statement s_1 is a *forward control-dependence predecessor* of s_2 in the CDG if s_2 is control dependent on s_1 and s_2 does not dominate s_1 in the CFG.

Statement s_2 is data dependent on statement s_1 if there is a definition of a variable v (i.e., a write of v) at s_1, a use of v (i.e., access with no write) at s_2, and there is a least one path from s_1 to s_2 in the CFG on which v is not redefined. The *program-dependence graph* (PDG) of program P is a directed graph whose nodes represent statements in P and whose edges represent control and data dependences. The graph is annotated with two special nodes, START and EXIT, which represent entry to and exit from P, respectively.

Informally, the *dynamic program dependence graph* (Dynamic PDG) is a directed graph constructed from a set of program executions in which nodes represent executed statements and edges represent executed control dependences and data dependences. Statement s_1 is a *dynamic forward control dependence predecessor* of s_2 if s_1 is a forward control-dependence predecessor of s_2 in the Dynamic-PDG. The Dynamic-PDG, which is a subgraph of the PDG, is similar to the graph obtained with Agrawal and Horgan's [2] technique (Approach 1) for dynamic slicing. However, the latter is created using one execution whereas the Dynamic-PDG described here is created using a set of executions. We define the *dynamic forward control dependence subgraph* as the subgraph of the Dynamic-PDG that contains only forward control-dependence edges.

2.3 Previous Fault Localization Model

To specify a causal model for statistical fault localization, it is necessary to indicate the form of the model, the treatment variable, and the covariates. Our initial causal model [5] includes a linear regression model for estimating the failure-causing effect of covering a program statement s:

$$Y = \alpha_s + \tau_s T_s + \beta_s C_s + \varepsilon_s \tag{6}$$

This model is fit separately for each statement in a program, using statement-coverage profiles from a set of passing and failing executions. In the model, Y is a binary variable that is 1 for a given execution if and only if the program failed; T_s is a binary treatment variable, which indicates whether s was covered (executed at least once) during the execution; C_s is a binary covariate, which indicates whether the dynamic forward control dependence predecessor $dfcdp(s)$ of s was covered; α_s is a constant intercept; and ε_s is a random error term that does not depend on the values of T_s and C_s. The average treatment effect of T_s upon Y is estimated by the fitted value $\hat{\tau}_s$ of the coefficient τ_s, which is used as a suspiciousness value for s.

A regression model such as Equation 6 describes only statistical relationships between variables. To obtain a full causal model, it must be augmented with additional information about causal relationships. This information can be represented by a *causal graph* [21], which is a directed acyclic

[2] In a *control-flow graph*, nodes represent program statements, and edges represent the flow of control between the statements.

	t_1 (-1,1)	t_2 (2,3)	t_3 (1,-3)	t_4 (0,5)	t_5 (3,4)	$\hat{\tau}$	$\hat{\tau}_{match}$
void Proc() {							
1 int x=read();	1	1	1	1	1	0.40	NA
2 int y=read();	1	1	1	1	1	0.40	NA
3 if(x > 0){	1	1	1	1	1	0.40	NA
4 if(y < 0)	0	1	1	0	1	0.67	0.67
5 y = 2;	0	0	1	0	0	-1.00	-1.00
6 print("Out:");	0	1	1	0	1	0.67	0.67
7 print(y+y);	0	1	1	0	1	0.67	1.00
8 }							
9 }							
	0	1	0	0	1		

Figure 1: Procedure with test cases, execution data, and causal-effect estimates. Error at statement 7; correct computation should be y×y.

graph (DAG) whose nodes represent random variables (corresponding to causes and effects) and whose edges represent causal relationships. An edge $A \rightarrow B$ in a causal graph indicates that A (potentially) causes B. Equation 6 is implicitly based on the causal graph obtained from a (structured) program's dynamic forward control dependence subgraph, by (1) associating with each node a coverage-indicator variable for the corresponding statement and (2) augmenting the dynamic forward control dependence subgraph with edges from each node to a new node for the failure indicator Y.

The role of the coverage indicator variable C_s for *dfcdp*(s) in Equation 6 is to control for confounding of the estimated failure-causing effect of s, due to coverage of other statements. Intuitively, conditioning on C_s reduces confounding because *dfcdp*(s) is the most immediate cause of s being covered or not being covered on a particular run. Pearl's well-known *Back-Door Criterion* [21] for causal graphs provides some formal justification for Equation 6, because *dfcdp*(s) blocks all "back-door paths" from T to Y in the augmented dynamic forward control dependence subgraph. (Such a path is actually a *semi-path*—one in which edges may point in either direction—whose first edge is of the form $T \leftarrow Z$ for some node Z.) Under the very strong assumption that the augmented dynamic forward control dependence subgraph is sufficient to model failure causation in a program, the Back-Door Criterion implies that T is conditionally independent of the potential outcomes Y^1 and Y^0 given the value of C_s, as required for Equation 4 to hold with T_s and C_s in place of T and X, respectively.

3. ADDRESSING BOTH DATA AND CONTROL DEPENDENCES

The causal model, given in Equation 6, which was used in our previous technique for statistical fault localization relies on the dynamic forward control dependence subgraph as a model of failure causation. However, the dynamic forward control dependence subgraph, and therefore Equation 6, does not adequately reflect failure causation in which data dependences play an important role. In this section, we present our new technique for estimating a statement's failure causing effect, which addresses confounding due to both dynamic data dependences and dynamic control dependences by matching executions based on information about both.

We begin with an example that illustrates the importance of incorporating data dependences into our causal model, and then, present the details of the model.

3.1 Motivating Example

Consider procedure `Proc` in Figure 1, which has a fault at line 7. `Proc` should print the square of the value of `y` at line 7 but instead prints two times the value of `y`. The first column shows `Proc` with line numbers associated with each of its statements. Columns 2 through 6 represent test cases t_1–t_5, respectively. The top entry of each column shows the values of `x` and `y` that are read at lines 1 and 2, respectively. The numbers in the column for a test case indicate whether the corresponding program statement is covered by the test case (1 for covered, 0 for not covered). The bottom row shows the outcome of each test-case execution, with 1 indicating a failing execution and 0 indicating a passing execution.

Suppose we want to compute the failure-causing effect of statement 7 using Equation 6. For statement 7, as Figure 1 shows, test cases t_2, t_3, and t_5 are in the treatment group, because they cover statement 7, and test cases t_1 and t_4 are in the control group, because they do not cover statement 7. The dynamic forward control dependence predecessor of statement 7 is statement 3. Variable C_s in Equation 6 corresponds to a coverage indicator C_3 for statement 3, which is covered by all tests. (Because C_3 is constant, it or the intercept α_s from Equation 6 can be dropped from the model for statement 7.) The column labeled $\hat{\tau}$ in Figure 1 indicates the failure-causing effect estimates obtained with Equation 6 for the statements in procedure `Proc`. The estimate for statement 7, which is faulty, is 0.67. However, the estimates for statements 4 and 6 are also 0.67, even though they are not faulty. Statements 4 and 6 have the same estimate as statement 7 because they are in the same control dependence region [10] and hence, are covered by the same tests. This example illustrates that serious confounding may occur even after conditioning on coverage of each statement's dynamic forward control dependence predecessor.

3.2 New Technique

Our new technique addresses the inadequacy of our previous technique for fault localization. The technique consists of two main components: a new causal model and a matching technique.

3.2.1 Overview

Algorithm `LocalizeFault`, shown in Figure 2, takes as input the dynamic program dependence graph (Dynamic-PDG) of a procedure and the coverage information (Coverage-Info) produced by executing the program containing the procedure on a set of test cases. `LocalizeFault` processes each statement s in the Dynamic-PDG; it initializes the causal estimate of each statement s, ($\hat{\tau}(s)$), to -1.0 (line 2). `LocalizeFault` computes the first major component of our technique, the causal model of s (Model(s)) (line 3). At line 4, the algorithm computes the predecessors of s (Pred(s)) from Model(s). After computing Pred(s), `LocalizeFault` then computes the second major component of our technique by matching on the Pred(s) in the Coverage-Info to produce the matched data, Mdata(s) (line 5). If matching is successful, the $\hat{\tau}(s)$ is estimated using Equation 1 (line 7); if matching is not successful Equation 5 is used to estimate $\hat{\tau}(s)$ (line 9). The algorithm computes $\hat{\tau}(s)$ for every state-

```
   LocalizeFault(Dynamic-PDG, Coverage-Info){
1    foreach s ∈ Dynamic-PDG do
2      τ̂(s) = -1.0
3      Model(s) = Compute causal model of s
4      Pred(s) = Compute predecessors of s from Model(s)
5      Mdata(s) = Match on Pred(s) in Coverage-Info
6      if (Mdata(s) ≠ ∅){
7        Compute τ̂(s) from Mdata(s) using Equation 1
8      }else{
9        Compute τ̂(s) using Equation 5
10     }
11   done
12   sorted_τ̂ = sort τ̂ in descending order
13   return (sorted_τ̂)
14 }
```

Figure 2: Algorithm for new technique

ment in the Dynamic-PDG. After the causal estimate for each statement has been computed, `LocalizeFault` sorts all the estimates in descending order at line 12. It then returns the sorted estimates at line 13 to the developer.

3.2.2 New Causal Model

Our new causal model extends our previous causal model (Equation 6) by addressing dynamic data dependences as well as dynamic control dependences. Dynamic data dependences are important because they carry the values that are used at a given statement. Whereas a statement's forward control dependence predecessor determines whether the statement is covered, the statement's data dependences determine the computation it carries out. Conceptually, the additional causal influences that we want to account for can be represented by including dynamic data dependences in the causal graph for a program, in addition to dynamic forward control dependences. A complication is that loop-carried data dependences [10] give rise to directed cycles in dependence graphs, whereas much of the theory of causal inference developed by Pearl [21] and other authors, including the Back Door Criterion, is based on causal graphs that are acyclic. However, to control confounding when estimating the failure-causing effect of a particular statement s_i, it suffices to consider acyclic dependence chains terminating at s, because if there is a causal path from s_j to s_i that contains one or more cycles, there must also be a cycle-free path from s_j to s_i. For example, consider a program loop of the form

```
1 while(...)
2    if (...)
3       x = f(y);
4    else
5       y = g(x);
```

Each edge in the data dependence cycle $3 \rightarrow 5 \rightarrow 3$ may be relevant to localizing a distinct fault. However, in seeking to control confounding while estimating the failure-causing effect of statement 3, we can ignore the edge (3, 5). Similarly, when estimating the failure causing effect of statement 5, we can ignore the edge (5, 3).

The kind of causal graph that is required can be conceptualized in terms of the *transitive reduction* of a digraph [3]. In essence, a transitive reduction of a digraph D is an acyclic, spanning subdigraph H of D with no redundant arcs such that the transitive closures of D and H are isomorphic [6].[3]

[3]Klamt and colleagues employ a form of transitive reduction to model causality in biological networks with cycles [14].

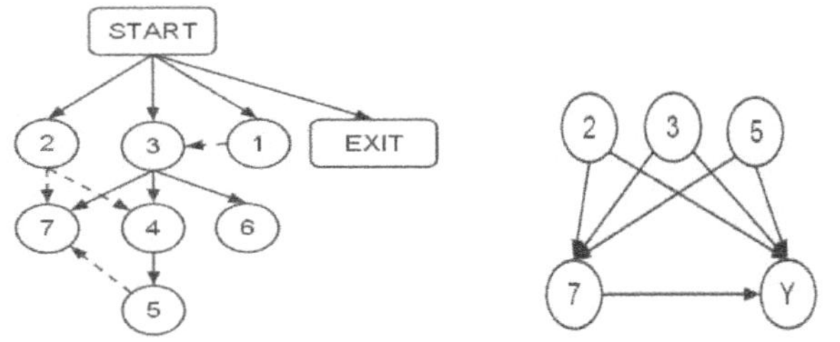

(a) Dynamic-PDG of `Proc`. (b) ICG of statement 7.

Figure 3: (a) Dynamic program dependence graph (Dynamic-PDG) of procedure `Proc`. (b) Integrated causal graph of statement 7.

Aho and colleagues [3] present a transitive reduction algorithm that, for a digraph with cycles, replaces each equivalence class of vertices appearing in the same cycle with a new vertex. Consider a slight variant of this algorithm, applied to a graph of dynamic data and control dependences between program statements. For a given statement s whose failure-causing effect we want to estimate, this variant preserves all nodes in s's equivalence class (if there is more than one) rather than collapsing them to a single node. However, it breaks any cycles involving s by deleting s's outgoing edges. Therefore, for each statement s in the dynamic program dependence graph, an acyclic subgraph H_s can be constructed that reflects all causal influences on s. H_s can be transformed into a proper causal graph by augmenting it as described in Section 2. We call the augmented H_s the *integrated causal graph* for s and denote it $ICG(s)$.[4]

In the integrated causal graph $ICG(s)$, there will be multiple back doors to s if it is dependent on multiple statements. Observe, however, that the set of predecessors of s ($Pred(s)$) blocks all back-door paths from s to the failure node Y. Thus, by conditioning on the coverage indicator variables associated with $Pred(s)$, we may be able to further reduce confounding when estimating the failure-causing effect of s. For example, Figure 3(a) shows the dynamic program dependence graph of `Proc`; dotted edges represent data dependences and solid edges represent control dependences. Figure 3(b) shows the ICG of statement 7, where nodes 2, 3, and 5 of statement 7 are nodes in the dynamic program dependence graph of `Proc`. As the graph shows, there are three back-door paths in the graph: $7 \leftarrow 2 \rightarrow Y$, $7 \leftarrow 3 \rightarrow Y$, and $7 \leftarrow 5 \rightarrow Y$.

3.2.3 Matching

Matching [18] is a technique that brings some of the benefits of randomized controlled experiments, in terms of reduced confounding bias, to observational studies. Matching involves mapping (if possible) each treatment unit from an observational study to one or more control units that are similar to it, in such a way that *balance* is achieved between the resulting treatment group and control group with respect to covariate values. Matching may involve removing

[4]One subtlety is that if a node n in $ICG(s)$ represents an equivalence class C of nodes from D, a set Z of coverage indicator variables should be associated with n. For each statement t represented in C, Z should contain a coverage indicator for t.

unmatched units or (in effect) duplicating certain units. We first describe a simple form of matching, called exact matching, before describing the more complex type of matching used with our new causal model.

In *exact matching*, each treatment unit is matched with one or more control units that have exactly the same covariate values as the treatment unit, if such control units exist. All matched treatment and control units are retained, and all unmatched units are discarded. The difference in the group means of the resulting treatment group and control group is an estimate of the treatment effect.

We now illustrate exact matching with reference to the procedure and data in Figure 1. Let the covariates for each statement s in procedure `Proc` be the coverage-indicator variables associated with the possible dynamic control and data dependence predecessors of s. For example, for statement 7, there are three predecessors: statement 2, which defines the value of `y` and may be used at statement 7; statement 3, which is statement 7's forward control dependence predecessor); and statement 5, which defines the value of `y` and may be used at statement 7. Figure 4 shows the treatment units and the control units with their associated test cases for statement 7. The treatment units, which are test cases that cover statement 7 are t_2, t_3, and t_5; the control units, which are test cases that do not cover statement 7 are t_1 and t_4. The vector of covariate values generated by the test cases is shown; a vector of the form [1, 1, 0] means that for that test case, statement 2 was covered, statement 3 was covered, and statement 5 was not covered, respectively. There is an arrow from each treatment unit to a matching control unit. Note that there is no match for t_3, because it is the only test case to cover each of statement 2, statement 3, and statement 5. Consequently, t_3 is not used to estimate the failure-causing effect of statement 7. Using Equation 1, the estimate for statement 7 is $(1 + 1)/2 - (0 + 0)/2 = 1.0$, which is the difference between the average outcome values for the treatment group and the average outcome values for the control group. The causal-effect estimates for the other statements are shown in Table 1, in the column labeled $\hat{\tau}_{match}$. (The NA for statement's 1, 2, and 3 reflects the fact that an estimate could not be computed for the statements because there were no control units for the statements.) The estimate for statement 5 is $0 - 1/1 = -1.0$ and the estimate for each of statements 4 and 6 is $(1+1+0)/3-(0+0)/2 = 0.67$. It can be seen that the faulty statement, statement 7, has the highest estimate.

Unfortunately, as the number of covariates increases, it becomes more difficult to find exact matches for treatment units. This difficulty results in more discarded units, which can increase bias[5] when computing causal estimates. Therefore, other forms of matching are typically used.

Matching with Mahalanobis Distance

To obtain more flexibility in matching treatment units with control units, our technique uses the *Mahalanobis distance* metric [18], which is a measure of the similarity $d_M(\mathbf{a}, \mathbf{b})$ between two random vectors $\mathbf{a}$ and $\mathbf{b}$. Let S be the covariance matrix of $\mathbf{a}$ and $\mathbf{b}$ and let the superscript T denote

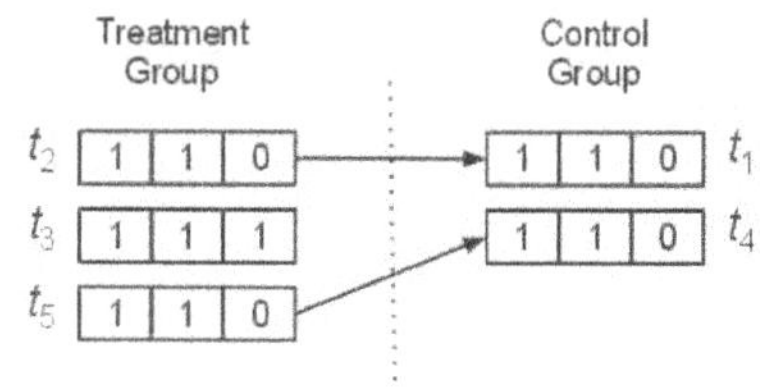

Figure 4: Units in treatment group and control group with their covariate values.

matrix/vector transpose. Then

$$d_M(\mathbf{a}, \mathbf{b}) = \sqrt{(\mathbf{a} - \mathbf{b})^T S^{-1} (\mathbf{a} - \mathbf{b})} \quad (7)$$

The matrix S is the sample covariance matrix for the treatment and control units. Each treatment unit (test case covering statement s) with covariate vector $\mathbf{a}$ is matched with a control unit (test case not covering s) with covariate vector $\mathbf{b}$ for which $d_M(\mathbf{a}, \mathbf{b})$ is minimal with respect to a threshold. In matching *without replacement*, the two units are then removed from further consideration. In matching *with replacement*, the control unit is retained to be matched with another treatment unit. Replacement is normally used if the number of treatment units exceeds the number of control units; matching with replacement also reduces bias[5] [29] in the causal estimate. A property of Mahalanobis-distance matching is that it regards all the components of the covariate vector as equally important [29]. This property is important when matching on the predecessors of s because in the absence of any prior information about the relative importance of the predecessors, our technique treats all predecessors of s as equally important.

4. EMPIRICAL EVALUATION

To evaluate the effectiveness of our technique for fault localization, we implemented it and performed empirical studies on a set of subjects. In this section, we first describe the set-up and then present the results of the studies.

4.1 Empirical Study Setup

For our studies, we used 16 programs with 272 faulty versions. We used seven programs from the Unix suite (Cal, Col, Comm, Spline, Tr, and Uniq), all programs in the Siemens suite (Print-tokens, Print-tokens2, Replace, Schedule, Schedule2, Tcas, and Tot-info), and programs Sed and Space.[6] Table 1 shows the characteristics of the subjects. For each subject, the first column gives the program name, the second column provides the ratio of the number of versions used to the number of versions available, the third column gives the number of lines of code for the subject, the fourth column gives the number of test cases, the fifth column shows the average number of vertices in the dynamic program dependence graph, and the last column provides a description. We omitted 25 faulty versions because either there were no syntactic differences between the C files of the correct version and the faulty version of the program or none of the test cases failed when executed on the faulty version of the program.

[5]This form of bias is different from confounding bias. The bias is the difference in an estimator's expected value and the true value of the parameter being estimated.

[6]We obtained the Unix programs from Eric Wong of University of Texas at Dallas and the Space and Sed programs from the Software-artifact Infrastructure Repository [9]. We obtained the Siemens suite from the Aristotle Research Lab.

Table 1: Subjects used for empirical studies.

Program	Number of Versions Used / Number of Versions	Number of Lines of Code	Number of Test Cases	Number of Nodes	Description
Cal	19 / 20	202	162	131.5	calendar printer
Col	29 / 30	102	156	240.0	filter-line reverser
Comm	10 / 12	167	186	116.1	file comparer
Look	8 / 14	170	193	140.9	word finder
Spline	13 / 13	338	700	247.0	curve interpolator
Tr	11 / 11	137	870	150.2	character translator
Uniq	17 / 17	143	431	131.3	duplicate line remover
Print-tokens	5 / 7	472	4130	423.6	lexical analyzer
Print-tokens2	10 / 10	399	4115	340.5	lexical analyzer
Replace	28 / 32	512	395	415.9	pattern replacement
Schedule	9 / 9	292	2710	216.3	priority scheduler
Schedule2	9 / 10	301	2650	225.9	priority scheduler
Tcas	41 / 41	141	1608	136.7	altitude separation
Tot-info	23 / 23	440	1052	249.0	information measure
Sed	10 / 10	14K	363	4151.0	stream editing utility
Space	30 / 38	6K	157	3851.9	ADL interpreter

For our implementation, we used the CIL framework [20], which supports the analysis of ANSI C programs, to analyze the subject programs. We implemented the algorithms to instrument the programs and to compute dynamic control-flow graphs in the *Object Caml Language* (OCaml), because OCaml is required to interface with CIL. Recall that our technique uses dynamic control-flow graphs to compute dynamic dependences, because the former contain only statements that are actually executed by a set of test cases.

We implemented all fault-localization algorithms in *R* [23], which is a statistical computation system with its own language and runtime environment. For matching on program dependences, we used the *R* package *Matching* [28]. We used matching with replacement and a default minimal distance of 0.00001. We also computed fault matrices that indicate, for each faulty program, which test cases pass and which test cases fail. We performed our studies on Mac OS X version 10.5.

4.2 Effectiveness Studies

To study the effectiveness of our technique for fault localization, we use a cost metric that has been used in previous studies [7, 25]. The metric, which we denote as *Cost*, measures the percentage of faulty statements a developer must examine before encountering the faulty statement. We assume that the statements are examined in a non-decreasing order of suspiciousness scores. If there are ties, we assume the developer must examine all the tied statements. For example, if there are n statements in a program and all n statements have the same suspiciousness score, we assume that the developer must examine all n statements. Therefore the *Cost* of finding the fault is 100%.

To compare the effectiveness of fault-localization techniques A and B with respect to a given program version P_i, we use B as a baseline, and compute the difference between the *Cost* of applying B to P_i and the *Cost* of applying A to P_i. A positive result implies that A performed better than B on P_i and a negative result implies that B performed better than A. The difference between the *Costs* corresponds to the magnitude of improvement. For example, if the *Cost* of A is 20% and the *Cost* of B is 60%, developers will examine 40% fewer statements if they use A for fault localization.

To reduce the uncertainty in the causal effect computed for each statement because of the matching technique, we computed a statement's causal effect 100 times and took the average of the 100 causal estimates. We found 100 to be an acceptable threshold for providing stable causal effects. Each computed causal effect has an associated standard error. We computed the average of the standard errors, and used it to construct a bound (one standard deviation) on the causal effect for each statement. For example, if the average of the causal effects of a statement on program failure is 0.3 and the average standard error is 0.1, then $[0.3 \pm 0.1]$ is the range of the causal effect over the 100 samples with 0.2 being the lower bound and 0.4 being the upper bound.

For brevity, we denote our new fault-localization technique, which matches executions based on data and control dependences, as PD; we denote a variant of the technique that matches only on data dependences as DD, and we denote our previous causal technique [5], which considered only control dependences, as CD. We also use PDmin and PDmax to represent variants of PD computed using the lower bounds and upper bounds of the causal-effect estimates of PD, respectively. For example, if for a statement the average causal estimate obtained with PD is 0.3 and the average standard error is 0.1 then PDmin and PDmax yield causal estimates of 0.2 and 0.4, respectively.

Table 2 summarizes the results of comparing fault-localization techniques. The first column (Fault Loc. Tech.) shows the two fault-localization techniques (i.e., A vs B) that are being compared; the second technique in each pair (i.e., B) is the baseline. The second column (Positive (%)) shows the percentage of faulty versions for which A performed better than B, the third column (Negative (%)) shows the percentage of faulty versions for which A performed worse than B, and the fourth column (Neutral (%)) shows the percentage of faulty versions for which there was no improvement. For example, the first row, which compares PD to CD, shows that PD performed better than CD on 61.4% of the faulty versions, performed worse on 13.97% of the faulty versions, and performed identically on 24.63% of the faulty versions.

Table 3 shows the minimum (Min), median (Med), maximum (Max), and mean (Mean) values of A's improvement over B. Half the faulty versions with positive improvement values have improvements between the minimum and the median, and the other half have improvements between the median and the maximum. For example, the first row, which compares PD to CD, shows that half of the 61.4%

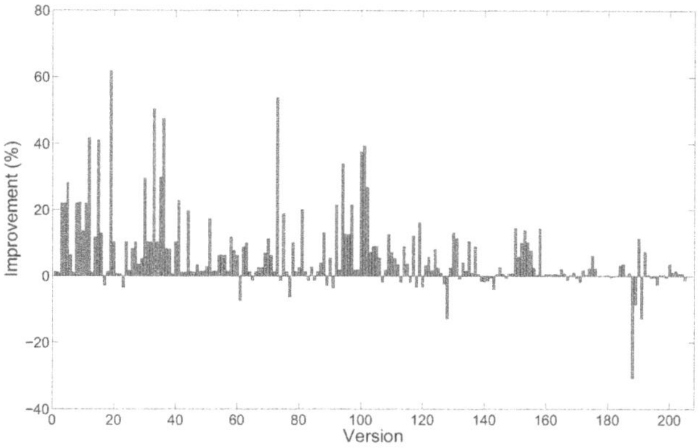

Figure 5: Comparison of new technique (PD) to old technique (CD).

of faulty versions with positive improvement values had improvements between 0.05% and 3.84% while the other half had improvements between 3.84% to 61.71%. The average positive improvement of PD over CD was 8.57%.

4.2.1 Study 1: New Technique vs Old Technique

The goal of this study is to compare the fault-localization effectiveness of our new technique PD to that of our previous causal technique CD, which considers control dependences but not data dependences. To do this, we compared the *Cost* values for the two techniques.

Figure 5 shows the bar graph that summarizes the comparison of PD to CD over all program versions. The horizontal axis (baseline) represents the *Cost* of using our previous technique CD, the vertical axis represents the magnitude of improvement of PD over CD. The graph contains a vertical bar for each faulty version for which there was positive or negative improvement on the horizontal axis; the vertical bar shows the difference in *Costs*. The bars above the horizontal axis represent faulty versions for which PD performed better than CD (positive improvement) and the bars below the horizontal axis represent faulty versions for which PD performed worse than CD (negative improvement). For example, for faulty-version 3 on the graph, PD performed better by about 21.87%. Figure 5 shows that PD performed better than CD overall. As indicated in Table 2, PD performed better than CD on 61.4% of the faulty versions, worse on 13.97% of the faulty versions, and showed no improvement on 24.63% of the faulty versions. The first row of Table 3 characterizes the degree of positive improvement of PD over CD. As the table indicates, half the 61.4% of the faulty versions with positive improvement values had improvements between 0.05% and 3.84%, and the other half had improvements between 3.84% and 61.71%. The average positive improvement of PD over CD was 8.57%.

We also compared the *Costs* of PDmin and PDmax to PD. As Table 2 shows, PDmin performed better than CD on 61.4% of the faulty versions, performed worse on 13.97% of the faulty versions, and performed identically on 24.63% of the faulty versions. The table also shows that PDmax performed better than CD on 60.29% of the faulty versions, performed worse on 14.71% of the faulty versions, and performed identically on 25% of the faulty versions. Table 3 shows that the performance of PD, PDmin, and PDmax are

Table 2: Comparison of fault-localization models.

Fault Loc. Tech.	Positive (%)	Negative (%)	Neutral (%)
PD vs CD	61.40	13.97	24.63
PDmin vs CD	61.40	13.97	24.63
PDmax vs CD	60.29	14.71	25.00
PD vs DD	49.26	23.16	27.57
DD vs CD	43.75	25.74	30.51
PD vs Tarantula	72.06	7.72	20.22
PD vs Ochiai	44.12	21.32	34.56
CO vs Ochiai	53.68	10.29	36.03

Table 3: Distribution of positive improvements.

Fault Loc. Tech.	Min (%)	Med (%)	Max (%)	Mean (%)
PD vs CD	0.05	3.84	61.71	8.57
PDmin vs CD	0.05	4.03	61.71	8.75
PDmax vs CD	0.05	3.94	62.29	8.60
PD vs DD	0.03	3.43	45.71	6.11
DD vs CD	0.05	5.07	59.43	9.54
PD vs Tarantula	0.05	6.41	70.29	11.44
PD vs Ochiai	0.03	4.79	54.86	7.77
CO vs Ochiai	0.03	4.28	54.86	7.45

similar. The results of PDmin and PDmax provide evidence of the stability of the causal estimates computed with PD.[5] Overall, the results indicate that PD improved the accuracy of fault localization over CD by further reducing confounding bias.

Although PD performed better overall, we wanted to see how much of the improvement resulted from data dependences. To do this, we compared DD to CD with respect to *Cost*. Table 2 indicates that DD had lower *Cost* than CD on 43.75% of the faulty versions and higher cost on only 25.74% of the versions. Thus most of the improvement seen with PD is due to considering data dependences. Considering both control and data dependences increases the accuracy of our technique by about 18%. Tables 2 and 3 indicate that causal models based on both data and control dependences are more effective than causal models based on either type of dependence alone. Overall, the results show that by blocking back-door paths created by program dependences in a faulty program, confounding bias can be reduced when estimating the failure-causing effect of a statement.

4.2.2 Study 2: New Technique vs Other Techniques

The goal of this study is to compare PD to two well-known statistical fault-localization techniques, Tarantula [13] and Ochiai [1], with respect to *Cost*. We used the *Costs* of Tarantula and Ochiai as baselines and subtracted the *Cost* of PD.

Figure 6 shows that PD performed better than Tarantula on most faulty versions. Table 2 indicates that PD performed better than Tarantula on 72.06% of the faulty versions, performed worse on 7.72% of the faulty versions, and performed identically on 20.22% of the faulty versions. Table 3 also shows that half the 72.06% with positive improvement values had improvements between 0.05% and 6.41% and that the other half had improvements between 6.41% and 70.29%. The average positive improvement of PD over Tarantula was 11.55%.

In our previous work [5], Ochiai performed better than our older technique (CD). However, Ochiai does not address confounding bias, so we incorporated CD into Ochiai (calling it Causal-Ochiai) and showed that Causal-Ochiai performed better than Ochiai. Here we show that PD performs better than Ochiai even when the techniques are not composed.

Figure 7 shows that PD performed better than Ochiai

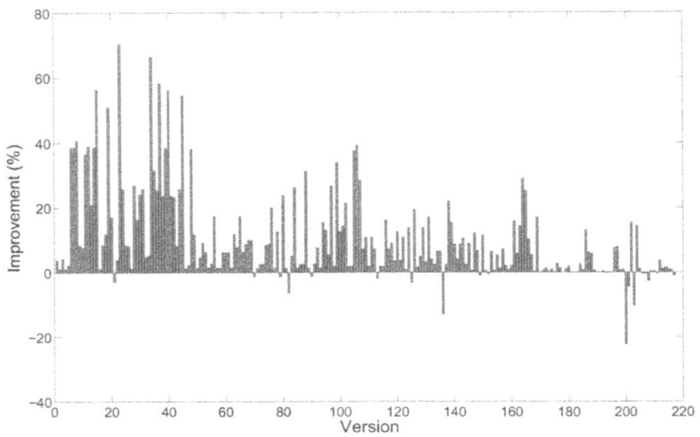

Figure 6: Comparison of our technique (PD) to Tarantula.

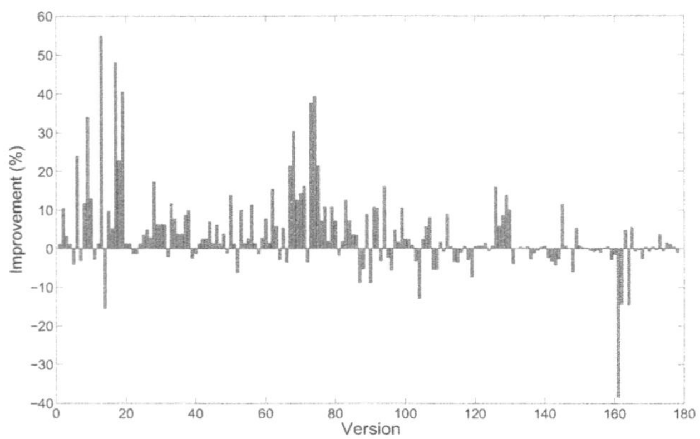

Figure 7: Comparison of our technique (PD) to Ochiai.

on most of the faulty versions. Table 2 indicates that PD performed better than Ochiai on 44.12% of the faulty versions, performed worse on 21.32% of the faulty versions, and performed identically on 34.56% of the faulty versions. Table 3 also shows that half the 44.12% of the faulty versions with positive improvement values had improvements between 0.03% and 4.79% and that the other half had improvements between 4.79% and 54.86%. The average positive improvement of PD over Ochiai was 7.77%. Tables 2 and 3 show that the performance of Ochiai was improved when PD was composed with it to produce Causal-Ochiai (CO). CO performed better on 53.68% of the faulty versions, performed worse on 10.29% of the faulty versions, and performed identically on 36.03% of the faulty versions. Also, half the 53.68% of faulty versions with positive improvement values had improvements between 0.03% and 4.28% and the other half had improvements between 4.28% and 54.86%. The average positive improvement of CO over Ochiai was 7.45%.

Overall, the results indicate that PD performs better than both Tarantula and Ochiai, and improves Ochiai.

4.2.3 Computation Time

In this section, we present the average computation time required to compute all the fault-localization results for one version of some of the subjects. We found that the computation time was largely dependent on the size of the test suite of a program. The Matching package [28] takes considerable time to invert the large covariance matrices. For Tcas, which had 1608 test cases, it took on average 8 minutes. For Schedule, which had 2710 test cases, it took on average 32.73 minutes. For Printtokens2, which had 4115 test cases, it took on average 2.3 hours.

4.3 Threats to Validity

There are three main types of threats to validity that affect our studies: internal, external, and construct. Threats to internal validity concern factors that might affect dependent variables without the researcher's knowledge. The implementations of the algorithms we used in our studies could contain errors. The Matching package we used in our studies is open source and has been used by other researchers for experimentation, which provides confidence that the algorithms in the package are stable. To address potential errors when constructing the dynamic program-dependence graph, we compared manually generated dynamic program-dependence graphs of smaller subjects to graphs generated automatically by our technique.

Threats to external validity occur when the results of a study cannot be generalized. In this work, such threats are greatly alleviated because our work is based on established causal inference theory and methodology. However, more empirical studies on additional subjects are needed to fully address this threat.

Threats to construct validity concern the appropriateness of the metrics used in our evaluation. We used the *Cost* metric to determine the effectiveness of our technique for fault localization. The *Cost* metric is a ranking metric that has been used to compare techniques in many fault-localization studies, though under a different name (*Score*). However, it is not established whether this metric is well suited for presenting fault-localization information to developers.

5. RELATED WORK

There are many techniques that attempt to locate the fault or faults in a failed program. This section discusses those most closely related to ours, and compares our new technique to them.

One category of fault-localization techniques are statistical fault-localization techniques (e.g., [1, 4, 13, 15, 16, 17, 27, 33]). These techniques compute the association between program entities and program failure. However, as we discussed in our previous work and demonstrated with analytical and empirical studies [5], statistical association does not imply causation. In contrast to these existing statistical fault-localization techniques, our technique for finding the cause of program failure is grounded in the theory of causal-inference methodology. Our empirical results in previous work and those presented in this paper demonstrate the effectiveness of our approach over the associative techniques.

Another category of fault-localization techniques are slicing techniques (e.g., [30, 32]). Slicing techniques compute the set of program entities (e.g., statements) that potentially or actually affect the values of variables at a given program point (e.g., the program output). One limitation of slicing techniques is that the techniques do not find the cause of the failure but instead compute the set of program entities associated with the failure. A second limitation is that the slicing techniques do not provide guidance as to how a developer is to examine the statements in the slice. In our work, we have demonstrated with analytical and empirical studies that such association does not imply causation. Our technique, which is grounded in causal theory is more effective at finding causes of failures and as such more effective than slicing techniques. Additionally, our technique provides guidance to developers on how to systematically examine program entities to find the cause of the fault.

A third category of fault-localization techniques are state-altering techniques (e.g., [7, 8, 31]). Like our technique, state-altering techniques are causal techniques. These techniques have a number of limitations that can make them difficult to apply. First, in performing experiments on programs, the techniques must ensure the semantic consistency of memory changes, which can be difficult and expensive. Second, in performing experiments on programs, the techniques require multiple re-executions of the program, which can also be expensive. Third, the techniques require the presence of an oracle (preferably automated) to determine the outcome (success or failure) of the program after each such re-execution, which in practice, can be difficult, if not impossible, to create. The main difference between our technique and state-altering techniques is that our causal technique is observational, whereas they are experimental. Our technique uses observational data (e.g., coverage information) that is often available by executing the program on test cases. Moreover, our technique does not require an automated oracle because the test cases have pre-determined outcomes, and it does not require multiple re-executions of the program. Finally, our technique avoids the semantic consistency problem encountered by state-altering techniques.

One other technique uses causal analysis and program slicing to generate graphs that explain unexpected behaviors produced by computational models [11]. This technique is similar to ours in that both are based on the theory of causal analysis. However, their technique does not find the location of faulty statements. Instead, their technique creates a causal graph that explains an unexpected behavior.

Yet another technique determines whether two versions of a program are the same, given that one of the versions has been transformed (e.g., code has been obsfucated) [19]. To do this, their technique performs dynamic matching on the control-flow graphs of the two versions. Their technique differs from ours in that we match on program dependences to reduce confounding bias for effective fault localization, whereas they match on control flow to determine whether the programs are the same.

Finally, in previous work [5], we presented a causal model that is based on only control dependences. In this work, we have augmented the causal model with data dependences and have shown through empirical studies the effectiveness of the new causal model for fault localization.

6. CONCLUSION AND FUTURE WORK

In this paper we have presented a novel statistically-based causal-inference technique for software fault localization that matches executions based on information about dynamic data and control dependences to obtain more accurate (less biased) estimates of a given statement's effect on the occurrences of program failures. The use of both covariate matching and data-dependence information in our technique are innovations. We also presented empirical results indicating that the new technique is more effective overall than other techniques—including our previous causal-inference technique, which does not consider data dependences.

Although the presented technique performed well overall, it performed relatively poorly on some faulty program versions, which indicates there is room for improvement. We mention three possible reasons for the technique's performance in some cases, and we suggest how it might be improved.

First, the results obtained with the new technique are subject to limitations of the test suite used for fault localization. Even if the test suite has desirable properties overall, it may be inadequate for accurately estimating the failure-causing effects of certain statements. This will be the case for any statement that is covered by very few test cases or for which it is not possible to extract two reasonably well-matched comparison groups of test cases that respectively cover and do not cover the statement. Suspiciousness scores computed for such statements cannot be trusted because they lack adequate support. To address this issue, we plan to investigate the automatic generation of test cases with the appropriate coverage characteristics.

Second, although matching using Mahalanobis distance was generally effective in our studies, it sometimes failed to yield balanced comparison groups. In the latter cases, the rankings produced by our technique are not consistent because they are based on valid causal estimates mixed with biased estimates. Using Mahalanobis distance for matching is also sometimes inefficient, because it is expensive to compute Mahalanobis distance when there are many program dependences. To address these issues, we plan to explore the use of other matching techniques, such as those based on propensity scores [18].

Finally, some faults cannot be effectively localized without considering the variable values carried by data dependences. For example, considering variables values may be the only way to determine that a check for an unusual condition is missing in a certain program location. Although the proposed technique considers data dependences it does not currently consider variable values. We are currently investigating how this can be done.

Acknowledgements

This research was supported in part by NSF award CCF-0725202 and an IBM Software Quality Innovation Award to Georgia Tech, by NSF awards CCF-0820217 and CCF 0702693 and by an award from ABB Corporation to Case Western Reserve University, and by a FACES (Facilitating Academic Careers in Engineering and Science) fellowship award to George Baah. The anonymous reviewers provided many helpful suggestions that improved the presentation of the paper.

7. REFERENCES

[1] R. Abreu, P. Zoeteweij, and A. J. van Gemund. On the Accuracy of Spectrum-Based Fault Localization. In *Proceedings of the Testing: Academic and Industrial Conference Practice and Research Techniques*, pages 89–98, September 2007.

[2] H. Agrawal and J. R. Horgan. Dynamic Program Slicing. In *Proceedings of the ACM SIGPLAN 1990 conference on Programming language design and implementation*, PLDI '90, pages 246–256. ACM, 1990.

[3] A. V. Aho, M. Garey, and J. D. Ullman. The transitive reduction of a directed graph. *SIAM Journal on Computing*, 1:131–137, 1972.

[4] S. Artzi, J. Dolby, F. Tip, and M. Pistoia. Directed Test Generation for Effective Fault Localization. In *Proceedings of the International Symposium for Software Testing and Analysis*, July 2010.

[5] G. K. Baah, A. Podgurski, and M. J. Harrold. Causal Inference for Statistical Fault Localization. In *Proceedings of the International Symposium on Software Testing and Analysis*, July 2010.

[6] J. Bang-Jensen and G. Gutin. *Digraphs: Theory, Algorithms and Applications*. Springer-Verlag, 2001.

[7] H. Cleve and A. Zeller. Locating Causes of Program Failures. In *Proceedings of the International Symposium on the Foundations of Software Engineering*, pages 342–351, May 2005.

[8] R. A. DeMillo, H. Pan, and E. H. Spafford. Critical Slicing for Software Fault Localization. In *ISSTA '96: Proceedings of the 1996 ACM SIGSOFT international symposium on Software testing and analysis*, pages 121–134, 1996.

[9] H. Do, S. Elbaum, and G. Rothermel. Supporting Controlled Experimentation with Testing Techniques: An Infrastructure and its Potential Impact. *Empirical Software Engineering*, 10(4):405–435, 2005.

[10] J. Ferrante, K. J. Ottenstein, and J. D. Warren. The Program Dependence Graph and Its Use in Optimization. *ACM Transactions on Programming Languages and Systems*, 9(3):319–349, July 1987.

[11] R. Gore and P. F. Reynolds, Jr. Causal program slicing. In *IEEE/SCS Workshop on Principles of Advanced and Distributed Simulation*, 2009.

[12] P. W. Holland. Statistics and Causal Inference. *Journal of American Statistical Association*, 81:945–970, 1986.

[13] J. Jones, M. J. Harrold, and J. Stasko. Visualization of Test Information to Assist Fault Localization. In *Proceedings of the International Conference on Software Engineering*, pages 467–477, May 2002.

[14] S. Klamt, R. J. Flassig, and K. Sundmacher. TRANSWESD: inferring cellular networks with transitive reduction. *Bioinformatics*, 26:2160–2168, 2010.

[15] B. Liblit, M. Naik, A. X. Zheng, A. Aiken, and M. I. Jordan. Scalable Statistical Bug Isolation. In *Proceedings of the Conference on Programming Language Design and Implementation*, pages 15–26, June 2005.

[16] C. Liu, X. Yan, L. Fei, J. Han, and S. P. Midkiff. SOBER: Statistical Model-based Bug Localization. In *Proceedings of the European Software Engineering Conference and ACM SIGSOFT Symposium on the Foundations of Software Engineering*, pages 286–295, September 2005.

[17] Lucia, D. Lo, L. Jiang, and A. Budi. Comprehensive Evaluation of Association Measures for Fault Localization. In *Proceedings of International Conference on Software Maintenance (ICSM)*, 2010.

[18] S. L. Morgan and C. Winship. *Counterfactuals and Causal Inference: Methods and Principles of Social Research*. Cambridge University Press, 2007.

[19] V. Nagarajan, R. Gupta, X. Zhang, M. Madou, and B. D. Sutter. Matching Control Flow of Program Versions. In *International Conference on Software Maintenance*, 2007.

[20] G. C. Necula, S. McPeak, S. P. Rahul, and W. Weimer. CIL: Intermediate Language and Tools for Analysis and Transformation of C Programs. In *Proceedings of the International Conference on Compiler Construction*, pages 213–228, April 2002.

[21] J. Pearl. *Causality: Models, Reasoning, and Inference*. Cambridge University Press, San Francisco, CA, USA, 2000.

[22] A. Podgurski and L. A. Clarke. A Formal Model of Program Dependences and Its Implications for Software Testing, Debugging, and Maintenance. *IEEE Transactions on Software Engineering*, 16(9):965–979, September 1990.

[23] R Development Core Team. *R: A Language and Environment for Statistical Computing*. R Foundation for Statistical Computing, Vienna, Austria, 2008.

[24] S. Rapps and E. Weyuker. Selecting Software Test Data Using Data Flow Information. *IEEE Transactions on Software Engineering*, SE-11, NO. 4:367–375, 1985.

[25] M. Renieris and S. Reiss. Fault Localization With Nearest Neighbor Queries. In *International Conference on Automated Software Engineering*, pages 30–39, November 2003.

[26] D. J. Richardson and M. C. Thompson. An Analysis of Test Data Selection Criteria Using the RELAY Model of Fault Detection. *IEEE Transactions on Software Engineering*, 19(6):533–553, 1993.

[27] R. Santelices, J. A. Jones, Y. Yu, and M. J. Harrold. Lightweight fault localization using multiple coverage types. In *International Conference on Software Engineering*, 2009.

[28] J. S. Sekhon. Multivariate and Propensity Score Matching Software with Automated Balance Optimization: The Matching Package for R. *Forthcoming, Journal of Statistical Software*, 2008. Forthcoming.

[29] E. A. Stuart. Matching Methods for Causal Inference: A Review and a Look Forward. *Statistical Science*, 25:1–21, 2010.

[30] M. Weiser. Program Slicing. In *Proceedings of the International Conference on Software Engineering*, pages 439–449, March 1981.

[31] A. Zeller. Isolating Cause-Effect Chains from Computer Programs. In *Proceedings ACM SIGSOFT 10th International Symposium on the Foundations of Software Engineering*, November 2002.

[32] X. Zhang, N. Gupta, and R. Gupta. Pruning Dynamic Slices With Confidence. In *Proceedings of the Conference on Programming Language Design and Implementation*, pages 169–180, June 2006.

[33] Z. Zhang, W. K. Chan, T. H. Tse, B. Jiang, and X. Wang. Capturing Propagation of Infected Program States. In *Proceedings of European Software Engineering Conference and the ACM SIGSOFT Symposium on the Foundations of Software Engineering*, pages 43–52. ACM, 2009.

Fault Localization for Data-Centric Programs

Diptikalyan Saha
IBM Research - India
diptsaha@in.ibm.com

Mangala Gowri Nanda
IBM Research - India
mgowri@in.ibm.com

Pankaj Dhoolia
IBM Research - India
pdhoolia@in.ibm.com

V. Krishna Nandivada
IBM Research - India
nvkrishna@in.ibm.com

Vibha Sinha
IBM Research - India
vibha.sinha@in.ibm.com

Satish Chandra
IBM T. J. Watson Research Ctr
satishchandra@us.ibm.com

ABSTRACT

In this paper we present an automated technique for localizing faults in data-centric programs. Data-centric programs primarily interact with databases to get collections of content, process each entry in the collection(s), and output another collection or write it back to the database. One or more entries in the output may be faulty. In our approach, we gather the execution trace of a faulty program. We use a novel, precise slicing algorithm to break the trace into multiple slices, such that each slice maps to an entry in the output collection. We then compute the semantic difference between the slices that correspond to correct entries and those that correspond to incorrect ones. The "diff" helps to identify potentially faulty statements.

We have implemented our approach for ABAP programs. ABAP is the language used to write custom code in SAP systems. It interacts heavily with databases using embedded SQL-like commands that work on collections of data. On a suite of 13 faulty ABAP programs, our technique was able to identify the precise fault location in 12 cases.

Categories and Subject Descriptors

F.3.2 [**Semantics of Programming Languages**]: Program Analysis; D.2.5 [**Testing and Debugging**]: Debugging aids

General Terms

Algorithms, Languages

Keywords

Automated debugging, Data-centric languages, Slicing, Semantic differencing

1. INTRODUCTION

Bug resolution is an important activity in any software maintenance project. Bug resolution for problems reported on applications already in use (in production) has two main implications. First, a client has discovered a bug in the field, and so it needs to be fixed urgently. Therefore, it is important to have good tool support that can help the programmer debug the program as quickly as possible, especially when the person who is debugging the code is not the programmer who originally wrote the code. Second, the bug has surfaced despite the fact that the code has been tested and has probably been running in the field for some time. That means it is likely to be an unanticipated corner case in otherwise correct code, and automated tools can focus their effort on identifying such corner cases.

The techniques presented in this paper, were developed to aid in faster resolution of programming errors reported for ABAP programs. ABAP is a widely used propriety language used in SAP-ERP systems, and is heavily data-centric in the tradition of PL/SQL and COBOL. Data-centric programs process large collections of data that typically originate from a database. ABAP contains both imperative and declarative syntax. The declarative syntax is similar to SQL and allows developer to do complex operations on collections of data. Henceforth, we refer to this declarative SQL-like commands in ABAP as database statements.

Figure 1 shows a sample program written in ABAP and Figure 2 explains the syntax of each of the commands. This program represents a business application that creates a report of orders placed by different customers. Figure 3(a) shows a sample input and output data combinations from the program. Each correct output row is followed by a $\surd$. The output row that is considered incorrect is marked with a $\times$ and is followed with the expected correct output. The `OrderTab` table contains the order details such as customer who placed the order `CstId`, item ordered `ItemId`, its price `Price` and year in which the order was placed

```
SELECT CstId ItemId Price Year from OrderTab INTO itab
SELECT CstId Discount Year from DiscountTab INTO stab

SORT itab CstId ItemId
DEL from itab where Year <= CurrentYear - 2.
LOOP AT itab INTO wa
  AT NEW CstId
    amount=0
  ENDAT
  amount = amount + wa.Price
  READ stab INTO fa WHERE CstId = wa.CstId
  IF subrc = 0
    amount = amount - fa.Discount
  ENDIF
  AT END CstId
    WRITE CstId amount
  ENDAT
ENDLOOP
```

Figure 1: Sample ABAP program

Permission to make digital or hard copies of all or part of this work for personal or classroom use is granted without fee provided that copies are not made or distributed for profit or commercial advantage and that copies bear this notice and the full citation on the first page. To copy otherwise, to republish, to post on servers or to redistribute to lists, requires prior specific permission and/or a fee.
ESEC/FSE'11, September 5–9, 2011, Szeged, Hungary.
Copyright 2011 ACM 978-1-4503-0443-6/11/09 ...$10.00.

Command	Description
`SELECT`	project selected columns from a persistent database table to an internal table in the program
`SORT`	sorts the specified internal table on specified key(s)
`DEL`	deletes rows from a table that satisfies the condition
`LOOP`	iterates over an internal table, reading one row at a time into a local record
`AT NEW` (`AT END`)	a predicate that is true for a given row and field name(s) when the row is the first (last) one in the table or when the field's value in the current row is different from the previous (next) row
`READ`	selects a row from table based on the `WHERE` clause. If more than one row matches, the last row is returned
`WRITE`	prints the specified data
`wa.f`	field `f` of structure `wa` (actual ABAP syntax `wa-f`)

Figure 2: Basic ABAP syntax

(a) `OrderTab/itab`

CstId	ItemId	Price	Year
1	I1	10.0	2010
1	I2	10.0	2011
2	I3	10.0	2011

`DiscountTab/stab`

CstId	Discount	Year
1	2.0	2010
2	3.0	2011

Output

CstId	Amount	
1	16.0	× [= 10.0 + 10.0 - 2.0 - 2.0] [18.0✓= 10.0 + 10.0 - 2.0]
2	7.0	✓[= 10.0-3.0]

(b)

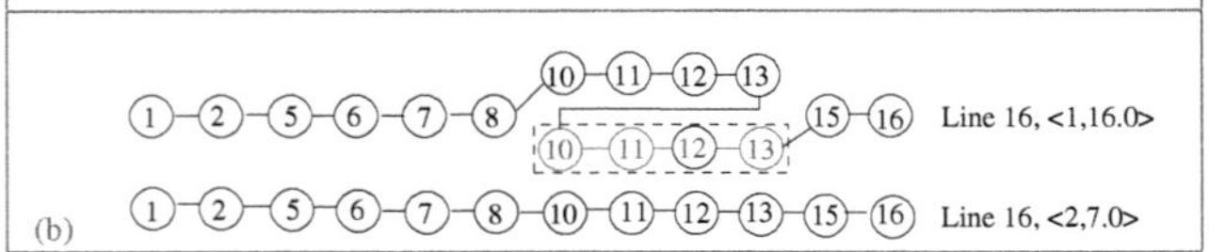

Figure 3: (a) Input and output for the ABAP program illustrated in Figure 1. (b) Dynamic slices for each output row.

`Year`. The `DiscountTab` table contains the discount applicable per customer per year. The output shows for each customer the total order amount. At the code level, the program first reads the input data from `OrderTab` and `DiscountTab` into internal tables `itab`, `stab` (lines 1,2), sorts table `itab` (line 4) and deletes records older than year `2010` (line 5). The `CurrentYear` variable is a parameter to the program and has value `2011`. The program then loops over the contents of `itab` (line 6), sums up the `Price` (line 10), subtracts any

(a) `OrderTab/itab-pre`

CstId	ItemId	Price	Year
1	I1	10.0	2009
1	I2	10.0	2011
2	I3	10.0	2011

`DiscountTab/stab`

CstId	Discount	Year
1	2.0	2011
2	3.0	2011

`itab-post`

CstId	ItemId	Price	Year
1	I2	10.0	2011
2	I3	10.0	2011

Output

CstId	Amt	
1	8.0	× [= 10.0-2.0] [16.0✓ = 10+ 10.0-2.0-2.0]
2	7.0	✓

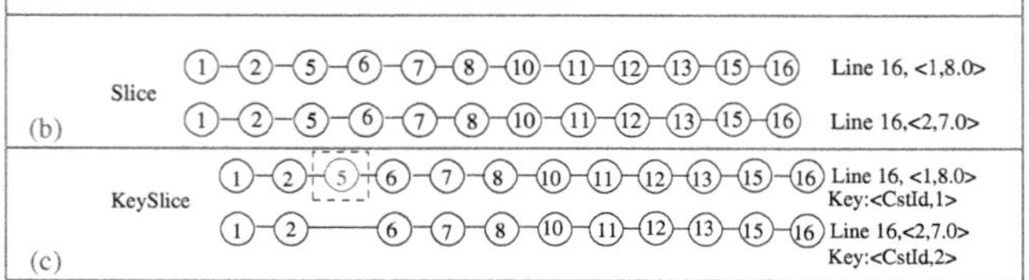

Figure 4: (a) Input and output for the ABAP program illustrated in Figure 1. (b) Dynamic slices for each output entry. (c) Key based slices for each output row.

(a) `OrderTab/itab`

CstId	ItemId	Price	Year
1	I1	10.0	2010
2	I3	10.0	2011

`DiscountTab/stab`

CstId	Discount	Year
1	2.0	2009
1	3.0	2010
2	3.0	2011

Output

CstId	Amount	
1	8.0	× [= 10.0 - 2.0] [7.0 ✓= 10.0 - 3.0]
2	7.0	✓

(b)

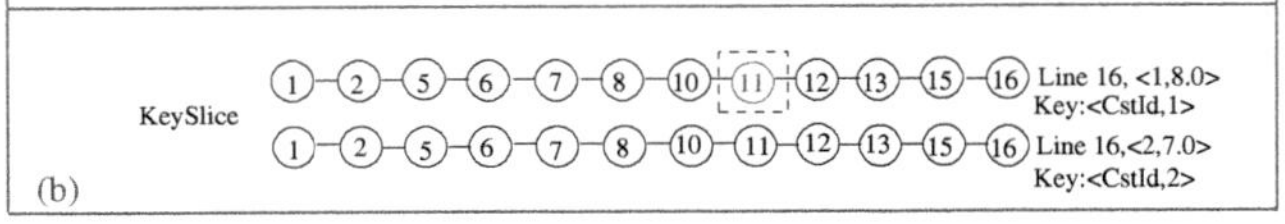

Figure 5: (a) Input and output for ABAP program illustrated in Figure 1. (b) Key-based slice for each output row.

relevant `Discount` (line 13) and prints out the total (line 16). One output entry is generated for each unique `CstId` present in the input `OrderTab`.

There are several challenges involved in developing fault localization techniques for these types of programs. The first challenge is that the analysis needs to handle both the imperative and declarative parts of the language. What should be the correct representative semantics for the different SQL-like commands in an ABAP program? Another challenge is that the analysis needs to be data driven, as the behavior of a command is very often dependent on the underlying data. Thus the same command at the same program point may run without any problems for most of the data and yet may throw an exception or generate incorrect output for some other data. As we shall see later in the paper, for the example shown in Figure 1, depending on the combinations of data available in the `OrderTab` and `DiscountTab` tables, three different bugs can manifest themselves in the output.

Problem resolution methodology. A large body of past work on fault localization relies on the usage of program slicing [1]. The basic idea in these techniques is that, when a program computes a correct value for a variable `x` and an incorrect value for variable `y`, the fault is likely to be in statements that are in the slice with respect to `y` but not in the slice with respect to `x` [14]. Similarly, if a program computes correct value for a variable `x` in a particular test case and computes incorrect value in another test case, then the potentially faulty statements would be in the difference between the slices of these two program executions [2, 22]. Our problem resolution methodology is motivated by these prior works and attempts to apply the same in the domain of data-centric programs.

One of the key challenges in applying any of the slicing based fault localization techniques in real world debugging scenarios is the lack of significant number of test cases that show the correct behavior of the program. These test cases are needed to collect the execution traces of correct examples that can be differentiated with the trace for the incorrect execution as reported in the bug description. However, in the context of data-centric programs, we can leverage the fact that a single run of the program yields an execution trace that can in turn be split into multiple independent slices, each of which is responsible for a single record in the output. This is because these programs typically loop over the input data records, aggregate the input depending on certain key fields and generate an output record per key value. In the case of the example discussed above, the key field was `CstId`. A defective program writes incorrect values for one or more key values. Further, if a user specifies that certain output rows are incorrect and we assume that the rest of the output is correct, we can associate a "incorrect" or a "correct" tag with each slice corresponding to each row of output. We can then compute the *difference* between the correct and incorrect slices to discover the statements that are potential sources of bugs.

To identify the bug reported in Figure 3(a), denoted by the output row postfixed with × mark, we first collect the dynamic trace by running it on the input that reveals the problem. We split the trace into multiple slices by applying dynamic slicing starting at each *instance* of line 16 (`WRITE`) in the execution trace. Figure 3(b) shows the slices. We then compute the difference between the slices to identify that line 10 through 13 are executed twice in the first slice versus once in the second slice. The lines are highlighted as fault inducing statements. This finding relates to the problem that the discount should have been given only once per customer. In the corrected code (done manually by the programmer), lines 11 through 14 were moved inside the `AT END` block (after line 15).

Key-based Slicing. It may appear that we can always generate incorrect and correct slices, and apply a differencing technique to this setting. However, this is not the case, as the dynamic slice based on simple data and control dependence may not differentiate between a correct and an incorrect execution slice. Consider the bug reported for the same program using input data in Figure 4(a). In this case the user was expecting to see the `amount` value as 16.0 for `CstId = 1` (considering that we have the code as it is in Figure 1). However, the code is deleting all order records that are older than 2 years (line 5). This means the conditional in `DELETE` statement in Line 5 is incorrect or incomplete. The slices for both the output rows are the same as shown in Figure 4(b) and hence differencing will not be able to identify any faulty lines. We resolve this by enhancing the existing dynamic slicing with the introduction of a key in the slicing predicate. The intuition for this is as follows. Usually in a data-centric program, as part of the output record, one or more input fields are written that together act as the identifier (or key) for the data and is unchanged from the input to output. For our example this field is the `CstId`. So, besides using an execution of a particular statement as the predicate for our slice, we also use the value of this key field as our slicing criterion. Figure 4(c) shows the key-based slices. Line 5 is only showing a side-effect for records in `OrderTab` with `CstId = 1`. The values in the table `itab` before (`Pre`) and after statement #5 (`Post`) are shown in Figure 4(a).

Once we do a differencing on these key-based slices, our technique highlights line 5 as the potential fault inducing code, as it effects the incorrect slice, and not the correct slice.

Semantic Differencing. In some cases even key-based slicing is not enough to differentiate between slices. Consider the input data in Figure 5(a) for the same program. Here the key slices for both the output records are the same. The actual difference is in the behavior of line 11 in its two different executions. The `READ` statement in ABAP returns only a single matching record. If there exist multiple records that match the selection criterion (`WHERE` clause), then it returns the first one. For `CstId = 1`, line 11 would need to select from two records, while for `CstId = 2`, there is only one matching record. Hence, the behaviors of the `READ` statement for these two keys are different. Our semantic differencing algorithm identifies such statements in the execution trace where different behavior of the command/statement have been exercised in the correct and incorrect key slices and highlights them as potential faults. For the example application, the fix is to change the `READ` (stmt 11) as `READ stab INTO fa WHERE CstId = wa.CstId and Year = wa.Year` such that appropriate year-wise discount is availed.

Novelty and Contributions. Key-based slicing and semantic differencing are novel generalizations of previous work on fault localization based on comparing program executions. Prior work in this area mostly takes into account just *whether* a statement appears in one slice but not in another one; but it does not take into account the *manner* in which it appears in a slice. Key-based slicing also takes into account the relevance of execution of statements to specific keys that were used in creating those slices; this is important in the context of data-centric programs. Semantic differencing contributes yet another attribute of statement execution, where the behavior of statement execution on specific input data is taken into account. We believe that our work is among the first to successfully adapt and extend fault-localization techniques to data-centric programs that occur in an industrial setting.

We have built a tool that takes an execution trace of an ABAP program and an indication of the buggy part of output. The tool then offers diagnosis of faults based on the techniques presented in this paper. In most cases, the diagnosis if found, was a single statement (for semantic differencing, we were looking for only a single statement difference).

Our experiments with the tool show that the above differencing techniques were able to accurately localize faults in 12 out of 13 ABAP programs provided to us by our colleagues in IBM Global Business Services. These ABAP programs were either old versions of some programs where there was a known defect that has since been fixed, or were programs in which a realistic defect was seeded by them. A baseline version of the tool that did not incorporate the generalizations of differencing mentioned above was effective only in 3 out of the 13 programs.

Organization. In the next section we give the details of our slicing algorithm. In Section 3, we elaborate on the differencing algorithm. In Section 4, we give the results of running our analysis on field bugs. Section 5 describes the related work and we conclude in Section 6 with some additional discussion on future work.

2. DYNAMIC SLICING

The efficacy of our differencing algorithm (cf. Section 3) depends on the accuracy of slicing. In this section we present an algorithm that performs precise backward dynamic slicing on execution traces containing database commands. Each slice is computed starting from a statement occurrence ($Line^{seq}$) that produces a row in the output, and on a set of variables (V), occurring in the statement. This constitutes the slicing criteria $\langle Line^{seq}, V\rangle$. We refer to the slices producing incorrect output as incorrect slices, and to the slices producing correct output as correct slices. The slices obtained in this way are analyzed with a differencing algorithm to reason about the possible faults present in incorrect slices.

Traditional slicing algorithms are oblivious to the rows and fields of tabular data (i.e., table accesses are treated as table[*].*). This results in overly conservative slices that are not effective in differencing data-centric programs. We obtain a row and field-sensitive algorithm based on the existing techniques of handling non-scalar data [29, 28, 19]. Our algorithm is built on top of precise (to the field-row level) dependency information, which can be obtained from the semantics of the statement and the data present in the execution trace. For example, the effect of a `DELETE` statement on a table is modeled such that it is possible to know the shift of indices of all the rows. The data effect of the `DELETE` statement will contain all those rows, whose table index is changed by the `DELETE` statement. In general, for each compound statement, its final effect is represented by a set of assignment statements, and a set of def-use pairs are identified from the assignment statements.

$1^1, 2^2, 4^3, 5^4, 6^5, 7^6, 8^7, 9^8, 10^9, 11^{10}, 12^{11}, 13^{12}, 14^{13}, 15^{14}, 16^{15}, 17^{16}, 18^{17}, 6^{18}, 7^{19}, 8^{20}, 9^{21}, 10^{22}, 11^{23}, 12^{24}, 13^{25}, 14^{26}, 15^{27}, 16^{28}, 17^{29}, 18^{30}$

(a) Execution Trace: List of $Line^{SequenceId}$

I^q	Statement	ϕ
16^{28}	`WRITE`	amount
15^{27}	`AT END` CstId	itab.length
13^{25}	amount = amount - fa.Discount	amount, fa.Discount, itab.length
12^{24}	`IF` subrc = 0	subrc, amount, fa.Discount, itab.length
11^{23}	`READ` stab into fa where CstId = wa.CstId	amount, stab[1].Discount, wa.CstId, itab.length
10^{22}	amount = amount+wa.Price	amount, wa.Price, itab.length stab[1].Discount, wa.CstId
8^{20}	amount = 0	wa.Price, itab.length, stab[1].Discount, wa.CstId
7^{19}	`AT NEW` CstId	wa.Price, itab.length, stab[1].Discount, wa.CstId itab[0].CstId, itab[1].CstId
6^{18}	`LOOP` at itab into wa.	itab[1].Price, stab[1].Discount, itab[1].CstId, itab.length itab[0].CstId
5^4	`DEL` from itab where ..	itab[2].Price, stab[1].Discount, itab[2].CstId, itab.length itab[1].CstId
2^2	`SELECT` .. from DiscountTab into stab	itab[2].Price, itab[2].CstId DiscountTab[1].Discount, itab.length, itab[1].CstId
1^1	`SELECT` .. from OrderTab into itab	OrderTab[2].Price DiscountTab[1].Discount, OrderTab[2].CstId, OrderTab[1].CstId

(b) Update of Data Dependency Set

Figure 6: Example: Slice Computation

The execution trace of the example in Figure 1 for input data specified in Figure 4, is presented in Figure 6(a). Figure 6(b) shows the update of the data dependency information after including each statement occurrence in the slice that is computed for the `amount` variable in the second row of the output, generated at statement occurrence 16^{28}.

Note that, due to shift of indices and its effect on the length of the table, the statement 5^4 is included in the slice. The `DELETE` statement actually does not affect the computation that is done for the second row of the output, as the addition is not performed on elements which have `Year` value $\leq$ 2009. Thus inclusion of `DELETE` statement in this slice makes it imprecise. Whereas, the slice computed with criteria $\langle 16^{15}, \{amount\}\rangle$ should include the `DELETE` statement, as the deleted rows, affect the computation, performed to compute the sum at 16^{15}.

2.1 Key-based Slicing

As discussed above, the row and field-sensitive slicing algorithm can result in imprecise slices. An important question to answer is, when does a statement occurrence become a part of the slice? Our dynamic slices represent the computations that affect specific rows in the output. A statement occurrence is not considered to be a part of the slice, if its absence has no effect on the *computation* of the variable values in the output row associated with the slice.

If a statement occurrence only affects the position of a row in the output, and not the values, we do not consider the statement to be part of the slice. In our experience it was the content of the row and not the order in which they occurred in the output that was more commonly observed to be at fault.

To determine whether a statement occurrence is effecting the variable values in the slicing criteria we need to check two conditions: ($C1$) if the statement occurrence is performing any operation that defines a variable in the dependency set, ($C2$) if the absence of the statement can change the dependency set in terms of addition or deletion of elements. If either of the conditions $C1$ or $C2$ is true, the statement is added to the slice. The statements that could change the dependency set by adding/deleting elements are called *db-change* statements. The `DELETE` statement in our running example does not satisfy the condition $C1$ for the slices corresponding to either row of the output. The condition $C2$ is satisfied for the first row of output: in the presence of the `DELETE` statement, the dependency set in the slice corresponding to `CstId=1` contains `OrderTab[1].Price` (as shown in Figure 6(b)), whereas in the absence of `DELETE` statement, that slice would have contained `OrderTab[0].Price` and `OrderTab[1].Price`. However, the condition $C2$ is not satisfied for the `DELETE` statement in the slice corresponding to the second output (corresponding to `CstId=2`), as in the absence of the `DELETE` statement, the dependency set would have still contained only `OrderTab[2].Price`.

The condition $C1$ is straightforward to check, and it is assumed that this check is precisely done as a part of field-row-sensitive algorithm for the non-db-change statements. We now present a criteria to check the condition $C2$ on the db-change statements. The purpose of this criteria is to remove a statement from the slice which otherwise would be included in the slice by a field-row-sensitive algorithm which takes conservative decision for inclusion of such database statements in the slice. The criteria has two parts 1) key-value condition and 2) sequence condition.

The first condition can be motivated by revisiting the running example. It is evident that the slices with respect to the criteria $\langle 16^{28}, \{\texttt{amount}\}\rangle$ and $\langle 16^{15}, \{\texttt{amount}\}\rangle$ have association with key-value pairs $\langle \texttt{CstId}, 2\rangle$ and $\langle \texttt{CstId}, 1\rangle$ respectively. With this association, whether to include the statement occurrence 5^4 can be easily checked by determining whether the deleted rows *match* the key-value pairs. In general, we say a row r matches a key-value pair (k, v) if the value of key k in row r is equal to v. A statement is not included in the slice if any change performed by the statement (such as added or deleted rows) does not match with the key-value pairs.

However, even if the change performed by a statement matches the key-value pair condition, the statement may not have any effect on the slice criteria, and thus, may not be included in the slice. The *sequence condition*, described next, is a condition that applies in the common `GROUP-BY/ORDER-BY` pattern in database processing. Consider an example pre-state and post-state of the `DELETE` statement 5^4.

```
          itab(Pre)                          itab(Post)
CstId ItemId Price Year          CstId    ItemId   Price Year
  1     I1    10.0 2009           1         I2       10.0  2011
  2     I1    5.0  2009           2         I3       10.0  2011
  1     I2    10.0 2011
  2     I3    10.0 2011
```

Here the `DELETE` statement does not affect the slicing criteria $\langle 16^{28}, \{\texttt{amount}\}\rangle$ as only the position of output row has changed, and not its values. The deleted rows could possibly effect the aggregated computations only if in the pre-state they were *adjacent* to the remaining undeleted rows. Sequence condition states that the table elements that are used to compute the values of the variables in the slicing criteria, are accessed in sequence. If the sequence condition is not met after key condition is met, the statement is not included in the slice. Note that the example does satisfy the key-value condition, so the sequence condition offers extra precision by eliding the `DELETE` statement from the slice.

There are multiple ways to identify key fields for association.

- The key fields may be specified by the user. This is not an unrealistic assumption. Observations on actual bug reports, indicate that the users find it more intuitive to describe the problem using the key fields associated with the row, i.e., they are more comfortable in specifying something like, "the unbilled amount for customer 2 is wrong", rather than, "the unbilled amount in the second row of the table is wrong"
- Fields in the internal table that are not modified before being written out into the output.
- Fields in the internal table that are used to select the rows to operate on (in `SELECT`, `DELETE`, `MODIFY`, etc.).

To summarize, we introduced, the key-value, and the sequence conditions, to more precisely evaluate condition $C2$ for verifying the inclusion of compound statements that process table elements, into a slice. It is important to describe here that as we move backward in the slice, the checking of one or both of these conditions may no longer remain applicable. For instance, say we encounter a statement such as `SORT`, which sorts the table elements based on the key-values, then as we move backward in the slice, we expect the table elements, to not be in sequence w.r.t. the key-values. Similarly, we may encounter a statement such as `APPEND`, backward to which, the key-value may not exist in the table elements.

The details of our key-based slicing algorithm are presented in Figure 7.

- Lines 1-6, 8-11, 15-16, 20-21 represent a basic field and row sensitive dynamic slicing algorithm.
- Function `get_def_use(s)` returns a set of def-use pairs representing def-use relationship between each pair.
- Function `field_row_sensitive_inclusion_check` performs checks like nonempty intersection of dependence set and defs in duSet to check data dependency and control dependency to include a statement occurrence in the slice.
- Once a statement is identified to be included in the slice, the dependency set is updated by removing the def and including use of each def-use pair in duSet (Line 16).
- Above the check done by field-row sensitive check, we add the key-value and sequence checking (Lines 12-13) to determine whether a statement occurrence chosen by the basic field-row sensitive algorithm will be part of the slice. These checks are only done for db-change statements.
- Function `check_kv_assumption` checks that all the non-scalar elements in the dependency set satisfy the key-value pairs
- Function `check_seq_assumption` checks that all the elements in the dependency set are in sequence, so that any statement occurrence which has a change outside this sequence will not have any effect for a particular key value.

Note that to highlight the interesting part of the algorithm we do not present the slicing algorithm in terms of dynamic dependence graph [1], used to express the data and control dependencies in the execution trace.

While, it is possible to give a necessary and sufficient condition to check the condition $C2$, the evaluation of such condition is not scalable, and thus not ideal for practical purpose. In this paper, we therefore restrict the presentation to the practical and scalable technique of key-based slicing.

3. SLICE DIFFERENCING

In this section we present the fault localization algorithms. We extend an existing approach to identify faults–to find the difference in behavior between *slices* that produce correct and incorrect output [14], and localize the faults at difference points. The novelty of our technique lies in the way we compute the differences between slices.

We apply two main differencing techniques. The first technique is relatively simple, where any control difference between two slices is determined (cf. Section 3.1). Such difference analysis typically determines the difference in sequences of statement occurrences in correct and incorrect slices. However, it is possible that sequence-based differencing may not produce any difference as the same sequences of statements can be present in both the slices. The second technique is particularly novel as it tries to find out the behavioral differences between two slices–finding statements that are present in both correct and incorrect slices but shows difference in their semantic behaviors (cf. Section 3.2). Note that, these differencing techniques are useful to localize faults when certain rows (not all) in the generated output have incorrect results.

```
1  Function KeySlice (I^q, V, S)
2  Input: int I^q /*sequenceid*/, Set V /*set of vars */
3  Output: List S /* List of statements */
4
5  Set φ = V
6  int i = I^q
7  key—value—pairs kvp = kvpairs// computed or user provided
8  while i>0
9    s = stmt.get(i)
10   duSet = get_def_use(s) // statement specific
11   if(field_row_sensitive_inclusion_check(s,duSet,φ)
12    ∧(!key_assumption_valid || (check_kv_constraint(kvp,s)
13     ∧(!sequence_valid||check_seq_constraint(kvp,s,φ))))
14     )
15      slice.add(s)
16      φ = update_dep_set(φ,duSet)
17      key_assumption_valid = check_kv_assumption(φ,kvp)
18      if key_assumption_valid
19        sequence_valid = check_seq_assumption(φ,kvp)
20   i − −
21 return slice;
22
23 check_kv_constraint kvp, s
24   if s is not a db—change statement
25      return true // condition C1
26   if any change by s satisfies kvp
27      return true
28   else
29      return false
30
31 check_seq_constraint kvp, s, φ
32   c = changes by s that satisfies kvp
33   if check_sequence_assumption ({c,φ},kvp)
34     return true
35   else
36     return false
37
38 check_kv_assumption φ, kvp
39   for each structure variable v.f
40     if f ∈ kvp.keySet
41        if value of v.f != kvp.getValue(f)
42             return false
43   return true
44
45 check_seq_assumption φ, kvp
46    for all itab
47       for any key f ∈ kvp.keySet
48         I = set of all i s.t. itab[i].f ∈ φ
49         if elements of I are not in sequence
50            return false
51    return false
```

Figure 7: Key-based Slicing

3.1 Sequence-based Differencing

The main aim of sequence-based differencing is to identify statements that contribute towards computation of the incorrect result and do not contribute to the computation of at least one correct result. To realize the presence of such statements we perform a two step process: 1) grouping correct and incorrect slices into equivalence classes, and 2) perform pair-wise differencing between the representative elements of the correct and incorrect equivalence classes.

In data-centric programs it is common to find the slices containing traces of same set of statements, but differing in the number of iterations of the some loops. Thus, while creating equivalence classes in correct and incorrect slices, we combine two slices into the same class if they are exactly same or if they have different number ($\geq$ 1) of iterations of the same statements in a loop. Generating equivalence classes in correct and incorrect slices reduces the number of pair-wise comparisons required to find differences between slices.

While sequence-based differencing of two slices, one from a correct equivalence class and another from an incorrect equivalence class, any difference of statements executed in the sequences of statement occurrences is noted. However, due to common nature of loop-iteration differences (such as, different number of loop iterations), these differences are given lower priority among all-sets of pair wise differences. The actual algorithm of sequence-based differencing in presence of loops is not presented here for brevity.

3.2 Semantic Differencing

As discussed above, an incorrect slice may not show any important difference compared to correct slices in sequence-based differencing. This is possible if a statement exhibits different "behaviors" in two slices due to the nature of input data to the statement. We call such difference in behavior as *semantic difference*. In this section, we illustrate such differences, and present algorithms to detect semantic differences. To the best of our knowledge, this is the first attempt to perform fault localization based on differences in the semantics as seen during the execution of program statements.

Consider the example program presented in Figure 1 and the corresponding test case shown in Figure 5(a). In this example corresponding to the `CstId=1` there are two rows in `stab`. In the `READ` statement at Line 11 when the selection condition is satisfied with multiple rows, then first (lowest index) matching row is selected based on ABAP semantics. In the example , the first row is selected with `Discount=2.0`, which results in output `8.0` instead of the correct output `7.0` corresponding to `CstId=1`. In this example, same slices exist for the two output rows as shown in Figure 5(b). So sequence-based differencing does not find any difference between slices.

In semantic differencing, we assume that there must exist a faulty statement in the program that appears both in the correct and incorrect slices, such that it *fortuitously* exhibits the intended semantics in the correct slices, but deviates from the intended semantics (based on programmer intent) in the incorrect slice. Remember that the fortuitous correct behavior in the correct slices is specific to the particular input data.

The important question is, how do we tell if a statement has deviated from its intended semantics? After all, programmers do not provide assertions after each statement to verify if the effect of the statement just executed is as they expected. We only know that the final effect, i.e. the intended output is present in the correct slices, and the unintended output in the incorrect slice.

In this paper, we use two kinds of heuristics to find the first statement in the incorrect slice which shows such a deviation.

Statement Type	Target Corner-case Difference
`READ` from itab into wa where C	Multiple/Unique rows are satisfied with C
`APPEND/INSERT` lines of jtab from idx1 to idx2 to itab.	The number of rows appended/inserted is different from idx2 - idx1 + 1
`INSERT`	The inserted row makes certain set of rows with same keys non-contiguous.
`APPEND/INSERT`	The inserted/appended row makes sorted data unsorted

Assignment
`MOVE`
`MOVE-CORRESPONDING`
transporting clause
	overflow
	overwriting same value

`LOOP` at itab. ... `ENDLOOP`.	the statement within loop contains delete from itab.
`AT NEW/END`	Whether `AT NEW` and `AT END` both is true for a single row.
`DEL ADJ` from itab comparing f1..fn.	the table is not sorted with f1..fn
`DELETE` from itab where C	Multiple/Single row selected by C.
selection condition $a \leq b$	$a = b$
selection condition $a \geq b$	$a = b$

Figure 8: Corner-case Differences

Corner Case Differencing. The first method of semantic differencing is called *corner-case differencing*. The semantics of some of the statements are classified into two separate categories: a normal case, and one or more corner cases. For example, in a `READ` statement, the `WHERE` condition could match multiple rows, or just one row. Since the first matching row is returned by the `READ`, the matching of just one row among several candidates is a corner case. A table of corner and non-corner cases for several statements is given in Figure 8. Given a trace, we can tell if a statement executed in a corner-case manner, or in a normal case manner.

Intuitively, this technique exploits the fact that most errors (typically seen in already tested code) occur due to non-handling of corner cases that are revealed in the incorrect slices, and not revealed in the correct slice. Key-based slicing determines whether there is *any* effect of a statement on a slice or not. Corner-case differencing tries to find out semantic difference of a statement with respect to correct and incorrect slices where the statement has *some* effect in both the slices.

In the example given in Figure 1 and data in Figure 5(a), we determine a corner-case difference in the `READ` statement, that in the case of correct slice only single row satisfies the selection condition, but in case of incorrect slice, the selection condition is satisfied with two rows. This difference is produced by looking at the semantics of `READ` statement and particularly evaluating the corner-case aspect in two slices. Note that, in this case, the difference in behavior of the `READ` statement is indeed this particular behavior found using behavioral differencing. The presence of this behavior (multiple satisfied selection) in `READ` is always a problem, as programmer may intend to get the first matching row always, and may not agree to specify an extra field in selection condition which increases the overhead of the operation. The fact that this difference in behavior showed in correct and incorrect slices is the key observation. Several other checks are presented in Figure 8.

Mutability Differencing. Our second method of differencing is called *mutability differencing*. Mutability differencing tries to make an intelligent guess on the correct form of the statement such that it produces different behavior than the observed behavior in the

Statement	Mutation
key constraint C in `READ/SELECT/DELETE` `APPEND/INSERT/MODIFY`	addition of key constraint deletion of key constraint
non-key constraint C in `READ/SELECT/DELETE/LOOP` `APPEND/INSERT/MODIFY`	modify C with post-condition imposed by a correct and all incorrect slices.
List of fields in `SORT`	addition and deletion of fields based on key constraint and field names in `DELETE ADJACENT` statement on the same table
`AT NEW` f. `AT END` f. on change f1..fn.	addition and deletion of fields to f based on key constraint and based on fields used in sort statement on the same table
`MOVE-CORRESPONDING`	`DELETE` or `INSERT` `MOVE` of other fields by breaking `MOVE-CORRESPONDING` to a set of `MOVE` statements

Figure 9: Mutation Operators

incorrect slice, expecting that the produced behavior after mutation is potentially same as the correct behavior. The important aspect of our technique is that we only consider mutation of the statements that do not change the behavior of the statement in the correct slice.

To diagnose the fault reported for Figure 5(a), we can also use mutability differencing. Consider the `READ` statement on line 11 in Figure 1. We apply a mutation to the `READ` statement at line 11 in Figure 1. `Year=wa.Year` is added to the selection condition in the `WHERE` clause. This is based on the observation that `READ` statement with key option is typically used as joining condition between two tables. There exist two common fields `CstId` and `Year` in the input tables `OrderTab`, `DiscountTab`. Any one of them or their combination could be used as the joining fields. However, in the buggy program only `CstId` is being used. After adding the common field `Year` in the joining condition, the analysis finds that the behavior in the correct slices remained same as same row is selected as before, but instead of selecting the record with values `<1, 2.0, 2009>` , the statement has now selected `<1, 3.0, 2010>` in the faulty slice. Indeed, the fix for this problem is the above change. A customer should only be given the discount applicable to the year in which the order was placed. Note that in general it is possible to get such a mutation after trying several number of mutations, and the applied mutation might not be the final fix, but could help to indicate the kind of fix to be made.

In general, the mutations we consider are based on identification of the key-fields. We identify the key-fields looking at similarity of field names in two joining tables (as above), matching fields names in sort, `DELETE ADJACENT`, and `AT NEW` statement, matching field names sort and binary search specification in `READ` statement. A complete list of patterns for ABAP language is not presented here for brevity. A list of mutation operators for different ABAP specific statements is presented in Figure 9.

Mutability differencing can be effective in cases where corner-case differencing is not. In Figure 10, minimum value for `f2` is computed for each distinct `f1` value. Before this computation, deletion occurred with a condition on `f2` values $f2 \leq 0$. In case (A), 1st and 4th rows are deleted by the `DELETE` statement. In case (A), say we want the second output to be `<2, 0>` instead of `<2, 2>`, and fix we need is $f2 < 0$ in delete condition. Corner-case differencing can find this error as for $f1 = 2$ the deletion of the row was done on the corner case of the condition $f2 \leq 0$, but for $f1 = 1$ the deletion was done on a non-corner case. Consider Case(B) where the first row reported is wrong as the expected output is `<1, -1>`. Here both the conditional evaluation for deletion went through a

```
1  DELETE itab where f2 <= 0
2  LOOP into itab into wa
3    AT NEW f1
4      min = MAXINT
5    ENDAT
6    IF wa.f2 < min
7     min  = wa.f2
8    AT END of f1
9      WRITE wa.f1, min
10   ENDAT
11 ENDLOOP
```

Case (A): `itab` (init)

f1	f2
1	-1
1	1
1	2
2	0
2	3
2	2

Output

1	1	✓
2	2	× [0✓]

Fix: at Line 1 where $f2 < 0$.

Case (B): `itab` (init)

f1	f2
1	-1
1	1
1	2
2	-2
2	3
2	2

1	1	× [-1✓]
2	2	✓

Fix: at Line 1 where $f2 < -1$.

Figure 10: Example: Mutability vs. Corner-case Differencing

non-corner cases. Thus, behavioral difference will not be able to perform any difference here. Mutability difference, on the other hand, can intelligently mutate looking at the post-conditions that is required $f2 \neq -2 \wedge f2 = -1 \wedge f2 \leq 0$.

However, mutability differencing is not strictly more powerful than corner-case differencing, as will be shown later in `ZROTC` experimental subject in Figure 12.

3.3 Extensions

The other kinds of bugs seen in data-centric programs are incorrect input data, unwanted rows, all incorrect rows, and missing rows. We briefly describe the approach we take for such description of bugs.

Missing rows. In this case the bug report contains the description of the missing rows in terms of their key-value pairs. Note that it is not possible to determine the slices corresponding to the missing rows as we cannot form slicing criteria for missing variables. However, the intuition that we follow here is that, if there is any row to be produced corresponding to the missing key-value pairs, their slices will be similar to the correct slices computed for some

```
1  SELECT * from zitr into table it_itr.
2  LOOP AT it_itr INTO wa_itr.
3      CLEAR : v_exrate.
4      v_exrate = 'READ_EXCHANGE_RATE'(wa_itr.waers)
5      IF subrc = 0.
6        IF v_exrate > wa_itr.exrate.
7          wa_itr.dispamt = wa_itr.amount * v_exrate.
8        ELSE.
9          wa_itr.dispamt = wa_itr.amount * wa_itr.exrate
10       ENDIF.
11       WRITE:/ wa_itr-matnr, 30 wa_itr-dispamt.
12     ELSE.
13       wa_itr.dispamt = wa_itr.amount * wa_itr.exrate.
14       ' Missing write here
15     ENDIF.
16 ENDLOOP.
```

`zitr`

matnr	amount	waers	exrate
1	50	USD	47
2	100	EUR	66
3	100	UK	75

Output

matnr	dispamt
1	2400
2	6600

Missing row: 3, 7500

Trace: $1^{1}, 2^{2}, 3^{3}, 4^{4}, 5^{5}, 6^{6}, 7^{7}, 11^{8}, 16^{9}, 2^{10}, 3^{11}, 4^{12}, 5^{13}, 6^{14}, 9^{15}, 11^{16}, 16^{17}, 2^{18}, 3^{19}, 4^{20}, 5^{21}, 13^{22}, 16^{23}$

Figure 11: Example: Missing Row

existing rows. Thus, we analyze (by stepping backward) each correct slice, to find the first statement occurrence (`s`) from end which has the missing key-value pairs in its `use` set, but not in its `def` set. If `s` does not occur in a loop, it is reported as a suspect as the selection operation in the statement has filtered out the missing key-value pairs. If `s` is in a loop, we determine all peer occurrences of `s` in different loop iterations, such that each of them (say `s'`) has the missing key-value pairs in its `use` and `def` set. The execution path starting from `s'` has the potential to produce the missing rows. Sequence-based difference of the execution path starting from `s'` and the execution path starting from `s` is presented to the user.

To explain the case in loop, we present the following example in Figure 11 along with the input data and trace. The row corresponding to key-value pair `<matnr,3>` is missing. The two slices corresponding to the generated rows with respect to the key `wa_itr-matnr` at write instances $11^8, 11^{16}$ are $\{1^1, 2^2\}$ and $\{1^1, 2^{10}\}$, respectively. Both the statement occurrences 2^2 and 2^{10} at line 2 contain the table `it_itr` in the `use` set which has the missing key-value pair, and do not contain the missing key-value pair in their `def` sets. Their peer statement occurrence 2^{18} has the missing key-value pair in both the `use` and `def` sets. 13^{22} is the difference between execution traces starting from 2^{18} and either of 2^2 and 2^{10}. This statement occurrence is presented to the user as fault suspect, which helps user to localize the missing write statement.

Incorrect input data. Along with the slice, we also highlight the variables that are defined in each statement occurrence in the slice and belong to the dependency set. This means for a select statement occurring in an incorrect slice, we identify the parts of the data selected which flow to the incorrect output. This information corresponding to the incorrect slices helps user to identify the incorrect input data.

Unwanted rows. In this case some (but not all) unwanted rows are found in the output. The fault localization problem is posed as an application of differencing where incorrect slices are computed based on key fields in the unwanted rows and correct slices are computed based on key fields in the rest of the rows. The key-based slicing, followed by sequence-based differencing, and, if required, semantic differencing is carried out to localize the fault.

Incorrect fields in all rows. In this case incorrect values in one or more fields for all rows in the output is reported as a bug. Incorrect slices are computed for each of the rows, and instead of computing sequence-based difference of them, the common statements in all the incorrect slices are computed. Furthermore, the mutation technique is applied to find a mutation of a statement (in the common statements set), such that the mutated behavior is different from all the existing behaviors of the statement in all incorrect slices. For each statement in the common set, corner-case differencing is applied to find a corner-case behavior of a statement which is present in all its occurrences in incorrect slices.

4. EMPIRICAL EVALUATION

We implemented our analysis algorithms for the ABAP language as a part of an analysis platform towards a joint program with IBM Global Business Services. We evaluate the effectiveness of our core contributions - key-based slicing, semantic differencing, and the analysis for missing rows in output. In our evaluation, the key-value pairs are obtained from the bug description. To perform semantic differencing, we implemented the semantics of several database statements of ABAP in Java, and hence could execute each database statement by mutating its original form.

4.1 Experimental Setup

We used a suite of 13 ABAP samples along with the bugs which were given to us by ABAP practitioners. 3 of these were client programs (SUTAX, ZQFPR, ZFR052). The other 10 bugs were replicas of bugs reported in client situations. As we did not have permission to use the client code, the bug was replicated on copies of similar SAP standard programs. Additionally, we also got 20 toy programs to test our algorithms. The fault relevant source snippets for all the subjects have been provided in the report [24]. To indicate the complexity of the subjects, lines of code and the size of execution (LOC/EXE) are provided in Figure 12. In the same table, we also report on the time it took to run the analysis (does not include trace collection time) for complete fault localization. The time includes sequence-based differencing of key-based slices followed by semantic differencing if required, or analysis for missing output. All the experiments are performed on a 2.53GHz PC with 4GB RAM, running Debian Linux 2.6. To conduct the experiments, we followed the method as given below -

- Execution trace was collected via an automated script, written using the SAP GUI Client scripting facility. The script simulates a step-thru debugging execution of an ABAP program, collecting use and def variable values.
- Fault observation was specified as a pair of precise slicing criteria and associated category (e.g. incorrect, missing).
- For problem categories incorrect and unwanted, we first identify the correct and incorrect slice criteria from user input. Then, we perform the sequence-based differencing on both field-row sensitive slices and key-based slices. If the sequence-based differencing does not yield any difference, we perform both the semantic differencing algorithms on key-based slices. For problems in missing category, we perform the missing algorithm described in subsection 3.3.
- The results were presented, as a navigable dynamic slice, mapped to the source, for the IBM GBS team to verify. The suspected faulty statement as identified by our algorithms was highlighted.

4.2 Results

In 12 cases out of 13, our analysis was able to localize to a single statement and it was manually verified that the line was the source of the fault. For the subject named SUTAX, we were not able to point out a single statement. Verification revealed that the program input was faulty and had to be fixed. The smallest key-based slice we reported was of size 12 (for ORDER program), and the input statement in the slice was related to the fault.

4.2.1 *Key-based Slicing*

In 5 cases sequence-based differencing yielded some difference. In 3 cases (RO13, IMAT, and IINV) the difference between field-row sensitive slices identified the fault. In 2 cases (MMAT and ORDER), the key-based slice was smaller than the field-row sensitive slice. The slice sizes are mentioned in the field-row, and key columns of Figure 12. A look at the relevant code snippets revealed that field-row sensitive slices had over-approximately included the `DELETE` statements. In case of ORDER this difference was vital in identifying the fault, as `DELETE` statement was key to the bug. In case of MMAT (* marked in Figure 12), field-row sensitive slice found a difference in the correct and incorrect slices, but that was not the exact faulty line. The sequence-based differencing of key-based slices showed the faulty line.

4.2.2 *Semantic Differencing*

In 5 cases sequence-based differencing (either just on field-row sensitive slices or key-based slices) was sufficient to identify the

Subject	LOC	EXE	Data Slice Size		Sequence Diff.		Semantic Diff.		Missing	Time in Secs
			Field-row	Key	Field-row	Key	Corner	Mutability [Space]		
RO13	1202	2948	8	8	✓	✓	-	-		23
IMAT	2661	3864	4	4	✓	✓	-	-		20
IINV	3154	5299	8	8	✓	✓	-	-		135
MMAT	1019	7251	5	4	✓	✓*	-	-		27
ORDER	1975	7386	13	12	×	✓	-	-		28
RLS	2013	569	4	4	×	×	✓	✓ [1]		1
ZROTC	1066	2397	4	4	×	×	✓	×		46
ZBMR	827	257	5	5	×	×	✓	✓ [1]		4
ZQFPR	1136	275	8	8	-	-	-	-	✓	1
ZFR052	944	520	4	4	-	-	-	-	✓	1
BABL	2795	367	6	6	-	-	-	-	✓	1
RV54	3492	1088	5	5	-	-	-	-	✓	1
SUTAX	1662	4028	12	12	-	-	-	-		2

Figure 12: Fault Localization Result

RLS

```
1  a: f1 f2 f3 f4 f5
2  b: f3 f4 f5 f6 f7
3  c: f1 f2  f3 f4 f5 f6 f7
4  LOOP into a
5    LOOP into b
6      MOVE—CORRESPONDING a to c
7      MOVE—CORRESPONDING b to c
8      MOVE a.f3 to c.f3
9      WRITE c
10   ENDLOOP
11 ENDLOOP.
```

(a)

ZROTC

```
1  SELECT from tab into table itab
2  LOOP at ktab
3    READ itab INTO w_itab
4         WITH KEY a = ktab.a
5    w_jtab.a = w_itab.a %overflow
6    APPEND w_jtab to jtab
7  ENDLOOP
8  ...
9  write_alv jtab.
```

(b)

ZBMR

```
1  SORT it_ekpo BY ebeln ebelp
2                 matnr werks
3  ...
4  LOOP AT it_ekbe INTO wa_ekbe
5    READ TABLE it_ekpo INTO wa_ekpo
6      WITH KEY
7           ebeln = wa_ekbe.ebeln
8           matnr = wa_ekbe.matnr
9           werks = wa_ekbe.werks
10                 BINARY SEARCH
11   ...
```

(c)

Figure 13: Code Snippets. (a) RLS, (b) ZROTC, (c) ZBMR

fault. In 3 cases, where the sequence-based differencing failed, semantic differencing was able to identify the fault. We now discuss in detail these 3 interesting cases -

RLS. In the example code snippet shown in Figure 13(a), the `MOVE-CORRESPONDING` X to Y statement moves the values from structure X to Y for the common fields. The Lines 1-3 show the fields for the structure. The correct assignments that needed to be done here are `c.f1=a.f1`, `c.f2=a.f2`, `c.f3=a.f3`, `c.f4=a.f4`, `c.f5=b.f5`, `c.f6=b.f6`, `c.f7=b.f7`. The assignment `a.f4` to `c.f4` was missing in the `MOVE` statement in Line 8. The error is only noticed when `a.f4` is different from `b.f4`. In an iteration which produced the correct output, both `a.f4` and `b.f4` were same. In an incorrect iteration `b.f4` had a non-zero value, whereas `a.f4` had a zero value. Both correct and incorrect slices had same sequence of statements having second `MOVE-CORRESPONDING` and not the first. So, sequence-based differencing failed to discover any difference. The corner-case differencing tried two corner (overflow and overwriting, cf. Figure 8) cases for the `MOVE-CORRESPONDING` statement. And the overwriting corner-case evaluation showed the following difference - `MOVE-CORRESPONDING` at Line 7 overwrites `c.f4` with its existing value in correct slice and with different value in the incorrect slice. This is also located using a mutation where the `MOVE-CORRESPONDING` statement in the slice is mutated to a sequence of `MOVE` statements and deleting the `MOVE-CORRESPONDING` to `c.f4=b.f4`. The assignment related to field `f4` is chosen for deletion as it is the common field between structure variables `a` and `b` that assigns values to structure variable `c`.

ZROTC. In Figure 13(b) Line 5 the overflow occurs in the assignment statement as size of $w\_jtab.a$ is smaller than that of $w\_itab.a$. The overflow is visible in incorrect slices as non-zero digits were truncated due to overflow. However, in correct slices only zeros were truncated, which did not produce any ill effect to the computed result. This statement was there in both correct and incorrect slices, and therefore sequence-based differencing was not able to catch this semantic difference. The corner-case differencing was able to catch this behavior as this is one of the corner-case that is determined in assignment statement (Figure 8). Note that, the fix to this bug is not a change the assignment statement, but requires a change in type in the declaration of the variables. As mutation only considers mutating a statement, this bug cannot be found using mutation.

ZBMR. The example shown in Figure 13(c) has the same flavor as our running example in Figure 1 with data in Figure 5. In this case the bug was the under-specification of the key constraint in the read statement. This resulted in the wrong row selection by the read statement in the incorrect slice. As explained in Section 3, both corner-case differencing and mutability differencing were able to find the error. Note that, in this case there was only one more common field (`ebelp`) between table `it_ekbe` and `it_ekpo` which was not present in the selection condition in the read statement. Thus mutability differencing considered only one mutation of the current statement.

The mutation space observed in our experiments was small as we use heuristics to restrict the mutation space.

4.2.3 *Missing Rows in Output.*

We explain a case for missing output with the code snippet of program `RV54` shown in Figure 14. The bug reported was that for some keys, corresponding rows were missing from the output. In the program, there was a `DELETE` statement, which was deleting the rows where the `f_new` field is null. Some computations were performed on the rows to produce output. We first obtained a key-based data slice which was of length 5 for an existing row in the

```
PERFORM batch_heading_babl
...
DELETE gt_output WHERE f_new IS INITIAL

PERFORM aendbelege_lesen
..
output gt_output
```

Figure 14: Code Snippet for Missing Row in RV54

output. Then by performing a backward traversal in the slice we found the DELETE statement that was deleting rows with the same key value as that of the reported missing data. As this statement was not in the loop, this was highlighted in the slice as the reason for the missing rows in the output. It was verified by the ABAP practitioners that, it was indeed the faulty line. The deletion should not have been to the gt_output table.

5. RELATED WORK

Static Program Slicing of ABAP Programs. Dor et al. [11] used static slicing to analyze how a given ABAP code uses data stored in different database tables. Their system PanayaAI, identifies all select statements in code and computes a forward static slice from these statements, to infer how the data returned from the select is being consumed in the program. They presented three algorithms; improving from a flow-field-context insensitive algorithm to field-sensitive, and finally to a flow-field sensitive algorithm. In their more recent work Litvak et al. [19] recognized the importance of field sensitive analysis in the ERP systems domain, and present an algorithm for efficient and precise computation of program dependences in the presence of large structure variables. In this paper we presented a backward dynamic slicing algorithm, which is field and row sensitive. We also observed that row-sensitivity plays an important role in reducing statement occurrences in dynamic slice.

Dynamic Program Slicing. There is significant work in the area of dynamic program slicing. Korel and Laski [18] had introduced the notion of a dynamic slice, way back in 1988. Agrawal and Horgan [1] significantly optimized the notion by dropping the executability constraints. Venkatesh [26] worked on separating the semantics based definition of a program slice from the semantic justification of an algorithm. Kamkar et al. [17] worked on interprocedural dynamic slices. Zhang and Gupta [29, 28] improvised the algorithms for dynamic slice computation in the presence of arrays, structures and pointers for complex real world programs.

Hainaut et al. [8] and Cleve [7] looked at applying dynamic analysis on data intensive systems, which contain embedded and dynamic SQL (such as in JDBC). The aim was to resolve the input queries being passed to a database as precisely as possible. The authors showed how just a static scan of the code for SQL statements does not suffice. The collected trace was used for program comprehension and to infer implicit referential constraints between database tables. We are similar to these papers as we also use dynamic analysis. However, our presented dynamic slicing techniques go a few steps further; in presence of integrated data intensive operations, we present row and field sensitive slicing, and extend it with key-based slicing.

Differencing based Fault Localization. Fault localization by differencing two program runs has been widely applied. The notion of spectrum (abstract trace) was introduced by Reps et al. [23] for acyclic, and intraprocedural path spectra. Harrold et al. [13] generalized the notion of spectrum and proposed spectra based on several program features - branch, complete-path, data-dependence, output, and execution trace. Tarantula [16] provides a visualization of various passing and failing test runs of a software system. Here the authors explored how visualizing the hit or miss count of various code statements in passing and failing runs can help users localize faults faster. Zeller [27] applied systematic delta changes to program input to generate guided passing and failing execution, that could be differenced to detect cause-effect chains more precisely. Renieris and Reiss [22] introduced distance spectrum. In a distance spectrum, a distance measure between the passing and failing spectra gives a measure of dissimilarity.

In the context of software verification, a number of techniques [25, 15] have been proposed to provide users with minimal information required to explain counter-examples resulting from model checking. Some techniques [4, 5] localize the errors in programs by identifying the diverging point between a counter-example and a *positive* example; a positive example is a sequence of statements in programs that does not lead to a violation of the property of interest. A similar approach is presented in [12] where errors are localized to program statements absent in all positive examples and present in all counter-examples leading to the same error condition.

In our approach, we difference between dynamic slices i.e. identify statements that have some effect in producing incorrect output but has different effect in producing correct output. However, we additionally, also identify if each executed statement showed similar behavior in each run.

Another novelty of our approach is that we split a single program execution into multiple slices that are further classified as correct or incorrect. We are able to do so because of the nature of the programs we are analyzing. Each program in a single run, produces some correct and some incorrect values. Mani et al. [21] applied a similar technique to retrieve passing and failing traces from a single execution to compute repair recommendations for model transforms. They used tainting to resolve how input data moved within a program to generate the output. However, their approach would not be applicable in our case where we need to handle data flows between code and external database. We used key based slicing to split a single execution run into multiple traces.

Mutation Analysis. In the area of testing, mutation technique is used to generate faulty programs from a correct program [10, 3, 20] to study the path divergence of faulty programs from the correct programs. Debroy et al. [9], use mutation based approach to suggest repairs to localized faults. The two classes of mutant operators used there are replacement of expression, replacement of assignment operator by another operator from the same class, and decision negation. Our mutation operators are specialized for database statements. Chandra et al. [6] determine alternate values of an expression to satisfy the goal of correcting the failing tests without breaking the correct traces. In comparison, we consider the syntactic mutations that change the outcome of a statement in the incorrect slices without changing its outcome in the correct slices. The space of syntactic mutations is managed due to the domain-specific nature of ABAP programs.

6. CONCLUSION

Fault localization using slicing and differencing have been identified as important techniques for performing fault localization in procedural programming languages. In this paper, we extend these techniques to data-centric programming languages which use embedded database specific statements to perform operations on in-memory and persistent data.

We present a new key-based dynamic slicing algorithm and two differencing techniques that use the underlying program semantics to localize faults in the data-centric programs. We applied our techniques on 13 real industrial programs and identified the underlying faults accurately in 12 of them.

We notice that, in data-centric programming paradigm the processing of data is separated out across different systems and languages. For example, many applications use the Java - JDBC - Stored Procedure framework to create a data-centric application. In future, we aim to check the applicability of our techniques in such paradigms.

Acknowledgment. We thank Anup Ghosh, Sugata Ghosal, Sourin Ghosh, Dhiman Ghosh, Anjan Nandy, Asidhara Lahiri, and Amitava Parui for many fruitful discussions and help in implementations of the project. We also thank Julian Dolby for sharing a version of the ABAP grammar. We also like to thank anonymous referees for their helpful comments on the earlier version of the paper.

7. REFERENCES

[1] H. Agrawal and J. Horgan. Dynamic program slicing. *ACM SIGPLAN Notices*, 25(6):246–256, 1990.

[2] H. Agrawal, J. R. Horgan, S. London, and W. E. Wong. Fault localization using execution slices and dataflow tests. In *International Symposium on Software Reliability Engineering*, 1995.

[3] J. H. Andrews, L. C. Briand, Y. Labiche, and A. S. Namin. Using mutation analysis for assessing and comparing testing coverage criteria. *IEEE Trans. Softw. Eng.*, 32:608–624, August 2006.

[4] T. Ball, M. Naik, and S. K. Rajamani. From symptom to cause: localizing errors in counterexample traces. In *Proceedings of POPL*, pages 97–105, New York, NY, USA, 2003. ACM.

[5] S. Basu, D. Saha, and S. A. Smolka. Localizing programs errors for cimple debugging. In *International Conference on Formal Techniques for Networked and Distributed Systems (FORTE)*, volume 3235, pages 79–96, Madrid, Spain, September 2004. Springer-Verlag.

[6] S. Chandra, E. Torlak, S. Barman, and R. Bodik. Angelic debugging. In *Proceedings of ICSE*, pages 121–130, New York, NY, USA, 2011. ACM.

[7] A. Cleve. Program analysis and transformation for data-intensive system evolution. In *Proceedings of ICSM*, pages 1–6, Washington, DC, USA, 2010. IEEE Computer Society.

[8] A. Cleve and J.-L. Hainaut. Dynamic analysis of sql statements for data-intensive applications reverse engineering. In *Proceedings of the 2008 15th Working Conference on Reverse Engineering*, pages 192–196, Washington, DC, USA, 2008. IEEE Computer Society.

[9] V. Debroy and W. E. Wong. Using Mutation to Automatically Suggest Fixes for Faulty Programs. In *Proceedings of ICST*, pages 65–74. IEEE, Apr. 2010.

[10] H. Do and G. Rothermel. On the use of mutation faults in empirical assessments of test case prioritization techniques. *IEEE Trans. Softw. Eng.*, 32:733–752, September 2006.

[11] N. Dor, T. Lev-Ami, S. Litvak, M. Sagiv, and D. Weiss. Customization change impact analysis for ERP professionals via program slicing. In *Proceedings of ISSTA*, pages 97–108. ACM, 2008.

[12] A. Groce and W. Visser. What went wrong: explaining counterexamples. In *Proceedings of SPIN*, pages 121–136, Berlin, Heidelberg, 2003. Springer-Verlag.

[13] M. Harrold, G. Rothermel, K. Sayre, R. Wu, and L. Yi. An empirical investigation of the relationship between spectra differences and regression faults. *Software Testing, Verification and Reliability*, 10(3):171–194, 2000.

[14] M. W. James R. Lyle. Automatic program bug location by program slicing. In *2nd International Conference on Computers And Applications*, pages 877–882, 1987.

[15] H. Jin, K. Ravi, and F. Somenzi. Fate and free will in error traces. In *Proceedings of the TACAS*, pages 445–459, London, UK, UK, 2002. Springer-Verlag.

[16] J. A. Jones and M. J. Harrold. Empirical evaluation of the tarantula automatic fault-localization technique. In *Proceedings of ASE*, pages 273–282, New York, NY, USA, 2005. ACM.

[17] M. Kamkar, N. Shahmehri, and P. Fritzson. Interprocedural dynamic slicing. In *Programming Language Implementation and Logic Programming*, pages 370–384. Springer, 1992.

[18] B. Korel and J. Laski. Dynamic program slicing. *Information Processing Letters*, 29(3):155–163, 1988.

[19] S. Litvak, N. Dor, R. Bodik, N. Rinetzky, and M. Sagiv. Field-sensitive program dependence analysis. In *Proceedings of FSE*, pages 287–296, New York, NY, USA, 2010. ACM.

[20] C. Liu, L. Fei, X. Yan, J. Han, and S. P. Midkiff. Statistical debugging: A hypothesis testing-based approach. *IEEE Trans. Softw. Eng.*, 32:831–848, October 2006.

[21] S. Mani, V. Sinha, P. Dhoolia, and S. Sinha. Automated support for repairing input-model faults. In *Proceedings of ASE*, pages 195–204. ACM, 2010.

[22] M. Renieres and S. Reiss. Fault localization with nearest neighbor queries. In *Proceedings of ASE*, pages 30–39, 2003.

[23] T. Reps, T. Ball, M. Das, and J. Larus. The use of program profiling for software maintenance with applications to the year 2000 problem. *Software Engineering—ESEC/FSE'97*, pages 432–449, 1997.

[24] D. Saha, M. G. Nanda, P. Dhoolia, V. K. Nandivada, V. Sinha, and S. Chandra. Fault localization in ABAP Programs. Technical Report RI11004, IBM, http://domino.research.ibm.com/library/cyberdig.nsf/index.html, March 2011.

[25] N. Sharygina and D. Peled. A combined testing and verification approach for software reliability. In *Proceedings of FME*, 2001.

[26] G. A. Venkatesh. The semantic approach to program slicing. In *Proceedings of PLDI*, pages 107–119, New York, NY, USA, 1991. ACM.

[27] A. Zeller. Isolating cause-effect chains from computer programs. *ACM SIGSOFT Software Engineering Notes*, 27(6):1–10, 2002.

[28] X. Zhang and R. Gupta. Cost effective dynamic program slicing. In *Proceedings of PLDI*, pages 94–106, New York, NY, USA, 2004. ACM.

[29] X. Zhang, R. Gupta, and Y. Zhang. Precise dynamic slicing algorithms. In *Proceedings of ICSE*, pages 319–329, Washington, DC, USA, 2003. IEEE Computer Society.

Proactive Detection of Collaboration Conflicts

Yuriy Brun[†], Reid Holmes[♦], Michael D. Ernst[†], David Notkin[†]
[†]Computer Science & Engineering, University of Washington, Seattle, WA, USA
[♦]School of Computer Science, University of Waterloo, Waterloo, ON, Canada
{brun,mernst,notkin}@cs.washington.edu, rtholmes@cs.uwaterloo.ca

Abstract

Collaborative development can be hampered when conflicts arise because developers have inconsistent copies of a shared project. We present an approach to help developers identify and resolve conflicts early, before those conflicts become severe and before relevant changes fade away in the developers' memories. This paper presents three results.

First, a study of open-source systems establishes that conflicts are frequent, persistent, and appear not only as overlapping textual edits but also as subsequent build and test failures. The study spans nine open-source systems totaling 3.4 million lines of code; our conflict data is derived from 550,000 development versions of the systems.

Second, using previously-unexploited information, we precisely diagnose important classes of conflicts using the novel technique of speculative analysis over version control operations.

Third, we describe the design of Crystal, a publicly-available tool that uses speculative analysis to make concrete advice unobtrusively available to developers, helping them identify, manage, and prevent conflicts.

Categories and Subject Descriptors: D.2.3 [Software Engineering]: Coding Tools and Techniques; D.2.6 [Software Engineering]: Programming Environments; D.2.8 [Software Engineering]: Metrics: process metrics

General Terms: Design, Human Factors, Experimentation

Keywords: collaborative development, collaboration conflicts, developer awareness, speculative analysis, version control, Crystal

1. Introduction

Each member of a collaborative development project works on an individual copy of the project files (source code, build files, etc.). Each developer repeatedly makes changes to his or her local copy of the files, shares those changes with the team, and incorporates changes from teammates.

The loose synchronization of these activities permits rapid development progress, but also allows two developers to make simultaneous, conflicting changes. Such *conflicts* [8, 11, 13, 17, 23, 34] are costly: they delay the project while the conflict is understood and resolved. Fear of conflicts is also costly. A developer may choose to postpone the incorporation of teammates' work because of a concern that a conflict may be hard to resolve [8, 13]. Ironically, this fear of *potential* conflicts can cause developer copies to diverge, making *real* conflicts more likely.

Conflicts can be *textual* or *higher-order*. A textual conflict arises when two developers make inconsistent changes to the same part of the source code. To prevent subsequent changes from overwriting previous ones, a version control system (VCS) allows the first developer to publish changes, but precludes the second developer from publishing until the conflict is resolved automatically (by the VCS) or manually (by a developer). Higher-order, and likely more damaging conflicts arise when the VCS can integrate the developers' textual changes, but the changes are semantically incompatible and can cause compilation errors, test failures, or other problems. Such conflicts are problematic to detect and resolve in practice [17].

As with errors in programs, it is generally easier and cheaper to identify and fix conflicts early, before they propagate in the code and the relevant changes fade away in the memories of the developers. Currently, this information is not readily available to developers [9].

Our approach, speculative analysis, unobtrusively provides information about the presence or absence of conflicts in a continual and accurate way. Our intent is for this information to allow developers make better-informed decisions about how and when to share changes, while simultaneously reducing the need for human processing and reasoning. We make the following contributions:

- We analyze nine open-source systems and show that, in practice, conflicts between developers' copies of a project are: (1) the norm, rather than the exception, (2) persist, on average, 10 days, and (3) are often higher-order.
- Using previously-unexploited information, we precisely diagnose important classes of conflicts and offer concrete advice about addressing them. We do this by introducing a novel technique called speculative analysis that anticipates actions a developer may wish to perform and executes them in the background. Reporting the consequences of these likely version control operations can improve the way in which collaborative developers identify and manage conflicts.
- We design and implement an open-source, publicly-available tool called Crystal[1]— `http://crystalvc.googlecode.com` — that implements the analyses and unobtrusively presents advice to developers, to aid them in identifying, managing, and preventing conflicts.

Section 2 provides a brief scenario of two collaborative developers, sketching how their development activities would differ with

Permission to make digital or hard copies of all or part of this work for personal or classroom use is granted without fee provided that copies are not made or distributed for profit or commercial advantage and that copies bear this notice and the full citation on the first page. To copy otherwise, to republish, to post on servers or to redistribute to lists, requires prior specific permission and/or a fee.
ESEC/FSE'11, September 5–9, 2011, Szeged, Hungary.
Copyright 2011 ACM 978-1-4503-0443-6/11/09 ...$10.00.

[1]Crystal "exceeded expectations" of the ESEC/FSE 2011 artifact evaluation committee.

Figure 1: A screenshot of the Crystal tool as run by a developer named George. The green arrow informs George that his changes can be published (uploaded) without conflict to the master repository. The red merge symbol indicates that Ringo's changes, if combined with George's, would cause a test ("T") failure.

and without the use of a Crystal-like tool. Section 3 presents VCS terminology. Section 4 details our retrospective analysis of the frequency and persistence of conflicts in practice. Section 5 describes the information that can help developers better manage their conflicts. Section 6 introduces the design of Crystal, an unobtrusive tool that computes and reports this information to developers. Section 7 surveys related work. Section 8 discusses threats to validity. Finally, Section 9 summarizes our results and contributions.

2. Scenario

Consider a simple scenario with George and Ringo adding features to a project. As part of George's feature, he makes changes to a library that Ringo also uses. When finished, George and Ringo each independently publish their changes to the master repository. Whenever the regression tests run after both have published, George and Ringo are notified about failing tests. At that time, they have to recollect their earlier changes and assumptions, and their fixes might force them to rework other code they had written in the meanwhile.

One way to lessen these difficulties is to use an awareness tool, which reports where in the code base teammates are working, allowing a developer to be more attentive to conflicts that may arise in those locations (see Section 7 for more details). For example, when George edits the library, an awareness tool may tell Ringo that someone else is editing code he depends on. However, if George's change to the library had not actually affected Ringo, the warning would have been a false positive. Furthermore, George might have been exploring some ideas and changes, without ever intended to share the intermediate changes with his team. Thus, awareness tools have the potential to give early warnings, but also the potential to give multiple types of false warnings.

By contrast, consider what would have happened if George and Ringo were using a speculative analysis tool, such as our tool Crystal, that proactively informs developers of version control conflicts. Figure 1 shows how Crystal informs George that his library changes' integration with Ringo's changes causes Ringo's test suite to fail. The tool encourages George and Ringo to address the impending conflict before their assumptions and understanding of the changes fade.

Speculative analysis [4] does not guess at possible conflicts. Instead, it speculatively performs the work and executes the VCS operations in the background on clones of the program: it actually merges George's and Ringo's committed code, builds it, and runs its tests. This allows speculative analysis to deliver precise information about conflicts: those that can be merged safely are not reported as potential conflicts, and textually-clean merges that fail to build or test properly are reported as conflicts. With respect to the issue of exploratory development and awareness tools, our approach assumes that when a developer commits code to the VCS, the developer decided to share that code with other developers. Overall, our approach provides precise and pertinent information available as soon as conflicts occur in the VCS.

3. Terminology

Our results are applicable in the context of both centralized version control systems (CVCSes) — such as CVS, Subversion, and Perforce — and distributed version control systems (DVCSes) — such as Git and Mercurial. This paper focuses on DVCSes to simplify the presentation. We first briefly present accepted DVCS terminology. We then introduce additional new terminology to allow us to precisely characterize seven pertinent relationships between repositories.

3.1 Version control terminology

Figure 2 shows a common [31] DVCS repository setup. There is a single *master* repository and four developers: George, Paul, Ringo, and John. Each developer makes a local repository *clone* from the master. Each local repository contains a complete and independent history of the master repository at the time it was cloned. In addition, each repository has a *working copy*, in which code is edited. Changing the working copy does not modify the local repository; to modify the local repository the developer *commits* a *changeset* to the local repository's history. Teammates are not privy to these changesets until the developer *pushes* them to the master repository from the local repository. After a push, another developer can perform a *pull* from the master, which updates that developer's local repository with the changesets. To refresh a working copy after a pull, the developer must apply the *update* operation. It is common for developers in a DVCS to commit multiple times before publishing through a push. It is uncommon for developers to pull without a corresponding update. A *merge* conflict can arise due to a pull operation, and the conflict must be *resolved* before proceeding. The terms used above are common, or have direct equivalents, across DVCS systems.

The discussion in this paper makes a few simplifying assumptions for clarity: one, it assumes that developers push to and pull from only the master repository; two, it assumes that developers only make a commit when all their tests pass. However, our approach in general, and the Crystal tool, in particular, handle arbitrary pushes, pulls, and commits.

3.2 Repository relationships

We have identified seven relevant relationships that can hold between two repositories. Figure 2 illustrates these relationships.

SAME: The repositories have the same changesets. For example, George's repository is the SAME as the master repository because they both consist of changesets 100 and 101.

AHEAD: The repository has a superset of the other repository's changesets. For example, George's repository is AHEAD of Paul's.

BEHIND: The inverse of AHEAD; for example, George's repository is BEHIND John's.

The remaining four relationships represent repositories that share an initial sequence of changesets followed by distinct sequences of changesets.

TEXTUAL✘: (pronounced "textual conflict") The distinct changesets necessitate human intervention as they cannot be automatically merged by the VCS. For example, if George's changeset 101 and Ringo's changeset 102 modify overlapping lines of code, they are in TEXTUAL✘.

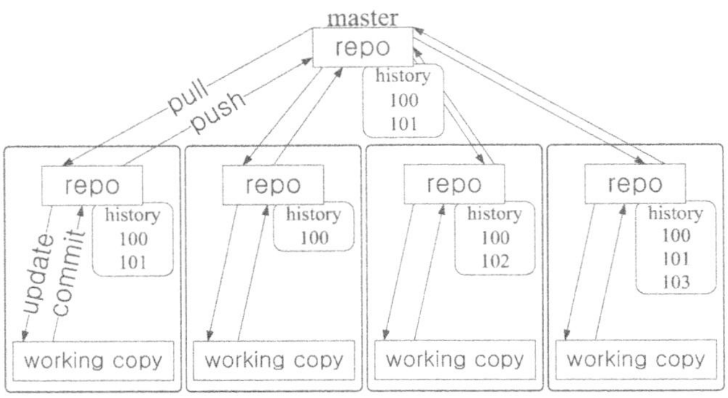

Figure 2: A DVCS with four clones of a master repository. The box labeled "history" lists those changesets currently in the repository. Each repository may have a working copy. The commit command creates a new changeset in its repository's history, and the update command incorporates changesets into the working copy. A developer can incorporate changesets from other repositories using the pull command and can share changesets using the push command.

BUILD✘: The repositories can be automatically merged by the VCS, but the resulting merged code fails to build.

TEST✘: The repositories can be automatically merged by the VCS and the resulting merged code builds but fails its test suite.

TEST✓: The repositories can be automatically merged by the VCS and the resulting merged code builds and passes its test suite.

Analogously to TEST✓, there there are relationships BUILD✓ and TEXTUAL✓ with the obvious meanings. The table header of Figure 4 illustrates the interrelation among the relationships. When build scripts and test suites are not available, we will distinguish only five relationships: SAME, AHEAD, BEHIND, TEXTUAL✓, and TEXTUAL✘.

Higher-order conflicts, such as BUILD✘ and TEST✘, are not considered by existing VCS systems. Although this paper discusses only these two higher-order relationships, others naturally arise for other analyses; for example, consider when a test suite passes but a performance analysis or code style checker does not.

4. Conflicts in practice

This section answers the following research questions. "How often do the TEXTUAL✘, BUILD✘, TEST✘, and TEST✓ relationships of Section 3.2 happen?" Section 4.1 focuses on the TEXTUAL✘ relationship, and Section 4.2 addresses BUILD✘, TEST✘, and TEST✓. Section 4.3 asks "How long do developers experience the conflict relationships such as TEXTUAL✘?" Section 4.4 asks "How damaging is it not to share changes with teammates, if those changes would currently merge cleanly?"

Anecdotally, conflicts are a serious problem. For example, in a private communication, an industrial manager expressed the following concerns to us about his two offshore teams and their collaboration with his local team:

> "The remote guys tend not to commit frequently enough to get leverage out of our continuous integration builds, even after prompting. It is a real challenge to know how far out of sync [the remote teams] are [with the local team] when their commits are not being merged in regularly.
>
> ...
>
> I want [my developers] to at least initiate a conversation with the relevant parties when the system says they have, or are just about to, walk into a conflicting situation. I also want the system to give them a certain level of **trust** of other developer's changes so that if [a merge] won't cause a problem, they should sync up."

system	KNCSL	devs	changesets	days	description
Gallery3	57	24	4,838	437	Web-based photo album
Git	267	27	20,785	1,741	Version control system
Insoshi	173	15	1,316	629	Social networking platform
jQuery	26	23	2,183	1,393	JavaScript library
MaNGOS	643	27	3,511	626	Online game server
Perl5	660	51	34,653	8,061	Programming language
Rails	141	50	12,342	1,875	Web application framework
Samba	1,363	59	58,802	5,001	File and print services
Voldemort	103	22	1,219	375	Structured storage system
Total	3,433	298	138,549	20,138	

Figure 3: Nine subject programs analyzed to address RQ1, RQ2, and RQ3 in collaborative development environments. KNCSL stands for thousands of non-comment source lines. The version control history ends on Feb 13, 2010.

There is little hard data on conflicts. Zimmermann's analysis of CVS repositories for four open source systems is the only work we could find that directly addresses this issue [34]. He reported that of all merges, 23% to 47% had textual conflicts (TEXTUAL✘) while the remainder could be merged automatically (TEXTUAL✓). Answering RQ1 and RQ2 requires analyses that significantly augment these data and anecdotes.

As subject programs (Figure 3), we chose Git itself and the eight most active projects on GitHub (`http://github.com`) that satisfy the following three criteria: (1) at least 10 developers, (2) at least 1000 changesets, and (3) not just a Git copy of a CVC repository (which would not contain sufficient information to answer our research questions).

4.1 Textual conflicts

> RQ1: How frequently do conflicts — textual and higher-order — arise across developers' copies of a project?

The answer to RQ1 is that conflicts are the norm: for each subject system, there were no times when all pairs of developers were in consistent relationships (SAME, AHEAD, or BEHIND) with each other.

Figure 4 shows how often developers merged their changes. (This is analogous to Zimmermann's result described above.) Of all the merges, one in six, or 17%, had textual conflicts as determined by Git's built-in merging mechanism, reflecting the TEXTUAL✘ relationship. (This number may be smaller than Zimmermann's 23–47% due to better merging algorithms in DVCSes.) The other 83% of the merges had no textual conflicts, meaning the relevant developers were in the TEXTUAL✓ (including BUILD✘ and TEST✘) relationship.

The importance of the frequency of the TEXTUAL✘ relationship is clear: an unrecognized TEXTUAL✘ between the repositories of two developers may cause problems. The importance of the frequency of the TEXTUAL✓ relationship is also material: a developer who is unsure whether others' changes can be incorporated safely might avoid doing so, allowing conflicts to persist and grow (as suggested in the manager's quotation above).

Figure 5 considers every commit at which developers who *did* eventually merge their changes *could* have done so earlier. On average, 19% of the potential merges would have resulted in a textual conflict. In other words, had the developers been using Crys-

system	merges	TEXTUAL✗		TEXTUAL✓					
				BUILD✗		BUILD✓			
						TEST✗		TEST✓	
Git	1,362	227	17%	2	.1%	53	4%	1,080	79%
Perl5	185	14	8%	7	4%	51	28%	113	61%
Voldemort	147	25	17%	15	10%	5	3%	102	69%
Gallery3	458	42	9%	416	91%				
Insoshi	93	23	25%	70	75%				
jQuery	15	1	7%	14	93%				
MaNGOS	192	81	42%	111	58%				
Rails	362	51	14%	311	86%				
Samba	748	100	13%	648	87%				
total	3,562	564	16%	2,998	84%				

Figure 4: Historical merges. Frequencies with which developers experienced TEXTUAL✗, BUILD✗, TEST✗, and TEST✓ relationships when they integrated their code. For three systems with non-trivial test suites in the repository, we measured the frequencies of all four relationships; for the other six (which had no non-trivial test suite that we could run), we measured only TEXTUAL✗ and TEXTUAL✓.

system	merges	TEXTUAL✗		TEXTUAL✓	
Git	179,249	15,965	9%	163,284	91%
Perl5	7,352	1,290	18%	6,052	82%
Voldemort	4,512	1,534	34%	2,978	66%
Gallery3	6,924	1,262	18%	5,662	82%
Insoshi	1,742	736	42%	1,006	58%
jQuery	74	13	18%	61	82%
MaNGOS	4,967	1,092	22%	3,875	78%
Rails	10,418	2,971	29%	7,447	71%
Samba	77,683	30,635	39%	47,048	61%
total	292,921	55,498	19%	237,423	81%

Figure 5: Potential early merges. The frequency with which developers would be informed of TEXTUAL✗ and TEXTUAL✓ relationships, if they had used Crystal throughout their development of nine open-source systems.

tal, it would have informed developers about TEXTUAL✗ relationships that resulted from 19% of the commits. Conversely, the 81% of clean merges indicate the likely benefit of notifying developers when a safe textual merge can be performed.

4.2 Higher-order conflicts

In our subject programs, 17% of merge operations required human assistance to resolve a textual conflict (Figure 4). This underestimates the human effort, since textually-safe merges are not always safe: an automatically merged change may suffer a build or test failure, for example. We computed the relationships at the time of each of the 5,355 merges that developers performed during the development of Git, Perl5, and Voldemort. We did not compute the information for the other six subject program because of the absence of a non-trivial test suite that we could run.

Figure 4 show that during the development of Git, Perl5, and Voldemort, 76% of merges completed cleanly, 16% of merges resulted in a textual conflict (TEXTUAL✗), 1% of merges resulted in a build failure (BUILD✗), and 6% of merges resulted in a test failure (TEST✗). The 266 textual conflicts reported by the version control system only represent 67% of all conflicts. Stated another way, 33% of the 399 merges that the version control system reported as being a clean merge, actually were a build or test conflict.

Few current awareness tools detect higher-order conflicts (see Section 7). Rather, they generally notify developers of all changes to the repository (e.g., FASTDash [3]) or of concurrent changes to ASTs (e.g., Syde [15]). In contrast, we use the project's tool chain to dynamically and precisely detect BUILD✗ relationships (via the build system) and TEST✗ relationships (via the test suite).

4.3 Persistence of conflicts

RQ2: How long do conflicts persist?

RQ2 asks how long developers experience the TEXTUAL✗ relationship. As we argue in Section 4.4, the longer a relationship persists, the more opportunities it has to change into a more severe relationship.

To measure the lifespan of a conflict, for each conflict that was eventually resolved, we found the first changeset that introduced the conflict and the changeset that resolved it. (We omitted all conflicts between changesets that were never actually merged in the history, such as those on dead-end branches.) Due to the sheer volume of the data and computation necessary to process it, we examined the development histories of only four of our subject programs: Gallery3, Insoshi, MaNGOS, and Voldemort.

On average, the TEXTUAL✗ relationship persisted for 9.8 days and involved 23.2 changesets — 11.6 per developer — (with median values of 1.6 days and 3 changesets) before incorporating (left side of Figure 6). A tool could have let developers know about these TEXTUAL✗ relationships immediately upon their creation. In the worst case, one TEXTUAL✗ relationship in MaNGOS persisted for 334 days and included 676 changesets by one of its developers.

If developers know that they can merge others' changes safely, they may do so quickly and thus prevent a future conflict. The longer a TEXTUAL✓ relationship persists, the more opportunities it has to change into a conflict. Accordingly, we asked "How long do developers experience the TEXTUAL✓ relationship?" We measured the lifespan of a TEXTUAL✓ relationship for each conflict-free merge in the history (again comparing the changeset that introduced the relationship to the one that resolved it).

On average, the TEXTUAL✓ relationship persisted for 11 days and spanned 23 changesets — 11.5 per developer — (with median values of 1.9 days and 3 changesets) before incorporation (right side of Figure 6). A tool could have helped developers learn immediately about the TEXTUAL✓ relationship, encouraging earlier, smooth incorporation. In the worst case, in terms of time, one TEXTUAL✓ relationship in Voldemort persisted for 138 days; in terms of changesets, one TEXTUAL✓ relationship in Gallery3 persisted for 232 changesets without a merge, while each of the possible merges along the way would have been textually clean and fully automated.

4.4 Escalation of clean merges into conflicts

RQ3: Do clean merges devolve into conflicting changes?

Parallel work enables faster progress, but also the creation of conflicts. We, and others, argue that developers should perform safe merges as frequently as possible. To determine how often, in practice, parallel editing escalates into a conflict, we used a methodology similar to that of Section 4.3.

Every conflict relationship develops from a situation in which a second developer makes a change without having incorporated and understood a first developer's work. We found that of all conflict relationships (TEXTUAL✗, BUILD✗, and TEST✗), 93% developed from a TEST✓ relationship; the other 7% of conflict relationships developed from a BEHIND relationship. In other words, in almost every case, both developers had already committed (but not shared)

system	TEXTUAL✗ relationships							TEXTUAL✓ relationships						
	number	length (days)			length (changesets)			number	length (days)			length (changesets)		
		mean	stddev	median	mean	stddev	median		mean	stddev	median	mean	stddev	median
Voldemort	39	25.7	35.0	8.9	12.8	16.4	6	128	35.0	46.6	7.3	9.7	15.1	3
Gallery3	80	3.1	9.4	0.7	7.5	19.7	3	483	7.1	12.5	1.0	14.3	30.0	3
Insoshi	27	11.8	21.2	4.8	9.4	16.3	3	87	7.7	13.5	3.7	6.3	8.5	3
MaNGOS	58	8.2	44.0	1.8	17.6	83.0	3	118	2.4	2.1	1.7	5.8	7.1	3
Total	204	9.8	30.3	1.6	11.6	96.9	3	816	11.0	23.8	1.9	11.5	24.2	3

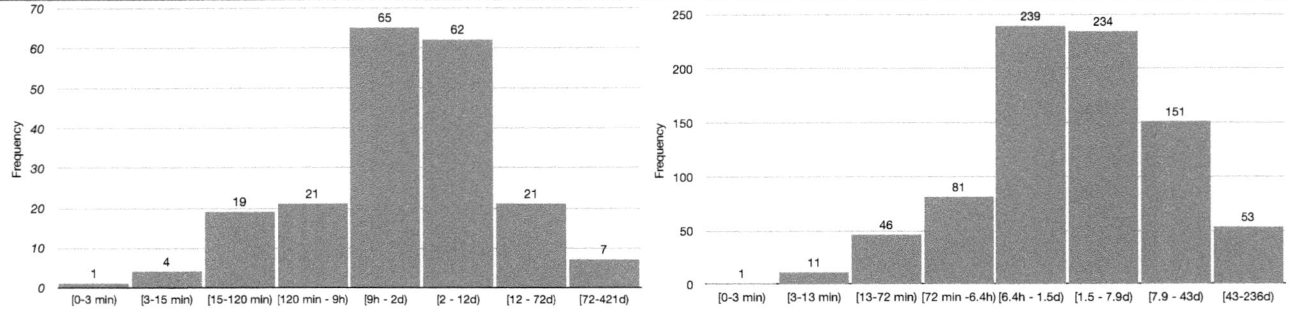

Figure 6: Persistence of the TEXTUAL✗ (left) and TEXTUAL✓ (right) relationships in historical data. The distributions are shown in eight-bucket geometric-progression histograms.

changes *before* the conflict developed. Every TEXTUAL✗ relationship could have been prevented by earlier incorporation of others' changes. Some BUILD✗ and TEST✗ relationships could also be prevented, and the others would at least be discovered locally and immediately, and would never be committed to the version control system.

We also found that 20% of TEST✓ relationships devolved into a conflict. The remaining 80% of TEST✓ relationships were merged successfully, preventing a conflict from developing. This suggests that what we call "safe merges" are actually at risk of devolving into conflicts that require human effort to resolve. Being aware of these merges early may prevent some such conflicts from arising.

While DVCSes record sufficient information to let us reconstruct how often a conflict arose from a BEHIND relationship, they do not record information that would allow us to determine how often a BEHIND relationship devolves into a conflict. We suspect that BEHIND relationships are also risky.

5. Information about conflicts

> RQ4: What information could developers use to reduce the frequency and duration of conflicts?

What kind of unexploited information is available from a VCS that is not yet leveraged to smooth collaboration? What information could help the developer make better-informed decisions, such as whether to perform a particular VC operation, to wait for a coworker to perform one, or to communicate directly with a coworker?

We explored this space systematically by analyzing a hypothetical global view of all version control information in all repositories. We then systematically analyzed this perspective by (1) enumerating all possible version control situations that can arise during collaborative development, (2) determining, based on the global perspective, the best course of action for the team, (3) identifying what information that decision depended on, and (4) classifying the advice for the team.

We made the following assumptions in our exploration:

- Without loss of generality, we considered all situations with three developers, using the third developer to represent arbitrary other developers and repository hierarchies.
- We limit our lookahead to two rounds of version control operations: one developer performs one VC operation and then the other developer may or may not perform one.

This approach has allowed us to identify key common and important use cases.

Section 5.1 describes five pertinent local states of a developer. We augment our classification of the relationships between developers' repositories (already described in Section 3.2) with two other categories of information: the developer's possible actions (Section 5.2) and guidance about those actions (Section 5.3). Finally, we describe the information available about higher-order conflicts, specifically build and test conflicts (Section 5.4).

5.1 Local states

The five possible local states are:

uncommitted There are uncommitted changes in the working copy.

in conflict The local repository is in conflict with itself; that is, it has two heads that are not automatically mergeable. This happens, for example, when pulled changesets conflict with local changesets.

build failure The repository's version of the code fails to build.

test failure The repository's version of the code builds but fails its test suite.

OK The repository's version of the code builds and passes its test suite.

These states are not mutually incompatible; for example, a user may have uncommitted changes, be in conflict with itself, and have different build/compile status for each head and for the working copy. Furthermore, these states obscure some information, such as whether the working copy has been updated to all of the changesets in the local repository. The list also omits some states, such as when the local repository has two heads that can be merged automatically. Our approach and tools can handle such situations. For simplicity of exposition, however, this paper classifies each developer's state as the first one in the list that holds. This is all the information about state that is needed to provide the generally best advice to the team.

5.2 Actions

Given two repositories A and B, the relationship between A and B as well as the local states determine the possible actions that developers can perform.

- SAME: Nothing to do.
- AHEAD: May push; the new relationship will be SAME.
- BEHIND: May pull; the new relationship will be SAME.
- TEXTUAL✗: May pull; will result in the "in conflict" state. May push; B will be in the "in conflict" state.
- BUILD✗: May pull and merge; will result in the "build failure" state. May push; B will be in the "build failure" state.
- TEST✗: May pull and merge; will result in the "test failure" state. May push; B will be in the "test failure" state.
- TEST✓: May pull and merge; the new relationship will be AHEAD. May push; B will be able to merge the changes cleanly.

The consequences of applying available actions can be tricky to understand and remember. One example is when the available actions are the same but the consequences differ. For example, the developer can cleanly pull in both the BEHIND and TEST✓ relationships. However, in the BEHIND case, the developer ends up in the SAME relationship, while in the TEST✓ case, the developer ends up in the AHEAD relationship. Another example is when there are side-effects of performing an operation intended to change the relationship between A and B, such as incorporating B's changes into A may put A and another repository C into a TEXTUAL✗ relationship. Using global version control information to help developers track such situations can be beneficial.

The local state also partially determines which version control operations can be executed in different situations.

If A's state is "uncommitted", then the "update" operation cannot be applied. If A's state is not "uncommitted", then the "commit" operation is inapplicable.

If A's state is "in conflict", then all operations except "merge" are discouraged. (DVCSes permit most operations at any moment, but discourage some of them, most commonly by aborting the operation unless the user supplies an extra confirmation flag.) If A's state is not "in conflict", then the "merge" operation is inapplicable. The "build failure" and "test failure" states do not limit the possible actions — VCSes are as yet unaware of such local states — although fixing these problems should likely be a priority. The "OK" state does not limit the possible actions.

5.3 Guidance

Information about how each action may affect the developer's state and relationships can help developers make better-informed decisions.

This section makes one common, generally realistic assumption: developers perform actions in a tree hierarchy, pushing only to and pulling only from a parent. This aligns with how developers predominantly interact with VCSes [31]. Further, we consider only information relevant to two developers who share a common parent repository (possibly that of one of the developers themselves), because in all other cases, the developers' relationship is dependent on actions by others.

We classify the guidance information into five types. One type of information concerns the relationship: *Committer*. The other four concern the possible action: *When*, *Consequences*, *Capable*, and *Ease*.

Committer: Who made the relevant changes?
Consider George and Ringo again, now working on a team with Paul. If George knows he is in the TEXTUAL✗ relationship with Ringo, George might decide to contact Ringo to discuss the situation. However, Ringo may not have made the conflicting changes; instead, Paul may have made and pushed the changes to the master, and Ringo then pulled them from the master. In this case, George should likely discuss the conflict with Paul rather than with Ringo. Knowing the committer facilitates communication between relevant parties, which in turn decreases the time required to fix conflicts [6].

When: Can an action that affects the relationship be performed now, or must it wait until later?
Ringo can be in the BEHIND relationship with George but may be unable to incorporate his changes because George may not have yet pushed them to the master. Thus, it may be helpful for Ringo to know that although he will need to pull at some point, he cannot get George's changes until George pushes. As another example, a developer may have to resolve an "in conflict" state before being allowed to push.

Consequences: Will an action — perhaps one on a different repository — affect a relationship?
The situation with Ringo BEHIND George illustrates this kind of guidance as well. Is Ringo BEHIND George because George has not yet pushed his changes to the master, or because George has pushed but Ringo has not yet pulled from the master? In the first case, even if Ringo pulls from the master, his relationship with George will not change. In the second case, if Ringo pulls, he will become SAME with George.

Capable: Who can perform an action that changes the relationship?
Consider a situation in which George is in the TEXTUAL✗ relationship with Ringo. If Ringo has already pushed his changes to the master, then George *must* be the one who resolves the conflict when he eventually pulls from the master. Conversely, if George has already pushed his changes, he *cannot* resolve the conflict any longer. And if neither has pushed, either of them *might* be the one to resolve the conflict.

Ease: Has anyone made changes that ease resolving an existing conflict?
Suppose George and Ringo created conflicting changes and Ringo has pushed his to the master. If George were to pull from the master, he would have to resolve the conflict. What if Ringo has made a set of follow-up changes that he has not yet pushed? If these changes resolve the conflict, then it is likely better for George to wait for Ringo to push his new changes. Ringo's pushing action would be the best way to resolve George's TEXTUAL✗ with the master.

By performing actions, developers can affect how long a conflict persists, or even prevent it from ever occurring. The guidance information can help developers decide which actions to perform. Knowing of a conflict relationship can encourage the developer to address it earlier, while the changes are fresh in the relevant developers' minds; this may reduce the conflict's duration as well as the effort necessary to resolve it. Knowing about BEHIND and TEST✓ relationships can reassure developers that it is safe to incorporate others' changes, which in turn keeps the development states closer together. In some cases, this may also allow the developer to prevent some potential conflicts altogether, which would also reduce conflict frequency. At a minimum, these relationships can prompt developers to communicate, which can reduce conflicts in the developers' mental models and work plans.

The *Committer* guidance informs the developers of who else is relevant to a conflict, reducing the time required to resolve it [6]. The *When* and *Capable* guidance can inform developers of the right time to perform an action, eliminating the overhead of manually figuring out if an action can be performed now and possibly having to undo actions later. The *Consequences* guidance can allow the developers a peek into the future, also limiting undoing and redoing of work. Finally, the *Ease* guidance can inform a developer if someone else may have an easier time resolving a conflict, thus helping reduce the effort needed to resolve it.

5.4 Examples of higher-order conflicts

Early identification of higher-order conflicts between developers reduces — or at the least is highly unlikely to increase — the time to resolve a conflict. We describe a TEST✗ and a BUILD✗ example from Voldemort.

Malformed non-code resource: On October 10, 2009, a developer successfully merged two branches ("tips" in Git), `50b74` and `00c35`. Branch `00c35` was edited 17 times while the branch was alive and the last changeset on this branch occurred only eight minutes before the merge. Branch `50b74` had not been edited in the previous 48 days. Although the patch between these two branches was very large (63,413 lines), Git successfully merged these changesets. Test `voldemort.store.http.HttpStoreTest::testBadPort()` did not fail either branch before the merge, but did in the merged system. Thus, some unintended behavioral interaction between the two branches' changes broke this test. In fact, the merge invalidated one of the metadata files, `cluster.xml`. In this case, if a tool had let the developers know that it was safe to merge earlier, the problem could have been avoided completely by sequentializing the changes to `cluster.xml` and/or by enabling earlier testing of the merged version.

Missing type: On November 9, 2009, a developer successfully merged branches `c77a4` and `7f776`. Branch `7f776` was edited 11 times while the branch was alive; branch `c77a4` was edited three times. Both branches had been modified within four days of the merge. While the merge had no textual conflicts, the code failed to build: four compilation errors resulted from referencing a missing type `ProtoBuffAdminClientRequestFormat`. Later, the developer merged in another branch (`68e3b`), which resolved the compilation problem.

In this case, a tool could have speculatively told the developer about the compilation error that would arise as the result of the merge. With this information, the developer may have chosen to do the merges in an alternate order, or manually, to avoid the problem and ensure other developers were not adversely affected.

6. Delivering version control advice

Given that version control conflicts are frequent and serious (Section 4) and that a global view of the VCS could detect conflicts and reduce their frequency and severity (Section 5), how can a tool effectively deliver that information and advice to developers?

The design of our tool, Crystal, has several ways to convey the key information without overwhelming or distracting the developer. (1) The main window *summarizes* all projects and relationships, allowing a developer to instantly scan it to identify situations that may require attention. (2) The main window is *compact* but *not needed* if the developer prefer to receive limited but critical information. (The main nor any other window is ever opened asynchronously.) (3) Full, detailed information about each relationship, action, and guidance is *available but hidden* until a developer shows specific interest in it.

Crystal uses (1) icons exploiting color and shape in stable locations in the main window (rather than, say, a textual list that a developer would have to read and interpret), (2) a taskbar icon in the system tray to report the most severe state for all tracked repositories, and (3) mouse-over tooltips that provide, on demand, all the information discussed in Section 5.

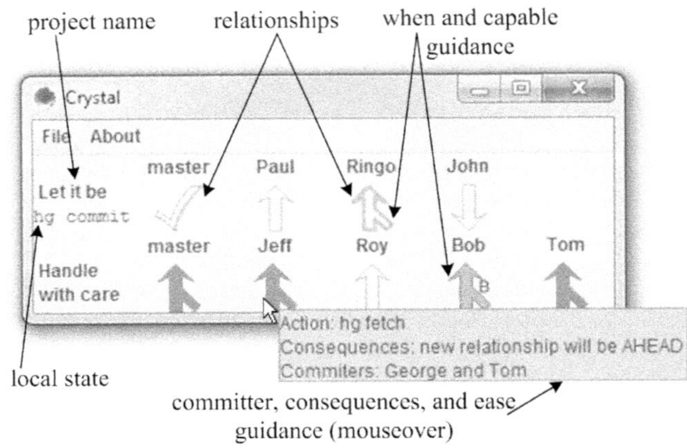

Figure 7: A screenshot of George's view of Crystal. George is following two projects under development: "Let it be" and "Handle with care". The former has four observed collaborators: George, Paul, Ringo, and John; the latter has five: George, Jeff, Roy, Bob, Tom. Crystal shows George's local state and his relationships with the master repository and the other collaborators, as well as guidance based on that information.

Crystal addresses scalability by allowing developers to select the repositories' relationships of interest. For example, a developer may be interested in the relationships with those in the same collaborative team and the main development repositories of the other teams. Crystal can provide information about relationships even with developers who are not using it, easing adoption by avoiding a requirement that the whole team uses the tool. Each developer can independently choose whether or not to run Crystal. Advantages accrue when more members of a team use Crystal, but this is not necessary.

Crystal allows developers to select a subset of the tests to execute, to integrate more smoothly into large development projects with extensive test suites. Naturally, for large projects with build scripts and test suites that take a long time to execute, Crystal will experience that latency. However, it would still identify relevant information sooner than other existing methods.

We have implemented our design in Crystal, a tool that performs speculative analysis of version control operations. Crystal currently works with the Mercurial DVCS; later versions of Crystal will support additional VCSes. Microsoft — in cooperation with us — is developing a version of Crystal. Crystal is an open-source, cross-platform, standalone tool and is available for download: `http://crystalvc.googlecode.com`. Our initial qualitative evaluation of Crystal is positive, but future work should evaluate it via both qualitative and quantitative user studies.

6.1 Crystal's UI

Figure 7 shows a screenshot of Crystal's main window. The window displays a row of icons (see Figure 8) for each of a developer's projects. In this example, there are two projects: "Let it be" and "Handle with care". The former has four collaborators: George (the developer running Crystal), Paul, Ringo, and John. The latter has five collaborators: George, Jeff, Roy, Bob, and Tom.

On the leftmost side of the row, underneath the project name, Crystal displays the local state. This tells George (in the native language of the underlying VCS) whether he must commit changes (`hg commit`, in Mercurial) or resolve a conflict. Then Crystal displays the relationship with the master and the collaborators' repositories.

If George has the ability to affect a relationship *now*, the icon is

SAME AHEAD BEHIND TEXTUAL✗ BUILD✗ TEST✗ TEST✓

Figure 8: Crystal associates an icon with each of the seven relationships. The color of each relationship icon represents the severity of the relationship (Section 3.2): relationships that require no merging are green, that can be merged automatically are yellow, and that require manual merging are red.

solid, which combines the *When* and *Capable* guidance. If George *cannot* affect the relationship, the icon is hollow. For example, consider John, who has made some changes in "Let it be" but has not yet pushed them to the master; George is BEHIND John, but the icon is hollow because George cannot affect this relationship until John pushes. Similarly, George's relationship with Ringo is a hollow TEST✓ because (1) George has the SAME relationship with the master, (2) Ringo had not pulled the latest changes from the master, and (3) Ringo has made some other changes, which he has not pushed but which can merge without human intervention. If the relationship is of the *might* variety — George might or might not have to perform an operation to affect the relationship — the icon is solid but slightly unsaturated (see the relationship with Bob in the "Handle with care" project).

These features allow George to quickly scan the Crystal window and identify the most urgent issues, the solid red icons, followed by other, less severe icons. George can also easily identify quickly whether there is something he can do now to improve his relationships (in the example, George can perform actions to improve his relationships in the "Handle with care" project, but not in "Let it be"), and whether there are unexpected conflicts George may wish to communicate with others about.

The most urgent relationship is displayed by Crystal as its system tray icon, which allows a developer to know at all times whether there is any action that requires attention without even having the Crystal window open.

Crystal also provides other guidance that is hidden unless a developer wants to see it. Holding the mouse pointer over an icon displays the action George can perform and the *Committer*, *Consequences*, and *Ease* guidance, when applicable. For example, when George holds the mouse over Jeff's TEXTUAL✗ icon, it tells him that he can perform a pull and a resolve (`hg fetch`, in Mercurial), that performing this action will resolve George's TEXTUAL✗ with Jeff, and that Tom and George committed the conflicting changesets.

Even though George asked for information about the relationship with Jeff, Crystal was able to correctly point George to Tom as the developer who was responsible for the conflicting changesets (which Jeff had pulled into his repository). In other situations, it is possible that George performing a pull and resolve operations with his parent would not resolve George's TEXTUAL✗ with Jeff (e.g., if Jeff and Tom had both created conflicting changesets but only Tom had pushed his changesets to the master). This is why the consequences guidance is important. As a final note, because no one else has merged these changesets, George must resolve this conflict and there is no *Ease* guidance for Crystal to display.

6.2 Initial experience

Crystal consists of 5,200 NCSL of Java and has been tested on Windows, Mac OS X, and several Linux distributions. The developer using Crystal must have read access to the collaborators' repositories; the Crystal manual (available at `http://crystalvc.googlecode.com`) describes several simple ways to accomplish this.

We deployed the beta-test version of the tool to a small number of developers and have been using it ourselves, and refining it, since early July 2010. One co-author uses Crystal to monitor 49 clones of 10 projects belonging to eight actively working collaborators.

Designing and deploying Crystal, along with frequent feedback from the handful of users, has helped us to better understand the issues and to improve the tool's design. Crystal user feedback enhanced our understanding of the need for guidance as well as which information is most pertinent to make available to the developer. For example, showing hollow and solid icons arose from a user's need to differentiate between relationships he or she could and could not affect. The feedback drove us to systematically explore the complete space, as described in Section 5.

Here is one example piece of feedback from an external user, via private communication:

> "Keeping a group of developers informed about the state of a code repository is a problem I have tried solving myself. My solution was an IRC bot that announced commits to an IRC channel where all of the developers on the project idled. This approach has many obvious problems. [...] The Crystal tool does not suffer from these problems. Crystal handles several projects and users effortlessly and presents the necessary information in a simple and understandable way, but it is only a start at filling this important void the in the world of version control."

Prior to developing Crystal, we surveyed 50 DVCS users about their collaborative development habits. Their use of highly heterogeneous operating systems, IDEs, VCSes, and languages informed Crystal's design. Even among this small group, there were vast differences in committing, pushing, and pulling styles, which further encouraged our research. We anticipate that future user studies will identify additional strengths and weaknesses that will allow us to further improve Crystal.

7. Related Work

This section places our research in the context of related work in evaluating the costs of conflicts, collaborative awareness, mining software repositories, and continuous development.

7.1 The cost of conflicts

Efficient coordination is important for effective software development. The number of defects rises as the amount of parallel work increases [23], but developers can more effectively manage risks to the consistency of their systems if they are aware of the consequences of their commits on other developers [11]. Developers eschew parallel work to avoid having to resolve conflicts when committing changes [13], or rush their work into the trunk to avoid being the developer who would have to resolve conflicts [8].

Several observational and laboratory experiments empirically assess the benefits of collaborative awareness for configuration management [3, 10, 30]. Augmenting these results, we performed a retrospective analysis on real projects to estimate the potential benefit. Our analysis is consistent with their studies in confirming the potential for better coordination of individual and team repositories.

Sarma provides a comprehensive classification of collaborative tools for software development [27]; in this classification, Crystal could be considered a seamless tool as it provides continuous awareness about development state and guidance about the consequences of potential future actions.

7.2 Collaborative awareness

The research most similar in intent to ours studies collaborative awareness — increasing awareness of the activities among team members. Such awareness can be a distraction unless a conflict is imminent, so awareness tools have adopted increasingly sophisticated methods for avoiding false positive warnings, as we now describe.

Palantír [29, 28, 1] shows which developers are changing which artifacts by how much. Palantír has similar motivations to ours: "providing workspace awareness to users will enable them to detect potential conflicts earlier, as they occur. Ideally developers can then proactively coordinate their actions to avoid those conflicts" [29, p. 444]. FASTDash [3] is similar: it is an interactive visualization — a spatial representation of which files each developer is editing — that augments existing software development tools with a specific focus on helping developers understand what other team members are doing.

Syde [15] reduces false positives via a fine-grained analysis of the abstract syntax trees (ASTs) modifications. Two potentially conflicting changes to the same file are flagged for a developer only when they also affect changes to the same parts of the underlying ASTs. For example, if two users have inserted, deleted, or changed the same method, the changes will be flagged "yellow"; if one of user had committed, the changes would instead be flagged "red", indicating that there may be a merge conflict. Syde examines files every time they are saved.

The most detailed analysis is done by tools like CollabVS and Safe-commit. CollabVS "detects a potential conflict when a user starts editing a program element that has a dependency on another program element that has been edited but not checked-in by another developer" [10]. Safe-commit [33] does the deepest program dependence analysis, identifying changes that are guaranteed not to cause tests to fail. This allows earlier publishing of some of a developer's changes, on the theory that increasing the publishing frequency can decrease the amount of duplicate development and the likelihood of merge conflicts.

Our approach suffers fewer false positives and fewer false negatives than previous awareness approaches [5] for several reasons. First, our approach computes actual pending conflicts rather than estimating potential ones. By speculatively doing exactly what a developer will actually do in the future — run a version control operation, then run the build script and, finally run the test script — our approach only reports problems that would actually happen while executing those steps. (A secondary benefit of using the underlying VCS directly is that users of Crystal can benefit immediately from any improvements to the VCS merging algorithm.) Second, Crystal does not report conflicts until they have been committed to some repository. This reduces false positives resulting from exploratory edits, such as for debugging: developers typically commit code that is consistent and is a candidate for sharing. This could delay delays Crystal's reports until a commit occurs, but commits tend to be frequent in a DVCS. Third, unlike most of the previous work, our approach aids developers in performing safe merges earlier, in addition to early isolation of conflicts. Fourth, also unlike most of the previous work, we consider and support multiple levels of conflicts — textual, build, and test.

7.3 Mining software repositories

Ball et al. [2] extracted metrics such as coupling — based on the probability that two classes are modified together — and used the metrics to assess the relationship between implementation decisions and the evolution of the resulting system. Later efforts mine version histories to determine functions that must likely be modified as a group [35], to identify common error patterns [19], to predict component failures [21], etc.

Our effort contrasts with these efforts in at least two dimensions. First, we are assessing a different property: opportunities to incorporate changes with others on a team. Second, the purpose of our mining was to determine whether building a tool like Crystal would be worthwhile. Other mining efforts generally aim to improve a team's software development process, such as by informing managers of a pattern so that they will allocate more quality assurance resources to more error-prone components.

7.4 Continuous development

Our approach can be characterized as continuous merging. Thus, it is related to a number of other approaches to continuous computation in the context of software development.

A programming environment, modeled on spreadsheets, can continuously execute the program as it is being developed [16, 18]. Modern programming environments focus instead on providing continuous compilation The environment maintains the project in a compiled state as it is edited, speeding software development in two ways. First, the developer receives rapid (and usually unobtrusive) feedback about compilation errors, allowing for quick correction while that code is fresh in the developer's mind. Second, the developer is freed from deciding when to compile, meaning that the developer is not distracted by the compilation task and that when it is time to run or test the code, no intervening compilation step is necessary.

Continuous testing [24, 25, 26, 12] applies the same idea to testing: it uses excess cycles on a developer's workstation to continuously run regression tests in the background. It is intended to reduce the time and energy required to keep code well-tested and prevent regression errors from persisting uncaught for long periods of time. The vision is that after every keystroke, the developer knows immediately (without taking any extra action) whether the change has broken the tests. Similar ideas are gaining traction in the development community.

Recent work has investigated supporting real-time integration to decrease developer's hesitation in committing changes using centralized version control [14]. Like FASTDash, this approach aims to help developers avoid conflicts but, in contrast to FASTDash and similarly to Crystal, it computes rather than predicts the presence of merge conflicts.

These continuous approaches are *reactive*, albeit very fast. In contrast, our notion of speculative VC relies instead on pre-computing (and perhaps presenting, depending on the user interface and user preferences) contingent information about VC operations *before* the programmer has even considered taking the associated speculative action.

8. Threats to validity

Our research, naturally, leaves open a set of potential concerns, which we present using the standard notions of threats to validity.

Construct.

The version control histories tell us when a TEXTUAL✘ or TEXTUAL✓ relationship first arose and when the developers resolved it. However, the histories do not tell us (1) when or how the developers found out about the relationship, (2) when the developers began trying to resolve the relationship, and (3) had the developers known about the relationship earlier, would they have done anything differently?

In addition, DVCS histories only contain information about incorporate operations from the TEXTUAL✓ and TEXTUAL✘ states; nothing is recorded when a developer pulls from the BEHIND state or pushes from the AHEAD state.

Internal.

Our experiments (Section 4) are in the context of DVCSes, which differ from CVCSes [7, 20, 22]. The effect of the VCS on developer behavior is not established: indeed, various researchers hypothesize the full spectrum — that a DVCS causes a developer to publish less often, more often, or the same amount as a CVCS. If DVCSes encourage more frequent branching and merging [32], that would provide additional opportunities for Crystal.

While our full retrospective analysis cannot be done on the histories of repositories built using existing CVCSes, we believe the data we find in DVCS projects is an approximation of what happens in development with CVCSes; the largely similar results to Zimmermann [34] justifies this belief.

External.

Another threat is that our retrospective study focused on nine open-source systems. The systems we selected may not be characteristic of other systems. Anecdotally, developers are all-but-universally worried about the problems that can arise from conflicts. The professional web (blogs, Q&A sites, etc.) is filled with examples of developers expressing this concern and suggesting ways to reduce it.

Usability and developer style.

While Crystal can answer important questions about the developers' relationships in a collaborative environment and aid those developers in making better-informed decisions, Crystal might also harm productivity by distracting developers or leading them to premature integration. To mitigate the issues of distraction, we have worked to reduce Crystal's intrusiveness. In particular, humans tend to be reasonably good at selecting which information to ignore, and we have designed Crystal to be consistent with that ability. Some developers may prefer to use the full Crystal view, while others may prefer the system-tray view most of the time. And a developer who is "heads-down" can simply quit Crystal for a while, just as many developers choose to, at times, ignore their email.

One challenge to Crystal's adoption may be that developers may fail to see its utility. One developer who attempted to use Crystal reported that he simply was not interested in seeing conflicts with unpublished changes and that he rarely experienced conflicts with others in his development. While he saw no harm to running Crystal, he anticipated it would provide him no benefit either. Crystal, indeed, may well not be appropriate for all classes of developers. Nonetheless, the data in Section 4 show that conflicts are common, not rare, suggesting strongly that most developers may well benefit from Crystal, regardless of their intuitions. We plan to test this hypothesis as part of a future user study.

Furthermore, conflicts are not the only reason to use Crystal. The developer who declined to use Crystal ended up doing redundant work. He noticed a problem and fixed it — but another developer had already made the same fix, and pushed it, six days earlier. The non-Crystal-user had forgotten to pull changes before beginning to work on the problem. Crystal would have reminded the user that he could pull changes, and had he followed Crystal's advice, he would have avoided the wasted effort of the duplicated bug fix.

9. Conclusions

Speculative analysis over version control operations provides precise information about pending conflicts between collaborating team members. These pending conflicts — including textual, build, and test — are guaranteed to occur (unless a developer modifies a committed change). Learning about them earlier allows developers to make better-informed decisions about how to proceed, whether it be to perform a safe merge, to publish a safe change, to quickly address a new conflict, to interact with another developer etc.

Our retrospective, quantitative study of over 550,000 development versions of nine open-source systems, spanning 3.4 million distinct (and a total of over 500 billion, over all versions) NCSL, confirms that (1) conflicts are the norm rather than the exception, (2) that 16% of all merges required human effort to resolve textual conflicts, (3) that 33% of merges that were reported to contain no textual conflicts by the VCS in fact contained higher-order conflicts, and (4) that conflicts persist, on average, for 10 days (with a median conflict persisting 1.6 days). Although there is a significant amount of qualitative and anecdotal evidence consistent with our findings, the only previous quantitative research we could find was Zimmermann's [34]. We expand on his work in several dimensions, including (1) comparing actual merges from project histories to merges that could have taken place successfully earlier than they did, and (2) considering not only textual conflicts but also higher-order conflicts, such as build and test conflicts.

Our speculative analysis tool, Crystal, provides concrete information and advice about pending conflicts while remaining largely unobtrusive. Our evaluation of Crystal is preliminary and qualitative; future work should evaluate it via both qualitative and quantitative user studies.

Collaborative development is essential but troublesome. Making pertinent and precise information available to developers, allowing them to identify and fix conflicts before they fester, is one useful and practical step in reducing some of the costs and difficulties of collaborative software development.

Acknowledgments

The Crystal beta users provided valuable feedback. This material is based upon work supported by the National Science Foundation under Grants CNS-0937060 to the Computing Research Association for the CIFellows Project and CCF-0963757, by a National Science and Engineering Research Council Postdoctoral Fellowship, and by Microsoft Research through a Software Engineering Innovation Foundation grant.

References

[1] Ban Al-Ani, Erik Trainer, Roger Ripley, Anita Sarma, André van der Hoek, and David Redmiles. Continuous coordination within the context of cooperative and human aspects of software engineering. In *CHASE*, pages 1–4, Leipzig, Germany, May 2008.

[2] Thomas Ball, Jung-Min Kim, Adam A. Porter, and Harvey P. Siy. If your version control system could talk... In *PMESSE*, Boston, MA, USA, May 1997.

[3] Jacob T. Biehl, Mary Czerwinski, Greg Smith, and George G. Robertson. FASTDash: A visual dashboard for fostering awareness in software teams. In *CHI*, pages 1313–1322, San Jose, CA, USA, Apr. 2007.

[4] Yuriy Brun, Reid Holmes, Michael D. Ernst, and David Notkin. Speculative analysis: Exploring future states of software. In *FoSER*, pages 59–63, Santa Fe, NM, USA, Nov. 2010.

[5] Yuriy Brun, Reid Holmes, Michael D. Ernst, and David Notkin. Crystal: Precise and unobtrusive conflict warnings. In *ESEC FSE Tool Demo*, Szeged, Hungary, Sep. 2011.

[6] Marcelo Cataldo, Patrick A. Wagstrom, James D. Herbsleb, and Kathleen M. Carley. Identification of coordination requirements: Implications for the design of collaboration and awareness tools. In *CSCW*, pages 353–362, Banff, AB, Canada, Nov. 2006.

[7] Reidar Conradi and Bernhard Westfechtel. Version models for software configuration management. *ACM Comput. Surv.*, 30(2):232–282, 1998.

[8] Cleidson R. B. de Souza, David Redmiles, and Paul Dourish. "Breaking the code", Moving between private and public work in collaborative software development. In *GROUP*, pages 105–114, Sanibel Island, FL, USA, Nov. 2003.

[9] Prasun Dewan. Dimensions of tools for detecting software conflicts. In *RSSE*, pages 21–25, Atlanta, GA, USA, Nov. 2008.

[10] Prasun Dewan and Rajesh Hegde. Semi-synchronous conflict detection and resolution in asynchronous software development. In *ECSCW*, pages 159–178, Limerick, Ireland, Sep. 2007.

[11] Jacky Estublier and Sergio Garcia. Process model and awareness in SCM. In *SCM*, pages 59–74, Oxford, England, UK, Sep. 2005.

[12] David Samuel Glasser. Test factoring with `amock`: Generating readable unit tests from system tests. Master's thesis, MIT Dept. of EECS, Aug. 21, 2007.

[13] Rebecca E. Grinter. Using a configuration management tool to coordinate software development. In *CoOCS*, pages 168–177, Milpitas, CA, USA, Aug. 1995.

[14] Mário Luís Guimarães and António Rito-Silva. Towards real-time integration. In *CHASE*, pages 56–63, Cape Town, South Africa, May 2010.

[15] Lile Hattori and Michele Lanza. Syde: A tool for collaborative software development. In *ICSE Tool Demo*, pages 235–238, Cape Town, South Africa, May 2010.

[16] Peter Henderson and Mark Weiser. Continuous execution: The VisiProg environment. In *ICSE*, pages 68–74, London, England, UK, Aug. 1985.

[17] Susan Horwitz, Jan Prins, and Thomas Reps. Integrating non-interfering versions of programs. *ACM TOPLAS*, 11:345–387, July 1989.

[18] R. R. Karinthi and M. Weiser. Incremental re-execution of programs. In *SIIT*, pages 38–44, St. Paul, MN, USA, June 1987.

[19] Benjamin Livshits and Thomas Zimmermann. DynaMine: Finding common error patterns by mining software revision histories. In *ESEC FSE*, pages 296–305, Lisbon, Portugal, Sep. 2005.

[20] Tom Mens. A state-of-the-art survey on software merging. *IEEE TSE*, 28(5):449–462, 2002.

[21] Nachiappan Nagappan, Thomas Ball, and Andreas Zeller. Mining metrics to predict component failures. In *ICSE*, pages 452–461, Shanghai, China, 2006.

[22] Bryan O'Sullivan. Making sense of revision-control systems. *Queue*, 7(7):30–40, 2009.

[23] Dewayne E. Perry, Harvey P. Siy, and Lawrence G. Votta. Parallel changes in large-scale software development: an observational case study. *ACM TOSEM*, 10:308–337, July 2001.

[24] David Saff and Michael D. Ernst. Reducing wasted development time via continuous testing. In *ISSRE*, pages 281–292, Denver, CO, USA, Nov. 2003.

[25] David Saff and Michael D. Ernst. Continuous testing in Eclipse. In *2nd Eclipse Technology Exchange Workshop (eTX)*, Barcelona, Spain, Mar. 2004.

[26] David Saff and Michael D. Ernst. An experimental evaluation of continuous testing during development. In *ISSTA*, pages 76–85, Boston, MA, USA, July 2004.

[27] Anita Sarma. A survey of collaborative tools in software development. Technical Report UCI-ISR-05-3, University of California, Irvine, Institute for Software Research, 2005.

[28] Anita Sarma, Gerald Bortis, and André van der Hoek. Towards supporting awareness of indirect conflicts across software configuration management workspaces. In *ASE*, pages 94–103, Atlanta, GA, USA, Nov. 2007.

[29] Anita Sarma, Zahra Noroozi, and André van der Hoek. Palantír: raising awareness among configuration management workspaces. In *ICSE*, pages 444–454, Portland, OR, May 2003.

[30] Anita Sarma, David Redmiles, and André van der Hoek. Empirical evidence of the benefits of workspace awareness in software configuration management. In *FSE*, pages 113–123, Atlanta, GA, USA, Nov. 2008.

[31] Chuck Walrad and Darrel Strom. The importance of branching models in SCM. *Computer*, 35(9):31–38, 2002.

[32] Chuck Walrad and Darrel Strom. The importance of branching models in SCM. *Computer*, 35(9):31–38, Sep. 2002.

[33] Jan Wloka, Barbara Ryder, Frank Tip, and Xiaoxia Ren. Safe-commit analysis to facilitate team software development. In *ICSE*, pages 507–517, Vancouver, BC, Canada, May 2009.

[34] Thomas Zimmermann. Mining workspace updates in CVS. In *MSR*, Minneapolis, MN, USA, May 2007.

[35] Thomas Zimmermann, Peter Weißgerber, Stephan Diehl, and Andreas Zeller. Mining version histories to guide software changes. In *ICSE*, pages 563–572, Edinburgh, Scotland, UK, 2004.

ADDiff: Semantic Differencing for Activity Diagrams *

Shahar Maoz, Jan Oliver Ringert, Bernhard Rumpe
Software Engineering
RWTH Aachen University, Germany
http://www.se-rwth.de/

ABSTRACT

Activity diagrams (ADs) have recently become widely used in the modeling of workflows, business processes, and web-services, where they serve various purposes, from documentation, requirement definitions, and test case specifications, to simulation and code generation. As models, programs, and systems evolve over time, understanding changes and their impact is an important challenge, which has attracted much research efforts in recent years.

In this paper we present *addiff*, a semantic differencing operator for ADs. Unlike most existing approaches to model comparison, which compare the concrete or the abstract syntax of two given diagrams and output a list of syntactical changes or edit operations, *addiff* considers the *semantics* of the diagrams at hand and outputs a set of *diff witnesses*, each of which is an execution trace that is possible in the first AD and is not possible in the second. We motivate the use of *addiff*, formally define it, and show two algorithms to compute it, a concrete forward-search algorithm and a symbolic fixpoint algorithm, implemented using BDDs and integrated into the Eclipse IDE. Empirical results and examples demonstrate the feasibility and unique contribution of *addiff* to the state-of-the-art in version comparison and evolution analysis.

Categories and Subject Descriptors

D.2.2 [**Software Engineering**]: Design Tools and Techniques; D.2.4 [**Software Engineering**]: Software/Program Verification

General Terms

Documentation, Verification

*S. Maoz acknowledges support from a postdoctoral Minerva Fellowship, funded by the German Federal Ministry for Education and Research. J.O. Ringert is supported by the DFG GK/1298 AlgoSyn.

Permission to make digital or hard copies of all or part of this work for personal or classroom use is granted without fee provided that copies are not made or distributed for profit or commercial advantage and that copies bear this notice and the full citation on the first page. To copy otherwise, to republish, to post on servers or to redistribute to lists, requires prior specific permission and/or a fee.
ESEC/FSE'11, September 5–9, 2011, Szeged, Hungary.
Copyright 2011 ACM 978-1-4503-0443-6/11/09 ...$10.00.

Keywords

software evolution, activity diagrams, differencing

1. INTRODUCTION

Activity diagrams (ADs) have recently become widely used in the modeling of workflows, business processes, and web-services, where they serve various purposes, from documentation, requirement definitions, and test case specifications, to simulation and code generation. Specifically, we are interested in a variant of the standard UML 2 ADs, which is rich and expressive, supporting guarded branches, parallel (interleaving) process executions, inputs, assignments, etc.

As models, programs, and systems evolve over time, during the development lifecycle and beyond it, effective change management and controlled evolution are major challenges in software development, and thus have attracted much research efforts in recent years (see, e.g., [1, 2, 6, 11, 14, 21, 23, 32]). Fundamental building blocks for tracking the evolution of software artifacts are diff operators one can use to compare two versions of a program or a model. Most existing approaches to differencing concentrate on matching between model elements using different heuristics related to their names and structure and on finding and presenting differences at a concrete or abstract syntactic level. While showing some success, most of these approaches are also limited. Models that are syntactically very similar may induce very different semantics (in the sense of 'meaning' [10]), and vice versa, models that semantically describe the same system may have rather different syntactic representations. Thus, a list of syntactic differences, although accurate, correct, and complete, may not be able to reveal the real implications these differences may have on the correctness and potential use of the models involved. In other words, such a list, although easy to follow, understand, and manipulate (e.g., for merging), may not be able to expose and represent the semantic differences between two versions of a model, in terms of the bugs that were fixed or the features (and new bugs...) that were added.

In this paper we present *addiff*, a semantic diff operator for ADs. Unlike existing differencing approaches, *addiff* is a *semantic diff operator*. Rather than comparing the concrete or the abstract syntax of two given diagrams, and outputing a list of syntactical changes or edit operations, *addiff* considers the semantics of the diagrams at hand and outputs a set of *diff witnesses*, each of which is an execution trace that is possible in the first AD and is not possible in the second. These traces provide concrete proofs for the meaning of the change that has been done between the two compared versions and for its effect on the use of the models at hand.

We specify ADs using a variant of standard UML 2 ADs [24], which can also be given textually using a grammar defined in MontiCore [13, 22]. The syntax of an AD consists of action nodes, pseudo nodes (initial, final, decision, merge, fork, join), transitions, input variables, and local variables. Transitions outgoing decision nodes are guarded with Boolean expressions over the input and local variables. Input variables values are set by the environment. Action nodes are labeled with action names and may include assignments to local variables.

We define the operational semantics of an AD using a translation to a finite automaton with variables over finite domains. This induces a trace-based semantics, i.e., a set of action traces from an initial node to a final node, considering also the values of input variables. Branches outgoing fork nodes describe parallel executions; they are used to succinctly specify concurrent interleaving traces. An overview of the syntax and semantics of our ADs is given in Sect. 3.

Given two ADs, ad_1 and ad_2, $addiff(ad_1, ad_2)$ is roughly defined as the set of execution traces possible in the first AD and not possible in the second. As there may be exponentially many diff traces, we are specifically interested in the shortest ones, i.e., ones that do not have a prefix which is a differentiating trace. In addition, we restrict the operator to provide only a single shortest diff trace for each possible assignment to input variables. To compute *addiff* we transform each of the ADs into a module in SMV, the input language of the SMV model checker [29]. We then present two algorithms: a concrete forward-search algorithm and a symbolic fixpoint algorithm. The second algorithm relies on the technologies of symbolic model checking [3] in order to address the state explosion problem of the first. We present them both in order to allow their comparison. The formal definition of *addiff* and the two algorithms are described in Sect. 4.

We have implemented the two algorithms for *addiff* using binary decision diagrams (BDDs), and integrated them into an Eclipse plug-in. The plug-in allows the engineer to compare two selected ADs, to check if they are equivalent, and to textually and visually browse the diff witnesses found, if any. We describe the plug-in implementation in Sect. 5. We have evaluated the plug-in against all examples shown in this paper and many other ADs. The results of our evaluation, including a performance comparison of the two algorithms, appear in Sect. 6.

In addition to finding concrete diff witnesses (if any exist), which demonstrate the meaning of the changes that were made between one version and another, *addiff* can be used to compare two ADs and decide whether one AD semantics includes the other AD semantics (the latter is a refinement of the former), are they semantically equivalent, or are they semantically incomparable (each allows executions that the other does not allow). When applied to the version history of a certain AD, as can be retrieved from a version repository, such an analysis provides a semantic insight into its evolution, which is not available in existing syntactic approaches.

Model and program differencing, in the context of software evolution, has attracted much research efforts in recent years. In contrast to our work, however, most studies in this area present syntactic differencing, at either the concrete or the abstract syntax level. We discuss related work in Sect. 7.

Finally, our work on semantic differencing does not come to replace existing syntactic differencing approaches. Rather, it is aimed at augmenting and complementing existing approaches with capabilities that were not available before. We discuss the combination of syntactic and semantic differencing as well as other future work directions in Sect. 6.

The next section presents motivating examples demonstrating the unique features of our work. Sect. 3 provides preliminary definitions of the AD language syntax and semantics as used in our work. Sect. 4 introduces *addiff* and the two algorithms to compute it. Sect. 5 presents the implementation, Sect. 6 presents an evaluation and a discussion, Sect. 7 considers related work, and Sect. 8 concludes.

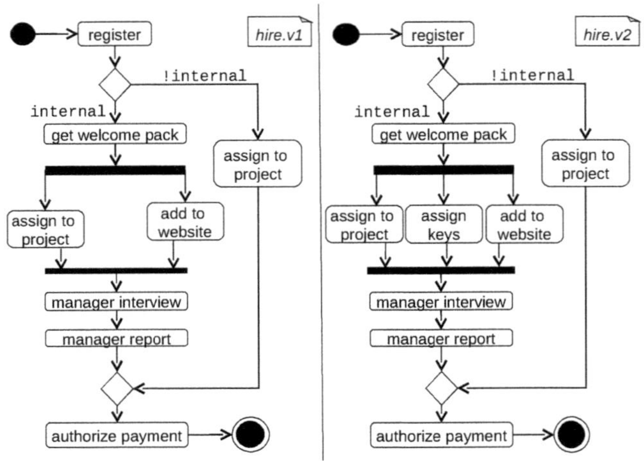

Figure 1: Versions 1 and 2 of the hire activity

2. EXAMPLES

We start off with motivating examples for semantic differencing of ADs. The examples are inspired by real-world ADs we have obtained from several sources (see Sect. 6).

2.1 Example I

AD *hire.v1* of Fig. 1 describes a company's workflow when hiring a new employee. Roughly, first the employee is registered. Then, if she is an internal employee, she gets a welcome package, she is assigned to a project and added to the company's computer system (in two parallel activities branching off a fork node), she is interviewed and gets a manager report, and finally her payments are authorized. Otherwise (note the decision node at the beginning of the AD), if the new employee is external, she is only assigned to a project before her payments are authorized.

After some time, the company deployed a new security system and every employee had to receive a key card. A revised workflow was created, as shown in *hire.v2* of Fig. 1.

Later, a problem was found: sometimes employees are assigned to a project but cannot enter the building since they do not have a key card yet. This bug was fixed in the next version, *hire.v3*, shown in Fig. 2. Finally, the company has decided that external employees should report to managers too. Thus, the merge between the two branches for internal and external new employees has moved 'up', in between the

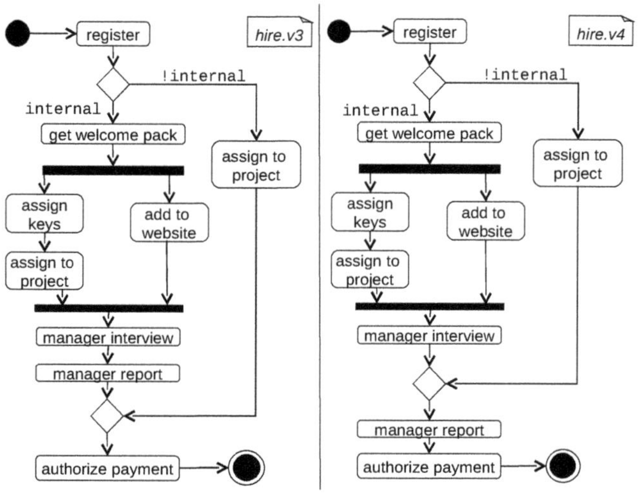

Figure 2: Versions 3 and 4 of the hire activity

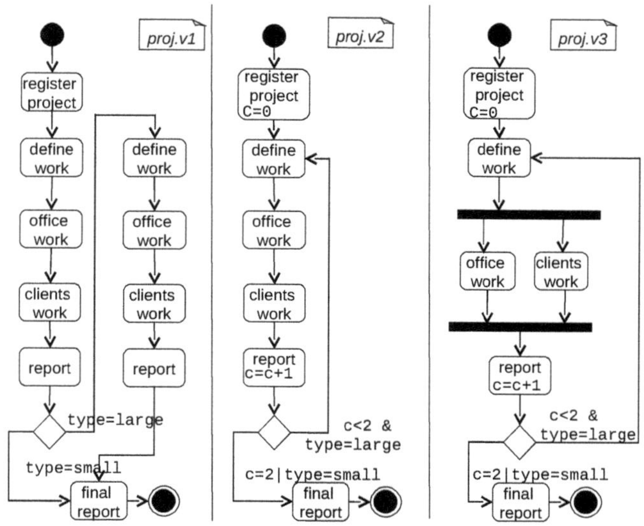

Figure 3: Versions 1-3 of the new project activity

interview and the report nodes. The resulting 4th version of the workflow, $hire.v4$, is shown in Fig. 2

Given these four versions of the activity, an evolution analysis is called for. Comparing $hire.v1$ and $hire.v2$ using *addiff* reveals that they are semantically incomparable: some executions of $hire.v1$ are no longer possible in $hire.v2$, and some executions of $hire.v2$ were not possible in $hire.v1$. Moreover, it reveals that handling of internal employees has changed, but handling of external ones remained the same between the two versions.

Comparing $hire.v2$ and $hire.v3$ reveals that the latter is a refinement of the former: $hire.v3$ has removed some traces of $hire.v2$ and did not allow new traces. In particular, *addiff*$(hire.v2, hire.v3)$ shows that the trace where a person is assigned to a project before she gets a key card was possible in $hire.v2$ and is no longer possible in $hire.v3$, i.e., it demonstrates that the bug was fixed.

Finally, comparing $hire.v3$ and $hire.v4$ using *addiff* reveals that although hiring of external employees has changed between the two versions, hiring of internal employees did not: *addiff*$(hire.v3, hire.v4)$ contains a single trace, where the employee is external, not internal. That is despite the syntactic change of moving the merge node from after to before the report node, which is also part of the trace of handling internal employees.

2.2 Example II

AD $proj.v1$ of Fig. 3 describes a company's workflow when receiving a new project. Roughly, first the project is registered. Then, the required work is defined, the office work is done, the clients work is done, and a report is written. If the project is of type small, the activity continues to final report and is completed. If the project is of type large, a second phase of the required work is defined, the office work is done, the clients work is done, and a report is written, before continuing to the final report and completion.

After some time, the activity designer suggested a refactoring: instead of the explicit duplication of the four work actions in the diagram, a loop will be defined. The designer added a local variable c, which is initialized when the project is registered and is incremented when writing the report. The guards of the decision node were changed accordingly. The resulting AD is $proj.v2$, shown in the same figure.

Before committing the new activity to the models repository, the designer used *addiff* to compare $proj.v1$ and $proj.v2$. Indeed, she found that *addiff*$(proj.v1, proj.v2) =$ *addiff*$(proj.v2, proj.v1) = \emptyset$. This proves that the refactoring did not change the semantics of the activity and the new version can be safely committed to the repository.

Finally, a consultant has examined the new project activity and suggested that in some cases, clients work can be done before the office work. Following this recommendation, the designer added fork and join nodes to the activity, to define the office work action and the clients work action on separate branches of a fork. The resulting AD is $proj.v3$, shown in the same figure.

Comparing $proj.v2$ and $proj.v3$ using *addiff* revealed that the new version has introduced several new traces that were not possible before: traces where clients work is done before office work (in the first or in the second iteration of the loop). Thus, the comparison demonstrated that the required enhancement was added. Moreover, the comparison showed that all traces of $proj.v2$ are still possible in $proj.v3$ (because *addiff*$(proj.v2, proj.v3) = \emptyset$). Thus, it proved that no behavior was lost.

The above examples are simple and thus immediately reveal the differences when looking at them. We use them in order to demonstrate our ideas. However, we have also done experiments with larger, synthetic and real-world AD's, where differences were manually much harder to find. See Sect. 6.

3. PRELIMINARIES

We define the AD language syntax and semantics as used in our work.

3.1 AD Language Syntax

An Activity Diagram is a structure $AD = \langle A, V^{inp}, V^{loc}, AN, PN, T\rangle$ where:

- A is a set of action names.

- V^{inp} is a (possibly empty) set of immutable input variables over finite domains.
- V^{loc} is a (possibly empty) set of local variables over finite domains.
- AN is a set of action nodes $an_1, \ldots, an_k$. Each action node an is labeled with an action name $acname(an) = ac \in A$, and a (possibly empty) set of assignment expressions to the variables in V^{loc}.
- PN is a set of pseudo nodes, consisting of initial nodes PN^{init}, final nodes PN^{fin}, decision nodes PM^{dec}, merge nodes PN^{mer}, fork nodes PN^{fork}, and join nodes PN^{join}.
- T is a set of transitions of the form $t = \langle n_{src}, n_{trg}, guard \rangle$ where $n_{src}, n_{trg} \in (AN \cup PN)$ and $guard$ is a Boolean expression over the variables in $V^{inp} \cup V^{loc}$. Unless n_{src} is a decision node, $guard = \texttt{true}$.

We do not formally capture here obvious well-formedness rules and context conditions such as: initial nodes have no incoming transitions, final nodes have no outgoing transitions, fork nodes must be followed by join nodes to remove all concurrency when reaching a final node, actions should not repeat in different forked branches, etc.

In addition, we assume that the Boolean expressions used as guards on transitions outgoing decision nodes are semantically exclusive, that is, no assignment to the diagram variables makes more than one of them true. Thus, the input variables provide external non-determinism, while except for forked branches, our ADs are internally deterministic.

We consider two concrete syntax definitions for ADs: a concrete visual syntax based on UML 2 ADs and a concrete textual syntax defined using MontiCore [13, 22]. We omit the concrete syntax definitions from this paper.

The implementation we present in Sect. 5 supports a subset of full UML 2 ADs: it supports action nodes and pseudo nodes: initial, final, fork, join, decision and merge; each AD has exactly one initial node but may have multiple final nodes. For simplicity reasons but without loss of generality, in our implementation no two pseudo nodes can follow each other directly. In addition, local and input variables have to be declared as such in the first action node; all variables' finite domains need to be given as SMV types or enumerations; and each local variable needs to be assigned a value in the first action node. We support Boolean guards specified in the rich SMV expression language [4]. Assignments to local variables can be made from any action node using values from SMV expressions.

3.2 AD Language Semantics

We distinguish operational semantics and trace-based semantics. The operational semantics is based on the definition of a state machine step, taking the AD from one state to another, where a state consists of a set of current action nodes and an assignment to all input and local variables.

The main idea of our operational semantics is to conceptually translate each $ad \in AD$ into a finite state machine (FSM). Each state is a configuration containing the values of all local variables and input variables (recall that variables range over finite domains), the executed action, and some extra variables with information on the control flow of the AD. Based on this state and evaluated guards possible transitions are computed that lead to the next state with an executed action, possibly changed local variables values, and a new configuration of the control flow tracking variables.

We formally define the operational semantics using a transformation of an AD to a module of SMV, the language of the SMV model checker [20, 29]. Our translation is inspired by the work of [7], but extends this previous translation with support for data. The complete translation, together with a detailed example, appears in a separate document [17].

Local variables assist the AD engineer together with guards to control the execution sequences of actions, e.g., by defining loops or activating/disabling branches of decision nodes. Input variables, in contrast to local variables, are initialized by the environment and do not change during the run of an AD. The runs of two ADs are compared with the same input, i.e., where common input variables of both ADs have the same values. We consider all possible input values of both ADs when comparing them.

Our semantics of ADs is rather expressive: it considers values of input variables to be set by the environment (external non-determinism). However, we only support internal non-determinism through interleaved execution of forked branches, and not through non-deterministic decision nodes; the current configuration and the next executed action determine the next configuration. Thus, for each assignment to the input variables there could be many possible executions due to the interleaving semantics of fork nodes.

We define a trace-based semantics that is induced by the operational semantics. Traces are sequences of states from the state space of the AD's FSM.

Definition 1 (AD state). *A state of an AD ad is an assignment to all variables defined in the* `VAR` *section of its SMV module. This includes the last executed node* `acnode` *and its action name* `ac`*, the values of variables $v \in ad.V^{inp} \cup ad.V^{loc}$ and the values of control flow tracking variables.*

AD states have a finite number of possible successor states that can be reached within one step. By construction, each such step executes an action or reaches a final node. We define the successors of an AD state s as $successors(s)$.

Definition 2 (Successor states). *For every AD state s, $successors(s)$ is the set of AD states reachable from s in one step of the SMV module.*

Each run of an AD starts with an initial state in the initial node. A sequence of successor states that describe a legal execution of the AD's FSM is a trace. A trace from the initial to a final node of the AD is an accepting trace.

Definition 3 (AD traces). *A sequence of AD states $tr = s_0, s_1, \ldots, s_k$ of AD ad with $s_{i+1} \in successors(s_i)$ and $s_0.acnode \in ad.PN^{init}$ is called a trace. The set of all traces of an AD ad is denoted by $traces(ad)$. A trace is called an accepted trace if its last state's node is a final node of the AD. The set of all accepted traces of an AD ad is denoted by $acceptedTraces(ad)$.*

4. ADDIFF

4.1 Definitions

Given two AD states, $s_1 \in ad_1$ and $s_2 \in ad_2$, we say that s_1 and s_2 are *corresponding*, iff the action names and values of equally named input variables of the two states are the same. Formally:

DEFINITION 4 (CORRESPONDING STATES). *Given two ADs, ad_1 and ad_2, and two states $s_1 \in ad_1$ and $s_2 \in ad_2$, we say that s_1 and s_2 are corresponding, denoted $s_1 \sim s_2$, iff the following conditions hold:*

1. $s_1.ac = s_2.ac$;
2. $\forall v \in V_1^{inp} \cap V_2^{inp}$, $s_1.val(v) = s_2.val(v)$.

The definition of corresponding states punctually extends to traces in a natural way.

Given two ADs, a trace of the first AD is a *diff trace* iff there exists a trace of the second AD where all states except the last correspond to the states of the first trace, but the last state of the first trace does not correspond to any possible successor state of the second trace. Formally:

DEFINITION 5 (DIFF TRACE). *Given two ADs, ad_1 and ad_2, a diff trace is a sequence of states $tr_1 = s_1^0, s_1^1, \ldots, s_1^k, s_1^{k+1}$ s.t.*

1. $tr_1 \in traces(ad_1)$
2. $\exists tr_2 = s_2^0, s_2^1, \ldots, s_2^k$ *s.t.* $tr_2 \in traces(ad_2)$
   $\wedge \forall i, 0 \leq i \leq k, s_1^i \sim s_2^i$
   $\wedge \nexists s_2^{k+1}$ *s.t.* $s_2^{k+1} \sim s_1^{k+1} \wedge s_2^0, s_2^1, \ldots, s_2^k, s_2^{k+1} \in traces(ad_2)$.

tr_2 is called a corresponding diff trace of tr_1.

We denote the set of all diff traces of ad_1 vs. ad_2 by *diffTraces*(ad_1, ad_2). Note that *diffTraces* is not symmetric.

We are now ready to present the definition of *addiff*. Note that we are interested only in shortest diff traces: we restrict *addiff* to diff traces that do not have another diff trace as prefix. Moreover, to make the set *addiff* succinct, for each initial state of ad_1, if there is a diff trace that starts at this initial state, we want only one such trace to be in *addiff*. Formally:

DEFINITION 6 (ADDIFF). *addiff(ad_1, ad_2) is a subset of diffTraces(ad_1, ad_2) s.t.*

1. $\forall tr \in addiff(ad_1, ad_2), \nexists tr'$ *s.t.* $tr' \in addiff(ad_1, ad_2) \wedge tr' \sqsubset tr$;
2. $\forall s_1^0 \in ad_1.initials$,
   if $\exists tr \in diffTraces(ad_1, ad_2)$ *s.t.* tr *starts at* s_1^0
   then $|\{tr \in addiff(ad_1, ad_2) | tr \text{ starts at } s_1^0\}| = 1$.

Finally, note that we do *not* require that diff traces can be extended into accepting traces (ones that end at a final node, see Def. 3). For an alternative definition, see the discussion in Sect. 6.

4.2 Computing ADDiff

We present two different algorithms, a concrete forward-search algorithm and a symbolic fixpoint algorithm.

4.2.1 Algorithm I

We compute *addiff*(ad_1, ad_2) using a BFS-like traversal of the state space of ad_1 that is used to 'guide' a BFS-like traversal of the state space of ad_2. Roughly, the algorithm uses a queue for corresponding states-pairs that have been reached but whose successors have not yet been traversed (the use of the queue guarantees that shortest paths will be found first). It also maintains a list of visited corresponding state-pairs and a list of rejecting state-pairs. Initially, all corresponding initial states-pairs are inserted in the queue, and all initial states of ad_1 that do not have a corresponding initial state in ad_2 are added to the list of rejecting state-pairs. Then, for each state-pair taken out from the queue, the algorithm checks that each successor state of the first element in the state-pair (the state in ad_1), has a corresponding successor state of the second element in the state-pair (the state in ad_2). Every corresponding pair found, if not visited before, is inserted to the queue. If no corresponding successor is found, we know we have found the end state of a (shortest) diff trace: we add it to the list of rejecting state-pairs and we remove from the queue all the state-pairs whose input variables values for ad_1 are the same as the ones for the state we have found. When the queue is empty, the list of visited state-pairs is used to construct the traces leading back from the rejecting state-pairs to the initial states.

A pseudo-code for the algorithm is given in Proc. 1, which uses Proc. 2 and 3. We describe these procedures below.

The algorithm uses a structure *Pair* made of two pairs of states: predecessor and current state in ad_1, pre_1 and cur_1, and predecessor and current state in ad_2, pre_2 and cur_2. Two pairs are considered equal if their current states are equal (ignoring predecessor states). *Pair* is used to keep track of pairs of visited states, one state from each AD, and of their predecessors, as found during the traversal of the state space. The predecessors are used in the reconstruction of the traces from the lists of rejecting and visited pairs.

Proc. 1 defines the required structures (l. 1-3): a queue of pairs, a list of visited pairs, a list of rejecting pairs, and a list of list of pairs, which will hold the computed diff traces. It iterates over all initial states of ad_1, and for each of them, looks for a corresponding initial state in ad_2. If a corresponding state is found, the new pair is inserted to the queue and to the visited list (l. 8). If no corresponding state is found, a pair where only the ad_1 current state is defined is added to the list of rejecting state pairs (l. 13).

After initialization, the algorithm calls *traverse* (Proc. 2), to iterate on the queue until it is empty. For each dequeued pair, the procedure iterates over all the successors of its current ad_1 state. For each successor, it tries to find a corresponding successor of the current ad_2 state. If a corresponding state is found, the new pair is inserted to the queue and to the visited list (l. 9). If no corresponding state is found, a pair where only the ad_1 current state is defined is added to the list of rejecting states (l. 15). In addition, all state-pairs whose current ad_1 state agrees with the current ad_1 state in the rejecting pair on input variables, are removed from the queue (l. 16-17). This ensures that no further searching of diff traces outgoing the same initial state will be done.

Finally, *trace* (Proc. 3) is used to reconstruct the traces leading from initial states to the rejecting states that have been found. The procedure works backward: it starts from the rejecting pairs and uses the predecessor states to build the required traces, from the rejecting states back to the initial states, using the pairs saved in the *visited* list. It continues as long as their predecessor states are defined, i.e., as long as it has not reached an initial state.

4.2.2 Algorithm II

We compute *addiff*(ad_1, ad_2) using a symbolic least-fixpoint algorithm. The algorithm relies on the technologies of symbolic model checking [3], and is inspired by the classic fixpoint algorithm to compute a maximal simulation relation, and, more specifically, by the synthesis algorithm of [26],

Procedure 1 concrete-addiff(ad_1,ad_2)

```
define queuePairs as queue of Pair
define visited, rejects as list of Pair
define traces as list of lists of Pair
for all ini_1 ∈ ad_1.initials do
   foundCorresponding ← false
   for all ini_2 ∈ ad_2.initials do
      if corresponding(ini_1, ini_2) then
         add Pair(−, ini_1, −, ini_2) to queuePairs, visited
         foundCorresponding ← true
      end if
   end for
   if not foundCorresponding then
      add Pair(−, ini_1, −, −) to rejects
   end if
end for
visited, rejects ← traverse(ad_1,ad_2)
traces ← trace(visited,rejects)
return traces
```

Procedure 2 traverse(ad_1,ad_2)

```
while queuePairs is not empty do
   p ← pair from queuePairs
   for all suc_1 ∈ p.cur_1.successors do
      foundCorresponding ← false
      for all suc_2 ∈ p.cur_2.successors do
         if corresponding(suc_1, suc_2) then
            newPair ← Pair(p.cur_1, suc_1, p.cur_2, suc_2)
            if newPair ∉ visited then
               add newPair to queuePairs, visited
            end if
            foundCorresponding ← true, break
         end if
      end for
      if not foundCorresponding then
         add Pair(p.cur_1, suc_1, p.cur_2, −) to rejects
         remove all pair from queuePairs
           where p.cur_1.inputs = pair.cur_1.inputs
      end if
   end for
end while
return visited, rejects
```

Procedure 3 trace($visited$,$rejects$)

```
for all rejectingPair ∈ rejects do
   define tr as list of Pair
   curPair ← rejectingPair
   while curPair is not null do
      add curPair to tr
      if curPair.pred_1 is not null then
         curPair ←
           getVisited(curPair.pred_1, curPair.pred_2, visited)
      else
         break
      end if
   end while
   add tr to traces
end for
return traces
```

Procedure 4 symbolic-addiff(ad_1,ad_2)

```
define traces as list of lists of Set
define mem as array of Set
mem ← least-fixpoint-with-mem(ad_1,ad_2)
if mem.last ∩ initials ≠ ∅ then
   traces ← build-traces-from-mem(ad_1,ad_2,mem)
end if
return traces
```

where intermediate values from the fixpoint computation are used in the construction of a concrete winning strategy.

Roughly, our symbolic algorithm starts with a representation of all non-corresponding states. It then moves 'backward', and adds to the current set of states, states from which there exists a successor in ad_1 such that for all successors in ad_2, the resulting successor pair is in the current set of states. Most importantly, to help in the construction of diff traces later, at each step backward, the algorithm remembers the newly computed set of added states. The steps 'backward' continue until reaching a least fixpoint, that is, until no more states are added.

When the fixpoint is reached, the algorithm checks whether the last computed set (the fixpoint set) includes initial states. For each such initial state, if any, the algorithm uses the sets of states computed during the backward steps to move forward (from the minimal position it can start from) and construct shortest diff traces.

We present our algorithm in general set notation, with the set-operations of union, intersection, and complementation. In the pseudo code below, sets with no subscript are sets of states over the union of all variables from ad_1 and ad_2. For $i \in \{1, 2\}$, sets with subscript i are sets of states over the variables of ad_i. The operator $S|_{ad_i}$ is used to restrict the variables of the set S to the variables of ad_i (all other variables are existentially quantified out). The operation `choose one` relates to choosing a single element from the relevant set (a single concrete assignment to the variables). The sets $corr$ and $initials$ are the set of corresponding states and the set of joint initial states, respectively. When intersecting a set S_i over the variables of ad_i with a set S over the union of all variables from both ADs, the result is a set over the union of variables where the variables of ad_i agree with their possible assignments in the set S_i.

In the implementation, the sets are represented using BDDs. A pseudo-code for the algorithm is given in Proc. 4, which uses Proc. 5 and 6.

Note that in the final iteration of the loop in Proc. 6, reached with $i = 1$, the assignment to $next_2$ is guaranteed to set $next_2 \leftarrow \emptyset$, because the first location in the memory array equals $\overline{corr}$. This guarantees that the last state in each diff trace assigns no values to the variables of ad_2: indeed, the last ad_1 state in the trace should have no corresponding ad_2 state in the trace.

If the user is interested only in checking the existence of differences but not in the set of all witnesses, we can stop the steps backward as soon as the set of added states includes an initial state (by checking whether $p \cap initials = \emptyset$ already after line 9 in Proc. 5). In some cases, as our evaluation shows (see Sect. 6), this is indeed much faster than waiting for the fixpoint to be reached and for all traces to be enumerated. Note that trace enumeration is not symbolic and thus may not scale well.

Finally, for both algorithms, the concrete and the symbolic, correctness and completeness are proved by induction on the length of the traces and rely on the fact that the ADs are internally deterministic.

5. IMPLEMENTATION AND USES

We have implemented *addiff* and integrated it into a prototype Eclipse plug-in. The input for the implementation are

Procedure 5 least-fixpoint-with-mem(ad_1,ad_2)

```
define mem as array of Set
define p, z, oldz as Set
define i as number
z ← corr̄, oldz ← ∅
i ← 0
mem[i] ← z
while z ≠ oldz do
    oldz ← z
    p ← { (s1, s2) | s1 ∈ ad1 ∧ s2 ∈ ad2 ∧ ∃suc1 ∈ s1.successors
      s.t. ∀suc2 ∈ s2.successors (suc1, suc2) ∈ z}
    z ← z ∪ p
    i ← i + 1
    mem[i] ← z
end while
return mem
```

Procedure 6 build-traces-from-mem(ad_1,ad_2,mem)

```
for all ini1 ∈ (mem.last ∩ initials)|ad1 do
    define tr as list of Set
    find minimal j s.t. ini1 ∩ mem[j] ≠ ∅
    ini2 ← choose one from (ini1 ∩ initials)|ad2
    CS ← CombinedState(ini1, ini2)
    add CS to tr
    for i = j down to 1 do
        next1 ← choose one from
            (CS|ad1.successors ∩ mem[i − 1]|ad1)
        next2 ← choose one from
            (next1 ∩ corr ∩ mem[i − 1])|ad2 ∩ (CS|ad2.successors)
        CS ← CombinedState(next1, next2)
        add CS to tr
    end for
    add tr to traces
end for
return traces
```

UML 2 ADs, drawn and parsed using Eclipse UML 2 APIs. The plug-in transforms the input ADs into SMV format. It then computes *addiff* via the APIs of JTLV [27], a framework for the development of verification algorithms, using bdd-based symbolic mechanisms. The underlying BDD package used is CUDD [30]. Both algorithms are implemented and the engineer can choose which one to use. The plug-in, together with all the example ADs we used in the evaluation, is available from [28].

5.1 Browsing diff traces

The plug-in allows the engineer to compare two selected ADs, and to textually and visually browse the diff traces found, if any. Fig. 4 shows an example screenshot, where the engineer has selected to compare diagrams *hire.v*2 (top) and *hire.v*4 (middle) (presented in Sect. 2), and is browsing one of the two diff traces that were found. Note the numbered and highlighted action nodes, which visually show the states along one of the diff traces that the plug-in has found: the trace `register`, `get welcome pack`, `assign to project` is possible in *hire.v*2 and is not possible in *hire.v*4.

A textual representation of the diff trace is displayed on the lower pane. This representation of a trace is a special case of a *model-based trace* (see [15, 16]). It shows the details of each state in the current diff trace in both ADs, consisting of the action name and all variable values. This textual representation is important because it is more detailed and because it scales better than the visual representation when handling long traces.

Clicking `Check Difference` checks whether the semantics of the second AD includes the semantics of the first. Clicking `Compute Witnesses` computes the diff traces and shows a message telling the engineer how many traces were found, if any. The `Next` and `Previous` buttons browse for the next and previous diff traces. The `Switch Direction` button switches the order of comparison. The `Concrete` and `Symbolic` buttons toggle between the two *addiff* algorithms.

5.2 High-level evolution analysis

Another application enabled by the plug-in is high-level evolution analysis. The plug-in supports a `compare` command: given two ADs, ad_1 and ad_2, the command checks whether one AD is a refinement of the other, are the two ADs semantically equivalent, or are they semantically incomparable (each allows traces the other does not allow). Formally, $compare(ad_1, ad_2)$ returns one of four answers:

$<$	if $addiff(ad_1, ad_2) = \emptyset$ and $addiff(ad_2, ad_1) \neq \emptyset$
$>$	if $addiff(ad_1, ad_2) \neq \emptyset$ and $addiff(ad_2, ad_1) = \emptyset$
$\equiv$	if $addiff(ad_1, ad_2) = \emptyset$ and $addiff(ad_2, ad_1) = \emptyset$
$<>$	if $addiff(ad_1, ad_2) \neq \emptyset$ and $addiff(ad_2, ad_1) \neq \emptyset$

Given a reference to a series of historical versions of an AD, as can be retrieved from the AD's entry in a revision repository (e.g., SVN), the plug-in can use the `compare` command to compute a high-level analysis of the evolution of the AD: which new versions have introduced new behaviors relative to their predecessors, which new versions have eliminated behaviors relative to their predecessors, and which new versions included only syntactical changes that have not changed the semantics of the AD. For example, applying this evolution analysis to the ADs presented in Sect. 2 reveals: $hire.v1 <> hire.v2$, $hire.v2 > hire.v3$, $hire.v3 <> hire.v4$, $proj.v1 \equiv proj.v2$ and $proj.v2 < proj.v3$.

6. EVALUATION AND DISCUSSION

6.1 Evaluation

We have tested our implementations of *addiff* against synthetic ADs and against real-world ADs, selected and adapted from several sources: (1) selected ADs from a library of more than 700 business process models by IBM [8] (our selection is representative of the size and complexity statistics of the models in this library, as described in [8]), (2) several models (with version history) we have obtained from Nokia Corp., Test Management, and (3) from a third company (which requested to remain unnamed). The IBM models did not include version history information so we have manually added some mutations (e.g., action additions and removals, change of branching conditions). The models from Nokia and the third company included version history. All the models we have used are available in a dedicated evaluation project that is attached to the plug-in so that all experiments we report on below can be reproduced. The experiments were performed on a regular laptop computer, Intel Dual Core CPU, 2.8 GHz, with 4 GB RAM, running Windows Vista. Running times are reported in milliseconds.

6.1.1 Quantitative evaluation

Table 1 (upper part) shows results from executing *addiff* over the examples presented in Sect. 2 and selected real-world ADs from the sources mentioned above. For each two versions we report the number of nodes, the size of the

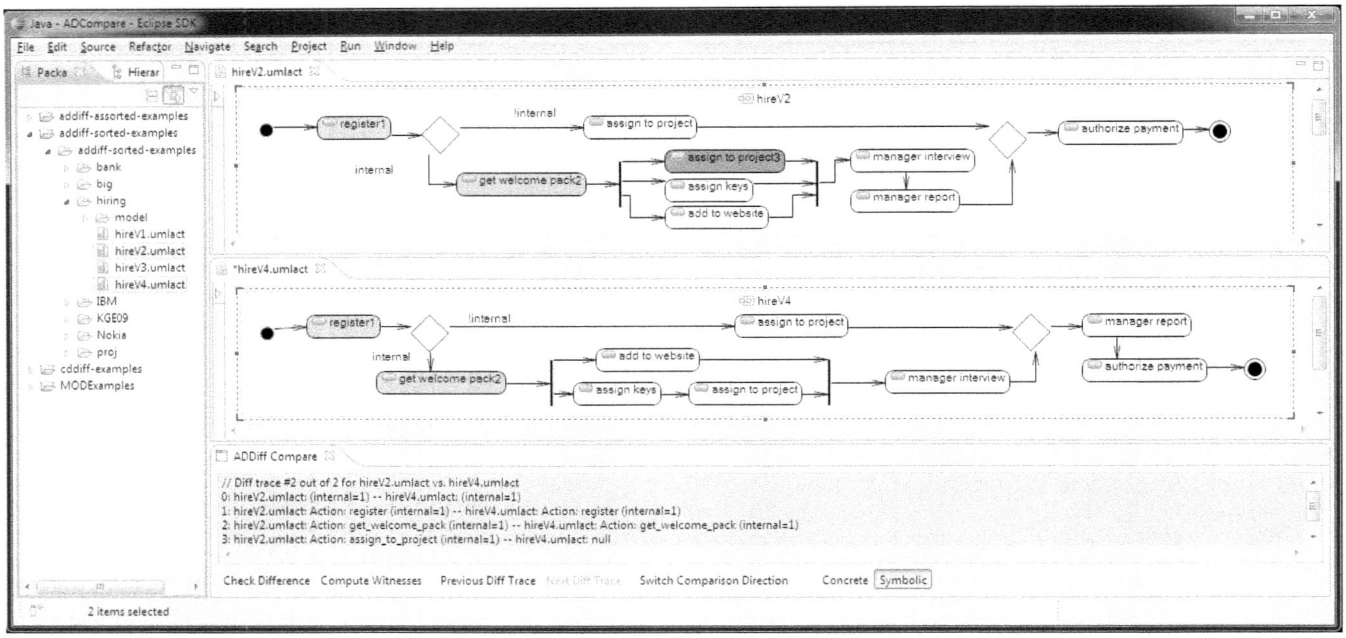

Figure 4: The prototype plug-in, comparing two ADs, $hire.v2$ and $hire.v4$. The highlighted and numbered nodes show one of the two diff traces found by *addiff*: for an internal employee, the trace `register`, `get welcome pack`, and `assign to project` is possible in $hire.v2$ and is not possible in $hire.v4$. A detailed textual representation of this diff trace is provided in the lower pane.

(reachable) state space, the number of diff traces found, the length of the shortest and longest diff traces found, and the times it took the concrete and the symbolic algorithms to (1) decide the existence of at least one diff trace and (2) to compute all diff traces.

To examine scalability, we used synthetic ADs of comparable or much larger size (in both number of action nodes and state space), divided into two families of 'worst case' ADs: a family of 'forking ADs' with concurrent section of length L and growing width W, and a family of 'linear ADs' with two linear fragments of length L seperated by a single decision over a domain of increasing size D. The lower part of Table 1 shows results from executing *addiff* on these ADs, with versions created using synthetic mutations: replacing, deleting, or moving of actions.

These results suggest the following observations. First, on small ADs, the two algorithms show similar performance results. However, as the ADs grow, the symbolic algorithm performs much better than the concrete one. On the largest ADs, the concrete algorithm performance is not practical while the symbolic algorithm stays within less than 4 seconds (on all real-world ADs). We believe this means *addiff* can be used by engineers in practice.

Second, checking for the existence of a difference is sometimes much faster than listing all diff traces, specifically when there are many diff traces or when the shortest one is much shorter than the longest one. Again, as the ADs grow, the symbolic algorithm outperforms the concrete one.

That said, we do have synthetic 'worst case' examples where the symbolic algorithm is not better than the concrete one. This happens, e.g., in the extreme case of a long linear AD with no branches or forks. It also happens when the number of diff traces is large and enumerating them takes much time. Moreover, the specific change done between the two ADs may have significant effect on both algorithms' performance: two very syntactically similar mutations (e.g., a rename in one branch or in another), may induce dramatic changes in the number of diff traces. Complete results of and models used in our experiments are available from [28].

6.1.2 Qualitative evaluation

As mentioned above, we have obtained several real-world ADs with version history information from Nokia Corp., Test Management, and from another company. We used our plug-in to compare different versions and analyze the evolution of these ADs. We have also used other publicly available diff tools (Eclipse default differencing mechanism and EMFCompare [5]) in the analysis and compared them with *addiff*. Screen captures from our analysis sessions are available from [28].

Classical textual differencing was, as expected, not helpful in comparing the ADs, as it merely compared their XMI representations. EMFCompare [5] reported correct addition and removal of actions and transitions and presented them on the abstract syntax tree structures of the two ADs. Still, this was not so helpful in understanding the differences between the ADs because (1) the comparison was done on the AST level and abstracted the control flow away, and (2) the results were shown on the AST and not on the ADs themselves: we saw the changes in the AST and had to manually search for their concrete manifestation on the ADs. Moreover, in many cases, the list of additions and removals reported by EMFCompare was too large to be useful, e.g., when comparing $hire.v2$ and $hire.v4$ (presented earlier), EMFCompare reported 23 additions and removals, much more than one would intuitively expect for these two

AD names	# Nodes	Reachable state spaces	# Wit.	Shortest/Longest	Alg. I decide/all (ms)	Alg. II decide/all (ms)
hireV1/hireV2	14/15	18/26	1	6/6	69/80	57/75
hireV2/hireV3	15/15	26/21	1	4/4	53/69	53/68
hireV3/hireV4	15/15	21/22	1	4/4	50/60	54/61
projV1/projV2	13/9	22/22	0	0/0	52/52	44/47
projV2/projV3	9/11	22/28	0	0/0	53/53	41/50
IBM3561-1/2	18/18	121/122	2	7/61	105/173	113/243
IBM2905-1/2	39/39	2680/2680	80	9/10	3010/7360	911/3667
IBM2568-1/2	50/50	3834/3834	128	5/5	2725/4503	1328/3508
IBM0863-1/2	23/23	1136/1136	76	5/8	1186/2970	200/844
IBM3735-1/2	16/15	118/99	5	4/9	57/101	57/89
IBM2557-1/2	17/15	275/175	6	7/7	66/95	74/120
NokiaAV1/2	15/17	38/44	4	4/9	48/67	47/71
NokiaAV2/3	17/23	44/96	4	7/7	71/101	76/111
NokiaAV3/4	23/23	96/76	4	7/7	84/119	98/137
AnonV1/2	15/15	37/37	2	6/6	50/64	47/61
AnonV2/3	15/19	37/80	1	8/8	67/72	57/70
forking(W1/L6)/mutated	12/12	11/11	1	9/9	57/79	49/58
forking(W2/L6)/mutated	18/18	89/89	1	15/15	121/135	100/138
forking(W3/L6)/mutated	24/24	887/887	1	21/21	1293/1332	496/667
forking(W4/L6)/mutated	30/30	8237/8237	1	27/27	88878/89399	5892/7757
lbl(L12/D16)/mutated	34/34	496/496	1	15/15	367/608	373/507
lbl(L12/D32)/mutated	34/34	992/992	1	15/15	698/1377	678/895
lbl(L12/D64)/mutated	34/34	1984/1984	1	15/15	2242/4874	1651/2161
lbl(L12/D128)/mutated	34/34	3968/3968	1	15/15	9867/23529	5789/6685

Table 1: Results from computing *addiff* for selected example, real-world, and synthetic ADs (see Sect. 6.1.1). For each two versions we report the number of nodes, the reachable state space, the number of diff traces found, the length of the shortest and longest diff traces found, and the times it took the concrete and the symbolic algorithms to (1) decide the existence of at least one diff trace and (2) to compute all diff traces.

ADs (*addiff* reports a total of three diff witnesses for this example (two in one direction, one in the other)).

In contrast, our plug-in computed diff traces and highlighted them, visually, on the ADs themselves. Thus, in addition to the semantic characteristics of the comparison, which shows the actual meaning of the changes that were done, we have also experienced the advantages of language-specific differencing over language-agnostic differencing as well as the advantage of showing the differences directly on the original diagrams rather than in a separate list.

The following lessons learned are noteworthy. First, in some cases the number of traces returned by *addiff* was large and the usefulness of the results was limited. To address this in the future we consider adding filters, e.g., to group together traces that agree on the list of actions and differ in the values of input variables, and present only a representative trace from each group. Similarly, we consider user interaction: the engineer would choose a node of interest and the plug-in would limit the results to diff traces that include/exclude this node.

Second, some of the ADs we have analyzed included 'swim lanes', which relate action nodes with roles. It seems that 'swim lanes', which are optional in the UML standard [24], are rather popular, so in the future it may be useful to add the role information to the semantics of ADs and consider it in computing the differences.

Finally, some of the ADs we have investigated were only semi-formal or included minor changes in action names, which seem to indeed be 'renames' rather than new actions with similar names. *addiff* considers such 'renames' as new actions, and we had to manually identify these cases and 'correct' them. To better address these cases in the future, a matching heuristics needs to be employed, based perhaps not only on syntactic structural similarity matching but also on natural language and domain-specific ontology.

6.2 Discussion

6.2.1 *Alternatives and extensions*

Our current definition of diff traces does not require that they can be extended into accepting traces (ones that end at a final node, see Def. 3). We have chosen not to require this, in order to support the comparison of incomplete and perhaps inconsistent ADs, ones where not all executions are eventually accepted. Such ADs may exist, mainly at the early stages of the version history of a model (indeed in our evaluation we have seen such 'incomplete' ADs). We could have given a more restrictive definition that limits diff traces to ones that can be extended to accepted traces. Adapting the algorithms we have presented to this restricted definition is not difficult.

Moreover, we have chosen to compute only a single shortest representative of the diff traces outgoing each initial AD state (that is, a single shortest diff trace for each assignment to input variables of the first AD). We consider this to be a good choice, as it keeps the *addiff* results relatively succinct and thus easy to read and understand by engineers, in most typical cases. Alternatively, one may suggest to compute a larger set, containing all diff traces. Adapting the algorithms to this more permissive definition is possible, however, as there may be exponentially many such traces, performance may be a problem. On the other hand, and in contrast, following the lesson learned in our evaluation we consider an alternative that would limit the number of diff traces to present: group them according to the list of actions they include and present a single representative trace of each group together with a predicate that describes the input variable values that are common to the traces in the group. We believe this may be computed symbolically, i.e., while avoiding the enumeration of all traces in the computation. We leave this for future work.

Finally, our current work supports a subset of the UML 2 AD language. In particular, we do not yet support structured activity nodes, which allow hierarchical nesting of action nodes or reference from a node to another activity. Hierarchy is useful in medium and large scale designs, so supporting it is important. Moreover, a hierarchy induces an abstraction mechanism, which a semantic comparison may take advantage of. Additional language features may be added. We leave these for future work.

6.2.2 *Syntactic differencing and matching*

Semantic differencing in general, and *addiff* in particular, do not come to replace existing syntactic differencing approaches. Rather, they are aimed at augmenting and complementing existing approaches with capabilities that were not available before. Thus, combining *addiff* with existing approaches to matching and syntactic differencing (see, e.g., [14, 32]), is an important direction for future work. For example, we may extend the applicability of semantic differencing in comparing diagrams whose elements have been renamed or moved in the course of evolution, by applying a syntactic matching before running the semantic differencing. The result of such an integrated solution would be a mapping plus a set of diff traces. As another example, we may use information extracted from syntactic differencing as a means to localize and improve the presentation and performance of the semantic differencing computation.

7. RELATED WORK

We discuss related work on AD formal semantics and analyses, and on model and program comparisons.

Eshuis [7] presents symbolic model checking of ADs. The work transforms ADs into SMV and uses the NuSMV model checker to verify LTL properties. The semantics given is partly inspired by the semantics of STATEMATE [9]. Our translation of ADs into SMV is somewhat similar to the two translations suggested in [7]. [7] does not handle data while our work does. The motivation of [7] is model checking while our motivation is model comparison. Störrle [31] defines a denotational semantics for UML 2 ADs as a mapping to procedural Petri nets. He also surveys and compares several previous studies that deal with a semantics for ADs, in terms of their semantic domain and expressiveness. Knieke and Goltz [12] present an executable semantics for UML 2 ADs with step semantics adapted from [9]. The works of [7, 12] support object nodes and several types of action nodes, while our current work supports only basic action nodes. Our work can be extended to support object nodes and other types of action nodes. Our focus is not on the different possible variants of ADs and their semantics but on the definition and the computation of the semantic diff operator we have presented, and on its use in evolution related tasks.

Model and program differencing, in the context of software evolution, has attracted much research efforts in recent years (see [1, 6, 14, 21, 23, 32]). In contrast to our work, almost all studies in this area, however, present syntactic differencing, at either the concrete or the abstract syntax level.

Alanen and Porres [1] describe the difference between two models as a sequence of elementary transformations, such as element creation and deletion and link insertion and removal; when applied to the first model, the sequence of transformations yields the second. Kuster et al. [14] investigate differencing and merging in the context of process models, focusing on identifying dependencies and conflicts between change operations. Engel et al. [6] present the use of a model merging language to reconcile model differences. Comparison is done by identifying new/old MOF IDs and checking related attributes and references recursively. Results include a set of additions and deletions, highlighted in a Diff/Merge browser. Mehra et al. [21] describe a visual differentiation tool where changes are presented using editing events such as add/remove shape/connector etc. Xing and Stroulia [32] present an algorithm for object-oriented design differencing whose output is a tree of structural changes, reporting differences in terms of additions, deletions, and moves of model elements, assisted by a set of similarity metrics. Ohst et al. [23] compare UML documents by traversing their abstract-syntax trees, detecting additions, deletions, and shifts of sub-trees.

As the above shows, some works go beyond the concrete textual or visual representation and have defined the comparison at the abstract-syntax level, detecting additions, removals, and shifts operations on model elements. However, to the best of our knowledge, no previous work considers model comparisons at the level of the semantic domain, as is done in our work.

Some works, e.g. [5, 32], use similarity-based matching before actual differencing. As our work focuses on semantics, it assumes a matching is given. Matching algorithms may be used to suggest a matching before the application of semantic differencing. The result of such an integration would be a mapping plus a set of differentiating traces.

We are aware of only a few studies of semantic differencing between programs. Jackson and Ladd [11] summarise the semantic diff between two procedures in terms of observable input-output behaviors. Apiwattanapong et al. [2] present a behavioral diff for object-oriented programs based on an extended control-flow graph, and a tool that implements it in the context of Java. Finally, Person et al. [25] suggest to compute a behavioral characterization of a program change using a technique called differential symbolic execution. We focus on model comparison and not on program comparison. Also, while our work is somewhat similar to these works in terms of motivation, it is very different in terms of technology.

8. CONCLUSION

We presented *addiff*, a semantic differencing operator for activity diagrams. Unlike existing approaches to model comparison, *addiff* performs a semantic comparison and outputs a set of diff witnesses, each of which is an execution trace that is possible in the first AD and is not possible in the second. We have formally defined *addiff*, described two algorithms to compute it, a concrete one and a more scalable symbolic one, and demonstrated its application in comparing ADs within the Eclipse IDE. *addiff* can help developers to understand and evaluate the differences between versions of ADs so that they can reason about the impact of changes. When applied to the version history of a given AD, *addiff* provides a semantic insight into its evolution, which is not available in existing syntactic approaches.

We suggested a number of future work directions in Sect. 6, among them, the development of more succinct, symbolic, or task-oriented representation of diff traces, the integration of *addiff* with existing approaches to matching and syntactic differencing, and the extension of *addiff* to cover a larger subset of the UML 2 AD language, in particular, handling hierarchical actions, which are useful when considering the specification of medium and large scale activities.

Finally, *addiff* is part of a larger project that applies the idea of semantic differencing and computation of diff witnesses to several modeling languages [19]. We have recently presented our work on semantic differencing for class diagrams [18] and hope to report additional results from this project in future papers.

Acknowledgements We are grateful to Tuula Pääkkönen for help in obtaining the models from Nokia Corp., to Dirk Fahland for suggesting the use of the library of process models by IBM, to Yaniv Sa'ar for advice on the implementation of the algorithms in JTLV, and to Smadar Szekely and Guy Weiss for advice on Eclipse plug-in development.

9. REFERENCES

[1] M. Alanen and I. Porres. Difference and union of models. In P. Stevens, J. Whittle, and G. Booch, editors, *Proc. 6th Int. Conf. on the UML*, volume 2863 of *LNCS*, pages 2–17. Springer, 2003.

[2] T. Apiwattanapong, A. Orso, and M. J. Harrold. JDiff: A differencing technique and tool for object-oriented programs. *Autom. Softw. Eng.*, 14(1):3–36, 2007.

[3] J. R. Burch, E. M. Clarke, K. L. McMillan, D. L. Dill, and L. J. Hwang. Symbolic model checking: 10^{20} states and beyond. *Inf. Comput.*, 98(2):142–170, 1992.

[4] R. Cavada, A. Cimatti, C. A. Jochim, G. Keighren, E. Olivetti, M. Pistore, M. Roveri, and A. Tchaltsev. NuSMV User Manual, 2005.

[5] EMF Compare. http://www.eclipse.org/modeling/emft/?project=compare.

[6] K.-D. Engel, R. F. Paige, and D. S. Kolovos. Using a model merging language for reconciling model versions. In A. Rensink and J. Warmer, editors, *ECMDA-FA*, volume 4066 of *LNCS*, pages 143–157. Springer, 2006.

[7] R. Eshuis. Symbolic model checking of UML activity diagrams. *ACM Trans. Softw. Eng. Methodol.*, 15(1):1–38, 2006.

[8] D. Fahland, C. Favre, B. Jobstmann, J. Koehler, N. Lohmann, H. Völzer, and K. Wolf. Instantaneous soundness checking of industrial business process models. In U. Dayal, J. Eder, J. Koehler, and H. A. Reijers, editors, *BPM*, volume 5701 of *LNCS*, pages 278–293. Springer, 2009.

[9] D. Harel and A. Naamad. The STATEMATE Semantics of Statecharts. *ACM Trans. Softw. Eng. Methodol.*, 5(4):293–333, 1996.

[10] D. Harel and B. Rumpe. Meaningful modeling: What's the semantics of "semantics"? *IEEE Computer*, 37(10):64–72, 2004.

[11] D. Jackson and D. A. Ladd. Semantic diff: A tool for summarizing the effects of modifications. In H. A. Müller and M. Georges, editors, *ICSM*, pages 243–252. IEEE Computer Society, 1994.

[12] C. Knieke and U. Goltz. An executable semantics for UML 2 activity diagrams. In *Proc. Int. Workshop on Formalization of Modeling Languages (FML)*, 2010.

[13] H. Krahn, B. Rumpe, and S. Völkel. MontiCore: a framework for compositional development of domain specific languages. *Int. J. on Software Tools for Technology Transfer (STTT)*, 12(5):353–372, 2010.

[14] J. M. Küster, C. Gerth, and G. Engels. Dependent and conflicting change operations of process models. In R. F. Paige, A. Hartman, and A. Rensink, editors, *ECMDA-FA*, volume 5562 of *LNCS*, pages 158–173. Springer, 2009.

[15] S. Maoz. Model-based traces. In M. R. V. Chaudron, editor, *MoDELS Workshops*, volume 5421 of *LNCS*, pages 109–119. Springer, 2008.

[16] S. Maoz. Using model-based traces as runtime models. *IEEE Computer*, 42(10):28–36, 2009.

[17] S. Maoz, J. O. Ringert, and B. Rumpe. An Operational Semantics for Activity Diagrams using SMV. Technical Report AIB 2011-07, RWTH Aachen University, Germany, 2011.

[18] S. Maoz, J. O. Ringert, and B. Rumpe. CDDiff: Semantic differencing for class diagrams. In M. Mezini, editor, *Proc. 25th Euro. Conf. on Object Oriented Programming (ECOOP'11)*, volume 6813 of *LNCS*, pages 230–254. Springer, 2011.

[19] S. Maoz, J. O. Ringert, and B. Rumpe. A manifesto for semantic model differencing. In J. Dingel and A. Solberg, editors, *MoDELS Workshops*, volume 6627 of *LNCS*, pages 194–203. Springer, 2011.

[20] K. McMillan. *Symbolic Model Checking*. Kluwer Academic Publishers, 1993.

[21] A. Mehra, J. Grundy, and J. Hosking. A generic approach to supporting diagram differencing and merging for collaborative design. In *ASE*, pages 204–213. ACM, 2005.

[22] MontiCore project. http://www.monticore.org/.

[23] D. Ohst, M. Welle, and U. Kelter. Differences between versions of UML diagrams. In *Proc. ESEC / SIGSOFT FSE*, pages 227–236. ACM, 2003.

[24] OMG. UML, version 2.2, OMG Specification, 2009.

[25] S. Person, M. B. Dwyer, S. G. Elbaum, and C. S. Pasareanu. Differential symbolic execution. In *SIGSOFT FSE*, pages 226–237. ACM, 2008.

[26] N. Piterman, A. Pnueli, and Y. Sa'ar. Synthesis of reactive(1) designs. In E. A. Emerson and K. S. Namjoshi, editors, *VMCAI*, volume 3855 of *LNCS*, pages 364–380. Springer, 2006.

[27] A. Pnueli, Y. Sa'ar, and L. Zuck. JTLV: A framework for developing verification algorithms. In T. Touili, B. Cook, and P. Jackson, editors, *CAV*, volume 6174 of *LNCS*, pages 171–174. Springer, 2010.

[28] Semantic diff project. http://www.se-rwth.de/materials/semdiff/.

[29] SMV model checker. http://www.cs.cmu.edu/~modelcheck/smv.html.

[30] F. Somenzi. CUDD: CU Decision Diagram package. http://vlsi.colorado.edu/~fabio/CUDD/, 1998.

[31] H. Störrle. Semantics of control-flow in UML 2.0 activities. In *VL/HCC*, pages 235–242. IEEE Computer Society, 2004.

[32] Z. Xing and E. Stroulia. Differencing logical UML models. *Autom. Softw. Eng.*, 14(2):215–259, 2007.

Semistructured Merge: Rethinking Merge in Revision Control Systems

Sven Apel, Jörg Liebig,
Benjamin Brandl, Christian Lengauer
University of Passau, Germany

Christian Kästner
Philipps University Marburg, Germany

ABSTRACT

An ongoing problem in revision control systems is how to resolve conflicts in a merge of independently developed revisions. Unstructured revision control systems are purely text-based and solve conflicts based on textual similarity. Structured revision control systems are tailored to specific languages and use language-specific knowledge for conflict resolution. We propose semistructured revision control systems that inherit the strengths of both: the generality of unstructured systems and the expressiveness of structured systems. The idea is to provide structural information of the underlying software artifacts — declaratively, in the form of annotated grammars. This way, a wide variety of languages can be supported and the information provided can assist in the automatic resolution of two classes of conflicts: ordering conflicts and semantic conflicts. The former can be resolved independently of the language and the latter using specific conflict handlers. We have been developing a tool that supports semistructured merge and conducted an empirical study on 24 software projects developed in Java, C#, and Python comprising 180 merge scenarios. We found that semistructured merge reduces the number of conflicts in 60 % of the sample merge scenarios by, on average, 34 %, compared to unstructured merge. We found also that renaming is challenging in that it can increase the number of conflicts during semistructured merge, and that a combination of unstructured and semistructured merge is a pragmatic way to go.

Categories and Subject Descriptors

D.2.8 [**Software Engineering**]: Distribution, Maintenance, and Enhancement—*Version control*; D.2.9 [**Software Engineering**]: Management—*Software configuration management*

General Terms

Management, Measurement, Experimentation

Keywords

Revision Control, Version Control, Software Merging, Semistructured Merge, FSTMERGE, FEATUREHOUSE

Permission to make digital or hard copies of all or part of this work for personal or classroom use is granted without fee provided that copies are not made or distributed for profit or commercial advantage and that copies bear this notice and the full citation on the first page. To copy otherwise, to republish, to post on servers or to redistribute to lists, requires prior specific permission and/or a fee.
ESEC/FSE'11, September 5–9, 2011, Szeged, Hungary.
Copyright 2011 ACM 978-1-4503-0443-6/11/09 ...$10.00.

1. INTRODUCTION

Revision control systems (a.k.a. version control systems) have a long tradition in software engineering and are a major means for managing revisions and variants of today's software systems [12, 14, 19]. A programmer creates a revision of a software system by deriving it from the base system or from another revision; a revision can be developed and evolve in isolation; and it can be merged again with the base system or another revision. A major problem of revision control is how to resolve merge conflicts that are caused by concurrent changes (e.g., when two developers independently change the same method) [17]. Zimmermann found in an empirical study of four large projects that 23 % to 46 % of all merge scenarios exhibit conflicts [22].

In recent years, two classes of revision control systems have emerged: (1) revision control systems that operate on plain text and (2) revision control systems that operate on more abstract and structured document representations. The first class is being used widely in practice because such systems are typically language-independent. Popular systems of this class are CVS, Subversion, and Git. Henceforth, we call them *unstructured revision control systems*. A problem of unstructured revision control systems is that, when conflicts occur, no knowledge of the structure of the underlying software artifacts is available. This makes it difficult to resolve certain kinds of conflicts, as we will illustrate.

The second class of revision control systems is explored mainly in academia with the goal of solving the conflict-resolution problems of unstructured revision control systems [11, 21]. The idea is to use the structure and semantics of the software artifacts being processed to resolve merge conflicts automatically [17]. These systems operate on abstract syntax trees or similar representations, rather than on plain program text, and incorporate all kinds of information on the underlying language. A drawback is that, relying on a particular language's syntax or semantics, they sacrifice language independence. Henceforth, we call them *structured revision control systems*.

There is a trade-off between generality and expressiveness of revision control systems [14]. A revision control system is general if it works with many different kinds of software artifacts. It is expressive if it is able to handle many merge conflicts automatically. Inspired by this trade-off, we propose a new class of revision control systems, called *semistructured revision control systems*, which inherit the strengths but not the weaknesses of unstructured and structured revision control systems. The idea is to increase the amount of information that a revision control system has at its disposal to resolve conflicts, while maintaining generality by supporting many languages. In particular, we concentrate on the merge process, so we speak of *semistructured merge*.

We developed a generic engine, called FSTMERGE, that merges different revisions of a software system based on the structure of the software artifacts involved. Users can plug a new language into FSTMERGE by providing a declarative specification of their language's syntax (i.e., a grammar) enriched with information for conflict resolution. While this approach is not entirely language-independent, it is still quite general. First, it enables to resolve conflicts that are caused by differing orderings of program elements independently of the language. Second, it allows the user to plug in dedicated conflict handlers in order to define further (possibly language-dependent) resolution strategies. If, for whatever reason, there is no grammar available for a certain language, FSTMERGE can use a fallback solution to parse software artifacts line by line, which makes it equivalent to the unstructured approach.

Overall, we make the following contributions:

- Based on an analysis of the trade-off between generality and expressiveness, we propose the concept of semistructured merge, which combines the strengths of unstructured and structured merge. It is able to resolve ordering conflicts independently of the language, and it can be extended by conflict resolution handlers to define additional (language-dependent) conflict resolution strategies.
- We provide the tool FSTMERGE for semistructured merge as an extension of the FEATUREHOUSE tool infrastructure for software composition [4].
- By using FSTMERGE on artifacts written in Java, C#, and Python, we demonstrate its applicability and generality.
- We report on an empirical study on 24 software projects to quantify the benefits of semistructured merge and to identify open issues. In a nutshell, we found that semistructured merge can reduce the number of conflicts in 60 % of the sample merge scenarios by 34 ± 21 %.[1] Furthermore, our study reveals that renaming is a challenge for semistructured merge that can increase the number of conflicts (in 26 % of the sample merge scenarios by 109 ± 170 %), which we discuss.
- A combination of unstructured and semistructured merge reduces the number of conflicts in our study by 35 % compared to pure unstructured merge.

The latter three contributions are novel compared to an earlier workshop paper [6]. The key contribution is the empirical study whose goal has been to explore how far we can get with an approach that is centered around ordering conflicts and conflict handlers — the results are encouraging, as we will discuss. The prototypical tool FSTMERGE is under ongoing development; in particular, it was a means to conduct the study.

2. BACKGROUND AND RELATED WORK

There is a large body of work on revision control systems [12, 14, 19] and conflict resolution in software merging [17]. The purpose of a revision control system is to manage different revisions of a software system. Usually, revisions are derived from a base program or from other revisions. Users can check out revisions from the repository, make asynchronous changes, and check them in again. By branching the main development line (or trunk), a programmer can create independent revisions, which can be changed and evolve independently (e.g., to add and test new features). Independent revisions can be merged back with the base program or with other revisions, which may have been changed in the meantime.

The key issue we address in our work is *merge conflict resolution*. Conflicts may occur while merging independent changes. A major goal of research on this problem is to empower revision control systems to resolve merge conflicts automatically, that is, to reduce the number of conflicts that otherwise have to be resolved manually by the user [17]. First, we illustrate the problem of conflict resolution in unstructured merge. Then, we illustrate the ability of structured merge to resolve conflicts better than unstructured merge.

[1] We write $m \pm s$ as an abbreviation for the mean value m of a data set and its standard deviation s.

2.1 Unstructured Merge

To illustrate the conflict resolution problem, we use the running example of a simple stack implementation, as shown in Figure 1 (top). Henceforth, we call this program the base program or simply STACK. It contains a class Stack that implements interface Cloneable and that contains a field items and the two methods push and pop.

Now, suppose a programmer would like to add a new method top to Stack, but would like to develop this feature in its own branch, independently of the main branch (i.e., the base program). To this end, the programmer creates a branch with a new revision TOP. Furthermore, suppose another programmer adds subsequently a method size directly to the main branch by creating revision SIZE of the base program. Figure 1 (middle) presents code for the two revisions, each of which adds a new method to class Stack. Finally, suppose that, at some point in time, the two branches are merged again to combine both revisions including the new methods.

Merging the two branches involves merging the two revisions TOP and SIZE (solid arrows) on the basis of the common ancestor, the base program STACK (dashed arrow). This process is called a *three-way merge* because it involves three revisions [19]. In our example, the merge process reports a conflict that cannot be resolved automatically with unstructured merge. Figure 1 (bottom) contains the output of the merge tool of CVS for this example. The output shows that the tool is not able to merge the two new methods top and size, such that both can be present in the merged program, because it cannot determine the desired order of both methods. Similar conflicts are reported by the merge tools of Subversion and Git — the user has to merge the revisions manually.

This example is very simple but it suffices to illustrate the problems of unstructured merge. An unstructured merge tool operates solely on the basis of text lines or tokens. It identifies new text fragments with regard to the common ancestor (base program) and stores the common fragments before and after the new fragments. If the two revisions change or extend text in the same region, the system reports a conflict. That is, it is not able to decide how to merge the changes or extensions. In our example, the merge tool knows that two independent text fragments (which actually implement the two methods top and size) are added to the same location of the base program (which is enclosed by the two fragments that implement the methods push and pop). The problem is that the unstructured merge tool does not know that these fragments are Java methods and that a merge of the two is actually straightforward because their order within their enclosing class can be permuted safely. If the tool knew this, it would be able to resolve the conflict automatically. There are actually two solutions: include method top first and then method size, or vice versa.

2.2 Structured Merge

In the past, many tools have been proposed that leverage information on the artifact language to resolve as many conflicts as possible [17]. Westfechtel and Buffenbarger pioneered this field by proposing tools that incorporate structural information such as the context-free and context-sensitive syntax in the merge process [11, 21]. Researchers proposed a wide variety of structural comparison and merge tools including tools specific to Java [8] and C++ [15]. Some tools even consult additionally semantic information of the language [10].

Let us illustrate the abilities of structured merge by a further ex-

Base Program STACK

```java
import java.util.LinkedList;
public class Stack<T> implements Cloneable {
  private LinkedList<T> items = new LinkedList<T>();
  public void push(T item) {
    items.addFirst(item);
  }
  public T pop() {
    if(items.size() > 0) return items.removeFirst();
    else return null;
  }
}
```

branch

Revision SIZE

```java
import java.util.LinkedList;
public class Stack<T>
    implements Cloneable {
  private LinkedList<T> items =
      new LinkedList<T>();
  public void push(T item) {
    items.addFirst(item);
  }
  public int size() {
    return items.size();
  }
  public T pop() {
    if(items.size() > 0) return
        items.removeFirst();
    else return null;
  }
}
```

Revision TOP

```java
import java.util.LinkedList;
public class Stack<T>
    implements Cloneable {
  private LinkedList<T> items =
      new LinkedList<T>();
  public void push(T item) {
    items.addFirst(item);
  }
  public T top() {
    return items.getFirst();
  }
  public T pop() {
    if(items.size() > 0) return
        items.removeFirst();
    else return null;
  }
}
```

merge

$merge_{unstructured}$(TOP, STACK, SIZE)

```java
import java.util.LinkedList;
public class Stack<T> implements Cloneable {
  private LinkedList<T> items = new LinkedList<T>();
  public void push(T item) {
    items.addFirst(item);
  }
<<<<<<< Top/Stack.java
  public T top() {
    return items.getFirst();
  }
=======
  public int size() {
    return items.size();
  }
>>>>>>> Size/Stack.java
  public T pop() {
    if(items.size() > 0) return items.removeFirst();
    else return null;
  }
}
```

Figure 1: Merging the revisions SIZE and TOP with unstructured merge

ample in Figure 2. Suppose we have the base stack implementation and we create two independent revisions, one that enables stack objects to be serialized (revision SERIALIZABLE) and another that allows programmers to flush the elements of the stack to a data stream (revision FLUSHABLE). Figure 2 depicts excerpts of the revisions. Merging the two revisions with the base program using unstructured merge causes two conflicts. First, the system is not able to merge the two new import statements and, second, it is not able to merge the implements clauses of the two revisions. Figure 2 (bottom) shows the conflicts as reported by the merge tool of CVS.

Base Program STACK

```java
import java.util.LinkedList;
public class Stack<T> implements Cloneable { ... }
```

branch

Revision FLUSHABLE

```java
import java.util.LinkedList;
import java.io.Flushable;
public class Stack<T>
    implements Cloneable,
    Flushable {
  ...
  public void flush() { ... }
}
```

Revision SERIALIZABLE

```java
import java.util.LinkedList;
import java.io.Serializable;
public class Stack<T>
    implements Cloneable,
    Serializable {
  private static final long
      serialVersionUID = 42;
  ...
}
```

merge

$merge_{unstructured}$(SERIALIZABLE, STACK, FLUSHABLE)

```java
import java.util.LinkedList;
<<<<<<< Serializable/Stack.java
import java.io.Serializable;
=======
import java.io.Flushable;
>>>>>>> Flushable/Stack.java
<<<<<<< Serializable/Stack.java
public class Stack<T> implements Cloneable, Serializable {
  private static final long serialVersionUID = 42;
=======
public class Stack<T> implements Cloneable, Flushable {
>>>>>>> Flushable/Stack.java
  private LinkedList<T> items = new LinkedList<T>();
  public void push(T item) {
    items.addFirst(item);
  }
  public T pop() {
    if(items.size() > 0) return items.removeFirst();
    else return null;
  }
  public void flush() { ... }
}
```

Figure 2: Merging the independently developed revisions FLUSHABLE and SERIALIZABLE with unstructured merge

In contrast, a structured revision control system that knows that the base program and the revisions are written in Java is able to resolve such conflicts automatically. It knows that the order of imports does not matter and that, in this case, implements clauses can be combined by union.

Beside the types of conflicts we have seen so far, there are other types of conflicts that can be resolved by structured revision control systems on the basis of language-specific knowledge. For example, a for loop in Java consists of a head and a body, and the head consists of three parts. This information is useful when two revisions modify disjoint parts of the head. Even if a structured merge cannot merge a conflict automatically, it may have information that assists the programmer in resolving the conflict (e.g., even if the heads of two for loops cannot be merged, a structured merge tool knows that the conflict occurs in a loop head and not in an arbitrary line of text).

2.3 Generality vs. Expressiveness

The previous discussion reveals that there is a trade-off between generality and expressiveness of revision control systems, as has been observed before [14]. Unstructured revision control systems are very general. They can be used with every kind of (textual) software artifact, but they are not able to resolve conflicts that require knowledge on the language of the artifacts involved. In contrast, a structured revision control system is typically tailored to a particular language. So, it would be possible to build a revision control system for Java that can resolve the conflicts we have discussed so far and, in addition, many other conflicts. However, such a system would be less useful in a setting in which a software system consists of artifacts written in many different languages (e.g., Java, JSP, Python, SQL, and Ant in a Web application).

This trade-off motivates us to explore the space between unstructured and structured revision control systems. Can we design a system that is able to handle a wide variety of software artifacts and that has enough information on these artifacts to resolve a reasonable number of conflicts automatically? A trivial solution would be to develop one structured revision control system for every artifact type that occurs in a software project, respectively. A problem with this naive approach is that it is very tedious and error-prone. Moreover, in many cases, not all artifact types can be anticipated.

2.4 Finding a Balance

Previous attempts to find a proper balance between structured and unstructured merge have some limitations. Niu et al. have proposed a merge approach that is both structured and independent of the language [18]. They represent programs as graphs and use graph morphisms to capture the relationships between the structural elements of the programs to be merged. The focus on graph structures, instead of on tree structures, is the biggest difference to our approach. The question of the scalability of graph-based algorithms may be raised, as general graph algorithms are usually more complex than tree algorithms. Niu et al. tested their approach only using a single C program of moderate size. It is not clear how their tool performs on larger programs and how difficult it is to provide support for new languages.

The approach of Dig et al. assumes a setting in which refactorings of the documents under revision control are recorded and replayed on demand [13]. That is, their approach is not applicable to scenarios in which this additional information is not available, which appears to be the rule rather than the exception in practice.

Other approaches require that the documents to be merged come with a formal semantics [9, 16], which is not always feasible in practice because, even for mainstream languages such as C++, there is no formal semantics available. We explore whether we can reduce the number of conflicts without these limitations.

3. SEMISTRUCTURED MERGE

3.1 Overview

Program Structure Trees. The basic idea of semistructured revision control systems is to represent software artifacts as trees and to provide information on how the nodes of a certain type (e.g., methods or classes) and their subtrees are merged. We call such a tree, which is essentially a parse tree, a *program structure tree* (or *feature structure tree* [4]). In Figure 3 (a), we show a simplified program structure tree of the base program STACK and, in Figures 3 (b) and 3 (c), simplified program structure trees of revisions TOP and SIZE. It is important to note that not all structural information is represented in the tree. For example, there are no nodes that represent statements or expressions. But this information is not lost; it is contained as plain text in the leaves (not shown). So a program structure tree is not necessarily a full parse tree; it abstracts from some details and contains them as text. In our setting, the order of child nodes of a common parent is arbitrary. That is, it may change without affecting the program semantics. This is a key property when resolving conflicts that rely on the element order, as we will explain shortly.

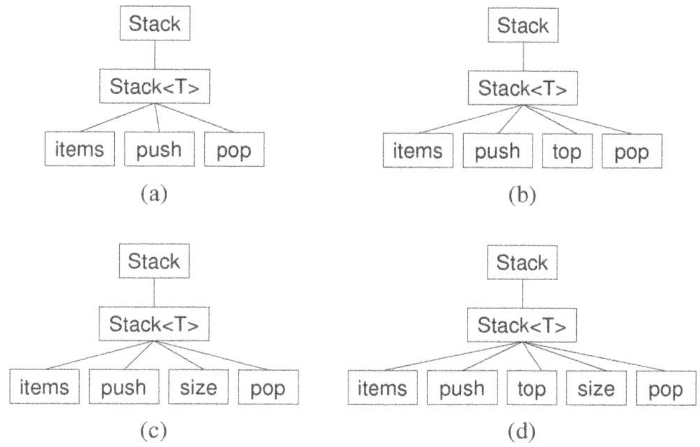

Figure 3: Revisions of the stack example as program structure trees

The choice of which kind of structural element is represented by a distinct node depends on the expressiveness which we want to attain with semistructured merge. Let us explain this choice by means of the stack example. Taking the three program structure trees as input, a merge tool can produce the desired output without conflict only by superimposing the trees, as shown in Figure 3 (d).[2] Why does this algorithm work? It works because the order of method declarations in Java does not matter, so superimposing the trees just adds the two new methods top and size in any possible order. If the two revisions added methods with identical signatures, the tool would have to merge the statements of their bodies. This would be more difficult since their order matters (and statements do not have unique names) [1, 5]. Even with all the knowledge on the Java language at our disposal, there remain cases in which we cannot say how to merge sequences of statements. This is the reason why we choose to represent methods as opaque leaves and their statements as text content; in other languages, we may choose a different granularity.

Conflict Types. The ability of semistructured merge to resolve certain conflicts is based on the observation that the order of certain elements (e.g., of classes, interfaces, methods, fields, imports, and so on) does not matter. We call such conflicts *ordering conflicts*. A merge algorithm that resolves just ordering conflicts automatically is defined more simply than a fully structured merge. A semistructured merge uses an *abstraction* of the structure of the document, which provides just enough information to identify ordered items.

Furthermore, in the example of Figure 2, we see that unstructured merge is not able to combine the differing implements clauses of two revisions of a class. With semistructured (and structured) merge, we are able to achieve this because we know that lists of types can be unified *in this case*. The routine that resolves conflicts of a special kind is called a *conflict handler*. To distinguish conflicts for which we use special conflict handlers from the conflicts that occur due to ordering issues, we call the former *semantic conflicts* and the latter, as before, ordering conflicts. We do not claim that it is possible to define a conflict handler for every case. However, at least, a conflict handler can assist the developer in identifying and resolving conflicts.

But what do we do with program elements which we do not

[2]Superimposition merges trees recursively, beginning from the root, based on structural and nominal similarities [4].

```
1  @FSTNonTerminal(name="{Type}")
2  ClassDecl : "class" Type ImplList "{"
3    (FieldDecl)∗ (ClassConstr)∗ (MethodDecl)∗
4  "}";
5  @FSTTerminal(name="Impl", merge="ImplUnion")
6  ImplList : "implements" Type ("," Type)∗
7  @FSTTerminal(name="{ID}({Params})", merge="LineBasedMerge")
8  MethodDeclaration : Type ID "(" (Params)? ")" "{"
9    (Statement)∗
10 "}"; ...
```

Figure 4: An excerpt of a simplified Java grammar with annotations

```
1 public class ImplUnion {
2   public final static String HANDLER = "ImplUnion";
3   public static void compose(FSTTerminal a, FSTTerminal b,
        FSTTerminal comp, FSTNonTerminal parent) {
4     String ifcA = a.getBody();
5     String ifcB = b.getBody();
6     String ifcComp = ifcB + ifcA;
7     ...
8   }
9 }
```

Figure 5: An excerpt of a conflict handler for merging implements lists in Java

know how to merge, such as method bodies with statements? The answer is simple: we represent the elements as plain text and use conventional unstructured merge. That is, if a conflict occurs inside a method body, we do not attempt to resolve it automatically — much like in unstructured merge.

Note that superimposition alone is not sufficient to implement semistructured merge because revisions may remove program elements. For example, one or both revisions of STACK may remove method push. The result should be a stack without this method. To this end, the merge algorithm has to check whether one or both revisions remove elements, and so on. In our tool, we implemented a set of standard rules for removing elements (following RCS's merge), whose description we omit here because they do not add anything to the discussion.

3.2 System Architecture and Annotations

Our system consists of two parts: (1) a generic engine that knows how to identify and resolve certain conflicts and (2) a small abstract specification — for each artifact language — of the program's or document's elements whose order does not matter or for which special conflict handlers are available. The abstract specification of a document structure is given by an annotated grammar of the language. Most of the work is done by the generic merge engine, using the grammar as a guide. This architecture makes it relatively easy to include new languages by providing proper abstract specifications, compared to implementing a complete structured merge tool from scratch.

To illustrate the role of annotations, consider the excerpt of a simplified Java grammar in Figure 4. It contains a set of production rules. For example, rule ClassDecl defines the structure of classes containing fields (FieldDecl), constructors (ClassConstr), and methods (MethodDecl). Production rules may be annotated with @FSTNonTerminal and @FSTTerminal. The former annotation defines that elements corresponding to the rule are represented as nodes in the corresponding program structure tree, there may be subnodes, and the order of elements or nodes is arbitrary. In our example, we annotate the rule for class declarations with @FSTNonTerminal because classes may contain further classes, methods, and so on, and the order of classes in a file or package may vary. The annotation parameter name is used to assign a name to the corresponding node in the program structure tree. Annotation @FSTTerminal is like annotation @FSTNonTerminal except that subelements are represented as plain text and that the developer can decide how code corresponding to the element in question is merged. For example, we annotate the rule for method declarations with @FSTTerminal to represent their inner statements by plain text, as explained before. Annotation parameter merge defines that the method's content is merged by a classic line-based merge algorithm, as used in unstructured merge.

A further interesting example is the rule for describing the syntax of implements lists (Fig. 4, Lines 5–6). This rule is annotated with @FSTTerminal, so the subelements (i.e., list of type names) are represented as plain text. But, in contrast to method declarations, we state that implements lists are merged by a special conflict handler that combines them by union (merge="ImplUnion"). This conflict handler is specific to Java's implements list and provided as a plugin for FSTMERGE (via FEATUREHOUSE's plugin mechanism). In Figure 5, we show an excerpt of a possible implementation in our tool. Note that the name of the handler, defined in constant HANDLER (Line 2), matches the name of the selected handler in the annotated grammar (Fig. 4, Line 5).

The example of Figure 5 illustrates the simplicity of defining conflict handlers. It is important to note that conflict handlers are not always language-independent but optional (if not provided, unstructured merge is used). Conflict handlers can be used not only to resolve conflicts, but also to provide structured and language-specific information on the kind of conflict and potential conflict resolution strategies, in the case a conflict cannot be resolved automatically using the information available. For example, we could use a conflict handler to specify how the parts of a for loop head are merged and, if this is not possible, to provide information on the kind and cause of the conflict.

3.3 Balancing Generality and Expressiveness

Semistructured merge is a combination of unstructured merge and structured merge. Elements whose order is arbitrary are represented by nodes and can be merged by superimposition. Elements whose order is not arbitrary are represented by text and merged either by unstructured merge or by special conflict handlers. That is, we have a choice per language of which elements are to be represented by nodes and which by text and which elements are treated by conflict handlers. With a coarse granularity, we have simple program structure trees (e.g., with Java classes as leaves) but cannot resolve conflicts at the method level. That is, the expressiveness of the merge algorithm is limited. A finer granularity leads to more complex trees (e.g., with Java fields and methods as leaves) but also allows a merge tool to resolve ordering conflicts automatically (or via conflict handlers). The result is a higher expressiveness of the merge algorithm.

As we have illustrated, an annotated grammar contains sufficient information to guide a revision control system in merging Java artifacts. But how does this approach facilitate generality? Indeed, for a language to be supported, we need some information in the form of an annotated grammar and, if desired, special conflict handlers, so the tool is not entirely language-independent. But, for many languages, such a grammar is easily provided, since standard grammars in Backus-Naur-Form are available on the Web for many languages, and adding annotations is a matter of hours, at most. Also, implementing special conflict handlers in the form of Java code is a matter of hours (e.g., for concatenating implements lists, a few lines of Java code are sufficient).

3.4 Summary

To summarize, semistructured merge is more expressive than unstructured merge, since certain conflicts can be resolved automatically based on information on the underlying languages. And semistructured merge is more general than structured merge, since a wide variety of languages can be supported on the basis of an annotated grammar, which needs to be provided only once per language. If, for whatever reason, no information on a given language is available, semistructured merge behaves exactly like unstructured merge, parsing the corresponding software artifact line by line.

4. IMPLEMENTATION

To demonstrate the feasibility of our approach, we implemented a semistructured-merge tool and used it to merge artifacts written in Java, C#, and Python.

4.1 Generic Merge Engine

We have implemented a first prototype of a semistructured-merge tool, called FSTMERGE, which is able to resolve ordering conflicts and which can be extended with special conflict handlers. FSTMERGE and the sample programs of our empirical study are publicly available on the project's Web site.[3]

FSTMERGE takes advantage of the existing tool infrastructure FEATUREHOUSE [4], as illustrated in Figure 6. The tool FSTGENERATOR generates almost all code that is necessary for the integration of a new language into FSTMERGE. FSTGENERATOR expects the grammar of the language in a specific format, called FEATUREBNF, of which we have already shown an example in Figure 4. We have extended FSTGENERATOR and FEATUREBNF to support annotations relevant to semistructured merge.

Using a grammar written in FEATUREBNF, FSTGENERATOR generates an LL(k) parser (that produces program structure trees) and a corresponding pretty printer, both of which are then integrated into FSTMERGE. Furthermore, developers have the opportunity to plug in special conflict handlers and to activate them in the grammar (using annotation parameter merge). After the generation step, FSTMERGE proceeds as follows: the generated parser takes the base program and two revisions written in the target language and produces a program structure tree for each program; FSTMERGE performs the semistructured merge as explained before (the trees are superimposed, deletions are handled separately, and special conflict handlers or a conventional unstructured merge are applied to the leaves); the generated pretty printer writes the merged revisions to disk.

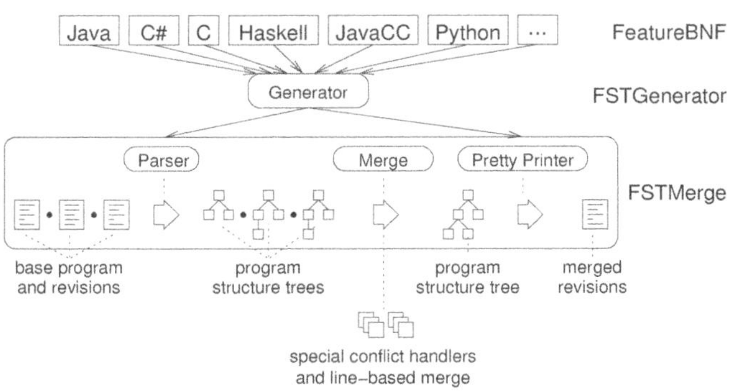

Figure 6: The architecture of FEATUREHOUSE

[3]http://www.fosd.de/SSMerge/

4.2 Language Plugins

We have tested FSTMERGE with three languages: Java, C#, and Python. All three languages are common in projects that use revision control systems and all are sufficiently complex and different from each other to demonstrate the practicality and generality of our approach. As a basis, we used publicly available grammars that we adapted and annotated for our purposes. Beside technical problems with the Python grammar (the Python grammar relies on indentation), plugging the three languages into FEATUREHOUSE and FSTMERGE was easy. Annotating and testing them was a matter of a few hours. Furthermore, we implemented special conflict handlers for merging implements, extends, and throws lists and for modifiers, mainly for displaying information on the conflicts. Typically, the implementation of a conflict handler requires only a few lines of well-separated Java code and follows the pattern of the handler shown in Figure 5.

5. EMPIRICAL STUDY

To quantify the benefits of our approach and to discover open issues, we conducted an empirical study on merging and conflict resolution in a number of software projects.

5.1 Motivation & Methodology

Due to our experience with FEATUREHOUSE in software product-line engineering [2–4, 7], we expect that integrating further languages is easy. The interesting issue is whether, in its current form, semistructured merge can play to its strengths in real software projects. The point is that concentrating on ordering and certain semantic conflicts is a fairly simple approach. By means of examples, we have demonstrated that semistructured merge is able to resolve conflicts that cannot be resolved with unstructured merge. But how frequently do such conflicts occur in real software projects? How far can we get with such a simple approach?

Hypothesis: *Many of the conflicts that occur in merging revisions are ordering conflicts, which can be resolved automatically with semistructured merge. An additional fraction of conflicts can be resolved with conflict handlers.*

Although there is some evidence that revisions often involve additions of larger structures such as entire functions [20], we need a substantial set of data to answer the question systematically. To this end, we used both semistructured merge and unstructured merge in a number of merge scenarios and compared the resulting numbers of conflicts, lines of conflicting code, and conflicting files. Unfortunately, we could not compare semistructured merge with structured merge because there are simply no practical tools available, least of all for Java, C#, and Python.[4] Also we could not compare our approach with tools that build on formal semantics [9, 16] or on refactoring replaying [13] because our approach aims at a broader scenario in which this information is not available.

Beside the quantitative analysis, we looked at selected samples of merged code in order to learn about the influence of the merge approach on the resulting code structure. We found a number of differences that may have an impact on code comprehension, which we discuss in Section 5.4.

[4]We are aware only of the *academic* prototypes for C of Westfechtel [21] and Buffenbarger [11]. These tools are not able to resolve ordering conflicts (personal communication with Westfechtel).

5.2 Sample Projects

Criteria. An important issue is how to select merge and conflict scenarios in a comparison of semistructured and unstructured merge. Developing our own case study would leave too much room for bias. Using only one or two scenarios would threaten external validity (i.e., we would not be able to generalize our findings). Thus, we decided to base our study on a substantial number of open-source projects developed by practitioners for real applications. We explored SourceForge, a popular open-source software portal, for candidates. We had two criteria: (1) the projects must be of reasonable but varying sizes and (2) either semistructured merge or unstructured merge must produce at least one conflict. To this end, we analyzed the revision history of the candidates including logs for real and realistic merges, which we call henceforth *merge scenarios*. Technically, we used Subversion to browse the revision histories and to check out revisions. In principle, we could have used any other state-of-the-art revision control system, but we were most familiar with Subversion.

Identifying Merge Scenarios. We have been considering two kinds of merge scenarios: (1) merges that have actually been performed in the revision history of a project and (2) merges that are realistic considering the history of a project.

Based on the logs, we were able to extract information on merges that actually have been performed by the developers and to obtain the revisions involved. Since Subversion has no standard log entry type for merges,[5] we used comments of the developers that point clearly to merges.

Beside merges that actually happened, we searched for merges that could have been performed (the logs are not clear about this) or that are realistic considering the revision history — to increase the sample size. One kind of indicator is a sequence of multiple, alternating changes in different branches (e.g., trunk → branch → trunk). This pattern indicates concurrent development and points to potential conflict scenarios (as long as the changes in different branches are not identical). A second indication is that developers evolve only a single branch in many revisions. Merging the branch back to the trunk is a classic scenario in revision control (e.g., to merge new features that have been added and tested in a separate branch with the trunk) and is likely to produce conflicts when the trunk has changed in between (typically, the more changes, the more conflicts).

Technically, a merge scenario is a triple consisting of a base revision, a left branch, and a right branch. The base revision marks the point in time in which the left or right branch was copied from the other. This way, we ensure that both branches have a common ancestor, which is necessary for a three-way merge. Furthermore, we check the two independently evolved branches out at the same point in the revision history, which is a prerequisite for merging them in practice.

In Table 1, we list information on the sample projects including name, domain, number of lines of code, number of merge scenarios, and programming language. Since Java is widely used, we were able to locate ten projects with ten conflict scenarios each. For C# and Python, we located fewer candidates with fewer conflict scenarios. Overall, our sample consists of 24 projects with, in summary, 180 merge scenarios comprising, summed over all scenarios, 50 million lines of code. All merge scenarios are available and documented on the project's Web site.

[5] This entry type is available since version 1.5, but all sample projects use earlier versions or did not take full advantage of this feature.

Project	Domain	LOC	MS	Lang.
AutoWikiBrowser	semi-autom. Wikipedia editor	63 K	9	C#
BitPim	mobile phone synchronization	180 K	7	Python
CruiseControl.NET	continuous integration server	148 K	9	C#
DrJava	development environment	89 K	10	Java
emesene	instant messaging client	29 K	1	Python
Eraser	secure data removal tool	18 K	6	C#
eXe	eLearning XHTML editor	98 K	9	Python
FreeCol	turn-based strategy game	86 K	10	Java
FireIRC	IRC client	17 K	1	C#
GenealogyJ	editor for genealogic data	56 K	10	Java
iFolder	directory synchronization	68 K	4	C#
iText	PDF library	71 K	10	Java
JabRef	BibTeX entry manager	75 K	10	Java
jEdit	programmer's text editor	107 K	10	Java
JFreeChart	chart library	149 K	10	Java
Jmol	viewer for chemical structures	135 K	10	Java
matplotlib	plotting library	86 K	10	Python
NASA WorldWind	virtual globe	193 K	8	C#
PMD	bug finder	71 K	10	Java
Process Hacker	process viewer	99 K	1	C#
RSS Bandit	news feeds reader	116 K	4	C#
SpamBayes	Bayesian anti-spam classifier	47 K	6	Python
SQuirrelSQL	graphical SQL client	218 K	10	Java
Wicd	network manager for Linux	5 K	5	Python

Table 1: Overview of the sample projects (all available on `http://sourceforge.net/`**); LOC: lines of code; MS: number of merge scenarios.**

5.3 Results

In Table 2, we depict the results of our analysis in terms of the numbers of conflicts, conflicting lines of code, conflicting files, and semantic conflicts. For the purpose of the study, we defined conflict handlers for 54 structural elements of Java, C#, and Python (implements lists, modifiers, and so on). Typically, the handlers are very simple and only flag a semantic conflict. So, we did not implement specific resolution strategies but we just counted situations in which they can be applied, which is sufficient for the quantitative analysis. Details on the conflict handlers are available on the project's Web site.

Due to the sheer amount of data, we provide for each project mean values over all merge scenarios. Detailed information on each merge scenario (including the number of conflicts, conflicting lines of code, conflicting files, and semantic conflicts per file and per merge scenario in the form of tables and diagrams) are available on the project's Web site.

Based on the results, we classify the projects into two categories, according to which numbers are reduced by semistructured merge compared to unstructured merge:

1. The number of conflicts, conflicting lines of code, and conflicting files are reduced or on the same order of magnitude.
2. The number of conflicts or conflicting lines is significantly increased (highlighted in Tab. 2), but other numbers are reduced.

We have highlighted projects that fall into the second category with a gray background in Table 2.

Compared to unstructured merge, semistructured merge (including conflict handlers) can reduce the number of conflicts in 60 % of the sample merge scenarios by 34 ± 21 % (the number of conflicting lines of code is reduced in 82 % of the sample merge scenarios by 61 ± 22 %; the number of conflicting files is reduced in 72 % of the sample merge scenarios by 28 ± 12 %).

Remarkably, in 26 % (46 of 180) of the sample merge scenar-

	conflicts		confl. LOC		confl. files		sem. confl.	
Project	UM	SM	UM	SM	UM	SM	UM	SM
AutoWikiBrowser	20	17	418	362	6	6	–	0
BitPim	29	25	5240	471	6	3	–	4
CruiseControl.NET	26	16	1133	279	14	8	–	5
DrJava	20	16	293	210	7	7	–	0
emesene	7	4	400	17	7	4	–	17
Eraser	24	24	2146	637	12	11	–	0
eXe	5	3	112	35	4	2	–	2
FireIRC IRC Client	5	3	36	23	3	2	–	0
FreeCol	237	213	4606	3265	63	58	–	1
GenealogyJ	19	9	489	146	9	6	–	0
iFolder	44	10	228	156	6	4	–	34
iText	219	706	113757	35109	216	179	–	262
JabRef	75	49	1701	1782	28	24	–	2
jEdit	7	6	105	80	3	3	–	0
JFreeChart	560	361	18142	5500	193	109	–	21
Jmol	94	112	20094	6869	40	33	–	4
matplotlib	57	15	500	466	13	9	–	16
NASA WorldWind	23	36	5946	2328	12	9	–	10
PMD	55	371	18469	6596	48	36	–	17
Process Hacker	1	1	4	4	1	1	–	1
RSS Bandit	65	51	4086	1478	12	8	–	32
SpamBayes	25	22	1166	343	10	7	–	2
SQuirrelSQL	26	24	2620	579	16	13	–	1
Wicd	10	9	1267	218	4	3	–	2

Table 2: Mean conflicts per scenario: numbers of conflicts, conflicting lines of code, conflicting files, and semantic conflicts for semistructured merge (SM) and unstructured merge (UM).

ios, semistructured merge increases the number of conflicts by 109±170 %. We found this result counter-intuitive at first: Why should additional information incur additional conflicts? In Section 5.4, we explain that renaming is the reason for the increased number of conflicts (and conflicting lines of code) in the projects of the second category.

To present more than just the mean values and to explore the reasons for the differences of the individual projects, we had a closer look at some representatives. In Figure 7, we display the numbers of conflicts and conflicting lines of code of all merge scenarios of CruiseControl.NET (first category).[6] The numbers show that semistructured merge can play to its strengths in CruiseControl.NET; the same applies to 18 other projects of our sample (all projects without gray cells in Table 2).

In Figure 8, we display the numbers of NASA WorldWind (second category). Interestingly, semistructured merge produces more conflicts than unstructured merge, which we did not expect initially. However, the number of conflicting lines of code is reduced significantly. This is similar for all projects in which the number of conflicts is increased. In Section 5.4, we discuss reasons for the diverging numbers.

Finally, we were surprised that the numbers of semantic conflicts are rather low compared to the numbers of ordering conflicts, especially when considering the quite high number of 54 elements that we handle with special conflict handlers. A notable difference is iText, which we discuss in Section 5.4.

[6]The name of a merge scenario is composed of the revision number of the base revision and the revision number of the left and right branch (which are equal, as explained in Sec. 5.2). For example, rev0815-4711 denotes a merge of the left and right branch of revision 4711 based on the base revision 0851.

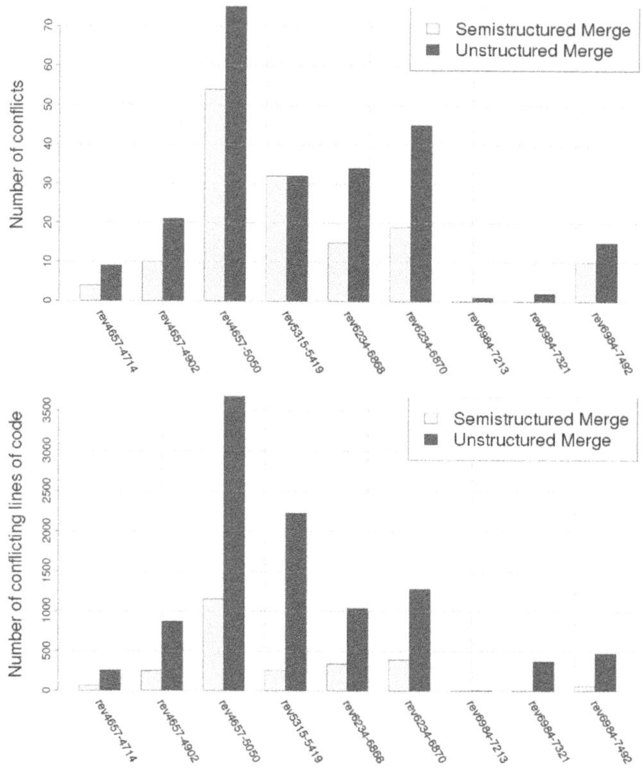

Figure 7: Results for CruiseControl.NET (first category)

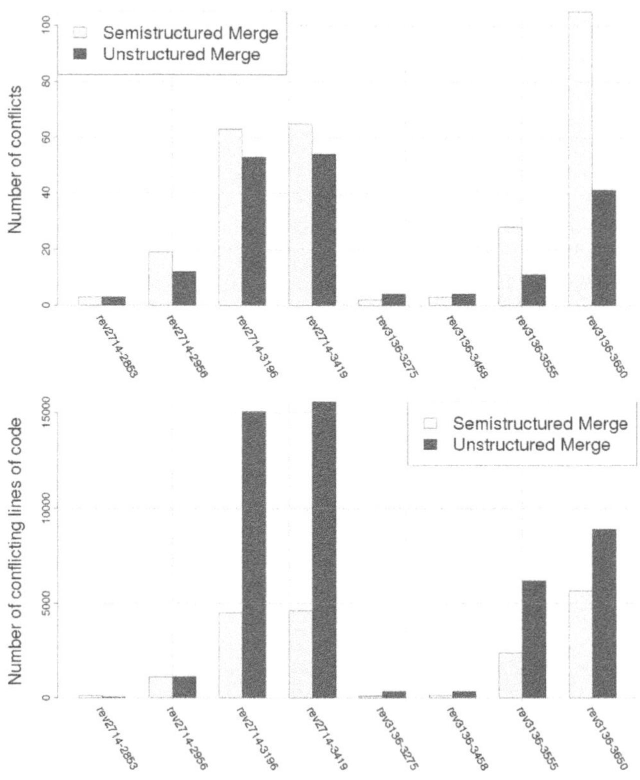

Figure 8: Results for NASA WorldWind (second category)

5.4 Discussion

We found many scenarios in which semistructured merge is superior to unstructured merge in that it reduces the number of conflicts, conflicting lines of code, and conflicting files. So, we can confirm our hypothesis: many of the conflicts that occur in merging revisions are ordering conflicts, which can be resolved automatically with semistructured merge. We also found that an additional fraction of conflicts can be potentially resolved with language-specific conflict handlers.

Nevertheless, the fact that, in some cases, semistructured merge increases the number of conflicts or conflicting lines of code surprised us. We had expected semistructured merge to be at least as good as unstructured merge. To address this issue and to learn more about the nature of semistructured merge, we reviewed the merged revisions of all projects manually. Next, we provide a summary of our findings.

Renaming. An analysis of the projects of the second category revealed that renaming poses a challenge for semistructured merge. The point is that semistructured merge uses superimposition to merge revisions. If a program element is renamed in one revision (in one of the branches), the merge algorithm is not aware of this fact and cannot map the renamed element to its previous version. This results in a situation in which we have in one branch an empty or non-existent element. In Figure 9, we illustrate a situation in which semistructured merge produces more conflicts and conflicting lines than unstructured merge. In the base revision, we have a simple stack. In revision SOMECHANGE, method push of Stack has been changed. In revision RENAMING, class Stack has been renamed to RenamedStack. Unstructured merge does not produce any conflicts because the changes to the method and the class name are located in different lines. Semistructured merge identifies merge partners by name, so it treats class Stack and class RenamedStack as distinct elements. The result of semistructured merge is shown at the bottom of in Figure 9. It contains a conflict comprising four lines of code.

The worst case is that a directory is renamed — instead of a class, as in the stack example. This happened, for instance, in PMD and Jmol. In these cases, unstructured merge reports, for each file of the directory, a large conflict because it cannot map the files of the renamed directory to the corresponding files of the other branch and uses empty files instead. The same happens in semistructured merge, except that the conflicts are not reported per file but per method or constructor in the file. This results in more conflicts but the overall number of conflicting lines is smaller than in unstructured merge. The reason is that unstructured merge flags entire files as conflicts and semistructured merge only individual structural elements such as methods. We discuss how to handle renaming better in Section 5.6.

Semantic Conflicts. We did not find many semantic conflicts, compared to other conflicts. An exception is iText. Examining iText's source code, we found that, at some point, the developers switched from Java 1.4 to Java 1.5. This transition involved renaming a large number of raw types to generic types (e.g., from LinkedList to LinkedList<String>). Thus, the cause for the exceptionally high number of semantics conflicts is again a form of renaming.

Structural Boundaries. An observation we made when examining the results of unstructured and semistructured merge is that semistructured merge, due to its structure-driven and fine-grained nature, leads always to conflicts that respect boundaries of classes, methods, and other structural elements. This is not the case for unstructured merge. We found that respecting structural boundaries

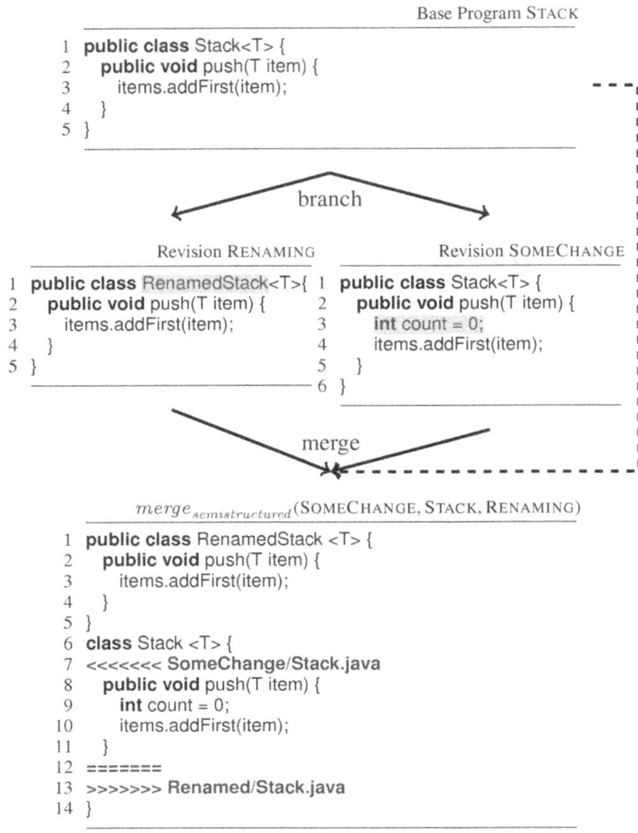

Figure 9: Semistructured merge in the presence of renaming

(i.e., aligning the merge with the program structure) is beneficial, because, this way, we could understand conflicts in terms of the underlying structure, even though this may result in more conflicts (e.g., one per method instead of one per file).

Automation. A goal of research on software merging is to minimize the number of conflicts that require manual intervention to be resolved [17]. However, an automatic resolution of conflicts has to be taken with a grain of salt. For example, if two developers add independently two methods that are intended to be the same, but the conflict resolution recognizes them as different, this mismatch goes unnoticed. This can happen in unstructured, structured, and semistructured merge. It is desirable to minimize the amount of manual intervention, but it is useful to keep information on conflict resolutions. Semistructured merge has benefits in this regard as it knows about the structural elements involved, not only about text.

5.5 Threats to Validity

Construct Validity. Although the output of semistructured merge in the presence of renaming is not satisfactory (cf. Fig. 9), it still allows us to detect conflicts properly and to incorporate them in our data. A threat to construct validity is that the number of conflicting lines of code may be estimated too low, because the renamed element is not considered (cf. Fig. 9). However, after code inspection we found that this fact is negligible for our conclusions.

Internal Validity. A threat to internal validity is that the results we obtained are influenced by (hidden) variables other than the kind of merge (which is the independent variable). Due to the simplicity of our setting, we can largely rule out such confounding variables. We applied semistructured and unstructured merge to the same set of merge scenarios and counted the number of conflicts subsequently on the merged code. Furthermore, we used a comparatively large sample (24 projects, 180 merge scenarios, 50 million lines of code) to rule out confounding variables such as programming experience, programming style, and the difference between domains.

A potential threat to internal (and external) validity is our approach of selecting conflict scenarios. The problem is that none of the projects we found contains explicit information on merges in its logs. So, we had to search the logs for comments that indicate merge scenarios (such comments are fortunately quite common). To increase the number of conflict scenarios, we considered further merge scenarios based on a number of patterns in the revision hierarchy (e.g., small alternating changes in two independent branches or branches that end abruptly) — see Section 5.2. Overall, we are confident that the conflict scenarios we selected reflect a broad spectrum of the current practice in revision control (due to the large sample) and thus our results are reliable in this respect.

One can speculate about the influence of the merge approach on patterns of concurrent development. Developers may avoid certain programming and change patterns in order not to run into conflicts when using unstructured merge. The availability of semistructured merge may influence developers in the choice of their patterns because more conflicts can be resolved.

Even though a comprehensive analysis of code quality is well beyond the scope of the paper, a look at samples of merged code made us confident that the resulting code structure of semistructured merge can aid code comprehension as the merge process follows the structural boundaries of the artifacts involved. However, a series of controlled experiments is necessary to provide a definite answer to this question.

External Validity. A common issue is to what extent the external validity of our study relies on the selection of samples. Can we generalize to other projects in other domain and written in other languages? To increase external validity, we collected a substantial number of projects and merge scenarios written in different languages and of different domains. This does not guarantee that we will arrive at the same picture in other projects, domains, and languages, but we are confident that we have covered a broad spectrum of merge scenarios.

5.6 Open Issues & Perspectives

We see some interesting open issues. A first issue is the role of refactoring. So far, we have not addressed changes, such as the renaming of methods or classes, systematically. We found that renaming can increase the number of conflicts substantially, compared to unstructured merge. The reason is that superimposition relies on nominal equality. We see two ways of dealing with this problem. First, we could use unstructured merge instead of semistructured merge for files that contain renamings. A merge tool can simply compare the numbers of conflicts produced by semistructured merge and by unstructured merge on a per-file basis and choose the better alternative. Since merging is done in linear time, the overhead should be acceptable. For our sample, the combination of unstructured and semistructured merge reduces the number of conflicts, in sum, by 35 % compared to pure unstructured merge (and by 50 % compared to pure semistructured merge). A merge in our setting takes about 15 min but, compared to the time for resolving conflicts manually, the overhead for applying both kinds of merge can be safely neglected.

Additionally, like in the approach of Dig et al. [13], we could trace renamings and pass this information to the revision control subsystem. This way, pairs of corresponding elements can be matched, even though they have different names, and the conflict of Figure 9 can be resolved automatically. This would further decrease the number of conflicts but is only applicable in specific scenarios.

Beside renaming, a further issue is that semistructured merge (much like structured merge) relies on structural information, so the revisions must be syntactically correct. Whereas it is best practice to commit only correct programs or documents, which has been confirmed by our study (we found only one Python project with a few problematic revisions), this is not a strict requirement of today's (unstructured) revision control systems. In such cases, the artifacts involved have to be parsed as plain text such that semistructured merge behaves exactly like unstructured merge. It is interesting to explore whether, in such cases, syntactically correct fragments can be represented by program structure trees and only the incorrect fragments as plain text.

In discussions at VAMOS'10 [6], some people asked how resolving ordering conflicts influences program comprehension. The background is that, in our approach, the merge tool decides the order (e.g., of method declarations in a class). An empirical assessment of this issue is well beyond the scope of this paper but an interesting avenue of further work. However, examinations of sample code make us believe that semistructured merge can aid program comprehension as it follows the structural boundaries of the artifacts involved in the merge process.

6. CONCLUSION

Both unstructured and structured revision control systems have strengths and weaknesses. The former are very general but cannot resolve certain kinds of conflicts. The latter are typically tailored to specific languages and thus can resolve conflicts better than the former. To reap the benefits of both worlds, we propose semistructured merge. Developers provide information on the artifact languages declaratively in the form of annotated grammars as well as in the form of pluggable conflict handlers. This way, a wide variety of different languages can be supported while taking advantage of the information provided during the merge process. We have implemented a tool for semistructured merge and plugged in support for Java, C#, and Python. In an empirical study, we found that semistructured merge can substantially reduce the number and size of conflicts that occur during merges, be it in terms of the number of conflicts (34 ± 21 %), the number of conflicting lines of code (61 ± 22 %), and the number of conflicting files (28 ± 12 %). We also found situations in which semistructured merge increases the number of conflicts or the number of conflicting lines of code. But, in every case, either the number of conflicting lines of code or the number of conflicts decreases. In the presence of renaming, semistructured merge produces more but often smaller conflicts than unstructured merge. In general, semistructured merge is finer-grained than unstructured merge and disallows conflicts across class or method boundaries.

Interestingly, a combination of unstructured and semistructured merge can reduce the number of conflicts further (by 35 % compared to pure unstructured merge). In the future, we would like to explore whether it is possible to trace renaming and to use this information during the merge process.

7. ACKNOWLEDGMENTS

We are grateful to Don Batory and William Cook (who was also an author of the workshop paper on which this paper is based) for fruitful discussions on the potential of semistructured merge. We thank Jens Dörre for preparing the grammars for FSTMERGE. Sven Apel's and Christian Lengauer's work is supported by the German Research Foundation (DFG – AP 206/2 and AP 206/4). Christian Kästner's work is supported by the European Research Council (ERC grant ScalPL #203099).

8. REFERENCES

[1] S. Apel and D. Hutchins. A Calculus for Uniform Feature Composition. *ACM Transactions on Programming Languages and Systems (TOPLAS)*, 32(5):Article 19, 2010.

[2] S. Apel, F. Janda, S. Trujillo, and C. Kästner. Model Superimposition in Software Product Lines. In *Proceedings of the International Conference on Model Transformation (ICMT)*, volume 5563 of *LNCS*, pages 4–19. Springer-Verlag, 2009.

[3] S. Apel, C. Kästner, A. Größlinger, and C. Lengauer. Feature (De)composition in Functional Programming. In *Proceedings of the International Conference on Software Composition (SC)*, volume 5634 of *LNCS*, pages 9–26. Springer-Verlag, 2009.

[4] S. Apel, C. Kästner, and C. Lengauer. FeatureHouse: Language-Independent, Automated Software Composition. In *Proceedings of the International Conference on Software Engineering (ICSE)*, pages 221–231. IEEE CS, 2009.

[5] S. Apel, C. Lengauer, B. Möller, and C. Kästner. An Algebraic Foundation for Automatic Feature-Based Program Synthesis. *Science of Computer Programming*, 75(11):1022–1047, 2010.

[6] S. Apel, J. Liebig, C. Lengauer, C. Kästner, and W. Cook. Semistructured Merge in Revision Control Systems. In *Proceedings of the International Workshop on Variability Modelling of Software-intensive Systems (VaMoS)*, pages 13–19. University of Duisburg-Essen, 2010.

[7] S. Apel, W. Scholz, C. Lengauer, and C. Kästner. Detecting Dependences and Interactions in Feature-Oriented Design. In *Proceedings of the International Symposium on Software Reliability Engineering (ISSRE)*, pages 161–170. IEEE CS, 2010.

[8] T. Apiwattanapong, A. Orso, and M. Harrold. JDiff: A Differencing Technique and Tool for Object-Oriented Programs. *Automated Software Engineering*, 14(1):3–36, 2007.

[9] V. Berzins. Software Merge: Semantics of Combining Changes to Programs. *ACM Transactions on Programming Languages and Systems (TOPLAS)*, 16(6):1875–1903, 1994.

[10] D. Binkley, S. Horwitz, and T. Reps. Program Integration for Languages with Procedure Calls. *ACM Transactions on Software Engineering and Methodology (TOSEM)*, 4(1):3–35, 1995.

[11] J. Buffenbarger. Syntactic Software Merging. In *Selected Papers from the ICSE SCM-4 and SCM-5 Workshops on Software Configuration Management*, volume 1005 of *LNCS*, pages 153–172. Springer-Verlag, 1995.

[12] R. Conradi and B. Westfechtel. Version Models for Software Configuration Management. *ACM Computing Surveys (CSUR)*, 30(2):232–282, 1998.

[13] D. Dig, K. Manzoor, R. Johnson, and T. Nguyen. Refactoring-Aware Configuration Management for Object-Oriented Programs. In *Proceedings of the International Conference on Software Engineering (ICSE)*, pages 427–436. IEEE CS, 2007.

[14] J. Estublier, D. Leblang, A. van der Hoek, R. Conradi, G. Clemm, W. Tichy, and D. Wiborg-Weber. Impact of Software Engineering Research on the Practice of Software Configuration Management. *ACM Transactions on Software Engineering and Methodology (TOSEM)*, 14(4):383–430, 2005.

[15] J. Grass. Cdiff: A Syntax Directed Differencer for C++ Programs. In *Proceedings of the USENIX C++ Conference*, pages 181–193. USENIX Association, 1992.

[16] D. Jackson and D. Ladd. Semantic Diff: A Tool for Summarizing the Effects of Modifications. In *Proceedings of the International Conference on Software Maintenance (ICSM)*, pages 243–252. IEEE CS, 1994.

[17] T. Mens. A State-of-the-Art Survey on Software Merging. *IEEE Transactions on Software Engineering (TSE)*, 28(5):449–462, 2002.

[18] N. Niu, S. Easterbrook, and M. Sabetzadeh. A Category-theoretic Approach to Syntactic Software Merging. In *Proceedings of the International Conference on Software Maintenance (ICSM)*, pages 197–206. IEEE CS, 2005.

[19] Bryan O'Sullivan. Making Sense of Revision-Control Systems. *Communication of the ACM*, 52(9):56–62, 2009.

[20] G. Stoyle, M. Hicks, G. Bierman, P. Sewell, and I. Neamtiu. Mutatis Mutandis: Safe and Predictable Dynamic Software Updating. In *Proceedings of the International Symposium on Principles of Programming Languages (POPL)*, pages 183–194. ACM Press, 2005.

[21] B. Westfechtel. Structure-Oriented Merging of Revisions of Software Documents. In *Proceedings of the International Workshop on Software Configuration Management (SCM)*, pages 68–79. ACM Press, 1991.

[22] T. Zimmermann. Mining Workspace Updates in CVS. In *Proceedings of the International Workshop on Mining Software Repositories (MSR)*, page 11. IEEE CS, 2007.

Testing Software In Age Of Data Privacy: A Balancing Act

Kunal Taneja
North Carolina State University
Raleigh, NC 27695
ktaneja@ncsu.edu

Mark Grechanik
Accenture Technology Labs
Chicago, IL 60601
mark.grechanik@accenture.com

Rayid Ghani
Accenture Technology Labs
Chicago, IL 60601
rayid.ghani@accenture.com

Tao Xie
North Carolina State University
Raleigh, NC 27695
xie@csc.ncsu.edu

ABSTRACT

Database-centric applications (DCAs) are common in enterprise computing, and they use nontrivial databases. Testing of DCAs is increasingly outsourced to test centers in order to achieve lower cost and higher quality. When proprietary DCAs are released, their databases should also be made available to test engineers. However, different data privacy laws prevent organizations from sharing this data with test centers because databases contain sensitive information. Currently, testing is performed with anonymized data, which often leads to worse test coverage (such as code coverage) and fewer uncovered faults, thereby reducing the quality of DCAs and obliterating benefits of test outsourcing.

To address this issue, we offer a novel approach that combines program analysis with a new data privacy framework that we design to address constraints of software testing. With our approach, organizations can balance the level of privacy with needs of testing. We have built a tool for our approach and applied it to nontrivial Java DCAs. Our results show that test coverage can be preserved at a higher level by anonymizing data based on their effect on corresponding DCAs.

Categories and Subject Descriptors

D.2.5 [**Software Engineering, Testing and Debugging**]: Testing tools; D.4.6 [**Software Engineering, Security and Protection**]: Information flow controls; K.4.1 [**Computers and Society, Public Policy Issues**]: Privacy

General Terms

Security, Verification

Keywords

Data anonymity, software testing, privacy framework, utility, PRIEST

1. INTRODUCTION

Large organizations today face many challenges when engineering software applications. Particularly challenging is the fact that many applications work with existing databases that contain confidential data. A large organization, such as a bank, insurance company, or government agency, typically hires an external company to develop or test a new custom software application. However, recent data protection laws and regulations [35] around the world prohibit data owners to easily share confidential data with external software service providers.

Database-centric applications (DCAs) are common in enterprise computing, and they use nontrivial databases [26]. When releasing these proprietary DCAs to external test centers, it is desirable for DCA owners to make their databases available to test engineers, so that they can perform testing using *original data*. However, since sensitive information cannot be disclosed to external organizations, testing is often performed with *synthetic input data*. For instance, if values of the field *Nationality* are replaced with the generic value "`Human`," DCAs may execute some paths that result in exceptions or miss certain paths [23]. As a result, test centers report worse test coverage (such as code coverage) and fewer uncovered faults, thereby reducing the quality of applications and obliterating benefits of test outsourcing [30].

Automatic approaches for test data generation [12, 17, 22, 29, 37] partially address this problem by generating synthetic input data that lead program execution toward untested statements. However, one of the main issues for these approaches is how to generate synthetic input data with which test engineers can achieve good code coverage. Using original data enables different approaches in testing and privacy to produce higher-quality synthetic input data [3][21, page 42], thus making original data important for test outsourcing.

A fundamental problem in test outsourcing is how to allow a DCA owner to release its private data with guarantees that the entities in this data (e.g., people, organizations) are protected at a certain level while retaining testing efficacy. Ideally, sanitized data (sanitized data or anonymized data is the original data after anonymization. We use the two terms interchangeably throughout this paper) should induce execution paths that are similar to the ones that are induced by the original data. In other words, when data is sanitized, information about how DCAs use this data should be taken into consideration. In practice, this consideration rarely happens; our previous work [23] showed that a popular data anonymization algorithm, called k–anonymity, seriously degrades test coverage of DCAs.

Naturally, different DCAs have different privacy goals and levels of data sensitivity – privacy goals are more relaxed for a DCA that manages a movie ticket database than for a DCA that is used within banks or government security agencies. Applying more relaxed protection to databases is likely to result in greater test coverage since a small part of the databases is anonymized; conversely,

Permission to make digital or hard copies of all or part of this work for personal or classroom use is granted without fee provided that copies are not made or distributed for profit or commercial advantage and that copies bear this notice and the full citation on the first page. To copy otherwise, to republish, to post on servers or to redistribute to lists, requires prior specific permission and/or a fee.
ESEC/FSE'11, September 5–9, 2011, Szeged, Hungary.
Copyright 2011 ACM 978-1-4503-0443-6/11/09 ...$10.00.

stricter protection makes it more difficult to outsource testing. The latter is the result of two conflicting goals: making testing as realistic as possible and hiding the original data from testers who need this data to make testing effective. Balancing these goals, i.e., to anonymize data while preserving test coverage of DCAs that use this data is emerging to be an important problem.

Given the importance of this problem, it may be surprising that there exists little prior research on this topic. There may be two main reasons for the lack of prior research. First, elaborate data privacy laws are a new phenomenon, and many of these laws [35, 38] have been introduced after the year 2000. Second, it is only in the past decade that applications are increasingly being tested by third-party specialized software service providers, which are also called test centers. Numerous test centers have emerged and often offer lower cost and higher quality when compared to in-house testing. In 2007, the test outsourcing market was worth more than USD 25 billion and growing at 20% annually, making test outsourcing the fastest growing segment of the application services market [7, 16].

To address this issue, we offer a novel approach, *PRIvacy Equalizer for Software Testing (PRIEST)* that combines a new data privacy framework with program analysis enabling business analysts to determine how anonymizing values of database attributes affects test coverage. With PRIEST, organizations can balance the goals of preserving test coverage, while releasing DCAs to external test centers with a controlled disclosure of sensitive information. The source code for PRIEST as well as its illustration video are publicly available[1]. Our work is unique; to the best of our knowledge, there exists no prior approach that addresses the problem that we pose in this paper. In summary, we make the following main contributions in this paper:

- We create a new privacy framework (described in Section 4) that includes a novel combination of guessing anonymity-based privacy metrics and a technique of data swapping anonymization to enable organizations to keep original values in sanitized data; keeping such values is important for improving the effectiveness of testing.
- We design and implement a technique using program analysis for determining how values of database attributes affect test coverage of DCAs that use this data (see Section 3.3).
- We combine our privacy framework with this technique in PRIEST to enable business analysts to balance data privacy with test coverage.
- We evaluate PRIEST using three open-source Java DCAs and one large Java DCA that handles logistics of one of the largest supermarket chains in Spain. We show that with PRIEST, test coverage can be preserved at a higher level by pinpointing database attributes that should be anonymized based on their effect on corresponding DCAs.

2. THE PROBLEM

In this section, we provide the necessary background on how DCAs interact with databases, show how sanitizing data affects test coverage of DCAs, describe the state of the art and practice, and formulate the problem statement.

2.1 Background

Majority of enterprise-level DCAs use programs that are written in general-purpose programming languages and relational databases to maintain large amounts of data. A primary way for these programs to communicate with databases is to use *call-level interfaces*, which allow DCAs to access database engines through standardized *application programming interfaces (APIs)*, e.g., Java DataBase Connectivity (JDBC). Using JDBC, programs pass SQL queries as strings to corresponding API calls to be sent to databases for execution.

```
recordset = db.execSql("SELECT␣*␣FROM␣TblPatient");
nationality = recordset.GetAttribute( i );
age = recordset.GetAttribute( j );
disease = = recordset.GetAttribute( "Disease" );
if (nationality=="Palauan" && age>60) f(disease);
```

Figure 1: An illustrative example that shows how replacing values of database attributes `Nationality` and `Age` of patients can make the function `f` unreachable.

Once these queries are executed, values of attributes of database tables are returned to DCAs using JDBC `RecordSet` objects and these values are stored in variables of the DCAs, which in turn use these variables as part of their application logic. In this way, values from a database may be used in branch decisions, and these values may therefore affect the subsequent execution of the DCAs. Depending on returned values, different paths can be taken in DCAs, and subsequently these values affect test coverage. Hence removing certain classes of values in database attributes may make some branches and statements in DCAs unreachable.

To see how anonymization affects test coverage of DCAs, consider a fragment of code shown in Figure 1. After executing JDBC API calls that submit an SQL query to a database and obtain the object `recordset`, the values of the attributes `Age`, `Nationality`, and `Disease` are put in the corresponding variables of the DCA `nationality`, `age`, and `disease`, respectively. If the values of the attribute nationality are replaced with the generic value "`Human`,", the function call `f()` becomes unreachable.

Certain classes of values of database attributes that contain non-sensitive information should be anonymized. These attributes, also called *quasi-identifiers (QI)* often contain information that can be linked with other data to infer sensitive information about entities (i.e., people, objects). For example, given the values of the QIs `Race`, `Sex`, `Height`, `ZipCode` and the attribute that contains sensitive data about diseases, it is possible to link a person to specific diseases, provided that the values of these QIs uniquely identify this person.

Existing data anonymization approaches are centered on creating models for privacy goals and developing algorithms for achieving these goals using particular anonymization techniques [15]. One of the most popular privacy goals is $k-$anonymity [34], where each entity in the database must be indistinguishable from $k-1$ others. Anonymization approaches use different anonymization techniques including suppression, where information (e.g., nationality) is removed from the data, and generalization, where information (e.g., age) is coarsened into sets (e.g., into age ranges) [15]. These and other techniques modify or suppress values of attributes, and a common side-effect of these modifications is non-covered statements in DCAs that are otherwise covered with the original data.

2.2 State of the Art and Practice

After interviewing professionals at IBM, Accenture, two large health insurance companies, a biopharmaceutical company, two large supermarket chains, and three major banks, we found that current test data anonymization is manual, laborious, and error-

[1] http://www.privacytesting.org

prone. In a few cases, client companies outsource testing using an especially expensive and cumbersome testing procedure called *cleanroom testing*, where DCAs and databases are kept on company premises in a physically secured environment [23]. Typically, business analysts and test managers from outsourcing companies come to the cleanrooms of their client companies to evaluate their clients' DCAs and to plan work. However, when better options to access data are not available, testers from outsourcing companies are also allowed in these cleanrooms to test software on their clients' premises. Actions of these test engineers are tightly monitored; network connections, phone calls, cameras, and USB keys are forbidden. Cleanroom testing requires significant resources and physical proximity of test outsourcing companies to their clients.

A more commonly used approach is to use tools that anonymize databases indiscriminately, by generalizing or suppressing all data. Even though this procedure is computationally intensive, it is appealing since it does not require sophisticated reasoning about privacy goals and protects all data.

But in many real-world settings, protecting all data blindly makes testing very difficult. When large databases are repopulated with fake data, it is likely that many implicit dependencies and patterns among data elements are missing, thereby reducing testing efficacy. Moreover, fake data is likely to trigger exceptions in DCAs, leading test engineers to flood bug-tracking systems with false bug reports. In addition, testers often cannot use such anonymized data because DCAs may throw exceptions that would not occur when the DCAs are tested with original data or other real data in field.

A more sophisticated approach is *selective anonymization*, where a team is assembled comprising of business analysts and database and security experts [25, page 134]. After the team sets privacy goals, identifies sensitive data, and marks database attributes that may help attackers to reveal this sensitive data (i.e., QIs), anonymization techniques are applied to these QIs to protect sensitive data, resulting in a sanitized database. A goal of all anonymization approaches is to make it impossible to deduce certain facts about entities with high confidence from the anonymized data [4, pages 137-156]. Unfortunately, this approach is subjective, manual, and laborious. In addition, it involves highly trained professionals and therefore this approach is very expensive. Currently, there exists no solution that enables these professionals to accomplish this task efficiently and effectively with metrics that clearly explain the cost and benefits of selective anonymization decisions.

2.3 Balancing Utility And Privacy

Utility of anonymized data is measured in terms of usefulness of this data for computational tasks when compared with how useful the original data is for the same tasks. Consider an example of the utility of calculating average salaries of employees. Adding random noise to protect salary information will most likely result in computing incorrect values of average salaries, thereby destroying utility of this computation. Recent cases with U.S. Census show that applying data privacy leads to incorrect results [5, 8]. Multiple studies demonstrate that even modest privacy gains require almost complete destruction of the data-mining utility [1, 9, 18, 19, 28].

Data swapping is an anonymization technique that is based on exchanging values of attributes among individual records while maintaining certain distribution properties [33, 32]. Data swapping is more effective in preserving utility than data suppression and generalization privacy algorithms since data swapping allows users to better preserve statistical information [21, page 42]. In this paper, we develop a data swapping privacy algorithm that allows analysts to balance privacy and utility goals, i.e., to choose appropriate levels of privacy that will guarantee certain basic test coverage.

2.4 The Problem Statement

The problem statement that we address in this paper is how to enable stakeholders to balance a level of test coverage for DCAs (i.e., utility) with privacy for databases that these DCAs use. The problem space is restricted by three fundamental constraints of software development and privacy-preserving data publishing as follows.

First, a chosen anonymization approach should preserve original data as much as possible since it is important for preserving the testing utility of DCAs. Anonymizing databases using data suppression techniques may result in a different behavior of the DCAs. Suppose that $N_o \subseteq N$ is the set of all covered nodes in the control flow graph of a DCA when the DCA is tested with the original data, and $N_a \subseteq N$ is the set of all covered nodes when the same DCA is tested with the anonymized data. In general, testing with anonymized data makes DCAs behave in ways that are different from specifications, and as a result new execution paths in DCAs with anonymized data may lead to exceptions or not-covered branches being covered originally. For example, the DCA logic handles suppressed values of `Nationality` by not covering the body of the `if` statement shown in Figure 1. Therefore, in the worst case $N_T = N_o \cap N_a = \oslash$, where N_T is the set of nodes of the preserved statement coverage. A problem is how to keep a good extent of the original data in databases for testing DCAs while guaranteeing certain levels of privacy.

Our goal is to ensure that all statements (i.e., nodes in the control flow graph) that are executed with original data will also be executed with anonymized data. Our goal is difficult to achieve since it is an undecidable problem to determine precisely how values of QIs are used in DCAs [27]. In addition, anonymization algorithms present a dilemma: suppressing attribute data with different values results in loss of test coverage, and keeping original data in the database results in loss of privacy. Balancing these conflicting outcomes is the problem that we address in this paper.

Second, as a result of software evolution [20, page 163], the code of the DCA is modified. In consecutive releases, the DCA may use different database attributes in different ways, thereby requiring the DCA owner to reanonymize data to ensure that the balance between privacy and utility is maintained. However, re-anonymization introduces a problem – if an attacker keeps the previous version of the anonymized data where values of some attributes are not sanitized, then this attacker can link original values in different releases, thus inferring sensitive information. A solution should enable stakeholders to repeatedly release anonymized data in such a way that both privacy and utility are guaranteed at certain levels.

Finally, a privacy metric should be linked directly to test coverage and vice versa, i.e., guaranteeing a certain level of test coverage should allow stakeholders to calculate bounds of the privacy level. For example, if some path is controlled by branch conditions that use values of database attributes, then it is possible to predict the effect of anonymization of these values on this path. In other words, the problem is to present business analysts with choices of predicted coverage levels for different anonymization goals.

3. OUR SOLUTION

In this section, we present core ideas behind our approach that we call *PRIvacy Equalizer for Software Testing (PRIEST)* and we describe the PRIEST architecture and its workflow. In this section, we concentrate on the overall architecture of PRIEST that uses our privacy framework that we describe in Section 4.

3.1 Core Ideas

At the core of our work are three major ideas. The first one is a privacy framework that enables organizations to keep original values in sanitized data. The framework is based on a data swapping anonymization technique to preserve original values of database attributes. As a result, test coverage is not affected so negatively as it happens when data suppression and generalization techniques are used. The technique swaps data based on a probability value provided by a user. Hence different levels of privacy can be achieved.

The second idea is our guessing anonymity privacy metric that allows stakeholders to quantify the level of privacy achieved in an anonymized database. In particular, the metric provides measurement of difficulty for an attacker to relate a sanitized record to the original record.

The third idea is an idea to statically determine how different database values affect the behavior of a DCA. This idea unifies DCAs and their databases in a novel way – database attributes are tied to the source code of the DCAs, and depending on how the DCAs use values of these attributes, business analysts and security experts can determine what anonymization strategy should be used to protect data without sacrificing much of test coverage. A key point is that often not all of the database attributes have to be anonymized to achieve a given level of data protection. Therefore, it is important to extend data protection strategies with information about how DCAs use their databases to which these strategies are applied.

As it often happens, control-flow decisions in DCAs are affected by a smaller subset of database attributes. In an extreme case, if some data in the database is not used in any control-flow decision of any DCAs, then anonymizing this data will have no effect on these DCAs. A more subtle point is that values of some attribute may not affect most branch conditions in DCAs, and therefore test coverage will not be affected much if this attribute is anonymized. Thus it is beneficial to focus anonymization on those aspects of the data that have minimal influence on deeply nested control-flow decisions.

3.2 PRIEST Architecture and Process

We propose a novel process for using PRIEST that partially involves the cleanroom testing that we described in Section 2.2. Recall that business analysts and test managers from outsourcing companies come to the cleanroom of their client company to evaluate their client's DCAs and to plan work. As part of their evaluation, these analysts and managers determine different sets of attributes of the database (i.e., QIs) that can be used by attackers to re-identify entities. In general, only a few subsets of these QIs should be anonymized, thus creating favorable conditions for preserving test coverage. With PRIEST, this QI selection procedure can be improved by pointing out the QIs that affect test coverage the least. These analysts and managers can use PRIEST as part of their evaluation and planning in order to determine how to maximize test coverage for DCAs while achieving desired privacy goals for databases that these DCAs use.

As the first step of the PRIEST process, programmers link program variables to database attributes using annotations, so that these annotations can be traced statically using control- and dataflow analyses. Tracing these attribute annotations is required to determine how the values of these attributes are used in conditional expressions to make branching decisions, thereby influencing the execution flow of the DCAs. Our goal is to quantify the effect of replacing values of database attributes on reachability of program statements.

At first glance, it appears to be tedious and laborious work for programmers to annotate program variables with the names of database attributes from which these variables obtain values. In reality, it is a practical and modest exercise that takes little time. Programmers annotate selected program variables only once, where these variables are first assigned values that are retrieved from recordset objects using specific database-related API calls. We observe that in many projects it is a small fraction of code that deals with obtaining values from databases, and most code is written to implement application logic that processes these values. This observation is confirmed by our previous study [24] that shows that out of 2,080 randomly chosen Java programs in Sourceforge, there is approximately one JDBC-related API call per 2,200 LOC on average that retrieves a value from a recordset object and assigns it to a program variable. Extrapolating this result means that programmers may have to annotate approximately 450 variables for a project with 1 Million LOC and such expense is acceptable.

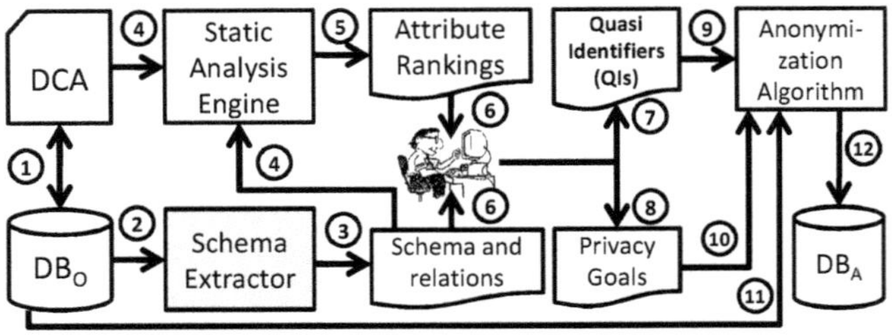

Figure 2: PRIEST architecture and workflow. Solid arrows depict the flow of command and data between components, numbers indicate the sequence of operations in the workflow.

In addition, a variety of *object-relational mapper (O/R mapping)* tools and frameworks bridge the gap between an application's object model and the relational schema of the underlying database by generating classes that represent objects in relational databases [6]. Since O/R mapping is done automatically, links between program variables and database attributes are recovered as a by-product of using O/R mapping tools. For example, one of our subject applications, a logistics application for handling one of the largest supermarket chains in Spain, is written using iBatis[2], an open-source O/R mapper.

Figure 2 shows the architecture of PRIEST. The inputs to PRIEST are the DCA bytecode and the original database DB_O that this DCA uses (1). With PRIEST, business analysts, test managers, and security experts connect to DB_O (2) to obtain its schema using the Schema Extractor that uses JDBC metadata services to obtain (3) database schema including all relations among different attributes. Next, PRIEST performs control and dataflow analyses (4) using the Soot toolkit[3] to establish how the DCA uses values of different database attributes. Values of some attributes are used in expressions to compute other values, which in turn are used in other expressions and statements. In some cases, these values are used in conditional statements, and they affect control flows of DCAs using control-flow dependencies. Ideally, attributes whose values affect many other expressions and statements in DCAs (in terms of statement coverage) should not be picked as QIs. The output (5) of this procedure is a list of attribute rankings that show how many statements are approximately encapsulated by branches whose conditions contain program variables that receive their values from database attributes.

At this point, PRIEST displays to the user (6) the list of ranked

[2]http://ibatis.apache.org

[3]http://www.sable.mcgill.ca/soot

attributes and their relations with other attributes in the database schema. The user selects (7) a subset of database attributes as QIs whose values should be anonymized to protect sensitive data based on certain privacy goals (8) that are required by the DCA owner. The selected QIs are supplied (9) to the Anonymization Algorithm along with (10) the required privacy level. In addition, the algorithm takes (11) DB_O as its input and outputs (12) the anonymized database DB_A.

3.3 Ranking Attributes

To understand which attributes affect DCAs the most, we rank these attributes by counting the numbers of statements that their values affect. To find the preceding information, our approach uses taint analysis to track the annotated variables (as described in Section 3.2) corresponding to each attribute. In particular, for each attribute, our approach uses control- and data-flow taint propagation [13] to find out branch conditions that are tainted by an annotated variable corresponding to the attribute. We then count the number of statements that are control-dependent on these branch conditions. We perform virtual-call resolution using static class hierarchy analysis, and we take a conservative approach by counting all the statements in all the target methods that can potentially be invoked.

Our experiments on subject applications show that this approach can predict the effect of anonymization on coverage within less than 8.3% error (see Section 5 and Table 6 for further details). Improving the precision to compute how many statements are affected by these attributes is a subject of future work.

4. PRIEST PRIVACY FRAMEWORK

In this section, we describe the PRIEST privacy framework. We discuss constraints, show how to connect different aspects of data privacy with the testing utility, and present a privacy metric and our anonymization algorithm.

4.1 Constraints and Goals

After discussions with a number of experts from different organizations who are involved in testing DCAs, we identified two main constraints for a successful anonymization solution: simplicity and consistency. A simple anonymization solution should not impose significant laborious manual or intellectual effort on stakeholders who are involved in protecting privacy. A case at hand is when using data suppression and generalization algorithms to achieve k-anonymity, a popular data privacy approach, users must specify generalization hierarchies that guide corresponding anonymization algorithms to replace data values with generalized substitutes to protect sensitive information. For example, a branch of the generalization hierarchy for the attribute `Nationality` could be $\{Canadian, Mexican, USA\} \rightarrow NorthAmerican \rightarrow American \rightarrow Human$. In general, identifying and properly using these hierarchies involves deep domain expertise and significant effort. Stakeholders want a high degree of automation where they are presented with choices for privacy levels and corresponding test coverages, making it easy for them to balance privacy and utility.

Consistency of data is the other constraint. Since data used in typical DCAs can span multiple tables in databases, any field that is used as a key to link entities across tables needs to be anonymized *consistently* so that the data can be linked correctly after anonymization. Thus, anonymization techniques should take into consideration different constraints among attributes that are imposed by the database schema for describing this data.

Preserving original data values is a goal of our anonymization framework – no new values for a data field should be introduced and the unique set of values in a field should be preserved after anonymization. This constraint is important because changing the values (such as generalizing a five digit zip code to first three digits, or replacing the city name with the state in the `City` field would result in new values for a field that the DCA may not be able to handle properly. Having new data values often results in extra effort to modify the DCA and may cause unintended consequences in production with real data; for example, exceptions that are thrown would not be thrown if the original data is used.

Random data generation would typically preserve only univariate properties (marginal distributions) of each attribute. Our approach can preserve distributions over conjunctions of attributes (Gender=Female, Diagnosis=Ovarian Cancer) that are useful for preserving test coverage when conditional statements containing variables linked to multiple attributes are concerned, and such cases are common in real-world DCAs.

Finally, in this paper, we assume that the developer or data owner cannot be an attacker. While other attack models are possible, we assume that since developers have direct access to all information that is needed to create software, it is reasonable to assume that developers enjoy a high level of trust.

4.2 Guessing Anonymity

Guessing anonymity [31] is a privacy metric that enables stakeholders to quantify the level of privacy using a guessing strategy of the attacker as a sequence of questions of the form "Are these the original values of quasi-identifiers that are used to generate a sanitized record?"

Definition: The guessing anonymity of the sanitized record is the number of guesses that the optimal guessing strategy of the attacker requires in order to correctly guess the record used to generate the sanitized record.

To illustrate this definition, consider an attacker with knowledge that Alice and Chris are in the database, and knowledge of their true ages shown in Table 1 that contains original data. Sanitized data is shown in Table 2 where names are replaced with "***" and the values of the attribute `Age` are perturbed with random noise. The guessing anonymity of each record is shown in the fourth column of Table 2. While the record that corresponds to Alice has a guessing anonymity of two, the sanitized record corresponding to Chris has a guessing anonymity of one due to the fact that his age is significantly higher than the ages in the other records. The distribution of guessing anonymity of the different records in a database can be used to define a variety of privacy metrics. *Mean guessing anonymity*, *Minimum guessing anonymity*, and *Fraction of records* with guessing anonymity greater than a certain value m are some metrics that we discuss later in this section. For our toy database shown in Table 1, those values would be 1.75, 1, and 0.75 (for m=1), respectively.

To further illustrate our definition of guessing anonymity, we link our definition to the definition of k-anonymity. Recall that in k-anonymity, a database is considered private if every record has at least k other records in the original database with which the released record is indistinguishable. k-anonymity can be achieved by different anonymization operators but typically suppression and generalization operators are the most commonly used ones.

Consider a released record that is anonymized such that there are exactly k records in the original database with which the released record is consistent. Without any further information, the optimal guessing strategy would choose among these k records with uniform probability for its first guess. The probability of the first

Table 1: Original Database

Name	Age	Procedure or Prescription
Alice	19	Antidepressants
Bob	15	Antibiotics
Chris	52	Chemotherapy
Diana	25	Abortion

Table 2: Sanitized Database

Name	Age	Procedure or Prescription	Guessing Anonymity
***	23.1	Antidepressants	2
***	19.4	Antibiotics	2
***	49.3	Chemotherapy	1
***	21.1	Abortion	2

Algorithm 1 The `PriestPrivacy` algorithm.

1: **PriestPrivacy**($\{QI\}$, p) $\{\{QI\}$ is the set of QIs, and p is the probability that the original data will remain unchanged in the anonymized set, $T\}$
2: $\|T\| \leftarrow$NULL {Initialize values of the anonymized matrix.}
3: **for** $j \leftarrow 1$ to # of attributes in $\|QI\|$ **do**
4: **DistinctValues**($\|QI\|_j$) $\mapsto \{V\}_j$ {Returns the set of distinct values for a given attribute.}
5: **for** $i \leftarrow 1$ to # of rows in $\|QI\|$ **do**
6: **Randomize**(QI^i_j, p) $\mapsto (\exists v \in \{V\}_j$ s.t. $T^i_j \leftarrow v)$
7: **end for**
8: **end for**
9: **return** $\|T\|$

Algorithm 2 Guessing anonymity metric calculation algorithm.

PrivacyMetric($\|QI\|$, $\|T\|$)
$\|D\| \leftarrow 0$ {Initialize values of the distance matrix, D.}
for $i \leftarrow 1$ to # of rows in $\|T\|$ **do**
  for $k \leftarrow 1$ to # of rows in $\|QI\|$ **do**
    for $j \leftarrow 1$ to # of attributes in $\|QI\|$ **do**
      if $T^i_j = QI^i_j$ **then**
        $D^i_k \leftarrow D^i_k + 1$
      end if
    end for
    $D^i_k \leftarrow \frac{D^i_k}{\#ofattributesinQI}$
  end for
end for
{Compute privacy metrics PM_1 and PM_2.}
$R \leftarrow 0$
$diffRecords \leftarrow 0$
$d \times d \leftarrow \|D\|$ {Dimensions of the similarity matrix.}
for $i \leftarrow 1$ to d **do**
  if $D(i,i) < 1$ **then**
    $diffRecords \leftarrow diffRecords + 1$ {For metric PM_2.}
  end if
  for $j \leftarrow 1$ to d **do**
    if $i \neq j \wedge D(i,j) \geq D(i,i)$ **then**
      $R \leftarrow R + 1$
    end if
  end for
end for
return $PM_1 = \frac{R}{d}$, $PM_2 = \frac{diffRecords}{d}$

guess being correct is $\frac{1}{k}$. If the first guess is incorrect, the second guess is chosen with uniform probability from among the remaining $k-1$ records. The probability of the second guess being correct is $\frac{1}{k-1}(1-\frac{1}{k})$. The expected number of guesses simplifies to $\frac{k+1}{2}$, so the expected guessing anonymity of a k-anonymized record is $\frac{k+1}{2}$.

4.3 The PRIEST Anonymization Algorithm

The algorithm `PriestPrivacy` is shown in Algorithm 1. We use a data swapping anonymization technique to preserve original values of database attributes. The goal is to preserve test coverage better than when data suppression and generalization techniques are used, while keeping the data usable by the DCA. To protect privacy, each value for each row for each attribute is swapped with some probability with a different value for the same attribute. For example, for the attribute `Gender` that contains two distinct values `M` and `F`, the user may choose to replace the value of a given cell with the other value with probability 0.5, i.e., an unbiased coin flip. Excluding an attribute from anonymization means that the probability of value replacement for this attribute is zero.

This algorithm takes as its inputs the matrix of QIs and their values, $\|QI\|$, whose columns include QIs and rows include different tuples for these QIs from the original database DB_O, and the value of the probability, p, that the original data will remain unchanged in the anonymized matrix, $\|T\|$. The matrix $\|T\|$ has the same dimensions and semantics as the matrix $\|QI\|$, and it contains anonymized values of QIs. $\|T\|$'s values are initialized to `NULL` in Line `2` and this matrix is returned in Line `9`.

The `for`-loop in Lines `3-8` iterates through attributes that are in $\|QI\|$, and the procedure `DistinctValues` is called to compute the set of distinct values for each QI, $\{V\}$. Next, in Lines `5-7` the nested `for`-loop iterates through all rows for the given QI and the procedure `Randomized` is invoked to replace the original value in a cell with one of the original distinct values of the given QI, and the replaced value is written in the corresponding location in the matrix $\|T\|$. Once the algorithm iterates over all QIs and all rows for each QI, it terminates and returns $\|T\|$ in Line `9`.

An example of application of the algorithm `PriestPrivacy` is shown in Table 3 that contains (for illustrative purposes) three attributes: `Age`, `Gender`, and `Race`. The first column of this table holds the record number. Original values are shown in each cell with their sanitized replacements shown as a superscript for each value. For example, record `1` contains original value `30` for the attribute `Age` that is anonymized and replaced with the value `40`, which is one of three distinct values for this attribute. The superscripted values populate the matrix $\|T\|$. Interestingly, the sanitized record `1` matches the original record `2`; however, since the attacker sees only the sanitized data, it is not possible for the attacker to know with certainty that the sanitized record matches some original record.

4.4 Privacy Metrics

We first calculate the probability distribution of guessing anonymity over all the database records. Specific privacy metrics are then defined as a function of that distribution. In this paper, we define three of them but the optimal metric may vary based on the task at hand.

A privacy metric measures how identifiable records in the sanitized table are with respect to the original table [21, page 43]. The privacy metrics that we propose in this paper are all motivated by the notion of guessing anonymity. We calculate guessing anonymity using the algorithm shown in Algorithm 2. We begin by creating a similarity matrix that shows the similarity between sanitized and original records. For each record R_o in the original table, the similarity of R_o to a record R_s in the sanitized table is

Table 3: A table with original and anonymized (superscript) data. For example, the original value of the attribute Age is 30 and the sanitized value is 40.

Record	Age	Gender	Race
Rec 1	30^{40}	F^M	W^B
Rec 2	40^{40}	M^M	B^H
Rec 3	45^{30}	M^F	H^W
Rec 4	30^{40}	F^M	W^H

Table 4: A similarity matrix for the table shown in Table 3. Each cell contains the value that shows the fraction of attributes values that are the same between original and sanitized records.

Anonymized \ Original	Rec 1	Rec 2	Rec 3	Rec 4
Rec 1	0	1	0.33	0
Rec 2	0	0.66	0.66	0
Rec 3	1	0	0	1
Rec 4	0	0.66	0.66	0

measured by the fraction of attributes whose values are the same between R_o and R_s. This computation is performed in Lines `3-12` of the privacy metric algorithm. This similarity matrix, $\|D\|$, shows similarities between rows in the original matrix, $\|QI\|$, and the anonymized matrix, $\|T\|$.

Table 4 shows an illustrative example for computing the similarity matrix $\|D\|$ for the data in Table 3. The similarity matrix $\|D\|$ has dimensions $d \times d$, where d is the number of records in the matrices $\|QI\|$ and $\|T\|$. Rows correspond to anonymized records and columns correspond to the original records in $\|D\|$. The values of the attributes `Age`, `Gender`, and `Race` are `30`, `F`, and `W` for the original record `1`, respectively, and the values for the sanitized record `1` are `40`, `M`, and `H`, respectively. Therefore, the similarity score is zero for the original and sanitized record `1`. In contrast, the similarity score is one for original record `2` and sanitized record `1` since all attribute values of the original record 2 match the values of their corresponding attributes for the sanitized record `1`.

We use the similarity matrix $\|D\|$ to compute how difficult it is for attackers to guess original records given sanitized records. Consider an extreme case where $\|D\|$ is a diagonal matrix, i.e., all entries outside the main diagonal are zero. In this case, each record is similar to itself only, that is, all records are unique and easily identifiable by attackers. The privacy level for this sanitized table is zero. The other extreme case is when all sanitized records are similar to all other records. In this case, it is very difficult for attackers to guess original data since all sanitized records are highly similar to one another. Correspondingly, the privacy level for this sanitized table is close to one. In practice, the privacy level is between zero and one, and our goal is to help analysts find the right balance between a privacy level and the utility of the sanitized database.

The distribution of guessing anonymity of the different records in a database can be used to define a variety of privacy metrics. In this paper, we propose three different privacy metrics that are derived from the guessing anonymity distribution, but do not focus on providing the *best* metric. We believe that different applications and risk tolerances of users would require the use of different derived metrics and leave the optimal metric determination as future work.

In this paper, we propose three metrics based on guessing anonymity: PM_1: *Mean guessing anonymity*, PM_2: *Fraction of records with guessing anonymity greater than a certain value m (where we set m to one in this paper)*, and *Unique Records*. The computation of these privacy metrics PM_1 and PM_2 is shown in Lines `14-27` of Algorithm 2, and their values are returned in Line `27`.

PM_1: The *Mean guessing anonymity* of a database is the arithmetic mean of the individual guessing anonymities for each record in the database. This metric gives us measurement of the overall privacy of the sanitized database and helps us compare different versions of sanitized databases. Naturally, a database with higher *Mean guessing anonymity* would be more difficult to attack and hence have higher privacy. Suppose that there is a record $r_o \in T_o$, where T_o is the table with original records. After T_o is sanitized, the table T_s with sanitized records is obtained, $r_s \in T_s$, and we compute the similarity matrix, $\|D\|$, for records in these tables. Then, for each $r_o \in T_o$, we increase the counter, R, by one if we find a record in the table T_s that has the similarity score in $\|D\|$ equal to or higher than the similarity score between r_o and its sanitized version, r_s, not counting the similarity score between r_o and r_s. The formula for the privacy metric is $PM_1 = \frac{R}{d}$, where d is the number of records.

PM_2: The fraction of records with guessing anonymity greater than m is our second metric. We set m to one for the work in this paper; such setting corresponds to measuring the fraction of original records that have been modified at all by the anonymization algorithm. PM_2 is calculated as the ratio of records that were sanitized and that differ from their original record in at least one attribute value to the total number of records. This metric is useful for a variety of reasons. If the fraction of records that have guessing anonymity greater than m is too low and the users are unsatisfied, they have the option to increase the level of privacy or remove the records that fall below the threshold from the sanitized database, thus making the database more private.

UniqueRecords is measured as part of PM_2 and it is defined as follows. Suppose that there is a record $r_o \in T_o$, where T_o is the table with original records. After T_o is sanitized, the table T_s with sanitized records is obtained. Let $r_s \in T_s$ be the sanitized record for $r_o \in T_o$. r_s is a unique record if there exists $r'_o \in T_o$, such that all attributes of r'_o have the same value as the attributes of r_s. A key idea of guessing anonymity is that although some records after applying data swapping may match some original records, the attacker still cannot know with certainty which ones do and whether sensitive information (that these records identify) was not changed. Ideally, the percentage of unique records in the anonymized database will be zero - that is what we would like to achieve. If the number of unique records is greater than zero and the desired goal is to have complete anonymity, the users will have to delete these unique records before releasing the database.

5. EXPERIMENTAL EVALUATION

In this section, we describe the results of the experimental evaluation of PRIEST on three open-source Java programs and one large commercial application that is used to manage logistics of one of the largest supermarket chains in Spain.

5.1 Research Questions

In this paper, we make one meta-claim – our privacy framework for managing the tradeoff between data privacy and test coverage for DCAs is "better" than other frameworks. We define "better" in two ways: *coverage* and *flexibility*. Achieving higher coverage with PRIEST means that for a given level of privacy, we can provide higher test coverage. We measure it using the area under the privacy-coverage curve. Flexibility means that we can give more choices to the business analyst to make informed decisions. If more data points in that curve can be created using PRIEST for a given range of privacy, we have a better framework for managing the tradeoff.

PRIEST does not compete with other anonymization techniques, such as k-anonymity since the latter is a metric, not a framework. Our claim is that our framework (that includes guessing anonymity) is a better framework to achieve coverage and flexibility. We seek to answer the following research questions.

RQ1 How much test coverage does PRIEST help achieve at given levels of privacy for subject applications?

RQ2 How effective is PRIEST in achieving different levels of data privacy while preserving original data?

RQ3 How effective is PRIEST in releasing different versions of anonymized databases for the same level of privacy and test coverage without enabling the attacker to link sensitive data?

With RQ1, we address our claim that we designed and implemented a technique using program analysis for determining how values of database attributes affect test coverage of DCAs that use this data. Our goal is to show that with PRIEST, the privacy metric is linked directly to test coverage and vice versa; in other words, guaranteeing a certain level of test coverage should allow stakeholders to calculate bounds of the privacy level.

With RQ2, we address our claim that using different levels of privacy enables business analysts to make trade-off decisions about privacy and utility.

With RQ3, we address our claim that PRIEST enables stakeholders to repeatedly release anonymized data in such a way that both privacy and utility are guaranteed at certain levels. Suppose that a technique of data suppression anonymization is applied to protect data and release the anonymized data with the DCA to testers. After some time, programmers produce the next release of this DCA that uses different attributes differently in its database. Suppose that the DCA does not use the attribute `Nationality` any more, and it uses the attribute `Race` instead. At this point, the database should be reanonymized, since the original values of the attribute `Race` should be left intact to preserve test coverage. However, in the previous anonymization, the values of the attribute `Nationality` are left unprotected. It means that the testers (the attackers) know original values of the attribute `Nationality` and now the testers will know the original values of the attribute `Race`. Together, these attributes enable the attackers to infer sensitive information from the released database.

5.2 Subject Programs

We evaluate PRIEST with three open-source and one large commercial Java programs that belong to different domains. Our selection of subject programs is influenced by several factors: sizes of the databases, size of the source code, presence of unit, system, and integration tests, and the presence of embedded SQL queries that these programs use.

We selected four subject programs that come with test cases. `N2A` is a program for handling logistics of one of the largest supermarket chains in Spain. `N2A` has a total of 77,828 LOC. `RiskIt` is an insurance quote program[4]. `DurboDax` enables customer support centers to manage customer data[5]. Finally, `UnixUsage` is a program for obtaining statistics on how users interact with Unix systems using their commands[6].

[4]https://riskitinsurance.svn.sourceforge.net as of March 10, 2011.

[5]http://se547-durbodax.svn.sourceforge.net as of March 10, 2011.

[6]http://sourceforge.net/projects/se549unixusage as of March 10, 2011.

DCA	App [kLOC]	Test	DB [MB]	Tbl	Att	IC %	ETC %
N2A	77.8	19.3	20	506	2514	53	50
DurboDax	2.8	2.0	49	27	114	77	59
UnixUsage	2.8	.9	21	8	31	61	53
RiskIt	4.3	2.6	628	13	57	62	48

Table 5: Characteristics of the subject DCAs. App = application code, Test = test cases, DB = database, Tbl = tables, Att = attributes in all tables, IC = initial test coverage with the original database, ETC = estimated worst test coverage with sanitized data using the approach described in Section 3.

Table 5 contains characteristics of the subject programs, their databases, and test cases. The first column shows the names of the subject programs, followed by the number of lines of code, LOC for the program code and accompanying test cases. The source code of the project ranges from 2.8 to 77.8 kLOC. The test cases range from 0.9 to 19.3 kLOC. Other columns show the size of the database, number of tables and attributes in the database, test coverage (statement coverage) that is obtained with the original database, and the estimated worst test coverage (statement coverage) with sanitized data using our approach described in Section 3.

5.3 Methodology

To evaluate PRIEST, we carry out experiments to explore its effectiveness in enabling users to determine how to balance test coverage while achieving different levels of data privacy (RQ1 and RQ2), and to show that it is possible to apply PRIEST to get privacy guarantees while releasing different sanitized versions of the database for the same privacy levels thereby supporting software evolution (RQ3).

5.3.1 Variables

The main independent variable is the value of p. Two main response variables are the time that it takes to anonymize data in the database to achieve the desired level of k to answer RQ2 and the test coverage in percentage of program statements to answer RQ1.

5.3.2 The Structure of the Experiments

For the experiments, we select as QIs all attributes whose values affect execution paths in the corresponding DCAs. It is physically not possible to carry out an experiment using all subsets of the powerset of attributes as QIs where we measure test coverage for subject DCAs while achieving anonymity, since it would require us to consider the powerset of all attributes. Given that databases of the subject DCAs contain between 31 and 2,514 attributes, it is challenging to select a subset of them as QIs to enable achieve the higher possible level of test coverage.

Our goal is to run experiments for different values of the independent variable p and report the effect of varying the values on p on dependent variables. To address RQ3, we anonymize databases for the subject DCAs for a given level of p, and we report and analyze privacy metrics between different sanitized versions of the same original database.

5.4 Threats to Validity

A threat to the validity of this experimental evaluation is that our subject programs are of small to moderate size because it is difficult to find a large number of open-source programs that use nontrivial databases. Large DCAs that have millions of lines of code and use databases whose sizes are measured in thousands of

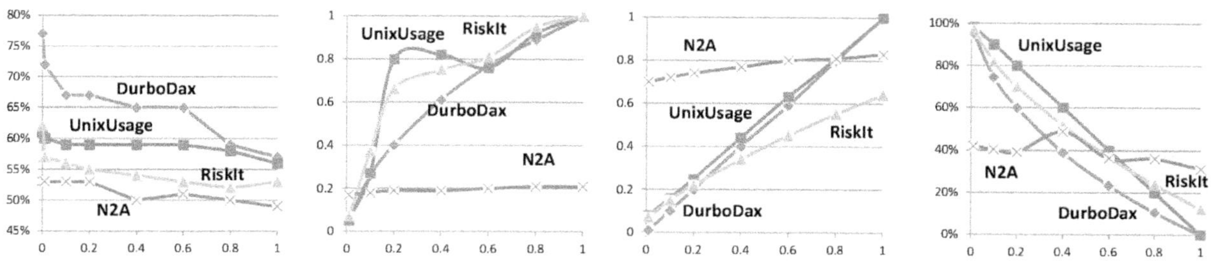

(a) Test coverage. (b) Privacy metric PM_1. (c) Privacy metric PM_2. (d) Unique records.

Figure 3: Experimental results for the subject DCAs. All graphs show the dependence on the probability of replacing original data value that is assigned to the horizontal axis. The vertical axis designates dependent variables that are given in the captions to these figures.

tables and attributes may have different characteristics compared to our small to medium size subject programs. Increasing the size of applications to millions of lines of code may lead to a nonlinear increase in the analysis time and space demand for PRIEST. Future work could focus on making PRIEST more scalable.

5.5 Results

The results of the experiments conducted to address $RQ1$ and $RQ2$ are shown in Figure 3 and Table 6. Dependency of test coverage on the probability p of replacing original values is shown in Figure $3(a)$. The maximum reduction in test coverage is close to 26% from the initial test coverage with $p = 1$ for application DurboDax. In our previous work [23], we showed that the maximum reduction in test coverage for the same applications reaches 80% from the initial test coverage when using a popular algorithm Datafly that is based on data suppression and generalization techniques [36]. We observed the biggest drop in test coverage with Datafly when $k = 7$, while much smaller maximum drop is observed with PRIEST for $p = 1$, which is the maximum value for the anonymization parameter.

The least drop in test coverage is observed for the application N2A, while the biggest drop is attributed to the application DurboDax. Our explanation is that N2A is least sensitive to values of the database attributes since it uses these values to compute results rather than in path conditions. We explain the sharper drop for DurboDax as a result of branch conditions that use conjunctions of multiple QIs, thereby making the application sensitive to joint distributions of values of different attributes that may be destroyed by anonymization. We also observe that the shape of the test coverage curves show gradual decline in test coverage rather than abrupt changes. The former makes it easier for stakeholders to balance privacy and coverage on a continuous scale.

Dependencies of privacy metrics PM_1 and PM_2 on the probability p of replacing original values are shown in Figure $3(b)$ and Figure $3(c)$. Combined with the test coverage curve shown in Figure $3(a)$, these dependencies enable business analysts to select a level of protection that also ensures a certain level of test coverage. While values of PM_1 are monotonically increasing for N2A, RiskIt, and DurboDax with the increase in p, the values of PM_1 for UnixUsage slightly drop when the values of p are increasing from 0.2 to 0.6. This result can be explained as an effect of the variations of random value replacement that may result in small changes in the numbers of similar records. The values for $PM1$ are relatively small for N2A since many of the selected QIs were involved in some primary or unique key. As a result, the sanitized

Table 7: Results for privacy metrics to compare two sanitized databases for $p = 0.6$ for subject DCAs

Subject DCA	PM_1	PM_2	Total Records	Unique Records	$UR, \%$
N2A	0.20	0.78	586801	265400	38.7
DurboDax	0.60	0.77	88450	20687	23.4
UnixUsage	0.61	0.60	250570	100422	40.1
RiskIt	0.47	0.76	1270792	512051	40.3

records contain distinct values for these QIs and fewer records (in the original database) are likely to be similar to a sanitized record.

Opposite to the dependencies of privacy metrics PM_1 and PM_2, the graph of the dependency of the percentage of unique records, UR shows corresponding decline in Figure $3(d)$. It means that the percentage of unique records between the original and sanitized databases is monotonically declining as the values of the probability p are increasing thereby making it more difficult for attackers to use these unique records to guess the original data. While values of UR are monotonically decreasing for UnixUsage, RiskIt, and DurboDax with the increase in p, the values of UR for N2A slightly increase when the values of p are increasing from 0.2 to 0.6. This result can be explained as an effect of the variations of random value replacement that may result in small changes in the numbers of unique records.

To address RQ3, we generated two sanitized databases for $p = 0.6$ and computed the privacy metrics $PM1$, $PM2$, and number of unique records between the two databases. These metrics quantify the difficulty of an attacker to relate records from the two sanitized databases. Since the same database is anonymized independently and the probabilities of replacing cell values are independent from one another, then resulting databases cannot be deterministically correlated since they are not used to produce each other. Thus, the attacker has to guess original data independently, meaning that the lowest guessing anonymity score can be used to quantify the difficulty of an attacker to guess records from both sanitized databases.

The values for $PM1$ are slightly lower to the values of $PM1$ for $p = 0.6$ in Table 6, while the values of $PM2$ are slightly higher to the values of $PM1$ for $p = 0.6$ in Table 6. This phenomenon is expected since the variation between the records of the two anonymized databases is expected to be more as compared to variation between the records of original and an anonymized database. The number of unique records is similar to the number of unique records for $p = 0.6$ in Table 6. It is also important to note that the overall privacy of multiple sanitized databases is only as good as the privacy of the least private version. If the first released version has $PM_2 = 3$ and the second version has $PM_2 = 5$, PM_2 for

Subject	QIs	Total Records	Initial Cov	Worst Exp Cov	Max Err Cov	Dependent Variable	The Probability of Value Replacement, p						
							0.01	0.1	0.2	0.4	0.6	0.8	1
N2A	61	586801	53%	50%	2.0%	PM_1	0.17	0.18	0.19	0.19	0.20	0.21	0.21
						PM_2	0.70	0.72	0.74	0.77	0.80	0.81	0.83
						TC,%	49.00	49.00	49.00	50.00	51.00	49.00	49.00
						UR,%	41.80	40.30	39.00	48.60	36.10	36.00	31.30
DurboDax	20	88450	77%	59%	3.6%	PM_1	0.05	0.26	0.40	0.61	0.77	0.89	1.00
						PM_2	0.01	0.10	0.20	0.40	0.59	0.80	1.00
						TC,%	72.00	67.00	67.00	65.00	65.00	59.00	57.00
						UR,%	95.20	74.40	60.00	38.90	23.30	10.60	0.00
UnixUsage	16	250570	61%	53%	5.7%	PM_1	0.05	0.27	0.80	0.82	0.76	0.92	1.00
						PM_2	0.08	0.16	0.25	0.44	0.63	0.81	1.00
						TC,%	60.00	59.00	59.00	59.00	59.00	58.00	56.00
						UR,%	98.30	90.00	80.00	60.20	39.90	20.00	0.01
RiskIt	28	1270792	62%	48%	8.3%	PM_1	0.07	0.37	0.66	0.75	0.81	0.95	1.00
						PM_2	0.07	0.15	0.22	0.34	0.45	0.55	0.64
						TC,%	57.00	56.00	55.00	54.00	53.00	52.00	53.00
						UR,%	96.90	81.70	69.90	51.60	36.70	23.80	12.30

Table 6: Results of experiments with subject DCAs for different values of the independent variable p that is shown in the last column header that spans seven subcolumns. The second column, QI, shows the number of QI whose values affect control-flow decisions in DCAs, the next two columns show the initial test coverage (statement coverage) with the original database and the estimated worst test coverage with sanitized data using the approach described in Section 3. The next column shows the error in the estimated test coverage that varies from 2.0% to 8.3%. Finally, the next column lists four dependent variables, privacy metrics PM_1 and PM_2, test coverage, TC, and the percentage of unique records, UR. Finally, the last seven subcolumns show values of these dependent variables for different values of p.

the two databases combined will be 3. In general, for two released databases D_i and D_j, the overall $PM_2 = \text{Min}(PM_2(D_i), PM_2(D_j))$.

Result summary. These results strongly suggest that PRIEST helps achieve higher test coverage for given levels of privacy for subject applications when compared with Datafly that is based on data suppression and generalization techniques, thereby addressing RQ1. PRIEST can also achieve different levels of data privacy while preserving original data as it is seen from Table 6, thereby addressing RQ2. Finally, the results shown in Table 7 strongly suggest that PRIEST is effective in releasing different versions of anonymized databases for the same level of privacy and test coverage, thereby addressing RQ3.

6. RELATED WORK

Our work is related to regression testing [39] since PRIEST is used to assess the impact of data anonymization on testing. Numerous techniques have been proposed to automate regression testing. These techniques usually rely on information obtained from the modifications made to the source code. These techniques are not directly applicable to preserving test coverage while achieving data anonymity for test outsourcing, since regression information is derived from changes made to the source code and not to how this code uses databases.

Closely related to PRIEST is $kb-$anonymity model that enables stakeholders to release private data for testing and debugging by combining the $k-$anonymity with the concept of program behavior preservation [10]. Unlike PRIEST, $kb-$anonymity replaces some information in the original data to ensure privacy preservation so that the replaced data can be released to third-party developers. PRIEST and $kb-$anonymity are complementary in using different privacy mechanisms to preserve original data thereby improving its testing utility.

Recently proposed is an anonymization technique for protecting private information in bug reports that are delivered to vendors when programs crash on computers of customers [11] and the follow-up work on this technique by Clause and Orso [14]. This technique provides software vendors with new input values that satisfy the conditions required to make the software follow the same execution path until it fails, but are otherwise unrelated with the original inputs. This technique uses symbolic execution to create new inputs that allow vendors to reproduce the bug while revealing less private information than existing techniques. The technique requires test cases, which are not present in our situation. In contrast, PRIEST does not require any test case.

There has been a lot of recent work to achieve general purpose (task-independent) data anonymization. We choose the guessing anonymity approach in this paper because guessing anonymity can be used to provide privacy guarantees for data swapping algorithms and can also provide an optimal noise parameter when implementing data swapping algorithms for anonymization. In contrast, approaches that aim to achieve k-anonymity do not allow the user to explicitly control how much each record is altered. Empirical results reported by Rachlin et al. [31] show that Guessing anonymity outperforms DataFly, a well-known k-Anonymity algorithm on specific data mining tasks, namely classification and regression, while at the same time providing a higher degree of control over how much the data is distorted.

Recent work on privacy introduced a similar definition of privacy for noise perturbation methods, known as k-randomization [2]. This work defines a record as k-randomized if the number of records that are a more likely match to the original is *at least* k. Although this notion is similar to the definition of guessing anonymity, the definition differs by not providing a lower limit on the number of records that provide a more likely match, and by explicitly establishing a connection between privacy and guessing functions.

7. CONCLUSION

We offer a novel and effective approach called PRIEST that helps organizations to remove an obstacle to effective DCA test outsourcing. With PRIEST, DCAs can be released to external testing organizations without disclosing sensitive information while retaining testing efficacy. We built a tool and applied it to nontrivial DCAs. The results show that PRIEST is effective in enabling users to determine how to balance test coverage while achieving different levels of data privacy, and that with PRIEST, users can release different sanitized versions of the database for the same privacy levels, thereby supporting software evolution.

Acknowledgments

We thank anonymous reviewers whose comments helped us to improve the quality of this paper. This work is supported in part by NSF CCF-0916139, CCF-1017633, CCF-0725190, CCF-0845272, CCF-0915400, CNS-0958235, an NCSU CACC grant, and ARO grant W911NF-08-1-0443, and Accenture. Any opinions, findings, and conclusions expressed herein are the authors' and do not necessarily reflect those of the sponsors.

8. REFERENCES

[1] C. C. Aggarwal. On k-anonymity and the curse of dimensionality. In *VLDB*, pages 901–909, 2005.

[2] C. C. Aggarwal. On randomization, public information and the curse of dimensionality. In *ICDE*, pages 136–145, 2007.

[3] C. C. Aggarwal and P. S. Yu. On static and dynamic methods for condensation-based privacy-preserving data mining. *ACM Trans. Database Syst.*, 33:2:1–2:39, March 2008.

[4] C. C. Aggarwal and P. S. Yu. *Privacy-Preserving Data Mining: Models and Algorithms*. Springer, 2008.

[5] J. T. Alexander, M. Davern, and B. Stevenson. Inaccurate age and sex data in the census pums files: Evidence and implications. Working Paper 15703, National Bureau of Economic Research, January 2010.

[6] S. Ambler. Robust persistence layers. *Softw. Dev.*, 6(2):73–75, 1998.

[7] W. Aspray, F. Mayades, and M. Vardi. *Globalization and Offshoring of Software*. ACM, 2006.

[8] C. Bialik. Census bureau obscured personal data – too well, some say. *The Wall Street Journal*, Feb. 2010.

[9] J. Brickell and V. Shmatikov. The cost of privacy: destruction of data-mining utility in anonymized data publishing. In *KDD*, pages 70–78, 2008.

[10] A. Budi, D. Lo, L. Jiang, and Lucia. *b*-anonymity: a model for anonymized behaviour-preserving test and debugging data. In *PLDI*, pages 447–457, 2011.

[11] M. Castro, M. Costa, and J.-P. Martin. Better bug reporting with better privacy. In *ASPLOS*, pages 319–328, 2008.

[12] L. A. Clarke. A system to generate test data and symbolically execute programs. *IEEE Trans. Softw. Eng.*, 2(3):215–222, 1976.

[13] J. Clause and A. Orso. Penumbra: Automatically identifying failure-relevant inputs using dynamic tainting. In *ISSTA*, pages 249–260, 2009.

[14] J. A. Clause and A. Orso. Camouflage: automated anonymization of field data. In *ICSE*, pages 21–30, 2011.

[15] G. Cormode and D. Srivastava. Anonymized data: generation, models, usage. In *SIGMOD*, pages 1015–1018, 2009.

[16] Datamonitor. Application testing services: global market forecast model. *Datamonitor Research Store*, Aug. 2007.

[17] R. A. DeMillo and A. J. Offutt. Constraint-based automatic test data generation. *IEEE Trans. Softw. Eng.*, 17(9):900–910, 1991.

[18] I. Dinur and K. Nissim. Revealing information while preserving privacy. In *PODS*, pages 202–210, 2003.

[19] J. Domingo-Ferrer and D. Rebollo-Monedero. Measuring risk and utility of anonymized data using information theory. In *EDBT/ICDT*, pages 126–130, 2009.

[20] A. Endres and D. Rombach. *A Handbook of Software and Systems Engineering*. Pearson Addison-Wesley, 2003.

[21] B. C. M. Fung, K. Wang, A. W.-C. Fu, and P. S. Yu. *Introduction to Privacy-Preserving Data Publishing: Concepts and Techniques*. Data Mining and Knowledge Discovery. Chapman & Hall/CRC, August 2010.

[22] P. Godefroid. Compositional dynamic test generation. In *POPL*, pages 47–54, 2007.

[23] M. Grechanik, C. Csallner, C. Fu, and Q. Xie. Is data privacy always good for software testing? In *ISSRE*, pages 368–377, 2010.

[24] M. Grechanik, C. McMillan, L. DeFerrari, M. Comi, S. Crespi, D. Poshyvanyk, C. Fu, Q. Xie, and C. Ghezzi. An empirical investigation into a large-scale Java open source code repository. In *ESEM*, pages 11:1–11:10, 2010.

[25] C. Jones. *Software Engineering Best Practices*. McGraw-Hill, Inc., New York, NY, USA, 1 edition, 2010.

[26] G. M. Kapfhammer and M. L. Soffa. A family of test adequacy criteria for database-driven applications. In *ESEC/FSE*, pages 98–107, 2003.

[27] W. Landi. Undecidability of static analysis. *ACM Lett. Program. Lang. Syst.*, 1(4):323–337, 1992.

[28] T. Li and N. Li. On the tradeoff between privacy and utility in data publishing. In *KDD*, pages 517–526, 2009.

[29] R. Majumdar and K. Sen. Hybrid concolic testing. In *ICSE*, pages 416–426, 2007.

[30] T. E. Murphy. Managing test data for maximum productivity. *http://www.gartner.com/DisplayDocument?doc_cd=163662&ref=g_economy_2reduce*, Dec. 2008.

[31] Y. Rachlin, K. Probst, and R. Ghani. Maximizing privacy under data distortion constraints in noise perturbation methods. In *PinKDD*, pages 92–110, 2008.

[32] S. P. Reiss. Practical data-swapping: the first steps. *ACM Trans. Database Syst.*, 9:20–37, March 1984.

[33] S. P. Reiss, M. J. Post, and T. Dalenius. Non-reversible privacy transformations. In *PODS*, pages 139–146, 1982.

[34] P. Samarati. Protecting respondents' identities in microdata release. *IEEE Trans. Knowl. Data Eng.*, 13(6):1010–1027, 2001.

[35] I. Shield. International data privacy laws. *http://www.informationshield.com/intprivacylaws.html*, 2010.

[36] L. Sweeney. k-anonymity: A model for protecting privacy. *International Journal of Uncertainty, Fuzziness and Knowledge-Based Systems*, 10(5):557–570, 2002.

[37] K. Taneja, Y. Zhang, and T. Xie. MODA: Automated test generation for database applications via mock objects. In *ASE*, pages 289–292, 2010.

[38] B. G. Thompson. *H.R.6423: Homeland Security Cyber and Physical Infrastructure Protection Act of 2010*. U.S.House, 111th Congress, Nov. 2010.

[39] S. Yoo and M. Harman. Regression testing minimisation, selection and prioritisation: A survey. *STVR, to appear*, 2011.

Strong Higher Order Mutation-Based Test Data Generation

Mark Harman
CREST Centre
University College London
Gower Street, London, UK

Yue Jia
CREST Centre
University College London
Gower Street, London, UK

William B. Langdon
CREST Centre
University College London
Gower Street, London, UK

ABSTRACT

This paper introduces SHOM, a mutation-based test data generation approach that combines Dynamic Symbolic Execution and Search Based Software Testing. SHOM targets strong mutation adequacy and is capable of killing both first and higher order mutants. We report the results of an empirical study using 17 programs, including production industrial code from ABB and Daimler and open source code as well as previously studied subjects. SHOM achieved higher strong mutation adequacy than two recent mutation-based test data generation approaches, killing between 8% and 38% of those mutants left unkilled by the best performing previous approach.

Categories and Subject Descriptors

D.2.5 [**Software Engineering**]: Testing and Debugging

General Terms

Experimentation

Keywords

Mutation testing, Test data generation

1. INTRODUCTION

Mutation testing is a fault based testing technique, first proposed by DeMillo et al. [7] and Hamlet [13] and widely studied since [22]. The idea underpinning mutation testing is to seed faults to assess the adequacy of the testing approach. The fault-seeded version of the original program is called a 'mutant'. Research activity in mutation testing is increasing and its tools and techniques are reaching a state of maturity and widespread applicability [22].

If a test case distinguishes the behaviour of the original program from that of one of its mutants, then the test case is said to 'kill' the mutant. If the test case merely causes the state to change after the mutation point is executed then the mutant is said to be 'weakly' killed. However, if the test case causes this state change to propagate to an output, where an observable failure is observed, then the test case is said to 'strongly' kill the mutant.

Permission to make digital or hard copies of all or part of this work for personal or classroom use is granted without fee provided that copies are not made or distributed for profit or commercial advantage and that copies bear this notice and the full citation on the first page. To copy otherwise, to republish, to post on servers or to redistribute to lists, requires prior specific permission and/or a fee.
ESEC/FSE'11, September 5–9, 2011, Szeged, Hungary.
Copyright 2011 ACM 978-1-4503-0443-6/11/09 ...$10.00.

Strong mutation testing embodies a more demanding test adequacy criterion than weak mutation testing, making it preferable that a test suite would be strong mutation adequate, where possible [41]. By definition a test that strongly kills a mutant must also weakly kill it, but not necessarily *vice versa*.

If a mutant and the original program are semantically identical then the mutant is said to be 'equivalent'; no test case can kill it. Equivalent mutants are a problem for mutation testing, because equivalence is undecidable, making it hard to know whether an unkilled mutant is killable.

Based on the types of faults seeded, mutation testing can classified as 'first order' or 'higher order'. First order mutation seeds only simple faults, generated by a single syntactic change to the original program. Higher order mutation combines simple first order faults to simulate more complex faults, motivated by a desire to capture subtle faults [21].

Higher Order Mutation Testing has been the subject of much recent attention [5, 16, 27]. As well as its ability to model more complex masking faults [20], there is evidence to suggest that it may reduce mutation effort [38] and also the proportion of mutants that are equivalent [25, 35].

There has been much work on different techniques and tools for generating mutants, with over 250 publications on mutation testing. However, the literature contains only 10 publications (about 4% of the total) that address the problem of automatically generating test data to kill mutants [22]. A summary of these 10 papers is presented in Table 1. While mutation generation remains important, it is also clearly desirable to be able to use mutation testing to generate test cases as well as to asses them.

Previous work on the generation of test data to kill mutants has used traditional structural-oriented test data generation techniques, for example, traditional symbolic execution [8, 26, 30, 31, 32], Dynamic Symbolic Execution (DSE) [34, 37, 42] and Search Based Software Testing (SBST) [4, 11]. However, all of the existing techniques are designed to achieve only weak mutation adequacy and only for first order mutants. There is neither existing work on killing higher order mutants, nor any work on generating strong mutation adequate test data.

This paper presents SHOM, a novel hybrid approach that draws on previous work from both DSE and SBST to achieve strong higher order mutation adequacy[1]. The paper presents evidence to support the claim that SHOM is efficient and effective for both first order and higher order mutation.

[1]A first order mutant is a special case of a higher order mutant so SHOM also achieves first order mutation adequacy.

The contributions of the paper can be summarised as follows:

1. We introduce a hybrid test data generation approach for strongly killing both first order and higher order mutants. We evaluate our approach on 17 subject programs, including 7 real world programs (four from two different closed source industrial systems and three for which source code is publicly available). For backward compatibility with comparable recent studies (that use C) and the older ones (that use Fortran) we also include C versions of 10 of the smaller programs studied in this previous work. However, our study also includes programs an order of magnitude larger than any of these smaller programs.

2. We report the results of an empirical evaluation of SHOM's efficiency and effectiveness for strong first order mutation adequacy. The results show that SHOM can kill up to 38% of the first order mutants left unkilled using reachability and infection, which in turn kills up to 36% of the mutants left unkilled using reachability alone.

3. We also report the results of a further empirical study of SHOM's efficiency and effectiveness for strong second order mutation adequacy. The results show that SHOM can kill up to 48% of the second order mutants left unkilled using reachability and infection, which in turn kills up to 41% of the mutants left unkilled using reachability alone.

The rest of this paper is organised as follows. Section 2 introduces our hybrid DSE/SBST approach, while Section 3 briefly describes implementation details. Section 4 explains the experimental method, the results of which are discussed in Section 5. Section 6 introduces related work, and the paper concludes with Section 7.

2. STRONGLY KILLING HIGHER ORDER MUTANTS USING DSE AND SBST

We first define a mutant and a higher order mutant and what it means to kill them, before explaining our approach to generating test data using a combination of DSE and SBST to strongly kill higher order mutants.

DEFINITION 1 (FIRST ORDER MUTANT). *A first order mutant p' of a program p is constructed by making a single syntactic change to p. A transformation that produces a mutant from the original program is called a 'mutation operator'.*

Of course there remains the question of what is a 'single syntactic change'. There are many definitions of such sets of mutation operators in the literature [1, 33]. For our purposes, it is only important to define first order mutation so that we can define higher order mutation in terms of it. Higher order mutation can only be formally defined with respect to a set of first order mutation operators.

DEFINITION 2 (HIGHER ORDER MUTANT). *Given a set of first order mutation operators M, if a mutant p' is created from a program p by the application of k operators from M then p' is said to be a kth order mutant of p.*

Definition 2 of Higher Order Mutation subsumes Definition 1 of first order mutation because setting $k = 1$ in Definition 2 yields Definition 1. In general, care will be required to ensure that all of the k mutation operations creates a distinct syntactic change when applied to p. It may also be necessary to define the order of application of the k mutation operators, since different application orders may produce different overall syntactic effect. However, we leave these topics for future studies on higher order mutation.

Higher order mutants are generally easier to kill than first order mutants. However, there also exists a small set of higher order mutants that is harder to kill than the first order mutants from which they are constructed. This type of higher order mutant is known as a subsuming higher order mutant [21]. Figure 1 shows a simple illustrative example of subsuming higher order mutant. Both mutant 1 and mutant 2 are so-called 'dumb' mutants (those which are very easy to kill). In this case both are killed by *any and every* test cases; the dumbest possible. However, the higher order mutants created by inserting both mutant 1 and mutant 2 together is far from dumb. It is much harder to kill than either of its first order mutants. Essentially, in this sort of situation, fault masking can create subtle higher order bugs from unsubtle first order bugs.

In order to (strongly) kill a first order mutant the killing conditions are well studied in the literature: A test input needs to satisfy following three conditions: Reachability, Infection and Propagation (RIP), each of which subsumes the preceding condition(s):

1. **Reachability**: The location of the mutant in the program must be executed by the test case. We say the mutant is 'reached'. Reaching all mutants of a program can be achieved by any branch adequate test set, so reachability is an instance of branch coverage, which is widely studied in literature [2, 12, 19, 39].

2. **Infection**: Immediately after mutant execution, the original program state and that of the mutant must differ. We say, the mutant 'infects' the state. A test case that achieves infection for a mutant m is also said to 'weakly kill' the m [8, 22, 28].

3. **Propagation**: The infected state must propagate to some point in the program at which it can be observed, such as an output statement. A test case that achieves propagation for a mutant m is also said to 'strongly kill' the m [8, 22, 28].

2.1 Weakly Killing Mutants

DSE has proved to be an effective means of satisfying both the reachability and infection conditions [12, 39] and, as a result, there has been work on DSE as a technique for achieving weak mutation adequacy [34, 37, 42]. However, it has not been adapted to handle strong mutation.

Our approach uses DSE to generate weakly killing constraints and test data that satisfy them. When generating mutants, properties denoting reachability infection are collected for each mutant. The reachability property is captured by the set of critical predicate nodes that transitively control mutant reachability. This property is generated by traditional control dependence analysis. The second property is the infection constraint which is determined by the specific type of mutant. We use the infection conditions found in the work of DeMillo and Offutt [8].

Table 1: Mutation-based Test Data Generation. In referring to study example sizes, 'tiny' refers to laboratory programs consisting of a single procedure, while 'small' refers to slightly less trivial laboratory programs. The term 'non-trivial' is reserved for real world programs, neither written by students, nor the experimenters themselves, nor drawn from the 'Siemens Suite'. (†)The work of Offutt et al. [31, 32] reported basic block and dataflow coverage, but not Mutation Score. (‡)The work of Fraser and Zeller achieved (R)eachability and (I)nfection and also a constrained form of (P)ropagation, because it sought to maximize the mutant's effect on assertions, providing a form of propagation and also a way to maximise mutant impact.

Authors [Ref]	Year	(R)eaches, (I)nfects, (P)ropagates	Technique	Tool Available?	Subjects Studied	Subject Language	Largest Subject	Average mutation score	(F)irst order / (H)igher order
DeMillo and Offutt [30, 8]	1991	R,I (Weak)	Static Domain Reduction	Yes	5 tiny examples	Fortran	55 Lines	98%	F
Offutt et al. [31, 32]	1994	R,I (Weak)	Dynamic Domain Reduction	Yes	12 tiny examples	Fortran	100 Lines	Not† given	F
Liu et al. [26]	2006	R,I (Weak)	Dynamic Domain Reduction	No	5 tiny examples	C	21 Lines	95%	F
Zhang et al. [42]	2010	R,I (Weak)	DSE	Yes	5 small examples	C#	472 Lines	90%	F
Papadakis et al. [36]	2010	R,I (Weak)	DSE	No	5 tiny examples plus 3 small Siemens suite examples	C	500 Lines	63%	F
SHOM [this paper]	**2011**	**R,I,P (Strong)**	**DSE&SBST**	**Yes**	**8 non-trivial examples in Table 2 and 10 of the above listed in Table 3 for comparability**	**C**	**9,564 Lines**	**First: 69% Second: 71%**	**F&H**
Ayari et al. [4]	2007	R (Weak)	SBST	No	2 tiny examples	Java	72 Lines	88%	F
Papadakis et al. [37]	2010	R (Weak)	DSE	Yes	10 tiny examples	Java	100 Loc	90%	F
Fraser and Zeller [11]	2010	R,I (Firm)‡	SBST	Yes	2 non-trivial examples: Commons-Math & Joda- Time	Java	412 Classes	72%	F

2.2 Handling Higher Order Mutants

We adopt and adapt the previous work on DSE for first order mutation testing, so that it is able to handle higher order mutants in addition to first order mutants. A higher order mutant, m, of order n is a is a composition of n first order mutants. We shall call these n first order mutants the 'constituent' mutants of m. For each higher order mutant, there are two important cases to consider: Case 1: There exists a path that traverses all constituent first order mutants. Case 2: There does not exist such a path.

If Case 1 applies, then it is possible that the higher order mutant is a subsuming higher order mutant. A 'subsuming' higher order mutant is one that is harder to kill than any of its first order constituents, due to fault masking among the constituent first order mutants [21]. In testing terms, we may say that 'the sum of the collection of first order mutants is more demanding to test than the union of its parts'. However, if there does not exist a path that passes through all constituent first order mutants then, by definition, they cannot all mask one another and so the 'sum is merely the union of its parts' and is, therefore, easier to kill.

Of course, in Case 2 there could be a path that traverses some subset, S, of the constituent first order mutants, but this would mean that there would also be a lower order mutant composed of precisely the S constituent mutants. If we seek to progressively increase the order of mutants considered, then such a case will already have been encountered. Therefore, we focus our attention on Cases 1 and 2 as defined above.

Suppose a higher order mutant that we seek to weakly kill is constructed from a set of constituent first order mutants $f_1, \ldots, f_n$. If there is a path in the control flow graph of the program that passes through all the critical predicate nodes of $f_1, \ldots, f_n$ then the higher order mutant may be subsuming. This is Case 1. For these higher order mutants, we define the critical predicate nodes of the higher order mutant to be the union of the critical predicate nodes of the $f_1, \ldots, f_n$. By extension, the infection constraint of the higher order mutant is the conjunction of the infection constraints of $f_1, \ldots, f_n$.

If there is no such path (Case 2), then it is not possible to find a test case that executes all the constituent first order mutants that combine to make the higher order mutant. In this situation, our approach treats the higher order mutant as merely a set of first order mutants; it is killed if any of the constituent first order mutants is killed.

We use a different variant of the DSE algorithm to that previously used for mutation testing [34, 37, 42]. Our reachability approach is the same as previous work and this is inherited from the standard DSE approach to branch coverage [12, 39]. However, we handle infection constraints differently, because we need to retain and extend the constraints for subsequent generation of strongly killing test cases.

Figure 1: Illustrative example: two dumb first order mutants combine to make a subtler second order mutant

```
intputs: a, x, y
1   z = x;
2   z = z + y;
3   if(a > 0)
4       return z;
5   else
6       return 2 * x + z;
```

mutant 1: changes line 1 to z = ++x
mutant 2: changes line 2 to z = z + - -y
mutant 12 (2nd order mutant): combines mutant1 and mutant2 together

inputs	output schema			
tests	original	mutant 1	mutant 2	mutant 12
$a > 0$	$x + y$	$x + y + 1$	$x + y - 1$	$x + y$
$a \leq 0$	$3x + y$	$3x + y + 3$	$3x + y - 1$	$3x + y + 2$
	n/a	killed by all	killed by all	killed by half

Previous work uses a testability transformation to transform the traditional branch adequacy problem, which is handled well by DSE, into weak mutation adequacy. This is done by simply replacing mutants with additional branches, the predicates of which capture the infection constraint.

Our approach does not transform the program. Rather, once a mutation point is reached, our DSE variant continues to generate test data to satisfy the weak killing constraint. This allows us to retain a mapping of mutants and the corresponding infection constraints, so that we can assess the fitness of each individual mutant when it subsequently comes to the task of propagating infections. The pseudo code of this DSE algorithm is shown in Algorithm 1.

If the DSE approach fails to generate weakly adequate test data for a mutant, we use standard SBST approaches to seek to weakly kill it. This is because it is known [23] that DSE and SBST achieve coverage of distinct, but overlapping, sets of branches. For example, SBST is well adapted to test data generation in the presence of floating point computation. This motivated work on a hybrid DSE–SBST approach, now incorporated into the Pex tool [24].

However, for our experiments (reported in Section 4), we switch off this search based weak killing feature of the SHOM implementation, so that weak adequacy is achieved by DSE alone. This was because we wish to compare the additional effort required and effectiveness achieved in terms of strong adequacy compared to the DSE–only approaches to weak adequacy.

Having used DSE to generate weakly adequate test data our hybrid DSE–SBST approach uses SBST to search for test inputs that propagate infected data states to outputs, thereby transforming weak mutation into strong mutation. The next section explains our SBST approach to strong higher order mutation testing, which lies at the heart of our overall SHOM approach.

2.3 Strongly Killing Mutants

In order to strongly kill a mutant, its infection must be propagated to an output so that the fault is manifested as a failure. The propagation problem has previously been considered to be hard because there may be infinitely many paths from the infection point to the point at which an output occurs. Therefore, the problem of propagation, *for each mutant*, can be reduced to the path coverage problem. Even if we approximate path coverage, this process would still have to be repeated for each mutant and so the cost would potentially be prohibitive.

Our approach uses SBST to search for paths from the infection point to the output that are *more likely* to propagate the infection, based on heuristic assumptions about the differences in paths taken by the original and the mutant, which we seek to maximise using the search.

Algorithm 1 The dynamic symbolic execution algorithm

Require: the set of critical predicate nodes N reaching the mutant
Require: the $InfectionConstraint$ of the mutant
  For program P, randomly generate concrete test input T
  while within execution upper bound **do**
    execution path $p \leftarrow$ dynamic execution (P, T)
    symbolic expression $sc \leftarrow$ symbolic execution (P, T)
    if p does not reach the mutant **then**
      current critical node $n \leftarrow$ get next critical node (N, p)
      $p \leftarrow$update constraints (p, n)
      $T \leftarrow$ constraint solver(p, sc)
    else
      break
    end if
  end while
  weak killing constraint $wkc \leftarrow InfectionContraint \wedge p$
  $T \leftarrow$ constraint solver(wkc)
  return T

In this way, we do not explicitly try all paths from infection to output. Rather, we *search* for those more likely to propagate, guided by a fitness function that measures control flow differences between original program and mutant.

We first use a testability transformation to ensure that the program has only a single return point; the return of the procedure in which the mutant resides. This simple transformation is always possible, because multiple return statements can be directed to a single 'gathered' return point.

We seek to maximally disrupt the path taken by the mutant version of the program from the infection point to this unique return statement. This increases the likelihood that any output statement that can be executed after the infection point will be executed differently (or even not at all). This, in turn, increases the likelihood that the mutant's output will be distinguishable from that of the original, thereby strongly killing the mutant.

We wish to favour tests that maximise disagreement on predicate choices made by the original program and mutant, thereby maximally disrupting the control flow path from the infection to the return. If a test makes the mutant follow a different path to the original after execution then it is very likely to produce a different value at the return point, thereby strongly killing the mutant. Let $Branch(p, i, t)$ denote the branch taken by program p at predicate i on input t. Let $inf(m)$ denote the infection point of mutant m and let $ret(m)$ denote the return point of the procedure containing m. Let $pred(p, x, y)$ denote all critical predicates between point x and point y in program p.

We define the decision function d for program p and mutant m at predicate i on input t as follows:

$$d(p,m,i,t) = \begin{cases} 1 & \text{if } Branch(p,i,t) = Branch(m,i,t) \\ 0 & \text{if } Branch(p,i,t) \neq Branch(m,i,t) \end{cases}$$

Our fitness $f(p,m,t)$ of a test case t executed on a mutant m of an original program p is defined to maximise the average 'predicate disagreement' between m and p:

$$f(p,m,t) = \frac{\sum_{i \in Pred(m,inf(m),ret(m))} d(p,m,i,t)}{n}$$

Recent results [18] have demonstrated that random restart hill climbing provides an effective and efficient way to generate test data using SBST. Motivated by this finding, we use a random re-start hill climbing algorithm to search for the test inputs that propagate the infection, as shown in Algorithm 2. However, the particular choice of SBST algorithm is a parameter to our approach and a pluggable component to its implementation.

2.4 Preserving Weak Adequacy Using Constrained Search

Our representation and move operations are designed to *guarantee* that the previously obtained reachability and infection constraints are also satisfied by any candidate input we consider during the SBST phase of our overall approach. To do this we represent an individual candidate solution to the problem of killing a mutant as a conjunction of constraints. This conjunction starts off as the reachability and infection constraints, to which we may subsequently only ever add additional conjuncts during the search process.

In order to express a potential move to a new test input in the search, we add an extra conjunct to the current constraint, representing the result in Conjunctive Normal Form (CNF). In this way we can only ever consider weakly killing test cases. The constraint solver is used to generate a candidate using the extended CNF consisting of the weakly killing constraint plus some candidate new constraint. The test input generated by the constraint solver is then evaluated for fitness and, if it improves fitness, it becomes the new current solution in the hill climb.

Our 'constrained search' approach to searching for test data is a novel aspect of our mutant killing technique that has not been used in any previous work on SBST. It may find other applications in more general work on SBST outside the domain of mutation testing. It allows us to combine constraint solving and SBST in a manner that preserves the value captured by the constraints, while extending it to achieve some additional aspiration using search.

Algorithm 2 Out hill climbing algorithm

```
Require: A weak killing test T
Require: The weak killing constraint wkc
  if T kills the mutant strongly then
    return T
  else
    while current evaluation < max evaluation do
      NeighboursTests ← neighbours(T)
      for all t in NeighboursTests do
        if t kills the mutant strongly then
          return t
        end if
        for all t in NeighboursTests do
          if fitness(t) > bestfitness then
            BestTest ← t
            bestfitness ←fitness(BestTest)
          end if
        end for
        if bestfitness ≤ fitness(T) then
          T ← get a weak killing test T
        else
          T ← BestTest
        end if
      end for
    end while
  end if
```

3. SHOM IMPLEMENTATION

Figure 2 depicts the architecture of SHOM, the implementation of our hybrid DSE–SBST approach to Strong Higher Order Mutation. To compute adequacy scores we use the tool MILU[20, 21]. MILU is a higher order mutant generation and assessment tool that supports general purpose first and higher order mutant generation for C. We used the subset of the Agrawal et al.'s 77 C mutation operators [1] that fall into the widely studied 'selective' mutation operators, defined and studied first by Offutt el al. [33]. We use our own implementation of the DSE phase so that we could extend it to include the subsequent SBST phase.

We use the CIL transformation system [29] to pre-process the program and its mutants for the DSE and SBST phases of our implementation. However, this is merely a testability transformation that reduces constraint and path analysis effort. It does not alter the semantics of the program under test, nor does it affect the test adequacy criteria involved. As illustrated in Figure 2, the test data generated using our approach is evaluated on the mutants generated by MILU, not the transformed versions.

Three transformation steps are performed. We first simplify the expressions denoting array indeces and other memory access operators. In this step, additional temporary variables are introduced to hold intermediate values for complex memory expressions which involve more than one memory reference. After this step, the lvalue of the simplified expression only contains a memory constructor. This simplifies our subsequent static analysis and dynamic symbolic , execution, by reducing the number of cases that have to be considered.

We also use CIL's standard transformations to simplify loop and switch statements, reducing all such control flow constructs to a simple canonical form, consisting of conditionals and branches. Once again, this leaves the semantics of the original unaltered, but eases the subsequent downstream analyses that we perform.

Finally, we transform each procedure to an equivalent single–entry/single–exit version, so that it contains exactly one single return statement, to which we seek to propagate the infection of all mutants that lie inside that procedure. As explained in the previous section, this simplifies strong mutation testing, since it means that our SBST phase need only consider a single exit node. For this single exist node, SBST seeks inputs that cause execution to flow from the infection point along a maximally disrupted control flow path to the exit node.

We also use CIL to perform our control dependence analysis. This collects the critical predicate nodes for each mutant, used to form the reachability and infection conditions. The dependence analysis is also used to identify those predicates for which SBST seeks to cause the mutant and original to disagree from infection to return.

The constraints for reachability and infection are represented in Conjunctive Normal Form. SHOM uses the Yices constraint solver [10] to solve these constraints. Yices is a Satisfiability Modulo Theories (SMT) constraint solver that uses a collection of advanced constraint solving techniques to find a satisfying assignment of values to variables in formulæ. We use it to satisfy the constraints for reachability and infection. Yices was chosen for two reasons:

1. Yices provides a C language application interface. This is necessary since we cannot simply use constraint solving as a 'black box' component. While this is possible for weak mutation killing techniques that simply use testability transformation to reformulate weak mutation as branch coverage, it is not possible for strong mutation. For strong mutation we require control over exactly which constraints need to be satisfied at each part of the overall SHOM process.

2. Yices provides state-of-the-art constraint solving. It supports a wide range of constraints, including linear expressions, scalar types, recursive datatypes, tuples, records, arrays and bit-vectors, all of which can arise in the constraints found in programming languages. It won first place for several of the categories of the 2005, 2006 and 2007 SMT-COMP competitions organised as part of the Computer Aided Verification Conference (CAV).

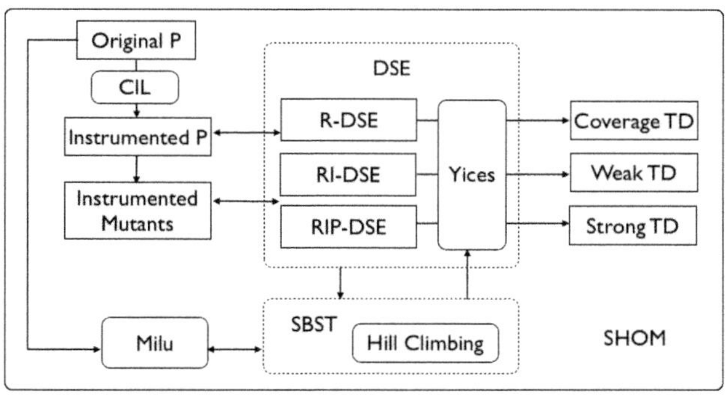

Figure 2: The SHOM Architecture. The DSE and SBST components were built from scratch. However, the DSE component delegates constraint solving to Yices [10]. It performs its analysis on transformed mutants, but all test data generated by SHOM is executed and evaluated by MILU**[20]. Transformation is performed CIL [29].**

4. EMPIRICAL STUDY

In our studies we consider, separately, first order mutation and higher order mutation, because first order mutation has been the subject of previous work, while no other previous study has considered test data generation to kill higher order mutants. We consider only second order mutants and, for larger programs, only sets of randomized samples from the set of all possible second order mutants. Sampling is required because of the infeasibility of considering all higher order mutants due to the explosion in mutant numbers that occurs at higher orders.

4.1 Subject Programs Studied

We applied SHOM to the example subjects in Tables 2 and 3. The examples in Table 2 are non-trivial real world programs. Four are modules from closed source industrial production code. Two of these, DeFroster and F1, come from Daimler and are used in automative control systems for a rear window defrosting system and an engine controller respectively and have been used in previous studies [14]. The other two, Hash and Buff, come from ABB and are used in robot controller systems.

We cannot provide the source code for these examples, because they are proprietary closed source code from industrial partners with which we have Non Disclosure Agreements in place. However, to support replication and more robust evaluation, we also include three additional larger programs, for which source code is readily available.

The program Space is a widely studied interpreter for an array definition language used by the European Space Agency. It is not open source, but its code is available from the Software-artifact Infrastructure Repository (SIR) [9]. The other two programs, Gzip (v1.5) and GArray (v2.26) are both open source. Gzip is the widely used compression program. GArray is an array data structure used in the GNU Glib. All programs in this non-trivial subject set of examples are summarised in Table 2.

The second set, summarised in Table 3, contains smaller laboratory programs that have been widely studied in the literature on mutation-based test data generation. We include this set of relatively small programs to provide backward compatibility with these previously studied examples.

The set includes three programs taken from SIR that originated in the Siemens suite: Tcas is an aircraft anti-collision system. Schedule is a program that prioritises schedulers. Replace performs pattern matching and substitution.

The remainder are a sample of some of the tiny programs used in previous studies. We make no attempt to infer findings from the results obtained using these tiny examples, but include them to facilitate replication. Triangle classifies the type of a triangle by the lengths of its three edges. Bubble is the standard bubble sort algorithm. Days calculates the number of days between two given days. Find locates and sorts the input array with a given index. Mid returns the middle value of three inputs. GCD is Euclid's GCD algorithm and MinMax returns the minimum and maximum values of the input array.

4.2 Mutant Generation

Some of the programs studied perform no output. For example, many of the tiny programs simply compute a single value as their result. For such programs we need to clarify what we mean by 'output'. If we took an overly pedantic and literal definition of output, for example: 'something that appears on an output device', then all mutants of such programs would be equivalent, because no mutation can change a non-existent output. Therefore, we allow 'output' include the result of the computation returned to the environment (such as a return value or the result computed in a global variable).

For the larger programs where the code is not a support routine, but an entire program, there is no such issue. These larger programs perform output, to screen and/or files and this is monitored and compared with the output of the original to determine whether the mutant is strongly killed.

4.3 Research Questions

Our study asks three research questions, which we define here, explaining how our experiments are designed to address them.

RQ1: How first-order-adequate is SHOM? To explore SHOM's test effectiveness for strong first order mutation, we compare SHOM with RI-DSE. We also report on the improvement RI-DSE achieves over R-DSE. In both cases we generate test sets for R-DSE and RI-DSE and compute the number of mutants each kills strongly and compare this to the number of mutants strongly killed by SHOM. This allows us to evaluate the degree to which a reached mutant is infected and propagates merely by reaching it using DSE and also the degree to which those mutants infected using DSE also already happen to propagate. We repeat all experiments ten times and take the average to cater for the stochastic nature of the search algorithm.

RQ2: How second-order-adequate is SHOM? The number of higher order mutants grows exponentially with the order k, presenting obvious experimental design challenges. For all of the ten programs from Table 3, the total number of second order mutants is 392,458 (which is manageable). However, for the real world programs in Table 2, the total number of second order mutants is 63,799,406 (which is unmanageable).

The quadratic increase in the number of second order mutants makes it impractical to consider all second order mutants. We therefore adopt a sampling approach. For programs with 0–4,999 second order mutants we use 100% of the mutants. For programs with 5,000–49,999 mutants, we sample 10%. For programs with 50,000–499,999 mutants, we sample 1%. For programs with 500,000–4,999,999 mutants, we sample 0.1%. For programs with 5,000,000 or more mutants, we sample 0.01%. To avoid sampling bias, we sample randomly from the set of all second order mutants. We also repeat the sampling experiment 10 times and compute the average levels of strong second order mutation adequacy achieved over all 10 samples.

To answer RQ2 we compare SHOM with RI-DSE and compare RI-DSE with R-DSE. However, there is no previous work on generating test data to kill second order mutants (either weakly or strongly). Therefore, to provide a baseline for comparison, we use the union of all test data generated for each of the two first order mutants from which the second order mutant is constructed as follows:

Suppose s is a second order mutant with constituent first order mutants f_1 and f_2. We use R-DSE to generate test data to kill f_1, creating a set of test data d_1. We then use R-DSE to generate test data to kill f_2, creating a second set of test data d_2. We define the result of applying R-DSE to s to be $d_1 \cup d_2$. Similarly, for RI-DSE, we generate two test sets, one for each of f_1 and f_2 and define the test set produced by RI-DSE for s to be the union of the two.

Using this approach, R-DSE and RI-DSE should be capable, in theory, of killing all those second order mutants that are coupled to their first order constituents in a way that killing either first order mutant kills the second order mutant. However, for second order mutants where fault masking may take place, a test set that kills both constituent first order mutants it not guaranteed to kill the second order mutant.

Table 2: The 7 larger programs used in the experiments. The upper 5 are industrial programs, while the lowest 2 are open source.

Program Name	Lines Of Code	Functions	Branches	1st order mutants	2nd order mutants
`DeFroster`	237	2	76	215	22,732
`F2`	511	1	42	212	22,113
`Hash`	1,011	12	76	465	107,211
`Space`	9,564	136	1,190	4,410	9,715,606
`Buff`	1,371	14	182	1,544	1,189,040
`GArray`	808	58	17	1,363	926,286
`Gzip`	7,933	97	1,717	10,182	51,816,418

Table 3: 10 smaller programs included for backward compatibility with previous studies.

Program Name	Lines Of Code	Functions	Branches	1st order mutants	2nd order mutants
Triangle	88	1	32	253	31,522
Bubble	35	1	6	80	3,032
Days	86	1	28	242	28,849
Find	88	1	22	201	19,791
Mid	43	1	10	65	1,970
GCD	43	1	6	73	2,526
MinMax	44	1	6	39	657
Tcas	166	8	66	223	24,496
Replace	595	23	176	714	253,585
Schedule	425	18	66	230	26,000

RQ3: How efficient is the SHOM data generation approach? The efficiency was measured using both the elapsed time for test data generation and the number of fitness evaluations required. Again, to cope with the stochastic nature of the search process, each experiment was repeated ten times and averages are reported.

The time was recorded using the Linux `time` utility. This is the elapsed time, so it includes all time taken to generate mutants, test data and to run test data on the program under test. As such, the timing information denotes a worst case upper bound on the total amount of time a tester would be expected to wait for test data to be produced by each technique. The experiments we undertaken on a Macbook pro laptop with Intel Duo2 2.6 GHz CPU, 4GB Memory in the Ubuntu 10.10 operating system.

5. RESULTS AND ANALYSIS

In this section we present the answer to each research question in turn, indicating how the results answer each. We consider strong first order effectiveness, followed by strong second order effectiveness and finally report on the efficiency of the SHOM implementation.

5.1 SHOM's First Order Adequacy

The results relating to RQ1 are summarised in Table 4. **Answer to RQ1**: As can be seen, SHOM produces increases in strong first order mutation adequacy compared to RI-DSE, which in turn produces noticable improvements on the strong adequacy achieved by R-DSE. For the smaller programs, the improvement in strong adequacy achieved by both RI-DSE and SHOM is less notable than it is for the larger programs.

Table 4: The complete results for all experiments. Columns labelled 'R-DSE' and 'RI-DSE' report, as percentages, the strong adequacy achieved by R-DSE and RI-DSE respectively for 1st and 2nd order mutants. Of the four columns labelled RI-DSE, the second two columns report the percentage of mutants left unkilled by R-DSE which are killed by RI-DSE. The four columns labelled 'SHOM' report the strong adequacy achieved by our new approach SHOM. The figures in the first two columns for SHOM report the average percentage of first and second order mutants killed over ten runs. The parenthetic numbers report the standard deviation. The figures in the second two columns for SHOM report the average percentage improvement of SHOM over RI-DSE for first and second order mutation. In these two columns the parenthetic numbers report the number of runs, out of ten, for which SHOM outperformed RI-DSE. The two columns labelled 'Time' report the average time taken by SHOM (in minutes). The final two columns, labelled 'Fitness' report the average number of kilo fitness evaluations required.

Program	**R**-DSE %		**RI**-DSE %				SHOM %				Time		Fitness	
	Order		Order		Imp. on **R**		Order (Std.)		Imp. on **RI** (# wins)		Order		Order	
	1st	2nd	1st	2nd	1st	2nd	1st	2nd	1st	2nd	1st	2nd	1st	2nd
Triangle	48	49	59	61	21	24	62 (1.6)	67 (3.8)	7 (10)	15 (10)	13	102	3	17
Bubble	76	77	76	77	0	0	76 (0.0)	77 (0.0)	0 (0)	0 (0)	22	141	0.2	8
Days	62	66	64	68	5	6	65 (0.5)	72 (2.6)	3 (10)	13 (10)	14	114	5	13
Find	64	59	69	60	14	2	69 (0.0)	61 (0.2)	0 (0)	3 (10)	28	191	2	9
Mid	65	62	66	73	3	29	82 (4.2)	82 (2.3)	47(10)	33 (10)	6	48	0.3	4
GCD	71	73	73	82	7	33	73 (0.0)	82 (0.0)	0 (0)	0 (0)	12	88	0.2	5
MinMax	75	64	77	75	8	31	77 (0.0)	76 (0.2)	0 (0)	4 (10)	22	84	0.1	3
Tcas	42	55	54	67	21	27	62 (2.1)	69 (9.1)	17 (10)	6 (10)	48	172	3	12
Replace	46	42	53	56	13	24	72 (2.2)	77 (11.5)	40 (10)	48 (10)	200	272	8	18
Schedule	55	57	57	62	4	12	69 (5.4)	70 (7.2)	28 (10)	21 (10)	110	202	4	15
Hash	51	54	56	61	10	15	63 (2.9)	64 (3.5)	16 (10)	8 (10)	81	128	5	8
Buff	63	64	71	73	22	25	82 (6.1)	85 (6.5)	38 (10)	44 (10)	152	176	11	7
GArray	64	68	77	81	36	41	82 (3.7)	86 (5.7)	22 (10)	26 (10)	95	131	2	3
DeFroster	53	55	62	63	19	18	66 (2.1)	68 (4.0)	11 (10)	14 (10)	102	272	2	11
F2	44	44	63	60	34	29	66 (1.2)	67 (8.4)	8 (10)	18 (10)	122	321	2	14
Space	30	32	46	51	23	28	52 (2.3)	57 (12.2)	11 (10)	12 (10)	1,423	884	43	18
Gzip	34	33	42	44	12	16	50 (1.5)	52 (13.4)	14 (10)	14 (10)	2,762	1,794	92	64
Average	55	56	62	65	15	21	69 (2.1)	71 (5.3)	15 (7.6)	16 (8.8)	307	301	11	13

This difference in behaviour is a further justification for including larger programs in the study of mutation-based test data generation. As we have seen, using only tiny examples may skew the results due to the relatively trivial nature of the test data generation problem for these tiny programs.

R-DSE and RI-DSE are entirely deterministic. SHOM builds on RI-DSE, but it is a randomised algorithm, so it can produce different values each time it is run. However, it is guaranteed to perform no worse than RI-DSE by construction, so we report the improvement it achieves (averaged over ten runs) together with standard deviation.

These are the first results reported for strong mutation test data generation so it is not possible to directly compare our results with previous findings, such as those in Table 1. Perhaps the closest work to ours is that of Frazer and Zeller [11].

Though Fraser and Zeller report on test data generation for Java, while we report on test data generation for C, their work is evaluated on two larger, non-trivial subjects and it achieves a form of propagation (to assertions in the program rather than outputs). Fraser and Zeller reported an overall average first order mutation score of 72% which lies between our weighted average strong first order mutation score for the whole programs (which was 59%) and that we achieved for the libraries (which is 76%).

There is a noticeable difference in the performance of all techniques for smaller and larger programs. For the smaller programs from Table 3, R-DSE is able to strongly kill between 42% and 76% of the first order mutants. RI-DSE can improve on this, but for some of the programs the test problem is so trivial that even weakly adequate test sets achieve high levels of strong mutation adequacy.

For the larger programs the results are more interesting. The behaviour of all three techniques falls into two distinct categories, depending on whether the larger program is a whole program or merely a collection of library routines to be called by some other program. Of the larger programs, Hash, Buff and GArray are each collections of routines to be called from elsewhere; these three programs consist of libraries of subordinate routines; they have no `main` function. The other four of the larger programs: DeFroster, F2, Space and Gzip, are invoked, in their entirety, from their `main` function so that the whole program is tested.

It has been known for some time [3] that whole program analyses are more challenging than inter-procedural analyses that focus on a single procedure. This is also true for test data generation. For the libraries, we need merely test each procedure in turn, thereby focusing the testing on a single procedure body rather than a whole program. The single procedure may call others in the library, so testing is still an inter-procedural activity, but it is not a 'whole program activity'.

This dichotomy between whole programs and libraries is borne out in the results. For the libraries, R-DSE is able to strongly kill between 51% and 64% of the first order mutants, whereas for the whole programs it kills between 30% to 53% of the mutants. RI-DSE improves on this, killing between 10% and 36% of the remaining mutants for the libraries and between 12% and 34% of the remaining mutants for the whole programs.

SHOM further improves strong first order mutation scores in all of the larger programs studied. For the library programs it manages to kill between 16% to 38% of the remaining mutants left unkilled by RI-DSE. For the whole programs, SHOM kills between 8% and 14% of the remaining mutants unkilled by RI-DSE.

5.2 SHOM's Second Order Adequacy

As can be seen from Table 4, on average, over all programs studied, all three techniques (R-DSE, RI-DSE and SHOM) are better at killing second order mutants than first order mutants. This is to be expected since second order mutants are, in general, coupled to first order mutants [22, 25]. These are the first results reported in the literature for automated test data generation to kill second order mutants, so they provide a baseline for future work.

The results also provide a baseline against which to evaluate SHOM. Over all programs studied, it produces an improvement in strong second order adequacy over RI-DSE, which, in turn, produces an improvement over R-DSE. Once again, we report average performance for SHOM (over ten runs) and standard deviation. Note that statistical tests such as the t-test or Mann Whitney test are not suitable here: The empirical evaluation is required to determine the size of this improvement, but SHOM is *guaranteed* to perform no worse than RI-DSE by construction.

For the larger programs from Table 2, the dichotomy between libraries and whole programs is evident for second order mutation (as it is for first order mutation). For whole programs, the adequacy of all techniques is reduced compared to that for libraries. Over all larger programs, RI-DSE kills between 15% and 41% of the second order mutants left unkilled by R-DSE, while SHOM further increases this effectiveness, killing between 8% and 44% of the mutants left unkilled by RI-DSE

5.3 SHOM's Efficiency

Table 4 reports the number of fitness evaluations and time required to kill all mutants. The number of fitness evaluations required is not dissimilar to that required for branch coverage of similar sized programs using search based techniques [2], so performance can be expected to be in line with previous work on SBST.

For the practicing software tester, the number of fitness evaluations, though machine-independent, will be of less interest; the results for the time taken to find an adequate test set are more important. The largest of the programs previously studied for mutation-based test data generation with C are the Siemen's suite examples (Schedule, Replace and Tcas from Table 3). For these programs we are able to generate a weakly killing test set in seconds.

It is not possible for us to compare these findings with the previously reported results from the literature on mutant test data generation for C. This is because the relevant papers for which a comparison would be meaningful reported in detail upon only the effectiveness (mutation score) of the approaches on which they reported and did not report the execution time details required for a comparison.

Of course, after two decades of Moore's Law, even were timing data available then, for those older studies from the 1990s, a head-to-head time-based comparison would have been grossly unfair to the achievements of previous work. For the more recently reported results (from 2010), even were timing data available, differences in techniques, platforms and configurations would also have made comparison problematic. In the present paper, we report on our execution times, configuration and platform details in order to support potential backward comparison in future work on strong and higher order mutation testing.

Mutation testing is generally regarded as a comparatively slow and expensive approach to testing. Despite this, it has endured through more than three decades as a research topic, perhaps because of results that demonstrate that it provides a particularly demanding test adequacy criterion and one that is attractively generic and flexible.

Given these historical perspectives, our timing findings are encouraging because they indicate that weak, strong and higher order mutation testing can all be used to generate test data within reasonable time on a standard laptop. Generation of test data by hand (the only currently available alternative for either strong or higher order mutation) would take considerably longer, and, using human effort rather than machine effort would be (perhaps prohibitively) more expensive.

6. RELATED WORK

Constraint Based Testing (CBT) was the first test data generation technique used for mutation testing. It was proposed by DeMillo and Offutt, based on the idea of control flow analysis and symbolic execution [8, 30]. Constraint based testing seeks to generate test data to kill mutants weakly by reaching and infecting mutants, thereby achieving the 'R' and 'I' of the 'RIP' framework described in Section 2. Offutt and DeMillo represent reachability as a set of path conditions, constructed using control flow analysis and symbolic execution and augment these path constraints with constraints that denote infection.

The initial approach to CBT suffered from several problems inherited from the state-of-the-art in symbolic evaluation available at the time and also from the static domain reduction technique used. It was unable to handle arrays, loops and nested expressions well. To overcome these restrictions, Offutt et al. proposed a dynamic domain reduction technique [31, 32]. The dynamic domain reduction technique uses a more sophisticated back-tracker to dynamically split domains.

Dynamic Symbolic Execution (DSE) [12, 39] is a more recent innovation that overcomes many of the limitations of traditional symbolic execution. Using DSE, non-linear path constraints are simplified by the instantiation of concrete runtime values, harvested from program execution. DSE has been used in several coverage based testing tools, such as DART [12], CUTE [39] and Pex [40].

DSE also provides a natural way to generate weakly adequate mutation-based test inputs. A simple testability transformation [15] can be used to augment the program with conditional statements, the predicates of which capture the infection constraints. By construction, covering the branches of the transformed program entails satisfying these infection constraints, thereby tranforming branch coverage into weak mutation coverage. This approach was first suggested by Liu et al. [26], and was implemented by Zhang et al. [42] and Papadakis et al. [36] who evaluated it on small programs, such as those found in Table 3.

Search Based Software Testing (SBST) [2, 17] has also been applied to the generation of weakly adequate mutation-based test data. Bottaci was the first to suggest using SBSE to kill mutants [6]. However, Search Based Mutation Test Generation remained unimplemented and unevaluated until the subsequent for work of Ayari et al. [4] and Fraser and Zeller [11], both of whom target Java. This previous work is not directly comparable to SHOM since SHOM targets C.

Ayari et al. evaluated their approach on small programs; essentially these are Java versions of those programs used in the previous work on mutant-based test data generation for Fortran and C, the largest of which is 70 Lines of Code. The more recent work by Fraser and Zeller reports results from a larger-scale study involving two Java programs, the larger of which contains 412 classes.

The SHOM approach introduced in this paper combines DSE and SBST. It uses DSE to achieve weak mutation adequacy and extends this with a constraint-aware search based approach that maintains weak adequacy, while seeking to propagate tests to achieve strong mutation adequacy. SHOM thus extends previous work by generating test data for strong mutation adequacy and by generating test data for higher order mutants. Like the recent work of Fraser and Zeller on Java, SHOM is evaluated on much larger examples; an order of magnitude larger than previous work on mutant-based test data generation for C.

7. CONCLUSIONS

In this paper we introduced a hybrid DSE and SBST approach to generate strongly adequate test data to kill first and higher order mutants. We implemented our approach in a tool called SHOM. We also implemented the two previously published approaches, based on reachability alone and reachability together with infection and used these implementations to evaluate our approach on 17 example programs. Our results show that SHOM is able to achieve higher levels of strong mutation coverage than either previously published approach for first order mutants. For second order mutants there is no previous work on test data generation so we compared our second order test sets with those composed from the union of the corresponding first order sets. Once again, SHOM was found to outperform approaches based on either reachability alone or reachability and infection.

8. REFERENCES

[1] H. Agrawal, R. A. DeMillo, B. Hathaway, W. Hsu, W. Hsu, E. W. Krauser, R. J. Martin, A. P. Mathur, and E. Spafford. Design of Mutant Operators for the C Programming Language. Technique Report SERC-TR-41-P, Purdue University, West Lafayette, Indiana, March 1989.

[2] S. Ali, L. C. Briand, H. Hemmati, and R. K. Panesar-Walawege. A Systematic Review of the Application and Empirical Investigation of Search-Based Test-Case Generation. *IEEE Transactions on Software Engineering*, 36(6):742–762, 2010.

[3] D. C. Atkinson and W. G. Griswold. The Design of Whole-Program Analysis Tools. In *International Conference on Software Engineering (ICSE '96)*, pages 16–27, 1996.

[4] K. Ayari, S. Bouktif, and G. Antoniol. Automatic Mutation Test Input Data Generation via Ant Colony. In *Proceedings of the Genetic and Evolutionary Computation Conference (GECCO'07)*, pages 1074–1081, London, England, 7-11 July 2007.

[5] F. Belli, N. Güler, A. Hollmann, G. Suna, and E. Yõldõz. Model-Based Higher-Order Mutation Analysis. In *Advances in Software Engineering*, volume 117 of *Communications in Computer and Information Science*, pages 164–173. Springer Berlin Heidelberg, 2010.

[6] L. Bottaci. A genetic algorithm fitness function for mutation testing. In *Proceedings of the 8th Wrokshop on Software Engineering using Metaheuristic INovative Algorithms (SEMINAL'01)*, pages 3–7, 2001.

[7] R. A. DeMillo, R. J. Lipton, and F. G. Sayward. Hints on Test Data Selection: Help for the Practicing Programmer. *Computer*, 11(4):34–41, April 1978.

[8] R. A. DeMillo and A. J. Offutt. Constraint-Based Automatic Test Data Generation. *IEEE Transactions on Software Engineering*, 17(9):900–910, September 1991.

[9] H. Do, S. Elbaum, and G. Rothermel. Supporting Controlled Experimentation with Testing Techniques: An Infrastructure and its Potential Impact. *Empirical Software Engineering*, 10(4):405 – 435, Oct. 2005.

[10] B. Dutertre and L. M. de Moura. A Fast Linear-Arithmetic Solver for DPLL(T). In *Proceedings of the 18th International Conference on Computer Aided Verification (CAV'06)*, pages 81–94, 2006.

[11] G. Fraser and A. Zeller. Mutation-driven generation of unit tests and oracles. In *Proceedings of the 19th International Symposium on Software Testing and Analysis (ISSTA'10)*, pages 147–158, Trento, Italy, 12-16 July ISSTA '10. ACM.

[12] P. Godefroid, N. Klarlund, and K. Sen. DART: Directed Automated Random Testing. In *Proceedings of the 2005 ACM SIGPLAN Conference on Programming Language Design and Implementation (PLDI'05)*, volume 40 of *6*, pages 213–223, Chicago, Illinois, USA, 11–15 June 2005. ACM.

[13] R. G. Hamlet. Testing Programs with the Aid of a Compiler. *IEEE Transactions on Software Engineering*, 3(4):279–290, July 1977.

[14] M. Harman, Y. Hassoun, K. Lakhotia, P. McMinn, and J. Wegener. The Impact of Input Domain Reduction on Search-Based Test Data Generation. In *ACM Symposium on the Foundations of Software Engineering (FSE '07)*, pages 155–164, Dubrovnik, Croatia, September 2007.

[15] M. Harman, L. Hu, R. M. Hierons, J. Wegener, H. Sthamer, A. Baresel, and M. Roper. Testability Transformation. *IEEE Transactions on Software Engineering*, 30(1):3–16, Jan. 2004.

[16] M. Harman, Y. Jia, and W. B. Langdon. A Manifesto for Higher Order Mutation Testing. In *Proceedings of the 5th International Workshop on Mutation Analysis (MUTATION'10)*, Paris, France, 6 April 2010. IEEE Computer Society. published with *Proceedings of the 3rd International Conference on Software Testing, Verification, and Validation Workshops.*

[17] M. Harman and B. F. Jones. Search-based Software Engineering. *Information and Software Technology*, 43(14):833–839, December 2001.

[18] M. Harman and P. McMinn. A Theoretical and Empirical Analysis of Evolutionary Testing and Hill Climbing for Structural Test Data Generation. In *International Symposium on Software Testing and Analysis (ISSTA'07)*, pages 73 – 83, London, United Kingdom, July 2007.

[19] M. Harman and P. McMinn. A Theoretical and Empirical Study of Search-Based Testing: Local, Global, and Hybrid Search. *IEEE Transactions on Software Engineering*, 36(2):226–247, 2010.

[20] Y. Jia and M. Harman. Constructing Subtle Faults Using Higher Order Mutation Testing. In *Proceedings of the 8th International Working Conference on Source Code Analysis and Manipulation (SCAM'08)*, pages 249–258, Beijing, China, 28-29 September 2008.

[21] Y. Jia and M. Harman. Higher Order Mutation Testing. *Journal of Information and Software Technology*, 51(10):1379–1393, October 2009.

[22] Y. Jia and M. Harman. An Analysis and Survey of the Development of Mutation Testing. *IEEE Transactions of Software Engineering*, Available online from IEEE Explore, 2011.

[23] K. Lakhotia, P. McMinn, and M. Harman. Automated Test Data Generation for Coverage: Haven't We Solved This Problem Yet? In 4th *Testing Academia and Industry Conference — Practice And Research Techniques (TAIC PART'09)*, pages 95–104, Windsor, UK, 4th–6th September 2009.

[24] K. Lakhotia, N. Tillmann, M. Harman, and J. de Halleux. FloPSy — Search-Based Floating Point Constraint Solving for Symbolic Execution. In 22nd *IFIP International Conference on Testing Software and Systems (ICTSS 2010)*, pages 142–157, Natal, Brazil, November 2010. LNCS Volume 6435.

[25] W. B. Langdon, M. Harman, and Y. Jia. Efficient multi-objective higher order mutation testing with genetic programming. *Journal of systems and Software*, 83:2416–2430, December 2010.

[26] M.-H. Liu, Y.-F. Gao, J.-H. Shan, J.-H. Liu, L. Zhang, and J.-S. Sun. An Approach to Test Data Generation for Killing Multiple Mutants. In *Proceedings of the 22nd IEEE International Conference on Software Maintenance (ICSM'06)*, pages 113–122, Philadelphia, Pennsylvania, USA, 24-27 September 2006.

[27] P. Madiraju and A. S. Namin. ParaMu - A Partial and Higher-Order Mutation Tool with Concurrency Operators. In *Proceedings of the 6th International Workshop on Mutation Analysis (Mutation 2011)*, Berlin, Germany, March 2011.

[28] L. J. Morell. A Theory of Fault-Based Testing. *IEEE Transactions on Software Engineering*, 16(8):844–857, August 1990.

[29] G. Necula, S. McPeak, S. Rahul, and W. Weimer. CIL: Intermediate Language and Tools for Analysis and Transformation of C Programs. In R. Horspool, editor, *Compiler Construction*, volume 2304 of *Lecture Notes in Computer Science*, pages 209–265. Springer Berlin / Heidelberg, 2002.

[30] A. J. Offutt. *Automatic Test Data Generation*. Phd thesis, Georgia Institute of Technology, Atlanta, GA, USA, 1988.

[31] A. J. Offutt, Z. Jin, and J. Pan. The Dynamic Domain Reduction Approach for Test Data Generation: Design and Algorithms. Technical Report ISSE-TR-94-110, George Mason University, Fairfax, Virginia, 1994.

[32] A. J. Offutt, Z. Jin, and J. Pan. The Dynamic Domain Reduction Procedure for Test Data Generation. *Software:Practice and Experience*, 29(2):167–193, February 1999.

[33] A. J. Offutt, A. Lee, G. Rothermel, R. H. Untch, and C. Zapf. An Experimental Determination of Sufficient Mutant Operators. *ACM Transactions on Software Engineering and Methodology*, 5(2):99–118, April 1996.

[34] M. Papadakis and N. Malevris. An Effective Path Selection Strategy for Mutation Testing. In *Proceedings of the 16th Asia-Pacific Software Engineering Conference (APSEC'09)*, pages 422 – 429, Penang, Malaysia, 1-3 December 2009. IEEE Computer Society.

[35] M. Papadakis and N. Malevris. An Empirical Evaluation of the First and Second Order Mutation Testing Strategies. In *Proceedings of the 5th International Workshop on Mutation Analysis (MUTATION'10)*, Paris, France, 6 April 2010. IEEE Computer Society. published with *Proceedings of the 3rd International Conference on Software Testing, Verification, and Validation Workshops*.

[36] M. Papadakis and N. Malevris. Automatic mutation test case generation via dynamic symbolic execution. In *Proceedings of the 21st International Symposium on Software Reliability Engineering (ISSRE'10)*, California, USA, November 2010.

[37] M. Papadakis, N. Malevris, and M. Kallia. Towards Automating the Generation of Mutation Tests. In *Proceedings of the 5th Workshop on Automation of Software Teste (AST'10)*, pages 111–118, Cape Town, South Africa, 3-4 May 2010. ACM.

[38] M. Polo, M. Piattini, and I. Garcia-Rodriguez. Decreasing the Cost of Mutation Testing with Second-Order Mutants. *Software Testing, Verification and Reliability*, 19(2):111 – 131, June 2008.

[39] K. Sen, D. Marinov, and G. Agha. CUTE: A Concolic Unit Testing Engine for C. In *Proceedings of the 13th ACM SIGSOFT International Symposium on Foundations of Software Engineering (FSE'05)*, pages 263–272, Lisbon, Portugal, 2005.

[40] N. Tillmann and J. de Halleux. Pex–White Box Test Generation for .NET. In *Proceedings of the 2nd International Conference on Tests and Proofs (TAP'08)*, volume 4966, pages 134–153, Prato, Italy, April 2008.

[41] M. R. Woodward. Errors in Algebraic Specifications and an Experimental Mutation Testing Tool. *Software Engineering Journal*, 8(4):221–224, July 1993.

[42] L. Zhang, T. Xie, L. Zhang, N. Tillmann, J. de Halleux, and H. Mei. Test generation via dynamic symbolic execution for mutation testing. In *Proceedings of the 26th International Conference on Software Maintenance (ICSM'10)*, Timisoara, Romania, September 2010.

Improved Multithreaded Unit Testing

Vilas Jagannath, Milos Gligoric, Dongyun Jin,
Qingzhou Luo, Grigore Roşu, Darko Marinov
Department of Computer Science, University of Illinois at Urbana-Champaign
Urbana, IL 61801, USA
{vbangal2, gliga, djin3, qluo2, grosu, marinov}@illinois.edu

ABSTRACT

Multithreaded code is notoriously hard to develop and test. A multithreaded test exercises the code under test with two or more threads. Each test execution follows some schedule/interleaving of the multiple threads, and different schedules can give different results. Developers often want to enforce a particular schedule for test execution, and to do so, they use time delays (`Thread.sleep` in Java). Unfortunately, this approach can produce false positives or negatives, and can result in unnecessarily long testing time.

This paper presents IMUnit, a novel approach to specifying and executing schedules for multithreaded tests. We introduce a new language that allows explicit specification of schedules as *orderings on events* encountered during test execution. We present a tool that automatically instruments the code to control test execution to follow the specified schedule, and a tool that helps developers migrate their legacy, sleep-based tests into event-based tests in IMUnit. The migration tool uses novel techniques for inferring events and schedules from the executions of sleep-based tests. We describe our experience in migrating over 200 tests. The inference techniques have high precision and recall of over 75%, and IMUnit reduces testing time compared to sleep-based tests on average 3.39x.

Categories and Subject Descriptors

D.2.5 [**Software Engineering**]: Testing and Debugging

General Terms

Verification, Reliability

Keywords

IMUnit, Unit Testing, Multithreaded Code

1. INTRODUCTION

Multicore processors are here to stay. To extract greater performance from multicore processors, developers need to write parallel code. The predominant paradigm for parallel code is that of shared memory where multiple threads of control communicate by reading and writing shared data objects. Shared-memory multithreaded code is often afflicted by concurrency bugs, which are hard to detect because multithreaded code can demonstrate different behavior based on the scheduling of threads, and the bugs may only be triggered by a small specific set of schedules.

To validate their multithreaded code, developers write multithreaded unit tests. A multithreaded test creates and executes two or more threads (and/or invokes code under test that itself creates and executes two or more threads). Each test execution follows some schedule/interleaving of the multiple threads, and different schedules can give different results. Developers often want to enforce a particular schedule for a test. For example, consider two threads, one executing a method m and the other executing a method m'. Developers may want to ensure in one test that m finishes before m' starts and in another test that m' finishes before m starts (and in more tests that m and m' interleave in certain ways). Without controlling the schedule, it is impossible to write precise assertions about the execution because the results can differ in the two scenarios, and it is impossible to guarantee which scenarios were covered during testing, even if multiple runs are performed.

To control the schedule of multithreaded tests, developers mostly use a combination of timed delays in the various test threads. In Java, the delay is performed with the `Thread.sleep` method, so we call this approach *sleep-based*. A sleep pauses a thread while other threads continue execution. Using a combination of sleeps, developers attempt to enforce the desired schedule during the execution of a multithreaded test, and then assert the intended result for the desired schedule. A sleep-based test can fail when an undesired schedule gets executed even if the code under test has no bug (false positive). Dually, a sleep-based test can pass when an unintended schedule gets executed even if the code under test has a bug (false negative). Indeed, sleeps are an unreliable and inefficient mechanism for enforcing schedules. To use sleeps, one has to estimate the real-time duration for which to delay a thread while the other threads perform their work. This is usually estimated by trial and error, starting from a small duration and increasing it until the test passes consistently on the developer's machine. The estimated duration depends on the execution environment (hardware/software configuration and the load on the machine). Therefore, when the same test is executed in a different environment, the intended schedule may not be en-

Permission to make digital or hard copies of all or part of this work for personal or classroom use is granted without fee provided that copies are not made or distributed for profit or commercial advantage and that copies bear this notice and the full citation on the first page. To copy otherwise, to republish, to post on servers or to redistribute to lists, requires prior specific permission and/or a fee.
ESEC/FSE'11, September 5–9, 2011, Szeged, Hungary.
Copyright 2011 ACM 978-1-4503-0443-6/11/09 ...$10.00.

forced, leading to false positives/negatives. Moreover, sleep can be very inaccurate even on a single machine [20]. In an attempt to mitigate the unreliability of sleep, developers often end up over-estimating the duration, which in turn leads to slow running multithreaded tests.

Researchers have previously noted the numerous problems with using sleeps to specify schedules in multithreaded tests and have developed frameworks such as ConAn [22, 23], ConcJUnit [27], MultithreadedTC [26], and ThreadControl [13] to tackle some problems in specifying and enforcing schedules in multithreaded unit tests. However, despite these frameworks, multithreaded unit testing still has many issues that could be categorized as follows:

Readability: Most current frameworks force developers to reason about the execution of threads relative to a global clock. This is unintuitive since developers usually reason about the execution of their multithreaded code in terms of event relationships (such as m finishing before m' starts). Some frameworks require users to write schedules in external scripts, which makes it even more difficult to reason about schedules. In other frameworks the schedule is implicit, as a part of the unit test code, and hence it is difficult to focus on the schedule and reason about it separately at a higher level.

Modularity: In some current frameworks, the intended schedule is intermixed with the test code and effectively hard-coded into a multithreaded unit test. This makes it difficult to specify multiple schedules for a particular unit test and/or to reuse test code among different tests.

Reliability: Some current frameworks, as well as the legacy sleep-based tests, rely on real time. As explained, this makes them very fragile, leading to false positives/negatives and/or slow testing time.

Migration Costs: Most current frameworks are very different from the traditional sleep-based tests. This makes it costly to migrate the existing sleep-based tests.

We present a new framework, called *IMUnit* (*pronounced "immunity"*), which aims to address these issues with multithreaded unit testing. Specifically, we make the following contributions:

Schedule Language: IMUnit introduces a novel language that enables natural and explicit specification of schedules for multithreaded unit tests. Semantically, the basic entity in an IMUnit schedule is an *event* that an execution can produce at various points (e.g., a thread starting/finishing the execution of a method, or a thread getting blocked). We call the IMUnit approach *event-based*. An IMUnit schedule itself is a (monitorable) property [10,24] on the sequence of events. More precisely, each schedule is expressed as a set of desirable *event orderings*, where each event ordering specifies the order between a pair of events (note that an IMUnit schedule need not specify a total order between all events but only the necessary partial order).

While the ideas of IMUnit can be embodied in any language, we have developed an implementation for Java. Syntactically, the IMUnit constructs are represented using Java annotations. A developer can use `@Event` and `@Schedule` annotations to describe the events and intended schedules, respectively, for a multithreaded unit test.

Automated Migration: We have developed two inference techniques and a tool to ease migration of legacy, sleep-based tests to IMUnit, event-based tests. Our inference techniques can automatically infer likely relevant events and schedules from the execution traces of existing sleep-based tests. We implemented our migration tool as an Eclipse plugin which uses the results of inference to automatically refactor a given multithreaded test into an IMUnit test.

Execution and Checking: We have implemented a tool for execution of IMUnit multithreaded unit tests. The tool can work in two modes. In the active mode, it controls the thread scheduler to enforce a given IMUnit schedule during test execution. In the passive mode, it checks whether an arbitrary test execution, controlled by the regular JVM thread scheduler, follows a given IMUnit schedule. To enforce/check the schedules, our tool uses the JavaMOP monitoring framework [10,24]. We also include a new runner for the standard JUnit testing framework to enable execution of IMUnit tests with our enforcement/checking tool.

Evaluation: To guide and refine our design of the IMUnit language, we have been inspecting over 200 sleep-based tests from several open-source projects. We manually translated 198 of those tests into IMUnit, adding events and schedules, and removing sleeps. As a result, the current version of IMUnit is highly expressive, and we were able to remove all sleeps from all but 4 tests.

We evaluated our inference techniques by automatically inferring events/schedules for the original tests that we manually translated (the subprojects on manual translation and automatic inference were performed by different authors to reduce the direct bias of manual translation on automatic inference). Computing the precision and recall of the automatically inferred events/schedules with respect to the manually translated events/schedules, we find our techniques to be highly effective, with over 75% precision and recall.

We also compared the execution time of the original tests and our translated tests. Because the main goal of IMUnit is to make tests more readable, modular, and reliable, we did not expect IMUnit to run faster. However, IMUnit did reduce the testing time, on average 3.39x, compared to the sleep-based tests, with the sleep duration that the original tests had in the code. As mentioned earlier, these duration values are often over-estimated, especially in older tests that were written for slower machines. In summary, IMUnit not only makes multithreaded unit tests more readable, modular, and reliable than the traditional sleep-based approach, but IMUnit can also make test execution faster.

This paper makes progress on our vision for improving multithreaded unit testing; our position paper [15] proposed the idea of event-based specification of schedules, but the IMUnit language and algorithms/tools for inference and execution are completely new.

2. EXAMPLE

We now illustrate IMUnit with the help of an example multithreaded unit test for the ArrayBlockingQueue class in `java.util.concurrent` (JSR-166) [17]. ArrayBlockingQueue is an array-backed implementation of a bounded blocking queue. One operation provided by ArrayBlockingQueue is `add`, which performs a non-blocking insertion of the given element at the tail of the queue. If `add` is performed on a full queue, it throws an exception. Another operation provided by ArrayBlockingQueue is `take`, which removes and returns the object at the head of the queue. If `take` is performed on an empty queue, it blocks until an element is inserted into the queue. These operations could have bugs that get triggered when the `add` and `take` operations execute on different threads. Consider testing some scenarios for these opera-

```java
1 @Test
2 public void testTakeWithAdd() {
3   ArrayBlockingQueue<Integer> q;
4   q = new ArrayBlockingQueue<Integer>(1);
5   new Thread(
6     new CheckedRunnable() {
7       public void realRun() {
8         q.add(1);
9         Thread.sleep(100);
10        q.add(2);
11      }
12    }, "addThread").start();
13  Thread.sleep(50);
14  Integer taken = q.take();
15  assertTrue(taken == 1 && q.isEmpty());
16  taken = q.take();
17  assertTrue(taken == 2 && q.isEmpty());
18  addThread.join();
19 }
```

(a) JUnit

```java
public class TestTakeWithAdd
    extends MultithreadedTest {
  ArrayBlockingQueue<Integer> q;
  @Override
  public void initialize() {
    q = new ArrayBlockingQueue<Integer>(1);
  }
  public void addThread() {
    q.add(1);
    waitForTick(2);
    q.add(2);
  }
  public void takeThread() {
    waitForTick(1);
    Integer taken = q.take();
    assertTrue(taken == 1 && q.isEmpty());
    taken = q.take();
    assertTick(2);
    assertTrue(taken == 2 && q.isEmpty());
  }
}
```

(b) MultithreadedTC

```java
@Test
@Schedule("finishedAdd1->startingTake1,
          [startingTake2]->startingAdd2")
public void testTakeWithAdd() {
  ArrayBlockingQueue<Integer> q;
  q = new ArrayBlockingQueue<Integer>(1);
  new Thread(
    new CheckedRunnable() {
      public void realRun() {
        q.add(1);
        @Event("finishedAdd1")
        @Event("startingAdd2")
        q.add(2);
      }
    }, "addThread").start();
  @Event("startingTake1")
  Integer taken = q.take();
  assertTrue(taken == 1 && q.isEmpty());
  @Event("startingTake2")
  taken = q.take();
  assertTrue(taken == 2 && q.isEmpty());
  addThread.join();
}
```

(c) IMUnit

Figure 1: Example multithreaded unit test for ArrayBlockingQueue

tions (in fact, the JSR-166 TCK provides over 100 tests for various scenarios for similar classes).

Figure 1 shows a multithreaded unit test that ArrayBlockingQueue exercises `add` and `take` in two scenarios. In particular, Figure 1(a) shows the test written as a regular JUnit test method, with sleeps used to specify the required schedule. We invite the reader to consider what scenarios are specified with that test (without looking at the other figures). It is likely to be difficult to understand which schedule is being exercised by reading the code of this unit test. While the sleeps provide hints as to which thread is waiting for another thread to perform operations, it is unclear which operations are intended to be performed by the other thread before the sleep finishes.

The test actually checks that `take` performs correctly both with and without blocking, when used with `add` from another thread. To check both scenarios, the test exercises a schedule where the first `add` finishes before the first `take` starts, and the second `take` blocks before the second `add` starts. Line 13 shows the first sleep that is intended to pause the `main` thread[1] while the `addThread` finishes the first `add`. Line 9 shows the second sleep which is intended to pause the `addThread` while the `main` thread finishes the first `take` and then proceeds to block while performing the second `take`. If the specified schedule is not enforced during the execution, there may be a false positive/negative. For example, if both `add` operations execute before a `take` is performed, the test will throw an exception and fail even if the code has no bug, and if both `take` operations finish without blocking, the test will not fail, even if the blocking `take` code had a bug.

Figure 1(b) shows the same test written using MultithreadedTC [26]. Note that it departs greatly from traditional JUnit where each test is a method. In MultithreadedTC, each test has to be written as a class, and each method in the test class contains the code executed by a thread in the test. The intended schedule is specified with respect to a global, logical clock. Since this clock measures time in *ticks*, we call the approach tick-based. When a thread executes a `waitForTick`, it is blocked until the global clock reaches the required tick. The clock advances implicitly when all threads are blocked (and at least one thread is blocked in a `waitForTick`). While a MultithreadedTC test does not rely on real time, and is thus more reliable than a sleep-based test, the intended schedule is still not immediately clear upon reading the test code. It is especially not clear when `waitForTick` operations are blocked/unblocked, because ticks are advanced implicitly when all the threads are blocked.

Figure 1(c) shows the same test written using IMUnit. The interesting events encountered during test execution are marked with `@Event` annotations[2], and the intended schedule is specified with a `@Schedule` annotation that contains a comma-separated set of *orderings* among events. An ordering is specified using the operator `->`, where the left event is intended to execute before the right event. An event specified within square brackets denotes that the thread executing that event is intended to block after that event. It should be clear from reading the schedule that the `addThread` should finish the first `add` before the `main` thread starts the first `take`, and that the `main` thread should block while performing the second `take` before the `addThread` starts the second `add`.

We now revisit, in the context of this example, the issues with multithreaded tests listed in the introduction. In terms of *readability*, we believe that making the schedules explicit, as in IMUnit, allows easier understanding and maintenance of schedules and code for both testing and debugging. In terms of *modularity*, IMUnit allows extracting the `addThread` as a helper thread (with its events) that can be reused in

[1] JVM names the thread that starts the execution `main` by default, although the name can be changed later.

[2] Note that `@Event` annotations appear on statements. The current version of Java (ver. 6) does not support annotations on statements, but the upcoming version of Java (ver. 7) will add such support. For now, `@Event` annotations can be written as comments, e.g., `/* @Event("finishedAdd1") */`, which IMUnit translates into code for test execution.

```
<Schedule>     ::= { <Ordering> [","] } <Ordering>
<Ordering>     ::= <Condition> "->" <Basic Event>
<Condition>    ::= <Basic Event> | <Block Event>
                 | <Condition> "||" <Condition>
                 | <Condition> "&&" <Condition>
                 | "(" <Condition> ")"
<Basic Event>  ::= <Event Name> ["@" <Thread Name>]
                 | "start" "@" <Thread Name>
                 | "end" "@" <Thread Name>
<Block Event>  ::= "[" <Basic Event> "]"
<Event Name>   ::= { <Id> "." } <Id>
<Thread Name>  ::= <Id>
```

Figure 2: Syntax of the IMUnit schedule language

other tests (in fact, many tests in the JSR-166 TCK [17] use such helper threads). In contrast, reusing thread methods from the MultithreadedTC test class is more involved, requiring subclassing, parametrizing tick values, and providing appropriate parameter values. Also, IMUnit allows specifying multiple schedules for the same test code (Section 4.3). In terms of *reliability*, IMUnit does not rely on real time and hence has no false positives/negatives due to unintended schedules. In terms of *migration costs*, IMUnit tests resemble legacy JUnit tests more than MultithreadedTC tests. This similarity eases the transition of legacy tests into IMUnit: in brief, add `@Event` annotations, add `@Schedule` annotation, and remove `sleep` calls. Section 4 presents our techniques and tool that automate this transition.

3. SCHEDULE LANGUAGE

We now describe the syntax and semantics of the language used in IMUnit's schedules.

3.1 Concrete Syntax

Figure 2 shows the concrete syntax of the implemented IMUnit schedule language. An IMUnit schedule is a comma-separated set of *orderings*. Each ordering defines a condition that must hold before a basic event can take place. A *basic event* is an event name possibly tagged with its issuing thread name when that is not understood from the context. An *event name* is any identifier, possibly prefixed with a qualified class name. There are two implicit event names for each thread, `start` and `end`, indicating when the thread starts and terminates. Any other event must be explicitly introduced by the user with the `@Event` annotation (see Figure 1(c)). A *condition* is a conjunctive/disjunctive combination of basic and block events, where block events are written as basic events in square brackets. A *block event* $[e']$ in the condition c of an ordering $c \to e$ states that e' must precede e and, additionally, the thread of e' is blocked when e takes place.

3.2 Schedule Logic

It is more convenient to define a richer logic than what is currently supported by our IMUnit implementation; the additional features are natural and thus may also be implemented in the future. The semantics of our logic is given in Section 3.3; here is its syntax:

$$\begin{array}{lll} a & ::= & \mathit{start} \mid \mathit{end} \mid \mathit{block} \mid \mathit{unblock} \mid \text{event names} \\ t & ::= & \text{thread names} \\ e & ::= & a@t \\ \varphi & ::= & [t] \mid \varphi \to \varphi \mid \text{usual propositional connectives} \end{array}$$

The intuition for $[t]$ is "thread t is blocked" and for $\varphi \to \psi$ "if ψ held in the past, then φ must have held at some moment before ψ". We call these two temporal operators the *block* and the *ordering* operators, respectively. For uniformity, all events are tagged with their thread. There are four implicit events: $\mathit{start}@t$ and $\mathit{end}@t$ were discussed above, and $\mathit{block}@t$ and $\mathit{unblock}@t$ correspond to when t gets blocked and unblocked[3].

For example, the following formula in our logic

$$\begin{array}{ll} & (a_1@t_1 \wedge ([t_2] \vee (\neg(\mathit{start}(t_2) \to a_1@t_1)))) \to a_2@t_2 \\ \wedge & (a_2@t_2 \wedge ([t_1] \vee (\mathit{end}(t_1) \to a_2@t_2))) \to a_2@t_2 \end{array}$$

says that if event a_2 is generated by thread t_2 then: (1) event a_1 must have been generated before that and, when a_1 was generated, t_2 was either blocked or not started yet; and (2) when a_2 is generated by t_2, t_1 is either blocked or terminated. As explained shortly, every event except for *block* and *unblock* is restricted to appear at most once in any execution trace. Above we assumed that $a_1, a_2 \notin \{\mathit{block}, \mathit{unblock}\}$.

Before we present the precise semantics, we explain how our current IMUnit language shown in Figure 2 (whose design was driven exclusively by practical needs) is a smaller fragment of the richer logic. An IMUnit schedule is a conjunction (we use comma instead of $\wedge$) of orderings, and schedules cannot be nested. Since generating *block* and *unblock* events is expensive, IMUnit currently disallows their explicit use in schedules. Moreover, to reduce their implicit use to a fast check of whether a thread is blocked or not, IMUnit also disallows the explicit use of $[t]$ formulas. Instead, it allows *block events* of the form $[a@t]$ (note the square brackets) in conditions. Since negations are not allowed in IMUnit, and since we can show (after we discuss the semantics) that $(\varphi_1 \vee \varphi_2) \to \psi$ equals $(\varphi_1 \to \psi) \vee (\varphi_2 \to \psi)$, we can reduce any IMUnit schedule to a Boolean combination of orderings $\varphi \to e$, where φ is a conjunction of basic events or block events. All that is left to show is how block events are desugared. Consider an IMUnit schedule $(\varphi \wedge [a_1@t_1]) \to a_2@t_2$, saying that $a_1@t_1$ and φ must precede $a_2@t_2$ *and* t_1 is blocked when $a_2@t_2$ occurs. This can be expressed as $((\varphi \wedge a_1@t_1) \to a_2@t_2) \wedge ((a_2@t_2 \wedge [t_1]) \to a_2@t_2)$, relying on $a_2@t_2$ happening at most once.

3.3 Semantics

Our schedule logic is a carefully chosen fragment of *past-time linear temporal logic (PTLTL)* over special well-formed multithreaded system execution traces.

Program executions are abstracted as finite traces of events $\tau = e_1 e_2 \ldots e_n$. Unlike in conventional LTL, our traces are finite because unit tests always terminate. Traces must satisfy the obvious condition that events corresponding to thread t can only appear while the thread is alive, that is, between $\mathit{start}@t$ and $\mathit{end}@t$. Using PTLTL, this requirement states that for any trace τ and any event $a@t$ with $a \notin \{\mathit{start}, \mathit{end}\}$, the following holds:

$$\tau \models \neg \diamondsuit (a@t \wedge (\diamondsuit \mathit{end}@t \vee \neg \diamondsuit \mathit{start}@t))$$

where $\diamondsuit$ stands for "eventually in the past". Moreover, except for $\mathit{block}@t$ and $\mathit{unblock}@t$ events, we assume that each

[3]It is expensive to explicitly generate *block*/*unblock* events in Java precisely when they occur, because it requires polling the status of each thread; our currently implemented fragment only needs, through its restricted syntax, to check if a given thread is currently blocked or not, which is fast.

event appears at most once in a trace. With PTLTL, this says that the following must hold ($\odot$ is "previously"):

$$\tau \models \neg \diamondsuit (a@t \wedge \odot \diamondsuit a@t)$$

for any trace τ and any $a@t$ with $a \notin \{block, unblock\}$.

The semantics of our logic is defined as follows:

$$\begin{array}{lll} e_1 e_2 \ldots e_n \models e & \text{iff} & e = e_n \\ \tau \models \varphi \ \wedge/\vee \ \psi & \text{iff} & \tau \models \varphi \text{ and/or } \tau \models \psi \\ e_1 e_2 \ldots e_n \models [t] & \text{iff} & (\exists 1 \leq i \leq n)\ (e_i = block@t \text{ and} \\ & & \quad (\forall i < j \leq n)\ e_j \neq unblock@t) \\ e_1 e_2 \ldots e_n \models \varphi \to \psi & \text{iff} & (\forall 1 \leq i \leq n)\ e_1 e_2 \ldots e_i \not\models \psi \text{ or} \\ & & (\exists 1 \leq i \leq n)\ (e_1 e_2 \ldots e_i \models \psi \text{ and} \\ & & \quad (\exists 1 \leq j \leq i)\ e_1 e_2 \ldots e_j \models \varphi) \end{array}$$

It is not hard to see that the two new operators $[t]$ and $\varphi \to \psi$ can be expressed in terms of PTLTL as

$$\begin{array}{rcl} [t] & \equiv & \neg unblock@t \ \mathcal{S} \ block@t \\ \varphi \to \psi & \equiv & \boxdot \neg \psi \ \vee \ \diamondsuit(\psi \wedge \diamondsuit \varphi) \end{array}$$

where $\mathcal{S}$ stands for "since" and $\boxdot$ for "always in the past".

4. MIGRATION

We now describe the process of migrating legacy, sleep-based tests to IMUnit, event-based tests. First we present the steps that are typically performed during manual migration and then we describe the automated support that we have developed for key steps of the migration.

4.1 Manual Migration

Based on our experience of manually migrating over 200 tests, the migration process typically follows these steps:

Step 1: Optionally add explicit names for threads in the test code (by using a thread constructor with a name or by adding a call to `setName`). This step is required if events are tagged with their thread name (e.g. `finishedAdd1@addThread`) in the schedule, because by default the JVM automatically assigns a name (e.g. `Thread-5`) for each thread created without an explicit name, and the automatic name may differ between JVMs or between different runs on the same JVM.

Step 2: Introduce `@Event` annotations for the events relevant for the intended schedule. Some of these annotations will be used for block events and some for basic events.

Step 3: Introduce a `@Schedule` annotation for the intended schedule. Steps 2 and 3 are the hardest to perform as they require understanding of the intended behavior of the sleep-based test. Note that a schedule with too few orderings can lead to failing tests that are false positives. On the other hand, a schedule with too many orderings may lead to false negatives whereby a bug is missed because the schedule is over-constraining the test execution.

Step 4: Check that the orderings in the introduced schedule are actually satisfied when running the test with sleeps (Section 5 describes the passive, checking mode).

Step 5: Remove sleeps.

Step 6: Optionally merge multiple tests with different schedules (but similar test code) into one test with multiple schedules, potentially adding schedule-specific code (Section 4.3).

4.2 Automated Migration

We have developed automated tool support to enable easier migration of sleep-based tests to IMUnit. In particular, we have developed inference techniques that can compute likely relevant events and schedules for sleep-based tests by inspecting the execution logs obtained from test runs. We next describe the common infrastructure for logging the test runs. We then present the techniques for inferring events and schedules.

```
enum EntryType { SLEEP_CALL, SLEEP_RETURN, BLOCK_CALL,
    BLOCK_RETURN, OTHER_CALL, OTHER_RETURN, TH_START,
    TH_END, EVENT }
class LogEntry { EntryType type; ThreadID tid; String info; StmtID sid; }
```

Figure 3: Log Entries

4.2.1 Lightweight Logging

Our inference of events and schedules from sleep-based tests is dynamic: it first instruments the test code (using AspectJ [19]) to emit entries potentially relevant for inference, then runs the instrumented code (several times, as explained below) to collect logs of entries from the test executions, and finally analyzes the logs to perform the inference.

Figure 3 shows the generic representation for log entries, although event and schedule inference require slightly different representations. Each log entry has a type, name/ID of the thread that emits the entry, potential info/parameters for the entry, and the ID of the statement that creates the entry (which is used only for event inference). The types of log entries and their corresponding `info` are as follows:

`SLEEP_CALL`: Invocation of `Thread.sleep` method. (Only used for inferring events.)

`SLEEP_RETURN`: Return from `Thread.sleep` method.

`BLOCK_CALL`: Invocation of a thread blocking method (`LockSupport.park` or `Object.wait`).

`BLOCK_RETURN`: Return from a thread blocking method.

`OTHER_CALL`: Invocation of a method (other than those listed above) in the test class. The `info` is the method name. (Only used for inferring events .)

`OTHER_RETURN`: Return from a method executed from the test class.

`TH_START`: Invocation of `Thread.start`. The `info` is the ID of the started thread. (Only used for inferring schedules.)

`TH_END`: End of thread execution.

`EVENT`: Execution of an IMUnit event. The `info` is the name of the event. (Only available while inferring schedules.)

Note that any logging can affect timing of test execution. Because sleep-based tests are especially sensitive to timing, care must be taken to avoid false positives. We address this in three ways. First, our logging is lightweight. The instrumented code only collects log entries (and their parameters) relevant to the inference. For example, `OTHER_CALL` is not collected for schedule inference. Also, the entries are buffered in memory during test execution, and they are converted to strings and logged to file only at the end of test execution. While keeping entries in memory would not work well for very long logs, it works quite well for the relatively short logs produced by test executions. Second, our instrumentation automatically scales the duration of sleeps by a given constant N to compensate for the logging overhead. For example, for $N = 3$ it increases all sleep times 3x. Increasing all the durations almost never makes a passing test fail, but it does make the test run slower. Third, we perform multiple runs of each test and only collect logs for passing runs. This increases the confidence that the logs indeed correspond to the intended schedules specified with sleeps.

4.2.2 Inferring Events

Figure 4 presents the algorithm for inferring IMUnit events from a sleep-based test. The input to the algorithm consists of a set of logs (as described in Section 4.2.1) and a `confidenceThreshold`. The output is a set of inferred events. Each event includes the code location where `@Event` annotation should be added and the name of the event. The intuition behind the algorithm is that `SLEEP_CALL` log entries are indicative of code locations for events. More precisely, a thread t calls `sleep` to wait for one or more events to happen on other threads (those will be "finished" events) before an event happens on t (that will be a "starting" event). Recall our example from Section 2. When the `main` thread calls `sleep`, it waits for `add` to finish before `take` starts, and thus `finishedAdd1` executes before `startingTake1`.

For each log, the algorithm first computes a set of *regions*, each of which is a sequence of log entries between `SLEEP_CALL` and the matching `SLEEP_RETURN` executed by the same thread. The log entries executed by other threads within a region are potential points for the "finished" events. Regions from different threads can be partially or completely overlapping, but regions from the same thread are disjoint (i.e., each `SLEEP_CALL` is followed directly by `SLEEP_RETURN` before any other statement is executed by the thread). Figure 5 shows two regions for a simplified log produced by our running example. In pseudo-code, each region is represented as a pair of `ints` that point to the beginning and end of the region in the list of log entries. For each region, the algorithm first calls `addFinishedEvents` to potentially add some "finished" events for threads other than the region's thread. If an event is added, the algorithm calls `addStartingEvent` to add the matching "starting" event.

The procedure `addFinishedEvents` potentially adds an inferred event for each thread that executes at least one statement in the region. For each such thread, the procedure first discovers a *relevant* statement, which is one of `SLEEP_CALL`, `BLOCK_CALL`, and `TH_END`. Only threads that have exactly one relevant statement in the region are considered. The intuition is that sleeps usually wait for exactly one event in each other thread. If a thread executes none or multiple relevant statements, it is most likely independent of the thread that started the region and therefore can be ignored. Figure 5 shows the relevant statements for each region. The procedure then finds the `OTHER_RETURN` statement immediately before the relevant statement for each thread. This statement determines the name for the new "finished" `StaticEvent`, whereas the relevant statement determines the location. Note that logging only method calls would not be enough to properly determine the previous statement since the call can come from a helper method in the test class. For our example, these before log entries are `OTHER_RETURN(add), addThread, 326` and `OTHER_RETURN(take), main, 336` (Fig. 5).

The procedure `addStartingEvent` adds an event for the thread that starts the region. The event is placed just before the first statement that follows the end of the region. The type of the statement can be any, including `OTHER_CALL`. The same statement is used for naming the event. In Figure 5, `OTHER_CALL(take), main, 336` and `OTHER_CALL(add), addThread, 330` are found following the algorithm.

```
// Input
Set⟨List⟨LogEntry⟩⟩ logs;
float confidenceThreshold;
// Output
class StaticEvent { StmtID sid; String name; }
Set⟨StaticEvent⟩ events;
// State
Bag⟨StaticEvent⟩ inferred := ∅;

class Region { int start; int end; }

void inferEvents() {
  foreach (List⟨LogEntry⟩ log in logs) {
    foreach (Region r in computeRegions(log)) {
      boolean addedFinished := addFinishedEvents(r, log);
      if (addedFinished) { addStartingEvent(r, log); }
    }
  }
  filterOutLowConfidence(confidenceThreshold);
  events := inferred.toSet();
}
Set⟨Region⟩ computeRegions(List⟨LogEntry⟩ log) {
  return { new Region(i, j) | log(i).type = SLEEP_CALL ∧
        j := min{ k | log(i).tid = log(k).tid ∧
        log(k).type = SLEEP_RETURN } }
}
boolean addFinishedEvents(Region r, List⟨LogEntry⟩ log) {
  boolean result := false;
  foreach (ThreadID t in { log(i).tid | i ∈ r } − { log(r.start).tid }) {
    Set⟨int⟩ relevant := { i ∈ r | log(i).tid = t ∧
        log(i).type ∈ { SLEEP_CALL, BLOCK_CALL, TH_END } ∧
          ¬(∃ j ∈ r | log(j).tid = t ∧
            log(j).type ∈ { SLEEP_RETURN, BLOCK_RETURN }) }
    if (relevant.size() ≠ 1) continue;
    int starting := max{ j < relevant | log(j).tid = t ∧
        log(j).type = OTHER_RETURN }
    addEvent(relevant, "finished", starting);
    result := true;
  }
  return result;
}
void addStartingEvent(Region r, List⟨LogEntry⟩ log) {
  int finished := min{ j > r.start | log(j).tid = log(r.start).tid ∧
      log(j).type ∈ { OTHER_CALL, TH_END } }
  addEvent(finished, "starting", finished);
}
void addEvent(int location, String namePrefix, int suffixIdx) {
    StmtID sid = log(location).sid;
    events ∪= new StaticEvent(sid, namePrefix +
        log(suffixIdx).info + sid);
}
```

Figure 4: Events-Inference Algorithm

```
           TH_START, main, 333
Region 0 ┌ SLEEP_CALL, main, 334
         │ OTHER_CALL(add), addThread, 326
         │ // calls/returns if add is a helper method
         │ OTHER_RETURN(add), addThread, 326
Region 1 ├┬ SLEEP_CALL, addThread, 328 // relevant in 0
         │└ SLEEP_RETURN, main, 334
         │ OTHER_CALL(take), main, 336
         │ OTHER_RETURN(take), main, 336
         │ OTHER_CALL(take), main, 339
         │ BLOCK_CALL, main, 155 // relevant in 1
         └ SLEEP_RETURN, addThread, 328
           OTHER_CALL(add), addThread, 330
           OTHER_RETURN(add), addThread, 330
           BLOCK_RETURN, main, 155
           OTHER_RETURN(take), main, 339
```

Figure 5: Snippet from a Log for Inferring Events

4.2.3 *Inferring Schedules*

Figure 6 presents the algorithm to infer an IMUnit schedule for a sleep-based multithreaded unit test that already contains IMUnit event annotations. These annotations can be automatically produced by our event inference or manually provided by the user. The input to the algorithm is a set of logs obtained from the passing executions of the sleep-based test. Figure 7 shows a snippet from one such log for our running example sleep-based test shown in Figure 1(a). The input also contains a `confidenceThreshold` which will be described later. The output is an inferred schedule, i.e., a set of orderings that encodes the intended schedule for the test. The main part of the algorithm is the `addSleepInducedOrderings` procedure. It captures the intuition that a thread normally executes a sleep to wait for the other active threads to perform events. Recall line 13 from our example in Figure 1(a) where the `main` thread sleeps to wait for the thread `addThread` to perform an `add` operation, and line 9 where `addThread` sleeps to wait for the `main` thread to first perform one `take` operation and then block while performing the second `take` operation.

For each log, the procedure scans for `SLEEP_RETURN` entries (line 31). As shown in Figure 7, the log for our example contains two `SLEEP_RETURN` entries, one each in the `main` thread and `addThread`. For each `SLEEP_RETURN` that is found, the procedure does the following:

1) Retrieves the next `EVENT` entry for the same thread (line 33). This event will be used as the `after` event in `Orderings` induced by the `SLEEP_RETURN`. In the example log, the two `after` events are `startingTake1` for the first `SLEEP_RETURN` and `startingAdd2` for the second `SLEEP_RETURN`.

2) Computes the other threads that were *active* between the `SLEEP_RETURN` and the `after` event (line 34). In the example, for the first `SLEEP_RETURN`, the only other active thread is `addThread` and for the second `SLEEP_RETURN`, the only other active thread is `main`.

3) Finds for each active thread the last `EVENT` entry that is before the `after` event. This event will be the `before` event in the `Ordering` induced by the `SLEEP_RETURN` with the corresponding active thread (line 38). Note that this `before` event on another thread can be even *before* the `SLEEP_RETURN`. Effectively, this event is the *current* last entry and not the last entry at the time of the sleep. In the example, the two `before` events are `finishedAdd1` and `startingTake2` for the first and second `SLEEP_RETURNs`, respectively.

4) Creates an `Ordering` for each `before` and `after` event pair and inserts it into the `inferred` bag. If a `before` event is followed immediately by a `BLOCK_CALL` (within entries for the same thread), a `BlockingOrdering` is created; otherwise, a `NonBlockingOrdering` is created (line 41). In the example, since `startingTake2` is followed by a `BLOCK_CALL`, the ordering between `startingTake2` and `startingAdd2` will be a `BlockingOrdering`, while the other ordering between `finishedAdd1` and `startingTake1` will be a `NonBlockingOrdering`.

Before the `addSleepInducedOrderings` procedure is invoked, each `log` is modified by the `preprocessLogs` procedure. This procedure looks for `SLEEP_RETURN` entries followed immediately by `TH_START` entries for the same thread. For every such instance, it swaps the `SLEEP_RETURN` and `TH_START` entries and sets the `tid` of the `SLEEP_RETURN` entry to be the ID of the thread that is *started* by the `TH_START` event. The intuition is that a `SLEEP_RETURN` followed by a `TH_START` signifies that the *started* thread, rather than the starting thread perform-

```
1  class Event { String eventName; ThreadID tid; }
2  abstract class Ordering { Event before; Event after; }
3  class NonBlockingOrdering extends Ordering {};
4  class BlockingOrdering extends Ordering {};
5  // Input
6  Set⟨List⟨LogEntry⟩⟩ logs;
7  float confidenceThreshold;
8  // Output
9  Set⟨Ordering⟩ orderings;
10 // State
11 Bag⟨Ordering⟩ inferred := ∅;
12
13 void inferSchedules() {
14   foreach (List⟨LogEntry⟩ log in logs) {
15     List⟨LogEntry⟩ preprocessed := preprocessLog(log);
16     addSleepInducedOrderings(preprocessed);
17   }
18   minimize();
19 }
20 List⟨LogEntry⟩ preprocessLog(List⟨LogEntry⟩ log) {
21   List⟨LogEntry⟩ result := log.clone();
22   foreach ({ i | log(i).type = SLEEP_RETURN }) {
23     int j := min{j > i | log(j).tid = log(i).tid };
24     if (log(j).type = TH_START) {
25       result(j) := new LogEntry(SLEEP_RETURN, _, log(j).info);
26       result(i) := log(j);
27     } }
28   return result;
29 }
30 void addSleepInducedOrderings(List⟨LogEntry⟩ log) {
31   foreach ({ i ∈ log.indexes() | log(i).type = SLEEP_RETURN }) {
32     ThreadID t := log(i).tid;
33     int j := min{ n > i | log(n).tid = t ∧ log(n).type = EVENT };
34     Set⟨ThreadID⟩ active := { t' | ( ∃ n < j |
35                   log(n).tid = t' ∧ log(n).type = EVENT ) ∧
36                   ( ∃ n > i | log(n).tid = t' ∧ log(n).type = TH_END
                     ) };
37     foreach (ThreadID t' in active − { t }) {
38       int j' := max{ n < j | log(n).tid = t' ∧ log(n).type = EVENT };
39       Event before := new Event(log(j').info, t');
40       Event after := new Event(log(j).info, t);
41       if (log(min{ n > j' | log(n).tid = t' }).type ≠ BLOCK_CALL) {
42         inferred ∪= new NonblockingOrdering(before, after);
43       } else { // before.type = BLOCK_CALL
44         inferred ∪= new BlockingOrdering(before, after);
45       } } } }
46 void minimize(List⟨LogEntry⟩ log) {
47   Set⟨Ordering⟩ graph := inferred.toSet() ∪ computeSeqOrderings(log);
48   removeCyclicOrderings(graph);
49   performTransitiveReduction(graph);
50   inferred.onlyRetainOrderingsIn(graph);
51   filterOutLowConfidence(confidenceThreshold);
52   orderings := inferred.toSet();
53 }
54 void Set⟨Ordering⟩ computeSeqOrderings(List⟨LogEntry⟩ log) {
55   return { new NonblockingOrdering(log(i), log(j)) |
56          i < j ∧ log(i).tid = log(j).tid ∧
57          log(i).type = log(j).type = EVENT ∧
58          ¬(∃ k | i < k < j ∧ log(j).tid = log(k).tid
59          ∧ log(k).type = EVENT) };
60 }
```

Figure 6: Schedule-Inference Algorithm

```
Ordering0
  TH_START(addThread), main
┌─EVENT(finishedAdd1), addThread
│ SLEEP_RETURN, main
└→EVENT(startingTake1), main
Ordering1
┌─EVENT(startingTake2), main
├─BLOCK_CALL, main
│ SLEEP_RETURN, addThread
└→EVENT(startingAdd2), addThread
```

Figure 7: Snippet from a Log for Inferring Schedules

ing the TH_START, should wait for the other active threads to perform events. Many of the sleep-based tests that we migrated included instances of this pattern. Effectively, this swap makes it appear as if the sleep was at the beginning of the run method for the started thread, although the sleep was actually before the start method.

After each log is processed by the preprocessLogs and addSleepInducedOrderings procedures, the inferred bag is populated with all the inferred orderings. However, the inferred orderings may contain cycles (e.g., a->b and b->a) and transitively redundant orderings (e.g., a->b, b->c, and a->c, where the last ordering is redundant). The minimize procedure removes such orderings. It first creates an ordering graph by combining the edges from the inferred orderings with the edges implied by the sequential orderings of events within each thread (the latter edges being computed by the computeSeqOrderings procedure). It then removes all the edges of the graph that participate in cycles. It finally performs a transitive reduction on the acyclic graph and updates the inferred bag by removing all orderings not included in the reduced graph. We use an open-source implementation [12] of the transitive reduction algorithm introduced by Aho et al. [1]. Since the transitive reduction is performed on an acyclic graph, we can use a simpler case of the general algorithm.

The last step of the minimize procedure is to remove the orderings that were inferred with low confidence. Recall that the input to our inference is a set of logs from several (passing) runs of the test being migrated. The confidence of an inferred ordering is the ratio of the count of that ordering in the inferred bag and the number of logs/runs. For example, an ordering may be inferred in only 60% of runs, say 3 out of 5. The confidenceThreshold defines the lowest acceptable confidence. All inferred orderings with confidence lower than the specified threshold are discarded.

4.2.4 *Eclipse Plugin*

We have developed a refactoring plugin for Eclipse to enable automated migration of existing sleep-based unit tests into event-based IMUnit tests. The plugin is implemented using the generic refactoring API provided by Eclipse. The refactoring automates the most important steps required to migrate a sleep-based test into an IMUnit test: introduction of events and schedule (using inference techniques) and checking of the introduced schedule. The refactoring can also help the user name the threads in the test.

4.3 Multiple Schedules

As mentioned in Step 6 of Section 4.1, after converting sleep-based tests to event-based IMUnit tests, developers can merge several similar tests with different schedules into one test with multiple IMUnit schedules. Recall our example sleep-based test from Figure 1(a). Its intended schedule is an add followed by a non-blocking take and a blocking take followed by another add. Suppose that the same test class contained another sleep-based test whose indented schedule is an add followed by a non-blocking take and another add followed by another non-blocking take. Although these two sleep-based tests would be almost identical (with the sleep at line 9 moved to before line 16), they cannot share the common code without using additional conditional statements to enable the appropriate sleeps during execution. In contrast, after both tests are migrated to IMUnit tests, they can be easily replaced by just one new test. This new test would have the same code as in Figure 1(a), with two added annotations: (1) @Event("finishedAdd2") added after the add(2) call, and (2) @Schedule("finishedAdd1->startingTake1, finishedAdd2->startingTake2") added before the test method.

5. ENFORCING & CHECKING

We now describe the IMUnit Runner, our tool for enforcing/checking schedules for IMUnit tests. It is implemented as a custom test runner for the JUnit testing framework. It executes each test for each IMUnit schedule and has two operation modes. In the *active mode*, it controls the thread scheduler to enforce an execution of the test to satisfy the given schedule. Note that this mode avoids the main problem of sleep-based tests, that of false positives and negatives due to the execution of unintended schedules. In the *passive mode*, our tool observes and checks the execution provided by the JVM against the given schedule.

Our runner is implemented using JavaMOP [10, 24], a high-performance runtime monitoring framework for Java. JavaMOP is generic in the property specification formalism and provides several such formalisms as *logic plugins*, including past-time linear temporal logic (PTLTL). Although our schedule language is a semantic fragment of PTLTL (Section 3), enforcing PTLTL specifications in their full generality on multithreaded programs is rather expensive.

Instead, we have developed a custom JavaMOP logic plugin for our current IMUnit schedule language from Figure 2. Since JavaMOP takes care of all the low-level instrumentation and monitor integration details (after a straightforward mapping of IMUnit events into JavaMOP events), we here only briefly discuss our new JavaMOP logic plugin. It takes as input an IMUnit schedule and generates as output a monitor written in pseudo-code; a *Java shell* for this language then turns the monitor into AspectJ code [19], which is further woven into the test program. In the active mode, the resulting monitor enforces the schedule by blocking the violating thread until all the conditions from the schedule are satisfied. In the passive mode, it simply prints an error when its corresponding schedule is violated.

A generated monitor for an IMUnit schedule observes the defined events. When an event e occurs, the monitor checks all the conditions that the event should satisfy according to the schedule, i.e., a Boolean combination of basic and block events (Figure 2). The status of each basic event is maintained by a Boolean variable which is true iff the event occurred in the past. The status of a block event is checked as a conjunction of this variable and its thread's blocked state. In the active mode, the thread of e will be blocked until this Boolean expression becomes true. If the condition contains any block event, periodic polling is used for checking thread states. Thus, IMUnit pauses threads only if their events are getting out of order for the schedule. Note that the user may have specified an infeasible schedule, which can cause a deadlock where all threads are paused. Our runner includes a low-overhead runtime deadlock detection that detects and reports deadlocks.

As an example, Figure 8 shows the active-mode monitor generated for the schedule in Figure 1(c). When events finishedAdd1 and startingTake2 occur, the monitor just sets the corresponding Boolean variables, as there is no condition for those events. For event startingTake1, it checks if there was an event finishedAdd1 in the past by checking the vari-

```
switch (event) {
case finishedAdd1:
  occurred_finishedAdd1 = true; notifyAll();
case startingTake2:
  thread_startingTake2 = currentThread();
  occurred_startingTake2 = true; notifyAll();
case startingTake1:
  while (!occurred_finishedAdd1)
    wait();
  occurred_startingTake1 = true; notifyAll();
case startingAdd2:
  while (!(occurred_startingTake2 &&
           isBlocked(thread_startingTake2)))
    wait();
  occurred_startingAdd2 = true; notifyAll(); }
```

Figure 8: Monitor for the schedule in Figure 1(c)

able `occurred_finishedAdd1`; if not, the thread will be blocked until `finishedAdd1` occurs. For event `startingAdd2`, in addition to checking the Boolean variable for `startingTake2`, it also checks whether the thread of the event `startingTake2` is blocked; if not, the thread of the event `startingAdd2` will be blocked until both conditions are satisfied.

6. EVALUATION

To evaluate the IMUnit contributions—schedule language, automated migration, and schedule execution—we analyzed over 200 sleep-based tests from several open-source projects. Table 1 lists the projects and the number of sleep-based tests that we manually migrated to IMUnit. We first describe our experience with the IMUnit language. We then present results of our inference techniques for migration. We finally discuss the test running time.

6.1 Schedule Language

It is hard to quantitatively evaluate and compare languages, be it implementation or specification languages, including languages for specifying schedules. One metric we use is how *expressive* the language is, i.e., how many sleep-based tests can be expressed in IMUnit such that *sleeps can be removed altogether*. Note that IMUnit conceptually subsumes sleeps: sleeps and IMUnit events/schedules can coexist in the same test, and developers just need to make sleeps long enough to account for the IMUnit schedule enforcement. While every sleep-based test is trivially an IMUnit test, we are interested only in those tests where IMUnit allows removing sleeps altogether.

We were able to remove sleeps from 198 tests, in fact all sleeps from all but 4 tests. While the current version of IMUnit is highly expressive, we have to point out that we refined the IMUnit language based on the experience with migrating the sleep-based tests. When we encountered a case that could not be expressed in IMUnit, we considered how frequent the case is, and how much IMUnit would need to change to support it. For example, blocking events are very frequent, and supporting them required a minimal syntactic extension (adding events with square brackets) to the initial version of our language. However, some cases would require bigger changes but are not frequent enough to justify them. The primary example is events in a loop. IMUnit currently does not support the occurrence of an event more than once in a trace. We did find 4 tests that would require multiple event occurrences, but changing the language to support them (e.g., adding event counters or loop indices to events) would add a layer of complexity that is not justified by the small number of cases. However, as we apply IMUnit

Subject	Tests	Events	Orderings
Collections [4]	18	51	32
JBoss-Cache [18]	27	105	47
Lucene [6]	2	3	4
Mina [7]	1	2	1
Pool [5]	2	8	3
Sysunit [11]	9	33	34
JSR-166 TCK [17]	139	577	277
Σ	198	779	398

Table 1: Subject Programs Statistics

to more projects, and gain more experience, we expect that the language could grow in the future.

6.2 Inference of Events and Schedules

To measure the effectiveness of our migration tool in inferring events/schedules, we calculated precision and recall of automatically inferred events/schedules with respect to the manually written events/schedules (i.e., the manual translations from sleep-based schedules). Calculating precision and recall requires comparing the automatically inferred and manually written events/schedules. For event inference, the input is a sleep-based test, and the output is a set of events. Our current comparison uses only the *source-code location* (line number) of the static events and not their name. For schedule inference, the input is a sleep-based test *with manually written (not automatically inferred) events*, and the output is a schedule. Our comparison considers all orderings from the automatically inferred and manually written schedules; two orderings match only if they have exactly the same *both before and after events* (including their name and type that can be basic or block). We performed the comparisons for all but 14 (discussed below) of our 198 tests. Table 2 shows for each project precision and recall values, averaged over the tests from that project.

Columns two and three show the results for event inference. In most cases, precision and recall are fairly high. We inspected the cases with lower precision and identified two causes for it. The first cause is due to our evaluation setup and not the algorithm itself. Namely, our current comparison requires the exact match of source-code locations. If the locations differ, the inferred event counts as a false negative, even if it was only a few lines from the manually written event, and even if those locations are equivalent with respect to the code. In the future, we plan to improve the setup by analyzing the code around the automatically inferred and manually written events to determine if their locations are equivalent. The second reason is that some tests use sleeps that are not relevant for the thread schedule (e.g., JBoss-Cache has such sleeps in the helper threads shared among tests, and Lucene has similar sleeps while interacting with the I/O library). These extra sleeps mislead our inference, which assumes that every sleep is relevant for the schedule and infers events for every sleep.

Columns four and five show the results for schedule inference. The results are even more impressive than for event inference, with precision and recall of over 75% in all cases. We identified two causes for misses. The first cause is that some threads can be independent. The algorithm always forms edges from all threads to the thread that invokes sleep method, but this should not be done for independent threads. In the future, we plan to consider an abstraction similar to regions (Figure 4) as a mechanism to detect inde-

Subject	Inferring Events		Inferring Schedules	
	Precision	Recall	Precision	Recall
Collections	0.75	0.82	0.96	0.97
JBoss-Cache	0.83	0.86	0.87	0.96
Lucene	0.75	1.00	1.00	0.75
Mina	0.22	1.00	1.00	1.00
Pool	0.90	1.00	1.00	1.00
Sysunit	0.76	0.87	0.89	0.89
JSR-166 TCK	0.67	0.74	0.98	0.98
Overall	0.75	0.79	0.96	0.94

Table 2: Precision and Recall for Inference

Subject	Original	CR	TR	LC
Collections	33	0	0	0
JBoss-Cache	39	2	3	0
Lucene	5	0	1	1
Mina	1	0	0	0
Pool	3	0	0	0
Sysunit	39	0	5	0
JSR-166 TCK	306	0	30	1

Table 3: Numbers of Removed Orderings

pendent threads. The second cause is the same as for event inference, namely unnecessary sleeps.

A known issue in information retrieval is that some result sets may be empty, which corresponds to infinite precision and zero recall. For 14 of 198 tests, our inference techniques returned empty sets of events/schedules because these tests do not use sleeps to control schedules. Instead, these tests use `while (condition) { Thread.sleep/yield }` or `wait/notify` or `CountDownLatch` and other concurrent constructs to control schedules. We excluded these 14 tests from the evaluation of our inference techniques.

Our inference algorithms use `confidenceThreshold` to select some of the events/schedules, with the default value of 0.5 (for Table 2). We performed a set of experiments to evaluate how sensitive our inference is to the value of `confidenceThreshold`. We found that the results are quite stable. For example, for schedule inference, when changing the value from 0.5 to 0.1, only for Lucene the precision drops from 1 to 0.75. When changing the value from 0.5 to 0.9, only for JBoss-Cache the precision and recall drop from 0.87 and 0.96 to 0.86 and 0.93, respectively. For all other cases, everything else is inferred exactly the same for the values 0.1 and 0.9 as for the default value 0.5.

The other input to our inference algorithms is the set of logs obtained from passing runs of the legacy tests. By default, we collect 5 passing logs for each test (for Table 2). Different runs of the legacy test can produce different logs that can in turn result in different sets of events/schedules being inferred. Therefore, depending on the number of logs, inferred events/schedules could differ. So we evaluated how sensitive our inference is to the number of logs. We found that the logs are quite stable, and almost identical results were obtained for 1, 5, and 10 logs. For instance, going from 5 to 10 logs only the recall for JBoss-Cache drops from 0.96 to 0.94, and everything else remains the same.

Lastly, our schedule-inference algorithm runs a minimization phase after processing all the logs. Table 3 summarizes the results of this phase. It tabulates, for each project, the number of schedule orderings originally inferred before minimization (Original) and the numbers of orderings removed by cycles removal (CR), by transitive reduction (TR), and due to low confidence (LC). As it can be seen, the minimization phase does not remove many orderings. However, it is important to remove the orderings it does remove. For example, without removing the cycle for JBoss-Cache, not only would inference have a lower precision but it would also produce a schedule that is unrealizable.

Subject	Original [s]	IMUnit [s]		Speedup	
		DDD	DDE	DDD	DDE
Collections	4.96	1.06	1.67	4.68	2.97
JBoss-Cache	65.58	31.25	31.76	2.10	2.06
Lucene	11.02	3.57	6.12	3.09	1.80
Mina	0.26	0.17	0.20	1.53	1.30
Pool	1.43	1.04	1.04	1.38	1.38
Sysunit	17.67	0.35	0.45	50.49	39.27
JSR-166 TCK	15.20	9.56	9.56	1.59	1.59
GeometricMean				3.39	2.76

Table 4: Test execution time. DDD - deadlock detection disabled; DDE - deadlock detection enabled

6.3 Performance

Table 4 shows the execution times of the 198 original, sleep-based tests and the corresponding IMUnit tests (for IMUnit, with deadlock detection both disabled and enabled). We ran the experiments on an Intel i7 2.67GHz laptop with 4GB memory, using Sun JVM 1.6.0_06. Our goal for IMUnit is to improve readability, modularity, and reliability of multithreaded unit tests, and we did not expect IMUnit execution to be faster than sleep-based execution. In fact, one could even expect IMUnit to be slower because of the additional code introduced by the instrumentation and the cost of controlling schedules. It came as a surprise that IMUnit is faster than sleep-based tests, on average 3.39x. Even with deadlock detection enabled, IMUnit was on average 2.76x faster. This result is with the sleep durations that the original tests had in the code.

We also compared the running time of IMUnit with MultithreadedTC on a common subset of JSR-166 TCK tests that the MultithreadedTC authors translated from sleep-based to tick-based [25]. For these 129 tests, MultithreadedTC was 1.36x faster than IMUnit. Although MultithreadedTC is somewhat faster, it has a much higher migration cost, and in our view, produces test code that is harder to understand and modify than the IMUnit test code. Moreover, we were surprised to notice that running MultithreadedTC on these tests, translated by the MultithreadedTC authors, can result in some failures (albeit with a low probability), which means that these MultithreadedTC tests can be unreliable and lead to false positives in test runs.

7. RELATED WORK

Three areas of work are related to IMUnit: (1) unit testing of multithreaded code, (2) enforcement of schedules, and (3) automated inference of specifications. We briefly discuss each of them. (1) ConAn [22, 23] and MultithreadedTC [26] introduce unit testing frameworks that allow developers to specify schedules to be used during the execution of multithreaded unit tests. However, the schedules in both frameworks are specified relative to a global clock (real time for ConAn and logic time for MultithreadedTC), which makes it difficult to reason about the schedules. Also, neither framework supports automated migration of sleep-based tests. ConcJUnit [27] extends JUnit to propagate exceptions raised by child threads up to the main thread and also checks whether all child threads have finished at the end of a test method. ThreadControl [13] proposes a tool to ensure that assertions are performed without interference from other threads. (2) There has been some previous work on using formally specified sequencing constraints to verify multithreaded programs [28]. The specifications are over sync events with LTL-like constraints, and the verification ensures that the implementation is faithful to the specification. In contrast, IMUnit schedule specifications are used to enforce ordering between user-specified events while the system is tested. Carver and Tai [9] use deterministic replay for concurrent programs. LEAP [14] is a more recent system using a similar record-and-replay approach to reproduce bugs. In comparison, our enforcement and checking mechanism targets ensuring the user-specified schedule rather than replaying a previously observed execution. (3) Work on automated mining of specifications for programs [2,3,8,21] is related to our automated inference of events and schedules. However, most existing work focuses on mining API usage patterns/rules in a single threaded scenario, while our techniques mine the intention of sleep-based tests i.e. interesting events and event orderings across multiple threads.

8. CONCLUSIONS

Current approaches for unit testing of multithreaded code have issues with readability, modularity, reliability, and/or migration cost. We presented IMUnit, a novel approach that addresses these issues. IMUnit includes a new language that makes tests more readable and modular as it allows explicitly specifying schedules on the events during test execution. We described inference techniques and a tool that can help in migrating sleep-based tests to IMUnit. We also described a tool that can reliably execute the specified schedule to avoid false positives/negatives. The promising results with IMUnit encourage us to further explore this approach, e.g., for automatic generation of multithreaded tests (both test code and schedules) only from the code under test, or for regression testing of code with IMUnit schedules [16].

Acknowledgements

We would like to thank Feng Chen, Steven Lauterburg and Traian Şerbănuţă for initial discussion on this work. Also, we would like to thank the participants of the IWMSE 2010 workshop for useful feedback. This work is partially supported by the National Science Foundation under Grant Nos. CCF-1012759, CNS-0958199, CCF-0916893, CCF-0746856, and CNS-0720512, by Intel and Microsoft via the Universal Parallel Computing Research Center (UPCRC), by NASA contract NNL08AA23C, by an NSA grant, by a UIUC Campus Research Board Award, and by a Samsung SAIT grant.

9. REFERENCES

[1] A. V. Aho, M. R. Garey, and J. D. Ullman. The transitive reduction of a directed graph. *SIAM Journal on Computing*, 1972.

[2] R. Alur, P. Cerný, M. Parthasarathy, and W. Nam. Synthesis of interface specifications for Java classes. In *POPL*, 2005.

[3] G. Ammons, R. Bodík, and J. R. Larus. Mining specifications. In *POPL*, 2002.

[4] Apache Software Foundation. Apache Commons Collections. `http://commons.apache.org/collections/`.

[5] Apache Software Foundation. Apache Commons Pool. `http://commons.apache.org/pool/`.

[6] Apache Software Foundation. Apache Lucene. `http://lucene.apache.org/`.

[7] Apache Software Foundation. Apache MINA. `http://mina.apache.org/`.

[8] J. Burnim and K. Sen. DETERMIN: Inferring likely deterministic specifications of multithreaded programs. In *ICSE*, 2010.

[9] R. H. Carver and K. Tai. Replay and testing for concurrent programs. *IEEE Software*, 1991.

[10] F. Chen and G. Roşu. Mop: An efficient and generic runtime verification framework. In *OOPSLA*, 2007.

[11] Codehaus. Sysunit. `http://docs.codehaus.org/display/SYSUNIT/Home`.

[12] S. Cotton. graphlib. `http://www-verimag.imag.fr/~cotton/`.

[13] A. Dantas, F. V. Brasileiro, and W. Cirne. Improving automated testing of multi-threaded software. In *ICST*, 2008.

[14] J. Huang, P. Liu, and C. Zhang. LEAP: Lightweight deterministic multi-processor replay of concurrent Java programs. In *FSE*, 2010.

[15] V. Jagannath, M. Gligoric, D. Jin, G. Rosu, and D. Marinov. IMUnit: Improved multithreaded unit testing (position statement). In *IWMSE*, 2010.

[16] V. Jagannath, Q. Luo, and D. Marinov. Change-aware preemption prioritization. In *ISSTA*, 2011.

[17] Java Community Process. JSR 166: Concurrency utilities. `http://g.oswego.edu/dl/concurrency-interest/`.

[18] JBoss Community. JBoss Cache. `http://www.jboss.org/jbosscache`.

[19] G. Kiczales, E. Hilsdale, J. Hugunin, M. Kersten, J. Palm, and W. G. Griswold. An overview of AspectJ. In *ECOOP*, 2001.

[20] Lassi Project. Sleep testcase. `http://tinyurl.com/4hk9zdr`.

[21] C. Lee, F. Chen, and G. Roşu. Mining parametric specifications. In *ICSE*, 2011.

[22] B. Long, D. Hoffman, and P. A. Strooper. A concurrency test tool for Java monitors. In *ASE*, 2001.

[23] B. Long, D. Hoffman, and P. A. Strooper. Tool support for testing concurrent Java components. *IEEE TSE*, 2003.

[24] P. O. Meredith, D. Jin, D. Griffith, F. Chen, and G. Roşu. An overview of the MOP runtime verification framework. *Springer STTT*, 2011.

[25] W. Pugh and N. Ayewah. MultithreadedTC - A framework for testing concurrent Java applications. `http://code.google.com/p/multithreadedtc/`.

[26] W. Pugh and N. Ayewah. Unit testing concurrent software. In *ASE*, 2007.

[27] M. Ricken and R. Cartwright. ConcJUnit: Unit testing for concurrent programs. In *PPPJ*, 2009.

[28] K. Tai and R. H. Carver. Use of sequencing constraints for specifying, testing, and debugging concurrent programs. In *ICPADS*, 1994.

Taming Uncertainty in Self-Adaptive Software

Naeem Esfahani
Department of Computer Science
George Mason University
nesfaha2@gmu.edu

Ehsan Kouroshfar
Department of Computer Science
George Mason University
ekourosh@gmu.edu

Sam Malek
Department of Computer Science
George Mason University
smalek@gmu.edu

ABSTRACT

Self-adaptation endows a software system with the ability to satisfy certain objectives by automatically modifying its behavior. While many promising approaches for the construction of self-adaptive software systems have been developed, the majority of them ignore the uncertainty underlying the adaptation decisions. This has been one of the key obstacles to wide-spread adoption of self-adaption techniques in risk-averse real-world settings. In this paper, we describe an approach, called *POssIbilistic SElf-aDaptation* (*POISED*), for tackling the challenge posed by uncertainty in making adaptation decisions. POISED builds on possibility theory to assess both the positive and negative consequences of uncertainty. It makes adaptation decisions that result in the best range of potential behavior. We demonstrate POISED's application to the problem of improving a software system's quality of service via runtime reconfiguration of its customizable software components. We have extensively evaluated POISED using a prototype of a robotic software system.

Categories and Subject Descriptors

D.2.10 [**Software Engineering**]: Design – *Methodologies.*

General Terms

Algorithms, Performance, Design.

Keywords

Uncertainty, Self-Adaptation, Software Architecture

1. INTRODUCTION

Self-adaptation is an effective approach in dealing with the changing dynamics of many application domains, such as mobile and pervasive systems. In response to changes in the environment or requirements, a self-adaptive software system modifies itself to satisfy certain objectives [2, 16]. While the benefits of such systems are plenty, their development has shown to be more challenging than traditional software systems [2]. One key culprit is that self-adaptation is subject to *uncertainty* [2].

We distinguish between the external and internal uncertainty. *External uncertainty* arises from the environment or domain in which the software is deployed. For example, external uncertainty for a software system deployed in an unmanned vehicle may include the likelihood of certain weather conditions occurring. Software self-adaptation is one approach in dealing with the effects of external uncertainty, e.g., in a snow storm the vehicle's navigator component may be replaced with a more conservative navigator to avoid a collision. On the other hand, *internal uncertainty* is rooted in the difficulty of determining the impact of adaptation on the system's quality objectives, e.g., determining the impact of replacing a software component on the system's responsiveness, battery usage, etc. While both sources of uncertainty are of great concern, in this paper we focus our attention on the challenges posed by *internal uncertainty*.

Permission to make digital or hard copies of all or part of this work for personal or classroom use is granted without fee provided that copies are not made or distributed for profit or commercial advantage and that copies bear this notice and the full citation on the first page. To copy otherwise, or republish, to post on servers or to redistribute to lists, requires prior specific permission and/or a fee.
ESEC/FSE'11, September 5–9, 2011, Szeged, Hungary.
Copyright 2011 ACM 978-1-4503-0443-6/11/09...$10.00.

Uncertainty can be observed in every facet of adaptation, albeit at varying degrees. It follows from the fact that the system's user, adaptation logic, and business logic are loosely coupled, introducing numerous sources of uncertainty [3]. A key observation is that while the level of uncertainty could vary, no self-adaptive software system is ever completely free of it.

The research community has made great strides in tackling the complexity of constructing self-adaptive software systems [2, 16]. However, as corroborated by others [2], there is a dearth of applicable techniques for handling uncertainty in this setting. A few researchers have recently begun to address uncertainty issues in requirements specification [1, 28] and resource prediction [23], but no approach that we are aware of has tackled the challenge posed by uncertainty in making adaptation decisions. We believe this has been one of the primary obstacles to wide-spread adoption of self-adaptation in risk-averse domains.

This is precisely the challenge we have aimed to address in this paper. We present a general quantitative approach for tackling the complexity of automatically making adaptation decisions under internal uncertainty, called *POssIbilistic SElf-aDaptation* (*POISED*). Estimates of uncertainty in the elements comprising a self-adaptation problem are incorporated in *possibilistic analysis* of the adaptation choices. Possibilistic analysis is founded on the principles of fuzzy mathematics [29], which provides a sound basis for representing uncertainty, as well as dealing with its negative and positive consequences on the adaptation choices. POISED redefines the conventional definition of optimal adaptation decision to one that has the best range of behavior. In turn, the selected solution has the highest likelihood of satisfying the system's quality objectives, even if due to uncertainty, properties expected of the system are not borne out in practice.

We demonstrate POISED by applying it to the problem of improving a software system's quality of service via runtime reconfiguration of its customizable software components. We have evaluated POISED under numerous circumstances and using a prototype of a robotic software system. The results demonstrate POISED's ability to deal with uncertainty by making adaptation decisions that are superior to those of the conventional approach.

This paper is organized as follows. Section 2 motivates the research. Section 3 provides an overview of POISED. Section 4 formalizes the self-adaptation problem used to describe and evaluate POISED. Section 5 describes techniques for quantifying uncertainty. Section 6 presents our possibilistic analysis approach, followed by detailed evaluation in Section 7. The paper concludes with a discussion of the related literature and future research.

2. MOTIVATING EXAMPLE

We use a subset of a robotic software system developed in another project [18] to motivate and describe this research. The robotic software is part of a distributed search and rescue system aimed at supporting the government agencies in dealing with emergency crises (e.g., fire, hurricane). Figure 1b provides an abridged view of the robotic system's architecture. The software components comprising the robotic system range from abstractions of the physical entities, such as software controlled sensors and actuators on board the robot, to purely logical functionalities, such as image detection and navigation. The bold path in Figure 1b indicates the *Maneuver* execution scenario, which aims to safely steer the robot. The *Camera* feed is sent to *Obstacle Detector*, which runs an image processing algorithm to identify obstacles. Obstacle information is used by *Navigator* to plan the direction and speed of movement, which are then put into effect by the *Controller*.

The software components comprising this system are *customizable* meaning that they can be configured to operate in different modes of operation. Figure 1a shows some of the available configuration dimensions. For instance, *Power* is a configuration dimension for the *Controller* component. A *Controller* could operate in either *Energy Saving* or *Full Power* mode. A component may have many configuration dimensions.

The configuration of a software component determines its quality attributes (e.g., response time) and resource usage (e.g., memory), which could also impact the properties of the entire system. For instance, given the resource constrained nature of the mobile robots, the configuration decisions of each component have a significant impact on the system's performance as well as its battery life. Such decisions can only be effectively made at

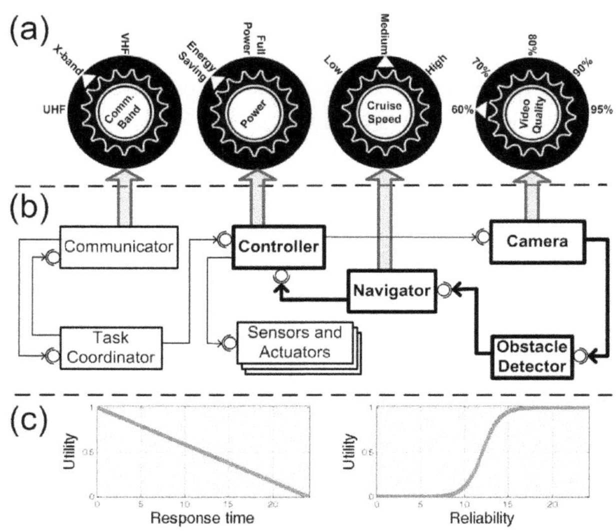

Figure 1. A subset of the robotic software: (a) configuration dimensions and alternatives for components of the robot, (b) software architecture, where the bold path indicates the components participating in the Maneuver execution scenario, and (c) utility functions defined in terms of quality attributes.

runtime, since the system properties (e.g., available bandwidth) are often not known at design-time and may change at runtime.

As shown in Figure 1c, for making runtime decisions, utility functions capturing the user's satisfaction with different levels of quality attribute (e.g., availability) are used. The adaptation logic uses analytical models to estimate the effect of configuration decision on the system's quality attributes, and in turn the resulting utility. For example, given the configuration of the robot's components, an analytical model, such as Queueing Network model [20], may be used to quantify the response time for its *Maneuver* scenario. The objective is to find a configuration that achieves the maximum overall utility.

The above approach is rather myopic, since it does not consider the uncertainty of information used in making adaptation decisions. Consider that almost every facet of the approach outlined above faces some form of uncertainty:

- *Uncertainty in System Parameters*: The monitoring data obtained from a running system rarely corresponds to a single value, but rather a distribution of values obtained over the observation period. For instance, a sensor monitoring the available network bandwidth may return a slightly different number every time a sample is collected. This variation could be either due to actual changes in the bandwidth or the error (noise) in the employed probes.
- *Uncertainty in Analytical Models*: Analytical models often make simplifying assumptions, and thus provide only estimates of the system's behavior. For instance, an analytical model quantifying the system's response time may account for the dominant factors, such as execution time of components, and ignore others, such as the transmission delay difference between TCP and UDP. Response time estimates provisioned by such a formulation are not only error-prone, but also the magnitude of error varies depending on the circumstances.
- *Uncertainty in User Preferences*: Eliciting user's preferences in terms of utility functions, such as those depicted in Figure 1c, is a well-known challenge [2]. Often users have difficulty expressing their preferences and thus the overall accuracy of the utility functions remains subjective, making the analysis based on them prone to uncertainty.

The uncertainty in these elements challenges the system's ability in making decisions that bring about the intended effects.

3. APPROACH

In this section, we first provide an intuitive description of our approach. Afterwards, we provide a brief background on the applicable mathematical techniques for realizing our approach, and justify our choices.

3.1 Underlying Insights

Figure 2a shows the typical behavior of a self-adaptive system that does not incorporate uncertainty in its analysis. We abstractly refer to this as the *traditional approach*. The system is initially executing with utility U_1 prior to time T_1. At time T_1, due to either an internal or external change, the system's utility drops to U_2. By time T_2, the self-adaptation logic detects this drop in utility, finds and effects an optimal configuration, which is conventionally defined as the one achieving the maximum utility. As shown in Figure 2a, this corresponds to U_3, which represents the *expected* utility of the best configuration for the system. In practice, however, the *actual* utility of the system may vary between the

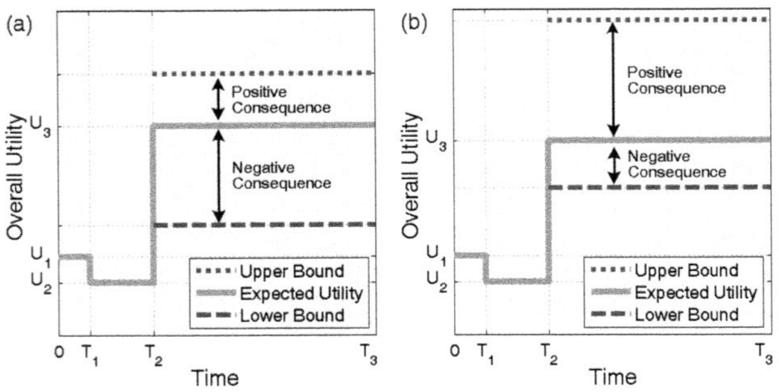

Figure 2. Impact of uncertainty on the utility of a self-adaptive system: traditional (part a) versus POISED's (part b) selection of optimal configuration.

two dashed lines, representing the likely positive and negative consequences of uncertainty. By not accounting for uncertainty, the approach is vulnerable to gross overestimation of the utility.

The centerpiece of POISED is the reconceptualization of what is traditionally considered as the optimal solution, such that the uncertainty is incorporated into the analysis. We illustrate the insights underlying POISED using Figure 2b. Similar to the scenario of Figure 2a, a new configuration is effected at time T_2, except POISED concurrently follows three objectives in selecting the new configuration: (1) maximizes U_3, which represents the most likely utility for the system under uncertainty; (2) maximizes the *positive consequence* of uncertainty, which represents the likelihood of the solution being better than U_3; and (3) minimizes the *negative consequence* of uncertainty, which represents the likelihood of the solution being worse than U_3.

The details of our approach, including how the likelihood of each objective is calculated, are described in Sections 5 and 6. Nevertheless, we can make a general observation. As depicted in Figure 2, concurrent satisfaction of the three objectives may result in a smaller value of *expected* utility (i.e., U_3) in POISED compared to that of the traditional approach. But since the information used to estimate the expected utility is uncertain, *expected* utility is not guaranteed to occur in practice. We argue the true quality of a solution is determined by the range of possible utility. As depicted here and evaluated in Section 7, POISED's objective is to find solutions with a better range.

3.2 Analysis Technique

The above discussion assumes one could quantify the range of utility under uncertainty. There are two general techniques to estimating uncertainty: *probability theory* and *possibility theory*. Probability theory is concerned with the analysis of random phenomena and forms the foundation of statistics. Possibility theory is founded on the concept of fuzzy set [30]. In a fuzzy set, the elements have a degree of membership. Degree of membership is a value between zero and one: a value of zero indicates the element is certainly not a member of the set, a value of one indicates the element is certainly a member of the set, and a value in between indicates the extent of certainty that the element is a member of the set. In possibility theory, the concept of *possibility* is defined as the degree of membership, which plays a similar role as that of probability in statistics. The *most optimistic* and *most pessimistic* values have a degree of membership of zero, while the *most possible* value has a degree of membership of one. The distinction between the two concepts is that *Probability theory* deals with the statistical characteristic of data, while *possibility theory* focuses on the meaning of data [30].

For an illustration of this difference, see Figures 3 and 4 in which the uncertainty in available network bandwidth is modeled using possibility and probability distributions, respectively. The details of how such functions can be obtained are described in Section 5. Possibility distribution models a *fuzzy variable*, while probability distribution models a *random variable*. Possibility distribution in Figure 3 returns the *degree of membership*, while probability distribution in Figure 4 returns the *probability density*.

While uncertainty can be represented using both approaches, the ability to make adaptation decisions is significantly impacted by the representation. The operations research technique for making decisions under probability theory is called *stochastic programming* [26]. When all the probability distributions follow normal distribution, by applying the central limit theorem [13], the problem can be solved effectively [14]. Central limit theorem allows for the definition of commonly used algebraic operations on the normally distributed variables. However, as further demonstrated in this paper, uncertainty in self-adaptive software systems rarely follows a normal distribution, which severely limits the application of stochastic programming.

An alternative approach that does not suffer from these limitations is *possibilistic programming*, which is founded on possibility theory. Possibilistic programming is widely used for making decisions under uncertainty in many fields of engineering, including control theory, robotics, and artificial intelligence. Advantages of possibilistic programming are twofold: generality and efficiency. Unlike stochastic programming, where simple algebraic operations require special considerations (e.g., central limit theorem), and not even always possible, in possibilistic programming, fuzzy variables can be simply operated on using traditional algebraic operators. This is true even if the distributions are complex and unique. Possibilistic programming problems can be solved much more efficiently than stochastic programming problems [14], making them desirable in many practical engineering problems, including self-adaptive systems. For these reasons we have adopted possibilistic programming as the technique for achieving POISED's objectives.

While the characteristics of our problem made possibility theory a better fit, probability theory has shown to be suitable in many areas of software engineering. Thus, the conclusions made here are only with respect to POISED's objectives. A more comprehensive analysis of the differences between the two theories can be found in the extensive body of literature [5, 7].

4. SELF-ADAPTATION PROBLEM

In this section, we provide a formal specification of the self-adaptation problem introduced in Section 2, which we use to demonstrate and evaluate POISED. However, note that the underlying concepts and techniques in POISED are generally applicable and not tied to the problem described here.

4.1 Configuration

A system like the one depicted in Figure 1b consists of several software components, which we denote as set C. Each component $c \in C$ may have several configuration *dimensions*, which we denote as set D_c. Configuration dimensions correspond to the knobs depicted in Figure 1a. Each configuration dimension $d \in D_c$ may have A_d configuration *alternatives*. For example, *Video Quality* dimension of the *Camera* component in Figure 1 is comprised of the following alternatives: *60%*, *70%*, *80%*, *90%*, and 95%. Configuration alternatives within the same dimension are mutually exclusive, e.g., *Video Quality* could be exactly in one of the 5 possible alternatives at any point in time.

We define the configuration space of component $c \in C$ as the Cartesian product of all the available configuration alternatives for that component:

$$ConfSpace_c \stackrel{\text{def}}{=} \otimes_{d \in D_c} \otimes_{a \in A_d} dom(x_{c,d,a})$$

Where x represents a decision variable with a binary domain and indicates whether an alternative has been selected or not.

A system may have several execution *scenarios* denoted as list $S \stackrel{\text{def}}{=} \langle s_1, s_2, \dots, s_n \rangle$, where each scenario $s_i \subseteq C$. A scenario represents a high-level functional capability involving the services provided by software components. For example, the components bolded in Figure 1b form a scenario dealing with the robot maneuvering a terrain. Same components can potentially form different scenarios, thus we represent execution scenarios as a list.

Configuration space of each scenario is the Cartesian product of the configuration space of all the components that participate in it:

$$ConfSpace_s \stackrel{\text{def}}{=} \otimes_{c \in s} ConfSpace_c$$

We use $ConfSpace$ with no subscript to denote the set of all possible configurations of components in a system (i.e., $s = C$):

$$ConfSpace \stackrel{\text{def}}{=} \otimes_{c \in C} ConfSpace_c$$

4.2 Configuration Constraint

Not all configurations for a software system are valid. There may be some constraints among the system's configuration dimensions. For example, one may not be able to configure the robot in a way that *Cruise Speed* is set to *High* and *Power* is set to *Energy Saving*. Another class of constraints are among the alternatives in a given configuration dimension, i.e., the fact that configuration alternatives are mutually exclusive (recall Section 4.1). We represent these constraints as follows:

$$ConfConstraints: ConfSpace \longrightarrow \{0,1\}$$

Where given a configuration, $ConfConstraints$ returns 0, if at least one constraint is violated, and 1, otherwise.

4.3 Quality Attribute

We use Q to denote the set of quality attributes, which are quantifiable non-functional properties of interest (e.g., response time). A quality attribute may take either discrete or continuous values, e.g., response time may take continuous values bigger than 0, while security may take an enumeration of discrete values.

The quality attributes of an execution scenario are determined by the configuration of components participating in that scenario. For example, the response time of the *Maneuver* scenario depicted in Figure 1b is affected by the configuration of its four components. Given a configuration of a scenario, a quality attribute is estimated via an analytical formula (model). These analytical formulas are used by the adaptation logic for making decisions. We represent an analytical formula estimating the configuration's impact on quality attribute $q \in Q$ of execution scenario $s \in S$ as:

$$\widetilde{QE_{s,q}}: ConfSpace_s \longrightarrow dom(q)$$

The tilde is the conventional notation for representing uncertainty. Description of analytical models for estimating quality attributes is beyond the scope of this paper. Numerous previous studies (e.g., [6, 9, 12, 21]) have developed analytical approaches for estimating quality attributes in terms of the system's architectural configuration. Regardless of the approach, the analytical models provide only estimates, and thus represent a source of uncertainty.

4.4 Resource

We use set R to denote the different computing resources utilized by the software system. For each resource $r \in R$, we use $\widetilde{Capacity_r}$ to represent the maximum available resource. While in some cases the available resource is a known constant (e.g., physical memory), in others the available resource may fluctuate (e.g., network bandwidth), and thus introduce uncertainty.

The configuration of a system determines its resource usage. For example, consider that in the robotics system, when the *Power* dimension of the *Controller* component is configured to operate at *Full Power*, the system's battery consumption increases. We represent an analytical formula estimating the configuration's impact on the system's resource $r \in R$ as follows:

$$\widetilde{RE_r}: ConfSpace \longrightarrow dom(r)$$

Numerous previous studies (e.g., [23-25]) have developed resource usage models that can be used in such setting. While sophisticated models may reduce the inaccuracy, they are not ever completely free of it, challenging the confidence with which adaptation decisions are made.

4.5 User Preference

Similar to the previous research [9, 23, 24, 27], we use utility functions to represent the user's preferences for changes in the quality attributes. A utility function representing the user's satisfaction with quality attribute $q \in Q$ of an execution scenario $s \in S$ is represented as:

$$\widetilde{UP_{s,q}}: ran(\widetilde{QE_{s,q}}) \longrightarrow [0,1]$$

A higher value indicates more user satisfaction with the system. Given a vector $\overrightarrow{cnf} \in ConfSpace$, we define the *overall utility* $\widetilde{U}$ to be the cumulative satisfaction of all the user preferences:

$$\widetilde{U} \stackrel{\text{def}}{=} \sum_{\forall s \in S} \sum_{\forall q \in Q} \widetilde{UP_{s,q}}\left(\widetilde{QE_{s,q}}(\overrightarrow{cnf_s})\right) \quad \text{Eq. 1}$$

Where $\overrightarrow{cnf_s}$ is defined as the *projection* of $\overrightarrow{cnf}$ from $ConfSpace$ onto $ConfSpace_s$: $\overrightarrow{cnf_s} = proj_{\overrightarrow{I_s}}(\overrightarrow{cnf})$, and $\overrightarrow{I_s}$ is the *identity* vector for $ConfSpace_s$. In other words, since not every component participates in every execution scenario of interest s, the above projection removes the unnecessary elements from vector $\overrightarrow{cnf}$ to derive $\overrightarrow{cnf_s}$. The assumption in the formulation of Eq. 1 is that if the user has not specified a preference for a quality attribute of an execution scenario, the corresponding utility function returns only zero.

4.6 Optimization Problem

The objective of the adaptation logic is to find a configuration that maximizes the system's overall utility:

$$argmax_{(\overrightarrow{cnf} \in ConfSpace)} \widetilde{U} \quad \text{Eq. 2}$$

The solution maximizing the above objective should satisfy two constraints. First, ensure that the solution satisfies the configuration constraints:

$$ConfConstraints(\overrightarrow{cnf}) = 1 \quad \text{Eq. 3}$$

Second, ensure that the resource usage does not exceed the available resources:

$$\forall r \in R, \quad \widetilde{RE_r}(\overrightarrow{cnf}) \leq \widetilde{Capacity_r} \quad \text{Eq. 4}$$

For simplicity, the above formulation assumes the capacity of all resources is uncertain. But as you may recall from Section 4.4, this may not always be the case.

5. QUANTIFYING UNCERTAINTY

Before uncertainty can be dealt with in the analysis, it needs to be quantified for a given configuration of the system. POISED's accuracy depends on the ability to: (1) identify the sources of uncertainty, and (2) estimate the level of uncertainty. To put it boldly, our approach addresses "known unknowns", not "unknown unknowns". However, even if the two conditions are partially satisfied (i.e., only some sources of uncertainty are identified and estimated), POISED produces better results than the traditional approach by incorporating the known uncertainties.

In this section, we first describe two ways of estimating uncertainty: eliciting it from the stakeholders (e.g., user, engineer), and observing it in the system. These techniques are not intended to be exhaustive, or even generally applicable, but rather concrete examples to illustrate the feasibility of our work. We then describe how uncertainty in the individual elements can be combined to quantify the overall uncertainty for the system.

5.1 Eliciting Uncertainty from Stakeholders

Stakeholders often provide inputs for different facets of a self-adaptive system. One of the most crucial and commonly elicited inputs is the user's quality preferences. It is commonly agreed that eliciting user's preferences in terms of complex utility functions is challenging [2]. The specification of such utility functions is highly subjective and inevitably prone to uncertainty. Engineers may also provide inputs for certain software properties that cannot be easily monitored. For instance, the maximum memory consumed by a software component is a property that may be available from the component's source code, but not easily obtainable through runtime monitoring. Similarly, engineers may provide inputs for certain systems parameters, such as the available network bandwidth, based on a combination of past experiences, hardware specifications, similar systems, etc.

For the inputs provided by the stakeholders, it is also reasonable to ask them to estimate the range of uncertainty based on the expected level of variation in the input. For illustration, Figure 3 shows how an engineer may estimate the range of uncertainty in the network bandwidth in the form of a *triangular* possibility distribution. Possibility distribution can be modeled in different ways (e.g., Gaussian, Triangular) [32], but for simplicity we use only triangular distribution in this paper. The horizontal axis marks the network bandwidth, while the vertical axis marks the possibility (i.e., degree of membership). This distribution indicates that the range of feasible values for network bandwidth is anywhere between the *most pessimistic*, denoted with $Capacity_{bw}^{p}$, and the *most optimistic*, denoted with $Capacity_{bw}^{o}$. In a triangular distribution, as we reach the boundaries, the possibility of getting the expected value drops to 0. The *most possible* value is $Capacity_{bw}^{m}$, which always has the value of 1.

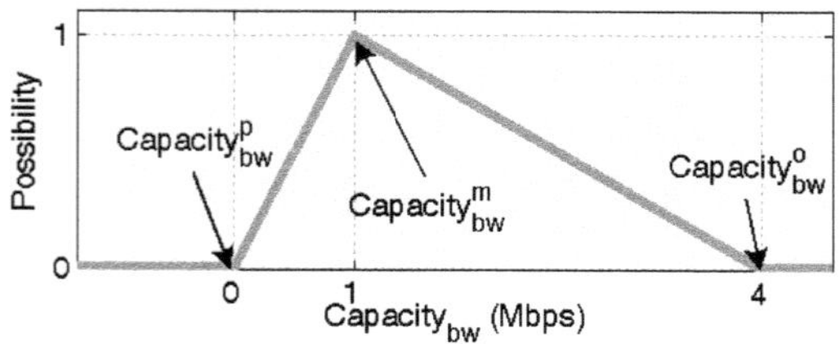

Figure 3. Triangular possibility distribution.

In the example of Figure 3, the engineer sets the most possible value to be the expected network bandwidth, which may be based on the engineer's past experiences, similar systems, etc. The most pessimistic value is set to 0, representing network failure, and the most optimistic value to the ideal network bandwidth, as advertised by the network provider. By connecting the most pessimistic and optimistic points with the most possible point, we arrive at a triangular possibility distribution representing the uncertainty in the network bandwidth. A similar approach could be used for eliciting and quantifying uncertainty with the other types of stakeholder provided inputs, such as utility functions.

5.2 Measuring Uncertainty via Monitoring

A self-adaptive software system often relies on monitoring to reason about changes in the execution condition. Dynamically fluctuating system parameters are one type of phenomena in this setting that are monitored. For instance, consider that while capacity of certain resources (e.g., available physical memory) may be known prior to system's deployment, other resources (e.g., available battery charge) may change at runtime, and thus would need to be sampled during the system's execution. On top of the uncertainty created by the fluctuations in the monitored phenomenon, monitoring is also impacted by the error in the sensors used for data collection. Such an error is in particular unavoidable with digital sensors that take samples of a continuous physical phenomenon. Even if the observed phenomenon is constant, the collected data may vary, due to noisy sensors.

System parameters may not be the only elements that need to be monitored. In [9] we showed that analytical models used for making self-adaptation decisions are abstractions of the system and by definition make simplifying assumptions, which if not held at runtime may make the estimates inaccurate. The inaccuracy of an analytical model could be determined by comparing its estimates (i.e., $\widetilde{QE}$, $\widetilde{RE}$) against the actual behavior of the system. This can be achieved either prior to system's deployment by benchmarking the system, or through runtime observation.

The uncertainty corresponding to any monitored phenomenon can be estimated as a probability distribution. For example, if the engineer is not able to use the technique from Section 5.1 to manually specify the uncertainty in network bandwidth, an alternative approach is to estimate it by monitoring the variations and constructing the equivalent probability distribution. Figure 4 shows the probability distribution corresponding to the data collected for variations in the network bandwidth (i.e., $Capacity_{bw}$). There are numerous approaches for deriving a *probability density function* [13] that represents the probability distribution of collected data, including Q-Q plot [13] that could be used to estimate well-known (e.g., *normal*, *beta*) distributions, and Quantile-Regression [15] that could be used to estimate arbitrary complex distributions. In our experiments, we found Q-Q plot to be sufficient, as monitoring data often follows one of the well-known distributions. For the parameters that only have

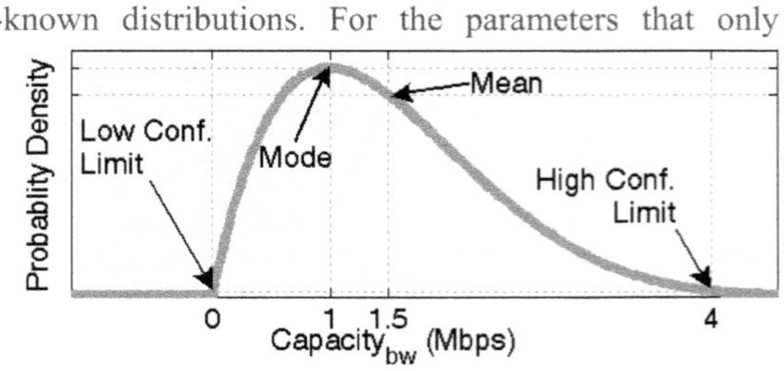

Figure 4. Probability distribution.

monitoring noise, we obtained approximate *normal* distribution. However, for most parameters, the distributions were skewed and best represented using *beta* distribution. As you may recall from Section 3.2, the fact that the majority of distributions were not normal was one of the primary motivations that led us to use possibilistic programming, as opposed to stochastic programming.

The majority of existing self-adaptive systems (e.g., [6, 9, 21, 24]) ignore the probability distribution of the collected data, and simply use the mean value in their analysis. By basing the analysis on the mean behavior, they essentially ignore the statistical characteristics of the data, and thus the underlying uncertainty.

5.3 Quantifying the Overall Uncertainty

From the estimates of uncertainty in the elements comprising a self-adaptive software system, we can estimate the overall uncertainty in the system's ability to satisfy its objectives (i.e., uncertainty in the overall utility). As mentioned in Section 3, for efficient and effective analysis of uncertainty, we have adopted the possibilistic model of uncertainty in POISED. However, to quantify the overall uncertainty under the possibility theory, and as a fuzzy variable, we also need the uncertainty associated with each of the elements to be expressed as a fuzzy variable.

As you may recall from Section 5.1, the approach for estimating uncertainty in the inputs provided by the stakeholder already produces fuzzy variables. Recall that a possibility distribution, such as the one depicted in Figure 3, defines a fuzzy variable. On the other hand, we need to transform the probability distribution representing the uncertainty in monitored elements to the equivalent possibility distribution.

We demonstrate this transformation via the network bandwidth example. From the probability distribution of Figure 4, we can derive the corresponding possibility distribution of Figure 3 as follows: (1) calculate the *confidence interval* [13] and *mode* [13] of probability distribution (*mode* is the value that occurs most frequently in a distribution), (2) set the most pessimistic value equal to the *low confidence limit* of the probability distribution, (3) set the most optimistic value equal to the *high confidence limit* of the probability distribution, (4) set the most possible value equal to the mode of probability distribution, (5) connect the most pessimistic and optimistic points with the most possible point to arrive at the triangular possibility distribution of the collected data. This approach could be used to derive the possibility distribution for all of the monitored elements.

The possibility distribution derived in this way is an approximation of the probability distribution. This is because the most pessimistic and optimistic values are determined based on the confidence limits, which are not the absolute pessimistic and optimistic values for a probability distribution. While in theory the two may not be identical, in practice, selecting a large confidence level (e.g., 99%) results in negligible difference.

Using the possibility distributions quantifying the uncertainty in the individual elements of our problem, we quantify the overall

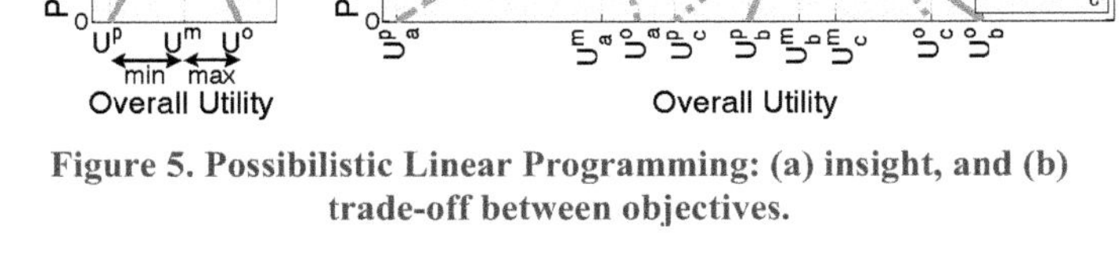

Figure 5. Possibilistic Linear Programming: (a) insight, and (b) trade-off between objectives.

uncertainty in system's ability to satisfy its overall utility (see Eq. 1) via a possibility distribution specified as follows:

$$\begin{cases} U^p \stackrel{\text{def}}{=} \sum_{\forall s \in S} \sum_{\forall q \in Q} UP^p_{s,q}\left(QE^p_{s,q}(\overrightarrow{cnf_s})\right) \\ U^m \stackrel{\text{def}}{=} \sum_{\forall s \in S} \sum_{\forall q \in Q} UP^m_{s,q}\left(QE^m_{s,q}(\overrightarrow{cnf_s})\right) \\ U^o \stackrel{\text{def}}{=} \sum_{\forall s \in S} \sum_{\forall q \in Q} UP^o_{s,q}\left(QE^o_{s,q}(\overrightarrow{cnf_s})\right) \end{cases}$$

Where $\overrightarrow{cnf} \in ConfSpace$, and U^p, U^m, and U^o denote the most pessimistic, possible, and optimistic values for the overall utility of the system, respectively. The insight is that the most pessimistic overall utility U^p occurs when all of the quality estimates QE and user preferences UP are also pessimistic. Similar insight holds for U^m and U^o. For simplicity, this formulation assumes the utility functions are monotonic, which is often the case with user-specified preferences [27]. If that is not the case, by taking the derivative of the functions we could find their extremums ; we elide the details for brevity.

6. POSSIBILISTIC ANALYSIS

We now describe our approach for formulating the problem of Section 4 as a Possibilistic Linear Programming (PLP) [14] problem, and solving it using conventional solvers [22].

6.1 Possibilistic Formulation of the Problem

As you may recall from Section 3, POISED manages the uncertainty by finding a solution that has the best range of overall utility, where the range depends on the level of uncertainty in the system. Figure 5a depicts the intuition behind our approach, which involves pursuing three concurrent objectives: (1) select a configuration that maximizes $z_m \stackrel{\text{def}}{=} U^m$, (2) minimize negative consequence of uncertainty $z_p \stackrel{\text{def}}{=} |U^m - U^p|$, and (3) maximize positive consequence of uncertainty $z_o \stackrel{\text{def}}{=} |U^o - U^m|$. In essence, the objective is to find a configuration that has the highest likelihood of satisfying the user's preferences given the level of uncertainty. We rewrite our objective (Eq. 2) as a PLP as follows:

$$\begin{cases} argmin_{(\overrightarrow{cnf} \in ConfSpace)}\, z_p \\ argmax_{(\overrightarrow{cnf} \in ConfSpace)}\, z_m \\ argmax_{(\overrightarrow{cnf} \in ConfSpace)}\, z_o \end{cases} \qquad \text{Eq. 5}$$

Figure 5b shows the two possible scenarios that could occur as PLP searches for the optimal solution among three hypothetical configurations. Each configuration corresponds to a possibility distribution in Figure 5b, which is unlike the traditional approach, where each configuration would be a point in the utility space. The first scenario occurs when a configuration is inferior to others with respect to all objectives. For instance, in Figure 5b, $Conf_a$ is inferior to $Conf_b$ and $Conf_c$ with respect to all three objectives. That is $Conf_a$ has a larger z_p, and a smaller z_m and z_o. The second scenario occurs when there are trade-offs. For instance, $Conf_b$ and $Conf_c$ present a trade-off, as $Conf_b$ is superior to $Conf_c$ with respect to z_o and z_p, and inferior with respect to z_m. Section 6.2 describes the process through which such trade-offs can be resolved.

The next step is the formulation of constraints with uncertainty, which in our problem corresponds to Eq. 4, ensuring the resource usage does not exceed the available capacity. In Section 5, we described how the range of uncertainty in resource estimate and capacity can be quantified in the form of a triangular possibility distribution. Since we are dealing with a constraint, we would like to assess it under the worst case.

Using the possibility distributions, we can reformulate Eq. 4 as follows:

$$\forall r \in R, \quad RE_r^p(\overrightarrow{cnf}) \leq Capacity_r^p \qquad \text{Eq. 6}$$

RE_r^p is the maximum resource usage, while $Capacity_r^p$ is the minimum resource capacity. While both RE_r^p and $Capacity_r^p$ represent the most pessimistic points in the corresponding possibility distributions, the two are semantically inverse of one another. Finally, as you may recall from Section 4.4, the capacity of certain resources may be a crisp value (e.g., available physical memory), in which case $Capacity_r^p = Capacity_r$.

6.2 Solving the Possibilistic Problem

The PLP problem is an instance of a multi-objective problem, and to solve it using commonly available linear programming solvers, we first need to transform it to an equivalent single-objective problem. This is necessary to allow us to reason about the objective trade-offs, such as those depicted in Figure 5b. Intuitively the transformation process entails (1) normalizing the objective functions, (2) combining the objective functions, and (3) if necessary, specifying priorities among the objectives. In this section, we describe the details of these three steps.

6.2.1 Normalizing the Objectives

Since the three PLP objectives are defined differently in terms of U, their range may not be the same. Therefore, to avoid one objective to dominate the other ones as we combine the three objectives, we first have to normalize them. We use normalizing linear membership function [17], which is a function μ that maps each objective z to a value between 0 and 1:

$$j \in \{p, m, o\}, \quad \mu_{z_j}: dom(z_j) \longrightarrow [0,1]$$

This allows us to have objective functions with the same range. However, for defining each function μ, we first need to determine the two extremums for each objective function z: given a configuration, the extremum maximizing the objective is called *Positive Ideal Solution* (PIS), and the one minimizing the objective is called *Negative Ideal Solution* (NIS). Note that the definitions of NIS and PIS are reversed when we are dealing with a minimization objective (i.e., z_p in Eq. 5).

We can obtain these values by performing the following six single objective optimizations:

$$z_p^{PIS} \overset{\text{def}}{=} \underset{(\overrightarrow{cnf} \in ConfSapce)}{argmin} z_p, \quad z_p^{NIS} \overset{\text{def}}{=} \underset{(\overrightarrow{cnf} \in ConfSapce)}{argmax} z_p$$

$$z_m^{PIS} \overset{\text{def}}{=} \underset{(\overrightarrow{cnf} \in ConfSapce)}{argmax} z_m, \quad z_m^{NIS} \overset{\text{def}}{=} \underset{(\overrightarrow{cnf} \in ConfSapce)}{argmin} z_m$$

$$z_o^{PIS} \overset{\text{def}}{=} \underset{(\overrightarrow{cnf} \in ConfSapce)}{argmax} z_o, \quad z_o^{NIS} \overset{\text{def}}{=} \underset{(\overrightarrow{cnf} \in ConfSapce)}{argmin} z_o$$

We specify μ to return 1 for the PIS value, 0 for the NIS value, and proportionally linear between the two extremums:

$$\mu_{z_p}\begin{cases} 1 & z_p < z_p^{PIS} \\ \dfrac{z_p^{NIS} - z_p}{z_p^{NIS} - z_p^{PIS}} & \begin{matrix} z_p^{PIS} \leq z_p \\ z_p \leq z_p^{NIS} \end{matrix} \\ 0 & z_p > z_p^{NIS} \end{cases} \qquad \mu_{z_m}\begin{cases} 1 & z_m > z_m^{PIS} \\ \dfrac{z_m - z_m^{NIS}}{z_m^{PIS} - z_m^{NIS}} & \begin{matrix} z_m^{NIS} \leq z_m \\ z_m \leq z_m^{PIS} \end{matrix} \\ 0 & z_m < z_m^{NIS} \end{cases}$$

Function μ_{z_o} is specified similar to μ_{z_m}. Figure 6 shows two instances of μ_{z_p} and μ_{z_m} that normalize the possible outputs of z_p and z_m, respectively. As the definitions of NIS and PIS are reversed for z_p, the normalizing function μ_{z_p} is decreasing, while

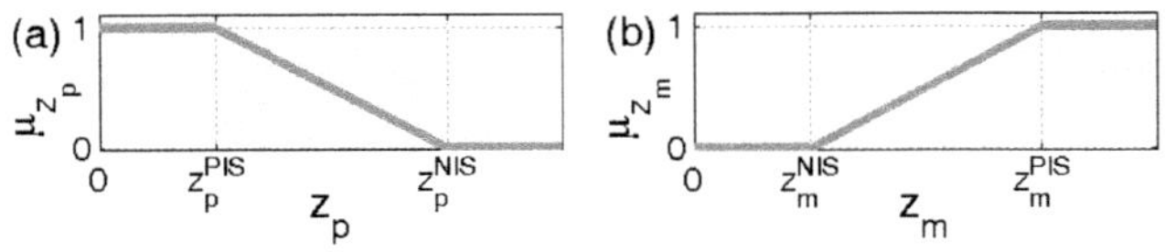

Figure 6. The normalizing linear membership functions for (a) z_p, and (b) z_m.

μ_{z_m} and μ_{z_o} are increasing. This is to transform the minimization objective (i.e., z_p in Eq. 5) into a maximization one.

6.2.2 Combining the Objectives

Given the maximization objectives with the same range, we use a well-known technique[1] to specify the single-objective problem equivalent to PLP problem of Eq. 5 as follows:

$$argmax_{(\overrightarrow{cnf} \in ConfSapce)} \varphi$$

Subject to: $\quad j \in \{p, m, o\}, \mu_{z_j} \geq \varphi$

In the above formulation, we have reformulated the objective to maximize the auxiliary decision variable $\varphi \in [0,1]$ representing the overall satisfaction with the three normalized objectives μ_{z_p}, μ_{z_m}, and μ_{z_o}. In other words, the auxiliary objective is to find a configuration that maximizes φ, which is constrained by the three normalized objectives, resulting first in their optimization.

6.2.3 Specifying Priorities

In the above formulation, the three objectives (expressed as constraints) have the same importance. But in certain domains, some of the objectives may have a higher priority. For instance, in a mission critical system, minimizing z_p may take precedence over maximizing z_o, since a solution capable of providing certain guarantees in the worst case scenario would be desirable. This may not be necessarily the case in other domains that are willing to tolerate higher risks with the potential of higher utility.

We achieve this by assigning weights w_p, w_m, and w_o to objectives μ_{z_p}, μ_{z_m}, and μ_{z_o}, respectively. The weights specify the importance of each objective, and $w_p + w_m + w_o = 1$. Thus, the final complete optimization problem, including the constraints (Eq. 3 and 6), can be formulated as follows:

$$argmax_{(\overrightarrow{cnf} \in ConfSapce)} \varphi$$

Subject to: $\quad j \in \{p, m, o\}, \quad (1 - w_j)\mu_{z_j} \geq \varphi$

$$ConfConstraints(\overrightarrow{cnf}) = 1$$

$$\forall r \in R, \quad RE_r^p(\overrightarrow{cnf}) \leq Capacity_r^p$$

To give a normalized objective μ_{z_j} more priority over others, we make the corresponding constraint (i.e., $\mu_{z_j} \geq \varphi$) more restrictive than others. For that reason, in the above formulation, we multiply each normalized objective μ_{z_j} with $1 - w_j$, where as the value of w_j increases, the related constraint becomes more restrictive.

7. EVALUATION

We have evaluated POISED on an extended version of the robotic software system that was developed in a previous project [18].

[1] *Canonical description of the mathematical technique for translating a maximization multi-objective problem to a maximization single-objective problem* (see [17, 31]): the problem of maximizing a set of objective functions $F = \{\mu_1, \mu_2, \cdots, \mu_n\}$, where all functions have the same range, is equivalent to the maximization of auxiliary variable φ, where $\forall \mu_i \in F, \mu_i \geq \varphi$.

The robotic software used in our experiments was comprised of 12 software components/connectors, and 50 configuration alternatives. POISED treats components and connectors the same, as they are both configurable. The self-adaptation logic was tasked with satisfying 5 user preferences in terms of utility expressed as sigmoid functions; therefore, the maximum achievable overall utility (recall Eq. 1) was 5. We used an implementation of the robotic software running on top of Prism-MW [19], which is a middleware platform with extensive support for runtime monitoring and adaptation. Interested reader can find additional details about the robotic software system in [18].

For the experiments we setup a controlled environment that allows us to create and measure the effect of uncertainty in the system. For that purpose, we used XTEAM [8], an architectural modeling, analysis, and simulation environment that has been integrated with Prism-MW [19]. Through this integration, the XTEAM models are kept in sync with the software running on top of Prism-MW, and vice versa. XTEAM can also be used to control the execution of the software running on Prism-MW. We used XTEAM to simulate uncertainty by controlling the extent of random changes in the system (e.g., available network bandwidth, memory consumption of configuration alternatives). However, neither the robotic software nor POISED was controlled, which allowed them to behave as they would in practice.

The analytical models used in our experiments were derived using the reinforcement learning technique developed in our recent work [9]. The adaptation logic was realized as a three step model interpreter engine that: (1) generates the PLP from the runtime model of the system, (2) solves it using the conventional linear programming solvers (e.g., [22]), and (3) changes the runtime model using the XTEAM's API [8], which automatically effects the changes to the software running on Prism-MW [19].

7.1 Quality Trade-Offs

We compared the quality of solutions selected by POISED with the traditional approach in 10 different experiments. In all of the experiments we applied both approaches on the same system. However, the components used in each experiment were instrumented to have different levels of uncertainty in their response time. As you may recall from Section 3, the traditional approach is representative of the majority of existing literature that ignore the uncertainty in the adaptation decisions (i.e., base the analysis on purely crisp values obtained by calculating the mean behavior of the system properties).

We performed two types of comparison: (1) For each experiment, we compared the expected quality of solutions (configurations) selected by each approach. We refer to these results as *expected*, since they are based on the calculated consequences of uncertainty in the solutions selected by POISED. (2) We then executed the software system in the selected configuration, and observed the actual quality of solution. We refer to these results as *actual*, since they are based on the data collected after the solution was put into effect.

We show the expected results in Figure 7a. The triangular possibility distribution values correspond to the solution selected by each approach. We observe a similar pattern to what was hypothesized in Figure 2. While POISED's solution may have a slightly lower *mode* [13] compared to that of the traditional approach, the overall range is always better—POISED's most pessimistic and optimistic points are higher than that of traditional approach. This is expected, since traditional approach aims to maximize the mean behavior of the system, while POISED aims to maximize the range of behavior.

We complemented the expected ranges of the system's behavior with the actual results obtained in 30 different executions of the system under each configuration. The results are shown in Figure 7b. For a fair comparison, in each experiment, we used XTEAM to fix the application workload, as well as the range of uncertainty in the execution context (e.g., network bandwidth). By "fixing the range of uncertainty" we mean controlling the range of random behavior within each source of uncertainty. Thus, different executions still resulted in different observed behaviors. We can see that the observed utilities are very closely correlated to the corresponding possibility distribution in Figure 7. The results show that in comparison to the traditional approach, POSIED is more likely to select a solution with better overall utility.

As the level of uncertainty in the system increases, it is more likely for POISED to select solutions that are better than the traditional approach. For instance, we instrumented the level of uncertainty in E4 to be higher than the level of uncertainty in E5. This can be gleaned from Figure 7a, as the utility range for the solutions selected by both POISED and traditional approach in E4 are larger than E5. Consequently, from Figure 7b we can see that the solution selected by POISED in E4 achieves more improvement over the traditional than in E5. The level of uncertainty, however, is not the only factor, as the structure of the problem also affects the amount of improvement over traditional.

For a meaningful comparison, in these experiments, we did not specify stringent resource constraints, which as shown next could significantly influence the outcome of both approaches.

7.2 Violation of Resource Constraints

We evaluated POISED's ability to satisfy the resource constraints

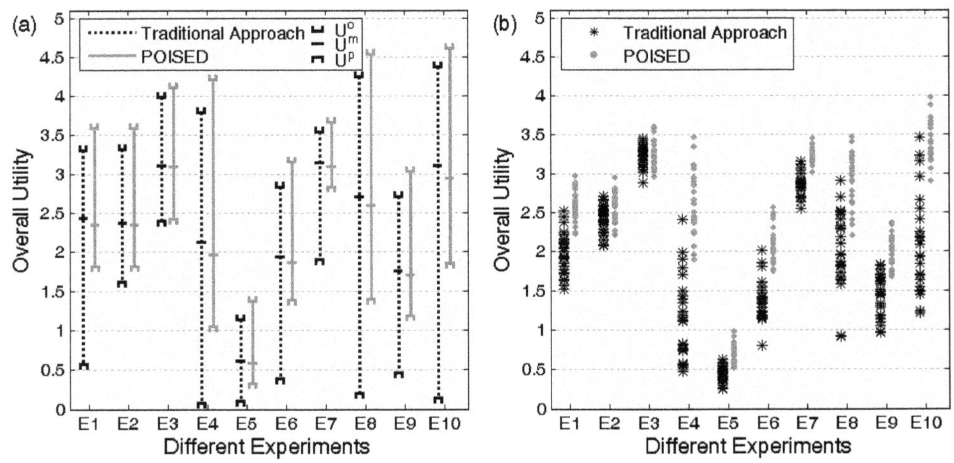

Figure 7. Comparison of POISED with traditional approach in 10 different experiments: (a) possibility distribution for the selected configuration, (b) 30 actual observations for each selected configuration.

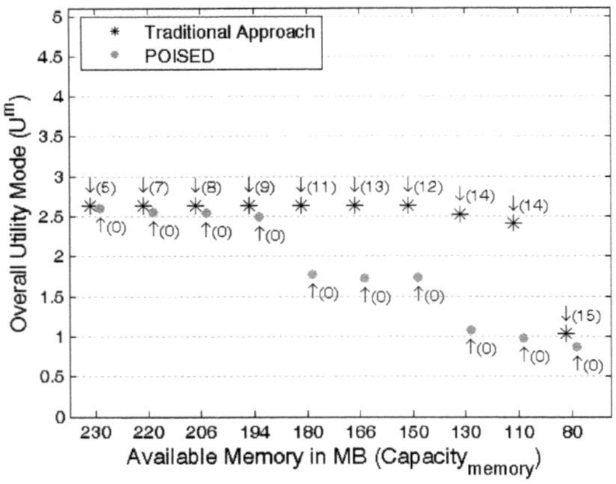

Figure 8. Impact of uncertainty on the overall utility and resource constraints. Number of violations is parenthesized.

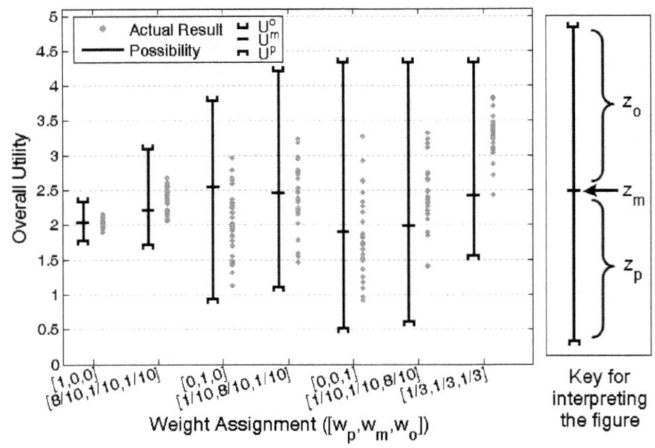

Figure 9. Impact of weights on the selected configuration.

under uncertainty, and compared its results against the traditional approach. We ran both approaches on the same adaptation problem but with varying levels of uncertainty in the available memory. The overall utility mode corresponding to the solution selected by each approach is shown in Figure 8. The robotic software system corresponding to each selected configuration was then executed 30 times. We instrumented our controlled environment to change the memory limit used by the adaptation logic (i.e., Capacity variable from Section 4.4). Parenthesized annotations in Figure 8 show the number of times a memory violation was observed in the actual executions of the system.

We can make several observations from these results. POISED incorporates the uncertainty in the resource usage estimates, and aims to satisfy the worst case (most pessimistic) formulation of resource constraints. Therefore, as the available memory decreases, POISED continues to select solutions that do not violate the memory constraint, but naturally have a lower utility compared to those of traditional approach. On the other hand, since the traditional approach ignores the underlying uncertainty in the estimates, as the available memory decreases, the likelihood of selecting configurations that would violate the memory constraint increases. This pattern persists until the available memory decreases to 80MB, which is less than the mean of the memory usage estimate for configurations with high utility. The traditional approach is thus forced to select configurations with a relatively low utility. But even then, since it does not consider uncertainty, 15 executions violate the memory constraint.

7.3 Effect of Weights

In previous experiments, we placed the same weight on all objectives (i.e., $w_p = w_m = w_o = \frac{1}{3}$). But as you may recall from Section 6.2.3, this may not always be the case. We evaluated POISED's sensitivity to these weights on an instance of the robotic software. For a meaningful comparison, with the exception of weights, all other attributes of the system were fixed, including the range of uncertainty. Figure 9 shows the overall utility for the experiments. The solid bar shows the possibility distribution corresponding to the selected configuration under each weight assignment. The dots depict the observed utility for 30 executions of the software in the selected configuration.

In the two experiments with high w_p, POISED selects a conservative solution, i.e., puts more emphasis on minimizing the negative consequence of uncertainty (z_p from Section 6.1). In the two experiments with high w_o, POISED selects a risky solution, i.e., puts more emphasis on maximizing the positive consequence of uncertainty (z_o from Section 6.1). Both approaches come at the cost of achieving mediocre overall utility mode (z_m from Section 6.1). In the two experiments with high w_m, POISED selects a solution with the best utility mode (z_m from Section 6.1), while ignoring the negative and positive consequences of uncertainty. In the last experiment, with a balanced assignment of weights, the solution achieves neither the best U^m, nor does it provide guarantees on the consequences of uncertainty. But since all of the objectives are given the same weight, it achieves a balanced set of trade-offs. However, as mentioned earlier, we can envision situations in which placing emphasis on one of the objectives may be more appropriate, which POISED allows for naturally.

7.4 Sensitivity to Uncertainty Estimates

We performed a set of experiments to evaluate how sensitive is POISED to the accuracy of uncertainty estimates. Figure 10 shows the results. For all of the experiments we used XTEAM to fix the range of uncertainty in the system parameters, as well as the workload. We changed the accuracy of uncertainty estimates used in our analysis. To that end, we simply changed the confidence level used for transforming the probability distribution corresponding to the monitored data to the equivalent possibility distribution (recall Section 5.3). As one decreases the confidence

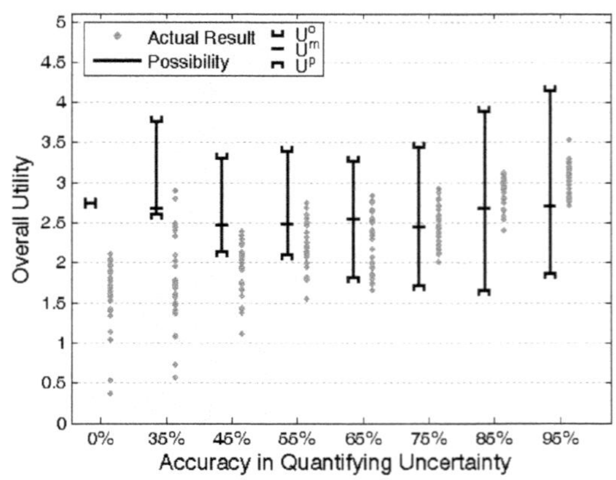

Figure 10. Impact of the accuracy of uncertainty estimates on the quality of POISED solutions.

level in a probability distribution, such as the one depicted in Figure 4, *low confidence* and *high confidence limits* converge to *mode*, resulting in underestimation of the range of uncertainty.

The confidence levels shown on the horizontal axis of Figure 10 denote the accuracy of uncertainty estimates. As we decrease the confidence level from 95% to 0%, thereby making the uncertainty estimates less accurate, POISED selects configurations for which overall utilities are not borne out in practice. More specifically, since by decreasing the confidence level we underestimate the uncertainty, the actual results are lower than the expected utility. Overestimating uncertainty would have the opposite effect.

Finally, in the experiment with 0% accuracy, the most pessimistic, possible, and optimistic points are overlapping. By not considering the uncertainty, POISED is behaving the same as the traditional approach. Comparing the results of experiment with 0% accuracy to others, corroborates our assertions in Section 5 that even with partially accurate estimates of uncertainty, POISED selects solutions that are better than the traditional approach.

7.5 Performance Trade-Offs

Table 1 shows the results of benchmarks comparing the execution time of traditional approach with that of POISED. It took POISED longer to compute the optimal solution, which is not surprising, since as you may recall from Section 6.2, POISED requires 6 additional optimizations to calculate PIS and NIS values pairs for the three objective functions. While it takes longer to execute POISED, we found its performance to be reasonable for our problem. It took 4.6 seconds to find the optimal configuration in the largest problem, consisting of 100 components and 20 different configuration alternatives, for a total of $20^{100} = 1.2 \times 10^{130}$ possible combinations.

8. RELATED WORK

The literature in this area of research is extensive. In lieu of enumerating all of the related studies, we refer the reader to [2, 16] for a comprehensive analysis of the state-of-the-art in self-adaptation. We focus our discussion here to those works that are of utmost relevance. The challenge posed by uncertainty in the construction of dependable self-adaptive software system is an established concept [2, 10]. A few works [1, 3, 4, 9, 23, 28] have aimed to tackle the different facets of this challenge as follows.

Whittle et al. [28] introduced RELAX, a formal requirements specification language that relies on Fuzzy Branching Temporal Logic to specify the uncertain requirements in self-adaptive systems. In a subsequent publication [1], Cheng et al. extended RELAX with goal modeling to specify the uncertainty in the objectives. Our approach is complementary to their work, as both RELAX and POISED are based on fuzzy mathematics, except RELAX targets requirements specification phase, while POISED targets decision making phase at runtime.

Chuang and Chan [4] presented a QoS management framework that uses a hierarchical fuzzy control model. Their work aims at making it easier for the users to specify their QoS requirements, which are then translated into fuzzy rules. Unlike POISED, their objective is QoS rule satisfaction, and does not target the challenge of making adaptation decisions under uncertainty.

Dynamic configuration of resource-aware services was studied by Poladian et al. [24], where they showed how to select an appropriate set of services to carry out a user task, and allocate resources among those services at runtime. Subsequently, the work was extended to make anticipatory decisions [23], and considered the inaccuracy of future resource usage predictions. Unlike POISED, their approach neither aims to satisfy a utility range, nor employs possibilistic analysis in incorporating the effect of uncertainty in decisions.

Table 1. Execution time of POISED versus traditional approach.

Problem		Exec. Time (ms)	
# of Comp	# of Conf	Tradit-ional	POISED
8	4	2	30
10	5	6	51
18	7	10	70
25	8	20	180
37	9	28	298
50	10	30	370
62	13	60	630
75	15	130	1520
88	17	290	3740
100	20	400	4600

Cheng and Garlan [3] described three specific sources of uncertainty (*problem-state identification*, *strategy selection*, and *strategy outcome*) in self-adaptation and provided high-level guidelines for mitigating them in Rainbow [11]. In this paper, we have presented a novel approach for tackling the challenge of *strategy outcome*, i.e., the impact of uncertainty on the selected solution, and techniques to deal with it.

Finally, in our recent work [9], we presented FUSION, a learning based approach to engineering self-adaptive systems. Instead of relying on static analytical models that are subject to wrong assumptions, FUSION uses machine learning to self-tune the adaptive behavior of the system to unanticipated changes, but does not address making adaptation decisions under uncertainty.

9. CONCLUSION AND FUTURE WORK

We presented a novel quantitative approach, called POISED, for making adaptation decisions under uncertainty. Unlike any other related work, POISED adopts a possibilistic method to assess the positive and negative consequences of uncertainty in its analysis. The centerpiece of our work is the reconceptualization of what is typically considered to be the optimal solution as one that has the best range of possible behavior. POISED's analysis can be made as risk-averse as desired via a set of knobs (weights). While POISED is a general approach that can be applied to many types of adaptation problems, it was described and extensively evaluated in the context of a self-adaptation problem aimed at improving a system's quality attributes via runtime reconfiguration of its customizable software components.

Our focus so far has been on the *internal uncertainty*, which is the uncertainty associated with adaptation decisions aimed at satisfying the system's internal quality objectives. In future, we plan to investigate applicability of POISED to *external uncertainty*, which is the uncertainty associated with decisions aimed at satisfying the domain objectives. We also believe POISED could complement the existing efforts aimed at alleviating uncertainty in other facets of self-adaptation. We envision an integration of RELAX [1, 28] with POISED to be a fruitful avenue of future work, as it would allow the traceability of uncertainty from the system's requirements specification to its execution. Proactively adaptive systems, such as those described in [6, 23], face another form of uncertainty—the inaccuracy of future predictions. Investigating the synergy between POISED and such approaches is another interesting avenue of future work.

10. ACKNOWLEDGMENTS

This work is partially supported by grants CCF-0820060 from the NSF and N11AP20025 from DARPA.

11. REFERENCES

[1] Cheng, B.H., Sawyer, P., Bencomo, N. and Whittle, J. 2009. A Goal-Based Modeling Approach to Develop Requirements of an Adaptive System with Environmental Uncertainty. *Int'l Conf. on Model Driven Engineering Languages and Systems* (Denver, Colorado, Oct. 2009), 468-483.

[2] Cheng, B. et al. 2009. Software Engineering for Self-Adaptive Systems: A Research Roadmap. *Software Engineering for Self-Adaptive Systems, LNCS Hot Topics*. 1-26.

[3] Cheng, S.W. and Garlan, D. 2007. Handling uncertainty in autonomic systems. *Int'l Wrkshp. on Living with Uncertainty* (Atlanta, Georgia, Nov. 2007).

[4] Chuang, S.-N. and Chan, A.T.S. 2008. Dynamic QoS Adaptation for Mobile Middleware. *IEEE Transactions on Software Engineering*. 34, 6 (Dec. 2008), 738-752.

[5] Coletti, G. and Scozzafava, R. 2004. Conditional probability, fuzzy sets, and possibility: a unifying view. *Fuzzy Sets and Systems*. 144, 1 (May. 2004), 227-249.

[6] Cooray, D., Malek, S., Roshandel, R. and Kilgore, D. 2010. RESISTing Reliability Degradation through Proactive Reconfiguration. *Int'l Conf. on Automated Software Engineering* (Antwerp, Belgium, Sep. 2010).

[7] Dubois, D. and Prade, H. 2001. Possibility Theory, Probability Theory and Multiple-Valued Logics: A Clarification. *Annals of Mathematics and Artificial Intelligence*. 32, (Aug. 2001), 35–66.

[8] Edwards, G., Malek, S. and Medvidovic, N. 2007. Scenario-Driven Dynamic Analysis of Distributed Architectures. *Int'l Conf. on Fundamental Approaches to Software Engineering* (Braga, Portugal, Mar. 2007), 125-139.

[9] Elkhodary, A., Esfahani, N. and Malek, S. 2010. FUSION: A Framework for Engineering Self-Tuning Self-Adaptive Software Systems. *Int'l Symp. on the Foundations of Software Engineering* (Santa Fe, New Mexico, Nov. 2010), 7-16.

[10] Garlan, D. 2010. Software Engineering in an Uncertain World. *FSE/SDP Wrkshp. on the Future of Software Engineering Research* (Santa Fe, New Mexico, Nov. 2010).

[11] Garlan, D., Cheng, S.W., Huang, A.C., Schmerl, B. and Steenkiste, P. 2004. Rainbow: Architecture-Based Self-Adaptation with Reusable Infrastructure. *IEEE Computer*. 37, 10 (Oct. 2004), 46-54.

[12] Ghezzi, C. and Tamburrelli, G. 2009. Predicting Performance Properties for Open Systems with KAMI. *Int'l Conf on the Quality of Software Architectures* (East Stroudsburg, Pensylvania, Jun. 2009), 70–85.

[13] Gibbons, J.D. and Chakraborti, S. 2003. *Nonparametric Statistical Inference (4th Edition)*. CRC Press.

[14] Inuiguchi, M. and Ramík, J. 2000. Possibilistic linear programming: a brief review of fuzzy mathematical programming and a comparison with stochastic programming in portfolio selection problem. *Fuzzy Sets Syst.* 111, 1 (Apr. 2000), 3-28.

[15] Koenker, R. 2005. *Quantile regression*. Cambridge University Press.

[16] Kramer, J. and Magee, J. 2007. Self-Managed Systems: an Architectural Challenge. *Int'l Conf. on Software Engineering* (Minneapolis, Minnesota, May. 2007), 259-268.

[17] Lai, Y.-J. and Hwang, C.-L. 1992. A new approach to some possibilistic linear programming problems. *Fuzzy Sets Syst.* 49, 2 (Jul. 1992), 121-133.

[18] Malek, S., Edwards, G., Brun, Y., Tajalli, H., Garcia, J., Krka, I., Medvidovic, N., Mikic-Rakic, M. and Sukhatme, G.S. 2010. An architecture-driven software mobility framework. *Journal of Systems and Software*. 83, 6 (Jun. 2010), 972-989.

[19] Malek, S., Mikic-Rakic, M. and Medvidovic, N. 2005. A Style-Aware Architectural Middleware for Resource-Constrained, Distributed Systems. *IEEE Trans. Softw. Eng.* 31, 3 (Mar. 2005), 256-272.

[20] Menasce, D.A., Dowdy, L.W. and Almeida, V.A.F. 2004. *Performance by Design: Computer Capacity Planning By Example*. Prentice Hall PTR.

[21] Menascé, D.A., Sousa, J.P., Malek, S. and Gomaa, H. 2010. QoS Architectural Patterns for Self-Architecting Software Systems. *Int'l Conf. on Autonomic Computing* (Washington, DC, Jun. 2010).

[22] NEOS Server for Optimization: *http://www-neos.mcs.anl.gov/*. Accessed: 2010-08-17.

[23] Poladian, V., Garlan, D., Shaw, M., Satyanarayanan, M., Schmerl, B. and Sousa, J. 2007. Leveraging Resource Prediction for Anticipatory Dynamic Configuration. *Int'l Conf. on Self-Adaptive and Self-Organizing Systems* (Boston, Massachusetts, Jul. 2007), 214-223.

[24] Poladian, V., Sousa, J.P., Garlan, D. and Shaw, M. 2004. Dynamic Configuration of Resource-Aware Services. *Int'l Conf. on Software Engineering* (Scotland, UK, May. 2004).

[25] Seo, C., Malek, S. and Medvidovic, N. 2008. Component-Level Energy Consumption Estimation for Distributed Java-Based Software Systems. *Int'l Symp. on Component Based Software Engineering* (Karlsruhe, Germany, Oct. 2008).

[26] Stochastic Programming Community Home Page: *http://www.stoprog.org/index.html?spintroduction.html*. Accessed: 2011-02-03.

[27] Walsh, W.E., Tesauro, G., Kephart, J.O. and Das, R. 2004. Utility Functions in Autonomic Systems. *Int'l Conf. on Autonomic Computing* (New York, New York, May. 2004).

[28] Whittle, J., Sawyer, P., Bencomo, N., Cheng, B.H.C. and Bruel, J.-M. 2009. RELAX: Incorporating Uncertainty into the Specification of Self-Adaptive Systems. *Int'l Requirements Engineering Conf.* (Atlanta, Georgia, Sep. 2009), 79-88.

[29] Zadeh, L.A. 1965. Fuzzy sets. *Information and control*. 8, 3 (Jun. 1965), 338–353.

[30] Zadeh, L.A. 1999. Fuzzy sets as a basis for a theory of possibility. *Fuzzy Sets Syst.* 100, (Jun. 1999), 9-34.

[31] Zimmermann, H.-J. 1978. Fuzzy programming and linear programming with several objective functions. *Fuzzy Sets and Systems*. 1, 1 (Jan. 1978), 45-55.

[32] Zimmermann, H.-J. 2001. *Fuzzy Set Theory and its Applications (4th Edition)*. Springer.

Version-consistent Dynamic Reconfiguration of Component-based Distributed Systems

Xiaoxing Ma[*†], Luciano Baresi[*], Carlo Ghezzi[*], Valerio Panzica La Manna[*], Jian Lu[†]
xxm|lj@nju.edu.cn, baresi|ghezzi|panzica@elet.polimi.it
[*]Politecnico di Milano, Dipartimento di Elettronica e Informazione, 20133 Milano, Italy
[†]Nanjing University, State Key Laboratory for Novel Software Technology, 210093 Nanjing, China

ABSTRACT

There is an increasing demand for the runtime reconfiguration of distributed systems in response to changing environments and evolving requirements. Reconfiguration must be done in a safe and low-disruptive way. In this paper, we propose version consistency of distributed transactions as a safe criterion for dynamic reconfiguration. Version consistency ensures that distributed transactions be served as if there were operating on a single coherent version of the system despite possible reconfigurations that may happen meanwhile. The paper also proposes a distributed algorithm to maintain dynamic dependences between components at architectural level and enable low-disruptive version-consistent dynamic reconfigurations. An initial assessment through simulation shows the benefits of the proposed approach with respect to timeliness and low degree of disruption.

Categories and Subject Descriptors

D.2.7 [**Distribution, Maintenance, and Enhancement**]

General Terms

design, reliability, management

Keywords

Dynamic reconfiguration, Version-consistency, Component-based distributed system

1. INTRODUCTION

Oftentimes component-based distributed systems (CBDSs) must cope with changes in the environment in which they are embedded and in the requirements they must satisfy. Such changes may be hard to predict at design time or they may be too expensive to identify and handle by the initially designed software. It is therefore necessary to modify existing parts of the implementation or add new functionality at runtime without blocking the system.

Permission to make digital or hard copies of all or part of this work for personal or classroom use is granted without fee provided that copies are not made or distributed for profit or commercial advantage and that copies bear this notice and the full citation on the first page. To copy otherwise, to republish, to post on servers or to redistribute to lists, requires prior specific permission and/or a fee.
ESEC/FSE'11, September 5–9, 2011, Szeged, Hungary.
Copyright 2011 ACM 978-1-4503-0443-6/11/09 ...$10.00.

Compared to off-line maintenance, dynamic modifications are more difficult since in addition to the correctness of the new version, they must also preserve the correct completion of on-going activities. At the same time, they should also minimize the interruption of system's service (usually called *disruption*) and the delay with which the system is updated (also called *timeliness*).

Dynamic reconfigurations (of CBDSs) are not trivial [15, 25, 27]. A safe approach that avoids the direct manipulation of application-specific states enables the reconfiguration of components after they have reached a *quiescence* status [15]. This approach has the advantage of a clear separation of concerns between computation and architectural (re)configuration. But since reconfiguration is oblivious to application states, it must be conservative. It blocks all potentially dependent computations before enabling any reconfiguration to ensure consistency, and thus it may bring more disruption than necessary.

The quiescence-based approach only considers *static* dependences between components specified by architectural configurations. Since these dependences pessimistically include all *potential* constraints among transactions, one can reduce disruption by considering *dynamic* dependences. These are temporal relationships between components caused by on-going transactions, and they only indicate the *current* constraints on the reconfigurability of the system. Multiple transactions are allowed to run during reconfiguration, thus reducing the degree of disruption and improving the timeliness of the reconfiguration.

Existing proposals ([4, 7, 25]) only use dynamic dependences to ensure some local consistency properties. In contrast, the approach presented in this paper exploits them to ensure the "global" consistency of multi-party distributed transactions through the notion of *version consistency.* Dynamic reconfigurations are seen as (sequences of) runtime updates of components; version consistency ensures that every transaction be entirely served by either the old versions of system's components or by the new ones, no matter when the reconfiguration happens. This approach introduces less disruption than the quiescence-based one since a component can be updated even when it is not quiescent, but it has not been used yet or it will not be used anymore by any on-going transaction.

Besides *version consistency* as a new criterion for the safe dynamic reconfiguration of CBDSs, the paper also proposes a management framework for multi-party distributed transactions. The framework exploits dynamic dependencies, a distributed algorithm to update the dependency model accordingly at runtime, and a locally checkable condition that is sufficient to ensure version-consistent dynamic reconfigurations.

The rest of the paper is organized as follows. Section 2 introduces our model of CBDS and the challenges posed by dynamic reconfiguration. Section 3 highlights the limitations of the two most representative approaches and paves the ground for our proposal. Section 4 presents version consistency and the management framework. Section 5 summarizes the main results of the assessment conducted to evaluate the proposal. Section 6 surveys related approaches and Section 7 concludes the paper.

2. PROBLEM SETTING

Similarly to UML component diagrams, a component-based distributed system may be described as a set of components (*nodes*) with in-ports and out-ports. *Components* are linked by directed edges from out-ports to in-ports. The resulting directed graph is called the system's static *configuration*, where each node is tagged with the current version of the component it represents. A static configuration can be described as follows:

Definition 1 (STATIC CONFIGURATION). *A static configuration of a component-based distributed system is a directed graph whose nodes represent versioned components with in-ports and out-ports. A directed edge, from the out-port of a given node N to the in-port of other node M, represents a static dependence, that is, the possibility for N to require a service provided by M.*

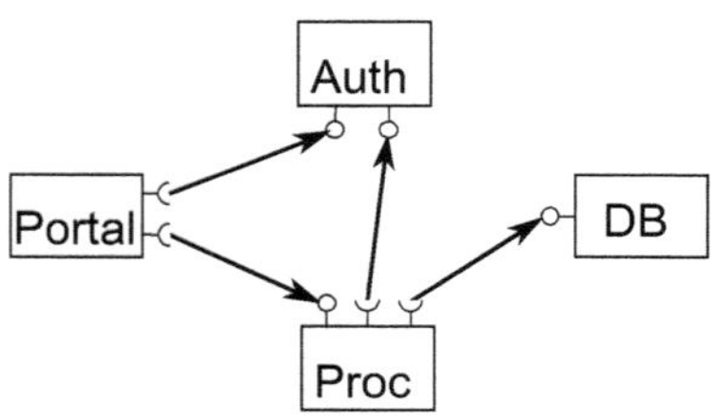

Figure 1: Our example system.

Figure 1 shows an example system used throughout the paper. A portal component (Portal) interacts with an authentication component (Auth) and a business processing component (Proc), while Proc interacts with both Auth and a database component (DB). This means that Portal statically depends on Proc and Auth, and Proc depends on Auth and DB.

Our approach supports the dynamic reconfigurations of CBDSs with transactional behavior, that is, systems whose execution evolves through atomic, separate tasks (transactions). This model is largely adopted in many applications: from systems implemented on top of component-based infrastructures (like EJBs or Spring) to service-oriented applications.

A *transaction* is a sequence of actions executed by a component that completes in bounded time. Actions include local computations and message exchanges. Transactions are described by the rectangles $T_0..T_4$ in the sequence diagram shown in Figure 2, which is used hereafter as an example. A transaction T can be initiated by an outside client or by another transaction T'. T is called a *root transaction* in the former case and a *sub-transaction* (of T') in the latter case. If a transaction T initiates sub-transactions, T, along with its sub-transactions, is said to be a *distributed transaction*. For example, T_4 is a sub-transaction of T_2 in the sequence diagram of Figure 2. The host component (node) of transaction T is denoted as h_T.

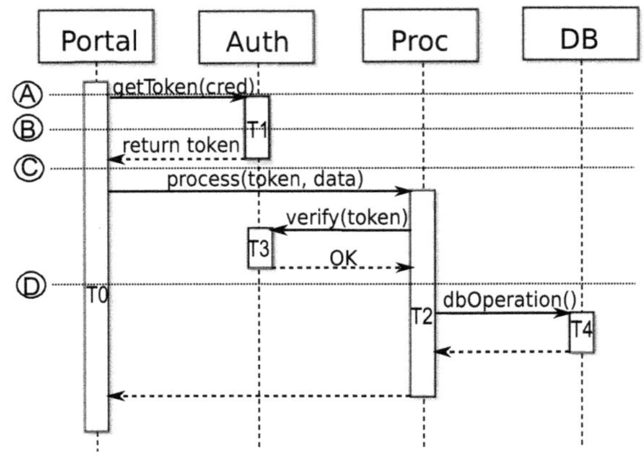

Figure 2: Detailed scenario.

The term $sub(T_1, T_2)$ denotes that T_2 is a direct sub-transaction of T_1. A transaction can only be a direct sub-transaction of one transaction. The set $ext(T) = \{x | x = T \vee sub^+(T, x)\}$ is the *extended transaction set* of T, which contains T and all its direct and indirect sub-transactions. The extended transaction set of a root transaction models the concept of *distributed transaction* that can span over multiple components. By definition, a root transaction is not a sub-transaction of any other transaction. A root transaction has a unique, system-wide identifier. For each transaction T, h_T must know $root(T)$, which is the identifier of the root transaction of T.

A transaction can initiate a sub-transaction on a neighbor component only when the host component of the initiating transaction is statically dependent on the neighbor component in charge of executing the sub-transaction. For example, the sequence diagram of Figure 2 illustrates a distributed transaction, where root transaction T_0 initiates T_1 and T_2. In turn transaction T_2 initiates T_3 and T_4. We also assume that transactions are also always notified of the completion of their sub-transactions and that a transaction cannot end before the termination of its sub-transactions. The other messages exchanged between h_T and h_{T_i} —because of T and its direct sub-transaction T_i— are temporally scoped between the two corresponding messages that initiate T_i and notify its completion.

Figure 2 shows a detailed usage scenario for the example system. The Portal first gets an authentication token from Auth and then uses it to require the service from Proc. Proc verifies the token through Auth and then starts computing, and interacting with DB. If we consider the root transaction T_0 at Portal, its extended transaction set is $ext(T_0) = \{T_0, T_1, T_2, T_3, T_4\}$, where T_1 at Auth is in response to the getToken request, T_2 at Proc in response to process, T_3 at Auth in response to verify, and T_4 at DB for T_2's request of database operations.

Different transactions may run concurrently in the system.

If the executions of two transactions on the same component do not interfere with each other, we assume they are safe. In contrast, if they compete for some resources, we rely on the *isolation* [11] provided by components to regulate the access.

2.1 Runtime updates

A dynamic reconfiguration policy defines *when* the update can be performed and *how* it must be accomplished to keep the system consistent.

A dynamic reconfiguration is an atomic sequence of runtime updates of components[1]. More rigorously, an update is specified as a tuple $< \Sigma, \omega, \omega', \mathcal{T}, s >$, where Σ is the original system's configuration and ω is the set of components that must be substituted by the new versions in ω'. The update happens when the system is in state s, and the state transformer $\mathcal{T}$ trasforms s into $s' = \mathcal{T}(s)$, which is a state of the updated system with configuration $\Sigma' = \Sigma[\omega'/\omega]$[2]. The system is expected to continue from s' with no externally-visible erroneous behavior. The (global) state of a CBDS comprises the local states of all components and all messages in transit. The state transformer is defined on global states, but in practice one can hardly manipulate states other than those local to the to-be-updated components.

We assume that given a runtime update $< \Sigma, \omega, \omega', \mathcal{T}, s >$, the corresponding off-line update $< \Sigma, \omega, \omega' >$ is correct. This means that the transactions running on Σ satisfy the old system specification $\mathbb{S}$ and the transactions on $\Sigma' = \Sigma[\omega'/\omega]$ satisfy the new specification $\mathbb{S}'$. Given the distributed nature of these transactions we can only adopt a *weak* definition of *correctness of a runtime update*, which is defined as follows:

- The transactions that end before the update satisfy $\mathbb{S}$;
- The transactions that begin after the update satisfy $\mathbb{S}'$;
- The transactions that begin before the update, and end after it, satisfy either $\mathbb{S}$ or $\mathbb{S}'$.

For example, if we consider the running example, one may assume that Auth be updated to exploit a stronger encryption algorithm to prevent security threats. Although the new algorithm is incompatible with the old one, the other components need not to be updated because all encryption/decryption operations are done within Auth. The specification of all other transactions remains unchanged; the off-line update would be "easy" and we assume it to be correct. The problem is that if we update Auth at runtime, we should ensure that all running transactions execute correctly before and after the update. If the update were allowed to happen any time, it would be difficult to ensure it [12]. An obvious restriction on *when* the update can happen is to impose that components targeted for update be *idle*.

Definition 2 (Idle Component). *A component is idle iff it is not currently hosting transactions and its current local state is equivalent to the initial one.*

[1]We consider any architectural change that can be treated as a replacement of components. For example, service rebindings can be seen as updates of the components that implement the services.

[2]This is to say that Σ' is equal to Σ where all components in ω have been substituted by the new versions in ω'.

Note that if we restrict updates to occur when components are idle then $\mathcal{T}$ only needs to be locally defined on the initial state of all substituted components. The initial state of the new component is assumed to be "equivalent" to the current state of the idle component being replaced.

The assumption that components can only be updated when they are idle is often insufficient to guarantee safe runtime updates. In fact, if we consider the scenario of Figure 2, and substitute Auth when idle, but after serving getToken (after time ©), the resulting system would behave incorrectly since the security token would be created with an algorithm and validated by another.

Since the correctness of arbitrary runtime updates is undecidable (even if the corresponding off-line update is correct and the runtime update only happens when to-be-updated components are idle [17]), we can only derive some automatically checkable conditions that are sufficient for the correctness by scoping the class of updates we consider. These conditions must be: (a) strong enough to ensure the correctness of runtime updates, (b) weak enough to allow for low-disruptive and timely changes, and (c) automatically checkable in a distributed setting (without enforcing unnatural centralized solutions).

3. QUIESCENCE AND TRANQUILLITY

In a seminal paper, Kramer and Magee [15] proposed a criterion called *quiescence* as a sufficient condition for a node to be safely manipulated in dynamic reconfigurations. They also model a distributed system as a directed graph, and define a transaction as "an exchange of information between two and only two nodes, initiated by one of the nodes. Transactions are the means by which the state of a node is affected by other connected nodes in the system. Transactions consist of a sequence of one or more message exchanges between the two connected nodes. It is assumed that transactions complete in bounded time and that the initiator of a transaction is aware of its completion". A transaction T may also depend on other (consequent) transactions T_i: the completion of T depends on the completion of all the T_i. This definition of transaction corresponds to our definition of distributed transaction between only two nodes. Through the notion of dependency between transactions, however, they also capture the concept of a distributed transaction involving multiple nodes.

Definition 3 (Quiescence). *A node is quiescent if:*

1. *It is not currently engaged in a transaction that it initiated;*
2. *It will not initiate new transactions;*
3. *It is not currently engaged in servicing a transaction;*
4. *No transactions have been or will be initiated by other nodes which require service from this node.*

A node satisfying the first two conditions is said to be *passive*. A node is required to respond to a passivate command from the configuration manager by driving itself into a passive state in bounded time. The last two conditions further make the node independent of all existing or future transactions, and thus it can be manipulated safely. To drive a node into a quiescent status, in addition to passivating it, all the nodes that statically depend on it must also be passivated to ensure the last two conditions.

According to this approach, a node cannot be quiescent before the completion of all the transactions initiated by statically dependent nodes. This means that the actual update could be deferred significantly. In our example, Auth cannot be quiescent before the end of the transactions hosted by Portal and Proc (T_0 and T_2). Moreover, all the other nodes that could potentially initiate transactions, which require service from Auth, directly or indirectly, are passivated, and their progress blocked till the end of the update. Again, in our example Portal and Proc are to be passivated before changing Auth. This means that the adoption of this approach could introduce significant disruption in the service provided by the system.

To reduce disruption, Vandewoude et al. [25] proposed the concept of *tranquillity*, as alternative to quiescence. The idea is that there is no need for waiting a transaction to complete if it will not request the service provided by the node targeted for update, even if the node has been involved in the transaction. It is also permitted to update a node even if some on-going transactions will require the service provided by the node in the future, but they have not interacted with it yet.

Definition 4 (TRANQUILLITY). *A node is tranquil if:*

1. *It is not currently engaged in a transaction that it initiated;*
2. *It will not initiate new transactions;*
3. *It is not actively processing a request;*
4. *None of its adjacent nodes are engaged in a transaction in which it has both already participated and might still participate in the future.*

While claimed to be "a sufficient condition for application consistency during a dynamic reconfiguration" [25], the notion of tranquillity is based on a rather strong assumption. If we used the definition of tranquillity in our model, the notion of distributed transaction could not be fully expressed as defined in Section 2. In fact, under the assumption imposed by tranquility, a distributed transaction initiated by a root transaction T at node N, could only contain sub-transactions hosted by (adjacent) nodes directly connected to N. This means that a sub-sub-transaction (i.e., a sub-transaction initiated by another sub-transaction), hosted by a node that is not directly connected to N, would not be part of the distributed transaction, and thus it could use any version of the components since it is an independent entity.

This limitation would permit unsafe updates in the scenario of Figure 2. In fact, after Auth returns the token to Portal, it will not participate in the session initiated by Portal anymore. In addition, before the request for verification is sent, Auth has not participated in the session initiated by Proc, and so Auth is tranquil at time Ⓒ. However, if Auth were updated at this time, the verification would fail because the token was issued by the old version of Auth, which might use a different encryption algorithm to validate the security token. This failure would not happen if the system entirely complied with either the old or the new system configuration.

To conclude, we can say that the quiescence-based approach is a general and safe solution, but it can be highly disruptive. The tranquillity-based approach is less disruptive, but its assumption is too restrictive to be applicable to a wide set of systems (e.g., our example). Our goal is to get the best of the two proposals and add efficiency and timeliness to safety.

4. DYNAMIC RECONFIGURATION

The notion of version consistency is proposed as a sufficient condition for the safety of dynamic reconfigurations.

Definition 5 (VERSION CONSISTENCY). *Transaction T is version consistent with respect to an update $< \Sigma, \omega, \omega', \mathcal{T}, s >$ iff $\nexists T_1, T_2 \in ext(T) \mid h_{T_1} \in \omega \wedge h_{T_2} \in \omega'$. A dynamic reconfiguration caused by an update $< \Sigma, \omega, \omega', \mathcal{T}, s >$ is version consistent if all transactions hosted by the current configuration Σ are version consistent.*

The definition is justified by the fact that we assume the new configuration to be correct and by the fact that any extant transaction with all its (direct and indirect) sub-transactions is entirely executed in the old or in the new configuration. Also note that a transaction that ends before (starts after) the update cannot have a direct or indirect sub-transaction hosted by the new (old) version of a component being updated.

For our example, if the update of Auth happens after transaction T_0 begins but before it sends a getToken request to Auth (time Ⓐ), all transactions in $ext(T_0)$ (i.e., all transactions in Figure 2) are served in the same way as if the update happened before they all began. If it happens at any time after Auth replies to the verify request issued by Proc (time Ⓓ), all transactions in $ext(T_0)$ are served the same way as if the update happened after they all ended. However, if it happens at time Ⓒ, then h_{T_1} = Auth, but h_{T_3} = Auth′. As both T_1 and $T_3 \in ext(T_0)$, T_0 would not be version-consistent.

In general, the tranquillity-based approach is not sufficient for version-consistent dynamic reconfigurations. It is equivalent to limiting the extended transaction set to $ext_{tran}(T) = \{x | x = T \vee sub(T, x)\}$. It only ensures a kind of local consistency, but not the global consistency of entire distributed transactions. The quiescence-based mechanism —if one takes dependent transactions into account— ensures version consistency because no distributed transactions depending on the node to be updated can exist when the node is quiescent. However, it would take a too pessimistic attitude.

4.1 Dynamic dependences

Since version consistency is not directly checkable, we need to identify a condition that is checkable on a component (or a set of components) and ensure that its (their) runtime update does not break version consistency; this condition must also allow for low-disruptive and timely reconfigurations.

Dynamic dependences are the means to define such a condition, and they can easily be added to the diagram of Figure 1 through properly-labelled edges. Dynamic edges, represented as dashed arcs, are added and removed dynamically and they are labelled as either future or past. A future edge represents the possibility for the source node to initiate a transaction on the target node; a past edge witnesses the fact that a transaction initiated by the source node has already been executed on the target node. Future and past edges are also labelled with the identifier of a root transaction. We use $C \xrightarrow[T]{future(past)} C'$ to denote a future (past) edge labelled with the identifier of root transaction T, from component C to component C'.

Definition 6 (VALID CONFIGURATION). *A static configuration decorated with edges representing dynamic dependences between corresponding components, hereafter, a configuration, is valid iff future and past edges are created and removed at runtime according to the following constraints:*

1. (HOST-VALIDITY) *The hosting component C of a transaction T is augmented with a pair of edges $C \xrightarrow[root(T)]{future} C$ and $C \xrightarrow[root(T)]{past} C$ as soon as T is initiated and till it ends;*
2. (LOCALITY) *Any* **future** *edge $C \xrightarrow[T]{future} C'$ (or* **past** *edge $C \xrightarrow[T]{past} C'$) cannot exist without a* **static** *edge $C \rightarrow C'$ connecting the same two nodes;*
3. (FUTURE-VALIDITY) *A* **future** *edge $C \xrightarrow[T]{future} C'$ must be added before the first sub-transaction $T' \in ext(T)$, with $T' \neq T$, is initiated, and it cannot be removed as long as transactions hosted by C will initiate further $T'' \in ext(T)$ on C'.*
4. (PAST-VALIDITY) *A* **past** *edge $C \xrightarrow[T]{past} C'$ must be added at the end of a transaction $T' \in ext(T)$ on C', initiated by a transaction hosted on a statically dependent node C and cannot be removed at least until the end of T.*

Figure 3 shows some configurations of the example system (two concentric cycles correspond to a pair of local future/past edges labelled with T_0). The configuration of Figure 3(a) corresponds to time Ⓐ in Figure 2: transaction T_0 just began on Portal. The dynamic edges indicate that (i) there may be a transaction in $ext(T_0)$ running on Portal; (ii) in order to serve transactions in $ext(T_0)$, Portal might use Auth and Proc in the future, and also Proc might use Auth and DB. Figure 3(b) corresponds to time Ⓑ and says that a transaction in $ext(T_0)$ (T_1) is currently running on Auth, but no further transactions in $ext(T_0)$ hosted by Portal will initiate any sub-transaction on Auth anymore because there is no T_0-labelled future edge between the two nodes. Figure 3(c), which corresponds to time Ⓒ in Figure 2, indicates that Auth might have hosted transactions in $ext(T_0)$ initiated by Portal in the past, and might host other transactions in $ext(T_0)$ initiated by Proc in the future. Figure 3(d) corresponds to time Ⓓ in Figure 2 and shows that Auth, although it might have hosted transactions in $ext(T_0)$, is not hosting and will not host them anymore.

Note that to keep a configuration valid, and consider alternative execution flows, one can adopt a conservative management of future/past edges between components. For example, if T_2 on Proc needed to evaluate the results from DB before deciding whether to ask Auth for verification, one could keep the future edge from Proc to Auth till T_2 does not need Auth anymore. In the worst case, this could be till the end of T_2.

On the other hand, with the validity of the configuration preserved, future (past) edges should be removed (created) as early (late) as possible to reduce spurious dependencies between components that could hinder actually legitimate dynamic reconfigurations. For instance, the future edge from Portal to Auth in Figure 3(a) is removed once Portal

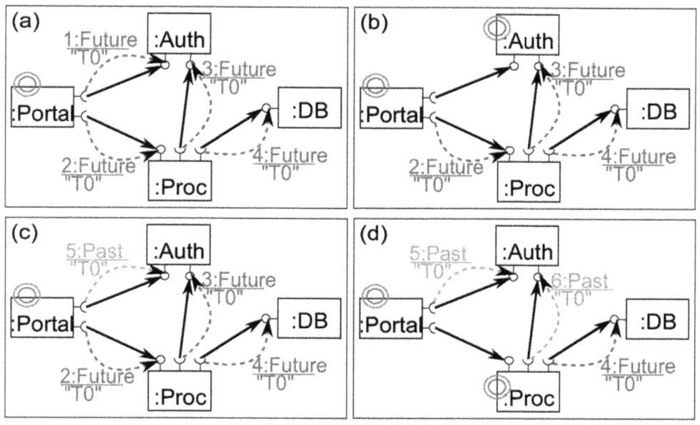

Figure 3: Some configurations of the example system with explicit dynamic dependences.

realizes that T_0 will not initiate sub-transactions on Auth anymore — this happens just after T_0 initiates T_1.

Given a valid configuration, we can identify a locally checkable condition that is sufficient for the version consistency of dynamic reconfigurations.

Definition 7 (FREENESS). *Given a configuration Σ, a component C (or a set of components ω) is said to be free of dependences with respect to a root transaction T iff there does not exist a pair of T-labelled future/past edges entering C (or ω). C (or ω) is said to be free in Σ iff it is free with respect to all the transactions in the configuration.*

Auth is free of dependences with respect to T_0 in the configurations of Figure 3(a) and 3(d), while the local dynamic edges at Auth trivially falsify its freeness in the configuration of Figure 3(b). Intuitively, for a valid configuration Σ, the freeness of a component C with respect to a root transaction T means that the distributed transaction modeled by $ext(T)$ either has not used C yet (otherwise there should be a past edge), or will not use C anymore (otherwise there should be a future edge). This leads to the following proposition.

Proposition 1. *Given a valid configuration Σ of a system, a dynamic reconfiguration of a set of its components ω is version consistent if it happens when ω is free in Σ.*

PROOF. If we suppose that version consistency does not hold, there is a transaction T that is not version-consistent, that is, $\exists\ T_1, T_2 \in ext(T) \mid h_{T_1} \in \omega \ \wedge\ h_{T_2} \in \omega'$.

1. There is no ongoing transaction hosted by any $C \in \omega$ when the update happens. This follows from the host-validity of Σ and the freeness of components in ω.
2. Let $\bar{\omega}$ be the set of unchanged components. Because T begins no later than T_1 and T_1 begins before the update since $h_{T_1} \in \omega$, T begins before the update. Similarly T ends after the update because of T_2. Since no transaction is hosted by any components in ω when the update happens, h_T must be in $\bar{\omega}$.
   (a) Consider the sub-transaction chain from T to T_1. There must be such T_i and T_j that $sub(T_i, T_j) \wedge h_{T_i} \in \bar{\omega} \wedge h_{T_j} \in \omega$. According to the past-validity of Σ and the fact that T_j must have already ended when the update happens (see point 1), there is a past T-labelled edge entering h_{T_j}.

(b) Because of the validity of the static configuration after the update, ω' must inherit all the incoming static dependence edges from ω. Without any loss of generality, let T_2 be the first transaction in $ext(T)$ initiated on a component in ω'. Consider the sub-transaction chain from T to T_2. There must be a T_k such that $sub(T_k, T_2) \wedge h_{T_k} \in \bar{\omega}$. Before T_k initiates T_2, all transactions from T to T_k in the chain will not be affected by the update because they are independent of transactions not in $ext(T)$, and T_2 is the first transaction in $ext(T)$ hosted by a component in ω'. According to the future-validity of Σ and the fact that T_2 is still to be initiated when the update happens, there is a future T-labelled edge from h_{T_k} to a component in ω.

So there is a pair of T-labelled past/future edges entering ω. This contradicts the freeness of ω. □

4.2 Distributed management of dependences

An advantage of specifying dynamic dependences with future and past edges is that the validity of a configuration can be achieved through the cooperation of components. Each component makes its decisions locally with limited information about the application logic; checking for freeness is also local to the part of the system to be updated.

The definition of *valid configuration* gives lower bounds for the time intervals during which dynamic dependence edges should exist to keep a configuration valid. One can satisfy all the conditions straightforwardly by creating all the dynamic edges at the beginning of a root transaction and by removing them at the end of it. However, although version consistency would be ensured, disruption could be too high.

We assume that given a transaction T, its host component h_T knows $f(T)$, the set of static edges through which it might initiate sub-transactions on neighbor components in the future, and $p(T)$, the set of static edges through which it has initiated sub-transactions in the past[3].

The overall configuration with dynamic dependences is maintained in a distributed way. Each component only has a local view of the configuration that includes itself and its direct neighbors. A component is responsible for the creation and removal of the dynamic edges leaving from it, but it is also always notified of the creation and removal of the dynamic edges entering it. Components exchange management messages, besides those related to transactions, to keep the consistency among the views of neighbor components. The maintenance of the distributed configuration may slightly delay the execution of the actual transactions, but it guarantees that no transactions will be blocked forever.

4.2.1 Management algorithm

The management of dynamic edges for different distributed transactions is independent of each other since these edges are labelled with the identifiers of the corresponding root transactions. If we consider a distributed transaction $ext(T)$, our algorithm consists of three steps: **set up**, **progress**, and **clean up**. Through these steps, the locality of the configuration is ensured by only creating dynamic edges that pair the existing static ones, and the host validity is preserved by always creating local future and past edges (if they do not already exist) when a transaction is initiated and by removing them only after the end of the transaction (if there are no other on-going transactions that need these edges).

In more detail, the three steps carry out the following actions and help preserve future and past validity as follows:

Set up: This step is carried out when the root transaction T is initiated and before it initiates any sub-transaction. During this phase, h_T creates a future edge for each of its out-going static edges that T might use to initiate sub-transactions according to $f(T)$, notifies corresponding neighbor components, and waits for their acknowledgements. Only after receiving all these acknowledgements, T is allowed to initiate its sub-transactions.

As soon as a component C is notified of the creation of an incoming future edge $fe = C' \xrightarrow[T]{future} C$ by C', it starts creating its own future edges, notifies neighbor components, waits for their acknowledgements, and then acknowledges C' back. The rationale is that by accepting the creation of fe, C "promises" C' to host some $T_C \in ext(T)$ in the future, but to make such a promise C first needs to get the promises from those components that T_C might need to use. Note that loops in the static configuration can be handled by avoiding the creation and notification of duplicated edges. This conservative way creates future edges to achieve a valid configuration with respect to T when the set up step finishes. Figure 3(a) shows the result of setting up future edges for transaction T_0 of Figure 2.

Progress: Due to the execution of transactions in $ext(T)$, future edges are gradually removed as soon as the algorithm knows that a component *will-not-use* another one anymore, and past edges are created to register *have-used* relationships.

In more detail, new *will-not-use* information can be available at various time instants including (1) when a transaction in $ext(T)$ hosted by C successfully initiates a sub-transaction on a neighbor component; (2) when a transaction in $ext(T)$ hosted by C ends; and (3) when C is notified of the removal of a T-labelled incoming future edge. No matter when the information is acquired, a non-local future edge $fe = C \xrightarrow[T]{future} C'$ is removed only when: (1) no on-going $T' \in ext(T)$ hosted by C will initiate any sub-transaction on C' through $C \xrightarrow{static} C'$ anymore; and (2) there is no incoming T-labelled future edge entering C, that is, no further $T'' \in ext(T)$ will be initiated on C anymore. This condition ensures future validity because once fe is removed, no sub-transactions in $ext(T)$ need to be initiated through $C \xrightarrow{static} C'$ anymore.

To record the *have-used* information, when a sub-transaction T originally initiated by T' ends, a corresponding past edge $pe = h_{T'} \xrightarrow[root(T)]{past} h_T$ is created *immediately*. This is done by letting h_T first notify $h_{T'}$ the end of T, and by removing the corresponding local edges only when pe is created by $h_{T'}$. This hand-shaking ensures that past validity holds despite the asynchrony of messages.

[3]It is safe to over estimate $f(T)$ and $p(T)$, but better accuracy means better timeliness and less disruption in the dynamic reconfiguration. This information can be extracted automatically from the component, but also by monitoring its transactions; the degree of accuracy of this information is up to the user. Note that similar information is also required to decide the actual tranquillity of components [25].

In our example scenario, Portal removes the future edge to Auth after it initiates T_1 on Auth as it is sure that T_0 will not initiate such transactions anymore (Figure 3(b)). When T_1 ends, Portal immediately creates a past edge to record the fact that it has used Auth (Figure 3(c)). Eventually, the system reaches the configuration of Figure 3(d), where Auth is free with respect to T_0.

Clean up: This step is carried out only when T ends. The algorithm recursively removes all remaining past and future edges. This step does not affect the validity of the configuration.

For the sake of readability, the algorithm has been described by taking the viewpoint of a distributed transaction, but the actual algorithm runs on each component without any centralized control. The underlying message delivery is assumed to be reliable, and the messages between two components are kept in order. Interested readers can refer to [17] for all details. Also note that since tracking dynamic dependences across the whole system can be expensive and unnecessary, a user can specify a portion of the system as scope for version consistency if the impact of the update is known to be limited. More details on this issue are also discussed in [17].

4.2.2 On-demand set up

The above algorithm assumes that configurations are always kept up-to-date no matter whether there is a request for dynamic reconfiguration. However, configuration management could introduce significant overhead. If reconfigurations are rare, a valid configuration can be set up on demand only when a request is planned or expected. To this end, dynamic edges must be created both for new transactions and for on-going ones.

The set up works as follows. The working *mode* of each component can be: NORMAL, ONDEMAND, or VALID. NORMAL means that the component is not supposed to manage dynamic dependences, while VALID requires it. ONDEMAND imposes that the component: (1) manages the dynamic dependences for all the new root transactions initiated locally, (2) blocks the initiation and termination of locally hosted sub-transactions temporarily, and (3) for each locally-hosted ongoing root transaction T, creates future (past) edges towards the components that might host in the future (might have hosted in the past) transactions in $ext(T)$ in a way similar to the one described above.

At the beginning, all components operate in mode NORMAL. When a component targeted for update receives a request for reconfiguration, it sends a request for set up to itself and waits for its mode to become VALID before using the approach we describe next to achieve freeness. Upon receiving a request for set up, a component C switches to mode ONDEMAND and sends set up requests to all the components C_i that statically depends on it. Once C has finished the set up of dynamic edges for its local root transactions, and has received all the acknowledgements from C_i, it switches to mode VALID, resumes all blocked transactions, and sends confirmations to all the nodes from which it received requests for set up. The whole on-demand set up procedure completes when the targeted component becomes VALID.

On-demand set up of dynamic dependencies also makes dealing with dynamic reconfigurations resulting in new dependencies straightforward, and thus multiple reconfiguration steps in sequence are supported. However, although our approach allows multiple components to be updated together (in a single reconfiguration step), it does not currently support concurrent reconfigurations, meaning independent updates of different components happening at same time without coordination.

4.3 Achieving freeness

Given a valid configuration maintained at runtime, checking for the freeness of ω —the set of components targeted for update— is straightforward since the condition is local to ω, but freeness can be achieved in different ways.

The first strategy, called *waiting for freeness (WF)*, is simply opportunistic. The system just waits for freeness to manifest itself. This strategy has no extra overhead other than setting up and maintaining the valid configuration and checking for the freeness of ω. However, although every transaction completes in finite time, the freeness of ω could never be reached —for example, there could always be transactions running on some components in ω.

To ensure the timeliness of runtime updates, a second strategy, called *concurrent versions (CV)*, lets the components in ω and ω' co-exist during the update process. The use of multiple versions of the same components is not new (e.g., HERCULES [8] and Upstart [1] adopt it), but our proposal can add version consistency as means to choose which version must serve a request and to decide when a version can be deleted. Given a valid configuration, one can choose a component $C \in \omega$ to serve the requests that come from a transaction T only if C has already an incoming past edge labeled with $root(T)$, and let the components in ω' serve the others. This means that components in ω cannot have incoming past edges labelled with new root transactions, and these components will eventually become free since old transactions will reach a stage where they will not use components in ω anymore. As soon as these components become free, they can be safely removed from the system.

However, if multiple versions cannot coexist, or it is preferable not to do it, the third strategy is called *blocking for freeness (BF)*. It requires that some of the requests to the components in ω be temporally blocked to avoid creating past edges labelled with new root transactions. These components will eventually become free when all existing transactions do not use them anymore. More precisely, the initiation of any transaction on any component in ω is blocked unless it belongs to an extended transaction set in which a member transaction has already been hosted by a component in ω. This comes from the fact that the first T-labelled past edge entering a component $C \in \omega$ is created the first time a transaction in $ext(T)$ is being initiated on C. As soon as all components in ω become free, they are substituted by the new versions in ω', and all blocked transactions are resumed.

Back to our example, if Auth receives the request for update before T_0 on Portal initiates T_1 on Auth, the initiation of T_1 is blocked because there is no T_0-labelled past edge entering Auth. Note that there can be T_0-labelled future edges entering Auth (e.g., see Fig. 3(a)), but by blocking the initiation of any $T \in ext(T_0)$ on Auth, the freeness of this component will not be hindered by T_0 since no T_0-labelled past edge needs to be created. However, if the request for update arrived at time ©, the initiation of T_3 by T_2 on Proc would be allowed because there is already a T_0-labelled past edge entering Auth (created when T_1 ended). In this case, Auth must wait all T_0-labelled future edges to be removed, that is, at time Ⓓ, which corresponds to the configuration presented in Fig. 3(d).

This last strategy relies on the assumption that executing transactions are independent of each other. If they are not, that is, the progress of a transaction in an extended transaction set can be blocked by a transaction in another extended transaction set, we may have deadlocks. For example, this happens when two transactions are concurrently hosted on the same component and need to access a shared resource protected by a mutual exclusion lock. If one blocked the transaction that holds the lock (to avoid creating new past edges to the component-to-update), the other would be blocked as well (since it does not hold the lock), blocks would never be released, and the system would enter a deadlock.

However we do not expect this situation to be very common because modern systems often use fine grained locks to avoid blocking a transaction to serve other business-irrelevant transactions. Even when this situation does occur, remedies are possible. One can rely on existing mechanisms for the avoidance, prevention, or detection of distributed deadlocks. For example, according to the Wait-for Graph used for deadlock detection [18], one can resume the initialization of blocked transactions if their initializers are waited for by some transactions that must proceed to free the targeted components. Note that such a mechanism is very likely already provided by the infrastructure since distributed deadlocks are an important, potential problem in distributed systems with shared resources protected by coarse-grained locks. One can also use a more conservative blocking policy, and delay the creation of future edges —instead of past edges— labelled with new root transactions. This method prevents the initialization of any new root transaction that may use the targeted component, thus introducing more disruption. In practice, one may first take an optimistic approach by ignoring the deadlock problem and exploit these remedies when the freeness is not achieved after a reasonable time interval.

Generally, CV is preferred when applicable. WF and CV do not introduce disruption to system's service other than that caused by setting up and maintaining the valid configuration, while BF imposes extra disruption due to its temporal blocking of some transactions. As for timeliness, CV and BF strategies are essentially equivalent.

5. SIMULATIONS

Besides ensuring safety, dynamic reconfiguration is expected to be timely and to cause limited disruption. This is why the objective of this section is to assess the timeliness and degree of disruption of our approach and to compare them with those offered by the quiescence-based solution. We also aim to evaluate the impact of different levels of network latency on both approaches. The tranquillity-based approach was not included in the comparisons because it only ensures a local consistency property while the two approaches above ensure global consistency. Timeliness is measured as the time span between receiving a request for dynamic reconfiguration and entering a state where the system is ready for the changes. The degree of disruption is measured as the loss of working time for business transactions with respect to the execution of these transactions without dynamic reconfiguration.

Figure 4 shows the framework we used for the experiments[4]. To make our simulation realistic, the topologies of the systems we wanted to simulate are directed scale-free graphs[5] randomly generated by means of the JUNG framework[6]. The behavior of a CBDS is mimicked through a discrete event simulator based on the DEUS framework [2]. Events from the simulator drive the management framework to maintain the configuration according to the algorithm described in the previous section. Configurations are maintained on demand, and components are assumed to have accurate $f(T)$ and $p(T)$ for each locally-hosted ongoing transaction T, but no information other than static dependences for transactions that have already completed or have not started yet. The quiescence-based approach is implemented on top of the same framework by recursively passivating all components that statically depend on the to-be-updated ones.

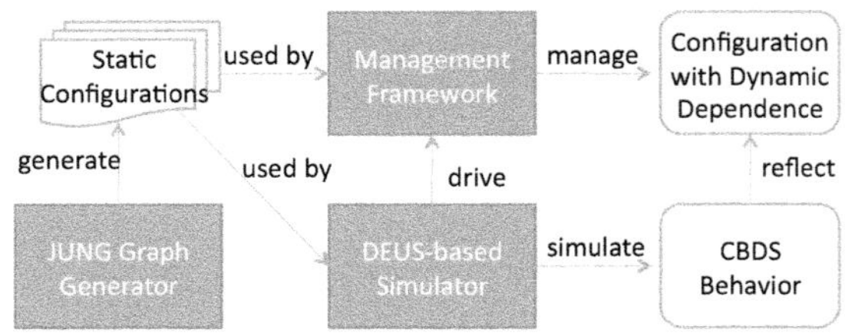

Figure 4: Simulation framework.

We also injected root transactions in all components with an activation pattern that satisfies Poisson distribution. Local processing times of transactions (not including the processing time of their sub-transactions) are normally distributed within a range of $(0, 2\mu)$ with a standard deviation of $\mu/5$, where μ is the mean local processing time. Transactions randomly initiate sub-transactions on the neighbor components of their host components. On average a transaction initiates one sub-transaction through each of its static outgoing edges. The actual system's workload for a particular configuration is given by the mean time interval between the activation of two root transactions at each component and the mean processing time of local transactions.

This framework allowed us to simulate systems with a different number of components and different workloads. The goal was to assess: (a) the impact of the system's size on the actual capabilities of ensuring version consistency, and (b) the performance of different strategies in achieving freeness with respect to different workloads.

5.1 Experiments

In our first experiment, we compared the timeliness and disruption of our approach[7] against those of the quiescence-based approach with systems of four different sizes: we generated 100 configurations of systems with 4, 8, 16, and 32

[4]The code of our experiments is available at: `http://vcsim.googlecode.com`.

[5]Scale-free graphs have been proposed as generic, universal models of network topologies that exhibit power law distributions in the connectivity of network nodes.

[6]`http://jung.sourceforge.net/index.html`.

[7]We used strategies CV and BF. For BF, the extended transaction sets are independent of each other as for liveness.

components. The mean processing time for local transactions was set to 50 time units[8], and the mean arrival interval between two root transactions at each component was set to 25 time units. The message delay between two neighbor components was set to 5 time units since the network delay between servers is often about an order of magnitude lower than the local processing time [14]. For each configuration, we randomly selected a component that had other components depending on it as the target for update, and probed the timeliness and disruption in the two cases.

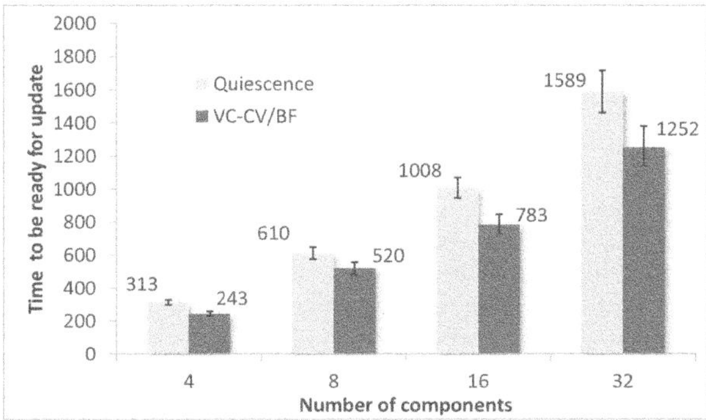

Figure 5: Timeliness of dynamic reconfiguration.

Figure 5 presents the mean timeliness of the two approaches and shows that freeness is achieved in a time that is some 20% less than the one needed to obtain quiescence.

Figure 6 shows that the degree of disruption of our approach with strategy BF is only about a half of that for the quiescence approach. With strategy CV, our approach only introduces negligible disruption, which is mainly due to the on-demand set up and maintenance of configurations. The standard errors of these values (shown by the error bars in the two figures) are relatively high, which indicates that the timeliness and disruption of both approaches are sensitive to the difference in the components targeted for update, the distribution of transactions on components, and the actual progressing of these transactions. However we observed that given the same configuration, even with strategy BF, our approach outperformed the quiescence-based one in 95% of the runs. These results then indicate that version-consistent dynamic reconfiguration, even with the overhead of handling dynamic edges introduced by the management algorithm, can be significantly less disruptive and more timely than the quiescence-based one.

The results also confirm the intuition that, for both ours and the quiescence-based approach, maintaining the consistency of dynamic reconfigurations becomes more and more expensive when the system scale increases.

Our second experiment was designed to evaluate the impact of network latency on the performance of the two approaches. In this experiment, we used the same settings introduced above with a couple of differences: we only show systems with 16 components —since the other configurations manifested the same trends— and message delay varied from 0 to 100. The results in Figure 7 show that our approach is consistently better than the quiescence-based one as far as

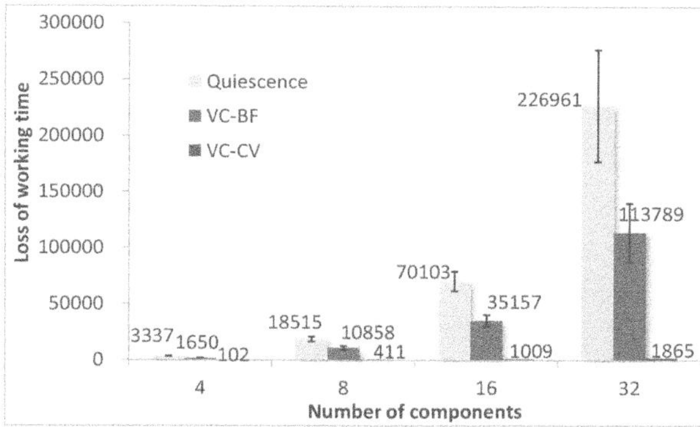

Figure 6: Disruption of dynamic reconfiguration.

disruption is concerned, but its gain in timeliness diminishes while message delay increases.

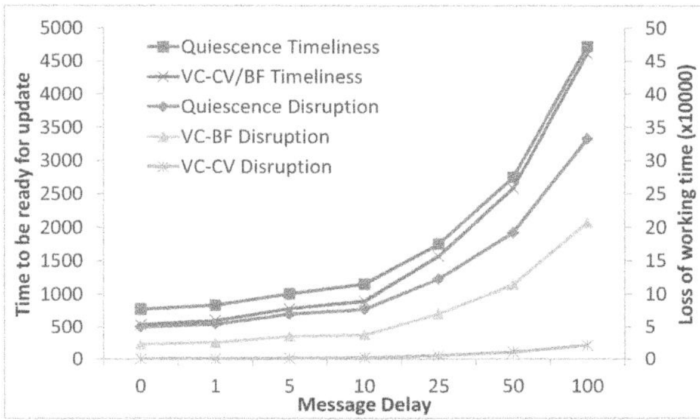

Figure 7: Impacts of network latency.

The third experiment presented here was aimed to analyze the impact of different strategies in achieving freeness on the timeliness of the actual reconfiguration. Especially, we want to see when strategy WF (simply based on waiting) can be applied and when we must use strategies CV (using concurrent versions) or BF (based on blocking). Intuitively the timeliness of strategy WF would be highly sensitive to the actual workload —more running transactions mean less opportunity for freeness. Figure 8 gives the time to freeness for strategies WF and CV/BF. The strategies were applied on the same 16-node configuration, and the same node was chosen as the target for update. The average local processing time was fixed to 50 time units, but with different intervals as for the arrival of root transactions, and thus different levels of workload. Figure 8 shows the average timeliness of 100 runs for each of the 9 different arrival intervals we selected (e.g., 1600 means that a new root transaction is initiated every 1600 time units). The results suggest that WF is preferable when the workload is rather light, but when it increases CV or BF ensures better timeliness.

6. RELATED WORK

The dynamic update of running applications has been extensively studied in multiple areas including programming languages [12, 13, 22, 23], operating systems [3, 10, 16], and software engineering [6, 21]. A common theme of these works

[8]Since the time is simulated, all time-related values in this section are in virtual time units unless otherwise specified.

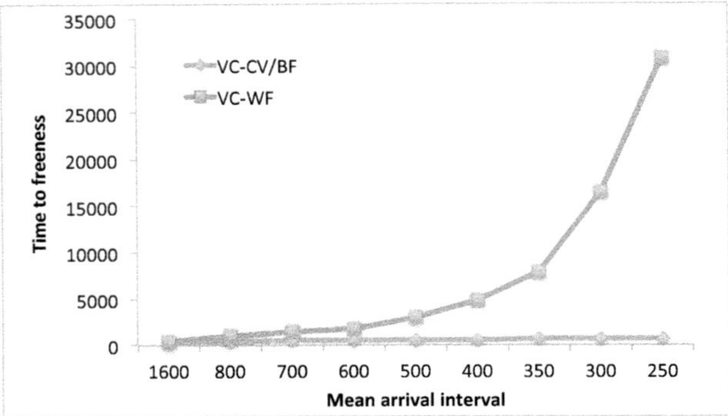

Figure 8: Timeliness: waiting vs. blocking.

is the selection of proper time points when the state of the system is steady and ready for applying a user-specified state transformation. The result is a new valid state from which the system is able to continue its evolution. Since generally the validity of the resulting state is undecidable [12], most research efforts focus on: (a) human-assisted identification of proper time points and state transformers by providing the necessary runtime support and (b) improving the timeliness of updates by automatically deriving further safe time points from those specified or known by the user.

Instead of switching from the old to the new version of the application, some works proposed intermediate versions to smooth the adaptation process. For example, Zhang and Cheng [27] proposed a model-based approach for the development of adaptive software. The behaviors of the different versions of an application are modeled by different state machines, and the adaptation behavior is rendered through states/transitions that connect them. Biyani and Kulkarni [5] used adaptation lattices to model transition paths from old to new programs, and introduced the concept of transitional-invariant lattice to verify the correctness of adaptations.

As for CBDSs, it is desirable and possible to avoid the direct manipulation of application-specific states of components and to maintain a clear separation of concerns between reconfiguration management and application logic. The focus is often on identifying suitable conditions (abstract states) under which components can be safely manipulated. The concept of quiescence by Kramer and Magee [15] is a prominent early work, but it may impose too high disruption on system's service. Subsequently, the dynamic reconfiguration service for CORBA by Bidan et al. [4], the proposal by Chen [7], and the idea of tranquillity by Vandewoude et al. [25] reduced disruption by means of considerations based on dynamic dependences, but they only guarantee some local consistency properties or impose stringent restrictions on the systems that can be updated.

It is also widely recognized that the dynamic adaptation of software systems should be modeled, analyzed, and managed at architectural level [9,20]. Architectural models provide abstract global views of systems and explicitly specify system-level integrity constraints that must be preserved by reconfiguration. However, these models do not usually provide information about the runtime dynamic dependences needed to perform safe and low-disruptive runtime reconfigurations. Wermelinger [26] et al. proposed a category theory-based approach for the uniform modeling of the computations performed by components and their architectural configurations. This proposal can be used as a formal foundation for the specification of and reasoning about dynamic reconfigurations. However its complexity prevents it from being directly used in any concrete runtime management framework. Taentzer et al. [24] proposed the use of distributed graph transformation to model configurable distributed systems, but the dynamic dependences among components are not specified directly. We chose to add future and past edges to architectural configurations because they provide a simple but powerful abstraction for dynamic dependences, and provide a good separation of concerns between application-specific computation and reconfiguration management.

As the name suggests, our version consistency criterion is inspired by the work on transactional version consistency by Neamtiu et al. [19]. This work focuses on the dynamic update of centralized applications at code level, and its notion of transaction is a user-defined scope in the code. Their approach ensures that the execution of the code in the scope complies with the same, single version, no matter when the update happens. However, in our work the notion of version consistency is defined for a distributed system model. Neamtiu et al.'s approach [19] relies on global static program analysis and cannot be used in a distributed setting. Moreover, we use the notion of version consistency as a sufficient condition for the correctness of dynamic reconfigurations, while they use it as a user-specified pre-requisite for dynamic updates.

7. CONCLUSIONS AND FUTURE WORK

Dynamic reconfiguration is widely desired but its application in practice is still limited, partly because of the complexity in balancing consistency (of changes) and disruption (of system's service). This is why we propose the use of version consistency as a criterion for safe dynamic reconfigurations of CBDSs. The approach does not compromise the correctness of distributed transactions, but it allows for better timeliness and lower disruption than previous approaches. The paper also proposes a distributed mechanism to manage dynamic dependences between components at runtime, and thus to support version consistent dynamic reconfigurations.

As for our on-going and future work, we are working on an implementation of our framework on top of a BPEL engine. We also have plans to explore to what extent our approach can be paired with other optimizations of dynamic reconfigurations, such as supporting the coordinated abortion of re-triable transactions.

Acknowledgment

This research has been partially funded by the European Commission, Programme IDEAS-ERC, Project 227977 SMScom. Xiaoxing Ma is also partially supported by the NSFC (60973044, 60736015, 61021062) and the 973 Program of China (2009CB320702).

8. REFERENCES

[1] S. Ajmani, B. Liskov, and L. Shrira. Modular software upgrades for distributed systems. In *European Conference on Object-Oriented Programming (ECOOP)*, July 2006.

[2] M. Amoretti, M. Agosti, and F. Zanichelli. DEUS: a discrete event universal simulator. In *Simutools '09: Proceedings of the 2nd International Conference on Simulation Tools and Techniques*, pages 1–9, ICST, Brussels, Belgium, Belgium, 2009. ICST (Institute for Computer Sciences, Social-Informatics and Telecommunications Engineering).

[3] A. Baumann, G. Heiser, J. Appavoo, D. D. Silva, O. Krieger, R. W. Wisniewski, and J. Kerr. Providing dynamic update in an operating system. In *ATEC '05: Proceedings of the annual conference on USENIX Annual Technical Conference*, pages 32–32, Berkeley, CA, USA, 2005. USENIX Association.

[4] C. Bidan, V. Issarny, T. Saridakis, and A. Zarras. A dynamic reconfiguration service for CORBA. In *CDS '98: Proceedings of the International Conference on Configurable Distributed Systems*, page 35, Washington, DC, USA, 1998. IEEE Computer Society.

[5] K. N. Biyani and S. S. Kulkarni. Assurance of dynamic adaptation in distributed systems. *J. Parallel Distrib. Comput.*, 68(8):1097–1112, 2008.

[6] H. Chen, J. Yu, R. Chen, B. Zang, and P.-C. Yew. POLUS: A powerful live updating system. In *ICSE '07: Proceedings of the 29th international conference on Software Engineering*, pages 271–281, 2007.

[7] X. Chen and M. Simons. A component framework for dynamic reconfiguration of distributed systems. In *CD '02: Proceedings of the IFIP/ACM Working Conference on Component Deployment*, pages 82–96, London, UK, 2002. Springer-Verlag.

[8] J. E. Cook and J. A. Dage. Highly reliable upgrading of components. In *ICSE '99: Proceedings of the 21st international conference on Software engineering*, pages 203–212, New York, NY, USA, 1999. ACM.

[9] D. Garlan, S.-W. Cheng, A.-C. Huang, B. Schmerl, and P. Steenkiste. Rainbow: Architecture-based self-adaptation with reusable infrastructure. *Computer*, 37(10):46–54, 2004.

[10] C. Giuffrida and A. S. Tanenbaum. Cooperative update: a new model for dependable live update. In *HotSWUp '09: Proceedings of the Second International Workshop on Hot Topics in Software Upgrades*, pages 1–6, New York, NY, USA, 2009. ACM.

[11] J. Gray and A. Reuter. *Transaction Processing: Concepts and Techniques.* Morgan Kaufmann Publishers Inc., San Francisco, CA, USA, 1992.

[12] D. Gupta, P. Jalote, and G. Barua. A formal framework for on-line software version change. *IEEE Transactions on Software Engineering*, 22(2):120–131, 1996.

[13] M. Hicks and S. Nettles. Dynamic software updating. *ACM Trans. Program. Lang. Syst.*, 27(6):1049–1096, 2005.

[14] U. Hoelzle and L. A. Barroso. *The Datacenter as a Computer: An Introduction to the Design of Warehouse-Scale Machines.* Morgan and Claypool Publishers, 2009.

[15] J. Kramer and J. Magee. The evolving philosophers problem: Dynamic change management. *IEEE Transactions on Software Engineering*, 16(11):1293–1306, 1990.

[16] K. Makris and K. D. Ryu. Dynamic and adaptive updates of non-quiescent subsystems in commodity operating system kernels. In *EuroSys '07: Proceedings of the 2nd ACM SIGOPS/EuroSys European Conference on Computer Systems 2007*, pages 327–340, New York, NY, USA, 2007. ACM.

[17] X. Ma, L. Baresi, C. Ghezzi, V. Panzica La Manna and J. Lu. Version-consistent Dynamic Reconfiguration of Component-based Distributed Systems. Technical Report, 2010. Available at http://home.dei.polimi.it/baresi/docs/vcdu-TR.pdf

[18] D. P. Mitchell and M. J. Merritt. A distributed algorithm for deadlock detection and resolution. In *Proceedings of the third annual ACM symposium on Principles of distributed computing 1984 (PODC '84)*, pages , 282–284, New York, NY, USA, 1984. ACM.

[19] I. Neamtiu, M. Hicks, J. S. Foster, and P. Pratikakis. Contextual effects for version-consistent dynamic software updating and safe concurrent programming. In *POPL '08: Proceedings of the 35th annual ACM SIGPLAN-SIGACT symposium on Principles of programming languages*, pages 37–49, 2008.

[20] P. Oreizy, N. Medvidovic, and R. N. Taylor. Runtime software adaptation: framework, approaches, and styles. In *ICSE Companion '08: Companion of the 30th international conference on Software engineering*, pages 899–910, New York, NY, USA, 2008. ACM.

[21] S. C. Previtali. Dynamic updates: another middleware service? In *MAI '07: Proceedings of the 1st workshop on Middleware-application interaction*, pages 49–54,2007.

[22] G. Stoyle, M. Hicks, G. Bierman, P. Sewell, and I. Neamtiu. Mutatis mutandis: Safe and predictable dynamic software updating. *ACM Trans. Program. Lang. Syst.*, 29(4):22, August 2007.

[23] S. Subramanian, M. Hicks, and K. S. McKinley. Dynamic software updates: a vm-centric approach. In *PLDI '09: Proceedings of the 2009 ACM SIGPLAN conference on Programming language design and implementation*, pages 1–12.

[24] G. Taentzer, M. Goedicke, and T. Meyer. Dynamic change management by distributed graph transformation: Towards configurable distributed systems. In *TAGT'98: Selected papers from the 6th International Workshop on Theory and Application of Graph Transformations*, pages 179–193, London, UK, 2000. Springer-Verlag.

[25] Y. Vandewoude, P. Ebraert, Y. Berbers, and T. D'Hondt. Tranquility: A low disruptive alternative to quiescence for ensuring safe dynamic updates. *IEEE Transactions on Software Engineering*, 33(12):856–868, 2007.

[26] M. Wermelinger, A. Lopes, and J. L. Fiadeiro. A graph based architectural (re)configuration language. In *ESEC/FSE-9: Proceedings of the 8th European software engineering conference held jointly with 9th ACM SIGSOFT international symposium on Foundations of software engineering*, pages 21–32.

[27] J. Zhang and B. H. C. Cheng. Model-based development of dynamically adaptive software. In *ICSE '06: Proceedings of the 28th international conference on Software engineering*, pages 371–380, 2006.

On Software Component Co-Installability

Jérôme Vouillon
CNRS, PPS UMR 7126
Univ Paris Diderot, Sorbonne Paris Cité
F-75205 Paris, France
jerome.vouillon@pps.jussieu.fr

Roberto Di Cosmo
Univ Paris Diderot, Sorbonne Paris Cité
PPS, UMR 7126 CNRS, and Inria
F-75205 Paris, France
roberto@dicosmo.org

ABSTRACT

Modern software systems are built by composing components drawn from large *repositories*, whose size and complexity is increasing quickly. A fundamental challenge for the maintainability and the scalability of such software systems is the ability to quickly identify the components that can or cannot be installed together: this is the *co-installability* problem, which is related to boolean satisfiability and is known to be algorithmically hard. This paper develops a novel theoretical framework, based on formally certified. semantic preserving graph-theoretic transformations, that allows to associate to each concrete component repository a much smaller one with a simpler structure, but with equivalent co-installability properties. This smaller repository can be represented graphically, giving a concise view of the co-installability issues in the original repository, or used as a basis for various algorithms related to co-installability, like the efficient computation of strong conflicts between components. The proofs contained in this work have been machine checked in Coq.

Keywords

component, dependencies, conflicts, co-installability, package management, open source

General Terms

Algorithms, Theory, Verification

Categories and Subject Descriptors

D.2.4 [**Software Engineering**]: Software/Program Verification—*Formal Methods*; G.2.2 [**Mathematics of Computing**]: Graph Theory—*Hypergraphs*

Partially supported by the European Community's 7th Framework Programme (FP7/2007-2013), grant agreement n°214898, "Mancoosi" project.
Work performed at the IRILL center for Free Software Research and Innovation (`http://www.irill.org`).

(c) 2011 Association for Computing Machinery. ACM acknowledges that this contribution was authored or co-authored by an employee, contractor or affiliate of the France national government. As such, the government of France retains a nonexclusive, royalty-free right to publish or reproduce this article, or to allow others to do so, for Government purposes only.
ESEC/FSE'11, September 5–9, 2011, Szeged, Hungary.
Copyright 2011 ACM 978-1-4503-0443-6/11/09 ...$10.00.

1. INTRODUCTION

The mainstream adoption of free and open source software (FOSS) has widely popularised component-based software architectures, maintained in a distributed fashion and evolving at a very quick pace. Components are typically made available via a *repository*, and each of these components is equipped with metadata, such as *dependencies* and *conflicts*, used to specify concisely the contexts in which a component can or cannot be installed.

A typical example of the metadata attached to a component, taken from the Debian GNU/Linux distribution, is shown in Example 1: the logical language used for expressing dependencies and conflicts is quite powerful, as it allows conjunctions (symbol '`,`'), disjunctions (symbol '`|`') and version constraints.

EXAMPLE 1. *The inter-package relationships of* **`postfix`**, *an Internet mail transport agent in the Debian GNU/Linux distribution (`http://www.debian.org`) currently reads:*

```
Package: postfix
Version: 2.5.5-1.1
Depends: libc6 (>= 2.7), libdb4.6, ssl-cert,
  libsasl2-2, libssl0.9.8 (>= 0.9.8f-5),
  debconf (>= 0.5) | debconf-2.0,
  netbase, adduser (>= 3.48), dpkg (>= 1.8),
  lsb-base (>= 3.0-6)
Conflicts: libnss-db (<< 2.2-3), smail,
  mail-transport-agent, postfix-tls
Provides: mail-transport-agent, postfix-tls
```

In most frameworks, determining whether a single component can be installed at all is already an NP-Complete problem, albeit the concrete instances arising in real-world systems, like GNU/Linux distributions, Eclipse plugins or OSGI component repositories, turn out to be tractable [1, 2, 3]. For the maintenance of component repositories, though, more sophisticated analyses are required. This includes identifying for each component the other components in the repository that it absolutely needs [4], and those that it can never be installed with [5].

More generally, a fundamental challenge for component based software maintainability is the study of the problem of *co-installability* of components, that involves identifying and visualising the relevant sets of components that can or cannot be installed together.

Indeed, from a maintenance point of view, one needs to identify which components cannot be installed together, in order to check whether these incompatibilities are justified or due to erroneous dependencies. The dependency graph

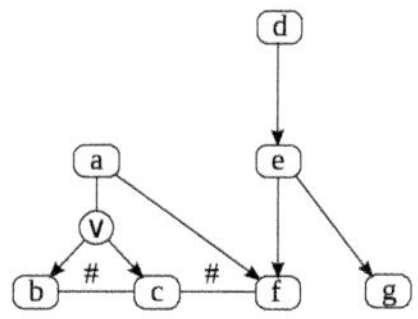

Figure 1: Graphical depiction of a repository

is also too rich for end users, which are interested in having a given set of functionalities provided by some components (for instance, they want a word processor and a Web browser) but do not care about the additional components also installed. This is illustrated by the fact that some package managers keep track of these additional components and automatically remove them when they are no more needed.

The sheer size of current mainstream repositories, with tens of thousands of components and hundreds of thousands of relations, makes it completely unfeasible to study such properties of a repository directly: visualising such large graphs is both technically challenging, and of little interest, as one would need to follow recursively a large number of dependency and conflict relations to understand how components relate to one other.

In this paper, we develop a novel theoretical framework, based on formally certified. semantic preserving graph-theoretic transformations, that allows to associate to each concrete component repository a much smaller repository with a simpler structure, but with equivalent co-installability properties. This smaller repository can be represented graphically, giving a concise view of the co-installability issues in the original repository, or used as a basis for various algorithms related to co-installability, like the efficient computation of the strong conflicts defined in [5].

We identified several bugs in the Debian distribution using the present work. For instance, the **harden-servers** package, meant to prevent the installation of unsafe packages, was in conflict with packages **proftpd** et **sendmail** but did not prevent the installation of the corresponding binaries which were in fact in packages **proftpd-base** et **sendmail-bin** (the first two packages were actually transitional packages used to ease the upgrade from a previous release).

The paper is organised as follows: Section 2 recalls the basic notions about packages and dependencies, and overviews the repository transformation developed in the paper, which achieves impressive results on real-world GNU/Linux distributions (Section 3). The technical development follows: repositories are equipped with a partial order in Section 4, put into a flattened form in Sections 5, 6 and 7, simplified by removing irrelevant dependencies and conflicts in Section 8 and quotiented in Section 9. Finally, we show how to draw a simplified graph of the kernel of a repository in Section 11. We discuss related works, and conclude in Section 13.

2. OVERALL APPROACH

While the concrete details may vary from one technology to the other, the core metadata associated to component based systems always allows to express a few fundamental properties: a component, called *package* in the following, may *depend* on a combination of components, expressed as a conjunction of disjunctions of components, and a component may *conflict* with a combination of components, expressed as a conjunction of components.

Extra properties like *provides* (e.g. `postfix-tls` in Example 1), or *versioned constraints* (e.g. `libc6 (>= 2.7)` in Example 1) can be easily preprocessed out [1], so that one can focus on a core dependency system that contains a binary symmetric conflict relation, and a dependency function $D(\pi) = \{\{\pi_1^1, ..., \pi_{n_1}^1\}, ..., \{\pi_1^k, ..., \pi_{n_k}^k\}\}$ that is satisfied when for each i at least one of the π_j^i is installed.

An example repository in this core dependency system is depicted in Figure 1, that also introduces the graphical notation used in the paper: package a has two dependencies, and can be installed only if, first, either package b or package c is installed, and second, package f is installed; package c conflicts with b and f: neither packages b and c, nor packages c and f, can be installed simultaneously; package d depends on package e, which in turn depends on both f and g.

2.1 Repositories

We follow the notations of earlier works [1, 6, 7, 8], that we recall here. A *repository* is a tuple $R = (P, D, C)$ where P is a finite set of *packages*, $D : P \to \mathcal{P}(\mathcal{P}(P))$ is the *dependency function* (we write $\mathcal{P}(X)$ for the set of subsets of X), and C, a symmetric irreflexive relation over P, is the *conflict relation*. An *installation* I of a repository (P, D, C) is a subset of P. An installation I is *healthy* when the following holds:

- *abundance*: every package has what it needs. Formally, for every package $\pi \in I$, and for every dependency $d \in D(\pi)$, we have $d \cap I \neq \emptyset$.

- *peace*: no two packages conflict, that is, $C \cap (I \times I) = \emptyset$.

We call *dependency* a set of packages d included in $D(\pi)$ for some package $\pi \in P$.

One can give a logical interpretation of the dependency function and the conflict relation. The logical variables are the packages $\pi \in P$. A set of packages $d \in \mathcal{P}(P)$ is interpreted as a disjunction:

$$[\![d]\!] = \bigvee_{\pi \in d} \pi.$$

A set of set of packages $D(\pi) \in \mathcal{P}(\mathcal{P}(P))$ is interpreted as a conjunction:

$$[\![D(\pi)]\!] = \bigwedge_{d \in D(\pi)} [\![d]\!].$$

A dependency function D is then interpreted as the set of formulas of the shape:

$$\pi \implies [\![D(\pi)]\!]$$

where π ranges over P, which can also be written:

$$\pi \implies \bigwedge_{1 \le i \le n} \bigvee_{1 \le j \le m_i} \pi_{i,j}$$

with $D(\pi) = \{d_i \mid 1 \le i \le n\}$ and $d_i = \{\pi_{i,j} \mid 1 \le j \le m_i\}$. A conflict relation C is interpreted as the set of formulas $\neg\pi \vee \neg\pi'$ for $(\pi, \pi') \in C$. A healthy installation is an assignment which simultaneously satisfies all these formulas.

2.2 Co-Installability

A package π is *installable* in a repository if it is included in a healthy installation I of this repository. A set of packages Π are *co-installable* in a repository if they are all included in some healthy installation I of the repository.

Checking co-installability has been shown equivalent to SAT by taking advantage of the logical interpretation of repositories [1]. However, our experience is that this problem is easy in practice: SAT-solver based tools are currently used routinely to identify non-installable components on repositories that contains dozens of thousands of packages, and hundreds of thousands of dependencies and conflicts.

2.3 Extracting a Co-Installability Kernel

Identifying all the sets of components that cannot be installed together is way more complex: even if we limit ourselves to the simplest case of sets of non co-installable components of size 2 (also known as *strong conflicts*), testing all possible pairs of packages is not a viable option, as the package number is in the tens of thousands. Even using all the optimisations described in [5], the computation takes almost a week on a modern workstation.

In the present work, we lay down the essential theoretical basis and algorithmic insight for tackling this *non co-installability* problem: the fundamental idea is to extract from the component repository a *kernel* repository which is equivalent to the original one, as far as co-installability is concerned, but which turns out in practice to be orders of magnitude smaller, and easily manageable.

The key steps of our approach are now summarised. The effect of each step on the example repository of Figure 1 is shown in Figure 2.

Flattening.

The recursive nature of dependencies is convenient for package developers, as it allows them to describe the dependencies among the different packages very concisely, in a modular way. To study the properties of a repository, though, it is way more convenient to use only a special *flattened* form $\widehat{D}$ of dependency functions that *directly* describes all dependencies of each package: if

$$\widehat{D}(\pi) = \{\{\pi_1^1, ..., \pi_1^{k_1}\}, ...\{\pi_n^1, ..., \pi_n^{k_n}\}\},$$

then the packages π_i^j are all the packages relevant for installing package π, and only them.

Any dependency function can be converted in this form by a sort of transitive closure that expands the dependencies of each intermediate package, and then converts the result again in a conjunction of disjunctions using distributivity: on our running example, this amounts to adding a dependency from d to f, and one from d to g (Figure 2b).

This transformation has some similarity with the conversion of logical formulae to conjunctive normal form, and is likewise subject to exponential blow-up (see for instance [9]): the dependency function of the repository in Figure 3 has size $3n$, and when expanded, gives rise to a repository whose dependency function has size 2^n.

This is a strong limiting result, but we are only interested in studying co-installability of packages, so we need not fully maintain the logical equivalence of repositories. In particular, we can prune the expanded dependency function by removing any dependency containing a package with no conflicts without changing the co-installability property. In

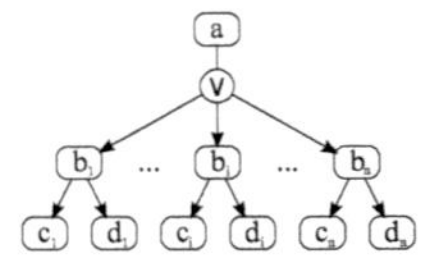

Figure 3: Repository that blows-up when flattened

practice, this suffices to avoid the exponential blow-up. On our running example, this pruning phase removes the dependencies from d to e, from d to g and from e to g, leading to the repository of Figure 2c.

We take a further action to render the repository more homogeneous: we add a self dependency to each package with conflicts. This sort of reflexive closure will be very useful when quotienting the repository, in a later phase. (There is no point in adding self dependencies to other packages as they would be removed by pruning.) We then find it convenient to draw the repository using a two-level structure: on the top, we have all packages; on the bottom, we have packages with conflicts; dependencies connects the top layer to the bottom layer; conflicts are between packages on the bottom layer. On our running example, this leads to the repository of Figure 2d.

The three phases of expansion, pruning and addition of self dependencies can be performed in a single pass, and we thereafter use the term *flattening* to denote all of them.

Elimination of irrelevant dependencies and conflicts.

As a second phase, we identify several classes of dependencies and conflicts that are irrelevant as far as co-installability is concerned, and remove them. In Figure 4, we can see some interesting examples (more are given in Section 8), in all of which the disjunctive dependency connecting package a to packages b and c can be dropped:

(a) if some branches of a disjunction are forced by a stronger dependency, all other branches can be dropped;

(b) a package with no conflict can be added to any installation, so dependencies on such a package are always satisfiable and all disjunctive dependencies containing it can be simplified out (this is the pruning defined above);

(c) if a package has a disjunctive dependency containing a package (here, b) that conflicts only with other packages in this dependency (here, c), this dependency is always satisfiable and can be dropped: either a package conflicting with package b is installed, or package b can be installed; in both cases, the dependency can be satisfied.

In Figure 5, the conflict between packages a and b is implied by the conflict between packages c and d and can be dropped.

Proving the soundness of such simplifications is far from trivial: in general, one has to rely on a peculiar structure of the repository to justify that a dependency can be removed, but removing a dependency may modify this very structure. Therefore, a suitable invariant has to be found, that allows to remove most, if not all, irrelevant dependencies.

On our example repository, we already removed dependencies corresponding to Figure 4b during flattening; the disjunctive dependency from package a to packages b and c, corresponding to Figure 4c, can be removed, yielding the repository of Figure 2e.

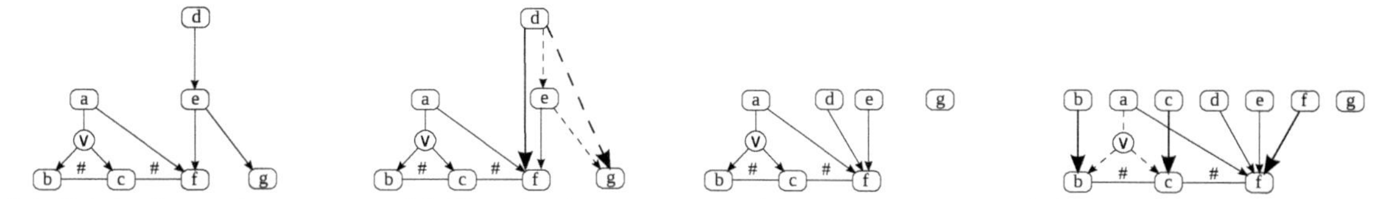

(a) Original repository (b) Transitivity (c) Pruning (d) Self dependency addition
(e) Simplification (f) Quotient (g) Drawing

Figure 2: Transformations of a repository (added dependencies are in bold, dotted ones are removed in the next phase)

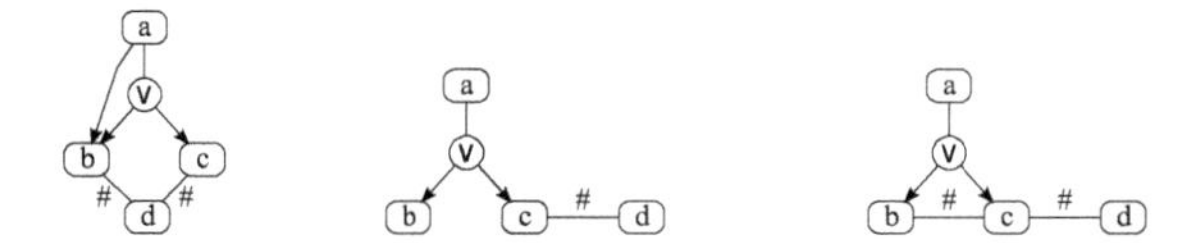

(a) Implied dependency (b) Dependency on package with no conflict (c) Dependency on package with only internal conflicts

Figure 4: Some irrelevant dependencies

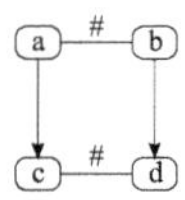

Figure 5: A redundant conflict

Quotienting equivalent packages.

It is now quite evident looking at Figure 2e, that packages a, d, e and f are, as far as co-installability is concerned, really equivalent: they share the very same set of dependencies (notice that this fact is easily detectable on the graph thanks to the self dependency of package f introduced during the flattening phase).

As many packages in a repository share the same behaviour with respect to co-installability, it is useful to quotient the final repository, identifying these packages; this step contributes greatly in reducing the size of the repository, as can be seen on our running example in Figure 2f.

After removing self dependencies, one gets the final repository of Figure 2g, where it is now quite easy to see which package can be installed with which other package, and which package cannot.

3. EXPERIMENTAL RESULTS

The transformations described in this paper have been proven correct, and all the proofs have been certified in Coq [10]. An OCaml program implementing these transformations has been run on several mainstream GNU/Linux distributions: Debian testing (full suite, amd64, snapshot taken August 22, 2010), Ubuntu 10.10 (main suite, x386) and Mandriva 2010.1 (main suite, x386). Running time were measured on a machine using a Intel Core 2 Duo Processor E6600 at 2.4GHz. The relevant statistics of the results are given on Table 1.

We can notice that the number of packages is greatly reduced: many packages share the same behaviour as far as co-installability is concerned, and the quotienting phase identifies them. In particular, many packages can *always* be installed, which is good news for the GNU/Linux distributions; they are thus mapped to a single equivalence class. The number of dependencies is reduced even more: many dependencies are not relevant to co-installability, and are removed by our transformations. The simplification shown in Figure 4c turns out to be essential; for example, in Debian, thousands of packages depend on `debconf` which depends on either `debconf-i18n` or `debconf-english`, these two last packages being mutually exclusive: removing the disjunctive dependency hugely reduces the size of the final repository.

Table 1: Repository sizes

	Debian		Ubuntu		Mandriva	
	before	after	before	after	before	after
Packages	28919	1038	7277	100	7601	84
Dependencies	124246	619	31069	29	38599	8
Conflicts	1146	985	82	60	78	62
Median cone size	38	1	38	1	59	1
Avg. cone size	66	1.7	84	1.3	153	1.1
Max. cone size	1134	15	842	4	1016	5
Running time (s)		10.6		1.19		11.6

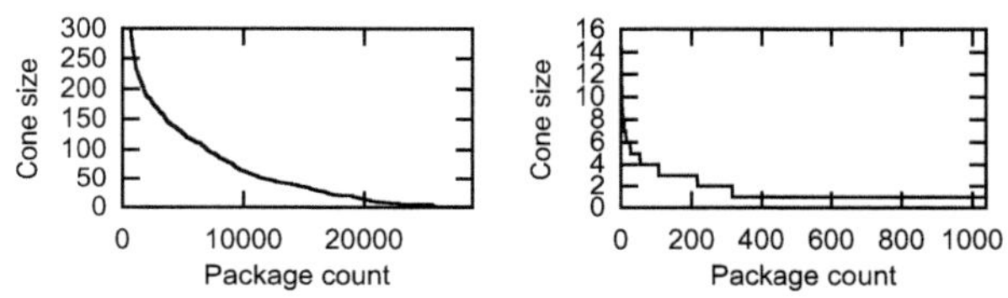

(a) before (b) after

Figure 6: Distribution of cone size (Debian testing)

As for conflicts, we notice that distributions contain only few of them, which explains that flattening is practical; most of them cannot be removed.

Finally, to each package p in a repository one can associate its *cone*, the set of packages that are reachable from p by following the dependency relations; the cone size of a package is typically quite large (Figure 6): two third of the packages have a cone of more than a hundred packages. On the other hand, after simplification, two third of the package equivalence classes have a cone of size one, meaning that they do not depend on any other package than themselves.

After simplification, the Ubuntu distribution fits on a letter size paper (see Figure 14 in Section 12) and can be easily inspected visually for errors. The corresponding graph

(a) $D(a) = \{\{b\}, \{b, c\}\}$ $\quad\sqsubseteq\quad$ (b) $D'(a) = \{\{b\}\}$

Figure 7: An example of dependency functions related by the preorder

for the Debian distribution is much larger, but it is our experience that it can still be displayed in a usable way with a suitable graph viewer: the visualisation of the Debian co-installability kernel can be tested online at `http://ocsigen.org/js_of_ocaml/graph/`.

As a consequence of the small size of the kernel extracted from a repository, many analyses can be performed very quickly. For example, it is easy to compute on the co-installability kernel of a repository the pairs of packages that can never be installed together, known as *strong conflicts* [5], which is the simplest case of co-installability. On the same data as [5], the computation takes a few seconds, instead of the several days reported there. This time is in fact included in the running times of Table 1 as we use this information when drawing the simplified repository to emphasise packages that prevent the installation of many other packages.

4. ORDERING REPOSITORIES

A large part of our work consists of finding constraints that can be removed while leaving co-installability invariant. We make the idea of removing constraints precise by defining a preorder on repositories.

We first define a preorder on dependency functions: $D \sqsubseteq D'$ iff for every package π, for every dependency $d \in D(\pi)$, there exists a dependency $d' \in D'(\pi)$ such that $d' \subseteq d$. As an example, the dependency function D of the repository shown in Figure 7a is subsumed by the dependency function D' of the repository shown in Figure 7b.

This preorder corresponds exactly to the converse of logical implication: $D \sqsubseteq D'$ if and only if the formulas $[\![D'(\pi)]\!] \implies [\![D(\pi)]\!]$ can be derived for all packages $\pi \in P$.

The preorder induces an equivalence relation over dependency functions, and a canonical representative of an equivalence class can be defined by taking the element which is point-wise the smallest. Given a dependency function D, its canonical representative can be explicitly defined as:

$$D'(\pi) = \{d \in D(\pi) \mid \forall d' \in D(\pi), d' \subseteq d \implies d' = d\}.$$

This provides a first way to simplify the dependency function (illustrated by Figure 4a), and our implementation aggressively put all dependencies in canonical form.

We can now define a preorder on repositories: $(P, D, C) \sqsubseteq (P', D', C')$ if and only if:

$$P = P', \qquad D \sqsubseteq D', \qquad C \subseteq C'.$$

Given two repositories related under this preorder, going from the right hand side one to the left hand side one consists in removing conflicts or relaxing dependencies, thus making it easier to install packages.

THEOREM 2. *When $(P, D, C) \sqsubseteq (P', D', C')$, any healthy installation I of repository (P', D', C') is also a healthy installation of repository (P, D, C).*

5. FLATTENING DEPENDENCIES

The *flattened* form of a dependency function, whose intuition has been given in the introduction, is formally defined as follows; given a repository (P, D, C), the *flattened* dependency function $\widehat{D}$ is the smallest function (with respect to point-wise inclusion) such that:

$$\textsc{Refl}\ \frac{(\pi, \pi') \in C}{\{\pi\} \in \widehat{D}(\pi)} \qquad \textsc{Trans}\ \frac{\{\pi_1, \ldots, \pi_n\} \in D(\pi) \qquad d_1 \in \widehat{D}(\pi_1) \quad \ldots \quad d_n \in \widehat{D}(\pi_n)}{\bigcup_{1 \leq i \leq n} d_i \in \widehat{D}(\pi)}$$

As the above rules are monotonous, such a function $\widehat{D}$ exists.

The rule TRANS expands the intermediate dependencies of a package π and converts the result back into a conjunction of disjunctions; this rule silently drops circular dependencies: adding a dependency $\{\pi\} \in D(\pi)$ has no effect on $\widehat{D}(\pi)$.

The rule REFL is designed to capture precisely the two properties we have outlined informally in the introduction: on one hand, we want to keep in $\widehat{D}(\pi)$ only dependencies on packages with at least a conflict (we prove in the next section that they are enough for keeping co-installability invariant); on the other hand, we want $\widehat{D}(\pi)$ to contain *explicitly* all the packages that are needed to install package π (so, if π has a conflict, it will also be an explicit dependency of itself).

The application of the transformation on the repository of Figure 1 gives the following result (illustrated by Figure 2e):

	D	$\widehat{D}$
a	$\{\{b, c\}, \{f\}\}$	$\{\{b, c\}, \{f\}\}$
b	$\emptyset$	$\{\{b\}\}$
c	$\emptyset$	$\{\{c\}\}$
d	$\{\{e\}\}$	$\{\{f\}\}$
e	$\{\{f\}, \{g\}\}$	$\{\{f\}\}$
f	$\emptyset$	$\{\{f\}\}$
g	$\emptyset$	$\emptyset$

Packages d, e and f now have the same dependencies, which reflects the intuition that they behave the same way as far as co-installability is concerned.

6. STRONGLY FLAT REPOSITORIES

A flattened repository satisfies two properties (Theorem 3 below): a reflexivity property (if a package has a conflict, then it depends on itself), and a transitivity property (dependencies are stable under composition). Co-installability in such repositories, that we call *strongly flat*, can be shown equivalent to a more convenient property, that we call *weak co-installability* (Theorem 4); this is instrumental to prove the key result of this section: a set of packages are co-installable in a repository if and only if they are co-installable in the corresponding flattened repository (Theorem 6).

We define precisely these two properties and study repositories that satisfies them.

We define the *composition* $D\,;D'$ of two dependency functions over a set of packages P as the smallest function (with respect to point-wise inclusion) such that for every package $\pi \in P$, for every set $\{\pi_1, \ldots, \pi_n\} \in D(\pi)$, for every sets $d_i \in D'(\pi_i)$, we have $\bigcup_{1 \leq i \leq n} d_i \in (D\,;D')(\pi)$.

To any conflict relation C, we associate a dependency

function Δ_C defined as follows:

$$\Delta_C(\pi) = \begin{cases} \{\{\pi\}\} & \text{if } (\pi, \pi') \in C \text{ for some } \pi' \in P \\ \emptyset & \text{otherwise} \end{cases}$$

A repository (P, D, C) is *strongly flat* when the following conditions hold:

- *reflexivity*: $\Delta_C \sqsubseteq D$ (every package with conflict depends on itself);
- *transitivity*: $D\,;D \sqsubseteq D$ (dependencies are closed under composition).

The flattening transformation produces strongly flat repositories.

THEOREM 3. *Let (P, D, C) be a repository. Let $\widehat{D}$ be the corresponding flattened dependency function. The repository $(P, \widehat{D}, C)$ is strongly flat.*

Intuitively, strongly flat repositories have a two level structure. Looking for instance at Figure 2e, we find all packages on the top layer, and typically only packages with conflicts (that we refer to as *features* in the following) at the bottom layer: thanks to transitivity, everything a package π may need to be installed is fully described by $D(\pi)$, without recursive traversal of dependencies; and thanks to reflexivity, conflicts need only be considered on the image of D.

We can take advantage of this to define a more convenient way of capturing co-installability:

A *configuration* is a pair (I, F) of a set I of packages and a set F of features; we say that it is *healthy* when the following conditions hold:

- *abundance*: every package has what it needs. Formally, for every package $\pi \in I$, and for every dependency $d \in D(\pi)$, we have $d \cap F \neq \emptyset$.
- *peace*: no two features conflict, that is, $C \cap (F \times F) = \emptyset$.

This is subtly different from the homonymous definitions regarding installations. Conflicts are only checked in F, and abundance only checked for packages in I w.r.t. F; the sets F and I might as well be disjoint, here.

A set of packages Π are *weakly co-installable* if there exists a set of features $F \subseteq P$ such that the configuration (Π, F) is healthy. In general, this is a weaker notion. In strongly flat repositories, though, the two notions are equivalent.

THEOREM 4. *Any set of packages Π weakly co-installable in a strongly flat repository are also co-installable.*

It is interesting to remark that the result of the flattening operation can be mathematically characterised as follows.

LEMMA 5. *The flattened dependency function $\widehat{D}$ associated to a repository (P, D, C) is the least dependency function D' (for preorder $\sqsubseteq$, and up to equivalence) such that:*

- $\Delta_C \sqsubseteq D'$
- $D\,; D' \sqsubseteq D'$.

The essential result of this section is that co-installability is left invariant by flattening.

THEOREM 6. *Let (P, D, C) be a repository. Let $\widehat{D}$ be the corresponding flattened dependency function. Let Π be a set of packages. The following propositions are equivalent:*

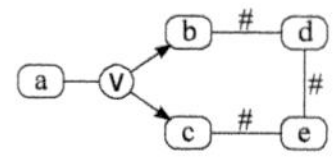

Figure 8: Illustration of monotony requirement

1. *Π is co-installable in (P, D, C);*
2. *Π is weakly co-installable in $(P, \widehat{D}, C)$;*
3. *Π is co-installable in $(P, \widehat{D}, C)$.*

7. FLAT REPOSITORIES

In this section, we focus on a particular class $\nabla_C \subseteq \mathcal{P}(P)$ of dependencies that can be safely removed (Theorem 11). Removing these dependencies may destroy the *strongly flat* structure of a repository, but we introduce the weaker notion of *flat* repository which is preserved (Theorem 11), and for which co-installability and weak co-installability still coincide (Theorem 10), thus enabling further simplifications introduced in Section 8.

We want to capture in the class ∇_C a set of dependencies that have the following two key properties:

always satisfiable any healthy configuration in the repository can be extended to satisfy these dependencies, so they are irrelevant for co-installability and we can remove them; formally, this means that if $d \in \nabla_C$, then for all $F \in \mathcal{P}(P)$ maximal with respect to set inclusion such that $C \cap (F \times F) = \emptyset$, we have $d \cap F \neq \emptyset$;

monotony a dependency which is in ∇_C must still be always satisfiable even if we remove some conflicts from the repository; formally, if $C' \subseteq C$, then $\nabla_C \subseteq \nabla_{C'}$.

The *monotony* property is necessary, because in the next section we introduce further simplifications that remove redundant conflicts. We want to be sure that removing a conflict later on does not invalidate the decision taken here of removing a dependency, as illustrated in Figure 8: the disjunctive dependency on packages b and c can always be satisfied because the conflict between d and e prevents the simultaneous installation of d and e; but this dependency is not in ∇_C since it is no longer satisfiable if the conflict between d and e is removed. This leads to the following:

DEFINITION 7. *Given a repository (P, D, C), the set ∇_C is the largest set such that $d \in \nabla_C$ if and only if, for all $C' \subseteq C$, for all $F \in \mathcal{P}(P)$ maximal with respect to set inclusion such that $C' \cap (F \times F) = \emptyset$, we have $d \cap F \neq \emptyset$.*

We can give a more explicit characterisation of the elements of ∇_C: these are *exactly* the dependencies that contain at least a package having only *internal* conflicts, like in Figure 4c.

THEOREM 8. *Let (P, D, C) be a repository. The set ∇_C is the set of dependencies d such that there exists a package $\pi \in d$ such that, for all pairs $(\pi, \pi') \in C$, we have $\pi' \in d$.*

Notice that, if a dependency d contains a package π with no conflict, then it is in ∇_C; so ∇_C also contains the redundant dependencies shown in Figure 4b.

As we shall see, weak co-installability is left invariant by the transformation that removes the elements of set ∇_C from a dependency function D of a strongly flat repository. But, in general, the strongly flat property is lost, so we need a weaker notion that is preserved by this simplification. We start by defining a coarser preorder on dependency functions that ignores dependencies in ∇_C :

> $D \prec_C D'$ if and only if for every package π, for every dependency $d \in D(\pi)$, *either* $d \in \nabla_C$ *or* there exists a dependency $d' \in D'(\pi)$ such that $d' \subseteq d$.

A repository (P, D, C) is *flat* when it satisfies the following properties:

- *reflexivity*: $\Delta_C \prec_C D$;
- *transitivity*: $D ; D \prec_C D$.

Flat repositories have a series of good properties: they include strongly flat repositories, co-installability and weak co-installability still coincide, removing ∇_C preserves flatness and keeps co-installability invariant.

LEMMA 9. *Any strongly flat repository is flat.*

THEOREM 10. *Any set of packages* Π *weakly co-installable in a flat repository are co-installable in this repository.*

THEOREM 11. *Let* (P, D, C) *be a flat repository and* D' *be the dependency function such that* $D'(\pi) = D(\pi) \setminus \nabla_C$ *for all* $\pi \in P$. *The repository* (P, D', C) *is flat, and co-installability is left invariant by this transformation.*

One can still reason on flat repositories, as far as co-installability is concerned, as if their dependency function was transitive: just choose installations (I, F) where F is maximal, and then any dependency obtained by composition is satisfied, even when it is not explicitly in the dependency function. (For strongly flat repositories, this holds for arbitrary sets F.)

8. IRRELEVANT CONSTRAINTS

We review now several classes of dependencies and conflicts that are redundant and can be simplified out.

8.1 Clearly Irrelevant Dependencies

The results of the previous section let us remove the dependencies in ∇_C from a flat repository while leaving weak co-installability invariant and keeping the repository flat.

8.2 Conflict Covered Dependencies

An example of another very interesting class of irrelevant dependencies is shown in Figure 9, where the dependency for package a can always be satisfied despite the conflict between packages e and f (we assume the other packages in this dependency also have conflicts, not explicited, so the dependency cannot be obviously removed): indeed, for this conflict to be relevant for the dependency, f needs to be installed; but if f is installed, at least one of packages c and d is installed as well, and thus the dependency is satisfied without needing to install e. This generalizes to the case where package e is in conflict with several packages with the same property as package f.

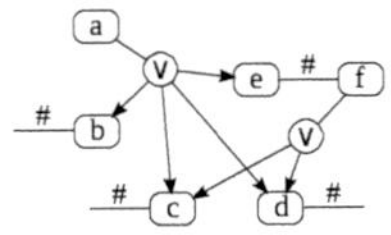

Figure 9: Dependency covered by the conflict requirements.

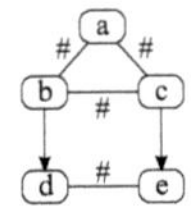

Figure 10: Redundant conflict belonging to a clique

More formally, we say that a dependency d is *conflict covered at* π if it contains a package π such that for all $(\pi, \pi') \in C$, there exists a dependency $d' \in D(\pi')$ such that $d' \subseteq d \setminus \{\pi\}$. Removing one such dependency leave co-installability invariant.

LEMMA 12. *Let* (P, D, C) *be a flat repository,* d *be a* conflict covered *dependency, and* D' *be the dependency function obtained by removing* d *from* D. *Any set of packages weakly co-installable in* (P, D', C) *is weakly co-installable in* (P, D, C).

Unfortunately, removing such dependencies may destroy the flatness of the repository, so we remove them one after another, in a greedy way, and only after checking that flatness is preserved by using the following result.

LEMMA 13. *Let* (P, D, C) *be a flat repository. Let* $\pi \in P$ *and* $d \in D$. *Let* D' *be the dependency function* D *where the dependency* d *of package* π *has been removed. If the following two conditions hold, then* (P, D', C) *is flat.*

- $d \not\subseteq \{\pi\}$;
- *for all* $d' \in (D' ; D')(\pi)$, *we have* $d \not\subseteq d'$.

In practice, it can be simpler to get all possible dependencies d' above by taking all dependencies $d'' \in D(\pi) \setminus \{d, \{\pi\}\}$ and composing them with dependencies in D.

The graph reduction rule defined by this simplification has unsolvable critical pairs, so the result of this simplification could depend on the order of removal. In practice, though, we remove all instances present in the initial repository.

8.3 Redundant Conflicts

We consider some of the conflicts that can be removed from a repository while leaving co-installability invariant. A conflicting pair $(\pi_1, \pi_1') \in C$ is *redundant* if there exists a dependency $d \in D(\pi_1)$ such that for all $\pi_2 \in d$, there exists a package π_2' such that:

- $(\pi_2, \pi_2') \in C$;
- $\{\pi_1, \pi_1'\} \neq \{\pi_2, \pi_2'\}$;
- there exists $d' \in D(\pi_2)$ such that $d' \subseteq \{\pi_2'\}$.

Redundant conflicts can be removed, but only one at a time: for example, if two conflicts are considered redundant thanks to the existence of one another, then removing both of them simultaneously is incorrect.

LEMMA 14. *Let* (P, D, C) *be a repository. Let* (π_1, π_2) *be a redundant conflict in this repository. Any healthy installation of repository* $(P, D, C \setminus \{(\pi_1, \pi_2), (\pi_2, \pi_1)\})$ *is healthy in repository* (P, D, C).

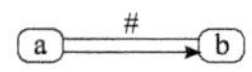

Figure 11: Dependence on conflicting package

Removing redundant conflicts involves a trade off. On one side, it may allow to remove some additional dependencies; on the other, it can also break some interesting structures. In Figure 10, the conflict between b and c is redundant, but removing it breaks the clique a, b, c, which is useful when drawing a simplified graph.

8.4 Dependence on Conflicting Packages

A special configuration may surface in the repository during simplification when the initial repository contains broken packages, as depicted in Figure 11: clearly, package a cannot be installed, and leaving such a configuration in the repository would pollute the graphical representation. In this case, we mark explicitly package a as broken by replacing its dependencies by the empty dependency $\emptyset$. All conflicts involving a can then be also removed, as they are redundant (Section 8.3). The transformation preserves healthiness.

LEMMA 15. *Let π be a package not installable in some repository (P, D, C). Let D' be the dependency function that coincide with D for all packages but π and such that $D'(\pi) = \{\emptyset\}$. Any healthy installation of repository (P, D, C) is also healthy in repository (P, D', C).*

The flatness of the repository may be destroyed, as some of the removed dependencies may be involved in transitivity. Thus, after applying such simplification, flattening should be performed again.

9. QUOTIENTING THE SET OF PACKAGES

In real-world repositories, many packages share the same behaviour as far as co-installability is concerned: for example, a lot of packages can always be installed, and some groups of packages only conflicts with a single other package.

In this section, we define an equivalence relation between packages, and show that the quotient w.r.t. this relation preserves all the good properties of a repository. We define two packages as equivalent in a repository (P, D, C) if they have the same dependencies:

$$\pi \equiv \pi' \text{ if and only if } D(\pi) = D(\pi').$$

We write $[\pi]$ for the equivalence class of package π, and extend this definition to set of packages: $[\Pi] = \{[\pi] \mid \pi \in \Pi\}$. The *quotient repository* (P', D', C') of a repository (P, D, C) is naturally defined as follows:

- P' is the set of all equivalence classes: $P' = P/{\equiv} = \{[\pi] \mid \pi \in P\}$;
- the dependency function D' is such that $D'([\pi]) = \{[d] \mid d \in D(\pi)\}$ for all $\pi \in P$;
- the conflict relation C' is defined by

$$C' = \{([\pi], [\pi']) \mid (\pi, \pi') \in C\}.$$

If the original repository does not contain dependencies of the form of Figure 11 nor redundant conflicts, then the quotient repository is indeed a repository (the key point to check is irreflexivity of the conflict relation).

LEMMA 16. *Let (P, D, C) be a flat repository such that, for all $\pi \in P$ and for all $d \in D(\pi)$, if $d \subseteq \{\pi'\}$ for some $\pi' \in P$, then $(\pi, \pi') \notin C$. Its quotient is indeed a repository.*

Quotienting preserves flatness and keeps co-installability invariant.

THEOREM 17. *A set of packages Π is weakly co-installable in the flat repository (P, D, C) if and only if the set $[\Pi]$ is weakly co-installable in the associated quotient repository.*

THEOREM 18. *If a repository is flat, then the corresponding quotiented repository is flat as well.*

10. REFLEXIVE TRANSITIVE REDUCTION

It would not be suitable to graph directly a repository after flattening as it would be polluted by dependencies which are not informative: due to reflexivity, we have packages π where $\{\pi\} \in D(\pi)$, and some dependencies can be deduced from others by transitivity. Thus, we perform a kind of reflexive transitive reduction of the dependency function: given a repository (P, D, C), we find a minimal dependency function D' with the same flattening (that is, $\widehat{D} = \widehat{D'}$).

Because of disjunctive dependencies, the complexity of finding an optimal solution is high [11, 12], in constract with the case of reflexive transitive reduction for graphs. As this is mostly a cosmetic issue for us, we use a simple non-optimal algorithm. As a first step, we iteratively remove dependencies which are implied from other dependencies by transitivity, in a greedy way. The second step is to remove all self dependencies, that is, dependencies $d \in D(\pi)$ such that $\pi \in d$. Co-installability is left invariant by these operations.

LEMMA 19. *Let (P, D, C) be a repository. Let $\pi \in P$ be a package and $d \in D(\pi)$ be a dependency of this package. Let $D' = D \setminus \{\pi \mapsto d\}$ be the dependency function D where the dependency has been removed. If $d \in (D' ; D')(\pi)$ then any healthy installation I of repository (P, D', C) is a healthy installation of repository (P, D, C).*

LEMMA 20. *Let (P, D, C) be a repository. Let D' be the dependency function defined by $D'(\pi) = \{d \in D \mid \pi \notin d\}$. Any healthy installation I of repository (P, D', C) is also a healthy installation of repository (P, D, C).*

11. PUTTING ALL TOGETHER

We now have all the ingredients at hand to perform on any repository (P, D, C) the transformations that allow to produce the final repository, which is suitable both for drawing a simplified graph, or performing efficiently various analysis related to co-installability.

11.1 Extracting a Co-Installability Kernel

The complete algorithm is shown in Figure 12. We first flatten the initial repository (Section 5), canonise the dependency function (Section 4), and remove the clearly irrelevant dependencies in ∇_C (Section 7). In our implementation, all these operations are performed simultaneously: this is significantly more efficient, as we have less dependencies to consider while flattening. Then, we set the dependencies of broken packages of the form of Figure 11 to the empty dependency $\emptyset$ (Section 8.4), and we remove redundant conflicts

repeat
  $(P, D, C) \leftarrow \mathit{flatten}(P, D, C)$
  $(P, D, C) \leftarrow \mathit{canonise}(P, D, C)$
  $(P, D, C) \leftarrow (P, D, C) \setminus \nabla_C$
  $(P, D, C) \leftarrow \mathit{remove\text{-}clearly\text{-}broken}(P, D, C)$
  $(P, D, C) \leftarrow \mathit{remove\text{-}redundant\text{-}conflicts}(P, D, C)$
until the last two steps above have no effect
$(P, D, C) \leftarrow \mathit{remove\text{-}conflict\text{-}covered\text{-}deps}(P, D, C)$
return $\mathit{quotient}(P, D, C)$

Figure 12: Simplifying the repository.

(a) Explicit representation (b) Compact representation

Figure 13: Conflict clique

(Section 8.3). As changing the dependencies of broken packages may break flatness and removing may grow ∇_C, these fives steps are iterated until no change occurs. The process terminates as at each iteration either $D(\pi)$ is set to $\{\emptyset\}$ for a package π or a conflict is removed. In practice, only two iterations are performed: more iterations are only needed in unlikely configurations where dealing with a broken package exposes another package as broken. Finally, we remove the conflict covered dependencies that can be safely dropped (Section 8.2) and the repository is quotiented (Section 9).

By combining the results of the previous sections, we obtain the fundamental result on the simplification performed by the algorithm.

THEOREM 21. *The transformation performed by the simplification algorithm leaves co-installability invariant. This algorithm produces a flat repository.*

As noticed above, on a repository with no broken package, it is not necessary to iterate the flattening phase, so the algorithm could run slighly faster; but finding all broken packages is slower than performing the whole simplification, as it requires to call a SAT solver repeatedly on large problems. On the other hand, repositories with good quality control should contain no broken packages, and a simpler version of the simplification algorithm could be used on them.

11.2 Drawing a Simplified Graph

Before drawing the final repository, we perform the transitive reflexive reduction of Section 10. The structure of the graph is then passed as input to the `dot` program of the Graphviz toolkit [13] that performs the layout.

It is important to name nodes using meaningful representatives of each equivalence class: we give preference to packages π that are directly involved in conflicts, as they have more chances to be relevant for the repository maintainers; these are easy to find by checking if $\{\pi\} \in D(\pi)$.

There can be many packages all mutually in conflict. For instance, this is the case of all mailer agents in Debian. We identify maximal such cliques and draw them in a more concise way, as shown in Figure 13.

We compute strong conflicts [5] (non-coinstallable pairs of packages) and use this information to emphasise packages that prevent the installation of many other packages.

12. VISUALIZING UBUNTU

In Figure 14 we can see the result of applying the simplifications described in this paper to the main section of release 10.10 of the Ubuntu GNU/Linux distribution; solid arrows indicate dependencies, dotted lines indicate conflicts, and conflict cliques are represented with a node containing a `#` connected with dotted lines to all packages in the clique. Of the thousands of packages, and dozens of thousands of relationships, only a handful are left, and it is possible to *read* interesting information directly on the graph.

We give here just a couple of examples. The isolated node in the middle left stands for 7049 packages that are *always* installable. The five conflict cliques are justified, as they all correspond to incompatible implementations of libraries which are compiled with different backends. One can see that package `libjpeg8-dev` is in conflict with 28 other packages, which is likely to make it unconvenient to use. The core package `ubuntu-desktop` is in conflict with a number of packages. These packages should either be removed from the main section, or the dependencies should be revised. For instance, packages `foomatic-db` and `libgd2-noxpm` should probably be removed. On the other hand, package `libsdl1.2debian-all` provides a superset of the functionalities of `libsdl1.2debian-pulseaudio`. Thus, it should not be in conflict with `ubuntu-desktop`. Overall, there are few issues with this repository. Our tool is most useful for detecting issues proactively when the distribution is in flux (during alpha and beta stages).

13. RELATED AND FUTURE WORK

Many relevant research issues stem from the concrete and widespread applications of software component repositories: identifying components that can never be installable has been shown NP-complete, but tractable in practice [1], and there is currently very active research on computing installations that optimise some given objective functions, organised around the Mancoosi International Solver Competition (`http://www.mancoosi.org/misc-2010/`); determining what other components a package will always need [4] and what pairs of packages are incompatible [5] have been shown to be relevant for quality assurance in package repositories; finally, since feature diagrams, used in software product lines, can be encoded as component repositories [14], all the problems related to configuration management can be equivalently stated in terms of repositories.

Component repositories have been in widespread use for quite a long time, but Little research work has been devoted to study the *formal* properties of component repositories: this situation is similar to what happened with the ubiquitous tool `make`, whose optimisations were only formalised and proven in [15].

Connections between component repositories and boolean satisfiability and constraint solving have been made only a few years ago in the framework of GNU/Linux distributions [1, 2] and the Eclipse platform [3], but these connections, and other recent developments such as [4, 5] do not exploit the *special structure* of the dependencies and conflicts found in a repository.

The underlying structure of software component repositories exposed here can also be seen as a generalisation of some known mathematical structures : prime event structure [16] correspond to repositories without loops and disjunctions; directed hypergraphs [11] correspond to repositories without conflict arcs, and Dual Horn theories correspond to repositories with conflicts [17].

In this paper, we have developed a theory and algorithms to extract from a repository a co-installability kernel, which can be seen as a minimal representation of the dependency and conflict relations: despite the apparent simplicity of the definition of the problem, and the intuitive appealing of the hypergraph transformations we have developed, the proofs of the crucial properties turned out to be surprisingly complex, so we decided to machine check them using Coq [10], and a long version of this paper containing all the proofs is available online as `http://hal.archives-ouvertes.fr/hal-00605491/`.

The results presented here pave the way to attacking significantly more complex problems concerning software component repositories. More generally, we believe this work clearly shows the interest of the mathematical objects underlying software repositories, which turn out to be amenable to an elegant formal treatment and of high practical interest.

Artifact evaluation: the tool `coinst` implemeting the analysis described in this article has been evaluated by the ESEC/FSE Artifact Evaluation Committee, and it has be found to *exceed expectations*; more information on this tool can be found online at `http://coinst.irill.org`.

14. REFERENCES

[1] F. Mancinelli, J. Boender, R. Di Cosmo, J. Vouillon, B. Durak, X. Leroy, and R. Treinen, "Managing the complexity of large free and open source package-based software distributions." in *Automated Software Engineering (ASE)*. IEEE Computer Society, 2006, pp. 199–208.

[2] C. Tucker, D. Shuffelton, R. Jhala, and S. Lerner, "Opium: Optimal package install/uninstall manager," *International Conference on Software Engineering (ICSE)*. IEEE Computer Society, 2007, pp. 178–188.

[3] D. L. Berre and A. Parrain, "On sat technologies for dependency management and beyond," in *Software Product Lines Conference (SPLC)*, S. Thiel and K. Pohl, Eds. Lero Int. Science Centre, University of Limerick, Ireland, 2008, pp. 197–200.

[4] P. Abate, J. Boender, R. Di Cosmo, and S. Zacchiroli, "Strong dependencies between software components," in *Empirical Software Engineering and Measurement (ESEM)*. IEEE Press, Oct. 2009, pp. 89–99. [Online]. Available: http://ieeexplore.ieee.org:80/search/wrapper.jsp?arnumber=5316017

[5] R. Di Cosmo and J. Boender, "Using strong conflicts to detect quality issues in component-based complex systems," in *ISEC '10: Proceedings of the 3rd India software engineering conference*. New York, NY, USA: ACM, 2010, pp. 163–172.

[6] R. Treinen and S. Zacchiroli, "Solving package dependencies: from EDOS to Mancoosi," in *DebConf8 (9th annual conference of the Debian project)*, Argentine, 08 2008, pp. 18–43. http://hal.archives-ouvertes.fr/hal-00340581/en/

[7] R. Di Cosmo, F. Mancinelli, J. Boender, J. Vouillon, B. Durak, X. Leroy, D. Pinheiro, P. Trezentos, M. Morgado, T. Milo, T. Zur, R. Suarez, M. Lijour, and R. Treinen, "Report on formal mangement of software dependencies,", Tech. Rep., Apr. 2006, EDOS project Deliverable 2.2, available as http://www.edos-project.org/xwiki/bin/download/Main/Deliverables/edos-wp2d2.pdf.

[8] R. Di Cosmo, B. Durak, X. Leroy, F. Mancinelli, and J. Vouillon, "Maintaining large software distributions: new challenges from the FOSS era," in *Proceedings of the FRCSS 2006 workshop*, 2006, eASST Newsletter.

[9] H. K. Buning and T. Lettmann, "Propositional logic: Deduction and algorithms," *Studia Logica*, vol. 71, pp. 247–258, 2002.

[10] The Coq Development Team, *The Coq Proof Assistant Reference Manual – Version V8.2*, 2008. http://coq.inria.fr

[11] G. Ausiello, A. D'Atri, and D. Saccà, "Graph algorithms for functional dependency manipulation," *Journal of the ACM*, vol. 30, no. 4, pp. 752–766, 1983.

[12] G. Ausiello, A. D'Atri, and D. Saccá, "Minimal representation of directed hypergraphs," *SIAM Journal of Computing*, vol. 15, no. 2, pp. 418–431, 1986.

[13] J. Ellson, E. Gansner, L. Koutsofios, S. North, and G. Woodhull, "Graphviz - open source graph drawing tools," in *Graph Drawing*, ser. Lecture Notes in Computer Science, P. Mutzel, M. Jünger, and S. Leipert, Eds. Springer Berlin / Heidelberg, 2002, vol. 2265, pp. 594–597. [Online]. Available: http://dx.doi.org/10.1007/3-540-45848-4_57

[14] R. Di Cosmo and S. Zacchiroli, "Feature diagrams as package dependencies," in *Software Product Lines Conference (SPLC)*, ser. Lecture Notes in Computer Science, J. Bosch and J. Lee, Eds., vol. 6287. Springer, 2010, pp. 476–480.

[15] C. A. Gunter, "Abstracting dependencies between software configuration items," *ACM Trans. Softw. Eng. Methodol.*, vol. 9, pp. 94–131, January 2000. [Online]. Available: http://doi.acm.org/10.1145/332740.332743

[16] G. Winskel, "Event structures," in *Petri Nets: Applications and Relationships to Other Models of Concurrency*, ser. Lecture Notes in Computer Science, W. Brauer, W. Reisig, and G. Rozenberg, Eds. Springer Berlin / Heidelberg, 1987, vol. 255, pp. 325–392. [Online]. Available: http://dx.doi.org/10.1007/3-540-17906-2_31

[17] W. F. Dowling and J. H. Gallier, "Linear-time algorithms for testing the satisfiability of propositional horn formulae," *Journal of Logic Programming*, vol. 1, no. 3, pp. 267–284, 1984.

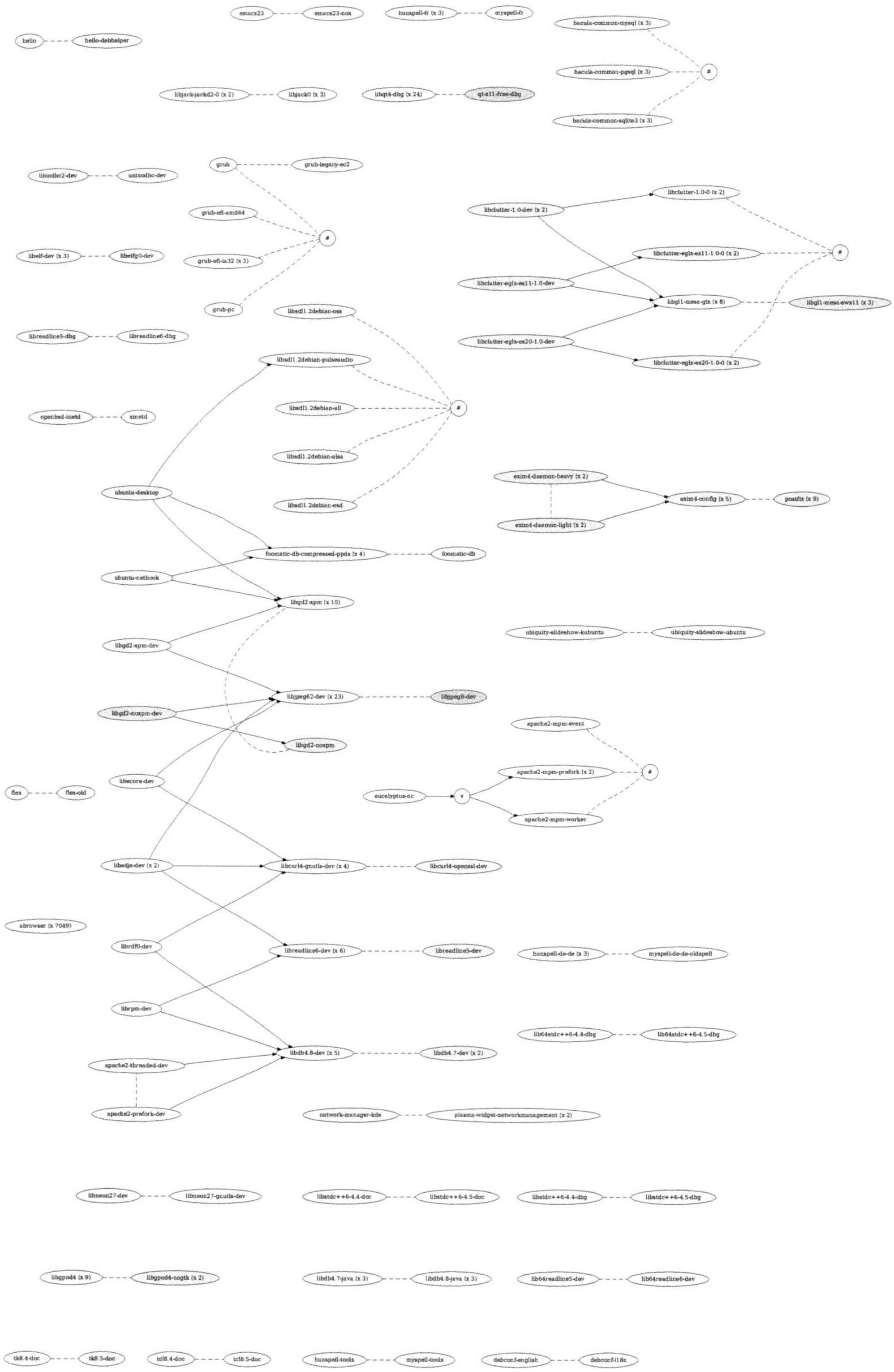

Figure 14: Output graph for Ubuntu 10.10 (main)

Leveraging Existing Instrumentation to Automatically Infer Invariant-Constrained Models

Ivan Beschastnikh[†] Yuriy Brun[†] Sigurd Schneider[∞] Michael Sloan[†] Michael D. Ernst[†]
[†]Computer Science & Engineering, University of Washington
[∞]Computer Science, Saarland University
{ivan,brun,mgsloan,mernst}@cs.washington.edu, sigurd@ps.uni-saarland.de

Abstract

Computer systems are often difficult to debug and understand. A common way of gaining insight into system behavior is to inspect execution logs and documentation. Unfortunately, manual inspection of logs is an arduous process and documentation is often incomplete and out of sync with the implementation.

This paper presents *Synoptic*, a tool that helps developers by inferring a concise and accurate system model. Unlike most related work, Synoptic does not require developer-written scenarios, specifications, negative execution examples, or other complex user input. Synoptic processes the logs most systems already produce and requires developers only to specify a set of regular expressions for parsing the logs.

Synoptic has two unique features. First, the model it produces satisfies three kinds of temporal invariants mined from the logs, improving accuracy over related approaches. Second, Synoptic uses refinement and coarsening to explore the space of models. This improves model efficiency and precision, compared to using just one approach.

In this paper, we formally prove that Synoptic always produces a model that satisfies exactly the temporal invariants mined from the log, and we argue that it does so efficiently. We empirically evaluate Synoptic through two user experience studies, one with a developer of a large, real-world system and another with 45 students in a distributed systems course. Developers used Synoptic-generated models to verify known bugs, diagnose new bugs, and increase their confidence in the correctness of their systems. None of the developers in our evaluation had a background in formal methods but were able to easily use Synoptic and detect implementation bugs in as little as a few minutes.

Categories and Subject Descriptors: D.2.5 [Testing and Debugging]: Debugging aids
General Terms: Algorithms, Reliability
Keywords: log analysis, temporal invariant mining, model inference, Synoptic

1. Introduction

Application of formal methods, such as specification and verification of systems during the design stage, is a promising means of preventing implementation bugs. Although such formal methods are popular in limited domains (e.g., avionics), only rarely do tools from the formal methods community get used by everyday developers. More commonly, developers rely on debugging.

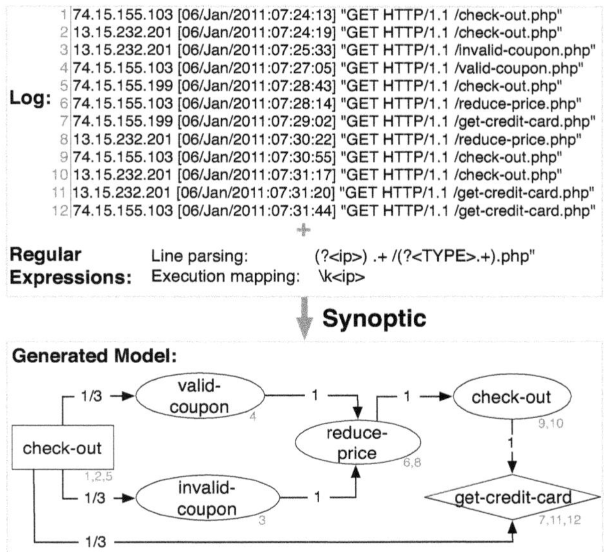

Figure 1: (Top) A log with line numbers for an online shopping cart, and two complete regular expressions for processing this log with Synoptic. (Bottom) The generated Synoptic model. In the model, rectangular/diamond/oval nodes indicate initial/terminal/intermediate nodes. Edge labels indicate transition probabilities. The subscript to the right of each node lists the log line numbers corresponding to the partition. This application contains a bug that is easily noticed in the generated model: processing an invalid coupon incorrectly reduces the shopping cart's total price.

Logging system behavior is one of the most ubiquitous, simple, and effective debugging tools. Developers instrument key locations in the code to gain insight into the state of a process, the execution sequence, and the presence or absence of certain events. Logging is so important that production systems at companies like Google are instrumented to generate *billions* of log events each day. These events are stored for weeks to help diagnose bugs [45].

However, logs are analyzed primarily by hand or with ad hoc tools. The goal of our work is to infer concise, accurate models of system behavior from logs. The inferred models aim to help developers in three ways: (1) help find bugs, (2) increase developers' confidence in the absence of certain bugs, and (3) improve developers' understanding of their systems. We present the design and evaluation of a tool called Synoptic, which processes the logs most systems

Permission to make digital or hard copies of all or part of this work for personal or classroom use is granted without fee provided that copies are not made or distributed for profit or commercial advantage and that copies bear this notice and the full citation on the first page. To copy otherwise, to republish, to post on servers or to redistribute to lists, requires prior specific permission and/or a fee.
ESEC/FSE'11, September 5–9, 2011, Szeged, Hungary.
Copyright 2011 ACM 978-1-4503-0443-6/11/09 ...$10.00.

already produce and requires developers only to specify a set of regular expressions for parsing the logs. Synoptic generates a model similar to a finite state machine that satisfies the temporal invariants mined from the logs. By leveraging existing logs, Synoptic produces models with details the developer already considers to be helpful in aiding understanding. More generally, Synoptic offers developers who have little expertise in formal methods a means to consider their systems more formally. Synoptic bridges the gap between the culture of the average developer who practices logging for debugging with advanced techniques developed by the formal methods community.

Synoptic differs from prior model-generation tools by its versatility and by imposing few requirements on the developer. To use the tool, developers neither need to specify their systems as part of the design, identify properties for the tool to verify, nor modify their code. Instead, Synoptic mines three kinds of temporal invariants from existing logs and uses these to generate a concise model satisfying the invariants. Developers only provide a set of regular expressions to parse events from the logs. With this approach, Synoptic (1) does not restrict developers to a particular log format and (2) allows developers to specify the events to include in the model.

Figure 1 shows a web server log for a shopping cart application. Using the two listed regular expressions, Synoptic parses the log into three traces, one for each of the three user IP addresses accessing the server (Figure 3). Synoptic then mines temporal invariants that hold in those traces and uses the invariants to infer a model of the system (bottom of Figure 1). The model clearly illustrates a bug that would be difficult to find by examining the log directly: applying an invalid coupon allows the user to reduce the price. Not only can Synoptic help a developer find this bug, it can also increase the developer's confidence that the bug has been successfully removed. For example, the developer can run Synoptic on logs generated by a new version of the system and compare the new model with the prior model.

We evaluated Synoptic both theoretically and experimentally. Section 3 formally proves that Synoptic produces a model that satisfies all the true temporal invariants mined from the log and none of the invariants that are not satisfied by the log. Further, we argue that Synoptic's exploration of the model space is efficient and produces concise models.

Additionally, to demonstrate Synoptic's ability to produce useful representations in practice, we evaluated it in two user experience studies (Section 4). We first report on a study with a developer working on reverse traceroute [23], a distributed system that determines the likely reverse Internet route between two hosts. Reverse traceroute has been in deployment for over 7 months, has handled a total of 3.6 million requests to date, and has been recently internally deployed by a large, popular, and ubiquitous Internet company. Second, we report on the experiences of 45 undergraduate students who used Synoptic in a distributed systems course. The students applied Synoptic to logs generated by their implementations of a distributed version of a cache coherence protocol [26].

In our evaluation, Synoptic generated models on logs up to 900,000 events that represent over 28,000 unique system executions. Most developers in our studies found the generated models helpful in understanding their systems. Synoptic models increased developer confidence in the correctness of their implementations, helped identify previously unknown bugs, and confirmed the existence of known bugs.

Next, we motivate and explain how Synoptic works by describing BisimH, the central algorithm Synoptic uses.

2. BisimH: Generating models from logs

Synoptic uses a hybrid refinement and coarsening algorithm called BisimH. Our prior workshop paper proposed this algorithm without

1 Input: log L, regular expressions $RegExps$
2 let traceGraph = `extract`(L, $RegExps$)
3 let I = `mineInvariants`(traceGraph)
4 let (V, E) = `partition`(traceGraph)
5 while (V, E) does not satisfy invariants I
6   // p: event → boolean, π: partition that will be split
7   let (p, π) = `selectSplit`($(V, E), I$)
8   let $\pi_1 = \{\text{event} \in \pi \mid p(\text{event})\}$
9   let $\pi_2 = \{\text{event} \in \pi \mid \neg p(\text{event})\}$
10   $V := (V - \{\pi\}) \cup \{\pi_1, \pi_2\}$
11   $E := \{(\pi_3, \pi_4, r) \in V \times V \times R \mid \exists\ \text{event}_1 \in \pi_3, \exists\ \text{event}_2 \in \pi_4$
12       $: \text{event}_1\ r\ \text{event}_2 \in \text{traceGraph}\}$
13 end while
14 (V, E) := `kTail`($(V, E), 0, I$)
15 Output: (V, E)

Figure 2: The BisimH algorithm. Section 2 describes the `extract`, `mineInvariants`, `partition`, `selectSplit`, and `kTail` procedures.

providing a formal analysis or reporting on user experience with the tool [39]. The rest of this section explains the algorithm in detail by walking through its pseudo-code listed in Figure 2, and by illustrating how Synoptic would process the log in Figure 1. For a more formal treatment see Section 3.

2.1 Log parsing

Synoptic constructs a system model from a set of observed system execution traces. It takes as input a log file containing the execution traces, and a set of user-defined regular expressions. Synoptic uses the regular expressions to parse the log file and extract from some of the log lines an *event instance*: a triplet containing: (1) a trace identifier, (2) a timestamp, and (3) an *event type*. Trace identifiers are used to group together event instances from the same *trace*. Synoptic requires that the event instances in a trace be totally ordered using their timestamps. Therefore, no two event instances in a trace may have identical timestamps. An event type can be an arbitrary string, and is usually defined by the developer as something that conveys important information about the system. For example, Section 4 presents two Synoptic-generated models in which an event type represents (1) an executed method's name, and (2) the state of a node in a distributed system.

A trace can be considered to be a linear graph — each vertex is an event instance, and the edges represent the total ordering. We term the union of such graphs a *trace graph*. The trace graph is built from the log using the provided regular expressions (line 2 in Figure 2).

Recall the shopping cart application. Figure 1 shows the log and the two complete regular expressions that Synoptic uses to parse the log into three traces, one per unique IP in the log; the php script names denote the trace event types. Figure 3 shows the three traces parsed from the log. For example, the trace corresponding to the IP 74.15.155.103 is ⟨0, check-out⟩, ⟨1, valid-coupon⟩, ⟨2, reduce-price⟩, ⟨3, check-out⟩, ⟨4, get-credit-card⟩. Here, the integer timestamp is derived implicitly from the order of lines in the log.

2.2 Mining invariants from the trace graph

To guide model generation, Synoptic mines three kinds of temporal invariants relating *event types* from the trace graph (line 3 in Figure 2):

- **a Always Followed by b** (written $a \to b$). Whenever the event type a appears, the event type b always appears later in the same trace.
- **a Never Followed by b** (written $a \not\to b$). Whenever the event

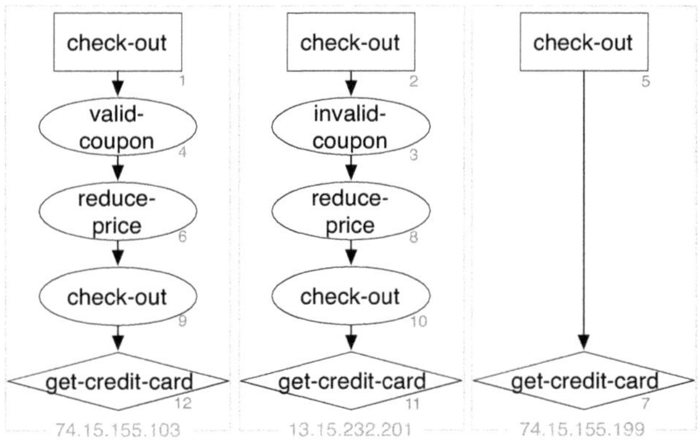

Figure 3: Trace graph parsed from the log in Figure 1. Each execution corresponds to an IP address that accessed the web application. The subscript to the right of each node lists the line number of the log line from which the event instance was extracted.

type a appears, the event type b never appears later in the same trace.

- **a Always Precedes b** (written $a \leftarrow b$). Whenever the event type b appears, the event type a always appears before b in the same trace.

The missing symmetrical invariant *Never Precedes*, defined as a Never Precedes b iff b can be generated only when no a was yet generated, is equivalent to the *Never Followed by* invariant.

We term these relations "invariants" because they succinctly capture temporal event type relationships that must hold true over all the input traces. The trace graph in Figure 3 yields 27 such invariants. Two examples are *reduce-price* $\not\rightarrow$ *valid-coupon*, and *invalid-coupon* $\rightarrow$ *check-out*. Section 2.5 justifies our use of these particular invariant types, and Section 3.2 explains how these invariants are mined. Next, we introduce Synoptic models.

2.3 Synoptic models and the initial model

The Synoptic model is a *partition graph* of the trace graph. Given a partitioning of the original vertices, each vertex in the model is one partition. Directed edges in the model are formed through existential abstraction. That is, a directed edge between two vertices indicates that there exists a pair of event instances in the corresponding partitions that are connected by an edge in the trace graph. A further constraint is that each partition contains event instances of only one particular event type. The resulting relational model makes minimal assumptions about the underlying process that produced the logged event instances. For a more complete discussion concerning our model choice see [39].

An important property of Synoptic models is that each trace in the input log is accepted by a model constructed from the corresponding event instances (in the sense that each trace maps to a valid path in the model). However, a Synoptic model is also generative — it may accept traces that were not present in the log.

The BisimH algorithm starts with an *initial model* (constructed using `partition` on line 4 of Figure 2). In this model, there is one partition per event type containing all the event instances of that type. Figure 4 shows the initial model for the trace graph in Figure 3.

By construction, the initial Synoptic model captures two important kinds of temporal properties for any two adjacent event instances in a trace in the log. First, if an event instance of type a is at some point immediately followed by an event instance of type b in the log, then there must be an edge from a to b. Second, if an event instance of type a is never immediately followed by an event instance of type b in the log, then there is no edge from a to b.

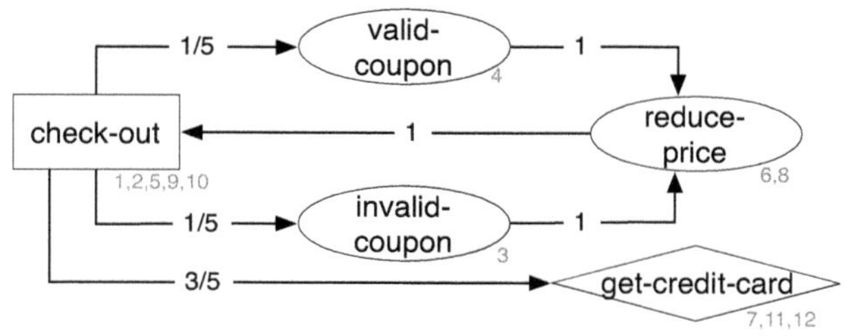

Figure 4: Initial model corresponding to the trace graph in Figure 3.

The initial model is therefore the most compact or abstract model plausible, based on the logged traces. The least compact (and most concrete) model is the trace graph, in which each partition contains a single event instance. This model makes no generalizations and overfits to the input traces.

2.4 Refinement and coarsening

Coarsening and refinement are dual operations on a Synoptic model. Starting with the initial model, Synoptic first performs model refinement, shown as an iterative process in lines 5–13 of Figure 2. This algorithm is a modification of a partition refinement algorithm introduced by Elomaa [13]. Synoptic refines (i.e., splits) partitions until it reaches a model that satisfies all the mined invariants. Next, Synoptic uses coarsening to merge those partitions that were needlessly refined due to an imperfect splitting heuristic (line 14 in Figure 2). The coarsening step is constrained to not violate the mined invariants satisfied during refinement. Synoptic outputs the model when it is unable to coarsen it any further.

2.4.1 *Refinement*

The refinement goal of BisimH is to pick a minimal sequence of splits, so that the resulting graph is the coarsest graph that satisfies a set of invariants. This problem is NP-hard [7], so an efficient algorithm might not yield the optimal result. For an example illustrating refinement suboptimality see [39].

BisimH performs splits as long as there exists some mined invariant that is not satisfied. BisimH uses an FSM-based model checker to check whether a model satisfies a mined invariant. It converts each invariant into a small FSM that accepts traces satisfying the invariant. It then updates the FSMs as it traverses the model graph. If the model does not satisfy an invariant, the model checker outputs a counterexample path. For example, the invariant *valid-coupon* $\not\rightarrow$ *invalid-coupon* mined from the log in Figure 1 is not true in the model in Figure 4 — Figure 5 shows a counterexample path.

Having identified a set of counterexamples that violate the mined invariants, BisimH follows the counterexample guided abstraction refinement (CEGAR) approach [7] to determine a set of *candidate partitions*, for each of which there exists a split that removes at least one of the counterexamples. BisimH identifies these partitions heuristically by tracing each counterexample, stepwise, in parallel, in the input traces and in the model. In the traces, only a prefix of the counterexample path will be present (otherwise the counterexample would not violate an invariant). BisimH finds the longest such prefix, and the last partition of this prefix in the model becomes a candidate for refinement — this partition allows a spurious transition in the model that allows for the counterexample path to exist. For example, the longest such prefix for the counterexample path in Figure 5 ends in the *check-out* partitions. This is because *check-out* stitches together two traces from the log (two left-most traces in Figure 3) into a trace that violates the *valid-coupon* $\not\rightarrow$ *invalid-coupon* invariant.

To refine a candidate partition (i.e., to eliminate the counterex-

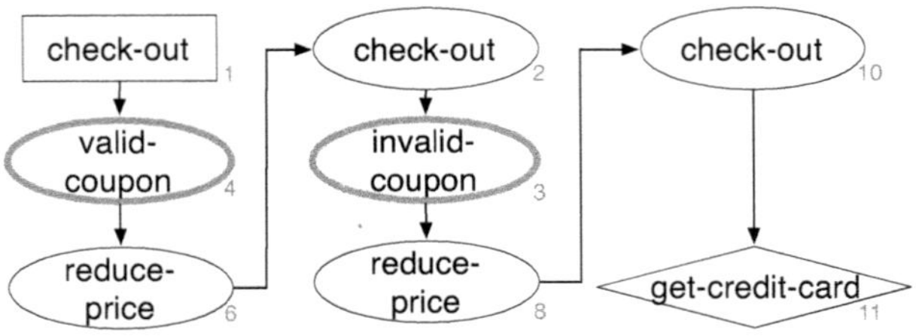

Figure 5: A path through the initial model in Figure 4 that violates the mined *valid-coupon* $\not\rightarrow$ *invalid-coupon* invariant.

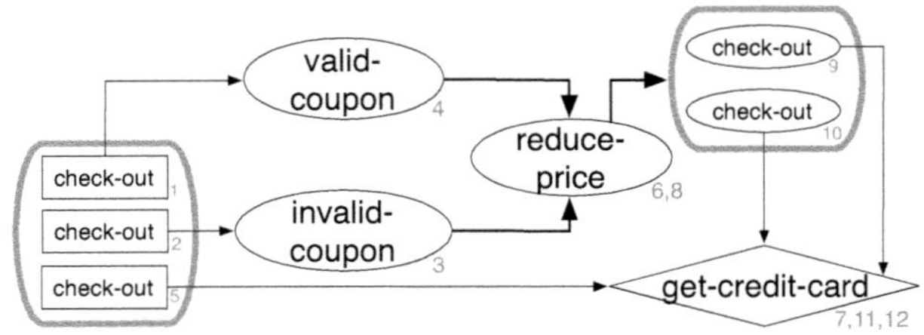

Figure 6: A refinement of the model in Figure 4 that eliminates the counterexample path in Figure 5. The edge between the *reduce-price* partition and the *check-out* partition induces a split of *check-out*: the *check-out* event instances reachable from *reduce-price* are split out. The two new *check-out* partitions, with the contained *check-out* event instances, are shown in bold. This model is equivalent to the final model shown at the bottom of Figure 1.

ample path), the event instances in this partition are divided into two sets based on whether they can or cannot be reached from the partition immediately preceding the candidate partition in the prefix. In line 7 of Figure 2, `selectSplit` obtains a predicate p that distinguishes these two event instance sets, and lines 8 and 9 introduce two new partitions, π_1 and π_2, corresponding to these two sets. Figure 6 illustrates a refinement of the initial model in Figure 4 to eliminate the counterexample in Figure 5. In this case, the predicate p separates the event instances in the *check-out* partition into those that can or cannot be reached from the *reduce-price* partition.

We experimented with two kinds of predicates. Synoptic uses the one described above: it separates event instances in the candidate partition based on an incoming edge from a partition that immediately precedes the candidate partition. We also tried a predicate that separates event instances in the candidate partition based on an outgoing edge representing the spurious transition — it separates event instances in the candidate partition into sets based on whether they can or cannot make the spurious transition. Though we did not show this formally, in practice, we found the second strategy to be less optimal than the first. It is also possible to split the candidate partition simultaneously on an incoming and on an outgoing edge. Though we have not tried this, we think this may work best. In our future work, we intend to further study the splitting predicate's impact on the algorithm.

Typically, the refined model violates several invariants and candidate partitions must be ranked to decide which one to split first. Synoptic employs a two-class ranking: it examines all counterexamples in an arbitrary order and performs the first split that validates an invariant (i.e., eliminates the last counterexample for that invariant). If no such split is available (because more counterexamples exist for each invariant), BisimH picks a split nondeterministically. This ranking introduces nondeterminism and BisimH might perform unnecessary splits.

2.4.2 *Coarsening*

BisimH may end up refining more than it needs to. When this happens, the model will contain partitions that can be merged without violating the satisfied invariants. After refinement, BisimH coarsens the model to merge such partitions (line 2 in Figure 2).

For coarsening, BisimH uses *kTail-equivalence* [5]. kTail is a coarsening algorithm that starts with the most fine-grained model. It stops once there is no pair of k-equivalent partitions, i.e., no two partitions that are roots of sub-graphs identical up to depth k. At each step, the algorithm merges one pair of *kTail-equivalent* partitions, chosen nondeterministically. BisimH runs kTail with $k = 0$ (label equivalence) to produce the most concise models. It starts with the final refined graph, under the extra constraint that all merges do not unsatisfy any invariants. The resulting merged model is locally minimal: merging any two partitions will violate some invariant.

2.5 The impact of mined invariants on BisimH

BisimH uses the mined invariants to establish a well-defined termination criterion for refinement, and also to guide refinement in its choice of partition to refine. This use of invariants is an important feature of BisimH. To see this, suppose the set of invariants is empty. In this case, refinement would terminate with a model that is the quotient under label-equivalence, i.e., the initial model. This model is often too compact to capture key properties of the log and is overly generative. On the other hand, suppose that the invariant set includes all possible temporal log invariants expressible in LTL. Then the algorithm will terminate when, for all partitions A, if an event instance in A has a successor event instance in a partition B, then every event instance in A has a successor event instance in B in the model. In this case, the final model is the quotient under bisimulation, i.e., a graph that satisfies the same set of LTL formulae as the trace graph. In our experience, the bisimulation quotient is usually too similar to the trace graph, and thus too fine-grained to be considered concise.

Our choice of the three invariant types is a compromise between the above two extremes. In our experience, the models derived using this set of invariants are accurate, yet sufficiently generative for the kinds of applications we are considering (e.g., improving developer understanding of how the system operates). These invariant types are also exactly the most frequently observed specification patterns formulated by Dwyer et al. [12], with scope constrained to a trace (i.e., global scope). The translation is not one-to-one: $a \rightarrow b$ is Dwyer's Existence pattern when a is *START* (see Definition 2 below), and is otherwise Dwyer's Response pattern. Another example is $\forall b, a \leftarrow b$, which is Dwyer's Universality pattern. In our experience, these invariants were sufficient for capturing key temporal properties of the systems that produced the logs we considered.

Users can write Java code to define custom Synoptic invariants. However, all of the users in our case studies (Section 4) successfully used Synoptic without even knowing about its use of invariants.

In the next section, we define log and model formalism and prove important positive results about the BisimH algorithm.

3. Formal evaluation

This section proves the correctness of our algorithm, and explains why it is efficient and is able to infer *concise* models in practice. Sections 3.1 and 3.2 define the formalisms. Section 3.3 proves that BisimH always halts and that the final model satisfies exactly the invariants mined from the input log. Section 3.4 proves an important result for improving model search efficiency, and Section 3.5 deals with model size.

3.1 Definitions

Two special event types — *START* and *END* — are added internally by Synoptic to keep track of initial and terminal events in the traces.[1]

Definition 1 (Event Types). A set of event types is a finite set (alphabet) $E \supseteq \{START, END\}$.

Definition 2 (Trace). Let E be a set of event types. Then for all $n \in \mathbb{N}_{\geq 2}$, a finite trace is an ordered sequence of event types $l \in E^n$ such that the first element of l is *START* and the last element is *END*. The length of l is $n-2$.

Definition 3 (Log). A log L is a set of traces.

The set of event instances in a log is the collection of elements in the traces in that log. Each trace element is a unique event instance, indexed by its trace and position within that trace.

Definition 4 (Event Instances). Let E be a set of event types. Let L be a log over E. Then an *event instance* is a triplet $\langle e, l, i \rangle$ such that $e \in E$ occurs in the log trace $l \in L$ at position $i \in \mathbb{N}$. $\hat{E}$ denotes the set of all such event instances for L.

An event instance relation is a set of pairs of elements of $\hat{E}$. For example, one representation (using "**0**" to represent the event instance $\langle \mathbf{0}, l, 1 \rangle$, etc.) of the event instance relation "next" on the log trace $l = \langle 0,1,2,3,4 \rangle$ is $\{\langle 0,1 \rangle, \langle 1,2 \rangle, \langle 2,3 \rangle, \langle 3,4 \rangle\}$. This paper's examples only use this "next" relation, although all the results generalize to arbitrary relations.

Definition 5 (Event Instance Relation). Let $\hat{E}$ be a set of event instances. Then $r \subseteq \hat{E}^2$ is an event instance relation.

A partitioning of a finite set of event instances $\hat{E}$ is a finite set of disjoint, exhaustive subsets of $\hat{E}$. Each subset is called a partition and contains event instances of the same event type.

Definition 6 (Partitioning). Let $\hat{E}$ be a set of event instances. Then $P \subset \mathcal{P}(\hat{E})$ is a partitioning of $\hat{E}$ if $\forall$ distinct $p, q \in P$, $p \cap q = \emptyset$, and $\hat{E} = \bigcup_{p \in P} p$, and $\forall p \in P$, all $\hat{e} \in p$ are of the same event type. Each $p \in P$ is called a partition. We enforce the condition that for a valid partitioning, all instances of the *START* event type are in a single partition and all instances of the *END* event type are in a single partition. That is, for all $\hat{e_1} \in p_1$, $\hat{e_2} \in p_2$: $\hat{e_1}, \hat{e_2}$ instances of *START* $\Rightarrow p_1 = p_2$ and $\hat{e_1}, \hat{e_2}$ instances of *END* $\Rightarrow p_1 = p_2$.

A relational model is a partition graph. The largest (most nodes) relational model for a log L is the trace graph: the set of disconnected subgraphs, one for each trace $l \in L$, with a vertex for each event instance and edges only between consecutive event instances in l. Other relational models can be generated by merging vertices that represent event instances of the same event type (and removing redundant edges).

Definition 7 (Relational Model). Let $\hat{E}$ be the set of event instances in a log. Let R_r be a family of relations over $\hat{E}$ indexed by r. Then the relational model is a directed graph $M = \langle M_V, M_A \rangle$, such that M_V is a partitioning of $\hat{E}$ and $a = \langle p_1, p_2, r \rangle \in M_A \subseteq M_V \times M_V \times R_r$ iff $p_1, p_2 \in M_V$ and $\exists \hat{e}_1, \hat{e}_2 \in \hat{E}$ such that $\hat{e}_1 \in p_1$, $\hat{e}_2 \in p_2$, and $\langle \hat{e}_1, \hat{e}_2 \rangle \in R_r$.

Definition 8 (Complete Path). A path in a model is complete if it starts at the *START* partition and ends at the *END* partition.

A relational model M accepts a trace if the event instances of the trace form a complete path in M.

[1]When viewing a model, the user can optionally hide these nodes, and instead have Synoptic specially mark the partitions containing any initial and terminal events as rectangles and rhombuses, respectively. The models pictured in this paper were all generated in this way.

Definition 9 (Trace Acceptance). Let $n \in \mathbb{N}$ and let $l = \langle START, \hat{e}_1, \ldots, \hat{e}_n, END \rangle$ be a trace of length n. Then a relational model M accepts l iff $\exists \Pi = \langle p_{START}, p_1, \ldots, p_n, p_{END} \rangle$ such that $\forall 1 \leq i \leq n$, $\hat{e}_i \in p_i$ and Π is a complete path in M.

Note that by construction a relational model M for a log L accepts all traces in L. To see this, consider a trace $l = \langle START, \hat{e}_1, \ldots, \hat{e}_n, END \rangle \in L$. The "next" relation, corresponding to R_{next}, holds for all pairs of adjacent event instances, that is $\forall 1 \leq i < n, \langle \hat{e}_i, \hat{e}_{i+1} \rangle \in R_{next}$ as well as $\langle START, \hat{e}_1 \rangle \in R_{next}$ and $\langle \hat{e}_n, END \rangle \in R_{next}$. This means that l maps to a complete path in M and therefore M accepts l.

3.2 Invariants

We consider three invariants that relate pairs of event types:

Definition 10 (Event Invariant). Let a and b be two event types. Then an event invariant is a property that relates a and b in one of the following three ways:

$a \rightarrow b$ **:** In a model, if some partition on a complete path contains an event instance of type a, then at least one later partition along that path contains an event instance of type b.

$a \not\rightarrow b$ **:** In a model, if some partition on a complete path contains an event instance of type a, no later partition along that path contains an event instance of type b.

$a \leftarrow b$ **:** In a model, if some partition on a complete path contains an event instance of type b, at least one earlier partition along that path contains an event instance of type a.

Definition 11 (Invariant Satisfiability). Let M be a relational model, and let i be an event invariant. M satisfies i iff $\forall$ Π, a complete path in M, i is true of Π.

Each of the three event invariants may relate any pair of event types. Thus, for a set of event types E there can be at most $3|E|^2$ invariants.

Synoptic mines the above invariants by collecting three kinds of counts across all the traces. Each trace is traversed once in the forward and once in the reverse direction to count:

- $\forall a$,Occurrences[a] : the number of event instances of type a,
- $\forall a, b$ Follows[a][b] : the number of event instances of type a that are followed by at least one event instance of type b, and
- $\forall a, b$ Precedes[a][b] : the number of event instances of type b that are preceded by at least one event instance of type a.

The invariants are then determined by using the following equivalences:

$$a \rightarrow b \Leftrightarrow \text{Follows}[a][b] = \text{Occurrences}[a]$$
$$a \not\rightarrow b \Leftrightarrow \text{Follows}[a][b] = 0$$
$$a \leftarrow b \Leftrightarrow \text{Precedes}[a][b] = \text{Occurrences}[b]$$

3.3 BisimH termination

This section proves that BisimH terminates (Theorem 1) and that the final model satisfies all the event invariants in the log (Theorem 2) and no others (Theorem 3).

Theorem 1 (BisimH Terminates). *BisimH makes a finite number of iterations (no more than the number of event instances).*

Proof of Theorem 1. After every BisimH iteration, the model has more partitions than the model before the iteration, as some partition is split into two new partitions. The maximal model has a finite number of partitions (each event instance is in its own partition, except the *START* and *END* instances) and satisfies all the mined invariants. Therefore, BisimH can make no more iterations than there are event instances. □

Theorem 2 (True Invariant Satisfiability). *BisimH produces a final model that satisfies all the event invariants that are true for a log.*

Proof of Theorem 2. The termination condition for BisimH is that the final model satisfies all the invariants mined from the log. The maximal model trivially satisfies all those invariants. Therefore, BisimH either terminates with that model or a smaller model that also satisfies the invariants. □

Theorem 3 (False Invariant Unsatisfiability). *Let L be a log with event instances $\hat{E}$ and event types E. Let $M = \langle M_V, M_A \rangle$ be a relational model over $\hat{E}$ with a family of relations R_r. Let i be an event invariant that is not true of L. Then M does not satisfy i.*

Proof of Theorem 3. Since i is not true for L, there must be a trace $l \in L$ for which i is not true. Since there exists a path in M corresponding to l, that path must start with *START* and end with *END* and must not satisfy i. Therefore, M does not satisfy i. □

3.4 Improving model search efficiency

The previous section proved that regardless of which partitions BisimH splits, the algorithm always finds a model that satisfies exactly the log invariants. This is an important theoretical result, but a splitting strategy must be efficient in practice since refinement is expensive — a log with dozens of event types will generally satisfy hundreds of invariants of the types we are considering. Checking these invariants is costly, especially when the model grows to a large size. In this section, we prove that once BisimH satisfies an invariant, it never again violates it (Theorem 4). Therefore, invariants that have been satisfied do not need to be re-checked in finer models. This reduces the number of model checking runs BisimH needs to perform, making it more efficient.

Theorem 4 (Invariant Preservation). *Let L be a log with event instances $\hat{E}$ and event types E. Let $M = \langle M_V, M_A \rangle$ be a relational model over $\hat{E}$ with a family of relations R_r. Construct a new relational model $M' = \langle M'_V, M'_A \rangle$ as follows:*

1. *Select one partition $p \in M_V$, $|p| \geq 2$.*
2. *Split p into two nonempty partitions p' and p''.*
3. *Let $M'_V = (M_V \setminus \{p\}) \cup \{p', p''\}$.*
4. *Compute M'_A using the family of relations R_r.*

For all event invariants i:

$$[(M \text{ satisfies } i) \wedge (i \text{ is true for } L)] \Rightarrow M' \text{ satisfies } i.$$

It is an immediate corollary that M' satisfies all invariants that M does and that are true in the log.

Proof sketch: The proof considers the differences between M and M', and relies on the fact that these differences are confined to the region around the refined partition p. Consider some path Π' in M' that might violate invariant i. That path is made up of edges, each of which comes from some trace, which means for each edge, there is a corresponding edge in M. Therefore, there is a corresponding path Π in M that goes through partitions of the same event types. Since the event types along both paths are identical, then either both or none of the paths satisfy i. But since M satisfies i, so must M'.

Proof of Theorem 4. Without loss of generality, let $\langle a, b \rangle$ be the pair of event types that i relates. We will now show that all paths in M' must satisfy i.

Consider a complete path Π' in M'. For any two partitions connected by an edge in Π' there must exist at least one pair of event instances, one in each partition, that is related by some relation in some trace. For each edge in Π' choose such a pair of event instances to construct a sequence of event instances s.

Now consider the unique path Π in M that corresponds to s. Every partition in Π contains event instances of the same type as the corresponding partition in Π' (in fact, Π's partition is a superset of Π''s).

Assume Π' violates i. Consider three cases:

Case 1: i is $a \rightarrow b$. There must be some partition in Π' with an event instance of type a such that no subsequent partition in Π' contains an event instance of type b. Therefore, no subsequent partition in Π contains an event instance of type b. But M satisfies i. Contradiction.

Case 2: i is $a \not\rightarrow b$. There must be some partition in Π' with an event instance of type b that follows a partition with an event instance of type a. Then Π must also violate i. Contradiction.

Case 3: i is $a \leftarrow b$. There must be some partition in Π' with an event instance of type b such that no earlier partition in Π' contains an event instance of type a. Then no earlier partition in Π contains an event instance of type a. But M satisfies i. Contradiction. □

3.5 Maintaining a small model size

Synoptic's aim is to present to a developer the smallest model (fewest nodes) satisfying the mined invariants. Large models are often too complex and no better than the raw log. In this section, we explain how the CEGAR [7] approach leads BisimH towards concise models. We argue that refinement always makes provable progress towards satisfying an invariant. Therefore BisimH rarely performs splits that make the model larger than it needs to be.

As a reminder, the CEGAR approach (detailed in Section 2.4.1) works as follows. First, BisimH generates a counterexample trace (e.g., Figure 5) that is accepted by the model and violates a mined invariant (*valid-coupon* $\not\rightarrow$ *invalid-coupon*). BisimH then traces along the counterexample trace in the model and in the input traces to find the longest prefix of partitions that exists as a sequence of corresponding event type instances in at least one input trace. The last partition in this prefix is refined (Figure 6). Two cases are possible:

Case 1: The refined model does not accept the counterexample trace. Consider the set of trace equivalence classes: two traces are in the same class if the paths of the two traces in the model are equivalent after removing all iterations through loops in the model. A split that eliminates one loop-free trace from an equivalence class, eliminates all traces in that class. Thus, eliminating a counterexample always eliminates an entire class of counterexamples that violate the invariant. Since there are a finite number of loop-free paths in a model, eliminating a class makes progress toward satisfying the invariant.

Case 2: The refined model accepts the counterexample trace. Consider the prefix corresponding to the counterexample trace in the refined model. This prefix is shorter than the previous prefix by at least one partition (the partition that was refined). Because any prefix must be finite, the refinement makes progress toward eliminating the counterexample trace from the model (towards Case 1).

Because BisimH considers one counterexample at a time, a refinement may split a partition suboptimally. That is, a split partition may need to be split again to help eliminate another counterexample, even though a single split might suffice to help eliminate both counterexamples. To counteract such suboptimal splits, BisimH uses coarsening (Section 2.4.2).

4. Experience with Synoptic

We performed two case studies to evaluate Synoptic's ability to produce concise and useful representations in practice. First, we carried out a user study with a developer working on the *reverse traceroute* system that determines the likely reverse route from an arbitrary destination on the Internet to a source host [23] (Section 4.1). Synoptic analyzed the coordinator node logs that contained debugging event instances generated by the system.

Second, we introduced Synoptic as a tool for use in an undergraduate distributed systems class of 45 students (Section 4.2). The students were tasked with designing and implementing a cache coherence protocol and had to (1) draw a finite state machine of their design, (2) run Synoptic on their implementation, and (3) explain any observed differences.

The students used Synoptic during development and testing, while the reverse traceroute developer used Synoptic on logs generated in production. We therefore believe that Synoptic can be helpful during all stages of a typical software engineering process. Overall, we found that Synoptic was useful for finding new bugs (Section 4.3), for increasing developer confidence (Section 4.4), and for building understanding (Section 4.5).

4.1 Reverse traceroute study

Reverse traceroute [23] is a distributed system that determines the likely reverse traceroute from an arbitrary destination on the Internet to a source host. Reverse traceroute relies on a distributed set of Internet vantage points hosted by PlanetLab [36], and uses a variety of methods to find each segment of the reverse route, such as IP record route and timestamp options [19, 20], and relies on IP spoofing from PlanetLab hosts.

Reverse traceroute has been in live deployment for over 7 months and since that time it has had hundreds of distinct users and has handled a total of 3.6 million requests. Today, it gets tens of thousands of requests per day. Recently, a large, popular, and ubiquitous Internet company has deployed the system internally.

We carried out a user study with a developer working on the system to study a log of 900,000 event instances. To generate this log, the developer spent a total of 15 minutes to add a total of 16 lines of logging code to the system. We then wrote four regular expressions to process the log. The log was divided into traces by measurement-based method names — a single trace corresponded to a sequence of method calls made to determine the reverse route for a particular ⟨source, destination⟩ pair.

Synoptic took 11.5 minutes to generate the final graph from the input log on an Intel i7 (2.8 GHz) OS X machine with 8GB of RAM. Because this graph contained many rare edges (i.e., edges with low transition probabilities), we showed the developer both the full graph, as well as a graph that omitted 62 edges with low transition probability. The second type of graph is shown in Figure 7. We then performed a talk-aloud user study with the developer by showing him Synoptic-derived graphs, explaining to him what they represent, and asking him to talk through his observations.

4.2 Distributed systems course assignment

In the University of Washington undergraduate distributed systems course[2], groups of 2–4 students designed and implemented a peer-to-peer Facebook-like social network. The project was divided into multiple assignments, one of which was to implement the distributed version of a cache coherence protocol [26] between a single master node and some number of replica clients. For this assignment, the students were to (1) record their design as a FSM diagram, (2) implement their design, (3) apply Synoptic to logs generated by their implementation, and (4) observe and explain any differences between the Synoptic output and their initial FSM diagram.

For testing, the students used a simulated environment in which all nodes executed in a single process, and communicated via a centralized simulator manager. The simulator provides the option of reordering, losing, and duplicating messages, as well as randomly failing and restarting nodes.

The simulator logged common event types like message sent, received, and lost and file read and written, and also allowed student node code to log user-defined event types. Although the simulated system was distributed, the simulator produced totally ordered logs — event instances were serialized through the central simulator manager. The students were also given a set of Synoptic regular expressions for processing logs generated by the simulator.

All 18 groups completed the assignment. Due to space constraints, Sections 4.3–4.5 showcase just a few of the Synoptic diagrams generated by the students, and quotes just a few of their reports on their experiences with Synoptic.

4.3 Finding bugs in code

Synoptic models capture event type orderings and co-occurrence frequencies among event types. The absence of an edge could indicate that the log is incomplete. However, if the behavior is supposed to occur at all times or with high frequency, an unexpected graph topology can be an indicator of a latent bug.

Reverse traceroute study.

The reverse traceroute developer identified one new and important bug using the Synoptic model within the first two minutes of seeing the model. All measurements made by the system must eventually terminate in either the `do_reach_callback` or the `do_fail_callback` methods. The developer thought that all traces reaching these methods terminated. The graph showed otherwise — some of the traces continued past these callbacks. The model in Figure 7 illustrates these buggy transitions with bold, dashed emphasis. The developer hypothesized that this bug is caused by concurrency in the measurement code. The developer also observed that the tool offers a light-weight means of verifying that some previously observed buggy behavior is not present after a bug fix, and that it may help to rule out bug fixes that fail to eliminate buggy behavior.

Distributed systems course.

Of the 18 groups, 3 groups found bugs in their implementations with Synoptic. Synoptic models effectively capture event type orderings and all three of the bugs had to do with illegal message orderings. One group observed that a transition that was expected never occurred — the node seemed to never execute the write command after processing it. They then fixed the bug and used Synoptic to confirm that it did not appear in the traces:

> "We did find a bug in the graph. If you follow the append path in the final graph you can see that it goes from append→send→write. In the old graph the append→send, but dies instead of passing it onto write."

A different group found a bug in which they mistakenly sent the wrong type of packet:

> "We had few places where we sent the wrong type of packet in the code. For example, we sent RDC when we had to send WDC. When looking at the Synoptic diagram, these kinds of mistakes were easy to find."

4.4 Increasing developer confidence

Synoptic models can succinctly represent thousands of execution traces with a few nodes in a graph. A single compact diagram that consolidates many executions gives developers confidence that they will not overlook any behaviors present in the log. Moreover,

[2]http://www.cs.washington.edu/education/courses/cse490h/11wi

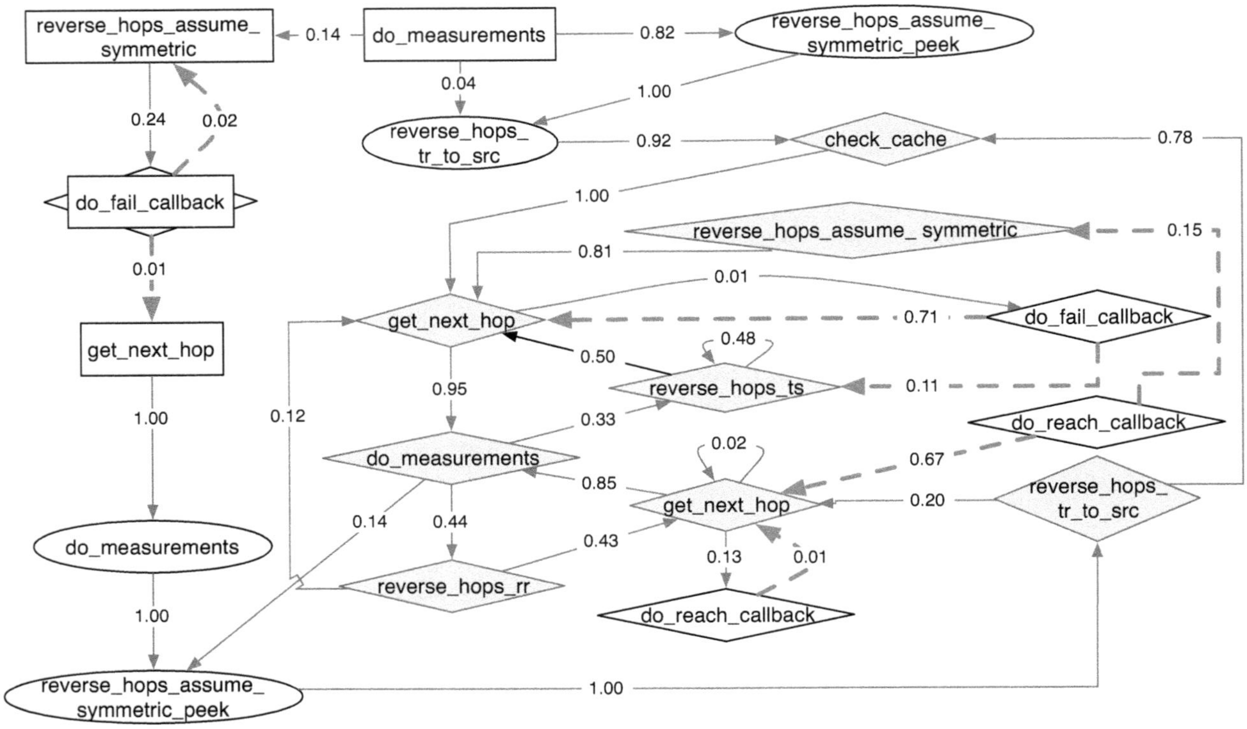

Figure 7: Synoptic model for a reverse traceroute input log of 900,000 event instances. Rectangular nodes are start nodes, and diamond nodes are terminal nodes. Edge labels indicate transition probability. For clarity certain edges and nodes are omitted. The (manually) bold, dashed lines indicate a new bug that was discovered by the developer. The (manually) shaded terminal nodes make up the set of methods exhibiting a bug known to the developer. Before viewing the Synoptic graph, the developer thought the bug affected only two of these eight nodes.

developers often recognized expected patterns and considered them to be important evidence that the system worked as expected.

Reverse traceroute study.
The reverse traceroute developer was often prompted by the model to try to explain various patterns. Patterns that were simpler and more noticeable, like self-loops on nodes, elicited more attention. For example, upon noticing a self-loop on one of the nodes the developer mentioned that this indicated that a specific type of measurement was re-tried and that this was correct behavior.

Distributed systems course.
Of the 18 groups in the class, 11 reported that Synoptic increased their confidence in their implementations. In many cases the students recognized expected patterns. Figure 8 illustrates two sets of diagrams generated by a group that felt that they acquired additional confidence in their system by using Synoptic. The figure shows four models, with each pair corresponding to a *Client* and *Server* processes in the system. The group decided to use a combination of messages and states for their event types — e.g., `create` is a file create request message sent by the client to the server, while e.g., `readonly_state` is the state of the client when it holds a shared read lock on the file. To more easily follow the sequence of event types the students generated two sets of models for two distinct scenarios (see Figure 8). By inspecting these models, the group confirmed that the messages were exchanged in the appropriate order and that the nodes transitioned between states correctly.

The following are some student quotes that indicate that Synoptic increased developers' confidence in their systems:

"[Synoptic] definitely let us know for sure that our code was functioning correctly."

"Using Synoptic did not help us find any bugs with our code, but it did help us to clarify that our code is doing what it should."

"We can confidently say that Synoptic helped confirm the correct behavior of our program, and certainly made us feel better about our code."

4.5 Building system understanding

Using the Synoptic model, the reverse traceroute developer was able to solidify his understanding about the system. For example, he knew that the system had a bug in which a reverse traceroute measurement terminates prematurely. Using the model, he was able to verify that this bug occurred — methods terminating prematurely appeared as terminal nodes in the model. However, as it turned out, the developer did not understand the full extent of this bug. He assumed that it affected only two methods. By inspecting the model, he found out that other methods were impacted as well. The model in Figure 7 illustrates the set of all the methods impacted by this known bug with a darker shading. This experience solidified the developer's understanding of where the bug manifested and he felt better prepared to resolve it.

Overall we found that Synoptic was useful for finding new bugs, for increasing developer confidence, and for building systems understanding.

4.6 Threats to validity

Our two user studies are limited in scope and have a number of inherent biases for which we were unable to control. The reverse traceroute system has been developed by about five developers, all of whom understand the entire system. Consequently, Synoptic models are straightforward for them to interpret. Developers who are new to a project or are working on a larger project may find it

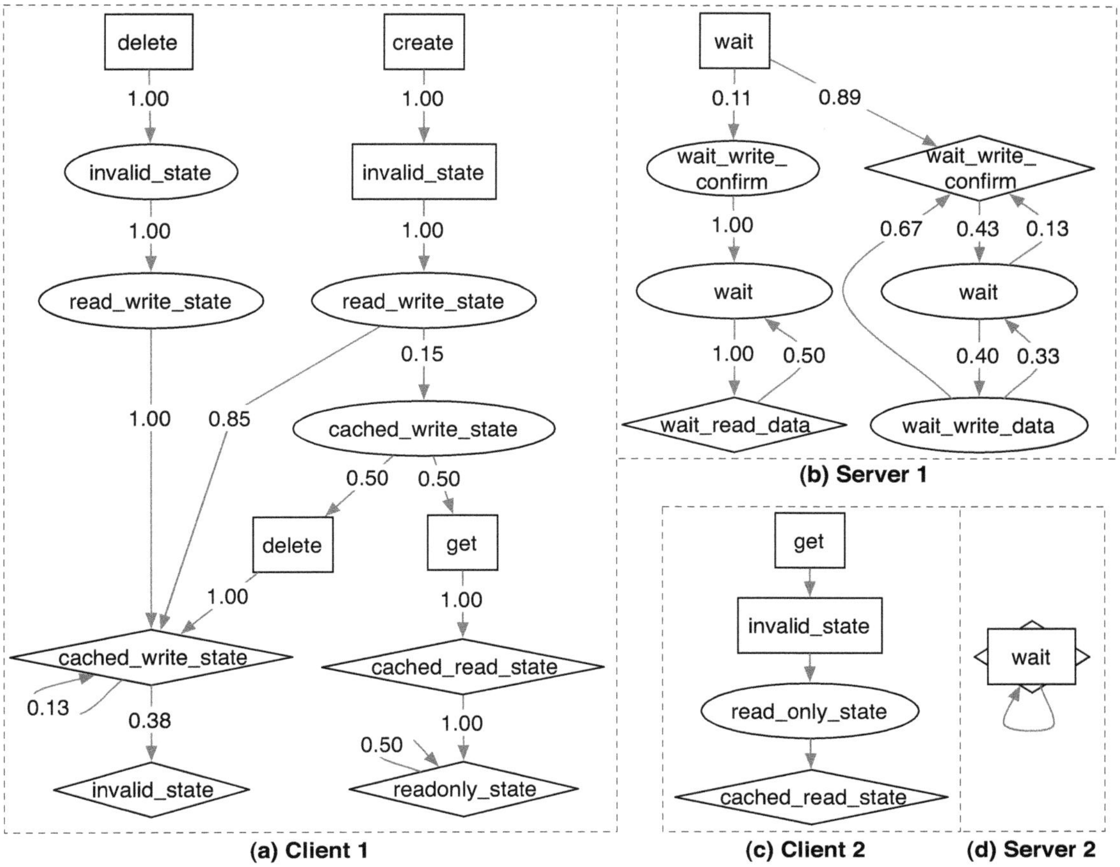

Figure 8: Two pairs of Synoptic models generated by a group of students in the distributed systems class for a distributed cache coherence assignment. Each pair of models has a server model and a client model. The **Client1** and **Server1** models correspond to a scenario in which the client host starts, and then deletes the file if it exists. Alternatively the client creates the file, and then either deletes it or reads from it. The **Client2** and **Server2** models correspond to the simpler scenario in which the client reads a file that is not currently accessed by any other client.

difficult to interpret Synoptic models, which may be larger and more complex. However, we believe that Synoptic may also be used to gain insight into components of larger systems, and because most sizable systems are developed in a modular fashion, there may still be value in using Synoptic in large projects. Lastly, our study with the developer implicitly emphasized bug findings, which may have primed the developer into thinking more about bugs. In a different context, he might have been less successful in identifying bugs.

Because the students in the distributed systems course were required to use Synoptic as part of the assignment, it is unknown whether they would have been motivated enough to learn about and use the tool without a mandate. Students might have also been attempting to please us and thereby reported only positive experiences with the tool. Finally, students are not representative of experienced developers and we do not know whether the bugs they found using Synoptic are problems for expert developers.

5. Related work

Work related to Synoptic falls into three main categories; (1) tools to mine logs generated by systems; (2) algorithms to create concise models of system executions; and (3) the study of bisimulations, which motivated our development of BisimH.

Mining systems logs

This paper extends our previous work [39] with a formal analysis of the BisimH algorithm and a report on user experiences with the Synoptic tool. An overview of the Synoptic tool from a user's perspective is given in [4]. Other prior work on mining systems logs focused on detecting dependencies [31], anomalies [22, 32, 46, 49], and performance debugging [40, 41]. That work does not target the problem of finding a concise model for an arbitrary system generating the log. For instance, SALSA [40] and Mochi [41] extract and visualize node behavior of Hadoop [17] node logs to support performance debugging. This line of work is MapReduce-specific. Perracotta [48] mines and visualizes temporal properties of event traces, and it has been used to study program evolution [47]. Unlike Synoptic, Perracotta does not use the mined temporal properties to infer a model of the system.

Inferring models

The problem of automata inference from positive examples of executions is computable [6], but is NP-complete [16, 3], and the FSA cannot be approximated by any polynomial-time algorithm [35].

The kTail algorithm [5], used extensively in related work, takes a finite state model and produces a more compact one by recursively merging states whose root subgraphs are identical up to a depth of *k*. Approaches that leverage kTail to infer models without developer supervision [1, 5, 27, 28, 30, 33, 37] can produce precise models for small and simple systems, but when complexity of the system increases, the precision of the inferred models decreases dramatically [27]. Lorenzoli et al. [30] developed GK-Tail, a variant of kTail, and applied it to logged sequences of method call invocations. Unlike BisimH, the GK-Tail algorithm does not preserve trace invariants. Lo et al. [29] augment the kTail algorithm by using temporal properties mined from execution traces to guide state merging while ensuring that the final model satisfies temporal constraints. Temporal-invariant-consistency greatly increases the model's precision. Synoptic produces similar high-precision models while leveraging refinement, as opposed to coarsening, to greatly increase the efficiency and scalability of the approach [39]. Krka et al. [25] have proposed, though have not yet implemented, using refinement and mined invariants to improve precision of inferred models beyond that of Lo et al.'s approach.

Numerous techniques leverage developer-written specifications to infer system models. Whittle and Schumann [44] generate component statecharts from scenarios and properties. Damas et al. [8] inductively infer labeled transition system (LTS) models from scenarios interactively provided by the developer. A later extension of this approach reduces the number of questions to the developer [9] by incorporating FLTL properties [15]. However, these techniques can synthesize overspecified models and require significant human input. Uchitel et al. [43] proposed using message sequence charts [21] to infer LTS models and discover implied scenarios. Harel et al. [18] synthesize statecharts from live sequence charts [10]. LTSs can also be constructed based on pre- and postcondition specifications [2, 11]. De Caso et al. [11] generate abstract models to support validation of the specifications. Alarjeh et al.'s technique [2] facilitates refinement of pre- and postconditions based on system goals and execution scenarios. Similarly, Krka et al.'s algorithm [24] synthesizes behavioral models from pre- and postcondition specifications and execution scenarios and can synthesize component-level models from system-level specification. Uchitel et al. [42] argued that it is crucial to consider the specifications' partiality when using developer-written specifications to infer models. In contrast to all these approaches, Synoptic requires much less input from the developer — the logs that are usually already generated by systems, and a small set of regular expressions. However, systems that are not instrumented to generate logs may require developers to change the implementation. However, logging is considered to be generally useful and adding such instrumentation leads to better software. Further, we hope that Synoptic's utility will motivate developers to increase their systems' logging capabilities.

Bisimulation

A bisimulation is a simulation relation that provides a strong notion of similarity for relational structures [38]. Its key feature is to preserve certain properties of the relational structure, for example, two strongly bisimilar transition systems are guaranteed to satisfy the same set of LTL formulae. An important application in model checking is model minimization [14]. Our BisimH algorithm is a modification of a partition refinement algorithm [34], which uses invariants to determine which state to split next and when to stop splitting, resulting in a coarser representation that is not bisimilar to the input structure. Our BisimH algorithm is also related to the partition refinement algorithms in [13], but BisimH uses invariants to guide exploration and termination.

6. Limitations and future work

While working on Synoptic, we observed a number of its limitations. Here, we detail the most important of these and connect some of them to our future work.

Applicability. Synoptic models capture ordering relationships between events observed in a log. It does not handle algebraic and logical relationships that may also be useful in modeling software (e.g., this.next $\neq$ this.prev). Synoptic is therefore best suited for studying logs of systems whose execution can be modeled as a sequence of elements, with the ordering, the presence, and absence of elements encoding some useful semantics about the system. We have observed that Synoptic can help with problems whose root causes can be deciphered using such semantic information. More advanced issues, however, would require richer and more complex models than Synoptic currently provides.

Invariants. Synoptic relies on three temporal invariants to determine when to terminate and how to proceed during refinement. A rigorous evaluation of the limitations and advantages of these invariant types is necessary. For example, we know that the invariants constrain Synoptic models in ways that are sometimes undesirable. For instance, the $\not\to$ invariant constrains Synoptic models to be less generative: e.g., if $a \not\to b$ is true, then the model is restricted from generating a path between a and b, even though this behavior might be valid and can appear in an execution that is not present in the input log. However, we do not know what kinds of systems or uses these invariants favor, and whether we should expand this set, or make it smaller.

Synoptic invariants are temporal. They do not involve the *data values* that are often present in logs. Extending Synoptic to mine and then preserve value-based invariants is a part of our future work.

Reliance on logs. To work well, Synoptic needs the input log to include as many different system executions as possible. This is because Synoptic models are at most as detailed as the input logs. If the user failed to log an important behavior, then this behavior will usually not be present in the Synoptic-generated model. However, generating all possible system behaviors is notoriously difficult, and may be infeasible, as illustrated by the following student quote:

> "However, we had to run specific simulation cases in order to produce the log, so while Synoptic was very useful, most of the debugging process involved trying commands in the simulator. We knew what cases we were testing, so running them through the terminal was an easier way to test for the bug. But Synoptic did confirm that we have the right message flows."

Handling concurrency. Synoptic cannot handle traces of concurrent systems as it assumes a totally ordered relation for ordering event instances in a trace. Concurrent systems may be modeled by Synoptic with explicit concurrency (e.g., by listing all possible event instance permutations), but this results in highly connected models that are difficult to interpret. Another alternative, which we are currently pursuing, is to extend Synoptic models and the semantics of the three invariants types to accommodate partially ordered traces.

Fault localization/interactive tool support. The feasibility of fault localization using Synoptic-generated models depends on the density and quality of the logging statements. Reconstructing execution paths based on logs is an active research area (e.g., SherLog [49]), and we hope to leverage this existing work in developing more automated fault localization techniques. However, fault localization fundamentally requires human insight. To this end, we are working on a Synoptic GUI that will support developers in this task. This GUI will allow developers to explore, query, and interact with the Synoptic models in real-time. For example, developers will be able to find out which of the logged traces pass through a set of partitions in the model and which event instances belong to a partition, as well as other information.

7. Conclusion

Logging is a popular debugging methodology. Unfortunately, large logs are often complex and difficult to analyze manually. This paper presented the design and evaluation of a tool called Synoptic, which builds a system model from its execution logs. Unlike other tools, Synoptic requires few inputs from the developer and can be applied to pre-existing logs.

The key to Synoptic's algorithm is its use of three types of mined temporal invariants to guide the model space exploration. Our formal evaluation showed that Synoptic's algorithm always makes progress and always finds a model that satisfies the mined invariants. Our case studies showed that Synoptic graphs improved developer confidence in the correctness of their systems, and were useful for finding bugs.

We believe that Synoptic bridges the gap between systems developed by developers with little to no training in formal methods, and a suite of methods developed by the formal methods community. Synoptic is an open-source tool (`http://synoptic.googlecode.com`) and has met the expectations of FSE artifact evaluation committee.

Acknowledgments

This work is supported by the National Science Foundation under grant CNS-0963754 and under grant #0937060 to the Computing Research Association for the CIFellows Project. This work is also supported by the Saarbrücken Graduate School of Computer Science, which receives funding from the DFG as part of the Excellence Initiative of the German Federal and State Governments.

References

[1] M. Acharya, T. Xie, J. Pei, and J. Xu. Mining API Patterns as Partial Orders from Source Code: From Usage Scenarios to Specifications. In *Proc. of FSE*, 2007.

[2] D. Alrajeh, J. Kramer, A. Russo, and S. Uchitel. Learning Operational Requirements from Goal Models. In *Proc. of ICSE*, 2009.

[3] D. Angluin. Finding Patterns Common to a Set of Strings. *Journal of Computer and System Sciences*, 21(1):46 – 62, 1980.

[4] I. Beschastnikh, J. Abrahamson, Y. Brun, and M. D. Ernst. Synoptic: Studying Logged Behavior with Inferred Models. In *Proc. of FSE*, 2011.

[5] A. W. Biermann and J. A. Feldman. On the Synthesis of Finite-State Machines from Samples of Their Behavior. *IEEE Trans. Comput.*, 21(6):592–597, 1972.

[6] L. Blum and M. Blum. Toward a Mathematical Theory of Inductive Inference. *Information and Control*, 28(2):125 – 155, 1975.

[7] E. Clarke, O. Grumberg, S. Jha, Y. Lu, and H. Veith. Counterexample-guided Abstraction Refinement. In *Computer Aided Verification*, pages 154–169. Springer, 2000.

[8] C. Damas et al. Generating Annotated Behavior Models from End-User Scenarios. *IEEE TSE*, 31(12), 2005.

[9] C. Damas, B. Lambeau, and A. van Lamsweerde. Scenarios, Goals, and State Machines: a Win-Win Partnership for Model Synthesis. In *Proc. of FSE*, 2006.

[10] W. Damm and D. Harel. LSCs: Breathing Life into Message Sequence Charts. *Form. Meth. Syst. Des.*, 19(1), 2001.

[11] G. de Caso, V. Braberman, D. Garbervetsky, and S. Uchitel. Validation of Contracts Using Enabledness Preserving Finite State Abstractions. In *Proc. of ICSE*, 2009.

[12] M. B. Dwyer, G. S. Avrunin, and J. C. Corbett. Patterns in Property Specifications for Finite-State Verification. In *Proc. of ICSE*, 1999.

[13] T. Elomaa. Partition-Refining Algorithms for Learning Finite State Automata. In *Proc. of ISMIS*, 2002.

[14] K. Fisler and M. Y. Vardi. Bisimulation Minimization and Symbolic Model Checking. *Formal Methods in System Design*, 21(1):39–78, 2002.

[15] D. Giannakopoulou and J. Magee. Fluent Model Checking for Event-Based Systems. In *Proc. of FSE*, 2003.

[16] E. M. Gold. Language Identification in the Limit. *Information and Control*, 10(5):447–474, 1967.

[17] Welcome to Apache Hadoop!, `http://hadoop.apache.org/`. Accessed March 9, 2011.

[18] D. Harel, H. Kugler, and A. Pnueli. Synthesis Revisited: Generating Statechart Models from Scenario-Based Requirements. *Form. Meth. in Soft. and Sys. Modeling*, 3393, 2005.

[19] IPv4 Specification, Record Route option. `http://www.ietf.org/rfc/rfc791.txt`. Pg. 20, 21. Accessed March 9, 2011.

[20] IPv4 Specification, Timestamp option. `http://www.ietf.org/rfc/rfc791.txt`. Pg. 22, 23. Accessed March 9, 2011.

[21] ITU. Message Sequence Charts, 2000.

[22] G. Jiang, H. Chen, C. Ungureanu, and K. Yoshihira. Multi-resolution Abnormal Trace Detection Using Varied-length N-grams and Automata. In *Proc. of ICAC*, 2005.

[23] E. Katz-Bassett, H. V. Madhyastha, V. K. Adhikari, C. Scott, J. Sherry, P. van Wesep, T. Anderson, and A. Krishnamurthy. Reverse Traceroute. In *Proc. of NSDI*, 2010.

[24] I. Krka, Y. Brun, G. Edwards, and N. Medvidovic. Synthesizing Partial Component-Level Behavior Models from System Specifications. In *Proc. of FSE*, 2009.

[25] I. Krka, Y. Brun, D. Popescu, J. Garcia, and N. Medvidovic. Using Dynamic Execution Traces and Program Invariants to Enhance Behavioral Model Inference. In *Proc. of ICSE*, 2010.

[26] K. Li and P. Hudak. Memory Coherence in Shared Virtual Memory Systems. *ACM Trans. Comput. Syst.*, 7:321–359, November 1989.

[27] D. Lo and S.-C. Khoo. QUARK: Empirical Assessment of Automaton-based Specification Miners. In *Proc. of WCRE*, 2006.

[28] D. Lo and S.-C. Khoo. SMArTIC: Towards Building an Accurate, Robust and Scalable Specification Miner. In *Proc. of FSE*, 2006.

[29] D. Lo, L. e. Mariani, and M. Pezzè. Automatic Steering of Behavioral Model Inference. In *Proc. of FSE*, 2009.

[30] D. Lorenzoli, L. Mariani, and M. Pezzè. Automatic Generation of Software Behavioral Models. In *Proc. of ICSE*, 2008.

[31] J.-G. Lou, Q. Fu, Y. Wang, and J. Li. Mining Dependency in Distributed Systems through Unstructured Logs Analysis. *SIGOPS Oper. Syst. Rev.*, 44:91–96, March 2010.

[32] J. G. Lou, Q. Fu, S. Yang, Y. Xu, and J. Li. Mining Invariants from Console Logs for System Problem Detection. In *Proc. of ATC*, 2010.

[33] L. Mariani and M. Pezzè. Dynamic Detection of COTS Component Incompatibility. *IEEE Software*, 24(5):76–85, September/October 2007.

[34] R. Paige and R. E. Tarjan. Three Partition Refinement Algorithms. *SIAM J. Comput.*, 16(6):973–989, 1987.

[35] L. Pitt and M. K. Warmuth. The Minimum Consistent DFA Problem Cannot be Approximated Within any Polynomial. *J. ACM*, 40(1):95–142, 1993.

[36] PlanetLab | An open platform for developing, deploying, and accessing planetary-scale services, `https://www.planet-lab.org`. Accessed March 9, 2011.

[37] S. P. Reiss and M. Renieris. Encoding Program Executions. In *Proc. of ICSE*, 2001.

[38] D. Sangiorgi. On the Origins of Bisimulation and Coinduction. *ACM Trans. Program. Lang. Syst.*, 31(4):1–41, 2009.

[39] S. Schneider, I. Beschastnikh, S. Chernyak, M. D. Ernst, and Y. Brun. Synoptic: Summarizing System Logs with Refinement. In *Proc. of SLAML*, 2010.

[40] J. Tan, X. Pan, S. Kavulya, R. G, and P. Narasimhan. SALSA: Analyzing Logs as StAte Machines. In *Proc. of WASL*, 2008.

[41] J. Tan, X. Pan, S. Kavulya, R. G, and P. Narasimhan. Mochi: Visual Log-Analysis Based Tools for Debugging Hadoop. In *Proc. of WASL*, 2009.

[42] S. Uchitel, J. Kramer, and J. Magee. Behaviour Model Elaboration Using Partial Labelled Transition Systems. In *Proc. of FSE*, 2003.

[43] S. Uchitel, J. Kramer, and J. Magee. Incremental Elaboration of Scenario-Based Specifications and Behavior Models Using Implied Scenarios. *ACM TOSEM*, 13(1), 2004.

[44] J. Whittle and J. Schumann. Generating Statechart Designs From Scenarios. In *Proc. of ICSE*, 2000.

[45] W. Xu, L. Huang, A. Fox, D. Patterson, and M. Jordan. Experience Mining Google's Production Console Logs. In *Proc. of SLAML*, 2010.

[46] W. Xu, L. Huang, A. Fox, D. Patterson, and M. I. Jordan. Detecting Large-Scale System Problems by Mining Console Logs. In *Proc. of SOSP*, 2009.

[47] J. Yang and D. Evans. Automatically Inferring Temporal Properties for Program Evolution. In *Proc. of ISSRE*, 2004.

[48] J. Yang and D. Evans. Dynamically Inferring Temporal Properties. In *Proc. of PASTE*, 2004.

[49] D. Yuan, H. Mai, W. Xiong, L. Tan, Y. Zhou, and S. Pasupathy. Sherlog: Error Diagnosis by Connecting Clues from Run-Time Logs. In *Proc. of ASPLOS*, 2010.

Path Exploration based on Symbolic Output

Dawei Qi, Hoang D.T. Nguyen, Abhik Roychoudhury
School of Computing, National University of Singapore
{dawei,nguyend1,abhik}@comp.nus.edu.sg

ABSTRACT

Efficient program path exploration is important for many software engineering activities such as testing, debugging and verification. However, enumerating all paths of a program is prohibitively expensive. In this paper, we develop a partitioning of program paths based on the program output. Two program paths are placed in the same partition if they derive the output similarly, that is, the symbolic expression connecting the output with the inputs is the same in both paths. Our grouping of paths is gradually created by a smart path exploration. Our experiments show the benefits of the proposed path exploration in test-suite construction.

Our path partitioning produces a semantic signature of a program — describing all the different symbolic expressions that the output can assume along different program paths. To reason about changes between program versions, we can therefore analyze their semantic signatures. In particular, we demonstrate the applications of our path partitioning in debugging of software regressions.

Categories and Subject Descriptors

D.2.5 [**Software Engineering**]: Testing and Debugging—*Testing tools, Symbolic execution*

General Terms

Experimentation, Performance, Reliability

Keywords

Path Exploration, Relevant Slice Condition, Symbolic Execution

1. INTRODUCTION

Programs follow paths. Indeed a program path constitutes a "unit" of program behavior in many software engineering activities, notably in software testing and debugging. Use of program paths to capture underlying program behavior is evidenced in techniques such as Directed Automated Random Testing or DART [8] - which try to achieve path coverage in test-suite construction.

Why do we attempt to cover more paths in software testing? The implicit assumption here is that by covering more paths, we are likely to cover more of the possible behaviors that can be exhibited by a program. However, as is well known, path enumeration is extremely expensive. Hence any method which covers various possible behaviors of a given program while avoiding path enumeration, can be extremely useful for software testing.

We note that software testing typically involves checking the program output for a given input - whether the observed output is same as the "expected" output. Hence, instead of enumerating individual program paths, we could focus on all the different ways in which the program output is computed from the program inputs. In other words, we can define an output as a symbolic expression in terms of the program inputs. Thus, given a program P, we seek to enumerate all the different possible symbolic expressions which describe how the output will be computed in terms of the inputs. Of course, the symbolic expression defining the output (in terms of the inputs) will be different along different program paths. However, we expect that the number of such symbolic expressions to be substantially lower than the number of program paths. In other words, a large number of paths can be considered "equivalent" since the symbolic expressions describing the output are the same.

To illustrate our observation, let us consider the program in Figure 1. The output variable `out` can be summarized as follows.

```
int x,y,z; // input variables
int out; // output variable
int a;
int b = 2;
scanf("%d %d %d",&x,&y,&z);
if(x - y > 0) //b1
    a = x;
else
    a = y;
if(x + y > 10) //b2
    b = a;
if(z*z > 3)  //b3
    printf("square(z) > 3 \n");
else
    printf("square(z) <=  3 \n");
out = b; //slicing criteria
```

Figure 1: Sample program

- If $x - y > 0$ and $x + y > 10$, then $out == x$
- If $x - y \leq 0$ and $x + y > 10$, then $out == y$
- If $x + y \leq 10$, then $out == 2$

The summary given in the preceding forms a "semantic signature" of the program as far as the output variable `out` is concerned. Note that there are *only three* cases in the semantic signature -

Permission to make digital or hard copies of all or part of this work for personal or classroom use is granted without fee provided that copies are not made or distributed for profit or commercial advantage and that copies bear this notice and the full citation on the first page. To copy otherwise, to republish, to post on servers or to redistribute to lists, requires prior specific permission and/or a fee.
ESEC/FSE'11, September 5–9, 2011, Szeged, Hungary.
Copyright 2011 ACM 978-1-4503-0443-6/11/09 ...$10.00.

whereas there are *eight paths* in the program. Thus, such a semantic signature can be much more concise than an enumeration of all paths.

In this paper, we develop a method to compute such a semantic signature for a given program. Our semantic signature is computed via dynamic path exploration. While exploring the paths of a program, we establish a natural partitioning of paths *on-the-fly* based on program dependencies - such that only one path in a partition is explored. Thus, for the example program in Figure 1 only three execution traces corresponding to the three cases will be explored. For test-suite construction, we can then construct only three tests corresponding to the three cases in the semantic signature.

How do we partition paths? The answer to this question lies in the computation of the *output* variable. We consider two program paths to be "equivalent" if they have the same relevant slice [9] with respect to the program output. A relevant slice is the transitive closure of dynamic data, control and potential dependencies. Data and control dependencies capture statements which affect the output by getting executed; on the other hand, potential dependencies capture statements which affect the program output by *not* getting executed. In Figure 1, even if line 11 is not executed, the output statement in line 16 is potentially dependent on the branch in line 10. This is to capture the fact that if line 10 is evaluated differently, the assignment in line 11 will be executed leading different values flowing to the output `out`. We base our path partitioning on relevant slices to capture all possible flows into the output variable - whether by the execution of certain statements or their non-execution.

The contributions of this paper can be summarized as follows. We present a mechanism to partition program paths based on the program output. The grouping of paths is done by efficient dynamic path exploration - where paths sharing the same relevant slice naturally get grouped together. We show that our smart path exploration is much more time efficient as opposed to full path exploration via path enumeration. Our efficient path exploration method has immediate benefits in software testing. Since our path exploration naturally groups several paths together - it is much more efficient than the full path exploration (as in Directed Automated Random Testing or DART) as evidenced by experiments. Moreover, since several paths are grouped as "equivalent" in our method (meaning that these paths compute the output similarly), the test-suite generated from our path exploration will also be concise.

Secondly, we show the application of our path partitioning method in reasoning about program versions, in particular, for debugging the root-cause of software regressions. While trying to introduce new features to a program, existing functionality often breaks; this is commonly called as software regression. Given two program versions P, P' and a test t which passes in P while failing in P' — we seek to find a bug report explaining the root cause of the failure of t in P'. In an earlier work [14], we presented the DARWIN approach for root causing software regressions. The DARWIN approach constructs and composes the path conditions of test t in program versions P, P' in trying to come up with a bug report explaining an observed regression. In this work, we show that computing and composing the logical condition over a relevant slice (also called *relevant-slice condition* throughout the paper) produces more pinpointed bug reports in a shorter time — as opposed to computing and composing path conditions. The reason for obtaining shorter bug reports in lesser time comes from the path conditions containing irrelevant information which are filtered out in *relevant-slice conditions*. Hence *relevant-slice conditions* are smaller formulae, which are constructed and solved (via Satisfiability Modulo Theory solvers) more efficiently.

2. OVERVIEW

We begin with a few definitions.

DEFINITION 1 (PATH CONDITION). *Given a program P and a test input t, let π be the execution trace of t in P. The path condition of π, say pc_π is a quantifier free first order logic formula which is satisfied by exactly the set of inputs executing π in program P. Clearly, $t \models pc_\pi$.*

The path condition is computed through symbolic execution. During symbolic execution, we interpret each statement and update the symbolic state to represent the effects of the statements (such as assignments) on program variables. At every conditional branch, we compute a branch constraint, which is a formula over the program's input variables which must be satisfied for the branch to be evaluated in the same direction as the concrete execution. The result of symbolic execution is a path condition, which is a conjunction of constraints corresponding to all branches along the path. Any input that satisfies the path condition generated by executing an input t is guaranteed to follow the same path as t. We take the following example to show that the effect of assignments is also considered in path conditions. The path condition for input $\langle x == 0 \rangle$ is $\neg(x - 1 > 0)$, that is, the effect of the assignment in line 4 is considered.

```
1 int x; //input variable
2 int a = 0;
3 scanf("%d",&x);
4 x = x - 1;
5 if(x > 0)
6     a = 1;
7 out = a;
```

Figure 2: Example to show path condition and *relevant-slice condition* computation

We now define slice conditions, which are path conditions computed over slices.

DEFINITION 2 (DYNAMIC SLICE CONDITION). *Given a program P, a test input t and a slicing criteria C — let π be the execution trace of t in P. Let $\pi\mid_C$ denote the projection of π w.r.t. the dynamic slice of C in π. In other words, a statement instance s in π is included in the projection $\pi\mid_C$ if and only if s is in the backward dynamic slice of C on π. The dynamic slice condition of C in π is the path condition computed over the projected trace $\pi\mid_C$.*

Slice conditions are weaker than path conditions, that is, $pc_\pi \Rightarrow dsc_{(\pi,C)}$ where $dsc_{(\pi,C)}$ is the dynamic slice condition of any slicing criteria C in π (see our technical report [13] for a simple proof of this claim). We now refine dynamic slice condition to *relevant-slice condition* - the central concept behind our path partitioning. But first, let us recall the notion of potential dependencies and relevant slices [1,9].

DEFINITION 3 (POTENTIAL DEPENDENCE [1]). *Given an execution trace π, let s be a statement instance and br be a branch instance that is before s in π. We say that s is potentially dependent on br iff. there exists a variable v used in s such that (i) v is not defined between br and s in trace π but there exists another path σ from br to s along which v is defined, and (ii) evaluating br differently may cause this untraversed path σ to be executed.*

An example of potential for the program in Figure 1 is shown in Figure 3.

We now introduce the notion of a relevant slice, and *relevant-slice condition*, a logical formula computed over a relevant slice.

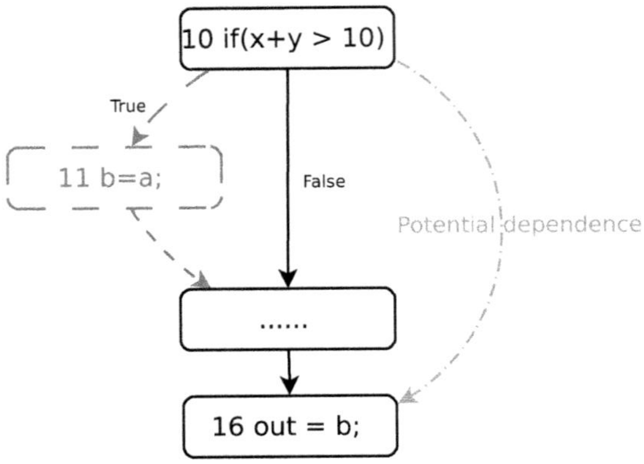

Figure 3: Example of potential dependence. The solid arrows denote the execution path. According to Definition 3, (i) the variable b is not defined between line 10 and line 16 but there exists a path (though line 11) along which b is defined, and (ii) evaluating the branch at line 10 differently may cause the path through line 11 to be executed. Therefore, line 16 is potentially dependent on line 10.

DEFINITION 4 (RELEVANT SLICE). *Given an execution trace π and a slicing criteria C in π, the relevant slice in π w.r.t. C contains a statement instance s in π iff. $C \rightsquigarrow s$ where $\rightsquigarrow$ denotes the transitive closure of dynamic data, control and potential dependence.*

Note that our definition of relevant slice is slightly different from the standard definition of relevant slice [1,9]. In standard relevant slicing algorithm, if a statement instance A is included only by potential dependence, the statement instances that are only control dependent by A are not included in the relevant slice. We have removed this restriction to simplify the definition of relevant slice, it is simply the transitive closure of three kinds of program dependencies — dynamic data dependencies, dynamic control dependencies and potential dependencies. In the rest of the paper, all appearances of relevant slice and *relevant-slice condition* refer to this simplified definition of relevant slice.

DEFINITION 5 (RELEVANT SLICE CONDITION). *Given an execution trace π and a slicing criteria C in π, the relevant slice condition in π w.r.t. criterion C is the path condition computed over the statement instances of π which are included in the relevant slice of C in π.*

We take the example program in Figure 2 to show that the effect of assignments is also considered in *relevant-slice condition* computation (just as assignments are considered in path condition computation). Let the slicing criteria be the value of `out` in line 7. The relevant slice for input $\langle x == 0\rangle$ is {2,3,4,5,7} and the corresponding *relevant-slice condition* is $\neg(x - 1 > 0)$. That is, the effect of the assignment in line 4 is considered.

We use the simple program in Figure 1 to illustrate the advantage of using *relevant-slice condition* in dynamic path exploration. The slicing criteria is the variable `out` at line 16. Since each statement is executed once, we do not distinguish between different execution instances of the same statement in this example.

We use the executed branch sequence annotated with directions to represent an execution trace. For example, the trace for input $\langle x == 6, y == 2, z == 2\rangle$ of the program in Figure 1 is denoted as $[b1^t, b2^f, b3^t]$. Let us take the input $\langle x == 6, y == 2, z == 2\rangle$ to see the differences between path condition, dynamic slice condition and *relevant-slice condition*. Given the trace $[b1^t, b2^f, b3^t]$ corresponding to input $\langle x == 6, y == 2, z == 2\rangle$, the path condition along this execution is $(x - y > 0) \wedge \neg(x + y > 10) \wedge (z * z > 3)$.

For the execution path of $\langle x == 6, y == 2, z == 2\rangle$, the dynamic backward slice result w.r.t. the slicing criteria at line 16 is {4,16} - it contains no branches. The path condition computed over the statements in the dynamic slice (or the dynamic slice condition) is simply the formula *true*.

Different from dynamic backward slicing, relevant slicing also includes the statement instances that could potentially affect the slicing criteria. For example, if evaluating a branch differently could affect the slicing criteria — such a branch is included in the relevant slice, even though it is not contained in the dynamic backward slice. In the example program, the branch at line 10 can potentially affect the value of *out* in the slicing criteria. This is because if the branch in line 10 is evaluated differently (to true), the variable b is re-defined (in line 11) which affects the output variable *out*. Hence the relevant slice contains line 10. The entire relevant slice is {4,5,10,16}, and the *relevant-slice condition* on it is $\neg(x + y > 10)$. Any input t satisfying the *relevant-slice condition* $\neg(x + y > 10)$ has the same symbolic expression for the output `out`, which in this case turns out be the constant value 2.

As mentioned earlier, program paths can be partitioned based on the input-output relation. *Relevant-slice condition* perfectly serves this purpose. If two paths have the same relevant slice with output being the slicing criteria, then they have the same input-output relation. The path partitions of the program in Figure 1 are shown in Figure 4. The grey nodes in Figure 4 are the statements that are contained in the relevant slice w.r.t. to the unique slicing criteria at line 16 in Figure 1. As we can see from Figure 4, based on the relevant slice, we can group the eight program paths into three path partitions.

Just like the DART approach [8] uses path conditions to dynamically explore paths in a program, *relevant-slice condition* can be used to explore the possible symbolic expressions that the program output can be assigned to. How would such an exploration proceed? Suppose we simply use *relevant-slice condition* to replace path condition in DART's path exploration. Given a *relevant-slice condition* $\psi_1 \wedge \psi_2 \wedge \ldots \wedge \psi_{k-1} \wedge \psi_k$ — we construct k sub-formulae of the form of $\psi_1 \wedge \psi_2 \ldots \wedge \psi_{i-1} \wedge \neg\psi_i$, where $1 \leq i \leq k$. The path exploration is done by solving these formulae to get new inputs and iteratively applying this process to the new inputs. Note that each sub-formula shares a common prefix with the *relevant-slice condition*. Now, we examine the effectiveness of this simple solution on the program in Figure 1. Depth-first exploration strategy is used, and path exploration terminates when no new sub-formulae are generated. Let the initial input be $\langle x == 6, y == 2, z == 2\rangle$, the path for this input is $[b1^t, b2^f, b3^t]$. The entire path exploration process is shown in Table 1. The "from" column of Table 1 can be understood as follows. If the "from" column contains $\alpha.\beta$, it means that the current input is generated by negating the βth branch constraint of the *relevant-slice condition* in the αth row.

Recall from Section 1 that we expect the following three symbolic expressions for *out* to be explored.

- $x - y > 0 \wedge x + y > 10$: `out` $== x$
- $\neg(x - y > 0) \wedge x + y > 10$: `out` $== y$
- $\neg(x + y > 10)$: `out` $== 2$

As we can see from Table 1, no path having *relevant-slice condition* $\neg(x - y > 0) \wedge (x + y > 10)$ is explored. Therefore, this feasible *relevant-slice condition* is missed by the exploration process. In addition, the *relevant-slice condition* $\neg(x + y > 10)$ is explored

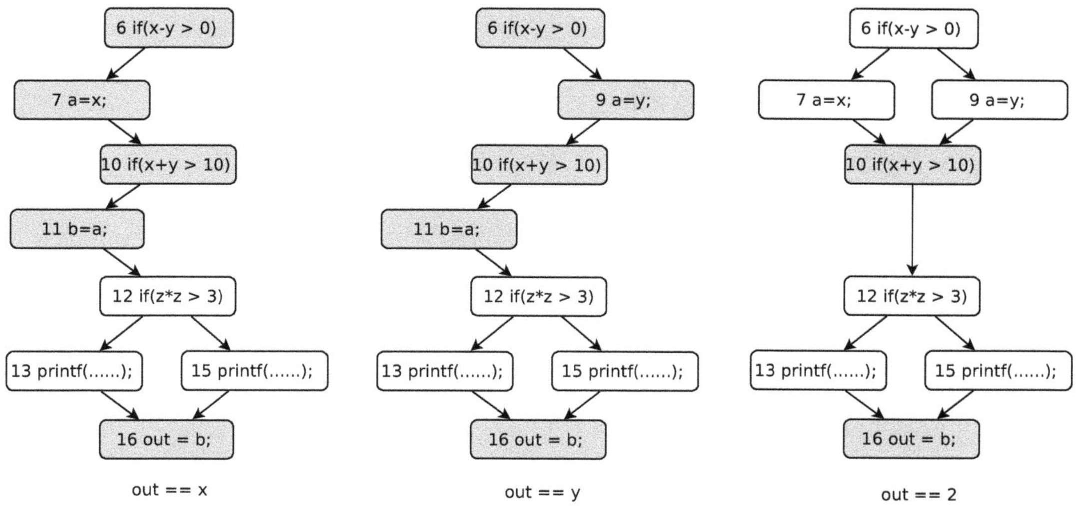

Figure 4: Path partitions of the example in Figure 1

several times. Thus, we cannot simply replace path condition with *relevant-slice condition* in DART's path exploration.

Let us examine closely what went wrong in the path exploration of Table 1. In particular, the input in the third row is generated by negating the second branch condition of the *relevant-slice condition* in second row in Table 1. That is, when we solve $(x - y > 0) \wedge \neg(x + y > 10)$, we get an input $\langle x == 6, y == 2, z == 2\rangle$ whose *relevant-slice condition* is $\neg(x + y > 10)$. The branch condition $(x - y > 0)$ disappears in the new *relevant-slice condition* because the corresponding branch is not contained in the relevant slice anymore. In contrast, DART follows certain path-prefixing properties — if $\psi_1 \wedge \psi_2 \ldots \wedge \psi_{i-1} \wedge \psi_i$ is the prefix of a path condition (for some program input), the path condition of any input satisfying $\psi_1 \wedge \psi_2 \ldots \wedge \psi_{i-1} \wedge \neg\psi_i$ will have $\psi_1 \wedge \psi_2 \ldots \wedge \psi_{i-1} \wedge \neg\psi_i$ as a prefix. Such a property does not hold for *relevant-slice condition*. Hence, simply replacing path condition with *relevant-slice condition* in DART not only causes redundant path exploration but also makes the exploration incomplete (in terms of possible symbolic expressions that the output variable may assume).

We have developed a path exploration method which avoids the aforementioned problems. While exploring (groups of) paths based on *relevant-slice condition*, our method re-orders the constraints in the *relevant-slice condition*. The path exploration is based on reordered *relevant-slice condition*. A reordered *relevant-slice condition* satisfies the following property (which also holds for path conditions): if $\psi_1 \wedge \psi_2 \ldots \wedge \psi_{i-1} \wedge \psi_i$ is a prefix of a reordered *relevant-slice condition*, the reordered *relevant-slice condition* of any input satisfying $\psi_1 \wedge \psi_2 \ldots \wedge \psi_{i-1} \wedge \neg\psi_i$ has $\psi_1 \wedge \psi_2 \ldots \wedge \psi_{i-1} \wedge \neg\psi_i$ as a prefix.

3. OUR APPROACH

In this section, we give our path exploration algorithm based on *relevant-slice condition*. We then give theorems on the completeness of our path exploration algorithm. Throughout the paper, we assume that the slicing criteria is in a basic block that post-dominates the entry of the program.

First we introduce the following notations.

Notations. We use C to denote the unique slicing criteria. When used in a dynamic context, C refers to the last executed instance of the slicing criteria. Given a test case t, we use $\pi(t)$ to denote the execution path of t. We use $rs(sc, \pi)$ to denote the relevant slice on path π w.r.t. slicing criteria sc. We use $rsc(sc, \pi)$ to denote the relevant slice condition on path π w.r.t. slicing criteria sc. We use $reordered\_rsc(sc, \pi)$ to denote the reordered sequence of $rsc(sc, \pi)$. We use $br(\psi)$ to denote the branch instance of a branch condition ψ.

3.1 Path exploration algorithm

We now present our path exploration method which operates on a given program P. All relevant slices and *relevant-slice conditions* are calculated on the same program P with respect to a slicing criteria C (which refers to the program output).

We group paths based on *relevant-slice condition*. As explained in the last section, a DART-like search based on *relevant-slice conditions* is incomplete, that is, not all possible symbolic expressions that the output may assume will be covered. For this reason, we reorder the *relevant-slice conditions*.

Our path exploration algorithm is shown in Algorithm 1. The core of the algorithm is the *reorder* procedure, which reorders the *relevant-slice conditions*. When we compute the *relevant-slice condition*, we get a sequence of branch conditions – ordered according to the sequence in which they are traversed. We use the $reorder$ function to reorder the branch conditions, after which the path exploration will be performed based on the reordered sequence of branch conditions.

The $reorder$ procedure is given in Algorithm 1. The reordering works in a quick-sort-like fashion. In each call to *reorder*, we split the to-be-reordered sequence into two sub-sequences. Suppose the last branch condition in the sequence is from branch instance b_k. Then b_k is used as the "pivot" in the splitting process. If a branch instance b is in the backward relevant slice of b_k, then the branch condition of b is placed before the branch condition of b_k. Otherwise, the branch condition of b is placed after the branch condition of b_k. Then we recursively call the *reorder* procedure to reorder the two sub-sequences.

We show the *reorder* procedure in action in Figure 5. Note that our reordering is done on branch conditions in a *relevant-slice condition*. Since there is a unique branch condition for each branch instance in the execution trace, the example in Figure 5 is on branch instances for simplicity. On the left of Figure 5, the dependencies among all the branch instances are provided. If there is an arrow

No.	from	input	path	RSC
1		$\langle 6,2,2\rangle$	$[b1^t, b2^f, b3^t]$	$\neg(x+y>10)$
2	1.1	$\langle 6,5,2\rangle$	$[b1^t, b2^t, b3^t]$	$(x-y>0)\wedge(x+y>10)$
3	2.2	$\langle 6,2,2\rangle$	$[b1^t, b2^f, b3^t]$	$\neg(x+y>10)$
4	2.1	$\langle 2,6,2\rangle$	$[b1^f, b2^f, b3^t]$	$\neg(x+y>10)$

Table 1: Path exploration based on *relevant-slice conditions* for example in Figure 1

No.	from	input	path	RSC	reordered RSC
1		$\langle 6,2,2\rangle$	$[b1^t, b2^f, b3^t]$	$\neg(x+y>10)$	$\neg(x+y>10)$
2	1.1	$\langle 6,5,2\rangle$	$[b1^t, b2^t, b3^t]$	$(x-y>0)\wedge(x+y>10)$	$(x+y>10)\wedge(x-y>0)$
3	2.2	$\langle 5,6,2\rangle$	$[b1^f, b2^t, b3^t]$	$\neg(x-y>0)\wedge(x+y>10)$	$(x+y>10)\wedge\neg(x-y>0)$

Table 2: Path exploration with reordered *relevant-slice conditions* for example in Figure 1

Algorithm 1 Path exploration using *relevant-slice condition*

Input:
P : The program to test
t : An initial test case for P
C : A slicing criterion
Output:
T: A test-suite for P

$Stack = null$ // The stack of partial rsc to be explored
$Execute(t, 0)$
while $Stack$ is not empty **do**
  let $\langle f, j\rangle = pop(Stack)$
  if f is satisfiable **then**
    let μ be one input that satisfies f
    put μ into T
    $Execute(\mu, j)$
  end if
end while
return T

procedure $Execute(t, n)$
  execute t in P and compute *relevant-slice condition* rsc w.r.t. C
  let $rsc = \psi_1 \wedge \psi_2 \wedge \ldots \wedge \psi_{m-1} \wedge \psi_m$
  let $rsc' = reorder(rsc)$
  suppose $rsc' = \psi'_1 \wedge \psi'_2 \wedge \ldots \wedge \psi'_{m-1} \wedge \psi'_m$
  for all i from n+1 to m **do**
    let $h = (\psi'_1 \wedge \psi'_2 \wedge \ldots \wedge \psi'_{i-1} \wedge \neg\psi'_i)$
    push $\langle h, i\rangle$ into $Stack$
  end for
  return
end procedure

procedure $reorder(seq)$
  if $|seq| == 0$ **then**
    return seq
  end if
  let seq be $\psi_1 \wedge \psi_2 \wedge \ldots \wedge \psi_{k-1} \wedge \psi_k$
  $seq_1 = true, seq_2 = true$
  for all i from 1 to k-1 **do**
    if $br(\psi_i)$ is in relevant slice of $br(\psi_k)$ **then**
      $seq_1 = seq_1 \wedge \psi_i$
    else
      $seq_2 = seq_2 \wedge \psi_i$
    end if
  end for
  return $reorder(seq_1) \wedge \psi_k \wedge reorder(seq_2)$
end procedure

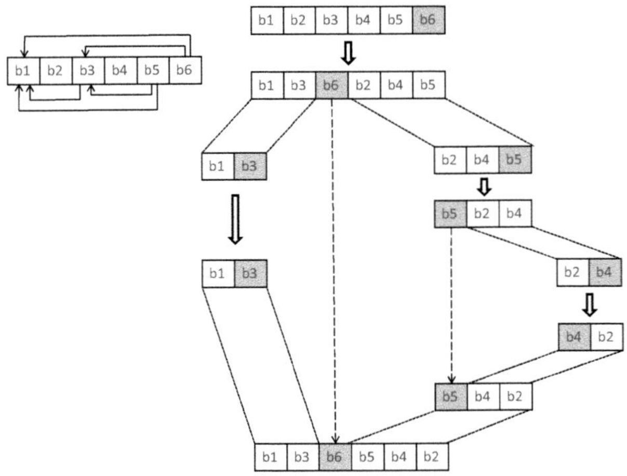

Figure 5: *Reorder* algorithm in action

from bj to bi, then bi is in the relevant slice of bj. The "pivot" in each reorder step is marked in dark; the other branches are reordered w.r.t to the "pivot". For example, initially `b6` is the pivot and we reorder `b1, ... b5` depending on whether they are in the relevant slice of `b6`.

In Algorithm 1, we use a stack to maintain the to-be-explored partial *relevant-slice conditions*. The main algorithm keeps on processing the formulae in the stack when it is not empty. In each iteration, the algorithm pops out one partial *relevant-slice condition* from the stack, and checks whether it is satisfiable or not. If it is satisfiable, we get a new input μ by solving the formula. The new input μ could lead to some unexplored *relevant-slice condition*. The *relevant-slice condition* for the execution trace of input μ is then explored, as shown by the procedure *Execute* in Algorithm 1. Given the execution trace of μ, the *relevant-slice condition* over this trace w.r.t. the slicing criteria C is first computed. The *relevant-slice condition* is reordered using the *reorder* procedure, and the to-be-explored partial *relevant-slice conditions* are pushed into the stack.

The second parameter of $Execute$ is used to avoid redundancy in path search. When $Execute$ is called with parameters t and n, let the reordered *relevant-slice condition* $reordered\_rsc(C, \pi(t))$ be $\psi'_1 \wedge \psi'_2 \wedge \ldots \wedge \psi'_{m-1} \wedge \psi'_m$. For any partial *relevant-slice condition* $\varphi_i = \psi'_1 \wedge \psi'_2 \wedge \ldots \wedge \psi'_{i-1} \wedge \neg\psi'_i$, $1 \leq i \leq n \leq m$, we know that φ_i has been pushed into the stack a-priori. So the for-loop in the *Execute* procedure starts from $n+1$ to avoid these explored partial *relevant-slice conditions*.

The path exploration of Algorithm 1 when employed on the program in Figure 1 leads to the *relevant-slice conditions* shown in Table 2. If the "from" column of Table 2 contains $\alpha.\beta$, it means that the current input is generated by negating the βth branch constraint of the reordered *relevant-slice condition* in the αth row. The path exploration based the reordered *relevant-slice condition* explores all possible *relevant-slice conditions* of the program.

3.2 Theorems

Due to space limit, the proofs of the theorems are omitted in this paper. The readers can refer to our technical report [13] for the proofs.

Assumptions. We assume that the SMT solver used to solve *relevant-slice conditions* is sound and complete. As mentioned earlier, we assume that the slicing criteria is in a basic block that post-dominates the entry of the program — this is the location of the program output. If the program contains *multiple outputs*, the slicing criteria can simply be a set of of primitive criteria of the form

$$\langle output\ variable, output\ location\rangle$$

Note that slicing can be performed on such a criteria (which is a set) without any change to our method.

THEOREM 3.1. *If the relevant-slice conditions of two paths π_1 and π_2 w.r.t. C are the same, then the variables used in the slicing criteria C have the same symbolic values in π_1 and π_2.*

In Theorem 3.1, we show that the *relevant-slice condition* determines the symbolic values of variables used in the slicing criteria — if the *relevant-slice conditions* of two paths are the same, the variables in the slicing criteria have the same symbolic values. Symbolic value can be computed by dynamic symbolic execution. Each symbolic value is an expression in terms of the program inputs. Let s be a statement instance in the path of input t, and v be a variable used in s. The symbolic value of v in s is an expression in terms of input variables. If the symbolic value of v is concretized with t, it must be the same as the value of v in s when the program is run concretely with input t.

THEOREM 3.2. *Given a program P and an execution trace $\pi(t)$ for input t in P, Algorithm 1 must explore an execution trace $\pi(t')$ for some input t' such that $\pi(t)$ and $\pi(t')$ share the same relevant-slice condition (irrespective of the initial test input with which Algorithm 1 is started) — provided the total number of relevant-slice conditions in P is bounded.*

In Theorem 3.2, given any feasible path π, we show that our path exploration algorithm is guaranteed to explore a path π' that shares the same *relevant-slice condition* with π. This establishes the completeness of our path search.

4. IMPLEMENTATION

In this section, we discuss our combined infra-structure for symbolic execution and dependency analysis of Java programs.

Our implementation is based on JSlice [17][1]. JSlice is an open-source dynamic slicing tool on Java bytecode. We have extended JSlice to compute *relevant-slice conditions*. The architecture of our extended JSlice is shown in Figure 6.

JSlice keeps the collected trace in a compressed form to achieve scalability. The compression is online — as the trace is generated it is simultaneously compressed and then slicing is done on

[1] http://jslice.sourceforge.net/

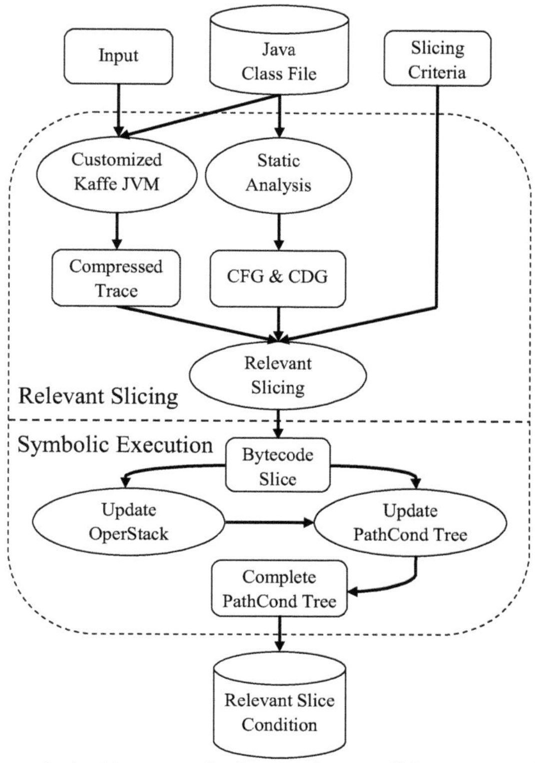

Figure 6: Architecture of *relevant-slice condition* computation

the compressed trace. The slicing algorithm works directly on the compressed trace. We design our extension of JSlice to retain this feature (of analyzing compressed traces without decompression).

In Figure 6, relevant slicing and symbolic execution are separated for ease of understanding. However, we do not need the entire relevant slicing result to start computing *relevant-slice condition* in the implementation. The process of constructing the *relevant-slice condition* is done along with the backward relevant slicing to achieve efficiency. Since the relevant slicing process is backward, we also compute the relevant slice condition via a backward symbolic execution which starts from the slicing criteria and stops at the beginning of the trace.

For backward symbolic execution, we keep a set of symbolic values which need to be explained. The symbolic value of a variable v is explained by either an assignment to v or by program input to v. Let us take the sample program in Figure 1 to show our backward symbolic execution on a relevant slice. Note that although we show this example at the source code level, our implementation is at the Java bytecode level. Suppose the input is $\langle x == 6, y == 5, z == 2\rangle$. The relevant slice for the execution trace of this input is $[5, 6, 7, 10, 11, 16]$. Backward symbolic execution along this trace is shown in Table 3.

To construct the *relevant-slice conditions*, we need to precisely represent the semantics of each bytecode type in the generated formula. There are more than 200 different bytecode types in the Java Virtual Machine instruction set, and all of them are handled in our implementation. Our implementation also handles native method calls (more details in the next paragraph). However, due to the JSlice version that our implementation is based on, currently we cannot handle programs with multi-threading and reflection.

In the original implementation of JSlice, the concrete operand values of most executed instructions are not stored in the compressed trace as they are not needed in the slicing process. How-

Relevant slice	Symbolic values	To be explained variables	Relevant slice condition
`16 out = b;`	$\{ out \to b \}$	$\{ b \}$	true
`11 b = a;`	$\{out \to a, b \to a \}$	$\{ a \}$	true
`10 if(x+y > 10)`	$\{out \to a, b \to a \}$	$\{ x, y \}$	$x + y > 10$
`7 a = x;`	$\{out \to x, b \to x, a \to x \}$	$\{ x, y \}$	$x + y > 10$
`6 if(x-y >0)`	$\{out \to x, b \to x, a \to x \}$	$\{ x, y \}$	$x - y > 0 \wedge x + y > 10$
`5 scanf("%d %d %d",&x,&y,&z);`	$\{out \to x, b \to x, a \to x \}$	$\{ x, y \}$	$x - y > 0 \wedge x + y > 10$

Table 3: Backward symbolic execution example

ever, these values are needed when the semantics of some operations cannot be precisely modelled. In such cases, we have to under-approximate the generated path condition/*relevant-slice condition* by concretizing certain symbolic values in the *relevant-slice condition*. For example, Java allows a program to use libraries written in other languages through native method call. Since the native calls cannot be traced in Java Virtual Machine, the symbolic return values from native calls cannot be precisely modelled. In this case, we simply concretize the symbolic return value from a native call using the concrete return value of the native call (therefore, the concrete return value of native calls are traced in our implementation).

In our implementation, we use the concept of execution index [20] to uniquely identify a statement instance across different paths. Two statement instances in different paths are the same iff. they have exactly the same "execution index". In its simplest form, we can use the path from root to a statement instance s in the Dynamic Control Dependence Graph of path π as the execution index of statement instance s in path π.

As mentioned in Section 3, we need to reorder the branch conditions in a *relevant-slice condition* in our path exploration process. Let $rs(C, \pi)$ be the relevant slice on trace π w.r.t. the slicing criteria C. Let $rsc(C, \pi)$ be the *relevant-slice condition* computed on $rs(C, \pi)$. To reorder the branch conditions in $rsc(C, \pi)$ using the *reorder* procedure shown in Algorithm 1, we need to compute a relevant slice using each branch instance in $rs(C, \pi)$ as the slicing criteria. Suppose there are m branch instances in $rs(C, \pi)$, our implementation traverses the trace π for m times to compute the m relevant slices. In future, we plan to speed up this process, by computing all m relevant slices at the same time of computing $rs(C, \pi)$. We also observe that there are a lot similarities among the slices w.r.t. different branch instances (used as slicing criteria) in the same trace. For example, if a branch instance b_i is in the relevant slice of branch instance b_j, then the relevant slice w.r.t. b_i is a subset of the relevant slice w.r.t. b_j. In future, we could exploit the similarities among these slices to further reduce the cost of our *reorder* procedure.

Our execution engine is a combined infra-structure for dynamic dependency analysis and dynamic symbolic execution. Thus, apart from computing *relevant-slice conditions*, we can simply disable the dependency analysis in our engine to compute path conditions. The path conditions and *relevant-slice conditions* generated from our tool are in the format of SMT2[2], which can be solved by various Satisfiability Modulo Theory or SMT solvers. In our implementation, we choose Z3 [4][3] as the SMT solver for our tool.

5. EXPERIMENTS

In the following, we first compare our *relevant-slice condition* based path exploration method with Directed Automated Random Testing (DART). We then present an application of *relevant-slice conditions* in the debugging of evolving programs.

5.1 Path exploration

We compare our path exploration algorithm with DART. The subject programs shown in Table 4 are from SIR [5] repository. The lines of code (LOC) in each program are also shown.

Recall that our path search is complete as supported by Theorem 3.2. However, the completeness is difficult to achieve in practice for several reasons. Two of the main reasons are the limited power of current SMT solvers and imprecise modelling of program semantics. Because of these reasons, our technique may miss a certain *relevant-slice condition* rsc_i when DART can explore a path whose *relevant-slice condition* is rsc_i. The example below explains how imprecise modelling of array can cause our implementation to be not as complete as DART in terms of *relevant-slice condition* coverage.

```
1  int x, y; //input
2  int out; //output
3  int a[2] = {0,1};
4  scanf("%d %d", &x, &y);
5  if(x > 0)
6      printf("x is greater than zero\n");
7  if(a[x]>0){
8      if(y > 0)
9          out = 1;
10     else
11         out = -1;
12 }else{
13     out = 0;
14 }
15 printf("%d\n", out);//slicing criteria
```

In our current implementation, we concretize symbolic array index using the value observed at execution time. Suppose the initial input for our method and DART are both $\langle x == 0, y == 0\rangle$. Due to the concretization of symbolic array index, the branch at line 7 cannot contribute a branch condition to either path condition or *relevant-slice condition*. The path condition and *relevant-slice condition* for $\langle x == 0, y == 0\rangle$ are $\neg(x > 0)$ and $true$ respectively. Since the *relevant-slice condition* for the initial input $\langle x == 0, y == 0\rangle$ is $true$ (containing no branch condition), our technique terminates. However, some *relevant-slice conditions* are missed by our technique. In particular, the *relevant-slice conditions* of paths that evaluate branch at line 7 to false are missed. In contrast, DART could explore all feasible paths (hence all *relevant-slice conditions*) of the above program. Although the branch at line 5 cannot directly affect the computation of *out*, it can help DART to negate the branch at line 7 due to the correlation between the two branches. If arrays are modelled precisely, this problem will disappear.

The "Completeness" column in Table 4 measures how much incompleteness in *relevant-slice condition* coverage is introduced

[2] http://combination.cs.uiowa.edu/smtlib/

[3] http://research.microsoft.com/en-us/um/redmond/projects/z3/

Subject prog.	Size (LOC)	Completeness	Time		#Testcases		Avg. formula size		#Solver calls	
			RSC	DART	RSC	DART	RSC	DART	RSC	DART
Tcas	113	100%	6.3s	13.1s	29	88	5744	64810	412	939
BinarySearchTree	175	75%	6.1s	58.6s	64	453	3836	49266	163	3188
OrdSet	211	79%	2.1s	7.4s	12	59	6444	55461	96	293
Schedule	257	100%	0.3s	15.4s	3	75	1808	13728	13	932
DisjointSet	102	100%	20.8s	64.8s	69	278	7643	170533	1192	3855

Table 4: Experiments in full program exploration

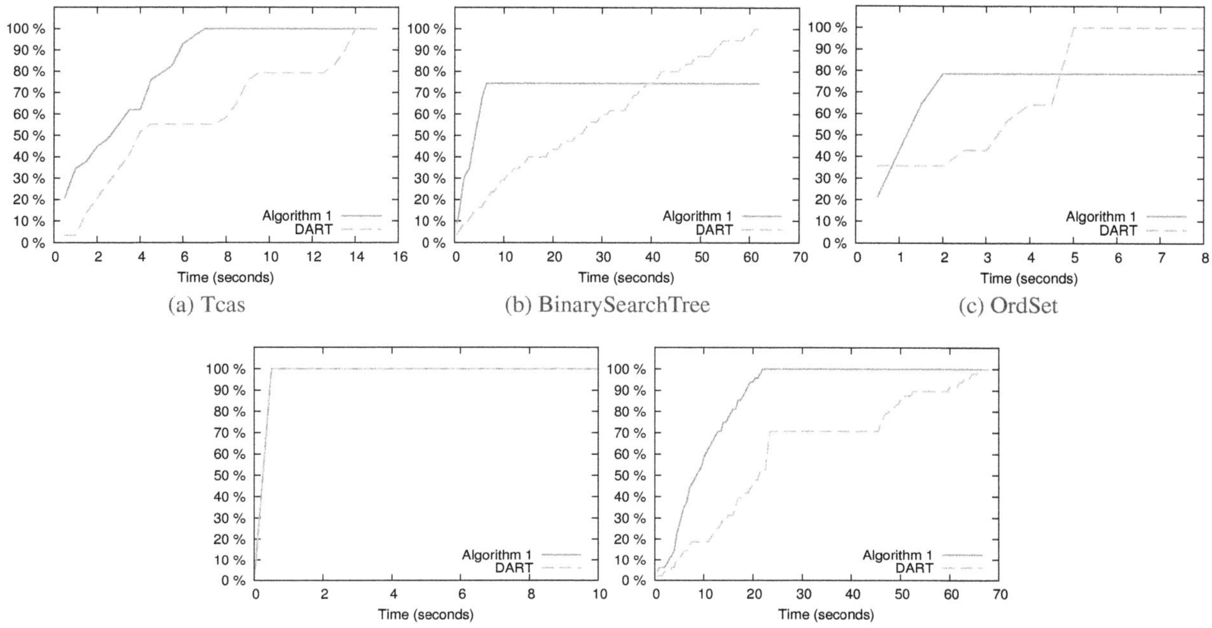

(a) Tcas (b) BinarySearchTree (c) OrdSet (d) Schedule (e) DisjointSet

Figure 7: Relevant-slice condition coverage comparison

by the imprecise modelling of program semantics in our implementation. The numbers in the "Completeness" column are computed as follows. Let the program being explored be P. We employ DART on P to explore program paths and construct a test-suite $T_{DART-ALL}$ which contains the set of all paths in P covered by DART. For each test case t in $T_{DART-ALL}$, we compute the *relevant-slice condition* on the execution trace of t and put this *relevant-slice condition* into a set $S_{DART-ALL}$. Similarly, we generate a test-suite T_{RSC} for program P using our path exploration method. For each test case t in T_{RSC}, we compute the *relevant-slice condition* on the execution trace of t and put this *relevant-slice condition* into a set S_{RSC}. Then the "Completeness" column in Table 4 is $\frac{|S_{RSC}|}{|S_{DART-ALL}|}$. As shown in Table 4, our method cannot always achieve 100 percent relevant slice coverage as compared to DART due to the imprecise modelling of program semantics in our implementation. Note that this does not affect the validity of the completeness claim in Theorem 3.2, the incompleteness is only in the implementation.

In columns 4-11 of Table 4, we compare the time, number of generated test cases, formula size and number of solver calls between our method and DART. The formula size is measured by the number of bytes in the SMT2 formula file. For getting these numbers, both our method (RSC) and the DART method are *run to completion*, and the running time is recorded. Note that the time reported in Table 4 includes the time taken in every steps of our method and DART. For example, the time taken by our method includes the time for program execution, relevant slicing, *relevant-slice condition* computation, branch condition reordering, formula solving, etc. As shown in Table 4, our technique takes much less time than DART. The efficiency comes from several sources. First, since we use *relevant-slice condition* instead of path condition, the formula size of our approach is much smaller than that of DART. This reduces the time taken by the solver. Second, the number of different *relevant-slice conditions* is considerably smaller than the number of path conditions. This reduces both the number of executions and the number of solver calls.

Figure 7 compares the *relevant-slice condition* coverage of our Algorithm 1 with Directed Automated Random Testing (DART) *under the same time limit.* Note that DART intends to achieve path coverage. However, as we have observed - several paths may have the same input-output relationship, and testing is always done by checking outputs. We check the number of *relevant-slice conditions* that are covered by the paths explored in DART search. As shown in Figure 7, our technique gets higher *relevant-slice condition* coverage then DART when the given time is short.

5.2 Debugging of evolving programs

The obvious application of *relevant-slice conditions* is in software testing - it groups program paths and can be used to efficiently generate a concise test-suite. We now show another application of *relevant-slice conditions* namely in the debugging of evolving pro-

Subject prog.	Stable version	Buggy version	Diff	Time		Debugging results	
				PC	RSC	PC	RSC
JLex	1.2.1 (7290 LOC)	1.1.1 (6984 LOC)	518 LOC	543 min	15 min	50 LOC	3 LOC
JTopas	0.8 (4514 LOC)	0.7 (5754 LOC)	2489 LOC	81 min	5 min	4 LOC	4 LOC

Table 5: DARWIN debugging results (LOC stands for Lines of Code)

grams. As a program evolves, functionality which worked earlier breaks. This is commonly known as software regressions. For any large scale software development, debugging the root-case of regressions is an extremely time consuming activity.

We applied our *relevant-slice conditions* on the DARWIN method for debugging evolving programs [14]. Given two program versions P and P', and a test case t which passes in P but fails in P', the work in [14] tries to find the root cause of the failure of t in P'. The debugging proceeds by computing and composing the path conditions of t in P and P', as follows.

First, the path conditions f and f' of t in P and P' are computed. We then compute the formula $f \wedge \neg f'$ as follows. Suppose f' is $f' = (\psi_1 \wedge \psi_2 \wedge \ldots \wedge \psi_m)$ where ψ_i are primitive constraints. The following m formulae $\{\varphi_i \mid 0 \le i < m\}$ are then solved where $\varphi_i \stackrel{def}{=} f \wedge \psi_1 \wedge \ldots \psi_i \wedge \neg\psi_{i+1}$. We invoke a Satisfiability Modulo Theory or SMT solver to solve the m formulae $\{\varphi_i \mid 0 \le i < m\}$. Finally, for every φ_i which is satisfiable, we can find a single line in the source code which is a potential error root cause — the branch corresponding to ψ_{i+1} (which is negated in φ_i).

We observe that the path conditions f and f' in the above method can be replaced by *relevant-slice conditions*. Path condition is not "goal-directed" — it contains the constraints of branches which are not "related" to the observable error. In particular, a path condition will typically contain constraints for branches which are not in the dynamic or relevant slice of the observable error. Consider the following example program

```
1   ... // input inp1, inp2
2   if (inp1 > 0)
3     x = inp1 + 1;
4   else
5     x = inp1 - 1;
6   if (inp2 > 0)
7     y = inp2 + 1
8   else
9     y = inp2 - 1;
10  ... // output x, y
```

Suppose the observed value of `x` is unexpected for `inp1 == inp2 == 0` because of a "bug" in line 2 (say, the condition should be `inp1 >= 0`). The path condition is $\neg(inp1 > 0) \wedge \neg(inp2 > 0)$. Clearly, the constraint $\neg(inp2 > 0)$ corresponding the the branch in line 6 is unrelated to the observable error (unexpected value of `x`). Indeed, line 6 is not in the dynamic slice or relevant slice of the slicing criterion corresponding to the output value of `x` in line 10.

Thus, due to the inherent parallelism in sequential programs, path conditions contain constraints for branches which are not in the slice of the observed error. Composing these path conditions for debugging then allows for such "unrelated" branches to be incorporated into the bug report (which is output by the debugging method). Indeed including these "unrelated" branch constraints increases the burden on the SMT solvers invoked by the DARWIN method, both in terms of the size of the formulae and the number of the formulae to solve. In addition, these "unrelated" branch constraints also introduce some false positives into the bug report produced by the DARWIN method.

Replacing path condition with *relevant-slice condition* in the DARWIN method resolves these issues. Thus, given a test case t that passes in the old version program P but fails in the new version program P' — we now compute g and g', the *relevant-slice condition* of t in P and P' respectively. We then solve $g \wedge \neg g'$ in a manner similar to the solving of $f \wedge \neg f'$ in DARWIN (where f, f' were the path conditions of t in programs P, P').

We compare the debugging result of DARWIN using *relevant-slice conditions* with the original DARWIN method (which uses path conditions) in Table 5.

Both methods are *fully* automated. We did not use the same SIR programs as used in Section 5.1 because debugging regression errors for SIR programs are usually trivial. This is because the difference between two SIR program versions is usually small. The first subject program being used is `JLex`[4]. `JLex` is a lexical analyzer generator written in Java. We use version 1.2.1 of `JLex` as the stable version, and version 1.1.1 as the buggy version. There are 6984 and 7290 lines of code in version 1.1.1 and version 1.2.2 respectively. The changes across version 1.1.1 and version 1.2.1 consist of 518 lines of code. In particular, the version 1.1.1 of `JLex` cannot recognize '\r' as the newline symbol, while in version 1.2.1 this bug is fixed. We use an input file manifesting this bug.

The experimental results from DARWIN using *relevant-slice conditions* vs. the original DARWIN method appears in Table 5. The original DARWIN method, which uses path conditions, takes 543 minutes (or 9 hours) to perform the debugging. The result of DARWIN is a bug report containing 50 lines of code, which are highlighted to the programmer as potential root-causes of the observable error. In contrast, DARWIN using *relevant-slice condition* takes only 15 minutes. The result is a bug report containing only 3 lines of code — potential root causes of the observed error. Indeed, the actual error root-cause lies in one of these three lines of code. Thus, by using *relevant-slice conditions* inside our DARWIN debugging method - we could avoid 47 false positives among the potential error causes which are reported to the programmer. Moreover, there is a huge savings in the debugging time (15 minutes vs 9 hours) which comes from the *relevant-slice conditions* being much smaller than path conditions.

We also conducted experiments using `JTopas` [5]as the subject program. `JTopas` is a Java library for parsing arbitrary text data. We use version 0.8 of `JTopas` as the stable version, and version 0.7 as the buggy version. There are 5754 and 4514 lines of code in version 0.7 and version 0.8 respectively. `JTopas` allows users to customize whitespace characters (i.e. characters that are considered as whitespace characters) by using function *setWhitespaces*. `JTopas` also uses a boolean field *_defaultWhitespaces* to control whether the default whitespace characters are used or the user-customized whitespace characters are used. To use the customized whitespace characters, *_defaultWhitespaces* has to be set to *false*. Unfortunately, the buggy `JTopas-0.7` does not reset the member *_defaultWhitespaces* leading to the default whitespace characters still being used instead of the customized ones although the user has specified the custom whitespace characters. In our experiment, we customize whitespace characters to {' ', '\r','\t'} ({' ', '\n', '\r','\t'} by default) and use an input file manifesting

[4] `http://www.cs.princeton.edu/~appel/modern/java/JLex/`

[5] `http://jtopas.sourceforge.net/jtopas/index.html`

the aforementioned bug. The debugging results of DARWIN using path condition and DARWIN using *relevant-slice condition* are shown in Table 5. The results from the original DARWIN method (using path condition) and DARWIN using *relevant-slice condition* are both four lines of code. They both contain the location where '\n' is treated differently between the two versions. The pinpointed location shows that the stable version does not consider '\n' as a whitespace. In contrast, the buggy version still treats '\n' as a whitespace because *_defaultWhitespaces* is *true* (even though whitespace characters have already been customized). From this clue, the programmer could easily infer that the member *_defaultWhitespaces* was not assigned to the correct value. Although using *relevant-slice condition* does not eliminate any false positives in the debugging result, it does reduce the time taken by DARWIN from 81 minutes to 5 minutes.

6. THREATS TO VALIDITY

Our path exploration does not try to cover all paths. Instead, we try to group paths based on symbolic outputs. This is done with the goal of test-suite construction, where testing will expose possible failures in the program. However, failure of a test case does not only come from unexpected outputs - it can also come from program crashes. Thus, for the paths which we do not explore if they contain program crashes - these will not be exposed by the test-suite computed by our technique. Realistically, our test-suite construction could be supplemented by techniques to statically detect possible program crashes, such as memory error detection [19].

Due to the conservative nature of static analysis used in computing relevant slice, our technique may under-approximate *relevant-slice conditions* in some situations. In that case, we may explore more than one paths that have the same *relevant-slice condition*. Consider the following program

```
101 if(x > 0){
102      p.num = 0;
103 }
104 out = q.num;
```

Suppose `p` and `q` never alias to each other. If the static analysis cannot determine the non-alias between `p` and `q`, line 104 is potential dependent on line 101 when the branch at line 101 is evaluated to false. Therefore, the branch at line 101 is included in relevant slice and our technique will try to explore both directions of the branch at line 101, which is unnecessary. Note that this under-approximation of *relevant-slice condition* only causes duplicated exploration of some *relevant-slice conditions*, it does not affect the completeness claim of our technique.

Although our technique considerably improves the efficiency of the path exploration, the path explosion problem still exist. In the worst case, the number of *relevant-slice conditions* grows exponentially with the size of the program.

7. RELATED WORK

The technique proposed in this paper is based on dynamic path exploration [8, 16] and relevant slicing [1, 9, 17]. Our technique improves existing dynamic path exploration techniques by grouping several paths together using *relevant-slice condition*. Existing dynamic path exploration tries to achieve path coverage. In contrast, our technique only selects one path from each *relevant-slice condition* to explore.

There are several works which focus on improving the efficiency of dynamic path exploration. In [6], function summaries are generated and exploited. In [7], the grammar of the input is used to avoid generating large percentage of invalid inputs. Our approach is orthogonal to these approaches, therefore, our approach can be combined together with any of these approaches to further improve the efficiency of the path search.

In [15], a program is statically decomposed into several path families, where each path family contains several paths that share similar behavior. Instead of analyzing each path individually, a program can be analyzed at the granularity of path family. The authors of [15] also compute a "path family condition" for each path family, which could characterize that path family. The path partition based on *relevant-slice condition* is different from the notion of "path family" in [15] in the sense that "path family" is more general. For example, all program paths in Figure 1 can be grouped into one path family, but they are grouped into three partitions by our technique. At the same time, "path family condition" does not guarantee the same input-output relationship, whereas *relevant-slice condition* does. The main difference between our work and [15] lies in the static vs. dynamic nature of the two techniques. The work in [15] statically computes their path family conditions, while we dynamically explore the *relevant-slice conditions*. Because of the dynamic nature of our method, we can under-approximate the *relevant-slice conditions* , while [15] over-approximates their "path family conditions" if needed. Clearly, the dynamic nature of our method makes it more suitable for test generation. Note that the effect of program statements written in real-life programming languages are hard to precisely model as symbolic formulae. In such a situation, under-approximation is a practical simplification, since it amounts to concretizing parts of the formula.

Other researches have also used the notion of "path equivalence" to alleviate the path explosion problem. However, what paths are considered equivalent are different between our work and earlier works. The difference in the definition of path equivalence originates from the different goals of our work and earlier works. In [2], the goal is to explore all possible program states. Based on this goal, two paths are equivalent if the symbolic states of all live variables are the same. In contrast, we only consider the variables that can affect the output – two paths are equivalent if they have the same symbolic expression for the output. In [11], the goal is to reach some critical locations in a program. Therefore, two paths are equivalent if they cannot reach any critical locations for the same reason (blocked by the same condition).

Apart from the application of *relevant-slice condition* in debugging mentioned in Section 5, there are many other path condition based techniques that could benefit from *relevant-slice condition*.

Our *relevant-slice condition* can be used to minimize an existing test-suite [10, 18]. If a test-suite contains two test cases that have the same *relevant-slice condition*, these two test cases compute the output in the same way. Therefore, we can choose to eliminate one of them to make the test-suite smaller.

The work in [3] explores paths to generate program invariants. For each path explored, the path condition serves as a pre-condition and the symbolic program output is treated as a post-condition. Thus, each explored path produces a program invariant which is defined as such a (pre-condition, post-condition) pair. Similar approaches are used in [6, 12] to generate method summaries. Instead of using path condition, we can generate such program invariants using *relevant-slice conditions* — the *relevant-slice condition* is the pre-condition and for each *relevant-slice condition* explored, there is a unique symbolic output which serves as the post-condition. Moreover, the invariants generated using *relevant-slice conditions* will be simpler (as *relevant-slice conditions* are smaller than path conditions) and fewer (since a single *relevant-slice condition* groups more paths).

8. DISCUSSION

In this paper, we have presented a novel path exploration method based on symbolic program outputs. Our path exploration dynamically groups paths on-the-fly, where two paths that have the same symbolic output are grouped together. Given such a path partitioning, we can generate a test case from each partition. This enables us to efficiently obtain a concise test-suite which stresses all possible input-output relationships in the program.

Our path exploration method is complete, that is, it covers all possible symbolic outputs in a given program. We also experimentally compare the efficiency and coverage of our method with respect to Directed Automated Random Testing, another path search method based on symbolic execution.

Apart from testing, the path partitioning computed by our method can be exploited in other software engineering activities. We have shown its use in the debugging of errors introduced by program changes, that is, in root-causing observable software regressions. By comparing the path partitioning in two program versions, we infer the semantic differences across the versions, leading to precise root cause identification.

Acknowledgements. This work was partially supported by a Ministry of Education research grant MOE2010-T2-2-073 (R-252-000-456-112 and R-252-100-456-112), as well as a Defence Innovative Research Programme (DIRP) grant (R-252-000-393-422) from Defence Research and Technology Office (DRTech).

9. REFERENCES

[1] H. Agrawal, J. R. Horgan, E. W. Krauser, and S. London. Incremental regression testing. In *Proceedings of the Conference on Software Maintenance*, ICSM '93, pages 348–357, Washington, DC, USA, 1993. IEEE Computer Society.

[2] P. Boonstoppel, C. Cadar, and D. Engler. Rwset: Attacking path explosion in constraint-based test generation. *Tools and Algorithms for the Construction and Analysis of Systems*, pages 351–366, 2008.

[3] C. Csallner, N. Tillmann, and Y. Smaragdakis. Dysy: dynamic symbolic execution for invariant inference. In *Proceedings of the 30th international conference on Software engineering*, ICSE '08, pages 281–290, New York, NY, USA, 2008. ACM.

[4] L. De Moura and N. Bjørner. Z3: An efficient smt solver. *Tools and Algorithms for the Construction and Analysis of Systems*, pages 337–340, 2008.

[5] H. Do, S. Elbaum, and G. Rothermel. Supporting controlled experimentation with testing techniques: An infrastructure and its potential impact. *Empirical Software Engineering*, 10(4), 2005.

[6] P. Godefroid. Compositional dynamic test generation. In *Proceedings of the 34th annual ACM SIGPLAN-SIGACT symposium on Principles of programming languages*, POPL '07, pages 47–54, New York, NY, USA, 2007. ACM.

[7] P. Godefroid, A. Kiezun, and M. Y. Levin. Grammar-based whitebox fuzzing. In *Proceedings of the 2008 ACM SIGPLAN conference on Programming language design and implementation*, PLDI '08, pages 206–215, New York, NY, USA, 2008. ACM.

[8] P. Godefroid, N. Klarlund, and K. Sen. DART: directed automated random testing. In *Proceedings of the 2005 ACM SIGPLAN conference on Programming language design and implementation*, PLDI '05, pages 213–223, New York, NY, USA, 2005. ACM.

[9] T. Gyimóthy, A. Beszédes, and I. Forgács. An efficient relevant slicing method for debugging. In *Proceedings of the 7th European software engineering conference held jointly with the 7th ACM SIGSOFT international symposium on Foundations of software engineering*, ESEC/FSE-7, pages 303–321, London, UK, 1999. Springer-Verlag.

[10] M. J. Harrold, R. Gupta, and M. L. Soffa. A methodology for controlling the size of a test suite. *ACM Trans. Softw. Eng. Methodol.*, 2:270–285, July 1993.

[11] K. McMillan. Lazy annotation for program testing and verification. In *Computer Aided Verification*, pages 104–118. Springer, 2010.

[12] S. Person, M. Dwyer, S. Elbaum, and C. Pasareanu. Differential symbolic execution. In *Proceedings of the 16th ACM SIGSOFT International Symposium on Foundations of software engineering*, pages 226–237. ACM, 2008.

[13] D. Qi, H. D. T. Nguyen, and A. Roychoudhury. Path exploration based on soymbolic output. Technical report, `http://dl.comp.nus.edu.sg/dspace/handle/1900.100/3347`, March 2011.

[14] D. Qi, A. Roychoudhury, Z. Liang, and K. Vaswani. DARWIN: an approach for debugging evolving programs. In *Proceedings of the the 7th joint meeting of the European software engineering conference and the ACM SIGSOFT symposium on The foundations of software engineering*, ESEC/FSE '09, pages 33–42, New York, NY, USA, 2009. ACM.

[15] R. Santelices and M. J. Harrold. Exploiting program dependencies for scalable multiple-path symbolic execution. In *Proceedings of the 19th international symposium on Software testing and analysis*, ISSTA '10, pages 195–206, New York, NY, USA, 2010. ACM.

[16] K. Sen, D. Marinov, and G. Agha. Cute: a concolic unit testing engine for c. In *Proceedings of the 10th European software engineering conference held jointly with 13th ACM SIGSOFT international symposium on Foundations of software engineering*, ESEC/FSE-13, pages 263–272, New York, NY, USA, 2005. ACM.

[17] T. Wang and A. Roychoudhury. Dynamic slicing on Java bytecode traces. *ACM Trans. Program. Lang. Syst.*, 30:10:1–10:49, March 2008.

[18] W. E. Wong, J. R. Horgan, S. London, and A. P. Mathur. Effect of test set minimization on fault detection effectiveness. In *Proceedings of the 17th international conference on Software engineering*, ICSE '95, pages 41–50, New York, NY, USA, 1995. ACM.

[19] Y. Xie, A. Chou, and D. Engler. Archer: using symbolic, path-sensitive analysis to detect memory access errors. In *Proceedings of the 9th European software engineering conference held jointly with 11th ACM SIGSOFT international symposium on Foundations of software engineering*, ESEC/FSE-11, pages 327–336, New York, NY, USA, 2003. ACM.

[20] B. Xin, W. N. Sumner, and X. Zhang. Efficient program execution indexing. In *Proceedings of the 2008 ACM SIGPLAN conference on Programming language design and implementation*, PLDI '08, pages 238–248, New York, NY, USA, 2008. ACM.

Synthesizing Data-structure Manipulations from Storyboards

Rishabh Singh
MIT CSAIL
Massachusetts, USA
rishabh@csail.mit.edu

Armando Solar-Lezama
MIT CSAIL
Massachusetts, USA
asolar@csail.mit.edu

ABSTRACT

We present the *Storyboard Programming* framework, a new synthesis system designed to help programmers write imperative low-level data-structure manipulations. The goal of this system is to bridge the gap between the "boxes-and-arrows" diagrams that programmers often use to think about data-structure manipulation algorithms and the low-level imperative code that implements them. The system takes as input a set of partial input-output examples, as well as a description of the high-level structure of the desired solution. From this information, it is able to synthesize low-level imperative implementations in a matter of minutes.

The framework is based on a new approach for combining constraint-based synthesis and abstract-interpretation-based shape analysis. The approach works by encoding both the synthesis and the abstract interpretation problem as a constraint satisfaction problem whose solution defines the desired low-level implementation. We have used the framework to synthesize several data-structure manipulations involving linked lists and binary search trees, as well as an insertion operation into an And Inverter Graph.

Categories and Subject Descriptors

D.1.2 [**Programming Techniques**]: Automatic Programming; I.2.2 [**Artificial Intelligence**]: Program Synthesis

Keywords

Program Synthesis, Storyboard Programming, Data structure manipulations

1. INTRODUCTION

When implementing complex data-structure manipulations, programmers must bridge the gulf that separates their intuitive understanding of how the manipulation works from the low-level code that actually implements it. The intuition behind these manipulations often takes the form of "boxes-and-arrows" diagrams which programmers might draw on a whiteboard to illustrate the evolution of the data-structure as it is manipulated. Unfortunately the visual intuition reflected in these diagrams is absent from the low-level pointer updates that make up the implementation. This semantic gap between intuition and implementation makes data-structure manipulations difficult to write and maintain.

To illustrate this gap, consider the example in Figure 1. Part (a) of the figure shows a graphical description of the removal of a node from a doubly linked-list. The diagram—we call it a *storyboard*—communicates very clearly the effect of the manipulation. By contrast, the imperative code in Figure 1(b) is short but not self-explanatory; understanding this code essentially requires one to mentally recreate the image from the storyboard in part (a). The system presented in this paper bridges this gap by using constraint-based synthesis technology to automatically implement data-structure manipulations that are provably correct with respect to high-level descriptions like the one illustrated by Figure 1.

a) Graphical intuition:

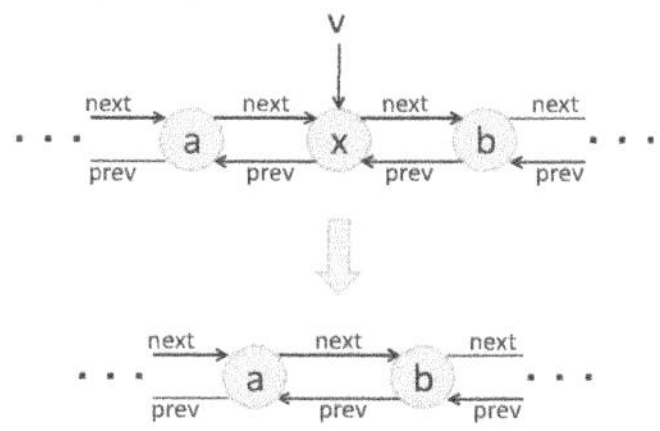

b) Code:

```
void dllRemove(Node v){
    v.n.p = v.p;
    v.p.n = v.n;
}
```

Figure 1: Doubly linked list deletion example

Our system is not yet a graphical programming system—it lacks a graphical user interface—but it brings closer to reality the promise of an effective graphical programming model for data-structure manipulations. It does so by supporting a form of *Programming by Example* (PBE) [6] where the manipulations are synthesized from partial descriptions of their effects. The main input to the system is a set of descriptions of the state of a data-structure before and after manipulation—essentially text descriptions of storyboards like the one in Figure 1. Two important features, however, distinguish our system from traditional PBE systems. The

Permission to make digital or hard copies of all or part of this work for personal or classroom use is granted without fee provided that copies are not made or distributed for profit or commercial advantage and that copies bear this notice and the full citation on the first page. To copy otherwise, to republish, to post on servers or to redistribute to lists, requires prior specific permission and/or a fee.

ESEC/FSE'11, September 5–9, 2011, Szeged, Hungary.

Copyright 2011 ACM 978-1-4503-0443-6/11/09 ...$10.00.

first is the ability to abstract away those parts of the data-structure that are not relevant to the manipulation, as is done in Figure 1 through the use of ellipsis. This form of abstraction gives our system a lot of expressive power, because it allows a single figure to succinctly describe the behavior of the algorithm on an infinite number of concrete inputs, turning a simple input-output pair into a partial specification. The second difference with PBE is that our system asks the user to provide information about the control-flow structure of the solution; this information reduces the space of possible implementations that the system needs to consider and makes it less likely that the system will produce a solution that only works for the given examples. These two features allow us to synthesize complex data-structure manipulations from relatively simple storyboards.

The system is made possible by a new synthesis algorithm that combines previous work on constraint-based synthesis [24, 29] with abstract interpretation. Our algorithm is not the first to do this [29], but it is the first to scale to the very large and complex abstract domains required to reason about data-structure manipulations. The key idea behind the algorithm is to use quantification to eliminate operations that require complex set-based reasoning, and to use the SKETCH solver [24] to solve these formulas(Section 5). The new synthesis algorithm allows us to combine constraint-based synthesis with a form of shape-analysis loosely based on TVLA [15]. The shape analysis algorithm used by our system is not as powerful as many of those found in the literature [21], but it is powerful enough to reason about most operations involving trees and lists. The strength of our particular form of shape analysis, however, lies in the ease with which we can take the abstractions expressed as part of the storyboard and use them as the basis for an abstract domain that is then used to verify each candidate implementation.

In summary, the key contributions of the paper are:

- Development of a new model of interaction between the synthesizer and the programmer, targeted at the domain of data-structure manipulations (Section 2).
- A novel synthesis algorithm that combines constraint-based synthesis with abstract interpretation to bridge the gap between high-level graphical specifications and their low-level implementation (Section 5).
- The development and evaluation of a tool to automatically synthesize data-structure manipulations involving linked lists and trees from high-level graphical specifications (Section 6).

So far, we have used our system to successfully synthesize several data structure manipulations such as insertion, deletion, search, reversal and rotation operations over singly linked list, doubly linked list and binary search tree data structures. We have also used our framework to synthesize small puzzle problems as well as some manipulations involving a tricky real-world And Inverter Graph [18] data-structure used in the ABC solver [3].

2. OVERVIEW: LINKED LIST REVERSAL

In this section, we present an overview of our framework through a textbook data-structure manipulation example: in-place linked list reversal. Reversing a list with a loop and using only a constant amount of additional memory is non-trivial; in fact, the algorithm for this manipulation is a common question in technical interviews. In the remainder of the section, we describe how the user describes this data-structure manipulation to the framework, and provide a high-level view of how the synthesizer uses this input to derive an implementation.

2.1 Storyboard

In order to synthesize the manipulation, our system takes as input a *storyboard* composed of three elements: a set of *scenarios*, each of which corresponds to an abstract input-output pair; a set of fold and unfold definitions, and a skeleton of the looping structure of the desired algorithm.

A scenario in our system is an input-output pair describing the effect of the manipulation on a potentially abstract data-structure, where abstraction is used to elide details of the data-structure that are not considered relevant. For example, Figure 2 below shows the main scenario describing the effect of reversing a linked list. Like the more informal

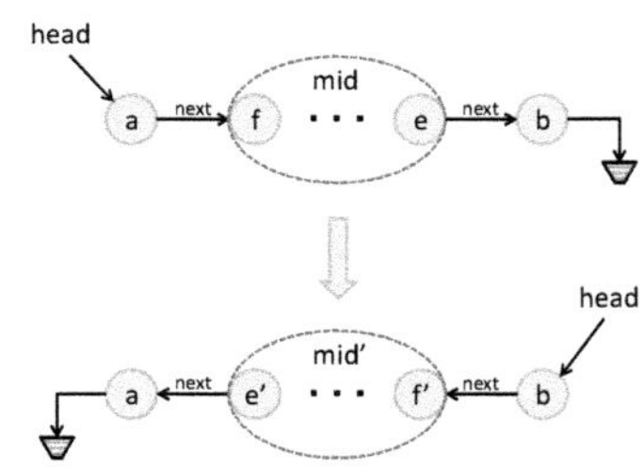

Figure 2: Graphical description of linked-list reverse

example in Figure 1, the scenario uses ellipses to abstract away part of the list. In our notation, however, the ellipses are formalized by using the concept of *summary nodes*. For this example, the scenario uses a summary node mid to represent the middle part of the list, which may vary in size for different runs of the algorithm. Out of all the nodes in the sub-list represented by mid, the first and last node deserve special attention because other nodes outside the sub-list mid may point to them. We call these special nodes *attachment points* of the summary node, and as we shall see, they play an important role in reasoning about scenarios.

Figure 3 shows the complete set of scenarios needed for this example, including scenarios to describe the behavior of the algorithm on lists of length zero, one and two. Figure 3(a) presents the text notation used by our system to describe one of the scenarios on the right. The storyboard consists of an environment description and a sequence of scenario descriptions. The environment defines the set of variables used in the implementation, the set of fields in the objects that make up the data-structure (which are called *selectors* in the shape analysis literature), and the set of concrete and summary locations. For this example there are only four program variables (head, temp1, temp2 and temp3), one selector corresponding to the field next, and eight concrete locations a, f, e, b, f' and e'. The concrete locations f and e (resp. f' and e') represent the two attachment points of the summary node mid (resp. mid'). The environment description also states a global invariant that the next pointers of locations f and f' point to mid and mid' respectively with a value of 1/2 in a 3-valued logic similar to TVLA [21]. Each scenario description, in turn, uses variable predicates, se-

Environment
vars Node head, temp1, temp2, temp3
selectors (Node,Node) next
locations Node a, f, e, b, f', e'
summary Node (mid,f,e), (mid',f',e')
invariant next(f,mid)=1/2, next(f',mid')=1/2

Scenario 1
input
head(a) //vars
next(a,f),next(e,b),next(b,null) //sels

output
head(b) //vars
next(b,f'), next(e',a), next(a,null) //sels

(a)

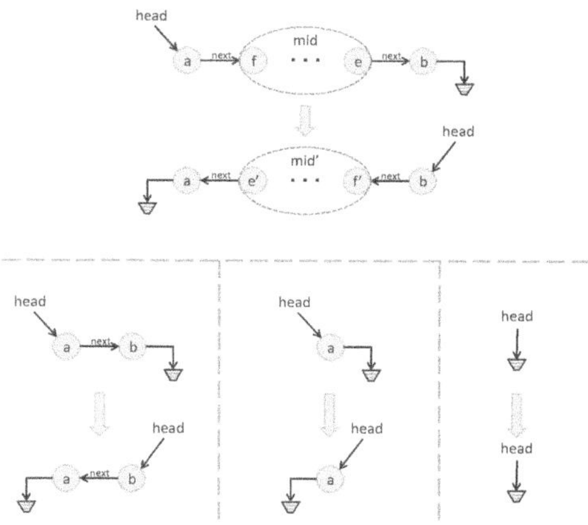

(b)

Figure 3: Storyboard for in-place linked list reversal

lector predicates and data constraint predicates to define a pair of input-output state configurations. The variable predicates of the form var(loc) denote that variable var points to location loc, and the selector predicates of the form sel(loc_1, loc_2) denote that the sel field of location loc_1 points to location loc_2. The data constraint predicates define additional constraints involving the data values of locations.

In order to make scenarios precise, it is often necessary to provide additional information about the structure of summary nodes. For example, in Figure 2, the summary node mid represents a set of nodes with a very particular structure; specifically, the scenario only makes sense under the assumption that node e is reachable from node f. Our system allows the user to provide this structural information through fold and unfold predicates. For example, Figure 4 shows the fold and unfold predicates used to describe the recursive structure of the mid summary node. The predicates describe the structure of summary nodes in terms of their attachment points, in a similar way as Fradet *et al.* [7] used context-free graph grammars to describe shape types.

The exact syntax and semantics of the predicates will be discussed in detail in Section 4.1; for now, it is enough to understand that the predicates in Figure 4(a) are precise text representations of the recursive definitions illustrated in Figure 4(b). For example, the unfold rule shows two alternatives for the summary node mid: either the attachment points f and e are actually the same node x', and this is the only node in mid, or f is a node x' whose next pointer points to the attachment point f' of another similar summary node mid'. For this example, fold is an inverse of unfold and could be derived automatically, but Section 4.1 will show other examples where it is useful to define fold and unfold independently as a way to guide the solver to a specific solution.

The scenarios and the fold and unfold definitions together describe the effects of the desired manipulation, but recall that our running example included some non-functional requirements, such as the requirement that the implementation use of a single loop. This requirement is expressed by providing a skeleton of the looping structure of the desired algorithm. Figure 5 shows the skeleton for list reverse, which states that the implementation should contain exactly one while loop with some blocks of code before and after it. The code produced by the synthesizer will have each of these blocks replaced by a series of guarded assignments of the form if(COND) then STMT. The conditional COND corresponds to expressions EXP op EXP, where EXP is either an expression of the form var(.sel?) or null and op ranges over the set of comparison operators. The set of assignment statements STMT corresponds to assignments of the form LHS = EXP where LHS is the same set as EXP but excluding null.

Each of these elements—the scenarios, the loop skeleton and the fold and unfold definitions—comprise a partial specification of the desired function. For example, the storyboard above is a partial specification because the abstraction does not define the relationship between mid in the input and mid' in the output. In this case, asking the synthesizer to produce a solution with a small number of statements is sufficient to ensure the correct answer, but sometimes the user may have to provide the system with additional information. In keeping with the PBE model, this additional information usually takes the form of additional scenarios with concrete examples, but it can also include providing intermediate state configurations, adding predicates in scenarios or providing a more detailed implementation sketch in place of the simple loop skeletons. The strength of our synthesis approach is that it can combine these different constraints into a concrete implementation. Moreover, as shown in Section 6, the constraints imposed by the storyboards are strong enough that in the few cases where the specification has to be strengthened, it only takes a few additional concrete scenarios or an intermediate state configuration to guide the framework to synthesize the correct implementation.

2.2 Synthesizing code from storyboards

Our synthesis strategy is based on constraint-based synthesis [24, 29]. The key idea behind this form of synthesis is to define a space of possible solutions to the synthesis problem and to represent it as a parameterized program. For example, in our case, each unknown assignment can be represented as a switch statement where an unknown parameter determines which assignment is actually performed. This means that the entire solution space can be represented as a program $P(in, c)$ where in is the input to the program and c is a vector of *control* parameters that determines which computations are performed. The goal of the synthesis process

```
unfold(f,{(f,in,x'),(e,out,x')},[true]);
unfold(f,{(f,in,x'),(e,out,e')},[x'.next = f']);
fold(x,{(x,in,f'),(x,out,e')},[true]);
fold(x,{(x,in,f'),(e,out,e')},[x.next = f]);
```

(a)

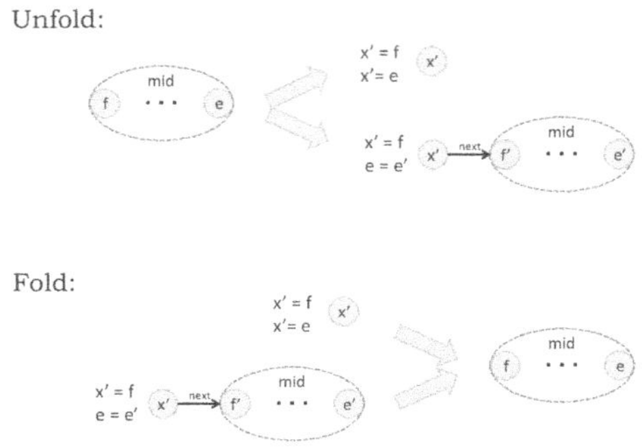

(b)

Figure 4: Unfold and fold predicate definitions for mid summary node

```
void llReverse(Node head){

        /* 1 */

        while(/*2*/){/*3*/}


        /*4*/
        return head;
}
```

Figure 5: Control flow sketch for list reversal. Each number corresponds to an unknown block of code.

is then to find a value c_{sol} such that the program $P(in, c_{sol})$ meets the storyboard specification for all inputs in.

This view of the synthesis problem is common to all constraint based synthesis approaches [24, 29]. In our framework, we derive these constraints from the storyboard by interpreting the input-output states in each scenario of the storyboard as abstract states in a specially crafted abstract domain. This allows us to use the theory of abstract interpretation [5] to frame the correctness condition as a set of equations. The fold/unfold predicates can be understood in the context of abstract interpretation as a way of defining instrumentation predicates for summary nodes. Once the correctness condition has been framed as a set of equations, the translation to constraints follows with only a small amount of effort.

2.2.1 *From storyboards to equations*

Our framework uses a powerset domain as an abstract domain where the state is represented as a set of shapes. Each shape, in turn, is represented as a set of predicates, following a formalism similar to TVLA [15, 21]. Given this abstract domain, the next step is to use the control flow sketch to derive a set of equations relating the abstract states at program points as described by Sharir and Pnueli in [23]. In these equations, each one of the unknown blocks of code in the control flow sketch is represented by a parameterized transition function $F_m(t_i, c)$ that maps an abstract state to an output abstract state for a given control value c. The control flow sketch then defines a set of equations involving the transition functions. For example, the control flow sketch in Figure 5 induces the following equations, where the transition function F_i corresponds to block i in the sketch.

$$t_0 = F_1(in, c); \quad (1)$$

$$t_1 = F_3(t_0 \cup t_2, c); \quad (2)$$

$$t_2 = F_2(t_1, c); \quad (3)$$

$$t_3 = \overline{F_2}(t_0 \cup t_2, c); \quad (4)$$

$$out = F_4(t_3, c); \quad (5)$$

If these equations came from a verification problem, each of the F_i would be a transition function, and we could use an iterative approach to find the least fixed point solution to the equations and check that out matched the solution required by the storyboard. But for synthesis, each F_i represents an unknown block of code, and the c values we are interested in finding do not form a lattice, so we cannot use a standard iterative solver find c_{sol}. Instead, we provide an efficient way to encode the problem in a form that an off-the-shelf constraint solver can efficiently solve.

Transition Functions: Each transition function $F_m(t_i, c)$ encodes the behavior of set of possible sequences of guarded assignments that can be used to complete the control flow skeleton. In addition to conditional statements, a transition function can also include two special kinds of statements: `unfold var` and `fold var`. The semantics of unfold and fold correspond to no-ops in the concrete domain; their sole purpose is to allow the abstract interpretation to reach a fixed point while allowing for very precise reasoning within the abstract domain. Figure 6 shows the role of the unfold and fold functions in materializing abstract nodes [21] to allow for more precise reasoning, and then collapsing multiple abstract shapes into a single one to allow the abstract interpretation to reach a fixed point. The semantics of fold and unfold will be described in detail in Section 4 after we formalize the overall abstract interpretation framework.

2.2.2 *Equations to Constraints*

So far, we have described how to encode the problem in terms of the least fixed point solution of a set of equations. Our framework translates these equations into a 2QBF formula, which in principle could be solved by any 2QBF solver, although in practice we have found that only our SKETCH solver scales to large synthesis problems. As we will show in Section 5, the key idea in the translation to constraints is that instead of having the transfer functions produce sets of states, we make the functions non-deterministically produce one element in the set. Therefore, by exploring all

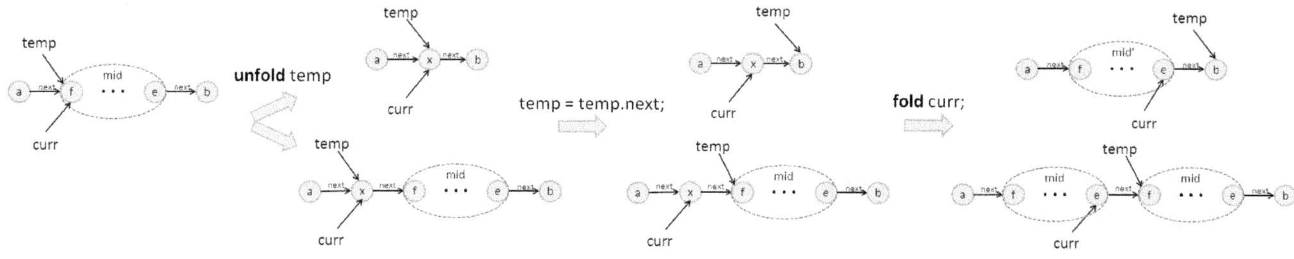

Figure 6: unfold and fold operations in action

```
Node llReverse(Node head){
  Node temp1 = null, temp2 = null;
  Node temp3 = null;

  temp1 = head;
  while(temp1 != null){
    // unfold temp1;
    head = temp1;
    temp1 = temp1.next;
    head.next = head;
    head.next = temp3;
    temp3 = head;
    // fold head;
} }
```

Figure 7: Synthesized list reverse implementation

non-deterministic choices, we guarantee that the entire set is considered.

2.3 Synthesized Implementation

From a satisfying assignment to the constraints, the framework derives the imperative implementation shown in Figure 7 for the linked list reverse manipulation. The conditionals (all true) from the conditional assignment statements have been removed for better readability of the code. It can be noted that the implementation did not use the program variable (temp2) and the loop body includes an extra *dead store* assignment statement (head.next = head). Aside from the additional assignment, the code is an efficient implementation of the desired algorithm, and the entire synthesis process takes only a couple of minutes.

3. DATA STRUCTURE CONFIGURATIONS

In this section we present the formalism used by our framework to encode and reason about the storyboard description. The formalism is based on abstract interpretation, and is similar to that of TVLA; the primary difference is our treatment of summary nodes with attachment points. But before we describe the abstract interpretation, we need to define the concrete domain over which programs operate. In this concrete domain, the state of the program is defined by a fixed set of local variables and a set of memory locations (also called nodes), where each location can have a number of fields pointing to other memory locations. Our framework currently does not support the allocation of memory by a synthesized routine, so the set of nodes that the program has to reason about does not grow as the routine executes.

Let $\mathcal{L}^{\#}$ represent the set of memory locations the synthesized program will operate on. Then, the state of the program is captured by two sets of predicates. First, for every variable v and location $l \in \mathcal{L}^{\#}$ there is a predicate $v(l)$ that indicates whether v points to location l. Then, for every field sel, there is a predicate $sel(l_1, l_2)$ that indicates whether a location l_1 has a field sel that points to location l_2. These two sets of predicates encode a *concrete shape* which defines the instantaneous configuration of the heap at any point in the execution.

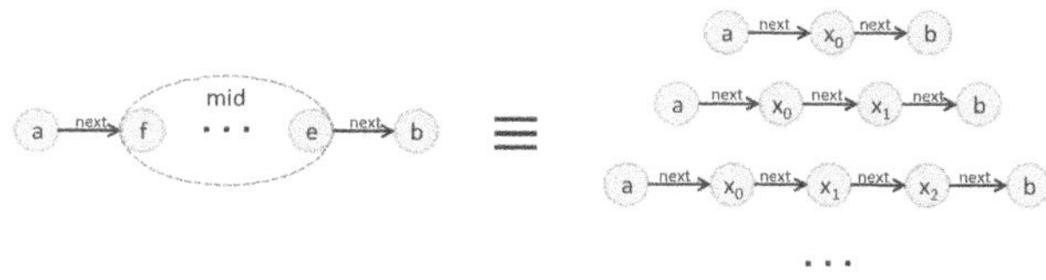

Figure 8: An abstract list representing infinite concrete lists

Shapes in the abstract domain.

The abstract domain consists of sets of *abstract shapes*, where each abstract shape itself represents a set of concrete shapes. The abstract shapes are defined in terms of a set of locations $\mathcal{L}$. Each location $loc \in \mathcal{L}$ can be either a summary location or a concrete location; we use the predicate $sm(loc)$ to indicate that loc is a summary location, so $\neg sm(loc)$ indicates that the location is concrete. As we have stated before, a concrete location loc may serve as an *attachment point* for a summary location u, which we express with the notation $loc \in \mathcal{A}(u)$; we use the predicate $apt(loc)$ to indicate the role of loc as an attachment point.

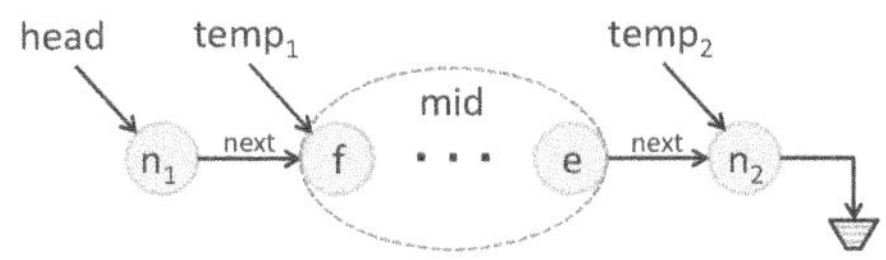

Figure 9: State configuration for a singly linked list

EXAMPLE 1. *The state configuration in Figure 9 is encoded as follows. The set of locations is given by* $\mathcal{L} = \{l_1, mid, f, e, l_2\}$, *with a summary node mid and attachment points* $\mathcal{A}(mid) = \{f, e\}$. *The set of program variables are* $\mathcal{V} = \{head, temp_1, temp_2\}$. *The variable predicates* $head(l_1)$, $temp_1(f)$ *and* $temp_2(l_2)$ *are true. The* next *selector predicates* $next(l_1, f)$, $next(e, l_2)$ *and* $next(l_2, null)$ *are true, and* $next(f, mid) = 1/2$.

To make the definition of the abstract domain more formal, consider a concrete shape $S^{\#}$ with a set of nodes $\mathcal{L}^{\#}$, a selector predicate $\mathsf{sel}^{\#}$ and a variable predicate $\mathsf{var}^{\#}$, together with an abstract shape S with a set of nodes $\mathcal{L}$, selector sel and variable predicate var. We say that shape $S^{\#}$ is in the concretization of S ($S^{\#} \in \gamma(S)$) when there exists a relation $\mathcal{M} : \mathcal{L}^{\#} \times \mathcal{L}$ that satisfies the following conditions.

- Every node in $S^{\#}$ maps to some node in S and vice versa: *i.e.* $\forall l_1 \in \mathcal{L}^{\#}\ \exists n_1 \in \mathcal{L}\ s.t.\ \mathcal{M}(l_1, n_1)$ and $\forall n_1 \in \mathcal{L}\ \exists l_1 \in \mathcal{L}^{\#}\ s.t.\ \mathcal{M}(l_1, n_1)$
- Nodes that do not map to summary nodes map to a single concrete node: *i.e.* for any $l_1 \in \mathcal{L}^{\#}$, if $\neg\exists n_2\ s.t.\ sm(n_2) \wedge \mathcal{M}(l_1, n_2)$ then $\mathcal{M}(l_1, n_a) \wedge \mathcal{M}(l_1, n_b) \Rightarrow n_a = n_b$.
- Summary nodes do not overlap: *i.e.* $sm(n_a) \wedge \mathcal{M}(l_1, n_a) \wedge \mathcal{M}(l_1, n_b) \Rightarrow (n_a = n_b \vee n_b \in \mathcal{A}(n_a))$.
- Edges between concrete nodes are preserved: *i.e.* given $l_1, l_2 \in \mathcal{L}^{\#}$ and $n_1, n_2 \in \mathcal{L}$ where $\neg sm(n_1)$ and $\neg sm(n_2)$, let $\mathcal{M}(l_1, n_1)$ and $\mathcal{M}(l_2, n_2)$; then, $\mathsf{sel}^{\#}(l_1, l_2) \Leftrightarrow \mathsf{sel}(n_1, n_2)$ and $\mathsf{var}^{\#}(l_1) \Leftrightarrow \mathsf{var}(n_1)$.
- Summary nodes own their associated attachment points: *i.e.* if $\mathcal{M}(l_1, n_2)$ and $n_2 \in \mathcal{A}(u)$ then $\mathcal{M}(l_1, u)$
- Any edge pointing to a summary node from the outside must point to one of its attachment points: *i.e.* let $\mathsf{sel}^{\#}(l_1, l_2) \wedge \mathcal{M}(l_2, n_b) \wedge sm(n_b)$, then either $\mathcal{M}(l_1, n_b)$ or $\exists n_a \in \mathcal{A}(n_b) s.t. \mathcal{M}(l_2, n_a)$, and for variables, $\mathsf{var}^{\#}(l_2) \wedge \mathcal{M}(l_2, n_b) \wedge sm(n_b)$, then $\exists n_a \in \mathcal{A}(n_b) s.t. \mathcal{M}(l_2, n_a)$
- Selector edges for summary nodes not originating in an attachment point are ignored: *i.e.* if $sm(n_a) \vee sm(n_b)$ then $\mathsf{sel}(n_a, n_b) = 0 \vee n_a \in \mathcal{A}(n_b)$.
- Selector edges from an attachment point to its enclosing summary node will have value 1/2: *i.e.* if $n_a \in \mathcal{A}(n_b)$ and $\exists l_1, l_2 \in \mathcal{L}^{\#}\ s.t.\ \mathsf{sel}^{\#}(l_1, l_2) \wedge \mathcal{M}(l_1, n_a) \wedge \mathcal{M}(l_2, n_b)$, and $\neg\exists n_c\ s.t.\ \mathcal{M}(l_2, n_c) \wedge \neg sm(n_c)$, then $\mathsf{sel}(n_a, n_b) = 1/2$.

In shape analysis it is common to use 3-valued logic to represent the values of selector and variable predicates in abstract shapes. However, notice that the rules above specifically require us to ignore most selector edges involving summary nodes. The restrictions imply that the only selector edges that will potentially have value equal to 1/2 are edges from an attachment point to its corresponding summary node; that is why we have next(f, mid) = 1/2 in the earlier example. As we shall see in the next section, the transition rules in the abstract semantics are defined in such a way that if the algorithm under analysis ever tries to dereference a field corresponding to one of these half edges, it will transition into an error state. This makes the analysis simpler at the expense of added imprecision, but our analysis compensates for this imprecision by relying on the unfold predicates to *materialize*[21] summary nodes.

4. ABSTRACT INTERPRETATION

Having defined the structure of the abstract domain, we now describe the transition rules used to model statements and conditionals, focusing on those aspects unique to our framework. Figures 10 and 11 show respectively the statements and conditionals considered by the synthesizer. The figures also show the formal definitions of the transition rules associated with each construct. The transition rules relate the state before the transition—the pre-state represented with non-primed predicates—with the post-state represented with primed predicates. It is assumed that the values of all other predicates not mentioned in the transition rule remain unchanged.

Statement	Transition rule
x = null	$\forall\, l \in \mathcal{L}:\ x'(l) = 0$
x = t	$\forall\, l \in \mathcal{L}:\ x'(l) = t(l)$
x = t.sel	assert $\neg\exists l_1, l_2 \in \mathcal{L} : t(l_1) \wedge sel(l_1, l_2) \wedge sm(l_2)$ $\forall\, l \in \mathcal{L}:\ x'(l) = \exists l_1\ t(l_1) \wedge sel(l_1, l)$
x.sel = null	assert $\neg\exists l_1, l_2 \in \mathcal{L} : x(l_1) \wedge sel(l_1, l_2) \wedge sm(l_2)$ $\forall\, l_1, l_2 \in \mathcal{L}:\ sel'(l_1, l_2) = \neg x(l_1) \wedge sel(l_1, l_2)$
x.sel = t	$\forall\, l_1, l_2 \in \mathcal{L}:\ sel'(l_1, l_2) = sel(l_1, l_2) \vee (x(l_1) \wedge t(l_2)))$
unfold x	$\mathsf{unfoldPred}(\mathsf{E}, \mathsf{M}, \mathsf{C})\ \wedge x(\mathsf{E})\ \Longrightarrow$ $((\forall\, l_1 \overset{\mathsf{in}}{\to} l_2 \in \mathsf{M} : \mathsf{fresh}(l_2) \wedge$ $\forall\, v \in \mathcal{V}:\ v'(l_2) = v(l_1)\ \wedge v'(l_1) = 0\ \wedge$ $\forall\, l \in \mathcal{L}:\ sel'(l, l_2) = sel(l, l_1)\ \wedge sel'(l, l_1) = 0) \wedge$ $(\forall\, l_1 \overset{\mathsf{out}}{\to} l_2 \in \mathsf{M} : \mathsf{fresh}(l_2) \wedge$ $\forall\, l \in \mathcal{L}:\ sel'(l_2, l) = sel(l_1, l)\ \wedge sel'(l_1, l) = 0)\ \wedge \mathsf{C})$
fold x	$\mathsf{foldPred}(\mathsf{E}, \mathsf{M}, \mathsf{C})\ \wedge (x(\mathsf{E}) \wedge \mathsf{C})\ \Longrightarrow$ $((\forall\, l_1 \overset{\mathsf{in}}{\to} l_2 \in \mathsf{M} : \mathsf{fresh}(l_2) \wedge$ $\forall\, v \in \mathcal{V}:\ v'(l_2) = v(l_1)\ \wedge v'(l_1) = 0\ \wedge$ $\forall\, l \in \mathcal{L}:\ sel'(l, l_2) = sel(l, l_1)\ \wedge sel'(l, l_1) = 0) \wedge$ $(\forall\, l_1 \overset{\mathsf{out}}{\to} l_2 \in \mathsf{M} : \mathsf{fresh}(l_2) \wedge$ $\forall\, l \in \mathcal{L}:\ sel'(l_2, l) = sel(l_1, l)\ \wedge sel'(l_1, l) = 0))$

Figure 10: Abstract semantics of statements manipulating pointers and pointer-valued fields

The rules follow a convention from shape analysis to assume that every statement of the form exp = t is preceded by a statement of the form exp = null, where exp is either x or x.sel. This assumption simplifies the rules because the transition rule for exp = t does not have to worry about destroying the value previously stored at exp [21]. The other important observation about the rules is the use of assertions for the two rules that do field dereferences. These assertions ensure that the system will transition into an error state when it tries to dereference a selector that points to a summary node, which in turn guarantees that 1/2 values corresponding to these selector predicates will not propagate through the representation.

The abstract semantics for the class of conditionals is shown in Figure 11. It can be noted that although the assignment statements in our target language of programs ignore data fields of the data-structure (.data as opposed to .sel), the conditionals can reason about the data constraints. We store data predicates using gt, gte, eq etc., which encode data constraints over the data values of locations. We do not consider conditionals involving selector dereferencing of variables, e.g. of the form x.next == null, as they can be reduced into a conditional of the form y == null where the variable y is first assigned by the statement y = x.next.

4.1 Fold/Unfold semantics

The unfold operation is described with a triple unfoldPred (E, M, C). The first argument E is called the enabling node, and it represents the summary node that is being expanded. The transition rule for the unfold x statement performs the unfold operation only if the variable x points to the enabling node E. The second argument M is the location mapping M : loc → loc, which describes how nodes before expansion relate to nodes after expansion. There are two kinds of location mappings in M: $\overset{\text{in}}{\rightarrow}$ mappings and $\overset{\text{out}}{\rightarrow}$ mappings. An $\overset{\text{in}}{\rightarrow}$ mapping maps a location loc_1 to loc_2 such that all variables and selector edges pointing to loc_1 in the pre-state should point to loc_2 in the post-state. An $\overset{\text{out}}{\rightarrow}$ mapping maps a location loc_1 to loc_2 such that all outgoing selector edges from loc_1 in the pre-state emanate from loc_2 in the post-state.

Finally, the description of unfold also includes a set of constraints C. These constraints describe how the new nodes will be connected together, and are asserted to hold in the post-state after unfolding. The transition rule for fold x statement works similarly to the unfold rule. The difference is that the fold operations are enabled only if the constraints C are also satisfied by the state configuration in addition to the requirement of x pointing to the enabling node E. The unfold and fold predicate definitions on the summary node mid are shown in Figure 4.

Another set of fold-unfold examples for the binary search tree (bst) case studies is shown in Figure 12. The goal of bst search is to search for a value x in the tree where r represents its root. The bst search (contains) manipulation assumes that the value x always exists in the tree. The three cases of bst search (contains) unfold are: i) $x < y.val$, ii) $x = y.val$ and iii) $x > y.val$ as shown in Fig 12(a), where y denotes the root node of the subtree being unfolded. The unfold definition for the more general case of bst search is shown in Figure 12(b). The tree summary nodes labeled *stuff* are given without any unfold rules, which means they cannot be materialized, so the verifier will not be able to reason about any implementation that tries to visit them. In this way, the unfold rule is providing algorithmic insights, telling the synthesizer that a given region of the tree should not be visited or manipulated.

One important thing to note about unfold is that a given shape can be expanded in many different ways, as illustrated in Figure 4. This is expressed by having multiple unfoldPred triples with the same enabling node. As a consequence, every abstract shape in the pre-state of an unfold operation may be expanded into a *set* of abstract shapes. This expansion allows the analysis to maintain precision, but having to represent sets of abstract shapes in the abstract interpreter will pose an interesting challenge when we turn the problem into a constraint satisfaction problem.

Another very important aspect about unfold is that the presence of unfold changes the concretization relation γ between abstract and concrete shapes. In the absence of unfold, any arbitrary set of concrete nodes can be mapped to a summary node by the relation $\mathcal{M}$ described in the previous section, but unfold has the effect of placing some structural constraints on the set of nodes that can be mapped to a summary node. This is a result of the requirement that unfold correspond to skip in the concrete domain; this means that if a given abstract shape S can be transformed by unfold into any shape in the set $\{S_i\}$, then the set of concrete shapes $\gamma(S)$ should equal $\bigcup_i \gamma(S_i)$. So we can refine the earlier definition of the concretization function to say that $S^{\#} \in \gamma(S)$ if it satisfies the requirements stated before *and* if $S^{\#} \in \bigcup_i \gamma(S_i)$, where S_i are all the shapes that can be derived from S through the application of unfold. The next section elaborates on how this definition relates to the instrumentation predicates used by TVLA to describe the structure of summary nodes.

Conditional	Transition rule
x == null	$\forall\, l \in \mathcal{L}:\ \neg x(l)$
x != null	$\exists\, l \in \mathcal{L}:\ x(l)$
x == t	$\forall\, l \in \mathcal{L}:\ x(l) \iff t(l)$
x.data > t.data	$\forall\, l_1, l_2 \in \mathcal{L} : x(l_1) \wedge t(l_2) \implies \mathsf{gt}(\mathsf{data}, l_1, l_2)$
x.data ≥ t.data	$\forall\, l_1, l_2 \in \mathcal{L} : x(l_1) \wedge t(l_2) \implies \mathsf{gte}(\mathsf{data}, l_1, l_2)$
x.data == t.data	$\forall\, l_1, l_2 \in \mathcal{L} : x(l_1) \wedge t(l_2) \implies \mathsf{eq}(\mathsf{data}, l_1, l_2)$
x.data != t.data	$\forall\, l_1, l_2 \in \mathcal{L} : x(l_1) \wedge t(l_2) \implies \neg\mathsf{eq}(\mathsf{data}, l_1, l_2)$

Figure 11: Abstract semantics of the conditionals involving the pointer variables

4.2 Relationship with TVLA

In order to understand some of the more subtle aspects of our formalism, it is useful to understand how it relates to the formalism in TVLA [15]. The two most apparent differences between the two formalisms are the use of attachment points as part of summary nodes and the use of fold and unfold.

In our system, the unfold definition serves two purposes: it provides a mechanism to convey structural properties of summary nodes, and it is also used to *materialize* summary nodes, *i.e.* to produce a set of more refined shapes that together represent the same set of concrete configurations as the original configuration. In TVLA, by contrast, structural properties are described through *instrumentation predicates*. These predicates are also used for materialization, but not directly; instead, a *focus* operation first expands a summary node into a set of possible shapes, and then a *coerce* operation uses the instrumentation predicates to refine the new shapes and to remove those that do not satisfy the required structural properties.

One can understand the unfold rules in our framework as a specialized way of describing instrumentation predicates. For example, from the unfold rule for mid we can derive the following instrumentation predicate:

$$\mathsf{isMid}(f, e) = (f = e) \vee \exists f'(f.next = f' \wedge \mathsf{isMid}(f', e)) \quad (6)$$

The predicate isMid encodes that every node in mid is reachable from the front attachment point, and therefore that the sub-list between f and e is acyclic. When we say that a summary node satisfies this predicate, it means that the summary node can only represent sets of nodes where we can find two nodes f and e that satisfy the predicate. The unfold operation induces this predicate because we want the effect of unfold in the abstract domain to be equivalent to the effect of skip in the concrete domain, and this will only be true if the summary nodes satisfy this predicate. It is interesting to see, however, that the structure of the predicate is very close to the structure of the unfold rules, with the attachment points serving as convenient parameters to the predicate.

Given such an instrumentation predicate, we can map our summary nodes with attachment points to a shape in TVLA; for example, Figure 13 shows how mid would look like as a shape in TVLA. Our unfold operation is equivalent to first applying materialization to partially concretize the summary node and then coerce to remove invalid shapes obtained after materialization.

The use of unfold in place of instrumentation predicates and the use of attachment points both have a number of advantages for the purpose of our framework. The first important advantage is that it simplifies the transition rules, because it eliminates the need to track instrumentation pred-

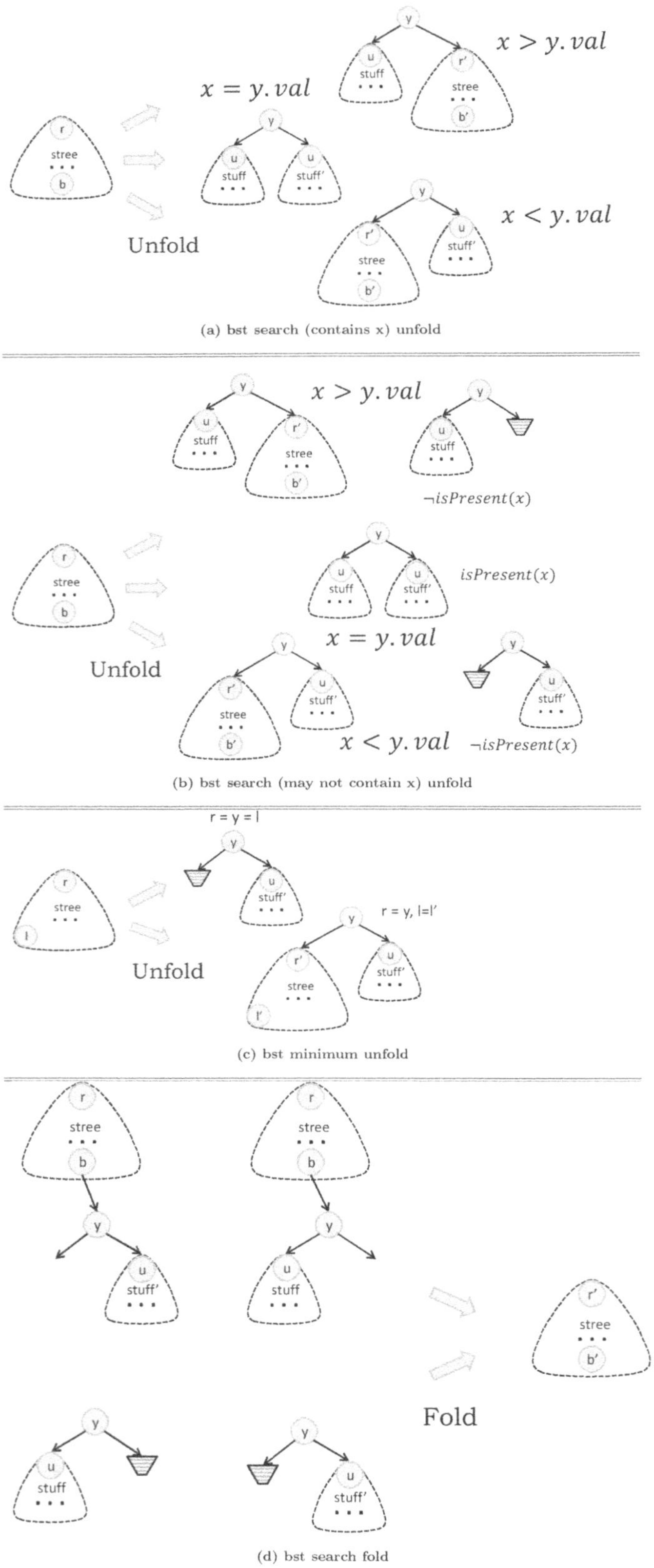

(a) bst search (contains x) unfold

(b) bst search (may not contain x) unfold

(c) bst minimum unfold

(d) bst search fold

Figure 12: Unfold and fold operations for different data structure manipulations

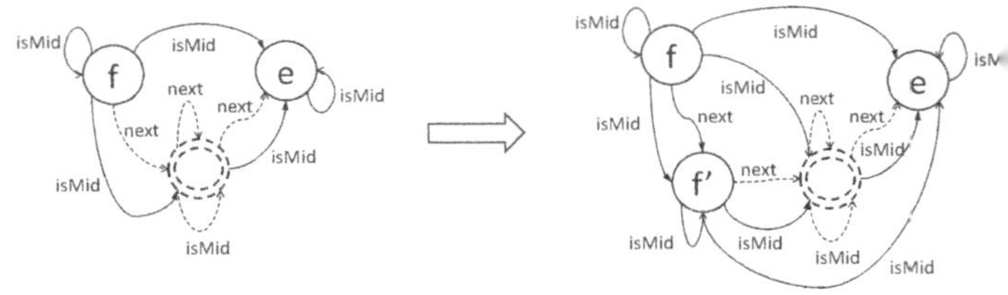

Figure 13: unfold in 3-valued shape analysis

icates. Another important benefit of using summary nodes with attachment points is that it simplifies the graphical representations, as can be readily appreciated by comparing Figure 13 with Figure 4. One clear difference between the two representations is that Figure 13 includes a number of selector edges with value 1/2 which are not present in the diagrams in Figure 4. This is partly by convention, since we omit from our representation the selector edges within summary nodes, and partly because the assumptions in Section 3 ensure that references from concrete to summary nodes always point to their attachment points.

Compared to TVLA, out formalism allows for a simpler analysis and more concise graphical representations. The downside, of course, is reduced expressive power. If one were trying to verify arbitrary programs, the shortcuts taken by our system would make the analysis impractical—it would be too easy for the user to write a program that could not be verified because it violated one of our assumptions. On the other hand, as Vechev *et al.* have pointed out [31], the combination of synthesis with abstract interpretation means that the synthesizer can work around the limitations of the abstract interpreter by producing programs that are easy to verify. In our case, the way the synthesizer works around the limitations imposed by our assumption is by using unfold statements to materialize nodes at the right time and ensure that the assumption is never violated.

5. CONSTRAINT BASED SYNTHESIS

Having defined our basic abstract interpretation framework, we can now describe how we frame the synthesis problem as a set of constraints whose solution will describe the implementation we are looking for. The starting point for this process is the control flow sketch together with the storyboard.

The control flow sketch Sk constitutes the control flow graph of the implementation; unlike a CFG, however, the vertices are not just basic blocks because they can contain conditional assignments. More formally, we represent the control flow sketch Sk as a directed graph $Sk = G(V, E)$ where V represents a set of blocks of code which can either be a sequence of conditional assignment statements or a conditional (for loop exit conditions); E in turn represents potential transitions between these blocks of code. By convention, we say that vertex v_0 is the entry point of the graph node and v_N is the exit point; neither the entry nor the exit blocks contain any code. As for scenarios, each of them is represented as a pair of input and output states $S_i = (In_i, Out_i)$.

We use standard techniques to encode each block of unknown statements as a parameterized function $F_i(in, c_i)$, where the parameter c_i selects which block of code out of the set of possible blocks of code F_i will represent. The inputs and outputs of F_i are elements of the abstract domain, which happen to be sets of shapes. Now, the set of possible sequences of conditional assignments is infinite, but bounding the maximum length of the statement sequence makes the set finite as there are a finite number of assignment statements and conditionals of the form shown in Figure 10 and Figure 11 respectively.

The goal of the synthesis process is to find values of c_i such that for each scenario S_k, the least fixed point solution to the following equation satisfies $t_N = Out_k$:

$$t_0 = In_k \ \wedge \ \forall v_i \in (V \setminus v_0) \ \ t_i = F_i(\bigcup_{j \in pred(v_i)} t_j, c_i) \quad (7)$$

The function $pred(v_i)$ in the equation above indicates the set of predecessors of node v_i. The equation above is fairly simple, but two challenges prevent us from solving it directly with an SMT solver. First, the equation above requires us to find not just any solution, but the least fixed point solution. Additionally, the t_i in the equation above are elements in the abstract domain, which is composed of sets of shapes. Such sets can get quite big given the nature of our domain, so representing them naïvely in an SMT solver is infeasible. In the rest of this section, we describe how our framework addresses both of these problems.

5.1 Computing Least Fixed Points

In order to find a least fixed point solution to Equation (7), we start from the assumption that an iterative method can reach a least fixed point after visiting each vertex in Sk at most K times. Now, let P^K be the set of all paths in Sk that visit each vertex at most K times.For each path $\mathsf{p}_i \in \mathsf{P}^K$, we can define a path transformer $\mathsf{p}_i(in, \vec{\mathsf{C}})$ which is just the composition of all the transfer functions $F_t(in, c_t)$ of all the vertices v_t in the path, where $\vec{\mathsf{C}} = [c_0, \ldots, c_N]$. Then, the least fixed point solution to the value of t_N in Equation (7) will be given by

$$\bigcup_{\mathsf{p}_i \in \mathsf{P}^K} \mathsf{p}_i(In_k, \vec{\mathsf{C}})$$

The equivalence follows from the distributivity of F (*i.e.* the fact that $F(a \cup b) = F(a) \cup F(b)$). Given a solution to the equation above, it is easy to check the assumption of K convergence by simply checking the solution against Equation 5.

5.2 Dealing with sets of abstract shapes

As we said before, in order to feed the constraints into a solver, we would like to avoid having to reason about sets of abstract shapes. Our strategy will be as follows. First, from a transfer function F, we can define a function F^j that returns a singleton set containing the jth element of the set returned by F, or an empty set if there is no j^{th} element. Thus, $F(a) = \cup_j F^j(a)$, where each F^j produces either singleton or empty sets.

The strategy even works when composing functions thanks to the distributivity of F. Because of this property, if we have a function $F(a)$ and a function $T(a)$, then the composition $F(T(a))$ can be computed as $\cup_{i,j} F^j(T^i(a))$.

In the case of our transfer functions $F_i(in, c)$, it is relatively easy to derive the functions $F_i^j(in, c)$. For example, one of the statements that can produce multiple shapes from a single one is unfold, so if we want a function to return only the jth shape produced by unfold, we only use the jth $\mathsf{unfoldPred}$ instead of using all of them. Composing the transfer functions for each block into path expressions, we get a path expression $\mathsf{p}_i^{\vec{j}}(In_k, \vec{\mathsf{C}})$, where instead of composing functions $F_i(in, c_i)$ in the path, we compose functions $F_i^{j_i}(in, c_i)$. With this transformation, the constraint we need to solve becomes:

$$\exists \vec{\mathsf{C}} \ \ (Out_k = \bigcup_{\vec{j}} \bigcup_{p_i \in \mathsf{P}} \mathsf{p}_i^{\vec{j}}(In_k, \vec{\mathsf{C}}))$$

The set unions in the equation above can be turned into universal quantifiers to produce the following equation:

$$\exists \vec{\mathsf{C}} \ \ (\forall_{\vec{j}} \forall_{p_i \in \mathsf{P}} \ \mathsf{p}_i^{\vec{j}}(In_k, \vec{\mathsf{C}}) \in Out_k \ \wedge$$
$$\exists_{\vec{j}} \exists_{p_i \in \mathsf{P}} \ \mathsf{p}_i^{\vec{j}}(In_k, \vec{\mathsf{C}}) = Out_k)$$

The universally quantified part of the equation forces the union of the path transformers to be a subset of Out_k, while the existentially quantified part of the constraint ensures that the singleton Out_k is a subset of the union of the path transformers. The equation above no longer has to reason about sets with more than one element, but in exchange for that, it has to cope with $\exists\forall$ quantifier alternation. However, the SKETCH system is very effective in dealing with such doubly quantified formulas, so our system actually translates the above equation into a sketch and uses the SKETCH solver to find a solution to all the unknowns.

5.3 Termination

Equation 5 only ensures partial correctness, so there is no termination guarantee for the synthesized implementation. However, we have found that adding a few additional constraints was enough to guarantee terminating solutions for all the examples we examined. The additional constraint was to require that for every state reachable inside any loop in the program it is possible to satisfy the loop exit condition in an additional K loop unrollings. If the unfold and fold predicates satisfy well-formedness constraints [19] and with the restriction of using only one unfold and fold operation per loop, the framework can guarantee termination of the synthesized implementation using a reasoning similar to [4]. This restriction works for data-structure manipulations that perform a single pass over the data-structure.

6. EXPERIMENTS

In our experiments with the Storyboard framework, the key questions we explored were: i) how does it scale for synthesizing reasonably complex data-structure manipulations, ii) how much additional information is required to be provided in the storyboards other than just the input-output scenarios, iii) how much having abstraction in the scenarios help and iv) can we use it to synthesize user-defined data-structure manipulations.

Table 1 presents the experimental results of the case studies that we performed with the framework. The experiments were run on an Intel Core-i7 1.87GHz CPU with 4GB of RAM. The first column in the table shows the name of the manipulation where ll refers to singly linked-list, dll refers to doubly linked-list and bst refers to binary search tree. The table presents the details about number of scenarios used in storyboard, the total time it took to synthesize the implementation, the number of clauses in the SAT translation of the constraints and the memory used. Even though this is not the most efficient encoding of the constraints, we were able to synthesize all the manipulations in less than 6 minutes using less than 1 GB of memory.

For reducing the search space in our experiments, we had to restrict the usage of unfold and fold statements to at most once at the beginning and end locations inside the loop respectively; which works well for single-pass algorithms. The case studies with the Interm column marked yes in Table 1 required some additional intermediate state configuration, *e.g.* in the storyboard for linked list insertion, we also had to provide intermediate state configuration after the loop body in the skeleton for helping the synthesizer to converge faster. These intermediate configurations present a natural interface for providing hints about the manipulation. Some case studies also required composition of storyboards (marked with a *), *e.g.* the bst-deletion storyboard required composition of bst-search and bst-find-min storyboards.

In some cases like bst-deletion, we found that the abstract input-output specification was too weak and allowed many undesired solutions; but it was easily fixed by providing a couple of concrete input-output bst instances. We also performed an experiment where we only provided concrete examples for these manipulations, the synthesizer either generated an undesired solution or got timed out and never converged for most of these case studies. This experiment shows the ability of abstract input-output examples to prune a big search space of undesired programs.

We have used our framework to synthesize manipulations for a complicated real-world AIG data structure. AIG is a DAG that encodes the structural implementation of the logical functionality of a circuit [18] using two-input AND gates and inverters. Each internal node of AIG represents an *and* gate and has two parents corresponding to the two inputs of the gate. The child list information for each node is overlayed inside the node itself by keeping a pointer to the first child and pointers to the sibling nodes. Even though our framework currently can not synthesize arbitrary graph manipulations, we exploit the listness property of the child lists of AIG nodes for synthesizing its manipulations.

Even for complicated data-structures like red-black trees, where it is difficult to draw a simple storyboard expressing the complex invariants about the data-structure, we found the storyboard framework helpful for synthesizing fragments of low-level code of different cases individually and then manually composing the synthesized code to obtain a complete implementation. Figure 14 shows the storyboard for red-black tree `fixInvariant` method (part of the `insertion` procedure) that we obtained from an online lecture note [1]. We used the framework to synthesize low-level code for the four cases, which were then easily composed manually inside the complete algorithm. Our tool and more details about the case studies can be found at the storyboard website [2].

7. RELATED WORK

Software synthesis has been an active research area at least since the early 80s when Waldinger and Manna [17, 16] did seminal work on deductive synthesis. A more algorithmic approach to synthesis was pioneered by Pnueli and

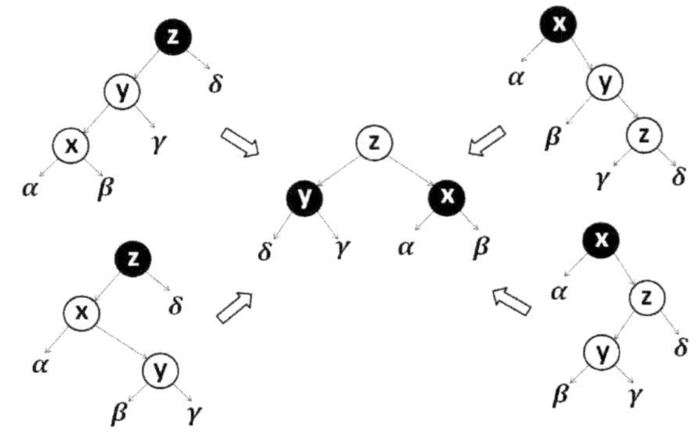

Figure 14: Red-black tree `fixInvariant` storyboard

Manipulation	#Scens	Time	#Clauses	Memory	Loops	Interm
ll-insertion	4	2m9s	1.99M	0.75GB	1	Yes
ll-deletion	4	1m48s	1.88M	0.54GB	1	Yes
ll-reversal	4	1m49s	1.3M	0.35GB	1	No
ll-find-last	4	0m56s	1.02M	0.29GB	1	No
ll-swap-first-last	4	4m18s	1.08M	0.31GB	1	Yes
dll-traversal	4	1m58s	1.72M	0.88GB	1	No
dll-reversal	4	3m47s	2.04M	0.49GB	1	No
bst-search(contains)	1	1m02s	0.62M	0.37GB	1	No
bst-search	1	6m07s	0.77M	0.45GB	1	No
bst-find-min	1	0m58s	0.63M	0.18GB	1	No
bst-find-max	1	0m23s	0.57M	0.16GB	1	No
bst-left-rotate	3	3m18s	1.41M	0.50GB	0	No
bst-right-rotate	3	3m15s	1.47M	0.43GB	0	No
bst-insertion*	3	1m52s	1.04M	0.46GB	1	Yes
bst-deletion*	6	3m13s	0.63M	0.62GB	2	Yes
aig-insertion*	4	1m04s	0.17M	0.31GB	1	Yes

Table 1: Experimental results for case studies

Rosner in the context of finite state controllers [20]. More recently, some of the ideas from the field of controller synthesis have been applied to software, for example, to synthesize program repairs [14]. For a recent survey, see [8].

The idea of using abstract interpretation for synthesis was recently introduced by Vechev, Yahav and Yorsh [31], as a follow up to earlier work on synthesis of concurrent data-structures [30]. Their system is designed to synthesize efficient synchronization for concurrent programs, and is very different from ours, both in its scope and in the algorithms it uses. Unlike their system, our synthesizer is based on a more general constraint-based approach that allows us to handle extremely large search spaces with no apparent structure.

The idea of using a constraint-based approach for abstract interpretation was previously introduced by Gulwani *et al.* [10]. Recently, their group has used similar techniques to synthesize invariants [11] and even complete programs [29]. Some important distinctions between their work and ours are the use of storyboards to capture insights, as well as our path-based representation of the constraints to support a very large and complex abstract domain.

The idea of using a sketch to define the structure of the implementation was adapted from the original work on sketch based synthesis [25]. The idea was originally applied to the domain of bit-stream manipulations [27], such as ciphers and error correction codes, and has been applied more recently to scientific programs [25] and concurrent data-structures [26]. Although SKETCH can synthesize some of the data-structure manipulations, it requires the programmer to provide detailed sketches and only provides bounded guarantees for the synthesized implementation. Additionally, writing specifications for data-structure manipulations tend to be harder, because they have to be written as tricky test harnesses.

Recent work in data representation synthesis [12] automatically synthesizes efficient data-structure representations for a given set of data usage patterns. The representations are built from a library of data-structure building-blocks and support only a fixed set of common interface methods. Our framework supports the implementation of more general data-structure manipulations, such as our list reverse example. The price of the generality is a more involved interaction model compared with the push-button interface provided by that system.

PINS [28] introduced the idea of focusing on individual paths when generating constraints. Their approach does not build upon abstract interpretation as ours and our framework lets the synthesizer select interesting paths automatically using the CEGIS algorithm unlike a heuristic technique used by PINS. Gulwani *et al.* [9, 13] have proposed component-based synthesis techniques for synthesizing tricky (but loop-free) code snippets from a given multi-set of components. These techniques are not applicable in our setting as we deal with loopy programs.

8. ACKNOWLEDGMENT

We would like to thank Rastislav Bodik, Zhilei Xu and the anonymous reviewers for their valuable comments and suggestions. This research was supported by the National Science Foundation grant CCF-1049406 and by MIT's Computer Science and Artificial Intelligence Lab (CSAIL).

9. REFERENCES

[1] http://cs.wellesley.edu/~cs231/fall01/red-black.pdf.

[2] http://people.csail.mit.edu/rishabh/storyboard/.

[3] Robert K. Brayton and Alan Mishchenko. ABC: An Academic Industrial-Strength Verification Tool. In *CAV*, pages 24–40, 2010.

[4] James Brotherston, Richard Bornat, and Cristiano Calcagno. Cyclic proofs of program termination in separation logic. In *POPL*, pages 101–112, 2008.

[5] Patrick Cousot and Radhia Cousot. Abstract interpretation: A unified lattice model for static analysis of programs by construction or approximation of fixpoints. In *POPL*, pages 238–252, 1977.

[6] Allen Cypher, Daniel C. Halbert, David Kurlander, Henry Lieberman, David Maulsby, Brad A. Myers, and Alan Turransky, editors. *Watch what I do: programming by demonstration*. MIT Press, Cambridge, MA, USA, 1993.

[7] Pascal Fradet and Daniel Le Metayer. Shape types. In *POPL*, pages 27–39. ACM Press, 1997.

[8] Sumit Gulwani. Dimensions in program synthesis. In *PPDP*, pages 13–24, 2010.

[9] Sumit Gulwani, Susmit Jha, Ashish Tiwari, and Ramarathnam Venkatesan. Synthesis of loop-free programs. In *PLDI*, pages 62–73, 2011.

[10] Sumit Gulwani, Saurabh Srivastava, and Ramarathnam Venkatesan. Program analysis as constraint solving. In *PLDI*, pages 281–292, 2008.

[11] Sumit Gulwani, Saurabh Srivastava, and Ramarathnam Venkatesan. Constraint-based invariant inference over predicate abstraction. In *VMCAI*, 2009.

[12] Peter Hawkins, Alex Aiken, Kathleen Fisher, Martin Rinard, and Mooly Sagiv. Data representation synthesis. In *PLDI*, pages 38–49. ACM, 2011.

[13] Susmit Jha, Sumit Gulwani, Sanjit A. Seshia, and Ashish Tiwari. Oracle-guided component-based program synthesis. In *ICSE*, pages 215–224, 2010.

[14] Barbara Jobstmann, Andreas Griesmayer, and Roderick Bloem. Program repair as a game. In *CAV*, pages 226–238, 2005.

[15] Tal Lev-Ami and Shmuel Sagiv. Tvla: A system for implementing static analyses. In *SAS*, 2000.

[16] Z. Manna and R. Waldinger. Synthesis: Dreams => programs. *IEEE Transactions on Software Engineering*, 5(4):294–328, 1979.

[17] Zohar Manna and Richard Waldinger. A deductive approach to program synthesis. *ACM Trans. Program. Lang. Syst.*, 2(1):90–121, 1980.

[18] A. Mishchenko, S. Chatterjee, R. Jiang, and R. K. Brayton. FRAIGs: A unifying representation for logic synthesis and verification. Technical report, EECS, UC Berkeley, 2005.

[19] Huu Hai Nguyen, Cristina David, Shengchao Qin, and Wei ngan Chin. Automated verification of shape and size properties via separation logic. In *In VMCAI*. Springer, 2007.

[20] Amir Pnueli and Roni Rosner. On the synthesis of an asynchronous reactive module. In *ICALP*, pages 652–671, London, UK, 1989. Springer-Verlag.

[21] Mooly Sagiv, Thomas Reps, and Reinhard Wilhelm. Parametric shape analysis via 3-valued logic. In *POPL*, pages 105–118. ACM, 1999.

[22] Horst Samulowitz and Fahiem Bacchus. Binary clause reasoning in qbf. In *SAT*, pages 353–367, 2006.

[23] M. Sharir and A. Pnueli. Two approaches to interprocedural data flow analysis. In *S. Muchnick, N. Jones (Eds.), Program Flow Analysis: Theory and Applications*, pages 189–234, 1981.

[24] Armando Solar-Lezama. *Program Synthesis By Sketching*. PhD thesis, EECS, UC Berkeley, 2008.

[25] Armando Solar-Lezama, Gilad Arnold, Liviu Tancau, Rastislav Bodik, Vijay Saraswat, and Sanjit Seshia. Sketching stencils. In *PLDI*, pages 167–178, 2007.

[26] Armando Solar-Lezama, Chris Jones, Gilad Arnold, and Rastislav Bodík. Sketching concurrent datastructures. In *PLDI*, 2008.

[27] Armando Solar-Lezama, Rodric Rabbah, Rastislav Bodik, and Kemal Ebcioglu. Programming by sketching for bit-streaming programs. In *PLDI*, 2005.

[28] Saurabh Srivastava, Sumit Gulwani, Swarat Chaudhuri, and Jeffrey S. Foster. Path-based inductive synthesis for program inversion. In *PLDI*, pages 492–503. ACM, 2011.

[29] Saurabh Srivastava, Sumit Gulwani, and Jeffrey Foster. From program verification to program synthesis. *POPL*, 2010.

[30] Martin Vechev and Eran Yahav. Deriving linearizable fine-grained concurrent objects. *SIGPLAN Not.*, 43(6):125–135, 2008.

[31] Martin Vechev, Eran Yahav, and Greta Yorsh. Abstraction-guided synthesis of synchronization. In *POPL*, New York, NY, USA, 2010. ACM.

High-Impact Defects: A Study of Breakage and Surprise Defects

Emad Shihab
Software Analysis and Intelligence Lab (SAIL)
Queen's University, Canada
emads@cs.queensu.ca

Audris Mockus
Avaya Labs Research
233 Mt Airy Rd, Basking Ridge, NJ
audris@avaya.com

Yasutaka Kamei, Bram Adams and Ahmed E. Hassan
Software Analysis and Intelligence Lab (SAIL)
Queen's University, Canada
{kamei, bram, ahmed}@cs.queensu.ca

ABSTRACT

The relationship between various software-related phenomena (e.g., code complexity) and post-release software defects has been thoroughly examined. However, to date these predictions have a limited adoption in practice. The most commonly cited reason is that the prediction identifies too much code to review without distinguishing the impact of these defects. Our aim is to address this drawback by focusing on *high-impact defects* for customers and practitioners. *Customers* are highly impacted by defects that break pre-existing functionality (breakage defects), whereas *practitioners* are caught off-guard by defects in files that had relatively few pre-release changes (surprise defects). The large commercial software system that we study already had an established concept of breakages as the highest-impact defects, however, the concept of surprises is novel and not as well established. We find that surprise defects are related to incomplete requirements and that the common assumption that a fix is caused by a previous change does not hold in this project. We then fit prediction models that are effective at identifying files containing breakages and surprises. The number of pre-release defects and file size are good indicators of breakages, whereas the number of co-changed files and the amount of time between the latest pre-release change and the release date are good indicators of surprises. Although our prediction models are effective at identifying files that have breakages and surprises, we learn that the prediction should also identify the nature or type of defects, with each type being specific enough to be easily identified and repaired.

Categories and Subject Descriptors

D.2.8 [**Software Engineering**]: Metrics—*Complexity measures, Performance measures*

General Terms

Software Quality Assurance

Keywords

High-Impact, Process Metrics, Defect Prediction

Permission to make digital or hard copies of all or part of this work for personal or classroom use is granted without fee provided that copies are not made or distributed for profit or commercial advantage and that copies bear this notice and the full citation on the first page. To copy otherwise, to republish, to post on servers or to redistribute to lists, requires prior specific permission and/or a fee.

ESEC/FSE'11, September 5–9, 2011, Szeged, Hungary.

Copyright 2011 ACM 978-1-4503-0443-6/11/09 ...$10.00.

1. INTRODUCTION

Work on defect prediction aims to assist practitioners in prioritizing software quality assurance efforts [6]. Most of this work uses code measures (e.g., [25, 35]), process measures (e.g., [11]), and social structure measures (e.g., [4]) to predict source code areas (i.e., files) where the post-release defects are most likely to be found. The number of pre-release changes or defects and the size of an artifact are commonly found to be the best indicators of a file's post-release defect potential.

Even though some studies showed promising performance results in terms of predictive power, the adoption of defect prediction models in practice remains low [10, 13, 29]. One of the main reasons is that the amount of code predicted to be defect-prone far exceeds the resources of the development teams considering inspection of that code. For example, Ostrand *et al.* [27] found that 80% of the defects were in 20% of the files. However, these 20% of the files accounted for 50% of the source code lines. At the same time, all defects are considered to have the same negative impact, which is not realistic, because, for example, documentation defects tend to be far less impacting than security defects. At the same time, model-based prediction tends to indicate the largest and the most changed files as defect-prone: areas already known to practitioners to be the most problematic.

In this work, we address the problem of predicting too many defects by focusing the prediction on the limited subset of *high-impact defects*. Since impact has a different meaning for different stakeholders, we consider two of the possible definitions in this paper: *breakages* and *surprises*. Breakages are a commonly accepted concept in industry that refer to defects that break functionality delivered in earlier releases of the product on which customers heavily rely in their daily operations. Such defects are more disruptive because 1) customers are more sensitive to defects that occur in functionality that they are used to than to defects in a new feature and 2) breakages are more likely to hurt the quality image of a producer, thus directly affecting its business. To ensure that we focus only on the highest impact defects, we only consider breakages that have severities "critical" (the product is rendered non-operational for a period of time) and "high" (the product operation has significant limitations negatively impacting the customer's business).

Whereas breakages have a high impact on customers, surprise defects are a novel concept representing a kind of defects that highly impact practitioners. Surprises are defects that appear in unexpected locations or locations that have a high ratio of post-to-pre release defects, catching practitioners off-guard, disrupting their already-tight quality assurance schedules. For example, post-release defects in files that are heavily changed or have many defects prior to the release are expected and scheduled for. However, when a defect appears in an unexpected file, the workflow of developers is disrupted, causing them to vacate their current work and shift focus to addressing these surprises.

The investigated project has used the concept of breakages for several decades but surprise defects are a new concept. Hence, we start by comparing the properties of breakage and surprise defects and qualifying the impact of surprises. We then build prediction models for breakages and surprise defects (RQ1), identify which factors are the best predictors for each type of defect (RQ2) and quantify the relative effect of each factor on the breakage and surprise-proneness (RQ3). Finally, we calculate the effort savings of using specialized defect prediction models and perform a qualitative evaluation of the usability of the prediction models in practice and propose ways to make such prediction more relevant.

We make the following contributions:

- **Identify and explore breakage and surprise defects.** We find that breakage and surprise defects are approximately one-fifth of the post-release defects. Only 6% of the files have both types of defects. For example, breakages tend to occur in locations that have experienced more defect fixing changes in the past and contain functionality that was implemented less recently than the functionality in locations with surprise defects.

- **Develop effective prediction models for breakage and surprise defects.** Our models can identify future breakage and surprise files with more than 70% recall and a two to three fold increase of precision over random prediction.

- **Identify and quantify the major factors predicting breakage and surprise defects.** Traditional defect prediction factors (i.e., pre-release defects and size) have a strong positive effect on the likelihood of a file containing a breakage, whereas the co-changed files and time-related factors have a negative effect on the likelihood of a file containing a surprise defect.

- **Measure the effort savings of specialized prediction models.** Our custom models reduce the amount of inspected files by 41 - 55%, which represents a 42 - 50% reduction in the number of inspected lines of code.

- **Propose areas and methods to make defect prediction more practical.** A qualitative study suggests that an important barrier to the use of prediction in practice is lack of indications about the nature of the problem or the ways to solve it. The method to detect surprise defects may be able to highlight areas of the code that have incorrect requirements. We propose that an essential part of defect prediction should include prediction of the nature of the defect or ways to fix it.

The rest of the paper is organized as follows. Section 2 highlights the related work. Section 3 compares the properties of breakages and surprise defects. Section 4 outlines the case study setup and Section 5 presents our case study results. Section 6 discusses the effort savings provided by the specialized models built in our study. Section 7 highlights the limitations of the study. Section 8 reflects on the lessons learned about the practicality of defect prediction and details our future work. We conclude the paper in Section 9.

2. RELATED WORK

The majority of the related work comes from the area of defect prediction. Previous work typically builds multivariate logistic regression models to predict defect-prone locations (e.g., files or directories). A large number of previous studies use complexity metrics (e.g., McCabe's cyclomatic complexity metric [19] and Chidamber and Kemerer (CK) metrics suite [5]) to predict defect-prone locations [3,12,24,26,32,35]. However, Graves *et al.* [11], Leszak *et al.* [18] and Herraiz *et al.* [15] showed that complexity metrics highly correlate with the much simpler lines of code (LOC) measure. Graves *et al.* [11] argued that change data is a better predictor of defects than code metrics in general and showed that the number of prior changes to a file is a good predictor of defects. A number of other studies supported the finding that prior changes are a good defect predictor and additionally showed that prior defect is also a good predictor of post release defects [1,14,17,18,23,33]. To sum up, this previous work showed that complexity metrics and hence size measured in LOC, prior change and prior defects are a good predictor of defect-proneness. The focus of the aforementioned work was to improve the prediction performance by enriching the set of metrics used in the prediction model. In this work, we incorporate the findings of previous work by using traditional defect prediction metrics/factors, in addition to other more specialized factors related to co-change and time properties to predict the location of highly impacting defects. However, we would like to note that our focus here is capturing high-impact defects rather than adding metrics to improve the performance of defect prediction models in general.

Although it has been shown that defect prediction can yield benefit in practice, its adoption remains low [10, 13]. As Ostrand *et al.* [27, 28] showed, 20% of the files with the highest number of predicted defects contain between 71-92% of the defects, however these 20% of the files make up 50% of the code. To make defect prediction more appealing to practice, recent work examined the performance of software prediction models when the effort required to address the identified defect is considered (i.e., effort-aware defect prediction) [2, 16, 20]. Although effort is taken into account, these models still predict the entire set of post-release defects, giving each defect equal impact potential.

Other work focused on reducing the set of predicted defects based on the semantics of the defect. For example, Shin *et al.* [31] and Zimmermann *et al.* [34] focused on predicting software vulnerabilities since they have high priority. Instead of narrowing down the set of defects vertically based on the semantics of the defects, we narrow down the defects horizontally across domains. For example, our models can predict high impact defects across many domains, whereas a model focused on vulnerability defects is only useful for one domain.

3. BREAKAGE AND SURPRISE DEFECTS

In this section, we provide background of the software project under study, and define breakages and surprise defects. We then characterize and compare breakage and surprise defects.

3.1 Background

Software Project: The data used in our study comes from a well-established telephony system with many tens of thousands of customers that was in active development for almost 30 years and, thus, has highly mature development and quality assurance procedures. The present size of the system is approximately seven million non-comment LOC, primarily in C and C++. The data used in our study covers five different releases of the software system.

Change Data: There are two primary sources of data used. Sablime, a configuration management system, is used to track Modification Requests (MR), which we use to identify and measure the size of a software release and the number of defects (pre-release and post-release). When a change to the software is needed, a work item (MR) is created. MRs are created for any modification to the code: new features, enhancements, and fixes. The project uses internally developed tools on top of the Source Code Control System (SCCS) to keep track of changes to the code. Every change to the code has to have an associated MR and a separate MR is created for different tasks. We call an individual modification to a single file a delta. Each MR may have zero or more deltas associated with it. Since the development culture is very mature, these norms are strictly enforced by peers.

For each MR, we extracted a number of attributes from Sablime and the SCCS: the files the MR touches, the release in which the MR was discovered, the date the MR was reported, the software build where the code was submitted, the resolution date (i.e., when the MR was fixed/implemented), resolution status for each release the MR was submitted to, the severity and priority of the MR, the MR type (e.g., enhancement or problem) and the general availability date of the release that includes the MR.

For each release, we classify all MRs into two types: pre-release changes (or defects if they are type problem), and post-release defects. MRs that are submitted to a release before the General Availability date (we refer to it as GA), are considered to be pre-release defects. Fixes reported for a particular release after the GA date, are considered to be post-release defects.

3.2 Defining Breakages and Surprise Defects

Breakage Defects: Defects are introduced into the product because the source code is modified to add new features or to fix existing defects. When such defects break, i.e., cause a fault or change existing functionality that has been introduced in prior releases, we call these defects breakages. The concept of breakages typically is familiar in most companies. For example, in the project studied in this paper, all severity one and two defects of established functionality are carefully investigated by a small team of experts. In addition to a root-cause analysis and suggestions to improve quality assurance efforts, the team also determines the originating MR that introduced the breakage. While other companies may use a different terminology than "breakages", most investigate such high-impact problems just as carefully, therefore similar data is likely to be available in other projects with mature quality practices.

Surprise Defects: Previous research has shown that the number of pre-release defects is a good predictor of post-release defects (e.g., [23, 35]). Therefore, it is a common practice for software practitioners to thoroughly test files with a large number of pre-release defects. However, in some cases, files that rarely change also have post-release defects. Such defects catch the software practitioners off-guard, disrupting their already-tight schedules. To the best of our knowledge, surprise defects have not been studied yet, and therefore are not recorded in issue tracking systems. Hence, for the purpose of our study, we use one possible definition of surprise. We define the degree to which a file contains surprise defects as:

$$Surprise(file) = \frac{No. of\ post\ release\ defects(file)}{No. of\ pre\ release\ defects(file)},$$

whereas in files without pre-release defects we define it as:
$Surprise(file) = No. of\ post\ release\ defects(file) * 2.$

Because our definition of surprise is given in terms of the ratio of post-to-pre release defects, we need to determine from what threshold the ratio should be considered significant. For example, if a file has one post-release defect and 10 pre-release defects, i.e., the defined surprise value is $\frac{1}{10} = 0.1$, should this file be flagged as being a surprise?

To calculate the surprise threshold, we examine all the files that had a defect reported within one month of the GA date of the previous release. The intuition behind this rule is that high impact defects are likely to be reported immediately after the software is released. Hence, we calculate the median of the ratio of all post-release defects and all pre-release defects for all files changed within one month of the previous GA date, then use this value as the surprise threshold for the next release. For example, the surprise threshold for release 2.1 is determined by the median ratio of post-to-pre-release defects of all files that had a post-release defect reported against them within a month after release 1.1.

3.3 Occurrence of Breakage and Surprise Defects

Before analyzing the characteristics of breakage and surprise defects, we examine the percentage of files that have breakages and surprise defects. To put things in context, we also show the percentage of files with one or more post-release defects. Table 1 shows that on average, only 2% of the files have breakages or surprise defects. That is approximately one fifth of the files that have post-release defects.

Having a small percentage of files does not necessarily mean less code, since some files are larger than others. Therefore, we also examine the amount of LOC that these files represent. Table 1 shows that on average, the amount of LOC that these breakage and surprise files make up is 3.2% and 3.8%, respectively. This is approximately one fourth the LOC of files with the post-release defects. The reduction is both promising, because it narrows down the set of files to be flagged for review, and challenging, because predicting such unusual files is much harder.

Table 1 also compares the percentages of MRs representing post-release, breakage and surprise defects. On average, the percentage of breakage and surprise MRs is much smaller than that of post-release MRs. Since we use the surprise threshold from the previous release to determine the surprise threshold, we are not able to calculate surprise defects for the first release (R1.1).

Breakage and surprise defects are difficult to pinpoint, since they only appear in 2% of the files.

3.4 Breakages vs Surprise Defects

As mentioned earlier, breakage defects are high severity defects that break existing functionality. They are a common concept in industry, and their impact is understood to be quite high. However, surprise defects are a concept that we defined based on our own industrial experience. In this section, we would like to learn more about the characteristics of surprise defects and verify our assumption that surprise defects highly impact the development organization, by addressing the following questions:

- Are surprise defects different than breakage defects? If so, what are the differences?
- Are surprise defects impactful?

Such verification helps us appreciate the value of studying surprise defects and to understand the implications of our findings for future research in the field.

Table 1: Percentage of Files, LOC and MRs containing Post-release, Breakage and Surprise defects.

Release	Post-Release			Breakage			Surprise		
	Files	LOC	MRs	Files	LOC	MRs	Files	LOC	MRs
R1.1	21.8	27	78.8	1.6	2.6	29.4	-	-	-
R2.1	6.5	8.4	48.6	2.1	2.6	27.1	0.2	0.4	1.5
R3.0	7.8	12.7	54.5	2.1	3.8	28.4	3.3	6.4	13.6
R4.0	11	18	79.7	1.4	1.3	25.6	3.0	5.2	11.5
R4.1	5.0	6.8	46.1	2.5	2.8	22.4	1.5	3.2	6.1
Average	**10.4**	**14.6**	**61.5**	**2.0**	**3.2**	**26.6**	**2.0**	**3.8**	**8.2**

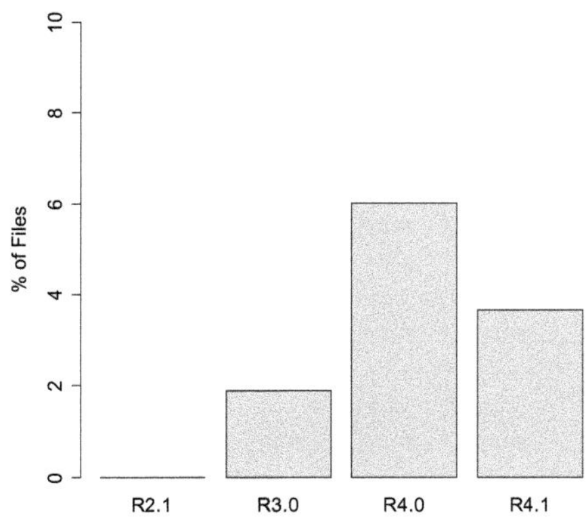

Figure 1: Percentage of Files Containing both, Surprise and Breakage Defects

Are surprise defects different than breakage defects? If so, what are the differences?

First, we look at the locations where breakage and surprise defects occur. If we, for example, find that breakage and surprise defects occur in the same location, then we can assume that the prediction models for breakage-prone files will suffice for surprise defect prediction.

To quantify the percentage of files that contain both types of defects, we divide the files into two sets: files with breakages and files with surprise defects. Then, we measure the intersection of the files in the two sets divided by the union of the files in the two sets:

$$\frac{Breakages \bigcap Surprise}{Breakages \bigcup Surprise}.$$

Figure 1 shows the percentage of files that have both breakages and surprise defects. At most 6% of the breakage and surprise files overlap. This low percentage of overlap shows that breakages and surprises are two very different types of defects. However, further examination of their specific characteristics is needed to better understand the potential overlap.

Therefore, we investigate the characteristics of breakage and surprise defects along the different defect prediction dimensions. For example, previous work showed that the amount of activity (i.e., number of pre-release changes) is a good indicator of defect-proneness, therefore, we look at the activity of breakage and surprise defects to compare and contrast. We summarize our findings, which are statistically significant with a p-value < 0.05, as follows:

Activity. Comparing the activity, measured in number of MRs, of breakage and surprise files to non-breakage and non-surprise files shows that breakage and surprise files have less activity. This could indicate that perhaps breakage and surprise files were inspected less.
MR size. Breakage and surprise files are modified by larger MRs. On average, a breakage MR touches 47 files as compared to 8 files touched for a non-breakage MRs. Surprise MRs touch 71 files on average as compared to 13 files touched by non-surprise MRs.
Time. The start times of MRs that touch breakage and surprise files show that for a particular release, breakage files are modified earlier than average, whereas surprise defect files are on average, worked on closer to the release date. This suggests that considerably less time was available for the development and testing of surprise files.
Functionality. By definition, breakage files are involved with legacy features (e.g., core features of the communication software), whereas surprise defect files are involved with more recent features (e.g., the porting of the studied software system to work in virtual environments).
Maintenance efforts. Breakage and surprise defect files are involved in more code addition MRs than the average non-breakage or non-surprise files. However, breakage files were involved in more fixes than surprise defect files.

Are surprise defects impactful?

The above comparisons show that breakage and surprise defects are different. To assess the impact of surprise defects we selected the five files with the highest surprise ratios in the last studied release of the software for an in-depth evaluation.

To evaluate the five files with the highest surprise score, we selected the latest changes prior to GA and the changes (defects) within one month after the GA for each of these files and investigated the nature and the origin of these defects by reading defect descriptions, resolution history and notes, inspection notes, as well as changes to the code. The five files were created eight, six, five, and, (for two files), one year(s) prior to GA. There were seven fixes within one month after the GA in these five files. Five defects had high severity and only two had medium severity, indicating that all of them were important defects. At least one fix in each of the five files was related to incomplete or inadequate requirements, i.e., introduced at the time of file creation or during the last enhancement of functionality.

For each post-GA defect in these five files, we traced back through changes to determine the first change that introduced the defect. Our intuition was that if the prediction can point to the change introducing the defect, it would limit the scope of the developers inspecting the flagged area to the kind of functionality changed and to the particular lines of code, thus simplifying the task of determining the nature of the potential defect or, perhaps, even highlighting the avenues for fixing it.

The results were surprising. In none of the cases the last pre-GA change could have been the cause of the defect. In the five defects related to inadequate requirements, we had to trace all the way to the initial implementation of the file. In the case of the two more recent files, at least we found a relationship between the pre-GA change (that was fixing inadequate requirements) and the post-GA fix that was fixing another shortcoming of the same requirements that was not addressed by the prior fix. For the two remaining defects introduced during coding or design phases, we had to trace back at least three changes to find the cause.

This qualitative investigation supports our intuition about the nature of surprise defects and our findings of the differences between breakages and surprise defects. The surprise defects appear to be an important kind of unexpected defect that appears to lurk in the code for long periods of time before surfacing. It also suggests a possible mechanism by which the prediction of surprise defects might work. As the usage profile or the intensity of usage changes over the years, early warnings are given by customers wanting to adjust a feature (one of the defects), or hard-to reproduce defects are starting to surface. Two of the defects appear to be caused by the increased use of multicore architecture that resulted in hard-to-reproduce timer errors and interactions with the system clock. At some point a major fault (surprise) is discovered (system restarting because of full message buffer, or because of data corruption) and the shortcomings of the requirements are finally addressed by the fix to the surprise defect.

Breakage and surprise defects are unique and different. Surprise defects also have high severity and appear to indicate problems in the requirements.

4. CASE STUDY SETUP

Now that we have analyzed the characteristics of breakage and surprise defects, we want to examine the effectiveness of predicting the locations of breakage and surprise defects. We address the following research questions:

RQ1. Can we effectively predict which files will have breakage/surprise defects?

RQ2. Which factors are important for the breakage/surprise defect prediction models?

RQ3. What effect does each factor have on the likelihood of finding a breakage/surprise defect in a file?

In this section, we outline and discuss the case study setup. First, we present the various factors used to predict breakage and surprise defects. Then, we outline the prediction modeling technique used. Finally, we outline how we evaluate the performance of our prediction models.

4.1 Factors Used to Predict Breakage and Surprise Defects

The factors that we use to predict files with breakage or surprise defects belong to three different categories: 1) traditional factors found in previous defect prediction work, 2) factors associated to co-changed files and 3) time-related factors (i.e., the age of a file and the time since the last change to the file).

These factors are based on previous post-release defect prediction work and on our findings in Section 3.4.

Traditional Factors: Previous work shows that the number of previous changes, the number of pre-release defects and the size of a file are good indicators of post-release defects [11, 35]. Since breakage and surprise defects are a special case of post-release defects, we believe that they can help us predict breakage and surprise defects as well.

Co-change Factors: By definition, breakage and surprise defects are not expected to happen. One possible reason for their occurrence could be hidden dependencies (e.g., logical coupling [9]). The intuition here is that a change to a co-changed file may cause a defect. Since more recent changes are more relevant, we also calculate for each factor its value in the three months prior to release, labeled as "recent".

Time Factors: To take into account the fact that breakage and surprise defects start earlier and later than average, respectively, we consider factors related to how close to a release a file is changed, as well as the file's age.

Each category comprises several factors, as listed in Table 2. For each factor, we provide a description, motivation and any related work.

4.2 Prediction Models

In this work, we are interested in predicting whether or not a file has a breakage or surprise defect. Similar to previous work on defect prediction [35], we use a logistic regression model. A logistic regression model correlates the independent variables in Table 2) with the dependent variable (probability of the file containing a breakage or surprise defect).

Initially, we built the logistic regression model using all of the factors. However, to avoid collinearity problems and to assure that all of the variables in the model are statistically significant, we removed highly correlated variables (i.e., any variables with correlation higher than 0.5). In the end, we were left with five factors that all had a Variance Inflation Factor (VIF) below 2.5, as recommended by previous work [4]. To test for statistical significance, we measure the p-value of the independent variables in the model to make sure that this is less than 0.1.

Altogether, we extracted a total of 15 factors. After removing the highly correlated variables, five factors were left that covered all three categories, i.e., pre_defects, file_size, num_co-changed_files, modification_size_co-changed_files and latest_change_before_release.

4.3 Performance Evaluation of the Prediction Models

After building the logistic regression model, we verify its performance using two criteria: Explanatory Power and Predictive Power. These measures are widely used to measure the performance of logistic regression models in defect prediction [6, 35].

Explanatory Power. Ranges between 0-100%, and quantifies the variability in the data explained by the model. We also report and compare the variability explained by each independent variable in the model. Examining the explained variability of each independent variable allows us to quantify the relative importance of the independent variables in the model.

Predictive Power. Measures the accuracy of the model in predicting the files that have one or more breakage/surprise defects. The accuracy measures that we use (precision and recall) are based on the classification results in the confusion matrix (shown in Table 3).

1. **Precision:** the percentage of correctly classified breakage/surprise files over all of the files classified as having breakage/surprise defects: Precision $= \frac{TP}{TP+FP}$.

2. **Recall:** the percentage of correctly classified breakage/surprise files relative to all of the files that actually have breakage/surprise defects: Recall $= \frac{TP}{TP+FN}$.

Table 2: List of Factors Used to Predict Breakage and Surprise Defects. Factors in italics are factors used in the final prediction models, i.e., after removing highly correlated factors.

Category	Factor	Description	Rationale	Related Work
Traditional Factors	*pre_defects*	Number of pre-release defects	Traditionally performs well for post-release defect prediction.	Prior defects are a good indicator of future defects [33].
	pre_changes	Number of pre-release changes	Traditionally performs well for post-release defect prediction.	The number of prior modifications to a file is a good predictor of future defects [1, 11, 18].
	file_size	Total number of lines in the file	Traditionally performs well for post-release defect prediction.	The lines of code metric correlates well with most complexity metrics (e.g., McCabe complexity) [11, 15, 18, 27].
Co-change Factors	(recent) *num_co-changed_files*	Number of files a file co-changed with	The higher the number of files a file co-changes with, the higher the chance of missing to propagate a change.	The number of files touched by a change is a good indicator of its risk to introduce a defect [22]. We apply this factor to the number of files co-changing with a file.
	(recent) size_co-changed_files	Cumulative size of the co-changed files	The larger the co-changed files are, the harder they are to maintain and understand.	The simple lines of code metric correlates well with most complexity metrics (e.g., McCabe complexity) [11, 15, 18, 27]. We apply this factor to co-changing files.
	(recent) *modification_size_co-changed_files*	The number of lines changed in the co-changed files	The larger the changes are to the co-changed files, the larger the chance of introducing a defect.	Larger changes have a higher risk of introducing a defect [22]. We apply this factor to a file's co-changing files.
	(recent) num_changes_co-changed_files	Number of changes to the co-changed files	The higher the number of changes to the co-changed file, the higher the chance of introducing defects.	The number of prior modifications to a file is a good predictor of its future defects [1, 11, 18]. We apply this factor to a file's co-changing files.
	(recent) pre_defects_co-changed_files	Number of pre-release defects in co-changed files	The higher the number of pre-release defects in the co-changed files, the higher the chance of a defect.	Prior defects are a good indicator of future defects [33]. We apply this factor to a file's co-changing files.
Time Factors	*latest_change_before_release*	The time from the latest change to the release (in days)	Changes made close to the release date do not have time to get tested properly.	More recent changes contribute more defects than older changes [11].
	age	The age of the file (from first change until the release GA date)	The older the file, the harder it becomes to change and maintain.	Code becomes harder to change over time [8].

Table 3: Confusion Matrix

	True class	
Classified as	Breakage	No Breakage
Breakage	TP	FP
No Breakage	FN	TN

A precision value of 100% would indicate that every file we classify as having a breakage/surprise defect, actually has a breakage/surprise defect. A recall value of 100% would indicate that every file that actually has a breakage was classified as having a breakage/surprise.

We employ 10-fold cross-validation [7]. The data set is divided into two parts, a testing data set that contains 10% of the original data set and a training data set that contains 90% of the original data set. The model is trained using the training data and its accuracy is tested using the testing data. We repeat the 10-fold cross validation 10 times by randomly changing the fold. We report the average of the 10 runs.

Determining the logistic regression model threshold value: The output of a logistic regression model is a probability (between 0 and 1) of the likelihood that a file belongs to the true class (e.g., a file is buggy). Then, it is up to the user of the output of the logistic regression model to determine a threshold at which she/he will consider a file as belonging to the true class. Generally speaking, a threshold of 0.5 is used. For example, if a file has a likelihood of 0.5 or higher, then it is considered buggy, otherwise it is not.

However, the threshold is different for different data sets and the value of the threshold affects the precision and recall values of the prediction models. In this paper, we determine the threshold for each model using an approach that examines the tradeoff between type I and type II errors [22]. Type I errors are files that are identified as belonging to the true class, while they are not. Having a low logistic regression threshold (e.g., 0.01) increases type I errors: a higher fraction of identified files will not belong to the true class. A high type I error leads to a waste of resources since many non-faulty files may be wrongly classified. On the other hand, type II error is the fraction of files in the true class that are not identified as being true when they should be. Having a high threshold can lead to large type II errors, and thus missing many files that may be defective.

To determine the optimal threshold for our models, we perform a cost-benefit analysis between the type I and type II errors. Similar to previous work [22], we vary the threshold value between 0 to 1 and use the threshold where the type I and type II errors are equal.

4.4 Measuring the Effect of Factors on the Predicted Probability

In addition to evaluating the accuracy and explanatory power of our prediction models, we need to understand the effect of a factor on the likelihood of finding a breakage or surprise defect. Quantifying this effect helps practitioners gain an in-depth understanding of how the various factors relate to breakage and surprise defects.

To quantify this effect, we set all of the factors to their median value and record the predicted probabilities, which we call the Standard Median Model (SMM). Then, to measure the individual effect of each factor, we set all of the factors to their median value, except for the factor whose effect we want to measure. We double the median value of that factor and re-calculate the predicted values, which we call the Doubled Median Model (DMM).

We then subtract the predicted probability of the SMM from the predicted output of the DMM and divide by the predicted probability of the SMM. Doing so provides us with a way to quantify the effect a factor has on the likelihood of a file containing a breakage or surprise defect.

The effect of a factor can be positive or negative. A positive effect means that a higher value of the factor increases the likelihood, whereas a negative effect value means that a higher value of the factor decreases the likelihood of a file containing a breakage/surprise defect.

5. CASE STUDY RESULTS

In this section, we address the research questions posted earlier. First, we examine the accuracy (in terms of predictive and explanatory power) of our prediction models. Then, we examine the contribution of each factor on the models in terms of explanatory power. Lastly, we examine the effect of the factors on the breakage- and surprise-proneness.

RQ1. Can we effectively predict which files will have breakage/surprise defects?

Using the extracted factors, we build logistic regression models that aim to predict whether or not a file will have a breakage or surprise defect. The prediction was performed for five different releases of the large commercial software system. To measure predictive power, we present the precision, recall and the threshold (Th.) value used in the logistic regression model, for each release. The last row in the tables presents the average across all releases.

Predictive power: Tables 4 and 5 show the results of the breakage and surprise defect prediction models, respectively. On average, the precision for breakage and surprise defects is low, i.e., 4.7% for breakages and 6.7% for surprise defects.

Table 4: Performance of Breakage Prediction Models

	Predictive Power			**Explanatory Power**
Release	Precision	Recall	Th. (pred)	Deviance Explained
R1.1	3.7	70.4	0.45	17.48%
R2.1	4.8	69.2	0.48	7.99%
R3	4.8	69.6	0.49	14.49%
R4	3.9	73.1	0.48	11.68%
R4.1	6.5	73.8	0.49	13.98%
Average	4.7	71.2	0.48	13.12%

Table 5: Performance of Surprise Prediction Models

	Predictive Power				**Explanatory Power**
Release	Precision	Recall	Th. (pred)	Th. (sup)	Deviance Explained
R1.1	-	-	-	-	-
R2.1	3.9	71.6	0.55	2.4	4.39 %
R3	7.3	69.0	0.44	1.7	10.79 %
R4	9.8	77.7	0.39	1.6	30.88 %
R4.1	5.7	78.0	0.38	1.5	25.27 %
Average	6.7	74.1	0.44	1.8	17.83 %

It is important to note that the low precision value is due to the low percentage of breakage and surprise defects in the data set (as shown earlier in Table 1). As noted by Menzies *et al.* [21], in cases where the number of instances of an occurrence is so low (i.e., 2%), achieving a high precision is extremely difficult, yet not that important. In fact, a random prediction would be correct 2.0% of the time, on average, whereas our prediction model more than doubles that precision for breakages and more than triples that for surprise defects. The more important measure of the prediction model's performance is recall [21], which, on average is 71.2% for breakage defects and 74.1% for surprise defects.

Explanatory power: The explanatory power of the models ranges between 8 - 17.5% (average of 13.1%) for breakage defects and between 4.4 - 30.9% (average of 17.8%) for surprise defects. The values that we achieve here are comparable to those achieved in previous work predicting post-release defects [4,30].

The explanatory power may be improved if more (or better) factors are used in the prediction model. We view the factors used in our study as a starting point for breakage and surprise defect prediction and plan to (and encourage others to) further investigate in order to improve the explanatory power of these models.

Other considerations: For each prediction model, we explicitly report the threshold for the logistic regression models as Th. (pred) in Tables 4 and 5. In addition, the surprise threshold, which we use to identify files that had surprise defects, is given under the Th. (sup) column in Table 5.

Since the number of pre-release defects is used in the dependent variable of the surprise model ($Surprise(file) = \frac{post\ defects}{pre\ defects}$), we did not use it as part of the independent variables in the prediction model. This makes our results even more significant, since previous work [23,35] showed that pre-release defects traditionally are the largest contributor to post-release defect prediction models.

> *Our prediction models predict breakage and surprise defects with a precision that is at least double that of a random prediction and a recall above 71%.*

RQ2. Which factors are important for the breakage/surprise defect prediction models?

In addition to knowing the predictive and explanatory power of our models, we would like to know which factors contribute the most to these predictions. To answer this question, we perform an ANOVA analysis to determine the contribution of the three factor categories. We summarize the findings in Tables 6 and 7 as follows:

Traditional Defect Prediction Factors: are major contributors for the breakage defect prediction models, however, they only have a small contribution in predicting surprise defects.

Co-Change Factors provide a small contribution to breakage defect prediction models, however, they make a major contribution to predicting surprise defects.

Time Factors provide a minor contribution to breakage defect prediction models, however, they make a major contribution in predicting surprise defects.

Although there are exceptions to the above mentioned observations (e.g., traditional defect prediction factors make a major contribution to the surprise defect model in R2.1), our observations are based on the trends observed in the majority of the releases.

As mentioned earlier in Section 3.4, breakage files were mainly involved with defect fixing efforts and are, by definition, defects that are found in the field. Perhaps these characteristics of breakage defects help explain why the traditional post-release defect prediction factors perform well in predicting breakages.

Furthermore, earlier observations in Section 3.4 showed that surprise defect files were worked on later than other files (i.e., MRs that touched surprise defect files were started later than other MRs). Our findings show that being changed close to a release is one of the best indicators of whether or not a file will have a surprise defect.

Traditional defect prediction factors are good indicators of breakage defects. The factors related to co-changed files and time-related factors are good indicators of surprise defects.

RQ3. What effect does each factor have on the likelihood of finding a breakage/surprise defect in a file?

Thus far we examined the prediction accuracy and the importance of the factors to these prediction models. Now, we study the effect of each factor on the likelihood of finding a breakage or surprise defect in a file. In addition to measuring the effect, we also consider stability and explanatory impact. If an effect has the same sign/direction for all releases (i.e., positive or negative effect in all releases), then we label it as highly stable. If the effect of a factor has the same sign in all releases except for one, then we label it as being mainly stable. A factor having a different sign in more than two of the five releases is labeled as being unstable. The explanatory impact column is derived from the values in Tables 6 and 7. If a factor belongs to a category that had a strong explanatory power, then we label it as having high impact, otherwise we consider it as having low impact.

We use the stability and impact measure to help explain the strength of our findings. For example, if we find that a factor has a positive effect and has high impact to the explanatory power of the model, then we believe this effect to be strong.

Breakage Defects: Table 8 shows the effect of the different factors on the likelihood of predicting a breakage defect in a file. We observe that in all releases, pre-release defects have a positive effect on the likelihood of a breakage defect existing in a file (i.e., highly stable). In addition, Table 6 showed that the traditional defect prediction factors contributed the most to the explanatory power of the model (i.e., high impact). File size and the number of co-changed files generally have a positive and negative effect, respectively. However, the impact of the number of co-changed files and recent modification size co-changed files is low (as shown in Table 6). Similarly, the latest change before release factor had low impact.

As stated earlier, our manual examination of the breakage files showed that breakage files were especially involved with fixing efforts. Therefore, the fact that pre-release defects and size have a strong positive effect was expected (since these factors are positively correlated with post-release defects). In fact, we found that the average file size of breakage files is 50% larger than non-breakage files. The rest of the factors had low impact on the explanatory power of the prediction model, therefore we cannot conclude any meaningful results from their effect.

Release 4 (R4) in our results seems to be an outlier. For example, contrary to the other releases, file size shows a negative effect in R4. After closer examination, we found that R4 was a large major release that added a large amount of new functionality. This could be the reason why the effect values for R4 are so different from the effect results of the remaining releases.

Surprise Defects: Table 9 shows the effect values for the surprise defect prediction model. In this model, file size has a large stable positive effect, however as shown earlier in Table 7 this factor category has very little contribution to the explanatory power of the model (i.e., low impact).

The number of co-changed files has a negative effect that is highly stable and highly impacting. This is counter-intuitive, especially since manual inspection showed that MRs that contained surprise files are larger than average. After closer examination, we found that although surprise files were part of large MRs, the number of surprise files in those MRs was low. In fact, the percentage of surprise files in those large MRs was 16.5% (15% in R2.1 and 17% in the remaining 3 releases). To sum up, we find that surprise defect files exist in large MRs, however these surprise files make up only a small portion of those MRs.

We find that the recent modification size of co-changed files has a negative effect that is mainly stable and highly impacting. Furthermore, as expected, making a change last minute increases the likelihood of a surprise defect (i.e., the negative effect of latest change before release). As shown in Section 3.4, in contrast to breakages, surprise defect files were worked on later than usual. We conjecture that starting late means less time for testing, hence the much higher effect of these late changes on surprise defect files compared to the breakage files.

Pre-release defects and file size have a positive effect on the likelihood of a file containing a breakage defect. The number of co-changed files, the modification size of recently co-changed files and the time since last change before release have a negative effect on the likelihood of a file having a surprise defect.

Table 6: Contribution of Factor Categories to the Explanatory Power of Breakage Prediction Models

	R1.1	R2.1	R3	R4	R4.1
Traditional Defect Prediction Factors	15.60%	6.80%	11.16%	8.92%	10.75%
Co-Change Factors	1.47%	1.09%	2.93%	0.62%	3.22%
Time Factors	0.39%	0.09%	0.39%	2.12%	0.00%
Overall Deviance Explained	**17.47%**	**7.98%**	**14.48%**	**11.67%**	**13.98%**

Table 7: Contribution of Factor Categories to the Explanatory Power of Surprise Prediction Models

	R1.1	R2.1	R3	R4	R4.1
Traditional Defect Prediction Factors	-%	2.94%	2.76%	0.68%	0.69%
Co-Change Factors	-%	1.11%	4.56%	9.80%	14.46%
Time Factors	-%	0.33%	3.46%	20.38%	10.11%
Overall Deviance Explained	-%	**4.39%**	**10.79%**	**30.87%**	**25.27%**

Table 8: Effect of factors on the likelihood of predicting a file with a breakage defect. Effect is measured by setting a factor to double its median value (1 if the median is 0), while the rest of the factors are set to their median value.

	R1.1	R2.1	R3	R4	R4.1	Stability	Explanatory Impact
pre_defects	136%	106%	85%	121%	154%	Highly Stable	High Impact
file_size	157%	68%	575%	-47%	39%	Mainly Stable	High Impact
num_co_changed_files_per_mr	-76%	-79%	-91%	629%	-89%	Mainly Stable	Low Impact
recent_modification_size_co_changed_files	3%	2%	13%	-4%	3%	Mainly Stable	Low Impact
latest_change_before_release	-47%	55%	85%	-88%	5%	Not Stable	Low Impact

Table 9: Effect of factors on the likelihood of predicting a file with a surprise defect. Effect is measured by setting a factor to double its median value (1 if the median is 0), while the rest of the factors are set to their median value.

	R1.1	R2.1	R3	R4	R4.1	Stability	Explanatory Impact
file_size	-	1113%	260%	184%	126%	Highly Stable	Low Impact
num_co_changed_files_per_mr	-	-57%	-75%	-71%	-85%	Highly Stable	High Impact
recent_modification_size_co_changed_files	-	6%	-3%	-28%	-19%	Mainly Stable	High Impact
latest_change_before_release	-	-50%	-65%	-97%	-92%	Highly Stable	High Impact

6. EFFORT SAVINGS BY FOCUSING ON SURPRISE AND BREAKAGE FILES

Thus far, we have shown that we are able to build prediction models to predict files that contain breakage and surprise defects. However, one question still lingers: what if we used the traditional post-release defect prediction model to predict breakage and surprise defects? Is it really worth the effort to build these specialized models?

To investigate whether building specialized prediction models for breakage and surprise defects is beneficial, we use defect prediction models that are trained to predict post-release defects, to predict files with breakages and surprise defects. Due to the fact that post-release defects are much more common than breakages or surprise defects, post-release defect models are more likely to say that most files have breakages or surprise defects. That will lead to a large amount of unnecessary work. Therefore, we use the number of false negatives to compare the performance of the post-release models and the specialized models. To make a meaningful comparison of effort (which is related to Type I error), we fix Type II error to be the same in both models.

Breakage Defects. Table 10 shows the results of the specialized prediction model (Breakage -> Breakage) and the post-release prediction model (Post -> Breakage) for release 4.1. Both of these

Table 10: Breakages in Release 4.1

	Breakage -> Breakage Predicted			Post -> Breakage Predicted	
Actual	0	1	Actual	0	1
0	1093	320	0	875	538
1	7	26	1	7	26

models predict files that have breakage defects. The false positives are highlighted (in grey) in Table 10. We observe that the specialized prediction model has approximately 41% (i.e., $\frac{538-320}{538}$) less false positives than the post-release model. This means that using the specialized model would reduce the inspection effort of files by 41%. We also convert this effort saving into LOC, which is approximately 42% of the total LOC.

Surprise Defects. Table 11 shows the results of the specialized model (Surprise -> Surprise) and the post-release prediction model (Post -> Surprise) for files that have surprise defects. In this case, the specialized models lead to approximately 55% (i.e., $\frac{525-235}{525}$) effort savings (i.e., less false positives). Comparing the savings in terms of LOC, we find that using the specialized prediction model

Table 11: Surprise in R4.1

	Surprise -> Surprise Predicted			Post -> Surprise Predicted	
Actual	0	1	Actual	0	1
0	1193	235	0	903	525
1	4	14	1	4	14

leads to approximately 50% effort savings compared to using a traditional post-release defect prediction model. This is a considerable amount of effort savings and shows the benefits of building a specialized prediction model of files with surprise defects.

Using our custom prediction models reduces the amount of files inspected by practitioners by 41% for breakages and 55% for surprise defects.

7. LIMITATIONS

Threats to Construct Validity consider the relationship between theory and observation, in case the measured variables do not measure the actual factors.

Breakage MRs were manually identified in our data by project experts. Although this manual linking was done by these project experts, some MRs may have been missed or incorrectly linked.

We used files in defects reported within one month after release to determine the surprise defect threshold. The assumption here is that defects reported within one month involve important functionality that is widely used after release. Defects that affect important functionality may be reported later than one month, however.

Threats to External Validity consider the generalization of our findings. The studied project was a commercial project written mainly in C/C++, therefore, our results may not generalize to other commercial or open source projects.

8. LESSONS LEARNED AND FUTURE WORK

After performing our study, we asked the opinions of the highly experienced quality manager in the project about the prediction results. The manager has a theory about the reported effect of our $last\_change\_before\_release$ factor. The theory is that the so called "late fix frenzies" that go on in organizations to bring down the number of open defects in a software system before the release, might have compromised the quality of inspections and other quality assurance activities. This suggests that prediction may help to quantify and confirm intuition about the relationships between the aspects of the development process and the high-impact defects.

However, when the quality manager considered the merits of our prediction by their utility for system verification she argued that identifying locations of defects is of limited use to system testers because they test system features or behaviors, not individual files. In addition, she doubted that the predicted location could be helpful even to developers doing inspections or unit tests without the additional information about the nature of the problem or how it should be fixed.

Despite the positive findings related to prediction quality, narrowing the scope, and effort savings, we still appear to be far from the state where the prediction results could be used in practice. Based on our quantitative and qualitative findings and experience we hypothesize that for defect prediction to become a practical tool, each predicted location has to also contain a clear suggestion on why the defect might be there and how it may be fixed.

To achieve this, we propose a procedure similar to the one we conducted to identify surprise defects, to classify defects into a variety of classes according to their nature, the ways they may have been introduced, and to the ways they may need to be fixed. We expect that each type of high-impact defect would have a different prediction signature, which, in turn, can be used to provide developers with a recommendation on where the defect may be, what nature it may have, and how it may be fixed. We can see an example of such a classification in the static analysis tools that not only provide a warning, but also give a reason why a particular pattern might be a defect and a clear suggestion on how the potential defect can be fixed. We are not aware of any similar patterns for defect prediction.

For example, our investigation of surprise defects could be used to provide a warning of the kind: "This file might contain a defect that has been introduced a while ago, perhaps because of incorrect requirements. Change patterns to this file suggest that the usage profile might have changed recently and the requirements may need to be reviewed to make sure they are accurate and complete." Obviously, a more extensive investigation may be needed to provide more specific recommendations and we believe that the defect prediction methods should be tailored not simply to predict defect locations, but, like basic static analysis tools such as `lint`, should also detect patterns of changes that are suggestive of a particular type of defect, and recommend appropriate remedies.

9. CONCLUSION

The majority of defect prediction work focuses on predicting post-release defects, yet the adoption of this work in practice remains relatively low [10, 13]. One of the main reasons for this is that defect prediction techniques generally identify too many files as having post-release defects, requiring significant inspection effort from developers.

Instead of considering all defects as equal, this paper focuses on predicting a small subset of defects that are highly impacting. Since there are many different interpretations of "high impact", we focus on one interpretation from the perspective of customers (breakage defects) and one from the perspective of practitioners (surprise defects). We find that:

- Both kinds of defects are different and that surprise defects, similar to the more established concept of breakage defects, have a high impact.
- Specialized defect prediction models can predict breakage and surprise defects effectively, yielding sizeable effort savings over using simple post-release defect prediction models.
- Traditional defect prediction factors (i.e., the number of pre-release defects and file size) are good predictors of breakage defects, whereas the number of co-changed files, the size of recently co-changed files and the time since the last change are good predictors of surprise defects.

Our findings suggest that building specialized prediction models is valuable to bring defect prediction techniques closer to adoption in practice.

However, our qualitative analysis of surprise defects and the feedback from the quality assurance manager clearly indicate that further work is needed to develop defect prediction into a practical tool. In particular, we found support for the idea of building specialized models that identify not only a defect's location, but also its nature, thus greatly simplifying the process of determining what the defect is and how it needs to be fixed.

10. REFERENCES

[1] E. Arisholm and L. C. Briand. Predicting fault-prone components in a java legacy system. In *Proc. Int'l Symposium on Empirical Softw. Eng. (ISESE'06)*, pages 8–17, 2006.

[2] E. Arisholm, L. C. Briand, and E. B. Johannessen. A systematic and comprehensive investigation of methods to build and evaluate fault prediction models. *J. Syst. Softw.*, 83(1):2–17, 2010.

[3] V. R. Basili, L. C. Briand, and W. L. Melo. A validation of object-oriented design metrics as quality indicators. *IEEE Trans. Softw. Eng.*, 22(10):751–761, 1996.

[4] M. Cataldo, A. Mockus, J. A. Roberts, and J. D. Herbsleb. Software dependencies, work dependencies, and their impact on failures. *IEEE Trans. Softw. Eng.*, 99(6):864–878, 2009.

[5] S. R. Chidamber and C. F. Kemerer. A metrics suite for object oriented design. *IEEE Trans. Softw. Eng.*, 20(6):476–493, 1994.

[6] M. D'Ambros, M. Lanza, and R. Robbes. An extensive comparison of bug prediction approaches. In *Proc. Int'l Working Conf. on Mining Software Repositories (MSR'10)*, pages 31–41, 2010.

[7] B. Efron. Estimating the error rate of a prediction rule: Improvement on Cross-Validation. *Journal of the American Statistical Association*, 78(382):316–331, 1983.

[8] S. G. Eick, T. L. Graves, A. F. Karr, J. S. Marron, and A. Mockus. Does code decay? assessing the evidence from change management data. *IEEE Trans. Softw. Eng.*, 27:1–12, 2001.

[9] H. Gall, K. Hajek, and M. Jazayeri. Detection of logical coupling based on product release history. In *Proc. Int'l Conf. on Software Maintenance (ICSM'98)*, pages 190–198, 1998.

[10] M. W. Godfrey, A. E. Hassan, J. Herbsleb, G. C. Murphy, M. Robillard, P. Devanbu, A. Mockus, D. E. Perry, and D. Notkin. Future of mining software archives: A roundtable. *IEEE Software*, 26(1):67 –70, 2009.

[11] T. L. Graves, A. F. Karr, J. S. Marron, and H. Siy. Predicting fault incidence using software change history. *IEEE Trans. Softw. Eng.*, 26(7):653–661, 2000.

[12] T. Gyimothy, R. Ferenc, and I. Siket. Empirical validation of object-oriented metrics on open source software for fault prediction. *IEEE Trans. Softw. Eng.*, 31(10):897–910, 2005.

[13] A. Hassan. The road ahead for mining software repositories. In *Frontiers of Software Maintenance (FoSM'08)*, pages 48–57, 2008.

[14] A. E. Hassan. Predicting faults using the complexity of code changes. In *Proc. Int'l Conf. on Softw. Eng. (ICSE'09)*, pages 78–88, 2009.

[15] I. Herraiz, J. M. Gonzalez-Barahona, and G. Robles. Towards a theoretical model for software growth. In *Proc. Int'l Workshop on Mining Software Repositories (MSR'07)*, pages 21–29, 2007.

[16] Y. Kamei, S. Matsumoto, A. Monden, K. Matsumoto, B. Adams, and A. E. Hassan. Revisiting common bug prediction findings using effort aware models. In *Proc. Int'l Conf. on Software Maintenance (ICSM'10)*, pages 1–10.

[17] T. M. Khoshgoftaar, E. B. Allen, W. D. Jones, and J. P. Hudepohl. Data mining for predictors of software quality. *International Journal of Software Engineering and Knowledge Engineering*, 9(5):547–564, 1999.

[18] M. Leszak, D. E. Perry, and D. Stoll. Classification and evaluation of defects in a project retrospective. *J. Syst. Softw.*, 61(3), 2002.

[19] T. J. McCabe. A complexity measure. In *Proc. Int'l Conf. on Softw. Eng. (ICSE'76)*, page 407, 1976.

[20] T. Mende and R. Koschke. Revisiting the evaluation of defect prediction models. In *Proc. Int'l Conf. on Predictor Models in Software Engineering (PROMISE'09)*, pages 7:1–7:10, 2009.

[21] T. Menzies, A. Dekhtyar, J. Distefano, and J. Greenwald. Problems with precision: A response to "comments on 'data mining static code attributes to learn defect predictors'". *IEEE Trans. Softw. Eng.*, 33:637–640, September 2007.

[22] A. Mockus and D. M. Weiss. Predicting risk of software changes. *Bell Labs Technical Journal*, 5(2):169–180, 2000.

[23] R. Moser, W. Pedrycz, and G. Succi. A comparative analysis of the efficiency of change metrics and static code attributes for defect prediction. In *Proc. Int'l Conf. on Softw. Eng. (ICSE'08)*, pages 181–190, 2008.

[24] N. Nagappan and T. Ball. Use of relative code churn measures to predict system defect density. In *Proc. Int'l Conf. on Softw. Eng. (ICSE'05)*, pages 284–292, 2005.

[25] N. Nagappan, T. Ball, and A. Zeller. Mining metrics to predict component failures. In *Proc. Int'l Conf. on Softw. Eng. (ICSE'06)*, pages 452–461, 2006.

[26] N. Ohlsson and H. Alberg. Predicting fault-prone software modules in telephone switches. *IEEE Trans. Softw. Eng.*, 22(12):886–894, 1996.

[27] T. J. Ostrand, E. J. Weyuker, and R. M. Bell. Where the bugs are. In *Proc. Int'l Symposium on Software Testing and Analysis (ISSTA'04)*.

[28] T. J. Ostrand, E. J. Weyuker, and R. M. Bell. Predicting the location and number of faults in large software systems. *IEEE Trans. Softw. Eng.*, 31(4):340–355, 2005.

[29] E. Shihab. Pragmatic prioritization of software quality assurance efforts. In *Proceeding of the 33rd international conference on Software engineering*, ICSE '11, pages 1106–1109, 2011.

[30] E. Shihab, Z. M. Jiang, W. M. Ibrahim, B. Adams, and A. E. Hassan. Understanding the impact of code and process metrics on post-release defects: A case study on the Eclipse project. In *Proc. Int'l Symposium on Empirical Softw. Eng. and Measurement (ESEM'10)*, pages 1–10, 2010.

[31] Y. Shin, A. Meneely, L. Williams, and J. Osborne. Evaluating complexity, code churn, and developer activity metrics as indicators of software vulnerabilities. *IEEE Trans. Softw. Eng.*, PP(99):1, 2010.

[32] R. Subramanyam and M. S. Krishnan. Empirical analysis of ck metrics for object-oriented design complexity: Implications for software defects. *IEEE Trans. Softw. Eng.*, 29(4):297–310, 2003.

[33] T.-J. Yu, V. Y. Shen, and H. E. Dunsmore. An analysis of several software defect models. *IEEE Trans. Softw. Eng.*, 14(9), 1988.

[34] T. Zimmermann, N. Nagappan, and L. Williams. Searching for a needle in a haystack: Predicting security vulnerabilities for windows vista. In *Proc. Int'l Conf. on Software Testing, Verification and Validation (ICST'10)*, pages 421–428, 2010.

[35] T. Zimmermann, R. Premraj, and A. Zeller. Predicting defects for Eclipse. In *Proc. Int'l Workshop on Predictor Models in Software Engineering (PROMISE'07)*, pages 1–7, 2007.

Micro Interaction Metrics for Defect Prediction

Taek Lee[†]*, Jaechang Nam[§], DongGyun Han[§], Sunghun Kim[§], Hoh Peter In[†]

[†]Department of Computer Science and Engineering
Korea University, Seoul, Korea
{comtaek, hoh_in}@korea.ac.kr

[§]Department of Computer Science and Engineering
The Hong Kong University of Science and Technology, Hong Kong
{jcnam, handk, hunkim}@cse.ust.hk

ABSTRACT

There is a common belief that developers' behavioral interaction patterns may affect software quality. However, widely used defect prediction metrics such as source code metrics, change churns, and the number of previous defects do not capture developers' direct interactions. We propose 56 novel micro interaction metrics (MIMs) that leverage developers' interaction information stored in the Mylyn data. Mylyn is an Eclipse plug-in, which captures developers' interactions such as file editing and selection events with time spent. To evaluate the performance of MIMs in defect prediction, we build defect prediction (classification and regression) models using MIMs, traditional metrics, and their combinations. Our experimental results show that MIMs significantly improve defect classification and regression accuracy.

Categories and Subject Descriptors

D.2.7 [**Software Engineering**]: Distribution, Maintenance, and Enhancement—*Restructuring, reverse engineering, and reengineering*; D.2.8 [**Software Engineering**]: Metrics—*Product metrics*; K.6.3 [**Management of Computing and Information Systems**]: Software Management—*Software maintenance*

General Terms

Algorithms, Measurement, Experimentation

1. INTRODUCTION

Defect prediction has been a very active research area in software engineering [10, 14, 15, 21, 26, 28, 36, 37]. Many effective new defect prediction models including new metrics have been proposed. Among them, source code metrics (CMs) and change history metrics (HMs) are widely used and yield reasonable defect prediction accuracy. For example, Basili et al. [3] used Chidamber and Kemerer metrics, and Ohlsson et al. [27] used McCabe's cyclomatic complexity for defect prediction. Moser et al. [23] used the number of revisions, authors, and past fixes, and age of a file as defect predictors.

In addition to software CMs and HMs, developers' behavioral patterns are also believed to be an important factor affecting software quality. Ko et al. [16] identified possible causes for programming errors using a breakdown model of cognitive chains. DeLine et al. [19] surveyed developers' work habits and found that work interruptions or task switching may affect programmer productivity. Their studies imply a correlation between developers' behaviors and software quality. Specifically, unexpected or abnormal behaviors may introduce bugs and cause software defects. Therefore, it is desirable to use developers' interaction information when building defect predictors. However, current defect metrics such as CMs and HMs do not directly capture developers' interactions, since current version control systems or bug report systems do not record developers' interactions.

We use Mylyn, a context storing and recovering Eclipse plug-in, to capture developers' interaction events. Examples of such events include selecting and editing software source files. Additionally, the order and time span of each event are also provided by Mylyn. Since developers' interaction patterns may affect software quality and developer productivity, metrics based on developers' interactions could be important indicators to predict defects.

In this paper, we propose 56 micro interaction metrics (MIMs) based on developers' interaction information stored in Mylyn. For example, *NumMultiTasks* measures task complexity by observing the number of ongoing tasks. *RepeatedlySelectedFileNum* and *RepeatedlyEditedFileNum* measure repeated work activities by counting selecting and editing events for the same file. (The full list of MIMs and their descriptions are shown in Appendix.)

To evaluate the performance of MIMs in defect prediction, we build defect prediction (classification and regression) models using MIMs, CMs, HMs, and their combinations. We evaluated various defect prediction models on Eclipse subprojects, which include the Mylyn data. Our evaluation results showed that MIMs significantly improve

*Taek Lee was a visiting PHD student at the Hong Kong University of Science and Technology when this work was carried out.

Permission to make digital or hard copies of all or part of this work for personal or classroom use is granted without fee provided that copies are not made or distributed for profit or commercial advantage and that copies bear this notice and the full citation on the first page. To copy otherwise, to republish, to post on servers or to redistribute to lists, requires prior specific permission and/or a fee.
ESEC/FSE'11, September 5–9, 2011, Szeged, Hungary.
Copyright 2011 ACM 978-1-4503-0443-6/11/09 ...$10.00.

prediction accuracy. The defect classification F-measure is 0.49 with MIMs, while it is only 0.26 with the combination of CM and HM. The mean square error of the defect regression model with MIMs is 0.76, while it is 0.81 with the combination of CM and HM.

These results concur with previous findings [16, 19]. Since developers' interactions affect software quality and programmer productivity, MIMs that capture a certain degree of developers' interactions play an important role in defect prediction. Our paper makes the following contributions:

- **56 MIMs**, which capture developers' interaction information from the Mylyn data.
- **Empirical evaluation** of the role of MIMs in defect prediction.

In the remainder of the paper, we start by presenting MIMs in Section 2. Section 3 describes our experimental setup including various defect prediction models, metrics used, and evaluation measures. Section 4 presents results of various defect models with/without MIMs. Section 5 discusses threats to validity of our study. We discuss related work in Section 6 and conclude the paper with future directions of our research in Section 7.

2. MICRO INTERACTION METRICS

This section proposes MIMs based on data collected by Mylyn, an Eclipse plug-in. We briefly introduce Mylyn and its data in Section 2.1, and describe the proposed MIMs in Section 2.2.

2.1 Mylyn

Mylyn is an Eclipse plug-in that records the context of developers' task such as editing or selecting files [8]. The recorded context is restored when developers want to resume the task. In this way, even after a task switching, developers can focus on the files they have previously worked on. The stored context can be shared among developers and help other developers understand what files were browsed and edited for the task.

The Mylyn data are stored as an attachment to the corresponding bug reports in the XML format. The data include events and their attributes performed by developers. Currently, Mylyn records six types of events: selection, edit, command, propagation, prediction, and manipulation as shown in Table 1. When a developer selects a file, a selection event occurs. Edit events are recorded when developers edit a file. Propagation events occur when a developer uses automatic refactoring features in Eclipse. For example, files can be modified automatically via Eclipse refactoring feature, and this is recorded as a propagation event.

Table 1: Event Type in the Mylyn Data [25]

Type	Description
Selection	Select a file in the explorer
Edit	Edit a file in the editor
Command	Invoke command by developer
Propagation	Propagated interaction
Prediction	Predict future interaction
Manipulation	Manipulate DOI value.

Each event is recorded with attributes including start-date, end-date, structure-handle, and degree-of-interest (DOI). The start-date and end-date attributes represent the starting and ending time of the event. The structure-handle attribute denotes corresponding files of the event. For example, for edit events, the structure-handle attribute indicates which file is edited. The DOI value indicates developer's interest in the corresponding file. The DOI value of a file increases when developers select or edit the file. DOI values help developers identify more/less important files for the task. Currently, DOI values are automatically computed based on the frequency of developers' interactions [11, 12].

When developers double click a file and open it in an editor, an edit event with no time spent, zero-time edit occurs. The time spent can be easily computed from end-date and start-date attributes. The zero-time edit event means the start-date and end-date of the event are the same. When developers change the content of the file, such events are recorded as non-zero-time events. We distinguish between these two types of events because it is important to separate real edits from simple double-clicks.

More information about the Mylyn data is available at the Mylyn Project home page[25].

2.2 Design of MIMs

The design principle of MIMs is quantifying the complexity and intensity of developers' interaction activities such as browsing or editing of files. Based on this principle, we designed two levels of MIMs, file-level and task-level.

The file-level MIMs capture specific interactions for a file in a task. For example, *NumEditEvent* represents the specific file edit events in one task. The task-level MIMs represent properties per task. For example, *TimeSpent* shows the time spent on a given task.

We designed three categories of file-level MIMs:

- **Effort**: Since Mylyn stores developers' interactions, this category measures developers' effort for a given file such as the number of events on a file.
- **Interest**: By using DOI value, we infer developers' interest in a specific file.
- **Intervals**: This category measures time intervals between events.

Task-level MIMs include six categories:

- **Effort**: Similar to the effort category in the file-level, we measure the effort made for a given task.
- **Distraction**: This measures developers' distraction for corresponding tasks such as low DOI events and non-java file edit events.
- **Work Portion**: All events in one task are divided into three event periods: Before beginning the first edit, edit, and after finishing the last edit sections. This category measures how much time was spent for each section.
- **Repetition**: There are some repeated events such as repeated selection or editing of the same file. This category counts this kind of repeated events.
- **Task Load**: This category measures the task load by observing the number of simultaneously on-going tasks (NumMultiTasks).
- **Event Pattern**: Since Mylyn contains interactions, we identify common patterns of sequential events. This cat-

egory captures the number of identified sequential patterns.

The complete list of MIMs with descriptions is shown in Appendix.

3. EXPERIMENTAL SETUP

This section describes our experimental setup including data collection, prediction models, and evaluation measures.

3.1 Bug Prediction Process

The commonly used file-level bug prediction process is used for our experiments as shown in Figure 1 [23, 28, 36].

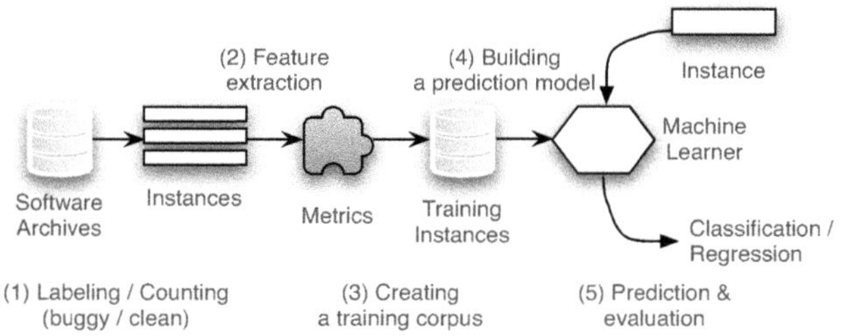

Figure 1: Overall steps of bug prediction process

First, we collect files as instances (in the machine learning sense) and count post-defects for each file. For the regression model, we predict the defect numbers. For classification, we label a file as *buggy* if it has any post-defect (post-defect number >= 1), or *clean* otherwise. The detailed post-defect counting process is described in Section 3.2.

Then, we extract MIMs, CM, and HMs for each instance as explained in Sections 3.3 and 3.4. Finally, we train prediction models using machine learning algorithms implemented in Weka [9]. The trained prediction models classify instances as *buggy* or *clean* (classification), or predict the post-defect numbers (regression). Detailed cross validation models and evaluation measures are explained in Section 3.5.

3.2 Data Collection

We extracted a total of 7,785 Mylyn tasks from Eclipse Bugzilla attachments between Dec 2005 [1] and Sep 2010.

To explicitly separate *metrics extraction* and *post-defect counting* periods, we set arbitrary time split points, P as shown in Figure 2. It is important not to collect any metrics from the post-defect counting period. Time P represents the present, and our model predicts future defects (after P) using metrics from the past to P. Thus, we computed all metrics (MIMs, CMs, and HMs) of instances before P, and counted post-defects after P. In our experiments, we used various time split points: 5:5, 7:3, and 8:2 to compare prediction results with different time split points. For example, Table 2 shows the number of instances and defect ratios for Eclipse subprojects from the 8:2 time split point. The goal of various time splits is evaluating MIM models by following the random split convention widely used in the literature [37, 38].

To collect metrics and count defects, instances must exist in both time periods (i.e. after and before Time P). If a file does not exist in the metrics collection period, there is

[1] Mylyn was released and widely used from Dec 2005.

Table 2: Collected file instances and post defects for the 8:2 split.

Subjects	# of instances (files)	% of defects
Mylyn	1061	14.3%
Team	239	35.5%
Etc.	1041	5.4%
All	2341	12.5%

no metrics to use for prediction. On the other hand, if a file does not exist in the post-defect counting period, the defect number for the file is always zero, which is misleading. To use only files which existed in both periods, we checked their existence using Eclipse CVS. For this reason, when we use different time split points, 5:5, 7:3, and 8:2, the number of instances changes.

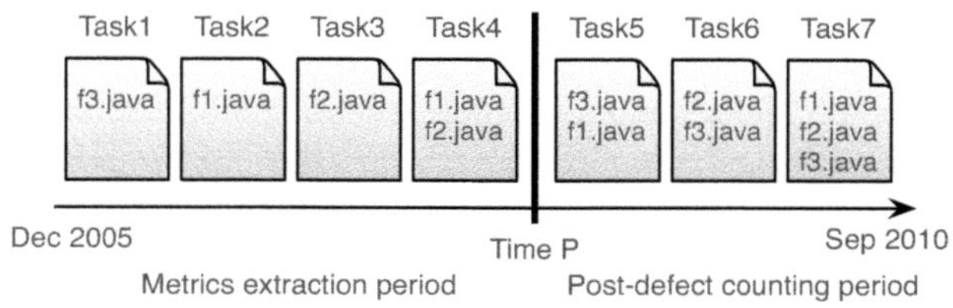

Figure 2: Time Split for metrics extraction and post-defect counting periods.

To count post-defects, we used edited file information in Mylyn tasks. Since each task is directly attached to a bug report, we checked if the corresponding bug report was a fixed bug. If it was not fixed or not a bug (such as feature-enhancement or trivial), we assumed the edited files for the particular bug report are not fixes. We marked the edited files only for fixed bug reports as fixed and increased the defect numbers for the files. For example, suppose Tasks 5 and 6 in Figure 2 were attached to fixed bug reports, and Task 7 is attached to a feature-enhancement bug report. In this case, the post defect number of 'f3.java' is two, since Task 7 is for feature enhancement. In this way, we could avoid false-positives in marking defects.

The following sections describe metrics extraction techniques and evaluation measures for prediction models in detail.

3.3 Extraction of MIMs

All MIMs listed in Appendix were extracted from the Mylyn data. Since our models are file-level defect predictors, we need to compute MIMs for each file.

Computation of file-level MIMs is straightforward. We first compute file-level MIMs for a given file. If the file is edited multiple times in the *metrics extraction period*, then it will have multiple metric values. We just average and total the multiple values and use the totaled values as features (in the machine learning sense) of the file.

For task-level MIMs such as *TimeSpent* of a task, first we propagate the metric values to all edited files in the task. Then, the propagated metric values are regarded as file level metrics. If a file is edited multiple times, and it has multiple metric values (propagated from tasks), we average the values and use them as features.

3.4 Extraction of CMs and HMs

We collected CMs at Time P as shown in Figure 2 since CMs can be extracted from a snapshot. We used the Understand tool [33] to extract CMs. The Understand tool extracts 24 file-level and 18 class-level metrics such as Chidamber and Kemerer [5] and Object-Oriented metrics. If a file has more than one class, we derived file-level metrics from multiple class-level metrics. The Understand tool mostly provides two kinds of metrics: Avg* and Count*. To generate file-level metrics from multiple classes in a file, we averaged Avg* class-level metrics. However, when we get file-level metrics from Count* classs-level metrics, we added the values together. We used all 42 CMs for our experiments. Selected CMs are listed in Table 3.

Table 3: List of selected source code metrics (CMs)

Metrics	Description
CountLineCode	Lines of code
CountSemicolon	# of semicolons
CountStmtDecl	# of declarative statements
SumEssential	Sum of essential complexity of methods
CntClassCoupled	Coupling between object classes (CBO)
CntClassDerived	# of Child classes (NOC)
CntDeclMethod	# of local methods (NOM)
CntDeclMethodPublic	# of local public methods (NOPM)
MxInheritanceTree	Depth of Inheritance Tree (DIT)
PcntLackOfCohesion	Lack of cohesion (LCOM)

In addition, we collected 15 HMs following Moser et al.'s approach [23]. All HMs were collected from the change history stored in Eclipse CVS repository[2] during the metrics extraction period as shown in Figure 2.

Table 4 lists 15 HMs used in our experiments. The *Refactorings* metrics indicates if a file change is refactoring [23]. This is determined by mining CVS commit logs: if they contain the keyword 'refactor', we assume it is a refactoring. We counted the number of all refactored revisions of a file in the metrics extraction period. The *Age* metric indicates the period of file existence [23]. The *BugFixes* metric represents the defect numbers in the metrics extraction period. To compute this, we mined commit logs to search explicit bug IDs in the logs. Then, we checked the bug reports, and if they were fixed bugs (not feature enhancement), we marked the change as bug-fix. In addition, we searched for specific keywords, *bug* or *fix*[3], which indicate bug fix changes [23]. If change logs had such keywords, we marked the changes as bug-fixes [23].

3.5 Performance Measures

In this section, we explain evaluation methods used in our prediction models. We compare the prediction performance of MIMs with other metrics. Thus, we build a model by each metrics (i.e. MIM, CM, HM) and combination of them (i.e. CM+HM). To evaluate our prediction models, we used 10-fold cross validation, which is widely used to evaluate prediction models [14, 23, 20]. We repeated 10-fold cross validation 100 times for each prediction model on each different time split to validate the prediction performance of MIMs by t-test.

[2]http://archive.eclipse.org/arch/

[3]The keywords, *postfix* and *prefix* are excluded [23].

Table 4: List of history metrics (HMs)

Metrics	Description
Revisions	# of revisions of a file
Refactorings	# of times a file has been refactored
BugFixes	# of times a file was involved in fixing bugs
Authors	# of distinct authors committing a file
LOC_Added	Sum of the lines of code added to a file
Max_LOC_Added	Maximum number of lines of code added
Ave_LOC_Added	Average lines of code added
LOC_Deleted	Sum of the lines of code deleted in a file
Max_LOC_Deleted	Maximum number of lines of code deleted
Avg_LOC_Deleted	Average lines of code deleted
CodeChurn	Sum of (added LOC - deleted LOC)
Max_CodeChurn	Maximum CodeChurn for all revisions
Ave_CodeChurn	Average CodeChurn per revision
Age	Age of a file in weeks
Weighted_Age	Age considering LOC_Added

3.5.1 Classification

To evaluate performance differences between different prediction models, we used F-measure. Usually, F-measure represents harmonic mean of precision and recall. We first computed precision and recall values of buggy instances, and then we obtained F-measures. The following outcomes were used to define precision, recall, and F-measure: (1) predicting a buggy instance as buggy (b→b); (2) predicting a buggy instance as clean (b→c); (3) predicting a clean instance as buggy (c→b). We use the above outcomes to evaluate the prediction accuracy of our prediction models with the following measures [1, 30]:

- **Precision:** the number of instances correctly classified as buggy ($N_{b\to b}$) over the number of all instances classified as buggy.

$$Precision\ P(b) = \frac{N_{b\to b}}{N_{b\to b} + N_{c\to b}} \quad (1)$$

- **Recall:** the number of instances correctly classified as buggy ($N_{b\to b}$) over the total number of buggy instances.

$$Recall\ R(b) = \frac{N_{b\to b}}{N_{b\to b} + N_{b\to c}} \quad (2)$$

- **F-measure:** a composite measure of precision *P(b)* and recall *R(b)* for buggy instances.

$$F\text{-}measure\ F(b) = \frac{2 * P(b) * R(b)}{P(b) + R(b)} \quad (3)$$

3.5.2 Regression

By using linear regression models, we predicted the number of post-defects. To compare the prediction performance of models of MIMs and other metrics, we calculated correlation coefficient, mean absolute error, and root mean squared error [34]. Correlation coefficient measures the correlation between predicted and real defect numbers. If the correlation coefficient is closer to 1, the metrics are more correlated to post-defects. Both mean absolute error and root mean squared error represent the difference between predicted and actual post-defects numbers. If both error values of a prediction model are less than others, it means the model has higher prediction accuracy. To compare the prediction model of MIMs with those of CMs, HMs and their combination, we measured these three values. We also repeated 10-fold cross validation 100 times to validate regression models for each metrics by t-test.

3.5.3 T-test

To check statistical significance of prediction performance of MIMs and CMs, HMs and CM+HM, the simple t-test was used [6]. We checked if mean of F-measure values of MIMs was not equal to the mean of F-measures of CM and HM. Specifically, the null and alternative hypotheses for t-test are:

- **H0** F-measure mean of CM+HM is *equal to* the F-measure mean of MIM.
- **H1** F-measure mean of CM+HM is *not equal to* the F-measure mean of MIM. (i.e. MIMs have better performance if the mean value is higher)

We rejected the null hypothesis *H0* and accepted the alternative hypothesis *H1* if the p-value was smaller than 0.05 (at the 95% confidence level) [6].

3.6 Dummy Classifier

To evaluate the performance of classifiers using MIMs, CM, and HMs, we introduce a baseline: *Dummy classifier* – guessing a change/file as buggy or clean in a purely random manner. Since there are only two labels, buggy and clean changes, the dummy predictor could also achieve certain prediction accuracy. For example, if there are 12.5% of changes in a project are buggy, by predicting all changes as buggy, the buggy recall would be 1, and the precision would be 0.125. It is also possible that the dummy predictor randomly predicts a change as buggy or clean with 0.5 probability. In this case, the buggy recall would be 0.5, but the precision will still be 0.125.

We used the F-measure of the dummy predictor as a baseline when showing the classification results. We computed the dummy F-measure assuming the dummy predictor randomly predicts 50% as buggy and 50% as clean. For example, for a project with 12.5% buggy changes as shown in Table 2, the dummy buggy F-measure is 0.2 ($2 \times \frac{0.5 \times 0.125}{0.5 + 0.125}$).

4. RESULTS

This section presents performance of bug prediction models using MIM, CM, HM, and their combinations.

4.1 Result Summary

This section provides a quick summary of results from different experiments. Details of settings and results are explained in subsections.

- MIM outperforms existing metrics (CM and HM) and their combination (CM+HM) for different subjects (Section 4.2.1).
- MIM outperforms CM, HM and CM+HM for different classification algorithms (Section 4.2.2).
- MIM outperforms CM+HM for different split points (Section 4.2.3).
- Among the top 56 important metrics for classification models, 44 (79%) are from MIMs. All top 42 important metrics are from MIMs (Section 4.2.4).
- MIM outperforms CM+HM for regression models (Section 4.3).

4.2 Predicting Buggy Files

4.2.1 Different Subjects

To evaluate the performance of MIMs for various subjects, we built defect prediction models using J48 Decision Tree for three Eclipse subprojects, *Mylyn*, *Team* and *Etc.* from the 8:2 split point as shown in Table 2. To build the models, MIM, CM, HM, CM+HM, and MIM+CM+HM were used.

We use F-measure to evaluate prediction performance as described in Section 3.5.3. The ten-fold cross validation is used to train and test models. Since ten-fold cross validation randomly samples instances and puts them in ten folds [1], we run the ten-fold cross validation 100 times to avoid sampling bias.

Figure 3 shows F-measure values for various Eclipse subjects and various metrics. F-measure values vary, but the trend is clear: MIM outperforms CM, HM, and their combination (CM+HM) for *All*, *Team*, and *Etc.* For *Mylyn*, the F-measure of MIM is slightly lower than that of CM+HM, but MIM+CM+HM outperforms CM+HM. In addition, the Dummy F-measure values are shown as a baseline, the solid line in Figure 3. Generally, CM and HM outperform the baseline, and MIM significantly outperforms the baseline.

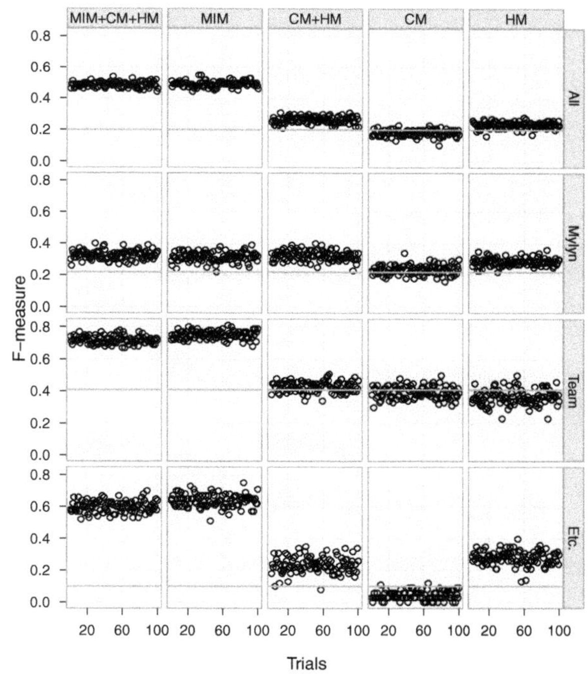

Figure 3: Performance comparison by different subjects (Classier: J48 decision tree). The Dummy F-measure is shown as a solid line.

Table 5 shows the mean of F-measure values from 100 ten-fold cross validations and their statistical significance. If F-measure values of MIM+CM+HM or MIM are significant (p-value < 0.05) in comparison to CM+HM, the corresponding values are in bold. For example, the F-measure (0.75) of MIMs in *Team* is better than that of CM+HM (0.43), and it is statistically significant. For *Mylyn*, the F-measure (0.31) of MIM is not better than that of CM+HM (0.32). However, MIM+CM+HM outperforms CM+HM, which indicates that MIM complements CM+HM to yield better prediction accuracy. Generally, the results in Table 5 indicate that MIM and/or MIM+CM+HM outperform traditional metrics (CM+HM). In addition, Dummy F-measures are shown in Table 5.

Table 5: F-measure mean values of each metrics in different subjects. (The F-measures in bold indicate the value difference in comparison to CM+HM is statistically significant. (p-value < 0.05))

Subjects	MIM+CM+HM	MIM	CM+HM	CM	HM	DUMMY
All	**0.49**	**0.49**	0.26	0.18	0.23	0.20
Mylyn	0.33	0.31	0.32	0.24	0.29	0.22
Team	**0.72**	**0.75**	0.43	0.39	0.36	0.41
Etc.	**0.60**	**0.64**	0.24	0.04	0.28	0.10

4.2.2 *Different Machine Learner*

This section compares the results of prediction models using three widely used classification algorithms, Bayesian Network, J48 decision tree, and logistics in Weka [9]. All instances with the 8:2 time split (in Table 2) are used for this experiment.

Figure 4 shows F-measures from 100 ten-fold cross validations. The F-measures vary, but they show a trend that MIM outperforms CM, HM, and their combination (CM+HM) in all algorithms.

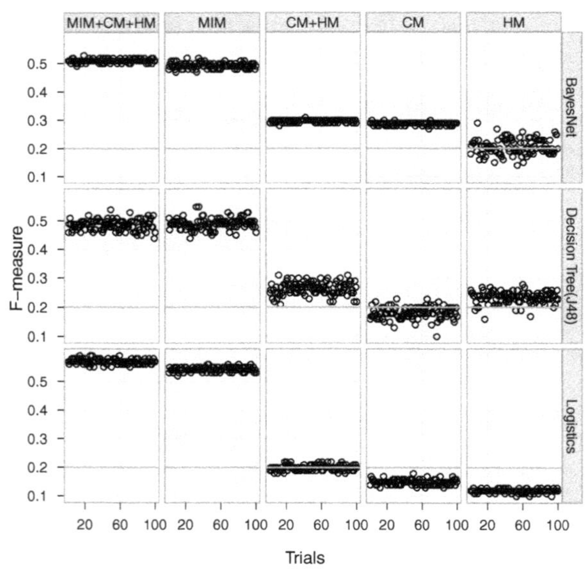

Figure 4: Performance comparison by different algorithms (All instances). The Dummy F-measure is shown as a solid line.

Table 6 shows mean F-measure values from 100 ten-fold cross validations. The F-measure mean (0.49) of MIMs in the BayesNet is better than that of CM+HM (0.30). If F-measure mean values of MIM+CM+HM or MIM are statistically significant in comparison to CM+HM, we mark the values in bold. For all algorithms, MIM outperforms CM+HM with statistical significance.

Table 6: F-measure mean values of each metrics in different algorithms. (The F-measures in bold indicate the value difference in comparison to CM+HM is statistically significant. (p-value < 0.05))

Measures	MIM+CM+HM	MIM	CM+HM	CM	HM	DUMMY
BayesNet	**0.51**	**0.49**	0.30	0.29	0.21	0.20
Decision Tree	**0.49**	**0.49**	0.26	0.18	0.23	0.20
Logistics	**0.57**	**0.54**	0.19	0.15	0.12	0.20

4.2.3 *Different Split Points*

To evaluate prediction performance of MIMs on different time splits, we built prediction models using three different time split points, 5:5, 7:3, and 8:2 as explained in Section 3.2. Table 7 shows corpus information. Since we collected instances before and after Time point P, the number of instances varies for different time split points (Section 3.2). The defect ratio varies, since we have different periods for post-defect counting as shown in Figure 2.

Table 7: Sample Conditions per Split Period

Time split point, P	# of instances	% of defects
Apr. 2008 (50:50)	1155	21.2%
Mar. 2009 (70:30)	2022	14.6%
Sep. 2009 (80:20)	2341	12.5%

Figure 5 shows F-measure values from 100 ten-fold cross validations. It indicates that MIM outperforms CM+HM for three different time split points.

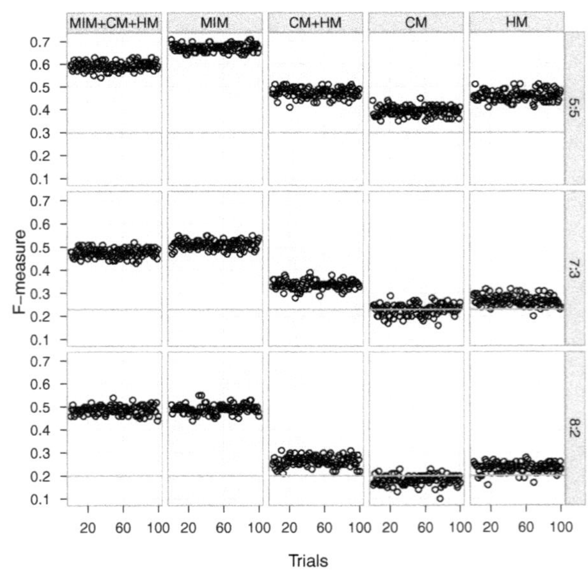

Figure 5: Performance comparison by time split (All instances, Classifier: J48 decision tree). The Dummy F-measure is shown as a solid line.

Table 8 shows F-measure mean values of MIMs, and values are in bold if they are statistically significant in comparison to CM+HM. For example, the F-measure mean (0.67) of MIM in the 5:5 time split point is better than that (0.47) of CM+HM, and it is statistically significant. As we observe in Table 8, MIM outperforms CM+HM for all time split points.

Table 8: F-measure mean values of each metrics at different split points. (The F-measures in bold indicate the value difference in comparison to CM+HM is statistically significant. (p-value < 0.05))

Measures	MIM+CM+HM	MIM	CM+HM	CM	HM	DUMMY
5:5	**0.59**	**0.67**	0.47	0.39	0.46	0.30
7:3	**0.48**	**0.51**	0.34	0.23	0.27	0.23
8:2	**0.49**	**0.49**	0.26	0.18	0.23	0.20

4.2.4 *Metrics Effectiveness Analysis*

To evaluate the effectiveness of each metric for classification, we measured the information gain ratio [18, 17] of MIMs, CMs, and HMs, and ranked them accordingly. All collected instances and post defects from the 8:2 split point as shown in Table 2 are used for this analysis. The information gain ratio indicates how well a metric distinguishes labels (i.e., buggy or clean) of instances. Even though the metrics effectiveness may differ based on machine learning algorithms, generally metrics with a high information gain ratio is regarded as important [13, 31].

Top 56 ranked metrics (among 113 metrics) based on the gain ratio are shown in Figure 6. Among the top 56 important metrics for classification models, 44 (79%) metrics are from MIMs. Especially, the top 42 metrics are MIMs. The best metric is *NumLowDOIEdit* followed by *NumPatternEXSX* and *TimeSpentOnEdit*. *NumLowDOIEdit* represents the number of low DOI file editing events, and editing low DOI files might affect software quality. *NumPatternEXSX* captures the event pattern of editing and selecting error-prone files consecutively. This pattern could be a defect prone interaction. The average time spent on editing events is also an important metric to predict defects.

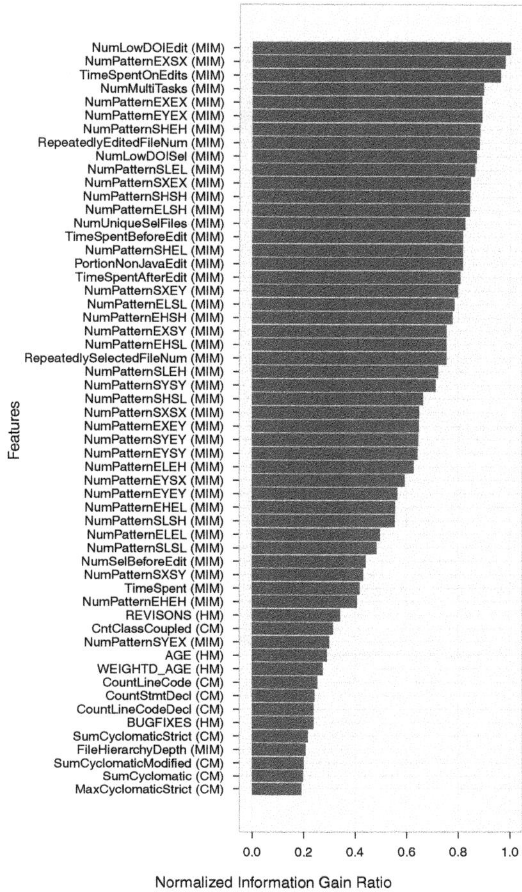

Figure 6: Top 56 ranked metrics (among 113 metrics) based on the gain ratio.

4.3 Predicting Defect Numbers

To evaluate the regression performance using MIMs, we built prediction models using linear regression [9] with the 8:2 time split point. MIM, CM, HM, and their combinations were used to build regression models. We repeated 10-fold cross validation 100 times and computed mean values of *correlation coefficient*, *mean absolute error*, and *root mean squared error*.

Figure 7 shows correlation coefficients of various metrics. The correlation coefficient of MIM is better than CM+HM, which indicates that prediction results using MIMs are more correlated to real defect numbers.

In terms of error, MIMs yield lower errors than CM+HM as shown in Figure 8.

Table 9 shows mean values of measures. Statistically significant values are in bold. For example, correlation coefficient (0.41) of MIMs is better than that (0.30) of CM+HM, and it is statistically significant. In terms of error, the mean absolute error (0.34) and root mean squared error (0.76) of MIM are lower than the values of CM+HM (0.37 and 0.81 respectively). These results show that MIM outperforms CM+HM in regression models.

4.4 Predicting CVS-log-based Defects

This section introduces prediction results using CVS-based defect counting. As explained in Section 3.2, we counted the number of post-defects based on edited files recorded in Mylyn tasks to avoid false positives in marking fixed files. However, it is possible that some developers may not have used Mylyn to fix bugs, i.e. these fixes are not recorded in the Mylyn data. This may lead to biased post-defect numbers.

To address this issue, we repeated experiments using the same instances but with a different defect counting method. We used traditional heuristics to count post-defects [22, 32] by searching for 'fix' or 'bug' keywords and bug report IDs in change logs. The change logs containing the keywords or bug IDs were marked as fix changes. After counting post-defects in this approach, we repeated ten-fold cross validation 100 times using three different classification algorithms used in Section 4.2.2. We used the 8:2 time split point for this experiment. The number of instances was 2341, the same number as in Table 7. However, the defect rate increased to 32.4%, since we counted defects by mining CVS change logs.

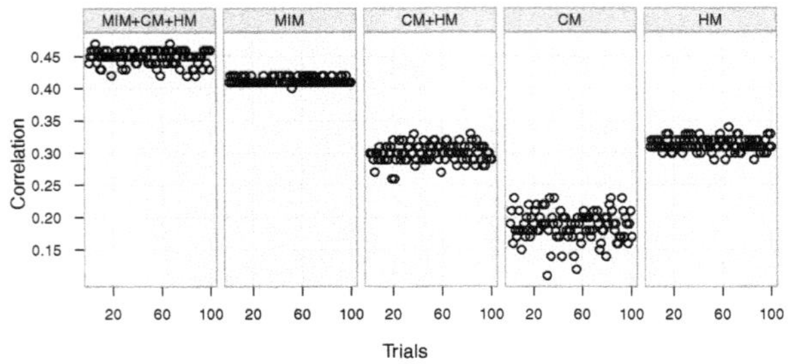

Figure 7: Correlation coefficient comparison (All instances, 8:2 split point, Linear Regression)

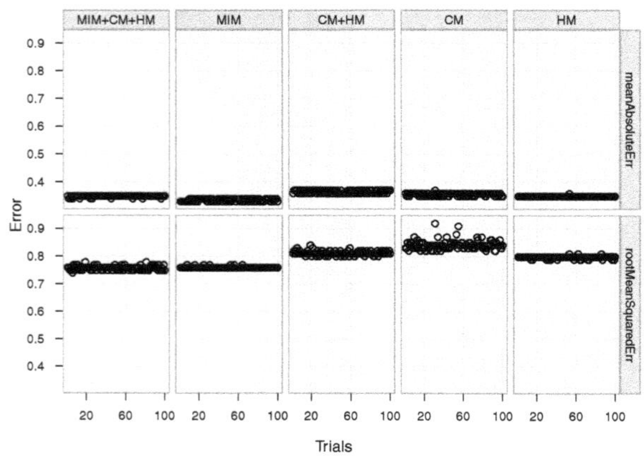

Figure 8: Error comparison (All instances, 80:20 split point)

Figure 9 and Table 10 show F-measure values for each metrics and classification algorithms. For *BayesNet* and *Logistics*, MIM+CM+HM turns out to have the best overall performance. For *Decision Tree*, HM is slightly better than MIM+CM+HM. We would like to point out that in this experiment, using MIMs alone does not yield better performance than CM or HM. One possible explanation is that even though Mylyn is widely used, some of the tasks are still performed without it. In this case, we lost developers' interactions for these tasks, and the information loss may affect the defect prediction performance. However, this issue will be automatically addressed when all files are edited using the Mylyn plug-in. Another reason could be the false positives in CVS-based defect counting [4], and they may affect the defect prediction performance.

5. THREATS TO VALIDITY

We have identified the following threats to validity.

- **Systems examined might not be representative.** Since MIMs rely on the Mylyn data, we intentionally chose subprojects which include the Mylyn data. We might have a project selection bias. In this sense, our approach using MIMs is not generally applicable for projects, which do not use Mylyn.

Table 9: Correlation Coefficient of MIM was validated against CM+HM metrics. (The values in bold indicate the value difference in comparison to CM+HM is statistically significant. (p-value < 0.05))

Measures	MIM+CM+HM	MIM	CM+HM	CM	HM
Correlation Coefficient	**0.45**	**0.41**	0.30	0.19	0.31
Mean absolute error	**0.35**	**0.34**	0.37	0.36	0.35
Root mean squared error	**0.76**	**0.76**	0.81	0.84	0.80

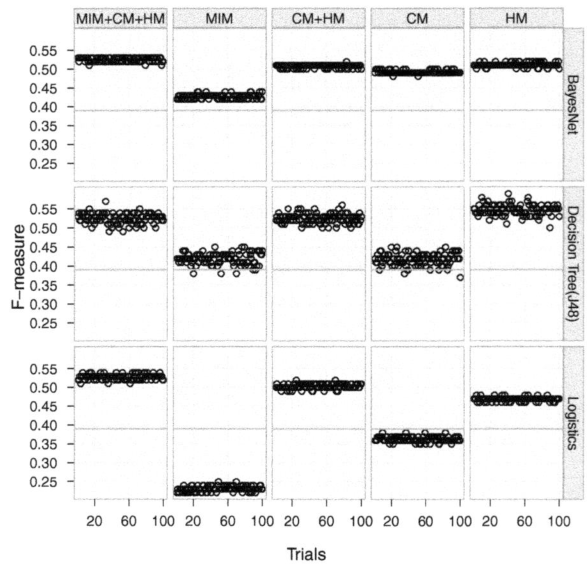

Figure 9: Performance comparison of prediction models by CVS-based labeling (All instances, 8:2 time split point). The Dummy F-measure is shown as a solid line.

- **Systems are all open source projects.** All subprojects examined in this paper are developed as open source projects. Hence they might not be representative of closed-source projects. Commercial software developers may have different micro-level interaction patterns.
- **Defect information might be biased.** We collected defect information from changed files in CVS and edited files recorded in the Mylyn data. In addition, we verified whether the corresponding bug reports were really fixed. However, our defect information might be biased, since some files are edited without using Mylyn and developers may not leave explicit bug IDs in CVS change logs.

Table 10: F-measure mean values of each metrics in CVS-based labeling. (The F-measures in bold indicate the value difference in comparison to CM+HM is statistically significant. (p-value < 0.05))

Measures	MIM+CM+HM	MIM	CM+HM	CM	HM	DUMMY
BayesNet	**0.525**	0.43	0.50	0.49	0.51	0.39
Decision Tree	0.525	0.42	0.525	0.42	0.55	0.39
Logistics	**0.528**	0.23	0.50	0.36	0.47	0.39

6. RELATED WORK

6.1 Defect Prediction

Software defect prediction is a very active research area [3, 14, 15, 27, 28, 37] in software engineering. Researchers have proposed new defect prediction algorithms and/or new metrics to effectively predict defects. Source code metrics such as complexity metrics are widely used for defect prediction, since there is a common understanding that complicated software may yield more defects. For example, Basili et al. [3] used Chidamber and Kemerer metrics, and Ohlsson et al. [27] used McCabe's cyclomatic complexity for defect prediction.

Recently, change history based metrics have been proposed and widely used for defect prediction. Nagappan et al. proposed the code churn metric, which is the amount of changed code, and showed that code churn is very effective for defect prediction. Moser et al. [23] used the number of revisions, authors, past fixes, and age of a file as defect predictors. Kim et al. used previous defect information to predict future defects. Hassan adopted the concept of entropy for change metrics, and found their approach is often better than the code churn approach and the approach based on previous bugs [10]. D'Ambros et al. conducted an extensive comparison of existing bug prediction approaches using source code metrics, change history metrics, past defects and entropy of change metrics [7]. They also proposed two noble metrics: churn and entropy of source code metrics.

Defect metrics other than CMs and HMs have also been proposed. Zimmermann and Nagappan predicted defects in Windows server 2003 using network analysis among binaries [37]. Bacchelli et al. proposed popularity metrics based on e-mail archives [2]. They assumed the most discussed files are more defect-prone. Meneely et al. proposed developer social network based metrics to predict defects [20].

These proposed metrics play an important role in defect prediction, and yield reasonable prediction accuracy. However, they do not capture developers' direct interactions. Proposed MIMs are the first metrics using developer interaction data to predict defects. We have also showed that developers' interaction based metrics outperform traditional metrics such as CMs and HMs.

6.2 Developer Interaction History

In recent years, researchers used developer's interaction history for facilitating software development and maintenance. Zou et al. proposed how to detect interaction coupling from task interaction histories [39]. Their case study showed the information of interaction coupling is helpful to comprehend software maintenance activities. Robbes and Lanza proposed a code completion tool based on programmer's code editing interaction history [29]. Ying and Robillard analyzed the influence of program change tasks based on developers' editing behavior and found editing patterns that are helpful for software tool designers [35].

Kersten et al. suggested task context model and implemented Mylyn to store/restore task context when developers switch their task context [11, 12]. As Mylyn is getting popular, there are many available developers' interaction history data captured by Mylyn. Murphy et al. analyzed statistics about IDE usage using the Mylyn data and showed the most used UI components and commands [24].

These approaches are similar to our work in that they are leveraging developer interactions to improve software quality. However, they do not address the software defect prediction issue using developers' interaction history, while we extract MIMs for defect prediction.

7. CONCLUSIONS

We proposed 56 micro interaction metrics, and showed that they significantly improve defect classification and regression accuracy. Our findings concur with previous studies [16, 19], which indicates developers' interaction patterns affect software quality.

In our experimental evaluation, MIM based defect prediction models are applied to Eclipse subprojects. We plan to extend our experiments by adding more subjects including industrial projects. Current MIMs depend on the Mylyn data, which may not be available for some projects. Therefore, we plan to extend MIMs leveraging other sources of developers' interaction data.

Overall, we expect that future defect prediction models will use more information from developers' direct and micro level interactions for effective defect prediction. MIMs are a first step in this direction.

All data we used in our experiments are publicly available at `http://www.cse.ust.hk/~jcnam/mim`.

8. ACKNOWLEDGEMENTS

Our thanks to Ananya Kanjilal, Seonah Lee, Yida Tao, Annie T.T. Ying, and the anonymous reviewers of ESEC/FSE for valuable and helpful suggestions on earlier versions of this paper.

This work was supported in part by Mid-career Researcher Program through NRF grant funded by the MEST (No. 2010-0000142) and in part by the R&BD Support Center of Seoul Development Institute and the South Korean government (Project title: WR080951, Establishment of Bell Labs in Seoul / Research of Broadband Convergent Networks and their Enabling Technologies).

9. REFERENCES

[1] E. Alpaydin. *Introduction to Machine Learning*. The MIT Press, 2nd edition, 2010.

[2] A. Bacchelli, M. D'Ambros, and M. Lanza. Are popular classes more defect prone? In *Fundamental Approaches to Software Engineering*, volume 6013, pages 59–73. 2010.

[3] V. R. Basili, L. C. Briand, and W. L. Melo. A validation of object-oriented design metrics as quality indicators. *IEEE Trans. Softw. Eng.*, 22:751–761, October 1996.

[4] C. Bird, A. Bachmann, E. Aune, J. Duffy, A. Bernstein, V. Filkov, and P. Devanbu. Fair and Balanced? Bias in Bug-Fix Datasets. In *ESEC/FSE'09*, 2009.

[5] S. R. Chidamber and C. F. Kemerer. A metrics suite for object oriented design. *IEEE Trans. Softw. Eng.*, 20:476–493, June 1994.

[6] P. Dalgaard. *Introductory statistics with R*. Springer, 2nd edition, 2010.

[7] M. D'Ambros, M. Lanza, and R. Robbes. An extensive comparison of bug prediction approaches. In *Mining Software Repositories (MSR), 2010 7th IEEE Working Conference on*, pages 31 –41, May 2010.

[8] Eclipse Mylyn. http://www.eclipse.org/mylyn.

[9] M. Hall, E. Frank, G. Holmes, B. Pfahringer, P. Reutemann, and I. H. Witten. The weka data mining software: an update. *SIGKDD Explor. Newsl.*, 11:10–18, November 2009.

[10] A. E. Hassan. Predicting faults using the complexity of code changes. In *Proceedings of the 31st International Conference on Software Engineering*, ICSE '09, pages 78–88, 2009.

[11] M. Kersten and G. C. Murphy. Mylar: a degree-of-interest model for ides. In *Proceedings of the 4th international conference on Aspect-oriented software development*, AOSD '05, pages 159–168, 2005.

[12] M. Kersten and G. C. Murphy. Using task context to improve programmer productivity. In *Proceedings of the 14th ACM SIGSOFT international symposium on Foundations of software engineering*, SIGSOFT '06/FSE-14, pages 1–11, 2006.

[13] D. Kim, X. Wang, S. Kim, A. Zeller, S. Cheung, and S. Park. Which crashes should i fix first?: Predicting top crashes at an early stage to prioritize debugging efforts. *IEEE Trans. Softw. Eng.*, 99, 2011.

[14] S. Kim, E. J. Whitehead, Jr., and Y. Zhang. Classifying software changes: Clean or buggy? *IEEE Trans. Softw. Eng.*, 34:181–196, March 2008.

[15] S. Kim, T. Zimmermann, E. J. Whitehead Jr., and A. Zeller. Predicting faults from cached history. In *Proceedings of the 29th international conference on Software Engineering*, ICSE '07, pages 489–498, 2007.

[16] A. J. Ko and B. A. Myers. A framework and methodology for studying the causes of software errors in programming systems. *J. Vis. Lang. Comput.*, 16:41–84, February 2005.

[17] S. Kullback. *Information Theory and Statistics*. John Wiley and Sons, 1959.

[18] S. Kullback and R. A. Leibler. On information and su ciency. In *The annals of Mathematical Statistics*, volume 22, pages 79–86, 1951.

[19] T. D. LaToza, G. Venolia, and R. DeLine. Maintaining mental models: a study of developer work habits. In *Proceedings of the 28th international conference on Software engineering*, ICSE '06, pages 492–501, 2006.

[20] A. Meneely, L. Williams, W. Snipes, and J. Osborne. Predicting failures with developer networks and social network analysis. In *SIGSOFT '08/FSE-16: Proceedings of the 16th ACM SIGSOFT International Symposium on Foundations of software engineering*, pages 13–23, 2008.

[21] T. Menzies, J. Greenwald, and A. Frank. Data mining static code attributes to learn defect predictors. *IEEE Trans. Softw. Eng.*, 33:2–13, January 2007.

[22] A. Mockus and L. G. Votta. Identifying reasons for software changes using historic databases. In *Proceedings of the International Conference on Software Maintenance*, 2000.

[23] R. Moser, W. Pedrycz, and G. Succi. A comparative analysis of the efficiency of change metrics and static code attributes for defect prediction. In *Proceedings of the 30th international conference on Software engineering*, ICSE '08, pages 181–190, 2008.

[24] G. C. Murphy, M. Kersten, and L. Findlater. How are java software developers using the eclipse ide? *IEEE Softw.*, 23:76–83, July 2006.

[25] Mylyn/Integrator Reference. http://wiki.eclipse.org/Mylyn_Integrator_Reference.

[26] N. Nagappan, T. Ball, and A. Zeller. Mining metrics to predict component failures. In *Proceedings of the 28th international conference on Software engineering*, ICSE '06, pages 452–461, 2006.

[27] N. Ohlsson and H. Alberg. Predicting fault-prone software modules in telephone switches. *IEEE Trans. Softw.*, 22(12):886 –894, Dec. 1996.

[28] T. J. Ostrand, E. J. Weyuker, and R. M. Bell. Predicting the location and number of faults in large software systems. *IEEE Trans. Softw. Eng.*, 31:340–355, April 2005.

[29] R. Robbes and M. Lanza. How program history can improve code completion. In *Automated Software Engineering, 2008. ASE 2008. 23rd IEEE/ACM International Conference on*, pages 317 –326, sept. 2008.

[30] S. Scott and S. Matwin. Feature engineering for text classification. In *Proceedings of the Sixteenth International Conference on Machine Learning*, ICML '99, pages 379–388, 1999.

[31] S. Shivaji, E. J. W. Jr., R. Akella, and S. Kim. Reducing features to improve bug prediction. In *Proceedings of the IEEE/ACM International Conference on Automated Software Engineering*, ASE '09, pages 600–604, 2009.

[32] J. Śliwerski, T. Zimmermann, and A. Zeller. When do changes induce fixes? In *Proceedings of the 2005 international workshop on Mining software repositories*, MSR '05, pages 1–5, 2005.

[33] Understand 2.0. http://www.scitools.com/products/understand/.

[34] I. H. Witten and E. Frank. *Data mining : practical machine learning tools and techniques*. Morgan Kaufmann, Amsterdam, 2 edition, 2005.

[35] A. T. Ying and M. P. Robillard. The influence of the task on programmer behaviour. In *Program Comprehension, 2011. ICPC '11. 19th IEEE International Conference on*, June 2011.

[36] H. Zhang. An investigation of the relationships between lines of code and defects. In *ICSM 2009*, pages 274 –283, 2009.

[37] T. Zimmermann and N. Nagappan. Predicting defects using network analysis on dependency graphs. In *Proceedings of the 30th international conference on Software engineering*, ICSE '08, pages 531–540, 2008.

[38] T. Zimmermann, R. Premraj, and A. Zeller. Predicting defects for eclipse. In *Proceedings of the Third International Workshop on Predictor Models in Software Engineering*, PROMISE '07, pages 9–, 2007.

[39] L. Zou, M. Godfrey, and A. Hassan. Detecting interaction coupling from task interaction histories. In *Program Comprehension, 2007. ICPC '07. 15th IEEE International Conference on*, pages 135 –144, June 2007.

APPENDIX: List of Micro Interaction Metrics

Level	Category	Name	Description
File Level	Effort	NumSelectionEvent NumEditEvent NumManipulationEvent NumPropagationEvent	The number of each kind of events of the file.
	Interest	AvgDOI VarDOI	Average and variance of Degree of Interest (DOI) values of the file.
	Intervals	AvgTimeIntervalEditEdit	The average time interval between two edit events of the file.
		AvgTimeIntervalSelSel	The average time interval between two selection events of the file.
		AvgTimeGapSelEdit	The average time interval between selection and edit events of the file
Task Level	Effort	NumUniqueSelFiles	The unique number of selected files in a task
		NumUniqueEdit	The unique number of edited files in a task.
		TimeSpent	The total time spent on a task.
	Distraction	NumLowDOISel	The number of selection events with low DOI (DOI < median of all DOIs).
		NumLowDOIEdit	The number of edit events with low DOI (DOI < median of all DOIs).
		PortionNonJavaEdit	The percentage of non-java file edit events in a task.
	Work Portion	TimeSpentBeforeEdit	The ratio of the time spent (out of total time spent) before the first edit.
		TimeSpendAfterEdit	The ratio of the time spent (out of total time spent) after the last edit.
		TimeSpentOnEdits	The ratio of the time spent (out of total time spent) between the first and last edits.
		NumSelBeforeEdit	The number of unique selections before the first edit event.
		NumSelAfterEdit	The number of unique selections after the last edit event.
	Repetition	RepeatedlySelectedFileNum	The number of files selected more than once in one task.
		RepeatedlyEditedFileNum	The number of files edited more than once in one task.
	Task Load	NumMultiTasks	The number of ongoing tasks at the same time.
		FileHierarchyDepth	The average depth of file hierarchy.
	Event Pattern	NumPatternSXSX NumPatternSXSY NumPatternSYSX NumPatternSYSY NumPatternSXEX NumPatternSXEY NumPatternSYEX NumPatternSYEY NumPatternEXSX NumPatternEXSY NumPatternEYSX NumPatternEYSY NumPatternEXEX NumPatternEXEY NumPatternEYEX NumPatternEYEY	The number of adjacent sequential event patterns in one task. S and E represent selection and edit events respectively. For example, S?E? describes adjacent sequential interactions of selecting a file and continuously editing a file. We classify files into two groups: X and Y. If a file satisfies one of the following three conditions, we mark them as Group X. 1) If the file has been ever fixed before due to a defect. 2) If the file is one of frequently edited files in a task. (frequency threshold: top 50% of file editing frequencies). 3) If the file has been recently selected or edited within $\pm n$ time spent of a given task, where $n = \frac{totaltime}{4}$ Otherwise, we put the file in the Y group. The group X implies high locality of file accessing with error-prone interaction. The hint of locality concept is from [15].
		NumPatternSLSL NumPatternSLSH NumPatternSHSL NumPatternSHSH NumPatternSLEL NumPatternSLEH NumPatternSHEL NumPatternSHEH NumPatternELSL NumPatternELSH NumPatternEHSL NumPatternEHSH NumPatternELEL NumPatternELEH NumPatternEHEL NumPatternEHEH	As explained above, S and E share the same meaning. But instead of X or Y encoding, H or L encoding is used here. If the DOI value of the edited or selected file is higher than the median of all the DOI values in a task, it is denoted by H. Otherwise, it is L.

BugCache for Inspections : Hit or Miss?

Foyzur Rahman Daryl Posnett Abram Hindle Earl Barr Premkumar Devanbu

Department of Computer Science
University of California Davis, Davis, CA., USA
{mfrahman,dpposnett,ajhindle,etbarr,ptdevanbu}@ucdavis.edu

ABSTRACT

Inspection is a highly effective but costly technique for quality control. Most companies do not have the resources to inspect all the code; thus accurate defect prediction can help focus available inspection resources. BugCache is a simple, elegant, award-winning prediction scheme that "caches" files that are likely to contain defects [12]. In this paper, we evaluate the utility of BugCache as a tool for focusing inspection, we examine the assumptions underlying BugCache with the aim of improving it, and finally we compare it with a simple, standard bug-prediction technique. We find that BugCache is, in fact, useful for focusing inspection effort; but surprisingly, we find that its performance, when used for inspections, is not much better than a naive prediction model — *viz.*, a model that orders files in the system by their count of closed bugs and chooses enough files to capture 20% of the lines in the system.

Categories and Subject Descriptors

D.2.5 [**Software Engineering**]: Testing and Debugging—*Code Inspections and Walk-Throughs*

General Terms

Experimentation; Measurement; Reliability; Verification

Keywords

Empirical Software Engineering, Fault Prediction, Inspection

1. INTRODUCTION

The later a bug is discovered, the more expensive and difficult it is to resolve [1]. Deployed bugs are the worst of all, requiring costly, embarrassing, and labor-intensive software updates in the field and/or re-deployments. Thus stakeholders, such as managers and quality assurance people, worry most about faults that escape into released and deployed products. Quality control methods such as inspection and testing aim to detect faults prior to release. Unfortunately, code inspection and testing are costly in terms of time and manpower, so managers seek to optimize their effectiveness. Bug prediction has been suggested as a means to this end. If one could predict which entities — modules, files or lines of code — are bug-prone, quality control teams might focus their effort on inspecting those entities.

In their award-winning paper on *BugCache* [12], Kim *et al.* hypothesized that past knowledge of fault occurrence can optimize testing and inspection effort. Their proposed cache-inspired models depend on the exploitable "locality" of faults. They hypothesized three types of locality. First, faults are more likely to occur in recently added/changed entities (churn locality). Second, if an entity contains a fault, then it is likely to contain more faults (temporal locality). Finally, entities that are logically coupled (by co-changes) with other faulty entities are more likely to contain faults (spatial locality).

To exploit fault locality, Kim *et al.* uses two types of changes, *bug-introducing* changes and *bug-fixing* changes, along with change history, to identify a subset of entities that are highly likely to contain defects. They implemented two types of caches: BugCache, a theoretical model, and FixCache, a practical prediction model. BugCache contains faulty entities and is updated when a bug, or fault, is introduced into a file. In reality, bug-introductions usually occur unnoticed, (and hopefully discovered later!) so BugCache is a theoretical model that can't be used until the full project history is known. FixCache, on the other hand, is a practical realization of BugCache that doesn't need oracular knowledge.

The evaluation of FixCache drew our attention: we wanted to replicate it from a different perspective, with an emphasis on inspection. FixCache was originally evaluated using the measure of "hit rate", which is the cumulative percentage of the successful cache probes through a project history. For *regression testing*, this measure is effective: if FixCache accurately identifies the defect-prone files, one can run tests only on defect-prone, modified files. However, our concern is *inspection efficiency*. Kim *et al.* wrote:

> "A manager then can use the list for quality assurance — for example, she can *test or review* the entities in the bug cache with increased priority" [12, §6] (our italics).

Thus we evaluate FixCache from the point of view of a stakeholder involved in code inspection — "how much effort does FixCache actually save inspectors?"

Code inspectors would prefer to focus their effort on buggiest of entities in order to achieve a greatest possible payoff

Permission to make digital or hard copies of all or part of this work for personal or classroom use is granted without fee provided that copies are not made or distributed for profit or commercial advantage and that copies bear this notice and the full citation on the first page. To copy otherwise, to republish, to post on servers or to redistribute to lists, requires prior specific permission and/or a fee.
ESEC/FSE'11, September 5–9, 2011, Szeged, Hungary.
Copyright 2011 ACM 978-1-4503-0443-6/11/09 ...$10.00.

of bug detection for a given investment in inspection time. Suppose, hypothetically, that FIXCACHE simply loaded the largest files into the cache. In this case, a high hit rate would not necessarily translate into an effective inspection process: a great many lines of code might have to be inspected to find bugs. Likewise, loading smaller files might lead to fewer hits, but might result in efficient inspection that discovers more bugs per unit of work.

To this end, we *first* evaluate FIXCACHE, not against hit rate (cache hits), but against defect density and the cost effectiveness of inspection. *Second*, we address the questions "What makes FIXCACHE work?" and "Of the different cache update policies it uses, which is most effective?" *Third*, we investigate whether certain modifications to these cache update policies would improve FIXCACHE's performance with respect to the inspection cost-effectiveness. *Finally*, we study whether FIXCACHE outperforms, in terms of inspection cost effectiveness, a very simple, standard bug prediction model.

This paper mounts a replicated study of FIXCACHE and makes the following contributions:

- We evaluate FIXCACHE using defect density. *We find that, in fact,* FIXCACHE *does indeed find more bug-dense entities.*
- We study how the different update and replacement policies applicable contribute to FIXCACHE's bug prediction and inspection efficiency, using an inspection cost-effectiveness measure. *We find that there is not much difference in the performance of different update and replacement policies.*
- We compare FIXCACHE with a simple prediction model, using the same inspection measure *and find that there is not much difference.*

2. THEORY

FIXCACHE is easily described. To start, the cache is primed with a set of files, typically the largest files. Then, the FIXCACHE algorithm monitors the commits to the system and updates its cache using a set of policies. A *hit* occurs when a file in the cache undergoes a bug fix; a *miss* occurs when a file outside the cache receives a bug fix. The cache's contents, at any one point in time, contains the target set of buggy files for testing or inspection. FIXCACHE uses 3 update policies.

When a bug-fix is committed, FIXCACHE immediately adds the modified files to its cache; this is the *temporal locality* policy. Next it retroactively finds and adds the file(s) from the commit(s) in which the bug was introduced, as well as the files that were most often committed together with these files at that time. This is the *spatial locality* policy. Finally, FIXCACHE adds recently added/changed files to the cache. We call this the *churn locality* policy. All these files are added to the cache, if they are not already present, when a bug-fix is observed in the anticipatory belief that they will require fixes soon.

Kim *et al.* empirically evaluated FIXCACHE using various cache sizes (most often 10% of the entities in the system) and found it very accurate (73%–95%) at identifying faulty files. They also evaluated FIXCACHE's accuracy at method granularity and found its accuracy to fall within 46%–72%. In this paper we only evaluate FIXCACHE at file granularity. Several papers [7, 19, 22, 24] have reported re-implementations of FixCache, for various applications; our implementation achieved performance levels similar to those reported in these earlier papers, roughly 60%–80% hit rate at file granularity, as we discuss below.

2.1 Cost-Effectiveness

Evidently, if we could inspect just 10% of the files in a project and find most of the project's defects, that would be terrific for the software industry. Unfortunately, unlike a hardware cache that contains fixed size cache lines, FIXCACHE contains source code entities, such as files, that can vary greatly in size. Thus, if the files in the FIXCACHE tend to be large and contain a disproportionately large portion of the project code, then focusing on the files in FIXCACHE may not be very helpful for code inspection. So, first, we ask what proportion of the lines of code are actually contained in the files that reside in the cache.

> **Research Question 1:** What proportion of the total lines of code are in the FIXCACHE?

Even if the entities in FIXCACHE include a very large proportion of the lines of code in the project, they might still be well worth inspecting, if those lines contain proportionately more bugs (*viz.*, higher defect density) than the lines not in the cache. When this happens, prioritizing the cached files increases inspection effectiveness. If, however, cached files turn out to have lower defect density than files that are not cached, then prioritizing files in FIXCACHE for inspection is unwarranted. This leads us to our next research question.

> **Research Question 2:** Do the cached files have higher defect density (defects per lines of code) than files not in the cache?

Answering this question will allow us to measure the efficacy of FIXCACHE. While this gives us a general idea of the possible benefits of using FIXCACHE, it does not tell us why it actually works (if it does). A good understanding of the mechanics of FIXCACHE may enable us to customize or enhance it. Thus arises the imperative to desconstruct the various "locality-based" update policies used by FIXCACHE, and evaluate their merits.

2.2 What Makes FIXCACHE Tick?

The operation of FIXCACHE is predicated upon several update policies. How do these update policies affect the performance of FIXCACHE? There are four sources of cache updates:

1. "Initial pre-fetch": Files added to the cache during cache initialization (following Kim *et al.* [12]).
2. "Temporal locality": Files added to the cache because they were changed to fix bugs.
3. "Spatial locality": Files co-changed with a buggy file, *viz.,* files that co-occur in many transactions where the buggy file was changed.
4. "Churn locality": Files that have recently been changed or added.

Of these four, we consider the first two to reflect core aspects of any cache, including FixCache. First, we must initialize the cache with some files, or else the initial hit rate would be low. Second, temporal locality adds a file to the cache, if it is not already present, when a defect is found in it. The other two sources, spatial locality and churn locality, provide additional policies for including files into the cache; it is these two policies that we evaluate empirically.

> **Research Question 3:** How do temporal and spatial locality policies affect FixCache performance?

With a detailed understanding of the relative influence of different FixCache update policies, future research may explore customizing FixCache to attain a different set of performance goals. For example, while Kim *et al.* used the "hit rate" measure to evaluate performance, one might, as we do, choose other measures, such as density or cost-effectiveness, a measure developed by Arisholm, Briand & Johannessen [3].

> **Research Question 4:** Can we improve FixCache to achieve better defect density?

This question raises additional interesting questions. What is the right way to optimize cache performance? Surely it will depend on a project's requirements and resource availability. Kim *et al.* measured FixCache performance in terms of predictive accuracy. Is this sufficient?

2.3 Evaluating Prediction Performance

Kim *et al.* use the measure "hit rate" to evaluate FixCache. "Hit rate" is the cumulative percentage of successful cache probes at the end of a run through a project's history. At any point in time, the cache may contain both defective and non-defective files. Only files that actually contain defects score hits, so the number of defective files in the cache bears some relation to the hit rate. FixCache considers files in the cache to be defective and those not in the cache to be non-defective. Consequently, the cache contains both *true positives* (TP), files that actually contain defects, and *false positives* (FP). The files not in the cache comprise the *true negatives* (TN), non-defective files, and *false negatives* (FN), defective files that are incorrectly classified. *Recall* measures the ratio of retrieved to relevant files:

$$\text{Recall} = \frac{TP}{TP + FN} = \frac{TP}{\text{Defective}}.$$

No matter how many false positives are in the cache, recall remains unaffected. In fact, we can achieve perfect recall simply by enlarging the cache to hold all files. Recall, however, only tells half the story of a successful prediction algorithm. We are also interested in the ratio of relevant files to those retrieved. If only 10% of the files are defective, then retrieving 100% of the files, which would naively yield perfect recall, is an inefficient way to identify the defective files and demonstrates the limitations of using recall in isolation. Thus, recall is usually paired with another measure that penalizes an algorithm for falsely predicting too many entities as defective. *Precision* is the ratio of correct predictions to the total predicted as defective

$$\text{Precision} = \frac{TP}{TP + FP} = \frac{TP}{\text{InCache}}.$$

When applied in this setting, however, both precision and recall treat all files equally. Effectively, they are indifferent to the number of *lines of code* (LOC) in the files being flagged as defective. When using a prediction tool as a guide for inspection, LOC is critical; smaller, buggy files may well have higher defect density, and consequently may yield a better return on inspection investment. When comparing different cache update policies, or different prediction models that select different numbers of files (and varying amounts of code) for inspection, we adopt a *cost-effectiveness* measure, specifically the area under the cost-effectiveness curve, or AUCEC. *Readers unfamiliar with this rather subtle measure may wish to read Section 2.4 below, before returning here.*

We apply these concepts to the evaluation of FixCache in order to build a more complete picture of its performance in an inspection setting. The extent to which FixCache exceeds the performance of standard models could suggest approaches for improving standard prediction models intended for use in inspection; perhaps an update policy, such as spatial locality, can be fruitfully incorporated into a traditional model. For this reason and to asses its efficacy, we use AUCEC to compare FixCache against a vanilla prediction model.

The FixCache algorithm imposes only a gross ordering of the files to be inspected, *viz.*, those files within the cache are to be inspected prior to those without. The calculation of cost effectiveness requires that we impose an order on the files within the cache so that we do not artificially penalize the FixCache algorithm in our evaluation.

To evaluate FixCache using AUCEC, we impose the same order on the files within the cache and those not in the cache — first by decreasing number of closed bugs, then by increasing size. This means that the smaller files with many closed bugs bubble up to the top.

This approach evaluates the cost-effectiveness of FixCache fairly with our naive algorithms: we found that this ordering provided the best performance for FixCache in every setting when compared with other simple orderings, *e.g.* density, file size, or previous defects.

> **Research Question 5:** Does FixCache outperform standard, simple prediction models, when used for inspection?

2.4 Cost-Effectiveness Curve

Here, we briefly define cost-effectiveness, then the area under the CE curve (AUCEC), measures which we use to investigate RQ5. If you are familiar with these measures, please feel free to skip this section.

Suppose defects are uniformly distributed throughout the source code. Then, if an inspection budget allows inspection of 10% of the source code, we might choose 10% of the lines at random and reasonably expect to find about 10% of the defects. This scheme requires no work or expertise in data gathering and defect modeling. It is therefore reasonable to expect that any useful defect prediction method should be able to improve on this result. This is the basis for the cost effectiveness (CE) metric defined by Arisholm *et al.* [2] to investigate defects in telecommunications software.

Suppose that source code is selected for inspection using a prediction algorithm that orders code entities (*e.g.*, files) in terms of predicted defectiveness. If the algorithm is good and the system has only a few defects, or well-clustered defects,

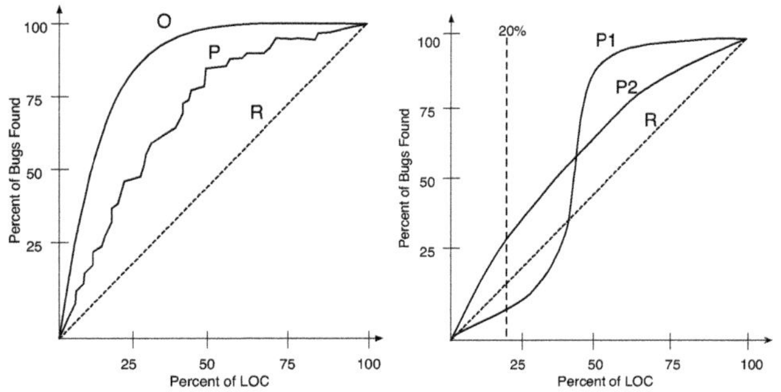

Figure 1: Cost Effectiveness Curve. On the left, O is the optimal, R is random, and P is a possible, *practical*, predictor model. On the right, we have two different models P1 and P2, with the same overall performance, but P2 is better when inspecting 20% of the lines or less.

this procedure would allow us to inspect just a few lines of code to find most of the defects. If the algorithm performs poorly and/or the defects are uniformly distributed in the code, we would expect to inspect most of the lines before we find all the defects. The CE curve (see Figure 1, left side) is a harsh but meticulous judge of prediction algorithms; it plots the proportion of identified faults (a number between 0 and 1) found against the proportion of the lines of code (also between 0 and 1) inspected. It is a way to evaluate a proposed inspection ordering. With a random ordering (the curve labeled R on the left side of Figure 1) and/or defects uniformly scattered throughout the code, the CE curve is the diagonal $y = x$ line. At file-granularity, the optimal ordering (labeled O in the Figure 1 left) places the smallest, most defective files first, and the curve climbs rapidly, quickly rising well above the $y = x$ line. A practical algorithm has a CE curve (labeled P in the Figure 1 left) that falls below the optimal ordering, but remains usefully above the $y = x$ line.

The CE curve represents a variety of operating choices: one can choose an operating point along this curve, inspect more or fewer lines of code and find more or fewer defects. Thus, to jointly capture the entire set of choices afforded by a particular prediction algorithm, one typically uses the *area under the CE curve*, or AUCEC, which is also a number between 0 and 1. An imaginary, utterly fantastical, prediction algorithm will have an area very close to 1, *viz.*, by ordering the *lines* so that one can discover all the defects by inspecting a single line; a superb algorithm will have a AUCEC value close to the optimal. Values of AUCEC below 1/2 indicate a poor algorithm. Thus, useful values of AUCEC lie between 1/2 and the optimum.

Consider two different prediction models with nearly identical AUCEC. On the right side of Figure 1, the two curves labeled P1 and P2 have very similar AUCEC values. However, if one were inspecting 20% of the lines or less, P2 offers a better set of operating points. This line budget is indeed quite realistic: inspecting 20% of the LOC in the system is definitely more realistic than inspecting all of it. Thus, the AUCEC, cut off at 20%, is a useful measure of the cost-effectiveness of a prediction model; this is what we use. Arisholm *et al.* [3] refer to a similar notion of AUCEC, conditioned on choosing 20% of the system. As it turns out, the preferred FixCache cache size setting of 10% of the overall number of files in the system, typically results in a cache that contains close to 20% *of the LOC in the system*. So we adopt AUCEC at 20% of the LOC, which we refer to as AUCEC_{20}.

3. EXPERIMENTAL FRAMEWORK

In this section, we define some terminology and present our experimental setup.

3.1 Revision

Source code management (SCM) systems provide a rich version history of software projects. This history includes all commits to every file. These commits have various attributes such as a timestamp, authorship, change content, and commit log message. In our study, a commit, or a revision, consists of an author, a timestamp and a set of files changed. We chose Git as our version control system, because of its excellent ability to track changes and find the origin of each line of code.

3.2 Bug-fixing Revision

Bugs are discovered and usually recorded into an issue-tracking system such as Bugzilla and subsequently rejected or fixed by the developers. Each bug report records its opening date, the date of the bug fix, a free-form textual bug description, and the final, triaged Bugzilla severity. For this research, we consider any severity other than an `enhancement` to be a bug.

Our study begins with links between Bugzilla bugs and the specific revision that fixes the bug — we call this a *bug-fixing revision*. We employed various heuristics to derive our data. We scan for keywords, such as "bug", "fixed", *etc.*, in the SCM commit log to flag bug-fixing revisions [16]. Also, numerical bug identifiers, mentioned in the commit log, are linked back to the issue tracking system's identifiers [8, 21]. Then these identifiers are crosschecked against the issue tracking system to see whether such an issue identifier exists and whether its status changed after the bug-fixing commit. Finally, we manually inspect the links to remove as many spurious links as possible. Each remaining *linked bug* has a bug-fixing revision. We gratefully acknowledge bug data we obtained from Bachmann *et al.* [4].

3.3 Bug-Introducing Change

We call the lines of code that are associated with the changes that trigger a bug fix "fix-inducing code", following Sliwerski *et al.* [20] (also see [11]), as it is the code that needed repair. For example, if `strcpy (str2,str1);` were changed to `strncpy(str2,str1,n);` then the original line is considered fix-inducing code. New lines may also be added in the bug-fixing revision, but we do not consider these "implicated", since they are part of the treatment, not the symptom. Kim *et al.* uses the term bug-introducing change to describe such fix-inducing code.

We use the popular Sliwerski-Zimmerman-Zeller *SZZ* [20] approach to identify bug-introducing changes. We start with data that links a bug to the revision where that bug was fixed. If a bug fix is linked to revision $n+1$, then n, the immediately preceding revision, contains the relevant buggy code. The `diff` of revision n and $n+1$ of each file changed in revision $n+1$ gives us the potentially buggy code. We call these lines the fix-inducing code. We then use the `git blame` command on the fix-inducing code; `git blame` produces accurate provenance annotations (author, date, revision number where they were last changed) for each line. With this information, we use the SZZ approach to rule out lines that could not have been involved in the defect, because of their time of introduction. For the rest, this approach identifies the commit that introduced the fix-inducing line.

3.4 Defect Density

We calculate two types of defect density: defect density based on open bugs and defect density based on closed bugs. At time t, we identify number of *closed bugs* of a file up to time t and divide that by the size of the file to calculate *closed bug density*. At time t, we identify *open bugs* as those reported before t and closed after t. *Open bug density* is the count of open bugs divided by file size. Note we use only the bugs that are linked to a file, since we cannot in general identify the culpable file of an unlinked bug. By using this density measure, we are assuming that files with higher *open* bug density are more profitable to inspect.

3.5 FixCache

We faithfully re-implemented FixCache as described in [12]. Following earlier evaluation studies [19, 22, 24] of FixCache, we implemented file-level FixCache, *i.e.* our implementation aims to predict defect-prone files.

Before running FixCache, for efficiency, we first identify all the bug-fixing revisions and chronologically order them. For each of these bug-fixing revisions, we also use the SZZ technique to identify the revision of the bug-introducing change. Now we are ready to run FixCache. We "prime" the cache with the largest files of a project during the *initial pre-fetch*, then scan its history. At every bug-fix revision, we probe the cache to see if the file being fixed is in the cache; if so, we score a hit, otherwise, we score a miss. If a probe results in a cache miss, we "fetch" that buggy file into the cache, and additionally determine all the spatially related files (files that were modified frequently with the buggy file in question). As described by Kim *et al.*, we go back in time to when a bug was introduced using SZZ, and determine *spatially local* files, files that were co-committed with the buggy file being probed at that time. We limit the fetch size of *spatially local* files to the block size parameter [12], prioritized by the frequency of co-commit (more often co-committed files get higher priority).

Regardless of cache hit or miss, we also fetch the recently changed/added files (files that were changed/added between two bug-fix revisions), subject to the pre-fetch size parameter [12].

As new files are added into the cache, we may need to evict old files. Following Kim *et al.*, we used two eviction policies — least recently used (LRU), to retain files recently involved in a bug-fix, and closed bugs, to retain files with the highest number of closed bugs. We did not implement the CHANGE [12] eviction policy as Kim *et al.* reported that it performs poorly.

The original FixCache presented results for 10% cache size. Prior evaluations [19, 22, 24] of FixCache also rely on 10% cache size. To ensure the sensitivity of our analysis, we experimented with several different cache sizes. We worked with 6, 10, 18 and 25% cache size. For these cache sizes, we set the block size to 2, 5, 9 and 13% respectively and pre-fetch size to 1, 1, 2 and 3% respectively.

3.6 Snapshot

As we described earlier, after each bug-fixing revision, we update the cached files. After updating the cache, we determine the state of the system, in particular the cached and uncached files. We also capture other system details such as the cache update source, the last hit time, *etc.* For each cached file, we determine its number of closed bugs, its size, *etc.* We call the overall system state after each bug-fixing revision a *snapshot* of the system.

4. THE DATA SETS

We chose 5 different medium to large-sized open-source projects for our study. All have long development histories, but are otherwise quite different. *Apache Httpd* is a widely used open source web server. *Gimp* is a popular open source image manipulation program. *Nautilus* is the default file manager for the Gnome desktop. *Evolution* is the default email client for the Gnome desktop with support for integrated mail, address book and calender functionality. *Lucene* is the most popular text search engine library. Except Lucene, all of our projects are written in C. Lucene is written in Java. We converted the Apache subversion repository to GIT and used the other projects' GIT repositories directly.

These systems span varied application domains: clients and servers, GUI applications, a file browsers, and libraries for text searching. All are of substantial size and complexity. Table 1 summarizes some descriptive statistics for each project studied. Project size ranges from 191k lines to about 800k lines. The table also presents the study period, the number of buggy files (which represents the number of cache probes made), the average number of source files (.c, .cpp, .h, or .java files) in bug fixing revisions, the average lines of code (as measured by `wc -l` Unix command) in bug fixing revisions, the number of commits made during the study period, the number of bug fixing commit made during this period and the number of bug-introducing commits (commits that introduced/changed some code that was changed/deleted later to fix some bug).

We determine all linked bugs and their associated bug-fixing revisions for all the subject projects. The corresponding bug-fixing change is found by using `diff` between a bug-fixing revision and its immediate preceding revision. After collecting all bug-fixing changes, we use GIT BLAME on each line of the bug-fixing change to identify its *last* modification time. This gives us all of the bug-introducing changes.

5. EVALUATION

We now present our results per each research question presented in Section 2. We only present plots from Apache and Lucene. Data from other projects is discussed in the text.

RQ1: *What is the line coverage of* FixCache*?*

Does FixCache achieve good hit-rates by simply caching a disproportionate fraction of the total LOC in the system? To check this, we plot the cached files' total LOC count in Figure 2 for 10% cache size and LRU based replacement policy. The time-series line plot shows that the FixCache caches a higher proportion of total line count when compared to the proportion of total file count within the cache. We found similar results for all projects. Moreover, we ran a sensitivity analysis by choosing the cache size to be 6, 10, 18

Name	Start Date	End Date	Number of Buggy Files	Avg. Number of Files	Avg. Number of LOC	Number of Commits	Number of Fix Commits	Number of Fix Inducing Commits
Apache	1996-07-03	2009-04-21	610	313	191303	18456	372	1108
Gimp	1997-01-01	2009-08-08	5291	2108	784529	25583	1727	6042
Nautilus	1997-01-02	2009-08-06	1235	312	136736	13462	656	1608
Evolution	1998-01-12	2009-08-08	3980	1146	432498	30528	1363	3733
Lucene	2001-09-11	2010-06-17	2453	1181	236672	5182	683	2369

Table 1: Summary of study subjects

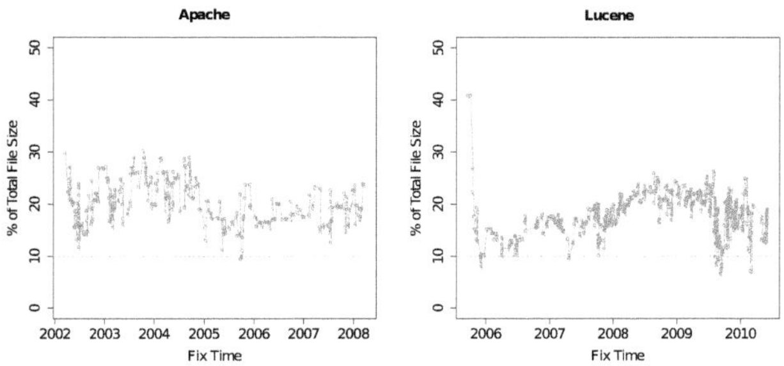

Figure 2: LOC in cached files for Apache and Lucene. If FixCache does not favor any particular size of file, then the dashed flat-line represents the *expected* fraction of total project line count in the cache for a 10% cache size. Time-varying line is the fraction of total project line count in the cache

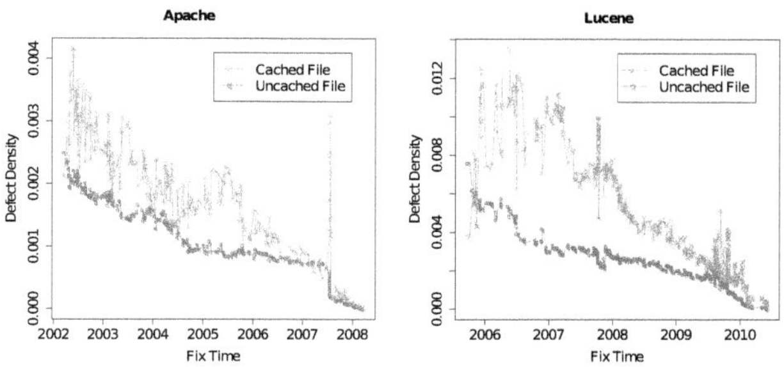

Figure 4: Defect Density in cached and un-cached files (10% cache size, LRU replacement) for Apache and Lucene.

and 25% of the overall files and using both LRU and Closed Bugs replacement policy. In all cases the FixCache retained a significantly greater (double to triple) proportion of lines, in comparison to the proportion of the total number of files held in the cache. This fact could undermine the efficacy of FixCache, when used to prioritize files for inspection.

These results suggest that the performance of FixCache, when used as an aid for targeting inspections, is not necessarily as good as suggested by the original hit rate measure. For inspection use, we need to consider file size to build a clearer picture of FixCache performance. We do this by comparing the defect density of cached files with that of the un-cached files.

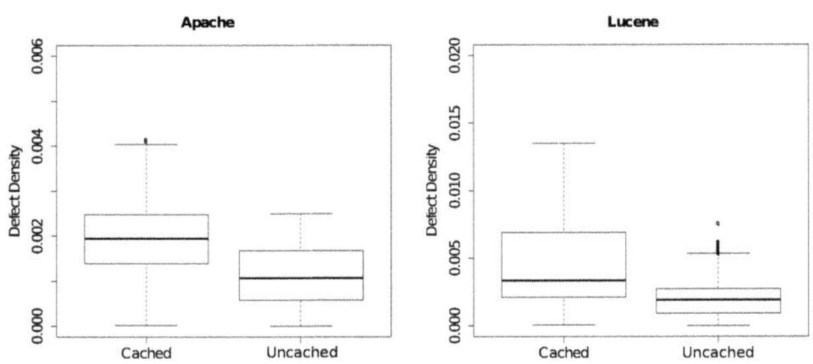

Figure 3: Defect Density boxplot in cached and un-cached files (10% cache size, LRU replacement) for Apache and Lucene.

RQ2a: *Do the cached files have higher defect density than files not in cache?*

Figure 3 shows the boxplot of defect density in cached and un-cached files for 10% cache size and LRU replacement policy. Clearly, files in the FixCache have higher defect density. We also ran an one sided paired Wilcoxon signed rank test with a *null hypothesis*: defect density in cached files is no greater than defect density in un-cached files. We found that the FixCache does indeed contain files with greater density (all the p-values were very small ($<< 0.001$)).

We also did a sensitivity analysis for different cache sizes. We found that the above result holds for all projects, for all cache sizes. Moreover, we found that the effect size varies little over all cache sizes for a given project.

Figure 4 shows the time-series line plot of density in cached and un-cached files (again for 10% cache size and LRU replacement policy). This figure highlights the right-censoring [14] effect in our data. We use bug fix information to determine opened/closed bugs for a given sets of files. We use our (*a posteriori*) knowledge of bug fixes to calculate the density of open bugs in the code at any given point in time. As we near the end of our data collection phase, we have fewer fixes; this gradually reduces the number of known, open bugs to zero. The cache, consequently, suffers from a diminishing defect density at the end of the run, which is really an artifact of right-censoring, not an indication that the performance of FixCache is getting worse.

There is a noteworthy, sudden spike in FixCache defect-density and hit rate in July, 2007 for Apache. We did a case study to understand this event. It turned out that on July 20, 2007, 15 distinct files were linked to 7 distinct bugs, resulting in a total of $15 * 7 = 105$ cache probes. This rapid succession of defects in the same files induced a a dramatic boost in the hit rate. Moreover, since each of these files had a large number of opened bugs, we also observed a higher cache defect density at that point. We observed similar (though less pronounced) sudden hit rate spikes for other projects as well. This suggests that FixCache may yield a higher return in response to certain events, while performing less well at other times.

Though files resident in FIXCACHE have higher density, one might argue that inspecting the entire set of files in the cache during each bug fix commit would induce redundant inspection effort, since some files would be inspected repeatedly. Rather, we could prefer to inspect files that are added or changed (we refer to such files as *churned files*) since the last inspection (the immediate prior bug fix). Thus we can ask, how well does FIXCACHE work if we only inspect the churned files? This immediately raises the question of FIXCACHE efficacy when considering only churned files. We therefore compare defect density of churned cached files against the defect density of churned un-cached files.

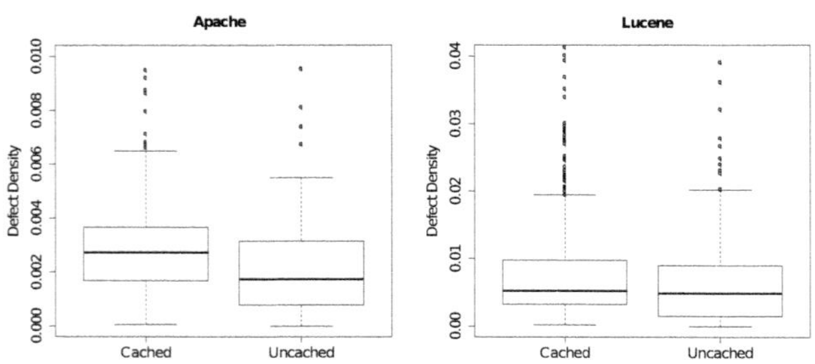

Figure 5: Defect Density boxplot in cached and un-cached *churned* (newly added or changed) files (10% cache size, LRU replacement) for Apache and Lucene.

RQ2b: *Do the churned files in the cache have higher defect density than churned files not in the cache?*

Figure 5 shows the boxplot of the calculated defect density of cached and un-cached churned files at 10% cache size for the LRU replacement policy. Not only the effect size dramatically diminished, it actually flipped for some projects, under some parameter settings. The Evolution project shows a lower defect density of cached files even at the typical 10% cache size. Moreover, Nautilus also shows lower defect density of cached files at all but the 10 and 18% cache size. Effect size is very small across the board; even so, some projects, for some parameter settings, show a statistically significant greater defect density for churned files.

Next, we evaluate the effect of each cache-replacement policy on the defect density achieved in FIXCACHE.

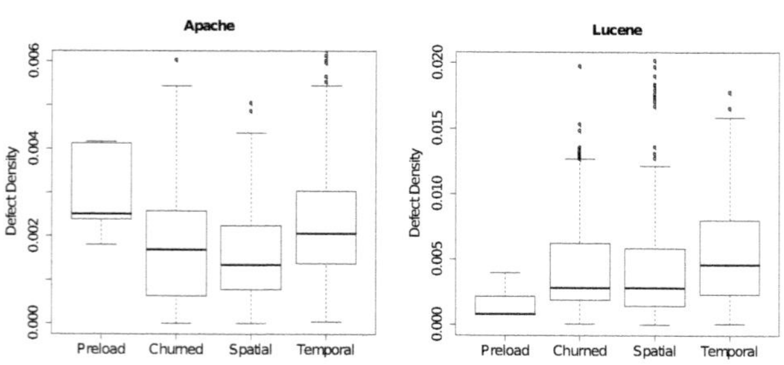

Figure 6: Defect Density by loading reason in cached and un-cached files for Apache and Lucene.

RQ3: *Do different sources of cache updates have different levels of influence on cache performance?*

Figure 6 shows the defect density as contributed by different sources of cache updates.

As is apparent from the figure, temporal locality is the highest contributor of defect density. We disregard the initial preloading of large files as we observe that, across all projects, they are evicted from the cache early in the run. Wilcoxon signed rank tests were used to check whether temporal locality consistently yields greater defect density across all cache sizes. We did find that temporal locality, for various cache sizes, and across all projects, exhibits higher defect density than spatial locality with only a few exceptions: Apache at 18 and 25% and Nautilus at 25% cache sizes. When compared to churn locality, however, temporal locality may not yield better performance.

This immediately raises a question: are temporally local entities are competing for cache space with spatially local or churn-local entities? In terms of defect density, can we do better if we selectively enable/disable the other sources of cache updates? This is a challenging question to answer as enabling and disabling different policies will change both the number of files and the number of lines in the cache. Consequently, we have to take into account the total number of lines to be inspected, as well as the open bug density. We use the aforementioned cost effectiveness measure AUCEC_{20} to consider this question.

To use AUCEC_{20}, we require a prediction model to provide an ordering in which the files should be inspected. As specified, the FIXCACHE algorithm provides only a gross ordering of files, *i.e.*, files in the cache should be inspected prior to files not in the cache. To compare FIXCACHE to other algorithms we tried various orderings to find the one most favorable to FIXCACHE, but, that only used data available to practitioners at the time of prediction. Specifically, we order the files within the cache and those not in the cache independently using the same ordering: order files first by decreasing number of closed bugs, then by increasing size. We found that this ordering provided the best performance for FIXCACHE in every setting. Given this ordering, we can then pick off files from the top of the ordering until we reach just over 20% of the overall line count in the system.

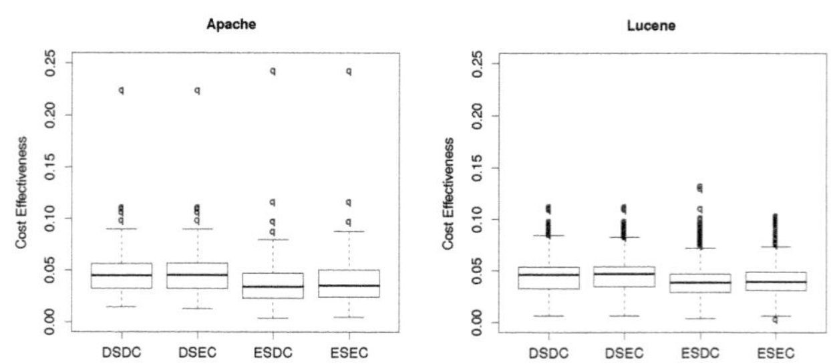

Figure 7: AUCEC_{20} cost effectiveness after enabling/disabling spatial/changed file locality (10% cache size, LRU replacement, 20% of lines inspected) for Apache and Lucene. EC/DC refers to enable/disable churn locality; ES/DS refers to enable/disable spatial locality. DSDC means disable both; all other combinations are labeled similarly

RQ4a: *Do spatial and churn locality update policies improve the cost-effectiveness of* FIXCACHE*?*

Figure 7 shows the AUCEC$_{20}$ measure after enabling and disabling spatial and churn locality.

In Figure 7, we use DS/ES to denote "Disable/Enable Spatial locality" and DC/EC for "Disable/Enable Churn locality". DSDC denotes "both disabled", while DSEC denotes "disable spatial, enable churn". This figure makes it abundantly clear that from the perspective of AUCEC$_{20}$ cost-effectiveness, adding spatial and churn locality to the FIXCACHE update policies provides little benefit.

We want to show that there is little to no practical difference in cost effectiveness across the different locality settings. The Kruskal-Wallis test is a non-parametric test which assess whether n independent samples are drawn from the same population. It is the non-parametric counterpart to a one-way Anova[13]. This test shows that for every project, there is no significant difference in cost-effectiveness observed when enabling or disabling churn and/or spatial locality. Thus, although Figure 6 suggests that churn and spatial locality potentially have some defect density to contribute, and may in fact cache additional files, they do not provide any benefit for inspection when inspecting 20% or fewer lines, (as per AUCEC$_{20}$). This clearly indicates that temporal locality (which caches files when defects are found) underlies most of the predictive power in FIXCACHE.

Finally, we focus on different cache replacement policies in FIXCACHE and compare their performance.

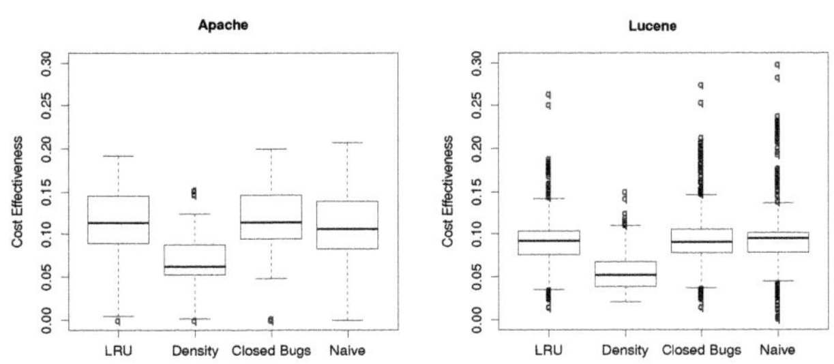

Figure 8: AUCEC$_{20}$ values for Apache and Lucene. The left 3 are FIXCACHE with different replacement policies, and right most is a naive prediction model, which simply order files by closed bug count. Only in Apache (of all) are any of the FIXCACHE version statistically better than the naive model, and even then the effect size is quite small

RQ4b: *Can we improve* FIXCACHE AUCEC$_{20}$ *performance by using a different cache replacement policy?*

The original FIXCACHE used two different policies. The first is an LRU based replacement policy, which keeps frequently hit files in the cache. The principle here is that files that haven't had bug fixes in a while are probably unlikely to have latent bugs. The second was a "closed bugs" policy, which replaced files with the least number of closed bugs first. For our evaluation, we added a third policy based on defect density,which replaced the file with the least density of closed bugs. The latter two policies are based on the theory that files with fewer bugs, or lower defect density, are likely to have fewer latent bugs. All of these policies *prima facie* appear to have merit, so it is reasonable to compare them to see which policies yield better AUCEC$_{20}$ performance.

The results are shown as the left most 3 boxplots in the two plots in Figure 8

For this question, we ran FIXCACHE with cache size set to 6%, 10%, 18% and 25% of the total file count, and consistently obtained results with all projects similar to those seen in Figure 8. The closed bugs policy generally showed the best performance, while the density policy was consistently the worst performer. This finding again, is strongly indicative that the raw count of closed bugs in a file is an excellent indicator of future latent bugs.

Our final question is in some sense the most critical evaluation of FIXCACHE. Does FIXCACHE perform better than a naive prediction model?

RQ5: *When used for inspections, is* FIXCACHE *doing better than a naive model that simply picks previously buggy files?*

For this question we chose a very simple, naive prediction model: *the model simply orders all the files in the system by the number of closed bugs*, and chooses enough files in order to capture 20% of the total line count. The results are shown as the rightmost boxplot in Figure 8.

Testing the hypothesis that the best FIXCACHE replacement policy (*viz* closed bugs) is better than the naive model, we find that, after Benjamini-Hochberg correction, only the Apache project data rejects the null hypothesis. However, as can be seen in Figure 8, even in this case, the effect size is fairly small.

This leads to a rather surprising, conclusion:

> *The naive model is actually about the same utility for inspections, under the* AUCEC$_{20}$ *measure, as the best possible setting for* FIXCACHE.

6. THREATS TO VALIDITY

Perry *et al.* [18] identify three forms of validity that must be addressed in research studies. We now examine threats to each form of validity in our study and the methods used to mitigate these threats where possible.

Construct validity refers to the degree to which the measurements are actually related to the concepts they are believed to represent. The main threat to construct validity come from bias in bug reporting. The bugs that are being reported might not be representative of actual bugs encountered in the system. Linking bias is certainly extant in the datasets, and can affect [5] the performance of FIXCACHE, and affect our evaluations of FIXCACHE and the merits of different update policies (RQ1-4). However, it is less likely that the result of comparing FIXCACHE and the simple standard prediction model (RQ5) is affected by bias.

Internal validity is the ability of a study to establish a causal link between independent and dependent variables regardless of what the variables are believed to represent. Our study is focused on examining a link between variables such as closed bugs per file, the FixCache prediction and the actually open bugs in a file. Threats to internal validity come from our choice of evaluation. We attempted to address this threat by using different, specifically tailored measures for different RQs: lines for RQ1, density for RQs 2a, 2b, and 3, and the very demanding AUCEC for the rest. We chose AUCEC at 20% of the lines, because it closely approximates the linecount of the files in FIXCACHE running with a cache size of 10%.

External validity refers to how these results generalize. Our study includes multiple projects, belonging to different software domains, and we find similar results among all projects studied. However, the sample size is only five projects. While this gives evidence of the ability of our results to generalize, further study on more projects will increase our confidence in these findings as answers to the research questions on a broad level. In particular we are concerned about projects that do not follow development processes similar to those of the projects that we studied.

7. RELATED WORK

Kim *et al.* took their inspiration from Hassan *et al.* who proposed the cache metaphor drawing on operating systems research [10]. BugCache principally differs from Hassan *et al.*'s "Top Ten List" in granularity: The top ten list contains modules, while BugCache contains files. BugCache performed better, even at the finer granularity. Our work mirrors this difference; we empirically evaluate the performance of FixCache, at *line granularity*, for prioritizing entities for inspection. In the course of this investigation, we compare FixCache to simple prediction models with an eye toward improving FixCache. Thus, there are two strands of work related to ours — FixCache evaluations and prediction models.

FixCache Evaluations Wikrstrand *et al.* used FixCache to dynamically select regression tests that run over modified, fault-prone (in cache) files. They found that in an embedded industrial system, the FixCache reached a weekly hit rate of 50–80% [24]. The study found that FixCache pre-population did not affect its hit rate and observed that daily updates quickly negate any pre-population effects. Engström *et al.* follow up Wikrstrand *et al.*'s and evaluate the effectiveness of Wikrstrand *et al.*'s algorithm at selecting regression tests. They found the fix-cache approach to be more efficient than its predecessor at selecting regression tests in four case studies [7]. Their work principally differs from ours in their focus on regression testing. Sadowski *et al.* investigated how FixCache's prediction performance varies over time and how much the set of buggy files changes [19]. They report that the hit rate is relatively stable and that, Apache `httpd`, the initial exception, stabilizes as the number of files approached the current project size. They find that most files that remain in the cache are correlated with a high hit rate, but that there is room for improvement. This evaluation differs from ours in the questions posed and our focus on cost-effectiveness, which is line-granular.

Prediction Models A large body of research into prediction models exits. Catal and Diri [6] have published a current survey. The Predictor Models in Software Engineering (PROMISE) series of events at ICSE are a well-known venue in this sub-discipline. The core idea is to build a statistical model, usually some type of linear, logistic, or count model, with either defect-proneness (binary response) or number of defects (count or continuous response) as the dependent variable. Predictors are measures such as size, number of authors [23], churn [17], social network measures [15], complexity [9], and a range of other measures. A full survey of this prolific sub-discipline would consume many pages; for our purposes here, it is sufficient to note that we chose a simple model as a straw-man for comparison, one that simply ordered files by number of closed defects found in that file.

8. CONCLUSION

In this paper, we evaluated the usefulness of FixCache as a tool for focusing code inspection effort. We found that FixCache tends to pull larger files into the cache; however, the bug density of files in FixCache is generally higher. We found, in addition, that of all the update policies in FixCache, temporal locality (recently closed bugs) contributed the most to increase bug density in the cache; indeed, when measured in terms of the demanding cost-effectiveness measure AUCEC_{20}, the other two policies, spatial and churn locality, did not contribute much. Furthermore, we compared three different cache replacement policies, *viz.*, based on LRU, closed bug density, and closed bugs, and found that closed bugs based replacement policy generally performs better in terms of cost-effectiveness.

Perhaps most surprisingly, we found that a very simple scheme — using the number of closed defects in a file to order the files — provides a AUCEC_{20} performance level that is in a statistical dead heat with the best performing configuration of FixCache. While *a priori* this might seem like a discouraging finding, it is in fact quite informative: this suggests that the most important aspect of FixCache, if one were to use it for inspection, is, in fact its temporal locality. Thus, the major conclusion of our paper is this:

> When used for inspection, FixCache gets most of its power by predicting that files that recently experienced a bug fix, do in fact contain additional, latent bugs.

Finally, we emphasize that our evaluation *targeted the utility of* FixCache *for inspections*. While the AUCEC_{20} measures the effectiveness of FixCache or other ordering algorithms when choosing 20% of the lines to inspect, it does not really say much about other possible uses of FixCache, for inspections, static analysis, formal verification, *etc.* We believe these are fruitful directions for further research.

References

[1] The economic impacts of inadequate infrastructure for software testing, www.nist.gov/director/planning/upload/report02-3.pdf.

[2] E. Arisholm, L. Briand, and M. Fuglerud. Data mining techniques for building fault-proneness models in telecom java software. 2007.

[3] E. Arisholm, L. C. Briand, and E. B. Johannessen. A systematic and comprehensive investigation of methods to build and evaluate fault prediction models. *Journal of Systems and Software*, 83(1):2–17, 2010.

[4] A. Bachmann and A. Bernstein. Software process data quality and characteristics: a historical view on open and closed source projects. In *IWPSE-Evol '09*, 2009.

[5] C. Bird, A. Bachmann, E. Aune, J. Duffy, A. Bernstein, V. Filkov, and P. Devanbu. Fair and balanced?: bias in bug-fix datasets. In *Proceedings of the the 7th joint meeting of the European software engineering conference and the ACM SIGSOFT symposium on The foundations of software engineering*, pages 121–130. ACM, 2009.

[6] C. Catal and B. Diri. A systematic review of software fault prediction studies. *Expert Systems with Applications*, 36(4):7346–7354, 2009.

[7] E. Engström, P. Runeson, and G. Wikstrand. An empirical evaluation of regression testing based on fix-cache recommendations. In *Software Testing, Verification and Validation (ICST), 2010 Third International Conference on*, pages 75–78. IEEE, 2010.

[8] M. Fischer, M. Pinzger, and H. Gall. Populating a release history database from version control and bug tracking systems. In *ICSM '03: Proceedings of the International Conference on Software Maintenance*, pages 23+, Washington, DC, USA, 2003. IEEE Computer Society.

[9] A. E. Hassan. Predicting faults using the complexity of code changes. In *Proceedings of the 31st International Conference on Software Engineering*, ICSE '09, pages 78–88, Washington, DC, USA, 2009. IEEE Computer Society.

[10] A. E. Hassan and R. C. Holt. The top ten list: Dynamic fault prediction. In *Proceedings of the 21st IEEE International Conference on Software Maintenance*, pages 263–272, Washington, DC, USA, 2005. IEEE Computer Society.

[11] S. Kim, T. Zimmermann, K. Pan, and J. Jr. Automatic identification of bug-introducing changes. In *ASE '06: Proceedings of the 21st IEEE/ACM International Conference on Automated Software Engineering*, pages 81–90, Washington, DC, USA, 2006. IEEE Computer Society.

[12] S. Kim, T. Zimmermann, E. Whitehead Jr, and A. Zeller. Predicting faults from cached history. In *Proceedings of the 29th international conference on Software Engineering*, pages 489–498. IEEE Computer Society, 2007.

[13] W. Kruskal and W. Wallis. Use of ranks in one-criterion variance analysis. *Journal of the American statistical Association*, 47(260):583–621, 1952.

[14] J. Lawless and J. Lawless. Statistical models and methods for lifetime data. 1982.

[15] A. Meneely and L. Williams. Secure open source collaboration: an empirical study of linus' law. In *Proceedings of the 16th ACM conference on Computer and communications security*, pages 453–462. ACM, 2009.

[16] A. Mockus and L. Votta. Identifying reasons for software changes using historic databases. In *Software Maintenance, 2000. Proceedings. International Conference on*, pages 120–130. IEEE, 2002.

[17] N. Nagappan and T. Ball. Use of relative code churn measures to predict system defect density. In *Software Engineering, 2005. ICSE 2005. Proceedings. 27th International Conference on*, pages 284–292. IEEE, 2005.

[18] D. Perry, A. Porter, and L. Votta. Empirical studies of software engineering: a roadmap. In *Proceedings of the conference on The future of Software engineering*, pages 345–355. ACM New York, NY, USA, 2000.

[19] C. Sadowski, C. Lewis, Z. Lin, Z. X., and E. J. Whitehead. An empirical analysis of the fixcache algorithm. In *Proceedings of the Eigth MSR Conference (to appear)*, 2011.

[20] J. Śliwerski, T. Zimmermann, and A. Zeller. When do changes induce fixes? In *MSR '05: Proceedings of the 2005 international workshop on Mining software repositories*, pages 1–5, New York, NY, USA, 2005. ACM.

[21] D. Čubranić and G. C. Murphy. Hipikat: recommending pertinent software development artifacts. In *ICSE '03: Proceedings of the 25th International Conference on Software Engineering*, pages 408–418, Washington, DC, USA, 2003. IEEE Computer Society.

[22] Z. Wang. Fix Cache Based Regression Test Selection. Master's thesis, Computer Science, Chalmers University of Technology, Sweden, 2010.

[23] E. Weyuker, T. Ostrand, and R. Bell. Do too many cooks spoil the broth? Using the number of developers to enhance defect prediction models. *Empirical Software Engineering*, 13(5):539–559, 2008.

[24] G. Wikstrand, R. Feldt, J. Gorantla, W. Zhe, and C. White. Dynamic regression test selection based on a file cache an industrial evaluation. In *Software Testing Verification and Validation, 2009. ICST'09. International Conference on*, pages 299–302. IEEE, 2009.

Inferring Data Polymorphism in Systems Code*

Brian Hackett
Stanford University
bhackett@cs.stanford.edu

Alex Aiken
Stanford University
aiken@cs.stanford.edu

ABSTRACT

We describe techniques for analyzing *data polymorphism* in C, and show that understanding data polymorphism is important for statically verifying type casts in the Linux kernel, where our techniques prove the safety of 75% of downcasts to structure types, out of a population of 28767. We also discuss prevalent patterns of data polymorphism in Linux, including code patterns we can handle and those we cannot.

Categories and Subject Descriptors

D.2.4 [**Software Engineering**]: Software/Program Verfication—*Assertion checkers*

General Terms

Verification, Experimentation

Keywords

type checking, type casting, static analysis

1. INTRODUCTION

Consider a typical Linux function, `saa7146_buffer_timeout`, which is part of the device driver for the saa7146 chipset:

```
// drivers/media/common/saa7146_fops.c
void saa7146_buffer_timeout(unsigned long data)
{
   struct saa7146_dmaqueue *q = (struct saa7146_dmaqueue*)data;
   struct saa7146_dev *dev = q->dev;
   unsigned long flags;
   ...
}
```

This function casts its integer parameter `data` to a pointer to type `saa7146_dmaqueue` and then accesses the contents of that structure. If `data` really is an integer, or if `data` is a pointer to an object that is not of type `saa7146_dmaqueue`, then these accesses will corrupt or crash the system. Type casts like this one are ubiquitous in Linux and other large C codebases. Analyzing these casts to determine their correctness requires deep reasoning about the heap, control flow and data flow of the system. In addition, many of these casts are used to implement polymorphism (including the above cast), and thus any successful analysis needs to model common patterns of polymorphism.

We have developed a static analysis that, augmented with 177 programmer annotations, proves the safety of 75% of the downcasts to structure types in Linux 2.6.17.1. The complete analysis consists of many components [11]; in this paper we focus on what we consider the most novel and difficult issue, the problem of analyzing *data polymorphism*, which is needed for 40% of the casts we are able to verify as well as most of the casts we are not able to verify. In Section 2 we expand the example, show why the cast is correct and motivate the problem of understanding data polymorphism. In Sections 3, 4 and 5 we reduce the problem of analyzing data polymorphism to discovering *structural relationships* and *structural correlations* and describe our algorithm. Section 6 presents experimental results, including examples that are beyond the reach of our fully automatic analysis, which we handle using programmer annotations. We postpone a discussion of our contributions until Section 3, after we have presented the extended example and the definition of structural relationships and structural correlations, the key ideas underlying our approach.

2. EXAMPLE

To verify the cast in `saa7146_buffer_timeout`, we must show the function's callers always pass a pointer to a value of type `saa7146_dmaqueue`. Now, `saa7146_buffer_timeout` is never called directly. In fact, it is mentioned in only two functions. The two cases are similar; one is shown below:

```
// drivers/media/common/saa7146_vbi.c
static void vbi_init(struct saa7146_dev *dev,
                     struct saa7146_vv *vv)
{
   INIT_LIST_HEAD(&vv->vbi_q.queue);
   init_timer(&vv->vbi_q.timeout);
   vv->vbi_q.timeout.function = saa7146_buffer_timeout;       (*)
   vv->vbi_q.timeout.data     = (unsigned long)(&vv->vbi_q);
   vv->vbi_q.dev              = dev;
   ...
}
```

The `timeout` field has type `timer_list`, a core kernel structure with a function pointer field `function` and an integer field `data`, among others. After the `function` field of the

*This work was supported in part by NSF grants CNS-050955 and CCF-0430378 with additional support from DARPA and gifts from Intel and IBM.

Permission to make digital or hard copies of all or part of this work for personal or classroom use is granted without fee provided that copies are not made or distributed for profit or commercial advantage and that copies bear this notice and the full citation on the first page. To copy otherwise, to republish, to post on servers or to redistribute to lists, requires prior specific permission and/or a fee.
ESEC/FSE'11, September 5–9, 2011, Szeged, Hungary.
Copyright 2011 ACM 978-1-4503-0443-6/11/09 ...$10.00.

timer_list is assigned saa7146_buffer_timeout, where can the function eventually be called? The function field never has its address taken and is only assigned to a local variable fn in the core kernel function __run_timers:

```
// kernel/timer.c
static inline void __run_timers(tvec_base_t *base)
{
   struct timer_list *timer;
   ...
   while (...) {
      ...
      void (*fn)(unsigned long);
      unsigned long data;
      timer = list_entry(head->next,struct timer_list,entry);
      fn = timer->function;
      data = timer->data;
      ...
      fn(data);
      ...
   }
}
```

Function __run_timers repeatedly pulls timer_lists off of lists and calls timer->function with timer->data. This exposes the design intent of the timer_list structure: whatever is stored in the function field of a timer_list is called with the data field of that same timer_list. The function field points to saa7146_buffer_timeout for timers whose data field was written by vbi_init. After such writes, the data field points to the vbi_q field of a saa7146_vv structure, which has type saa7146_dmaqueue, which is just what saa7146_buffer_timeout expects. Thus, we know that if the function saa7146_buffer_timeout is only called with vbi_q for its data parameter, then the cast it performs is safe.

So, might saa7146_buffer_timeout be called with a parameter other than vbi_q? Two possibilities must be considered. First, the data field could be assigned another value (of a possibly different type) between the calls to vbi_init and __run_timers. Second, the function field could be called somewhere outside __run_timers with a parameter other than the data field of the timer_list. It turns out *both* possibilities actually occur (see below), but neither affects any timer_list containing saa7146_buffer_timeout in the function field.

Normally the function and data fields of a timer_list are written at the same time, shortly after the timer_list is created—after all, __run_timers requires both fields to be set. However, in a few places the data field is written without any corresponding write to the function field, such as in tlclk_interrupt:

```
// drivers/char/tlclk.c
static irqreturn_t tlclk_interrupt(...)
{
   ...
   if (int_events & HOLDOVER_01_MASK) {
      alarm_events->pll_holdover++;
      switchover_timer.expires = jiffies + msecs_to_jiffies(10);
      switchover_timer.data = inb(TLCLK_REG1);
      add_timer(&switchover_timer);
   }
   ...
}
```

Under certain circumstances tlclk_interrupt changes the data field of the global switchover_timer variable to a non-pointer integer value. But switchover_timer cannot alias a timer_list containing saa7146_buffer_timeout — switchover_timer is a statically allocated timer_list, while the timer manipulated by vbi_init is embedded in another structure.

The other way saa7146_buffer_timeout might receive a value other than vbi_q is if the function field is invoked with an argument other than the data field. There are five places in the kernel where the function field is invoked, and __run_timers is the only one where the data field is passed. The function ctnetlink_del_conntrack is representative of the other four:

```
// net/ipv4/netfilter/ip_conntrack_netlink.c
static int ctnetlink_del_conntrack(...)
{
   struct ip_conntrack *ct;
   ...
   ct = tuplehash_to_ctrack(h);
   ...
   if (del_timer(&ct->timeout))
      ct->timeout.function((unsigned long)ct);
   ip_conntrack_put(ct);
   return 0;
}
```

Instead of passing ct->timeout.data to ct->timeout.function, ct itself is passed, exploiting knowledge that ct->timeout.data == ct in this context. We know ct->timeout cannot alias the timer from vbi_init: the two timers are embedded in different types of structures. Thus, ct->timeout.function cannot invoke saa7146_buffer_timeout.

3. ANALYZING POLYMORPHISM

When saa7146_buffer_timeout is called by __run_timers, the data passed is provably generated by a previous call to vbi_init, not any of the hundreds of other assignments to the data field of a timer_list in the Linux kernel. The proof relies on two facts. First, the indirect call in __run_timers exploits a *structural relationship* between the function pointer target and function argument: these are fields of the same timer_list structure. In general, a structural relationship is a pair of locations reachable (via zero or more field accesses and dereferences) from a common base structure, or two locations reachable from the arguments to a common function. Second, the possible values of the locations in a structural relationship have *structural correlations* with one another: the function field of a timer_list is saa7146_buffer_timeout if and only if the data field was set by vbi_init, and similarly for the hundreds of other functions that may be used in a timer_list.

Structural relationships are related to the standard notion of type polymorphism in languages with more advanced type systems than C; commonly (but not exclusively) fields in a structural relationship would have related polymorphic types in statically typed functional or object-oriented languages. However, solving our problem requires more than identifying polymorphic fields, as we must also understand the actual contents of those fields, which means finding and correlating the field assignments. In the example the correlation is easily identified, as the structural correlation involves only two fields of a single structure and both fields are assigned in vbi_init. In more complex scenarios the structural relationship may span chains of dereferences across several structures, and the correlated assignments to the fields of the structural relationship may also be spread across multiple functions. It is the combination of identifying polymorphic data structures and the correlated side-effects to different parts of these structures in the heap that makes understanding data polymorphism a challenging problem.

Structural correlations are also related to standard notions in points-to analysis. Consider a field `a` that can take on values in set A and field `b` that can take on values in set B. Context-insensitive points-to analyses are often too inaccurate in the sense that the cross-product $A \times B$ contains too many possibilities to be useful. By adding some form of context we split the fields `a` and `b` into multiple abstract locations `a1`, `a2`, ..., `b1`, `b2` ... representing smaller sets of runtime values, which will have analysis sets $A_1, A_2, \ldots, B_1, B_2, \ldots$ associated with them. The client of the points-to analysis must still consider the cross-products of values in these sets, but by adding context we hope that the set of pairs $\bigcup_{i,j} A_i \times B_j$ will be much smaller than the original cross product $A \times B$. The major difference with our approach is that structural correlation defines the desired output directly, without committing to a particular implementation strategy. Points-to analysis, in contrast, defines a particular framework in which the approach to improving precision is to refine (increase) the set of abstract locations.

No context-sensitive points-to methods have been shown to scale to programs the size of the Linux kernel, and based on the efforts that have tried [4], we believe it is necessary to take a different approach. The space consumption of a global points-to graph, particularly a context sensitive one, is difficult to control. Thus, our method does not build a global points-to graph. Instead, we first perform only local analysis of each function (which is in fact much more detailed than a points-to computation). At the interprocedural level we trade time for space, using an escape analysis to follow values through the program. This analysis queries the local analysis information, but does not build a global points-to graph, construct explicit contexts, or refine abstract locations. Because we do not build a global points-to graph or any global structures except for the structural correlations that are the output of the data polymorphism analysis, we do not encounter the memory consumption problems that appear to limit the scalability of context-sensitive points-to analyses.

Structural relationships and correlations are sufficiently general to tackle our polymorphism problem, the algorithm for which we break into two phases. First, we scan all indirect call sites to identify the important structural relationships holding between the function pointer used to invoke the call and the data (or other function pointers) reachable from the arguments to the call (Section 4). Second, we take in turn all the structural relationships identified for some indirect call site by the first phase, and for each of these identify all the possible structural correlations between particular functions and values which could exist for that relationship (Section 5).

Our algorithm is sound in the sense that if it identifies a structural relationship and associated structural correlations, it is guaranteed that *all* of the possible structural correlations for that structural relationship have been discovered; the algorithm has a complete view of the possible combinations of values that can be assigned to the fields involved in the structural relationship. Our algorithm is conservative in that it is not guaranteed to discover every structural relationship with non-trivial correlations, and even for the structural relationships it identifies as important it may fail to compute a set of structural correlations. Any field not in a structural relationship, or in a structural relationship that could not be successfully analyzed, is conservatively assumed to be able to take on any possible value for the field, independent of the values of other fields.

In summary, our main contributions are:

- We introduce structural relationships and structural correlations, which characterize the desired output of any analysis of data polymorphism without implying a particular implementation technique.
- We present an algorithm for computing structural correlations that is substantially different from conventional points-to analyses and has advantages for analyzing very large systems. In particular, we combine very precise but separate local analysis of individual functions with demand-driven and space-efficient interprocedural search algorithms.
- The core component of our search algorithm is an interprocedural escape analysis that may be of independent interest. The novel aspect is tunable precision, allowing us to conduct escape analysis at different granularities and use the most precise analysis which terminates with acceptable cost. Because both the cost and precision of an escape analysis query is unpredictable, the ability to try different strategies is very important.
- We give numerous examples of data polymorphism from the very simple to the very involved, including examples that our system cannot handle fully automatically. While the simple examples can be expressed in modern languages using parametric polymorphism, the most involved examples are not readily expressible in any static type system known to us, and furthermore, we are unaware of any previous literature where such coding patterns are described. These examples point out future challenges for both static analysis and static type systems in obtaining more expressive and automated systems for checking properties of large systems.
- We give the results of a large experiment in which we are able to statically verify 75% of downcasts to structure types in a version of the Linux kernel, out of a population of 28767.

Most of the components of our system have been described previously. It is the system architecture, the way the components are assembled, that is new. Thus, with a few exceptions for key aspects of our approach (structural relationships, correlations, and some aspects of the interprocedural escape analysis), we describe our approach at a relatively high level; details may be found in [11].

4. STRUCTURAL RELATIONSHIPS

A *trace* is an access path: a series of field accesses and pointer dereferences beginning with a global variable, local variable, function parameter, or allocation site. For example, `x->f.g->h` is a trace starting from variable `x`. A *relative trace* (or *rtrace*) drops the starting variable or allocation site: it is a pure sequence of field accesses and dereferences.

Structural relationships are recorded in two maps, one for structural relationships on types and one for functions:

$$\begin{aligned} \text{SR\_Type} &: (\mathit{callsite} \times \mathit{trace}) \Rightarrow 2^{(\mathit{type} \times \mathit{rtrace} \times \mathit{rtrace})} \\ \text{SR\_Func} &: (\mathit{callsite} \times \mathit{trace}) \Rightarrow 2^{(\mathit{trace} \times \mathit{trace})} \end{aligned}$$

Consider a function g with an indirect call f(x) at call site I. Let AT be the trace which the call uses to access x (in this case a function argument, and more generally a sequence of field selections/dereferences from an argument). Now (C, RFT, RT) $\in$ SR_Type(I, AT) if there is a structure of type C such that the function pointer f is at relative trace RFT from C and x is at relative trace RT from C. Also, (FT, T) $\in$ SR_Func(I, AT) if the function pointer f is reachable from an argument to g with trace FT and x is also reachable from one of g's arguments with trace T. For the indirect call in __run_timers and the call's first argument, a single structural relationship is found for SR_Type:

(timer_list, .function, .data)

Computing structural relations is a straightforward intraprocedural analysis. Taking a tuple (I,AT) as input, we determine the trace FT through which the indirect call is invoked, and the trace T passed as argument AT to the indirect call (the memory model accounts for all prior assignments and control flow in the function invoking I [19, 12]). Occasionally there may be multiple different values for FT or T, depending on the path taken to reach I (an example of this, __dentry_open, is shown in Section 5.3). In such cases we compute the relationships separately for each possible FT/T.

There is a problem, however. While using the plain arguments is sufficient for __run_timers, some calls are concerned not with an argument, but a field or transitive field of an argument (again, see Section 5.3). In general the amount of data reachable from each argument, and thus the number of possible structural relationships, is unbounded. To bound the number of structural relationships, we focus on relationships between function pointers and untyped data—void* pointers and integers which could be pointers in disguise (such as the argument to saa7146_buffer_timeout). These relationships are the most likely to have meaningful structural correlations, as well as being the most useful to the casting analysis. The argument traces AT we consider are:

- void* call arguments,
- void* fields of call arguments (or fields of fields, transitively, without following dereferences),
- any trace that might be cast by a target of the indirect call, as determined by a separate interprocedural analysis to determine possible function pointer targets and a prepass to look for casts in each function.

5. STRUCTURAL CORRELATIONS

For each structural relationship for some function call we represent the correlations that may hold:

$$\text{SC\_Type} \;:\; (name \times rtrace \times rtrace) \Rightarrow 2^{(name \times name \times trace)} + \top$$

$$\text{SC\_Func} \;:\; (name \times trace \times trace) \Rightarrow 2^{(name \times name \times trace)} + \top$$

Each (FNPTR, FN, DT) $\in$ SC_Type(C, FT, T) is a possible correlation for the (C,FT,T) structural relationship. For a value of type C, the value assigned to trace FT may be the function FNPTR, and the value assigned to trace T may be the value of DT when accessed from some call to FN; the function name FN is needed to give the context in which trace DT is interpreted.

The relation SC_Func is similar. For the timer_list relationship (timer_list,.function,.data), there is a single correlation introduced by vbi_init:

(saa7146_buffer_timeout, vbi_init, &vv->vbi_q)

There are hundreds of correlations for this relationship, but no other uses saa7146_buffer_timeout for the function pointer.

To compute correlations for a structural relationship R, we first compute tuples (WFN,WFT,WT), where function trace WFT and trace WT may be set for R within function WFN. For SC_Type, WFN includes functions that write the fields of the relationship, and WFT and WT are the possible pairs of values written to those fields. If only one field is written, the other reflects the field's initial value. For SC_Func, WFN includes functions calling the function containing the indirect call I, and WFT and WT are the corresponding values passed at that call site in WFN.

The actual correlations (FNPTR,FN,DT) are computed from the triples (WFN,WFT,WT) by converting the trace WFT to one or more concrete function names FNPTR via any of the following methods:

- Use an escape analysis to determine where WFT came from and which functions it could refer to (Section 5.1).
- Follow transitive structural relationships between WFT and WT (Section 5.2). If WFT and WT are derived from the same structure, or both passed into the current function, they share a relationship whose correlations are a superset of the possible values for WFT and WT.
- If WFN is always invoked through an indirect call, look for structural relationships between WFT and the function pointer used to invoke WFN (Section 5.3).

Each of these approaches either fails or generates an overapproximation of the values of WFT and WT. If all approaches fail, we set SC_Type or SC_Func to $\top$; we could not capture the effect of all writes affecting the relationship. Otherwise, we take the intersection of all the result sets to get the tightest overapproximation we can for the correlations on (WFN,WFT,WT).

5.1 Escaped Correlations

We have developed an escape analysis determining where a value escaped from or where it may escape to. As mentioned in Section 3, we use escape analysis to avoid the unpredictable space consumption of a global points-to graph. The escape analysis' most novel aspect is tunable precision, which we discuss further below.

Our escape analysis is built upon a path-sensitive, intraprocedural memory and alias analysis that computes all aliases for each memory location accessed within a function body or loop in the manner of [19, 12]. Given a pair of traces, this per-function analysis returns the path-sensitive condition within that function under which the two traces alias. Note that if the condition is *false*, the traces cannot alias.

The escape analysis is demand driven, flow insensitive and has limited context sensitivity, but suffices for determining the functions referred to by many values of WFT. Consider a function trace WFN in function f. Escape_Backward(f,WFN), the set of functions that could flow to WFN, is calculated as follows (we do not describe Escape_Forward(,) which is symmetric). First, f's local information is queried to determine traces WFN is equivalent to, and in particular whether

WFN is derived from a global or local variable, an argument of f, a field of a heap-allocated data structure, or a constant (a concrete function name). The most interesting cases are handled as follows:

- If WFN aliases a function name, we return a singleton set containing that function.
- If WFN aliases an argument x of f, we return the union over all the following sets. Without loss of generality, assume x is the only argument of f.
  - For any direct call f(e) occurring in a function g, we compute Escape_Backward(g,ET), where ET is the trace for e.
  - If the address of f is taken in function h, we also compute the set of indirect call sites of f via Escape_Forward(h,FFN), where FFN is the trace of the location to which f is assigned. We add to the output Escape_Backward(k,AT) for each such indirect call in a function k with argument trace AT.
- If WFN aliases a structure field, then we must compute both forwards and backwards escape information for that field to see what assignments to the field may flow to WFN.

The output of the escape analysis is the set of concrete function names that can flow to WFN. In the simplest cases, such as in vbi_init, WFT is already a named function and the escape analysis gives us an exact singleton set. Now consider the function vbi_init without the write to vv->vbi_q.timeout.function (i.e., the line marked (*) is removed). In this case, the value of WFT is the value of the function pointer on entry to vbi_init, which is simply *(vv->vbi_q.timeout.function). To compute the correlations, we need to know what values this function pointer can have. There are several ways to determine which concrete functions escape to this value: we can examine values assigned to the .function field of a timer_list anywhere in the program, values assigned to the field .timeout.function of a saa7146_dmaqueue, or to .vbi_q.timeout.function of a saa7146_vv, or values passed to vbi_init through the function argument vv->vbi_q.timeout.function. These are ordered by increasing precision: any value assigned to the .timeout.function field of a saa7146_dmaqueue is also assigned to the .timeout field of a timer_list, but not vice versa. A low level of precision may be too imprecise. However, the escape analysis cannot always determine the set of concrete functions for a value at a higher level of precision, because it may be too expensive to explore all the possibilities at a very fine level of granularity. In practice the best level of precision varies widely; we try several and use the most precise result that succeeds.

In this example, escape analysis using .function finds every function that could be assigned to *any* timer_list, a uselessly imprecise overapproximation. On the other hand, using vv->vbi_q.timeout.function follows vv everywhere it is passed in the code, and the escape analysis fails after exceeding a resource threshold. Escaping using .timeout.function or .vbi_q.timeout.function yields the correct result, finding the only value that is assigned directly to this field chain is saa7146_buffer_timeout and that the address of .timeout is not passed anywhere which will lead to the function field being written.

5.2 Transitive Correlations

Sometimes structural relationships are dependent on one another. Consider this code from the Linux IRQ subsystem:

```
// kernel/irq/manage.c
int request_irq(unsigned int irq,
      irqreturn_t (*handler)(int, void *, struct pt_regs *),
      unsigned long irqflags, const char * devname, void *dev_id)
{
   struct irqaction * action;
   ...
   action = kmalloc(sizeof(struct irqaction), GFP_ATOMIC);
   if (!action) return -ENOMEM;
   action->handler = handler;   (*)
   action->flags = irqflags;
   cpus_clear(action->mask);
   action->name = devname;
   action->next = NULL;
   action->dev_id = dev_id;     (*)
   ...
}
```

Type irqaction has a function pointer handler called when a specific interrupt is received. The handler field is passed, among other things, the void* field dev_id, so .handler and .dev_id have a structural relationship R. Each irqaction is created within request_irq; note the function arguments handler and dev_id. There is thus another structural relationship R' between variables handler and dev_id, and because of the assignments marked (*) any correlations in R' are also correlations of R. We detect such dependencies between structural relationships in a manner similar to the handling of indirect call sites (Section 4). When computing structural correlations for the handler and dev_id fields of irqaction, we notice the assignments to those fields in request_irq participate in R' and add all correlations for R' to R. Because there may be cycles in the graph of dependencies between structural relationships, this process is iterated to a fixed point (i.e., until no new transitive correlations are discovered).

5.3 Dominating Indirect Calls

More complicated types of data polymorphism correlate data with multiple function pointers. These function pointers often manage the data's contents, and we can recover correlations from calls to these functions. Consider this function in the saa7146 driver:

```
// drivers/media/common/saa7146_fops.c
static ssize_t fops_read(struct file *file,
            char __user *data, size_t count, loff_t *ppos)
{
   struct saa7146_fh *fh = file->private_data;
   switch (fh->type) {
      ...
   }
}
```

The file->private_data pointer has type void*, and thus fops_read performs a cast we are interested in checking for type safety. What's going on with this function?

In keeping with Unix practice, user applications in Linux interact with many devices as if they were regular files. Linux has a common interface for defining new files: the file_operations structure, a table of 27 function pointers (though not all are used by each driver or filesystem).

```
// include/linux/fs.h
struct file_operations {
   struct module *owner;
   loff_t (*llseek) (struct file*, loff_t, int);
```

```
    ssize_t (*read) (struct file*, char __user*, size_t, loff_t*);
    ssize_t (*aio_read) (...);
    ssize_t (*write) (...);
    ssize_t (*aio_write) (...);
    ...
    int (*open) (struct inode *, struct file *);
    int (*flush) (struct file *);
    int (*release) (struct inode *, struct file *);
    ...
};
```

Interaction with a `file` is primarily through the function pointers in the `f_op` field pointing to the file's `file_operations`. For example, `vfs_read` reads out of a file:

```
// include/linux/fs.h
struct file {
    ...
    struct dentry                *f_dentry;
    struct vfsmount              *f_vfsmnt;
    const struct file_operations *f_op;
    ...
    void              *private_data;
    ...
};

// fs/read_write.c
ssize_t vfs_read(struct file *file,
                 char __user *buf, size_t count, loff_t *pos)
{
    ...
    ret = security_file_permission (file, MAY_READ);
    if (!ret) {
        if (file->f_op->read)
            ret = file->f_op->read(file, buf, count, pos);
        ...
    }
    return ret;
}
```

The system call `sys_read` invokes `vfs_read` directly. To allow `vfs_read` and other top-level file operations to interact with `saa7146` devices, the `saa7146` driver creates a `file_operations` structure whose `read` field is set to `fops_read`. Note `vfs_read` will indirectly call `fops_read`.

```
// drivers/media/common/saa7146_fops.c
static struct file_operations video_fops =
{
    .owner      = THIS_MODULE,
    .open       = fops_open,
    .release    = fops_release,
    .read       = fops_read,
    .write      = fops_write,
    ...
};
```

Now that `fops_read` can be invoked, why is the cast it performs correct? Interestingly, `video_fops` is never directly assigned to any `file->f_op`, and writes to the `f_op` field are never directly correlated with writes to the `private_data` field. A more elaborate mechanism is in use. Function `__dentry_open`, which opens a file, sets the `f_op` field and calls its `open` method.

```
// fs/open.c
static struct file *
__dentry_open(struct dentry *dentry, struct vfsmount *mnt,
              int flags, struct file *f,
              int (*open)(struct inode *, struct file *))
{
    ...
    f->f_dentry = dentry;
    f->f_vfsmnt = mnt;
    f->f_op = fops_get(inode->i_fop);
    ...
    if (!open && f->f_op)
        open = f->f_op->open;
    if (open) {
        error = open(inode, f);
        if (error)
            goto cleanup_all;
    }
    ...
}
```

Returning to the `video_fops` used to store `fops_read`, we see the corresponding open function is `fops_open`, which sets the `private_data` field of the file to the value expected by `fops_read`.

```
// drivers/media/common/saa7146_fops.c
static int fops_open(struct inode *inode, struct file *file)
{
    struct saa7146_fh *fh = NULL;
    ...
    fh = kzalloc(sizeof(*fh),GFP_KERNEL);
    if (NULL == fh) {
        ...
        goto out;
    }
    file->private_data = fh;
    fh->dev = dev;
    fh->type = type;
    ...
}
```

For the polymorphic data analysis we need to correlate the `f_op->read` field of a `file` with the `private_data`. We cannot do this by looking for matched writes of `f_op` and `private_data`, but instead by matching up the `f_op->open` function and the writes it performs with the `f_op->read` function.

The write we are most concerned with is in `fops_open` to `file->private_data`. We are interested in the possible values for `file->f_op->read` here, and while that value is not written in `fops_open` we can get information about it from the call stack. Now, `fops_open` is only called indirectly through `__dentry_open` and a few similar functions. In each such function we can prove `fops_open` is only called through `file->f_op->open`: the code is some variant of `file->f_op->open(inode, file)`. We thus know in `fops_open`, `file->f_op->open == fops_open`. When this equality holds, what are the possible values for `file->f_op->read`? If we track the structural relationship for type `file_operations` between its `open` and `read` fields, we can answer this question with the resulting correlations.

Finding the correlations for this `file_operations` relationship is straightforward, as the `open` and `read` fields are always written in synchronization with each other, almost always in a global initializer. With `fops_open` in the `open` field, the only value for the `read` field is `fops_read`, which is thus correlated with the value written to `private_data` in `fops_open`.

This dominating-caller technique is geared towards relationships involving function pointer tables with an `open`-type method that fills in private data for other methods in the table to access. The technique in whole is:

1. For a function FN, find a function pointer trace XFT such that FN is called only when XFT is a particular function XFNPTR. This dominance relation holds for FN if either:

    - FN is only called indirectly and XFT is the invoked function pointer at each parent call site. In this case XFNPTR = FN.

- Each PFN that can invoke FN is itself dominated by calls where XFNPTR = YFT for some YFT in PFN.

   Searching for dominators is k-limited to avoid unbounded call graph exploration; using $k = 5$ has been sufficient.

2. Look for a structural relationship on a `struct` type between XFT and WFT. Normally the type is a function pointer table like `file_operations`.

3. If there is such a relationship, then for each correlation between XFNPTR and some ZFT, the possible values for WFT are the union over the the ZFT. Normally each ZFT is a particular function; if not, resolve with the escape analysis as in Section 5.1.

6. RESULTS

The version of Linux we analyzed, 2.6.17.1, contains about 4.4 million lines of code and 11976 indirect call sites. Of these call sites, 7850 (66%) involve structural relationships—a parameter to the call was either a `void*` pointer or was a structure containing a `void*` field. From these call sites, 8830 structural relationships were identified, and an additional 5939 relationships were added by transitive correlations (see Section 5.2), for a total of 14769 structural relationships. Of these, 9601 were between structure fields, and 5168 between the arguments to a function.

We successfully found the correlations for 10416 (71%) relationships, including 5750 (60%) structure field relationships and 4666 (90%) function argument relationships (the remainder were marked as failed). Of the 7850 call sites with relationships, correlations were found for at least one relationship at 6883 (88%) sites.

Our parallel implementation of the analysis took 3 hours and 42 minutes to run on a 50 core cluster, using 130 hours of CPU time (the analysis was written using a logic programming language [11], which in our experience is much easier to develop analyses in than C, but incurs a 20x to 40x slowdown over C). Analysis timed out on 522 functions, or .5% of all functions analyzed; these timeouts can cause us to unsoundly underapproximate the correlations. We examined many of these timeouts, which were generally caused by functions where the analysis would have ultimately failed anyway and thus did not affect the generated correlations.

The results of this analysis are crucial for our broader analysis for proving the safety of type casts [11]. Out of a population of 28767 downcasts, we prove the safety of 21637, 75.2% of the total. Of the proved casts, 8754 or 40% require the polymorphic relationships identified here.

A small group of structures with polymorphic relationships are responsible for most proved casts: 173 different structures have some associated relationship used to prove at least one cast. Of the 8754 casts proved using polymorphism, 7521 (86%) use relationships from a set of 26 structures used to prove 50 or more casts each, and 6000 (69%) use relationships from a set of 10 structures used to prove 200 or more casts each. This latter set includes both the `file` structure (used to prove 736 casts) and `timer_list` structure (used to prove 408 casts).

Analyzing polymorphic relationships with sufficient precision for the casting analysis required 177 annotations (for several million lines of code). These annotations are trusted: they are assumed by the analysis and must be checked manually. Annotations are needed for three broad reasons:

- General analysis imprecision leading to results too imprecise for the casting analysis. This imprecision accounts for about 75% of the annotations we needed.

- The initialization of a structure may not fit the inference techniques our analysis uses to find correlations. The fit is often close, and we can use annotations to adjust the inference to match the initialization.

- The structure's polymorphism might not fit the model of structural relationships our analysis uses. We can sometimes fit these cases so that we can capture the needed correlations, even if our analysis of the structure's internals is largely incomplete.

The following subsections give examples of each category.

6.1 Analysis Overapproximation

When initialization of multiple fields of a data structure is split across many functions, we need precise knowledge of which fields are uninitialized, NULL, or non-NULL at various control points to generate precise correlations. Consider again the `__dentry_open` function from Section 5.3. In this example, we are interested in structural relationships between the `private_data` field of a `file` and the `read` and other fields of that file's `f_op` table. The `f_op` is written in `__dentry_open`, and `private_data` is written in the indirect call to `open`.

Our analysis sees the `f_op` write in `__dentry_open` and no `private_data` write, and so correlates all possible values of `f_op->read` (all file `read` functions in existence) with the input value `f->private_data`. Simply inlining the possible targets of `open` cannot help; some `open` methods do not set `private_data`, as those filesystems never use that field. Now, `__dentry_open` is only called during initialization of `f`, and the only possible value for `f->private_data` at entry to `__dentry_open` is `NULL`. Unfortunately, our system misses that `f->private_data` is `NULL` due to tricky initialization code. Usually `__dentry_open` is called through `dentry_open`, which directly allocates a `file` with `NULL` contents through `get_empty_filp`; this case is easy to analyze.

```
// fs/open.c
struct file *dentry_open(struct dentry *dentry,
                         struct vfsmount *mnt, int flags)
{
   struct file *f;
   ...
   f = get_empty_filp();
   if (f == NULL) {  ...  }
   return __dentry_open(dentry, mnt, flags, f, NULL);
}
```

The difficult case is `lookup_instantiate_filp`, another caller of `__dentry_open`, which passes in as the file argument `nd->intent.open.file`, a pointer to data allocated by its own callers.

```
// fs/open.c
struct file *lookup_instantiate_filp(struct nameidata *nd,
                struct dentry *dentry,
                int (*open)(struct inode *, struct file *))
{
 ...
 nd->intent.open.file = __dentry_open(dget(dentry), mntget(nd->mnt),
        nd->intent.open.flags - 1, nd->intent.open.file, open);
 ...
}
```

While the nd->intent.open.file pointer is always either NULL or points to an empty file in this function, it is allocated several levels up the call chain and across potentially multiple indirect calls. We use one annotation to disable correlations between fields of the file structure within __dentry_open.

In general, the annotations we used to fix imprecision either disable a portion of the analysis for some function (where doing so will not cause the correlations to be under-approximated) or correct some intermediate analysis information to increase the precision of the correlations.

6.2 Unhandled Initialization

Some data structures have important structural relationships but the initialization is a poor fit for our inference algorithm. For example, in some sound PCM layer structures snd_pcm_ops is a function pointer table used by snd_pcm and its children:

```
// include/sound/pcm.h

struct snd_pcm {
   struct snd_card *card;
   ...
   struct snd_pcm_str streams[2];
   ...
   void *private_data;
   void (*private_free) (struct snd_pcm *pcm);
   ...
};

struct snd_pcm_str {
   int stream;
   struct snd_pcm *pcm;
   unsigned int substream_count;
   unsigned int substream_opened;
   struct snd_pcm_substream *substream;
   ...
};

struct snd_pcm_substream {
   struct snd_pcm *pcm;
   struct snd_pcm_str *pstr;
   void *private_data;
   ...
   struct snd_pcm_ops *ops;
   ...
   struct snd_pcm_substream *next;
   ...
};
```

Each snd_pcm has two child snd_pcm_str structures in its streams field; each snd_pcm_str has a list substream of snd_pcm_substream structures that are linked through the next field. Each object has pointers back to its parents.

There are important structural relationships between the function pointers in the ops field of a snd_pcm_substream and its private_data field. Writes to the ops and private_data fields of snd_pcm_substream are not correlated in the usual way. Instead of writing both fields together, functions initializing the parent snd_pcm write to the ops field of *all* the associated substreams with the snd_pcm_set_ops helper function, but only write to the private_data of the parent snd_pcm. An example is in snd_atiixp_pcm_new, which is called during device probe and allocates and initializes a new snd_pcm.

```
// sound/core/pcm_lib.c
void snd_pcm_set_ops(struct snd_pcm *pcm, int direction,
                     struct snd_pcm_ops *ops)
{
   struct snd_pcm_str *stream = &pcm->streams[direction];
   struct snd_pcm_substream *substream;
   for (substream = stream->substream; substream != NULL;
        substream = substream->next)
      substream->ops = ops;
}

// sound/pci/atiixp_modem.c
static int __devinit snd_atiixp_pcm_new(struct atiixp_modem *chip)
{
   struct snd_pcm *pcm;
   int err;
   ...
   err = snd_pcm_new(chip->card, ..., &pcm);
   if (err < 0) return err;
   snd_pcm_set_ops(pcm, SNDRV_PCM_STREAM_PLAYBACK,
                   &snd_atiixp_playback_ops);
   snd_pcm_set_ops(pcm, SNDRV_PCM_STREAM_CAPTURE,
                   &snd_atiixp_capture_ops);
   pcm->dev_class = SNDRV_PCM_CLASS_MODEM;
   pcm->private_data = chip;
   ...
}
```

After initialization, the substream's ops is set but not its private_data. This state persists until the substream is opened in snd_pcm_open_substream, which looks up the substream via snd_pcm_attach_substream, which scans the substreams in the snd_pcm, finds one that is not in use, and sets its private_data to the private_data of the parent snd_pcm.

```
// sound/core/pcm_native.c
int snd_pcm_open_substream(struct snd_pcm *pcm, int stream,
                           struct file *file,
                           struct snd_pcm_substream **rsubstream)
{
   struct snd_pcm_substream *substream;
   int err;
   err = snd_pcm_attach_substream(pcm, stream, file, &substream);
   if (err < 0) return err;
   ...
   if ((err = substream->ops->open(substream)) < 0) goto error;
   ...
}

// sound/core/pcm.c
int snd_pcm_attach_substream(struct snd_pcm *pcm, int stream,
                             struct file *file,
                             struct snd_pcm_substream **rsubstream)
{
   struct snd_pcm_str * pstr;
   struct snd_pcm_substream *substream;
   ...
   pstr = &pcm->streams[stream];
   if (pstr->substream == NULL || pstr->substream_count == 0)
      return -ENODEV;
   ...
   for (substream = pstr->substream; substream;
        substream = substream->next)
      if (!SUBSTREAM_BUSY(substream)) break;
   if (substream == NULL) return -EAGAIN;
   ...
   substream->private_data = pcm->private_data;
   substream->ffile = file;
   pstr->substream_opened++;
   *rsubstream = substream;
   return 0;
}
```

By correlating a write to snd_pcm->private_data with calls to snd_pcm_set_ops, a PCM driver ensures when the substream is opened the correlation between private_data and the ops used in snd_pcm_set_ops is introduced as a correlation in the snd_pcm_substream structural relationship. Our annotations add correlations for snd_pcm_substream when snd_pcm->private_data is written or snd_pcm_set_ops is called, not when the ops or private_data fields of the snd_pcm_substream itself are written.

6.3 Unhandled Polymorphism

The most interesting uses of polymorphism are those our analysis cannot even express. There are not many of these, but they are generally important. We have annotated one such case, the Sysfs filesystem, providing a mechanism to check the casts performed by clients of Sysfs with the usual limitation that the annotations are trusted; we assume Sysfs follows the annotated behavior. In this section we describe the interface Sysfs uses to expose its polymorphism, which we have annotated, and the internal invariants Sysfs maintains for this interface, which our analysis has little understanding of.

Sysfs provides a mechanism for userspace programs to query and update attributes of the drivers and associated devices by accessing files in the `/sys` directory. To the driver writer, this functionality is behind a simple polymorphic interface, which relates a kernel object `kobj` (each device used in Sysfs has its own kernel object) with an attribute with a name and access mode (read, read/write, etc.).

```
// include/linux/sysfs.h
int sysfs_create_file(struct kobject * kobj,
                      const struct attribute * attr);

struct attribute {
   const char       * name;
   struct module    * owner;
   mode_t           mode;
};
```

The driver uses `sysfs_create_file` by passing the device's kernel object and the attribute to associate with the device.

```
// drivers/block/aoe/aoeblk.c
static ssize_t aoedisk_show_state(struct gendisk * disk, char *page)
{
   struct aoedev *d = disk->private_data;
   return snprintf(page, PAGE_SIZE, ...);
}

static struct disk_attribute disk_attr_state = {
   .attr = {.name = "state", .mode = S_IRUGO },
   .show = aoedisk_show_state
};

static void aoedisk_add_sysfs(struct aoedev *d)
{
   sysfs_create_file(&d->gd->kobj, &disk_attr_state.attr);
   sysfs_create_file(&d->gd->kobj, &disk_attr_mac.attr);
   sysfs_create_file(&d->gd->kobj, &disk_attr_netif.attr);
   sysfs_create_file(&d->gd->kobj, &disk_attr_fwver.attr);
}
```

In this example, there is a correlation where the `disk` parameter to `aoedisk_show_state` is equal to the `d->gd` value as passed into a call to `aoedisk_add_sysfs`. We need to know this correlation to show that the cast of `disk->private_data` performed by `aoedisk_add_sysfs` is correct. We use a total of 17 annotations to capture the correlations introduced by calls to `sysfs_create_file` and several wrappers which create Sysfs files for particular kinds of devices.

These annotations do not address the internal invariants of Sysfs, the machinery hidden behind `sysfs_create_file` and the filesystem itself which ensures `aoedisk_show_state` is called with the right value. The remainder of this section describes these invariants. Calling `sysfs_create_file` eventually leads to a file with the following file operations (see Section 5.3 for a description of `file_operations`).

```
// fs/sysfs/file.c
const struct file_operations sysfs_file_operations = {
   .read      = sysfs_read_file,
   .write     = sysfs_write_file,
   .llseek    = generic_file_llseek,
   .open      = sysfs_open_file,
   .release   = sysfs_release,
   .poll      = sysfs_poll,
};
```

When a user tries to read this file, the `sysfs_read_file` function is called, which invokes `aoedisk_show_state` on the correct `disk` argument to get the state of the disk.

```
// fs/sysfs/file.c
static ssize_t sysfs_read_file(struct file *file, char __user *buf,
                               size_t count, loff_t *ppos)
{
   struct sysfs_buffer * buffer = file->private_data;
   ...
   if (buffer->needs_read_fill) {
      fill_read_buffer(file->f_dentry,buffer);
   }
   ...
}

static int fill_read_buffer(struct dentry * dentry,
                            struct sysfs_buffer * buffer)
{
   struct attribute * attr = to_attr(dentry);
   struct kobject * kobj = to_kobj(dentry->d_parent);
   struct sysfs_ops * ops = buffer->ops;
   ...
   count = ops->show(kobj,attr,buffer->page);
   ...
}

// fs/sysfs/sysfs.h
static inline struct attribute * to_attr(struct dentry * dentry)
{
   struct sysfs_dirent * sd = dentry->d_fsdata;
   return ((struct attribute *) sd->s_element);
}

static inline struct kobject * to_kobj(struct dentry * dentry)
{
   struct sysfs_dirent * sd = dentry->d_fsdata;
   return ((struct kobject *) sd->s_element);
}

// block/genhd.c
#define to_disk(obj) container_of(obj,struct gendisk,kobj)

static ssize_t disk_attr_show(struct kobject *kobj,
                              struct attribute *attr, char *page)
{
   struct gendisk *disk = to_disk(kobj);
   struct disk_attribute *disk_attr =
      container_of(attr,struct disk_attribute,attr);
   if (disk_attr->show) disk_attr->show(disk,page);
}

static struct sysfs_ops disk_sysfs_ops = {
   .show  = &disk_attr_show,
   .store = &disk_attr_store,
};
```

Now the function `sysfs_read_file` calls the helper function `fill_read_buffer`, which gets an `attribute` and `kobject` from the file and performs an indirect call `ops->show` to fill in the data from the attribute which will be returned by the file read. If the attribute read is `disk_attr_state.attr` (or any other attribute of a `gendisk`), the `ops` points to `disk_sysfs_ops`, and `ops->show` calls `disk_attr_show`, which backs out the kernel object pointer to the containing `gendisk` (`d->gd` in the call to `aoedisk_add_sysfs`) and the attribute pointer to the containing `disk_attribute` (`disk_attr_state`). Finally, `disk_attr_state.show` points to `aoedisk_show_state`, completing the call chain from `sysfs_read_file`.

This example assumes numerous data invariants which must hold or else the indirect calls will break. Our analysis can capture some of these invariants, but user annotations are required for the rest; for more details, see [11]. More complete automatic checking for these properties at this scale is well beyond what is currently feasible with existing techniques.

7. RELATED WORK

Our analysis can be characterized as simultaneously scaling to large programs (millions of lines of code), being a verifier (i.e., proving properties, in contrast to finding bugs), and being highly *heap sensitive*, meaning simply that to be successful it requires a relatively deep understanding of the relationships between data structures in the heap. Several bug-finding (non-verifying) efforts have scaled to systems of the size we consider; representative examples include [13, 19, 3]. Fewer verifiers have been demonstrated to work on million line programs and these have focused on finite-state properties; these systems are subject to the caveat (as is our system) that portions of the analysis may be unsound due to time-outs and other resource limits for a small portion of the analysis [8, 14, 4]. We are not aware of any previous work on verifying type casts that scales to programs of the size that we analyze, and more generally we are not aware of any verification system that is heap sensitive on multi-million line programs.

C and C++ are alone among widely used typed languages today in not providing type safety guarantees. Consequently, research has sought to ensure that C programs are type safe, or to replace C with similarly expressive type safe alternatives. Most work focuses not just on type safety, but memory safety as well (ensuring `NULL` or dangling pointers are not dereferenced, buffers do not overrun, and so forth).

Siff et. al. [18] describe rules for physical subtyping in C and examine the casts in several hundred thousand lines of code. They find that about 85% of the downcasts involving structure types in C are between `void*` or `char*` and a structure, rather than between different structure types. In the Linux kernel version we analyzed we found far fewer casts involving structure subtyping — just 459 out of 44910 casts, or 1%, and involving just 44 different supertypes. For these casts we use the same physical subtyping rules as [18] to determine compatibility between the structures. However, rather than just counting the number of downcasts in a program our interest is in proving these casts correct.

Loginov et. al. [16] compute type information for C programs at runtime and check the program's behavior against these types to find type safety violations. Since virtually any access in C might be type unsafe, virtually all memory accesses are instrumented by this method, leading to an average slowdown of greater than 20 times the original program's runtime.

HAVOC [15] is a static analysis system for C programs that uses function preconditions, postconditions, and loop invariants to perform modular verification of memory safety and other properties. HAVOC has recently been used to verify type safety for a few Windows device drivers [5]. HAVOC provides far stronger guarantees about a program than the casting analysis we present; we are only checking downcasts to structure types, while HAVOC checks these as well as downcasts to other types, use of the `container_of` macro to jump to a structure's base pointer, buffer overflows, and all other ways type safety might be violated. However, to completely verify 5000 lines of code, HAVOC requires 35 changes to the code, 36 trusted annotations (annotations which, like our annotations, are not checked for correctness), and 153 untrusted annotations (which are checked for correctness). At these rates, annotating and checking a system the size of the Linux kernel would require several hundred thousand lines of annotations.

CCured [17, 7] uses pointer type qualifiers in combination with runtime checks to check type and memory safety in C with fairly low overhead. Pointers used in downcasts are transformed into 'fat' `WILD` pointers, structures which contain both the pointer and additional bounds and runtime type information to perform the appropriate checks at accesses to the pointer. The initial version of CCured [17] would mark as `WILD` any pointer whose value might have been used in a downcast or might in the future be downcast (according to a global flow- and context-insensitive algorithm). For polymorphic structures such as `file` and `timer_list`, this would encompass all uses of the data which at any point were stored in their `void*` data fields. An improvement [7] allows most pointers which are downcast to be less than fully `WILD` at the cost of limited runtime type information attached for checking the downcast is safe. After the downcast and checks are performed, the result is a `SAFE` pointer which can be accessed in the future with few additional checks.

Deputy [6] is a type system for C that uses a more lightweight approach than CCured, inserting runtime assertions where necessary without changing the in-memory layout of pointers and other structures. When dealing with downcasts from one type to another, Deputy soundly checks the cast at compile time provided the pointers are annotated with correct dependent types. The dependent types used by Deputy cover the parametric polymorphism as used in many of the Linux kernel data structures [2], but not other, rarer constructs such as pointers whose type depends on a program condition. Moreover, even if suitable polymorphic types are assigned for the various polymorphic structures in Linux, it is not clear that the Deputy checker can deal with many of the intricacies found in initialization of these structures; for example, the `f_op` field of a `file` may be freely changed so long as its `private_data` is `NULL` (Section 6.1).

Cyclone [10] is a C-like language that ensures memory and type safety, sharing many of the same features as CCured and Deputy. Pointers used in arithmetic can be either fat as in CCured, or be associated with a specific length as in Deputy. Casts are allowed in Cyclone, but only from a subtype to a supertype [1]; downcasts are disallowed. Types in Cyclone can be polymorphic [9] in a similar fashion to Deputy, again handling many of the polymorphic structures we have seen in Linux and removing the need for many downcasts. Still, Cyclone requires that the type over which a polymorphic structure is instantiated be set at the creation point of the structure, which breaks on initializers such as the `file` open example (Section 6.1).

Our approach to modeling polymorphic structures is more indirect than the approaches used by Deputy and Cyclone, and does not try to associate type variables with the structure declarations and concrete type instantiations at each point the structure is used. This allows us to handle cases such as the `file` open example, as we do not have to fix a type to a `file` at the points where it in fact has no type.

Finally, more modern languages than C, such as C++ and Java, have richer type systems that can directly express polymorphic interfaces a C programmer must construct by hand. For example, `timer_list` could be implemented as a C++ template structure, and `file_operations` could be implemented as virtual methods in a C++ class. Whether such languages are appropriate for a full-fledged operating system is a divisive topic; we observe, though, that the `file` open example illustrates the flexibility of C to write code which falls outside the usual approach of a C++ or Java program.

8. CONCLUSION

Big software systems are tremendously complex with all their details taken together. By focusing on downcasts we are able to peel away and characterize a small portion of this complexity. The combination of polymorphic data structures and initialization via assignment leads to important and sometimes complex relationships that are critical to proving basic safety properties of large systems. Understanding these heap invariants is a challenging static analysis problem, and we have shown that it can be solved automatically for many, but not all, of the common idioms in the Linux kernel. We suspect the results apply beyond Linux and C; in particular, we expect large systems written in untyped scripting languages will display similar phenomena, and we even suppose that similar implicit structural correlations can be found in large systems written in strongly typed languages such as Java, at least for properties of fields that are not directly enforced by the strong type system.

9. REFERENCES

[1] *Cyclone: User Manual.* http://cyclone.thelanguage.org/wiki/User Manual.

[2] *Deputy Manual.* http://deputy.cs.berkeley.edu/manual.html.

[3] Alex Aiken, Suhabe Bugrara, Iisil Dillig, Thomas Dillig, Peter Hawkins, and Brian Hackett. An overview of the saturn project. In *Workshop on Program Analysis for Software Tools and Engineering*, 2007.

[4] Suhabe Bugrara and Alex Aiken. Verifying the safety of user pointer dereferences. In *IEEE Symposium on Security and Privacy*, pages 325–338, 2008.

[5] Jeremy Condit, Brian Hackett, Shuvendu Lahiri, and Shaz Qadeer. Unifying type checking and property checking for low-level code. In *Principles of Programming Languages*, 2009.

[6] Jeremy Condit, Matthew Harren, Zachary Anderson, David Gay, and George Necula. Dependent types for low-level programming. In *European Symposium on Programming*, 2007.

[7] Jeremy Condit, Matthew Harren, Scott McPeak, George C. Necula, and Westley Weimer. CCured in the real world. In *Programming Language Design and Implementation*, 2003.

[8] Manuvir Das, Sorin Lerner, and Mark Seigle. Program verification in polynomial time. In *Conference on Programming Language Design and Implementation*, pages 57–68, 2002.

[9] Dan Grossman. Quantified types in an imperative language. *ACM Transactions on Programming Languages and Systems*, 28, 2006.

[10] Dan Grossman, Michael Hicks, Trevor Jim, and Greg Morrisett. Cyclone: a type-safe dialect of C. In *C/C++ Users Journal*, volume 23, 2005.

[11] Brian Hackett. *Type Safety in the Linux Kernel.* PhD thesis, Stanford University, 2010.

[12] Brian Hackett and Alex Aiken. How is aliasing used in systems software? In *Foundations of Software Engineering*, 2006.

[13] Seth Hallen, Benjamin Chelf, Yichen Xie, and Dawson Engler. A system and language for building system-specific, static analyses. In *Conference on Programming Language Design and Implementation*, pages 69–82, 2002.

[14] Robert Johnson and David Wagner. Finding user/kernel pointer bugs with type inference. In *USENIX Security Symposium*, pages 119–134, 2004.

[15] Shuvendu Lahiri and Shaz Qadeer. Back to the future: Revisiting precise program verification using SMT solvers. In *Principles of Programming Languages*, 2008.

[16] Alexey Loginov, Suan Hsi Yong, Susan Horwitz, and Thomas Reps. Debugging via run-time type checking. In *In Proceedings of FASE 2001: Fundamental Approaches to Software Engineering*, pages 217–232. Springer, 2001.

[17] George C. Necula, Scott McPeak, and Westley Weimer. CCured: Type-safe retrofitting of legacy software. In *Principles of Programming Languages*, 2002.

[18] Michael Siff, Satish Chandra, Thomas Ball, Krishna Kunchithapadam, and Thomas Reps. Coping with type casts in C. In *Foundations of Software Engineering*, 1999.

[19] Yichen Xie and Alex Aiken. Scalable error detection using boolean satisfiability. In *Principles of Programming Languages*, 2005.

Boosting the Performance of Flow-sensitive Points-to Analysis using Value Flow

Lian Li Cristina Cifuentes Nathan Keynes
Oracle Labs
Brisbane, Australia
{lian.li,cristina.cifuentes,nathan.keynes}@oracle.com

ABSTRACT

Points-to analysis is a fundamental static analysis technique which computes the set of memory objects that a pointer may point to. Many different applications, such as security-related program analyses, bug checking, and analyses of multi-threaded programs, require precise points-to information to be effective. Recent work has focused on improving the precision of points-to analysis through *flow-sensitivity* and great progress has been made. However, even with all recent progress, flow-sensitive points-to analysis can still be much slower than a flow-insensitive analysis.

In this paper, we propose a novel method that simplifies flow-sensitive points-to analysis to a general graph reachability problem in a value flow graph. The value flow graph summarizes dependencies between pointer variables, including those memory dependencies via pointer dereferences. The points-to set for each pointer variable can then be computed as the set of memory objects that can reach it in the graph. We develop an algorithm to build the value flow graph efficiently by examining the *pointed-to-by* set of a memory object, i.e., the set of pointers that point to an object. The pointed-to-by information of memory objects is very useful for applications such as escape analysis, and information flow analysis.

Our approach is intuitive, easy to implement and very efficient. The implementation is around 2000 lines of code and it is more efficient than existing flow-sensitive points-to analyses. The runtime is comparable with the state-of-the-art flow-insensitive points-to analysis.

Categories and Subject Descriptors

F3.2 [**LOGICS AND MEANINGS OF PROGRAMS**]: Semantics of Programming Languages–Program analysis

General Terms

Precision, Efficiency

1. INTRODUCTION

Permission to make digital or hard copies of all or part of this work for personal or classroom use is granted without fee provided that copies are not made or distributed for profit or commercial advantage and that copies bear this notice and the full citation on the first page. To copy otherwise, to republish, to post on servers or to redistribute to lists, requires prior specific permission and/or a fee.
ESEC/FSE'11, September 5–9, 2011, Szeged, Hungary.
Copyright 2011 ACM 978-1-4503-0443-6/11/09 ...$10.00.

Points-to analysis is a fundamental static analysis technique which computes the set of memory objects (abstract locations) that a pointer variable may point to. The points-to information is often represented in the form of points-to sets [1] or points-to graphs [5] and such information is a prerequisite for many important problems, including security analysis [13], bug checking [26], hardware synthesis [39], and the analysis of multi-threaded programs [30]. The effectiveness and efficiency of such techniques depend heavily on the precision of the pointer information provided.

Recent researches have focused on improving the precision of points-to analysis through *flow-sensitivity.* Compared to flow-insensitive approaches, flow-sensitive points-to analyses respect the execution order of program statements and compute different points-to graphs at different program points. Flow-sensitive points-to analysis has been shown to be beneficial for the above important problems. However, traditionally flow-sensitive analysis [21], based on the iterative data-flow analysis framework, is too costly to be applied. It is not scalable because of the high cost of conservatively propagating and computing large amounts of pointer information along the control flow graph (CFG) of a program.

Recent research efforts on flow-sensitive points-to analysis [18, 19, 37] hence have emphasized in avoiding the propagation and computation of unnecessary pointer information to improve performance. One of the key insights is to employ the *static single assignment* (SSA) [10] representation, which enables *sparse analysis* and propagates pointer information from the definition of a variable directly to its corresponding uses (i.e., following the *def-use* chain), thus avoiding over-conservatively propagation of pointer information. Based on this observation, previous work has successfully sped up flow-sensitive points-to analysis by more than 100X [18, 19, 37]. However, even with this improvement, flow-sensitive points-to analysis can still be much slower compared to its flow-insensitive counterpart [19]. We evaluated the state-of-the-art flow-sensitive points-to analysis [18] in our experiments: for the three benchmarks that it can run to completion, it is on average 7× slower than a flow-insensitive one.

In this paper, we introduce a novel method for flow-sensitive points-to analysis based on value flow. Our approach is intuitive, easy to implement and very efficient. The implementation is around 2000 lines of code and it is much more efficient than existing flow-sensitive points-to analyses. The runtime is comparable with the state-of-the-art flow-insensitive points-to analysis algorithm [16].

We achieve the large performance improvement by simplifying flow-sensitive points-to analysis to a general graph reachability problem in a *value flow* graph. The value flow graph (VFG) monitors how memory objects *flow* to pointer variables. Variable a is said to *flow* to variable b if a is assigned to b directly (via assign statements b = a) or indirectly (via pointer dereferences), represented as an edge a → b in the graph. Both direct and indirect flows are represented in the graph. In the VFG, for each pointer variable, its points-to set is the set of memory objects that can reach it. Similarly, the set of nodes that are reachable from a memory object node is the set of pointers that can point to it, denoted as the *pointed-to-by* set of the memory object.

PROPERTY 1. *Variable a can flow to variable b indirectly via pointer dereferences, only if a is stored to a memory object first and b is loaded from the same memory object afterwards.*

Property 1 highlights the key observation of our approach. Based on this property, we can build the value flow graph with indirect flows efficiently by computing and examining the pointed-to-by set for each memory object: a stored value can flow to a loaded value only if both targets point to the same memory object, i.e., both targets are from the same pointed-to-by set of a memory object. Note that the pointed-to-by information for memory objects is also very useful for many applications, such as escape analysis and information flow analysis. With the value flow graph representation, we avoid propagating large points-to information along the CFG node or def-use chains as in most existing flow-sensitive points-to analyses and significantly improve the performance.

Our analysis is flow sensitive and so is the value flow graph. Different definitions of the same variable in the original program are represented as distinct nodes in the graph (as in SSA). The execution order of statements is also respected when computing direct and indirect value flows.

We have developed an efficient value-flow based flow sensitive points-to analysis algorithm and implemented it in LLVM [27]. Experimental results against several large applications, including the OpenSolaris™Operating system and Networking (ON) consolidation with over 8 millions of lines of code (LOC), show that the analysis is as precise as existing flow-sensitive analyses for the benchmarks we studied, and that it is significantly more efficient than previous work [18]: the runtime is comparable with the state-of-the-art flow-insensitive points-to analysis. To summarize, our contributions are as follows:

- We propose a novel method for flow-sensitive points-to analysis based on value flow. Our approach not only computes the standard points-to information, it also computes the pointed-to-by information for each memory object. In this work, we focus on flow-sensitivity only and we do not distinguish different calling contexts at different call sites (i.e., it is context-insensitive). However, the proposed method can be naturally extended to be context-sensitive.

- We highlight the major challenges in our approach and develop an efficient algorithm to build the flow-sensitive value flow graph, with both direct and indirect value flows of a program. The algorithm can be easily implemented and adopted in modern compilers. The value flow graph built by our analysis can be used in many value-flow based applications, including compiler optimizations [4], error detection [7] and software validation [11].

- We implement our algorithm in LLVM and demonstrate that it is significantly more efficient than previous approaches. The performance is comparable with the state-of-the-art flow-insensitive points-to analysis algorithm [16].

The rest of the paper is organized as follows: Section 2 reviews related work. Section 3 introduces flow-sensitive pointer analysis in general and explains how it is optimized in SSA. We describe our proposed approach in Section 4 and highlight the major challenges. Section 5 introduces an efficient implementation in detail. We evaluate our implementation using several large applications in Section 6 and Section 7 concludes this paper.

2. RELATED WORK

Points-to analysis is a fundamental static analysis that has been studied extensively in the past [33, 1, 5, 12, 15]. Most existing work focuses on improving the precision of points-to analysis by being context-sensitive [6, 28, 40, 24, 35, 31], while flow-sensitivity was previous considered not to be as important [22]. Its importance is only recognized recently and great progress has been made, including [18, 19, 37, 25] and some references therein.

In [22], Hind and Pioli formalized flow-sensitive points-to analysis using a classic iterative dataflow analysis framework. They eliminated unnecessary propagation and computation of pointer information by using a sparse evaluation graph [8], a graph derived from the CFG with only nodes manipulating pointer information. With this optimization, they were able to scale flow-sensitive points-to analysis to applications with tens of thousands of LOC. The idea of using a sparse graph is also adopted and applied in [18]. Goyal [14] optimized the formulation of Hind and Pioli using a fine-grained work-list. The optimized formulation runs in asymptotically cubic time and cubic space in the worst case. A similar algorithm with the same complexity is designed and implemented by Staiger-Stöhr in [32]. In [25], Lhoták et al. applied an effective tradeoff that focuses flow sensitivity only on pointers with strong updates. The technique is efficient like flow-insensitive analysis, and almost as precise as a fully flow-sensitive analysis.

A number of papers [5, 20, 34, 18, 19, 37] try to optimize flow-sensitive points-to analysis by employing the SSA representation, which enables efficient sparse analysis and avoids unnecessary propagation of pointer information along the CFG. Hasti and Horwitz [20] propose a scheme that firstly uses a flow-insensitive analysis to gather pointer information, then the program is transformed into SSA with the provided pointer information and fed back into the analysis to improve precision. This process can be iteratively applied until convergence. In [5] and [34], the authors implement a similar idea to dynamically transform the program into SSA during the course of the flow-sensitive pointer analysis. However, it was in 2009 that Hardekopf and Calvin [18] successfully applied flow-sensitive points-to analysis to large benchmarks with hundreds of thousands of LOC for the first time. They made the observation that many program variables are

```
     main() {
1       char A[...], B[...];
2       char *a, *b, **t1, **t2;
3       t1=&a;
4       t2=&b;
5       a=&A;
6       b=&B;
7       if (...)
8          *a='A';
9       else{
10         swap(t1, t2);
11         *a='B';
12      }
13       *a = '?';
     }

     void swap (void *p, void *q){
14      void tmp = *p;
15      *p = *q;
16      *q = tmp;
     }
```

(a) An example

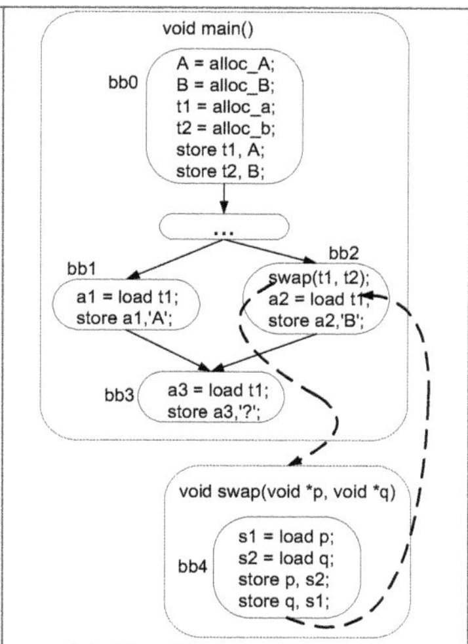

(b) The SSA representation

pts(t1), pts(p)	{alloc_a}
pts(t2), pts(q)	{alloc_b}
pts(a1)	{alloc_A, alloc_B}
pts(a2)	{alloc_A, alloc_B}
pts(a3)	{alloc_A, alloc_B}
pts(s1)	{alloc_A, alloc_B}
pts(s2)	{alloc_A, alloc_B}

(c) The flow-insensitive points-to set

pts(t1), pts(p)	{alloc_a}
pts(t2), pts(q)	{alloc_b}
pts(a1)	{alloc_A}
pts(a2)	{alloc_B}
pts(a3)	{alloc_A, alloc_B}
pts(s1)	{alloc_A}
pts(s2)	{alloc_B}

(d) The flow-sensitive points-to set

Figure 1: An example.

never referenced by pointers, and thus can be represented in SSA without any pointer information. Hence sparse analysis can be applied to these SSA variables, and the sparse evaluation graph can be largely reduced by removing nodes with only SSA pointer variables. This optimization can greatly improve the scalability and performance of flow-sensitive points-to analysis. Later in his thesis [19], Hardekopf proposed a more efficient algorithm which enables full sparse analysis by using an auxiliary flow-insensitive analysis to represent all program variables in SSA [9]. This approach is further extended in [37], where the authors partition the program variables into different points-to levels using a flow-insensitive analysis. Pointer information is enforced to flow uni-directionally from the higher level to the lower level. The analysis is then efficiently implemented by processing variables level by level, from the highest to the lowest where the analyzed results of higher level variables can be used in building the SSA representation of variables in the lower level. This level-by-level idea is also adopted in [23, 38, 19]. Our approach differs from all these in that we enable efficient sparse analysis by building a flow-sensitive value flow graph, and we avoid propagation of pointer information by making use of the pointed-to-by information of memory objects, instead of relying on the points-to information of pointers.

Optimizations that can be applied, but not restricted to flow-sensitive points-to analysis include [2, 40, 23, 13]. The authors in [2] and [40] propose an efficient representation of points-to relation using Binary Decision Diagrams (BDDs). Kahlon [23] bootstraps the more precise and costly flow-sensitive pointer analysis by using cheaper and less precise analyses to partition programs into small sections that can be analyzed independently. Fink et al [13] use a technique that applies more precise pointer analyses only to portions of the program which requires that level of precision. These optimizations can be applied in our approach to further improve performance.

Value flow analysis computes which program variable holds which value of interest and it has been studied in many different areas, including compiler optimizations [4, 3], error detection [7], software validation [11], and symbolic evaluation [29]. Existing value flow analyses rely on external points-to analysis to handle memory dependencies with aliases. In this paper, we present a new flow-sensitive points-to analysis using value flow. Our results can be used in existing value flow analyses to make them more effective.

3. BACKGROUND

In this section, we give a brief introduction to the SSA representation as our implementation is based on SSA and it motivates most of recent researches on flow-sensitive points-to analysis [18, 19, 37]. Note that our method itself does not rely on SSA. We also introduce flow-sensitive points-to analysis in general using the example in Figure 1(a).

In Figure 1(a), initially we have t1 points to a, t2 points to b, a points to array A, and b points to array B. The function swap takes two input pointers and swaps the values they point to. As a result, after swapping the two pointers t1 and t2 at line 10, variable a points to array B at line 11.

3.1 The SSA representation

The CFG and the SSA representation of the example is given in Figure 1(b). In SSA, all variables are defined exactly once and different definitions for the same variable in the original program are represented as distinct variables. If a variable is defined along two different paths then at the join point in the CFG where the two paths merge, a ϕ instruction is introduced to represent the combination of these definitions. SSA enables sparse analysis and its benefits are widely acknowledged: dataflow analysis can be more efficiently computed by following the def-use chain of each variable, avoiding propagation of unnecessary information in the CFG.

As variables can be defined indirectly through pointers (e.g., in Figure 1(a), *p=*q at line 15), pointer information is required to build the SSA representation for a given program. This is also the major challenge of employing SSA for points-to analysis. To overcome this issue, in practice, modern compilers such as GCC and LLVM [27] use *partial SSA* form, where only these variables whose addresses are never taken are represented in SSA. Without loss of generality, variables which might be referenced via pointers (e.g., a and b in the example) are memory objects represented by alloc instructions and they are accessed via load and store instructions. Each load instruction (e.g., a1=load,t1 in bb1) defines a distinct variable.

As in Figure 1, there are four memory objects representing the four address-taken variables a, b, A and B in the original program. All memory objects are accessed via load and store instructions. References to address-taken variable a at line 8 and 11 in Figure 1(a) are represented as two distinct load instructions in bb1 and bb2 (Figure 1(b)), respectively.

3.2 Flow-Sensitive Points-to Analysis

Traditional flow-sensitive points-to analysis [21] is based on the classic iterative dataflow analysis framework. Conceptually, the analysis is applied to every node in the CFG of a program. Each CFG node k is associated with a transfer function that computes its outgoing points-to graph OUT_k from its input points-to graph IN_k. The transfer function is summarized as:

$$\begin{aligned} IN_k &= \bigcup_{x \in pred(k)} OUT_x \\ OUT_k &= GEN_k \cup (IN_k - KILL_k) \end{aligned} \quad (1)$$

where GEN_k and $KILL_k$ represent the set of pointer information generated by the node and killed by the node, respectively. The analysis iteratively computes the above two functions for all nodes in the CFG until convergence. As required by the iterative dataflow analysis framework, a lattice of points-to graphs is defined by introducing a partial order on the points-to graphs (according to set relations). The meet and join operators of points-to graphs are thus defined based on set union operations.

Compared to the flow-insensitive approach, the precision of points-to analysis is greatly improved in two ways:

- Points-to information generated in node k is considered in node p only if p is reachable from k in the CFG. Thus the execution order of program statements is respected.
- Unnecessary points-to information is removed by the $KILL$ set. When we are certain that the left-hand side of an assignment definitely points to a single memory location v, the points-to relations $v \rightarrow x$ prior to the assignment can be replaced with a new set of points-to relations. This is referred to as *strong update*. Accordingly, if the left-hand side cannot be determined to point to a single memory location, the conservative *weak update* rule is applied. The $KILL$ set is set to $\emptyset$ and all existing points-to relations are preserved.

Figure 1(c) and Figure 1(d) compare the points-to sets for all pointer variables when flow-sensitivity is or not considered. As shown in the graph, flow-sensitive analysis is more precise. With flow-sensitivity, we can conclude that a1 only points to alloc_A, while a flow-insensitive analysis will assume it can point to both alloc_A and alloc_B.

Since it is in general not possible to determine where variables are defined or used without pointer information, the analysis must conservatively propagate the pointer information generated at each node to all its successors. As a result, large points-to sets are involved in the two flow functions in Equation 1, making the analysis both time-consuming and memory-consuming. Many research efforts hence have focused on reducing the propagation and computation of unnecessary pointer information. One of the most effective ways [18, 19, 37] is to employ the SSA representation as discussed in detail in Section 2.

4. THE METHODOLOGY

In this work, we propose a new method for flow-sensitive points-to analysis. The method is sound and as precise as the traditional flow-sensitive points-to analysis [21] introduced above. Our approach enables efficient sparse analysis by computing the def-use information for all pointer variables, summarized as a value flow graph (VFG). Nodes in the VFG represent memory objects and pointer variables, and edges represent value flows between them. For flow-sensitive points-to analysis, the graph also needs to be flow-sensitive: different definitions to the same variable in the original program are represented as distinct nodes in the graph, and a definition can flow to a use only if the definition can reach the use in the CFG without being killed by another definition.

Flow-sensitive points-to analysis is then formulated as a general graph reachability problem in the VFG: the points-to set of each pointer variable is the set of memory objects that can reach it, and the pointed-to-by set of each memory object is the set of nodes that are reachable from the memory object.

4.1 Value Flow Graph

Instruction		Type	Value flow
a = alloc_o	Base	Direct	alloc_o → a
a = b	Assign		b → a
store x, b	Store	Indirect	∃alloc_o|alloc_o → $x \wedge$
a = load y	Load		alloc_o → $y \Longrightarrow b \rightarrow a$

Table 1: Value flow rules.

Table 1 summarizes the value flow rules, where alloc_o denotes a memory object. In our representation (Section 3.1), memory objects are accessed via load and store instructions, and they are represented in the VFG as source nodes without incoming edges.

Following previous work [1], it suffices to analyze the four types of instructions listed in the table. Nested pointer dereferences are eliminated by introducing auxiliary variables. Data aggregates such as arrays and structs are regarded as monolithic objects, heap objects are modeled by representing the allocation site p by an instruction of the form x=alloc_p. Branches are uninterpreted and treated as non-deterministic. Call instructions are translated to a set of base or assign instructions between function arguments and parameters as explained in Section 5.2. Function pointers are analyzed by regarding functions as a special object.

Figure 2 shows the VFG for the example in Figure 1. Each store or load instruction is represented as a node in the VFG (annotated with the instruction) if it stores or loads a pointer. For a store node, there is a direct flow edge from the stored pointer to it, e.g., A → (store t1, A) in Figure 2. Indirect flows are those from store to load nodes as highlighted in dashed lines. According to Table 1, we have (store t1, A) → (s1 = load p) as both t1 and p refer to the same memory object alloc_a.

The indirect flow rule in Table 1 highlights our observation (Property 1). It suggests that we can build the VFG efficiently by examining the pointed-to-by set for each mem-

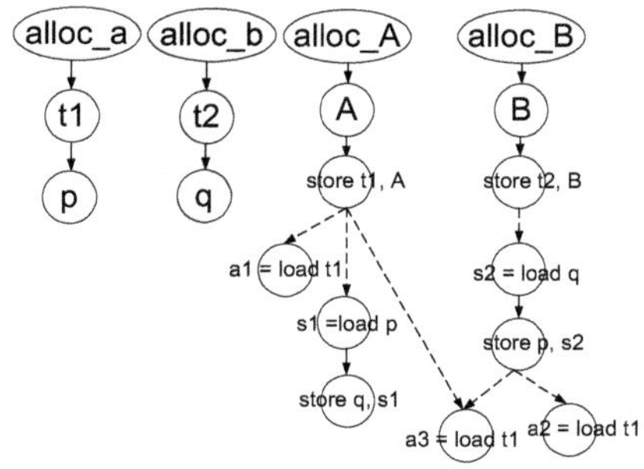

Figure 2: VFG for the example in Figure 1. Memory objects are represented as ovals and pointer variables as circles. Solid lines represent direct flows and indirect value flows are highlighted in dashed lines.

ory object: a store node can flow to a load node only if both targets refer to the same memory object, i.e., both targets are from the same pointed-to-by set of a memory object. The pointed-to-by set of a memory object can be computed with standard graphical traversal algorithms on the VFG, then the VFG is updated by computing indirect value flows of the memory object, i.e., introducing indirect flows between those stores and loads that refer to it. In the end, the analysis terminates at a fixed point where the VFG is complete and no more direct or indirect value flows can be introduced. The points-to set for each pointer variable, and the pointed-to-by set for each memory object, are thus computed.

4.2 Flow-sensitivity

For flow-sensitive analysis, the VFG needs to be flow-sensitive: we need to respect the execution order of program instructions in computing value flows. Direct value flows via base and assign instructions can be represented in SSA with common practices first then trivially processed. Indirect value flows from store to load instructions cannot be directly represented in SSA. We not only need to check whether they refer to the same memory object or not, also we need to check whether the store can reach the load in the CFG or not. This becomes even more challenging with the strong update rule, where a store instruction can be *killed* by another store instruction and the killed store cannot flow further to a load. The key challenge is discussed in Section 4.3.

In our method, the strong update rule is defined as:

DEFINITION 1. *For scalar memory object* alloc_o *with a single memory location, the instruction* (store X, ...) *will kill all previous store instructions to the object if the referring pointer variable* X *only points to* alloc_o.

For the example in Figure 1(b), the instruction (store p, s2) in bb3 will kill all previous store instructions to alloc_a, e.g., (store t1, A) in bb0, as p only points to the scalar object alloc_a.

Hence flow-sensitivity can be achieved in computing indirect flows by ensuring that a store can flow to a load only if it can reach the load in the CFG without being killed. Compared to existing points-to analysis algorithms, we do not rely on the points-to information of pointer variables to handle indirect references with pointers. As a result, our approach does not need to propagate points-to information along the CFG or def-use chains, where large points-to set often need to be propagated and expensive set operations are involved. This optimization is very effective in improving the performance as shown in our experimental results in Section 6.

4.3 The Challenge

The challenge lies in how to precisely and efficiently compute indirect flows of a memory object. Since the VFG is dynamically updated during the analysis, the computed pointed-to-by information and points-to information may not be complete. As a result, indirect value flows may be incorrectly computed based on the incomplete information, leading to both inefficiency and imprecision.

Imprecision can happen due to missed strong updates. During the analysis, the VFG is updated by introducing indirect value flows from store to load instructions that refer to a same memory object. With incomplete pointed-to-by information of the memory object, some store instructions may not be considered in computing its indirect flows since we do not know yet they actually refer to it. If these missed store instructions happen to be strong updates, unnecessary value flows will be introduced into the VFG, making the analysis imprecise. For the example in Figure 1, if we are not aware that p also refers to alloc_a, the store instruction (store p, s2) in function swap will not be considered in computing the indirect flows of alloc_a. As a result, we will falsely conclude that (store t1, A) in bb0 can flow to (a2 = load t1) in bb2 since both refer to the same pointer variable, although it will be killed by the call to function swap.

On the other hand, incompleteness can happen due to false strong updates. Some strong updates may be incorrectly applied where weak updates should be used instead. With incomplete points-to information, we may falsely assume that a store only refers to one memory object and kills all other stores to that object, resulting in incomplete results.

While the incompleteness problem can be handled by updating and recomputing the indirect flows of the memory object a store refers to when it is no longer a strong update (when it can also refer to another memory object), the imprecision problem is much more difficult to address. The solution as employed in most previous works is to conservatively assume that a store instruction can kill all other stores (no matter which objects they refer to) when it refers to a pointer with unknown points-to information. However, this may result in recomputing the indirect flows for all memory objects when the points-to set of the referring pointer gets updated, which could be very inefficient. We need to avoid unnecessary and frequent re-computation of indirect flows in order to efficiently solve the problem.

4.4 Escape Order

In this section, we introduce an efficient optimization technique to avoid unnecessary re-computation of indirect flows. The idea is to compute the indirect flows of a memory object only if its pointed-to-by set is complete. This is achieved by following an *escape order* in computing indirect flows. We prove that precision can be guaranteed if the escape order is enforced. Furthermore, we show that in practice there typically exists an escape order for scalar memory objects with strong updates and the analysis is precise if their indirect flows are computed in escape order.

We introduce a partial order relation, the escape order $\trianglelefteq$, between memory objects.

Definition 2. *For two objects alloc_A and alloc_B, alloc_B escapes to alloc_A if there exists an instruction (store X, Y) such that alloc_A → X and alloc_B → Y, denoted as alloc_A $\trianglelefteq$ alloc_B.*

The escape order states whether an memory object can escape to another or not. In another word, it indicates whether we could access a memory object by dereferencing another memory object or not. Since memory objects are accessed via load and store instructions, a memory object can escape to another only via store instructions. For our example in Figure 1, we have {alloc_a, alloc_b} $\trianglelefteq$ {alloc_A,alloc_B}. By definition, the escape order is transitive and antisymmetric. Two memory objects are said to be in a *cyclic escaping relation* if they escape to each other.

Observation 1. *Scalar memory objects with strong updates often are not in a cyclic escaping relation.*

The above observation is often enforced by static type checking rules. In programming languages such as C, one can write arbitrary type castings that may violate the property. However, we have studied several very large open source applications, including OpenSolaris with more than 8M LOC, and have not found a violation of this observation.

Theorem 1. *We can guarantee precision if the indirect flows for all scalar memory objects with strong updates are computed in escape order.*

Proof. Imprecision can only occur if some strong updates are not considered in computing the indirect flows of a memory object. For scalar memory object alloc_A, let $\mathcal{S}$ be the set of objects such that $\{\forall \text{alloc\_o} \in \mathcal{S} | \text{alloc\_o} \trianglelefteq \text{alloc\_A}\}$. The indirect flows of alloc_A are computed only if the indirect flows for all objects in $\mathcal{S}$ are computed. Thus the pointed-to-by set for alloc_A is completely computed since alloc_A can be referenced only via direct flows and indirect flows of memory objects in $\mathcal{S}$. Hence all strong updates will be considered in computing the indirect flows of alloc_A, and the analysis is precise. □

In our implementation, the escape order is computed according to existing pointed-to-by and points-to information during the analysis. As discussed in Section 4.3, the computed order may not be the exact order due to the incomplete pointer information. If we are not certain whether the exact escape order can be enforced or not, we can always guarantee precision by conservatively assuming that a store referring to a pointer with unknown points-to set will kill all other store instructions. However, this turns to be unnecessary for the benchmarks we studied.

5. AN IMPLEMENTATION

In this section, we present an algorithm to build the flow-sensitive value flow graph very efficiently. Our algorithm is able to detect the situations when imprecision might happen, i.e., when indirect flows of scalar memory objects with strong updates are not computed in escaping order. For all the benchmarks we have evaluated (Table 3), no such situation is detected.

VFG	Value flow graph	<N, E>
alloc_o	Memory Object	*pted*(alloc_o) *esp*(alloc_o)
P	Pointer node	*pts*(*P*)

Table 2: Notations used in the algorithm.

Table 2 highlights the notations used throughout our algorithm. The value flow graph VFG includes nodes for both memory objects and pointer variables, with memory objects being source nodes without incoming edges. For a memory object alloc_o, we use *pted*(alloc_o) and *esp*(alloc_o) to denote the set of pointers point to it and the set of memory objects it escapes to, respectively. The set *pts*(P) represents the set of memory objects pointed to by pointer P.

In this section, we first show how to compute the pointed-to-by set of a memory object by traversing the VFG and how to efficiently compute indirect flows using a sparse reachability analysis. Then in Section 5.3, we explain how the escape order is enforced and how the VFG is updated by introducing indirect flows of memory objects.

5.1 Compute Pointed-to-by Set

Algorithm 1 Traverse the value flow graph

```
1: procedure ComputePtedSet(alloc_o)
2:     Let 𝒫 be the set of nodes reachable from alloc_o in VFG
3:     for each node P in 𝒫 do
4:         pted(alloc_o) := pted(alloc_o) ∪ {P}
5:         pts(P) := pts(P) ∪ {alloc_o}
6:     end for
7: end procedure
8: procedure ComputeEspSet(alloc_o)
9:     for each node P in pted(alloc_o) do
10:        if P a store instruction then
11:            Let P' be the pointer P refers to
12:            if ptsTo(P') = ∅ then
13:                esp(alloc_o) := {All memory objects}
14:            else
15:                esp(alloc_o) := esp(alloc_o) ∪ pts(P')
16:            end if
17:        end if
18:    end for
19: end procedure
```

As shown in Algorithm 1, the pointed-to-by set of object alloc_o is computed by traversing the VFG from its representative source node. During the traversal, each visited pointer node P is added to *pted*(alloc_o), and its points-to set $pts(P)$ is updated by including the object alloc_o.

The set of objects alloc_o escapes to, *esp*(alloc_o), is computed in ComputeEspSet. When a pointer P in *pted*(alloc_o) represents a store instruction, alloc_o escapes to the pointer P refers to. The set *esp*(alloc_o) is updated accordingly (lines 10 - 17). Note that when the set of memory objects that P refers to is not computed (line 12), *esp*(alloc_o) is set to include all memory objects, suggesting that its indirect flows is not ready to be computed.

5.2 Compute Indirect Flows

The procedure ComputeIndirectFlow in Algorithm 2 outlines how to compute indirect flows of a memory object. It is also the key of our approach. The indirect flows of a memory object is computed by examining the set of store and load instructions that refer to it, and checking whether a store can reach a load or not.

The set of store and load instructions referring to a same memory object can be trivially computed based on its pointed-to-by set. To check whether a store can flow to a load instruction or not, the procedure PREPROCESSGLOBALFLOW is firstly invoked to handle inter-procedural indirect flows. Then a sparse reachability analysis is applied to every function where the object is referenced to compute its local flows.

Algorithm 2 Compute Indirect Flows

1: **procedure** COMPUTEINDIRECTFLOW(alloc_o)
2: PREPROCESSGLOBALFLOW(alloc_o)
3: **for** each function f where alloc_o is referenced **do**
4: COMPUTELOCALFLOW(f, alloc_o)
5: **end for**
6: **end procedure**
7: **procedure** PREPROCESSGLOBALFLOW(alloc_o)
8: **for** each inter-procedural flow arg → para of alloc_o **do**
9: Let c be the callsite
10: Let f be the callee function
11: Introducing the following four instructions

ref.arg = load arg	before callsite c
store para, ref.arg	at the entry of function f
ref.para = load para	at the exit of function f
store arg, ref.para	after callsite c

12: **end for**
13: **end procedure**
14: **procedure** COMPUTELOCALFLOW(f, alloc_o)
15: Let $\mathcal{S}$ be the set of store instructions in f refer to alloc_o
16: Let $IDF((S)$ be the iterated dominance frontier of $\mathcal{S}$
17: Build the simplified CFG $\mathcal{G}$ of f as follows
$\mathcal{G} := \{\mathcal{S} \cup IDF(\mathcal{S})\}$
add edge $S_1 \longrightarrow S_2$ to $\mathcal{G}$ if
S_2 is the dominance frontier of S_1 or
S_1 is the most immediate dominator of S_2 in $\mathcal{G}$
18: Solve the following dataflow equation in $\mathcal{G}$

$$IN_k = \bigcup_{x \in pred(k)} OUT_x$$
$$OUT_k = \begin{cases} GEN_k & \text{strong update} \\ GEN_k \cup IN_k & \text{otherwise} \end{cases} \tag{2}$$

where GEN_k is the store instruction in k
19: Let $\mathcal{L}$ be the set of load instructions in f refer to alloc_o
20: **for** each load instruction L in $\mathcal{L}$ **do**
21: Let S be the most immediate dominator of L in $\mathcal{G}$
22: OUT_S is the set of store instructions that can reach L
23: **end for**
24: **end procedure**

5.2.1 *Inter-procedural Indirect Flows*

As shown in PREPROCESSGLOBALFLOW, inter-procedural indirect flows are modeled as value flows between auxiliary variables introduced for objects passed into a function by reference. Global variables are handled by creating a local copy at each function where it is used then processed in the same fashion. The idea is to translate *passing by reference* into *passing by value*. For every inter-procedural value flow arg → para, we introduce two variables ref.arg and ref.para to represent dereferences of arg and para, respectively. The value flows between ref.arg and ref.para are enabled by the four instructions introduced as highlighted at line 11. As a result, inter-procedural indirect flows of alloc_o are modeled as value flows between the introduced variables.

The value flow edge (ref.arg=load arg) → (store para, ref.arg) models all indirect flows of alloc_o from callsite c into function f. A store instruction S in the caller function can flow to a load L in f if 1) S can reach the callsite, i.e., $S \rightarrow$ (ref.arg=load arg), and 2) L is reachable from the entry of f, i.e., (store para, ref.arg) $\rightarrow L$. Similarly, indirect flows returning from the callee function f to its caller function via dereferences of alloc_o are enabled by the flow edge (ref.para=load para) → (store arg, ref.para).

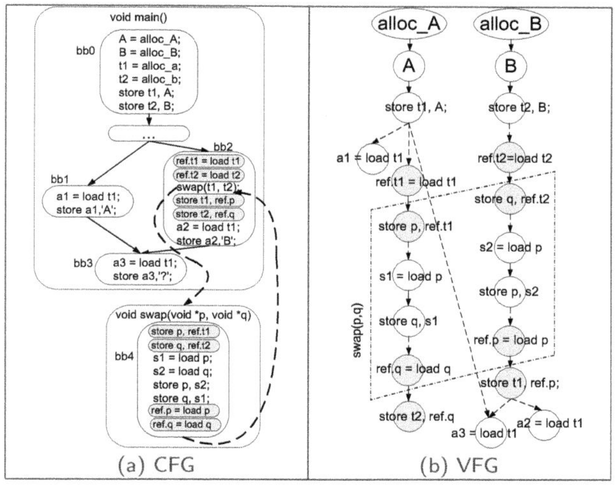

Figure 3: CFG and VFG of the example in Figure 1 after introducing auxiliary variables for inter-procedural indirect value flows.

In our example (Figure 1), object alloc_a and alloc_b are passed into function swap at the callsite in bb2 via pointer t1 and t2, respectively. There are two inter-procedural value flow edges: t1 → p, and t2 → q. As a result, eight instructions (four for each) are introduced as highlighted in Figure 3(a). The corresponding VFG is given in Figure 3(b). For simplicity, only the value flows of alloc_A and alloc_B are presented. The VFG in function swap is highlighted in the box. It is connected with the VFG in the caller function main via the introduced auxiliary variables.

5.2.2 *Local Indirect Flows*

Local indirect flows of object alloc_o are computed by applying a sparse reachability analysis (COMPUTELOCALFLOW) in every function where it is referenced. It can be proved that a store can reach a load in the CFG only if the load is dominated by the store or one of its iterated dominance frontiers. Hence the analysis first builds a sparse graph $\mathcal{G}$ including only store instructions referring to alloc_o and their iterated dominance frontiers (lines 15 - 17). The dataflow equation 2 is then efficiently solved in the sparse graph to compute the reachable store set (i.e., the set of store instructions that can reach an instruction) for $\mathcal{G}$ (line 18). The reachable store set of a load instruction is computed by finding its most immediate dominator in $\mathcal{G}$ (lines 19 - 23). Since the simplified graph $\mathcal{G}$ is very sparse and the reachable store set that we try to compute is in general very small with only local store instructions referring to alloc_o, the analysis is very efficient.

Figure 4(a) gives the simplified CFG $\mathcal{G}$ when computing

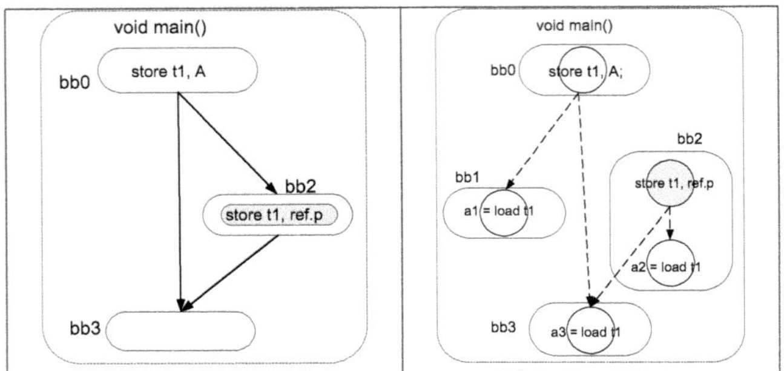

(a) Simplified CFG (b) Indirect flows

Figure 4: Compute local indirect flows of alloc_a in function main.

the local indirect flows of alloc_a in function main. There are two store instructions referring to alloc_o, (store t1, A) in bb0 and (store t1, ref.p) in bb2. The later is introduced in PREPROCESSGLOBALFLOW for inter-procedural indirect flows of alloc_o. The two store instructions and their iterated dominance frontier bb3 are included in $\mathcal{G}$.

The local indirect flows of alloc_a are given in Figure 4(b). As the only dominator in $\mathcal{G}$, the store in bb0 (store t1, A) flows to the load (a1=load t1) in bb1. The store instruction (store t1, ref.p) in bb2 kills all its previous stores and only it can reach the load (a2=load t1) in the same block. The most immediate dominator of (a3 = load t1) in the simplified CFG is bb3. Hence its reachable store set is OUT_{bb3}, including both store instructions in bb0 and bb2.

5.3 Put It Together

Algorithm 3 presents the top level algorithm. The VFG is initialized with direct value flows only, then is dynamically updated by introducing indirect flows until a fixed point. To follow the escape order in computing indirect flows, we maintain three mutually exclusive lists for all memory objects: *processedList* for those whose indirect flows already computed, *updateList* for those whose pointed-to-by set and indirect flows are to be computed, and *waitList* for those whose indirect flows are not ready to be computed. Initially, all memory objects are in *updateList* and the other two lists are set to $\emptyset$.

In lines 4 - 6, the pointed-to-by set for each memory object, and the points-to set for each pointer variable are computed in the function call to COMPUTEPTEDSET. Lines 7 - 9 address the incompleteness problem and the set of objects that an object escapes to is calculated in lines 10 - 12. The indirect flows of a memory object will not be computed if it escapes to another object whose indirect flows are not computed yet. It will be put into *waitList* instead (lines 17 - 19). Otherwise, the procedure UPDATEVFG is called at line 22 to compute its indirect flows and update the VFG. Lines 25 - 30 handles the situation when no further updates can be made (due to cyclic escaping relations). The indirect flows of all non-scalar memory objects will be computed, and the VFG is updated accordingly. This guarantees termination if Observation 1 holds. In case when it does not hold, we can select to compute the indirect flows of a scalar object. But it never happens in our experiments.

In UPDATEVFG, the VFG is updated by including indirect flows of alloc_o (line 37). As a result, the pointed-to-by sets of those memory objects that flow to the source of the

Algorithm 3 Flow-sensitive Points-to Analysis using Value Flow Graph

```
    processedList := ∅
    waitList := ∅
    updateList := {All memory objects}
 1: procedure ComputePointsToVFG
 2:     Initialize VFG with direct value flows only
 3:     while updateList ≠ ∅ ∨ waitList ≠ ∅ do
 4:         for every object alloc_o in updateList do
 5:             ComputePtedSet(alloc_o)
 6:         end for
 7:         for any pointer P that is no longer strong update do
 8:             Move pts(P) to updateList
 9:         end for
10:         for every object alloc_o in updateList do
11:             ComputeEspSet(alloc_o)
12:         end for
13:         updated := false
14:         toUpdateList := ∅
15:         for every object alloc_o in updateList do
16:             updateList := updateList \ {alloc_o}
17:             if esp(alloc_o) ∩ {updateList ∪ waitList} ≠ ∅ then
18:                 waitList := waitList ∪ {alloc_o}
19:             else
20:                 updated := true
21:                 Move alloc_o to processedList
22:                 UpdateVFG(alloc_o, toUpdateList)
23:             end if
24:         end for
25:         if updated = false then
26:             for every non-scalar object alloc_o in waitList do
27:                 updateList := updateList ∪ {alloc_o}
28:                 UpdateVFG(alloc_o, toUpdateList)
29:             end for
30:         end if
31:         Move toUpdateList to updateList
32:     end while
33: end procedure
34: procedure UpdateVFG(alloc_o, toUpdateList)
35:     ComputeIndirectFlow(alloc_o)
36:     for each indirect flow S → L of alloc_o do
37:         if S → L ∉ VFG then
38:             Add S → L to VFG
39:             toUpdateList := toUpdateList ∪ pts(S)
40:         end if
41:     end for
42: end procedure
```

newly introduced indirect flows need to be updated (line 38). Note that if escape order is enforced, no processed object needs to be updated. In our experiments, scalar objects with strong updates are never updated once their indirect flows are computed. Hence our algorithm is precise for the benchmarks we studied. In the end, the algorithm terminates when all memory objects are in *processedList* and no more indirect flows can be introduced.

For our example, we have {alloc_a, alloc_b} $\trianglelefteq$ {alloc_A, alloc_B}. The indirect flows of alloc_a and alloc_b are computed first and the VFG is updated as shown in Figure 3 (b). Then the pointed-to-by set of alloc_A and alloc_B are updated. In the end, the points-to set is computed as in Figure 1 (d).

6. EXPERIMENTAL RESULTS

We implemented our value-flow based flow-sensitive points-to analysis (VF-PA) in LLVM [27] and evaluated its efficiency using the six benchmarks in Table 3. The results reported use the LLVM intermediate representation (bitcode files) as the starting point. The runtime includes the

Benchmark	IPA		SS-PA		VF-PA	
	Time (min:sec)	Mem	Time (min:sec)	Mem	Time (min:sec)	Mem
sendmail 8.12.3	0:57	228 MB	2:15	292MB	1:09	881 MB
httpd 2.0.63	0:32	428 MB	8:24	487MB	0:18	655 MB
400.perlbench	0:40	637 MB	-	-	6:48	10 GB
403.gcc	7:31	2590 MB	22:15	1466 MB	3:05	8147 MB
MySQL 4.1.22	36:40	4003 MB	-	-	61:30	4525 MB
OpenSolaris ON b93	232:23	6672 MB	-	-	76:27	14 GB

Table 4: Performance: runtime and memory consumption for the insensitive analysis (IPA), the semi-sparse flow-sensitive points-to analysis (SS-PA), and our value-flow based flow-sensitive analysis (VF-PA).

Benchmarks	#Objs	Initial VFG		Final VFG			
		#Nodes	#Edges	#Nodes	#Edges		
					Total	Direct	Indirect
sendmail 8.12.3	1418	54211	48988	154291	233723	138712	95011
httpd 2.0.63	3727	96221	80921	96677	82919	81231	1688
400.perlbench	2150	164122	137889	2092368	2681002	1864585	816417
403.gcc	5229	563528	516215	1506878	1845397	1369374	476023
MySQL 4.1.22	8324	263393	217865	482363	191856971	390728	191466243
OpenSolaris ON b93	5931	275135	241251	2590295	2633313	2171245	462068

Table 5: Statistics of the VFG at the beginning and end of the analysis.

Benchmark	NC-LOC (lines of code)			Bitcode files
	C	C++	Total	
sendmail 8.12.3	84.2K	0	84.2k	8.9MB
httpd 2.0.63	174.8K	0	174.8k	9.1MB
400.perlbench	126.3K	0	126.3K	11.9MB
403.gcc	236.3K	0	236.3K	39.4MB
MySQL™ 4.1.22	473.4K	413.3K	886.7K	69.0MB
OpenSolaris ON b93	8.5M	87K	8.6M	1.44GB

Table 3: Summary of the benchmark data.

time in loading the bitcode files to memory, building the intermediate representation, as well as the time in performing our analysis. Several large applications in different areas are selected in our evaluation: sendmail and httpd are two popular applications used in previous points-to analysis work [37, 23]. 400.perlbench and 403.gcc are two large benchmarks from CPU2006. MySQL is a popular open source database and OpenSolaris is a general-purpose operating system. For each benchmark, we list its version or build number, the number of non-commented lines of C/C++ code (NC-LOC) generated by the SLOCCount [36] tool, and the size of the bitcode files generated by the LLVM frontend.

We compare our analysis with two different points-to analysis algorithms: the semi-sparse flow-sensitive (SS-PA) points-to analysis [19] and the insensitive points-to analysis (IPA) in LLVM. SS-PA is one of the latest flow-sensitive points-to analysis techniques. IPA is an Anderson-style analysis with several recent optimization techniques [16, 17] implemented and it is regarded as the state-of-the-art insensitive points-to analysis implementation. SS-PA represents points-to sets using BDDs, while in both VF-PA and IPA, pointer information is represented using sparse bitmaps. Table 4 summarizes the runtime and memory usage for the six benchmarks on an AMD Opteron 2.9GHz processor with 16G of memory.

The implementation of SS-PA is downloaded from the website of its developer. It cannot pass the three benchmarks 400.perlbench, MySQL, and OpenSolaris due to assertion failure. For the other three benchmarks, our analysis is 28X faster in httpd, 7X faster in 403.gcc and twice as fast in sendmail.

As shown in the table, our approach also outperforms the insensitive analysis (IPA) in httpd, 403.gcc, and OpenSolaris. The runtime is similar for both analyses in sendmail. The biggest performance improvement is in OpenSolaris, where we achieve more than three times speedup. The large performance improvements come from the following three facts: 1) we do not propagate large points-to information in the VFG, 2) flow-sensitivity can be cheaply achieved by solving the simple flow equation 2 in the sparse graph, and 3) we avoid frequent re-computation of indirect flows by following the escape order. For example, in 403.gcc, we have to compute the indirect flows of all non-scalar memory objects only once (lines 23 - 28 in Algorithm 3). Note that when recomputing the indirect flows of an object, only its local flows in those functions where the set of instructions dereferencing it have changed need to be recomputed.

On the other hand, we observe some slowdowns in MySQL and 400.perlbench. The worst case is 400.perlbench, in which we are almost an order of magnitude slower than IPA. The reason is that there are many global variables in this benchmark. In our approach, these global variables are cloned in every function where they are used when computing their indirect flows (Section 5.2.1). As a result, a large number of local copies are introduced as shown in Table 5: the number of nodes in the final VFG is much larger than in the initial VFG. A manual spot inspection suggests that most of those copies are not necessary. Hence there is scope for further optimizations of our approach.

The introduced auxiliary variables for inter-procedural indirect flows is also one of the reasons why VF-PA consumes more memory than IPA for all benchmarks. The other reason is that we need to represent each store instruction as a distinct node in the VFG for the sake of flow-sensitivity. Hence our approach consumes more memory although it is more precise and the points-to set sizes are smaller. One effective way to optimize the memory footprint would be to use BDDs to represent pointer information. As shown in the table, SS-PA consumes much less memory with the BDD representation.

Table 5 compares the initial VFG with the final VFG. For each benchmark, we list the number of memory objects, as well as the number of nodes and edges of the initial and final VFGs. OpenSolaris and sendmail are built into multiple modules and for the two benchmarks, we show the largest VFG in the table. The initial VFG has only direct flow edges. In the final VFG, the number of both indirect and direct flow edges, as well as the total number of edges are presented.

As shown in Table 5, the final VFG is much larger than the initial VFG. For 400.perlbench, there are 12 times more nodes and almost 20 times more edges in the final VFG. Most of these extra nodes are introduced local copies of global variables. The benchmark httpd has the smallest number of nodes and edges in the final VFG, and it can be analyzed very efficiently as shown in Table 4. On the other hand, the benchmark MySQL has the largest number of indirect flow edges due to its C++ code, and it takes a long time for both IPA and VF-PA to analyze.

7. CONCLUSION AND FUTURE WORK

In this paper, we presented a new method that applies value flow analysis to compute flow-sensitive pointer information. The method is intuitive and can be easily adopted in modern compilers. We demonstrated the efficiency of our approach by showing that the performance is comparable with the state-of-the-art flow-insensitive points-to analysis implementation.

Our future work includes optimizing the memory consumption of our approach by using BDDs and extending the analysis to be context-sensitive. We are also looking into applying our analysis together with other value flow analyses to make them more effective.

References

[1] L. O. Andersen. *Program Analysis and Specialization for the C Programming Language.* PhD thesis, DIKU, University of Copenhagen, Fall 1994.

[2] M. Berndl, O. Lhoták, F. Qian, L. Hendren, and N. Umanee. Points-to analysis using bdds. In *Proceedings of the ACM SIGPLAN 2003 conference on Programming language design and implementation*, PLDI '03, pages 103–114, New York, NY, USA, 2003. ACM.

[3] R. Bodik. *Path-sensitive, value-flow optimizations of programs.* PhD thesis, Pittsburgh, PA, USA, 1999.

[4] R. Bodik and S. Anik. Path-sensitive value-flow analysis. In *Proceedings of the 25th ACM SIGPLAN-SIGACT symposium on Principles of programming languages*, POPL '98, pages 237–251, New York, NY, USA, 1998. ACM.

[5] D. R. Chase, M. Wegman, and F. K. Zadeck. Analysis of pointers and structures. In *Proceedings of the ACM SIGPLAN 1990 conference on Programming language design and implementation*, PLDI '90, pages 296–310, New York, NY, USA, 1990. ACM.

[6] R. Chatterjee, B. G. Ryder, and W. A. Landi. Relevant context inference. In *Proceedings of the 26th ACM SIGPLAN-SIGACT symposium on Principles of programming languages*, POPL '99, pages 133–146, New York, NY, USA, 1999. ACM.

[7] S. Cherem, L. Princehouse, and R. Rugina. Practical memory leak detection using guarded value-flow analysis. In *Proceedings of the 2007 ACM SIGPLAN conference on Programming language design and implementation*, PLDI '07, pages 480–491, New York, NY, USA, 2007. ACM.

[8] J.-D. Choi, R. Cytron, and J. Ferrante. Automatic construction of sparse data flow evaluation graphs. In *Proceedings of the 18th ACM SIGPLAN-SIGACT symposium on Principles of programming languages*, POPL '91, pages 55–66, New York, NY, USA, 1991. ACM.

[9] F. C. Chow, S. Chan, S.-M. Liu, R. Lo, and M. Streich. Effective representation of aliases and indirect memory operations in ssa form. In *Proceedings of the 6th International Conference on Compiler Construction*, pages 253–267, London, UK, 1996. Springer-Verlag.

[10] R. Cytron, J. Ferrante, B. K. Rosen, M. N. Wegman, and F. K. Zadeck. Efficiently computing static single assignment form and the control dependence graph. *ACM Transactions on Programming Languages and Systems*, 13(4):451–490, October 1991.

[11] N. Dor, S. Adams, M. Das, and Z. Yang. Software validation via scalable path-sensitive value flow analysis. In *Proceedings of the 2004 ACM SIGSOFT international symposium on Software testing and analysis*, ISSTA '04, pages 12–22, New York, NY, USA, 2004. ACM.

[12] M. Fähndrich, J. S. Foster, Z. Su, and A. Aiken. Partial online cycle elimination in inclusion constraint graphs. In *Proceedings of the ACM SIGPLAN 1998 conference on Programming language design and implementation*, PLDI '98, pages 85–96, New York, NY, USA, 1998. ACM.

[13] S. J. Fink, E. Yahav, N. Dor, G. Ramalingam, and E. Geay. Effective typestate verification in the presence of aliasing. *ACM Trans. Softw. Eng. Methodol.*, 17:9:1–9:34, May 2008.

[14] D. Goyal. Transformational derivation of an improved alias analysis algorithm. *Higher Order Symbol. Comput.*, 18:15–49, June 2005.

[15] B. Hackett and A. Aiken. How is aliasing used in systems software? In *Proceedings of the 14th ACM SIGSOFT international symposium on Foundations of software engineering*, SIGSOFT '06/FSE-14, pages 69–80, New York, NY, USA, 2006. ACM.

[16] B. Hardekopf and C. Lin. The ant and the grasshopper: fast and accurate pointer analysis for millions of lines of code. In *Proceedings of the 2007 ACM SIGPLAN conference on Programming language design and implementation*, PLDI '07, pages 290–299, New York, NY, USA, 2007. ACM.

[17] B. Hardekopf and C. Lin. Exploiting pointer and location equivalence to optimize pointer analysis. In *In International Static Analysis Symposium (SAS)*, pages 265–280, 2007.

[18] B. Hardekopf and C. Lin. Semi-sparse flow-sensitive pointer analysis. In *Proceedings of the 36th annual ACM SIGPLAN-SIGACT symposium on Principles of programming languages*, POPL '09, pages 226–238, New York, NY, USA, 2009. ACM.

[19] B. C. Hardekopf. *Pointer analysis: building a foundation for effective program analysis.* PhD thesis, Austin, TX, USA, 2009.

[20] R. Hasti and S. Horwitz. Using static single assignment form to improve flow-insensitive pointer analysis. In *Proceedings of the ACM SIGPLAN 1998 conference on Programming language design and implementation*, PLDI '98, pages 97–105, New York, NY, USA, 1998. ACM.

[21] M. Hind, M. Burke, P. Carini, and J.-D. Choi. Interprocedural pointer alias analysis. *ACM Trans. Program. Lang. Syst.*, 21:848–894, July 1999.

[22] M. Hind and A. Pioli. Assessing the effects of flow-sensitivity on pointer alias analyses. In *Proceedings of the 5th International Symposium on Static Analysis*, SAS '98, pages 57–81, London, UK, 1998. Springer-Verlag.

[23] V. Kahlon. Bootstrapping: a technique for scalable flow and context-sensitive pointer alias analysis. In *Proceedings of the 2008 ACM SIGPLAN conference on Programming language design and implementation*, PLDI '08, pages 249–259, New York, NY, USA, 2008. ACM.

[24] C. Lattner, A. Lenharth, and V. Adve. Making context-sensitive points-to analysis with heap cloning practical for the real world. In *Proceedings of the 2007 ACM SIGPLAN conference on Programming language design and implementation*, PLDI '07, pages 278–289, New York, NY, USA, 2007. ACM.

[25] O. Lhoták and K.-C. A. Chung. Points-to analysis with efficient strong updates. In *Proceedings of the 38th annual ACM SIGPLAN-SIGACT symposium on Principles of programming languages*, POPL '11, pages 3–16, New York, NY, USA, 2011. ACM.

[26] L. Li, C. Cifuentes, and N. Keynes. Practical and effective symbolic analysis for buffer overflow detection. In *Proceedings of the eighteenth ACM SIGSOFT international symposium on Foundations of software engineering*, FSE '10, pages 317–326, New York, NY, USA, 2010. ACM.

[27] LLVM. Low Level Virtual Machine. `http://www.llvm.org`, detail on website.

[28] E. M. Nystrom, H.-S. Kim, and W. mei W. Hwu. Bottom-up and top-down context-sensitive summary-based pointer analysis. In *SAS'04*, pages 165–180, 2004.

[29] J. H. Reif and H. R. Lewis. Symbolic evaluation and the global value graph. In *Proceedings of the 4th ACM SIGACT-SIGPLAN symposium on Principles of programming languages*, POPL '77, pages 104–118, New York, NY, USA, 1977. ACM.

[30] A. Salcianu and M. Rinard. Pointer and escape analysis for multithreaded programs. In *Proceedings of the eighth ACM SIGPLAN symposium on Principles and practices of parallel programming*, PPoPP '01, pages 12–23, New York, NY, USA, 2001. ACM.

[31] M. Sridharan and R. Bodík. Refinement-based context-sensitive points-to analysis for java. In *Proceedings of the 2006 ACM SIGPLAN conference on Programming language design and implementation*, PLDI '06, pages 387–400, New York, NY, USA, 2006. ACM.

[32] S. Staiger-Stöhr. Implementing sparse flow-sensitive andersen analysis. Technical report, UniversitÃd't Stuttgart, 2009.

[33] B. Steensgaard. Points-to analysis in almost linear time. In *Proceedings of the 23rd ACM SIGPLAN-SIGACT symposium on Principles of programming languages*, POPL '96, pages 32–41, New York, NY, USA, 1996. ACM.

[34] T. B. Tok, S. Z. Guyer, and C. Lin. Efficient flow-sensitive interprocedural data-flow analysis in the presence of pointers. In *In 15th International Conference on Compiler Construction*, pages 17–31. Springer, 2006.

[35] J. Whaley and M. S. Lam. Cloning-based context-sensitive pointer alias analysis using binary decision diagrams. In *Proceedings of the ACM SIGPLAN 2004 conference on Programming language design and implementation*, PLDI '04, pages 131–144, New York, NY, USA, 2004. ACM.

[36] D. A. Wheeler. SLOC Count User Guide. `http://www.dwheeler.com/sloccount/`. Last accessed: 16 March 2009.

[37] H. Yu, J. Xue, W. Huo, X. Feng, and Z. Zhang. Level by level: making flow- and context-sensitive pointer analysis scalable for millions of lines of code. In *Proceedings of the 8th annual IEEE/ACM international symposium on Code generation and optimization*, CGO '10, pages 218–229, New York, NY, USA, 2010. ACM.

[38] B. Zheng and P. chung Yew. A hierarchical approach to context-sensitive interprocedural alias analysis, 1999.

[39] J. Zhu. Towards scalable flow and context sensitive pointer analysis. In *Proceedings of the 42nd annual Design Automation Conference*, DAC '05, pages 831–836, New York, NY, USA, 2005. ACM.

[40] J. Zhu and S. Calman. Symbolic pointer analysis revisited. In *Proceedings of the ACM SIGPLAN 2004 conference on Programming language design and implementation*, PLDI '04, pages 145–157, New York, NY, USA, 2004. ACM.

On the Congruence of Modularity and Code Coupling

Fabian Beck Stephan Diehl
Computer Science
University of Trier, Germany
{beckf,diehl}@uni-trier.de

ABSTRACT

Software systems are modularized to make their inherent complexity manageable. While there exists a set of well-known principles that may guide software engineers to design the modules of a software system, we do not know which principles are followed in practice. In a study based on 16 open source projects, we look at different kinds of coupling concepts between source code entities, including structural dependencies, fan-out similarity, evolutionary coupling, code ownership, code clones, and semantic similarity. The congruence between these coupling concepts and the modularization of the system hints at the modularity principles used in practice. Furthermore, the results provide insights on how to support developers to modularize software systems.

Categories and Subject Descriptors

D.2.8 [**Software Engineering**]: Metrics—*Software science*

General Terms

Design, Experimentation, Measurement

1. INTRODUCTION

Applying the age-old warfare strategy of *divide and conquer* to a software system, its complexity can be managed by modularizing it into smaller parts. Every non-trivial software system is modularized on different levels of abstraction and employing different techniques. For instance, classes enclose related functionalities, packages summarize classes into subsystems, components provide reusable units of source code, or aspects represent cross-cutting features.

When modularization came up, Parnas [19] introduced the concept of information hiding, which became a fundamental paradigm for designing software systems. Shortly thereafter, Stevens et al. [23] proposed the principle of low coupling and high cohesion: While modules should only be loosely coupled, the elements of a module are supposed to be highly cohesive. Moreover, Conway [11] observed that modularity of a product is connected with the structure of the organization that designs the product. These principles and theories put forward different criteria to modularize a system. *But we do not know which design principles are really used in practice.*

In this paper we want to approach this question and validate known design principles by looking at the different types of relationships that connect the entities of a software system. These relationships, which we call *code couplings*, may explain the design decisions that constitute the modularization of a system. In particular, we will compare a set of different code coupling concepts to the package structures of Java systems. This comparison will be based on a metric that measures the congruence between coupling and modularity. We will show that different principles impact the studied software systems, but none of them dominates the modular structures.

In the rest of this paper, we first briefly review different principles on modularizing software systems as well as different code coupling concepts (Section 2). Then, we present our study analyzing the relationship between the coupling concepts and the modularization of the systems (Section 3): We contrast the information contained in the coupling concepts (Section 3.1). Based on a measure of congruence between the coupling concepts and modularity, we compare the coupling types to find out which concepts impact the modularization most (Section 3.2). By classifying the modules of the systems, we furthermore derive coupling patterns for different module types (Section 3.3). While the discussion shows some limitations of the study, it also raises possible implications of the results for designing and maintaining software systems (Section 4). Finally, we present related research (Section 5) and conclude the paper (Section 6).

2. MODULARITY AND COUPLING

> "For human beings, the only way to manage a complex system or solve a problem is to break it up." [3]

Modularizing a system to manage its complexity is not unique to software engineering, but is part of every engineering or design process. Baldwin and Clark [3] summarize this idea in an interdisciplinary theory on modularity. They argue that a well-modularized system or design allows concurrently working on different parts in parallel, makes a larger complexity manageable, and hides uncertainties into modules.

Permission to make digital or hard copies of all or part of this work for personal or classroom use is granted without fee provided that copies are not made or distributed for profit or commercial advantage and that copies bear this notice and the full citation on the first page. To copy otherwise, to republish, to post on servers or to redistribute to lists, requires prior specific permission and/or a fee.
ESEC/FSE'11, September 5–9, 2011, Szeged, Hungary.
Copyright 2011 ACM 978-1-4503-0443-6/11/09 ...$10.00.

2.1 Modularity Principles

In software engineering, different design principles were proposed on how to create a good modular structure of software systems. We will briefly outline these principles in the following.

2.1.1 *Low Coupling and High Cohesion (P1)*

Stevens et al. propose to focus on the data communication dependencies of a program [23]. The target characteristic of good modularization is that the elements of each single module are highly cohesive (i.e., connected by many dependencies), while elements belonging to different modules should be low coupled (i.e., connected by few dependencies)—short, *low coupling and high cohesion*. This principle might be considered as the default approach when analyzing or retrieving the modularization of a software system.

2.1.2 *Information Hiding (P2)*

Parnas introduced the principle of *information hiding* [18, 19]—hiding design decisions inside modules. Slim interfaces should represent the facade of the module. The design starts with identifying a set of important design decisions that may change during development. Each of these decisions should be encapsulated in an independent module. As a result of this process, changes in the software system should be limited within the boundaries of a module. Information hiding later on became one of the main principles of the object oriented paradigm [16].

2.1.3 *Conway's Law (P3)*

Conway formulated a general law on the congruence between organizations and the products they design [11]: "[...] organizations which design systems [...] are constrained to produce designs which are copies of the communication structures of these organizations."

Conway's law does not directly state guidelines to modularize a software system. Nevertheless, it implies the principle that the design of a system, and hence its modularization as a part of the design, should match the structure of the organization. Otherwise, the intended design would conflict with the social preconditions and may not be enforceable in practice.

2.1.4 *Others (P4)*

Besides these three often cited principles, there are other explicit modularity principles or principles that at least impact modularity.

a) Martin [15] introduced three package design principles: the *reuse-release equivalence principle*, the *common-reuse principle*, and the *common-closure principle*. These principles propose that the package reflects the granule of reuse, release, and change.

b) Architectural styles like *client-server* or *pipes-and-filters* provide a tight framework for modularization; layered architectures impose rules on the structural dependencies of the modules.

c) The idea of separating concerns, which led to the development of aspect-oriented programming [25], could govern the modular structure of a software system in form of non-cross-cutting concerns.

d) Domain knowledge is one of the key strategies to identify classes in object-oriented analysis [16].

In summary, various principles exist on how to modularize software systems. They focus on different aspects of software engineering: While the principle of low coupling and high cohesion looks at the source code, information hiding and Conway's law take the development process into account. In turn, others reflect the domain the software is part of (identification of classes) or consider the ecosystem around the software (common-reuse principle). It is reasonable to assume that these principles are not independent but interact with each other. A consistent theory or framework to formally summarize or compare these principles, however, does not exist.

2.2 Code Coupling Concepts

If applied, modularity principles, as those discussed above, leave traces in the structure and evolution of a software system. Since modularizing a system means grouping its elements based on their connecting properties, the principles are closely related to the relationships of code entities. We will use the general term *coupling* to refer to such a relationship. While the frequently used term *dependency* implies a cause and effect of the connecting property, the term *coupling* is not necessarily directed and is neutral with respect to causality. Please note, that *code coupling* has here a different meaning than the term *coupling* as used in the principle of low coupling and high cohesion (*P1*): While, in the principle, it only denotes cross-module relationships, we will use the term in general for relationships.

In this study, we focus on object-oriented software systems, namely, systems mainly written in Java. Such systems are modularized into packages that themselves may include further packages. These hierarchically organized packages form a mid-level of abstraction and will be considered as the modularization of a system in this study.

Classes and interfaces are the basic elements of a package. As a matter of simplification, we will use the term *class* interchangeable for *classes and interfaces*. Together with a coupling concept, the classes form a graph data structure. The package modularization defines a hierarchy on the classes. Formally, this data structure can be described as a five-tupel $G = (\mathcal{C}, P, E, I, \mu)$—called a *directed weighted compound graph*—where $\mathcal{C}$ is the set of classes, P is the set of packages, $E \subset \mathcal{C} \times \mathcal{C}$ is the set of directed couplings, $I \subset (\mathcal{C} \cup P) \times (\mathcal{C} \cup P)$ contains the inclusion edges of the package hierarchy, and $\mu : E \rightarrow \mathbb{R}_0^+$ is the coupling weight function. Furthermore, $((\mathcal{C} \cup P), I)$ forms a tree with leaves $\mathcal{C}$ and inner vertices P.

Quite a number of different coupling concepts have been proposed in software engineering literature. In the following we will introduce the set of coupling concepts that we will analyze in our study. We will also discuss possible relationships between the coupling concepts and the modularity principles as conjectures.

2.2.1 *Structural Dependencies (SD)*

A method calls another method, a class extends another class, or a class aggregates objects of another class—all this creates a direct dependency between two classes. These static structural code dependencies are most frequently used when analyzing or leveraging code coupling.

In our study we distinguish the following three types of structural dependencies.

SD.Inh *Two classes are coupled (directed) if one class extends the other class. If coupled, the coupling weight is 1.*

SD.Agg *Two classes are coupled (directed) if one class aggregates another by having class variables using the other class. The coupling weight is the number of class variables relying on the other class.*

SD.Use *Two classes are coupled (directed) if one class uses the other class in a method as a local variable, a method parameter, or by calling a method of the other class. The coupling weight is the number of methods using the other class.*

We use the tool *DependencyFinder* to retrieve these structural dependencies from compiled Java bytecode.

Conjecture: Structural dependencies are a straightforward approach to measure the data communication for the principle of low coupling and high cohesion (*P1*). Introduced prior to object-oriented design, it is, however, not clear how to rate the different types of the object-oriented structural dependencies when applying the principle.

2.2.2 Fan-Out Similarity (FO)

Structural dependencies might not only *directly* couple two code entities but also *indirectly*: Two entities connected to the same set of other entities might indicate a similar purpose or functionality of these two entities. We refer to these indirect structural couplings as *fan-out similarity*.

A feature vector describes the fan-out for each class. Each feature represents the number of direct structural dependencies (SD) to a particular class. If two vectors of two classes are similar, the classes reference similar other classes. To quantify the similarity, we employ the cosine similarity measure, which computes the angle between the vectors but does not take their lengths into account [24].

We again distinguish three types of structural information. Orthogonally, external fan-out similarity (abbreviated *E*), which is based on references to external libraries, contrasts internal fan-out similarity (abbreviated *I*), which only considers the dependencies between the classes of the system.

FO.InhE, FO.IhnI *Two classes are coupled (undirected) if they extend the same class or implement a similar set of interfaces. The coupling weight is the cosine similarity of the* **inheritance** *feature vectors.*

FO.AggE, FO.AggI *Two classes are coupled (undirected) if they aggregate a similar set of classes. The coupling weight is the cosine similarity of the* **aggregation** *feature vectors.*

FO.UseE, FO.UseI *Two classes are coupled (undirected) if they use a similar set of classes. The coupling weight is the cosine similarity of the* **usage** *feature vectors.*

Conjecture: Rather than optimizing coupling and cohesion (P1), grouping together similar classes with respect to fan-out similarity aligns the structural dependencies of the grouped classes. High similarity regarding external fan-out shows the common use of the same external functionality, which might hint at being covered by the same concern (*P4c*)—cross-cutting concerns have been detected based on this idea [8].

If we assume that a class of the system reflects a design decision, then, depending on the same class means depending on that design decision. Following the principle of information hiding (*P2*), the two elements depending on the same internal class should be placed into the same module to hide the design decision. Hence, similar internal fan-out similarity could be an indicator for information hiding as Schwanke argues [22].

2.2.3 Evolutionary Coupling (EC)

If two classes are frequently changed together during development, this reveals an implicit dependency. Since this information stems from the evolution of the software, we call the coupling concept *evolutionary coupling*, which is also known as *co-change coupling* or *logical coupling*.

We measure evolutionary coupling in terms of two established measures, *support* and *confidence*. The support value of a coupling counts how often the two coupled software artifacts were changed together. Additionally, the confidence value of a coupling normalizes the support by the total number of changes of one of the artifacts. While *support* is a symmetric metric, *confidence* is not because of its asymmetric normalization (see [4] for details). Support and confidence produce two coupling variants that relate the same classes but differ concerning their weights.

EC.Sup *Two classes are coupled (undirected) if they were changed together during development. The coupling weight reflects the number of common changes (***support***).*

EC.Conf *Two classes are coupled (directed) if they were changed together during development. The coupling weight reflects the number of common changes relative to the number of changes of the first compared class (***confidence***).*

We use the approach by Zimmermann and Weißgerber [28] to extract the evolutionary class dependency graphs from the version archives. As common when mining software repositories, we omit large transactions (transactions including more than 25 classes) to reduce noise.

Conjecture: Information hiding (*P2*) argues that hiding design decisions increases the changeability of a system because changing a design decision causes only local changes in one module [19]. Hence, information hiding should rather lead to local changes, which result in local evolutionary coupling. Conversely, if the changes are local, this could also have other reasons, for instance, a strict module ownership policy, where each package has an owner who is responsible for it.

2.2.4 Code Clones (CC)

Code clones are fragments of code that are equivalent or similar. They introduce another concept of coupling: For example, changing a cloned code fragment often requires to change the other fragments of the clone group, too.

Comparing two classes, we take their overlap in terms of cloned code into account to get a similarity measure. Liviery et al. [14] introduced a coverage metric for this purpose. We employ this metric in a slightly adapted version:

$$\mu_{cc}(c_1, c_2) = \frac{\|cc(c_1, c_2)\|}{\|c_1\| + \|c_2\|}$$

where $\|c\|$ is the size of class c measured in number of tokens and $cc(c_1, c_2)$ denotes the set of code fragments covered by common clones between classes c_1 and c_2.

We use the code clone detection API *JCCD* [5] and apply two configurations: The first one detects Type I clones—exact matches of code fragments ignoring code layout and comments. The second one detects Type II clones—code fragments that are equivalent when generalizing from identifier names and also ignoring code layout and comments [20].

CC.I *Two classes are coupled (undirected) if they share* **Type I clones***. The coupling weight is the clone coverage* μ_{cc}

CC.II *Two classes are coupled (undirected) if they share* **Type II clones***. The coupling weight is the clone coverage* μ_{cc}

Conjecture: It may sound strange that the *bad* smell of duplicated code should indicate a *good* design principle. But code clones are often introduced for good reasons, for example, performance improvement, forking, generative programming, or reducing dependencies [20]. Depending on the purpose, code clones may disguise other couplings. For instance, copied code could replace an inheritance connection (*SD.Inh*) or a method call that would otherwise lead to a usage dependency (*SD.Use*) or a similar fan-out (*FO*).

2.2.5 Code Ownership (CO)

The main author of a code entity is the expert to be contacted when there is a problem or question concerning this code. If two code entities have the same author or authors, they could be covered by the same expertise.

To compare classes based on their owner, we list the developers who have ever changed a particular class and transform this list into a binary vector. In a more elaborate approach, we proportionally quantify the code ownership: For each class, the number of changes made by a particular author is divided by the total number of changes. Both metrics produce couplings relating the same classes but with different weights.

CO.Bin *Two classes are coupled (undirected) if they share common authors. The coupling weight is the cosine similarity of the* **binary** *ownership vectors.*

CO.Prop *Two classes are coupled (undirected) if they share common authors. The coupling weight is the cosine similarity of the* **proportional** *ownership vectors.*

Conjecture: Bowman and Holt [7] argue that, if two code entities have a common author, communication between the developers of two entities is likely. Hence, code ownership similarity is a way to map parts of the communication structure of the development team into the source code. Referring to Conway's Law (*P3*), the design of the system is said to follow this communication structure.

2.2.6 Semantic Similarity (SS)

Interpreting the source code of classes as plain text documents, the classes are coupled, like text documents, by their common vocabulary. In this case, the vocabulary consists of the identifiers used in the code and the words in the comments. Standard information retrieval methods for semantically relating documents can be applied.

Each class is described as a bag of words which is transformed into a vector where each dimension counts the number of occurrences of a particular term. To counterbalance the importance of frequently occurring terms across documents, we apply the *tf-idf* measure. Furthermore, we use *latent semantic indexing* (*LSI*) to consider related terms as a concept and to reduce noise.

SS.Tfidf *Two classes are coupled (undirected) if they share a similar vocabulary. The coupling weight is the cosine similarity of the* **tf-idf** *document vectors.*

SS.LSI *Two classes are coupled (undirected) if they share a similar vocabulary. The coupling weight is the cosine similarity of the* **LSI** *document vectors.*

In particular, we implemented an approach very similar to the one used by Kuhn et al. to cluster source code documents [13]: From the source code of a class including comments, we excluded the license text and, much more important in our scenario, the package name and the names of its ancestor packages. The preprocessing splits camel-case words into their components, removes meaningless words based on Java key words and a list of English stop words, and normalizes the words by reducing them to their stem based on the *Porter* algorithm. The resulting document vector is balanced by applying *tf-idf*, and finally transformed into an *LSI* model with 30 dimensions. We applied the Python APIs *stemming* and *gensim* to implement the process.

Conjecture: Among the presented coupling concepts, the domain knowledge incorporated in the package design (*P4d*) might be best reflected in the vocabulary used in the source code text. The terms describing a domain concept should also appear in the code as identifier names or in comments. The problem, however, could be that, besides these domain-related terms, many other circumstances influence the vocabulary, like reference to other code entities, information on the author, applied design patterns that bring in a certain terminology, etc.

3. STUDY

Based on the source code and its accompanying information, it is hard to directly conclude what principles were used to design the modular structure of a software system. Hence, we abstract the software project by reducing it to a set of different coupling concepts between the classes of the system. Analyzing the coupling concepts and their impact on modularity builds the foundation for indirectly drawing conclusions on principles applied. In particular, we want to empirically answer three questions:

- How do the different coupling concepts relate to each other? (Section 3.1)
- What is the impact of each coupling concept on the modularization? (Section 3.2)
- Are there specific differences in this impact for different package types? (Section 3.3)

The study examines the modularity of 16 open source software projects—Table 1 provides a complete list. Each of these projects is mainly written in Java and hosted at *sourceforge.net*. We selected a broad spectrum of application types, varying from small to mid-size projects. The number of packages that directly contain classes shows the size of the hierarchy, the number of classes provides an estimate of the size of the project. *CVS* or *SVN* repositories provide data about the development history of the projects. For the studied projects, the available development activity spans 10 months to up to 9 years or 126 to up to 4602 check-in transactions (only counting the transactions where relevant Java classes were checked in) involving up to 23 developers. To extract the coupling information, we mirrored the repositories and downloaded a compiled version of the software in form of a *jar* file. The structural dependencies (*SD*) as well as the fan-out references (*FO*) were derived from the *jar* file. By the date of release, we determined the corresponding version of the Java source code. This version is used to retrieve the code clone information (*CC*) and the semantic similarity (*SS*). Finally, the extraction of evolutionary coupling (*EC*) and code ownership coupling (*CC*) required to process the whole repository from the first check-in up to the version corresponding to the selected release. We used the released *jar* file as a reference to determine the set of classes considered for analysis (excluding contained third-party libraries). Other classes possibly contained in the repository like test classes, experimental functionality,

Table 1: Properties of the sample of software projects and their repositories.

Project	Description	Version	#Pack.	#Classes	Repos.	Time frame	#Trans.	#Dev.
Checkstyle	coding conventions	5.1	21	261	SVN	2001-06-22 – 2010-02-16	1335	6
Cobertura	test coverage	1.9.4.1	19	99	SVN	2005-02-12 – 2010-03-03	226	6
CruiseControl	continuous integration	2.8.4	27	295	SVN	2001-03-26 – 2010-09-16	1615	10
iText	PDF library	5.0.5	24	402	SVN	2007-12-20 – 2010-11-02	817	7
JabRef	BibTeX management	2.6	37	499	SVN	2003-10-16 – 2010-04-14	1348	23
JEdit	text editor	4.3.2	28	488	SVN	2001-09-03 – 2010-05-09	2927	23
JFreeChart	chart library	1.0.13	37	587	SVN	2007-06-19 – 2009-04-20	551	2
JFtp	FTP client	1.0	7	78	CVS	2002-02-06 – 2003-03-23	155	5
JHotDraw	GUI framework	7.6	65	679	SVN	2006-11-22 – 2011-01-09	302	2
JUnit	regression testing	4.5	23	119	CVS	2007-12-07 – 2008-08-08	126	2
LWJGL	gaming library	2.7.1	27	564	SVN	2002-08-09 – 2011-02-10	1557	11
PMD	code problems	4.2	47	565	SVN	2002-06-24 – 2008-03-26	2041	18
Stripes	web framework	1.5.5	19	238	SVN	2005-09-07 – 2011-01-04	812	7
SweetHome3D	interior design	3.1	8	167	CVS	2006-04-11 – 2011-02-13	1807	1
TV-Browser	program guide	2.7.6	62	485	SVN	2003-04-25 – 2010-12-19	4602	12
Wicket	web framework	1.2.2	86	622	SVN	2004-12-21 – 2006-08-27	3456	12

SD Inh	0.012	0.009	0.0014	0.0041	0.015	0.0045	0.0047	0.058	0.053	0.071	0.022	0.024	0.0048	0.011	0.12	0.094
0.012	SD Agg	0.31	0.0018	0.015	0.028	0.0007	0.0065	0.011	0.056	0.04	0.022	0.025	0.0019	0.0027	0.052	0.039
0.009	0.31	SD Use	0.00024	0.022	0.013	5.6e-05	0.014	0.017	0.043	0.019	0.0066	0.0073	0.0009	0.0007	0.034	0.025
0.0014	0.0018	0.00024	FO InhE	0.044	0.064	0.11	0.073	0.0029	0.052	0.061	0.14	0.14	0.097	0.15	0.17	0.13
0.0041	0.015	0.022	0.044	FO AggE	0.30	0.047	0.15	0.092	0.095	0.059	0.063	0.057	0.032	0.15	0.13	0.12
0.015	0.028	0.013	0.064	0.30	FO UseE	0.15	0.07	0.17	0.13	0.13	0.10	0.10	0.11	0.18	0.22	0.21
0.0045	0.0007	5.6e-05	0.11	0.047	0.15	FO InhI	0.13	0.30	0.085	0.12	0.042	0.044	0.18	0.21	0.25	0.24
0.0047	0.0065	0.014	0.073	0.15	0.07	0.13	FO AggI	0.23	0.064	0.045	0.09	0.077	0.0021	0.032	0.13	0.13
0.058	0.011	0.017	0.0029	0.092	0.17	0.30	0.23	FO UseI	0.093	0.084	0.071	0.067	0.17	0.19	0.29	0.31
0.053	0.056	0.043	0.052	0.095	0.13	0.085	0.064	0.093	EC Sup	0.42	0.15	0.17	0.015	0.049	0.23	0.19
0.071	0.04	0.019	0.061	0.059	0.13	0.12	0.045	0.084	0.42	EC Conf	0.19	0.20	0.043	0.068	0.28	0.22
0.022	0.022	0.0066	0.14	0.063	0.10	0.042	0.09	0.071	0.15	0.19	CO Bin	0.93	0.0097	0.069	0.14	0.13
0.024	0.025	0.0073	0.14	0.057	0.10	0.044	0.077	0.067	0.17	0.20	0.93	CO Prop	0.0084	0.065	0.15	0.14
0.0048	0.0019	0.0009	0.097	0.032	0.11	0.18	0.0021	0.17	0.015	0.043	0.0097	0.0084	CC I	0.82	0.32	0.24
0.011	0.0027	0.0007	0.15	0.15	0.18	0.21	0.032	0.19	0.049	0.068	0.069	0.065	0.82	CC II	0.33	0.26
0.12	0.052	0.034	0.17	0.13	0.22	0.25	0.13	0.29	0.23	0.28	0.14	0.15	0.32	0.33	SS Tfidf	0.83
0.094	0.039	0.025	0.13	0.12	0.21	0.24	0.13	0.31	0.19	0.22	0.13	0.14	0.24	0.26	0.83	SS LSI

Figure 1: Correlation between coupling graphs.

or unused legacy code are skipped. For simplification, we ignored anonymous and inner classes by considering them just as parts of the containing class.

3.1 Dimensions of Coupling

The first part of our analysis will compare the different coupling concepts themselves, yet ignoring the modular structure of the system. We may consider each concept as one dimension to describe a software system. If two concepts share some information, these dimensions would not be orthogonal, but correlated.

3.1.1 Method

For a project, each coupling concept provides a graph on the same set of classes. To compare the concepts, we describe each concept as a vector. A dimension of such a vector represents a pair of classes; its value reflects the weight of the edge between the two classes or is zero if there is no edge for this combination. Hence, a project consisting of n classes is described as an n^2-dimensional vector for each coupling concept. Concatenating theses vectors for all projects, we get a summarized vector $\vec{v}_{co}$ describing the coupling concept co. To equally weigh each project, we align the number of dimensions by randomly sampling 20,000 dimensions (with repetition) for each project. Finally, the Pearson correlation of two vectors $\vec{v}_{co_1}$ and $\vec{v}_{co_2}$ provides a measure of similarity for two concepts co_1 and co_2.

3.1.2 Results

We computed the pairwise correlation for all combinations of coupling concepts and visualize the resulting correlation matrix in Figure 1. High values indicate a strong (positive) correlation between two coupling concepts, which means, if two classes are coupled by the first concept, it is likely that they are also coupled by the second concept and vice versa.

The first, quite surprising observation is that the matrix is sparsely filled with high correlations—only few combinations of concepts near the diagonal are strongly correlated. These strong relationships can be identified as similarities between metrics measuring variants of the same concept, for instance, the two code ownership metrics *CO.Bin* and *CO.Prop*. But it is not always true that variants of the same concept provide similar data as the inheritance dependencies show: *SD.Inh* is only weakly correlated to the other variants of the structural dependencies. Such a statistical independence advocates to consider inheritance dependencies as an independent concept.

Off the diagonal, we mostly observe very weak correlations, which indicates that the coupling concepts indeed provide different coupling information. Though based on the same underlying information, structural dependencies are not considerably correlated with fan-out similarity. Analyzing the few somewhat stronger cross-concept correlations (0.10 – 0.35), we observe some interesting relationships:

- Ownership couplings (*CO*) correlate with evolutionary couplings (*EC*). An explanation is that both are based on the check-in information. Two files can only be coupled by evolution if they share at least one common author.
- Coupling by code clones (*CC*) shares some information with internal and external inheritance and us-

age fan-out (*FO.InhE*, *FO.UseE*, *FO.InhI*, *FO.UseI*) but clearly less with aggregation fan-out (*FO.AggE*, *FO.AggI*). The relationship to inheritance could be caused by code that implements or overrides the same methods in the same or similar way in two sibling classes of the inheritance hierarchy. Furthermore, the references used in code clones are necessarily equal and lead to a certain usage similarity, but do not directly imply similar aggregation.

- Semantic similarity (*SS*) is linked to most other coupling metrics, only structural aggregation and usage dependencies form an exception (*SD.Agg*, *SD.Use*). Since this similarity is based on the raw source code text, it partly aggregates other source code based coupling concepts (*SD*, *FO*, *CC*). Often the name of the author is also mentioned in the source code, which explains the correlation to code ownership (*CO*). For the correlation to evolutionary coupling (*EC*), we could not find an evident explanation.

In summary, the correlation matrix shows that the different coupling concepts are quite independent and thus each represents different coupling information. The correlations between metrics for variants of the same concept confirm the grouping of the metrics—except inheritance dependencies, they should not be equated with other structural dependencies.

3.2 Coupling-Modularity Congruence

The central part of this study is to relate the different coupling concepts to the modularity of the software systems. Thus, we have to find a measure of the congruence between a coupling concept and the modularization. This comes down to the problem of how to relate a graph structure (the coupling graph) and a hierarchy (the modularization).

3.2.1 Method

Usually, the extent to which the structure of a system matches its call graph is measured by coupling and cohesion as proposed by the modularity principle of low coupling and high cohesion (*P1*). Since we capture each concept as a graph $G = (\mathcal{C}, P, E, I, \mu)$ (Section 2.2), we are able to apply the same approach to measuring the congruence between coupling and modularity for all coupling concepts. Hence, in the following, *coupling* and *cohesion* are general properties independent of a coupling concept and do not extend the terms used in the modularity principle of low coupling and high cohesion.

An edge connecting two classes of the same package contributes to the cohesion of the package and moreover to the cohesion of the whole system. Just as well, an edge connecting two classes of different packages contributes to the coupling. This model, however, disregards the hierarchical structure of the packages. A more elaborate model also considers the distance of two packages in the hierarchy. Now, an edge e partly accounts to coupling and cohesion depending on the distance it spans.

$$cohesion(e) = \frac{weight(e)}{distance(e)}$$

$$coupling(e) = weight - cohesion(e)$$

The distance function $distance(e)$ counts the number of intermediate nodes on the shortest path through the package hierarchy that connects the source and target of an edge e. Thus, the distance is 1 if the source and target class are in the same package, 2 if, for instance, the source is in a sub-package of the package of the target, etc. The sum of cohesion and coupling always is equal the weight of the edge.

To express coupling and cohesion for a set of classes $C \subseteq \mathcal{C}$ (e.g., a package or the whole system), we sum up the respective cohesion and coupling values for all outgoing edges $out(C)$ and incoming edges $in(C)$ of the classes in the set.

$$cohesion(C) = \sum_{e \in out(C)} cohesion(e) + \sum_{e \in in(C)} cohesion(e)$$

$$coupling(C) = \sum_{e \in out(C)} coupling(e) + \sum_{e \in in(C)} coupling(e)$$

Finally, the cohesion in relation to the coupling expresses the congruence of the coupling graph and the modular structure of the system for a set of classes C, which we denote as *coupling-modularity congruence* (short, *congruence*).

$$congruence(C) = \frac{cohesion(C)}{cohesion(C) + coupling(C)}$$

High congruence values indicate high consistency between coupling and modularity. If the coupling graph is totally independent of the modularity the congruence, however, is not zero but larger because $\forall e \in E : cohesion(e) > 0$. Hence, we have to compute the congruence of such a graph for every project to get a project-specific baseline of the congruence metric. To this end, we take the complete graph which fulfills the independence of the coupling structure and the modularity—every other graph fulfilling the independence condition is just a modularity-independent random sample of the complete graph.

The congruence metric measures the quality of the coupling information with respect to modularity in the graph but not the richness or density of this information. This is intended because we do not want to mix quality and density. Nevertheless, we need a further metric to also measure the density of the congruence information.

The congruence density is high for a set of classes C if the congruence information is good for each class of the set. Hence, we take the average of this class-specific congruence to get a density measure, which we denote as *average class coupling-modularity congruence* (short, *average congruence*).

$$congruence_{avg}(C) = \frac{1}{|C|} \sum_{c \in C} congruence(\{c\})$$

When there is no information available for a class c, hence $out(\{c\}) = in(\{c\}) = \emptyset$, the function $congruence(\{c\})$ is undefined because $cohesion(\{c\})$ and $coupling(\{c\})$ are undefined. In that case, we consider instead the respective baseline value for $\{c\}$ to define the average.

3.2.2 Results

To analyze the relationship between coupling concepts and modularity, we compute the congruence and average congruence for all combinations of projects and coupling concepts,

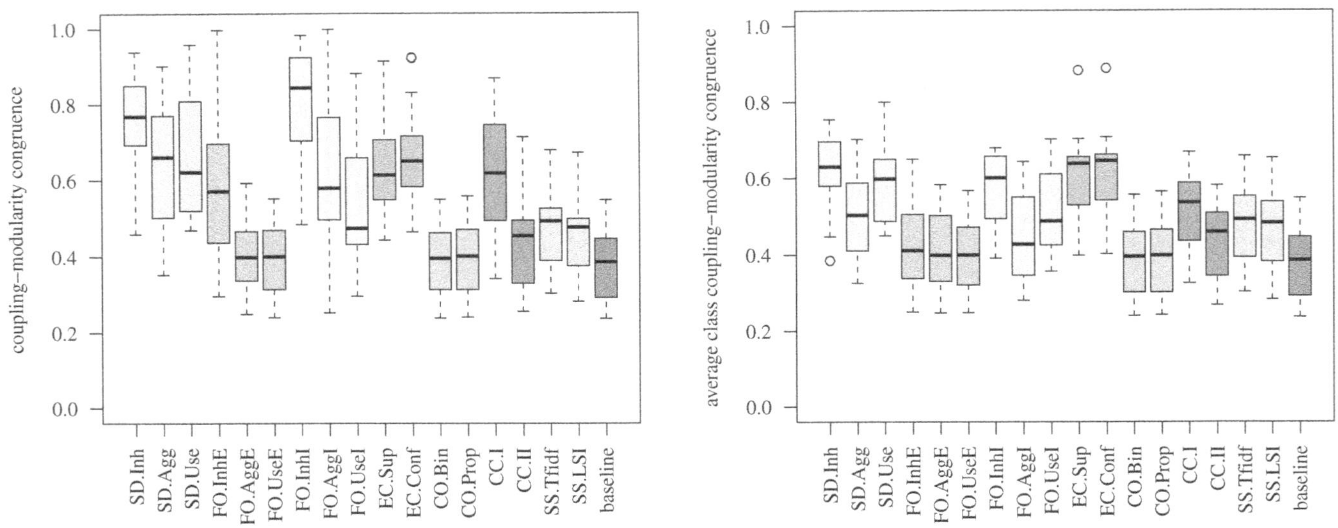

Figure 2: Coupling-modularity congruence and average class coupling-modularity congruence.

in each case considering all classes of the project. Summarized by concept, the result hence is a distribution of congruence values. We present these distributions as box plot diagrams in Figure 2—one diagram for congruence, the other for the average congruence. Such box plot diagrams sketch a distribution by plotting its main characteristic values: the median (horizontal line), the two mid-quartiles (filled box), and the outliers (dashed lines and circles).

The results of structural dependencies (*SD*) show high coupling-modularity congruence values clearly exceeding the baseline congruence. Hence, structural dependencies seem to preferably link classes of the same or neighboring packages. Among the three variants, the inheritance dependencies (*SD.Inh*) provide the best results. Taking also the information density into account, the average congruence values of structural dependencies are also among the overall best results. The usage dependencies gain against the aggregation dependencies.

For the fan-out similarity (*FO*), we observe large differences between external and internal fan-out. While the internal fan-out provides good congruence values, only the inheritance variant of the external fan-out (*FO.InhE*) is able to compete. External aggregation (*FO.AggE*) and usage fan-out (*FO.UseE*) do not seem to be a relevant criterion for modularity because they do not notably top the baseline values. The overall best congruence is reached by taking the internal inheritance fan-out (*FO.InhI*) into account. This fan-out similarity is also among the best average congruence values. Similar to the structural dependencies, again the usage information (*FO.UseI*) gains with respect to density and, together with the inheritance information (*FO.InhI*), shows competitive results for internal fan-out.

Evolutionary coupling (*EC*) is also congruent to the modularity of the systems—the congruence metric shows about equally high values as for structural aggregation and usage dependencies (*SD.Agg*, *SD.Use*). The difference between the two variants of the concept of evolutionary coupling is small but consistently better for the confidence metric (*EC.Conf*) than for the support metric (*EC.Sup*). Relating the common number of changes to the number of total changes as it is done in the confidence metric here shows a positive effect. With respect to density, the results for both evolutionary coupling metrics are very good—the median even is the highest compared to all other concepts.

Code ownership similarity (*CO*) does not impact modularity as clearly as most other analyzed coupling concepts. The congruence and average congruence only slightly exceed the baseline. This is, by the way, no problem of granularity—ignoring the lowest levels of packages, the congruence does not improve with respect to the baseline.

Instances of the same Type I clone can be often found in the same package as indicated by the high congruence values for this metric (*CC.I*). This is not true to the same extent for the more lax Type II clones (*CC.II*). Surprisingly, the density of Type I clones is high enough to also provide good average congruence values. Here, the inherently denser Type II clone information shows at least medium results.

Finally, the semantic similarity (*SS*) turns out to only be a second class factor for modularity. Though the congruence and average congruence clearly rise above the baseline, they cannot compete with the high values of other concepts. Notably, the more elaborate *LSI* variant of the semantic similarity (*SS.LSI*) consistently falls below the simpler *tf-idf* variant (*SS.Tfidf*). The negative impact of loosing some information by dimension reduction seems to outweigh the positive effect of noise reduction.

In general, we got the best coupling-modularity congruence for structural dependencies (*SD*), internal fan-out similarity (*FO.*I*), evolutionary coupling (EC), and Type I code clones (*CC.I*). Among the structural information, inheritance information outperforms for structural dependencies as well as for fan-out similarity especially with respect to quality. Since inheritance is nearly uncorrelated to the other structural information (Section 3.1), we observe here different highly congruent independent coupling concepts.

3.3 Module Type Congruence

The third and last part of the study investigates whether there are individual differences in the coupling-modularity congruence between different types of modules. A variation

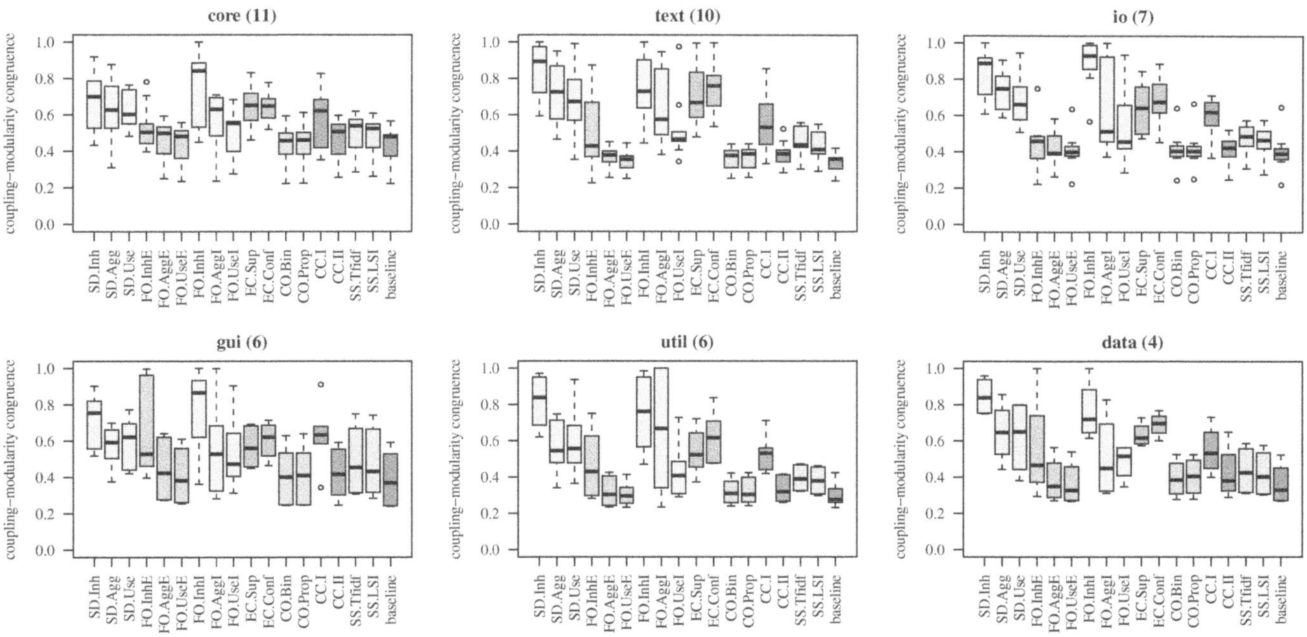

Figure 3: Coupling-modularity congruence for the most frequently occurring package types.

Table 2: Package types.

Type	Description
core	*implements the core functionality*
data	*encapsulates data and manages data structures*
event	*handles temporal events, actions, messages or exceptions*
graphics	*draws 2D or 3D graphics*
gui	*creates and controls the graphical user interface*
io	*reads or writes data from/to a device*
text	*parses, transforms, or creates textual data*
util	*provides supporting functionality*

could indicate that different design principles are used in different contexts.

3.3.1 Method

The first step towards such a module type congruence is to manually classify the packages of the software systems into distinctive types. We identified a set of package types that repeatedly appear in the projects (Table 2) and applied this classification to the main packages of the 16 software projects—sub-packages of the classified ones are assumed to belong to the same type. Some packages could not be unambiguously assigned to a type, but they can be safely omitted because the following analysis process does not rely on a complete classification.

For each project, we evaluate $congruence(C_t)$ where C_t is the set of classes included in a package assigned to type t to get a congruence value specific for a package type. We summarize each package type by considering all projects that at least contain 6 classes of this type.

3.3.2 Results

We present the results of this analysis by showing box plots of the six most frequently found package types (Figure 3). Each box plot depicts one type, the value in parentheses refers to the number of projects this type was detected in. The interpretation of the congruence values again depends on the baseline, and thus, the diagrams cannot be compared without considering the slightly different baseline values.

The box plot diagrams roughly show similar patterns compared to each other. This pattern reflects most of the observations we already described in the previous part of the study (Section 3.2). Hence, these general results virtually sustain for the different package types. Even utility packages, which are said to follow different laws than other packages [26], show this pattern together with considerably high congruence values. Nevertheless, there are small differences between the package types:

- Packages of type *io* and *gui* are exceptionally congruent with respect to the internal inheritance fan-out similarity (*FO.InhI*). Together with a high congruence value for *SD.Inh* this could hint at a special significance of inheritance in these packages.
- Overall the *core* packages show somewhat lower congruence values compared to the baseline. Here, factors that could not be grasped by the selection of coupling concepts might impact their design.
- For *text* packages, some metrics particularly exceed the baseline, including structural dependencies (*SD*), internal fan-out similarity (*FO.*I*), and evolutionary coupling (*EC*). This type of package seems to be particularly related to these coupling concepts.

4. DISCUSSION

So far, we have analyzed the results of the study with respect to the congruence of the coupling concepts and modularity. To finally get back to the modularity principles introduced in Section 2.1, we will next discuss the limitations of the results and interpret the results with respect to these principles. Beyond that, we will provide an outlook on how the results could be directly leveraged in applications regarding modularity.

4.1 Threats to Validity

The generalizability of the results is limited by the restricted set of software projects as well as by other design decisions of the study. The 16 software projects are open source systems written in Java and consist of up to 86 packages and up to 679 classes. Closed source projects might lead to different results especially with respect to evolutionary and code ownership couplings because they might follow a fundamentally different development process. Larger open-source projects may as well be organized differently. Furthermore, the results cannot be directly transferred to non-object-oriented systems because, there, concepts like inheritance do not exist.

We looked at modularity at a mid-level of abstraction and equate *module* with *package*. Hence, our results only apply to this level. For example, grouping methods into classes could follow totally different standards.

Though we covered many important coupling concepts, we did not exhaustively include all established concepts, for instance, dynamic dependencies or coupling by bug reports. Furthermore, the applied metrics are only heuristics to measure the respective concept. Although we tried to use established metrics, there could exist more appropriate metrics. Analogously, the introduced congruence metric might be unsuitable.

4.2 Modularity Principles

We must beware of over-interpreting the results with respect to modularity principles because we can only conjecture about the relationship of the principles to the coupling concepts. A high congruence for a particular concept might be caused by the application of a modularity principle, but could also be the consequence of another, unknown property. Furthermore, low congruence values do not necessarily indicate the absence of a particular modularity principle, but could also stem from weaknesses in measuring the principle by this concept. Nevertheless, the following implications can be considered as circumstantial evidence on the practical relevance of modularity principles and might be used as hypotheses for future research.

The high congruence values for structural dependencies (*SD*) suggest that the principle of low coupling and high cohesion (*P1*) is used to modularize software systems in practice as one of the dominating principles. The particularly high congruence values for inheritance (*SD.Inh*) together with its independence of the other structural dependencies (Section 3.1) highlights the role of inheritance. It appears to be the prevailing structural dependency type to implement the principle.

Also Information hiding (*P2*) seems to play a major role in the analyzed projects as the high congruence values for internal fan-out similarity (*FO*) and evolutionary coupling (*EC*) suggest. Again inheritance (*FO.InhI*) is outstanding as it provides the overall best coupling-modularity congruence result and might also be a distinguished aspect in the application of information hiding.

Code ownership (*CO*) does not play an important role in the package design of the investigated projects. A likely conclusion is that the impact of Conway's Law (*P3*) is small in contrast to other principles.

The external fan-out similarity (*FO.*E*), which we assume to be related to the separation of concerns (*P4c*), notably impacts modularity only with respect to inheritance (*FO.InhE*). The low result matches the observation that often concerns cross-cut the hierarchical structure of the system [25]. It would be interesting to also take aspects into account and compare the congruence of aspect-oriented and non-aspect-oriented systems with respect to external fan-out.

The role of domain knowledge (*P4d*) is hard to judge from the results of our study. The semantic similarity (*SS*) provides medium congruence. On the one hand, we may assume that domain knowledge is irrelevant and the medium congruence is just a result of the correlation to other high congruent coupling concepts (Section 3.1). On the other hand, we may assume that domain knowledge is a driving factor, but it is not appropriately reflected in the applied metric.

Finally, code clones (*CO*) clearly relate to the modular structure of the systems and are frequent enough to also provide medium data density (average congruence). Hence, they may significantly impact modularity principles, but we do not know their relation to the principles because code clones could hide different types of code coupling.

Concerning the module-type-specific properties, we were surprised by the stable congruence patterns that we observed for different types (Section 3.3). This is an indicator, that the the same modularity principles or guidelines are applied regardless of the package type.

4.3 Modularity Applications

Many tasks and problems in software engineering are related to modularity. First of all, finding a good modularization is a major part of designing a software system. The initial modularization might degenerate during the development process or could prove to be flawed so that a later remodularization would be necessary. In general, documenting the modularization is helpful for navigating and understanding the code.

Tools based on code couplings might support the developer in these modularity-related applications. Such tools, however, often considered coupling a one-dimensional concept, for instance, equating coupling with structural dependencies. In contrast, our results clearly show that coupling consists of several dimensions (Section 3.1), many of them impacting the modularity (Section 3.2). Exploiting combinations of coupling concepts could improve modularity tools like tools for software clustering, aspect mining, or component extraction. For instance, in the domain of software clustering, combining a few data sources has been already successfully applied [2, 4, 6]. Moreover, it is to assume that other applications of coupling data besides modularity are neither dominated by one coupling concept and could also profit from integrating different coupling concepts.

In detail, this study contains some findings that might be of particular interest for designing automatic modularization tools:

- It seems to be useful to discriminate structural dependencies (*SD*) further. At least inheritance (*SD.Inh*) should be considered as an independent concept because otherwise aggregation and usage dependencies might weaken the high impact of the inheritance dependencies.

- Including the highly congruent and dense Type I clone information (*CO.I*) is likely to have a positive effect because clones may disguise parts of the relevant coupling information.
- Using fan-out information (*FO*), it could be beneficial to discern external and internal fan-out because of its clearly different congruence to modularity that we observed in this study.

The conjectured relationships between the code coupling concepts and the modularity principles provide the opportunity to check whether the development team follows a certain principle. This could be a useful instrument for monitoring the development process. The congruence results of our study provide a reference of how modularity relates to coupling concepts in other projects.

We did not observe large differences for the coupling-modularity congruence between different package types (Section 3.3). This supports the decision of many existing automatic modularization approaches to handle all types of modules alike.

5. RELATED WORK

Abreu and Goulão [1] present an approach to find out whether coupling and cohesion are the driving forces for the modularity of a software system. They optimized the modularization with respect to this principle. The resulting modularization significantly exceeded the metric value of the original modularization. The authors conclude that "*the ideal of minimal coupling and maximal cohesion [...] does not match practitioners' reality at least in what concerns the modularity of object-oriented systems.*" Based on our new results, we can qualify this statement further: Coupling and cohesion still seem to be an important factors for modularity, but there appear to be other about equally important ones.

Sarkar et al. [21] discuss different principles used in module design, namely, *similarity of purpose*, *published API*, *compilability*, *extendibility*, *testability*, *acyclic dependencies*, and *module size*. They propose a set of metrics to quantify to what extent a modular structure follows these principles. The results of their case study validate the metrics with respect to measure modularity improvements. The applied metrics thoroughly investigate different kinds of couplings based on structural dependencies. By concluding that a single metric is not sufficient to estimate the quality of a modularization, they back our result that code coupling is a multi-dimensional construct. In contrast to our work, they focus on creating modularity quality metrics but do not aim at comparing different coupling concepts.

Evaluating different code coupling concepts to automatically retrieve the modular structure of a system by clustering, Beck and Diehl [4] compared structural dependencies and evolutionary couplings. They retrieved better results for structural dependencies because of a higher data density. Combining structural dependencies and evolutionary couplings improved the clustering result. Andritsos and Tzerpos [2] added meta information like developer, directory, number of lines of code, and the time stamp of the file to structural dependencies and were also able to improve the quality of the clustered modularization. Wierda et al. [27] showed how combining structural dependencies from multiple versions can be used to improve the clustering result. Bittencourt et al. [6] enhance the assignment of new classes to modules by enqueing semantic similarity and structural dependencies in the assignment process. These different improvements in automatically modularizing software systems by integrating different coupling concepts already exploit the multi-dimensionality of code couplings. Our study predicts that more rigorously integrating coupling concepts could lead to further improvements.

Comparisons between coupling concepts have been conducted not only to explain or construct modules. For instance, Cataldo et al. [9] found that high congruence between code couplings and the communication between developers leads to better productivity—for structural dependencies as well as for evolutionary couplings. In a further study [10], they focus on the impact of different coupling types on failures and conclude that evolutionary and work-related couplings have a higher impact on failures than structural dependencies.

The introduced congruence metric is similar to some metrics applied in software clustering. If we assume the package structure to be flat instead of hierarchical, our metric is closely related to the *clustering factor* metric used in the software clustering tool Bunch [17], to the *score of a cluster* defined for the *EVM* metric [12], or to the *intra modular coupling density* [1].

6. CONCLUSION

This work is a first step towards understanding, based on conjectured relationships to code couplings, how modularity principles are used in practice. We compared a broad spectrum of coupling concepts on a substantial set of software projects. The introduced measure of congruence connects code coupling and modularity while also taking the hierarchical structure of the modularization into account. The results of the study provide hints how modularity principles are applied in object-oriented open source software systems today. These findings could be used as hypotheses for future research. The study furthermore yields recommendations to enhance existing modularization approaches and tools.

Overall, we observed that none of the principles is exclusively dominating the modularity of the studied systems. Among the coupling concepts, a similar internal inheritance fan-out, in other words, the sibling relation in the internal inheritance hierarchy has the highest impact on modularity.

Acknowledgment

We like to thank Benjamin Biegel, Artur Lipinski, and Alexander Voskoboinik, who helped us retrieve the various kinds of coupling data.

7. REFERENCES

[1] F. B. Abreu and M. Goulão. Coupling and Cohesion as Modularization Drivers: Are We Being Over-Persuaded? In *CSMR '01: Proceedings of the Fifth European Conference on Software Maintenance and Reengineering*, pages 47–57. IEEE Computer Society, 2001.

[2] P. Andritsos and V. Tzerpos. Information-Theoretic Software Clustering. *IEEE Transactions on Software Engineering*, 31(2):150–165, 2005.

[3] C. Y. Baldwin and K. B. Clark. *Design Rules, Vol. 1: The Power of Modularity*. The MIT Press, 1st edition, Mar. 2000.

[4] F. Beck and S. Diehl. Evaluating the Impact of Software Evolution on Software Clustering. In *WCRE '10: Proceedings of the 17th Working Conference on Reverse Engineering*, pages 99–108. IEEE Computer Society, 2010.

[5] B. Biegel and S. Diehl. Highly Configurable and Extensible Code Clone Detection. In *WCRE'10: Proceedings of the 17th Working Conference on Reverse Engineering*, pages 237–241. IEEE Computer Society, 2010.

[6] R. A. Bittencourt, G. J. S. Santos, D. D. S. Guerrero, and G. C. Murphy. Improving Automated Mapping in Reflexion Models using Information Retrieval Techniques. In *WCRE'10: Proceedings of the 17th Working Conference on Reverse Engineering*, pages 163–172. IEEE Computer Society, 2010.

[7] I. T. Bowman and R. C. Holt. Software Architecture Recovery Using Conway's Law. In *CASCON '98: Proceedings of the 1998 Conference of the Centre for Advanced Studies on Collaborative Research*, pages 6+. IBM Press, 1998.

[8] S. Breu and T. Zimmermann. Mining Aspects from Version History. In *ASE '06: Proceedings of the 21st IEEE/ACM International Conference on Automated Software Engineering*, pages 221–230. IEEE Computer Society, 2006.

[9] M. Cataldo, J. D. Herbsleb, and K. M. Carley. Socio-Technical Congruence: a Framework for Assessing the Impact of Technical and Work Dependencies on Software Development Productivity. In *ESEM '08: Proceedings of the Second ACM-IEEE International Symposium on Empirical Software Engineering and Measurement*, pages 2–11. ACM, 2008.

[10] M. Cataldo, A. Mockus, J. A. Roberts, and J. D. Herbsleb. Software Dependencies, Work Dependencies, and Their Impact on Failures. *IEEE Transactions on Software Engineering*, 35(6):864–878, Nov. 2009.

[11] M. Conway. How do Committees Invent? *Datamation Journal*, pages 28–31, 1968.

[12] M. Harman, S. Swift, and K. Mahdavi. An Empirical Study of the Robustness of two Module Clustering Fitness Functions. In *GECCO '05: Proceedings of the 2005 Conference on Genetic and Evolutionary Computation*, pages 1029–1036. ACM Press, 2005.

[13] A. Kuhn, S. Ducasse, and T. Girba. Enriching Reverse Engineering with Semantic Clustering. In *WCRE '05: Proceedings of the 12th Working Conference on Reverse Engineering*, pages 133–142. IEEE Computer Society, 2005.

[14] S. Livieri, Y. Higo, M. Matsushita, and K. Inoue. Very-Large Scale Code Clone Analysis and Visualization of Open Source Programs Using Distributed CCFinder: D-CCFinder. In *ICSE '07: Proceedings of the 29th International Conference on Software Engineering*, pages 106–115. IEEE Computer Society, 2007.

[15] R. C. Martin. *Agile Software Development, Principles, Patterns, and Practices*. Prentice Hall, 1st edition, Oct. 2002.

[16] B. Meyer. *Object-Oriented Software Construction, 1st editon*. Prentice-Hall, 1988.

[17] B. S. Mitchell and S. Mancoridis. On the Evaluation of the Bunch Search-Based Software Modularization Algorithm. *Soft Computing*, 12(1):77–93, Aug. 2007.

[18] D. L. Parnas. Information Distribution Aspects of Design Methodology. In *IFIP Congress (1)*, pages 339–344, 1971.

[19] D. L. Parnas. On the Criteria to be Used in Decomposing Systems into Modules. *Communications of the ACM*, 15(12):1053–1058, Dec. 1972.

[20] C. K. Roy and J. R. Cordy. A Survey on Software Clone Detection Research. Technical report, Queen's University at Kingston, Ontario, Canada, 2007.

[21] S. Sarkar, G. M. Rama, and A. C. Kak. API-Based and Information-Theoretic Metrics for Measuring the Quality of Software Modularization. *IEEE Transactions on Software Engineering*, 33(1):14–32, 2007.

[22] R. W. Schwanke. An Intelligent Tool for Re-Engineering Software Modularity. In *ICSE '91: Proceedings of the 13th International Conference on Software Engineering*, pages 83–92. IEEE Computer Society, 1991.

[23] W. P. Stevens, G. J. Myers, and L. L. Constantine. Structured Design. *IBM Systems Journal*, 13(2):115–139, 1974.

[24] P.-N. Tan, M. Steinbach, and V. Kumar. *Introduction to Data Mining*. Addison Wesley, May 2005.

[25] P. Tarr, H. Ossher, W. Harrison, and S. M. Sutton. N Degrees of Separation: Multi-Dimensional Separation of Concerns. In *ICSE '99: Proceedings of the 21st International Conference on Software Engineering*, pages 107–119. ACM, 1999.

[26] Z. Wen and V. Tzerpos. Software Clustering based on Omnipresent Object Detection. In *IWPC '05: Proceedings of the 13th International Workshop on Program Comprehension*, pages 269–278, Washington, DC, USA, 2005. IEEE Computer Society.

[27] A. Wierda, E. Dortmans, and L. L. Somers. Using Version Information in Architectural Clustering - A Case Study. In *CSMR '06: Proceedings of the Conference on Software Maintenance and Reengineering*, pages 214–228. IEEE Computer Society, 2006.

[28] T. Zimmermann and P. Weißgerber. Preprocessing CVS Data For Fine-Grained Analysis. In *MSR '04: Proceedings of the 1st International Workshop on Mining Software Repositories*, pages 2–6. IEEE Computer Society, 2004.

Fuzzy Set and Cache-based Approach for Bug Triaging

Ahmed Tamrawi
atamrawi@iastate.edu

Tung Thanh Nguyen
tung@iastate.edu

Jafar M. Al-Kofahi
jafar@iastate.edu

Tien N. Nguyen
tien@iastate.edu

Electrical and Computer Engineering Department
Iowa State University
Ames, IA 50011, USA

ABSTRACT

Bug triaging aims to assign a bug to the most appropriate fixer. That task is crucial in reducing time and efforts in a bug fixing process. In this paper, we propose Bugzie, a novel approach for automatic bug triaging based on fuzzy set and cache-based modeling of the bug-fixing expertise of developers. Bugzie considers a software system to have multiple technical aspects, each of which is associated with technical terms. For each technical term, it uses a fuzzy set to represent the developers who are capable/competent of fixing the bugs relevant to the corresponding aspect. The fixing correlation of a developer toward a technical term is represented by his/her membership score toward the corresponding fuzzy set. The score is calculated based on the bug reports that (s)he has fixed, and is updated as the newly fixed bug reports are available. For a new bug report, Bugzie combines the fuzzy sets corresponding to its terms and ranks the developers based on their membership scores toward that combined fuzzy set to find the most capable fixers. Our empirical results show that Bugzie achieves significantly higher accuracy and time efficiency than existing state-of-the-art approaches.

Categories and Subject Descriptors

D.2.9 [**Software Engineering**]: Management

General Terms

Algorithms, Human Factors, Management, Reliability

Keywords

Bug Triaging, Fuzzy Set, Developers' Expertise

1. INTRODUCTION

Software bugs are inevitable and bug fixing is an essential, yet costly phase during software development. To improve its efficiency and reduce its cost, one should assign a bug report, which describes some technical issue(s), to the right fixer. This process is known as *bug triaging* [3].

Permission to make digital or hard copies of all or part of this work for personal or classroom use is granted without fee provided that copies are not made or distributed for profit or commercial advantage and that copies bear this notice and the full citation on the first page. To copy otherwise, to republish, to post on servers or to redistribute to lists, requires prior specific permission and/or a fee.
ESEC/FSE'11, September 5–9, 2011, Szeged, Hungary.
Copyright 2011 ACM 978-1-4503-0443-6/11/09 ...$10.00.

To support developers in this task, we propose Bugzie, a novel fuzzy set and cache-based approach for automatic bug triaging. Bugzie considers a software system to have a collection of technical aspects/concerns, which are described via the corresponding technical terms appearing in software artifacts. Among the artifacts, a bug report describes an issue(s) related to some technical aspects/concerns via the corresponding technical terms. Therefore, in Bugzie, the key research question is that *given a bug report, how to determine who have the most bug-fixing capability/expertise with respect to the reported technical aspect(s)/issue(s).*

The key idea of Bugzie is to model the *fixing correlation/association* of developers toward a technical aspect via fuzzy sets [25]. The fixing correlation/association represents the bug-fixing capability/expertise of developers with respect to the technical aspects in a project. To realize that, the fuzzy sets are defined for the corresponding technical terms and built based on developers' past fixing bug reports and activities. Then, Bugzie recommends the most potential fixer(s) for a new bug report based on such information.

For a specific technical term t, a *fuzzy set* C_t is defined to represent the set of developers who have the bug-fixing expertise relevant to t, i.e. the most capable/competent ones to fix the bugs on the technical aspects described via the term t. The membership score of a developer d to the set C_t, i.e. the degree of certainty that d is a capable fixer for the bugs on the technical aspect(s) corresponding to t, is calculated via the similarity of the set of fixed bug reports containing t, and the set of bug reports that d has fixed. That is, the more distinct and prevalent the term t in the bug reports d has fixed, the higher the degree of certainty that d is a competent fixer for the technical issue(s) corresponding to t. Then, for a new bug report B, the fuzzy set C_B of capable developers toward the technical aspect(s) reported in B is modeled by the union set of all fuzzy sets corresponding to all the terms extracted from B.

To cope with the large numbers of active developers and technical terms in large and long-lived projects, Bugzie has two design strategies on selecting the *fixer candidates* and *significant terms* for the computation. Conducting an empirical study on several bug databases of real-world projects, we discovered the locality of the fixing activity: "the recent fixing developers are likely to fix bug reports in the near future". For example, in Eclipse, 81% of actual fixers belong to the 10% of developers having the most recent fixing activities. Thus, we can apply a filtering technique [21] to select a portion of recent fixers as the candidates for fixing a new bug report. In addition, instead of using all extracted words as

Table 1: Statistics of All Collected Bug Report Data

Project	Time	Report	Fixer	Term
Firefox	04/07/98 - 10/28/10	188,139	3,014	177,028
Eclipse	10/10/01 - 10/28/10	177,637	2,144	193,862
Apache	05/10/02 - 01/01/11	43,162	1,695	110,231
NetBeans	01/01/08 - 11/01/10	23,522	380	42,797
FreeDesktop	01/09/03 - 12/05/10	17,084	374	61,773
Gcc	08/03/99 - 10/28/10	19,430	293	63,013
Jazz	06/01/05 - 06/01/08	34,228	156	39,771

terms for its computation, Bugzie is flexible to use only the terms that are highly correlated with each developer as the most significant terms to represent his/her fixing expertise.

To adapt to software evolution, Bugzie updates its model regularly (e.g. the lists of fixer candidates and terms, and membership scores) as new fixing information is available.

Our evaluation results on large-scale subject systems show that Bugzie achieves significantly higher levels of efficiency and correctness than existing state-of-the-art approaches. For example, it could process the whole Eclipse bug dataset, containing around 178K bug reports and having more than 2,100 active developers, in 12 minutes with 45% and 83% accuracy on top-1 and top-5 recommendations, respectively. That means, in almost half of the cases, the single recommended developer is the actual fixer of the given bug report, and in 83% of the cases, (s)he is in the list of 5 recommended developers. In 7 subject projects, Bugzie's accuracy for top-1 and top-5 recommendations is generally in the range of 31-51% and 70-83%, respectively. It selects about 10-40% of recent fixers as candidates, and characterizes/profiles each candidate with 3-20 most significant terms. Importantly, while existing approaches take from hours to days (even almost a month) to finish training as well as predicting, in Bugzie, training time is from tens of minutes to an hour, while it still consistently achieves higher accuracy. Bugzie's top-1 and top-5 accuracy levels are higher than those of the second best approach from 4-15% and 6-31%, respectively.

In summary, the key contributions of this paper include:

1. A scalable, fuzzy set and cache-based automatic bug triaging approach, which is significantly more efficient and accurate than existing state-of-the-art approaches;
2. The finding of the *locality* of fixing activity: one of the recent fixers is likely to be the fixer of the next bug report;
3. A comprehensive evaluation on the efficiency and correctness of Bugzie in comparison with existing approaches;
4. An observation/method to capture a small, yet significant set of terms describing developers' bug-fixing expertise.

Section 2 presents an empirical study and a motivating example for Bugzie. Sections 3 and 4 describe our approach and algorithm. Section 5 presents our empirical evaluation. Related work is in Section 6. Conclusions appear last.

2. EMPIRICAL STUDY AND MOTIVATION

This section presents our empirical study and an analysis that motivates our approach.

2.1 Data Collection

Our datasets contain bug reports, corresponding fixers, and related information (e.g. summary, description, and creation/fixing time). Table 1 shows our collected datasets of seven projects: FireFox (FF) [14], Eclipse (EC) [13], Apache (AP) [2], Netbeans (NB) [30], FreeDesktop (FD) [15], Gcc (GC) [17], and Jazz (JZ). All bug reports and their data are available and downloaded from the bug tracking systems of the corresponding projects, except that Jazz data is available for us as a grant from IBM Corporation. We collected bug records noted as *fixed* and *closed*. Duplicate and unresolved (open) bug reports were excluded. For the duplicate bug reports, only the master ones were assigned to the fixers. Thus, we kept the master ones and removed all other reports marked as their duplicates. Re-open/un-finished bug fixes were not included either. In Table 1, Column Time shows the time period of the fixed bug reports. Columns Report and Fixer show the number of fixed bug reports and that of the corresponding fixing developers, respectively.

For each bug report, we extracted its unique bug ID, the actual fixing developer's ID, email address, creating and fixing time, summary, and full description. Comments and discussions are excluded. We merged the summary and description of each bug report, extracted their terms and preprocessed them, such as stemming for term normalization and removing grammatical and stop words. Column Term in Table 1 shows the total numbers of terms in all datasets.

AssignedTo:James Moody
Summary:New Repository wizard follows implementation model, not user model.
Description:The new CVS Repository Connection wizard's layout is confusing. This is because it follows the implementation model of the order of fields in the full CVS location path,...

Figure 1: Bug report #6021 in Eclipse project

AssignedTo:James Moody
Summary:Opening repository resources doesn't honor type.
Description:Opening repository resource always open the default text editor and doesn't honor any mapping between resource types and editors. As a result it is not possible to view ...

Figure 2: Bug report #0002 in Eclipse project

2.2 A Motivating Example

Let us present a motivating example in our collected data. Figure 1 depicts a bug report from Eclipse, with the relevant fields including the fixing developer (AssignedTo), a short summary (Summary), and a description (Description) of the bug. The bug report describes an issue that the layout of the wizard for CVS repository connection was not properly implemented. Analyzing Eclipse's documentation, we found that this issue is related to a technical aspect: *version control and management* (VCM) for software artifacts. This aspect of VCM can be recognized in the report's contents via its descriptive terms such as CVS, repository, connection, path, etc. Checking the corresponding fixed code in Eclipse, we found that the bug occurred in the code implementing an operation of VCM: CVS repository connection. The bug was assigned to and fixed by a developer named James Moody.

Searching and analyzing other Eclipse's bug reports, we found that James also fixed several other VCM-related bugs, for example, bug #0002 (Figure 2). The description states that the system always used its default editor to open any resource file (e.g. a GIF file) regardless of its file type. This aspect of VCM is described via the terms such as repository, resource, and editor. This observation suggests that James Moody probably has the expertise, knowledge, or capability with respect to fixing the VCM-related bugs in Eclipse.

2.3 Implications and our Approach

This example suggests us the following:

1. A software system has several technical aspects. Each could be associated with some descriptive technical terms. A bug report is related to one or multiple technical aspects.

2. If a developer frequently fixes the bugs related to a technical aspect, we could consider him to have *bug-fixing expertise/capability* on that aspect, i.e., he could be a capable/competent fixer for a future bug related to that aspect.

Based on those two implications, we approach to solve the problem of automated bug triaging using the following *key philosophy*: *"who have the most bug-fixing capability/expertise with respect to the reported technical aspect(s) in a given bug report should be the fixer(s)"*.

Since technical aspects could be described via the corresponding technical terms, our solution could rely on the modeling of the fixing capability of a developer toward a technical aspect via the *association/correlation of that developer with the technical terms for that aspect*. Specifically, we will determine the most capable developers toward a technical aspect in the project based on their past fixing activities. Then, when a new bug is reported, we will recommend those developers who are most capable of fixing the corresponding technical issue(s) in the given bug report.

Our solution is different from existing approaches to automatic bug triaging [3, 5, 10, 28]. The first line of ideas from existing machine learning (ML)-based approaches [3, 5] is that if a new bug report is closest in characteristics/similarity with a set of bug reports fixed by a developer, (s)he should be suggested. The second line is from existing ML and information retrieval (IR) approaches [28, 10], which aim to profile a developer's expertise by a set of characteristic features (e.g. terms) in his fixed bug reports, and then match a new bug report with such profiles to find the fixer(s). Bugzie is aligned more with the second line of ideas, however, it is centered around the modeling of the correlation/association between two sets: *developers* and *terms*. Thus, we have to address the question of how to make the selections and take into account relevant terms and developers.

As shown in Table 1, for large projects with long histories, the numbers of terms (after stemming and filtering) are still very large (e.g. 200K words for FireFox). More importantly, not all terms appearing in a bug report would be technically meaningful and relevant to the fixers or reported technical issues. Thus, using all of them would be computationally expensive, and even worse, might reduce the fixer recommendation accuracy by introducing noise to the ranking. The motivating example suggests that such term selection could be based on the level of association, i.e. a word having high correlation with some developers could be a significant term for bug triaging, e.g. the association of repository and James Moody (Details will be presented in Section 3).

The selection of developers is also needed because in a large and long-lived project, the number of developers could be large and some might not be as active in certain technical areas as others any more. Moreover, considering all developers as the fixer candidates for a bug report could be computationally costly. Next, we will describe an empirical study that motivates our developers' selection strategy.

2.4 Locality of Fixing Activity

Analyzing several bug reports fixed by the same person in our datasets, we found that (s)he tends to have recent fixing activities. For example, bug reports #312322, #312291, #312466, and #311848 were fixed by the same fixer Darin Wright in two days 05/10 and 05/11/2010. We hypothesize that, *the fixing activity has locality: the recent fixing developers are likely to fix bug reports in the near future.*

Table 2: % of Actual Fixers Having Recent Fixes

Recent	EC	FF	JZ	GC	AP	FD	NB
10%	81%	82%	62%	84%	71%	73%	69%
20%	87%	92%	74%	92%	81%	89%	87%
30%	92%	96%	83%	95%	89%	94%	94%
40%	96%	97%	92%	97%	92%	96%	96%
50%	98%	98%	97%	98%	94%	97%	97%
60%	98%	98%	99%	98%	95%	98%	98%
70%	99%	98%	99%	98%	96%	98%	98%
80%	99%	98%	100%	99%	96%	98%	98%
90%	99%	98%	100%	99%	96%	98%	98%
100%	99%	98%	100%	99%	96%	98%	99%

To validate this hypothesis, we have conducted an experiment in which we analyzed the collected datasets to compute how often a fixer of a bug report is the one who has some recent fixing activity. First, we chronically sorted the bug reports in a project by their fixing time. For a bug report b that was fixed at time t by a developer d, we sorted all developers having fixing activities before t based on their most recent fixing time, i.e. a developer performing a fix more recently to time t was sorted higher. Then, if d belongs to the top x% fixers of that list, we count this as a *hit*. Finally, we compute $p(x)$ as the percentage of hits over the total number of analyzed bug reports. Table 2 shows the result.

As seen, it is consistent in all systems that $p(x)$ is quite large even at a small x. For example, in Eclipse, at $x = 10\%$, $p(x) = 81\%$, i.e. in around 81% of the cases, the fixer of a bug report is in the top 10% of the developers who have most recent fixing activities. At $x = 50\%$, $p(x)$ exceeds 97% in 6 systems. Note that, at $x = 100\%$, $p(x)$ might not reach 100% since there are always new fixers who have no historical fixing activity, thus, (s)he does not belong to the list of developers with recent fixing activities.

Implications. The result confirms our hypothesis on the locality of fixing activity. This result enables us to apply the filtering technique for recommender systems [21]: instead of selecting all available developers as fixer candidates for a bug report, we could select a small portion of them based on their recent fixing activities. This selection would significantly improve time efficiency without losing much accuracy.

3. Bugzie MODEL

3.1 Overview

In Bugzie, the problem of automatic bug triaging is modeled as follows: given a bug report, find the developer(s) with the most fixing capability/expertise with respect to the reported technical issue(s). Thus, Bugzie determines and ranks *the fixing capability/expertise* of the developers *toward the technical aspects* by modeling the *correlation/association of a developer and a technical aspect*. That is, if a developer has higher fixing correlation with a technical aspect, (s)he is considered to have higher capability/expertise on that aspect, and will be ranked higher.

Because "technical aspect" is an abstract concept, with potential different levels of granularity, Bugzie models them via their corresponding descriptive technical terms. That is, a technical aspect is considered as *a collection of technical terms* that are extracted directly from the software artifacts in a project, and more specifically from its bug reports.

Bugzie utilizes fuzzy set theory [25] to model the *fixing correlation/association between developers and the technical terms*, which is used to recommend the most capable fixers for a given bug report. Bugzie also uses the locality of fixing activity to select the fixer candidates, and uses the levels of correlation between the fixers and terms to identify the most correlated/important terms to model developers' expertise.

3.2 Association of Fixer and Term

DEFINITION 1 (CAPABLE FIXER TOWARD A TERM). *For a specific technical term t, a fuzzy set C_t, with an associated membership function $\mu_t()$, represents the set of capable fixers toward t, i.e. the developers who have the bug-fixing expertise relevant to the technical aspect(s) described by t.*

In fuzzy set theory, fuzzy set C_t is determined via a membership function μ_t with the values in the range of [0,1]. For a developer d, the membership score $\mu_t(d)$ determines the certainty degree of the membership of d in C_t, i.e. how likely d belongs to the fuzzy set C_t. In this context, $\mu_t(d)$ determines the degree to which d is capable of fixing the bug(s) relevant to the technical aspect(s) associated with t. The membership score also determines the ranking, i.e. if $\mu_t(d) > \mu_t(d')$ then d is considered to be more capable than d' in the technical issue(s) related to t. $\mu_t(d)$ is calculated based on d's past fixing activities as follows:

DEFINITION 2 (MEMBERSHIP SCORE TOWARD A TERM). *The membership score $\mu_t(d)$ is calculated as the correlation between the set D_d of the bug reports that d has fixed, and the set D_t of the bug reports containing term t:*

$$\mu_t(d) = \frac{|D_d \cap D_t|}{|D_d \cup D_t|} = \frac{n_{d,t}}{n_t + n_d - n_{d,t}}$$

In this formula, n_d, n_t, and $n_{d,t}$ are the number of bug reports that d has fixed, the number of reports containing the term t, and that with both, respectively (counted from the available training data, i.e. given fixed bug reports).

With this formula, the value of $\mu_t(d) \in [0,1]$. The higher $\mu_t(d)$ is, the higher the degree that d is a capable fixer for the bugs related to term t. If $\mu_t(d) = 1$, then only d had fixed the bug reports containing t, thus, d is highly capable of fixing the bugs relevant to the technical aspects associated with term t. If $\mu_t(d) = 0$, d has never fixed any bug report containing t, thus, might not be the right fixer with respect to t. In general cases, the more frequently a term t appears in the reports that developer d has fixed, the higher $\mu_t(d)$ is, i.e. the more likely that developer d has fixing expertise toward the technical aspects associated with t.

The membership value $\mu_t(d)$, representing the *fixing correlation of a developer toward a technical term*, is an intrinsically gradual notion, rather than a concrete notion as in conventional logic. That is, the boundary of the set of developers who are capable of fixing the bugs relevant to t is fuzzy.

Definition 2 gives us $\mu_t(d) = \frac{1}{\frac{n_t+n_d}{n_{d,t}}-1}$. Thus, Bugzie favors (ranks higher) the developers who have emphasized their fixing activities toward some technical aspect/term t (i.e. specialists) over the ones with less specialization with their fixing activities on multiple other technical issues (i.e. generalists). That is, if both d and d' have similar levels of fixing activities on t, i.e. $n_{d,t}$ and $n_{d',t}$ are similar, but d' has fixed several other technical issues while d emphasizes mostly on t, then $n_{d'}$ will be much larger than n_d, and $\mu_t(d')$ will be smaller than $\mu_t(d)$. Thus, Bugzie will favor the specialist d. In general, if $\frac{n_t+n_d}{n_{d,t}}$ is smaller, $\mu_t(d)$ will be higher. Therefore, Bugzie favors the specialists who have fixed more bug reports relevant to t (i.e. large $n_{d,t}$) and have emphasized their fixing more on t (i.e. large $n_{d,t}/n_d$).

Because a bug report might contain multiple technical issues/aspects, and each technical aspect could be expressed via multiple technical terms, Bugzie needs to model the capable fixers with respect to a bug report based on their correlation values toward its associated terms. This is done using the union operation in fuzzy set theory as follows.

DEFINITION 3 (CAPABLE FIXER FOR A BUG REPORT). *For a given bug report B, fuzzy set C_B, with associated membership function $\mu_B()$, represents the set of capable fixers for B, i.e. the developers who have the bug-fixing expertise relevant to technical aspect(s) reported in B. C_B is computed as the union of the fuzzy sets for the terms extracted from B*

$$C_B = \bigcup_{t \in B} C_t$$

In fuzzy set theory, union is a flexible combination, i.e. the strong membership to some sub-fuzzy set(s) will imply the strong membership to the combined fuzzy set. Especially, the more sub-fuzzy sets with strong membership degrees exist, the stronger the membership toward the combined fuzzy set is. According to [25], the membership score of d with respect to the union set C_B is calculated as the following:

DEFINITION 4 (MEMBERSHIP SCORE FOR A REPORT). *The membership score $\mu_B(d)$ is computed as the combination of the membership scores $\mu_t(d)$ of its associated terms t:*

$$\mu_B(d) = 1 - \prod_{t \in B}(1 - \mu_t(d))$$

$\mu_B(d)$ represents the fixing correlation of d toward bug report B. As seen, $\mu_B(d)$ is also within [0,1] and represents the degree in which developer d belongs to C_B, i.e. the set of capable fixers for the bug(s) reported in B. The value $\mu_B(d) = 0$ when all $\mu_t(d) = 0$, i.e. d has never fixed any report containing any term in B. Thus, Bugzie considers that d might not be as suitable as others in fixing the technical issues reported in B. Otherwise, if there is one term t with $\mu_t(d) = 1$, then $\mu_B(d) = 1$, and d is considered as the capable developer (since only d has fixed bug reports with term t before). In general cases, the more the terms in B with high $\mu_t(d)$ scores, the higher $\mu_B(d)$ is, i.e. the more likely d is a capable fixer for bug report B. Using this formula, after calculating fixing correlation scores $\mu_B(d)$s for candidate developers, Bugzie ranks and recommends the top-scored developers as the most capable fixers for bug report B.

The union operation allows Bugzie to take into account the co-occurring/correlated terms associated with some technical aspects and reduce the impact of noises. Generally, a technical aspect could be expressed in some technical terms, e.g., the concern of version control in Eclipse might be associated with the terms like t = repository and t' = cvs. Thus, these two terms tend to co-occur in the bug reports on version control and if a concrete bug report B contains both terms, B should be considered to be more relevant to version control than the ones containing only one term. That means, if d is a developer with fixing expertise in version control, $\mu_t(d)$ and $\mu_{t'}(d)$ should be equally high, and $\mu_B(d)$ must be higher than either of them. Those are actually true in our model. Since t and t' tend to co-occur, bug reports contain t, including the ones fixed by d, might also contain t'. Thus, two sets D_t and $D_{t'}$ are similar, and because d has fixing expertise on version control, $\mu_t(d)$ and $\mu_{t'}(d)$ will be similarly high. Assume that $\mu_t(d) = 0.7$ and $\mu_{t'}(d) = 0.6$. Then, $\mu_B(d) =$ 1 - (1-0.7)*(1-0.6) = 0.88, i.e. higher than $\mu_t(d)$ and $\mu_{t'}(d)$.

$\mu_B(d)$ is also not affected much by noises, i.e. the terms irrelevant to developers' expertise/technical aspects (e.g. misspelled words). Assume that B contains t and a noise e. Since e rarely occurs in the bug reports that d had fixed, d has a small membership score toward e, e.g., 0.1. Then, $\mu_B(d)$=1-(1-0.7)*(1-0.1)= 0.73, i.e. not much larger than $\mu_t(d)$= 0.7.

3.3 Fixer Candidate and Term Selection

Let us discuss our selection strategies for fixers and terms.

3.3.1 Selection of Fixer Candidates

The locality of fixing activity suggests the actual fixer for a given bug report is likely the one having recent fixing activity. Thus, for each bug report, Bugzie chooses the top x% of developers sorted by their latest fixing time as the fixer candidates $F(x)$ for its computation. This is a trade-off between performance and accuracy. If x = 100%, all developers will be considered, accuracy could be higher, however, running time will be longer. Importantly, in general, the locality of fixing activity suggests that the loss in accuracy is acceptable. For example, by selecting x = 50%, we can reduce in half the computation time, while losing at most 1-3% of accuracy for all subject systems (lines 50%, 100% of Table 2).

3.3.2 Selection of Descriptive Terms

Bugzie measures the term significance based on the fixing correlation, i.e. the membership scores. That is, for a developer d and a term t, the higher their correlation score $\mu_t(d)$, the higher significance of t in describing the technical aspects that d has fixing capability/expertise. Thus, Bugzie selects the descriptive terms as follows. For each developer d, it sorts the terms in the descending order based on the correlation scores $\mu_t(d)$, and selects the top k terms in the sorted list as the significant terms $T_d(k)$ for developer d. The collection $T(k)$ of all such terms selected for all developers is considered as the set of technical terms for the whole system. Then, when recommending, Bugzie uses only those terms in its ranking formula. In other words, if a term extracted from the bug report under consideration does not belong to that list, Bugzie will discard it in the formulas in Section 3.2.

Table 3 shows such lists of top-10 terms having highest correlation scores with some Eclipse's developers produced by our tool. As seen, Bugzie discovers that James Moody has many fixing activities toward VCM technical aspect.

4. ALGORITHM

This section describes the key algorithm in Bugzie. With two adjustable parameters x (for fixer candidates) and k (for selected term lists), Bugzie operates in three main phases: 1) **initializing**, i.e. building the fuzzy sets for the technical terms collected from the initially available information (e.g. already-fixed bug reports); 2) **recommending**, i.e. producing a ranked list of developers capable of fixing an unfixed bug report, and 3) **updating**, i.e. updating the fuzzy sets as new information is available (i.e. newly fixed bug reports).

Table 3: Term Selection for Eclipse's developers

Ed Merks	Darin Wright	Tod Creasey	James Moody
xsd	debug	marker	outgoing
ecore	breakpoint	progress	vcm
xsdschema	launch	decoration	itpvcm
genmodel	console	dialog	repository
emf	vm	workbench	history
xsdecorebuild	memory	background	ccv
xmlschema	jdi	font	team
eobject	suspend	view	cvs
xmlhandler	config	ui	merge
ecoreutil	thread	jface	conflict

4.1 Initial Training

In this phase, Bugzie uses a collection of already-fixed bug reports to build its initial internal data, including 1) the fuzzy sets of capable fixers for the available technical terms, 2) the fixer candidate list $F(x)$, 3) the individual term lists $T_d(k)$, and 4) the system-wide term list $T(k)$. While modeling the fuzzy sets, it stores only the counting values n_d, n_t, and $n_{d,t}$ (see Definition 2) for any available developer d and technical term t. The values $\mu_t(d)$ are computed on-demand to reduce the memory needed to store membership scores, and make the updating phase simpler (since only those counting numbers need to be updated).

4.2 Recommending

In this phase, Bugzie recommends the most capable developers for a given unfixed bug report B. First, it extracts all terms from B and keeps only terms belonging to the selected term list $T(k)$. Then, it computes the membership scores of all developers in the candidate list $F(x)$ using Definition 2. The values $\mu_t(d)$ are computed as needed using the counting values n_d, n_t, and $n_{d,t}$. Finally, Bugzie ranks those membership scores and recommends the top-n developers.

4.3 Updating

In this phase, Bugzie incrementally updates its internal data with newly available information (i.e. new bug reports are fixed by some developers). First, it updates the counting values n_d, n_t, and $n_{d,t}$ using newly available fixed bug reports by adding new corresponding counts for the new data. For example, if developer d just fixed a bug report B, Bugzie increases the counting number n_d by 1 and increases $n_{d,t}$, and n_t by 1 for any term t extracted from B. If a new term or a new developer just appears in new data, Bugzie creates new counting numbers n_t or n_d, and $n_{d,t}$.

After updating the counting numbers, Bugzie updates the lists $F(x)$, $T_d(k)$, and $T(k)$. Instead of re-sorting all available developers and terms to update those lists, Bugzie uses a caching strategy: it stores $F(x)$ as a cache (called *developer cache*). Thus, for each fixed bug report in the updating data, if the fixer does not belong to the cache, Bugzie will add it to the cache, and if the cache is full, it will remove from the cache the developer(s) having the *least* recent fixing activity. Similarly, Bugzie also stores $T_d(k)$ as caches (called *term cache*), and updates them based on the membership scores. $T_d(k)$ is stored as a descendingly sorted list.

During updating, if a term t does not belong to the cache and its score $\mu_t(d)$ is larger than that of some term currently in the cache, Bugzie will insert it to the cache, and if the cache is full, it will remove the least-scored term.

This updating and caching strategy makes Bugzie's incremental training efficient. Importantly, it fits well with software evolution. The membership score $\mu_t(d)$ is computed on-demand with the most recently updated counting numbers n_d, n_t, and $n_{d,t}$. The cache $F(x)$ always reflects the developers with most tendency for fixing bugs. The lists $T_d(k)$ always consist of the terms having highest association with the developers. Existing bug triaging approaches are not sufficiently flexible to support such caching of developers and terms. In Bugzie, time-sensitive knowledge on developers' fixing activities and important terms during software evolution can be taken into account. In future, other cache replacement strategies as in BugCache [23] could be explored, e.g., caching recent buggy terms and their co-occurring terms.

5. EMPIRICAL EVALUATION

We evaluated Bugzie on our collected datasets (Section 2), some of which were used in prior bug triaging research [3, 28, 5]. We evaluated it with various parameters for developers' and terms' selections, and compared it with state-of-the-art approaches [11, 3, 28, 5]. All experiments were on a Windows Vista, Intel Core 2 Duo 2.10Ghz, 4GB RAM desktop.

5.1 Experiment Setup

To simulate the usage of Bugzie in practice, we used the same longitudinal data setup as in [5]. That is, all extracted bug reports from each bug repository in Table 1 were sorted in the chronological order of creation time, and then divided into 11 non-overlapped and equally sized frames.

Initially, frame 0 with its bug reports were used in initial training. Then, Bugzie used that training data to recommend a list of top-n developers to fix the first bug report $BR_{1,1}$ in frame 1. After that, we performed updating for our training data with tested bug report $BR_{1,1}$, and started recommending for the next bug report $BR_{1,2}$ in frame 1. After completing frame 1, the updated training data was then used to test frame 2 in the same manner. We repeated this process until all the bug reports in all frames were consumed.

If a recommendation list for a bug report contains its actual fixer, we count this as a *hit* (i.e. a correct recommendation). For each frame under test, we calculated *prediction accuracy* as in [5], i.e. the ratio between the number of hits over the total number of prediction cases. We calculated the average accuracy value on all 10 frames for each choice of the top-ranked list of n. We also measured the training (initial training and updating) and recommending time.

5.2 Selection of Fixer Candidates

In this experiment, we tuned different options for the selection of fixer candidates (i.e. developer cache). Bugzie allows to choose $x\%$ of top fixers having most recent fixing activities. We ran it with various values of $x\%$, from 1-100% (at x=100%, all developers in the project's history were chosen). For each value of x, we measured prediction accuracy and total *processing time* (for training and recommending). The same process was applied for all datasets in Table 1.

Figures 3 and 4 show the graphs for the top-1 and top-5 prediction accuracy for different values of x for all datasets. As seen, all graphs exhibit the same behavior. The accuracy

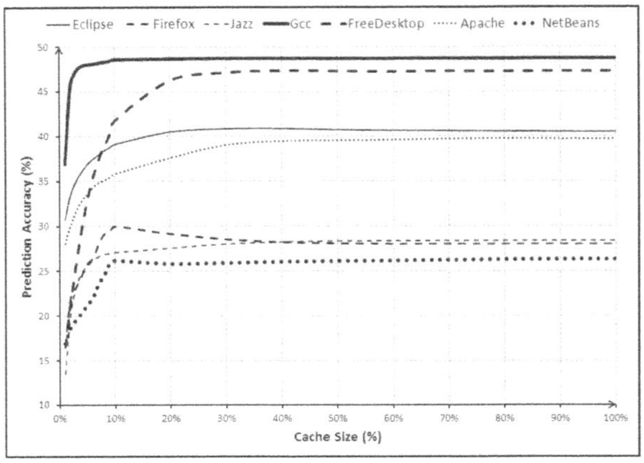

Figure 3: Top-1 Accuracy with Various Cache Sizes

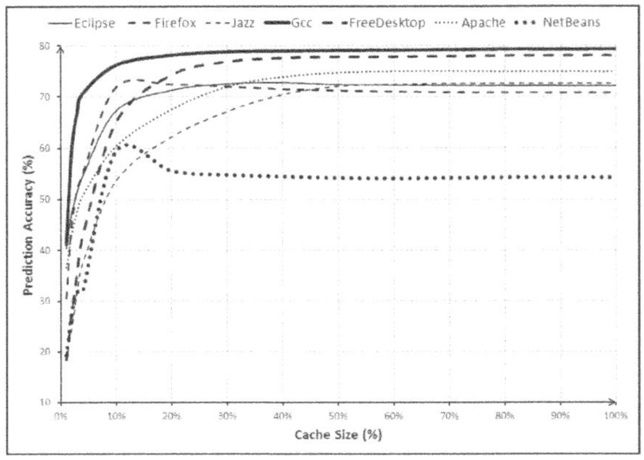

Figure 4: Top-5 Accuracy with Various Cache Sizes

peaks at some value x that is quite smaller than 100%. In all 7 projects, accuracy reaches its peak at $x < 40\%$. This implies that selecting a suitable portion of recent fixers as candidates actually does not lessen much the accuracy. In some cases, it *improves* the prediction accuracy. For example, in FireFox, at $x = 20\%$, Bugzie has top-5 accuracy of 72.4%, while top-5 accuracy at $x = 100\%$ is only 70.7%, i.e. when considering all available fixers as candidates. Definitely, selecting only a portion of available fixers as candidates also significantly improves time efficiency. Figure 5 displays the total processing time. Since in prediction/recommendation phase, Bugzie just needs to compute membership scores based on the stored counting values, prediction time is just a few tens of seconds for all cases. As seen, the processing time for FireFox and Eclipse is higher than that for other projects due to their larger datasets. However, for FireFox, at $x = 20\%$, with caching, Bugzie can reduce the processing time around 2.7 times less. The processing time is also linear with respect to the cache size of fixer candidates.

This result suggests that the selection of fixer candidates (i.e. developer cache) significantly improve time efficiency because Bugzie just needs to process a smaller number of developers. In some cases, it even helps improve prediction accuracy. We examined those cases and found that Bugzie fits well with the nature of the locality in fixing activity: the appropriate cache was able to capture the majority of actual

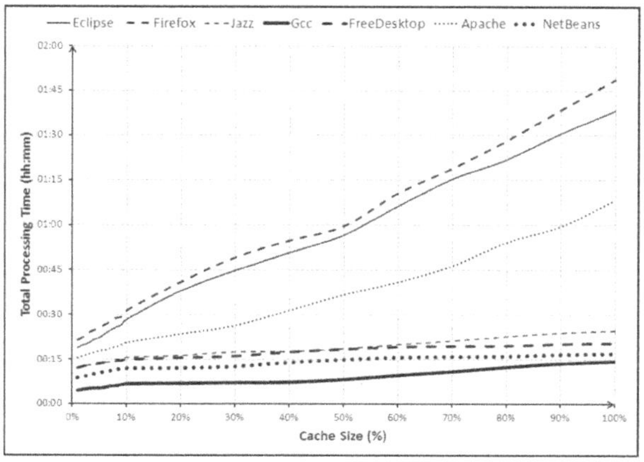

Figure 5: Processing Time with Various Cache Sizes

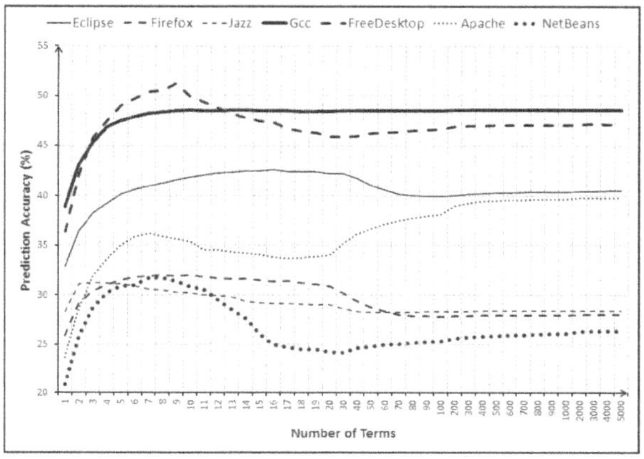

Figure 6: Top-1 Accuracy - Various Term Selection

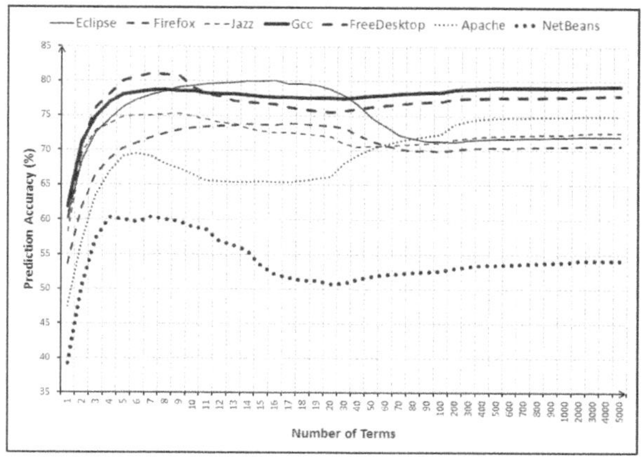

Figure 7: Top-5 Accuracy - Various Term Selection

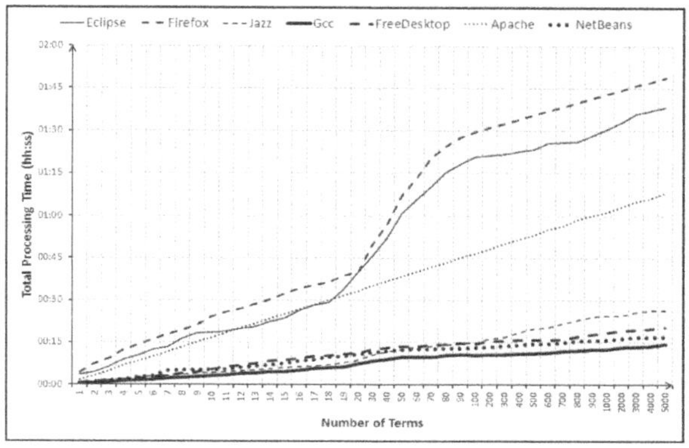

Figure 8: Processing Time - Various Term Selection

fixers. Also, it did not include the developers who had high fixing expertise in some technical aspect in a very long time ago, but do not handle much that technical issue anymore. When including such developers and their past fixing terms, ranking could be imprecise since more irrelevant developers and terms are considered. As seen in Figure 4, the appropriate size of developer cache depends on individual projects.

5.3 Selection of Terms

We conducted a similar experiment for the selection of terms. Bugzie is flexible to allow the selection of only top-k terms that are most correlated with each fixer (Section 3.3.2). We ran Bugzie with different values of k, increasing from 1-5,000. With k=5,000 for each developer, the system-wide term list $T(k)$ covers most of available terms in all bug reports. If a developer has the number of terms less than k, all of his associated terms with non-zero correlation scores are used. For each value of k, we measured top-n prediction accuracy and the total processing time.

Figures 6 and 7 show the results of top-1 and top-5 prediction accuracy on all datasets, with different values of k. As seen, for most projects, the graphs have similar shapes. This exhibits a very interesting phenomenon: accuracy increases and reaches its peak in the range of *3-20 terms*, and when more terms are used, accuracy slightly decreases to a stable level. Thus, selecting a small yet significant set of terms for ranking computation in fact *improves* prediction accuracy. For example, for Eclipse, at $k = 16$, we have top-5 accuracy of 80%, while at $k = 5,000$, top-5 accuracy is only 72%.

This result shows that the selection of terms could improve much prediction accuracy. The result also suggests that one just needs *a small, yet significant set of terms for each developer* to describe his bug-fixing expertise. Bugzie with term selection is flexible to capture those significant terms representing the technical issues handled by each developer. For example, analyzing Eclipse's bug reports, we verified the core bug-fixing technical expertise of the fixers listed in Table 3. Bugzie also enables the exclusion of a large number of un-important terms in bug reports, as well as the terms with small correlation scores to developers. Those terms could have brought noises to the computation in Bugzie.

More importantly, selecting only a small portion of available terms significantly improves time efficiency. Figure 8 shows the graph for the total processing time. As seen, in Eclipse, at $k = 16$ (the system-wide term list $T(k)$ has 6,772 terms), Bugzie is four times faster than at $k = 5,000$ ($T(k)$ has 193,862). Moreover, the processing time is also linear with respect to the cache size of selected terms, showing that Bugzie is scalable well to large projects.

5.4 Selection of Developers and Terms

To evaluate the impacts of both types of selection, we conducted another experiment and tuned the model with dif-

Table 4: Eclipse: Accuracy - Various Parameters

Tuning Parameters	top-1	top-2	top-3	top-4	top-5	Time
$x = 40\%$, $k = 16$	45.0	61.2	71.2	78.2	83.2	12:00
$x = 100\%$, $k =$ All	40.5	53.7	61.7	67.5	72.0	1:39:12

Table 5: FireFox: Accuracy - Various Parameters

Tuning Parameters	top-1	top-2	top-3	top-4	top-5	Time
$x = 10\%$, $k = 10$	34.6	50.9	61.8	70.3	76.7	6:16
$x = 10\%$, $k = 17$	33.8	50.4	61.8	70.3	76.8	8:57
$x = 10\%$, $k = 18$	33.6	50.3	61.7	70.2	76.7	9:51
$x = 20\%$, $k = 10$	34.1	50.5	61.8	70.7	77.7	9:17
$x = 20\%$, $k = 17$	33.2	50.1	61.8	70.8	77.8	12:04
$x = 20\%$, $k = 18$	33.0	49.9	61.7	70.8	77.7	13:10
$x = 100\%$, $k =$ All	28.0	44.7	55.8	64.1	70.7	1:50:04

ferent sizes of developer cache and term cache. Two caches are used together in which Bugzie computes the scores and ranks only the developers in the developer cache for recommendation, and uses only the terms in the term cache for its computation (Section 3.3). We ran Bugzie on all datasets in Table 1 with all combinations of the best values we discovered in the previous experiments as the model's parameters. Tables 4 and 5 show the accuracy and total processing time (hh:mm:ss) with different parameters for Eclipse and FireFox.

As seen, Bugzie could be tuned to achieve very high levels of accuracy and efficiency. For example, for Eclipse, the best configured model processes the whole Eclipse's bug dataset (with about 178K bug records and 2K developers) in only 12 minutes and achieves 83% top-5 prediction accuracy. That is about 8.3 times faster, and 11% more accurate than the base model ($x = 100\%$ and all terms). For FireFox, the respective numbers are 12 minutes, 78% top-5 accuracy, 9 times faster and 7% more accurate than the base model (Table 5).

Table 6 shows top-1 and top-5 best accuracy when we ran Bugzie with 4 types of configurations: base model with all developers and all terms (Column Base), base model with candidate selection (Column C.S.), base model with term selection (Column T.S.), and base model with both (Column Both).

Generally, the top-5 accuracy achieves the best results in the range of 75-83% for all projects (except for NetBeans - 61.3%). That is, approximately in 5 out of 6 cases, the correct fixer is in Bugzie's recommending list of 5 developers. The best results for top-1 accuracy are from 31-51%. That is, in one out of 2-3 cases, the single recommended developer by Bugzie is actually the fixer of the given bug report. Importantly, comparing with the base model, the models with tuned parameters (C.S., T.S., and Both) significantly improve time efficiency, while maintaining the high levels of accuracy. Even in 5 out of 7 systems, tuned parameters help increase top-1 accuracy levels from 3-7% and top-5 ones from 3-11%.

5.5 Comparison Results

For comparison, we used Weka [38] to re-implement existing approaches [11, 3, 5, 28] following the descriptions in their papers. Cubranic and Murphy [11] use Naive Bayes. Anvik *et al.* [3] use Naive Bayes, SVM, and C4.5 classifiers. Bhattacharya and Neamtiu [5] use Naive Bayes and Bayesian Network with and without incremental learning. We re-implemented Matter *et al.* [28]'s vector-space model (VSM) with the terms being extracted only from the bug reports.

Table 7: 3-Year Fixing History Data

Project	Time	Record	Fixer	Term
Firefox	01/01/08 - 10/28/10	77,236	1,682	85,951
Eclipse	01/01/08 - 10/28/10	69,829	1,510	103,690
Apache	01/01/08 - 01/01/11	28,682	1,354	80,757
NetBeans	01/01/08 - 11/01/10	23,522	380	42,797
FreeDesktop	01/01/08 - 12/05/10	10,624	161	37,596
Gcc	01/01/08 - 10/28/10	6,865	161	20,279
Jazz	06/01/05 - 06/01/08	34,228	156	39,771

Since some machine-learning approaches (e.g. C4.5) realized in Weka can not scale up to the full datasets, we prepared smaller datasets, which have 3-year histories of the full ones (Table 7). Table 8 shows the comparison result for top-rank accuracy. Table 9 shows training and prediction time.

As seen, Bugzie consistently outperforms other approaches in term of both prediction accuracy and time efficiency for all subjects. For example, for Eclipse, in term of top-5 accuracy, the second best model is SVM, which has almost 18 hours of processing time and achieves 53% top-5 accuracy, while Bugzie takes only 22 minutes and achieves 72% top-5 accuracy. That is, Bugzie is about 49 times faster and relatively 19% more accurate. In term of processing time, the second best model for Eclipse is VSM, which takes 14 hours and achieves 31% top-5 accuracy, i.e. it is 38 times slower, and 41% less accurate than Bugzie. Generally, ML-based approaches takes from hours to days (even almost a month) to finish training as well as predicting. Bugzie has its training time of tens of minutes to half an hour and prediction time of only seconds, while still achieves higher accuracy.

Decision tree approach (C4.5) has low time efficiency: it takes nearly 28 days for training on Eclipse dataset (with about 70K bug reports). Naive Bayes (NB) model takes less time for training (around 9 hours), but much more time for recommending (5.5 days). It is also less accurate than Bugzie: 24% versus 39% (top-1) and 47% versus 72% (top-5). It is similar for Bayesian Network (BN) (15 hours for training and 7.5 days for predicting, with 13% and 28% of top-1 and top-5 accuracy). Generally, the respective accuracy of incremental NB and BN is from 7-21% and 15-38% less than Bugzie's accuracy for top-1 and top-5 prediction.

5.6 Discussions and Comparisons

Our results suggest that machine learning classification models are less efficient for very large numbers of bug records/fixers. Especially, tree induction models (e.g. C4.5) require all training data to fit in the memory to be efficient [18].

Using SVM, for a developer d, one needs to train a *classifier* SVM_d to distinguish the bug reports that d is able to fix (i.e. $SVM_d(B) = 1$) from the others (i.e. $SVM_d(B) = -1$). Using it to rank developers, one needs another measure $R_d(B)$ to measure the confidence on the event that d is able to fix B, which is computed as the distance from the vector representing B to the separate hyperplan of SVM_d. Since the classifiers are trained independently, the ranking functions $R_d()$ are not trained competitively together to reflect the actual ranking they should provide (e.g. if both d and d' are viewed as capable to fix a bug report B, $R_d(B) > R_{d'}(B)$ might not imply that d is more capable than d' in fixing B). In contrast, Bugzie actually models/learns the ranking functions, i.e. $\mu_t(d)$ and $\mu_B(d)$. Thus, $\mu_B(d) > \mu_B(d')$ does imply that d is more capable than d' in fixing B.

Table 6: Top-1 & Top-5 Prediction Accuracy (%) - C.S: Fixer Candidate Selection, T.S: Term Selection

	Top-1				Top-5				Time			
Project	Base	C.S	T.S	Both	Base	C.S.	T.S.	Both	Base	C.S.	T.S.	Both
FireFox	28.0	30.0	32.1	34.6	70.7	72.4	73.9	77.8	1:50:04	31:24	24:14	12:04
Eclipse	40.5	40.9	42.6	45.0	72.0	72.7	80.1	83.2	1:39:12	50:47	26:28	12:00
Apache	39.8	39.8	39.8	39.8	75.0	74.9	75.0	75.0	1:08:23	46:24	1:05:00	36:59
Netbeans	26.3	26.3	31.8	32.3	54.2	59.5	60.4	61.3	17:04	11:51	4:49	2:30
FreeDesktop	47.1	47.3	51.2	51.2	77.9	78.0	81.1	81.1	20:35	17:26	3:03	2:07
Gcc	48.6	48.7	48.6	48.7	79.2	79.3	79.2	79.6	14:37	7:08	11:44	7:08
Jazz	28.4	28.4	31.3	31.3	72.6	72.6	75.3	75.3	24:45	21:12	1:37	1:37

In Naive Bayes (NB), given a bug report B as a set of terms, the probability that this bug report belongs to the class of bug reports associated with a developer d is:

$$P(d|B) \propto P(d).P(B|d) = P(d).\prod_{t \in B} P(t|d) \ (*)$$

In this formula, $P(d)$ is the probability of observing developer d in the fixing data and $P(t|d)$ is the probability of observing term t in the bug reports fixed by d. This formula is used to rank the developers for recommendation.

However, there are two reasons that NB is less suited for automatic bug triaging. First, the probability of assigning developer d to a bug report $P(d|B)$ is proportional to $P(d)$. That is, the more frequently d fixes, the higher chance he is assigned to a new report. This might not fit well with the locality of fixing activity. For example, in practice, there often happens that a developer has been active in bug-fixing for certain technical areas in a period of time, and moves on to other areas. He might have extensive past fixing activities, but does not handle those technical issues anymore. NB still tends to give him higher probability due to his past activities. In contrast, Bugzie will not have him in its candidate list, if it finds that he has not fixed any bug for a long time.

Second, an important assumption in NB is the independence of the features (i.e. terms), which gives $P(B|d) = \prod_{t \in B} P(t|d)$, while in bug reports, the terms, especially those relevant to a technical issue, tend to co-occur, i.e. are highly correlated. Let d be a developer with fixing expertise on version control, t = repository and t' = cvs be two terms associated with that concern. t and t' highly co-occur in the bug reports on version control. However, for a bug report B containing both terms, NB will have $P(B|d) = P(t|d) * P(t'|d)$, which is likely different from $P(t, t'|d)$. Thus, the feature independence assumption reduces the probability $P(B|d)$. Moreover, that product formula is also sensitive to noises. For example, if B contains t and a misspelled word e, which rarely occurs in bug reports fixed by d ($P(e|d)$ is very small). Then, $P(B|d) = P(t|d) * P(e|d)$ is much smaller than $P(t|d)$.

For Bayesian Network models, the assumption for feature independence is not enforced. However, they still face the same issue, i.e. $P(d|B)$ is proportional to $P(d)$. Thus, BN models are not well suited with the locality of fixing activity.

In Vector Space Model (VSM), all terms in bug reports are collected into a corpus. It builds the term-fixer matrix in which a fixer is profiled by a vector whose entries equal to the frequencies of the terms in his fixed bug reports. Developers whose vectors have highest similarity to the vector for a new report are suggested. VSM is less suitable for bug triaging than Bugzie. First, term selection is less flexible because VSM requires all vectors to have the same size. Moreover, all terms in a bug report are assumed to be independent.

In brief, comparing to those models, Bugzie is better suited to bug triaging because it is adapted to the ranking nature of the problem, the *locality* of fixing activity, the *co-occurrences* (i.e. dependency) of technical terms associated with the same technical aspect, and the *evolutionary nature* of software development. In addition to significantly higher accuracy, Bugzie also has significantly higher efficiency than existing approaches because 1) training/recommending relies on simple arithmetic calculations on counting values (Section 3), 2) updating is fast and truly incremental, and 3) selections of terms and developers reduce processing time.

In Bugzie, technical terms are selected based on their levels of direct association to developers. One could use other feature selection methods such as information theoretic measures (e.g. information gain). Topic-modeling [9] could be used to identify technical topics and associated terms. Also, other developers' selection strategies [32] could be applied.

Threats to Validity. Since the tools of existing approaches are not available, we re-implemented them via Weka [38]. However, our code is strictly based on their descriptions.

6. RELATED WORK

There exist machine learning (ML) and information retrieval (IR) approaches to automatic bug triaging. In Cubranic and Murphy [11]'s, the titles, descriptions, and keywords are extracted from the bug reports to build a classifier for developers using Naive Bayes. The classifier suggests potential fixers based on the classification of a new report. Its prediction accuracy is up to 30% on an Eclipse's bug dataset from Jan to Sep-2002. Anvik *et al.* [3] follow similar ML approach and improve Cubranic *et al.*'s work by filtering out unfixed bug reports and inactive developers. With 3 different classifiers using SVM, Naive Bayes, and C4.5, they achieve a precision of up to 64%. Comparing to those ML approaches, Bugzie has some advances. First, it is able to provide more precisely the ranked list of potential fixers. The outcome of a classifier has the assignment of a bug report to one specific fixer, thus, an additional ranking scheme was needed with the classifier. Second, simple fuzzy set computation with its counting values is much more time efficiency than ML approaches in training/prediction. Importantly, Bugzie's truly incremental training and caching fits well with software evolution and improves its performance. Finally, it can handle the co-occurrences of terms of the same technical issue.

Another approach is from Bhattacharya and Neamtiu [5]. They use Bayesian Network and Naive Bayes. Those models are less precise than Bugzie since they cannot handle co-occurrent technical terms, and suffer other limitations as in ML approaches (Section 5.6). To improve ranking, they utilize *bug tossing graphs*, which represent the re-assignments of a bug to multiple developers before it gets resolved. As shown, Bugzie outperformed (incremental) NB and BN from

Table 8: Comparison of Top-1 and Top-5 Prediction Accuracy (%)

	Top-1								Top-5							
Project	NB	InB	BN	InBN	C4.5	SVM	VSM	Bugzie	NB	InB	BN	InBN	C4.5	SVM	VSM	Bugzie
Firefox	19.8	21.7	12.9	13.2	24.1	25.7	13.4	29.9	43.5	45.8	29.4	30.5	32.6	54.8	33.6	71.8
Eclipse	23.7	25.9	12.2	14.1	23.8	27.4	12.2	38.9	47.1	49.8	27.9	31.9	33.0	53.0	30.9	71.7
Apache	24.3	24.7	11.3	11.6	21.6	26.2	12.0	40.0	45.3	46.0	26.6	28.4	32.4	47.6	30.7	78.0
NetBeans	16.8	2.7	7.2	5.8	17.9	21.8	8.0	29.2	38.5	11.6	21.9	18.9	26.9	45.2	20.8	59.8
FreeDesktop	37.1	38.1	31.8	32.6	35.3	42.2	23.2	52.7	63.5	65.2	57.2	59.1	47.9	69.0	54.5	80.0
Gcc	32.8	33.3	44.2	45.6	39.3	43.0	10.2	45.7	71.3	72.5	69.6	71.5	57.5	77.0	37.3	88.8
Jazz	19.9	20.4	22.6	22.7	20.5	27.9	6.4	30.0	50.3	50.1	55.4	55.8	34.6	67.4	18.9	73.2

Table 9: Comparison of Processing Time (s: seconds, m: minutes, h: hours, d: days)

	Train Time								Pred. Time							
Project	NB	InB	BN	InBN	C4.5	SVM	VSM	Bugzie	NB	InB	BN	InBN	C4.5	SVM	VSM	Bugzie
FF	9 h	22 h	12 h	33 h	26 d	6 h	42 m	28 m	3 d	3 d	4 d	4.5 d	9 m	8 h	8 h	30 s
EC	9 h	37 h	15 h	2 d	28 d	6 h	39 m	21 m	5.5 d	5 d	7.5 d	8 d	14 m	12 h	13 h	18 s
AP	3 h	8 h	7.5 h	19 h	25 d	2.5 h	1 m	17 m	10 h	2 d	25 h	4 d	1 m	48 m	6 h	31 s
NB	1 h	4 h	2 h	6 h	10 d	1 h	14 m	10 m	14 h	11 h	22 h	15 h	2 m	1 h	1.5 h	5 s
FD	18 m	39 m	27 m	1 h	2 d	19 m	13 m	6 m	4 h	4 h	6 h	5.5 h	48 s	15 m	23 m	3 s
GC	5 m	14 m	8 m	22 m	27 h	9 m	13 m	5 m	40 m	40 m	35 m	25 m	14 s	4 m	8 m	4 s
JZ	3 h	4 h	3.5 h	6 h	22 h	4 h	2 m	9 m	6.5 h	6.5 h	7 h	7 h	10 s	31 m	5 m	5 s

6-20% and 13-35% for top-1 and top-5 accuracy, respectively. Despite of incremental learning, the training and prediction time of those models for Eclipse is from 9-15 hours and 5.5-7.5 days, while Bugzie takes only minutes to an hour.

The idea of bug tossing graphs was introduced by Jeong *et al.* [22]. Their Markov-based model learns from the past the patterns of bug tossing from developers to others after a bug was assigned. Their goal is more toward reducing the lengths of bug tossing paths, rather than addressing the question of who should fix a given bug as in an initial assignment.

Lin *et al.* [27] use ML with SVM and C4.5 classifiers on both textual and non-text fields (e.g. bug type, submitter, phase ID, module ID, and priority). Running on a proprietary project with 2,576 bug records, their models achieve the accuracy of up to 77.64%. The accuracy is 63% if module IDs were not considered. Bugzie has higher accuracy and can integrate non-text fields for further improvement. Podgurski *et al.* [31] utilize ML to classify/prioritize bug reports, but not directly support bug triaging. Di Lucca *et al.* use Bayesian and VSM to classify maintenance requests [12].

Other researchers use IR for automatic bug triaging. Canfora and Cerulo [10, 8] use the terms of fixed change requests to index source files and developers, and query them as a new change request comes for bug triaging. The accuracy was not very good (10-20% on Mozilla and 30-50% on KDE).

In Develect [28], VSM is used to model a developer's expertise by a vector of frequencies of the terms extracted from his contributed source code. The vector for a new bug report is compared with the vectors for developers for bug triaging. Testing on 130,769 bug reports in Eclipse, the accuracy is not as high as Bugzie (up to 71% with top-10 recommendation list). Compared to Develect, Bugzie's fuzzy sets first enable more *flexible computation and modeling* of developers' bug-fixing expertise. All vectors in Develect must have the same length. With fuzzy set nature, Bugzie allows to select a small yet significant set of terms for each developer. Second, Develect assumes the independence of features/terms. Moreover, as *a project evolves*, VSM must *recompute* the entire vector set, while Bugzie incrementally updates its data with high efficiency. Baysal *et al.* [4] proposed to enhance VSM in modeling developers' expertise with preference elicitation and task allocation. Rahman *et al.* [32] measure the quality of assignment by matching the requested and available competence profiles from bug reports and developers.

Other researchers categorize/assess bug reports based on their quality, severity levels, duplications, fixing time, and relations [7, 34, 36, 33, 19, 20, 29, 6, 26, 16, 24, 37].

Our preliminary Bugzie [35] takes into account all extracted terms and developers in a project's history. Taking advantage of our new finding on the locality of fixing activity and the use of two caching techniques, new Bugzie greatly improves over the old model: reducing processing time about 10 times, and improving up to 12% in top-5 prediction accuracy (Table 6). The improvement is confirmed in our new comprehensive, empirical evaluation on 7 large-scale, long-lived projects, while the preliminary results were only on 3-year Eclipse data. TagRec [1] uses fuzzy set theory to recommend the most relevant software tags (i.e. terms) to software artifacts. It is based on the term-to-term correlation, i.e. modeling the association among terms, which belong to the same space. In contrast, Bugzie is based on the developer-to-term correlation, i.e. modeling the association of developers and terms, which are the entities in different spaces. Caching also helps it fit with bug triaging problem.

7. CONCLUSIONS

We propose Bugzie, a fuzzy set and cache-based approach for automatic bug triaging. A fuzzy set represents the capable developers of fixing the bugs related to a technical issue. The membership score of a developer to a fuzzy set is calculated based on his fixed bug reports, and is incrementally updated. With flexible caching of developers and terms, Bugzie can accommodate the locality of fixing activity, the co-occurrences of the terms of same technical aspects, and software evolution. Our evaluation shows that it achieves higher accuracy and efficiency than existing approaches.

Acknowledgment. This project is funded in part by NSF CCF-1018600 grant.

8. REFERENCES

[1] J. Al-Kofahi, A. Tamrawi, T. Nguyen, H. Nguyen, and T.N. Nguyen. Fuzzy Set Approach for Automatic Tagging in Evolving Software. In ICSM'10. IEEE CS, 2010.

[2] Apache. https://issues.apache.org/jira/

[3] J. Anvik, L. Hiew, and G. C. Murphy. Who should fix this bug? In ICSE '06, pages 361–370. ACM Press, 2006.

[4] O. Baysal, M. W. Godfrey, and R. Cohen. A bug you like: A framework for automated assignment of bugs. In ICPC'09, pages 297-298. IEEE CS, 2009.

[5] P. Bhattacharya and I. Neamtiu. Fine-grained incremental learning and multi-feature tossing graphs to improve bug triaging. In *ICSM'10*. IEEE CS, 2010.

[6] N. Bettenburg, S. Just, A. Schröter, C. Weiss, R. Premraj, T. Zimmermann. What makes a good bug report? In FSE'08, pages 308-318. ACM Press, 2008.

[7] N. Bettenburg, R. Premraj, T. Zimmermann, S. Kim. Duplicate bug reports considered harmful... really? In ICSM' 08, pages 337-345. IEEE CS, 2008.

[8] G. Canfora and L. Cerulo. How software repositories can help in resolving a new change request. In *Workshop on Empirical Studies in Reverse Eng.*, 2005.

[9] D. Blei, A.Y. Ng, and M. Jordan. Latent Dirichlet Allocation. J. Mach. Learn. Res. 3 (2003), 993-1022.

[10] G. Canfora and L. Cerulo. Supporting change request assignment in open source development. In SAC'06: ACM symposium on Applied computing, pages 1767–1772. ACM Press, 2006.

[11] D. Cubranic and G. Murphy. Automatic bug triage using text categorization. In SEKE'04: the 16th International Conference on Software Engineering and Knowledge Engineering, pages 92–97. KSI Press, 2004.

[12] G. Di-Lucca, M. Di-Penta, and S. Gradara. An approach to classify software maintenance requests. In ICSM'02, pages 93-102, IEEE CS, 2002.

[13] Eclipse. https://bugs.eclipse.org/bugs/

[14] FireFox. https://bugzilla.mozilla.org/

[15] FreeDesktop. https://bugs.freedesktop.org/

[16] M. Fischer, M. Pinzger, H. Gall. Analyzing and relating bug report data for feature tracking. In WCRE'03, pages 90-99. IEEE CS, 2003.

[17] Gcc. http://gcc.gnu.org/bugzilla/

[18] J. Han, M. Kamber, and J. Pei. Data Mining: Concepts and Techniques. The Morgan Kaufmann Series in Data Management Systems, 2006.

[19] L. Hiew. Assisted detection of duplicate bug reports. Master's thesis, University of British Columbia, 2006.

[20] P. Hooimeijer, W. Weimer. Modeling bug report quality. In ASE '07, pages 34–43. ACM Press, 2007.

[21] D. Jannach, M. Zanker, A. Felfernig, G. Friedrich. Recommender Systems: An Introduction. Cambridge University Press, 2011.

[22] G. Jeong, S. Kim, T. Zimmermann. Improving bug triage with bug tossing graphs. In *FSE'09*, pages 111-120. ACM Press, 2009.

[23] S. Kim, T. Zimmermann, J. Whitehead Jr., and A. Zeller. Predicting faults from cached history. In *ICSE'07*, pages 489-498. IEEE CS, 2007.

[24] S. Kim, E.J. Whitehead, Jr. How long did it take to fix bugs? In MSR '06, pages 173-174. ACM Press, 2006.

[25] G.J. Klir and Bo Yuan. Fuzzy Sets and Fuzzy Logic: Theory and Applications. Prentice Hall, 1995.

[26] A.J. Ko, A.B. Myers, D.H. Chau. A linguistic analysis of how people describe software problems. In VLHCC'06, pagess 127-134. IEEE CS, 2006.

[27] Z. Lin, F. Shu, Y. Yang, C. Hu, and Q. Wang. An empirical study on bug assignment automation using Chinese bug data. In *ESEM'09*, pages 451–455. IEEE CS, 2009.

[28] D. Matter, A. Kuhn, and O. Nierstrasz. Assigning bug reports using a vocabulary-based expertise model of developers. In *MSR'09*, pp. 131–140. IEEE CS, 2009.

[29] T. Menzies, A.Marcus. Automated severity assessment of software defect reports. In ICSM'08, pages 346–355. IEEE CS, 2008.

[30] Netbeans. http://netbeans.org/bugzilla/

[31] A. Podgurski, D. Leon, P. Francis, W. Masri, M. Minch, J. Sun, B. Wang. Automated support for classifying software failure reports. In ICSE'03, pages 465-475. IEEE CS, 2003.

[32] M. Rahman, G. Ruhe, T. Zimmermann. Optimized assignment of developers for fixing bugs an initial evaluation for Eclipse projects. In ESEM'09, pages 439-442. IEEE CS, 2009.

[33] P. Runeson, M. Alexandersson, O. Nyholm. Detection of duplicate defect reports using natural language processing. In ICSE '07, pp. 499–510. IEEE CS, 2007.

[34] C. Sun, D. Lo, X. Wang, J. Jiang, S.C. Khoo. A discriminative model approach for accurate duplicate bug report retrieval. In ICSE '10, pages 45-54. ACM Press, 2010.

[35] A. Tamrawi, T. Nguyen, J. Al-Kofahi, and T.N. Nguyen. Fuzzy Set-based Automatic Bug Triaging. In ICSE'11 (NIER). ACM, 2011.

[36] X. Wang, L. Zhang, T. Xie, J. Anvik, J. Sun. An approach to detecting duplicate bug reports using natural language and execution information. In ICSE'08, pages 461-470. ACM Press, 2008.

[37] C. Weiss, R. Premraj, T. Zimmermann, A. Zeller. How long will it take to fix this bug? In MSR'07, IEEE CS, 2007.

[38] Weka: Data mining software in Java. http://www.cs.waikato.ac.nz/ml/weka/.

Mining Development Repositories To Study the Impact of Collaboration on Software Systems

Nicolas Bettenburg
Software Analysis and Intelligence Lab (SAIL)
Queen's University, School of Computing
Kingston, Ontario K7L 3N6, Canada
nicbet@cs.queensu.ca

ABSTRACT

Software development is a largely collaborative effort, of which the actual encoding of program logic in source code is a relatively small part. Yet, little is known about the impact of collaboration between stakeholders on software quality. We hypothesize that the collaboration between stakeholders during software development has a non-negligible impact on the software system. Information about collaborative activities can be recovered from traces of their communication, which are recorded in the repositories used for the development of the software system. This thesis contributes the following: 1) to make this information accessible for practitioners and researchers, we present approaches to distill communication information from development repositories, and empirically validate our proposed extractors. 2) By linking back the extracted communication data to the parts of the software system under discussion, we are able to empirically study the impact of communication, as a proxy to collaboration between stakeholders, on a software system. Through case studies on a broad spectrum of open-source software projects, we demonstrate the important role of social interactions between stakeholders with respect to the evolution of a software system.

Categories and Subject Descriptors

D.2.7 [**Software Engineering**]: Distribution, Maintenance, and Enhancement; D.2.8 [**Software Engineering**]: Metrics; D.2.9 [**Software Engineering**]: Management

General Terms

Management, Measurement, Human Factors

Keywords

Collaboration, Empirical Studies, Software Repositories, Unstructured Data, Socio-Technical Congruence

Permission to make digital or hard copies of all or part of this work for personal or classroom use is granted without fee provided that copies are not made or distributed for profit or commercial advantage and that copies bear this notice and the full citation on the first page. To copy otherwise, to republish, to post on servers or to redistribute to lists, requires prior specific permission and/or a fee.
ESEC/FSE'11, September 5–9, 2011, Szeged, Hungary.
Copyright 2011 ACM 978-1-4503-0443-6/11/09 ...$10.00.

1. INTRODUCTION

Software development as a social activity.
Non-trivial software development is a complex task based on the combined social and technical efforts of software engineers. Modularization makes this complexity manageable [2, 27], and managers use high-level information about the software system to divide the development effort into work teams [15]. This conception is formalized in Conway's Law, who notes in his original work that the source code of a software system stands in direct relation with the organizational structure of the development team, as design decisions require communication among the stakeholders making those decisions [18]. Since software development requires a great amount of social and interpersonal interactions, it comes to no surprise that software engineers typically spend a large fraction of their workday communicating with their co-workers [3]. Lately, research begins to understand that the intricacies of these interactions, such as the forming of social networks and sub-communities [13, 31], work dependencies [16], or daily routines [29] stand in a direct relation to the quality of the final software product [15].

The role of communication in software development.
De Souza et al. provided evidence that communication among software developers is critical for the success of software systems: information hiding led development teams to be unaware of other teams' work, resulting in coordination problems [20]. Bird et al. and Grinter et al. have reported similar findings for distributed software development [11, 22], which highlight communication as the most referenced problem in distributed software development.

Research Hypothesis.
Motivated by the empirical evidence provided in past research, this dissertation proposes to study the impact of collaboration between stakeholders on the quality of a software system more closely. We believe that the quality of a software, is impacted not only by the condition of the source code, but also by the collaborative activities of the stakeholders responsible for the development of the software system. Furthermore, we believe that these collaborative activities also impact the community of developers involved in producing the software system. These believes have led to the formulation of our research hypothesis, which we state as follows:

The collaboration between stakeholders impacts the code quality and development community of a software system.

We conjecture that the communication between stakeholders is a valuable proxy to their collaborative activities. To validate our research hypothesis, we propose the following methodology. First, we develop tools and techniques to extract communication data from development repositories, and empirically validate the proposed approaches through case studies on development repositories provided by open-source software systems. Next, we perform a linking of the extracted communication data back to the parts of the software system referenced within the data. These links enable us to investigate the impact of collaboration between stakeholders on quality and the development community.

The rest of this paper is organized as follows: we present our proposed approach to validating our research hypothesis in Sections 2-4. In each section, we present our motivation, current progress and future research opportunities. In Section 5, we expand on the describing the state of the art beyond the research work presented in Section 1. We conclude our work in Section 6 by outlining the prospective contributions of our work.

2. EXTRACTING COLLABORATION DATA FROM SOFTWARE DEVELOPMENT REPOSITORIES.

Through publicly available data from open-source systems, researchers have access to the rich development repositories of large software systems that are developed by hundreds of developers over extended periods of time. Some of these repositories, such as developer mailing lists, record communication data *explicitly*. At the same time, communication data is also captured *implicitly* in development repositories meant for other tasks, for example developers have been observed to chat through the transaction logs in version control repositories [32].

However, the extraction of communication data from development repositories is a challenging task [4], as communication data was never designed to be pulled out of development repositories. Such data exists mainly in the form of *unstructured data*: arbitrary combinations of natural language text and technical artifacts like source code entities, references to parts of the software system, stack traces, patches, code examples, and other project specific vocabulary. Conventional data and text mining approaches were designed for proper natural language text, as one would find for example in newspaper articles. As such, we cannot readily apply these approaches to mine communication data [8].

Co-organized by Dr. Bram Adams and me, we initiated the 2010 Workshop on Mining Unstructured Data (MUD'10) [4] as a forum for researchers and developers for discussing and sharing the existing work on mining unstructured data into a common reference frame and to discuss the techniques for mining unstructured data.

Within the same line of work presented in the MUD'10 workshop [4], we proposed a lightweight approach based on morphological language analysis to uncover technical artifacts, such as source code examples, stack traces, class and function names, patches, identifiers, and other development specific lingo within unstructured data [5].

We are currently continuing this line of work by extending our empirical validation of the proposed tool. In addition, we are investigating different approaches, including heuristics based on regular expressions, fuzzy text search and vector space models for linking the extracted technical artifacts back to the software system. Through these links we are able to establish a connection between communications and the parts of the software system they talk about.

3. STUDYING THE IMPACT OF COLLABORATION ON THE QUALITY OF A SOFTWARE SYSTEM.

Using the extracted communication data from development repositories, we are able to investigate the impact of collaboration on quality of software systems more closely.

As a first step into this direction, we mined the discussions surrounding the maintenance efforts recorded in the issue trackers of the `Eclipse` and Mozilla `Firefox` software systems. We linked the discussions to the software system through the unique issue report identifiers, which are often referenced by developers when carrying out corrective changes. Through a case study we demonstrated the impact of both, the contents, as well as the dynamics of the communication surrounding corrective maintenance efforts on future software quality [7].

In this line of work, we investigated the relative impact of different aspects of this communication on post-release defects through statistical models. Similar approaches have been successfully used in the past to study the relationship between source code measures and defects [16, 23, 25, 26, 28, 34]. Through our results we observed that the discussions of source code and proposed patches correlate with the risk of future bugs in the areas of source code they reference. Similarly, we discovered that inconsistency in communication flow among stakeholders, for example extended periods of silence, stand in a strong relation with the risk of introducing defects in the software system.

Additionally, we demonstrated that measurements of the communication surrounding corrective maintenance can not only explain post-release defects as well as traditional models based on code metrics, but also that a combination of traditional models based on code metrics, and models based on communication metrics explains post release defects better than each model separately [6].

We are currently investigating the possibilities of increasing the performance of traditional defect prediction methods through the use of collaboration measures.

4. STUDYING THE IMPACT OF COLLABORATION ON THE DEVELOPMENT COMMUNITY.

In the first line of our contributions we propose to analyze the relationships between collaboration and the quality of a software system. However, evidence reported by past research, such as the findings of Bird et al. on the forming of sub-communities [10], led us to strongly believe that collaboration does impact software systems beyond source code: as software development requires a large amount of social and interpersonal interactions, we hypothesize that there is also an impact on the development community responsible for the creation of the software.

Since the quality of a software system is influenced by both, the state of the source code, as well as the people producing the source code, we propose to investigate the impact of collaboration on the stakeholders responsible for providing source code changes.

Within this line of work, we are currently studying the contribution management processes of several successful open-source systems and the communication surrounding these processes. Open-source systems rely on a thriving community surrounding the software system that carries out much of the adaptive development effort [9]. As software systems are constantly changing [24], the management of new source code, contributed by the development community takes on important role in the development of open-source software. Contribution management requires communication between a variety of different stakeholders, including the discussion of the design and implementation of contributions, peer-reviews carried out for means of software quality assurance, and the integration of the proposed changes into future releases. We conjecture that irregularities in the communication surrounding these processes are potentially disruptive to the integration of future changes into the software. For example, a member of that development community who does not get timely feedback on his proposed source code changes in a timely fashion might get discouraged to contribute to the software system in the future and leave the community.

Our preliminary findings suggest the existence of several strong relationships between the way an open-source software community collaborates and the evolution of their organizational structure.

5. STATE OF THE ART

Beyond the research work presented in Section 1, we recognize the following lines of research that are closely related to the work presented in this thesis.

Socio-Technical Congruence.
Literature documents a variety of factors leading to communication problems in software development, such as frequency [3], the number of stakeholders involved [14,17], the non-sharing of knowledge [19], and architectural modularity [21]. Amrit et al. were the first to propose a formalization of developer communication in so-called "affiliation networks" [1], within the context of validating Conway's law. This idea has been picked up by Valetto et al., who examine socio-technical networks, which merge social networks mined from communication meta-data with collaboration networks mined from source code [30]. In this line of work, Valetto et al. propose the notion of socio-technical congruence as a degree of fit between communication and coordination of developers related to the same software component [30]. Cataldo et al. studied the relation between socio-technical congruence and the software development process [15,17].

Use of collaboration metrics in defect prediction.
Research has since picked up social networks and social network analysis to describe developer collaboration. To date, most research effort is based on both social network analysis and socio-technical networks. Some notable instances include the work by Bird et al., who use social network analysis on social networks mined from email repositories [10,13]. These social networks lay the foundation for the use of socio-technical networks to predict software defects [12]. Similarly, Zimmermann et al. use social network measures on dependency graphs to predict defects [33], and Wolf et al. present a case study on the use of social network analysis measures obtained from inter-developer communication in the IBM Jazz repository to predict build failures [31].

6. CONCLUSIONS AND CONTRIBUTIONS

Traces of collaborative software development activities can be found in the repositories, developers use on a day to day basis, such as version control systems, issue tracking systems and email discussion lists. By extracting communication data from development repositories and linking them back to the software system, we are able to investigate the impact of collaboration on the quality and the development community of a software system.
The *technical contributions* of our work center around the development and empirical validation of methods to extract communication information from development repositories. In particular, we propose the following contributions:

- **Tools and techniques for mining communication information from development repositories.** As a first step towards making communication data hidden in development repositories accessible for researchers and practitioners, this dissertation presents tools and methods to distill communication information from development repositories, such as mailing list archives, version control systems, or issue tracking databases.

- **Empirical validation of the applicability of the presented tools and heuristics.** We demonstrate the applicability of these tools by empirically validating the proposed methods and heuristics through case studies on a wide range of development repositories of different software systems. We propose tools and techniques for the automated extraction of communication data from software development repositories.

The *conceptual contributions* of our work center around using the extracted communication information to investigate the impact of collaboration on software quality. In particular, we propose the following contributions:

- **Empirical validation of the impact of collaboration on the quality of a software system.** Through an empirical study on the impact of communication surrounding the software development process and the quality of a software system we uncovered several factors influencing the risk of post-release defects.

- **Empirical validation of the impact of collaboration on the development community.** Through an empirical study on the communication surrounding the process of contribution management in open source software systems, we demonstrate the impact of collaboration on the community developing the software system, which in return effects the integration of adaptive, corrective and prescriptive changes into the software.

7. REFERENCES

[1] C. Amrit, J. Hillegersberg, and K. Kumar. A social network perspective of conway's law. In *Proceedings of the CSCW Workshop on Social Networks*, Chicago, IL, 2004.

[2] C. Y. Baldwin and K. B. Clark. *Design Rules: The Power of Modularity Volume 1*. MIT Press, Cambridge, MA, USA, 1999.

[3] A. Begel, Y. P. Khoo, and T. Zimmermann. Codebook: discovering and exploiting relationships in software repositories. In *Proceedings of the 32nd ACM/IEEE International Conference on Software Engineering - Volume 1*, ICSE '10, pages 125–134, New York, NY, USA, 2010. ACM.

[4] N. Bettenburg and B. Adams. Workshop on Mining Unstructured Data (MUD), because "mining unstructured data is like fishing in muddy waters"! In *Proceedings of the 17th IEEE Working Conference on Reverse Engineering*, pages 277 -278. IEEE Computer, 2010.

[5] N. Bettenburg, B. Adams, A. E. Hassan, and M. Smidt. A lightweight approach to uncover technical artifacts in unstructured data. In *ICPC'11: Proceedings of the 19th IEEE International Conference on Program Comprehension*, page to appear, Kingston, Ontario, Canada, 2011. IEEE Computer.

[6] N. Bettenburg and A. E. Hassan. Studying the impact of social structures on software quality. In *ICPC'10: Proceedings of the 18th IEEE International Conference on Program Comprehension*, pages 124–133, Braga, Portugal, 2010. IEEE.

[7] N. Bettenburg and A. E. Hassan. Studying the impact of social structures on software quality. *submitted to the Editorial Office of Empirical Software Engineering*, 2011.

[8] N. Bettenburg, E. Shihab, and A. E. Hassan. An empirical study on the risks of using off-the-shelf techniques for processing mailing list data. In *Proceedings of the 25th IEEE International Conference on Software Maintenance*, Edmonton, Alberta, Canada, 2009. IEEE Computer.

[9] C. Bird, A. Gourley, and P. Devanbu. Detecting Patch Submission and Acceptance in OSS Projects. In *Proceedings of the Fourth International Workshop on Mining Software Repositories*. IEEE Computer Society, 2007.

[10] C. Bird, A. Gourley, P. Devanbu, M. Gertz, and A. Swaminathan. Mining Email Social Networks in Postgres. In *Proceedings of the Third International Workshop on Mining software repositories (Challenge Track)*. ACM, 2006.

[11] C. Bird, N. Nagappan, P. Devanbu, H. Gall, and B. Murphy. Does Distributed Development Affect Software Quality? An Empirical Case Study of Windows Vista. *Communications of the ACM*, 52(8):85–93, August 2009.

[12] C. Bird, N. Nagappan, P. Devanbu, H. Gall, and B. Murphy. Putting it All Together: Using Socio-Technical Networks to Predict Failures. In *Proceedings of the 17th International Symposium on Software Reliability Engineering*, 2009.

[13] C. Bird, D. Pattison, R. D'Souza, V. Filkov, and P. Devanbu. Latent social structure in open source projects. In *Proceedings of the 16th ACM SIGSOFT International Symposium on Foundations of software engineering*, SIGSOFT '08/FSE-16, pages 24–35, New York, NY, USA, 2008. ACM.

[14] F. P. Brooks, Jr. *The mythical man-month (anniversary ed.)*. Addison-Wesley Longman Publishing Co., Inc., Boston, MA, USA, 1995.

[15] M. Cataldo, J. D. Herbsleb, and K. M. Carley. Socio-technical congruence: a framework for assessing the impact of technical and work dependencies on software development productivity. In *Proceedings of the Second ACM-IEEE international symposium on Empirical software engineering and measurement*, ESEM '08, pages 2–11, New York, NY, USA, 2008. ACM.

[16] M. Cataldo, A. Mockus, J. A. Roberts, and J. D. Herbsleb. Software dependencies, work dependencies, and their impact on failures. *IEEE Transactions on Software Engineering*, 35(6):864–878, 2009.

[17] M. Cataldo, P. A. Wagstrom, J. D. Herbsleb, and K. M. Carley. Identification of coordination requirements: implications for the design of collaboration and awareness tools. In *Proceedings of the 2006 20th anniversary conference on Computer supported cooperative work*, CSCW '06, pages 353–362, New York, NY, USA, 2006. ACM.

[18] M. Conway. How do committees invent. *Datamation*, 14(4):28–31, 1968.

[19] B. Curtis, H. Krasner, and N. Iscoe. A field study of the software design process for large systems. *Commun. ACM*, 31:1268–1287, November 1988.

[20] C. R. B. de Souza, D. Redmiles, L.-T. Cheng, D. Millen, and J. Patterson. How a good software practice thwarts collaboration: the multiple roles of apis in software development. *SIGSOFT Softw. Eng. Notes*, 29(6):221–230, October 2004.

[21] C. R. B. de Souza, D. Redmiles, and P. Dourish. "breaking the code", moving between private and public work in collaborative software development. In *Proceedings of the 2003 international ACM SIGGROUP conference on Supporting group work*, GROUP '03, pages 105–114, New York, NY, USA, 2003. ACM.

[22] R. E. Grinter, J. D. Herbsleb, and D. E. Perry. The geography of coordination: dealing with distance in r&d work. In *Proceedings of the international ACM SIGGROUP conference on Supporting group work*, GROUP '99, pages 306–315, New York, NY, USA, 1999. ACM.

[23] A. E. Hassan. Predicting faults using the complexity of code changes. In *ICSE '09: Proceedings of the 31st International Conference on Software Engineering*, pages 78–88. IEEE Computer Society, 2009.

[24] M. M. Lehman. On understanding laws, evolution, and conservation in the large-program life cycle. *Journal of Systems and Software*, 1:213–221, 1980.

[25] N. Nagappan and T. Ball. Use of relative code churn measures to predict system defect density. In *ICSE '05: Proceedings of the 27th International Conference on Software Engineering*, pages 284–292. ACM, 2005.

[26] N. Nagappan and T. Ball. Using software dependencies and churn metrics to predict field failures: An empirical case study. In *ESEM '07: Proceedings of the First International Symposium on Empirical Software Engineering and Measurement*, pages 364–373. IEEE Computer Society, 2007.

[27] D. L. Parnas. On the criteria to be used in decomposing systems into modules. *Commun. ACM*, 15:1053–1058, December 1972.

[28] A. Schröter, T. Zimmermann, and A. Zeller. Predicting component failures at design time. In *ISESE '06: Proceedings of the 2006 ACM/IEEE International Symposium on Empirical Software Engineering*, pages 18–27. ACM, 2006.

[29] J. Śliwerski, T. Zimmermann, and A. Zeller. When do changes induce fixes? In *MSR '05: Proceedings of the 2005 International Workshop on Mining Software Repositories*, pages 1–5. ACM, 2005.

[30] G. Valetto, M. Helander, K. Ehrlich, S. Chulani, M. Wegman, and C. Williams. Using software repositories to investigate socio-technical congruence in development projects. In *Proceedings of the Fourth International Workshop on Mining Software Repositories*, MSR '07, pages 25–, Washington, DC, USA, 2007. IEEE Computer Society.

[31] T. Wolf, A. Schröter, D. Damian, and T. Nguyen. Predicting build failures using social network analysis on developer communication. In *ICSE '09: Proceedings of the 31st International Conference on Software Engineering*, pages 1–11. IEEE Computer Society, 2009.

[32] A. T. T. Ying, J. L. Wright, and S. Abrams. Source code that talks: an exploration of eclipse task comments and their implication to repository mining. In *Proceedings of the 2005 international workshop on Mining software repositories*, MSR '05, pages 1–5, New York, NY, USA, 2005. ACM.

[33] T. Zimmermann and N. Nagappan. Predicting defects using network analysis on dependency graphs. In *ICSE '08: Proceedings of the 30th international conference on Software engineering*, pages 531–540. ACM, 2008.

[34] T. Zimmermann, R. Premraj, and A. Zeller. Predicting defects for eclipse. In *Proceedings of the Third International Workshop on Predictor Models in Software Engineering*, May 2007.

Reputation-based Self-management of Software Process Artifact Quality in Consortium Research Projects

Christian R. Prause
Fraunhofer FIT
Schloss Birlinghoven, Sankt Augustin, Germany
christian.prause@fit.fraunhofer.de

ABSTRACT

This paper proposes a PhD research that deals with improving internal documentation in software projects. Software developers often do not like to create documentation because it has few value to the individual himself. Yet the purpose of internal documentation is to help others understand the software and the problem it addresses. Documentation increases development speed, reduces software maintenance costs, helps to keep development on track, and mitigates the negative effects of distance in distributed settings. This research aims to increase the individuals' motivation to write documentation by means of reputation. The CollabReview prototype is a web-based reputation system that analyzes artifacts of internal documentation to derive personal reputation scores. Developers making many good contributions will achieve higher reputation scores. These scores can then be employed to softly influence developer behavior, e.g. by incentivizing them to contribute to documentation with social rewards. No strict rule enforcement is necessary.

Categories and Subject Descriptors

D.2.7 [**Software Engineering**]: Documentation; D.2.9 [**Management**]: Software quality assurance

General Terms

Documentation, Human Factors, Management, Measurement

Keywords

software quality, documentation, collaboration, reputation

1. INTRODUCTION AND BACKGROUND

Source code is the most precise description of a software [9]. It contains all the detailed knowledge. Other artifacts of the software process like requirements, designs, rationale and so forth are no less important to humans for understanding. This *internal documentation* encompasses all information that originated from the development of a software product. It is bound for developers and maintainers, and is internal to the organization and project [11]. (External documentation is not treated here.) Due to complexity, a large software system is difficult to understand. But a certain understanding is necessary to modify it. Working on it is therefore a continuous learning process. Documentation is the learning material that provides developers with the knowledge that enables them to modify and extend a software [18]. It serves as a reference to the original developer but is especially valuable to others [25].

In general, research must deliver results that are well usable in the next phase of the innovation process. Fundamental research delivers proven concepts; applied research creates prototypes and runs pilots to demonstrate that a certain design is suitable and works as expected. Prototypes bridge the gap between research and industrial products.

Prototypes are cheap and light-weight versions of software that can later be extended into full-fledged products [13]. They may have bugs, miss features and look crude but the knowledge obtained through them must be preserved. The nearer development draws to its product phase, the more important becomes engineering and the precise knowledge of construction details and design rationale. Only then is incremental refinement possible, and can lead to products.

The majority of projects co-funded under the European Union (EU) Framework Programmes (FPs) are applied research projects, i.e. projects conducting ambitious research with the goal of subsequent industrial exploitation. Research consortia bring together universities, research institutes and small to large industry partners from several different countries. However, documentation is a particularly intricate matter in this environment (see Section 2).

The thesis research deals with improving software development in distributed, multi-partner research projects by motivating developers to contribute more to documentation. It applies reputation and economic theory elements to the software process to enable self-management of documentation. Documentation is considered as a common property that is subject to the "tragedy of commons" (see [8]) – the decay of a valuable resource due to a misalignment between individual and social cost: Documentation has few value to the individual developer but costs him his own precious time to produce [25]. Yet for the whole team, the total "social" cost of not having good documentation is much higher [24].

There are two strategies for preventing poor documentation quality: one is to enforce strict regulations on the usage of the common property, the other one is to *internalize* social

Permission to make digital or hard copies of all or part of this work for personal or classroom use is granted without fee provided that copies are not made or distributed for profit or commercial advantage and that copies bear this notice and the full citation on the first page. To copy otherwise, to republish, to post on servers or to redistribute to lists, requires prior specific permission and/or a fee.
ESEC/FSE'11, September 5–9, 2011, Szeged, Hungary.
Copyright 2011 ACM 978-1-4503-0443-6/11/09 ...$10.00.

cost [4]. Most current approaches follow the first strategy (see Section 3). This research focuses on the second strategy.

The idea is to assign personal responsibility for collaboratively created and used artifacts (source code, wiki pages, ...), and thus internalize common property. *Internalizing* means that the social cost of degeneration is partially transferred to individuals that consequently have a higher interest in preventing degeneration [4]. The CollabReview platform was developed as tool-support for automatically internalizing common properties in a software project (Section 4).

Improving internal documentation reduces project costs and increases quality, [24] and thereby makes industrial exploitation easier and more probable. Compared to approaches based on regulation, internalizing common properties could lessen the need for strict quality prescriptions and instead give developers more flexibility. Additionally, fewer quality control would be necessary, reducing quality control costs and, more importantly, being more suitable in consortium-based projects with flat hierarchies (see Section 6).

2. PROBLEM DESCRIPTION

A lack of high quality documentation is a pervasive problem in software projects. For example, a study of 500 data processing organizations finds that poor documentation is one of the biggest problems [14]. The role and maintenance of documentation is either poorly understood, or documentation does not exist at all because of other project pressures [7, 5]. Software developers are famous for their dislike of documentation, often trying to avoid doing it altogether [25]. Wray asks "Why do we persist in poor programming practices when we know they're poor?" [30]. Boehm calls it the "cowboy role model" of young developers [2]. Even for prototype projects in research, insufficient documentation is a problem when a later project continues the initial research but the original developers and their knowledge are not available anymore [21].

During the last years, I gained insight into a family of projects where improving software processes is difficult. With its FPs, the European Commission (EC) co-funds hundreds of so-called "cooperative projects" with an average cost of more than 5M Euros each year. These projects are signified by a high degree of distributedness because they involve multiple partners by definition. The partners come from several countries, and have different organizational backgrounds: small- and medium-sized enterprises, large corporations, universities and research institutes [22]. Obtaining high quality documentation is challenging but nonetheless important for the demanded industrial exploitation.

In a consortium project, partners will try to minimize their own problems at the expense of others [5] and prioritize practices differently. For example, writing documentation can be considered overly bureaucratic by some, too clumsy by others or just unsuitable. However, as consortium management has a weaker position here than project management in projects conducted by a single entity, agreed documentation standards are difficult to establish.

For example, towards the end of one project, telephone conferences and email discussions were held frequently to try to jointly reconstruct knowledge of the actual workings of the system. Meanwhile, since commercial exploitation opportunities increased, even a reimplementation was discussed. A software system from an earlier project was in such a bad condition that one developer, when leaving for a new job, recommended "to fight tooth and nail" to never have to maintain that system. In another project, some partners had never worked with a wiki before, and prevented that it was established as a primary point of reference. So it contained only few documentation while other documentation was distributed over reports delivered to the EC. One partner resigningly noted that getting documentation from partners was like "trying to get blood out of stone". Developers mostly avoided writing messages when committing source code to revision control, or rarely committed twice a year. Entering bug reports into a tracker was seen as bureaucratic. Therefore not a single report was filed, although issue tracking is pivotal for knowledge management [1].

Poor quality and the non-existence of certain software process artifacts means that knowledge is not (adequately) preserved. When it fades from the developers minds, it is either lost forever, or has to be recovered or recreated in a costly process. For instance, understanding a software architecture from source code only is extremely difficult, guessing non-functional requirements from an implementation comes close to impracticality, and throwing away code means to lose all the implementation subtleties. The thorough use documentation therefore actually speeds implementation and reduces total cost in the long run [24].

3. RELATED WORK

Organizational operation is characterized by the dimensions certainty and agreement. Where there is low certainty of the effects of actions and low agreement between agents about the nature of an issue, processes are difficult to establish, or can even be harmful [27]. EU projects operate in this area. Heavy-weight processes are therefore not suitable.

Approaches like the "Don't repeat yourself" [26] principle aim at reducing the developers' effort when creating documentation. Similarly, tools like Javadoc can generate certain documentation by analyzing source code, or relate existing pieces of documentation [16]. However, manually created documentation that explains the complex backgrounds of software will always be necessary [24].

It seems that a certain amount of continuous pressure to force a change in developer behavior — either through rules and enforcement, or incentives — is necessary [20]. Pair programming has been identified as a source of pair-pressure that reduces bad habits [29]. Also, Extreme Programming reduces the need for documentation through an active direct exchange of knowledge in the team, and with customers. But in EU projects, team sizes at each partner's site are often less than five people [22]. Here, knowledge transfer between sites has to take different forms. Similarly, coding and documentation rules are difficult to enforce across sites.

Relevant to this research are furthermore concepts that attempt to alter user behavior through rewards. Successful examples exist in very different domains: One example is the "Thief of the Week award" that rewards developers who re-use code instead of developing it anew [15]. In pervasive computing, Yamabe et al. showed that micro-payments can have a significant impact on user behavior [31]. Since the advent of the Internet, reputation systems have become an important factor in online communities to alter user behavior [12]. Social rewards are applied to wikis in work places to motivate employees to contribute [10, 6]. Although metrics are important in software development, they have to be used with care because they might be perceived as threats to developers' careers. Also, metrics might fail and not tell the truth, or be manipulated by developers [28].

4. THESIS STATEMENT

There is no universal documentation method. This holds true for research projects, too, where the predominant form of organization is self-organization. Only the individual developer can effectively decide what is worth documenting and what not. As the purpose of documentation is to impart knowledge in its audience, it has to be judged based on this ability. It may, for instance, be incomplete and still be appreciated, as long as the necessary information is conveyed [7]. By adding a little motivation to do documentation, developers may be willing to contribute more. I claim that...

> *"Internalizing software process artifacts with a reputation-based software tool in combination with suitable rewards, encourages the individual developer himself to care more for the quality of the project team's common property."*

To allow researching this claim, the CollabReview platform has been developed. CollabReview is a reputation system that analyzes how developers interact with the common properties. A developer who often makes high-quality contributions will consequently receive a high reputation score. The scores are then exploited to influence developer behavior. For example, publishing all developers' scores to the team can reward well-behaving developers. But also social games, computing personal technical debt with respect to documentation [3], or tangible rewards are possible.

In order to compute reputation scores, CollabReview assesses the quality of each artifact of documentation, and determines who contributed to it. The quality of an artifact of documentation is determined by voting (called review). Feedback from developers as well as results of automatic analyses (e.g. static analysis) are collected, and then averaged to compute the quality rating for that artifact. To account for out-of-date reviews, reviews are weighted according to their timeliness. Timeliness is based on how much the reviewed artifact has changed since the review [19].

The developers' contribution to an artifact is calculated by CollabReview through authorship. Text that is contributed to the artifact by a developer, is said to be authored by that developer. A developer who owns much of the text of an artifact, has a high responsibility for the artifact. For instance, if half of the text of an artifact was written by a certain developer, then that developer will have half of the responsibility for the artifact. CollabReview compares different revisions of an artifact to determine authorship.

Each new revision of an article is compared with several of its probable ancestors. When an optimal candidate has been found, the algorithm determines an author for the newly added or modified lines; unmodified lines will retain their authorship information. If a non-trivial line (e.g. one that contains only whitespace) is found to be a clone of an already existing line, authorship information is copied from there. Otherwise the revision's creator is author of the line [17].

5. APPROACH AND CONTRIBUTIONS

The thesis research interconnects different scientific areas. At a technical level, there are analyses of project common property to obtain authorship, and quality information through static analysis and reviews. At a higher level, software processes, collaboration, motivation and economic aspects must be considered. A solution cannot be purely technical, theoretical or conceptional.

The research therefore loosely follows a user-centered design approach. Yet the proposed solution was not explicitly demanded by users. Instead, it is developed to exploit potential for improvement. However, concept and prototype are developed iteratively with frequent user involvement.

Years of project experience led to the observation of problems as described in Section 2. Conventional software process improvement techniques were difficult to establish in these environments. An empirical study involving 100 respondents from 50 EU projects was conducted to define a frame of reference for the personal project experiences [22].

An initial set of requirements was gathered from personal experience. They were used to draft a solution concept, and were discussed with colleagues. Refinements to the concept were based on existing literature [20]. After this, the initial CollabReview prototype was implemented [19]. The concept was presented and discussed in three expert rounds to generate conceptual feedback. This feedback led to refinements of the concept, and further requirements and constraints.

CollabReview was tested with source code from two real projects (one EU and one open source project). The goal was to show that the prototype can handle real-world data and produce sensible results. Adaptations were necessary to make the prototype capable of handling the large datasets that occur in reality. A source code evolution algorithm was developed to improve handling of moved code, and to increase the tampering resistance of CollabReview's authorship analysis [17]. For source code, CollabReview's way of computing reputation has been validated. Validation was possible because static analysis can cheaply generate objective quality data. The validation first computed developers' reputation scores, and then used the reputation scores to predict source code quality in a 10-fold cross validation. The results showed a significant, substantial correlation of $r \approx 0.4$. While prediction is not highly accurate, it shows that reputation scores work as indicators for prediction, and are therefore sound. (Publication pending.)

In parallel to this, a survey of rewards used in practice was conducted. From this survey, twelve dimensions of the *incentives space* were identified and aligned with the responses of 16 subjects working in EU projects [23]. This information directed the search for a suitable rewarding mechanism.

Moknowpedia, the knowledge management wiki of the Mobile Knowledge workgroup, was chosen as a first field-test environment for the CollabReview platform. The prototype was adapted to process wiki articles instead of source code. Its user interfaces were reworked for seamless integration with the wiki. In a two months trial, the effects of the extensions to Moknowpedia were evaluated. Significant improvements to article quantity and quality were measurable as well as perceived by the users [6]. The reception of the platform was mostly positive, and it keeps being in use even after the evaluation has ended. The experiences gathered with the enhanced Moknowpedia informed further design decisions. Work is in progress to improve the reputation-based rewarding scheme to make it more effective.

6. EVALUATION

This section details the plans for the final evaluation of the concept. (Section 5 lists validations and evaluations that were already conducted.) The final evaluation is scheduled for 2011. It concludes the thesis research with field-tests in EU projects, and a laboratory experiment.

CollabReview is currently being integrated with the GForge software project infrastructure that is used in several EU projects. The integration with GForge will enable field-tests in two EU projects with up to 100 developers from different European countries. In these field-tests, the effects on both source code quality and wiki articles are investigated, and developer reactions are studied.

The laboratory experiment will test the researched concept under controlled conditions. Two groups of users, control groups and experimental groups, will implement the same, specified, small software. While the experimental group will be using CollabReview, CollabReview will not be installed in the control group.

Acknowledgment

This work is co-funded by the *ebbits* EU FP7 project under grant agreement no. 257852.

7. REFERENCES

[1] D. Bertram, A. Voida, S. Greenberg, and R. Walker. Communication, collaboration, and bugs: the social nature of issue tracking in small, collocated teams. In *CSCW*, pages 291–300. ACM, 2010.

[2] B. Boehm. Get ready for agile methods, with care. *Computer*, 35:64–69, 2002.

[3] N. Brown, Y. Cai, Y. Guo, R. Kazman, M. Kim, P. Kruchten, E. Lim, A. MacCormack, R. Nord, I. Ozkaya, R. Sangwan, C. Seaman, K. Sullivan, and N. Zazworka. Managing technical debt in software-reliant systems. In *FoSER*. ACM, 2010.

[4] R. H. Coase. The problem of social cost. *The Journal of Law and Economics*, 3(1):1–44, 1960.

[5] B. Curtis, H. Krasner, and N. Iscoe. A field study of the software design process for large systems. *Communications of the ACM*, 31:1268–1287, 1988.

[6] S. Dencheva, C. R. Prause, and W. Prinz. Dynamic self-moderation in a corporate wiki to improve participation and contribution quality. In *Eur. Conf. Comp.-Supp. Coop. Work*, ECSCW. Springer, 2011.

[7] A. Forward and T. C. Lethbridge. The relevance of software documentation, tools and technologies: a survey. In *DocEng*, pages 26–33. ACM, 2002.

[8] G. Hardin. The tragedy of the commons. *Science*, 162:1243–1248, 1968.

[9] M. Harman. Why source code analysis and manipulation will always be important. In *SCAM*. IEEE, 2010.

[10] B. Hoisl, W. Aigner, and S. Miksch. Social rewarding in wiki systems — motivating the community. In *Online Communities and Soc. Comp.* Springer, 2007.

[11] A. Hunt and D. Thomas. *The Pragmatic Programmer*. Addison-Wesley Longman, 1999.

[12] A. Jøsang, R. Ismail, and C. Boyd. A survey of trust and reputation systems for online service provision. *Decision Support Systems*, 43(2):618–644, 2007.

[13] W. E. Lewis. *Software Testing and Continuous Quality Improvement*. Auerbach, 2005.

[14] B. P. Lientz and E. B. Swanson. Problems in application software maintenance. *Communications of the ACM*, 24(11):763–769, 1981.

[15] J. S. Poulin. Populating software repositories: Incentives and domain-specific software. *Journal of Systems and Software*, 30:187–199, 1995.

[16] C. Prause, J. Kuck, S. Apelt, R. Oppermann, and A. B. Cremers. Interconnecting documentation - harnessing the different powers of current documentation tools in software development. In *Ninth ICEIS*, volume ISAS, pages 63–68. INSTICC, 2007.

[17] C. R. Prause. Maintaining fine-grained code metadata regardless of moving, copying and merging. In *9th International Working Conference on Source Code Analysis and Manipulation*, SCAM. IEEE, 2009.

[18] C. R. Prause. A software project perspective on the fitness and evolvability of personal learning environments. In *Exploring the Fitness and Evolvability of Personal Learning Environments*, 2011.

[19] C. R. Prause and S. Apelt. An approach for continuous inspection of source code. In *International Workshop on Software quality*, WoSQ. ACM, 2008.

[20] C. R. Prause and M. Eisenhauer. Social aspects of a continuous inspection platform for software source code. In *Workshop on Cooperative and Human Aspects of Software Engineering*, CHASE. ACM, 2008.

[21] C. R. Prause, M. Jentsch, and M. Eisenhauer. Mica - a mobile support system for warehouse workers. *International Journal of Handheld Computing Research (IJHCR)*, 2(1):1–24, January-March 2011.

[22] C. R. Prause, R. Reiners, and S. Dencheva. Empirical study of tool support in highly distributed research projects. In *5th International Conference on Global Software Engineering*, ICGSE, pages 23–32. IEEE Computer Society, 2010.

[23] C. R. Prause, R. Reiners, S. Dencheva, and A. Zimmermann. Incentives for maintaining high-quality source code. In *Psychology of Programming Work in Progress Meeting*, PPIG WiP, 2010.

[24] J. Raskin. Comments are more important than code. *ACM Queue*, 3(2):64–62 (sic!), 2005.

[25] B. Selic. Agile documentation, anyone? *IEEE Software*, 26(6):11–12, Nov/Dec 2009.

[26] D. Spinellis. Code documentation. *IEEE Software*, 27:18–19, 2010.

[27] R. D. Stacey. *Strategic Management and Organisational Dynamics: the challenge of complexity*. Financial Times, 1999.

[28] M. Umarji and F. Shull. Measuring developers: Aligning perspectives and other best practices. *IEEE Software*, 26(6):92–94, Nov./Dec. 2009.

[29] L. Williams and B. Kessler. The effects of "pair-pressure" and "pair-learning" on software engineering education. In *13th Conference on Software Engineering Education & Training*. IEEE, 2000.

[30] S. Wray. How pair programming really works. *IEEE Software*, 27:50–55, 2009.

[31] T. Yamabe, V. Lehdonvirta, H. Ito, H. Soma, H. Kimura, and T. Nakajima. Applying pervasive technologies to create economic incentives that alter consumer behavior. In *UbiComp*. ACM, 2009.

An Architecture-centric Approach for Goal-driven Requirements Elicitation

Zoya Durdik
Research Center for
Information Technology (FZI)
76131 Karlsruhe, Germany
durdik@fzi.de

ABSTRACT

Software system development typically starts from a requirement specification followed by stepwise refinement of available requirements while transferring them into the system architecture. However, the granularity and the amount of requirements to be elicited for a successful architectural design are not well understood. This paper proposes a process concept to support system development with the help of an architecture-centric approach for goal-driven requirements elicitation. The process focuses on multiple quality dimensions, such as performance, reliability and scalability, and at the same time shall reduce costs and risks through early decision evaluation. The main contribution of this paper is a novel process where not only requirements can drive architectural design, but also architectural design can selectively drive requirement elicitation with the help of hypotheses connected to the selected architectural solutions. The paper concludes with a discussion on its possible empirical validation.

Categories and Subject Descriptors

D.2.1 [**Software Engineering**]: Requirements/Specifications; D.2.11 [**Software Engineering**]: Software Architectures; D.2.9 [**Software Engineering**]: Management

General Terms

Design, Documentation

Keywords

Requirements elicitation, software architecture, architectural modelling, architectural solutions, design patterns, architectural decisions, development process

1. PROBLEM STATEMENT

Because of the high complexity, strict time and resource constraints, the derivation of a complete requirement specification before proceeding to the architectural design is probably impossible in practice [10]. This fact is especially common for non-functional requirements, but also includes high-priority functional requirements [21]. Moreover, it is not clear how many requirements and shall be elicited and at which level of detail before the process can proceed to the architectural design. An architect usually starts the software design process with such incomplete requirements specification. He transforms available requirements stepwise into elements of the architecture, which in this case are drivers of architectural design. Even already available requirements can be misinterpreted or be inconsistent [10]. The later such inconsistencies and new important requirements are discovered, the higher is the cost and overhead connected to the required system refactorings and implementation [21]. In this case, success of the design process strongly depends on architects experience, quality of the initial requirements and complexity of the system to be developed.

However, not only requirements can drive architectural design, but also architectural design can drive requirement elicitation. Given a catalogue of architectural solutions (architectural styles, patterns, components, services, domain specific solutions, etc.), the solutions could be annotated with sets of questions unique for each solution. Questions would serve for the identification of a solution satisfying a subset of selected requirements, and for the validation of solution suitability and applicability at architectural design. These specific questions sets are referred to as hypotheses in this paper. Answering the hypotheses would contribute to implementation of the available requirements (and trace link creation), and to the elicitation of the new requirements (which are then captured and traced). The advantages would be the following: faster recognition of new relevant requirements, right level of granularity, early detection of contradictions between requirements, and less time spent on at the moment unnecessary requirement elicitation.

In this paper I propose a process concept to support system development with the help of an architecture-centric approach for goal-driven requirements elicitation. The process focuses on multiple quality dimensions, such as sustainability, performance, reliability, security and scalability, and at the same time shall reduce costs and risks through early decision evaluation. Explicit architecture modelling drives selective requirement elicitation through the hypotheses connected to the selected solutions.

This paper is organized as follows: Section 2 presents research objectives and Section 3 the proposed process; Section 4 describes research status. Section 5 provides an overview of related work, and Section 6 concludes.

Permission to make digital or hard copies of all or part of this work for personal or classroom use is granted without fee provided that copies are not made or distributed for profit or commercial advantage and that copies bear this notice and the full citation on the first page. To copy otherwise, to republish, to post on servers or to redistribute to lists, requires prior specific permission and/or a fee.
ESEC/FSE'11, September 5–9, 2011, Szeged, Hungary.
Copyright 2011 ACM 978-1-4503-0443-6/11/09 ...$10.00.

2. RESEARCH OBJECTIVES

The goal is to improve the requirements elicitation phase by establishing a stronger connection between architecture decisions and requirements, and to support system development with focus on multiple quality dimensions, such as sustainability, performance, reliability, security and scalability, reducing costs and risks.

In order to achieve this goal I propose a novel architecture-centric tool-supported software development process described in Section 3. The expected contributions of the process are the following:

- active driving of selective requirements elicitation at the appropriate level of granularity, and early detection of contradictions between requirements through the use of available solutions in the architecture solutions repository;
- reduced risks and costs through early decision evaluation and reuse of architectural knowledge;
- explicit focus on multiple quality dimensions through reuse of specific solutions (e.g. patterns targeting scalability or performance)
- support explicit architecture modelling, documentation of system design and design rationale building up trace links between solutions, decisions, requirements and architecture model elements.

I argue that the approach is beneficial for domains where explicit modelled architecture design plays a significant role, such as business information systems domain (e.g. SAP system).

3. PROPOSED APPROACH

The process consists of iterations of the three major phases: initialisation, architectural solutions selection (architectural styles and patterns, existing services and components, domain specific solutions, etc.) and design implementation, as illustrated on Fig. 1. Selection and implementation phases are themselves iterative and incremental (both alone and in combination), and shall be executed as Scrum Sprints [20]. In the following the process foundations, and major phases are described in detail.

Foundations. The process builds upon Scrum, extendible and relatively lightweight agile method of software development [20], and a process proposed by me in [3], [4], and summarized in [5] (this earlier proposed process was targeting agile architecture modelling). For definition and modelling of software architectures I build upon the Palladio Component Modelling approach (PCM) that is a component-based architecture model approach and tool-chain [1]. PCM has five views on software architecture: repository, assembly, behaviour, deployment and usage. It is implemented as a set of Eclipse plug-ins for prediction of non-functional properties (performance and reliability) at the architectural level, thus enabling early architecture decision validation. It will be additionally enhanced with a requirements view for requirements capture and management, and a trace links mechanism. The decomposition of the problem domain is based on [22] and the extended problem frames approach [17, 2]. The idea to extend focus from reliability and performance to multiple other quality dimensions was inspired by [18].

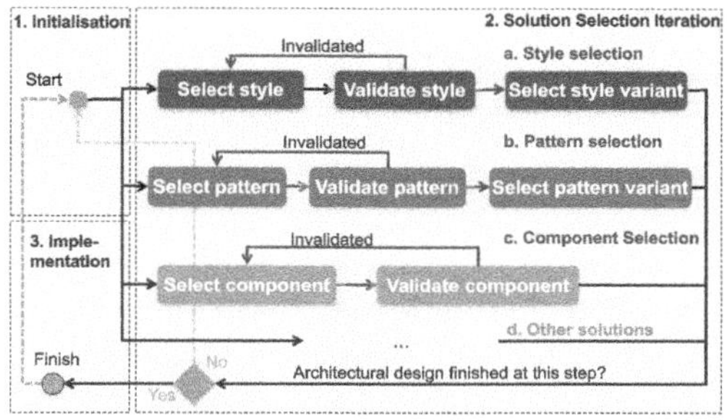

Figure 1: Collaboration between process phases

Initialisation. The process does not consider initial requirements elicitation, assuming it could be successfully executed before start. The initially elicited requirements shall be recorded and prioritised conforming to the special requirements description template and requirements meta-model (both currently in development) and shall be managed in PCM requirements view. The template is the enhancement of Scrum Product Backlog [20] and Architecture Backlog, developed in the [19] under my supervision. After initialisation work the architect can proceed to the solution selection. In later process iterations during initialisation phase the architect goes on with the refinement of the next most important requirements that are not yet implemented and described with the help of the template.

Solution selection. To support requirements refinement into architecture, I propose a rule-based expert system containing a repository of architectural solutions (styles, architecture-relevant patterns, existing components, services, domain specific solutions, etc.). Each of the solutions is stored in the solution repository together with the detailed description of its goal, context, instantiation details and hypotheses. *Hypothesis* is a set of questions specific for a solution, aiming not only to discern between similar solutions, but also to validate the suitability of the selected solution. Solutions are annotated with information about their relevance to the quality dimensions (e.g. improves security, reduces performance).

While there is a rather limited number of architectural styles, the number of e.g. architecture relevant patterns or services can be next to unlimited. The system has to support several solution selection mechanisms to scale and to propose a limited number of only the most relevant solutions.

First, the initial set of available solutions is reduced through the selection of a category (e.g. pattern, style, component, categories within patterns), predefined keywords and the most relevant and prioritized quality dimensions. Solution annotations support the focus on the desired quality dimensions. The non-functional properties of the designed system can be later evaluated with the help of PCM, as solution annotations are not sufficient to make conclusions on the overall expected system quality.

Second, the architect will be able either to browse through the reduced choice of solutions, or answer special questions narrowing the choice towards one possible solution group, and then a particular solution in the group. These questions target the difference between groups of solutions and

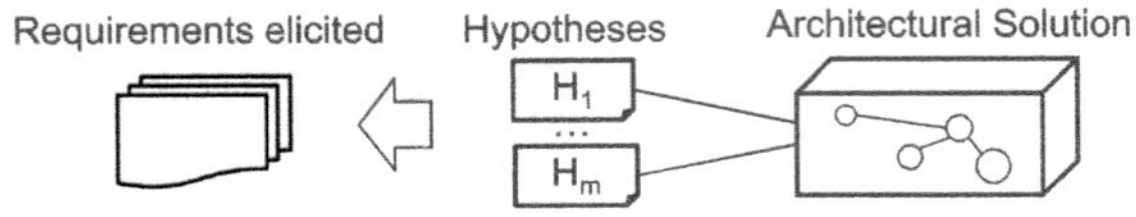

Figure 2: Requirements elicitation from hypotheses

solutions within these groups solving the same problem. For example, concrete table inheritance, single table inheritance and class table inheritance patterns solve the same problem of mapping from objects to relational database tables as they do not support inheritance [7]. Such patterns would belong to one group in the repository. To discern between them in the group, more specific questions contained in the connected hypotheses are required (e.g. questions concerning performance or database technology preference).

Moreover, answering questions contained in the hypotheses can help to elicit new requirements that were otherwise not evident, as shown in Fig. 2. Coming back to the example: it might become clear that due to the performance issues in the database, the access load shall be spread between different tables (concrete table inheritance), or that the database does not have an optimisation and any loss of space shall be avoided (single table inheritance). In this case a new requirement is elicited that otherwise might have remained undiscovered till the point where consideration of it would have been highly expensive. This example requirement is non-functional, but the approach also supports elicitation of functional requirements.

When the architectural style is selected, one goes on analysing requirements having the highest priority and implementing them in the design, refining the architecture and also architecture model. An expert system that proposes suitable solutions shall reduce architecture design overhead at the same time stimulating explicit architecture modelling and its further refinement. Ideally, modelled architectural solutions could be imported directly into PCM. An architecture model created in PCM can than be simulated to predict e.g. the system's performance or reliability. This prevents unsuitable architecture solutions from being implemented and, therefore, reduces risks and makes development more agile. Thus, the focus on quality dimensions is supported by the solution quality annotations at the one side, and PCM at the other side.

Additionally, using hypotheses to validate the solution enables traces between architecture elements, requirements and decisions, including their rationale. The rationale contains information on requirements that were crucial for the selection of one particular solution. An advantage is that requirements that are crucial for the making of a concrete decision, and therefore are the most relevant for certain architectural elements, can be filtered and marked automatically. This helps to avoid having a forest of trace links themselves requiring a lot of maintenance effort (e.g. when architecture needs to be refactored).

Implementation and next iterations. A design draft (partial or complete) created within architecture design iterations shall be presented and explained to the implementation team that can start implementing identified tasks with the highest priority (Scrum). Architect goes on with the architectural design iterations refining architecture. This paper does not touch upon the issue of implementation itself, assuming that design decisions can be successfully broken down into tasks, and then implemented in Sprints.

4. RESEARCH STATUS

In [3] I initially proposed a process targeting agile architecture modelling, and in [4] its validation concept. These proposals are summarized in [5] (to appear). Current work in progress incorporates: 1) development of the requirements description template and a corresponding meta-model, and 2) development of the expert system prototype. The prototype containing an initial set of solutions (only architectural styles in the first version) shall be finished till the end of 2011. The hypotheses for the prototype base on the literature and existing patterns catalogues (e.g. [7, 9]). The preliminary validation is planned for the beginning of 2012.

This work is supervised by Prof. Dr. Ralf H. Reussner, Karlsruhe Institute of Technology.

5. RELATED WORK

The process proposed in this abstract supposes decisions to be captured through the hypotheses and questions connected to them. It differentiates it from majority of approaches dealing with the design decisions and their capture, e.g. [24, 11]. A Goal Solution Scheme [18] maps quality goals and goal refinements to architectural principles and solutions, and can be used complementary to my approach. It focuses on non-functional requirements and architectural solutions, similar to the ones proposed in this paper, but does not consider requirements elicitation, and early decision evaluation. The main drivers of the approach are quality goals that serve as weights when proposing a solution. These arguments are also valid for the [10, 9, 12, 8] and [15], the latter evaluates multiple available design decisions basing on selected quality attributes.

Studies in [14, 13, 6] confirmed influence of existing software architecture on the requirements engineering, however they do not consider using this influence for the requirement elicitation. The idea to use architecture as a basis for further requirement discovery and determination of the alternative design solutions is presented in [16]. However, authors propose to use the view on models and prototypes and commercially available software to emerge new requirements. Design patterns are a way of implementation. The authors give very few details about the method itself. To my best knowledge, the author has no further publications directly to this topic. Another method using similar idea is [23]. It uses information extraction to improve the architecture evolution process by mining architecture and design patterns, however, its goal is to support the system's evolution and to extract general scenarios for it.

6. CONCLUSION

I argue that architectural design can be a driver for a goal-oriented requirement elicitation. First, an expert system containing various solutions shall support architect transforming requirements into architecture. Second, architectural solutions themselves contribute to goal-oriented requirement elicitation through unique hypotheses connected to each solution in the repository. Validation or invalidation of this hypotheses leads to refinement or implementation of existing requirements or to the elicitation of new ones. Thus, not only requirements lead to architectural decisions, but also architectural decisions lead to new requirements that are may be crucial for the system sustainability and would be otherwise discovered much later.

A solution repository supports architectural knowledge reuse through use of patterns, styles, services, etc. contained in a solution repository. No expert knowledge of possible architectural solutions is required by a person using the expert system, as he is supported by the expert system, which can be also used as a knowledge repository itself. Selection of solutions from the repository leads to the creation and continues refinement of architectural models. These models can then be evaluated in the PCM for the violation of non-functional requirements, such as performance and reliability.

Although not all architectural decisions can be derived from available architectural solutions and not all requirements are architecture relevant, the semi-automated proposal and integration of solutions can improve overall system quality targeting sustainability, design speed, and assure that design decisions are validated before implementation. The proposed Backlog modification will enable dealing with and management of requirements that are irrelevant to the architecture. Additionally, I plan to include some non-architectural best practices into the solution repository, that are important to support the selected quality dimensions .

The cost of efficiency benefits of software processes are hard to empirically demonstrate by nature. Therefore, I plan to validate that (a) the process leads to less wasted requirements, (b) more precise formulated requirements (c) traceability between requirements and implementing architectures through series of planned case studies. Of course, controlled empirical experiments would have a higher validity, but are practically hard to perform due to the high effort for the participants. Therefore, I plan to perform studies, where participants (students and researchers colleagues) have to do only specific subtasks in existing documents, such as finding ambiguities or lacking requirements. From a comparison of this process with a process without architectural feedback on requirements elicitation, I plan to extrapolate from finding on such subtasks to the general effect of the process. Additionally, the sufficiency of scalability mechanism will to be tested on the larger set of requirements.

I am thankful for the support of the German Federal Ministry of Education and Research (BMBF), grant No.01BS0822.

7. REFERENCES

[1] S. Becker, H. Koziolek, and R. Reussner. The palladio component model for model-driven performance prediction. *Journal of Systems and Software*, 82:3–22, 2009.

[2] C. Choppy and M. Hatebur, D.and Heisel. Architectural patterns for problem frames. *Software, IEE*, 152:198 – 208, 2005.

[3] Z. Durdik. Architectural modeling in agile methods. volume 2010-14 of *Interne Berichte*, pages 23–30, Karlsruhe, Germany, June 2010. Awarded with CompArch Young Investigator Award.

[4] Z. Durdik. A Proposal on Validation of an Agile Architecture-Modelling Process. In *Proceedings of Software Engineering 2011, Dokt.-Symposium*, 2011.

[5] Z. Durdik. Towards a process for architectural modelling in agile methods. In *7th Int. Conf. on the Quality of Software Architectures (QoSA'11)*, 2011.

[6] R. Ferrari, O. Sudmann, C. Henke, J. Geisler, W. Schafer, and N. H. Madhavji. Requirements and systems architecture interaction in a prototypical project: Emerging results. *16th Int. Working Conf. on Requirements Engineering*, 6182/2010:23 – 29, 2010.

[7] M. Fowler. *Patterns of Enterprise Application Architecture*. Addison-Wesley Professional, 2005.

[8] M. Galster, A. Eberlein, and Moussavi. Systematic selection of software architecture styles. *Software, IET*, 4 Issue:5:349 – 360, 2010.

[9] H. Garbe, C. Janssen, C. Moebus, H. Seebold, and H. de Vries. KARaCAs: Knowledge Acquisition with Repertory Grids and Formal Concept Analysis for Dialog System Construction. In *Managing Knowledge in a World of Networks*. Springer, 2006.

[10] P. Grünbacher, A. Egyed, E. Egyed, and N. Medvidovic. Reconciling software requirements and architectures with intermediate models. In *Software and Systems Modeling*, pages 202–211. Springer, 2003.

[11] L. Lee and P. Kruchten. Customizing the capture of software architectural design decisions. In *Canadian Conf. on Electrical and Computer Engineering*, 2008.

[12] J. Madison. Agile-architecture interactions. *Software, IEEE*, 27 , Issue 2:41 – 48, 2010.

[13] J. Miller, R. Ferrari, and N. Madhavji. Architectural effects on requirements decisions: An exploratory study. *Seventh Working IEEE/IFIP Conf. on Software Architecture*, pages 231 – 240, 2008.

[14] J. A. Miller, R. Ferrari, and N. H. Madhavji. Characteristics of new requirements in the presence or absence of an existing system architecture. *17th Int. Requirements Engineering Conf.*, pages 5 – 14, 2009.

[15] M. Nowak, C. Pautasso, and O. Zimmermann. Architectural decision modeling with reuse: challenges and opportunities. In *Proceedings of the 2010 ICSE Workshop on Sharing and Reusing Architectural Knowledge*, SHARK '10, pages 13–20. ACM, 2010.

[16] B. Nuseibeh. Weaving together requirements and architectures. *Computer*, 34 , Issue 3:115 – 119, 2001.

[17] L. Rapanotti, J. G. Hall, M. Jackson, and B. Nuseibeh. Architecture-driven problem decomposition. *In Proceedings of the 12th IEEE Int. Requirements Engineering Conf.*, pages 80 – 89, 2004.

[18] M. Riebisch. Problem-Solution Mapping for Evolution Support of Software Architectural Design. In *Proceedings of Software Engineering 2011*, 2011.

[19] F. Schad. Enhancement of an agile process model through a software architecture artefact. Student research thesis, KIT, 2010.

[20] K. Schwaber and M. Beedle. *Agile Software Development with Scrum*. Pearson Studium, 2008.

[21] I. Sommerville. *Software Engineering*. Addison Wesley, 2006.

[22] W. Wang and J. E. Burge. Using rationale to support pattern-based architectural design. In *Proceedings of the 2010 ICSE Workshop on Sharing and Reusing Architectural Knowledge*, SHARK '10, pages 1–8, 2010.

[23] L. Zhu, M. A. Babar, and R. Jeffery. Mining patterns to support software architecture evaluation. *Fourth Working IEEE/IFIP Conf. on the Software Architecture*, pages 25 – 34, 2004.

[24] O. Zimmermann. Architectural decisions as reusable design assets. *Software, IEEE*, 28 Issue 1:64 – 69, 2010.

Experimental Specification Mining for Enterprise Applications

Matthias Schur*
SAP Research
Darmstadt, Germany
matthias.schur@sap.com

ABSTRACT

Specification mining infers abstractions over a set of program execution traces. Whereas inductive approaches to specification mining rely on a given set of execution traces, experimental approaches systematically generate and execute test cases to infer rich models including uncommon and exceptional behavior. State-of-the-art experimental mining approaches infer low-level models representing the behavior of single classes. This paper proposes an approach for inferring models of built-in processes in enterprise systems based on systematic scenario test generation. The paper motivates the approach, sketches the relevant concepts and challenges, and discusses related work.

Categories and Subject Descriptors

D.2.1 [**Software Engineering**]: Requirements/Specifications

General Terms

Algorithms, Documentation, Experimentation, Verification

Keywords

Specification Mining, Test Case Generation, Model-based Testing, Enterprise Applications

1. INTRODUCTION

In recent years a multitude of software engineering techniques based on explicit models such as formal verification and model-based testing (MBT), have been developed. These techniques can be used to verify certain properties of complex software systems, but they rely on formal specifications of the systems to verify. However, in software engineering practice, specifications are often informal, outdated or entirely missing, elevating the implementation to the single source of truth. As large enterprise application vendors start to address the mid-market segment with core business functionality that can be extended by numerous partners, reliable system models become critical to ensure operational reliability. In general, the success of model-based software engineering (SE) techniques in industry largely depends on the tradeoff between modeling effort (incl. the effort for keeping the models up-to-date) and the expected benefit. Modeling large industrial software systems is a complex and time-consuming task, hampering broad adoption of model-based SE techniques in industry. Automated techniques actively supporting the modeling process are an essential prerequisite for the success of model-based SE techniques. By utilizing the advances in model-based testing, techniques for automatically inferring models from implementations could significantly decrease the modeling effort and thus make the adoption of additional model-based SE techniques such as formal verification more interesting for industry. Furthermore, inferred models could also be beneficial to documentation, monitoring and change management activities. From an industrial point of view, specification mining also can support the integration of legacy systems that have been adapted and modified over the years and come with outdated documentation.

This paper presents an approach for inferring models of built-in processes in enterprise systems by utilizing MBT methodology. It is organized as follows. *Section 2* discusses the problem to be solved in this research, as well as the underlying research hypothesis. *Section 3* sketches the proposed approach and briefly discusses some challenges. *Section 4* presents the research plan and planned contributions. *Section 5* discusses the state of the art in mining specifications. *Section 6* concludes the paper.

2. RESEARCH QUESTION

In state-of-the-art enterprise systems, most of the functionality is implemented in so called business objects (BOs) such as *Sales Quote* (SQ) and *Sales Order* (SO). BOs are classes with a well defined interface and an internal model describing the state of the object (e.g. *submitted* or *approved*) and the actions that are enabled in each state (e.g. *submit*, *approve* or *reject*) [9]. State-of-the-art approaches to specification mining can infer such models either based on a given set of execution traces or by generating and executing test cases. Especially the latter one, establishing a feedback loop between specification mining and test case generation, is a promising approach, where the quality of models can be improved based on the results of generated test cases and vice versa. (cf. [14])

*Advised by Andreas Zeller, Saarland University, Saarbrücken, Germany, zeller@cs.uni-saarland.de

Permission to make digital or hard copies of all or part of this work for personal or classroom use is granted without fee provided that copies are not made or distributed for profit or commercial advantage and that copies bear this notice and the full citation on the first page. To copy otherwise, to republish, to post on servers or to redistribute to lists, requires prior specific permission and/or a fee.
ESEC/FSE'11, September 5–9, 2011, Szeged, Hungary.
Copyright 2011 ACM 978-1-4503-0443-6/11/09 ...$10.00.

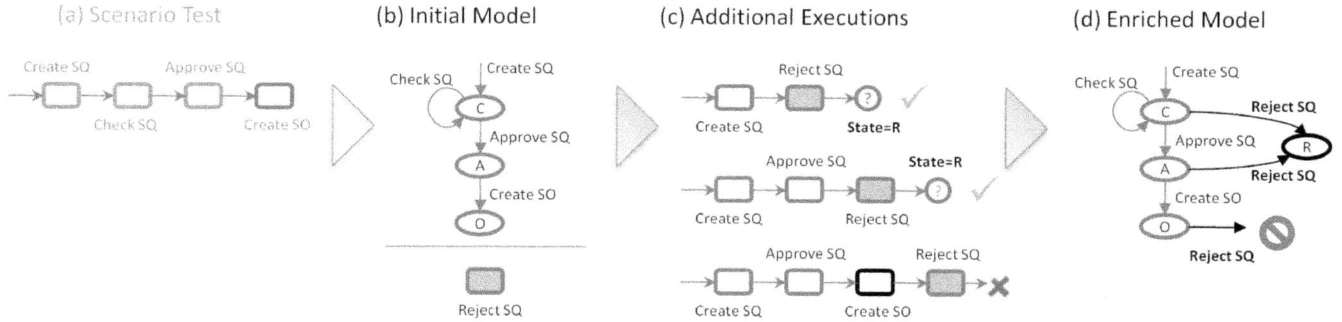

Figure 1: Example. An executable scenario step *Reject SQ* is selected to extend an initial model of the application behavior (b), which can optionally be inferred from a scenario test execution (a). Based on the initial model, scenario tests are generated that execute the selected step in each state of the model; after successful scenario test executions, state information is extracted (c). The initial model is enriched with the observed behavior (d).

Another kind of model that is more common to enterprise systems are business process models. These models represent common business processes implemented by the enterprise system. Figure 1 (a) illustrates such a process: a sales clerk creates a quote for a customer (step 1). The system checks the quote for consistency (step 2). The sales manager approves the quote (step 3). The customer accepts the quote and the sales clerk creates a sales order with reference to the quote (step 3). Despite the importance of process models in enterprise applications, in the majority of enterprise systems, process models are used solely for documentation while there is no direct link to the implementation like in business process execution engines. Compared to models inferred by state-of-the-art specification mining approaches, business process models have a much higher abstraction level; due to the heavy involvement of frameworks for persistency, access and life cycle control, a single process step usually comprises hundreds of method calls on several objects. The proposed research addresses the question *how to automatically enrich models of built-in processes in enterprise systems without relying on a given set of execution traces.* The underlying research hypothesis is that this goal can be achieved by *systematically generating and executing high-level scenario tests* for testing cross-unit functionality. Not relying on a given set of execution traces has several advantages: (1) the approach is also useful for non-productive systems, with no or only a small set of execution traces. (2) The approach is not restricted to a given set of traces. (3) Execution traces are produced in a controlled way. On the other side, this implies a number of challenges that will be discussed in the following section.

3. APPROACH

In enterprise application development, scenario tests are one of the major quality assurance techniques. Software vendors maintain large repositories of scenario tests, usually constructed with the same degree of abstraction as business process models. Scenario tests comprise multiple steps, where each step is an abstract test script that can be equipped with test data and executed on the system under test (SUT). Each step may provide arguments for following steps.

The general idea of the presented approach is to leverage scenario tests to infer models of built-in processes in enterprise systems. In a nutshell, the approach works as follows (see Figure 1). A domain expert selects an executable scenario step e.g. *Reject Sales Quote* (SQ) to extend an initial model of the application behavior (b). Since executable process models are often missing in industrial practice, the initial model can optionally be inferred from a given scenario test (a), which consists of several steps such as creating a sales quote, checking the quote for consistency, approving the quote and creating a *sales order* (SO) with reference to the quote. Therefore the scenario test is executed and after each step the state of the core objects affected by the current step is extracted from the SUT using the tracing functionality provided by modern enterprise systems. States in the initial model represent the state of the main objects the scenario steps operate on such as *SalesQuote(submitted|approved|rejected)* and transitions are labeled with scenario step names such as *Approve SQ*. Based on the initial model, additional scenario tests are generated that execute the selected step in each state of the model; after successful scenario test executions, state information is extracted (c). The observations made from the execution of the generated scenario tests are used to enrich the initial model (d). Note that step (c) and (d) are executed iteratively, i.e. that for each new legal state discovered by the generated scenario tests, further tests are generated that execute the selected step in the new state, until no new states are discovered by the generated tests. If each of the selected scenario steps has been executed in each state of the inferred model or a predefined timeout has been reached, the mining process stops. The inferred model can then be used to compare the implemented system behavior with the intended behavior.

There are a number of challenges that will be briefly discussed in following.

Combinatorial explosion: a naïve approach that generates and executes all combinations of a set S of selected scenario steps has to execute $|S|!$ scenario tests. For the small example in Figure 1 with $|S| = 5$ this means a total of 120 tests comprising of 600 scenario steps to execute. This is only feasible for scenarios with a small number of selected steps and a short average step runtime.

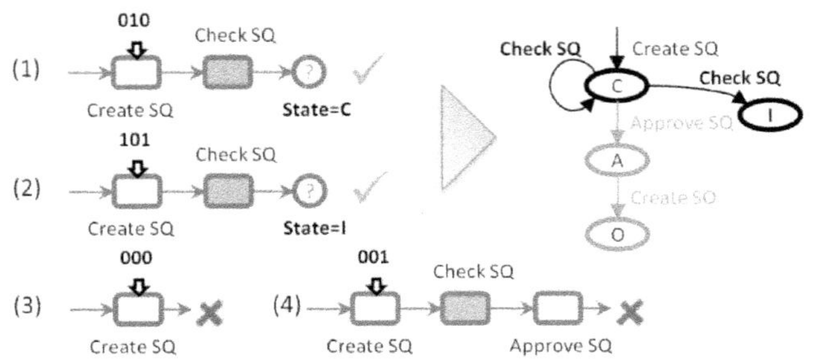

Figure 2: Influence of test data. Executing the same steps may lead to different states (1, 2), or even fail (3, 4), which results in nondeterministic models.

Long running test scripts: unlike existing approaches that leverage test case generation to infer models, this approach generates and executes scenario tests instead of unit tests. A scenario test consists of several steps that typically comprise a multitude of operations. This allows abstracting from single operations, but also increases the runtime of the approach compared to approaches that mine models with transitions representing single method calls.

Test data provisioning: scenario tests comprise multiple steps, i.e. parameterized test cases that have to be provided with concrete arguments to execute them. Figure 2 illustrates the influence of test data on experimental specification mining approaches. Depending on the selected test data for the scenario step parameters, executing the same steps may lead to different states - *consistent* (1) or *inconsistent* (2), or even fail (3). Another, more business related example where test data influences test execution is the approval step in scenario test (4); depending on the order value provided as an argument for the *Create SQ* step, an approval may become unnecessary and the execution of the *Approve SQ* step may even fail. If test data is not fixed and data dependencies are not inferred, this results in nondeterministic models. However, inferring relations over arguments requires executing each scenario test multiple times with different test data. For a scenario with s parameterized steps and n argument lists for each step, testing all data combinations results in n^s executions for a single scenario test.

Parameter mapping: another challenge that is an exacerbated version of the previous one is to find arguments for steps that are not represented in the initial model such as *Reject SQ* in Figure 1 (b), and therefore are missing a parameter mapping; this means it is not clear which arguments are generated by preceding steps (e.g. *SQ Id*), and which arguments are independent from previous steps (e.g. rejection comments). Searching for script usage in existing scenario tests and comparing parameter naming and types could help but may not solve the problem in all cases. Therefore user interaction might be necessary where automated techniques do not provide good results.

Anonymous vs. labeled states: a number of specification mining approaches [3, 1] define states solely by their outgoing transitions, i.e. states are anonymous and provide no information except for their outgoing transitions. Approaches with anonymous states do not need to extract state information from the SUT, but the algorithm for building the FSM and merging states is more complex [2]. For the approach presented in this paper, inferring FSMs with anonymous states increases the number of scenario steps to execute in order to distinguish states, whereas an approach based on explicit state information requires extracting the system state after each scenario test execution.

State abstraction: considering an approach based on explicit state information leads to the question of finding the right level of abstraction for the system state. Due to the enormous state space of business application systems, it is hardly possible to extract and represent the full system state. Apart from that the inferred models would be too detailed to be useful.

4. RESEARCH PLAN

Being at the beginning of my research, I did some first experiments with SAP enterprise systems. I achieved to extract selected state information from the system; the aforementioned long runtime of single scenario steps turned out to be a major challenge.

I plan to proceed by implementing a tool in the domain of enterprise systems. In the first iteration I will exclude the test data aspect by fixing the data. In order to evaluate the proposed approach, I plan to analyze a number of processes in SAP enterprise systems, using the tool and comparing the results with manually created models.

The expected contributions of this research are: (1) a technique to mine high-level models of built-in processes from enterprise systems. (2) A tool implementing the mining technique for SAP enterprise systems. (3) An evaluation of the technique based on experiments with the tool.

5. RELATED WORK

The first approach that infers finite-state machines (FSMs) from process event traces was published by Cook and Wolf [3]; the *Ktail* algorithm, which builds upon the work of Biermann and Feldman [2], mines FSMs with anonymous states and transitions labeled with process events. States reached by process events are defined by the future behavior that can occur from it, i.e. events whose successor events are equal belong to the same equivalence class and therefore lead to the same state in the FSM. Ammons et al. [1] mine nondeterministic finite automata (NFAs) with anonymous states capturing temporal and data dependencies of API call. They use a variation on the classic *k-tails* algorithm [2] to mine probabilistic finite state automata (PFSAs) from execution traces annotated with flow dependencies; each edge in the PFSA is labeled with an interaction and weighted by how often it is used. The PFSA is then transformed into an NFA by removing rarely-used edges, unreachable states and the weights. The *GK-Tail* algorithm by Lorenzoli et al. [10] mines extended FSMs from execution traces that capture the relations between data values and component interactions. The algorithm uses *k-tails* [2] to mine interaction patterns and extends the inferred FSMs with invariants over data values extracted with the *Daikon* tool by Ernst et al. [6].

The *ProM* framework [12] provides an extensible environment for analyzing process event logs and comes with a multitude of plug-ins for process model inference: the *α-algorithm* by van der Aalst et al. [11] mines Petri nets. The *fuzzy miner* [8] infers abstractions over less structured processes by aggregating and abstracting less significant behavior based on several metrics. The *flexible heuristics miner* [13] infers dependency graphs with the most frequent dependencies between events in the log and annotates less frequent dependencies in form of causal nets, making the algorithm robust to noise.

The specification mining approaches [3, 1, 10, 11, 8, 13] can be classified as inductive approaches (cf. [16]), i.e. they build abstractions over a given set of program executions. In contrast, the proposed approach systematically generates and executes scenario tests and therefore does not rely on a given set of execution traces. The idea of building a feedback loop between specification inference and test generation was first published by Xie and Notkin [14]. The *Obstra* tool [15] implements this idea by executing a given test case to infer an initial specification. This specification is used to automatically generate new test cases, which are executed in a subsequent iteration to extend the specification. The *Tautoko* tool by Dallmeier et al. [4] mines typestate automata based on systematic test case generation. Typestates are FSMs with anonymous states and transitions labeled with method names that encode the legal usage of a class under test. The approach builds on their previous work [5] for inferring *object behavior models* (OBMs), which have a lower level of state abstraction than typestates. Given a Java program and a concrete test case, Tautoko infers an initial OBM by executing the test case; the initial OBM is enriched by observing the execution of additional test cases generated by mutating the given test case such that each method in the test case is called in each state of the OBM. The enriched OBM is then transformed into a typestate automaton by replacing each state label, except for *start* and *exception*, with a unique number. The proposed approach as well as [14, 15, 4] control program executions by generating test cases and therefore can be considered as experimental techniques to program analysis (cf. [16]). However, the proposed approach infers models with a higher level of abstraction granularity.

Another field related to the proposed approach is model-based robustness testing [7], which mutates an initial system specification to produce test cases violating the initial specification. While the purpose of robustness testing is checking that certain behavior is inhibited by the system e.g. a high volume sales quote may not be released without manager approval, the proposed approach observes the test case execution and extends the specification accordingly.

6. CONCLUSION

To the best of my knowledge, the proposed approach is the first one that infers models of built-in processes in enterprise systems based on systematic scenario test generation and therefore does not rely on a given set of process execution logs. The approach builds on research in specification mining and model-based testing and will be implemented and evaluated in the domain of enterprise systems.

Acknowledgments. I would like to thank Andreas Zeller, Andreas Roth, Sebastian Wieczorek, Wei Wei and the anonymous reviewers for their valuable comments.

7. REFERENCES

[1] G. Ammons, R. Bodik, and J. R. Larus. Mining Specifications. *ACM Sigplan Notices*, 37(1):4–16, 2002.

[2] A. W. Biermann and J. A. Feldman. On the Synthesis of Finite-State Machines from Samples of Their Behavior. *IEEE Transactions on Computers*, C-21(6):592–597, 1972.

[3] J. E. Cook and A. L. Wolf. Discovering Models of Software Processes from Event-based Data. *ACM Transactions on Software Engineering and Methodology*, 7(3):215–249, July 1998.

[4] V. Dallmeier, N. Knopp, C. Mallon, S. Hack, and A. Zeller. Generating Test Cases for Specification Mining. In *Proc. of the 19th International Symposium on Software Testing and Analysis*, ISSTA '10, pages 85–96, New York, NY, USA, 2010. ACM.

[5] V. Dallmeier, C. Lindig, A. Wasylkowski, and A. Zeller. Mining Object Behavior with Adabu. In *Proc. of the 2006 International Workshop on Dynamic Systems Analysis*, WODA '06, pages 17–24, New York, NY, USA, 2006. ACM.

[6] M. D. Ernst, J. Cockrell, W. G. Griswold, and D. Notkin. Dynamically Discovering Likely Program Invariants to Support Program Evolution. *IEEE Trans. on Software Engineering*, 27(2):99–123, 2001.

[7] J.-C. Fernandez, L. Mounier, and C. Pachon. A Model-based Approach for Robustness Testing. In *TestCom*, pages 333–348, 2005.

[8] C. W. Günther and W. M. P. van der Aalst. Fuzzy Mining - Adaptive Process Simplification Based on Multi-perspective Metrics. In *Proc. of BPM*, pages 328–343, 2007.

[9] S. Kätker and S. Patig. Model-driven Development of Serviceoriented Business Application Systems. In *Wirtschaftsinformatik (1)*, pages 171–180, 2009.

[10] D. Lorenzoli, L. Mariani, and M. Pezzè. Automatic Generation of Software Behavioral Models. In *Proc. of the 30th International Conference on Software Engineering*, ICSE'08, pages 501–510, Leipzig, Germany, 2008.

[11] W. M. P. van der Aalst, T. Weijters, and L. Maruster. Workflow Mining: Discovering Process Models from Event Logs. *IEEE Trans. Knowl. Data Eng.*, 16(9):1128–1142, 2004.

[12] B. F. Van Dongen, A. K. A. De Medeiros, H. M. W. Verbeek, A. J. M. M. Weijters, and W. M. P. Van Der Aalst. The ProM Framework. *Lecture Notes in Computer Science*, 3536/2005:1105–1116, 2005.

[13] A. J. M. M. Weijters and J. T. S. Ribeiro. Flexible Heuristics Miner. 2011. Accepted for the SSCI2011.

[14] T. Xie and D. Notkin. Mutually Enhancing Test Generation and Specification Inference. In *Proc. 3rd International Workshop on Formal Approaches to Testing of Software*, FATES 03, volume 2931 of *LNCS*, pages 60–69, October 2003.

[15] T. Xie and D. Notkin. Automatic Extraction of Object-oriented Observer Abstractions from Unit-Test Executions. In *Proc. 6th International Conference on Formal Engineering Methods*, ICFEM 2004, pages 290–305, November 2004.

[16] A. Zeller. Program Analysis: A Hierarchy. In *Proc. Workshop on Dynamic Analysis*, May 2003.

Search Based Hierarchy Generation for Reverse Engineered State Machines

Mathew Hall
2nd *year PhD, Supervisor: Phil McMinn*
m.hall@dcs.shef.ac.uk
University of Sheffield
Sheffield
UK

ABSTRACT

Abstraction is a valuable tool that can play an important role in reducing the cost of maintenance of software systems. Despite the cost reduction abstract documentation can provide, the cost of generating documentation that offers an implementation-independent overview of the system often outweighs it. This has been the motivating force for tools and techniques that reduce the cost of documentation generation, including this work.

State machines offer an ideal level of abstraction and techniques to infer them from machines are already mature. Despite this, the abstraction state machines provide is restricted as they become unmanageable when they are of any significant size. As a result, inference tools are only ideal for those who are already familiar with the system.

This work focuses on making state machines useful for larger systems. In order to do so the complexity of a machine needs to be reduced; this is realised by introducing a hierarchy to the machine, making them closer to Harel's Statechart formalism (without concurrency).

Categories and Subject Descriptors

D.2.2 [**Software Engineering**]: Design Tools and Techniques—*State diagrams*; D.2.7 [**Software Engineering**]: Distribution, Maintenance, and Enhancement—*Documentation, reverse engineering*

General Terms

Algorithms, design, experimentation

Keywords

State machines, search-based clustering, hill-climbing, Bunch, hierarchy generation

1. INTRODUCTION

It is common for quality and accuracy of software documentation to deteriorate, particularly with legacy systems. Although documentation has been shown to result in more rapid and accurate development (as well as increased quality and volume of new documentation) [10] the cost of addressing a deficiency of documentation is often too great.

State machines, the focus of this work, are a simple way of expressing the behaviour of a system, independent of the implementation. Their downside is the (exponential in some cases) complexity increase with size, which is due to the lack of provisions for allowing repeating or commonly occurring elements to be reduced. This imposes an effective upper bound on the size of machines, making them unsuitable for all but small components of software systems.

The statechart formalism [3] extends state machines to include provisions for concurrent as well as orthogonal composite "superstates". Each of these composite states define a higher-level state, comprised of one or more "sub-states"; during execution, if a statechart is in a state, it is also said to be in the superstate of that state (if any). Concurrent superstates also allow the machine to be in more than one substate of the superstate simultaneously, although they are not addressed in this work.

Superstates may also have transitions themselves; this is simply a shorthand notation that defines the same transition to originate from every substate. By using this shorthand notation, the cyclomatic complexity of the machine can be reduced. Cyclomatic complexity gives an estimation of how complex a given graph is. Normally used in control flow graphs of programs, it can be applied to any graph and is defined as $E - N + 2$ [6], where E is the number of transitions and N is the number of states.

By providing a hierarchy for a state machine, its behaviour can be abstracted, with superstates conveying higher-level analogies of the behaviour expressed by its substates. This enables a developer to analyse the machine at a more general level, allowing them to focus on detailed substates of the superstates relevant to the task at hand. It also effectively reduces the number of states the machine has, and therefore its complexity, (when viewed only at the superstate level) allowing larger state machines to be used for documentation.

Intended Contributions

This work seeks to provide a solution to the problem of state machine complexity by introducing a hierarchy, specifically, using clustering to identify groups of states to form superstates.

The specific contribution this work will provide is a set of methods that use clustering to produce the hierarchy; the fundamental difficulty of the problem arises from the require-

Permission to make digital or hard copies of all or part of this work for personal or classroom use is granted without fee provided that copies are not made or distributed for profit or commercial advantage and that copies bear this notice and the full citation on the first page. To copy otherwise, to republish, to post on servers or to redistribute to lists, requires prior specific permission and/or a fee.
ESEC/FSE'11, September 5–9, 2011, Szeged, Hungary.
Copyright 2011 ACM 978-1-4503-0443-6/11/09 ...$10.00.

ment to automatically identify groups of states that will form a superstate.

2. BACKGROUND

Chu et al. propose an XOR rule [1] which allows a statechart to be built from a state machine. This rule simply dictates that any subset of states in the machine may be grouped in a composite state if and only if the transitions from each are the same (excepting transitions between the states in the subset).

Kumar proposes a similar method [4], whereby the labels of transitions are examined for two states; if the set of transition labels for each state have a non-empty intersection then they may be placed within a composite state.

These two techniques, however are limited to a subset of cases where their rules can be applied; in general, hierarchy generation is not constrained by these rules and is driven by the similarity of one state to another. Thus, hierarchy generation is a problem of clustering — where a cluster is analogous to a superstate.

Once this hierarchy has been found, a form of Kumar's technique can be applied; wherever all substates of a superstate have a common transition, it can be rewritten as a single superstate transition, thus lowering the cyclomatic complexity of the machine.

Clustering algorithms have been applied with a varying level of success to many problems in software engineering, perhaps the most significant being the Bunch clustering tool [8].

Clustering-Based Techniques

Bunch is a tool that generates a hierarchy of a set of software modules when provided with a module dependency graph (MDG). It employs a "search-based" approach, where, instead of exhaustively considering all possible solutions, it makes small changes to a solution with the hope of improving it. Over many iterations it optimises a "fitness value" which roughly rates the overall quality of a solution, allowing for selection of the best candidate one the algorithm has seen.

This is known as a "hill climbing" search, named so because the search aims to take the step that increases the fitness, eventually arriving at a maximum value. Another example of a search-based approach is the genetic algorithm, which uses a population of candidate solutions which are recombined, taking parts from each in the hope of generating a better (more fit) solution.

Bunch uses this hill climbing search for the best grouping of modules, driven by a fitness function named "modularisation quality" (MQ). MQ favours cluster assignments that have a high ratio of edges within a cluster to those that leave (or enter) it.

Bunch been used to generate a hierarchy for two state machines which were obtained by flattening a statechart [2]. Results showed that Bunch was able to recover the hierarchy of a small, uniformly structured machine using MQ. A second example, a larger more complex machine, caused Bunch to assign states to superstates differently to the original assignments. If anything, this study demonstrates the viability of the use of clustering and that the method of evaluation needs to be carefully selected.

Beyond Bunch there are other instances where clustering has been used to infer a hierarchy. The minimum description length principle [9] from Information Theory has been applied to infer hierarchies for software modules [5], this was achieved in a similar way to Bunch, using a genetic algorithm to minimise the length of the bit-string required to express hierarchical representation of a module dependency graph.

Work using less application-specific clustering methods has also been done to infer classes for variables in COBOL software [11]. In this work, each variable was given a number of features, which were set to either 0 or 1 based on their presence in several programs. A vector for each variable was formed using this and the Euclidean distance between each vector used as the similarity measure.

3. HIERARCHY GENERATION FOR FINITE STATE MACHINES

This work applies clustering to a previously unaddressed problem: hierarchy generation for state machines. Although clustering has been used in closely related fields it is yet to be applied to state machines.

To cluster a given state machine, the method chosen deploys a search-based approach. The genetic algorithm represents solutions as a sequence of merges applied to an initial clustering, consisting of a single cluster containing each state of the input machine. The algorithm then takes a population of these solutions and recombines them, using an fitness function to evaluate their performance. This is implemented in a tool, Crunch, which is built upon the JGAP genetic algorithms package [7]. Crunch was designed to address Bunch's shortcomings with dealing with state machines, as it does not support directional or reflexive edges.

Multiple fitness functions have been developed for use in Crunch and are detailed below. In some cases these are search-based versions of algorithms that are normally run exhaustively. By using a search-based approach issues of computational complexity can be avoided (where necessary) as well as maximising re-use of code.

In addition to the fitness functions running within Crunch, a random hierarchy generator has also been produced to offer a baseline comparison.

Fitness Functions

A number of fitness functions have been implemented for use on the tool; as well as methods outside the tool, they are detailed below. Each of these functions serves to guide the tool, providing a number representing the quality of each individual.

MQ

The original "TurboMQ" fitness function implemented in Bunch. This fitness function allows the comparison of the performance of other functions against MQ without considering the search method of each tool.

The MQ value for k clusters is given by:

$$MQ = \sum_{i=1}^{k} CF_i$$

$$CF_i = \begin{cases} 0 & \mu_i = 0 \\ \dfrac{2\mu_i}{2\mu_i + \sum\limits_{\substack{j=1 \\ j\neq i}}^{k} (\epsilon_{i,j} + \epsilon_{j,i})} & \text{otherwise} \end{cases}$$

Where μ_i is the number of edges within a cluster (intra edges) and $\epsilon_{i,j}$ is the number of edges from cluster i to cluster j (the inter edges).

XOR

A fitness function based on Chu et al's work. It is given by:

$$\sum_{c \in C} \sum_{n \in c} \epsilon_n / \epsilon_c$$

where $C = \{\{n_1, n_2\}, \{n_3\}, \{n_i\}\}$ is the set of clusters, each element containing a set of states. ϵ_x is defined as the set of transitions leaving x whose destination is in a different cluster.

HMD

Lutz's Hierarchical Module Decomposition [5] method fitness function. Based on the minimum description length principle from Information Theory. This assigns a number of bits required to express a given clustered state machine using a formula; the less complex the hierarchical machine, the lower the number of bits required to express it.

Cyclomatic

A cyclomatic complexity (CC) fitness function; given by $E - N + 2$. This can be seen to approximate Kumar's method (detailed in section 2). A transformation is applied that removes transitions occurring from every state in a superstate, replacing them with a single transition from the superstate (this transformation is available to other fitness functions should one be developed that needs it). The superstates themselves are ignored in this calculation, such that N never changes, although E decreases when this rewriting occurs.

Levenshtein

Levenshtein distance provides a mapping of a pair of strings to their "edit distance", the textual difference between two strings represented by an integer, which is 0 when they are identical. In this fitness function, the following calculation is applied to the labels of each state:

$$\frac{1}{\sum_{c \in C} \sum_{n,m \in c} led(n, m)}$$

using the same definitions as in section 3, where $led(n, m)$ returns an integer representing the Levenshtein edit distance between the labels of states n and m.

This fitness function therefore favours solutions where superstates that contain similarly named states and therefore requires that state labels are meaningful (which may not be the case in reverse engineering scenarios).

Edge Similarity

This fitness function assigns each state a coordinate based on its connectivity to other states, based on van Deursen and Kuipers' method [11]. The coordinates of a state s are given as a vector of 1s and 0s which denote the existence or non-existence of a transition from s to each $t \in N$.

The similarity of two states s and t is defined as the euclidean distance between them. This is given by

$$\sqrt{\sum_{i=0}^{n} (u[i] - v[i])^2}$$

where u and v represent the coordinates of states s and t respectively.

This distance is then calculated for all pairs of states in the machine. If the pair is in the same cluster, the reciprocal is added to the fitness; if the pair's states are in different clusters then the difference is added to the fitness. The best solution in this case is one where the distance between every pair of states in a cluster is 0, and the distance between states in different clusters is non-zero.

4. EXPERIMENT: PERFORMANCE OF SEVERAL TECHNIQUES

An experiment was carried out in order to quantify the effectiveness of some of the fitness functions at minimising top-level complexity. As the case studies (detailed below) were reverse engineered, they lacked state labels, making the use of the Levenshtein fitness function unnecessary.

The final set of methods used in this experiment were: MQ, cyclomatic complexity (CC), Edge Similarity (ES), Lutz, XOR and Random (Rand).

4.1 Case Studies

In order to produce these machines, traces of them were obtained using AspectJ `http://www.eclipse.org/aspectj/`. These traces were then be passed to StateChum [12], which synthesises a state machine that will accept, at the very least, every sequence in a set of traces supplied to it. As StateChum operates only on the traces supplied to it, state names are not available and the machine is built on the assumption that every method call changes the state. Transition names are simply the name of the method that causes the change in state.

These machines are ideal for testing this technique, as they are not necessarily the correct machine for the program that generated the traces (as all input values cannot possibly be considered). This makes them very close, if not identical to, machines that would be generated in a real reverse engineering scenario.

Two pieces of software, detailed below, were used in this experiment. Their machines were obtained as described in this section.

Collections HashBag The Apache Commons Collections library (`http://commons.apache.org`) is an open source implementation of several data structures for storage of elements. One member of this library is the HashBag class. A small Java class was written that randomly calls insert, delete and getCount methods in a HashBag instance a random number of times was traced to obtain this machine.

Colt OpenLongObjectMap The CERN Colt library contains (amongst other things) a collection of data storage classes. This machine was obtained using a similar class that randomly inserted, deleted and counted data stored in a randomly generated LongObjectMap. It is available at `http://acs.lbl.gov/software/colt`.

Due to the size of each machine, they are shown in this paper at a small size; full size PDFs (as well as DOT files) are available at `http://staffwww.dcs.shef.ac.uk/people/M.Hall/fse`. Figure 1 provides an overview of each machine.

4.2 Method

Each case study was clustered 10 times using each of the fitness functions. The results were then pruned to remove all clusters containing nothing other than a single child cluster.

Case Study	Transitions	States	Cyclomatic complexity
Collections	38	26	14
Colt	63	53	12

Figure 1: An overview of each case study.

FF	Inter-edges		CC of top level		Num. of Clusters		MQ	
	Avg	Std Dev.	Avg	Std Dev.	Avg	Std Dev.	Avg	Std Dev.
Collections								
MQ	14.9	2.6437	9.8	2.5298	7.1	0.9944	4.1298	0.5546
CC	28.9	3.3813	23.9	2.2336	7	1.633	0.9141	0.1831
ES	9.1	5.8963	8.6	5.9104	2.5	0.527	0.9179	0.0652
Lutz	14.8	9.7957	13.9	9.122	2.9	0.9944	0.9355	0.1714
XOR	28.5	1.5092	28.5	1.5092	2	0	0.4826	0.0776
Rand	20	8.5635	18.4	7.6478	3.6	1.3499	0.8742	0.1041
Colt								
MQ	34.1	2.1833	19.7	3.093	16.4	2.8363	7.4454	1.0444
CC	57.1	2.079	39.8	2.6162	19.3	1.767	0.7594	0.3458
ES	50.6	6.3105	38.7	5.697	13.9	2.5582	0.9359	0.3319
Lutz	50.5	3.7193	38.5	2.9533	14	2.1082	1.0499	0.4274
XOR	52.4	2.8363	46.3	3.653	8.1	3.604	0.7508	0.3582
Rand	25.8	13.7097	24.2	12.994	3.6	1.1738	0.945	0.2067

Figure 2: Results for each case study.
Due to space constraints only the average and standard deviation are given. Full results are available at `http://staffwww.dcs.shef.ac.uk/people/M.Hall/fse`

Metrics were then calculated for each result. These consisted of the number of transitions leaving a superstate (inter-edges), the cyclomatic complexity of the top level of the hierarchy (treating the top superstates as a node and looking only at the inter edges) and the number of clusters in the graph. Additionally, the MQ values of each of the results was performed to provide a comparison of each fitness function's results with those obtained using Bunch's MQ.

4.3 Results

Figure 2 shows the results of the experiments. The FF column contains the name each fitness function.

The results show, perhaps most interestingly that MQ outperforms other fitness functions in terms of the complexity of the top level; however they also show that in many cases the top level complexity of a hierarchy can be higher than the flat machine, even when it contains far fewer nodes.

In some cases, the number of clusters was particularly small. Although this produced low values for complexity, these results are also unlikely to convey much about the machine without the display of deeper levels in the hierarchy.

5. CONCLUSIONS & FUTURE WORK

The results obtained through this work demonstrate that, of the fitness functions surveyed, MQ is the best function to minimise the cyclomatic complexity of the top level of a hierarchy for a state machine. The results show that the top level of a hierarchy it generates may actually be more complex than the original machine.

The results only portray half of a picture, however. They do not compare the level of abstraction the hierarchies generated, nor do they quantify to what extent the clustered machine is better than the non-clustered machine (or vice-versa) beyond the cyclomatic complexity of the top level of the hierarchy.

These results lead to several conclusions; firstly and most significantly that a set of metrics specifically defined for hierarchy complexity evaluation needs to be defined for future studies. Additionally, a human-based study into the abstraction provided by the hierarchy is necessary before any claims of the utility of this technique in real-world scenarios can be made.

In addition to work on the analysis of the output of these clustering techniques, the results also suggest that an application specific fitness function is still yet to be developed; although this task depends entirely on availability of a better suite of metrics.

In summary, this work demonstrates a novel application of clustering algorithms to state machines in order to generate a hierarchy and the potential reduction in complexity of reverse engineered state machines this hierarchy can provide. The principal contribution of this work beyond this study is the open source tool (Crunch) and the implementation of the fitness functions mentioned earlier.

Acknowledgements

Mathew Hall is supported by the EPSRC grant EP/F065825/1 (REGI: Reverse Engineering State Machine Hierarchies by Grammar Inference).

6. REFERENCES

[1] H. Chu, Q. Li, S. Hu, and P. Chen. An approach for reversely generating hierarchical uml statechart diagrams. *Fuzzy Systems and Knowledge Discovery*, pages 434–437, 2006.

[2] M. Hall, P. Mcminn, and N. Walkinshaw. Superstate identification for state machines using search-based clustering. *Proceedings of the 12th Anuual Conference on Genetic and Evolutionary Computation*, pages 1381—1388, Jul 2010.

[3] D. Harel. Statecharts: A visual formalism for complex systems. *Science of Computer Programming*, 8:231–274, 1987.

[4] A. Kumar. Schaem: A method to extract statechart representation of fsms. *IEE International Advance Computing Conference 2009*, Jan 2009.

[5] R. Lutz. Evolving good hierarchical decompositions of complex systems. *Journal of systems architecture*, 47(7):613—634, Jan 2001.

[6] T. McCabe. A complexity measure. *IEEE Transactions on Software Engineering*, 2(4):308—320, Jan 1976.

[7] K. Meffert et al. JGAP - Java Genetic Algorithms and Genetic Programming Package. `http://jgap.sf.net`.

[8] B. Mitchell and S. Mancoridis. On the automatic modularization of software systems using the bunch tool. In *IEEE Transactions on Software Engineering*, 2006.

[9] J. Rissanen. Modeling by shortest data description. *Automatica*, 14, Jan 1978.

[10] E. Tryggeseth. Report from an experiment: Impact of documentation on maintenance. *Empirical Software Engineering*, Jan 1997.

[11] A. van Deursen and T. Kuipers. Identifying objects using cluster and concept analysis. *21st International Conference on Software Engineering (ICSE)*, Jan 1999.

[12] N. Walkinshaw and K. Bogdanov. Improving dynamic software analysis by applying grammar inference principles. *Journal of Software Maintenance and Evolution: Research and Practice - Special Issue on Program Comprehension through Dynamic Analysis (PCODA)*, Jan 2008.

Automatic Test Suite Evolution*

Mehdi Mirzaaghaei
Faculty of Informatics
University of Lugano, Switzerland
mehdi.mirzaaghaei@usi.ch

ABSTRACT

Software evolves continuously, and developers need to retest it frequently. To save time and effort, developers often reuse existing test cases to verify the functionality of software systems after changes, but they often need to adapt or augment the test cases to match the new characteristics of the software systems. Adapting test cases is tedious and expensive. Current automated techniques often generate invalid and incomplete test cases, and require manual inspection and correction of the generated test cases.

My research aims to introduce new automated approaches for evolving and generating test cases, to keep them aligned with the corresponding software evolution. The new approach is based on the observation that software developers follow common patterns to identify changes and adapt test cases. I experimentally identified patterns that developers use in presence of specific changes, and I am working on an automated approach that generalizes these patterns into a set of test adaptation patterns that can automatically evolve existing test cases and generate new ones. My preliminary evaluation shows the applicability and effectiveness of the approach.

Categories and Subject Descriptors

D.2.5 [**Software Engineering**]: [Testing and Debugging]

General Terms

Test case generation, Test case maintenance, software evolution, Automated testing process

1. INTRODUCTION

Software systems continuously evolve, and developers must adapt test suites to verify the unmodified, revised, and new functionality. Software developers rerun existing test cases on modified software, repair obsolete test cases, and generate new test cases to verify the new functionality that has been introduced. This process is expensive and time consuming. Test maintenance techniques try to reduce this cost by partially automating the activities involved in test case generation, augmentation, and repair.

Automatic test case generation techniques like symbolic [7, 10], concolic [4], and random execution [9] do not use domain information, and thus tend to generate test cases that may be both incomplete and difficult to understand. These techniques often do not identify the setup actions necessary to execute the test cases, and generate a large amount of test inputs without distinguishing between valid and invalid inputs, thus causing invalid failures. Even if the generated test cases are filtered by mining source code [13, 1], these difficulties persist. Furthermore, they do not generate test oracles, thus forcing developers to inspect the generated test cases to write oracles [6].

Test suite augmentation techniques [14, 11] generate test cases that cover execution paths that belong to the modified software and are not covered by existing test cases. These techniques present the same kind of limitations of test generation approaches: They do not identify the setup actions necessary to execute the test cases, generate a large amount of test inputs without distinguishing between valid and invalid inputs, and do not generate test oracles.

Although researchers proposed many test case generation techniques, automatically generated test cases do not substitute manually generated test cases, which are still more readable, maintainable and effective [14].

Test suite repair techniques focus on repairing obsolete test cases. The existing approaches either focus on simple fixes, like the plugins available in Eclipse, or deal with specific problems, like *ReAssert* that suggests fixes of test oracles that are broken by changes in the software system [3, 2]. *ReAssert* computes likely fixfes by re-executing the failing test cases of the system through either concrete [3] or symbolic execution [2]. *ReAssert* modifies the test cases that fail in the current version to produce cases that succeed. In this way, *ReAssert* may fix a problem in the test case, but also erroneously mask a failure, thus, the suggestions of *ReAssert* must be validated by software developers. *ReAssert* repairs test oracles, but does not fix test inputs, thus, developer still needs to manually update the test inputs.

My work aims to define an approach that automates the generation of test cases for evolving software to successfully repair test cases that cannot be repaired by current tech-

*This research is supervised by Mauro Pezzè, University of Lugano, Switzerland (mauro.pezze@usi.ch). The results produced so far have been published in [8]

Permission to make digital or hard copies of all or part of this work for personal or classroom use is granted without fee provided that copies are not made or distributed for profit or commercial advantage and that copies bear this notice and the full citation on the first page. To copy otherwise, to republish, to post on servers or to redistribute to lists, requires prior specific permission and/or a fee.
ESEC/FSE'11, September 5–9, 2011, Szeged, Hungary.
Copyright 2011 ACM 978-1-4503-0443-6/11/09 ...$10.00.

niques. The main underlying idea is that existing test cases encapsulate domain knowledge, and thus can be reused to generate new test setup actions, inputs, and oracles without the need of complete specifications. In particular, I focus on the test cases written in the same language of the software under test, for example JUnit test cases for Java. The main hypothesis of my Ph.D. Thesis is that *existing test suites can be reused to test modified and extended functionality by repairing and adapting existing test cases.*

In the first part of my research, I examined several fixes in open source systems, and I inferred that when repairing test cases, software developers often follow some repetitive sets of actions to address some classes of problems that recur quite frequently. I noticed that some of these actions can be formalized as repair patterns that can be applied automatically. The preliminary investigation showed that it is indeed possible to define repair patterns that successfully fix some faults in test cases not addressed by current repairing techniques. These observations lead to detailing the main research hypothesis into the following research question:

RQ1: *Can test maintenance activities be formalized into reproducible patterns?*

RQ2: *To what extent can test suite maintenance activities be automated?*

RQ3: *How do automatically generated test cases compare with manually generated test suites and state of the art techniques?*

RQ1 focuses on the possibility of formalizing test maintenance activities: I ask whether test maintenance activities are generalizable, and whether they can be categorized into a set of reproducible patterns. To address *RQ1* I performed an empirical study over a set of open source software systems. I identified common activities that developers perform to generate test cases from existing ones, and I call such activities *test adaptation patterns*. For example, to generate test cases for classes that extend a class hierarchy, software developers usually copy the test case of another class of the hierarchy, replace the instances of the original class with the instances of the new one, replace previous test inputs with new ones that are valid for the new class, and update the test oracles. Section 2 describes the test adaptation patterns that I discovered so far, and Section 4 evaluates the completeness of these pattens in real software systems.

RQ2 focuses on the possibility of developing automated test evolution algorithms starting from the identified test adaptation patterns. To address *RQ2* I developed a technique to automatically generate test cases for an initial set of patterns. The technique is presented in Section 3.

RQ3 investigates the effectiveness of the generated test cases. To address *RQ3* I defined a validation methodology to compare the test cases generated by the proposed approach both with the test cases generated by the state of the art techniques and with the test cases written by the developers. Section 4 presents the preliminary evaluation results and outlines my evaluation plans.

2. TEST ADAPTATION PATTERNS

I started addressing *RQ1* by conducting an empirical study on some open source projects. I inspected different pairs of consecutive versions of `JFreeChart` (www.jfree.org), `PMD` (pmd.sourceforge.net), and `JodaTime` (jodatime.sourceforge.-net), and identified similarities, differences and common patterns. I identified common activities that developers typically perform, and generalized them to create the initial set of reproducible *test adaptation patterns* described below.

Modification of Method Declaration: Software developers often change method signatures while refactoring a software system. As a consequence, they need to update the existing test cases to fix the compilation errors induced by the changes in the signature. I observed that changes in method signatures are among the most frequent non trivial causes of errors in the test cases, and thus addressing such type of changes would fix a relevant amount of non trivial problems. I discovered that most changes in method declarations can be reduced to some key actions that include adding, removing and changing the type of method parameters, and changing the return type. I found the mechanisms that developers use to evolve the test cases to cope with changes in method declarations, and generalized them as *modification of method declaration* pattern.

Extension of Class Hierarchy: In object oriented systems, developers regularly extend software functionality by extending class hierarchies. Whenever a new class is introduced, developers need to generate new test cases to verify the functionality of the new class. To save testing effort, often software developers reuse existing test cases and adapt test inputs and oracles to the specification of the new class. Since the new class shares some behavior with its sibling and parent classes, existing test cases that verify sibling and parent classes can be often reused successfully to test the new class. I discovered that the test cases designed for the similar sibling classes can be reused as a template to derive the test cases for the new class. Software developers use their domain knowledge to identify the similar sibling of the class under test, copy the test case for that class, and finally modify the test inputs and outputs to fit the specifications of the new class.

Implementation of Interface: The test cases developed to verify two classes that implement the same interface usually share common behavior, but they differ in terms of input values and oracles. Software developers often reuse the test cases developed for a first class that implements a given interface to test new classes that implement the same interface by adapting the old test inputs and oracles.

Introduction of Overloaded Method: The overloaded methods of a class share their name but not the number and/or type of parameters, and usually present slight changes in the implemented functionality. Software developers reuse the test cases developed for an overloaded method to generate the test cases for the other overloaded methods by modifying the input parameters according to the signature of the new method and by altering the oracles according to the implementation of the new method.

Introduction of Overridden Method: When developers override a method, they generate a new method with the same signature of a method defined in a parent class. Software developers reuse the test cases developed for the method of the parent class to test the new method, for example, they change the oracles to verify the expected behavior of the child class.

Introduction of New Component: When a new component extends the functionality of the system without altering the existing functionality, software developers typically reuse existing test cases by updating the setup and the inputs of the test cases embodying their domain knowledge.

3. TEST SUITE EVOLUTION

I started addressing *RQ2* by designing algorithms to generate test cases for the test adaptation patterns identified so far. I propose an approach, TestCareAssistant (*TcA*), that works on the original and the modified source code along with the original test cases, and applies a set of algorithms that implement the test adaptation patterns to generate new test cases for the modified code. So far, I designed algorithms to generate test cases for the *modification of method declaration* and *extension of class hierarchy* patterns.

Modification of Method Declaration

In the presence of changes in a method declaration, for example the addition and removal of a parameter, or the change of the type of a parameter and return value, *TcA* adapts related test cases by combining source code diff-ing and data flow analysis techniques (a detailed description of *TcA* is provided in [8]). *TcA* works in three steps:

Step 1. Identify the variables to initialize: When a test case does not compile due to changes in parameters or return values, *TcA* identifies the parameters or the return values that cause the compilation error by diff-ing the original and modified versions of the source code. To identify the *variables to initialize*, *TcA* locates the *first use* of the modified parameter in the new version of the software system by means of data flow analysis.

Step 2. Identify Initialization Values: After identifying the *variables to initialize*, *TcA* determines the proper initialization values, i.e., the values that preserve the test behavior, by looking for the corresponding values used in the test cases for the original software. For the *first use* of each of the *variables to initialize* identified in the previous step, *TcA* looks for a *corresponding line* in the original code. *TcA* identifies the *corresponding line* by diff-ing the original and the modified source code of the method. Then *TcA* determines the value of the *corresponding term* in the original software by statically navigating its definition-use chain [5]. If the static approach does not succeed, *TcA* identifies the runtime value of the *corresponding term* by means of dynamic analysis.

Step 3. Generate Fixes for Test Cases: *TcA* repairs test compilation errors by changing the invocation of the modified method to match the new method signature. For new or modified method parameters, *TcA* adds an instruction to define the updated parameter. If the modification consists of adding, changing, or removing a parameter, *TcA* also assigns a value to the *variables to initialize.* If the modification consists of a return type change, *TcA* retrieves data from test objects instead of using the original return value.

Extension of Class Hierarchy

When a new class is added to a class hierarchy, TcA looks for sibling classes that have been already tested and generates test cases for the new class by reusing the test cases of its siblings. *TcA* creates test cases for a new class by copying and adapting all the test cases of its siblings and by filtering out the test cases that do not improve coverage. After copying the original test cases, *TcA* adapts them by repairing compilation errors, replacing inputs with valid ones, and removing invalid assertions. *TcA* repairs parameter mismatch compilation error by applying the *modification of method declaration* pattern. The errors that cannot be repaired with *modification of method declaration* pattern are removed by commenting out the statements causing the error. Once *TcA* obtains a set of compilable test cases it adapts the inputs of the copied test cases to the new class specifications.

Currently, *TcA* handles literals, constants, and static fields. Here I overview the approach for literals, the approaches for constant and static fields are similar. For each literal used in the test cases of the sibling classes, *TcA* looks for instructions in the sibling class that use the same literal. It finds the corresponding statement in the new class by applying the algorithm defined for the modification of method declaration pattern. The statement in the new class and the corresponding instruction in the sibling class should be the same except for the modified literal that *TcA* uses to replace all the occurrences of the literal in the copied test cases. *TcA* then removes invalid assertions by running the generated test cases and disabling the failing assertions. We assume that failures depends on the functional differences among the classes.

The generated test cases are then filtered to obtain an effective test suite without redundant test cases. *TcA* runs all the generated test cases, and measure their coverage. *TcA* then ranks siblings on the basis of their similarity with the new class[1]. Then, *TcA* inspects the coverage of each test case, starting from the ones of the most similar sibling, and discards the test cases that do not improve coverage.

4. EVALUATION

I plan to evaluate my research questions by measuring the results on representative open source programs referring to the three research questions discussed in the introduction. I will address *RQ1* and *RQ2* by considering the history of different software systems and by measuring the percentage of changes manually performed by software developers that could have been automated with the identified patterns. I will address *RQ3* by comparing the test cases generated by a Java implementation of *TcA*, with the ones written by developers and those generated using standard automatic test generation techniques based on symbolic, random, and concolic execution.

Following paragraphs report the preliminary results obtained for the algorithms designed for *modification of method declaration* and *extension of class hierarchy* patterns.

Modification of Method Declaration

To measure the applicability of *TcA* for the *modification of method declaration* pattern, I analyzed 80 versions of 10 open source projects of the Apache Software Foundation[2]. I used *JDiff*[3] to automatically extract the changes between two consecutive releases of each project. I focussed on the changes that lead to compilation errors in method calls: methods deleted/renamed, parameters and return values added/removed/renamed. In my experiments, *JDiff* identified 312,271 differences, 27.96% of which regarded parameter and return value declarations. These results indicate that modifications of method declarations generally impacts on the test cases maintenance costs.

To evaluate the effectiveness of *TcA* using the method declaration pattern, I conducted a study on 138 test cases of 3 software systems `JFreeChart`, `PMD` and `JodaTime`. The

[1] *TcA* calculates similarity by counting the number of fields and methods that share the same name or signature.

[2] Apache Software Foundation, www.apache.org

[3] http://www.jdiff.org/

test cases failed because of the following changes: 24 parameter types changed, 68 parameters added, 23 parameters removed, 21 return types changed. I evaluated *TcA* by executing the tool on test cases and inspecting the generated fixes. The fixes that *TcA* produced automatically, resolved all compilation errors and produced 128 (almost 90%) valid test cases. It repaired 105 (more than 70%) test cases in the same way as of the developers.

Extension of Class Hierarchy

To evaluate the applicability of *TcA* for *extension of class hierarchy* pattern, I performed an empirical investigation to count the classes that extend hierarchies in `Jodatime` and `JFreeChart`. The obtained results indicate that this pattern can be highly applicable in software systems: 84% of the 524 classes of the two projects extends a hierarchy.

I evaluated the effectiveness of *TcA* in generating test cases for the extension of class hierarchies by using *TcA* to generate the test cases for five different classes of `JodaTime`. I compared the test cases generated by *TcA* both with the ones manually written by software developers and with the ones generated by a well known random testing technique, Randoop [9]. For the comparison I focused on the capability of the generated tests to cover the software behavior by measuring the statements coverage of the test cases, and the effectiveness of the generated test suite to identify faults by applying mutation testing using Javalanche [12]. The test cases generated by *TcA* cover 80.5% of the statements of the class under test, while test cases generated by developers and Randoop cover 75.0% and 72.6% respectively. As for mutation results, the test cases generated by *TcA* identify 75% of the faults injected in the software, the test cases generated by developers and Randoop identify 68.9% and 32.4% of the injected faults respectively. These results indicate that the approach can be effective in practice.

5. RESEARCH PLAN

The results achieved so far indicate that there is a relevant amount of test cases that can be automatically evolved by applying test adaptation patterns that generalize classic test maintenance activities. The research conducted so far identified several test maintenance activities that can be formalized into test adaptation patterns and showed that some of the identified patterns can be automated to adapt many test cases. In the remaining of the Ph.D., I plan to extend the set of discovered patterns by studying test maintenance activities in open and well as close source projects, designing algorithms and tools for all of the discovered patterns, and thoroughly evaluating the approach by comparing it with state of the art test case generation techniques as well as manually generated test cases by software developers.

This research will make the following contributions: (1) a catalog of test adaptation patterns (i.e., activities usually performed by software developers to generate test cases by reusing and adapting existing ones), (2) a set of techniques to automatically generate test cases for newly introduced functionality by generalizing the identified patterns, (3) a prototype implementation of the techniques to validate the approach, (4) a set of empirical data that demonstrates the validity and the limitations of the technique with respect to state of art approaches.

6. REFERENCES

[1] M. d'Amorim, C. Pacheco, T. Xie, D. Marinov, and M. D. Ernst. An empirical comparison of automated generation and classification techniques for object-oriented unit testing. In *International Conference on Automated Software Engineering*, pages 59–68, 2006.

[2] B. Daniel, T. Gvero, and D. Marinov. On test repair using symbolic execution. In *International Symposium on Software Testing and Analysis*, pages 207–218, 2010.

[3] B. Daniel, V. Jagannath, D. Dig, and D. Marinov. Reassert: Suggesting repairs for broken unit tests. In *International Conference on Automated software engineering*, pages 433–444, 2009.

[4] P. Godefroid, N. Klarlund, and K. Sen. Dart: directed automated random testing. In *Conference on Programming language design and implementation*, pages 213–223. ACM, 2005.

[5] M. J. Harrold and M. L. Soffa. Efficient computation of interprocedural definition-use chains. *ACM Transactions on Programming Languages and Systems*, 16(2):175–204, 1994.

[6] V. Jagannath, Y. Y. Lee, B. Daniel, and D. Marinov. Reducing the costs of bounded-exhaustive testing. In *International Conference on Fundamental Approaches to Software Engineering*, pages 171–185, 2009.

[7] J. C. King. Symbolic execution and program testing. *Communications of ACM*, 19(7):385–394, 1976.

[8] M. Mirzaaghaei, F. Pastore, and M. Pezzè. Automatically repairing test cases for evolving method declarations. In *International Conference on Software Maintenance*, pages 1–5, 2010.

[9] C. Pacheco and M. D. Ernst. Randoop: feedback-directed random testing for java. In *Conference on Object-oriented programming systems and applications*, pages 815–816, 2007.

[10] C. S. Păsăreanu, P. C. Mehlitz, D. H. Bushnell, K. Gundy-Burlet, M. Lowry, S. Person, and M. Pape. Combining unit-level symbolic execution and system-level concrete execution for testing nasa software. In *International Symposium on Software testing and analysis*, pages 15–26, 2008.

[11] R. Santelices, P. Chittimalli, T. Apiwattanapong, A. Orso, and M. Harrold. Test-suite augmentation for evolving software. In *International Conference on Automated Software Engineering*, pages 218–227, 2008.

[12] D. Schuler and A. Zeller. Javalanche: Efficient mutation testing for java. In *International Symposium on Foundations of Software Engineering*, pages 297–298, 2009.

[13] S. Thummalapenta, T. Xie, N. Tillmann, J. de Halleux, and W. Schulte. Mseqgen: object-oriented unit-test generation via mining source code. In *Symposium on the foundations of software engineering*, pages 193–202, 2009.

[14] Z. Xu, Y. Kim, M. Kim, G. Rothermel, and M. B. Cohen. Directed test suite augmentation:techniques and tradeoffs. In *Foundations of Software Engineering Conference*, pages 257–266, 2010.

Automatic Structural Testing with Abstraction Refinement and Coarsening*

Mauro Baluda
Faculty of Informatics
University of Lugano, Switzerland
mauro.baluda@usi.ch

ABSTRACT

White box testing, also referred to as structural testing, can be used to assess the validity of test suites with respect to the implementation. The applicability of white box testing and structural coverage is limited by the difficulty and the cost of inspecting the uncovered code elements to either generate test cases that cover elements not yet executed or to prove the infeasibility of the elements not yet covered.

My research targets the problem of increasing code coverage by automatically generating test cases that augment the coverage of the code or proving the infeasibility of uncovered elements, and thus eliminating them from the coverage measure to obtain more realistic values. Although the problem is undecidable in general, the results achieved so far during my PhD indicate that it is possible to extend the test suites and identify many infeasible elements by suitably combining static and dynamic analysis techniques, and that it is possible to manage the combinatorial explosion of execution models by identifying and remove elements of the execution models when not needed anymore.

Categories and Subject Descriptors

D.2.5 [**Software Engineering**]: Testing and Debugging—*Testing Tools (E.G., Data Generators, Coverage Testing)*

General Terms

Algorithms, Verification

1. PROBLEM STATEMENT

Testing is the most popular quality assurance technique in the software industry. One of the challenges of testing is to evaluate the adequacy of a test suite, that is, establishing whether a test suite exercises the software to a sufficient extent, or must be augmented with other test cases. One of the ways proposed by researchers to quantify the adequacy of testing is to measure code coverage, defined as the amount of code elements of a given type (for example, statements, branches or data flow uses) exercised by a test suite, with respect to the number of those elements in the program [12].

Despite the large body of scientific literature on code coverage, only simple coverage metrics find some practical interest, and their industrial application is still limited. The main problem that reduces the applicability of coverage metrics amounts to the high effort needed for manually devising test cases that execute specific code elements, especially if the coverage domain is huge and includes infeasible elements, that is, elements that belong statically to the code but cannot be executed for any possible input. Infeasible elements both divert the testing effort, since testers may waste resources to prove that they cannot be executed, and weaken the meaningfulness of the coverage metrics, since achieving high coverage rates can be impossible when the portion of undetected infeasible elements is large, as is often the case when considering advanced coverage metrics (for example data-flow criteria) and complex code (for example code that include OTS components and exploit defensive programming).

The problem of augmenting test suites and improving code coverage is attracting a lot of interest. Recent work proposes techniques for either generating test cases by exploring the program paths in some order, or proving the reachability of specific faulty statements, but no proposal addresses both goals in a synergistic fashion yet [10, 11, 5, 9, 13].

My PhD research focuses on synergistic solutions that increase code coverage, while identifying as many infeasible code elements as possible. Identifying infeasible elements can both speed up the convergence of the analysis, by avoiding to be stuck in the impossible attempt of covering an infeasible element, and strengthen the precision of the coverage measurements, by pruning the infeasible elements out of the coverage counts.

2. RELATED WORK

So far researchers have investigated automatic test generation and code reachability as separate problems. Test generation has been addressed with approaches based on input space search and symbolic execution. Code reachability has been explored in the domain of software model checking.

Random testing samples the input space randomly. It can quickly produce large test suites that cover part of the code, but typically fails to cover code that depends on corner val-

*This research is supervised by Mauro Pezzè, University of Lugano, Switzerland (mauro.pezze@usi.ch).
During my research I coauthored two publications that present the initial results of my PhD work [1, 2].

Permission to make digital or hard copies of all or part of this work for personal or classroom use is granted without fee provided that copies are not made or distributed for profit or commercial advantage and that copies bear this notice and the full citation on the first page. To copy otherwise, to republish, to post on servers or to redistribute to lists, requires prior specific permission and/or a fee.
ESEC/FSE'11, September 5–9, 2011, Szeged, Hungary.
Copyright 2011 ACM 978-1-4503-0443-6/11/09 ...$10.00.

ues or rare behaviors. More elaborate search strategies proposed in literature, for example based on genetic algorithms, may outperform random testing in some circumstances, but share similar problems in the general case [10].

Symbolic execution computes logic formulas that characterize the inputs that drive the execution along sets of program paths, and finds inputs that execute given paths by satisfying these formulas by means of automatic solvers [11]. Concolic execution exploits the interplay between symbolic execution and dynamic concrete analysis to overcome the limitations of theorem provers and progress the analysis. Popular tools that exploit concolic execution, like DART [5] and PEX [9], proceed through a depth-first analysis of program paths, which may lead to explore only a small portion of the program state space. Different search heuristics have been proposed, but none of them seems to perform consistently better then the others. Neither Random/genetic searches nor symbolic execution account for infeasible code.

Techniques for proving reachability properties of programs have been developed in the area of software model checking. Counter-Example Guided Abstraction Refinement (CEGAR) addresses the unreachability of faulty statements by conservatively over-approximating a program state space to a finite model, and then refining the model incrementally up to the precision needed for the proof [7].

The approaches closest to my research are the one proposed by Beckman et al., who combine CEGAR and testing in a verification approach that generates test cases and triggers suitable abstraction refinement when the test generation fails [6, 3], and McMillan, who proposes a similar procedure that exploits an interpolating prover [8]. Both approaches can prove the reachability of specific faulty statements, but do not apply well to the problem of identifying infeasible elements within large coverage domains, since this problem requires to simultaneously solve many reachability problems, becoming intractable even for small size programs, as demonstrated experimentally when we tried to apply CEGAR based techniques to cover the code coverage problem.

3. RESEARCH OBJECTIVES

My PhD research tackles the problem of both increasing code coverage and identifying unreachable code elements by combining static and dynamic techniques and complementing analysis with a new technique that we call *coarsening* and that contrasts the state explosion of CEGAR by unrolling the refinement steps as soon as the analysis satisfies any intermediate reachability goal [1, 2].

I plan to meet the main goal of my thesis by exploring the following research directions:

- Assessing existing and novel analysis techniques to generate test cases that exercise code elements not yet covered and identify unreachable ones.
- Studying how techniques for generating test cases, which typically reason at the level of the control flow of the program under analysis, can be adapted and extended to efficiently address coverage domains based on different program abstractions, such as, data-flow models.
- Conducting extensive experimental campaigns to identify the best balance between precision and efficiency of the proposed solutions. This is of paramount importance for the approach to scale to practical software, and then be useful in practice.

4. TECHNICAL CHALLENGES

The main technical challenges relate to the research directions outlined above: suitably combining and extending static and dynamic analysis techniques to efficiently generate test cases and rule out infeasible elements, tackling advanced coverage metrics, and instantiating the approach into an efficient analysis framework.

Symbolic and concolic execution are well known techniques for generating test cases, and are implemented in several robust tools. The main bottleneck for the applicability of symbolic and concolic executors is the underlying constraint solvers. Automatic solvers can reason efficiently about basic arithmetic constructs, but do not perform well when tackling non linear operations, and cannot deal with the complexity of floating point representation. The first challenge of my PhD work is to leverage on existing techniques for overcoming the limitation of current constraint solvers in the scope of the problem of interest.

The performance of current approaches for proving code reachability depends on the specific problem instance. For example, the relative qualities of popular approaches to devise the state predicates needed for abstraction refinement, for instance weakest precondition calculus and Craig interpolants [3, 8], are still unclear. My research will address the challenge of identifying an effective combination of analysis techniques by empirically investigating the performance of different approaches, to find a suitable adaptation to the specificity of structural testing. In the first part of my PhD, I experimentally investigated the applicability of CEGAR and I found out that CEGAR performs well when analyzing the reachability of single program statements, but does not perform equally well when analyzing the reachability of a whole coverage domain as required by our problem. The performance problems derive from the complexity of the models maintained during analysis that easily goes out of memory. In the first part of my PhD, I proposed a novel technique (called coarsening) to control memory consumption while CEGAR progresses [1]. Tackling the state explosion problem by leveraging the specificity of test case generation is a crucial challenge to my research.

Generating test cases for a wide range of coverage criteria challenges the path exploration strategies available in the literature. Current symbolic test generation techniques are control flow directed and do not target complex criteria like data flow based structural coverage, which would greatly benefit from the approach, since a large portion of the coverage domain is typically infeasible with such criteria.

The availability of an efficient analysis tool can show the potential of the approach in supporting fault detection and quality assessment activities for software of industrial interest. A remarkable engineering and optimization effort is required to exploit the characteristics of modern machines like complex memory hierarchies and parallelism in the implementation of the tool.

5. CURRENT STATUS

In the first part of my PhD I focused mostly on the challenge of evaluating, combining and complementing existing analysis techniques to deal with branch coverage. I refer to the approach as *ARC (abstraction refinement and coarsening)*, and to the prototype tool that works for branch coverage as (ARC-B).

The ARC approach works on what we call the *frontier* between covered and not-covered code elements, the frontier includes the transitions that connect elements of the two groups in the execution tree of the program under test. The frontier plays a key role in exploiting the interplay of static and dynamic analysis techniques effectively.

ARC identifies the current frontier by referring to the **coverage domain model**, which is a state transition system that represents all the elements of the coverage domain as abstract states (the coverage targets), and overapproximates the possible program flows as transitions between the abstract states. ARC combines in a unitary framework four static and dynamic analysis components:

Coverage frontier monitoring: a dynamic analysis technique that traces sets of executions against the coverage domain model, measures the current coverage, and identifies the *frontier* between the reached and the unreached abstract states. The frontier indicates promising program flows to be explored to reach coverage targets not yet covered.

Coverage frontier analysis: an analysis technique that reasons on the frontier of the coverage domain model. This analysis aims to identify new test cases that can traverse the frontier towards uncovered targets, reach abstract states not reached yet and possibly increase the code coverage. The current ARC-B prototype exploits symbolic execution techniques as a support for coverage frontier analysis. When the coverage frontier analysis fails in generating a test case that traverses the frontier, it triggers the coverage frontier refinement analysis technique that refines the model to identify and eliminate unreachable flows.

Coverage frontier refinement: an abstraction refinement analysis technique that increases the level of precision of the coverage domain model with respect to a set of frontier transitions. This analysis aims to transform (possibly recompute) the current model either to better characterize the set of executions that can reach a given frontier transition, or to remove such transition from the model when the analysis can conclude that no program execution may reach that transition. The increased precision can allow test generation to progress, while removing transitions can detect unreachable abstract states, and possibly identify infeasible coverage targets. The current ARC-B prototype exploits CEGAR model checking as a support for coverage frontier refinement.

Coarsening: a maintenance analysis technique that contrasts the state explosion problem caused by reiterated abstraction refinement. While coverage frontier analysis and refinement alternate to explore the execution space of the program and move the frontier further in the coverage domain model, many elements created during refinement become irrelevant. Coarsening alleviates the state explosion problem by eliminating redundant elements from the coverage domain model. Coarsening tracks the relation between the refinements due to the analysis of the transitions leading to a given abstract state and the abstract state itself, and deletes the information produced by the refinement step when the corresponding abstract state is either reached or removed from the model. Coarsening is triggered by the frontier monitoring component upon reaching abstract states, and by the frontier refinement component upon removing unreachable abstract states.

The prototype tool ARC-B helped me in collecting a preliminary set of empirical data on the validity of the approach for branch coverage. In ARC-B, the abstract states of the coverage domain model correspond to the branches in the program execution. ARC-B initializes the coverage domain model based on the control-flow graph of the program, and while the test generation progresses it augments the abstract states with constraints on the values of the program variables, to assist the reachability analysis. ARC-B implements frontier monitoring evaluating the abstract states against the program execution during the test runs. ARC-B implements frontier analysis in the style of concolic execution, that is, by performing lightweight symbolic execution on a concrete path up to a frontier, and then using a solver to compute a test case for traversing the frontier. ARC-B implements frontier refinement in the style of template-based abstract refinement [3], that is, by augmenting the pre-frontier abstract states with the weakest precondition to reach the post-frontier abstract states. By doing this, it incrementally improves the precision of the analysis done by the test generation stage, and it can eventually detect contradictory preconditions and thus determine the possibility of removing transitions. Finally, ARC-B includes an implementation of coarsening that removes the conditions generated by the refinements upon traversing or removing the frontier transitions.

The empirical data collected with ARC-B on 12 sample C programs indicate that ARC-B generated test cases that cover most branches (543 out of 588), and identified most unreachable branches (34 out of at most 45). The coverage obtained with ARC-B spans from 96% to 100% of the branches in the programs and outperforms state of the art tools. Additional details of the experiments are reported in [1].

6. RESEARCH PLAN

My research activity is conceived as an incremental process driven by experimental evaluation of the proposed solutions with respect to the research objectives. The need to experiment with existing analysis techniques to evaluate their effectiveness in practical settings suggested the design of a general architectural framework to simplify their integration and evaluation. The proposed framework identifies a small number of analysis steps that can be embodied by different combinations of static and dynamic techniques allowing innovative combinations and their empirical evaluation.

My future plan is articulated in two main phases. In the first phase I plan to extend the initial results obtained so far to increase branch coverage of large programs. The results obtained with ARC-B show that the approach is potentially interesting and useful, but are limited to small size programs, and thus do not generalize yet. To understand the applicability and the limits of the analysis techniques embedded in ARC-B, I plan to work experimentally, and I need to both extend the approach and the prototype tool, to deal with a larger subset of the C language, and ameliorate the constraint solver support that seems to be the bottleneck of the current prototype.

Currently the template-based Coverage frontier refinement implemented in ARC-B treats pointer aliases with imprecision (making the detection of infeasible elements reliable only for programs that do not contain aliases) and is limited to intra-procedural analysis. I plan to investigate the use of recently proposed algorithms to precisely account for aliases during symbolic execution and abstraction refinement [3, 4]. I also plan to integrate support for inter-procedural analysis by extending the current coverage domain model according to the program call graph, and designing call-return context sensitiveness in the current algorithms. I finally plan to integrate other techniques for abstraction refinement, and in particular I will study the applicability of interpolant based predicate refinement [8].

To improve the constraint solving power, I need to compare the performances of the different kinds of solvers in the context of the target problem. I plan to work experimentally by designing a parametric interface to integrate different kinds of solvers in the ARC-B prototype tool and compare the solvers experimentally in the filed. I am currently introducing an homogeneous interface for SMT solvers and implementing ad hoc techniques to treat specific nonlinearities like the ones arising from the application of modulo and division operators between integer variables and constants.

The improvement in the technique and in the prototype tool will enable the collection of further experimental data on the efficiency of the approach, while the identification of possible bottlenecks will indicate the elements of the analysis that require further refinement. A key element for the scalability of the approach is the new coarsening technique that I introduced in the first part of my PhD, and that succeeded in removing redundancy from the model and controlling the state explosion issue. I believe that the core technique can be further improved by introducing strategies to prioritize and parallelize the selection of the frontier transitions to be traversed. An aggressive preprocessing step to the analysis of the software could also improve the approach considerably, in particular I will consider precise program dependence analysis as a means to reduce the number of transitions in the coverage domain model.

This first phase will result in an approach to increase branch coverage up to approximating 100% coverage. In the second and last phase, I plan to extend the approach towards finer grain coverage criteria. In particular, I aim to cover data flow criteria, since I expect the ARC approach to be particularly suitable for these criteria that suffer greatly from the presence of infeasible elements. Extending the approach to a wider class of coverage criteria would require only the definition of different coverage domain models and the adaptation of the coverage frontier monitor to the new models. Coverage frontier analysis, refinement and coarsening depend only on the coverage frontier monitor and are independent from the coverage criteria. Thus this second phase should not be too demanding.

A continuous validation effort will highlight strengths and weaknesses of the different analysis combinations and new directions of improvement. The possibility to compare results from different analysis techniques on the same subjects will increase confidence in the correctness of their implementation. I will evaluate the effectiveness of ARC against increasingly large programs from open source domains (e.g., common UNIX utilities). Through all experiments, I will evaluate the failure detection ability of the test suites computed by the ARC framework, as the objective of any novel testing method is to be effective in failure detection.

In the final evaluation I will try to quantify the testing effort and effectiveness induced by ARC, and I will compare the results both with other automated techniques (for instance, random testing) and manual test-design strategies.

7. REFERENCES

[1] M. Baluda, P. Braione, G. Denaro, and M. Pezzè. Structural coverage of feasible code. In *Proceedings of the 5th Workshop on Automation of Software Test*, AST '10, pages 59–66, New York, NY, USA, 2010.

[2] M. Baluda, P. Braione, G. Denaro, and M. Pezzè. Structural coverage of feasible code. In *Software Quality Journal*, 2011, to appear.

[3] N. E. Beckman, A. V. Nori, S. K. Rajamani, and R. J. Simmons. Proofs from tests. In *Proceedings of the 2008 international symposium on Software testing and analysis*, ISSTA '08, pages 3–14, New York, NY, USA, 2008. ACM.

[4] B. Elkarablieh, P. Godefroid, and M. Y. Levin. Precise pointer reasoning for dynamic test generation. In *Proceedings of the eighteenth international symposium on Software testing and analysis*, ISSTA '09, pages 129–140, New York, NY, USA, 2009. ACM.

[5] P. Godefroid, N. Klarlund, and K. Sen. Dart: directed automated random testing. In *Proceedings of the 2005 ACM SIGPLAN conference on Programming language design and implementation*, PLDI '05, pages 213–223, New York, NY, USA, 2005. ACM.

[6] B. S. Gulavani, T. A. Henzinger, Y. Kannan, A. V. Nori, and S. K. Rajamani. Synergy: a new algorithm for property checking. In *Proceedings of the 14th ACM SIGSOFT international symposium on Foundations of software engineering*, SIGSOFT '06/FSE-14, pages 117–127, New York, NY, USA, 2006. ACM.

[7] T. A. Henzinger, R. Jhala, R. Majumdar, and G. Sutre. Lazy abstraction. In *Proceedings of the 29th ACM SIGPLAN-SIGACT symposium on Principles of programming languages*, POPL '02, pages 58–70, New York, NY, USA, 2002. ACM.

[8] K. McMillan. Lazy annotation for program testing and verification. In T. Touili, B. Cook, and P. Jackson, editors, *Computer Aided Verification*, volume 6174 of *Lecture Notes in Computer Science*, pages 104–118. Springer Berlin / Heidelberg, 2010.

[9] N. Tillmann and J. De Halleux. Pex: white box test generation for .net. In *Proceedings of the 2nd international conference on Tests and proofs*, TAP'08, pages 134–153, Berlin, Heidelberg, 2008. Springer-Verlag.

[10] P. Tonella. Evolutionary testing of classes. In *Proceedings of the 2004 ACM SIGSOFT international symposium on Software testing and analysis*, ISSTA '04, pages 119–128, New York, NY, USA, 2004. ACM.

[11] W. Visser, C. S. Păsăreanu, and S. Khurshid. Test input generation with java pathfinder. In *Proceedings of the 2004 ACM SIGSOFT international symposium on Software testing and analysis*, ISSTA '04, pages 97–107, New York, NY, USA, 2004. ACM.

[12] E. J. Weyuker. The evaluation of program-based software test data adequacy criteria. *Communications of The ACM*, 31:668–675, June 1988.

[13] Z. Xu, Y. Kim, M. Kim, G. Rothermel, and M. B. Cohen. Directed test suite augmentation: techniques and tradeoffs. In *Proceedings of the eighteenth ACM SIGSOFT international symposium on Foundations of software engineering*, FSE '10, pages 257–266, New York, NY, USA, 2010. ACM.

Understanding Failures Through Facts

Jeremias Rößler
Saarland University, Saarbrücken, Germany
roessler@cs.uni-saarland.de

ABSTRACT

"Why does my program crash?"—This ever recurring question of software debugging drives the developer during the analysis of the failure. Complex defects are impossible to automatically identify; this can only be left to human judgment. But what we can do is empower the developer to make an informed decision, by helping her understand the failure. To fully comprehend a failure, one may need to consider many different aspects such as the range of the input parameters and the program's structure and runtime behavior. I propose an approach that gathers a variety of such *facts* from a given failing execution. To examine the correlation of those facts to the failure, it produces additional executions that differ in as few facts as possible. Then the approach creates generalizations and abstractions over the correlating facts. These explain different aspects of the failure and thus help the developer understand and eventually fix the underlying defect.

Categories and Subject Descriptors

D.2.5 [**Software Engineering**]: Testing and Debugging—*Diagnostics, Symbolic execution, Testing tools*

General Terms

Experimentation

Keywords

Automated debugging, test case generation, failure classification, statistical debugging

1. INTRODUCTION

What is special about Brazil as a time zone in regard to a particular date? And why does this make my program crash? These are the questions a developer might ask in order to understand the failure that is reproduced by the test case shown in Figure 1. This test case produces a certain

```
public class JodaTest extends TestCase {
  public void testBrazil() {
    DateTimeZone dtz =
      DateTimeZone.forID("America/Sao_Paulo");
    LocalDate date =
      new LocalDate(2009, 10, 18);
    Interval interval = date.toInterval(dtz);
  }
}
```

Figure 1: JODA TIME bug 2487417: toInterval() fails when processing October 18, 2009, Brazil time.

date and transforms this date to a time interval that represents the 24 hours of that date in the Brazilian time zone. If a developer wants to write a fix for the underlying defect or even only assess it, she has to investigate the code and do some manual debugging to understand how the failure comes into existence. And since this three lines long test case invokes 367 methods and executes 1,465 lines of code (ignoring JAVA system libraries), she might have a hard time doing so.

The state of the art in automated debugging focuses on defect localization—the reporting of individual faulty lines of code. The evaluation of those approaches usually assumes an "ideal user" [28], who immediately recognizes the defect on sight. This convenient assumption allows for an easy and objective evaluation. But this assumption is also very questionable [25]: After some time has passed, developers usually do not understand their own code, let alone someone else's. If only the problematic lines of code are presented without explanation or context, *developers won't recognize the defect.* And even if the code is almost correct and the fix is simple, without understand the failure *developers cannot write the fix.* As for the example in Figure 1: in such a case defect localization does not help at all. The fix involves an API change with deprecation of several methods and classes, and the development of new classes and methods to replace them. For such cases most approaches to defect localization do not even fail well—they are not designed to detect when the fix involves more than a single line of code.

In contrast, little effort has been spent to help developers understand a failure. And for an obvious reason: the evaluation depends on human feedback and thus is much more laborious and much less objective. Yet this is a much better indicator of the overall goal of developer productivity. In the following, I will introduce an approach that is capable of extracting different *facts*: structural and behavioral runtime information that helps the developer understand different aspects of the failure.

Permission to make digital or hard copies of all or part of this work for personal or classroom use is granted without fee provided that copies are not made or distributed for profit or commercial advantage and that copies bear this notice and the full citation on the first page. To copy otherwise, to republish, to post on servers or to redistribute to lists, requires prior specific permission and/or a fee.
ESEC/FSE'11, September 5–9, 2011, Szeged, Hungary.
Copyright 2011 ACM 978-1-4503-0443-6/11/09 ...$10.00.

2. EXPLANATORY FACTS

In previous work [29] the goal was to extract failure conditions in the form of constraints on the input. These constraints are helpful when assessing the frequency and severity of the failure. Yet they do not suffice to explain the failure in terms of the internals of the program. To fully understand a failure, one has to take into account various aspects, such as input, program structure and runtime behavior both in terms of control flow and data flow. Information about these aspects is represented by *facts* of different types that complement and confirm each other and are helpful in diverse scenarios. Such facts are:

Constraints on the input: The input-related path conditions, as they are encountered during execution, form constraints on that input. The proposed approach tries to extract 1-minimal [35] failure conditions that explain the failure in terms of the input (as shown by previous work [29]). For the initial example as given in Figure 1, these failure conditions are

$$\mathit{isDaylightCutDay}() \wedge (\mathit{cutoverTime} = \mathit{00{:}00{:}00})$$

That is, the failure occurs whenever the chosen date is a daylight cut day in the corresponding time zone and the cutover time is midnight.

Variable values: The relations and abstractions of the values of variables may also point to the underlying problem. For the initial example, the value of

```
dateTZ.nextTransition(date.getLocalMillis())
```

has always the same relation to the chosen date: It is the date of the next daylight savings time transition, whenever that transition is at 00:00:00. That is in line with the constraints on the input as mentioned above.

Invariants: Program invariants [13] that hold for failing runs, but never for passing runs or vice versa often reveal some interesting properties. For the initial example, invariants of passing runs that are violated by failing runs are:

$$\mathit{millisLocal} = \mathit{millisUTC} + \mathit{getOffset}(\mathit{millisUTC})$$
$$\mathit{millisUTC} = \mathit{millisLocal} - \mathit{getOffsetFromLocal}(\mathit{millisLocal})$$

This means that the local time is always the universal time plus offset, where the universal time is always the local time minus local offset. For the faulty runs, this mapping is inconsistent, since the created local time maps to some universal time, but this universal time in turn maps back to a different local time.

Definition-usage pairs: The definition and later usage of a variable in the code gives a good understanding of how the data flows through an execution of the program and what data dependencies exist. If the problematic definition and later usage of a value are far away from each other, which is especially common in object oriented programs, that connection can be important to show. For the initial example, such definition-usage pairs could be used to show the origin of the invariant violation as given above:

```
getOffsetFromLocal(millisLocal) !=
        getOffset(millisLocal -
          getOffsetFromLocal(millisLocal))
```

This is the guarding condition of an internal consistency check which realizes that the start of the day (midnight) does not exist in the chosen time zone and raises an exception.

Executed branches: The correlation between executed branches (branch coverage) and defects is an often chosen indicator to single out problematic code. Yet for the given example, this shows a problem that arises when only considering a single aspect of the execution: the code has several places where daylight savings time transitions are treated differently, and due to the nature of the problem, all those branches are highly correlated to the failure. Only when also considering other aspects, it becomes clear which of these branches are really relevant for the failure and which are just coincidentally correlated.

Number of loop-iterations: When it comes to loops, path conditions may not be enough information; the developer might also want to know how often a loop was executed. For example, in JODA TIME, there is a piece of code where two dates from different APIs are aligned:

```
while (date.getDate() == dom) {
  date.setTime(date.getTime() - 1000);
}
```

In that situation, the developer wants to know whether the number of loop iterations is correlated to the failure. For instance, it would be interesting if the loop is always executed 3.600 times (representing one hour).

The facts are gathered during execution. Every execution produces many facts of each type. As most of them are irrelevant for the failure, the next step is to identify facts that are related to the failure and discard facts that are not. To achieve this, I propose an approach of systematic experimentation that works for all types of facts: for each fact it tries to come up with an execution that differs in only the selected fact. If the failure still occurs, the fact is not related; otherwise it is. Of course, for many cases such an execution does not exist. The solution is to generate several executions where each differs in as few facts as possible, but those facts are as divers among the executions as possible. These executions can be used to calculate the correlation of the facts to the failure [2].

This approach is an extension of previous work [29]. The idea to examine the constraints individually by generating additional executions nicely generalizes to all types of facts. Formerly this was done by changing the inputs to the program under test using a constraint solver. Now the constraint solver is embedded into a genetic algorithm [24] to also change the test. This approach partly explores the execution space. The alternative is to explore the complete execution space by applying symbolic execution [20]. Symbolic execution suffers from the problem of state explosion [31]. For most real-life programs the execution space is infinite and its complete exploration infeasible. Because of this, concrete executions were chosen over symbolic execution. But since the execution space is only partly explored, the proposed approach is not complete. For instance it generates a set of constraints on the input that could possibly be further reduced; thus it does not produce the weakest precondition [12]. In return the approach scales much better and is applicable to programs of any size. It starts with a concrete failure and iteratively expands to additional executions, adding more information and increasing the precision in the process. This allows to abort at any stage and still get some results.

After identifying correlating facts, the approach generalizes over them and tries to find abstractions. This is done differently for every type of fact. In many cases, one can leverage the names of the methods the facts are generated in, as well as names of variables and constants. The idea is to reuse as much domain specific semantic information from the code as possible.

The less non-related facts there are to start with, the faster and more precise are the results. Thus techniques that reduce the size or the trace of the execution could be applied to improve the approach. One way to do this is to create the dynamic backward slice [33] of the failing statement. Another approach as proposed by Burger and Zeller [7] minimizes object interactions. After the general applicability of the initial approach has been shown, such techniques could be used to increase its efficiency and the precision of the results.

3. RESEARCH HYPOTHESES

The overall goal is to extract different *facts* and abstractions thereof, that help the developer understand the failure. Of course, helpfulness is not a measurable quantity so it is not directly and objectively verifiable whether the approach meets its goal. Perhaps this is one of the reasons, why this goal has received so little attention in the past. For the proposed approach, two things are done to remedy the problem: A quantitative evaluation is performed on defects for which the fix is available. And a qualitative evaluation is performed manually on defects that are resolved and the reason for the failure is filed.

The ground truth in automated debugging is always the fix. All the facts that the approach reports are somehow related to the failure, meaning that they are part of the chain of causation. The fix breaks this chain such that the failure does not occur anymore. This leads to the first falsifiable research hypothesis. **RH1: Once the fix is applied, the reported facts are not observable anymore**. So the strategy to quantitatively evaluate the proposed approach is to apply it to some defects for which a fix is available. Such defects are contained in the iBugs project [11], which provides a benchmark of real-life subjects with real bugs. When the approach is applied to the defects of that project, the results and the generated executions are recorded. Then the fixes are applied to the defects and the generated executions are performed again. Now the previously reported facts should not be observable anymore. However, this evaluation strategy has a problem: the reported facts might stem from earlier in the chain of causation than where the fix is later applied. This means that the chain is only broken after the facts are observed. So even though the failure is not observable anymore, the facts still are. It is yet unclear how prevalent this problem is. Therefore it will be dealt with when it occurs during evaluation.

Since the generalizations and abstractions produced in the last step involve domain specific semantic information, they cannot be verified automatically. Therefore, I perform a manual and subjective investigation to confirm the last research hypothesis. **RH2: The generalizations and abstractions over the facts are correct and helpful to understand the failure.** For a body of known faults, I manually inspect the results of the approach and, only using that information, try to understand the failure. Then I compare this understanding to the description of the defect as I find it in the bug database and how it was fixed in the code. This non-repeatable evaluation qualitatively indicates the success of the approach.

4. RELATED WORK

Automated debugging is a very dense field and depending on which aspects are emphasized, the proposed approach is related or comparable to many others.

The intuition of informative *facts* about the runs that are presented to the developer is comparable to the facts LaToza and colleagues [22] observed when monitoring developers as they tried to understand foreign code. This notion is mirrored in other contexts as "spectra", "features" or "execution profiles". Harrold and colleagues [16] give a very good overview and classification of the different possible types of program spectra. Santelices and colleagues [30] find that for a set of lightweight fault-localization techniques, a combination of different types of program spectra (such as we use) outperforms individual approaches.

Much work in the context of debugging is targeted at defect localization. Since most of these approaches are evaluated on the Siemens Suite [17] their performance and thus the rising precision of the state of the art is easy to follow. Agrawal and colleagues [3] created a tool termed χslice that produces dices (set difference of dynamic slices) to localize defects. Renieris and Reiss [28] try to localize the fault by comparing the coverage spectra of a failing run to its "nearest" passing run (according to their distance metric). Pytlik and colleagues [26] do preliminary work with two types of simple variable invariants. Given a counterexample trace of a model checker, Groce's Explain tool [14] creates a passing run with minimal distance and extracts a specialized dynamic slice. Liblit and colleagues [23] do statistical debugging with remotely recorded predicate evaluations. Chilimbi and colleagues [8] do the same, but use path profiles instead. Dallmeier and colleagues [10] use method call sequences to identify defective classes. Zeller [34] and Cleve and Zeller [9] transfer data from a healthy to an infected program state to extract cause-effect chains and cause transitions. Jones and colleagues [18] changed their Tarantula tool to localize the defect according to the number of passing and failing test cases a certain block of code participates in. Abreu and colleagues [2] perfect this approach by creating a detailed mathematical probabilistic model of a component chain. Qi and colleagues [27] use the path conditions of a correct and a faulty version of a program to generate an additional execution path and present differences as possible locations of the defect. The Deputo tool of Abreu and colleagues [1] combines a spectrum-based approach with model-based diagnosis. Baah and colleagues [6] use a probabilistic program dependence graph whose probabilities are based on observed executions and causal effect estimation to rank executed statements. The approaches to defect localization show an impressive advancement in the field and many of the ideas can be reused in the context of defect explanation.

Current research takes this idea even one step further: Instead of only locating the failure, some approaches try to automatically come up with fixes for it. For instance Weimer and colleagues [32] use genetic programing to generate fixes and Arcuri and Yao [4] try to co-evolve the program and its test suite. Naturally these approaches suffer from the same shortcomings as defect localization approaches. For a developer to accept a proposed fix, he first has to understand the underlying problem—which is not facilitated.

In contrast to the maturity of the defect localization discipline, only few approaches try to help the developer understand a failure. Originally, "Tarantula" should visualize test information and highlight suspicious code [19], but without further explanation. The cause-effect chains and cause transitions of Cleve and Zeller [9] explain a failure in terms of how the data flows through a program execution but ignore other important aspects. The probabilistic program dependence graphs from Baah and colleagues [5] can also be used to comprehend a fault but need further improvement in that regard. Other techniques aim at the same goal, but take a dialog-oriented approach, rendering them completely different. Whyline is a tool from Ko and colleagues [21] that allows developers to ask questions about the visual output of the program based on a recorded execution. Hao and colleagues [15] implemented a tool that suggests breakpoints to the developer for an interactive localization of the defect.

5. CONCLUSIONS

In this paper I argued for the need to help the developer understand a failure, enabling her to make informed decisions. The contribution of this paper is the proposal of a new approach that, given a failing execution, gathers *facts* that capture important aspects of the input, the structure and the runtime behavior of the program. Additional executions are generated to examine the correlation of those facts to the failure. The approach reuses semantic information found in the source code of the program to abstract and generalize over the correlating facts. Those abstractions and generalizations help the developer understand the failure. The overall goal is an explanation rather than a localization of the underlying defect.

6. ACKNOWLEDGEMENTS

I want to thank my advisors Andreas Zeller and Alessandro Orso for their continuing support and patience. I had valuable discussions with Kevin Streit, Clemens Hammacher and Kim Herzig. David Schuler and Yana Mileva provided helpful comments on earlier revisions of this paper. The anonymous reviewers pointed out some additional related work.

7. REFERENCES

[1] R. Abreu, W. Mayer, M. Stumptner, and A. J. C. van Gemund. Refining spectrum-based fault localization rankings. In *SAC*, pages 409–414, 2009.

[2] R. Abreu, P. Zoeteweij, and A. J. C. van Gemund. An observation-based model for fault localization. In *WODA*, pages 64–70, 2008.

[3] H. Agrawal, J. R. Horgan, S. London, and W. E. Wong. Fault localization using execution slices and dataflow tests. In *ISSRE*, pages 143–151, 1995.

[4] A. Arcuri and X. Yao. A novel co-evolutionary approach to automatic software bug fixing. In *IEEE Congress on Evolutionary Computation*, pages 162–168, 2008.

[5] G. K. Baah, A. Podgurski, and M. J. Harrold. The probabilistic program dependence graph and its application to fault diagnosis. In *ISSTA*, pages 189–200, 2008.

[6] G. K. Baah, A. Podgurski, and M. J. Harrold. Causal inference for statistical fault localization. In *ISSTA*, pages 73–84, 2010.

[7] M. Burger and A. Zeller. Minimizing reproduction of software failures. In *ISSTA*, 2011. to appear.

[8] T. M. Chilimbi, B. Liblit, K. K. Mehra, A. V. Nori, and K. Vaswani. Holmes: Effective statistical debugging via efficient path profiling. In *ICSE*, pages 34–44, 2009.

[9] H. Cleve and A. Zeller. Locating causes of program failures. In *ICSE*, pages 342–351, 2005.

[10] V. Dallmeier, C. Lindig, and A. Zeller. Lightweight defect localization for java. In *ECOOP*, pages 528–550, 2005.

[11] V. Dallmeier and T. Zimmermann. Extraction of bug localization benchmarks from history. In *ASE*, pages 433–436, 2007.

[12] E. W. Dijkstra. *A Discipline of Programming*. Prentice Hall, Inc., 1976.

[13] M. D. Ernst. *Dynamically Discovering Likely Program Invariants*. PhD thesis, University of Washington, 2000.

[14] A. Groce. Error explanation with distance metrics. In *TACAS*, pages 108–122, 2004.

[15] D. Hao, L. Zhang, T. Xie, H. Mei, and J. Sun. Interactive fault localization using test information. *J. Comput. Sci. Technol.*, 24(5):962–974, 2009.

[16] M. J. Harrold, G. Rothermel, R. Wu, and L. Yi. An empirical investigation of program spectra. In *PASTE*, pages 83–90, 1998.

[17] M. Hutchins, H. Foster, T. Goradia, and T. J. Ostrand. Experiments of the effectiveness of dataflow- and controlflow-based test adequacy criteria. In *ICSE*, pages 191–200, 1994.

[18] J. A. Jones and M. J. Harrold. Empirical evaluation of the tarantula automatic fault-localization technique. In *ASE*, pages 273–282, 2005.

[19] J. A. Jones, M. J. Harrold, and J. T. Stasko. Visualization of test information to assist fault localization. In *ICSE*, pages 467–477, 2002.

[20] J. C. King. Symbolic execution and program testing. *Commun. ACM*, 19(7):385–394, 1976.

[21] A. J. Ko and B. A. Myers. Finding causes of program output with the java whyline. In *CHI*, pages 1569–1578, 2009.

[22] T. D. LaToza, D. Garlan, J. D. Herbsleb, and B. A. Myers. Program comprehension as fact finding. In *ESEC/SIGSOFT FSE*, pages 361–370, 2007.

[23] B. Liblit, M. Naik, A. X. Zheng, A. Aiken, and M. I. Jordan. Scalable statistical bug isolation. In *PLDI*, pages 15–26, 2005.

[24] J. Malburg and G. Fraser. Combining search-based and constraint-based testing. In *ISSTA*, 2011. to appear.

[25] C. Parnin and A. Orso. Are automated debugging techniques actually helping programmers? In *ISSTA*, 2011. to appear.

[26] B. Pytlik, M. Renieris, S. Krishnamurthi, and S. P. Reiss. Automated fault localization using potential invariants. In *AADEBUG*, pages 273–276, 2003.

[27] D. Qi, A. Roychoudhury, Z. Liang, and K. Vaswani. Darwin: an approach for debugging evolving programs. In *ESEC/SIGSOFT FSE*, pages 33–42, 2009.

[28] M. Renieris and S. P. Reiss. Fault localization with nearest neighbor queries. In *ASE*, pages 30–39, 2003.

[29] J. Rößler, A. Orso, and A. Zeller. When does my program fail? In *CSTVA*, 2011. to appear.

[30] R. A. Santelices, J. A. Jones, Y. Yu, and M. J. Harrold. Lightweight fault-localization using multiple coverage types. In *ICSE*, pages 56–66, 2009.

[31] A. Valmari. The state explosion problem. *Lecture Notes in Computer Science: Lectures on Petri Nets I: Basic Models*, 1491:429–528, 1998.

[32] W. Weimer, T. Nguyen, C. L. Goues, and S. Forrest. Automatically finding patches using genetic programming. In *ICSE*, pages 364–374, 2009.

[33] M. Weiser. Program slicing. *IEEE Trans. Softw. Eng.*, 10:352 –357, July 1984.

[34] A. Zeller. Isolating cause-effect chains from computer programs. In *SIGSOFT FSE*, pages 1–10, 2002.

[35] A. Zeller and R. Hildebrandt. Simplifying and isolating failure-inducing input. *IEEE Trans. Softw. Eng.*, 28:183–200, February 2002.

QoS Verification and Model Tuning @ Runtime

Antonio Filieri
DEI-DeepSE Group - Politecnico di Milano
via Golgi, 42 - Milan, Italy
filieri@elet.polimi.it

Categories and Subject Descriptors:
D.2.4 Software/Program Verification: Formal Methods
General Terms: Algorithms,Reliability,Verification.

1. INTRODUCTION

Unpredictable changes continuously affect software systems and may have a severe impact on their quality of service, potentially jeopardizing the system's ability to meet the desired requirements. Changes may occur in critical components of the system, clients' operational profiles, requirements, or deployment environments. As a consequence, software engineers are increasingly required to design software as a *(self-) adaptive system*, which automatically detects and reacts to changes.

In order to detect significant changes in the execution environment, effective monitoring procedures are not enough since their outcome can seldom provide a direct support for reasoning and verification on the state of the system and its changes. The adoption of software models and model checking techniques at run time may support automatic reasoning about such changes, detect harmful configurations, and potentially enable appropriate (self-)reactions. However, traditional model checking techniques and tools may not be simply applied as they are at run time, since they may not meet the constraints imposed by on-the-fly analysis, in terms of execution time and memory occupation. The key idea to deal with verification complexity as proposed in this research consists of splitting the problem in two steps: 1) precomputing a set of closed formulae corresponding to desired properties and depending on relevant system's variables, and then 2) quickly evaluate such formulas every time a variation is detected.

This continuous verification of QoS requirements can support continuous adaptation of the software system. The term continuous here subsumes that reactions should be completed before a new variation invalidates their utility. A special, though large, class of systems behaves depending on a finite set of parameters, e.g. possible configurations, routing options, third party components selection and so on. Many control-theory based approaches have been studied to manipulate control parametersin order to reach or keep desired goals, but this continuous verification is an extremely hard task since software is usually very complex to formalize as a dynamic system, and even when it is possible, it usually shows a very complex, often non-linear, structure, which control-theory can hardly deal with. The claim of this research is that by exploiting software models at runtime, control can be made feasible and efficient. The key idea is to measure and control the system through models capturing its relevant aspects.

The goal of this research is to study new solutions for runtime efficient verification of non-functional properties and to exploit them for self-tuning.

Permission to make digital or hard copies of all or part of this work for personal or classroom use is granted without fee provided that copies are not made or distributed for profit or commercial advantage and that copies bear this notice and the full citation on the first page. To copy otherwise, to republish, to post on servers or to redistribute to lists, requires prior specific permission and/or a fee.
ESEC/FSE'11, September 5–9, 2011, Szeged, Hungary.
Copyright 2011 ACM 978-1-4503-0443-6/11/09 ...$10.00.

2. RUNTIME VERIFICATION

The goal on this topic is to define a set of methodologies allowing for *time-efficient verification* of non-functional properties of software systems.

The focus of this research is on system models where the parameters that describe runtime variability are explicitly represented. Furthermore, it is assumed that phenomena reflected as changes are measurable by monitors and/or runtime predictors as values of models' parameters. The property of interest depends on all or part of those variable parameters and thus its truth must be re-verified every time a relevant parameter changes.

2.1 State of The Art

A number of methods have been proposed to support reasoning on non-functional properties of software based on models that are analyzed at run-time by relying on monitor data (e.g.[9, 19, 20]). Unfortunately most of them can be computationally expensive, which implies that detection of requirements violation may require a time frame that is incompatible with an effective reaction.

Concerning reliability, the research was up to now focused on properties formally expressed by means of Probabilistic Computational Tree Logic (PCTL) [16] assertions checked against Discrete Time Markov Chains (DTMC) [18]. The most popular way to verify the truth of PCTL assertions on DTMC models is by Probabilistic Model-Checking [1]. Model-Checking may be unsuitable for self-adaptive systems because it may require minutes or more to evaluate properties over large models, thus hindering planning and reconfiguration capabilities that must respond to tighter time bounds. In [5] Daws proposed a procedure to first convert the DTMC into a finite automaton from which it is possible to obtain a corresponding regular expression. This expression can be evaluated to produce a mathematical formula, which represents any arbitrary reachability property. Daws' approach is restricted to formulae without nested probabilistic operators and the outcoming regular expression grows quickly with the number of states composing the DTMC ($O(n^{log(n)})$). In [15] Hahn et al. propose a refinement of the approach presented in [5] for reachability formulae, which combines state space reduction techniques and early evaluation of the regular expression in order to improve actual execution times when only a few variable parameters appear in the model. The improvement in [15] requires n^3 arithmetic operations among polynomials, performing better than [5] in most practical cases, although still leading to an expression whose length is $O(n^{log(n)})$ in the worse case.

In [14] the opposite approach is followed. Instead of trying to produce a closed formula corresponding to a reachability property, the goal is to find the sets of parameter values for which a formula is true. Such an approach essentially proceeds through an iterative refinement of an initial partition of parameter values spaces. The performance of the algorithm is quite formula-dependent, and for complex formulae it seems to take longer than [15] and [12]. Still [14] is correct and complete with respect to reachability formulae (i.e. concerning the probability of reaching a certain set of execution states) and is still under improvement.

In [17], an incremental approach for quantitative verification of Markov Decision Processes (MDPs) is proposed. Given that (D)MDPs are a superclass of DTMCs, the approach is of interest for this research. It introduces an incremental verification method, which allows for reuse of previous partial results, by exploiting the presence of Strongly Connected Components (SCCs). The approach in [17] reduces model-checking time, on average, of one order of magnitude on popular large case studies. Such a reduction might already be sufficient for a number of self-adaptive systems.

2.2 Current Achievements

The initial achievements on this research are going to appear in [12], and is focused on reliability properties. In this section the main concepts summarized.

DTMCs are defined as state-transition systems augmented with probabilities. *States* represent possible configurations of the system. *Transitions* among states occur at discrete time and have an associated probability. DTMCs are discrete stochastic processes with the Markov property, according to which the probability distribution of future states depend only upon the current state.

Formally, a (labeled) DTMC is tuple (S, S_0, P, L) where

- S is a finite set of states
- $S_0 \subseteq S$ is a set of initial states
- $P : S \times S \rightarrow [0, 1]$ is a stochastic matrix ($\sum_{s' \in S} P(s, s') = 1 \ \forall s \in S$). An element $P(s_i, s_j)$ represents the probability that the next state of the process will be s_j given that the current state is s_i.
- $L : S \rightarrow 2^{AP}$ is a labeling function which assigns to each state the set of *Atomic Propositions* which are true in that state.

This definition is here implicitly extended by also allowing transitions to be labeled with variables (in the range 0..1) instead of constants. A state $s \in S$ is said to be an *absorbing state* if $P(s, s) = 1$. If a DTMC contains at least one absorbing state, the DTMC itself is said to be a *absorbing*.

In an absorbing DTMC with r absorbing states and t transient states, rows and columns of the transition matrix P can be reordered such that P is in the following *canonical form*:

$$\mathbf{P} = \begin{pmatrix} Q & R \\ 0 & I \end{pmatrix}$$

where I is an r by r identity matrix, 0 is an r by t zero matrix, R is a nonzero t by r matrix and Q is a t by t matrix.

In the simplest model for reliability analysis, the DTMC will have two absorbing states, representing the correct accomplishment of the task and the task's failure, respectively. The use of absorbing states is commonly extended to modeling different failure conditions. For example, different failure states may be associated with the invocation of different external services. Notice that, for a sufficiently long execution time, every run of an absorbing DTMC is going to be absorbed in one of the absorbing states [18].

Due to the lack of space, PCTL is not recalled here. The interested reader can refer to [16, 1]. The most important properties of PTCL are *reachability properties*, which predicate on the probability of reaching a certain desired state. It can be shown that all the other properties can be reduced to reachability ones on properly manipulated versions of the DTMC they are being checked on [1].

Contribution. The goal is to precompute, once for all, parametric closed formulae corresponding to PCTL properties over given DTMCs; closed formulae can then be efficiently evaluated at runtime, when parameters' values will be available from monitors. As shown in [18], the probability of reaching an absorbing state s_j given that the execution of the DTMC started in s_i corresponds to the entry b_{ij} of the matrix $B = N * R$, where $N = (I - Q)^{-1}$. In an analogous way, it can be proved that the probability of passing through a state s_j before being absorbed (and given that the execution started in the transient state s_i) corresponds to the value $f_{ij} = n_{ij}/n_{jj}$.

The computation of b_{ij} and f_{ij} in the field of polynomials multivariate by parameters could be, in general, computationally expensive. But, this operation has to be done once for all. Additionally, it can be heavily parallelized as well known from matrix algorithms. Finally, there are special situations in which complexity can be reduced. One of these situations appears when the number of variable components c (i.e. components parametric outgoing transitions) is small and the matrix describing the DTMC is sparse, as very frequently happens in practice.

Let $W = I - Q$. The elements of its inverse N are:

$$n_{ij} = \frac{1}{det(W)} \cdot \alpha_{ji}(W)$$

where $\alpha_{ji}(W)$ is the cofactor of the element w_{ji}. Thus:

$$b_{ik} = \sum_{x \in 0..t-1} n_{ix} \cdot r_{xj} = \frac{1}{det(W)} \sum_{x \in 0..t-1} \alpha_{xi}(W) \cdot r_{xj}$$

Computing b_{ik} requires the computation of t determinants of square matrices with size $t - 1$. Let τ be the average number of outgoing transitions from each state ($\tau << n$ by assumption). Each of the determinants can be computed by means of Laplace expansion. Precisely, by expanding first the c rows representing the variable states (each has τ symbolic terms), we need to compute at most τ^c determinants and then linearly combine them. Each submatrix of size $t - c$ does not contain any variable symbol, by construction, thus its determinant can be computed with $(t - c)^3$ operations among constant numbers (LU-decomposition), thus much faster than the corresponding ones among polynomials. The final complexity is thus $\tau^c \cdot (t-c)^3 \sim \tau^c \cdot t^3$, which significantly reduces the original complexity and makes the design-time pre-computation of *reachability properties* feasible in a reasonable time, even for large values of t.

Similar considerations lead to the definition of $f_{ij} = n_{ij}/n_{jj} = \alpha_{ji}(W)/\alpha_{jj}(W)$ and to the estimation of their complexity.

The approach can be generalized, significantly increasing pre-computation complexity but still keeping the option of high-parallelism, to cover the entire PCTL [12]. To the best of the author's knowledge, none of the other approaches to parametric model-checking of PCTL are able expressions with nested temporal operators, as this contribution can do.

The validity of this approach has been proved via simulation and comparison with other model-checking tools [12].

2.3 Future Directions

The approach can be improved at different levels. One concerns the realization of a more efficient implementation by exploiting state-of-the-art mathematical algorithms for matrix manipulation. A distributed version could also be interesting in order to verify the scalability of the approach in case of very large systems.

Other levels of improvement and extension consist in: 1) using PCTL*, which is more expressive than PCTL and allows the expression of more complex reliability requirements, and 2) the extension to different models, e.g. CTMCs for performance and Reward models, in order to support basic cost metrics. The integration of the procedure within an established model-checker would instead lead to a comprehensive tool for DTMC-based reliability analysis.

The identification of significant benchmarks in order to compare this approach with others in the field is also a needed step toward a deeper understanding of strengths and pitfalls of each one.

3. PARAMETER TUNING

Self-adaptive software systems interact with their environment. A number of them embed control parameters which allow to "tune" the behavior of the system in different ways. Example of those systems are:

- routing algorithms for networks
- graphical user interfaces that adapt to the user
- caching strategies for OS memory management
- load-balancing procedures

The goal is to identify appropriate tuning strategies suitable for the adaptation of software systems at runtime, once the need for adaptation is discovered, as explained in the previous section. The novelty of the author's approach consists in observing and controlling an model of the software, kept alive by proper methodologies [9]. Verifying QoS properties on and controlling a proper abstraction instead of the software itself could make the complexity of software manageable, at least to some reasonable extent.

3.1 State of The Art

In recent time, Control Theory has captured a large interest from the community of Software Engineering (SE) interested in self-management as a mean to meet QoS requirements [6]. There were a number of attempts in the field of web servers, data centers, storage systems. Nevertheless Control Theory is still not a widely present practice in SE. This is largely due to the fact that developing accurate system models for software is in fact hard. Moreover, strong mathematical skills are needed in order to deal with complex non-linear dynamics o real systems [8, 6, 21]. These difficulties usually lead to the design of controllers focused on particular operating regions or conditions. Such "local" controllers can than be combined in order to be able to switch from one to another as the operating region changes.

3.2 Current Achievements

In the current stage two directions have been explored. The simplest one is a reliability-driven load-balancer; the second is a general methodology for optimal control of software systems through their DTMC representation.

Reliability-driven Load-balancing. The research issue in this case is how to design a load-balancer aware of the reliability of possible providers as well as of users' requirements. The goal for the load-balancer (LB) is to keep the desired reliability, avoiding higher failure rates, that would turn in contract violation, and higher reliability, that would imply higher costs and would reduce the market value of higher reliability solution. Another strong requirement for the LB concerns its performance: it must be fast and its computational overhead negligible.

The solution can be an adaptive feedback control with the following features:

- Linear hierarchical control: the LB exposes the same interface of the service to be provided, thus it is itself an instance of the service. Such a structure allows for hierarchical load-balancing in a natural way: each LB has only 2 possible choices, each of them can in turn be lower level load-balancer. Keeping the hierarchy as balanced as possible, requires to make $log_2(n)$ choices in order to select the proper provider. Each of these choices is as fast as rolling a dice: each load balancer knows with which fraction of the incoming requests has to be routed toward each of the two available alternatives and can behave consequently.
- PI control + Auto-Tuning: LB behavior, determined by the probability of choosing the first or second alternative, is controlled by a Proportional Integral (PI) controller [8]. Desired reliability to be provided to the users is the set-point of the PI. Variation in the nominal reliability of providers (revealed via monitoring) and variation in reliability requirements are considered "disturbs", in the sense that they are able to alter *the*unpredictably ability of the LB to meet its requirements. Controller's performance, in terms of *disturb rejection*, *spike reduction*, *convergence time to set-point* and *overshoots* are determined by two parameters, namely the proportional and the integral coefficients. These two values are hard to guess for a non expert. As part of this work an automatic tuning procedure has been design for the controller. Notice that this case concerns the tuning of the controller, not the system (which will be tuned by the LB).
- As close as possible to the goal: in real life it could happen that, due to temporary or permanent external conditions, goals become unreachable. In this case the expected behavior of the LB is to take the system as close as possible to its requirements, and to signal the unfeasibility of them to whom it may concern. These features are currently provided by this pilot project.

Controlling software through DTMC abstractions. In many practical cases, the actual behavior of a system can be modeled as a stochastic process. This can be due either to an intrinsically random behavior or, more often, to the dependency of the deterministic procedure on external uncertainties, e.g. user decisions, communication failures, load conditions, or non-determinism of distributed systems.

Many of these behaviors can be suitably modeled by DTMCs [2]. Some transitions of the DTMC will represent observable (misurable) *disturbs*, such as monitored reliability of external services or the current usage profile expressed as a probabilistic characterization of users' choices. Other transitions will represent *control inputs*, that is, tunable configuration parameters of the system, for example the selection of a specific user interface or a certain set of advertisement banners. The goal of the controller is to continuously correct the value of control inputs in order to make the system meet its requirements, compensating the effects of disturbs. In general the number of control inputs may be different from the number of the goals, and this setting suffers an increased mathematical complexity of the controller [8]. Also, there are not automatic techniques to produce a strictly linear controller, in general. Leaving out details, the core of the problem is that possibly infinite assignments of the control inputs can make the controlled system reach its goals. This indeterminism requires appropriate techniques to be managed, since the controller must provide one single directive.

The solutions proposed in this research make use of optimal-control. In practice, a cost function is introduced as index of the quality of an assignment above the others. Costs may depend on any reasonable factor, e.g. service cost per invocation or average overhead. In case it does not make sense in the specific domain to talk about cost of the configuration, any convex, possibly linear, function of the control input can be provided. Minimizing this function would anyway make the assignment unique and the control feasible.

The entire solution is implemented in Wolfram Mathematica and shown to be effective and general.

3.3 Future Directions

Transposition of Control Theory principles into Software Engineering is becoming increasingly popular. The idea of controlling models of the software system and delegating the actuation to a synchronization layer seems promising.

The next step on the Load-Balancer topic is the extension to multiple QoS metrics and thus the adoption of model more complex than DTMCs. Also a support for some cost metrics could be interesting. Concerning the tuning methodology, the current effort is toward controlling a general CTMC model, thus including both reliability, performance and eventually rewards. There is some preliminary result that defined a first thread of exploration.

Both of the topics can benefit from the application of more advanced control techniques. First of all the adoption of some prediction model that would give to the controller a longer time to take decisions, thus possibly allowing for the realization of more effective strategies that are also more expensive to be found.

Another application field under exam concerns the control of virtual machines farms. Appropriate resource allocation strategies could reduce costs while still ensuring required QoS. An adaptive controller can do the job: based on preliminary results, it should be possible to produce adaptive controllers that allocate as much as needed, with minimal overshoots.

4. ACKNOWLEDGMENTS

Author's advisors is Prof. Carlo Ghezzi (carlo.ghezzi@polimi.it), DeepSE Group @ DEI, Politecnico di Milano.
This research has been partially funded by the European Commission, Programme IDEAS- ERC, Project 227977-SMScom.
Other publications of the author include [10, 4, 7, 3, 12, 13, 11]. He is also co-author of the Dagstuhl proceedings book "Model Driven Quality Prediction" (Springer ed.)

5. REFERENCES

[1] C. Baier and J. P. Katoen. *Principles of Model Checking*. The MIT Press, 2008.
[2] R. C. Cheung. A user-oriented software reliability model. *IEEE TSE*, 6(2):118–125, 1980.
[3] A. Ciancone, A. Filieri, M. L. Drago, R. Mirandola, and V. Grassi. Klapersuite: an integrated model-driven environment for non-functional requirements analysis of component-based systems. In *TOOLS 2011 - to appear*. 2011.
[4] A. Ciancone, A. Filieri, and R. Mirandola. Mantra: Towards model transformation testing. In *QUATIC 2010*, pages 97–105. IEEE, 2010.
[5] C. Daws. Symbolic and parametric model checking of discrete-time markov chains. *ICTAC*, pages 280–294, 2005.
[6] Y. Diao, J. Hellerstein, S. Parekh, R. Griffith, G. Kaiser, and D. Phung. Self-managing systems: a control theory foundation. In *ECBS '05*, pages 441 – 448, 2005.
[7] S. Distefano, A. Filieri, C. Ghezzi, and R. Mirandola. A compositional method for reliability analysis of workflows affected by multiple failure modes. In *CBSE 2011 - to appear*. 2011.
[8] R. Dorf and R. Bishop. *Modern control systems*. Prentice Hall, 2008.
[9] I. Epifani, C. Ghezzi, R. Mirandola, and G. Tamburrelli. Model evolution by run-time parameter adaptation. In *ICSE*, 2009.
[10] A. Filieri, C. Ghezzi, V. Grassi, and R. Mirandola. Reliability analysis of component-based systems with multiple failure modes. In *CBSE 2010*, volume 6092, pages 1–20. 2010.
[11] A. Filieri, C. Ghezzi, R. Mirandola, and G. Tamburrelli. Conquering complexity via seamless integration of design-time and run-time verification, to appear.
[12] A. Filieri, C. Ghezzi, and G. Tamburrelli. Run-time efficient probabilistic model checking. In *ICSE - to appear*, 2011.
[13] A. Filieri, C. Ghezzi, and G. Tamburrelli. A formal approach to adaptive software: Continuous assurance of non-functional requirements. *Formal Aspects of Computing*, under revision.
[14] E. Hahn, T. Han, A. Mereacre, and L. Zhang. Synthesis for pctl in parametric markov decision processes. *NFM - to appear*, 2011.
[15] E. Hahn, H. Hermanns, and L. Zhang. Probabilistic reachability for parametric markov models. *Model Checking Software*, pages 88–106, 2009.
[16] H. Hansson and B. Jonsson. A logic for reasoning about time and reliability. *Formal Aspects of Computing*, 6(5):512–535, 1994.
[17] M. Kwiatkowska, D. Parker, and H. Qu. Incremental quantitative verification for markov decision processes. In *IEEE/IFIP DSN-PDS*. IEEE CS Press, 2011. To appear.
[18] S. Ross. *Stochastic Processes*. Wiley New York, 1996.
[19] J. Zhang and B. H. C. Cheng. Model-based development of dynamically adaptive software. In *ICSE*. ACM, 2006.
[20] T. Zheng, M. Woodside, and M. Litoiu. Performance model estimation and tracking using optimal filters. *IEEE TSE*, 34(3):391–406, 2008.
[21] X. Zhu, M. Uysal, Z. Wang, S. Singhal, A. Merchant, P. Padala, and K. Shin. What does control theory bring to systems research? *SIGOPS Oper. Syst. Rev.*, 43:62–69, January 2009.

A Software Lifecycle Process for Context-Aware Adaptive Systems *

Marco Mori
IMT Institute for Advanced Studies Lucca
Lucca, Italy
marco.mori@imtlucca.it

ABSTRACT

It is increasingly important for computing systems to evolve their behavior at run-time because of resources uncertainty, system failures and emerging user needs. Our approach supports software engineers to analyze and develop context-aware adaptive applications. The software lifecycle process we propose supports static and dynamic decision making mechanisms, run-time consistent evolution and it is amenable to be automated.

Categories and Subject Descriptors

D.2.4 [**Software Engineering**]: Software/Program Verification; D.2.9 [**Software Engineering**]: Management

General Terms

Design, Verification

1. RESEARCH PROBLEM AND MOTIVATION

As ubiquitous computing systems are becoming increasingly popular, software engineers have to deal with different variability dimensions such as the heterogeneity of the underlying communications, executing environment and changing user needs. In addition even the system may be modeled as a source of changes taking into account the possible software failures [2].

In the software engineering arena, adaptive systems are studied in order to define methodologies and theories to efficiently and consistently support their evolutions at run-time [31, 7]. Context plays a key role for the evolution since it represents the portion of the environment that is beyond the control of the system but it may influence the system behavior. Designers define a set of alternative behaviors at design time while the actual evolution decisions are taken at run-time when the context information are available. Since the context is not always predictable it is necessary to support also dynamic adaptations by providing mechanisms to update the logic of evolution [28]. To this end, the context needs to be explicitly modeled as proposed in contemporary research of context-aware systems [5, 18, 25].

We propose context-aware adaptive systems to deal with the uncertainty shown by the environment, the user and the system itself. Indeed, their main ability is to perform run-time adaptations driven by the "context" thus promoting software evolution to the norm rather than considering it as an exception. Context is characterized by foreseen and unforeseen variations to which correspond foreseen and unforeseen system evolutions. In the foreseen case the system evolves in order to keep satisfied a fixed set of requirements while in the unforeseen case the system evolves in order to respond to requirements variations that are unknown at design-time.

A consensus is emerging in the SE community that these kind of applications demand for a different software engineering process where the traditional distinction in phases and their characterization as static activities versus dynamic ones is disappearing [14, 23]. A challenging research problem is to define a software lifecycle process to enable software engineers to design context-aware adaptive applications resilient to context and user needs variations. This process should support consistent system evolutions, thus maintaining the system goal satisfaction in the face of new environmental conditions. To this end, evolutions should be both functional and non-functional. Run-time and consistent evolutions are achieved exploiting traceability links among system models at the different software engineering phases. Requirements, design and implementation artifacts have to be preserved at run-time along with a unified context model that supports the management of the evolution logic.

2. BACKGROUND AND RELATED WORK

The notion of context has been exploited in the software engineering field in order to define context-aware requirement models, context-aware architectural models and context-aware implementation models. In the literature different approaches address requirement engineering problems for context-aware adaptive systems. In [3] the authors have proposed a framework to explain the relations among the main concepts concerning requirement engineering for context-aware adaptive services. The approaches presented in [12] and [8] describe two different attempts to deal with the requirement elicitation problem for context-aware adaptive systems. They define requirement artifacts by means of

*My research is under the supervision of prof. Paola Inverardi, Università dell'Aquila (paola.inverardi@di.univaq.it)

Permission to make digital or hard copies of all or part of this work for personal or classroom use is granted without fee provided that copies are not made or distributed for profi or commercial advantage and that copies bear this notice and the full citation on the firs page. To copy otherwise, to republish, to post on servers or to redistribute to lists, requires prior specifi permission and/or a fee.
ESEC/FSE'11, September 5–9, 2011, Szeged, Hungary.
Copyright 2011 ACM 978-1-4503-0443-6/11/09 ...$10.00.

first-class context entities. In [36] and [34] the authors propose two different formal representations of context-aware requirements by including a notion of uncertainty. In [30] the authors define a complete framework for requirement engineering to distinguish activities at design-time from activities at run-time. They provide a mechanism to evolve the requirement specification at run-time driven by the user. In [32] it is claimed that requirements represent the adequate level to enact the system evolution, thus systems should be requirement-aware. The authors also show how to achieve the traceability from requirements to the design in order to actually achieve the reconfiguration.
Architectural representations for context-aware system have been surveyed in [5, 11]. Finally at implementation level Hirschfeld et al. [17] propose a new programming technique called Context-oriented Programming (COP) in order to adapt the behavior of software entities to the current execution context. They surveyed different mechanisms to treat the context explicitly and to achieve the consequent adaptation for the implementation artifacts at run-time.
Several frameworks address the problem of achieving system evolution at different granularity level. The Rainbow framework [13] enables architecture-based self-adaptation for software systems. It proposes adaptation rules to specify how to reconfigure system components whenever certain situations arise. The framework supports non-functional adaptation whereas it does not consider requirements management at run-time. In addition there is no notion of consistency check for the system evolution and there is no explicit definition of context. The PLASTIC approach [4] applies reconfiguration strategies at implementation level by exploiting an explicit definition of context. The approach supports non-functional reconfiguration to statically defined Java artifacts driven by current context variations. Nevertheless a notion of consistency check is still missing. A common aspect for the above mentioned frameworks [13, 4] is that whatever is the grain of reconfiguration, they do not support evolutions arising at run-time. They only consider evolution strategies that are statically analyzed at design-time; thus making the system unable to achieve reconfigurations required by unanticipated user need variations arising at run-time.
In [35] the authors present a three-layered conceptual model to support the architectural reconfiguration of self-managing systems. This model entails a Component layer, a Change Management layer and a Goal Management layer. The Goal layer identifies the action to perform while the Change layer executes the required action and interacts with the Component layer to add/remove/reconnect components. Through the Goal Management layer, requirements are managed at run-time by generating new plans to perform whenever the deployed ones are not suitable for the current context situation. This feature supports reconfigurations required by new requirements arising at run-time. Even if the framework provides functional and non-functional evolutions there is no definition of context and a definition of consistency check for the composition of components is still missing.
To the best of our knowledge the frameworks presented in the literature do not consider a complete software lifecycle process for context-aware adaptive systems. They address only a few of the issues arising from the three software engineering phases. Moreover most approaches are not based on an explicit context model to support system evolution in all phases of the software lifecycle process.

3. APPROACH AND UNIQUENESS

My research work concentrates in defining a framework to support a general lifecycle process for the development and the evolution of context-aware adaptive systems. We focus on context-aware requirements, context-aware design models and context-aware implementations mechanisms.
We have identified two different types of evolutions each one addressing a different nature of context variability. On one hand, designers deal with foreseeable context variations by providing the required system evolutions at design-time. They statically define the logic of evolution to the foreseeable context by means of different system variants that have to be deployed and un-deployed at run-time in order to keep satisfied a fixed set of system requirements. The selection among the system variants is driven by the context requirements and the non-functional properties that characterize each variant. On the other hand, the context may change unpredictably thus causing the change of user needs that can be expressed as a variation to the requirement set to satisfy. The user may specify a new requirement as a consequence of the unforeseen context variation. Therefore the evolution logic should be revisited at run-time by updating the space of system variants provided by the designer at design time. We refer to the first case as *foreseen evolution* because the evolution logic is embedded inside the system models and the foreseeable contexts have been completely characterized at design time. The second case is called *unforeseen evolution* as the evolution logic and the context is not known at design time and the user is placed into the evolution feedback loop. Fig.1 shows how the context affects system evolutions. While in the foreseen evolution the system evolves to keep satisfied a fixed set of system requirements in different known contexts, the unforeseen evolution is driven by new requirements arising from unforeseeable contexts.

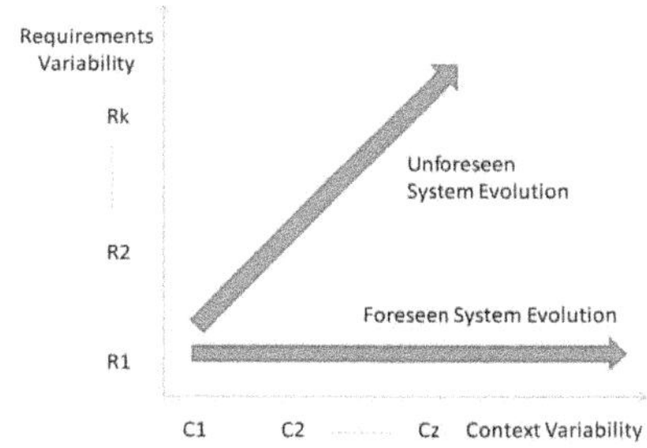

Figure 1: System Evolutions

Our approach to support context-aware adaptive applications is inspired by the Software Product Line Engineering (SPLE) perspective. Among the possible ways to model a system, SPLE is amenable to represent system variability and it supports a notion of consistency. In SPLE the basic unit of behavior is the so called feature that is the smallest part of a service that can be perceived by the user. The system variability is expressed through the space of the system variants. Each variant is obtained by putting together two or more features and it shows the feature interaction phenomenon if its features run correctly in isolation but they give rise to undesired behavior when jointly executed [26, 1, 6]. The work [10] has already shown common research questions between SPLE and adaptive system and the necessity to dynamically manage features at run-time. Most

recently, Dynamic Software Product lines (DSPL) have been presented as a new direction in SPL engineering field to deal with software capable of adapting to changing user needs and evolving context environment at different binding time [16, 29]. However in the DSPL field dealing with evolutions arising at runtime is still an open issue.
Our intention is to take advantage of the methodologies proposed in SPLE to support consistent evolutions for context-aware adaptive systems. We define a context-aware adaptive application in terms of sets of features each one implemented with a component and / or a service. We define a feature as composed by a context-independent requirement, a context-dependent requirement, and an implementation part. The notion of requirements we adopt is inspired by the taxonomy proposed by Glinz in [15]. A feature is a triple $f_i = (R_i, C_i, I_i)$ where each element is defined as follows:

- R_i is a conjunction of functional, performance and specific quality requirements (context-independent)
- C_i is a context-dependent constraint requirement
- I_i is the feature implementation expressed as Java code.

The definition above is inspired by [9] which has been in turn inspired by the Problem Frame approach defined in [24]. Differently from these approaches we refer to C as the context requirement instead of the domain assumption.
Each *system variant* is represented as a different combination of features expressed as $G_F = (R_F, C_F, I_F)$. At this level of description we do not explain how to combine features. We just suppose to have an abstract union operator among features which is defined in terms of union operators for context-independent requirements, context-dependent requirements and implementation components. In concrete instantiations of the framework these operators will take a precise form.
We represent the space of admissible system variants by using the *feature diagram* defined in the SPLE with a tree structure [33]. We adopt the absence of feature interaction as the notion of *consistent evolution* for a system variant. A certain variant G_F shows a feature interaction phenomenon if the features in F run correctly in isolation but they give rise to undesired behavior when they are jointly executed. The feature interaction for G_F is checked as: $I_F, C_F \vdash R_F$. This formula is automatically verified at design time to cope with foreseen evolutions and at run-time in order to support the unforeseen evolutions. We have defined the consistency check formula by means of three different problems: the satisfiability for the context requirement C, the satisfiability for the requirement R and the validation/verification problem of I against R. The context model is a key aspect in performing the system evolution; it has to be monitored and updated at each evolution step. It entails the set of entities based on which our context requirements are defined. Since in ubiquitous computing the unpredictability of the context is the main cause of system failures, we believe that the problem of checking the satisfiability for the context requirements plays a key role in supporting consistent evolutions. In addition we consider the three problems to be run-time problems since we support a notion of run-time unforeseen evolution. As a consequence computational issues become important to actually achieve the consistency check at run-time. Furthermore we assume that requirements artifacts are available.

4. RESULTS AND CONTRIBUTIONS

We have defined a general lifecycle process for context-aware adaptive systems in order to support the consistent evolutions based on two decision making mechanisms. The static decision making mechanism supports foreseen evolutions whereas the dynamic decision making mechanism supports unforeseen evolutions. As shown in our preliminary work [19] we have provided easy-to-use modeling techniques for software engineers along with preliminary ideas to enact run-time evolutions. We have presented an explicit model of context and we have shown how the system can evolve its behavior at run-time based on context changes and changing user needs. We have dealt with the problem of selecting and executing the most suitable system configuration in a given context and how to reconfigure the system to augment it with un-anticipated behavior arising from new requirements at run-time. We have formalized a notion of consistent evolution based on the context-dependent requirements.
In [22] we have designed and partially implemented a framework that supports our general lifecycle process for context-aware adaptive systems. We have defined a generic interface architecture that can be implemented by any evolution framework to support our kinds of evolution.
Our framework is generic and it is amenable to augment the system with new requirements arising at run-time. Since new requirements may interact with deployed requirements we have provided the support to keep those entities at run-time and check their correctness jointly. In [21] we have formalized three consistency checks to provide high-assurance guarantee to the evolution. In this paper we have also proposed a technique to check context requirements at run-time with respect to the variations of context resources. In [20] we have shown how to verify context-independent requirements with respect to implementation artifacts. We have defined a practical technique which exploits the Java Path Finder tool[1].
As far as static decision making mechanisms are concerned in [27], we have proposed a practical support for context-aware system reconfiguration based on changing user preferences. In order to select the best configuration to deploy we have defined a multi-criteria selection problem by means of an aggregative objective function that combines user benefit and cost. This function accumulates the perceived current user benefit and the probable future user benefit evaluated exploiting a state-based context prediction model. The reconfiguration cost measures the distance between two system variants in terms of features to deploy and un-deploy. We have validated this approach by simulating the reconfiguration process at large scale in order to capture the relevance of considering future contexts. The proposed selection algorithm performed satisfactory in the set of experiments that we carried out.
Currently, we are implementing an instance of our framework with specific technologies to define requirements specifications and implementation artifacts and technologies to carry out the consistency check. We will also extend the PLASTIC approach [4] to achieve system reconfigurations on Java implementation artifacts at run-time for our unforeseen evolution. My research will result in a new methodological approach in developing and evolving context-aware adaptive applications. I will show the applicability of the

[1]http://babelfish.arc.nasa.gov/hg/jpf/jpf-core

proposed lifecycle process by applying the target framework to large scale systems.

5. REFERENCES

[1] M. Alférez, A. Moreira, U. Kulesza, J. Araújo, R. Mateus, and V. Amaral. Detecting feature interactions in spl requirements analysis models. In *FOSD*, pages 117–123, 2009.

[2] J. Andersson, R. de Lemos, S. Malek, and D. Weyns. Modeling dimensions of self-adaptive software systems. In *SEAMS*, pages 27–47, 2009.

[3] A. F. Andrea and A. Savigni. A framework for requirements engineering for context-aware services. In *STRAW 01*, pages 200–1, 2001.

[4] M. Autili, P. D. Benedetto, and P. Inverardi. Context-aware adaptive services: The plastic approach. In *FASE*, pages 124–139, 2009.

[5] M. Baldauf, S. Dustdar, and F. Rosenberg. A survey on context-aware systems. *IJAHUC*, 2(4):263–277, 2007.

[6] J. Bisbal and B. H. C. Cheng. Resource-based approach to feature interaction in adaptive software. In *WOSS*, pages 23–27, 2004.

[7] B. H. C. Cheng, R. de Lemos, H. Giese, P. Inverardi, and J. Magee, editors. *Software Engineering for Self-Adaptive Systems*, volume 5525 of *LNCS*, 2009.

[8] J. Choi. Context-driven requirements analysis. In *ICCSA (3)*, pages 739–748, 2007.

[9] A. Classen, P. Heymans, and P.-Y. Schobbens. What's in a feature: A requirements engineering perspective. In *FASE*, pages 16–30, 2008.

[10] A. Classen, A. Hubaux, F. Sanen, E. Truyen, J. Vallejos, P. Costanza, W. De Meuter, P. Heymans, and W. Joosen. Modelling variability in self-adaptive systems: Towards a research agenda. In *Proc. of McGPLE at GPCE08*, pages 19–26, 2008.

[11] P. D. Costa, L. F. Pires, and M. van Sinderen. Architectural patterns for context-aware services platforms. In *IWUC*, pages 3–18, 2005.

[12] B. Desmet, J. Vallejos, P. Costanza, W. D. Meuter, and T. D'Hondt. Context-oriented domain analysis. In *CONTEXT*, pages 178–191, 2007.

[13] D. Garlan, S.-W. Cheng, A.-C. Huang, B. R. Schmerl, and P. Steenkiste. Rainbow: Architecture-based self-adaptation with reusable infrastructure. *IEEE Computer*, 37(10):46–54, 2004.

[14] C. Ghezzi, P. Inverardi, and C. Montangero. Dynamically evolvable dependable software: From oxymoron to reality. In *Concurrency, Graphs and Models*, pages 330–353, 2008.

[15] M. Glinz. On non-functional requirements. In *RE*, pages 21–26, 2007.

[16] S. Hallsteinsen, M. Hinchey, S. Park, K. Schmid, and T. Sintefict. Dynamic software product lines. *IEEE Computer*, 41(4):93–95, 2008.

[17] R. Hirschfeld, P. Costanza, and O. Nierstrasz. Context-oriented programming. *Journal of Object Technology*, 7(3):125–151, 2008.

[18] J. Hong, E. Suh, and S.-J. Kim. Context-aware systems: A literature review and classification. *Expert Syst. Appl.*, 36(4):8509–8522, 2009.

[19] P. Inverardi and M. Mori. Feature oriented evolutions for context-aware adaptive systems. In *EVOL/IWPSE*, pages 93–97, 2010.

[20] P. Inverardi and M. Mori. Model checking requirements at run-time in adaptive systems. In *ASAS at ESEC/FSE*, 2011.

[21] P. Inverardi and M. Mori. Requirements models at run-time to support consistent system evolutions. In *Technical Report, University of L'Aquila, Department of Computer Science*, 2011.

[22] P. Inverardi and M. Mori. A software lifecycle process to support consistent evolutions. In *Tec. Rep. Univ. of L'Aquila, Department of Computer Science*, 2011.

[23] P. Inverardi and M. Tivoli. The future of software: Adaptation and dependability. In *ISSSE*, pp 1–31, 2008.

[24] M. Jackson. *Problem Frames: Analyzing and structuring software development problems.* Addison-Wesley Longman Publishing Co., Inc. Boston, MA, USA, 2000.

[25] G. M. Kapitsaki, G. N. Prezerakos, N. D. Tselikas, and I. S. Venieris. Context-aware service engineering: A survey. *JSS*, 82(8), 2009.

[26] D. O. Keck and P. J. Kühn. The feature and service interaction problem in telecommunications systems. a survey. *IEEE TSE*, 24(10):779–796, 1998.

[27] M. Mori, F. Li, C. Dorn, P. Inverardi, and S. Dustdar. Leveraging state-based user preferences in context-aware reconfigurations for self-adaptive systems. In *SEFM*, 2011.

[28] P. Oreizy, N. Medvidovic, and R. N. Taylor. Runtime software adaptation: framework, approaches, and styles. In *ICSE Companion*, pages 899–910, 2008.

[29] C. A. Parra, X. Blanc, and L. Duchien. Context awareness for dynamic service-oriented product lines. In *SPLC*, pages 131–140, 2009.

[30] N. A. Qureshi and A. Perini. Requirements engineering for adaptive service based applications. In *RE*, pages 108–111, 2010.

[31] M. Salehie and L. Tahvildari. Self-adaptive software: Landscape and research challenges. *TAAS*, 4(2), 2009.

[32] P. Sawyer, N. Bencomo, J. Whittle, E. Letier, and A. Finkelstein. Requirements-aware systems: A research agenda for re for self-adaptive systems. In *RE*, pages 95–103, 2010.

[33] P.-Y. Schobbens, P. Heymans, J.-C. Trigaux, and Y. Bontemps. Generic semantics of feature diagrams. *Computer Networks*, 51(2):456–479, 2007.

[34] V. E. Silva Souza, A. Lapouchnian, W. N. Robinson, and J. Mylopoulos. Awareness requirements for adaptive systems. In *SEAMS*, pages 60–69, 2011.

[35] D. Sykes, W. Heaven, J. Magee, and J. Kramer. From goals to components: a combined approach to self-management. In *SEAMS*, pages 1–8, 2008.

[36] J. Whittle, P. Sawyer, N. Bencomo, B. H. C. Cheng, and J.-M. Bruel. Relax: Incorporating uncertainty into the specification of self-adaptive systems. In *RE*, pages 79–88, 2009.

EvoSuite: Automatic Test Suite Generation for Object-Oriented Software

Gordon Fraser
Saarland University – Computer Science
Saarbrücken, Germany
fraser@cs.uni-saarland.de

Andrea Arcuri
Simula Research Laboratory
P.O. Box 134, 1325 Lysaker, Norway
arcuri@simula.no

ABSTRACT

To find defects in software, one needs *test cases* that execute the software systematically, and *oracles* that assess the correctness of the observed behavior when running these test cases. This paper presents EvoSuite, a tool that automatically generates test cases with assertions for classes written in Java code. To achieve this, EvoSuite applies a novel hybrid approach that generates and optimizes whole test suites towards satisfying a coverage criterion. For the produced test suites, EvoSuite suggests possible oracles by adding small and effective sets of assertions that concisely summarize the current behavior; these assertions allow the developer to detect deviations from expected behavior, and to capture the current behavior in order to protect against future defects breaking this behavior.

Categories and Subject Descriptors

D.2.5 [**Software Engineering**]: Testing and Debugging; I.2.8 [**Artificial Intelligence**]: Problem Solving, Control Methods, and Search

General Terms

Experimentation

Keywords

Test case generation, assertion generation, search based software testing

1. INTRODUCTION

When writing programs in object-oriented languages such as Java, one typically performs unit testing to identify defects in the software and to capture the current behavior, such that future defects breaking the behavior are detected.

Test cases can be generated automatically, but there is the issue of the *oracle*, i.e., how to verify that the outputs of the test cases are the expected ones. Faults can sometimes be automatically detected if they lead to program crashes, deadlocks, or violate a formal specification. In many cases, however, there are no formal specifications, and the faults do not lead to program crashes or deadlocks. Therefore, there is the need to provide small test suites (in terms of both test data and assertions) to the user that can be manually verified, i.e., are the assert statements consistent with the semantics of the program?

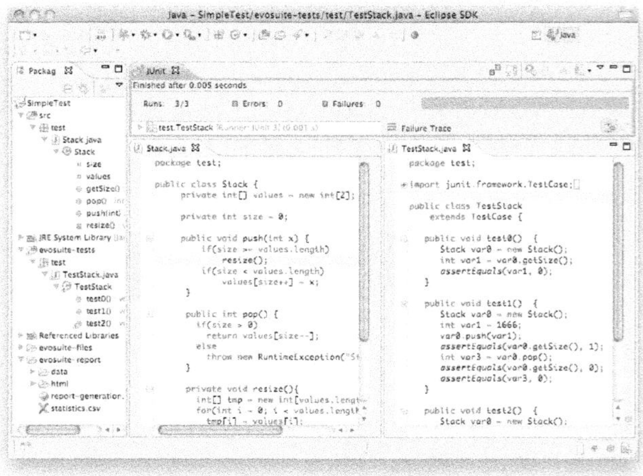

Figure 1: EvoSuite can be used as a command line tool or as an Eclipse plugin, producing coverage test suites for Java classes fully automatically.

EvoSuite is a tool that automates this task by systematically producing test suites that achieve high code coverage, are as small as possible, and provide assertions (see Figure 1). EvoSuite uses a search-based approach integrating state-of-the-art techniques such as for example hybrid search [9], dynamic symbolic execution [7] and testability transformation [8]. Furthermore, EvoSuite implements several novel techniques to efficiently achieve its objectives:

Whole test suite generation: EvoSuite uses an evolutionary search approach that evolves whole test suites with respect to an entire coverage criterion at the same time [3]. Optimizing with respect to a coverage criterion rather than individual coverage goals achieves that the result is neither adversely influenced by the order nor by the difficulty or infeasibility of individual coverage goals.

Mutation-based assertion generation: EvoSuite uses mutation testing to produce a reduced set of assertions that maximizes the number of seeded defects in a class that are revealed by the test cases [5]. These assertions highlight the

Permission to make digital or hard copies of all or part of this work for personal or classroom use is granted without fee provided that copies are not made or distributed for profit or commercial advantage and that copies bear this notice and the full citation on the first page. To copy otherwise, to republish, to post on servers or to redistribute to lists, requires prior specific permission and/or a fee.
ESEC/FSE'11, September 5–9, 2011, Szeged, Hungary.
Copyright 2011 ACM 978-1-4503-0443-6/11/09 ...$10.00.

relevant aspects of the current behavior in order to support developers in identifying defects, and the assertions capture the current behavior to protect against regression faults.

EvoSuite fully automatically produces these test suites for individual classes or entire projects, without requiring complicated manual steps. The tool is freely available, and can be used on the command line, as a plugin to the Eclipse development platform, or through a web interface.

2. WHOLE TEST SUITE OPTIMIZATION

In white box testing, when no automated oracles are available, a common systematic approach to test generation is to select one coverage goal for a given coverage criterion at a time (e.g., a program branch or a control flow path), and to derive a test case that exercises this particular goal (e.g., [9,13]). Although feasible, there is a major flaw in this strategy, as it assumes that all coverage goals are equally important, equally difficult to reach, and independent of each other. Unfortunately, none of these assumptions holds.

Many coverage goals are simply infeasible, meaning that there exists no test that would exercise them; this is an instance of the undecidable infeasible path problem. Even if feasible, some coverage goals are simply more difficult to satisfy than others. Therefore, given a limited amount of resources for testing, a lucky choice of the order of coverage goals can result in a good test suite, whereas an unlucky choice can result in all the resources being spent on only few test cases. Furthermore, a test case targeting a particular coverage goal will mostly also satisfy further coverage goals by accident. Again the order in which goals are chosen influences the result – even if all coverage goals are considered, collateral coverage can influence the resulting test suite. There is no efficient solution to predict collateral coverage or the difficulty of a coverage goal.

To overcome these problems, whole test suite generation [3] is an approach that does not produce individual test cases for individual coverage goals, but instead focuses on test *suites* targeting an entire coverage criterion. Optimizing with respect to a coverage criterion rather than individual coverage goals achieves that the result is neither adversely influenced by the order nor by the difficulty or infeasibility of individual coverage goals. In addition, the concept of collateral coverage disappears as all coverage is intentional.

EvoSuite implements whole test suite generation as a search based approach, improving significantly over previous search based approaches (see Figure 2). In evolutionary search, a population of candidate solutions is evolved using operators imitating natural evolution such as crossover and mutation. Individuals are selected for reproduction based on their fitness, i.e., an estimation of how close they are to the optimal solution, and with each generation the fitness improves until a solution is found or the allotted resources are used up.

A candidate solution in EvoSuite is a test suite, consisting of a variable number of individual test cases. Each of these test cases is a sequence of method calls again of variable length, exercising the unit under test (UUT) and setting up complex objects in order to do so. Crossover between two test suites exchanges test cases based on a randomly chosen crossover position. This type of crossover removes the difficulties of crossover on method sequences (e.g., [13]) due to dependencies between statements of a test case. Mutation of a test suite may add new test cases, or mutate individual

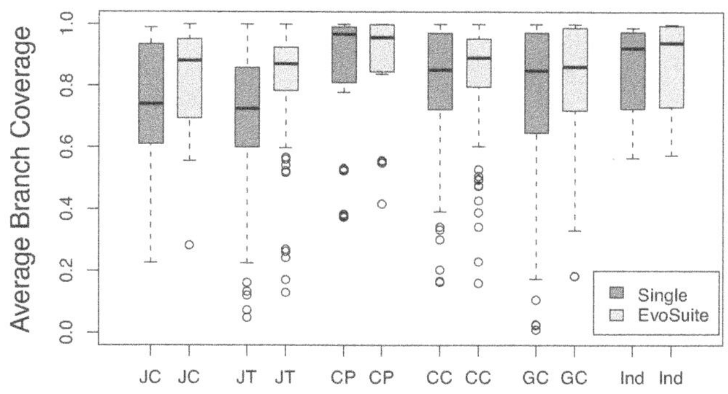

Figure 2: Average branch coverage achieved with EvoSuite on six case study libraries, compared to the standard approach of targeting one branch at a time ("Single"): Even with an evolution limit of 1,000,000 statements, EvoSuite achieves higher coverage [3].

tests. Test cases, in turn, are mutated by adding, deleting, or changing individual statements and parameters. To help the generation of appropriate input data, EvoSuite also makes use of focused local searches and dynamic symbolic execution after every predefined number of generations.

The fitness of individuals is measured with respect to an entire coverage criterion. For example, for branch coverage the fitness calculates the sum of the individual (normalized) branch distances of all the branches in the UUT. The branch distance is a commonly used estimation of how far an individual execution is from having a branch evaluate to true or to false; for example, the condition $x = 42$ with the value 10 for x has a branch distance of $|42 - 10| = 32$ of becoming true. Consequently, an individual has fitness 0 if it covers all branches of a UUT.

As longer method sequences make it easier to reach coverage goals, EvoSuite allows the search to dive into long sequences, but applies several bloat control techniques [4] to ensure that individuals do not become excessively large. At the end of the search, test suites are minimized such that only statements contributing to coverage remain.

3. MUTATION-BASED ASSERTION GENERATION

The aim of producing a coverage test suite is to provide the developer with a representative set of test cases. This allows the software engineer to check and capture the functional correctness of the UUT that cannot be captured with automated oracles. In order to do so, test cases need some kind of manual oracles, which in the case of unit tests typically are assertions. The test oracle problem is one of the main problems in traditional white-box test generation.

Given an automatically generated unit test, there is only a finite number of things one can assert — the choice of assertions is defined by the possible observations one can make on the public API of the UUT and its dependent classes. For example, one can write assertions on return values, compare objects with each other, or call inspector methods on objects. Consequently, synthesizing the possible assertions is easily possible [14]. However, presenting all assertions to

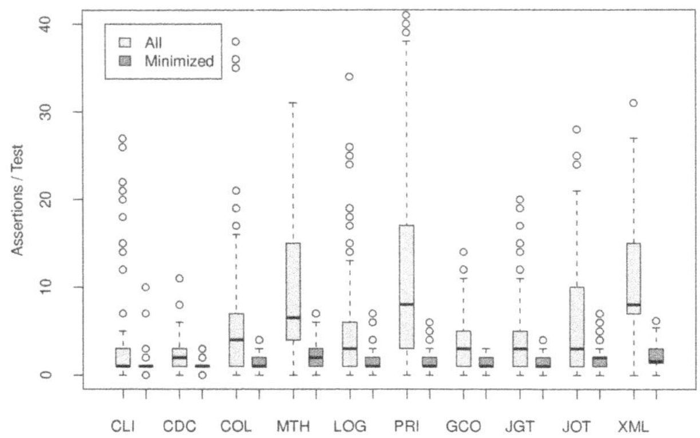

Figure 3: Effectiveness of the mutation-based assertion minimization, evaluated on 10 open source projects [5]. The boxplots summarize the statistics on assertions before ("All") and after ("Minimized") applying the mutation-based minimization.

the developer is problematic, as there might be too many of them, and many of them will be irrelevant: A fault in the current version of the program can only be detected if the developer verifies the correctness of the synthesized assertion and identifies a problem. Similarly, a test case might fail at a later point, indicating a regression failure, when in fact having too many assertions might simply overspecify the test case, leading to false alarms.

In order to determine the important and effective assertions, EvoSuite applies mutation testing. This was originally developed as part of the tool μTest [5], which is now a component of EvoSuite. In mutation testing, artificial defects (mutants) are seeded into a program, and test cases are evaluated with respect to how many of these seeded defects they can distinguish from the original program. A mutant that is not detected shows a deficiency in the test suite and indicates in most cases that either a new test case should be added, or that an existing test case needs a better test oracle. A mutant is detected if an assertion fails; conversely, if an assertion does not detect any of the mutants of a program, it is likely irrelevant to the test case, similarly in principle to a vacuously satisfied property in verification.

After the test case generation process EvoSuite runs each test case on the unmodified software as well as all mutants that are covered by the test case, while recording information on which mutants are detected by which assertions. Then, EvoSuite calculates a reduced set of assertions that is sufficient in order to detect all the mutants of the UUT that the given test case may reveal. Figure 3 shows how effective this reduction is, evaluated on a set of open source libraries. The theory of mutation testing suggests that using only these assertions is sufficient to detect most other possible faults in the UUT [10].

4. IMPLEMENTATION

To generate test suites for Java classes, EvoSuite requires only the Java bytecode of the class under test and its dependencies. The bytecode is analyzed and instrumented, and at the end of the search EvoSuite produces a JUnit test suite for a given class. EvoSuite works fully automatically; it can generate test suites for entire packages without requiring user intervention.

For a given package, EvoSuite considers one class at a time, and tries to produce a test suite maximizing branch coverage for this class. EvoSuite is not restricted to primitive datatypes, but can handle arrays and objects of any class. To produce instances of classes, EvoSuite considers all possible methods and constructors that produce an instance of a required type, and recursively tries to satisfy all dependencies. EvoSuite treats the `String` class specially, by replacing calls to string comparison methods with calls to its own helper methods that calculate string distances based on the Levenshtein distance. This allows the search to also evolve strings towards desired values to satisfy conditions on strings. As another improvement, EvoSuite uses a pool of constant primitive and string values it determines statically in the Java bytecode. However, EvoSuite is currently limited to single threading applications.

As test cases are repeatedly executed as part of the search to measure fitness values, interactions of the code under test with the environment can be unwanted and even dangerous: Random sequences accessing data on the filesystem can result in clutter in the best case, and data loss in the worst case; random accesses to networking or databases are usually not desirable either. EvoSuite provides its own security manager, which can be configured to prohibit unwanted access to the environment. To overcome the problem that random values can lead to very long execution times, EvoSuite uses timeouts and penalizes long executing test cases during the search. To overcome problems with unstoppable very long executions, EvoSuite applies a combination of bytecode instrumentation, thread handling and, in the worst case, restarting the virtual machine.

EvoSuite can be used as a command line tool that produces test suites for individual classes or entire packages, and produces HTML reports for further analysis. For convenience, EvoSuite can also be used with an experimental plugin to the Eclipse development platform (see Figure 1), where test cases can be created with a simple mouse click. Finally, EvoSuite can also be used through a webservice, allowing simple experimentation without any installation.

5. RELATED WORK

Recent advances allow modern testing tools to efficiently derive test cases for realistically sized programs fully automatically. Often, these test cases are generated randomly with the objective to detect program crashes [2] or to find contract violations [11]. To improve over random testing and its variants, which usually achieve low code coverage, techniques based on dynamic symbolic execution have been presented [7]. In contrast to such tools, EvoSuite not only tries to find test cases that violate the automated oracles, but it also aims at producing compact test suites achieving high code coverage, such that developers can use them to evaluate functional correctness.

When using code coverage, a common systematic approach is to select one coverage goal at a time (e.g., a program branch or a control flow path), and to derive a test case that exercises this particular goal (e.g., [9,13]). In contrast, EvoSuite evolves entire test suites targeting all coverage goals at the same time, leading to several advantages as discussed in Section 2.

A popular tool for unit testing C# code is Pex [12], which generates input values for parameterized test cases using dynamic symbolic execution. Pex can also produce assertions based on return values of methods, but is limited with respect to classes that require complex method sequences. There are several tools for Java producing JUnit test cases: Randoop [11] is well known for its ease of use, but in contrast to EvoSuite it randomly tests software without guidance in covering complex code structures, reporting violations of predefined contracts.

TestFul [1] and eToc [13] are perhaps the most related tools. Both use a search-based approach to generate JUnit test suites to maximize structural coverage. However, eToc is an old tool that has not been updated for several years, and therefore does not feature the most recent advances in test data generation. On the other hand, TestFul differs from EvoSuite in many critical details, and it is not fully automated. For example, TestFul requires the manual editing of XML files for each class under test, which led its empirical evaluation to be just on 15 classes. On other hand, because EvoSuite is fully automated like Randoop, it was possible to evaluate it on thousands of classes [3].

In terms of assertion generation, Randoop [11] allows annotation of the source code to identify observer methods to be used for assertion generation. Orstra [14] generates assertions based on observed return values and object states and adds assertions to check future runs against these observations. While such approaches can be used to derive efficient oracles, they do not serve to identify which of these assertions are actually useful, and such techniques are therefore only found in regression testing. In contrast, through the μTest tool, EvoSuite uses mutation testing to select an effective subset of assertions.

6. CONCLUSIONS

EvoSuite is a tool that automatically produces test suites for Java programs that achieve high code coverage and provide assertions. EvoSuite implements several novel techniques, leading to higher structural coverage and an efficient selection of assertions based on seeded defects, which is a critical feature that other Java tools miss.

EvoSuite currently supports branch coverage and mutation testing as test objectives, but we are also working on adding further criteria, such as criteria based on data flow, and a further focus of our research is to produce more readable test cases [6].

To learn more about EvoSuite, visit our Web site:

`http://www.st.cs.uni-saarland.de/evosuite/`

Acknowledgments. We thank Andrey Tarasevich, Andre Mis, Sebastian Steenbuck, and David Schuler for their support in developing EvoSuite. This project has been funded by Deutsche Forschungsgemeinschaft (DFG), grant Ze509/5-1, and by a Google Focused Research Award on "Test Amplification". Gordon Fraser is funded by the Cluster of Excellence on Multimodal Computing and Interaction at Saarland University, Germany. Andrea Arcuri is funded by the Norwegian Research Council.

7. REFERENCES

[1] L. Baresi and M. Miraz. Testful: automatic unit-test generation for java classes. In *Proceedings of the 32nd ACM/IEEE International Conference on Software Engineering - Volume 2*, ICSE '10, pages 281–284, New York, NY, USA, 2010. ACM.

[2] C. Csallner and Y. Smaragdakis. JCrasher: an automatic robustness tester for Java. *Software Practice and Experience*, 34:1025–1050, September 2004.

[3] G. Fraser and A. Arcuri. Evolutionary generation of whole test suites. In *QSIC'11: Proceedings of the 11th International Conference On Quality Software*, 2011.

[4] G. Fraser and A. Arcuri. It is not the length that matters, it is how you control it. In *ICST'11: Proceedings of the 4th International Conference on Software Testing, Verification and Validation*, pages 150–159. IEEE Computer Society, 2011.

[5] G. Fraser and A. Zeller. Mutation-driven generation of unit tests and oracles. In *Proceedings of the 19th International Symposium on Software Testing and Analysis*, ISSTA'10, pages 147–158, New York, NY, USA, 2010. ACM.

[6] G. Fraser and A. Zeller. Exploiting common object usage in test case generation. In *ICST'11: Proceedings of the 4th International Conference on Software Testing, Verification and Validation*, pages 80–89. IEEE Computer Society, 2011.

[7] P. Godefroid, N. Klarlund, and K. Sen. DART: directed automated random testing. In *PLDI'05: Proc. of the 2005 ACM SIGPLAN Conference on Programming Language Design and Implementation*, pages 213–223, New York, USA, 2005. ACM.

[8] M. Harman, L. Hu, R. Hierons, J. Wegener, H. Sthamer, A. Baresel, and M. Roper. Testability transformation. *IEEE Transactions on Software Engineering*, 30(1):3–16, 2004.

[9] M. Harman and P. McMinn. A theoretical and empirical study of search based testing: Local, global and hybrid search. *IEEE Transactions on Software Engineering*, 36(2):226–247, 2010.

[10] A. J. Offutt. Investigations of the software testing coupling effect. *ACM Trans. Softw. Eng. Methodol.*, 1:5–20, January 1992.

[11] C. Pacheco and M. D. Ernst. Randoop: feedback-directed random testing for Java. In *OOPSLA '07: Companion to the 22nd ACM SIGPLAN conference on Object-oriented programming systems and applications companion*, pages 815–816, New York, NY, USA, 2007. ACM.

[12] N. Tillmann and J. N. de Halleux. Pex — white box test generation for .NET. In *TAP 2008: International Conference on Tests And Proofs*, volume 4966 of *LNCS*, pages 134 – 253. Springer, 2008.

[13] P. Tonella. Evolutionary testing of classes. In *ISSTA'04: Proceedings of the 2004 ACM SIGSOFT International Symposium on Software Testing and Analysis*, pages 119–128, New York, USA, 2004. ACM.

[14] T. Xie. Augmenting automatically generated unit-test suites with regression oracle checking. In *ECOOP 2006: Proceedings of the 20th European Conference on Object-Oriented Programming*, pages 380–403, 2006.

SCORE: A Scalable Concolic Testing Tool for Reliable Embedded Software

Yunho Kim and Moonzoo Kim
Computer Science Department
Korea Advanced Institute of Science and Technology
Daejeon, South Korea
kimyunho@kaist.ac.kr, moonzoo@cs.kaist.ac.kr

ABSTRACT

Current industrial testing practices often generate test cases in a manual manner, which degrades both the effectiveness and efficiency of testing. To alleviate this problem, concolic testing generates test cases that can achieve high coverage in an automated fashion. One main task of concolic testing is to extract symbolic information from a concrete execution of a target program at runtime. Thus, a design decision on how to extract symbolic information affects efficiency, effectiveness, and applicability of concolic testing. We have developed a Scalable COncolic testing tool for REliable embedded software (SCORE) that targets embedded C programs. SCORE instruments a target C program to extract symbolic information and applies concolic testing to a target program in a scalable manner by utilizing a large number of distributed computing nodes. In this paper, we describe our design decisions that are implemented in SCORE and demonstrate the performance of SCORE through the experiments on the SIR benchmarks.

Categories and Subject Descriptors

D.2.5 [**Software Engineering**]: Testing and Debugging

General Terms

Algorithms, Experimentation

1. INTRODUCTION

Dynamic testing is a de-facto standard method for improving the quality of software in industry. Conventional testing methods, however, often fail to detect faults in programs. One reason for this is that a program can have an enormous number of different execution paths due to conditional and loop statements. Thus, it is practically infeasible for a test engineer to manually create test cases sufficient to detect subtle bugs in specific execution paths. In addition, it is a technically challenging task to generate effective test cases in an automated manner. An alternative approach, concolic (CONCrete + symbOLIC) [17] testing (also known as dynamic symbolic execution [19] or white-box fuzzing [8]) combines concrete dynamic analysis and static symbolic analysis to *automatically* generate test cases to explore execution paths of a program, to achieve full path coverage (or at least, coverage of paths up to some bound).

A concolic testing tool extracts symbolic information from a concrete execution of a target program at runtime. In other words, to build a corresponding symbolic path formula, a concolic testing tool monitors every update of symbolic variables and branching decisions in an execution of a target program. Thus, a design decision on how to extract symbolic information affects efficiency, effectiveness, and applicability of concolic testing.

We have developed a Scalable COncolic testing tool for REliabile embedded software (SCORE) that targets sequential embedded C programs. SCORE instruments a target C source code by inserting probes to extract symbolic information at runtime. This concolic testing approach has several advantages when applied to embedded C programs compared to a modified virtual machine approach (Section 2). In addition, to reduce a time cost to explore a large number of execution paths, SCORE utilizes a scalable distributed concolic algorithm that involves a large number of computing nodes dynamically with high efficiency (Section 3). Currently, SCORE is implemented on the Amazon EC2 cloud computing platform [6]. In this paper, we describe our design decisions that are implemented in the SCORE tool for applying concolic testing in a practical and scalable manner to embedded C programs. In addition, we demonstrate the performance of SCORE through the experiments on the SIR benchmarks

2. INSTRUMENTATION-BASED CONCOLIC TESTING FOR EMBEDDED C PROGRAMS

A core idea behind concolic testing is to obtain symbolic path formulas from concrete executions and solve them to generate test cases by using constraint solvers. Various concolic testing tools have been implemented to realize this core idea (see [15] for a survey). Existing tools can be classified into two groups in terms of the approach they use to extract symbolic path formulas from concrete executions.

The first approach for extracting symbolic path formulas is to use modified virtual machines (VM). The concolic testing tools that use this approach are implemented as modified VMs on which target programs execute. An advantage of this approach is that the tools can exploit all execution information at run-time, since a VM possesses all necessary information. PEX [19] targets C# programs that are compiled into Microsoft .Net bytecode, KLEE [4] targets LLVM [14] bytecode, and jFuzz [10] targets Java bytecode on top of Java PathFinder [20].

The second approach for extracting symbolic path formulas is to instrument the target source code to insert probes that ex-

Permission to make digital or hard copies of all or part of this work for personal or classroom use is granted without fee provided that copies are not made or distributed for profit or commercial advantage and that copies bear this notice and the full citation on the first page. To copy otherwise, to republish, to post on servers or to redistribute to lists, requires prior specific permission and/or a fee.
ESEC/FSE'11, September 5–9, 2011, Szeged, Hungary.
Copyright 2011 ACM 978-1-4503-0443-6/11/09 ...$10.00.

tract symbolic path formulas from concrete executions at runtime. Tools that use this approach include CUTE [17], DART [7], and CREST [3], which operate on C programs, and jCUTE [16], which operates on Java programs. This approach is more suitable for embedded C programs compared to the first approach, since embedded software often has different development/runtime environments from those of non-embedded software due to limited computational power and physical constraints. Advantages of the instrumentation-based concolic testing for embedded C programs are as follows:

1. Embedded software is often developed for a specific hardware/OS platform (or tested on a customized simulation environment such as Scratchbox [1]) (see [12][1]). Therefore, the first approach using a VM requires to port a modified VM that supports concolic testing to a specific hardware/simulator platform, which is expensive.
2. An embedded program often contains native binary code to access hardware devices directly, which cannot be interpreted using the VM approach. Most concolic testing tools of the first approach simply stop/ignore a current symbolic execution when they encounter such native binary code and try another execution path, which can miss bugs related with low-level I/O operations that are often the focus of embedded programs. Although the second approach cannot symbolically interpret native binary code either, it still executes such binary code and continues to analyze an execution path using concrete values.
3. A target program written in C can be compiled into a binary executable program that can run on hardware directly. A binary executable program that is compiled from a C source code can run order of magnitude faster than the corresponding bytecode runs on a VM. Thus, this second approach can test an embedded C program much faster than the first approach does, which is an important advantage, since concolic testing takes a large amount of time.

Therefore, SCORE utilizes the second approach for embedded C programs. As shown in Figure 1, a target C program is instrumented by the SCORE instrumentor (implemented in CIL with an extension module). To alleviate difficulty of extracting symbolic information from a concrete execution, SCORE transforms a target C program into an equivalent one that has no side-effect and a single atomic predicate at each conditional statement (i.e., every conditional statement with a compound predicate is transformed into combination of conditional statements with atomic predicates). Then, SCORE inserts probes into a target C program that invoke symbolic execution library to extract symbolic information to build a corresponding symbolic path formula at run-time. Lastly, the instrumented target program is compiled into an executable binary through gcc.

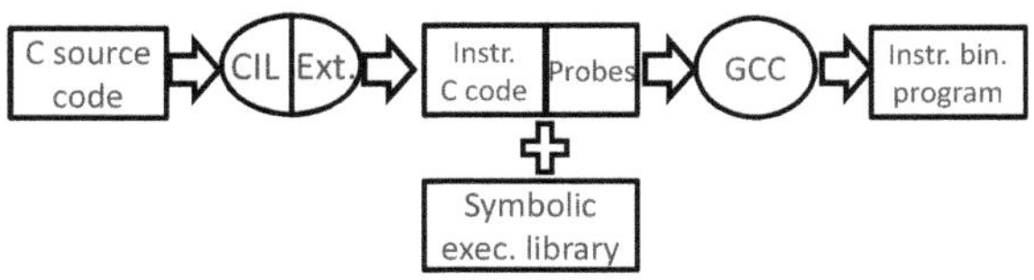

Figure 1: Instrumentation Process of SCORE

[1]We could not apply SCORE to the industrial project with Samsung Electronics, since we were not allowed to utilize Amazon EC2 due to the security policy of Samsung Electronics.

3. DISTRIBUTED CONCOLIC TESTING FRAMEWORK

3.1 Overview

SCORE consists of one server, multiple clients, and a user interface program through which a user can control SCORE. For efficient communication between computing nodes, SCORE adopts a hybrid architecture of a client-server architecture and a peer-to-peer architecture by utilizing a central server that handles control messages to keep track of the status of the clients and to direct load-balancing between the clients (i.e., test cases are transferred between clients in a well-balanced manner) (see Figure 2).

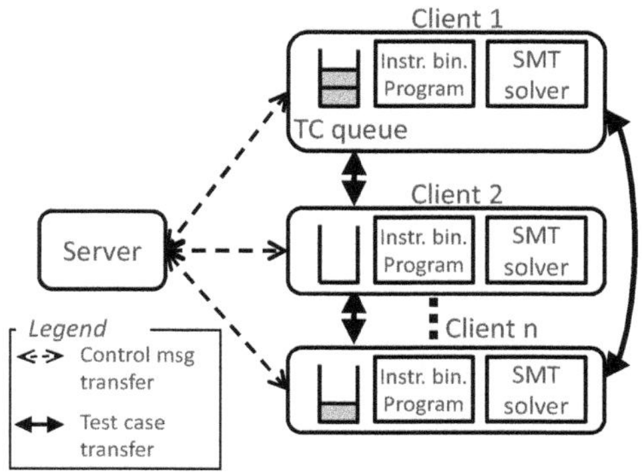

Figure 2: SCORE architecture

Each client has its own copy of an instrumented target binary program (possibly with a platform simulator) and applies concolic testing to the target program to generate test cases, which are stored in a test case queue. After a client pops a test case from the queue, it generates further test cases by solving symbolic path formulas that are obtained by negating branch conditions of the execution path on the test case. If a client has an empty test case queue, it requests new test cases from the server and the server commands another client that has test cases to send test cases to the requesting client. [2] Although SCORE utilizes a large number of computing nodes, a user can manage these nodes conveniently through the automated initialization (Section 3.2) and dynamic management of nodes (Section 3.3) features.

There are several concolic testing tools utilizing distributed platforms such as Staats et al. [18], King [13] and Cloud9 [2], all of which utilize a VM-based approach. However, these tools do not consider characteristics of embedded software and they are not adequate for embedded software due to the reasons explained in Section 2. In addition, except Cloud9, these tools do not achieve linear speed-up in terms of a number of computing nodes.

3.2 Initialization of Distributed Clients

Before starting distributed concolic testing, SCORE automatically instantiates virtual nodes and installs copies of an instrumented target binary program on the virtual nodes. This automated initialization process is desirable, since SCORE utilizes virtual nodes of 'spot-instance' type of Amazon EC2 whose storages are destroyed when virtual nodes are turned off. SCORE utilizes virtual nodes of spot-instance type, because a price for virtual node of spot-instance is cheaper (US$ 0.06/hour) than a price for a virtual node of persistent storage (US$ 0.17/hour). In addition, only

[2]The distributed concolic algorithm of SCORE, detailed communication protocol, and complete experimental results can be found in [11].

20 virtual nodes of persistent storage type can be instantiated in one user account while 100 virtual nodes of spot-instance type can be instantiated in one user account.

For this automated initialization, we have built an Amazon AMI (Amazon Machine Instance) for SCORE, which is used to instantiate virtual node. Amazon AMI for SCORE is based on a 32 bit minimal version of Fedora Core 8 and contains basic development libraries, a ftp client (to download an instrumented target program), a SMT solver (Z3), and a monitoring tool (to measure CPU usage and network traffic).

Distributed concolic testing is initiated by invoking a SCORE server with an instrumented binary target program. The server instantiates clients and establishes network connections to the clients. Then, the clients download the target program from the server and start distributed concolic testing. Although the clients can share the target program on Network File System (NFS) without downloading the target program from the server, it will cause significant overhead due to a large number of concurrent network accesses to the target program on NFS.

3.3 Dynamic Management of Nodes

SCORE can add and remove clients dynamically at run-time. This dynamic resource management feature is useful, because SCORE utilizes a large number of computing nodes. This dynamic management feature supports flexible management of multiple testing tasks and thus assigns computing resources to multiple testing tasks in a globally efficient manner. In addition, flexible management of multiple testing tasks is beneficial in an economic sense. For example, the price for using computing nodes at night may be cheaper than the price during the day (this is true for Amazon EC2's spot-instance computing nodes, which are purchased by bidding).

For example, suppose that a user applies concolic testing to a target program using SCORE. The user commands a server to assign n clients to the testing task initially. In addition, during the testing process, SCORE allows a user to both increase or decrease n at run-time. To add a new client, the server instantiates a new computing node through the underlying Amazon EC2 API and remotely starts a client on the node. The client begins to participate in the testing task by sending a request packet to the server. To remove a client, a user can specify a number of clients to remove, or conditions by which to select a client such as the number of test cases in the client, execution time spent so far, and so on. For example, suppose a user requests removal of all clients that have fewer than five test cases. The server searches the status table of all clients and selects those that satisfy the condition. For each such client, the server sends a termination packet to the client. Then, the client transfers test cases generated so far, covered path/branch information, and statistics on testing activities to another designated client.

3.4 Non-redundant Test Case Generation

SCORE uses a depth-first search (DFS) strategy to explore a symbolic execution tree. In theory, the DFS strategy explores one execution path exactly once; it would generate redundant test cases (i.e., test cases running a same execution path) otherwise. However, when a target program contains external library calls and floating-point arithmetics that cannot be reasoned by SMT solvers, the DFS strategy may execute the same path multiple times in practice.

For example, suppose that a target program has `if(x == abs(x)) exit(); else {...}` where `abs()` is an external C library function. The program will terminate if a test case TC1 (`x=0`) is given. Then, SCORE negates this branch condition to generate TC2 to explore the `else` branch. Since the external library invocation `abs(x)` is *concretized* to its current concrete return value (i.e., 0), the negated symbolic path formula is `x != 0`. Although a new test case TC2 (`x=1`) is generated by solving the negated formula, TC2 executes the same execution path explored by TC1. Note that if a newly generated test case is redundant, all test cases that are derived from it can be also redundant. Thus, SCORE detects such redundant test cases and does not generate further test cases from these redundant test cases.

To detect such redundant test cases, SCORE checks whether a newly generated test case executes a *predicted* execution path $c_1 \wedge c_2 ... \wedge c_{k-1} \wedge \neg c_k$ (c_i is a branch condition and c_i is executed immediately before c_{i+1}) that has common prefix (i.e., $c_1 \wedge ... c_{k-1}$) with the previous execution path until the negated branch condition (i.e., $\neg c_k$). For this purpose, SCORE keeps information on the previous execution path, since this prediction test can be done by comparing a current execution path and the previous execution path. [3] This prediction test applies to the distributed clients by transferring test cases with common prefixes of their previous execution paths (i.e., $c_1 \wedge c_2 ... \wedge c_{k-1}$) and negated branch conditions (i.e., c_k).

3.5 Implementation

SCORE is written in C/C++ and contains 7600 lines of code with 24 classes and 265 functions. For n clients, the server creates n threads, each of which communicates with one client. To minimize communication overhead, each client is implemented as two separate threads. One thread generates test cases through concolic testing. The other thread communicates with other computing nodes to receive/send test cases or control messages. Each client stores testing outcomes such as test cases generated, covered branches, and covered execution paths on the local hard disk. When the testing process terminates or a user requests to stop the concolic testing, these outcomes are collected by the server automatically.

SCORE is implemented to operate on distributed computers connected through TCP/IP networks, since the framework may be deployed on a large scale computing platform such as cloud computing platforms or P2P networks where communication might not be reliable. SCORE uses CREST 0.1.1 [3] to instrument a target C program and to obtain symbolic formulas from concrete execution paths at run-time. However, we have extended the instrumentation tool and the symbolic execution engine of CREST to support symbolic path formulas in bit-vector theory while the original CREST supports only linear-integer arithmetic symbolic path formulas. In addition, SCORE uses Z3 2.15 as a underlying SMT solver instead of Yices (a SMT solver used by CREST), since Z3 provides richer C APIs for bit-vector theory than Yices does (for example, Z3 provides C API for bit-vector division and modular operators, which are not directly supported by C API of Yices) and user community are more active.

3.6 Experimental Results

To demonstrate efficiency and effectiveness of SCORE, we applied SCORE to well-known benchmark programs. As objects of experiments, we selected six programs from the SIR repository [5], including three of the Siemens programs [9], and three non-trivial real-world programs (`grep` 2.0, `sed` 1.17, and `vim` 5.0). [4]

All experiments were performed on the Amazon EC2 cloud computing platform. The server of the SCORE framework ran on a virtual node that had 7GB of memory and 8 CPU cores of 20 ECU computing power in total (1 ECU is equivalent to a 1Ghz Xeon pro-

[3] A test case that exercises an execution path that does not match a predicted execution path may not be a redundant test case. However, since such a test case can be a redundant one, we conservatively consider the test case as a redundant one.

[4] The experimental results are taken from [11]

cessor). Each client ran on a virtual node that was equipped with 1.7 GB memory and 2 CPU cores of 5 ECU in total. The server and clients ran on Fedora Core Linux 8. All virtual nodes are connected through a 1 gigabps Ethernet.

For each target program, we executed CREST on a node and SCORE on each of the five client number levels for 5 minutes. To control for potential differences in runs due to the randomization inherent in the techniques, we repeated the experiments 30 times and reported the mean value of 30 runs.

We begin by comparing SCORE to CREST. In these experiments, we set SCORE to use linear-integer arithmetic symbolic path formulas for fair comparison to CREST. Figure 3 illustrates the effectiveness (i.e., number of non-redundant test cases generated) increase achieved by SCORE as the client number level increased, in a manner that compares the two tools. The figure compares effectiveness results obtained by SCORE at all five client number levels to the results obtained by CREST, per program, in terms of the ratio of numbers of test cases generated by each. Effectiveness appears to increase *linearly* with client number level, but the rate of increase does vary per program.

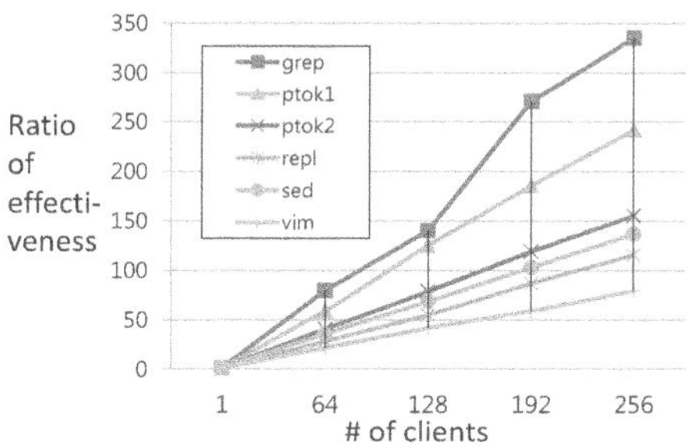

Figure 3: Ratio of effectiveness between CREST and SCORE, per client number level

4. CONCLUSION AND FUTURE WORK

We have developed the SCORE framework that targets embedded C programs to decrease the time cost of concolic testing by utilizing a large number of distributed computing nodes. The framework enables distributed nodes to generate test cases independently, and in so doing it achieves scalability. In addition, SCORE utilizes instrumentation-based approach that is suitable for testing embedded C programs. We demonstrated linear speedup of SCORE on distributed systems through the experiments.

As future work, we intend to apply SCORE to industrial embedded C programs, to analyze advantages and weakness of the framework in practice. In addition, we plan to develop additional distributed concolic algorithms that aim higher branch coverage in a fast manner instead of path coverage pursued by DFS, which may facilitate its earlier adoption in industrial software development. Finally, we plan to release SCORE as an open-source project for researchers and testing practitioners to utilize SCORE in their research platforms and projects freely and to improve SCORE with support from open source community.

Acknowledgements

This research was partially supported by the ERC of Excellence Program of Korea Ministry of Education, Science and Technology(MEST) / National Research Foundation of Korea) (Grant 2011-0000978), and Basic Science Research Program through the NRF funded by the MEST (2010-0005498). We would like to thank Matt Staats for his feedback and comments.

5. REFERENCES

[1] Scratchbox - cross-compilation toolkit. `http://www.scratchbox.org/`.

[2] S. Bucur, V. Ureche, C. Zamfir, and G. Candea. Parallel symbolic execution for automated real-world software testing. In *6th ACM SIGOPS/EuroSys*, 2011.

[3] J. Burnim and K. Sen. Heuristics for scalable dynamic test generation. Technical Report UCB/EECS-2008-123, EECS Department, University of California, Berkeley, Sep 2008.

[4] C. Cadar, D. Dunbar, and D. Engler. KLEE: Unassisted and automatic generation of high-coverage tests for complex systems programs. In *Operating System Design and Implementation*, 2008.

[5] H. Do, S. Elbaum, and G. Rothermel. Supporting controlled experimentation with testing techniques: An infrastructure and its potential impact. *Empirical Software Engineering Journal*, 10(4):405–435, 2005.

[6] Amazon Elastic Compute Cloud (Amazon EC2). `http://aws.amazon.com/ec2/`.

[7] P. Godefroid, N. Klarlund, and K. Sen. DART: Directed automated random testing. In *Programming Language Design and Implementation*, 2005.

[8] P. Godefroid, M. Y. Levin, and D. Molnar. Automated whitebox fuzz testing. In *Network and Distributed Systems Security*, 2008.

[9] M. Hutchins, H. Foster, T. Goradia, and T. Ostrand. Experiments of the effectiveness of dataflow- and controlflow-based test adequacy criteria. In *International Conference on Software Engineering*, pages 191–200, 1994.

[10] K. Jayaraman, D. Harvison, V. Ganesh, and A. Kiezun. jFuzz: A concolic whitebox fuzzer for Java. In *NASA Formal Methods Symposium*, 2009.

[11] M. Kim, Y. Kim, and G. Rothermel. A scalable distributed concolic testing approach. In *Automated Software Engineering*, 2011. under review.

[12] Y. Kim, M. Kim, and Y. Jang. Concolic testing on embedded software - case studies on mobile platform programs. In *Foundations of Software Engineering (FSE)*, 2011.

[13] A. King. Distributed parallel symbolic execution. Technical report, Kansas State University, 2009. MS thesis.

[14] C. Lattner and V. Adve. LLVM: A compilation framework for lifelong program analysis & transformation, 2004.

[15] C. Pasareanu and W. Visser. A survey of new trends in symbolic execution for software testing and analysis. *Software Tools for Tech. Transfer*, 11(4):339–353, 2009.

[16] K. Sen and G. Agha. CUTE and jCUTE : Concolic unit testing and explicit path model-checking tools. In *Computer Aided Verification*, 2006.

[17] K. Sen, D. Marinov, and G. Agha. CUTE: A concolic unit testing engine for C. In *European Software Engineering Conference/Foundations of Software Engineering*, 2005.

[18] M. Staats and C. Pasareanu. Parallel symbolic execution for structural test generation. In *International Symposium on Software Testing and Analysis*, 2010.

[19] N. Tillmann and W. Schulte. Parameterized unit tests. In *European Software Engineering Conference/Foundations of Software Engineering*, 2005.

[20] W. Visser, K. Havelund, G. Brat, and S. Park. Model checking programs. In *Automated Software Engineering*, September 2000.

SMutant: A Tool for Type-Sensitive Mutation Testing in a Dynamic Language

Milos Gligoric Sandro Badame Ralph Johnson
Department of Computer Science
University of Illinois, Urbana, IL 61801, USA
{gliga, badame1, rjohnson}@illinois.edu

ABSTRACT

A mutation testing tool takes as input a system under test and a test suite and produces as output the mutation score of the test suite. The tool systematically creates mutants by making small syntactic changes to the system under test and executes the test suite to determine which mutants give different results from the original system. Almost all mutation testing tools have been developed for statically typed languages. The lack of tools for dynamically typed languages may be rooted in additional challenges that are caused by the lack of precise type information until the program is executed. Existing tools for dynamically typed languages mostly focus on mutation of literals because the type of literals are known statically.

This paper presents SMutant, the first mutation testing tool for Smalltalk programs. In addition to literal replacement, SMutant supports many mutation operators that are commonly seen in tools for statically typed languages, such as operator replacement. Instead of applying mutations statically, SMutant postpones mutating until execution and applies mutations dynamically, when the types are available. Also, SMutant enables the user to define new mutation operators by sending a single message. The tool automatically generates code to support new mutation operators.

Categories and Subject Descriptors: D.2.5 [Software Engineering]: Testing and Debugging—*Testing tools*

General Terms: Reliability

Keywords: Mutation testing, dynamic languages

1. INTRODUCTION

Mutation testing [1, 3, 4] is a method for measuring the quality of a test suite. A mutation testing tool takes as input a *system under test* (SUT) and a *test suite*, then proceeds in two phases: (1) systematically creates *mutants* in the SUT and (2) executes the test suite to check how many mutants are *killed*; a mutant is killed if the result of the mutated code differs from the result that is obtained by running the original SUT, otherwise the mutant is *live*. In the first phase, mutants are created by applying *mutation operators* that perform small syntactic changes in the SUT. For example, a mutation operator can be defined to replace + with -. In the second phase, a tool tracks killed mutants. The ratio of the killed mutants to all mutants, known as *mutation score*, is used to measure the effectiveness of a test suite.

Mutation testing for statically typed languages has been actively researched since its introduction [3, 4]. The main focus was on measuring the effectiveness of mutation operators. In particular, mutation operators have been proposed and evaluated for a number of languages including Ada, C, Cobol, C#, Fortran, Java, and SQL. A few of the mutation testing tools that have been developed are Mothra (Fortran), Javalanche (Java), and CREAM (C#). These tools perform mutations *statically*, since type information is known before a program is executed. The survey report by Jia and Harman [7] gives an overview of mutation testing.

In contrast, mutation testing for dynamically typed languages has been little explored. The key reason for this may lay in the nature of these languages – *type information is not available until a program is executed.* Therefore, existing tools for dynamically typed languages ignore mutation operators that require type information and are commonly used for statically typed languages. For instance, the same operator + can be used for string concatenation and number addition, but there is no - for strings; thus, an expression v1 + v2 cannot be replaced with v1 - v2 until we know that v1 and v2 are numbers rather than strings. For example, a mutation testing tool for Python, Pester [9], focuses on literal replacement. Similarly, a tool for Ruby, Heckle [5], focuses on literal replacement and expression replacement (e.g., replace "while" with "unless"). In both cases no type information is used. Recently [2], there has been work on defining mutation operators for JavaScript and proposal that mutations should be applied *dynamically*, during the execution of a program. However, no tool was developed.

This paper presents our tool, SMutant, for mutation testing of Smalltalk programs. In addition to replacement of literals, the tool supports many mutation operators commonly used for statically typed languages [7], such as arithmetic operator replacement. Instead of applying mutations statically, SMutant waits until the type information is available (at runtime) and *dynamically* applies mutations [2]. To the best of our knowledge, SMutant is the first tool that performs this kind of mutation testing. Another novelty that comes with SMutant is a support for defining new mutation

Permission to make digital or hard copies of all or part of this work for personal or classroom use is granted without fee provided that copies are not made or distributed for profit or commercial advantage and that copies bear this notice and the full citation on the first page. To copy otherwise, to republish, to post on servers or to redistribute to lists, requires prior specific permission and/or a fee.
ESEC/FSE'11, September 5–9, 2011, Szeged, Hungary.
Copyright 2011 ACM 978-1-4503-0443-6/11/09 ...$10.00.

operators by sending a single message[1] to SMutant. The tool *automatically* generates the code that is needed to support new mutation operators as described in detail in Section 3.3.

The design goals for SMutant were: (1) support for mutation operators for dynamic languages that are common for statically typed languages; (2) support for extending the set of predefined mutation operators without knowing details of the tool; (3) no modifications are required to the base Smalltalk image; and (4) making the tool practical by implementing known techniques from other tools (e.g. running mutation in a separate thread to avoid infinite looping).

SMutant is publicly available at the most popular site for Smalltalk: `http://www.squeaksource.com/smutant/`.

2. SMALLTALK BACKGROUND

Before we discuss SMutant in more detail, we provide a brief, high-level overview of the characteristics of Smalltalk that are relevant for the following sections.

Smalltalk is an object-oriented, dynamically typed, reflective programming language. As opposed to most programming systems, Smalltalk does not separate application data (objects) and code (classes). Smalltalk systems store objects and classes in an *image*, that can be loaded by the virtual machine to restore an earlier state. Therefore, Smalltalk can be seen as a "living" system, which can be extended at run time, saved, and loaded at later point.

Being a "pure" object-oriented language, everything – including code – is an object in Smalltalk. Querying or modifying a state of an object is performed by sending messages that can be seen as being equivalent to a method invocation in Java. Unlike many other languages, Smalltalk does not have primitive types or predefined messages; for example, + is only the name of a message and it can be defined for any object in the system. Any message can be sent to any object. When a message is sent, the system checks if a message is defined in the receiving object; if the message is not defined, the `doesNotUnderstand` message is invoked by the system, which throws an exception by default.

Commonly, code is written as a body of a message. However, the Smalltalk image provides a *Workspace* that can be used for evaluating snippets of code. A Workspace is similar to a "Read-eval-print loop" available for many languages (e.g., Python). Note that code evaluated in Workspace can affect the state of the system.

A typical Smalltalk image comes with many frameworks and tools. One of the available frameworks is *SUnit*, a unit testing framework. SUnit allows for writing tests and assertions in Smalltalk. It has served as a basis for all xUnit tools, including JUnit. As in JUnit (version 3), SUnit requires (1) a class, which extends `TestCase`, that defines test cases; and (2) each test case in a separate method, whose name starts with "test". Optionally, the user can define `setUp` and `tearDown` methods that are executed before and after each test case, respectively. Just as with many other frameworks, SUnit is accompanied with a GUI, called TestRunner, that enables the user to easily select and execute test cases. The following sections describe similarities (Section 3.2) and the dependency between SMutant (MutationTestRunner) and SUnit (TestRunner) (Section 3.7).

[1]Sending a message in Smalltalk can be seen as equivalent to a method invocation in Java (see Section 2).

```
MatrixMutationScenario>>classesToMutate
    ^ { Matrix }
MatrixMutationScenario>>classesWithTests
    ^ { MatrixTest }
MatrixMutationScenario>>mutationFactories
    ^ {RetroReplacementOperatorFactory singleton
                    original: #+ replacement: #-}
MatrixMutationScenario>>isCopy
    ^ false
```

Figure 1: Mutation scenario for `MatrixTest` class.

3. SMUTANT DETAILS

We next describe some features, design decisions, and implementation of SMutant in more detail.

3.1 Mutation Scenario

A *mutation scenario* is used to specify (1) which classes belong to the SUT (classes to be mutated) and (2) which classes belong to the test suite (classes for which mutation score is measured). To define a mutation scenario, the user has to extend the `MutationScenario` class and to override two methods to specify (1) and (2). As an example, suppose that the goal is to measure the mutation score of `MatrixTest`, which is a test suite for the `Matrix` class. (Both classes are available in the Pharo Smalltalk image [10].) The `MatrixMutationScenario` class, which is shown in Figure 1, specifies classes that belong to a SUT by overriding `classesToMutate` and classes that belong to a test suite by overriding `classesWithTests`. The user can also specify which mutation operators should be used by overriding `mutationFactories` (default implementation includes all implemented operators). The method `isCopy` is described in Section 3.6.

Note that SMutant has requirements similar to those of SUnit, which are described in Section 2. However, defining a mutation scenario is much simpler, since the user only has to select proper classes to mutate and the mutation operators from the appropriate/available sets.

3.2 GUI Design Inspired by TestRunner

As mentioned, SUnit includes TestRunner, a GUI that can be used to select test suites to run and obtain details about the results. Similarly, SMutant includes MutationTestRunner, a GUI that can be used to select mutation scenarios to run and obtain details about the results. Figure 2 shows MutationTestRunner. The left-most pane lists all the categories that include mutation scenarios. When a particular category is selected, appropriate mutation scenarios appear in the middle pane (e.g., `MatrixMutationScenario`). The status bar (top-right pane) shows number of all mutants, number of killed mutants, number of live mutants, and mutation score. These numbers are updated dynamically as mutation testing is in progress (similar to TestRunner). The red color of the status bar indicates that there are live mutants, which is analogous to the red color in TestRunner when some tests do not pass. A green color is used when all mutants are killed. If some mutants are alive, the middle right-most pane lists the live mutants with the location where the mutant was created (including class and method name). The right-most pane at the bottom can be used to specify mutation factories for the selected mutation scenarios (Section 3.8). Finally, the button at the bottom can be used to execute the selected mutation scenarios.

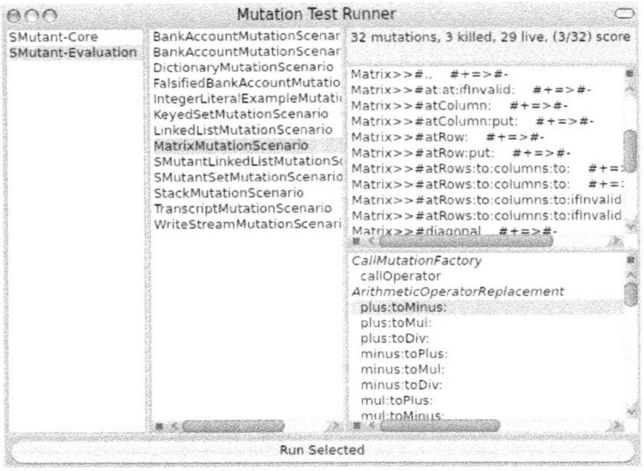

Figure 2: MutationTestRunner can be used to select mutation scenarios to run and show details about the results. The design closely mimics the design of TestRunner.

3.3 Applying Mutations Dynamically

When a mutation scenario is run, by either using MutationTestRunner or invoking the appropriate method from SMutant, the tool proceeds with the three steps.

Analysis. The tool analyzes the code under test (i.e., list of classes that are returned by the `classesToMutate` method) to find potential places to create mutants (e.g., + symbols, if the mutation operator "arithmetic replacement operator: + to - if arguments are Numbers" is selected). It is important to note that a set of mutants is created statically. Namely, this phase is performed before any code is executed. In other words, *a set of mutants does not depend on the test suite and the types that are used in test cases.* Unlike mutants in statically typed languages, each mutant is surrounded with proper type checks. This approach ensures consistent calculation of mutation score to those reported by the tools for statically typed languages. As in existing tools, the test suite does not have to be executed for the mutants that would be created at the locations that are not executed when running the test suite with the original SUT.

Insert type checks. SMutant integrates additional checks at the places of potential mutants to ensure that the arguments of messages are of appropriate type. In this phase, rather than copying the class that is mutated, we use powerful Smalltalk reflection mechanism and replace only mutated method. The changes are automatically reverted when the mutation testing is done, so the user neither has to worry about implementation details nor about saving/copying/restoring the code.

Execution. For each potential mutant, identified in the first phase, the test suite is executed and mutation is *applied* only if one of the inserted checks is satisfied (e.g., invokes - instead of + if both arguments are Numbers). Note that the same message (e.g., +) at the same place in code can be sent with arguments of different types during the same execution. The tool applies mutation only (and always) when types are appropriate. This approach closely mimics mutation testing for statically typed languages; the mutant is created at a specific location in the code and is applied whenever the mutated code is executed.

An alternative to dynamic mutation testing would be mutation testing with support of a type inferencer. The first step would include type inference of the SUT. In the second step, mutants would be created in the same fashion as for statically typed languages wherever the type of arguments is unique (e.g., it is always Number).

3.4 Is Type Checking Necessary?

Do we need to surround mutants with type checks as described in the previous section? In some cases, we do not. Recall from Section 2 that any message can be sent to any object. When the message is inappropriate for the receiver object, the system sends `doesNotUnderstand` message to the same object, which throws an exception by default. If a mutant leads to `doesNotUnderstand`, it can be killed either because of the exception or likely incorrect result if `doesNotUnderstand` is overridden. However, this approach is not applicable in general. First, granularity of mutation operators is lost. Namely, it would be impossible to define: "arithmetic replacement operator: + to - if arguments are Numbers". Therefore, the analogy with mutation testing tools for statically typed languages would be lost. Which granularity is actually necessary remains to be seen, and SMutant enables performing the experiment. Second, although type checking may not be needed for some mutation operators, for others it is mandatory. For example, "logical negation of boolean variable" [2] requires type information.

3.5 User-Defined Mutation Operators

SMutant supports many mutation operators that are commonly implemented in the tools for statically typed languages, such as literal replacement, arithmetic operator replacement, or relational operator replacement. While implementing SMutant, the following became obvious: (1) some traditional mutation operators can be merged into a single mutation operator in Smalltalk and (2) defining replacement operators follows a pattern that is easy to automate.

Some traditional mutation operators can be merged in one mutation operator in Smalltalk because operators such as + or -, which have a special treatment in most programming languages, are treated the same as other messages. In other words, + or - are just names of the messages and can be defined for any type. This fact makes "arithmetic replacement operators" and "method replacement" the same mutation operators in Smalltalk. We implemented only one (generic) mutation operator for this case. Additional analysis of traditional mutation operators is needed to detect other similar cases that may hold in Smalltalk.

Implementation of replacement mutation operators, such as arithmetic and logical mutation operators, follows the same pattern. Since the number of operators (e.g., arithmetic) is limited in most statically typed languages, the replacement mutation operators are commonly written manually. Defining replacement mutation operators in Smalltalk is somewhat different, because one message (including what other languages commonly consider to be operators) can be replaced with any other message (provided that they have the same number of arguments). Therefore, defining all possible replacement mutation operators is not practical due to the number of possible replacements. SMutant includes standard sets of replacement mutation operators (e.g., arith-

```
defineUserOperator := DefineUserOperator new.
defineUserOperator original: #+.
defineUserOperator replacement: #-.
defineUserOperator runtime: #plusToMinus.
defineUserOperator firstType: Number.
defineUserOperator secondType: Number.
defineUserOperator define.
```

Figure 3: Code to evaluate in Workspace in order to define new mutation operator.

metic replacement operators) and includes support for user-defined mutation operators. User can decide, based on the application, which mutation operators to define. User only has to specify the name of the original message (i.e., the message to be replaced), replacement message, and type of the arguments that must hold to enable application of mutation. The code in Figure 3 can be used to define "arithmetic replacement operator + to - when arguments are Numbers".

It is important to mention that the list of mutation operators, available in MutationTestRunner (Figure 2), is automatically updated, after the message (Figure 3) is sent. Also code that is needed to support new operators is automatically generated.

3.6 Mutation Testing Library Classes

Mutation Testing of library classes (e.g., Set) introduces an additional challenge since these classes may be in use by the image, the runtime, or the mutation testing tool itself. Therefore, direct application of mutation testing on library classes could result in unpredictable and usually incorrect behavior. Existing tools do not specifically deal with this issue, but leave it up to the user to copy the class and perform necessary changes (e.g., renaming). SMutant comes with support for testing classes that are used by the image. Instead of direct application of mutation testing as described earlier, the tool copies the classes (`classesToMutate` and `classesWithTests`), and performs necessary changes to the new classes before applying the mutations. The user can easily turn this feature on by returning "true" from `isCopy` method (see Figure 1). Caution is needed with `isCopy` option; whenever possible this option should be off, since it introduces additional overhead. Note that the classes are copied only once, at the beginning of a mutation testing run.

3.7 Implementation Details

SMutant is developed in Pharo [10] Smalltalk. Nevertheless, we expect that the tool should work, after minor modifications (e.g., renaming), with the Squeak [11] implementation of Smalltalk. It is important to mention that no single line of code has to be modified/deleted/added in the base image in order to support SMutant. Changes that are needed to support GUI, which is optional, are made automatically when the tool is installed by the user. These changes are reverted when the tool is uninstalled. In addition, SMutant, as many other tools for mutation testing [6,8], runs mutated version of the code in a separate thread and kills the thread if it did not finish in the given amount of time, which prevents infinite loops, deadlocks, and livelocks. SMutant deploys SUnit framework, described in Section 2, to perform mutation testing: for each mutant, SMutant creates a test case with the appropriate values that is executed by SUnit.

3.8 Limitations

There are several features that can be improved. First, specification of mutation scenarios should be separated from running mutation scenarios (Figure 2). We have designed a separate GUI, which has to be integrated in SMutant, for specifying mutation scenarios, because manually writing a list of mutation operators may be quite tedious, although not difficult. Second, at this point, defining new mutation operators can be done only by sending a single message (Figure 3). We plan to design a simple GUI to simplify defining new mutation operators. Finally, the applicability of defining new mutation operators is to be determined.

4. CONCLUSIONS

We presented SMutant, a tool for mutation testing of programs written in Smalltalk. Because the type information is not known before the program is executed, SMutant applies mutations dynamically (at run-time), when information about the types becomes available. Also, SMutant supports defining new mutation operators without requiring the user to know any of the implementation details of SMutant. The code that is needed to support new mutation operators is automatically generated. SMutant is available at `http://www.squeaksource.com/smutant/`.

Acknowledgments

We thank Vilas Jagannath and Darko Marinov for great comments on this work. Aleksandar Milicevic and Rohan Sharma provided comments on an early draft of this paper. We also thank the fellow students of CS 598REJ at the University of Illinois at Urbana-Champaign for constructive discussions on the material presented in this paper. This material is based upon work partially supported by the US National Science Foundation under Grant Nos. CCF-0746856, CNS-0958199, and CCF-1012759.

5. REFERENCES

[1] P. Ammann and J. Offutt. *Introduction to Software Testing*. 2008.

[2] L. Bottaci. Type Sensitive Application of Mutation Operators for Dynamically Typed Programs. In *ICST Workshops*, 2010.

[3] R. A. DeMillo, R. J. Lipton, and F. G. Sayward. Hints on Test Data Selection: Help for the Practicing Programmer. *Computer*, 4(11), 1978.

[4] R. G. Hamlet. Testing Programs with the Aid of a Compiler. *IEEE TSE*, 3(4), 1977.

[5] Heckle. `http://seattlerb.rubyforge.org/heckle/`.

[6] S. A. Irvine, T. Pavlinic, L. Trigg, J. G. Cleary, S. Inglis, and M. Utting. Jumble Java Byte Code to Measure the Effectiveness of Unit Tests. In *MUTATION*, 2007.

[7] Y. Jia and M. Harman. An Analysis and Survey of the Development of Mutation Testing. *IEEE TSE*, 99(6), 2010.

[8] D. Marinov. *Automatic Testing of Software with Structurally Complex Inputs*. PhD thesis, MIT, 2004.

[9] Pester. `http://jester.sourceforge.net/`.

[10] Pharo. `http://www.pharo-project.org/`.

[11] Squeak. `http://squeak.org/`.

jStar-eclipse: An IDE for Automated Verification of Java Programs

Daiva Naudžiūnienė
University of Cambridge
da319@cam.ac.uk

Matko Botinčan
University of Cambridge
mb741@cam.ac.uk

Dino Distefano
Queen Mary Univ. of London
and Monoidics Ltd
ddino@eecs.qmul.ac.uk

Mike Dodds
University of Cambridge
md466@cam.ac.uk

Radu Grigore
Queen Mary Univ. of London
radu.grigore@eecs.qmul.ac.uk

Matthew J. Parkinson
Microsoft Research
mattpark@microsoft.com

ABSTRACT

jStar is a tool for automatically verifying Java programs. It uses separation logic to support abstract reasoning about object specifications. jStar can verify a number of challenging design patterns, including Subject/Observer, Visitor, Factory and Pooling. However, to use jStar one has to deal with a family of command-line tools that expect specifications in separate files and diagnose the errors by inspecting the text output from these tools.

In this paper we present a plug-in, called **jStar-eclipse**, allowing programmers to use jStar from within Eclipse IDE. Our plug-in allows writing method contracts in Java source files in form of Java annotations. It automatically translates Java annotations into jStar specifications and propagates errors reported by jStar back to Eclipse, pinpointing the errors to the locations in source files. This way the plug-in ensures an overall better user experience when working with jStar. Our end goal is to make automated verification based on separation logic accessible to a broader audience.

Categories and Subject Descriptors

D.2.4 [**Software/Program Verification**]: Formal methods

General Terms

Verification

Keywords

Automated verification, Separation logic, Java, Eclipse

1. INTRODUCTION

Software verification helps in developing more reliable programs. Although initially focused on verifying low-level mission critical programs, a variety of techniques and tools have been developed recently for verifying common everyday programs written in object-oriented programming languages [2, 4, 6]. However, bringing such techniques and tools to become a part of the standard software development process has proved difficult.

In recent years, separation logic has emerged as a highly successful approach to software verification. Separation logic enables concise specifications and the verification techniques based on it were shown to scale to large code bases such as Linux kernel [5]. However, these verification efforts have universally been led by the developers of the tools. As a result, in comparison to other approaches, e.g. Spec$^{\#}$ [1], there has been little or no effort to make separation logic tools accessible to a broader audience of software developers.

jStar [6] is a verification tool for Java programs based on principles of design-by-contract and separation logic. The aim of jStar has been to generalise and simplify the verification of Java programs. It abstracts away the details of objects implementation and can verify tricky Java programs such as commonly used design patterns, including Subject/Observer, Visitor, Factory and Pooling [7].

In this paper, we pursue the jStar agenda further by developing a developer-friendly interface to jStar. To this end, we have built a plug-in for the widely used Eclipse development environment. Our plug-in allows writing function contracts within the source code. Each time a developer saves the file, the plug-in maps the annotated Java programs to jStar specifications, and propagates jStar error reports back to the original Java program, enabling error diagnosis. This makes writing a program and verifying it in one place possible. We present **jStar-eclipse** by demonstrating two examples: a simple binary tree example and a more interesting and challenging example using Iterator and Decorator patterns.

2. JSTAR-ECLIPSE

Fig. 1 shows the high level structure of **jStar-eclipse** and its workflow. We write contracts for Java class methods as Java annotations (`@Spec` in Fig. 1). The contracts are function pre- and post-conditions written using our syntax based on separation logic. For a given Java file we extract these contracts to a specification file. Using the Soot tool [10] we convert the Java program into the Jimple intermediate representation (which is easier to analyse than Java). Finally we pass the specifications and the Jimple file to jStar which tries to verify the code against the specification.

Permission to make digital or hard copies of all or part of this work for personal or classroom use is granted without fee provided that copies are not made or distributed for profit or commercial advantage and that copies bear this notice and the full citation on the first page. To copy otherwise, to republish, to post on servers or to redistribute to lists, requires prior specific permission and/or a fee.
ESEC/FSE'11, September 5–9, 2011, Szeged, Hungary.
Copyright 2011 ACM 978-1-4503-0443-6/11/09 ...$10.00.

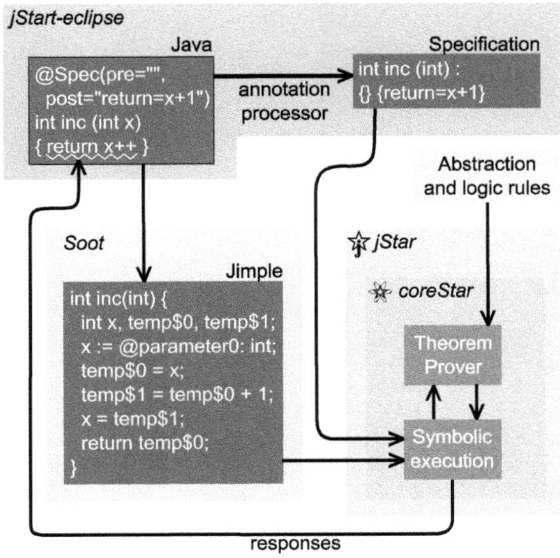

Figure 1: jStar-eclipse and its workflow

jStar is built on top of the separation logic based verification framework coreStar [3]. In addition to specifications and program code, coreStar takes collection of logic and abstraction rules (the former used by the internal theorem prover, the latter used by the internal abstract interpreter). jStar translates Jimple programs to the coreStar intermediate language. coreStar performs symbolic execution of the input program in a fix-point loop, applying abstraction and synthesising loop invariants automatically to allow termination. At the end, it checks whether each symbolic execution path satisfies the postcondition. Responses, such as error messages, are returned to the Eclipse plug-in.

2.1 New highlights of jStar-eclipse

To increase the productivity of the user, jStar-eclipse introduces several new valuable features which improve and simplify the verification process done in the jStar command line tool.

Specifications in the source file.
Java annotations are a natural way to write specifications: their purpose is to add metadata to Java source code. Writing specifications usually requires looking at the code that is being specified. Having them contained in the source code makes the verification process easier. After writing the method with its specification and saving the source file, **jStar-eclipse** automatically checks if the code satisfies its specification and shows an error message if it does not.

Error messages for verification failures.
One of the key difficulties in the verification process is understanding why the verification has failed. jStar itself returns only the part of its internal representation that it failed to verify. Relating this error back to the original Java program is difficult for non-experts. **jStar-eclipse** simplifies this debugging burden. When Java code is converted to the Jimple language, the Java source code positions are saved. This information is also kept when translating Jimple into the coreStar input language. Hence in the case of a counterexample we are able to locate the position of the Java code causing the error. The problematic source code is underlined in **jStar-eclipse**. Hovering over underlined code pops up a tooltip containing the error description.

Project-based organisation.
The files containing specifications, logic and abstraction rules are organised in the same way as Java source files. This simplifies navigation and file handling for larger projects.

3. SEPARATION LOGIC

The key benefit of separation logic is in its support for local reasoning: when we are giving a specification of a piece of code, we only need to supply information about what the code actually uses and need not to worry about the context the code is used in. To support local reasoning, separation logic introduces a new logical connective, the separating conjunction $*$, which represents disjointness of resources. The formula $P * Q$ asserts that we can split resources into two disjoint parts: one of them satisfying P and the other one Q. If we have a program C with a specification $\{P\}\ C\ \{Q\}$, then we can extend P and Q by arbitrary resource F that C does not access. This is known as the *frame rule*.

The specification $\{P\}\ C\ \{Q\}$ asserts that if we start at the state satisfying precondition P and the program C terminates then the resulting state satisfies postcondition Q. We can specify postconditions for exceptions as $\{P\}\ C\ \{Q\}$ $\{exception\ class:\ E\}$. If an exception is thrown, we end up in a state satisfying postcondition E.

jStar uses *abstract predicates* to reason about object oriented programs [8, 9]. Abstract predicates can represent encapsulated properties of an object by a separation logic formula. Writing specifications in terms of abstract predicates does not expose the inner structure outside the class and thus provides us with modular reasoning and information hiding. For example, for the `Tree` class given in Fig. 2 we define an abstract predicate *Tree(x,{sum=s})* which encapsulates the inner structure of the object.

4. EXAMPLES

In order to demonstrate how to verify code with **jStar-eclipse** we describe two examples. We start with a simple binary tree example and continue with a more challenging iterator example taken from the Apache Commons library.

4.1 Binary tree

Let us consider a class `Tree` representing a binary tree. Each node in a `Tree` object has left and right subtrees and a value. The method `treesum()` computes the total sum of the whole tree. Fig. 2 gives the source code, annotated with **jStar-eclipse** specifications.

We first define an abstract predicate *Tree(x,{sum=s})* representing a non-empty binary tree at location x, with property *sum*. The definition of *Tree* is given in the class annotation *@Predicate*. This annotation asserts that the `Tree` object has three fields: an integer field `value` that stores some value *_v* and two subtrees `left` and `right` that are either *null*, or store some values *_l* and *_r*. We also have a derived predicate *TreeOrNull(x,{sum=s})*, meaning that either *x=null* (i.e, it is an empty tree) or *Tree(x,{sum=s})*. To constrain *_l* and *_r* to be trees we use the *TreeOrNull*

```
@Predicate(predicate="Tree(x,{sum=s})",
  formula = "x.value |-> _v *
             x.left |-> _l * x.right |-> _r *
             TreeOrNull(_l,{sum=_ls}) *
             TreeOrNull(_r,{sum=_rs}) *
             s=((_v+_ls)+_rs)")

public class Tree {
  int value; Tree left, right;

  @Spec(pre="TreeOrNull(l,{sum=_ls}) *
             TreeOrNull(r,{sum=_rs})",
        post="Tree$(this,{sum=((v+_ls)+_rs)})")
  public Tree(int v, Tree l, Tree r) {
    super(); value = v; left = l; right = r;
  }

  @Spec(pre="Tree$(this,{sum=_s})", post="return=_s")
  int treesum() {
    int r = value;
    if (left != null) r += left.treesum();
    if (right != null) r += right.treesum();
    return r;
  }
}
```

Figure 2: Binary tree

predicate. Finally we assert that *sum* is equal to the sum of the tree, i.e., its value plus the sums of the subtrees.

Method specifications are written using the *@Spec* annotation. The specification of the class constructor asserts that, given two trees `l` and `r`, the constructor returns a tree with *sum* that is equal to the sum of the given trees and `v`. The specification of the method `treesum()` says that given a tree, it returns the value of the *sum* of the tree. By the definition of the predicate *Tree* we know that the returned value is the sum of the whole tree. These are all annotations needed to verify this example with **jStar-eclipse**.

4.2 Iterator

The second example we consider uses the Iterator and Decorator design patterns [7]. Fig. 3 gives the source code of the `FilterIterator` class[1] from Apache Commons library[2]. The `FilterIterator` decorates another `iterator` by filtering its collection values with a given `predicate`. It implements the `java.util.Iterator` interface with two methods: `hasNext()`, which returns `true` if there are more elements in the filtered collection, and `next()`, which returns the next element from the filtered collection if it exists, otherwise it throws an exception. To implement the interface, the class has two auxiliary fields: `nextObject` and `nextObjectSet`. `nextObject` works as a buffer of one cell corresponding to the next element in the collection. `nextObjectSet` says if the buffer is empty or full. We can have two possible situations as shown in Fig. 4. If `nextObjectSet` is `true`, then the first element of the filtered collection is contained in `nextObject`, otherwise, we do not use `nextObject`.

Due to limited space, we use the shorthand notation *method name: {precondition} {postcondition}* to write specifications in this example. Before specifying methods of the `FilterIterator` class, we give the specification of `java.util.Iterator` in Fig. 5. We use the abstract predicate *It(this,{collection=_c})* to abstract away the interface from the implementation. The specification of `hasNext()` says that it does not change the collection of the iterator, and the returned value is `true` if the collection has at least one element, otherwise it is `false`. The specification of `next()` says that the method returns the first element from the collection. However, it throws `NoSuchElementException` if the collection is empty.

We also need the specification of the `Predicate` interface:

```
interface Predicate {
  boolean evaluate(Object object):
  {Pred(this,{function=_f})}
  {Pred(this,{function=_f}) * return=satisfies(_f,object)}
}
```

Now we can specify the `FilterIterator` class. First we define the abstract predicate It^3 for this class:

```
It(x, {collection=c; under=i; underCollection=uc; pred=p;
     predFn=f; nextOb=nob; nextObSet=nobs}) =
  x.iterator |-> i * x.predicate |-> p *
  x.nextObject |-> nob * x.nextObjectSet |-> nobs *
  It(i, {collection=uc}) * i != null *
  Pred(p, {function=f}) * p != null *
  ( (nobs = true * c = cons(nob, _ct) *
    (Filter(f, uc, _ct)) * satisfies(f, nob) = true)
    ||
    (nobs = false * Filter(f, uc, c))) )
```

The definition says that we have four fields: `iterator`, `predicate`, `nextObject`, `nextObjectSet`. The field `iterator` satisfies `java.util.Iterator` interface, the field `predicate` satisfies `Predicate` interface. The last two disjuncts encode the two states in Fig. 4. *Filter(f, c1, c2)* means that if we filter the collection *c1* with the function *f* we get the collection*c2*. Specifications for `FilterIterator` methods are given in Fig. 6. The specification of `hasNext()` says that either the method returns `true` and the next object is set, or the method returns `false`, the next object is not set, and the collection is empty. The specification of `next()` says that we return the first element of the collection or we get the `NoSuchElementException` if the collection is empty. And finally, the specification of `setNextObject()` restricts calling this method only when `nextObjectSet` is `false`. The method tries to set next object and returns true if it succeeds. If it returns `false`, it must be that the underlying collection is empty.

We have used mathematical objects in the specifications, e.g. *cons*, *satisfies*, *Filter*. Here we give just their informal meanings, however to use them in the tool we have to formally define them using logic rules. Recall our informal definition of *Filter(f, c, fc)* which says that filtering the collection *c* with the function*f* we get*fc*. An example of a logic rule is an axiom saying that filtering an empty collection gives us an empty collection: $\vdash$*Filter(f, empty, empty)*.

5. CONCLUSIONS

The aim of **jStar-eclipse** was to integrate jStar within an IDE in order to support performing verification together with code writing. We have collected all that is required by the jStar command-line tool into one convenient framework. That is (1) specifications are included in the source file and automatically converted to jStar input specification files, (2) Java source is automatically converted into the intermediate representation used by jStar, and (3) error messages are

[1]For simplicity we have omitted constructors, setters, getters and remove function.
[2]http://commons.apache.org/collections/

[3]For readability we use the shorthand notation *It(x,{c,i,uc,p,f,nob,nobs})* later in the paper.

```
public class FilterIterator implements Iterator {
  private Iterator iterator;
  private Predicate predicate;
  private Object nextObject;
  private boolean nextObjectSet = false;

  public boolean hasNext() {
    if (nextObjectSet) { return true;}
    else { return setNextObject(); }
  }

  public Object next() {
    if (!nextObjectSet) {
      if (!setNextObject())
        { throw new NoSuchElementException(); }
    }
    nextObjectSet = false;
    return nextObject;
  }

  private boolean setNextObject() {
    while (iterator.hasNext()) {
      Object object = iterator.next();
      if (predicate.evaluate(object)) {
        nextObject = object;
        nextObjectSet = true;
        return true;
      }
    }
    return false;
  }
}
```

Figure 3: FilterIterator class

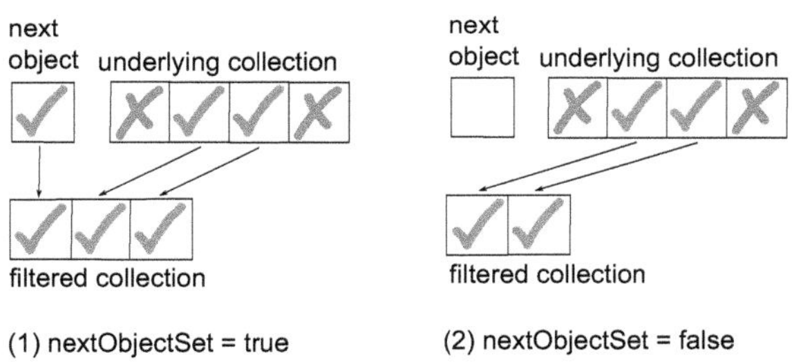

Figure 4: FilterIterator states

```
interface java.util.Iterator {
  boolean hasNext():
  {It$(this,{collection=_c})}
  {It$(this,{collection=_c}) *
   ((_c=empty * return=false) ||
    (_c=cons(_x,_ct) * return=true))}

  java.lang.Object next():
  {It$(this,{collection=_c})}
  {It$(this,{collection=_ct}) *
   _c=cons(_x,_ct) * return=_x}
  {NoSuchElementException:
   It$(this,{collection=empty}) * _c=empty}
}
```

Figure 5: Specification of java.util.Iterator

presented directly on top of the Java source code. Though **jStar-eclipse** is still at an early stage of development, already these features greatly simplify the workflow with jStar. We see development of **jStar-eclipse** as the first step

```
class FilterIterator {
  boolean hasNext():
  {It$(this,{_c;_i;_;_p;_f;_;_})}
  {It$(this,{_c;_i;_;_p;_f;_nob;_nobs}) *
   ((_c=empty * return=false * _nobs=false) ||
    (_c=cons(_nob, _ct) * _nobs=true * return=true))}

  java.lang.Object next():
  {It$(this,{_c;_i;_;_p;_f;_;_})}
  {It$(this,{_ct;_i;_;_p;_f;_;false}) *
   _c=cons(_x, _ct) * return=_x}
  {NoSuchElementException :
   It$(this,{empty;_i;empty;_p;_f;_;false}) * _c=empty}

  boolean setNextObject() static:
  {It$FilterIterator(this,{_c;_i;_;_p;_f;_;false})}
  {It$FilterIterator(this,{_c;_i;_uc;_p;_f;_;_nobs}) *
   (return=_nobs * (return=true || _uc=empty))}
}
```

Figure 6: Specification of FilterIterator

towards a user-friendly verification tool based on jStar, the first one that aims to bring separation logic based verification to a daily mainstream development.

Acknowledgments

We acknowledge funding from EPSRC H011749 (Grigore and Distefano) and H010815 (Dodds, Naudžiūnienė and Parkinson) and RAEng research fellowships (Distefano and Parkinson). Parkinson's work on jStar was carried out while at the University of Cambridge.

6. REFERENCES

[1] M. Barnett, M. Fähndrich, K. Leino, P. Müller, W. Schulte, and H. Venter. Specification and verification: The spec$^{\#}$ experience. *Communications of the ACM*, 54(6):81–91, 2011.

[2] M. Barnett, K. Leino, and W. Schulte. The Spec$^{\#}$ programming system: An overview. *CASSIS*, 2005.

[3] M. Botinčan, D. Distefano, M. Dodds, R. Grigore, D. Naudžiūnienė, and M. J. Parkinson. coreStar: The Core of jStar. In *Boogie 2011: 1st Intl. Workshop on Intermediate Verification Languages*, 2011.

[4] L. Burdy, Y. Cheon, D. Cok, M. Ernst, J. Kiniry, G. Leavens, K. Leino, and E. Poll. An overview of JML tools and applications. *International Journal on STTT*, 7(3):212–232, 2005.

[5] C. Calcagno, D. Distefano, P. W. O'Hearn, and H. Yang. Compositional shape analysis by means of BI-abduction. In *POPL*, 2009.

[6] D. Distefano and M. J. Parkinson. jStar: Towards practical verification for Java. In *OOPSLA*, 2008.

[7] E. Gamma, R. Helm, R. Johnson, and J. Vlissides. *Design Patterns: Elements of Reusable Object-Oriented Software.* Addison–Wesley, 1995.

[8] M. J. Parkinson and G. M. Bierman. Separation logic and abstraction. In *POPL*, 2005.

[9] M. J. Parkinson and G. M. Bierman. Separation logic, abstraction and inheritance. In *POPL*, 2008.

[10] R. Vallée-Rai, L. Hendren, V. Sundaresan, P. Lam, E. Gagnon, and P. Co. Soot-a Java optimization framework. In *CASCON*, 1999.

Static Deep Error Checking in Large System Applications using Parfait

Cristina Cifuentes, Nathan Keynes, Lian Li, Nathan Hawes,
Manuel Valdiviezo, Andrew Browne, Jacob Zimmermann,
Andrew Craik, Douglas Teoh and Christian Hoermann
Oracle Labs
Brisbane, Australia
http://labs.oracle.com/project/downunder
{cristina.cifuentes,nathan.keynes, lian.li}@oracle.com

ABSTRACT

In this paper, we introduce Parfait, a static bug-checking tool for C/C++ applications. Parfait achieves precision and scalability at the same time by employing a layered program analysis framework. In Parfait, different analyses varying in precision and runtime expense can be invoked on demand to detect defects of a specific type, effectively achieving higher precision with smaller runtime overheads.

Several production organizations within Oracle have started to integrate Parfait into their development process. Feedback from various production teams suggests that it is precise and scalable: the tool is able to analyze the OpenSolaris™ operating system and network consolidation (ON) with more than 6 million lines of code in 1 hour, and report thousands of defects with a false positive rate of close to 10%.

Categories and Subject Descriptors

D.2.5 [**Software Engineering**]: Testing and Debugging–Testing tools

General Terms

Precision, Scalability

1. INTRODUCTION

Parfait is a static bug-checking tool for C/C++ applications, designed to be both scalable and precise. Requirements for this tool were derived from interactions with different production teams within Oracle: the tool must be able to check large applications consiting of millions of lines of source code (MLOC), such as the OpenSolaris™ operating systems, in a time-efficient manner and at the same time find deep program errors without producing too much noise (i.e., false positives).

The design of Parfait [2] was presented at the Static Analysis Workshop in 2008: it defines an extensible framework composed of layers of program analyses that vary in complexity and runtime expense. Program analyses are designed to be demand-driven and ordered from the least to most time expensive, ensuring that each buggy statement is detected with the cheapest program analysis capable of detecting it, effectively achieving higher precision with smaller runtime overheads. For each defect-type, Parfait compiles a list of potentially buggy statements for the framework to process. Each analysis that relates to that defect-type can then either confirm that the statement is a defect, reject it as a non-defect, or pass it to the next analysis. At the end of the process, the user is presented with the list of defects and optionally can view (and manually verify) entries in the remainder list of potential defects.

The core of Parfait consists of a suite of static analyses, including data-flow analyses, pointer analyses [12], symbolic analyses [11], and taint analyses [14]. These analyses compute various properties of a program which are used in client analyses that detect specific defect types. For example, a client analysis for buffer overflow detection may require the results from symbolic analysis and from pointer analysis. Each type of core analysis comes in several different implementations of varying precision and efficiency. Specifically, we developed an efficient intra-procedural data-flow analysis framework, a precise inter-procedural, path-sensitive data-flow analysis framework, several different versions of pointer analysis, from simple local alias analysis to the more precise context- and flow-sensitive points-to analysis; similarly for taint analysis and symbolic analysis. These analyses make it easier to develop multiple client analyses for a given defect type, with different tradeoffs between precision and run time. Less precise but faster versions are used by default, the more precise ones are used when the analysed code is too complex to be solved by the faster versions.

Based on the core analyses in Parfait, various client analyses are developed to detect different types of defects. The defect types supported in Parfait include common language-specific errors in C/C++ such as buffer overflow, integer overflow, memory leak, double free, null-pointer dereferences, as well as application-specific errors requested by different production organizations, such as application-specific coding standards and library API miss-usage. To meet the scalability and precision requirements, each client analysis is thoroughly tested before being deployed in Parfait. We built a benchmark suite, BegBunch [1], which includes an accuracy suite with more than 1000 marked-up bug kernels

Permission to make digital or hard copies of all or part of this work for personal or classroom use is granted without fee provided that copies are not made or distributed for profit or commercial advantage and that copies bear this notice and the full citation on the first page. To copy otherwise, to republish, to post on servers or to redistribute to lists, requires prior specific permission and/or a fee.
ESEC/FSE'11, September 5–9, 2011, Szeged, Hungary.
Copyright 2011 ACM 978-1-4503-0443-6/11/09 ...$10.00.

and a scalability suite composed of several large open source applications, to automatically exercise a given client analysis in order to test its precision and scalability. We also manually verify the reports of each client analysis over large codebases such as OpenSolaris and OpenJDK™. Currently Parfait is able to analyze the OpenSolaris Operating system and Network Consolidation (ON) with more than 6 MLOC in 1 hour and reports thousands of defects with an overall false positive rate of close to 10%.

2. RELATED WORK

In the last decade a variety of bug checking tools based on static analysis techniques have become available in academia and industry. These tools mainly support popular languages such as C, C++ and the Java™ as well as a variety of types of defects, such as buffer overflows, cross-site scripting, SQL injection, deadlocks and race conditions. Tools vary in accuracy, performance and cost.

Popular commercial tools include Coverity Prevent [4], Klocwork Insight [16], GrammaTech CodeSonar [9], Fortify 360 [8] and PolySpace [6]. PolySpace focuses on embedded real time systems code, while the other tools focus on general application code.

Research/academic tools include FindBugs [10], ASTRÉE [3], Splint [7], Uno [15], Orion [5], Saturn [17], and Clang [13]. Those tools that are publicly available have been evaluated against Parfait in our previous paper [11].

3. USING PARFAIT IN LARGE SYSTEM APPLICATIONS

Much effort has been put into improving the usability of Parfait, including generating clear and easy-to-understand defect reports, and keeping track of reports across different versions of a user's codebase. Managing this information centrally enables a collaborative development environment. These capabilities allow Parfait to be easily integrated at several points in a software development process.

3.1 Use Cases

An important design goal for Parfait was to be flexible, in order to facilitate widespread acceptance by development teams. In practice, different teams have required Parfait to support a variety of use cases to fit into their established development processes.

The first use case is using Parfait at compile time in a standalone manner, without integration into the development process. A developer can receive useful defect reports without involving the rest of their team. This use case includes users trying Parfait for the first time.

Commit time integration consists of including a Parfait analysis as part of the commit process. Changesets may only be pushed to the repository if they do not add any new Parfait defect reports. This use case aims to prevent any new defects from being introduced into the repository.

Other teams choose to integrate Parfait as part of their regression tests, typically as a nightly run. This has the advantage of reporting defects present in the central repository, as opposed to an uncommitted changeset. Parfait results from nightly regression tests constitute a convenient baseline to identify defects added or removed during development. Teams often chose to use Parfait both as part of a commit process and as a regression testing process, to monitor defects in the central repository and to prevent changes from introducing new defects.

3.2 Defect Reports

The Parfait tool can present defect reports either textually on the command-line, or graphically in a web-based interface.

A simple example of the Parfait command-line output showing four buffer overruns is shown in Figure 1.

```
Error: Buffer overrun
   Buffer overflow (CWE 120): In array dereference of *p \\
      defined as buffer[(i + 1)] with index '(i + 1)'
      Array size is 100 elements (of 4 bytes each), index <= 100
        at line 19 of /example.cpp in function 'main'.
   Read outside array bounds (CWE 125): In array dereference \\
      of buffer[(i + 1)] with index '(i + 1)'
      Array size is 100 elements (of 4 bytes each), index <= 100
        at line 13 of /example.cpp in function 'main'.
        at line 17 of /example.cpp in function 'main'.
Error: Buffer overrun
   Buffer overflow (CWE 120): In array dereference of \\
      buffer[i] with index 'i'
      Array size is 100 elements (of 4 bytes each), index >= 0 \\
        and index <= 100
        at line 25 of /example.cpp in function 'main'.
```

Figure 1: Parfait command-line output.

When a particular Parfait analysis finds two or more defects with the same root cause (i.e., *structurally equivalent* defects that are detected with identical dependence information) in the same function, it groups them together. In the case of the first report in Figure 1, for example, three buffer overruns are grouped in a single report: one buffer write at line 19 and two reads at lines 13 and 17. All of these defects are real off-by-one array accesses/stores of the same array at the same index, and all can be corrected by changing a single enclosing loop condition.

The structural equivalence of all defects in a group proves beneficial on two fronts. Firstly, because all defects within a group share a common cause (structurally), they can be verified together and a common fix can often be used to correct them. This effectively reduces the total number of reports and translates into a time saving for the user. Secondly, it provides an effective mechanism to track repeated defect reports generated from multiple Parfait runs: instances of the same defect report are identified by their structural equivalence instead of their source locations. This is very useful in practice as software changes throughout the development process and often multiple versions of a codebase need to be maintained at the same time. This functionality enables effective integration of Parfait at commit time and regression time, where defect reports can be compared with those from previous Parfait runs and new defects highlighted.

Nevertheless for large codebases such as OpenSolaris, Parfait still generates a large number of reports (approx. 4000 in the case of OpenSolaris). In these cases, the web-based interface often proves more useful than the command-line output. The web interface provides a broad overview of defect reports, allowing the user to see at a glance what types of defects were detected in the codebase and where. Two simple visualisations are provided: a bar graph of reports sorted by type, and a tag cloud of the source files where most of the detected defects occur. The graph of defect reports by type helps to identify common faults that developers may need to be more aware of, while the tag cloud makes it easy to identify files that need attention.

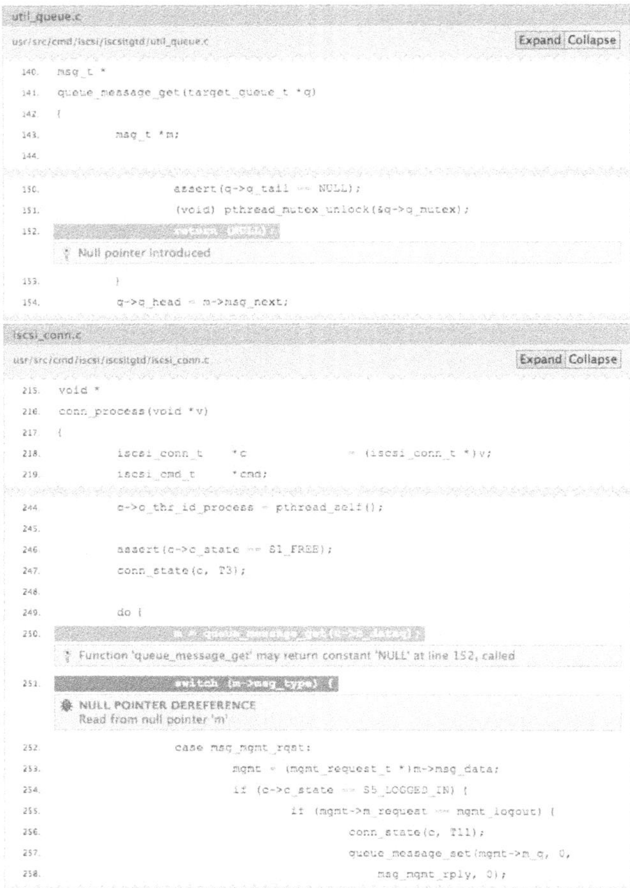

Figure 2: Parfait web-based bug report.

From this high-level overview, users can then navigate to the individual defect reports that interest them by selecting a defect type or a source file. At the individual report level, the web interface presents each report in context, surrounded by the relevant source code excerpt where it was detected. The line that contains the defective statement and the statements that Parfait considered during its analysis are highlighted and annotated with a short explanation. Figure 2 shows an example null pointer dereference defect report in the web-interface.

3.3 Managing Defect Reports

Managing defect reports from multiple Parfait runs can be error prone and time consuming. To provide development groups with an easy way to store, organise and access these reports, we have developed the Parfait Server. Parfait Server is a web application designed to facilitate the management of defect reports. Figure 3 depicts its high level architecture. The main features include the collection of defect reports uploaded directly from the Parfait bug-checking tool in a centralized database (DB), comparison between reports from multiple Parfait runs, defect browsing and flagging via the web-based interface, as well as source code management (SCM) and bug tracking system integration.

Parfait Server can automatically receive defect reports

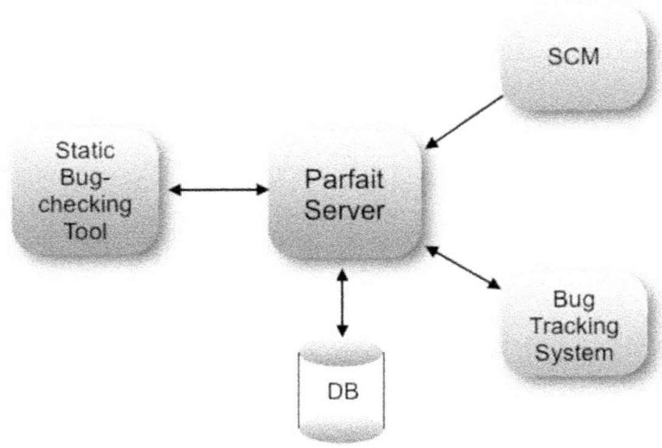

Figure 3: The Parfait Server.

generated by the bug-checking tool. Teams usually configure their nightly Parfait runs to upload results to a Parfait Server instance. These reports are thus stored in a central defect report database and team members can easily review the reported defects. The server also allows users to search for defects in the source code, since it is integrated with the most common software configuration management systems. Additionally, reports can be organised in multiple groups. For example, reports generated by different types of Parfait runs (e.g., nightly, weekly) can be displayed together. Once the server collects a sufficient number of reports, teams can observe and examine defect trends in their source code.

One of the most useful features of Parfait Server is report comparison. The mechanism used to group defect reports, introduced in previous section, is used in tracking repeated defect reports. There are two use cases where the comparison is employed: regression and commit time. Since Parfait Server usually stores reports from regression tests, teams can view the introduced and removed defects of a report with respect to any previous report in the database. This allows them, for example, to easily identify any new bug in the central repository and to quickly request a fix. Secondly, the commit time integration lets developers know if their changes in the source code introduce a new defect, before pushing their changes to the central repository. This is achieved by retrieving a report from the server (usually from the last regression test) and comparing it to the Parfait run over the new version of the source code.

Additionally, the server provides a web-based interface to let users browse defects and flag them as 'Unverified', 'Verified', 'False' or 'Won't fix'. All new defects are 'Unverified' by default, meaning that the defect hasn't been confirmed by a developer. Defects that are incorrectly reported by the bug-checking tool (i.e., false positives) should be flagged as 'False'. These bugs won't be computed in the statistics of reports. Valid defects can be marked as 'Verified' or 'Won't fix', if the bug will not be corrected. In addition, Parfait Server allows team members to add comments to defects, so more detail or possible solutions can be attached to bugs.

Finally, the server can be integrated with a bug tracking system. Defects reported by Parfait can be automatically submitted (individually or by batch) to the tracking system. Information such as defect type, location and user comments are included in the submission. Parfait Server shows the status of defects in the bug tracking system, so that teams can see the progress of the fixes without leaving the web interface.

Defect type	Reported	True	False	Unverified
Buffer overrun	335	258	22	55
Double free	18	10	2	6
Integer overflow	18	18	0	0
Memory leak	933	732	39	162
Null pointer dereference	869	32	3	829
Uninitialised variable	89	23	4	62
Use after free	72	50	1	21

Table 1: Number of defect groups reported in OpenSolaris (snv_93)

Defect type	Reported	True	False	Unverified
Buffer overrun	10	10	0	0
Double free	0	0	0	0
Integer overflow	12	12	0	0
Memory leak	26	12	0	14
Null pointer dereference	307	1	0	306
Uninitialised variable	2	0	0	2
Use after free	0	0	0	0

Table 2: Number of defect groups reported in OpenJDK (b94)

As an alternative to using Parfait Server, the bug-checking tool can also use a text file as the bug database. This file contains the flags and comments of defects which can be updated from a tool-generated web-based report interface. Also, the bug database file can be used as a baseline to compute the introduced defects in a new changeset.

4. RESULTS

Tables 1 and 2 show the defects of the eight different types reported from running Parfait over OpenSolaris ON (snv_93) and OpenJDK (b94). For each defect type we present the total number of grouped defects reported by Parfait and the number of these verified as true or false. Due to the large number of reports and limited time we have not verified all reports. For some defect types, a sample of reports were checked.

Overall, Parfait is able to identify defects in large codebases with relatively few false positives. In addition to OpenSolaris and OpenJDK, Parfait has also been used by various product organizations within Oracle. Feedback from these teams indicates that Parfait is a useful tool that is able to find a large number of real defects with relatively small false positive rates, and can be easily integrated into their development process.

5. CONCLUSION

To summarise, Parfait is a useful static error detection tool for large commerical system applications. To ensure Parfait can be efficiently integrated into product organizations, much effort has been put into improving the usability of the tool, such as generating clear and easy-to-understand defect reports, and integrating with source code management and bug tracking systems. For the users of Parfait, these usability features are as important as developing sophisticated and efficient analysis techniques.

References

[1] C. Cifuentes, C. Hoermann, N. Keynes, L. Li, S. Long, E. Mealy, M. Mounteney, and B. Scholz. BegBunch: Benchmarking for C bug detection tools. In *Proceedings of the 2009 international workshop on Defects in large software systems*, July 2009.

[2] C. Cifuentes and B. Scholz. Parfait – designing a scalable bug checker. In *Proceedings of the ACM SIGPLAN Static Analysis Workshop*, pages 4–11, 12 June 2008.

[3] P. Cousot, R. Cousot, J. Feret, L. Mauborgne, A. Miné, D. Monniaux, and X. Rival. The ASTRÉE analyser. In *Proceedings of the 2005 European Symposium on Programming*, pages 21–30. Springer, April 2005.

[4] Fortify Static Code Analysis (SCA). `http://www.coverity.com/products/coverity-prevent.html`. Last accessed: 1 June 2011.

[5] D. Dams and K. S. Namjoshi. Orion: High-precision methods for static error analysis of c and c++ programs. In *FMCO'05: Proceedings of the 4th International Symposium on Formal Methods for Components and Objects*, volume 4111 of *Lecture Notes in Computer Science*, pages 138–160. Springer, 2005.

[6] A. Deutsch. Static verification of dynamic properties. PolySpace White Paper, February 2004.

[7] D. Evans and D. Larochelle. Improving security using extensible lightweight static analysis. *IEEE Software*, pages 42–51, January/February 2002.

[8] Fortify Static Code Analysis (SCA). `http://www.fortify.com/products/sca/`. Last accessed: 1 June 2011.

[9] GrammaTech CodeSonar. `http://www.grammatech.com/products/codesonar/overview.html`. Last accessed: 1 April 2008.

[10] D. Hovemeyer and W. Pugh. Finding bugs is easy. In *Companion to the 19th conference on Object-oriented Programming Systems, Languages, and Applications*, pages 132–136. ACM Press, 2004.

[11] L. Li, C. Cifuentes, and N. Keynes. Practical and effective symbolic analysis for buffer overflow detection. In *Proceedings of the eighteenth ACM SIGSOFT international symposium on Foundations of software engineering*, FSE '10, pages 317–326, New York, NY, USA, 2010. ACM.

[12] L. Li, C. Cifuentes, and N. Keynes. Boosting the performance of flow-sensitive points-to analysis using value flow. In *Proceedings of the eighteenth ACM SIGSOFT international symposium on Foundations of software engineering*, FSE '11, New York, NY, USA, 2011. ACM.

[13] LLVM/Clang Static Analyzer. `http://clang.llvm.org/StaticAnalysis.html`. Last accessed: 1 December 2010.

[14] B. Scholz, C. Zhang, and C. Cifuentes. User-input dependence analysis via graph reachability. In *Proceedings of the Eighth IEEE Working Conference on Source Code Analysis and Manipulation*, pages 25–34, 28-29 September 2008.

[15] Uno Tool Synopsis. `http://spinroot.com/uno/`. Last accessed: 26 October 2010.

[16] M. Webster. Leveraging static analysis for a multidimensional view of software quality and security: Klocwork's solution. White paper, IDC, Sept. 2005.

[17] Y. Xie and A. Aiken. Saturn: A scalable framework for error detection using boolean satisfiability. *ACM Transactions on Programming Languages and Systems*, 29(3):16, 2007.

Querypoint : Moving Backwards on Wrong Values in the Buggy Execution

Salman Mirghasemi
École Polytechnique Fédérale de Lausanne (EPFL), Switzerland
salman.mirghasemi@epfl.ch

John J. Barton
IBM Research - Almaden
bartonjj@us.ibm.com

Claude Petitpierre
École Polytechnique Fédérale de Lausanne (EPFL), Switzerland
claude.petitpierre@epfl.ch

ABSTRACT

As developers debug, they often have to seek the origins of wrong values they see in their debugger. This search must be performed backwards in time since the code causing the wrong value is executed before the wrong value appears. Therefore, locating the origin of wrong values with breakpoint- or log- based debuggers demands persistence and significant experience.

Querypoint, is a Firefox plugin that enhances the popular Firebug JavaScript debugger with a new, practical feature called *lastChange*. *lastChange* automatically locates the last point at which a variable or an object property has been changed. Starting from a program suspended on a breakpoint, the *lastChange* algorithm applies queries to the live program during re-execution, recording the call stack and limited program state each time the property value changes. When the program halts again on the breakpoint, it shows the call stack and program state at the last change point. To evaluate the usability and effectiveness of *Querypoint* we studied four experienced JavaScript developers applying the tool to two test cases.

Categories and Subject Descriptors

D.2.5 [**Testing and Debugging**]: Debugging aids; D.2.6 [**Programming Environments**]: Integrated environments

General Terms

Algorithms, Human Factors, Languages

Keywords

Debugging, Locating Defects, Querypoint, LastChange, Breakpoint, Watchpoint, Logging

1. INTRODUCTION

According to [5], developers spend about fifty percent of their time on debugging. To fix a bug, developers typically reproduce and monitor the buggy execution several times to understand the program's unexpected behavior. Trial-and-error, guess-work, and analyzing complicated data make debugging difficult and time-consuming. Thus enhanced debugging operations are highly needed to save time, reduce development costs and improve software quality.

In a common strategy for locating defects, the developer starts from the bug symptoms and traces the execution backwards, moving from a point in the program execution where a value appears to be incorrect back to the point where that value was set. Two conventional approaches, breakpoint-based and log-based debugging, require tedious steps to select the data to be collected, collect these data and, then analyzing the results.

Locating the origin of wrong values becomes even harder when developers deal with weakly-typed dynamic languages such as JavaScript. First, due to weakly-typed nature of these languages the search space that the developer should consider is considerably larger than with traditional languages such as Java and C#. Second, the dynamics features of these languages limit the value of traditional compile-time program analysis.

Querypoint, is a Firefox plugin that enhances the popular Firebug JavaScript debugger with a new, practical feature called *lastChange* [8]. *lastChange* makes it possible to locate the origin of a wrong value by making queries about the running program. This feature allows the developer to navigate through dynamic data dependency without requiring a full trace, unlike other interfaces based on dynamic slicing. The proposed technique builds on the existing breakpoint approach and it does not require any special environment to create identical, instruction by instruction, re-executions. *Querypoint* also provides a mechanism to automate the bug reproduction, and a novel user interface that summarizes the data of the investigated execution points and the collected results.

2. RELATED WORK

Most tools developed to enhance developers' navigation on a buggy execution can be classified in two main groups: replay-based and logging-based. Replay-based approaches capture limited data during execution and replay the buggy execution to reach past points. In contrast, logging-based approaches collect enough data during execution to relieve the developer from re-executing.

Two replay-based debuggers, bdb [3] and reverse watchpoint [7], rely on deterministic executions and employ a step counter to locate the requested point from the beginning of

Permission to make digital or hard copies of all or part of this work for personal or classroom use is granted without fee provided that copies are not made or distributed for profit or commercial advantage and that copies bear this notice and the full citation on the first page. To copy otherwise, to republish, to post on servers or to redistribute to lists, requires prior specific permission and/or a fee.
ESEC/FSE'11, September 5–9, 2011, Szeged, Hungary.
Copyright 2011 ACM 978-1-4503-0443-6/11/09 ...$10.00.

execution. These tools incur two to four times runtime overhead.

Among logging-based debuggers are *omniscient* debuggers (e.g., ODB [6], TOD [9], and WhyLine [4]) and time-travelling debuggers (e.g., Nirvana [1]). Logging-based debuggers suffer from different issues. First, the recording phase is time expensive (20-120 times) and it must be repeated in case of changes in the program. Second, the execution log cannot fully replace the live execution. There are other aspects of execution (e.g., program user interface, file system, database tables, etc.) that are also important in debugging and are not available to the developer in logging-based debuggers. Third, querying collected data (e.g., to restore the program state at a certain point) may not be efficient enough to debug realistic programs.

Querypoint resembles the operational model of replay-based debuggers and the query approach of logging-based debuggers. However, contrary to other replay-based debuggers, which require exactly the same re-executions (deterministic executions), *Querypoint* only requires the *reproducibility* of the bug, so that a test case reproduces the bug and a way to halt the execution reliably after the reproduction is available. Unlike logging-based debuggers *Querypoint* selectively collects data which significantly reduces runtime overhead incurred by logging.

3. QUERYPOINT

Let us illustrate the *Querypoint* functionality by a simple example. This example demonstrates a buggy JavaScript code in a HTML page (Figure 1). This page contains a button (line 40) that shows the value of `myObject.myProperty`. When the user clicks on the button, the `onClick` function (line 13) is called. This function increases the value of `myObject.myProperty` by one (line 15) and calls the `updateButton` function that updates the button's text to the new value (line 22). When the page is loaded for the first time, the button shows `1` as the initial value of `myObject.myProperty`. In practice when the user clicks on the button, `0` appears instead of `2`: there is a bug.

```
1 <html>
...
5   <script type="text/javascript">
6     myObject = {myProperty : 1};
7     myCondition = {value : 1};
...
13    function onClick(){
14      foo();
15      myObject.myProperty++;
16      bar();
17      ...
18      updateButton();
19    }
20    function updateButton(){
21      var myParagraph =
          document.getElementById("myButton");
22      myButton.innerHTML = myObject.myProperty;
23    }
24    function foo(){
25        myCondition.value = oldValue;
26    }
27    function bar(){
28      if (!myCondition.value)
29          myObject.myProperty = 0;
30    }
31  </script>
...
40  <button id="myButton" onclick="onClick()">
41      1
42  </button>
43 </html>
```

Figure 1: A Web page containing JavaScript code. Some lines not related to our paper have been elided.

By browsing through the code,the developer determines that the value displayed on the button is set at line 22. Since the displayed value is incorrect they know the bug occurred before the program hit this line. To start debugging, the developer sets a breakpoint on line 22. Once the button is clicked, the execution is paused at line 22. Figure 2(a) shows the Firebug debugger while the execution is paused. Firebug has several panels (e.g., HTML, CSS, Script, DOM, etc.) each one demonstrating one aspect of the Web page. The Script panel on the left side contains the list of all loaded source files and regular debugging facilities such as setting breakpoints and stepping. On the right of the script panel, the Watch panel shows the program state that displays the scopes and the variable values. In our case, the `myObject.myProperty` value at the paused point is `0`. We expected this value to be `2`.

To apply the backward search strategy to locate defects, the developer first needs to know the origin of the wrong value. Then they muse use breakpoints, and look through the code to find all possible places where `myObject.myProperty` might get a new value and set a breakpoint at these locations. However, an object and property can be accessed and changed through different names and methods. There is no simple way to identify these aliases or even their total number. The developer is limited to make a good guess and to set breakpoints on lines where the property seems to be changed, to re-execute the program and to examine the state looking for values that may lead to the incorrect value observed at line 22. All this work must be repeated if new aliases are discovered or if some information related to the buggy result was missed while suspended on one of the breakpoints.

In our proposal, we have added a high-level function in the debugger, *lastChange*, that provides the answer without tedious manual effort from the developer. By right clicking on `myObject.myProperty` in the Watch panel, the developer can run the *lastChange* command (Figure 2(a)). The debugger re-executes the program and halts again at the breakpoint on line 22. However, it shows a new panel, called QP, centered on the source at line 29 (Figure 2(b)), the point of *lastChange*. To the right, the TraceData panel shows the values of properties of the program state when it passed through line 29. These two panels resemble the Script and Watch panels, but they show data collected by the debugger at one execution point that is now in the past: these data are *traces* or *logs* collected during the re-execution.

Looking at line 29, the developer concludes that something is wrong with `myCondition.value` which leads to the execution of line 29. The developer then examines `myCondition.value` and noticed that it is `undefined`. The next step the developer performs is to know when this property got this value. To do so, they run the *lastChange* command on `myCondition.value` from this point. The debugger re-executes the program and breaks again on line 22, analyzes the queries and shows the developer line 25-the place `oldValue` is assigned to `myCondition.value`. If the developer asks for *lastChange* on `oldValue`, the debugger can notify

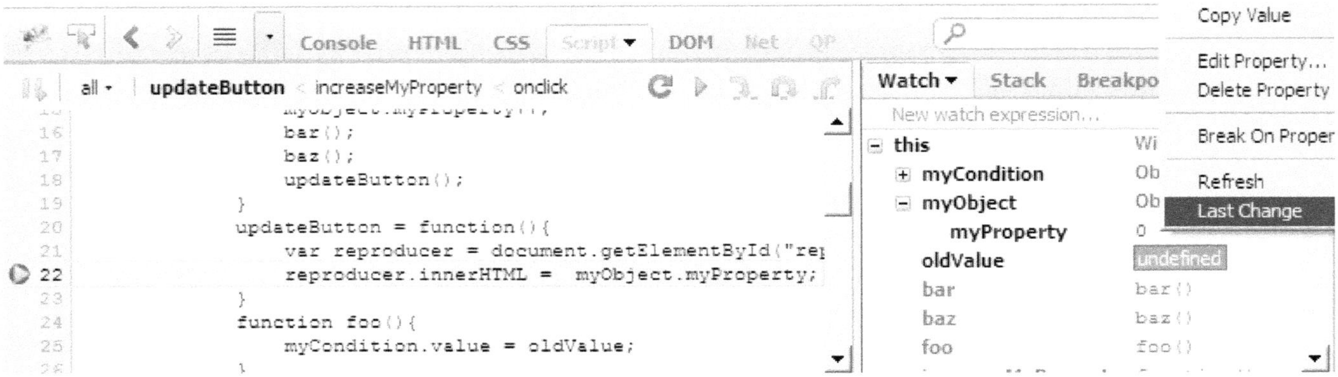

(a) A screen shot of the Firebug debugger while running the example code from Fig. 1. The Script panel is selected; it gives access to all loaded source files and allows breakpoints to be set on lines. In this figure, the execution is paused at line 22 by a regular breakpoint. The Watch panel on the right shows the program state at the breakpoint. The developer can query *lastChange* on `myObject.myProperty` by right-clicking on the value of `myProperty`.

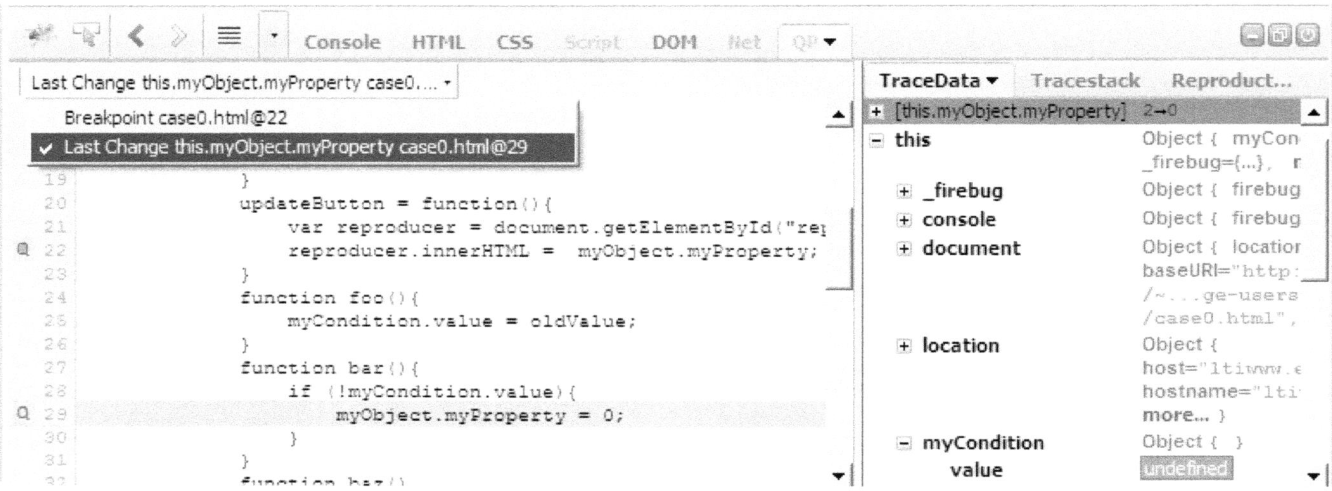

(b) The result of *lastChange* query for `myObject.myProperty`. The left panel, QP, shows the source code at the point of *lastChange*; The right panel, TraceData, shows the collected data at the point.

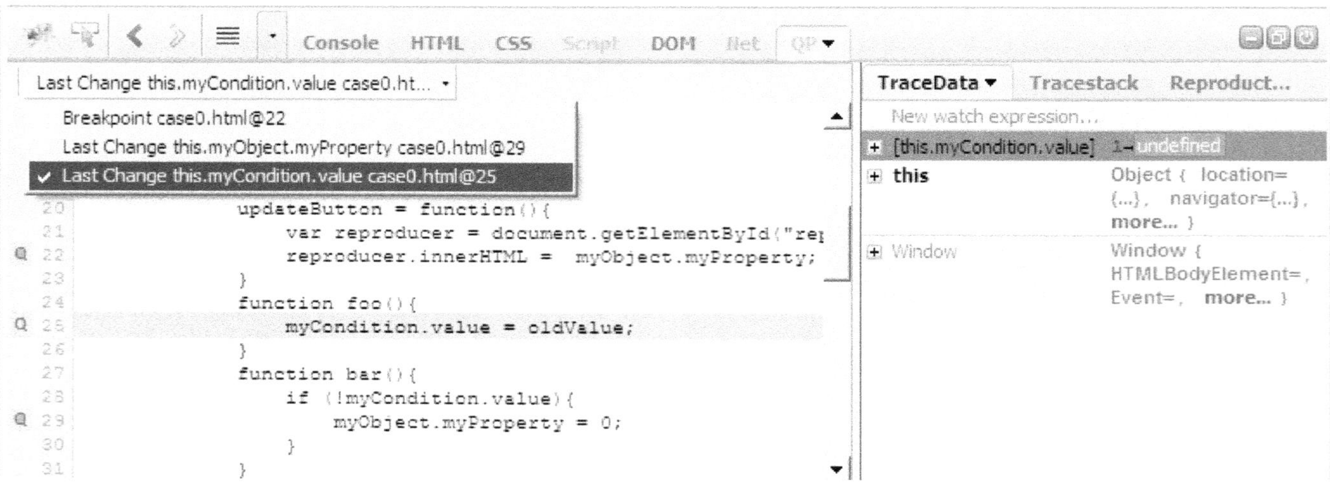

(c) The result of *lastChange* query for `myCondition.value`. To evaluate an expression (e.g., oldValue) at this point, the developer can enter the expression in the watch box and after a re-execution the result is available. The opened list on the top of the left panel shows the visited execution points. Clicking on each point in the list shows the corresponding code and data.

Figure 2: The stages of locating the defect using *lastChange* feature.

the developer that this variable has never been assigned a value. Now it is clear that the bug occurs because `oldValue` is `undefined` when the execution reaches line 25 (Figure 2(c)).

The developer has examined three points of execution, but set one explicitly. We call the latter breakpoint the *reproduction point*. The second and third points precede the reproduction point in the execution sequence. All three points correspond to the history of the search for the defect. They are available through the debugger's interface. At the top of the left panel in Figure 2(c) there is an opened list that shows all three examined points. Moreover, the source lines related to these points are marked with red **Q** icons.

Querypoint needs a test case to reproduce the execution and conditions to correctly recognize the reproduction point. Although both elements can be directly provided by developer, *Querypoint* is also able to automatically create them from the first execution.

To replay an execution, *Querypoint* keeps track of breakpoint and single steps the execution went through. *Querypoint* supports two mechanisms for automatic re-execution: callstack-reproduction and record-replay. In callstack reproduction the function from the bottom frame of the call stack is called with the same parameters. The record-replay execution uses two phases. In the record phase, it stores the initial page url and the events and parameters corresponding to user actions. In the replay phase, it opens the same url and simulates events as if they were user actions.

In addition to the data collected at every change event for identifying the *lastChange* result, *Querypoint* partially stores values in program state. There is a trade-off between the amount of data collected at every change event and the number of re-executions. If the developer asks for some values that have not been stored, *Querypoint* re-executes and collects the requested data.

4. USER STUDY

We supplied four experienced Javascript developers with *Querypoint* integrated in an extended Firebug debugger[1]. Following a tutorial and a practice case, we observed them as they applied both conventional breakpoint and *lastChange* on two small programs we provided. The first program, Shapes, calculates the area and perimeter values for a list of shapes. The bug happens when one of the calculated numbers is zero. The second program, Moving Circle, randomly scales and moves a circle in the page. The bug happens once the circle becomes invisible after an exception occurs. This case represent a reproducible non-deterministic execution. The developers were asked to locate the defects that caused these bugs. All four developers successfully applied *lastChange* to the test programs and understood how it could help debugging. To find the defect location with breakpoints, all four users took more steps[2] and more time (Figure 3).

5. CONCLUSION AND FUTURE WORK

Querypoint provides critical information for debugging JavaScript programs: the location and state at the point where a questionable value was assigned. It only requires bug reproducibility and is built on the existing breakpoint technology.

In our next iteration we plan to merge the query and breakpoint results. *Querypoint* shows the results of *lastChange* in a similar but different view from breakpoint debugging. This focuses attention on value changes, but it makes studying control flow more difficult.

[1] http://ltiwww.epfl.ch/~mirghase/lastchange-userstudy

[2] A step is a button push, either single stepping the debugger or running a *lastChange* query.

Programs \ Developers	DEV1	DEV2	DEV3	DEV4
Shapes	**3 (85 s)**	13 (182 s)	39 (318 s)	**3 (80 s)**
Moving Circle	9 (215 s)	**4 (40 s)**	**3 (195 s)**	12 (234 s)

Figure 3: The number of steps (and time in seconds) required before locating a defect, for each test subject and test program. Cells with a white background report values with conventional debugging; Cells with a colored background use *lastChange*.

6. REFERENCES

[1] S. Bhansali, W. Chen, S. de Jong, A. Edwards, R. Murray, M. Drinić, D. Mihočka, J. Chau. Framework for instruction-level tracing and analysis of program executions. In *International Conference on Virtual Execution Environments(VEE)*, June, 2006.

[2] M.D. Bond, N. Nethercote, S.W. Kent, S.Z. Guyer, and K.S. McKinley. Tracking bad apples: reporting the origin of null and undefined value errors. In *22nd annual ACM SIGPLAN conference on Object-oriented programming, systems, languages, and applications(OOPSLA)*, October, 2007.

[3] B. Boothe. Efficient algorithms for bidirectional debugging. In *Conference on Programming Language Design and Implementation(PLDI)*, June, 2000.

[4] A.J. Ko, and B.A. Myers. Debugging reinvented: asking and answering why and why not questions about program behavior. In *30th international conference on Software engineering(ICSE)*, May, 2008.

[5] T.D. LaToza, G. Venolia, and R. DeLine. Maintaining mental models: a study of developer work habits In *28th international conference on Software engineering(ICSE)*, May, 2006.

[6] B. Lewis, and M. Ducasse. Using events to debug Java programs backwards in time. In *Companion of the 18th annual ACM SIGPLAN conference on Object-oriented programming, systems, languages, and applications(OOPSLA)*, 2003.

[7] K. Maruyama, and T. Kazutaka. Debugging with Reverse Watchpoint. In *Proceedings of the Third International Conference on Quality Software*, 2003.

[8] S. Mirghasemi, J.J. Barton, and C. Petitpierre. Debugging by lastChange. Technical Report. EPFL-REPORT-164250, 2011.

[9] G. Pothier, É. Tanter, and J. Piquer. Scalable omniscient debugging. In *22nd annual ACM SIGPLAN conference on Object-oriented programming, systems, languages, and applications(OOPSLA)*, October, 2007.

Sydit: Creating and Applying a Program Transformation from an Example

Na Meng* Miryung Kim* Kathryn S. McKinley*†
* The University of Texas at Austin †Microsoft Research
* Austin, TX † Seattle, WA
mengna09@cs.utexas.edu, miryung@ece.utexas.edu, mckinley@cs.utexas.edu

ABSTRACT

Bug fixes and feature additions to large code bases often require *systematic edits*—similar, but not identical, coordinated changes to multiple places. This process is tedious and error-prone. Our prior work introduces a systematic editing approach that creates generalized edit scripts from exemplar edits and applies them to user-selected targets. This paper describes how the SYDIT plug-in integrates our technology into the Eclipse integrated development environment. A programmer provides an example edit to SYDIT that consists of an old and new version of a changed method. Based on this one example, SYDIT generates a *context-aware, abstract edit script*. To make transformations applicable to similar but not identical methods, SYDIT encodes control, data, and containment dependences and abstracts position, type, method, and variable names. Then the programmer selects target methods and SYDIT customizes the edit script to each target and displays the results for the programmer to review and approve. SYDIT thus automates much of the systematic editing process. To fully automate systematic editing, future tool enhancements should include automated selection of targets and testing of SYDIT generated edits.

Categories and Subject Descriptors

D.2.6 [**Software Engineering**]: Programming Environments—*integrated environments*

General Terms

Design, Experimentation, and Measurement

Keywords

Software evolution, program transformation and differencing

1. INTRODUCTION

A software life cycle begins with design, prototyping, and writing code. After the initial burst of development, programmers continue to fix bugs, refactor code, and add new features. Recent work observes that many changes during a maintenance phase are *systematic*—programmers add, delete, and modify code in numerous classes in similar, but not identical ways [9]. Manually making these edits is tedious and error prone.

We recently introduced a flexible systematic editing approach that consists of two algorithms: (1) *transformation creation*, which derives a generalized *context-aware, abstract* edit script from an exemplar edit, and (2) *transformation application*, which applies and customizes the derived transformation to target methods specified by the user [7]. Our prior work describes and evaluates this approach in detail. Our empirical evaluation used version histories from five Java open source projects and showed that (1) SYDIT produces syntactically valid transformations for 82% of target methods, (2) it perfectly mimics developer edits on 70% of the targets, and (3) syntactic program differencing judges the human generated version and the SYDIT generated version as 96% similar. We argue that working from examples is intuitive and this level of accuracy is sufficient to make it appealing for programmers as well.

This paper describes an Eclipse IDE plug-in implementation of the SYDIT technology in an interactive programming tool. To use SYDIT, users provide an *exemplar* edit. SYDIT then generates a program transformation that is more general than the concrete edit, which makes the edit applicable to similar but not identical target methods. Users next specify one or more target methods to apply the transformation and SYDIT produces a new version of each target method. Users examine each new version, edit them further, and/or accept the new versions as correct. To ease this process, SYDIT presents a *diff-style* comparison of each original target and its suggested versions. Users may examine, name, and store transformations for later use. Our initial experiences suggest that interactive refinement of the derived transformations and automated selection of targets are important features for future work.

Compared to prior work for helping programmers systematically fix and enhance software, SYDIT is more effective, convenient, and automated [7]. For instance, existing refactoring engines in Integrated Development Environments (IDEs), such as Eclipse, automate repetitive edits, but are confined to pre-defined semantic-preserving transformations. Source transformation languages and tools such as iXJ [1] and TXL [2] force programmers to prescribe systematic edits in a formal syntax in advance. Search-and-replace in text editors is the most popular approach, but it typically only supports simple text replacements and does not han-

Permission to make digital or hard copies of all or part of this work for personal or classroom use is granted without fee provided that copies are not made or distributed for profit or commercial advantage and that copies bear this notice and the full citation on the first page. To copy otherwise, to republish, to post on servers or to redistribute to lists, requires prior specific permission and/or a fee.
ESEC/FSE'11, September 5–9, 2011, Szeged, Hungary.
Copyright 2011 ACM 978-1-4503-0443-6/11/09 ...$10.00.

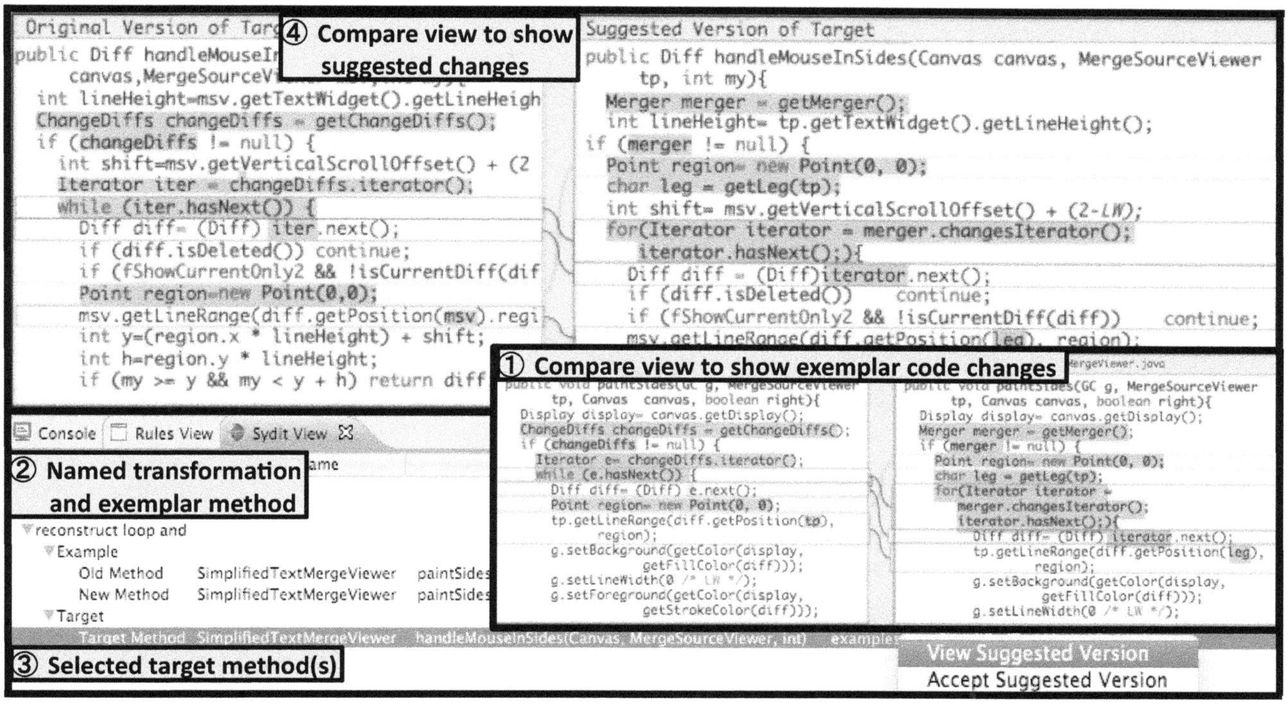

Figure 1: A screen snapshot of SYDIT Eclipse plug-in and its features

dle non-contiguous edits nor edits that require customization for different contexts. Clone detection and approaches do suggest edit locations, but leave the task of editing the code manually to programmers [9, 6]. With *simultaneous editing*, programmers edit pre-specified clones in parallel, naïvely propagating exactly the same edit to all clones without regard to context, which leads to errors [11, 8, 3]. In the work closest to SYDIT, Lanza et al. monitor the evolution of a code fragment, deriving a sequence of change operations to represent this transformation [10]. Developers then specify any generalization of position and names by hand. In contrast, SYDIT automatically derives a general edit script from the original and final version of an exemplar changed method, which makes it convenient for programmers to use, and our prior evaluation shows SYDIT is effective.

Whereas our prior publication focused on the algorithms and evaluation, this tool paper makes new contributions by presenting SYDIT's instantiation as an Eclipse plug-in, workflow architecture, user interfaces, and implementation details. The next section contains some background [7]. Section 2 illustrates the SYDIT Eclipse plug-in features and user interface with an example scenario. Section 3 describes the implementation.

Background

This section summarizes SYDIT's two key algorithms: (1) generating program transformations from an example and (2) applying the resulting context-aware abstract transformations to new code.

SYDIT transformation generation algorithm takes an *exemplar edit* as input, which consists of the original and modified versions of a changed method. It first performs program differencing on the original and modified versions to generate a sequence of Abstract Syntax Tree (AST) node *additions, deletions, updates,* and *moves.* For each edit in the sequence, SYDIT computes control, data, and containment dependences and then combines them to describe the edit's *context*, i.e., other program statements on which the edits depend, and statements that depend on the edits. SYDIT then abstracts edit positions and the names of variables, methods, and types. This abstraction process generalizes edit positions and names. The result of this algorithm is an abstract context-aware edit script.

SYDIT's transformation application algorithm takes as input this edit script and a target method. SYDIT tries to establish a map of the edit context to the target method for exact and approximate matches of statements, dependences, positions, and names. If SYDIT establishes a map, it next customizes the abstract edit script by replacing the matched abstract identifiers with the corresponding names used by the concrete AST nodes in the target method. Similarly, it calculates concrete edit positions based on the target. SYDIT then generates a new version of the target by applying the customized concrete edit script to the target method.

2. SYDIT FEATURES

Consider a simplified example from the Eclipse `compare` project. Suppose Alice wants to replace the use of class `ChangeDiffs` with `Merger` and refactor iteration over `diff` objects in two methods: `paintSides` and `handleMouseInSides`. Part ① on the right-hand side of Figure 1 shows the exemplar edit, and ④ on the left-hand side shows SYDIT's suggestion modification on a different target. Though both methods use the same API for `ChangeDiffs` and iterate `diff` objects, they use different variables names (`Iterator e` versus `Iterator iter`), and contain different code. For example, `paintSides` lays out the `diff` information while `handleMouseInSides` captures mouse activities over the `diff` layout. The required edits for these changes are not exactly the same with respect to edit content and position, but they are very similar.

In this example, both edits involve complex coordinated changes. To replace the use of `ChangeDiffs` with `Merger`, Alice needs to remove the declaration of `ChangeDiffs` and insert one for `Merger`. She also needs to replace all uses of `changeDiffs` with `merger` and its method invocations. To refactor the `diff` object iterator, Alice needs to replace the `while` loop with a `for` loop, move the declaration of variable `region` from inside to outside of the loop, and adjust the API usage. We use this relatively complicated example to show the power of SYDIT. Since each method needs multiple non-contiguous edits and the edit content is different for each method, `search-and-replace` is not very helpful to Alice.

Alice reviews and tests her changes to `paintSides` as shown in ① in Figure 1. She next provides this example edit to SYDIT. Using syntactic program differencing, SYDIT computes a set of edits that transform the old version to the new version. In this case, SYDIT computes: delete the `changeDiffs` declaration, insert the `merger` declaration, update the `if` condition `changeDiffs != null` with `merger != null`, move the `region` declaration out of the `while` loop, insert the `leg` declaration on the true branch of the `if` statement, delete the `e` declaration, update the `while` loop with a `for` loop, update the `diff` declaration, and update the argument of the `tp.getLineRange()` method invocation.

SYDIT next generalizes these edits, abstracting position and names. The result is an abstract, context-aware edit script. Alice names this script, *reconstruct loop and change API*, and stores the **Old Method** and **New Method** of `paintSides` as an example edit (see Figure 1 ②).

Alice then selects one or more target methods to which she wants to apply the derived script. Alice selects `handleMouseInSides` (see Figure 1 ③). SYDIT suggests similar but not identical edits, e.g., delete `iter`'s declaration instead of `e`'s, and update the argument of method invocation `msv.getLineRange()` instead of `tp.getLineRange()`.

Alice inspects the suggested version of `handleMouseInSides` using Eclipse's `compare` view (see Figure 1 ④). After Alice examines the suggested edits, she approves SYDIT's suggestion by choosing **Accept Suggested Version**.

Although the target method `handleMouseInSides` and the source method `paintSides` have different structures and use different identifier names, SYDIT correctly identifies a reusable, abstract transformation and applies it. SYDIT ignores concrete names in the edit content and computes edit positions relative to the edit context. These abstraction features make the edit application problem harder, but are key to replicating similar but not identical program transformations.

3. SYSTEM ARCHITECTURE

This section describes the system architecture and implementation details of SYDIT. SYDIT currently targets Java programs and consists of five components: (1) program differencing, (2) edit context extraction through dependence analysis, (3) identifier and edit position abstraction, (4) context matching, and (5) program transformation through AST rewrites. As shown in Figure 2, the first three components correspond to program transformation creation while the last two correspond to program transformation application.

Program Differencing. SYDIT compares the syntax trees

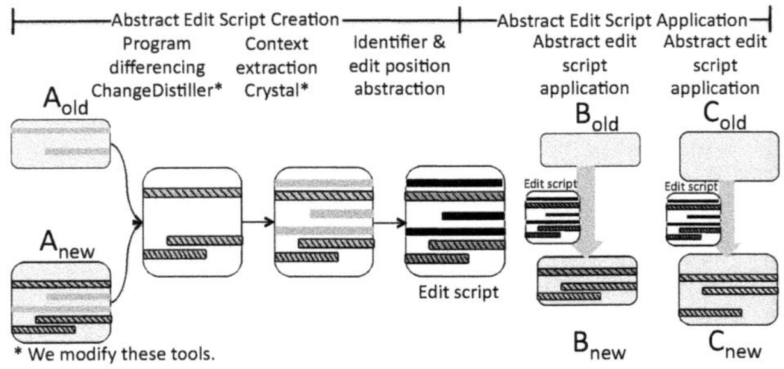

Figure 2: Sydit User and Tool Workflow

of two versions of the same method to derive a sequence of AST node edits. It performs this task with a modified version of ChangeDistiller [4]. For example, Figure 3 shows the derived edits for `paintSides` in Figure 1. We modify ChangeDistiller's algorithms in two ways. First, instead of allowing any inner nodes to match if their children nodes match, we also require the inner nodes should at least be similar control-flow constructs, such as `while` and `for` loops. Second, we match leaf nodes and inner nodes to handle cases such as matching a `catch clause` with an empty body (a leaf node) to a `catch clause` with a non-empty body (an inner node).

Edit Context Extraction. SYDIT extracts a change context from both the old and new versions using control, data, and containment dependence analysis. By *context*, we mean other program statements on which the edits depend or those that depend on the edits. The context nodes serve as anchors to position edits correctly in a new target location. We implement the context analysis in the Crystal static analysis framework [5]. SYDIT takes an input a parameter k, which indicates the dependence chain length, i.e., the *hop* distance from edits to context nodes. When k is set to 1, SYDIT selects only unchanged nodes on which the edits are directly dependent upon or statements that direct depend on the edit. In Figure 3, the gray boxes represent the found contextual nodes when $k = 1$. Setting k to 2 selects unchanged directly dependent nodes and unchanged nodes that transitively depend on these nodes, i.e., dependences with a 2 hop distance.

Edit Position and Identifier Abstraction. SYDIT then replaces concrete identifiers of variables, methods, and types with corresponding symbolic names, `v$n`, `m$n`, and `T$n` in the edits and extracted context, creating conversion mappings between them. It then recalculates the position of each edit with respect to the extracted context.

Context Matching. Given a target method, SYDIT uses context matching to establish a mapping between the AST nodes in the edit script and the target method. The mapping problem is similar to a labeled graph isomorphism problem and we invented a specialized tree matching algorithm customized to the needs of this problem. The intuition behind our algorithm is that it first finds candidate leaf matches and then uses them to match inner nodes. We find as many candidate matches as possible between leaf nodes in the abstract context and the target tree. Starting from these candidate leaf matches, we determine a best match in the target context for each path. This algorithm is described in detail

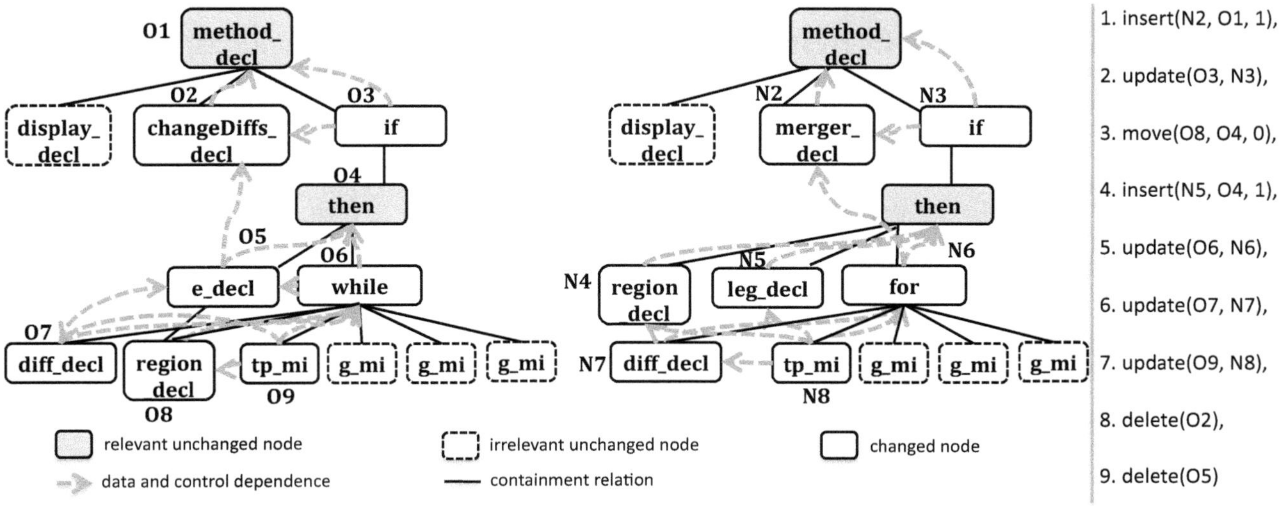

Figure 3: Concrete AST edits of paintSides

in reference [7]. If every node in the abstract script finds a unique correspondence in the target tree, SYDIT collects the identifier mappings based on the node matches and proceeds to the next step.

Program Transformation. To generate concrete edits for a target method, SYDIT replaces symbolic names used in the abstract edit script with corresponding concrete identifiers found in the target context. It also recalculates each edit position with respect to the concrete target method. SYDIT translates the resulting edits to a sequence of AST rewrite operations step by step using the Eclipse ASTRewrite API, and provides suggested edits to a user.

4. SUMMARY

SYDIT helps developers perform systematic editing tasks that involve similar but not necessarily identical changes to multiple places. The SYDIT plug-in makes it easier for developers to specify an exemplar changed method and multiple target methods to change similarly. It assists programmers by showing them the suggested changes for each target method and only using them if the programmer approves. In future, we plan to support developers to edit the generated abstract transformations for better flexibility. We also plan to simplify target method selection by searching for candidates which are similar to the exemplar changed method and providing potential candidates to programmers.

5. ACKNOWLEDGMENTS

This work was supported in part by the National Science Foundation under grants CCF-1043810, SHF-0910818, and CCF-0811524. We thank anonymous reviewers for their thorough comments on our earlier version of the paper.

6. REFERENCES

[1] M. Boshernitsan, S. L. Graham, and M. A. Hearst. Aligning development tools with the way programmers think about code changes. In *CHI '07*, pages 567–576, New York, NY, USA, 2007. ACM.

[2] J. R. Cordy. The txl source transformation language. *Science of Computer Programming*, 61(3):190–210, 2006.

[3] E. Duala-Ekoko and M. P. Robillard. Tracking code clones in evolving software. In *ICSE '07: Proceedings of the 29th International Conference on Software Engineering*, pages 158–167, Washington, DC, USA, 2007. IEEE Computer Society.

[4] B. Fluri, M. Würsch, M. Pinzger, and H. C. Gall. Change distilling—tree differencing for fine-grained source code change extraction. *IEEE TSE*, 33(11):18, November 2007.

[5] C. Jaspan, K. Bierhoff, and J. Aldrich. Crystal tutorial notes. 2009.

[6] T. Kamiya, S. Kusumoto, and K. Inoue. CCFinder: A multilinguistic token-based code clone detection system for large scale source code. *IEEE TSE*, 28(7):654–670, 2002.

[7] N. Meng, M. Kim, and K. S. McKinley. Systematic Editing: Generating Program Transformations from an Example. In *PLDI '11*, pages 329–342, San Jose, CA, 2011. ACM.

[8] R. C. Miller and B. A. Myers. Interactive simultaneous editing of multiple text regions. In *Proceedings of the General Track: 2002 USENIX Annual Technical Conference*, pages 161–174, Berkeley, CA, USA, 2001. USENIX Association.

[9] T. T. Nguyen, H. A. Nguyen, N. H. Pham, J. Al-Kofahi, and T. N. Nguyen. Recurring bug fixes in object-oriented programs. In *ICSE '10*, pages 315–324, New York, NY, USA, 2010. ACM.

[10] R. Robbes and M. Lanza. Example-based program transformation. In *Proceedings of the 11th international conference on Model Driven Engineering Languages and Systems*, MoDELS '08, pages 174–188, Berlin, Heidelberg, 2008. Springer-Verlag.

[11] M. Toomim, A. Begel, and S. L. Graham. Managing duplicated code with linked editing. In *VLHCC '04*, pages 173–180, Washington, DC, USA, 2004. IEEE Computer Society.

Crystal: Precise and Unobtrusive Conflict Warnings

Yuriy Brun[†], Reid Holmes[♦], Michael D. Ernst[†], David Notkin[†]

[†]Computer Science & Engineering
University of Washington
Seattle, WA, USA

[♦]School of Computer Science
University of Waterloo
Waterloo, ON, Canada

{brun,mernst,notkin}@cs.washington.edu, rtholmes@cs.uwaterloo.ca

Abstract

During collaborative development, individual developers can create conflicts in their copies of the code. Such conflicting edits are frequent in practice, and resolving them can be costly. We present Crystal, a tool that proactively examines developers' code and precisely identifies and reports on textual, compilation, and behavioral conflicts. When conflicts are present, Crystal enables developers to resolve them more quickly, and therefore at a lesser cost. When conflicts are absent, Crystal increases the developers' confidence that it is safe to merge their code. Crystal uses an unobtrusive interface to deliver pertinent information about conflicts. It informs developers about actions that would address the conflicts and about people with whom they should communicate.

Categories and Subject Descriptors: D.2.3 [Software Engineering]: Coding Tools and Techniques; D.2.6 [Software Engineering]: Programming Environments

General Terms: Design, Human Factors

Keywords: collaborative development, collaboration conflicts, developer awareness, speculative analysis, version control, Crystal

1. Introduction

Developers working collaboratively on a team can find themselves in conflicting states with one another. These conflicts generally manifest themselves in concrete artifacts within the version control (VC) repository. Such conflicts occur in practice and are costly [5, 7, 8, 10, 11, 12].

This paper describes Crystal, a tool that proactively identifies conflicts in version-controlled artifacts. Crystal provides developers with information about the presence and severity of conflicts as soon as they occur, before the relevant artifacts and changes fade in their minds. Crystal helps developers make well-informed decisions about how to identify and prioritize their tasks, particularly VC operations, and about when and with whom to communicate.

Consider an illustrative scenario in which two developers are enhancing a single program (Figure 1). On Monday, Melinda and Bill start working on different program features, periodically checkpointing their work locally. Melinda takes a week to finish her changes, test them to her satisfaction, and share them with the master code repository. Bill takes two weeks to finish his work, avoiding the distraction of potential conflicts by opting not to incorporate work from Melinda and the master repository. When he does incorporate Melinda's work (which she has shared with the master) after two weeks, he discovers a conflicting interaction between the implementations of the two features. Bill, unable to resolve the conflict on his own, meets with Melinda. Melinda, who has shifted her focus to yet another feature, has to reconstruct her thought process and assumptions. Their schedules are delayed as they understand the interaction, resolve the conflicts, and produce versions of the features that integrate properly.

Suppose, instead, that Bill were using Crystal. Crystal continuously and unobtrusively reports what would happen *if* he were to share his work and incorporate that of others. The right side of Figure 1 shows Bill's view of Crystal. After his first checkpoint on Monday, he is ahead of (has done strictly more work than) both the master repository and Melinda, and he could share (akin to upload, and signified by an up arrow) his changes to either one. After Melinda's checkpoint on Tuesday, Bill is still ahead of the master repository, but Melinda's work would require a merge, which would proceed cleanly (yellow "merge" icon). Bill's work on Wednes-

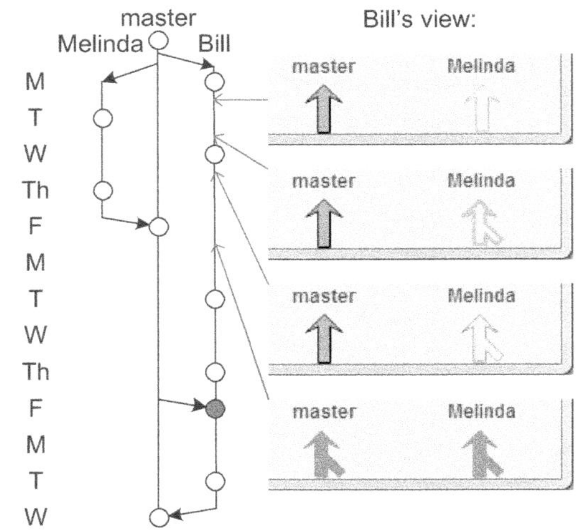

Figure 1: A collaborative development scenario in which Crystal would have enabled Bill to avoid a costly conflict resolution.

On the left is the revision history for Melinda, Bill, and the master repository. Each circle in the history is a code checkpoint. The filled circle indicates the need for manual resolution of conflicts.

On the right is the view Crystal would provide Bill at various points in time. (Shown are actual partial screenshots of our tool. Section 3 describes Crystal's icons.) In the Crystal screenshots, a solid icon represents to Bill a relationship that Bill can affect by performing an action, and a hollow icon represents a relationship that will persist until someone else addresses it.

Permission to make digital or hard copies of all or part of this work for personal or classroom use is granted without fee provided that copies are not made or distributed for profit or commercial advantage and that copies bear this notice and the full citation on the first page. To copy otherwise, to republish, to post on servers or to redistribute to lists, requires prior specific permission and/or a fee.
ESEC/FSE'11, September 5–9, 2011, Szeged, Hungary.
Copyright 2011 ACM 978-1-4503-0443-6/11/09 ...$10.00.

day conflicts with Melinda's in a way requiring human intervention (red "merge" icon). Once Melinda shares her work with the master repository on Friday, Bill's relationship with the master changes.

Using existing VC tools, Bill could, at any time, choose to determine his relationship with the master repository (the left part of each screenshot); however, he is unlikely to do so as he is trying to avoid distractions. Crystal provides earlier information that enables more effective behaviors without significant interruption. On Tuesday, Bill can see that Melinda is working in parallel. On Wednesday, upon checkpointing his change, Bill can see that it conflicts with Melinda's work. Given that information, Bill may choose to contact Melinda to discuss the unintended feature interaction.

This scenario sketches how Crystal might encourage Bill and Melinda to discover and interact about this conflict as much as $1\frac{1}{2}$ weeks before Bill finishes his feature and $\frac{1}{2}$ week earlier than in the best case using the VC system (VCS) alone.

In some cases, Crystal may help *prevent* such conflicts from occurring. Suppose that on Tuesday, Bill noticed that Melinda was working and asked her to share her work so far. Seeing Melinda's changes, Bill might proceed differently on Wednesday. Even if he does not, resolving the conflict then would be easier, as it would be small and fresh in both Bill's and Melinda's minds.

In addition to textual conflicts identified by the underlying VCS, Crystal can also proactively discover higher-order conflicts. For example, suppose Bill's and Melinda's code merged cleanly from the VCS's point of view, but the merged code failed to compile, or failed its test suite. Crystal accurately identifies such conflicts and reports them to the developers as soon as they occur. In the absence of Crystal, these conflicts are likely to be discovered even later, sometime after the code is merged, incurring even more effort to resolve them. Crystal explicitly checks for compilation and testing conflicts; a future version could perform other kinds of analyses, e.g., to identify performance degradation.

Crystal is open-source, platform-independent, available for download — `http://crystalvc.googlecode.com` — and works with the Mercurial distributed VCS (DVCS). We are extending Crystal to work with Git. Crystal could be made to work with a centralized VCS (CVCS) in two ways: (1) Crystal could speculatively merge branches similarly to the way it currently merges repositories, and (2) Crystal could speculatively merge changes in the developers' working copies. In fact, Microsoft, in collaboration with us, is developing a similar tool for a CVCS.

We have previously evaluated Crystal's potential for helping developers by examining 550,000 development versions of nine open-source systems. We found that both textual and higher-order conflicts occur often and last, on average, for 10 days [3]. In this paper, we focus on how Crystal precisely detects conflicts and effectively communicates information to the developers.

The rest of this paper is structured as follows. Section 2 discusses how Crystal precisely detects conflicts. Section 3 describes how Crystal's user interface reports conflicts without distracting the developer. Finally, Section 4 describes how Crystal's implementation scales to large projects and efficiently detects conflicts.

2. Early and precise conflict detection

Crystal precisely reports actual conflicts, determining the relationship between two developers' states by actually creating the merged artifact. In other words, to find out what would happen if Bill and Melinda merged their code, Crystal, in the background, makes a copy of Bill's code and incorporates Melinda's changes. Similarly, once Crystal creates the merged code artifact, it attempts to compile and to execute the test suite on that artifact. Again, Crystal only reports a compilation or testing conflict when the build or

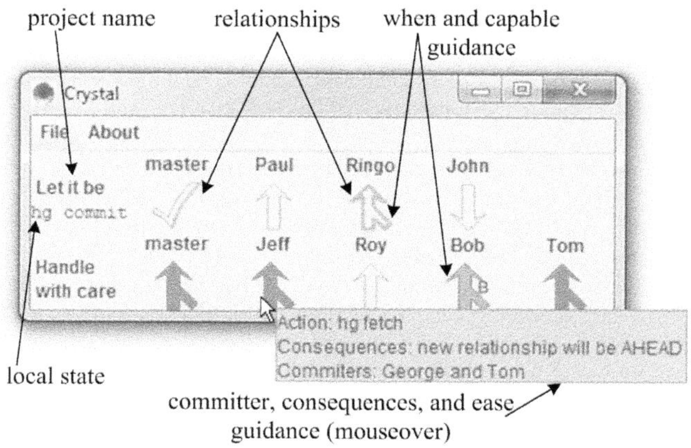

Figure 2: A screenshot of George's view of Crystal. George is following two projects under development: "Let it be" and "Handle with care". The former has four observed collaborators: George, Paul, Ringo, and John; the latter has five: George, Jeff, Roy, Bob, and Tom. Crystal shows George's local state and his relationships with the master repository and the other collaborators, as well as guidance based on that information.

a test actually fails. Because the computation happens in the background, the developers can continue to work without interruption; in certain situations, we expect the developers to ignore Crystal, much as they sometimes ignore project bulletin boards and email.

We refer to the idea of attempting a set of actions on the developer's state in the background and reporting on the outcomes of those actions as *speculative analysis* [2].

Awareness tools [1, 6, 9] notify developers when they *might* have conflicting changes. This approximation is computed differently in various tools. Some determine if a co-developer is working in the same file, some report any change to the repository (e.g., FASTDash [1]), others report concurrent changes to the AST (e.g., Syde [9], etc. These approaches can lead to the inclusion of false positives — reporting potential conflicts that do not evolve into actual conflicts. Furthermore, few current awareness tools try to automatically detect higher-order merge conflicts; again, Crystal is precise as it uses the project's tool chain to dynamically detect conflicts by execution of the build system and test suites. We refer the reader to [3] for a more detailed description of related work.

Crystal can, in rare situations, also report false positives. Checkpointed changes that are later *discarded* can cause a teammate to see a pending conflict that later disappears. This can happen when a developer checkpoints exploratory code or a partial change.

3. Reporting conflicts

Crystal unobtrusively reports four kinds of information: the developer's local state, relationships with other developers or repositories, the possible actions (which is derived from the local state and relationship with the master repository, and which we omit from this paper for brevity), and guidance about those actions. The remainder of this section summarizes Crystal's interface and the information it reports; more details on both are available in [3].

3.1 Example Crystal use

Figure 2 shows a screenshot of Crystal's main window. The window displays a row of icons for each of a developer's projects. In this example, there are two projects: "Let it be" and "Handle with care". The former has four collaborators: George (the developer running Crystal), Paul, Ringo, and John. The latter has five collaborators: George, Jeff, Roy, Bob, and Tom. Each developer can independently choose whether or not to run Crystal.

On the left-most side of each row, underneath the project name, Crystal displays the local state (Section 3.2). This tells George, in the native language of the underlying VCS, whether he must checkpoint changes (`hg commit`, in Mercurial) or resolve a conflict. Then, for each repository (master and other collaborators', whether or not they are running Crystal), Crystal displays the relationship with that repository (Section 3.3). If George has the ability to affect a relationship *now*, the icon is solid, which combines the *When* and *Capable* guidance (Section 3.4). If George *cannot* affect the relationship, the icon is hollow. If the relationship is of the *might* variety — George might or might not have to perform an operation to affect the relationship — the icon is solid but slightly unsaturated (see the relationship with Bob in the "Handle with care" project). These features allow George to quickly scan the Crystal window and identify the most urgent issues — the solid red icons — followed by other, less severe icons. George can also quickly identify whether there is something he can do now to improve his relationships (in the example, George can perform actions to improve his relationships in the "Handle with care" project, but not in "Let it be"), and whether there are unexpected conflicts George may wish to communicate with others about. Holding the mouse pointer over an icon displays the action George can perform and the *Committer*, *Consequences*, and *Ease* guidance (Section 3.4), when appropriate.

3.2 Local states

There are five possible local states for a developer.

uncommitted There are uncommitted changes in the working copy.

in conflict The local repository is in conflict with itself; that is, (in DVCS terminology) it has two heads that are not automatically mergeable. This happens, for example, when incorporated and local changesets conflict.

build failure The repository's version of the code fails to build.

test failure The repository's version of the code builds but fails its test suite.

OK The repository's version of the code builds and passes its test suite.

3.3 Repository relationships

We have identified seven relevant relationships that can hold between two repositories. Figure 3 displays the icons Crystal uses to denote each relationship.

SAME The repositories have the same changesets.

AHEAD The repository has a superset of the other repository's changesets.

BEHIND The inverse of AHEAD.

The remaining four relationships represent repositories that share an initial sequence of changesets followed by distinct sequences of changesets.

TEXTUAL✘: (pronounced "textual conflict") The distinct changesets cannot be automatically merged by the VCS.

BUILD✘: The repositories can be automatically merged by the VCS, but the resulting merged code fails to build.

TEST✘: The repositories can be automatically merged by the VCS and the resulting merged code builds but fails its test suite.

TEST✓: The repositories can be automatically merged by the VCS and the resulting merged code builds and passes its test suite.

Higher-order conflicts, such as BUILD✘ and TEST✘, are not considered by existing VCSes. Although this paper discusses only

SAME AHEAD BEHIND TEXTUAL✘ BUILD✘ TEST✘ TEST✓

Figure 3: Crystal associates an icon with each of the seven relationships. The color of each relationship icon represents the severity of the relationship: relationships that require no merging are green, that can be merged automatically are yellow, and that require manual merging are red.

these two higher-order relationships, others naturally arise for other analyses; for example, consider when a test suite passes but a performance analysis or code style checker does not.

3.4 Guidance

Knowing how each action may affect the developer's state and relationships can help developers make better-informed decisions.

We classify the guidance information into five types. One type concerns the relationship: *Committer*. The other four concern the possible action: *When*, *Consequences*, *Capable*, and *Ease*.

Committer: Who made the relevant changes?
For example, two developers may be in the TEXTUAL✘ relationship, but the cause of the conflict could be a change made by a third developer. This information is important to identify with whom the developers looking to resolve this conflict should communicate, which, in turn, decreases the time required to fix technical problems [4].

When: Can an action that affects the relationship be performed now, or must it wait until later?
For example, a developer may not be able to affect a TEXTUAL✘ relationship until the other relevant developer shares his changes with the master repository.

Consequences: Will an action — perhaps one on a different repository — affect a relationship?
For example, a developer may be BEHIND because she has not yet incorporated from or because another developer has not yet shared with the master. In the former case, an incorporate action would affect the relationship. In the latter case, it would not.

Capable: Who can perform an action that changes the relationship?
For example, of two developers in TEXTUAL✘, the one who shares with the master first can no longer resolve the conflict, whereas the other developer can.

Ease: Who can most easily resolve a conflict?
Suppose two developers created conflicting changes and one has shared his with the master. If the other were to incorporate the changes, she would have to resolve the conflict. What if the first developer has made a set of follow-up changes that he has not yet shared? If these changes resolve the conflict, then it is likely better for the second developer to wait until the first one shares.

3.5 Limiting distractions

We designed Crystal to convey important information without being overwhelming or distracting. Towards this end, we used the following principles:

- do not asynchronously open windows,
- do not require the developer to keep the main window open,
- keep the main window compact,
- summarize all projects and relationships (allowing for quick visual identification of those that may require attention), and
- make all relationship, possible action, and guidance information available, but hidden until a developer shows specific interest.

Crystal's icons convey urgency and ability through use of color, shape, and saturation in fixed locations in the main window, and mouseover tooltips provide the rest of the information. The system tray icon summarizes the most urgent state and is available at all times, including when the main window is closed.

4. Scalability

This section describes how Crystal's design allows it to scale to large projects and compute the relevant information efficiently.

4.1 Large projects

Crystal scales to large projects that involve many developers and repositories. A developer explicitly instructs Crystal (via a GUI or a configuration file) which repositories to observe. For example, a developer may be interested in only the relationships with other developers in his collaborative team and the per-team development repositories of the other teams.

Crystal can provide information about relationships even with developers who are not using it, easing adoption by avoiding a requirement that the whole team uses the tool. Each developer can independently choose whether or not to run Crystal. Advantages accrue when more members of a team use Crystal, but this is not necessary.

Crystal allows developers to select a subset of the tests to execute, to integrate more smoothly into large development projects with extensive test suites. Naturally, for large projects with build scripts and test suites that take a long time to execute, Crystal will experience that latency. However, it would still identify relevant information sooner than other existing methods.

4.2 Computation efficiency

Crystal provides a developer with information on his development state and the relationships between his repository and collaborators' repositories. Thus, Crystal needs access to that developer's repository and working copy (if the working copy is inaccessible, Crystal does not report certain local states, e.g., uncommitted), and the locations of the other repositories. In some development environments, access to others' repositories is trivial. For example, many corporate development configurations include a common file system. In other environments, it is possible for developers to have their local repositories on machines that are often offline. For such environments, we leverage Dropbox[1] to enable developers to easily share their development states by symbolically linking their working copy to their Dropbox shared folder.

To limit the computation necessary to extract the relationships between repositories, Crystal follows the following algorithm. First, Crystal checks the history of the two repositories to identify the changesets each contains, and only re-computes the relationship if at least one history has changed. If the sets of changesets are the same, then the relationship is SAME. If one repository contains strictly more (respectively fewer) changesets, it is AHEAD (respectively BEHIND). If both repositories contain changesets the other does not (and Crystal has not previously computed their relationship), Crystal makes a local clone of one repository and uses the VCS to attempt to incorporate the changesets from the other repository. If the VCS reports a problem with incorporation, the relationship is TEXTUAL✘. If the integration succeeds, Crystal runs the build script. If that script fails, the relationship is BUILD✘. Finally, if the build script succeeds, Crystal runs the test suite and determines whether the relationship is TEST✘ or TEST✓.

Cloning repositories, especially remote ones, can be costly. To address this issue (and to enable faster start-up times), Crystal keeps a cached clone of each project, bringing it up to date before updating the relevant relationship. This has significantly increased Crystal's performance in all common cases. In the rare and discouraged situation of changing existing VC history (e.g., rebasing), the cache may contain changesets that no longer exist in a repository. This can cause problems and require the developer to clear the cache.

[1] http://www.dropbox.com

5. Contributions

We have described Crystal, a tool that proactively detects and reports on collaboration conflicts. Crystal identifies conflicts precisely and reports them unobtrusively. Developers quickly learn if there are actions they should perform and with whom they should communicate. As a result, they can limit the severity of, or even prevent, costly conflicts.

Acknowledgments

The Crystal beta users provided valuable feedback. This material is based upon work supported by the National Science Foundation under Grants CNS-0937060 to the Computing Research Association for the CIFellows Project and CCF-0963757, by a National Science and Engineering Research Council Postdoctoral Fellowship, and by Microsoft Research through a Software Engineering Innovation Foundation grant.

References

[1] J. T. Biehl, M. Czerwinski, G. Smith, and G. G. Robertson. FASTDash: A visual dashboard for fostering awareness in software teams. In *CHI*, pages 1313–1322, San Jose, CA, USA, Apr. 2007.

[2] Y. Brun, R. Holmes, M. D. Ernst, and D. Notkin. Speculative analysis: Exploring future states of software. In *FoSER*, pages 59–63, Santa Fe, NM, USA, Nov. 2010.

[3] Y. Brun, R. Holmes, M. D. Ernst, and D. Notkin. Proactive detection of collaboration conflicts. In *ESEC FSE*, Szeged, Hungary, Sep. 2011.

[4] M. Cataldo, P. A. Wagstrom, J. D. Herbsleb, and K. M. Carley. Identification of coordination requirements: Implications for the design of collaboration and awareness tools. In *CSCW*, pages 353–362, Banff, AB, Canada, Nov. 2006.

[5] C. R. B. de Souza, D. Redmiles, and P. Dourish. "Breaking the code", Moving between private and public work in collaborative software development. In *GROUP*, pages 105–114, Sanibel Island, FL, USA, Nov. 2003.

[6] P. Dewan and R. Hegde. Semi-synchronous conflict detection and resolution in asynchronous software development. In *ECSCW*, pages 159–178, Limerick, Ireland, Sep. 2007.

[7] J. Estublier and S. Garcia. Process model and awareness in SCM. In *SCM*, pages 59–74, Oxford, England, UK, Sep. 2005.

[8] R. E. Grinter. Using a configuration management tool to coordinate software development. In *CoOCS*, pages 168–177, Milpitas, CA, USA, Aug. 1995.

[9] L. Hattori and M. Lanza. Syde: A tool for collaborative software development. In *ICSE Tool Demo*, pages 235–238, Cape Town, South Africa, May 2010.

[10] S. Horwitz, J. Prins, and T. Reps. Integrating noninterfering versions of programs. *ACM TOPLAS*, 11:345–387, July 1989.

[11] D. E. Perry, H. P. Siy, and L. G. Votta. Parallel changes in large-scale software development: an observational case study. *ACM TOSEM*, 10:308–337, July 2001.

[12] T. Zimmermann. Mining workspace updates in CVS. In *MSR*, Minneapolis, MN, USA, May 2007.

Synoptic: Studying Logged Behavior with Inferred Models

Ivan Beschastnikh Jenny Abrahamson Yuriy Brun Michael D. Ernst

Computer Science & Engineering
University of Washington
{ivan,jabrah,brun,mernst}@cs.washington.edu

Abstract

Logging is a powerful method for capturing program activity and state during an execution. However, log inspection remains a tedious activity, with developers often piecing together what went on from multiple log lines and across many files. This paper describes Synoptic, a tool that takes logs as input and outputs a finite state machine that models the process generating the logs. The paper overviews the model inference algorithms. Then, it describes the Synoptic tool, which is designed to support a rich log exploration workflow.

Categories and Subject Descriptors: D.2.5 [Testing and Debugging]: Debugging aids
General Terms: Algorithms, Reliability
Keywords: log analysis, temporal invariant mining, model inference, Synoptic

1. Introduction

Examining logs is one of the most popular means of gaining insight into program execution. Developers add logging statements to record events and state transitions. The resulting logs are then inspected to find anomalies, verify correctness, debug performance, and for other tasks.

Unfortunately, developers find it difficult to inspect and reason about logged information. As an example of this consider Figure 1, which lists two log snippets based on a real log of security-related events on an OS X system. Each snippet represents a sequence of login attempts resulting in authorization. One of the two snippets contains a bug, but it is difficult to tell which one.

This paper describes Synoptic[1] — a tool that takes a log as input and infers a compact finite state machine model of the process that generated the log. Previous work has referred to this procedure as model inference, specification mining, and process discovery. For example, a longer log consisting of login attempts like the ones listed in Figure 1 can be processed with Synoptic to derive the model in Figure 4(b). This model captures the essential information necessary to understand basic temporal relationships between the logged events and can be used for various tasks by the developer. For example, this model makes it easier to notice the aforementioned bug — a failed authentication attempt sometimes results in an authorized login. The developer can also be more confident that the bug has been successfully removed by inspecting the model generated with Synoptic for a log of a system with the bug fix.

```
loginwindow[35]: Login Window Started Security Agent
May 20 16:15:27 my-mac SecurityAgent[130]: Showing Login Window
May 20 16:29:19 my-mac SecurityAgent[130]: User info context values set for jenny
May 20 16:29:19 my-mac authorizationhost[129]: Failed to authenticate user <jenny> (tDirStatus: -14090)
May 20 16:29:22 my-mac SecurityAgent[130]: User info context values set for jenny
May 20 16:29:22 my-mac SecurityAgent[130]: Login Window Showing Progress
May 20 16:29:22 my-mac SecurityAgent[130]: Login Window done
May 20 16:29:22 my-mac com.apple.SecurityServer[23]: Succeeded authorizing right
'system.login.console' by client '/System/Library/CoreServices/loginwindow.app' for authorization created
by '/System/Library/CoreServices/loginwindow.app'
```

(a)

```
loginwindow[35]: Login Window Started Security Agent
May 22 07:24:18 my-mac SecurityAgent[130]: Showing Login Window
May 22 07:25:13 my-mac SecurityAgent[130]: User info context values set for ivan
May 22 07:25:13 my-mac authorizationhost[129]: Failed to authenticate user <ivan> (tDirStatus: -14090).
May 22 07:25:15 my-mac SecurityAgent[130]: Login Window Showing Progress
May 22 07:25:15 my-mac SecurityAgent[130]: Login Window done
May 22 07:25:16 my-mac com.apple.SecurityServer[23]: Succeeded authorizing right
'system.login.console' by client '/System/Library/CoreServices/loginwindow.app' for authorization created
by '/System/Library/CoreServices/loginwindow.app'
```

(b)

Figure 1: Two log snippets based on the `/var/log/secure.log` file found in OS X 10.6.8. Each snippet represents a sequence of login attempts resulting in authorization. One of the snippets contains a security bug. Can you figure out which one? Answer is in the footnote.[2] Synoptic helps with the task of understanding what is in a log by generating a model that describes it (Figure 4(b)).

Synoptic works on logs of systems that can be modeled as a finite state machine. In particular, Synoptic cannot yet reason about concurrency. Further, the log must contain sufficient information to effectively model the system. The efficacy of a given model depends on its intended use. More concretely, Synoptic requires an input log that (1) contains one or more system executions, each of which can be thought of as a path through a finite state machine; (2) totally orders the log lines belonging to the same execution (e.g., with respect to a time field, or the ordering of lines in the file); and (3) captures the abstract event type or abstract state of the system on each line belonging to an execution.

We have previously formally evaluated Synoptic's algorithms and showed that Synoptic-generated models can help developers discover bugs [3]. In this paper, we briefly summarize Synoptic's model inference algorithm (Section 2). We then focus on the design of the Synoptic tool (Section 3) and describe how Synoptic supports a workflow in which developers spend most of their time analyzing the derived Synoptic models (Section 4). We end with a survey of related tools and techniques (Section 5).

2. How Synoptic works

Figure 2 summarizes how Synoptic works. This section overviews Synoptic's mechanisms by working through an example log based

[1] `http://synoptic.googlecode.com`

[2] The two snippets differ structurally in a single place — `User info context...` line appears twice in snippet (a) and once in snippet (b). Snippet (b) contains the bug since the user is authorized even though he failed to authenticate.

Permission to make digital or hard copies of all or part of this work for personal or classroom use is granted without fee provided that copies are not made or distributed for profit or commercial advantage and that copies bear this notice and the full citation on the first page. To copy otherwise, to republish, to post on servers or to redistribute to lists, requires prior specific permission and/or a fee.
ESEC/FSE'11, September 5–9, 2011, Szeged, Hungary.
Copyright 2011 ACM 978-1-4503-0443-6/11/09 ...$10.00.

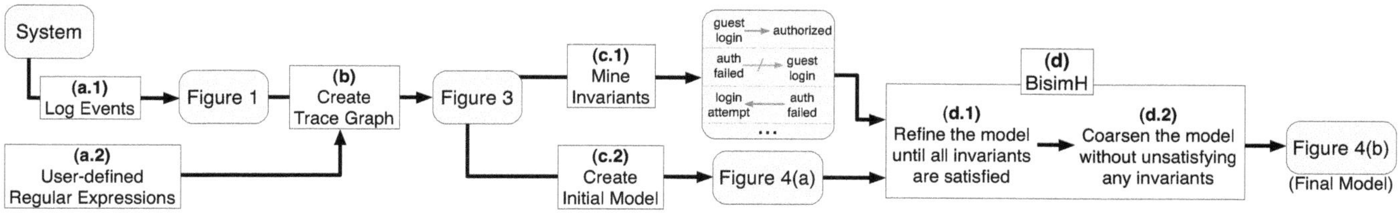

Figure 2: A step-by-step depiction of how Synoptic works.

on Figure 1. We refer the reader to [3] for a more detailed treatment of the algorithm, as well as proofs of several of its key properties.

2.1 Constructing the trace graph

Synoptic constructs a model from a set of system execution traces. It takes as input a log file containing the traces and a set of regular expressions. The log is parsed using the expressions to extract from some of the lines an *event instance*, a triplet of: (1) a trace identifier, (2) an optional timestamp, and (3) an *event type*. Trace identifiers group event instances into *traces* — linear graphs with vertices representing event instances and edges capturing their ordering. Synoptic requires event instances in a trace to be totally ordered. Timestamps may be used for this or the order could be derived implicitly from the order of lines in the log. Lastly, an event type is an arbitrary string, defined by the developer as something that conveys important information about the system.

The union of traces is a *trace graph*. Figure 3 shows a trace graph with five traces for a log based on Figure 1: a trace represents a series of login attempts ending with authorization. The traces are extracted with an implicit log line ordering and four regular expressions:

```
.+User info.+guest$(?<TYPE=>guest login)
.+User info.+(?<TYPE=>login attempt)
.+Failed to authenticate.+(?<TYPE=>failed auth)
.+Succeeded authorizing.+(?<TYPE=>authorized)
```

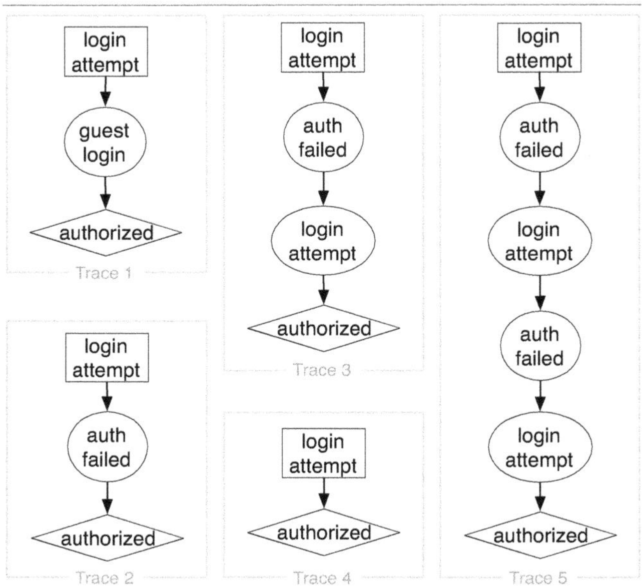

Figure 3: A trace graph representing executions parsed from a log based on Figure 1. Rectangular/diamond/oval nodes indicate initial/terminal/intermediate events. An execution represents some login attempts terminating in authorization. Trace 2 contains a bug.

2.2 Mining invariants from the trace graph

To guide model generation, Synoptic mines three kinds of temporal invariants relating *event types* from the trace graph:

a Always Followed by b ($a \to b$). Whenever the event a appears, the event b must follow later in the same trace.

a Never Followed by b ($a \not\to b$). Whenever the event a appears, the event b never appears later in the same trace.

a Always Precedes b ($a \leftarrow b$). Whenever the event b appears, the event a always appears before b in the same trace.

We term these relations "invariants" because they succinctly capture temporal event type relationships that hold true over all the input traces. These invariants are based on the most frequently observed specification patterns in Dwyer et al. [7]. In practice, we found these invariants to be sufficient for capturing key temporal properties of systems whose logs we've considered. The trace graph in Figure 3 yields 16 such invariants. One example is *auth failed* $\not\to$ *guest login*.

2.3 Synoptic models and the initial model

A Synoptic model is a *partition graph* of the trace graph. Given a partitioning of the original vertices with each partition containing event instances of the same event type, each vertex in the model represents one partition. A directed edge between two vertices indicates that there is a pair of event instances in the corresponding partitions that are adjacent with respect to the total order relation in at least one of the input traces. This model makes minimal assumptions about the underlying process that produced the logged events [9].

An important property of a Synoptic model is that each trace in the input log is accepted by a model constructed from the corresponding event instances (a trace maps to a valid path in the model). However, a Synoptic model is also generative: it may accept traces that were not present in the log.

Synoptic's core algorithm (BisimH) starts with an *initial model* in which there is one partition per event type containing all the event instances of that type. This is the most compact or abstract model. Figure 4(a) shows the initial model for the trace graph in Figure 3. BisimH then refines the initial graph until it satisfies all the invariants mined from the trace graph.

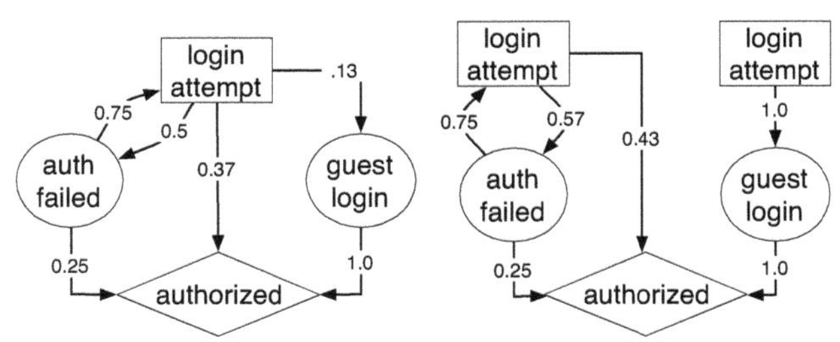

(a) Initial model (b) Final model

Figure 4: **(a)** Initial mode and **(b)** final model for the trace graph in Figure 3. Edge labels indicate transition probabilities. Note how the *login attempt* node in (a) is refined in (b).

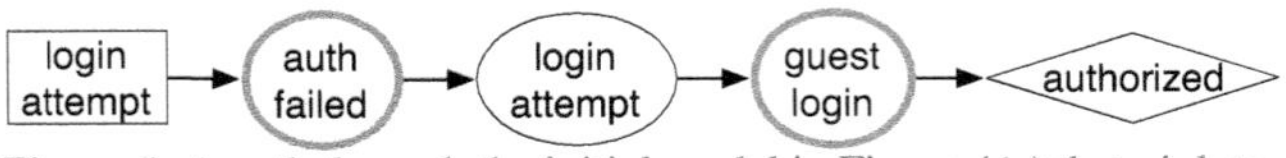

Figure 5: A path through the initial model in Figure 4(a) that violates the mined *auth failed* $\not\to$ *guest login* invariant.

2.4 Refining models to satisfy invariants

BisimH attempts to pick a minimal sequence of partition refinements (i.e., splits), to produce a smallest graph satisfying the mined invariants. This problem is NP-hard [5] so BisimH uses heuristics to produce a result that is good in practice.

BisimH performs refinement as long as some mined invariant is not satisfied by all paths in the model. It uses a model checker to check if a model satisfies a mined invariant. The checker produces a counterexample path when the model does not satisfy an invariant. For example, the invariant *auth failed* $\not\to$ *guest login* mined from the trace graph in Figure 3 is not satisfied by the initial model in Figure 4(a). Figure 5 shows the corresponding counterexample path.

Having identified a set of counterexamples that violate the mined invariants, BisimH follows the counterexample guided abstraction refinement approach [5] to identify a set of *candidate partitions*, for each of which there exists a split that removes at least one of the counterexamples. BisimH finds these partitions heuristically by tracing each counterexample, simultaneously in the initial traces and in the model. In the traces, only a prefix of the counterexample path will be present. BisimH finds the longest such prefix, and the last partition of this prefix in the model becomes a candidate for refinement — this partition allows a spurious transition in the model creating the counterexample path. The candidate partition is refined to eliminate the spurious transition. For example, to eliminate the counterexample path in Figure 5 from the model in Figure 4(a), the *context set* partition is split into the set of events that can and cannot reach any events in the *guest login* partition. Figure 4(b) shows the resulting refined model.

2.5 Compacting the model with coarsening

The BisimH algorithm may end up refining more than is necessary. When this happens, the model will contain partitions that can be merged without violating the satisfied invariants. After refinement, BisimH merges such partitions using *kTail-equivalence* [4] (k=0). The resulting merged model is locally minimal: merging any two partitions will violate some invariant. In the running example, no coarsening is necessary. Figure 4(b) is the final model.

3. Synoptic design

We designed Synoptic as a public web service that can be accessed with a browser, and also as a stand-alone application that can be downloaded to and run on a user's personal computer (both are available at `http://synoptic.googlecode.com`). These two approaches provide different trade-offs, and we support both for greater user flexibility.

Synoptic web service. A web service allows us to transparently update the code and to improve the user's experience without requiring users to download a new software version. Another important benefit is that we can transparently parallelize many of the Synoptic algorithms on the back-end, thus providing users with better performance than if Synoptic were to run on a single machine. Users can also more easily share Synoptic output with others (e.g., by sharing a URL). We also provide users with the option of downloading and running a Synoptic web service instance of their own.

Logs can be uploaded to the service as files. Or, if the developer is using log4j or log4net, the stream of logged messages can be directed to the web service using a TCP socket. The second option is preferable when the final log is too large for local storage, or if the logs are generated by and must be collected from multiple machines.

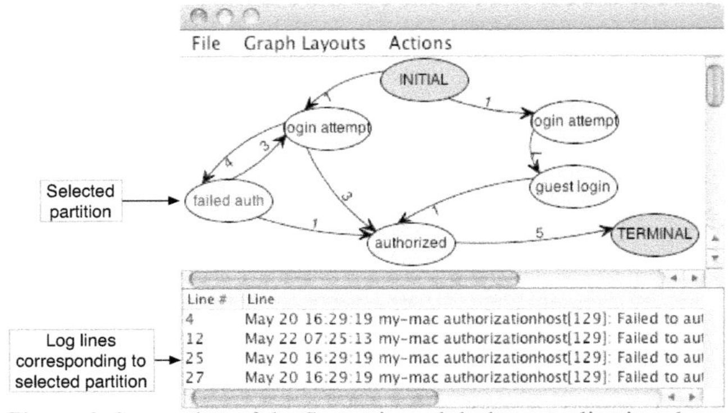

Figure 6: Screenshot of the Synoptic tool desktop application showing the final model in Figure 4(b).

Synoptic desktop application. One drawback of a web service is the latency associated with uploading large logs — the user may want a quick analysis of a log that is local. Users with proprietary logs likely also cannot use a public web service. For these reasons, Synoptic is also available as a platform-independent desktop application. It can be used from a command line or from within a GUI (see screenshot in Figure 6). However, the Synoptic's web service includes more features than the desktop version.

Next, we detail how a user interacts with Synoptic.

4. Synoptic workflow

Synoptic's workflow targets effective support of log exploration through the lens of the generated model. The workflow aims to simplify the task of log parsing, so that users can spend most of their time analyzing the derived models. This section describes how logs are parsed, and some of the model analyses that Synoptic supports.

4.1 Extracting event instance triplets

Synoptic uses regular expressions [1] to extract event instance triplets from log lines the user considers relevant (see Section 2.1).

Division into executions. A single log file may record multiple executions of a system. Synoptic provides the user with two methods for breaking up a log into executions. The user may provide *delimiter* regular expressions, in which case an execution is a contiguous set of log lines between two matched delimiters. The user may also specify some number of *mapping* regular expressions, in which case fields parsed from the log line are mapped to some trace id. Lines mapping to a trace with the same id are interpreted as belonging to the same execution. For example, the traces in Figure 3 use the `Succeeded authorizing...` line as a delimiter.

Event abstraction. Users provide regular expressions to match log lines of interest. These regular expressions must all define a capturing group named `TYPE`, which indicates the abstract event-type that will be associated with the log line. This group's value may be a hard-coded string, a concatenation of multiple groups parsed from the log line, or a combination of the two.

Ordering events in an execution. To mine temporal event invariants from executions, events in an execution must be totally ordered. Users may specify the value to use for ordering as a built-in regular expression capturing group (e.g., `FTIME` for a float-based ordering), or use the order implicit in the log file line numbers.

4.2 Invariant selection

Synoptic mines three types of temporal invariants (Section 2) to guide refinement. The choice of invariants is important because they constrain the executions a derived model may generate. By default, Synoptic uses all of the mined invariants. However, users may know that some invariants are false because the logs do not sufficiently represent possible system behavior. Synoptic assumes that the user knows more about the system than is present in the log and allows users to mark some of the mined invariants as false so that Synoptic does not use them to over-fit the model to the log.

4.3 Model exploration

Synoptic presents users with interactive models. Users can tweak and explore them in pursuit of goals ranging from a more complete understanding of their system to identifying the source of unexpected behavior. A number of features are available to aid users in manipulating the models for these purposes.

4.3.1 Matching abstract and concrete information

The user can select a partition in the model and view the log lines that correspond to this partition (Figure 6). This is useful when the user wants to unpack the partition and identify the set of events that were actually logged at this point. The user can use this information to browse to a specific line in the log file that contains the interesting event. This operation is a kind of drilling down, mapping abstract information in the model to concrete events in the log.

Synoptic models are generative — they may accept traces that are not present in the input log. A user may want to know if a trace accepted by the model was observed in the log or not. For example, to a user, a generated trace may resemble buggy behavior, and the user may want to know whether the behavior actually occurred (if so, the system contains a bug). If a generated trace is invalid, it indicates that the input log is incomplete. This may lead the user to expand the test suite to invalidate an overfitted temporal invariant, which both improves the test suite and allows Synoptic to exclude the invalid generated path from the model.

To help users distinguish these two kinds of traces, users may select multiple partitions and consider the set of concrete traces that pass through the selected partitions. Synoptic either lists all the observed traces that pass through these partitions or lets the user know that the selected sub-trace was not observed. For example, the user may select the left most *login attempt* node, along with *auth failed* and *authorized* nodes in the model in Figure 6, and find out that there is indeed an observed trace that passes through these nodes (Trace 2 in Figure 3). This more advanced capability proved to be of particular use to developers in practice. It helped them understand unexpected paths in the model by exposing the associated concrete traces from the input log.

4.3.2 Filtering rare and common behavior

Sometimes Synoptic-generated models are large and contain more information than is necessary. For example, a developer may be interested in a section of the model when seeking to pinpoint a rarely-occurring behavior. To support this use-case, Synoptic allows the developer to filter out high/low probability edges from her view of the model. More generally, the user may be interested in high/low probability traces admitted by the model. Synoptic lets the user select a start and end node, and specify the maximum/minimum path probability to use for hiding all paths between the two nodes that have a path probability outside of the desired range.

4.3.3 Comparing models

A common use-case for Synoptic models is to study how the models change with different log inputs. Log inputs may differ because of additional executions in the log, a change to the mined set of invariants, a modification to the codebase, or because of added or removed logging statements.

Synoptic displays two models side by side and highlights their differences. These may be topological (e.g., the node count is different), or statistical (e.g., the transition probability of certain edges may have increased/decreased). By studying model differences, developers can check whether system behavior is the same or different — either over different traces or different system settings.

5. Related work

Numerous log analysis tools exist; however, we know of no freely-available tool to extract finite state machine models from console logs. A popular tool choice in the enterprise is Splunk[2], which supports various analyses and understands many common log formats. Splunk's main advantage is the scalability of its analyses due to MapReduce [6]. Popular tools that are similar to Splunk are Sawmill[3] and AWStats[4]. Synoptic supports log exploration, which is a more general goal than what is targeted by tools that have a tighter focus, such as Sisyphus[5], which targets anomaly detection.

Due to space constraints, we only briefly summarize related work that deals with specification mining. We introduced the basic BisimH algorithm in a workshop paper [9], and provided a rigorous evaluation of the approach, as well as positioned it among related work, in [3]. Perracotta [10] mines and visualizes temporal properties of event traces, and has been used to study program evolution. Unlike Synoptic, Perracotta does not use the mined temporal properties to infer a model of the system. The kTail algorithm [4], used extensively in related work (e.g., [2]), takes a finite state model and produces a more compact one by recursively merging states whose root subgraphs are identical up to a depth of k. Lo et al. [8] augment the kTail algorithm with temporal properties mined from execution traces to guide state merging while ensuring that the final model satisfies temporal constraints. Synoptic produces similar high-precision models while leveraging refinement, as opposed to coarsening, to greatly increase the efficiency and scalability of the approach.

Acknowledgments

This work is supported by the National Science Foundation under grants CNS-0963754, CCF-1016701, and under grant #0937060 to the Computing Research Association for the CIFellows Project.

References

[1] Pattern (Java Platform SE 7 b141) http://download.oracle.com/javase/7/docs/api/java/util/regex/Pattern.html. Accessed July 1, 2011.

[2] M. Acharya, T. Xie, J. Pei, and J. Xu. Mining API Patterns as Partial Orders from Source Code: From Usage Scenarios to Specifications. In *Proc. of FSE*, 2007.

[3] I. Beschastnikh, Y. Brun, S. Schneider, M. Sloan, and M. D. Ernst. Leveraging Existing Instrumentation to Automatically Infer Invariant-Constrained Models. In *Proc. of FSE*, 2011.

[4] A. W. Biermann and J. A. Feldman. On the Synthesis of Finite-State Machines from Samples of Their Behavior. *IEEE Trans. Comput.*, 21(6):592–597, 1972.

[5] E. Clarke, O. Grumberg, S. Jha, Y. Lu, and H. Veith. Counterexample-guided Abstraction Refinement. In *Proc. of CAV*, 2000.

[6] J. Dean and S. Ghemawat. MapReduce: Simplified Data Processing on Large Clusters. *Commun. ACM*, 51(1):107–113, 2008.

[7] M. B. Dwyer, G. S. Avrunin, and J. C. Corbett. Patterns in Property Specifications for Finite-State Verification. In *Proc. of ICSE*, 1999.

[8] D. Lo, L. e. Mariani, and M. Pezzè. Automatic Steering of Behavioral Model Inference. In *Proc. of FSE*, 2009.

[9] S. Schneider, I. Beschastnikh, S. Chernyak, M. D. Ernst, and Y. Brun. Synoptic: Summarizing System Logs with Refinement. In *Proc. of SLAML*, 2010.

[10] J. Yang, D. Evans, D. Bhardwaj, T. Bhat, and M. Das. Perracotta: Mining Temporal API Rules from Imperfect Traces. In *Proc. of ICSE*, 2006.

[2] http://www.splunk.com

[3] http://www.sawmill.net

[4] http://awstats.sourceforge.net

[5] http://www.cs.sandia.gov/~jrstear/sisyphus

Cross-Layer Modeler – A Tool for Flexible Multilevel Modeling with Consistency Checking

Andreas Demuth
Institute for Systems Engineering and Automation
Johannes Kepler University
Linz, Austria
andreas.demuth@jku.at

Roberto E. Lopez-Herrejon
Institute for Systems Engineering and Automation
Johannes Kepler University
Linz, Austria
roberto.lopez@jku.at

Alexander Egyed
Institute for Systems Engineering and Automation
Johannes Kepler University
Linz, Austria
alexander.egyed@jku.at

ABSTRACT

Model-driven engineering has become a popular methodology in software engineering. Most available modeling tools support the creation of models based on a fixed metamodel. Typically, tool users cannot change the metamodel to reflect domain changes or newly emerged requirements. As a consequence, an updated version of the tool with an evolved metamodel must be developed and models as well as constraints that ensure model consistency have to be co-evolved, often manually, to conform to the new metamodel. Both, tool evolution and the necessary co-evolutions, are time consuming and error prone tasks. Furthermore, common tools often restrict the number of metalevels that can be modeled and force modelers to use workarounds to express certain facts. To overcome these issues we present the *Cross-Layer Modeler (XLM)*, a modeling tool that supports multilevel modeling and allows co-evolution of metamodels and models. The XLM automatically performs co-evolution of constraints and gives instant feedback about model consistency. We illustrate the novel modeling approach of our tool and discuss its main capabilities.

Categories and Subject Descriptors

I.6.5 [**Simulation and Modeling**]: Model Development

General Terms

Design, Experimentation

Keywords

Consistency checking, metamodeling, multilevel modeling

1. INTRODUCTION

Model-driven engineering (MDE) has become a popular practice to reduce development effort and to improve product quality by automatically generating artifacts from models [8]. Even though most common modeling tools use sophisticated metamodels (e.g., the *Unified Modeling Language (UML)* [7]) that allow the modeler to describe various aspects of systems in different notations, there can still arise the need for special language constructs that are not provided by the metamodel. However, modeling tools typically do not support metamodel modifications because they internally use a fixed implementation of the metamodel and rely on an immutable set of classes and their properties.

Metamodeling tools can be used to easily create domain-specific modeling tools with a metamodel that reflects a single domain. Although this simplifies updating the metamodel, there are several issues that arise with the updated version of the modeling tool. Namely, old models are likely to no longer conform to the new metamodel and require co-evolution.

Changes of metamodels do not only require tools and existing models to be updated, they can also mean that existing constraints can become syntactically incorrect or that they are checking wrong properties because of modified semantics.

In this paper, we present the *Cross-Layer Modeler (XLM)* that addresses these issues by allowing the user to modify metamodels and models at the same time. Our tool provides consistency checking and automatically updates constraints to keep them valid after metamodel changes.

In the next section, we illustrate the problems that can arise with the use of conventional modeling tools. Then, we show how the use of our tool can avoid these problems in Section 3. We give a detailed description of how our tool can be used to model an arbitrary number of metalevels at the same time, explain how we add constraints and discuss different aspects of the tool's architecture.

2. MOTIVATION

As a motivating example, we use a simple feature model of a car product line inspired by [2].

Fig. 1(a) depicts the metamodel of the used feature model. There are `Feature` elements that can be linked by `Association` elements. Every `Association` connects a `source` feature to at least one `target` feature. Features can be the source of an arbitrary number of associations. There are different kinds of associations: `Xor`, `Or`, `Mandatory`, and `Optional`. `Xor` and `Or` associations are respectively used when exactly one or at least one of several `target` sub-features

Permission to make digital or hard copies of all or part of this work for personal or classroom use is granted without fee provided that copies are not made or distributed for profit or commercial advantage and that copies bear this notice and the full citation on the first page. To copy otherwise, to republish, to post on servers or to redistribute to lists, requires prior specific permission and/or a fee.
ESEC/FSE'11, September 5–9, 2011, Szeged, Hungary.
Copyright 2011 ACM 978-1-4503-0443-6/11/09 ...$10.00.

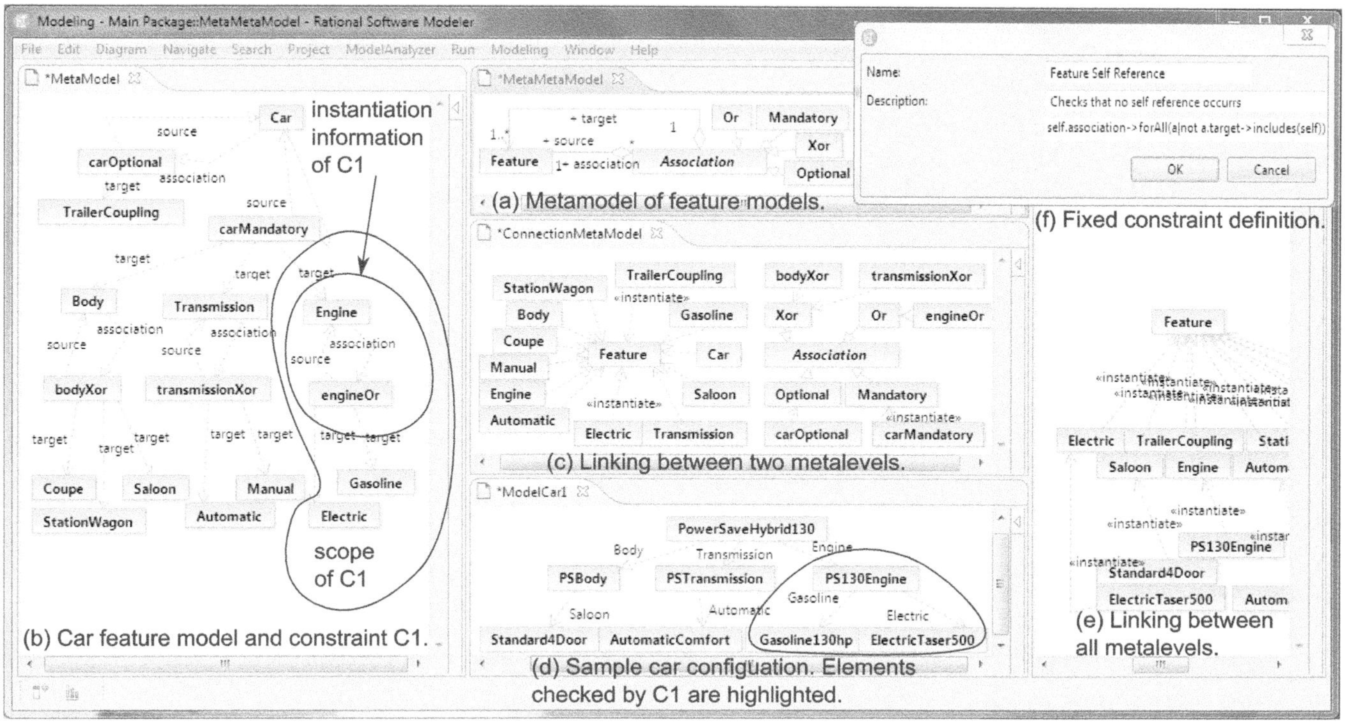

Figure 1: Screenshot of the Cross-Layer Modeler.

must be selected. The `target` of `Mandatory` associations must be selected and `target` features of `Optional` associations can be selected.

Based on this metamodel, we create the feature model of our car product line as depicted by the diagram in Fig. 1(b). A `Car` needs a `Body`, a `Transmission`, an `Engine` and can have a `TrailerCoupling`. The `Transmission` can be either `Automatic` or `Manual`. The `Engine` can be `Electric` or `Gasoline` powered, hybrid models can have both. One of three different `Body` types must be used: `Convertible`, `Saloon`, or `Coupe`. Note that for readability reasons we displayed only references from `Association` elements to features and omitted reference names.

Now that we have created a metamodel and a feature model for our small product line, we want to model a product configuration that consists of concrete realizations of the defined features. At this point, we face a challenge: modeling more than two metalevels (e.g., the metamodel and the feature model).

When we create an instance of a metamodel element (e.g., `Feature`) to define a feature (e.g., `Body`), the actual class of the created objects is the UML type `InstanceSpecification`, which means that we cannot create instances of `Body`, for example to describe a concrete feature realization.

The typical workaround is to define a class `FeatureRealization` and create a reference to the realized `Feature`. However, this approach leads to a counterintuitive situation where features and their realizations are situated at the same metalevel, namely they are all defined and also instantiated at the `M1` (User Model) level directly underneath the `M2` (UML) level (as discussed in [1]). Next, we explain how we addressed this issue.

3. CROSS-LAYER MODELER

The Cross-Layer Modeler allows multilevel modeling of arbitrary numbers of modeling layers. Every model element, regardless of its metalevel, can be instantiated to create an element at the next metalevel underneath. It should be noted that our tool does not impose any restrictions in terms of instantiations or connections between model elements at different levels. In contrast to the UML where different elements have different meanings and properties (e.g., `Usage` and `Generalization` connections), in XLM model elements and connections do not have a meaning unless it is assigned by the addition of type information (e.g., `Body` is an instance of `Feature`) or constraints (e.g., every `Feature` instance can have an arbitrary number of `Association` instances assigned to it).

Most parts of modeling, including instantiations, are performed visually. The user can decide whether the modeling of various aspects of the system is done in a single or in multiple diagrams, the latter allows a clear visual separation of metalevels or other concerns. Instances of selected model elements as well as all of its attributes are displayed in a separate view to provide a quick overview even when the information is not explicitly shown in the diagram. We will illustrate the modeling by extending our sample product line by a product configuration next.

3.1 Building models

As it can be seen in Fig. 1(b), we use UML `Class` elements instead of `InstanceSpecification` elements to define various features such as `Body` or `Engine`. Since we want to keep model and metamodel in different diagrams to achieve a clear visual separation, we use a separate diagram for instantiations between the two levels. Fig. 1(c) depicts how we use UML `Usage` elements (dashed connections) with an `instantiate` stereotype to model instantiations of features (left side) and associations (right side) (most stereotype labels are omitted in the figure for readability reasons).

Now we create a concrete configuration that is assembled from several artifacts that implement different features, this configuration is shown in Fig. 1(d). The `PowerSaveHybrid130` has a body (`PSBody`), a transmission (`PSTransmission`) and an engine (`PS130Engine`) designed especially for the PowerSave series. The body is a `Standard4Door` version, the `PSTransmission` is based on the `AutomaticComfort` transmission and the `PS130Engine` is a combination of the `Gasoline130hp` and the `ElectricTaser500` engines. In this configuration, the car does not provide a trailer coupling. In the same way we did it in Fig. 1(c), we can use a separate diagram to define that the used model elements are realizations of features. We use the same kind of connection to indicate that a model element follows the concepts defined by another element, like instantiations of classes or realizations of features, as shown in Fig. 1(e).

For references between model elements we use UML `Dependency` connections. The source element of the connection owns a reference with the connection's name to the target. For example, `PS130Engine.Gasoline` refers to `Gasoline130hp`.

Note that the modeling we have done so far, except for the instantiations, does not add any semantics to model elements and that there are no rules that restrict the addition of connections between arbitrary elements. Next, we describe how we add semantics and restrict the freedom of modeling to only allow correct models.

3.2 Adding constraints

In our tool, there are two ways of adding constraints to models: i) add a *constraint template* or ii) add a *fixed constraint*. Constraint templates are automatically instantiated to create constraints that check properties that are not known in advance. For example, we can define a template `T1` to ensure that for every `Or` association and its source `Feature` we check that realizations of the `Feature` have references to realizations of the association's `target` features. This template generates a specific constraint for every `Or` association and its `source` in the model.

A template consists of the *instantiation context*, the types of the elements that are needed for an instantiation (e.g., `Feature` and `Or` in case of `T1`). We specify the desired *abstract constraint* with a rule language statement (e.g., in OCL [9]), parts of the constraint that are different for every instantiation of the template are expressed with placeholders. For example, we define the abstract constraint of `T1` as:

```
context FEATURE inv:  not self.allReferences->
excludesAll(TARGETS).
```

Then, we define how concrete values for the placeholders are retrieved. We can use the elements required for instantiation - called the *instantiation information* - to retrieve the values `Feature.name` for `FEATURE` and `Or.target->collect(name)` for `TARGETS`. The resulting *concrete constraint* is:

```
context Engine inv:  not self.allReferences->
excludesAll({'Gasoline', 'Electric'}).
```

Fig. 1(b) shows the instantiation information (`Engine` and `engineOr`) and the elements that are additionally accessed

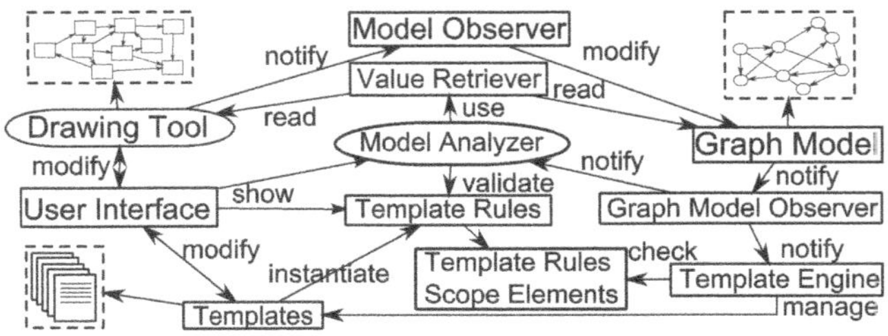

Figure 2: Architecture of Cross-Layer Modeler.

(`Gasoline` and `Electric`) when `T1` is instantiated to create `C1`. As it can be seen highlighted in Fig. 1(d), our sample configuration is consistent with `C1` because `PS130Engine` has a reference named `Gasoline` to `Gasoline130hp` and a reference named `Electric` to `ElectricTaser500`.

Fixed constraints are used to check properties that are equal for all instances of a type, for example a constraint could check that every `FeatureModel` does not contain two different features with the same name.

Our tool provides several wizards for the definition of templates and fixed constraints, as seen in Fig. 1(f). There are also various views that inform the user about constraints defined on selected model elements, all defined constraints, model inconsistencies and more. Because we perform the consistency checking incrementally, feedback about model consistency is provided instantly after every model change.

In addition to the creation of different metalevels at the same time and consistency checking, another key aspect of our tool is the flexibility in terms of model evolution.

3.3 Evolving models

The XLM does not only allow the user to perform typical modifications like adding and removing elements from the model, but it also supports changes of the types of model elements at runtime. As an example, lets assume that because of new laws our `Standard4Door` feature realization is now legally treated as a station wagon. We can easily adapt to this new situation by changing the type from `Saloon` to `StationWagon` without the need of creating a new element or performing any other changes (note that in standard modeling tools, changing the type of an instance is typically not possible). However, changing the type means that our sample configuration in Fig. 1(d) is no longer valid because `PSBody` must refer to `Standard4Door` via `StationWagon` now.

Constraints derived from constraint templates are automatically updated if model elements that provided specific information for the constraint are modified. For example, changing the name of the element `Gasoline` to `Gas` in Fig. 1(b) triggers an update of the constraint `C1` because the modified element is part of the constraint's *scope*, the set of elements that are accessed during template instantiation (illustrated by the highlighted area in Fig. 1(b)). The updated constraint then requires a reference named `Gas` instead of `Gasoline`.

Now that we have presented the most important features of the XLM, we will have a look at its architecture in the next section.

3.4 Tool Architecture

Fig. 2 illustrates the overall architecture of the Cross-Layer Modeler. Encircled we indicate the connections of our tool with other existing components, dashed boxes indicate artifacts (e.g., models and template files). We employed the *IBM Rational Software Modeler (RSM)* as a front-end drawing tool. We addressed the issues previously highlighted in Section 2 by using a graph-oriented model (`GraphModel`) that consists of `Node` and `Association` elements. Every model element, independent from the type it models or the metalevel it resides on, is an instance of `Node`. Instantiation of modeled types is emulated by a reference `type` between two nodes. This means that we can treat every element at every metalevel equally without having to deal with different classes and their properties. The graph model is kept up to date by the `Model Observer`, which is notified about changes of the drawing tool and performs the required steps to reflect these changes in the graph model.

The templates that describe the desired behavior of models are managed by the `TemplateEngine` component. The engine handles the creation of `Template Rules` (i.e., rules that were created through template instantiation) and is also responsible for updates of outdated rules. Rules are considered as outdated by the template engine when parts of their scopes (i.e., the model elements that were used during instantiation to derive concrete values to replace the variables in the abstract specification of a template) are changed.

The `Model Analyzer` [5] component is responsible for validating rules and checking the model's consistency. Note that the component also handles rules that were not derived from templates but directly added by the user, which is omitted in Fig. 2. We use a `Value Retriever` component to extract values required during rule validation.

The `Graph Model` informs the `Graph Model Observer` about changes. This observer generates change notifications and notifies both the `Template Engine` and the `Model Analyzer` so that they can start a re-validation of affected rules or trigger the creation or an update of `Template Rules`.

3.5 Preliminary Evaluation

We performed several tests with our tool and compared its consistency checking performance to the reference implementation of the *Model Analyzer* [5] consistency checker. The results show that the higher complexity of our implementation – based on the template mechanism and more complex type handling – does not impose noticeable performance drawbacks as feedback about model consistency is provided within milliseconds after a model change occurred. For the future, we plan to do extensive analysis of this impact with large-scale industrial models.

4. RELATED WORK

Even though there are various approaches that address the issue of model and metamodel co-evolution (e.g., *Epsilon Flock* by Rose et al. [6]), less work has focused on the co-evolution of (meta)models and constraints.

In terms of flexible modeling, the *Generic Modeling Environment (GME)* is a well known configurable environment that allows the modeler to specify metamodels and generate domain-specific modeling environments [3]. They use a sophisticated, yet fixed, set of concepts to describe these metamodels, therefore there are still possible restrictions.

Another tool that focuses on flexibility is the *Business Insight Toolkit (BITKit)* developed by IBM [4]. It allows the user to create diagrams and add semantics to graphical elements afterwards. This approach is also used in our tool where we can create elements and change their type anytime, although we do not provide such a visual experience yet.

5. CONCLUSIONS AND FUTURE WORK

In this paper we have shown that the Cross-Layer Modeler supports the modeling of multiple metalevels and gives the user the freedom to change types of model elements as well as semantics at any time. The simple notation and the clear design principles enable even novice users to work with our tool. Currently our tool is in an early prototype stage, nevertheless it provides full functionality in terms of modeling multiple metalevels and checking the conformance of models to their metamodels.

For future releases we plan to enrich the visual experience during modeling and to add more flexibility and guidance regarding the definition of constraints, for example dynamic code-completion during constraint or template authoring.

Even though we focused on a small product line example, we believe that our tool is suitable for modeling various domains where it is necessary to use multiple metalevels or where aspects of the domain are likely to change.

6. ACKNOWLEDGMENTS

We would like to gratefully acknowledge the Austrian Science Fund (FWF) through grant P21321-N15 and the EU Marie Curie Actions – Intra European Fellowship (IEF) through project number 254965.

7. REFERENCES

[1] Colin Atkinson and Thomas Kühne. The essence of multilevel metamodeling. In *UML*, pages 19–33. Springer, 2001.

[2] Krzysztof Czarnecki and Ulrich W. Eisenecker. Components and generative programming. In *ESEC / SIGSOFT FSE*, pages 2–19. Springer, 1999.

[3] Ákos Lédeczi, Arpad Bakay, Miklos Maroti, Péter Völgyesi, Greg Nordstrom, Jonathan Sprinkle, and Gabor Karsai. Composing domain-specific design environments. *IEEE Computer*, 34(11):44–51, 2001.

[4] Harold Ossher, Rachel K. E. Bellamy, Ian Simmonds, David Amid, Ateret Anaby-Tavor, Matthew Callery, Michael Desmond, Jacqueline de Vries, Amit Fisher, and Sophia Krasikov. Flexible modeling tools for pre-requirements analysis: conceptual architecture and research challenges. In *OOPSLA*, pages 848–864. ACM, 2010.

[5] Alexander Reder and Alexander Egyed. Model/analyzer: a tool for detecting, visualizing and fixing design errors in UML. In *ASE*, pages 347–348. ACM, 2010.

[6] Louis M. Rose, Dimitrios S. Kolovos, Richard F. Paige, and Fiona A. C. Polack. Model migration with epsilon flock. In *ICMT*, pages 184–198. Springer, 2010.

[7] James Rumbaugh, Ivar Jacobson, and Grady Booch. *The Unified Modeling Language Reference Manual (2nd Edition)*. Pearson Higher Education, 2004.

[8] Douglas C. Schmidt. Guest editor's introduction: Model-driven engineering. *IEEE Computer*, 39(2):25–31, 2006.

[9] Jos Warmer and Anneke Kleppe. *The Object Constraint Language: Precise Modeling with UML*. Addison Wesley Longman, Inc., 1999.

Tool Support for UML-Based Specification and Verification of Role-Based Access Control Properties

Lionel Montrieux Michel Wermelinger Yijun Yu
Centre for Research in Computing & Computing Department
The Open University, Milton Keynes, UK
L.M.C.Montrieux@open.ac.uk M.A.Wermelinger@open.ac.uk Y.Yu@open.ac.uk

ABSTRACT

It has been argued that security perspectives, of which access control is one, should be taken into account as early as possible in the software development process. Towards that goal, we present in this paper a tool supporting our modelling approach to specify and verify access control in accordance to the NIST standard Role-Based Access Control (RBAC). RBAC is centred on mapping users to their roles in an organisation, to make access control permissions easier to set and maintain.

Our modelling approach uses only standard UML mechanisms, like metamodels and OCL constraints, and improves on existing approaches in various ways: designers don't have to learn new languages or adopt new tools or methodologies; user-role and role-permission assignments can be specified separately to be reused across models; access control is specified over class and activity diagrams, including 'anti-scenarios'; access control is automatically verified. The tool is built on top of an existing modelling IDE and allows for automatic verification of models according to our RBAC modelling approach, while providing users with the ability to easily identify and correct errors in the model when they are detected.

Categories and Subject Descriptors: D.2.2 [**Software Engineering**]: Design Tools and Techniques — *Computer-Aided Software Engineering*

General Terms: Security, Verification.

Keywords: Security, UML, RBAC, model, verification, OCL, Model-Driven Engineering.

1. INTRODUCTION

Security is a growing concern in the software engineering community [8]. As software systems are increasingly connected and handle more and more sensitive data, making sure that access is restricted to only those who are authorised becomes a crucial concern. Giving users access to too much data or processes will increase the risk of misuse, while not giving users the permissions they actually need will prevent them from getting their work done.

Too often is security dealt with at the end of a software development project, leading to ill-designed systems with poor protection of data and other assets. As Fernandez-Medina et al. point out [4], security would greatly benefit from being taken into account as early as possible in the software development process, for example as part of a Model-Driven Engineering process. This would make it easier to: keep track of security requirements and to make sure that the security measures that have been selected actually enforce those requirements; handle change and its impact on security; communicate the security measures to the stakeholders who do not have a computer science background and are not able or not willing to read code.

This paper presents tool support for modelling RBAC configurations and properties on several UML diagrams, and for verifying that the model actually does enforce those access control properties. The tool is a part of a modelling IDE, allowing users to use it in a familiar environment, together with their usual modelling activities.

The paper is organised as follows: we present background and related work in Section 2, then introduce the tool and the approach it supports in Section 3. We discuss future work in Section 4 and conclude in Section 5.

2. BACKGROUND

In this section, we present the RBAC standard, as well as existing Model-Driven Security approaches.

2.1 RBAC

RBAC is an access control model that has been standardised by the NIST [9]. The main idea behind RBAC is to map users to roles and roles to permissions, instead of mapping users to permissions directly. Roles are supposed to match the users' actual roles in an organisation. Since roles, and not users, are assigned permissions, it makes access control configuration easier to maintain within an organisation: when a new person joins, the administrator only has to assign her to the roles she needs to get her work done. If that person's responsibilities within the organisation change later, then it's just a matter of adding and/or removing roles. If a role's responsibilities change, then changing the role's permissions accordingly will be reflected in what all the users assigned to that role can and cannot do.

The RBAC standard is divided in four different levels, each level adding new functionalities on top of the previous one. Level 0 defines user-role assignments as well as

Permission to make digital or hard copies of all or part of this work for personal or classroom use is granted without fee provided that copies are not made or distributed for profit or commercial advantage and that copies bear this notice and the full citation on the first page. To copy otherwise, to republish, to post on servers or to redistribute to lists, requires prior specific permission and/or a fee.
ESEC/FSE'11, September 5–9, 2011, Szeged, Hungary.
Copyright 2011 ACM 978-1-4503-0443-6/11/09 ...$10.00.

Level	Features
0	users, roles, permissions
1	role hierarchies
2	constraints (Separation of Duty)
3	review

Table 1: RBAC features for each level

role-permission assignments. Each user can be assigned any number of roles, and each role can be assigned any number of permissions. Level 1 adds role hierarchies: these are partial orders in which roles can inherit other roles' permissions. Level 1a, also called General Hierarchical RBAC, supports arbitrary partial orders, while level 1b, also called Limited Hierarchical RBAC, comes with limited partial orders. The limitation depends on the vendor's choice. Next, level 2 adds Separation of Duty (SoD) constraints: to prevent conflicts of interest, it is possible to forbid a user to be granted two roles at the same time. This enforcement can be done either at the user-role assignment level, using static constraints, or within a session, using dynamic constraints. Finally, level 3 adds a permission-role assignment review requirement: it must be possible to review which roles are assigned to a specific permission, and which permissions are assigned to a specific role. Table 2.1 summarises each level's requirements.

2.2 Model-Driven Engineering

Model-Driven Engineering (MDE) is the software engineering approach that is built around the principle that *everything is a model.* Models are defined according to a metamodel, but the growing number of metamodels led to another higher level to describe metamodels: meta-metamodels [3]. Several organisations and companies propose platforms to support MDE. One of them, arguably the most widely used, is the OMG's Model-Driven Architecture approach [10], which includes UML (Unified Modeling Language) models, OCL (Object Constraint Language) constraints and MOF (Meta-Object Facility) metamodels and meta-metamodels.

In the security world, Fernandez-Medina et al. point out that "*current approaches which take security into consideration from the early stages of software development do not take advantage of Model-Driven Development*"[4], but it is a direction that is being developed, including by Basin et al. [2], who define Model-Driven Security (MDS) as a specialisation of MDE, where "*a designer builds a system model along with security requirements, and automatically generates from this a complete, configured security infrastructure*".

2.3 Modelling RBAC properties on UML

Several approaches exist for modelling RBAC properties on UML. UMLsec [6] uses UML's extension mechanisms to express security properties. It is not limited to access control, but its support of RBAC is limited, as it does not support all the levels of the standard. RBAC properties can be defined on activity diagrams only. Tool support exists to verify models against the RBAC properties.

Another approach, SecureUML [7], uses class diagrams instead of activity diagrams to express access control configurations and properties. Classes are used to model users and roles, and association classes give permissions. SecureUML can also generate EJB code enforcing the RBAC properties.

Finally, authUML [1] allows one to define RBAC properties on use case diagrams, which are usually used early in the development cycle. authUML modelling is done in three consecutive steps: first, defining and processing access control requirements, by transforming the requirements into predicates; second, ensuring consistency, completeness and conflict-free accesses of Use Cases; third, ensuring consistency, completeness and conflict-free accesses for operations. We are not aware of any tool support for authUML.

3. OUR APPROACH

Our approach differs from the other ones in that it allows one to model RBAC configurations and properties on several UML diagrams. We use the standard UML extension mechanisms to provide extra annotation capabilities to existing UML diagrams: class diagrams, activity diagrams, and access control diagrams, that are a custom version of class diagrams to model users, roles, permissions, and their assignments.

It is also different from other approaches by including anti-scenarios: while other approaches focus only on verifying that a specific user has access to a specific resource, we also allow one to model anti-scenarios, where a specific user *must not* have access to a specific resource.

3.1 RBAC profile

The access control configuration can be seen on the access control diagram: users, roles and permissions are represented using stereotyped classes. Associations between users and roles and between roles and permissions are the assignments. The entire RBAC standard is supported: role hierarchies can be represented using class generalisation, and SoD constraints can be expressed using OCL constraints.

The class diagram allows one to stereotype operations whose access should be restricted. These stereotypes must come with at least one association to a permission in the access control diagram. The set of associations represents the permissions needed to perform the operation.

Finally, the activity diagram is the place where the access control properties are defined: stereotyped partitions represent users, and those stereotypes must come with an association with a user in the access control diagram. Stereotyped partitions also come with associations to roles: these are the roles that the user represented by the partition has activated before the activity starts. This set of roles must necessarily be a subset of the roles assigned to the user. Then, actions in the diagram can also be stereotyped. An action that a user needs to be able to perform is stereotyped with «**`granted`**», while an anti-scenario, i.e. an action that a user can never be able to perform is stereotyped with «**`forbidden`**». Both these stereotypes come with associations to operations in the class diagram, that describe the operations involved in the action. Actions can also be stereotyped with «**`activateRoles`**» (resp. «**`deactivateRoles`**») to express that a set of roles is activated (resp. deactivated) before the action starts, and deactivated (resp. re-activated) right after it finishes.

Figure 1 is a sample model annotated using our approach. It represents a system allowing professors and teaching assistants to fill a database with students' marks. The students are only able to read their marks. There is a hierarchy relationship between professors and teaching assistants so that users assigned with the Professor role inherit from the permissions assigned to the Teaching Assistant role. The model is made of one access control diagram, one class diagram and one activity diagram. In the activity diagram, the user Doe starts the activity with no role activated, and activates the Student role to perform an action. This is to demonstrate the possibility to activate roles for a specific action. Associations between stereotypes are normally not visible on the diagrams, but we have represented them as notes for the reader's convenience.

3.2 Consistency

Because we use several types of diagrams, it is essential to ensure that they do not contradict each other. To enforce consistency between diagrams, we have defined a set of 20 OCL constraints. For example, one of them makes sure that an action stereotyped with «**granted**» is not also stereotyped with «**forbidden**»: it would not make sense to have an action that a user must at the same time *always* be able to perform and *never* be able to perform.

SoD constraints can be added by the user to the profile. While static SoD ensures that the same user can not be assigned both of two roles, dynamic SoD only enforces that these two roles can not be activated in the same time. Static SoD is verified on the access control diagram, by checking the user-role assignments while taking role hierarchies into account. Dynamic SoD is verified on activity diagrams, by making sure that the two conflicting roles are not activated in the same time on a single action.

3.3 Verification

The verification of RBAC properties is done using two similar OCL contraints: one for actions stereotyped with «**granted**», and another one for actions stereotyped with «**forbidden**». In both cases, we compute two sets: the set $Perm_{needed}$ of permissions required for the action to be performed, and the set $Perm_{activated}$ of permissions that the user has activated when s/he tries to perform the action. For actions stereotyped with «**granted**», the verification succeedes if the user has activated at least all the permissions required, i.e. if $Perm_{needed} \subseteq Perm_{activated}$. For actions stereotyped with «**forbidden**», the verifications suceeds if the user has not activated all the required permissions, i.e. if $Perm_{needed} \nsubseteq Perm_{activated}$.

3.4 Implementation

Our approach has been implemented as a UML profile for IBM Rational Software Architect [5]. The profile, together with a few sample models, are available online[1].

During the modelling process, the model will go through stages where it violates one or several constraints. Live evaluation, i.e. evaluation of the constraints every time a change is performed to the model, is therefore not suitable for this approach, as it would trigger a lot of unnecessary errors. The OCL constraints are therefore verified in batch mode. The tool then issues errors and warning that indicate which OCL constraint has been violated and where, both in the console and in the diagram, as one can see in Figure 2. The verification of the example in Figure 1 takes about 3 seconds on a computer with a 2.53GHz Intel i5 M 460 CPU and 4GB of RAM, using Rational Software Architect version 8.0.1

Our RBAC profile can simply be added to an existing modelling project, and it is possible to use it immediately.

[1]http://computing-research.open.ac.uk/rbac

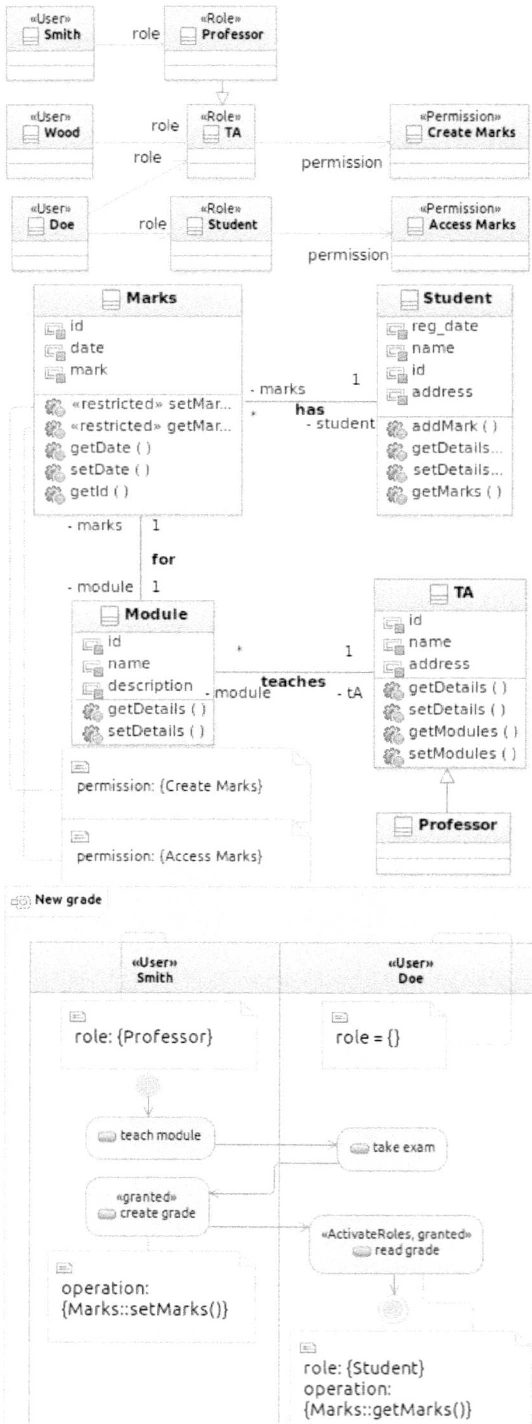

Figure 1: A sample model of a students' mark system

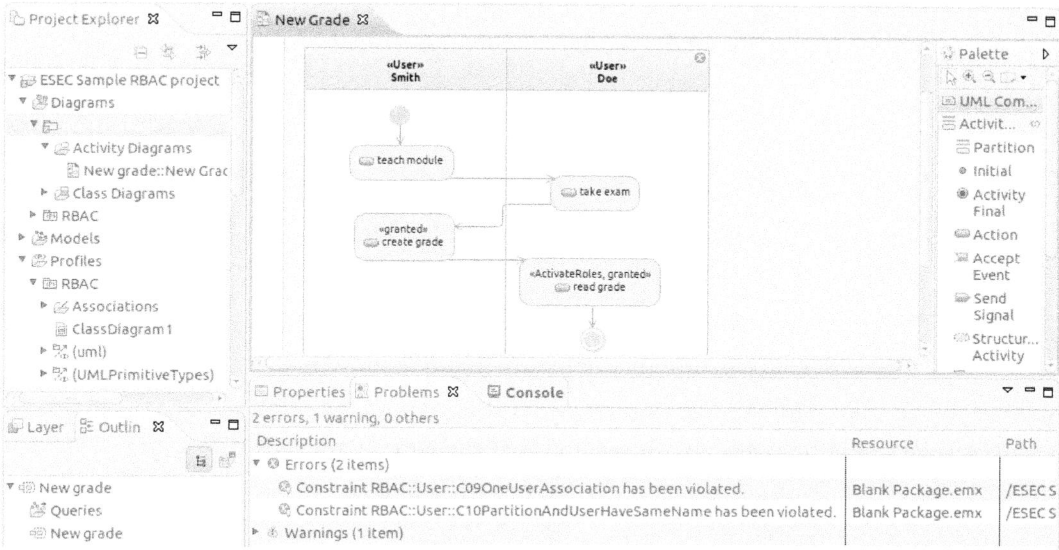

Figure 2: Screenshot of the tool showing errors in the model

The OCL validation command will then verify the annotated model against the RBAC properties specified on the activity diagrams. If errors are found, they are reported both on the graphical representation of the model and in an error message. The combination of both notifications makes it easy to identify where a problem lies, and what constraint the model violates. The tool stays out of the way of the user, allowing her to proceed with her modelling activities, especially those not directly related to access control concerns.

4. FUTURE WORK

Future releases of the software will extend the metamodel and support model evolution.

The extension of our approach's metamodel will allow us to support more UML diagrams, such as sequence diagrams. Each type of diagram provides a different view on the software, and it is important to be able to represent access control in each of the views in which it makes sense to do so.

Software evolution is the other direction we will follow to improve our tool, both for step-by-step evolution and for software merging. After a sequence of changes, only the OCL rules whose evaluation may have been impacted should be re-checked. Repair actions will then be suggested when a model is found insecure, in order to fix it.

Merge situations typically arise when two organisations become one. They will eventually have to merge their access control configurations and properties. We will provide support to help users during the merge operations, by detecting potential conflicts as well as similar elements that might be merged, and by providing repair actions to make the resulting model satisfy the merged properties.

5. CONCLUSION

We presented a UML profile for Rational Software Architect that allows one to model RBAC configurations and properties on a UML model, using three different types of diagrams. The profile contains OCL constraints that ensure that the RBAC-related annotations are consistent, and will raise both textual and visual errors when they are violated. OCL constraints can also be used to enforce static and dynamic SoD constraints. The verification of the RBAC properties expressed on activity diagrams is performed with two OCL constraints that make use of the annotations in the three supported types of diagrams to make sure that the annotated model does enforce the properties expressed. Although the profile has been developed for use with Rational Software Architect, the fact that we only use standard technologies makes it easy to port to other modelling IDEs that support modelling of UML models, extensions of the UML metamodel, and verification of OCL constraints.

6. REFERENCES

[1] K. Alghathbar and D. Wijesekera. authUML: a three-phased framework to analyze access control specifications in use cases. In *Proceedings of the 2003 ACM workshop on Formal methods in security engineering*, FMSE '03, pages 77–86, 2003.

[2] D. A. Basin, J. Doser, and T. Lodderstedt. Model driven security for process-oriented systems. In *SACMAT*, pages 100–109. ACM, 2003.

[3] J. Bézivin, F. Jouault, and D. Touzet. Principles, Standards and Tools for Model Engineering. In *ICECCS*, pages 28–29. IEEE Computer Society, 2005.

[4] E. Fernández-Medina, J. Jürjens, J. Trujillo, and S. Jajodia. Model-Driven Development for secure information systems. *Information & Software Technology*, 51(5):809–814, 2009.

[5] IBM. Rational Software Architect 8.1, 2010.

[6] J. Jürjens. *Secure Systems Development with UML.* Springer-Verlag, 2005.

[7] T. Lodderstedt, D. A. Basin, and J. Doser. SecureUML: A UML-Based Modeling Language for Model-Driven Security. In *Proceedings of the 5th International Conference on The Unified Modeling Language*, UML '02, pages 426–441, 2002.

[8] J. Münther. On the Security of Security Software: Invited Position Paper. *Electr. Notes Theor. Comput. Sci.*, 142:5–10, 2006.

[9] R. S. Sandhu, D. F. Ferraiolo, and D. R. Kuhn. The NIST model for role-based access control: towards a unified standard. In *ACM Workshop on Role-Based Access Control*, pages 47–63, 2000.

[10] R. Soley and the OMG staff. Model Driven Architecture. white paper, November 2000. http://www.omg.org/cgi-bin/doc?omg/00-11-05 (Last accessed 14 June 2010).

SafeSlice: A Model Slicing and Design Safety Inspection Tool for SysML

Davide Falessi[1,2] Shiva Nejati[1] Mehrdad Sabetzadeh[1] Lionel Briand[1] Antonio Messina[2]

[1]Simula Research Laboratory
Oslo, Norway

[2] University of Rome (Tor Vergata)
Rome, Italy

{falessi,shiva,mehrdad,briand}@simula.no ant.messina@gmail.com

ABSTRACT

Software safety certification involves checking that the software design meets the (software) safety requirements. In practice, inspections are one of the primary vehicles for ensuring that safety requirements are satisfied by the design. Unless the safety-related aspects of the design are clearly delineated, the inspections conducted by safety assessors would have to consider the entire design, although only small fragments of the design may be related to safety. In a model-driven development context, this means that the assessors have to browse through large models, understand them, and identify the safety-related fragments. This is time-consuming and error-prone, specially noting that the assessors are often third-party regulatory bodies who were not involved in the design. To address this problem, we describe in this paper a prototype tool called, SafeSlice, that enables one to automatically extract the safety-related slices (fragments) of design models. The main enabler for our slicing technique is the traceability between the safety requirements and the design, established by following a structured design methodology that we propose. Our work is grounded on SysML, which is being increasingly used for expressing the design of safety-critical systems. We have validated our work through two case studies and a control experiment which we briefly outline in the paper.

Categories and Subject Descriptors

D.2.1 [**Software Engineering**]: Requirements/Specifications

General Terms

Design, Verification

Keywords

Safety Certification, SysML, Traceability, Model Slicing

1. INTRODUCTION

Models have long been used for capturing the design of safety-critical software in domains such as avionics, railways, maritime, and automotive. In addition to being one of the main drivers of the development process, models in these domains further serve as a key source of information for third-party assessment activities, particularly certification, where an external professional or regulatory body needs to verify that a system does not pose unacceptable risks to people or the environment. An important step in the certification process is for the assessing body to review (inspect) the design models and ensure that the design meets the safety requirements.

The tool we describe in this paper, SafeSlice, was motivated by the difficulties we observed during third-party inspections of the design of safety-critical software. The focus of our investigation was on the inspections performed during the certification of integrated control systems in the maritime and energy sector, but similar problems can be expected in other safety-critical domains, such as the automotive sector, where (software) safety certification is an emerging topic. In particular, we observed that the design models could be large and their safety-related aspect not clearly identifiable. Subsequently, checking compliance between the safety requirements and the design turned into a time-consuming endeavor, often forcing the inspector to browse through large models and manually analyzing a large numbers of dependencies before the safety-related design aspects could be determined.

To address this problem, we have developed a model slicing algorithm that enables inspectors to automatically extract model slices (fragments) related to safety requirements. This reduces inspection effort, and further makes it less likely that safety issues would be overlooked. Of course, this automation does not come for free and requires the development team to follow certain guidelines to link the safety requirements to the design. In [4], we elaborate a design methodology which ensures that the traceability links required for automated slicing are properly established. The methodology and the slicing algorithm in [4] are the basis for the SafeSlice tool that we describe in this paper.

Specifically, SafeSlice enables users to: 1) specify the traceability links envisaged by our design methodology, 2) check the consistency of the established links, and 3) automatically extract slices of design with respect to requirements. These slices can then be used for conducting inspections and ensuring that the design satisfies the safety requirements. In addition to implementing our proposed traceability mechanism and slicing algorithm, SafeSlice provides facilities for managing inspections and report generation.

We ground our work on the Systems Modeling Language (SysML) [7], as SysML is becoming the de-facto modeling standard for systems engineering [6]. Since safety is a system issue, and not just a software issue, this was a natural choice to ease the adoption of our approach in practice.

The rest of the paper describes the SafeSlice tool and summarizes the evaluation we have done to validate the approach behind it.

2. TOOL OVERVIEW

Figure 1 shows a high-level view of the process implemented by the SafeSlice tool. The process consists of three main steps: (1) Establishing traceability between safety requirements and SysML

Permission to make digital or hard copies of all or part of this work for personal or classroom use is granted without fee provided that copies are not made or distributed for profit or commercial advantage and that copies bear this notice and the full citation on the first page. To copy otherwise, to republish, to post on servers or to redistribute to lists, requires prior specific permission and/or a fee.

ESEC/FSE'11, September 5–9, 2011, Szeged, Hungary.

Copyright 2011 ACM 978-1-4503-0443-6/11/09 ...$10.00.

Figure 1: Method of use for SafeSlice.

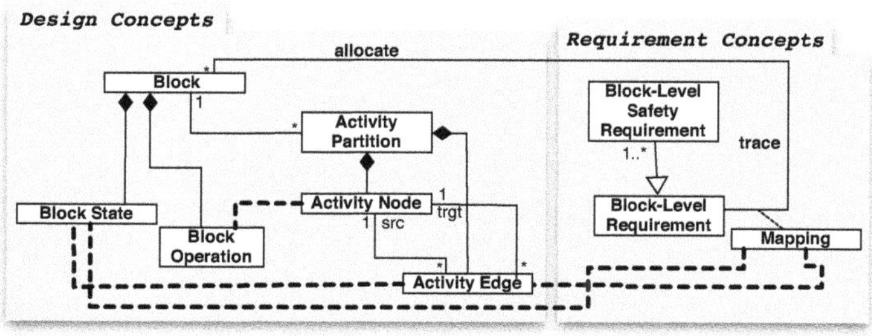

Figure 2: A Fragment of SafeSlice's traceability information model.

```
ERROR - RULEID: 1
     -> DESCRIPTION: "The 'Safety Relevant' or 'Non-Safety Relevant' requirement
        should have 'Level' tagged value specified ('System level' or 'Block level')"
     -> CATEGORY: Requirement tagged value unexpected/not specified
     -> HOW TO FIX: "Choose a value for selected Requirement's 'Level' tagged value"
     -> FIND THE ELEMENT (otElement): click here to select specified element
---- CHECK SUMMARY ---
Number of analyzed elements: 496
Number of checked rules: 177
Nymber of checked diagrams: 66
Elapsed scan time (sec): 22 (0 hours, 0 min, 22 sec).
----- Total Violations ----
Errors: 1
Warnings: 0
```

Figure 3: Example output from Rules Assistant.

design diagrams, (2) Generating design slices based on the traceability links, and (3) Inspection of design slices by assessors. We require that the traceability links defined in the first step should conform to a traceability information model. This information model (discussed later in this section) provides a SysML adaptation of the traceability information requirements gleaned from observing actual certification meetings, consultation with certification experts, and reviewing major safety standards (most notably IEC 61508 [2]). The traceability links between safety requirements and the SysML design (defined in accordance with the information model) are used in the second step to automatically extract minimized slices for the safety requirements. These slices are then reviewed by the assessors to ensure that the safety requirements are met by the design. In the rest of this section, we elaborate the three steps of the process shown in Figure 1.

2.1 Establishing Traceability

SafeSlice is implemented as a plug-in for the Enterprise Architect tool (`http://www.sparxsystems.com/ea`) which, like other tools with support for SysML, has an environment for building SysML models and creating SysML's built-in traceability links. However, as we argue in our earlier work [4], existing SysML traceability mechanisms do not provide adequate support for addressing all the traceability information requirements mandated by safety standards and asked for by the assessors during certification. In [4], we provide methodological guidelines on how to extend and use SysML traceability links for the purpose of safety certification. These guidelines led to an information model, a small fragment of which is shown in Figure 2 – see [4] for the complete model. The fragment shown characterizes the links from requirements to SysML blocks and activity diagrams (the diagram types used later in the paper for illustration) along with the rationale for the links.

"*Rule Assistant*" is a feature of SafeSlice that enables guided and validated application of our proposed traceability information model. Our information model yields a set of 20 multiplicity and compatibility relational constraints (rules). We encoded these rules into a spreadsheet that can be easily edited by users to add new rules or to modify/delete the existing ones. Rule Assistant loads the entire set of rules in the spreadsheet at every invocation and executes the rules using the EA built-in rule engine. If a violation is detected, Rule Assistant provides diagnostic information about the violated rule, the model element(s) involved, and the action(s) to be taken to resolve the issue. As an example, in Figure 3, we show the diagnostic information generated by the Rule Assistant for the situation where a safety requirement has been defined but it is unspecified whether the requirement is at the system level or at the block level. In this example, the user can read the "How to fix" field and then click on "Find the element" to quickly navigate to the element in question and apply the necessary fix.

Rule Assistant can check the information model rules in two modes: *investigator* and *listening*. In the investigator mode, the compliance of an entire project is checked. In this mode, the user waits until the compliance checking process is finished and then applies the suggested changes if violations are detected. In the listening mode, Rule Assistant is always active in the background and monitors every change made by the user and checks that the change is consistent with the information model. If a violation is detected, feedback is immediately shown in the diagnostic window. The time required by Rule Assistant to check all the rules is small. On a standard laptop, it took less than half a minute to check a SysML design with about a thousand elements (blocks, relations, activities, transitions, states, attributes, and operations) against all the 20 rules.

2.2 Slice Generator

"*Slice Generator*" is an implementation of the slicing algorithm proposed in [4]. A high-level overview of algorithm is shown in Figure 4. Briefly, a system safety requirement is refined into safety requirements at the level of blocks. If necessary, more detailed safety-relevant requirements could be defined in order to satisfy block-level safety requirements. In our tool, slices are constructed for atomic requirements, i.e., requirements that are directly related to design via traceability links. System-level requirements are never related to the design directly, because even in the simplest case where these requirements do not need to be decomposed, they still need to be allocated to some block and restated as a block-level requirement. If a block-level safety requirement is atomic, then our tool will generate a slice directly for the block-level requirement; otherwise, one slice will be generated for each of the atomic safety-relevant requirements contributing to the satisfaction of a block-level safety requirement. For example, Figure 5 shows a safety requirement, the traces, and the generated slices in terms of block and activity diagrams. The system underlying the example is a well-known benchmark embedded system, named the Production Cell System (PCS) [3], whose function is the transformation of metal blanks into forged plates by means of a press and their transportation from a feed belt into a container. We use PCS as a benchmark case study for our approach (see Section 3).

2.3 Inspection Assistant

The "*Inspection Assistant*" feature aims to help users in better managing the inspection process. In particular, Inspection Assistant can record the decisions made during (1) inspections of atomic requirements (conducted over design slices), and (2) inspections done to ensure that the atomic requirements together lead to the satisfaction of higher-level requirements and ultimately the system-level safety requirements.

Algorithm. *GenerateSlice*

Input: Requirement *R*, and a set of SysML design diagrams conforming to the input traceability information model

Output: Design slices related to *R*.

Step 1. Find design elements (indirectly) related to *R*.

Step 2. Extract block diagram slices:

- **Step 2.1** Remove operations, and attributes that are not related to *R*.
- **Step 2.2** Include relations between the blocks linked to *R*.

Step 3. Extract activity diagram slices:

- **Step 3.1** Identify activity partitions related to the blocks linked to *R*.
- **Step 3.2** Remove activity nodes and edges not related to *R* from these partitions.
- **Step 3.3** Add stuttering edges to maintain the connectivity between the diagram nodes.
- **Step 3.4** Identify new initial activity nodes.

Step 4. Extract state machine diagram slices:

- **Step 4.1** Identify state machines related to the blocks linked to *R*.
- **Step 4.2** Remove states and transitions not related to *R*.
- **Step 4.3** Add stuttering transitions to maintain the connectivity between the states.

Figure 4: Overview slicing algorithm in SafeSlice

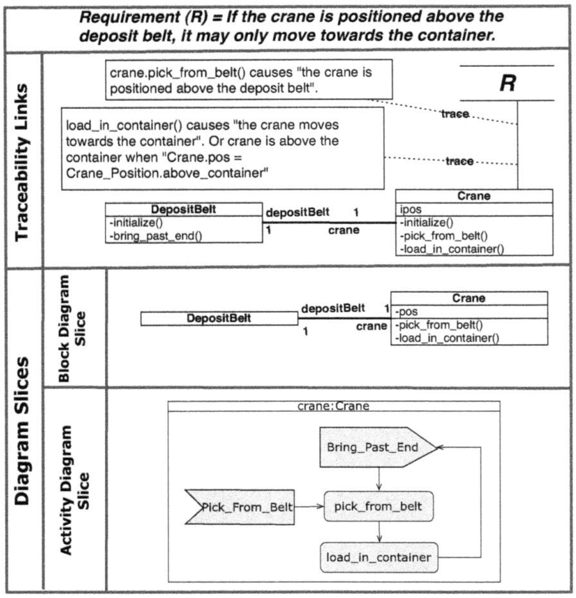

Figure 5: A safety requirement (R), the traces, and resulting slices.

Figure 6 shows the various states an atomic requirement can go through during the inspection process. The initial state is "Yet to approve". The user then reviews the design and marks the requirement as "Approved" or "Not approved", depending on whether she deems the design as satisfying the requirement or not. Because the design evolves over time, it is important to check the impact of design changes on safety requirements. Based on the traceability information, Inspection Assistant detects the requirements that need to be re-inspected due to changes. Specifically, if there is a change made to any of the block operations or attributes to which an atomic requirement is traced, then that requirement needs to be re-inspected. The status of an atomic requirement that needs to be re-inspected is set to "Out of date"; the status of the related higher-level requirements is set to "Out of date" as well. In addition, any change to the textual description of a requirement (at any level) would render the state of that requirement "Out of date" and the state will be propagated up to all the higher-level requirements.

To facilitate monitoring the progress of the inspection activities, Inspection Assistant can generate pie charts to visualize the relative proportion of requirements in different states. An example is shown in Figure 7. This pie chart depicts the status of the safety-relevant requirements that contribute to a selected system-level requirement (intermediate block-level requirements were filtered in this chart).

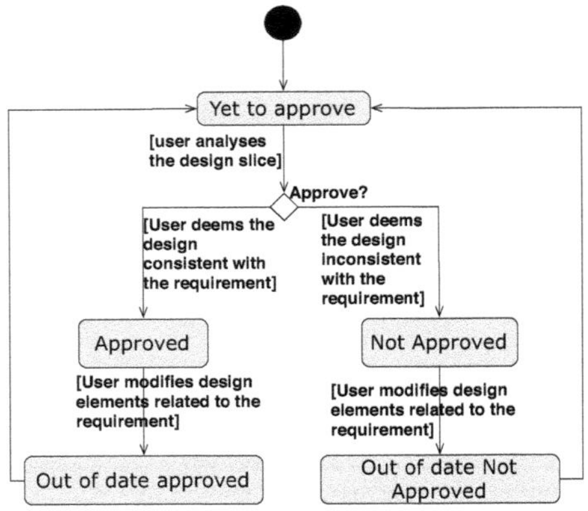

Figure 6: Inspection states for an atomic requirement.

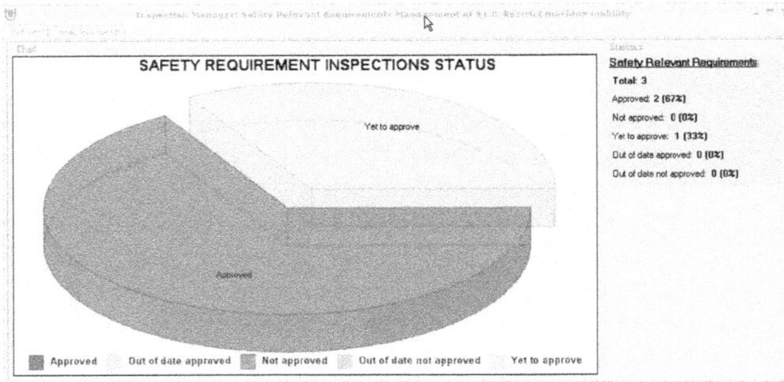

Figure 7: Monitoring the inspection progress using pie charts.

The chart indicates that there are three safety-relevant requirements for the given system-level requirement and of these, two have been already approved and the third is awaiting inspection. To make re-inspections more efficient, our tool keeps the previously-generated slices and allows the user to compare the new slices against the old ones. In this way, users can better investigate the differences.

2.3.1 Report Generator

Report generation is an important feature for supporting safety inspections. Reports are useful, for example, when a printed document needs to be signed off for legal obligations or simply for sequential reading of the inspection material. SafeSlice supports the automated generation of reports in PDF format. In particular, the tool allows the user to select the information to include in the report (e.g. design slice, whole design, statistics, pie charts). For instance, it is possible to generate a document reporting the inspection details of a given requirement or one that reports all the inspection details of all the requirements in a project.

2.3.2 Advanced Navigator

To make the inspection process more effective, SafeSlice supports advanced search and navigation of model elements. The Advanced Navigator feature allows the user to select an element x (e.g., a requirement, class, block, etc.) and retrieve the elements of given types (e.g., specific requirements, classes, blocks, etc.) that have a given type of relationship with x (e.g., satisfy, trace, derive, etc.). The user specifies the element/relation types to search for from a pre-defined list. This list can be modified by the user if needed, e.g., when a new SysML stereotype is defined for capturing new types of elements.

3. EVALUATION

We have evaluated the traceability and slicing techniques implemented in SafeSlice in several ways using a combination of formal methods [4], benchmark and industrial case studies [4], and a controlled experiment [1]. We outline our evaluation work below.

First, we provide a formal analysis of our slicing algorithm whereby we show that the generated design slices are sound for temporal safety properties [4]. That is, if a requirement holds over a design slice, it holds over the original (non-sliced) design as well. This ensures that the design slices will not be providing misleading information to the assessors.

Second, we have used SafeSlice in two case-studies [4]: the first case study is a benchmark case, the Production Cell System (PCS) [3], mentioned earlier in the paper (see Figure 5). The second case study is a real-world industrial system from the maritime and energy domain. The PCS design consisted of 58 diagrams with 479 elements, 419 relations, and 189 attributes. The industrial case study included 23 diagrams, with 194 elements, 186 relations, and 57 attributes. In both case studies, SafeSlice was used for creating traceability links, checking their compliance, and generating design slices. Our case studies indicated that: (1) The cost of applying our methodology, which mostly depends on the cost to establish traceability links, was reasonable. In particular, this was confirmed in the second case study by our industry partner. (2) Our slicing technique yields a substantial reduction in the amount of information that needs to be inspected to check that a given safety requirement is met by the design.

Lastly, we executed a controlled experiment to assess the impact of our traceability and slicing mechanism on inspectors' conformance decisions and effort [1]. Results clearly show benefits in terms of increasing the correctness of conformance decisions (from 50% to 63%), decreasing the proportion of uncertain decisions (-45%), and reducing the effort of inspections (-27%).

In summary, our evaluation suggests that our approach is effective for improving design safety inspections and thus of value in realistic settings for improving accuracy and reducing costs in software safety certification.

4. DESIGN AND IMPLEMENTATION

As stated earlier, SafeSlice is implemented as a plugin for Enterprise Architect (EA), which is a versatile and mature modeling environment. This makes it possible to seamlessly introduce SafeSlice into real development settings and further simplifies tool evolution and maintenance. Among the possible alternatives for modeling environments, EA was chosen due to its usability, wide industrial adoption (confirmed by our industrial partners), availability of detailed guidelines for plugin construction, and built-in support for storing and linking heterogeneous development artifacts (e.g., natural language requirements specifications, UML/SysML models, Word documents, source code).

Figure 8 shows the architecture of the SafeSlice tool. It communicates asynchronously with EA via events. All the information related to a development project is stored by EA in a database. The plugin can read from and write to this database via EA's API. In particular, the additional traceability information required in our methodology, previously-generated design slices and reports, and the decisions made by users during inspections are all stored and retrieved by the plugin via the API; this communication layer thus simplifies the implementation by hiding the underlying database technology.

SafeSlice builds on Microsoft ActiveX COM technology. We used Microsoft .NET Framework 2.0 and Visual Studio 2008 as the development platform. SafeSlice is written in Visual C# and is

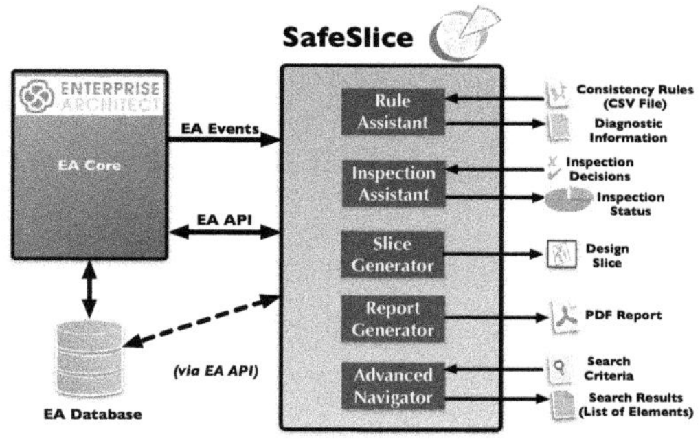

Figure 8: SafeSlice tool architecture

roughly 10,000 lines of code excluding comments and third-party libraries. SafeSlice was publicly released in May 2011. The tool is available at: http://sites.google.com/a/simula.no/safeslice/

5. CONCLUSION

We presented a tool, SafeSlice, for extraction and inspection of design slices (where the design is expressed in SysML) for use in certification of safety-critical software systems. The tool enables users to specify the traceability links envisaged by a given traceability information model, check the consistency of the established links, automatically extract slices of design with respect to safety requirements, and manage the design inspection process. Our evaluation indicates that the use of design slices substantially reduces the amount of information that needs to be inspected for ensuring that a given safety requirement is met by a SysML design model.

In the future, we plan to conduct studies to more conclusively quantify the gains in budget, time, and quality resulting from the use of design slices in the software safety certification process. Specifically, the quality of the slices generated by SafeSlice is related to the completeness and accuracy of the traceability information available. In the future, we plan to investigate whether the quality of the traceability information impacts the effectiveness of the inspection process.

SafeSlice is implemented as part of a larger research effort to build model-based support for software safety certification. A complementary part is a project aimed at developing conceptual models that precisely characterize the interpretation of dependability standards, such as IEC 61508, and recommended practices [5].

6. REFERENCES

[1] L. Briand, D. Falessi, S. Nejati, M. Sabetzadeh, and T. Yue. Traceability and SysML design slices to support safety inspections: A controlled experiment. Tech repo, Simula Research Lab, January 2011.

[2] IEC 61508: Functional Safety of Electrical / Electronic / Programmable Electronic Safety-related Systems, 2005. International Electrotechnical Commission: International Electrotechnical Commission.

[3] C. Lewerentz and T. Lindner, editors. *Formal Development of Reactive Systems - Case Study Production Cell*, volume 891 of *LNCS*. Springer, 1995.

[4] S. Nejati, M. Sabetzadeh, D. Falessi, L. Briand, and T. Coq. A SysML-based approach to traceability management and design slicing in support of safety certification: Framework, tool support, and case studies. Tech repo, Simula Research Lab, May 2011.

[5] R. K. Panesar-Walawege, M. Sabetzadeh, L. Briand, and T. Coq. Characterizing the chain of evidence for software safety cases: A conceptual model based on the IEC 61508 standard. In *ICST*, 2010.

[6] W. Schafer and H. Wehrheim. The challenges of building advanced mechatronic systems. In *FOSE '07*, pages 72–84, 2007.

[7] OMG Systems Modeling Language (OMG SysML). 2008. Object Management Group (OMG), version 1.1.

Design and Validation of Feature-based Process Model Tailoring – A Sample Implementation of PDE

Daniela Costache, Georg Kalus, Marco Kuhrmann
Technische Universität München – Software & Systems Engineering
Munich, Germany
{daniela.costache, kalus, kuhrmann}@in.tum.de

ABSTRACT

A comprehensive software development process needs some adjustment before it can be used: It needs to be tailored to the particular organization's and project's setting. The definition of an appropriate tailoring model is a critical task. Process users need tailoring that enables them to trim the process to reflect the actual needs. Process engineers need a method and a tool to define a valid model. The SE Book of T-Systems contains a feature model to describe variable parts of the process model and relations and constraints between these parts. The notation and semantics of feature models can be used to visually author a consistent and valid tailoring model. In this paper we present a tool for visual modeling and validation of process model tailoring based on feature models using the SE Book of T-Systems as an example. The tool is based on a domain-specific language that represents the process model. It leverages the semantics of feature models to provide an easy-to-use editor for tailoring-enabled process models.

Categories and Subject Descriptors

D.2.2 [**Design Tools and Techniques**]: Programmer workbench; D.2.6 [**Programming Environments**]: Graphical environments, Integrated environments

Keywords

development process, feature-model, visual modeling

1. INTRODUCTION

Software development process models summarize and formalize experience, knowledge, and best practices of successful projects. Standard processes such as the the Rational Unified Process (RUP, [7]) are designed as a superset of development processes to be applicable in many different software development projects. Before such a generic process model can be used, it has to be tailored to reflect the circumstances of a concrete project. As a process model is of limited value without project-specific customization, a tailoring method can be considered a critical part of the process itself.

The so-called *SE Book* is the in-house development process of T-Systems International GmbH[1]. It uses a feature model known from Software Product Line engineering [2] to describe the mandatory and the variable parts of the process model. The process user can customize the process to the project's circumstances using a tool that makes use of the feature model.

1.1 Problem Statement

Similar to RUP or the V-Modell XT, the SE Book is very large. It consists of a couple of thousand elements with relations between them. Virtually every one of those elements can be subject to tailoring, meaning that it is affected by the selection or deselection of a feature in the feature-model. To avoid configurations where two features would have conflicting effects, the process engineer needs to keep in mind potentially the whole model during design. The process engineer could be relieved from dealing with some of this complexity by appropriate tool support.

1.2 Contribution & Context

In this paper we present a tool that supports the process engineer during the design of a feature model for tailoring. The tool is based on the platform PDE [8, 17], which supports process engineers during the design- and authoring phases of process model development and maintenance. PDE is a generic platform. We show how the problems of design and validation of a comprehensive feature model can be approached using an integrated process modeling tool generated from the metamodel definition of the development process.

1.3 Outline

The remainder of this paper is organized as follows: We give an overview over state of the art and state of practice with regards to process tailoring and process model design in Sect. 2. We then introduce the SE Book in Sect. 3, focusing on the parts of the model that are involved in tailoring. In Sect. 4 we give an overview over PDE, the tool infrastructure that we are using as a basis for the tool presented in this paper. The tool itself is subject of Sect. 5. We conclude the paper in Sect. 6 with a summary and an outlook.

[1]We did not include a reference as this development process model is property of T-Systems International GmbH and has not been published.

Permission to make digital or hard copies of all or part of this work for personal or classroom use is granted without fee provided that copies are not made or distributed for profit or commercial advantage and that copies bear this notice and the full citation on the first page. To copy otherwise, to republish, to post on servers or to redistribute to lists, requires prior specific permission and/or a fee.
ESEC/FSE'11, September 5–9, 2011, Szeged, Hungary.
Copyright 2011 ACM 978-1-4503-0443-6/11/09 ...$10.00.

2. RELATED WORK

Rich process models, such as RUP, V-Modell XT [4], or SE Book, are well suited for tool support, as their *metamodel* [14] can be used to structure the tool's "data models". A couple of comprehensive process metamodels (SPEM [15], V-Modell XT [18], ISO/IEC 24744 [5]) have been developed. Yet, there are just a handful of tools to support process engineering: The tool to edit SPEM/EPF is the *EPF Composer* based on Eclipse. The equivalent tool for the V-Modell XT is the *V-Modell XT Editor*, which is also used to work with the SE Book. For the ISO 24744 metamodel we are currently not aware of any accepted tool support.

Tailoring and Feature Modeling. In process models based on SPEM, tailoring can be regarded a "constructive" activity. Customizing the process means to "build" a process model that reflects the organization's and project's needs. The tailoring philosophy realized in the SE Book and in the V-Modell XT assumes a ready process model that through the specification of a number of project characteristics gets "pruned" to reflect the needs. Although it seems natural to adapt product line *modeling* techniques [2] to tailoring of process models, we are not aware of other implementations than the SE Book. In some respect, the tool presented in this paper is a proof of concept for the applicability of Feature-Oriented Domain Analysis (FODA) [6] to process model tailoring.

Discussion. Tool support for working with development process models is essential. The V-Modell XT Editor, which is the tool used to work with the SE Book, is basically a specialized XML editor. It's advantage is that it can be used to work with any kind of XML-based model. The flexibility comes at a price, however: the tool does not use the "meaning" of the model structures to provide editing capabilities that would feel more natural than working natively with the XML structure. The SE Book's feature model is a good example where one would expect to work with a graphical representation of the feature tree instead of with the underlying XML nodes. The fact that the existing editor ignores the meaning the model structures also means that it cannot perform sanity checks [10] and validation, making editing the SE Book fairly error-prone. Mistakes made during the design of the process model often occur much later in the tool chain, for example when generating process documentation from the model.

3. TAILORING THE SE BOOK

Whenever the SE Book is instantiated for a project, it does exhibit a number of traits depending on the project's characteristics. It does for example contain rules and regulations about how to deal with sub-contractors *if* these play a role in the project – otherwise it would not contain this content. Recommendations for the design of a mobile user interface may or may not play a role in the project but they certainly do not make sense if the project does not include a user interface at all. Generally, some of the traits *imply* or *exclude* each other.

The SE Book uses a feature model to express the traits of the process model and relations between them. The approach is roughly sketched in Fig. 1: Each feature of the feature tree represents a trait that the instantiated process model may or may not have. The structure of the tree determines the relations between the traits. Each *leaf-feature* is associated with a set of *operations* to manipulate the process content (currently, the operations are: add a process content element to the resulting process model instance, remove a content element and all it's dependencies from the resulting instance). The feature "high safety-requirements" for example leads to the inclusion of a couple of extra activities and artifacts into the resulting instance – process content elements that would otherwise not be part of the process model instance.

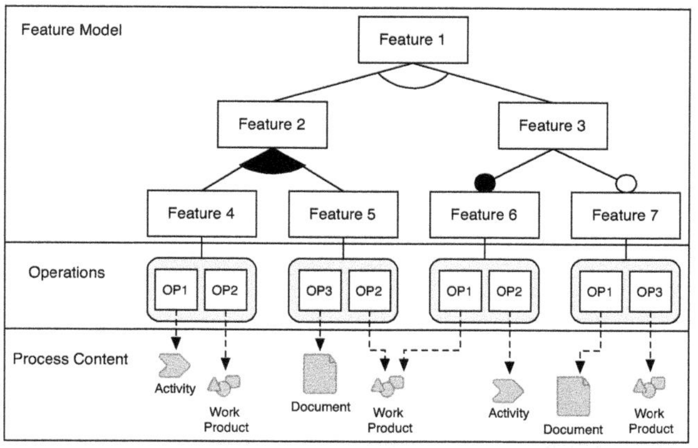

Figure 1: Tailoring using a feature-model

The SE Book, including the feature model, associated operations and the process content, is defined in an XML file (the name SE "Book" may give a slightly wrong impression: although there exists a printed version of the process documentation, the SE Book is first and foremost a process "model"). Designing the process model basically means to edit the XML file. With over 6 MB the file is so large that it cannot be edited with standard XML editors. The *Process Development Environment* is a flexible tool that we have built to edit large development process models in general. For the SE Book we built a specialized instance of PDE. The resulting tool is covered in Sect. 5 after a brief description of the PDE platform.

4. THE PDE PLATFORM

The Process Development Environment (PDE) is a platform based on domain-specific languages and has served as a basis for the specialized editor for the SE Book and particularly for it's tailoring. It allows the definition of a process metamodel and the generation of a (visual) process model editor. PDE consists of several components, the most important of which are briefly described in the following (for details cf. [8], [17]).

4.1 Technical Foundation

PDE is built using the Microsoft DSL toolkit [3], which provides the basic infrastructure for the definition of DSLs. Metamodels, in terms of DSLs, are developed using a Visual Studio 2010 plugin. The Windows Presentation Foundation (WPF) [13] is used to develop/define the "end-user" application. Runtime plugins are realized using the Managed Extensibility Framework (MEF) [12].

4.2 Platform Architecture

Figure 2 shows the architecture of the PDE. The framework consists of two parts: (1) the *PDE Language*, which is the extension of the DSL tools, and (2) an *PDE Editor Framework* that provides the basic features to edit a designed process model. A concrete process language (a process metamodel) is a DSL based on the PDE Language.

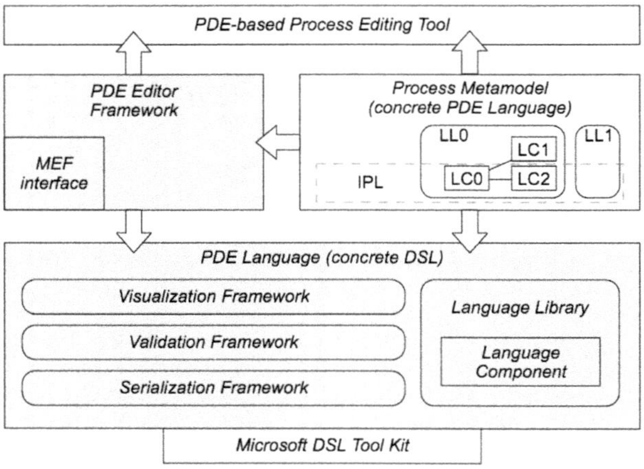

Figure 2: PDE Architecture Overview

Modular Languages. The language elements (fragments, which can be later model elements, validation routines, images etc.) are stored in *Language Components* (LC). Components are comprised in *Language Libraries* (LL) and can be developed and maintained independently (close to SME). Components can be preconfigured within a library. If there are components that have dependencies, they can refer to each other, can reuse and/or extend content of other components. A library itself is a container to hold certain components. An *Integrated Process Language* (IPL) is a configuration of components $lc_1, \ldots, lc_n$, where usually an initial component lc_0 is the root of the IPL.

Visual Languages. PDE is focused on visual languages [9]. If, for example, a process contains state entities and transition relations between states, the corresponding language/metamodel elements *State* and *Transition* contain information on how to visualize these elements, e.g., by simple shapes or images. The platform provides assistance to the process language engineer to add visual elements. The advantage of visual editing is also a limitation of PDE: textual DSLs/process languages are not supported.

Validation. PDE supports two kinds of validation. Firstly, so-called *hard constraints* are language properties that are used for structural validation. If, for example, a language element Workflow requires exactly one starting point, PDE can check this constraint without additional logic by just using the metamodel properties. The editors get their basic functionality from those hard constraints and forbid operations on the model which are not covered by the metamodel. The second validation style is realized by *soft constraints*. Soft constraints are properties of the model instance and can provide semantic validation e.g., naming rules, cycle freeness, and fulfillment of dependencies. In an experimental prototype [19] a sample validation of modular processes according to [1] using Petri-Nets was realized using this validation style. In addition, PDE provides several plugin mechanisms [16] that allow the injection of extra validation logic by external libraries. The hooks for soft-constraints were used in the editor for the SE Book feature-tree to see if it contains any deficiencies (see Sect. 5.2).

5. THE SE BOOK IN PDE

The editor tool for the feature model of the SE Book is built on top of the PDE platform and extends the default functionality by adding a custom visual editor for the feature tree and by hooking in to the validation extension points to validate the feature tree.

5.1 Visual Design

As mentioned in Sect. 3, the SE Book is defined in an XML file. If used without extensions, PDE displays the hierarical structure of the XML file in a tree view with a property grid for the individual elements. This generic user interface works for any kind of process content, independent of it's meaning. For the feature-model that is part of the SE Book we have decided to extend default PDE with a visual designer. Figure 3 displays a rough impression of the designer. It uses the accepted notation for feature models and allows the user to manipulate the feature tree with drag and drop.

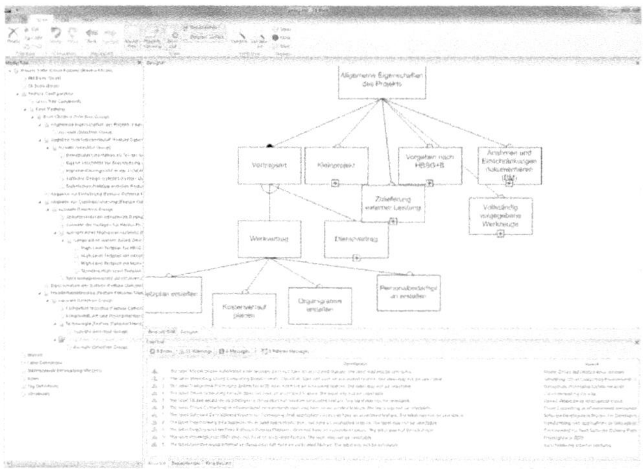

Figure 3: Visual Editor for SE Book Tailoring

5.2 Validation

Validation plays an important role in generating consistent product (process) configurations. To ensure a valid feature model, the tool looks for deficiencies in the tree as described in [10]. The paper describes three classes of deficiencies, namely redundancy, anomalies and inconsistencies. A typical deficiency for example would be "*A mutual exclusion is modeled between alternative child features. As the alternative relation implies a mutual exclusion between the child features the dependency is superfluous.*"

By extending the default validation using custom soft constraints, PDE detects all these types of deficiencies by using the feature tree representation generated from the process model DSL. When implementing the validation, we found that some checks seem redundant at first sight, as some deficiencies represent a specialized case of a more general one. In these cases, the tool detects both the general case (e.g., anomaly: "*An optional feature is mutual exclusive to a full-mandatory feature*") and the specialized case (e.g., anomaly: "*An alternative-child feature is mutual exclusive to a full-mandatory feature*"; the alternative-child feature is an optional feature).

The deficiencies in [10] are described in their most simple form, usually for the first "child-parent" level of the feature tree. The SE Book tool also deals with identifying deficiencies where the source of the problem is located "farther away" in the tree, for example for features situated on different levels in the tree. The reason behind this implementation is given by the previous example, where validation may seem redundant, but in specific configurations only the specialized case can be detected, due to the complexity of the feature model.

If the tool recognizes a deficiency pattern, it outputs a message to the output pane, similar to compiler warnings in an IDE. We have decided to classify the messages as *warnings*, allowing the user to save a faulty model. We have yet to decide whether to promote some of the deficiencies to *errors*, which would mean that such deficiencies would have to be resolved before the process model can be saved.

6. CONCLUSIONS AND FUTURE WORK

We have presented a special-purpose tool for editing the SE Book – a proprietary software development process of T-Systems International GmbH. The tool is built using the Process Development Environment (PDE) platform, which in turn is built on top of the Microsoft DSL toolkit.

For a particular area of the development process model, namely the feature-model-based tailoring, we have extended the default PDE functionality to provide a visual editor for the tailoring feature tree and for validation of this tree. The metamodel extension using feature-model-based tailoring is included in the recent release of SE Book. The PDE-based implementation was originally planned for evaluation purposes, and is, still, subject to ongoing research.

6.1 Future Work

We have an implementation for a couple of sanity checks concerning the relation between the feature tree, associated operations and the process content (see Sect. 3 for details). We also have an implementation that translates the feature model into a propositional formula which serves as input into a SAT solver to determine valid configurations [11]. Both implementations are in Java and have yet to be translated to our PDE-based implementation of the process model editor.

While the presented tool offers a comfortable way to edit the tailoring-related parts of the SE Book, other parts of the process model still have to be edited using the default PDE functionality. We are considering to add more visual designers for other parts of the process model, such as the artifact model and the milestone configuration.

7. REFERENCES

[1] K. Bergner and J. Friedrich. Using Project Procedure Diagrams for Milestone Planning. In *Proceedings of International Conference on Software Process (ICSP 2010)*, 2010.

[2] CMU Software Engineering Institute. Software product lines. Online: `http://www.sei.cmu.edu/productlines`, 2011. Visit: 2011-06-06.

[3] S. Cook, G. Jones, S. Kent, and A. C. Wills. *Domain-Specific Development with Visual Studio DSL Tools*. Addison-Wesley, 2007.

[4] J. Friedrich, U. Hammerschall, M. Kuhrmann, and M. Sihling. *Das V-Modell XT - Für Projektleiter und QS-Verantwortliche kompakt und übersichtlich*. Springer, 2. edition, 2009.

[5] Joint Technical Committee ISO/IEC JTC 1, Subcommittee SC 7. Software engineering – metamodel for development methodologies. Technical Report ISO/IEC 24744:2007, International Organization for Standardization, 2007.

[6] K. C. Kang, S. G. Cohen, J. A. Hess, W. E. Novak, and A. S. Peterson. Feature-Oriented Domain Analysis (FODA) Feasibility Study. Technical Report CMU/SEI-90-TR-021, Software Engineering Institute, Carnegie Mellon Univerisity, 2000.

[7] P. Kruchten. *The Rational Unified Process: An Introduction*. Addison-Wesley Longman, 3 edition, 2003.

[8] M. Kuhrmann, G. Kalus, M. Then, and E. Wachtel. From Design to Tools: Process Modeling and Enactment with PDE and PET. In *Third International Workshop on Academic Software Development Tools and Techniques*, 2010.

[9] M. Kuhrmann, G. Kalus, E. Wachtel, and M. Broy. Visual Process Model Design using Domain-specific Languages. In *Proceedings of SPLASH Workshop on Flexible Modeling Tools 2010*, 2010.

[10] T. Maßen and H. Lichter. Deficiencies in Feature Models, 2004.

[11] M. Mendonca, A. Wąsowski, and K. Czarnecki. Sat-based analysis of feature models is easy. In *Proceedings of the 13th International Software Product Line Conference*, SPLC '09, pages 231–240, Pittsburgh, PA, USA, 2009. Carnegie Mellon University.

[12] Microsoft Corporation, CodePlex. Managed Extensibility Framework. Online: `http://mef.codeplex.com`, 2010.

[13] A. Nathan. *WPF 4 Unleashed*. Sams, 2010.

[14] OMG. Meta Object Facility (MOF) Core Specification Version 2.0. Technical report, Object Management Group, 2006.

[15] OMG. Software & Systems Process Engineering Metamodel Specification (SPEM) Version 2.0. Technical report, Object Management Group, 2008.

[16] L. Surhone, M. Timpledon, and S. Marseken, editors. *Managed Extensibility Framework*. Betascript Publishing, 2010.

[17] Technische Universität München. Process Development Environment (PDE) – Project Homepage. Online: `http://pde.codeplex.com`, 2010.

[18] T. Ternité and M. Kuhrmann. Das V-Modell XT 1.3 Metamodell. Research Report TUM-I0905, Technische Universität München, 2009.

[19] E. Wachtel, M. Kuhrmann, and G. Kalus. A Domain Specific Language for Project Execution Models. In *39th Annual Conference of the German Computer Society*, 2009.

PSPWizard: Machine-assisted Definition of Temporal Logical Properties with Specification Patterns

Markus Lumpe, Indika Meedeniya
Faculty of ICT
Swinburne University of Technology
Hawthorn, VIC 3122, Australia
{mlumpe,imeedeniya}@swin.edu.au

Lars Grunske
Faculty of Computer Science & Center for Mathematical and Computational Modelling (CM)[2]
University of Kaiserslautern, D-67653, Germany
grunske@cs.uni-kl.de

ABSTRACT

Model checking provides a powerful means to assert and verify desired system properties. But, for the verification process to become feasible, a correct formulation of these properties in a temporal logic is necessary – a potential barrier to application in practice. Research on property specification has supplied us with rich pattern catalogs that capture commonly occurring system properties in different temporal logics. Furthermore, these property specification pattern catalogs usually offer both a structured English grammar to facilitate the pattern selection and an associated template solutions to express the properties formally. Yet, the actual use of property specification patterns remains cumbersome, due to limited tool support. For this reason, we have developed the Property Specification Pattern Wizard (PSPWizard), a framework that defines an interface for the currently accepted property specification pattern libraries. PSPWizard consists of two main building blocks: a mapping generator that weaves a given pattern library with a target logic and a GUI front-end to the structured English grammar tailored to those patterns that are supported in the target logic.

Categories and Subject Descriptors

D.2.4 [**Software Engineering**]: Software/Program Verification—*Formal methods*; D.2.6 [**Software Engineering**]: Programming Environments—*Programmer workbench*; F4.1 [**Mathematical Logic and Formal Languages**]: Mathematical Logic—*Temporal logic*

General Terms

Design, Languages, Verification

Keywords

Specification Patterns, Temporal Logic, Structured English Grammar

Permission to make digital or hard copies of all or part of this work for personal or classroom use is granted without fee provided that copies are not made or distributed for profit or commercial advantage and that copies bear this notice and the full citation on the first page. To copy otherwise, to republish, to post on servers or to redistribute to lists, requires prior specific permission and/or a fee.
ESEC/FSE'11, September 5–9, 2011, Szeged, Hungary.
Copyright 2011 ACM 978-1-4503-0443-6/11/09 ...$10.00.

1. INTRODUCTION

An effective verification of a system requires both an appropriate system model and a correct set of attributes capturing the systems's properties. But Dwyer *et al.* [3] realized that, specifically for practitioners, the correct and formal specification of system properties is a major challenge and they developed, therefore, the concept of *property specification pattern* as a solution. A property specification pattern describes a generalized recurring system attribute (that needs to be verified independently) and offers a solution in the form of a formal specification in different temporal logics. In their work, Dwyer *et al.* [3] studied so-called *qualitative* specification patterns and their representation in linear and branching time temporal logics. As a result, a set of 8 patterns, occurring within 5 generic scopes each, has been identified. Today, property specification catalogs for: *qualitative* properties [3], *real-time* properties [1, 5, 7], and *probabilistic* properties [6] have been developed.

Property specification patterns are defined in mathematical and temporal logical terms and at a granularity quite different from *natural language*. For this reason, corresponding *structured English grammars* have been developed [4,6,7] to facilitate the use of property specification patterns. Each pattern is represented by a natural language *phrase* in the structured English grammar. Moreover, if the structured English grammar is paired with a set of corresponding temporal logic mappings, then we obtain, as result, a set of isomorphisms between patterns and temporal formulae that allow for a *syntax-directed* translation of property specifications to the designated target formalism [4, 6, 7].

However, pairing a structured English grammar with a target logic is not an easy task. Moreover, the capabilities of specific patterns, target logics, and verification tool may not align. We need, therefore, some means to assist the system engineer in this process. In particular, we wish to automate the process of *weaving* target logic mappings into the structured English grammar phrases. This is the domain of the Property Specification Pattern Wizard (PSPWizard), a framework for machine-assisted definition of temporal formulae capturing pattern-based system properties. PSPWizard supports the currently available specification pattern catalogs and also provides a mechanism to accommodate new emergent property specification patterns. Once instantiated with a concrete target logic mapping, PSPWizard guides the system engineer through the property specification pattern catalog, in a top-down fashion, to indicate which patterns and subordinate attributes are supported in the selected target formalism.

2. THE FRAMEWORK

With PSPWizard we aim at two objectives: (i) ease the use of property specification patterns, and (ii) enable the discovery or incorporation of new patterns to foster the application of property specification patterns in industry. We achieve the former by equipping PSPWizard with a configurable user interface that allows for an incremental refinement of the property specification being defined by the system engineer. Hence, with PSPWizard, the system engineer is free to elect subordinate attributes (*e.g.*, time or probability constraints, even additional events) in any order. Traditionally [6,7], a system engineer has to commit to a specific category (*i.e.*, qualitative, real-time, or probabilistic specification) as the first action.

Our second objective targets *pattern discovery* and *pattern evaluation*. Specification patterns do not only assist system engineers in capturing properties in a concise and correct manner, but also provide the means to perform property specifications at the right level of abstraction. The mapping generator embedded in PSPWizard allows new patterns and logic formulae to be integrated into the framework on demand. In particular, system engineers can alter the underlying pattern definitions by proactively enabling or disabling specific specification options in order to adjust patterns and the corresponding phrases in the structured English grammar to the capabilities of the target logic.

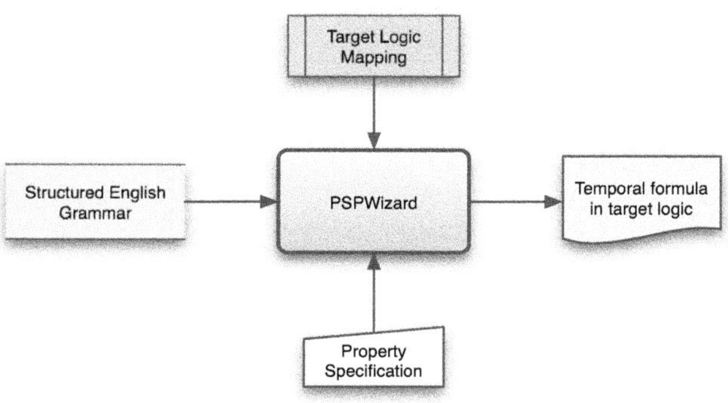

Figure 1: Property specification in PSPWizard.

A conceptual overview of the use of PSPWizard for property specification is shown in Figure 1. Before a property specification can be supplied to PSPWizard, we need to define the associated pattern first. This step requires the construction of a suitable natural language phrase (*i.e.*, a structured English grammar rule) and the formulation of a mapping to the target logic (*i.e.*, a term rewriting rule that translates the natural languages phrase into a formula of the target logic). We use XML for both. More precisely, the structured English grammar and the mapping to a target logic are captured in XML-files that are parsed by PSPWizard's mapping generator to yield an executable runtime representation. Once loaded, that representation serves as a means to configure the GUI front-end of PSPWizard. The dialog elements of the GUI are made up of the input patterns definitions. If a specific pattern or subordinate attribute is not supported by the target logic, then the corresponding dialog elements in the GUI are disabled. This is to inform the system engineer of the level of support for the selected pattern catalog in the chosen target logic.

Property specification is through a guided dialog in PSPWizard. The system engineer enters a property specification by selecting *pattern scope*, *pattern category*, and *pattern*. Then a pattern editor becomes available that allows for the specification of individual state formulae and for the configuration of subordinate constraints, if available, of the selected pattern. The process is a accompanied by a simultaneous translation of the pattern (or its fragments) into a logic formula of the target language. Once the property specification is complete, the computed logic formula can be copied for post processing (*i.e.*, supplied to a secondary verification tool or document).

2.1 Encoding of Patterns

Mathematical logic, though the most effective means to capture systematically system properties, is too strict and most software engineers prefer natural language to formulate their system requirements. Konrad & Cheng [7] as well as Grunske [6] utilized this very observation when defining language support for their respective specification pattern catalogs.

A schematic overview of the syntax of the structured English grammar for Property Specification Patterns is shown in Table 1. In the grammar terminal strings are written in **bold** font, whereas non-terminal symbols are given in `true type` font. We use `[]` to denote an optional symbol. For example, we write [**holds**] to express that the English verb "holds" can be omitted from a concrete pattern specification, if the resulting sentence is closer to natural language.

`Property`	`::=`	`Scope , Pattern .`
`Scope`	`::=`	**Globally** | **Before** R | **After** Q | **Between** Q **and** R | **After** Q **until** R
`Pattern`	`::=`	`Occurrence` | `Order`
`Occurrence`	`::=`	`Absence` | `Universality` | `Existence` | `TransientState` | `SteadyState` | `Recurrence` | `MinimumDuration` | `MaximumDuration`
`Order`	`::=`	`Precedence` | `Response` | `PrecedenceChain1-2` | `PrecedenceChain2-1` | `ResponseChain1-2` | `ResponseChain2-1` | `ResponseInvariance` | `Until`
`Universality`	`::=`	**it is always the case that** P [**holds**] [$\mathtt{Time}_{\mathrm{O}}$] `[Prob]`
	...	

Table 1: Structured English grammar overview.

For the encoding of the structured English grammar we use an *attribute grammar*. Attribute grammars allow for the specification of *inherited attributes*, which we can employ to capture dependencies between different parts of a grammar. For example, such a dependency exists within the `Universality` pattern. Its subordinate time constraint (*i.e.*, $\mathtt{Time}_{\mathrm{O}}$) captures a possible time bound. If specified, the value of this time bound is *pushed* into the runtime variable (*e.g.*, `TBO`, as shown Table 3 below) that PSPWizard uses to populate the corresponding time bounds in target logic formulae, if necessary.

In order to process the structured English grammar, we have developed an XML-based interchange format. XML offers two compelling benefits: (i) XML separates data from presentation, a feature that allows us to choose freely which information to make available to the system engineer in PSPWizard, and (ii) XML enables easy data exchange between applications, a feature that allows us, for example, to run PSPWizard within a Web-browser also. The schematic

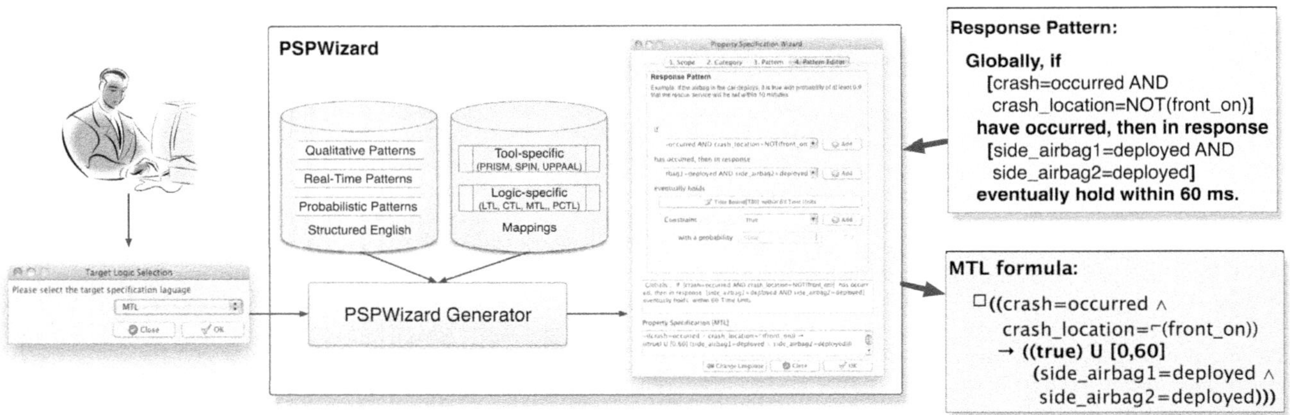

Figure 2: The PSPWizard workflow

overview of the XML document format for the encoding of property specification patterns is shown in Table 2.

catalog	::=	scope*, category*, pattern*
scope	::=	scope_id, description
category	::=	category_id, description
pattern	::=	id, category_id, example, pattern_specification*
pattern_specification	::=	spec_element*
spec_element	::=	type, id, property*
type	::=	label | state_formula | time_bound | probability_bound | constraint | formula_ref
property	::=	property_type, value

Table 2: XML encoding of structured English grammar.

The elements shown in Table 2 all denote proper XML elements. A given pattern catalog contains a, possibly empty, sequence of scope, category, and pattern tags. Each of those tags can contain a variable number of elements and attributes. We use *id* attributes to uniquely identify elements. These identifiers provides us with a means to fetch pattern-specific values in order to construct the corresponding target logic formula. The XML encoding of the *Existence* pattern [3] is shown in Table 3.

```
<pattern id="Existence" name="Existence" category="PC_OCCSF">
  <property name="description" type="string">Existence Description
    </property>
  <property name="example" type="string">An ambulance must arrive
      at the accident scene within 15 min in 95% of the cases.
     </property>
  <patternspecification>
    <specelement type="stateformula" id="P"></specelement>
    <specelement type="label" id="LBL1">
      <property name="value" type="string">eventually holds
         </property>
    </specelement>
    <specelement type="time" id="TBO" ></specelement>
    <specelement type="probabilitybound" id="PB"></specelement>
  </patternspecification>
</pattern>
```

Table 3: XML encoding of *Existence* pattern.

2.2 Encoding of Target Logic Mappings

The second set of XML documents provides the mappings to different target logics. These mappings have to be defined by domain experts. There are two types of mappings: (i) tool-specific (*e.g.*, PRISM) and (ii) logic-specific (*e.g.*, PCTL) translations. Whether or not a specific pattern can be mapped to the target logic depends on its capabilities. Also, we may not wish to provide mappings for all patterns. In both cases, patterns for which no translation is given in the target logic encoding will be disabled in the GUI of PSPWizard. The structure of the mapping encoding XML documents is shown in Table 4, where the XML elements:

Mapping	::=	name, logic_property*, operator_mapping*, construct*
operator_mapping	::=	id, string
construct	::=	construct_id, construct_element*
construct_element	::=	string | state_formula | time_bound | constraint | invocation
state_formula	::=	spec_element_id
constraint	::=	spec_element_id
time_bound	::=	spec_element_id
invocation	::=	class, function, argument*
argument	::=	name, type, value

Table 4: XML encoding of target logic mappings.

- `logic_property` contains customizations that inform the PSPWizard about specific target logic capabilities (*e.g.*, whether the target logic supports the notion of time or probability);
- `operator_mapping` defines the characters that denote Boolean operators in the target logic. For example AND in MTL is $\wedge$, whereas Prism uses &;
- `construct` specifies the mappings from the structured English pattern templates to target logic. The attribute `construct_id` consists of two components: the scope and pattern identifier. A specific pattern may be defined for 5 unique scopes [3]. So, up to 5 `construct`-mappings for the same pattern may exist in a particular target logic mapping. We use the scope component in the `construct_id` to disambiguated them. But only those variants need to be specified that can be represented in the target logic;
- `invocation` defines a *gateway* to the underlying Java runtime environment of PSPWizard. XML is a data definition language not a full-featured programming

language *per se*. However, especially the mapping of subordinate attributes in pattern definitions requires additional computational power. To achieve this, we exploit Java's reflection mechanism and equip each target logic mapping with a *support class* [8] that provides string-based auxiliary methods to perform the required transformations. At runtime, the GUI front-end of PSPWizard dynamically loads the external support class and binds the `invocation` tag to a method in the support class.

2.3 Graphical User Interface

The GUI front-end of PSPWizard is a dynamically generated when the target logic is selected. The PSPWizard generator uses the XML documents defined for the structured English grammars and the target logic, and processes both to yield an interface configuration for the GUI front-end.

Consider, for example, the requirement: *"Whenever a crash has occurred and the crash is not front-on, then within 60ms both side airbags shall be deployed."* This temporal property corresponds to the real-time *Response* pattern [7] and can be captured in structured English as follows:

```
Globally,
    if [crash=occurred AND crash_location=NOT(front_on)],
    then [side_airbag1=deployed AND side_airbag2=deployed]
         within 60 ms.
```

We can use PSPWizard to rewrite this property to a suitable target logic mapping (*e.g.*, MTL) as illustrated in Figure 2.

The specific level of support that PSPWizard offers for the definition of system properties depends on the available target logics mappings. We have experimented with both tool-specific and logic-specific mappings. Our approach allows for a seamless integration of either type of mapping into PSPWizard. The structured English grammar of a given pattern catalog can result in a temporal logical formula that is represented by a CTL, MTL, PCTL, a LaTeX formula, or in an property specification formalism of a model checking tool like SPIN, UPPAAL, or PRISM.

2.4 Maturity and Availability

PSPWizard is open source and available here: `http://mercury.it.swin.edu.au/g_archeopterix/pspwizard/`. The current distribution of the tool consists of a collection of state-of-the-art property specification pattern catalogs including probabilistic and real-time extensions (*e.g.*, MTL and PRISM). The tool is also accompanied by a Perl script that can be used to automatically generate the XML mapping specification from a textual specification.

3. CONCLUSION AND FUTURE WORK

Specification pattern systems [1,3,5–7] have improved the acceptance of formal verification techniques and have been demonstrated their usefulness [2,9] in a variety of domains. To continue this development we have developed the Property Specification Pattern Wizard (PSPWizard), a framework that provides a feasible solution to the problem of pairing the structured English grammar of different specification pattern catalogs with suitable temporal logic mappings. As a result, we obtain an approach that assists system engineers in their task to capture system properties formally, while at the same time allowing them to use a natural language format to formulate those properties.

The front-end of PSPWizard is dialog-oriented and mimics the design choices necessary to capture system properties. Whether or not a specific attribute can be expressed in the target logic is an information that is readily available in the user interface of PSPWizard. Moreover, the automated translations of property specifications to temporal logic formulae enables the system engineer to focus on the system attribute rather than how that system attribute must be encoded in the target logic. This increases productivity.

The presented tool demonstrates the feasibility of a machine-assisted selection and parametrization of temporal logical properties in terms of specification patterns. At present, PSPWizard is a stand-alone application. In the future, we envision to embed it in a Web-browser and operate its functionality as a Web service that provides managed access to both the specification pattern catalogs and the associated mappings to target logics. Moreover, we plan to explore options that would allow to PSPWizard to interact with suitable verification engines directly.

4. REFERENCES

[1] P. Bellini, P. Nesi, and D. Rogai. Expressing and organizing real-time specification patterns via temporal logics. *Journal of Systems and Software*, 82(2):183 – 196, 2009.

[2] J. Corbett, M. Dwyer, J. Hatcliff, C. Pasareanu, Robby, S. Laubach, and H. Zheng. Bandera: Extracting finite-state models from Java source code. In *Proc. 22nd International Conference on Software Engineering, ICSE 00*, pages 439–448. IEEE Computer Society, 2000.

[3] M. B. Dwyer, G. S. Avrunin, and J. C. Corbett. Patterns in property specifications for finite-state verification. In *Proceedings of the 1999 International Conference on Software Engineering (ICSE'99)*, pages 411–421, New York, 1999. Association for Computing Machinery.

[4] S. Flake, W. Müller, and J. Ruf. Structured English for Model Checking Specification. *Methoden und Beschreibungssprachen zur Modellierung und Verifikation von Schaltungen und Systemen, Frankfurt/M*, pages 99–108, 2003.

[5] V. Gruhn and R. Laue. Patterns for timed property specifications. *Electr. Not. Theor. Comp. Sci*, 153(2):117–133, 2006.

[6] L. Grunske. Specification patterns for probabilistic quality properties. In Robby, editor, *30th International Conference on Software Engineering (ICSE 2008)*, pages 31–40. ACM, 2008.

[7] S. Konrad and B. H. C. Cheng. Real-time specification patterns. In G.-C. Roman, W. G. Griswold, and B. Nuseibeh, editors, *27th Int. Conf. on Software Engineering, ICSE 05*, pages 372–381. ACM, 2005.

[8] M. Lumpe. Applications = Components + GLoo. *Electronic Notes in Theoretical Computer Science*, 182:123–138, June 2007.

[9] J. Yu, T. P. Manh, J. Han, Y. Jin, Y. Han, and J. Wang. Pattern based property specification and verification for service composition. In K. Aberer et al., editor, *Proc. 7th Int. Conference on Web Information Systems Engineering, WISE 06*, volume 4255 of *LNCS*, pages 156–168. Springer, 2006.

Using Social Media to Study the Diversity of Example Usage Among Professional Developers

Ohad Barzilay
Blavatnik School of Computer Science
Tel-Aviv University
Tel-Aviv, Israel
ohadbr@tau.ac.il

Orit Hazzan
Department of Education in Technology and Science
Technion – IIT
Haifa, Israel
oritha@techunix.technion.ac.il

Amiram Yehudai
Blavatnik School of Computer Science
Tel-Aviv University
Tel-Aviv, Israel
amiramy@tau.ac.il

ABSTRACT
Socio-professional websites such as LinkedIn use various mechanisms such as network of colleagues, groups and discussions to assist their users in maintaining their professional network and keeping up with relevant discussions. Software professionals post hundreds of thousands of comments each week in these group discussions regarding technological and methodological aspects of their work. Analyzing these comments enables us, the software community at large, to better understand the state of the practice of many aspects of software development. In this paper we describe a case study in which we use such LinkedIn group discussion to learn about developers' perception of using code examples.

We show how the discussion participants' online profile could be used for research purposes and to provide the data with additional context. Our preliminary findings suggest that although many developers advocate the usage of code examples in their work, many of them use examples in a limited way. We also show that some developers oppose using examples altogether. The implications of this work are twofold; we pose research questions and suggest future work both in order to leverage further the tools offered by social media websites, as well as to explore further aspects involved in example usage.

Categories and Subject Descriptors
D.2.3 [**Software Engineering**]: Coding Tools and Techniques. K.7 [**Computing Milieux**]: The Computing Profession.

General Terms
Human Factors, Measurement.

Keywords
Social media, LinkedIn, Example usage, Virtual focus group.

1. INTRODUCTION AND MOTIVATION
As part of our comprehensive research on the use of code examples by professional programmers, we conducted an online survey in which we asked programmers about their examples usage practices and techniques. To encourage developers to participate in the survey, we used social network sites [5] and posted invitation on the LinkedIn[1] ".NET People" discussion group. We received 134 comments in this discussion thread, written by 67 separate subjects, and it became a virtual focus group on the developers' perceptions of example usage.

This emergent use of socio-professional media for research purposes was surprising to us (the original post was only meant to solicit developers' participation in our online survey). Nevertheless, we found that using the services offered by LinkedIn we could extract additional data points in the analysis process. Specifically, we used the discussion participants' background such as years of experience, size of company and role to examine whether their views regarding example usage correlate to these factors.

2. BACKGROUND AND RELATED WORK
In this paper we use social media, namely LinkedIn, to study how developers use code examples. Hence the work related to this research can be divided respectively into work on social websites, and work that studies developers' use of code examples.

Bougie *et al.* [4] investigate the use of Twitter by software engineers. They found that software engineering-related topics are discussed over Twitter (about 23% of the tweets that were qualitatively analyzed) and they outline some of the challenges in exploring this type of data. Skeels and Grudin [12] found that LinkedIn is widely used to build and maintain external professional networks and report that social networking software has found professional uses. Finding high quality content in social media was investigated by Agichtein *et al.* [1]. They investigate methods for exploiting community feedback to automatically identify high quality content in Yahoo! Answers[2], a large community question/answering portal. In a related project, Shah and Pomerantz [11] found that contextual information such as a user's profile can be used to predict content quality. In our work we also use the user's profile; however, we do not use it in order to determine the *quality* of the answer but rather in order to provide *additional context* to the data.

Developers' use of code examples was studied mainly in the context of using designated recommender systems such as the Strathcona system [8], EG [7], Blueprint [6] and Mica [13]. While these studies highlight the benefit of example usage, they do not address some the challenges involved in extensive example usage. In our study we find that some developers avoid extensive example usage; some of them explicitly and others are not aware of additional opportunities of using examples. These results support our previous findings regarding developers' lack of attentiveness to example usage [3].

Permission to make digital or hard copies of all or part of this work for personal or classroom use is granted without fee provided that copies are not made or distributed for profit or commercial advantage and that copies bear this notice and the full citation on the first page. To copy otherwise, or republish, to post on servers or to redistribute to lists, requires prior specific permission and/or a fee.
ESEC/FSE'11, September 5–9, 2011, Szeged, Hungary.
Copyright 2011 ACM 978-1-4503-0443-6/11/09...$10.00.

[1] http://www.linkedin.com/

[2] http://answers.yahoo.com/

3. LINKEDIN.COM

LinkedIn.com is a business-oriented social networking website, hosting more than 100 million professionals worldwide, and rapidly growing at roughly one million new LinkedIn members every week (as of March 2011[3]). The network is global, 56% of the users are outside of the United States. High tech is the second largest sector represented in LinkedIn with 9% of the members (largest sector is Service with 20%), and 5 out of the 6 most represented companies in LinkedIn are technological.

The volume of LinkedIn, as well as its rich engagement mechanisms, makes it a suitable tool for data gathering regarding professional communities. In this paper we investigate professional developers' views regarding example usage by analyzing LinkedIn group discussions.

3.1 LinkedIn Groups

LinkedIn allows members to form and join groups based on professional or shared interest. Users may take active parts in discussions and quickly discover the most popular discussions in their area of interest. Members have an active part in determining the top discussions by liking and commenting, and may find interesting discussions by seeing who liked a discussion and how many people commented.

More than 17 million LinkedIn users are members in groups, there are more than 1.5 million new group memberships per week, and more than 1.2 million weekly posts and comments (including likes, jobs, news, and shares).

LinkedIn group discussions may form an online virtual focus group [9]. They have some interesting properties that make them suitable to be used for research purposes, as is explained in what follows.

3.1.1 Subjects

All LinkedIn users have an online profile. This profile includes their employment history, experience, education, social network, recommendations and more. Since some users use this profile also for job hunting, the data there is detailed and accurate. This fact has some important implications for researchers:

- Researchers are able to cross check participants' answers and backgrounds (educational or professional) and reveal some interesting correlations.
- Barriers of research participation is lower (compared to online surveys), since subjects are not required to fill in their details before answering the survey questions.
- Subjects are traceable: the researchers may contact a specific subject for follow-up purposes, via email or the site's internal inbox.

3.1.2 Reaching potential subjects

The following properties can help researchers reach potential subjects:

- Specific LinkedIn groups exist in many fields and interests, which allow researchers to address a segmented community which is not only the most relevant for the research purposes, but also might find interest in participating in the discussion.
- Using social platforms might provide participants with an incentive to take part in a discussion in order to increase their Web presence in some areas of interest.
- LinkedIn promotes new topics and hot topics to the group's front page, which assists researchers in reaching broader audiences if the community finds interest in their topic.

3.1.3 Discussion visibility

In discussion groups, unlike online surveys, the discussion is visible both during and after the research period. Some of the implications of this fact for researchers, participants, and the rest of the community are as follows:

- *Participants* can see each other's responses, which may further promote the discussion. Participants can relate to statements made by others and can fine-tune their arguments accordingly. Participants may change their mind over time and may be influenced by peer pressure.
- Other *researchers* can review the discussion later on and may re-validate the conclusions independently.
- The discussion is also visible to other members of the *community*; hence a practitioner in the field may contribute to a discussion in that field in order to increase his or her Web visibility.

4. RESEARCH METHODOLOGY

This study is part of a larger ongoing research on the use of code examples by professional programmers. The research investigates the following questions:

1a. Do professional developers use code examples in their work? What are their reasons for using or avoiding them?

1b. Do developers support extensive example usage? Do they associate example usage with a specific kind of development task?

1c. What challenges are involved in example usage? What techniques are used to overcome them?

However, the emergence of social media usage for research purposes added another set of research questions as follows:

2a. What can be learned from social media on developers opinions?

2b. What mechanisms provided by social media web sites could be leveraged for research purposes?

2c. What are the characteristics of the different social media channels?

In this short paper, we partially address questions 1a, 2a and 2b.

The data analysis included manual qualitative coding of the discussion transcript (134 posts, including 12 that were later deleted by their authors) and the public profile of all 67 discussion participants. Discussion transcript appears in [2].

5. CASE STUDY: EXAMPLE USAGE

5.1 Discussion Participants

We used the online profile of the discussion participants to extract relevant data about their background. We went over the professional experience section of their LinkedIn profile and checked the *size* of the companies they work for, the *role* they filled in these companies, and the total length of their relevant *employment period*. This data is summarized in Figures 1-3. Participants who work in multiple companies and/or in multiple roles appear multiple times in Figures 1-2.

[3] http://blog.linkedin.com/2011/03/22/linkedin-100-million/

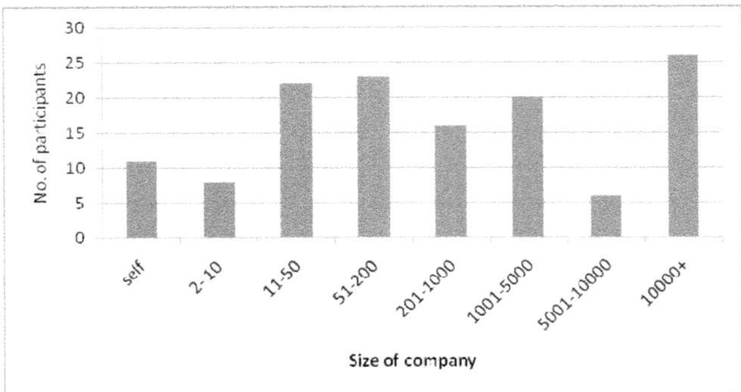

Figure 1: Size of companies in which participants work

Working in large companies is sometimes associated with the awareness of rigorous methods and inner protocols. For example, public companies often have a strict policy regarding using open source code, in order to protect their own intellectual property. Thirty nine percent (39%) of the participants have worked for large companies (more than 10,000 employees).

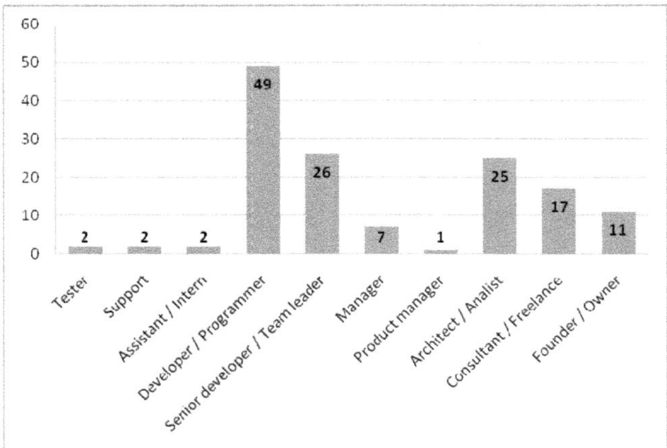

Figure 2: Professional experience of participants (job title)

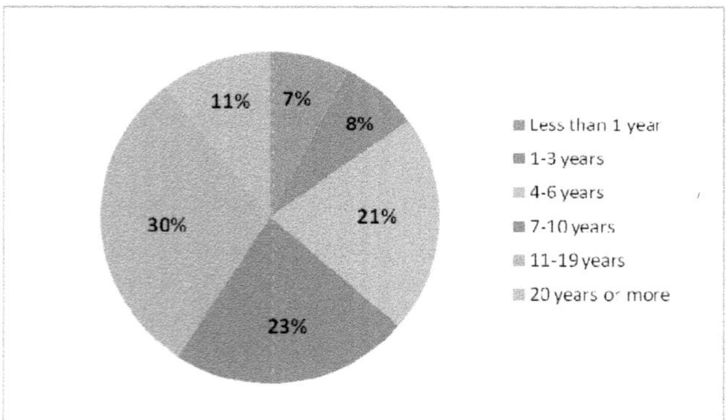

Figure 3: Professional experience of participants (in years)

Most of the discussion participants served in multiple roles and in multiple companies, only one of them had no relevant background (HR person who used the discussion thread for job hunt). The most frequent positions were: software developer, senior developer and analyst. Sixty four percent (64%) of the participants have more than 7 years of experience (41% have more than 11 years), and the average experience was 10 years. This data also implies the age of the participants.

5.2 Preliminary Findings

Based on the participants' responses, we categorized them into 3 major groups according to their approach to example usage:

(1) **Supporters**: Habitual example users – 35%

(2) **Opposers**: Those who oppose using examples altogether due to their inherent pitfalls – 14%

(3) **Limited**: Those who use examples only in a limited context: only examples of certain size, only for learning purposes, only from specific sources etc. – 51%.

As Figure 4 shows, similar proportion was kept across different roles, with the following two exceptions: there were no managers who oppose example usage altogether, and there were more founders who support extensive example usage than those who use examples only in a limited way. This could be explained by the fact that managers and founders are more attentive to the business and organizational perspective of software engineering and therefore see the benefit of example usage in a wider context.

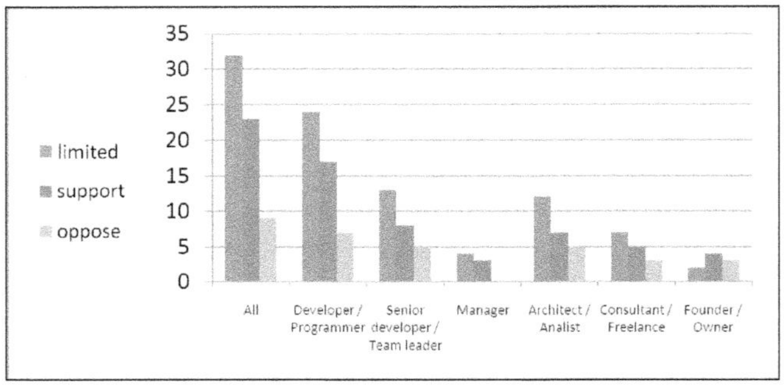

Figure 4: Dividing participants into groups according to their approach to example usage and to their job title. Participants who work in multiple roles appear multiple times.

In Figure 5 the participants are partitioned by their years of professional experience. Although not statistically significant, it can be seen that the 11-19 group is the only one in which there are more example supporters than limited example users. In addition, in this group the proportion of example opposers is smaller than the overall proportion of example opposers. If we ignore the participants with experience period of less than 3 years and or more than 20 years (less than 6 participants in each subgroup) we see that example supporters proportion increases as the engineers are more experienced. We propose few explanations for this observation: first, since there are some challenges involved with extensive example usage, novice developers, who lack the tools to address these challenges, do not leverage the full potential of code examples. The more experienced a developer is – the more tools he or she acquires that could assist him or her in addressing these challenges, and uses examples in additional ways. This also conforms previous empirical findings [10] showing that reuse-related experience is one of the two major factors (together with self-efficacy) affecting software developers' intention to reuse software assets.

Also, experienced developers might have been exposed to different programming style than their own and developed their example usage attentiveness. In our previous study [3] we found that example usage level of attentiveness could be easily increased.

Another explanation is related to the fact that many of the experienced developers are promoted to managerial positions, or at least are assigned managerial responsibilities. As discussed earlier, such responsibilities make them consider example usage in a wider perspective.

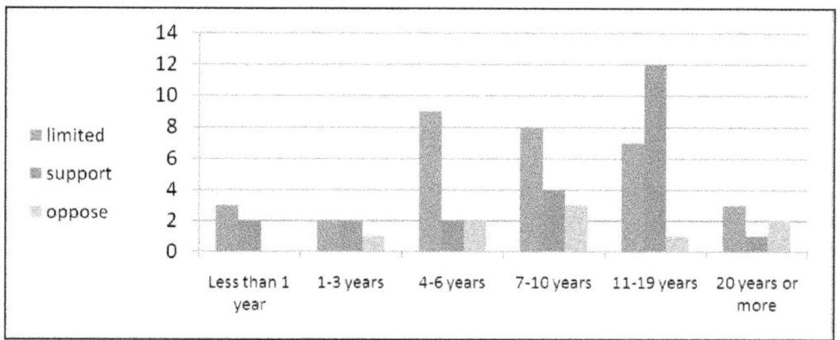

Figure 5: Dividing participants into groups according to their approach to example usage and to their professional experience period.

6. DISCUSSION

The data presented above suggests that developers are diverse in their approach to using examples. Many developers use examples only in a limited way and others oppose example usage altogether.

These results are rather surprising to us and dramatically different (definitely more intense) than the sporadic comments we were used to get. However, this fact also made this discussion thread an excellent opportunity to investigate further the more profound reasons that dominate developers approach towards example usage.

7. LIMITATIONS

One threat to the validity of this research stems from the relatively small number of participants and their homogeneous technological interest (.net) which do not represent the entire developers' community. This is true. However, we do not draw any quantitative conclusions from this research, but rather, use it as a motivation for further research. In Section 5.2 we indeed use percentages; however, they are only used to summarize this specific discussion thread.

Another threat is that since users are posting on a public forum there may be bias of the volunteers - i.e., only those people who feel strongly about this topic (or employees from very small companies who do not have restrictions) have commented. This limitation is also related to a more general limitation of focus groups, in which the dynamics of the discussion can be easily diverged by few dominant voices.

Another threat related to the publicity of the medium is participants that do not write what they really think, but what they think is expected from them to think (e.g. by future employers). If this is true, it does not make the results less surprising – it implies that many of the participants think that they'd better express opinions that oppose example usage then to support it.

Another threat is related to the licensing issue (though mentioned by only one participant) – in some large companies developers *are not allowed* to use open source code due to copyright laws. These developers would not confess using open source code, even if they actually do so.

8. IMPACT AND FUTURE WORK

In this paper we shared our preliminary results of studying developers' perception of example usage using social media. We showed that developers are diverse in their views of example usage; however we did not provide yet any explanation for the reasons of this diversity. In future work we intend to further analyze these results, as well as using additional research tools in order to address our other research questions.

Furthermore, now that we have encountered the rich data that resides in social media regarding developers' views, we could probe this data source more extensively, e.g. by using the LinkedIn API[4], in order to extract and process larger amount of data regarding additional aspects of software engineering.

9. REFERENCES

[1] E. Agichtein, C. Castillo, D. Donato, A. Gionis, and G. Mishne. Finding high-quality content in social media. In *Proceedings of the international conference on Web search and web data mining*, WSDM '08, pp 183–194, 2008. ACM.

[2] O. Barzilay. Do .NET People Use Examples? Virtual focus group transcript: http://tinyurl.com/FocusGroupData, 2010.

[3] O. Barzilay, A. Yehudai, and O. Hazzan. Developers attentiveness to example usage. In *Human Aspects of Software Engineering*, HAoSE '10, pp 1–8, 2010. ACM.

[4] G. Bougie, J. Starke, M.-A. Storey, and D. M. German. Towards understanding twitter use in software engineering: preliminary findings, ongoing challenges and future questions. In *Proc of the 2nd international workshop on Web 2.0 for software engineering*, Web2SE '11, pp 31–36, 2011.

[5] d. m. boyd and N. B. Ellison. Social network sites: Definition, history, and scholarship. *Journal of Computer-Mediated Communication*, 13(1):210–230, 2007.

[6] J. Brandt, M. Dontcheva, M. Weskamp, and S. R. Klemmer. Example-centric programming: integrating web search into the development environment. In *Proceedings of the 28th international conference on Human factors in computing systems*, CHI '10, pp 513–522, 2010. ACM.

[7] J. Edwards. Example centric programming. *SIGPLAN Not.*, 39(12):84–91, 2004.

[8] R. Holmes and G. C. Murphy. Using structural context to recommend source code examples. In *ICSE '05: Proceedings of the 27th international conference on Software engineering*, pages 117–125. ACM, 2005.

[9] J. Kontio, J. Bragge, and L. Lehtola. The focus group method as an empirical tool in software engineering. In *Guide to Advanced Empirical Software Engineering*, pp 93–116. Springer London, 2008.

[10] V. Mellarkod, R. Appan, D. R. Jones, and K. Sherif. A multi-level analysis of factors affecting software developers' intention to reuse software assets: An empirical investigation. *Information & Management*, 44(7):613 – 625, 2007.

[11] C. Shah and J. Pomerantz. Evaluating and predicting answer quality in community qa. In *Proc of the 33rd international conference on Research and development in information retrieval*, SIGIR '10, pp 411–418, 2010. ACM.

[12] M. M. Skeels and J. Grudin. When social networks cross boundaries: a case study of workplace use of facebook and linkedin. In *Proc of the ACM 2009 international conference on Supporting group work*, GROUP '09, pp 95–104, 2009.

[13] J. Stylos and B. Myers. Mica: A web-search tool for finding api components and examples. In *Visual Languages and Human-Centric Computing, 2006. VL/HCC 2006. IEEE Symposium on*, pp 195 –202, 2006.

[4] http://developer.linkedin.com/community/overview

Social Sensing: When Users Become Monitors

Raian Ali, Carlos Solis, Mazeiar Salehie, Inah Omoronyia
Lero - University of Limerick, Ireland

Bashar Nuseibeh
Lero - University of Limerick, Ireland
The Open University, UK

Walid Maalej
Technische Universität München, Germany

ABSTRACT

Adaptation requires a system to monitor its operational context to ensure that when changes occur, a suitable adaptation action is planned and taken at runtime. The ultimate goal of adaptation is that users get their dynamic requirements met efficiently and correctly. Context changes and users' judgment of the role of the system in meeting their requirements are drivers for adaptation. In many cases, these drivers are hard to identify by designers at design time and hard to monitor by the use of exclusively technological means by the system at runtime. In this paper, we propose *Social Sensing* as the activity performed by users who act as monitors and provide information needed for adaptation at runtime. Such information helps the system cope with technology limitations and designers' uncertainty. We discuss the motivation and foundations of Social Sensing and outline a set of research challenges to address in future work.

Categories and Subject Descriptors
D.2.2 [**Software Engineering**]: Design Tools and Techniques
General Terms
Design, Human Factors, Management
Keywords
Requirements Engineering; Social Software Engineering; Models at Runtime; Adaptive Software Engineering.

1. INTRODUCTION

Self-adaptive systems are increasingly expected to cope with the volatile nature of the environment in which the system operates. Different categories of environmental changes trigger different categories of responses [1]. For example, security breaches and attacks could trigger certain self-protection actions, or changes in the available resources could trigger self-optimization actions. The ultimate goal of this so-called *self-** computing paradigm is that users' dynamic requirements are met efficiently and effectively, and adaptation is done autonomously by the system so that computing transparency is maximized and humans' (designers and users) effort is minimized [2].

The adaptation loop [3] consists of monitoring changes in the system operational environment, analysis of changes, planning an action, executing it, monitoring back the effects, and so on. Focusing on the monitoring stage, the system should monitor its context, i.e. the state of the environment in which it operates [4]. Moreover, the system has to monitor if its executed actions were performed successfully. Self-healing deals with incorrect execution in a way that allows a system to handle faults and errors autonomously. However, the technical correctness of system execution (bug-free, no connection errors happens, etc.) does not necessarily mean that users' requirements are met [5]. For example, sending an invitation to a meeting can be done via one of two system alternatives: by SMS or email. A successful sending of an invitation to a meeting via email does not necessarily mean that the invitee was notified on time as the invitee might miss the email or misinterpret it. That is, monitoring should primarily be concerned with determining if users find the system execution a valid and effective way for reaching their requirements, and adaptation should respond to how users judge each system execution against the meeting of their requirements.

Monitoring context changes and the quality of each system alternative is not always achievable with the use of solely technological means and might require users to collaborate with the system. For example, in a driver-assistant system, the traffic level in the area is a context attribute that affects to which park the system should guide the driver. Such context might be un-monitorable due to the lack of necessary infrastructure. As a solution, the system could rely on the information obtainable through the drivers' community in that area. The system could have different alternatives to interact with a driver while assisting him (voice commands, maps, street view, etc.). For instance, a quality attribute such as "readability" could be judged differently in different contexts for each of these alternatives. However, neither the designers at design time nor the system at runtime can decide with certainty how the drivers judge "readability" for each alternative. As a solution, drivers may be asked to provide such quality judgments at runtime after an alternative is executed.

Besides monitoring the values of context attributes and quality attributes, users could also be involved in identifying such attributes. Users act as monitors to decide relevant context and quality attributes to add to the design of the system and irrelevant ones to remove from it as well. For example, drivers might add "straightness of the road" as a context attribute which influences the quality of each interaction alternative (voice command, map, street view, etc.) against the quality attribute "readability". Moreover, drivers might add "minimum noise" as a relevant quality attribute, which the designers did not consider when designing the system, so that each system alternative is also qualified against it. Thus, users are also monitors for identifying drivers for adaptation, i.e. mainly context and quality attributes.

Maalej et al. [6] discuss how to make the user's involvement a first order concern in software projects, moving from a transactional to a social engineering process. In line with this view, the involvement of users can also be done at runtime as an integral part of the system operation and not only the engineering process. Ali et al [7] propose to weave together the variability of context and the space of alternatives designed to reach the requirements. However, context is presumed monitorable by the system at runtime and the relation between context and alternatives is specified under certainty. These two design assumptions are hard to achieve in certain systems, which might need humans to monitor context and its influence on the activation, adoptability, and quality of each system alternative.

Permission to make digital or hard copies of all or part of this work for personal or classroom use is granted without fee provided that copies are not made or distributed for profit or commercial advantage and that copies bear this notice and the full citation on the first page. To copy otherwise, or republish, to post on servers or to redistribute to lists, requires prior specific permission and/or a fee.
ESEC/FSE'11, September 5-9, 2010, Szeged, Hungary.
Copyright 2011 ACM 978-1-4503-0443-6/11/09...$10.00.

In this paper, we propose *Social Sensing* as a system development technique which involves users, at runtime, in the monitoring activity of the adaptation loop. The goal is that limitations of technological devices as well as uncertainty and incompleteness of the system design are faced via the involvement of users' perception as an integral part of the system monitor. Social Sensing treats users as a primitive component of the system instead of pure consumers of its functionalities. We discuss Social Sensing foundations in Section 2, list research challenges in Section 3, and conclude the paper in Section 4.

2. SOCIAL SENSING: FOUNDATIONS

Social Sensing is based on exploiting users' perception as an integral part of the computation. The system relies on the users' community to get information which is un-monitorable by automated means and/or unspecifiable under certainty by designers at design time. The users play the monitor role and provide input to the system so that the right decision and response will be planned and enacted during the operation. This is particularly important when dealing with systems involving a community of users. For example, when volunteer drivers provide context information, e.g. the traffic level in a specific area, other drivers will benefit from it when the system executes for them. The information provided by the volunteer drivers about the quality of a system behavior, e.g., the comfort level of each interaction technique for guiding a driver, is the main ingredient for the collective judgment of the drivers' community about each alternative so the system can act accordingly.

We discuss Social Sensing in the context of adaptive systems. In such systems, the context monitoring as well as the validity and quality of system alternatives are essential to guide adaptation. Moreover, we focus on the problem space rather than the solution space taking the users' satisfaction about the role of system in meeting their requirements as the main goal of adaptation.

Social Sensing advocates that users can play a role in establishing the monitoring process. Users understand the system as a means to solve their problems and can collaborate with it as monitors providing information using their own terms, which belong to the problem domain (requirements, quality, context, validity, etc.) not the technical solution domain (bug, error, protocol, proxy, etc.). Thus, one of the ideal domains of Social Sensing is requirements-driven adaptation. In the rest of this section, we discuss the meta-model of this domain (represented in Figure 1) as a baseline for our Social Sensing method.

Variability is the cornerstone for adaptation. A system provided with only one alternative is unable to adapt when context changes. A system alternative is a synthesis between automated and human activities intended to reach certain requirements. In adaptive systems, a requirement could be reached via different system alternatives. For example, considering the driver-assistant system, the system could have two main system alternatives "guide to a public park" and "guide to a paid park". The interaction with a driver for guiding him to a suitable park can be also achieved via different alternatives such as voice commands, an interactive map, or a street view. Adaptation is seen as the selection of the system alternative which best fits to the current context. The fitness of a system alternative is measured via both its validity as a means to reach the requirements and its quality degree as well.

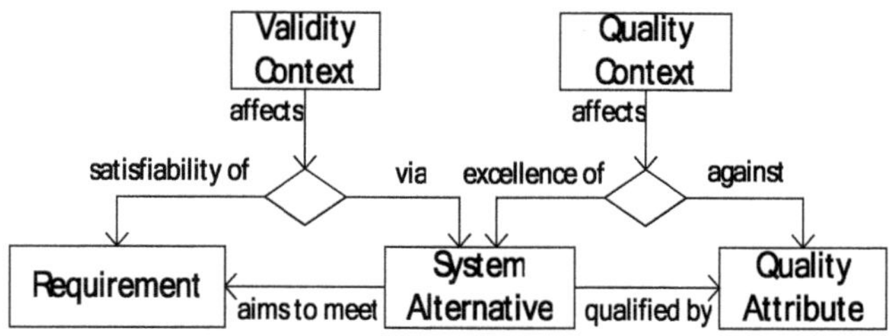

Figure 1 Meta-model of Requirements-driven Adaptation Artifacts

The validity of a system alternative is a binary property referring to its success/failure in reaching the requirement it is intended for. For example, using the guidance of the driver-assistance via one alternative, the driver either reaches (valid) or does not reach (invalid) a free parking place. The quality of a system alternative is captured via a number of quality attributes each representing a distinguished characteristic of the degree of excellence of an alternative. For example, the quality of each way of interacting with a driver could be refined to "readability", "fast", or "less distraction". The assessment of a system alternative against a quality attribute could fall into a designated scale (e.g. [very poor, poor, acceptable, good, very good], or [low, medium, high]). The validity and the quality of the operation of a system alternative in the past are main factors to consider when adaptation is planned so that the best alternative will be selected and applied.

The validity and the quality of a system alternative are context-dependent. Context is represented via context attributes, each one representing a distinguished characteristics of the environment in which the system operates, e.g., driving speed, driver age, traffic level, etc. Certain context attributes might influence the validity of a system alternative and/or its quality against certain quality attributes. For example, suppose the following context attributes (Driver is in a *hurry*, The distance to the public park is *far*, Traffic level is *high*) then most probably the system alternative "guide to public park" is invalid. Certain context attributes might influence the quality assessment of a system alternative against certain quality attribute. For example, the level of driving experience, the complexity of the road and the traffic level in the area are context attributes which influence the assessment of each alternative of communicating with a driver against a quality attribute like "less distraction".

Social Sensing plays a major role within the above settings and is characterized by the following four distinct contributions:

1. **Context values**. Users play a role in obtaining values of context attributes that affect the validity and quality of system alternatives, which are not monitorable for reasons such as limitations or failure of technology, lack of infrastructure, etc. Using these values, a system can decide applicable alternatives by analyzing the history of each alternative in similar values of context in the past. As a result, the alternative which best fits the current values of context will be applied. For example, a context attribute like "there is an accident in a certain area" may not be monitorable by the driver-assistant system due to the lack of access to the official traffic management system or because no such system exists. Thus when volunteer drivers passing close to the accident's location provide such information, the system will benefit from it for guiding other drivers.

2. **Quality and validity assessment**. Uncertainty is inherent when designing a system. The validity of a system alternative and its quality assessment against each quality attribute is not always decidable under certainty by designers at design time. In Social Sensing, the users play the role of monitors of the validity and quality of each system alternative. For example, whether guiding a driver with medium driving experience via an interactive map is a valid interaction method, is unknown unless the system operates in practice and drivers themselves decide that. Moreover, designers might not be able to decide the quality of guiding a driver, who is familiar with the area, via voice commands against the quality attribute "less distraction". Moreover, validity and quality are not static properties. What is known to be a valid and high-quality alternative at one point in time may lose these characteristics as time passes. Social Sensing allows for a continuous evaluation of the system alternatives by involving the users' community. For example, "voice recognition" might be judged as low quality interaction alternative compared to a quality attribute such as "ease of use" by drivers. In the future, when the drivers become more familiar with this technology, their judgment of its quality might be different. Social Sensing allows for capturing changes in the users' community judgment of the system alternatives so that adaptation is up-to-date.

3. **Context attributes identification**. Uncertainty concerns also the identification of the context attributes which affect the validity and the quality of each system alternative. Designers might be uncertain if their identification is correct and complete. Social Sensing allows users to act as designers while the system is operating, by dropping context attributes that they judge to be irrelevant and adding others which they believe to be relevant for the validity and the quality of each system alternative. In Social Sensing, users can engage with this process throughout the life of a system. This is essential to cope with the fact that relevance itself is not a static property and what is judged to be relevant at the moment might become irrelevant in the future, and vice versa. For example, unlike the designers' specification, the drivers' community might identify "the existence of a staff assistant" as a relevant context attribute that affects the quality attribute "reliability" of the system alternative "guide to paid parking". However, this attribute may turn out to be irrelevant when the drivers' community becomes more competent about the use of new technology and trusts it more. Moreover, the designers might specify that "the existence of traffic lights inside the park" is a context attribute which affects all alternatives against the quality attribute "less distraction". On the other hand, this decision might be seen as a wrong one by the drivers' community and they may decide collectively to drop this context attribute and consider it irrelevant.

4. **Quality attributes identification**. Similarly to the above discussion about context attributes, designers might miss quality attributes which the users' community finds relevant. Also, designers might include quality attributes that may be deemed irrelevant by the user community. Social Sensing gives users a voice and allows them to be a part of the decision making team. It allows them to continuously play the role of monitor to decide relevant quality attributes to add and irrelevant ones to drop when appropriate. For example, "reduced pollution" might be considered by the drivers' community as a relevant quality attribute when evaluating each system alternative so that the system might choose park place that is not ideal in terms of time and effort required to reach it but good for reducing the pollution in the area. Thus, if the drivers' community decides that this attribute is relevant, it will be added to the list of quality attributes defined initially by the designers. Moreover, the users' community might drop some attributes from that list if they are found to be irrelevant. For example, in a city where traffic is often low and the need to reduce pollution is not critical, the drivers' community might collectively decide to drop the attribute "reduced pollution".

Social Sensing allows users to express their opinion so the system analyzes it and takes decisions which reflect the collective intelligence of the users' community. The information provided by the users' community at runtime is a main ingredient for planning and enacting adaptation. On the one hand, it helps the system to cope with the limitations of the technological means of monitoring the environment and the uncertainty and incompleteness in the designers' decisions. On the other hand, it allows the users to drive the adaptation and maximize its correctness so that their requirements are reached in the best available way when changes happen.

3. RESEARCH CHALLENGES

While Social Sensing is powerful for crowd-sourcing users and enabling them to act as monitors, it brings several software engineering challenges.

1. **Users' subjectivity**. Social Sensing relies on the existence of a certain degree of similarity in the perception of different users. That is, Social Sensing requires that the perception of users of the values and relevance of the adaptation drivers (context and quality attributes, etc.) are similar. However, this is not always the case and users might perceive adaptation drivers subjectively. For example, the value of a context like "traffic level" could be monitored by one driver as "medium" and by another as "high". The same subjectivity could arise when assessing the system alternatives against a quality attribute. Devising methods and analysis mechanisms to normalize the different users' perception is a challenging problem of Social Sensing.

2. **Trust management**. Social Sensing requires users to provide information and thus implies dealing with trustworthiness of information and users. The benefits of the openness-to-the-crowd might be sacrificed if untrusted users, who might intentionally or unintentionally cause harm to the system or misuse it, are not detected and dealt with. Moreover, users need to trust the system itself before collaborating with it. Developing systems that adopt Social Sensing and are able to inspire users' trust is another socio-technical challenge, and achieving such trust has to be engineered as a first class requirement of the whole system.

3. **Security and Privacy**. Depending on the criticality and sensitivity of monitored information, security goals such as confidentiality, integrity, and availability might become concerns in Social Sensing. For example, Social Sensing might not be ideal for a driver-assistant system for an ambulance that is typically assigned to critical missions, unless information provided by the driver's community in

the area is strictly verified and secured. Moreover, while Social Sensing relies on crowd-sourcing a large number of users, it also opens the door for malicious users to attack the system. For example, some drivers might provide wrong information that leads to less traffic in the areas where they drive. Furthermore, it is notable that some of the security requirements in Social Sensing could be in conflict with other categories of requirements such as privacy ones. For example, if a driver refuses to provide his location for privacy reasons, the system might not be able to help him avoid traffic, thereby making the main system service practically unavailable.

4. **Transparency**. An important goal of adaptation is to minimize humans' (users and designers) effort and maximize computers' transparency. Social Sensing implies the intervention of users as monitors and thus users are required to provide input not necessarily used for their own immediate benefit. This means that Social Sensing, if not designed effectively, may provide adaptation capabilities for one group of people while potentially violating adaptation of another. For example, the evaluation of a system alternative may be provided by a user after the operation terminates, so that the system benefits in next operations executed for benefit of different drivers. Devising mechanisms to encourage users to act as monitors and feel some gain by doing this task is therefore a research challenge to address.
5. **Volatility.** The validity of information provided by users, especially context changes, is volatile. Context may change rapidly so that information, which was true when the users provided it, might become false when the system starts to plan and enact adaptation. Social Sensing design has either to deal with this volatility or to avoid taking decisions based on information having highly volatile validity. For example, when the car needs to be refueled, the driver-assistant activates the requirement "guide the driver to filling station". When the system receives information from other drivers that there is a filling station close to the driver location and starts to plan and execute adaptation (notifying the driver, getting his confirmation, choosing the right interaction method, etc.), the driver would have passed the station. That is, the system has to deal with the liveness of sensed information.
6. **Implementation**. There are major challenges regarding the implementation of Social Sensing. These challenges include the way to represent context and quality attributes and the values and judgments provided by users, the way to capture this information efficiently and independently from the applications, the decision about what information to collect exactly and how long this data should be stored, etc [6]. Moreover, involving users in dealing with large volume of information might compromise the applicability of Social Sensing. For example, the list of quality attributes provided by the users' community could increase to an extent where users find it tedious to assess a system alternative against all attributes included in it. This means that the system might need iterative maintenance so that applicability is not sacrificed. Ideally, the system has to help designers when maintaining the system by pointing out loci where designers need to fix errors or take some other altering actions.

4. CONCLUSIONS AND FUTURE WORK

In this paper, we proposed Social Sensing as a system development technique in which users' perception is part of the system computation. We advocated that users are a powerful source for information that drives adaptation. In Social Sensing, users act as monitors, increasing the ability of the system and designers for capturing the values and the relevance of certain adaptation drivers. Out of these drivers, we discussed context, quality and validity. Social Sensing implies a direct interaction with users. Thus, users interact using their own terms, i.e. their problem domain terms, and this explains the focus of our discussion of Social Sensing from a requirements engineering perspective.

Our future work includes developing a methodology (models, development process, analysis techniques, and a software framework for Social Sensing) for incorporating the role of users in the design of requirements at runtime. Our ultimate goal is to develop capabilities that make Social Sensing viable and useful from two perspectives. First, the users' interaction with the system should be facilitated and the awareness of users about the consequences and the benefits of their interaction should be maximized. In other words, engineering the awareness of users and facilitating and encouraging their collaboration with the system represent the first main thread of research we plan to conduct. Second, the system has to be provided with analysis techniques to process the information gathered from its users' community and make use of it at runtime. These include deciding about the significance of information provided by users and formulating the community's collective judgment, autonomously or with a minimum intervention of designers.

ACKNOWLEDGMENTS. This work has been partially funded by the EU Commission through the FastFix project, and by Science Foundation Ireland grant 10/CE/I1855. We also thank Vinny Cahill, Siobhán Clarke and Gavin Doherty for the discussions which enriched the idea presented in this paper.

5. REFERENCES

[1] Mazeiar Salehie, Ladan Tahvildari. Self-adaptive software: landscape and research challenges. ACM Transactions on Autonomic and Autonomic Systems, 4:2, pp. 1-42, 2009.

[2] Richard Murch. Autonomic computing. IBM Press, 2004.

[3] Robert Laddaga. Self-adaptive software. Tech. Rep. 98-12, DARPA BAA. 1997.

[4] Anthony Finkelstein, Andrea Savigni. A framework for requirements engineering for context-aware services. In STRAW 2001.

[5] Raian Ali, Fabiano Dalpiaz, Paolo Giorgini, Vitor E. Silva Souza. Requirements Evolution: From Assumptions to Reality. In EMMSAD 2011.

[6] Walid Maalej, Hans-Jörg Happel, Asarnusch Rashid. When Users Become Collaborators: Towards Continuous and Context-Aware User Input. In OOPSLA 2009

[7] Raian Ali, Fabiano Dalpiaz, Paolo Giorgini. A goal-based framework for contextual requirements modeling and analysis. Requirements engineering, Springer, 2010, 15, 439-458.

Cross-Library API Recommendation using Web Search Engines

Wujie Zheng, Qirun Zhang, Michael Lyu
Computer Science and Engineering
The Chinese University of Hong Kong, China
{wjzheng,qrzhang,lyu}@cse.cuhk.edu.hk

ABSTRACT

Software systems are often built upon third party libraries. Developers may replace an old library with a new library, for the consideration of functionality, performance, security, and so on. It is tedious to learn the often complex APIs in the new library from the scratch. Instead, developers may identify the suitable APIs in the old library, and then find counterparts of these APIs in the new library. However, there is typically no such cross-references for APIs in different libraries. Previous work on automatic API recommendation often recommends related APIs in the same library. In this paper, we propose to mine search results of Web search engines to recommend related APIs of different libraries. In particular, we use Web search engines to collect relevant Web search results of a given API in the old library, and then recommend API candidates in the new library that are frequently appeared in the Web search results. Preliminary results of generating related C# APIs for the APIs in JDK show the feasibility of our approach.

Categories and Subject Descriptors

D.2.7 [**Software Engineering**]: Distribution, Maintenance, and Enhancement

General Terms

Documentation, Reliability

1. INTRODUCTION

Code reuse is one of the primary techniques to improve the productivity of building software systems. Due to the requirement changes of a software system, developers may need to replace an old library with a new library. Working with complex APIs in the new library presents many barriers, such as selecting the appropriate APIs and figuring out how to use the selected APIs. Since the developers often can identify the suitable APIs in the old library easily, a possible solution is to find counterparts of the old APIs in the new library. However, there is typically no such cross-references for APIs in different libraries, and thus it can still take much time of developers to look for the suitable API counterparts.

There has been much work on automatically generating cross-references for APIs. Doxygen [4] and Javadoc [3] are well-known for generating cross-references and documentations from developers' comments in source code. However, there are few, if any, comments that talk about the relationship of APIs in different libraries. Many approaches recommend related APIs in the same library by analyzing the source code of the library [8, 9, 11] or the client code [7, 10, 13]. These approaches rely on the assumption that two related APIs are structurally or statistically connected in some source code, which are not valid for APIs in different libraries. Zhong et al. [12] mine API mappings from Java to C# from the same projects' different implementations in these two languages (based on these languages' basic libraries). However, for two arbitrary libraries, there may not be implementations of the same project in these two libraries, and the APIs used in such projects may be limited.

In this paper, we propose to mine search results of Web search engines to recommend related APIs of different libraries. The idea is that developers often share their knowledge of related APIs of different libraries in the Web. For example, the following question illustrates a case that developers ask about equivalent APIs in C# (more exactly, the .NET Framework) for the "HashMap" class in Java (more exactly, the Jave Development Kit) (http://stackoverflow.com/questions/1273139/c-java-hashmap-equivalent).

- "Coming from a Java world into a C# one is there a HashMap equivalent? If not what would you recommend?"

There can be many similar questions and discussions in the Web. However, such knowledge is often described in unstructured web pages that are spread in the Web. Moreover, the results can be different and many unrelated APIs may also be discussed. To mine the knowledge of developers for cross-library API recommendation, we use Web search engines to collect relevant Web search results of a given API query, and then extract API candidates that are frequently appeared in the Web search results. For a library, after getting the results of each API, we also re-rank the related APIs based on the whole distributions to reduce false positives. We have built a prototype for the proposed approach and applied it to generate related APIs in .NET Framework for the APIs in JDK.

Permission to make digital or hard copies of all or part of this work for personal or classroom use is granted without fee provided that copies are not made or distributed for profit or commercial advantage and that copies bear this notice and the full citation on the first page. To copy otherwise, to republish, to post on servers or to redistribute to lists, requires prior specific permission and/or a fee.
ESEC/FSE'11, September 5–9, 2011, Szeged, Hungary.
Copyright 2011 ACM 978-1-4503-0443-6/11/09 ...$10.00.

2. RELATED WORK

In this section we discuss the related work, including the most related work by us and by others. We also point out the novelty of our approach.

There have been many approaches to recommend related APIs in the same library by analyzing the source code of the library [8, 9] or the client code [7, 10, 13]. Robillard [9] proposed an approach named Suade to automatically rank program elements for an investigation task based on the structural dependencies in a program. Long et al. [8] developed a tool Altair that ranks related API methods for a given method according to the share variables between methods. Li and Zhou [7] developed a tool named PR-Miner that uses frequent itemset mining to extract implicit API usage patterns from source code. Zhong et al. [13] proposed a tool named MAPO that combines the frequent subsequence mining technique with the clustering technique to mine code snippets with respect to programming contexts. Thummalapenta and Xie [10] developed a tool named PARSEWeb that uses Google code search engine [2] to collect relevant code snippets and then mines code snippets for a given target object type.

We [11] have augmented the call graph with control flow analysis to capture the significance of the caller-callee linkages for API recommendation. In the previous work, we focus on recommending related APIs in the same library using static analysis techniques. While in this work, we would like to recommend related APIs in different libraries using information retrieval and statistical analysis techniques. Both the usage scenarios and the required techniques are very different.

The single most related work by others is the MAM approach, proposed by Zhong et al. [12]. MAM mines API mappings from Java to C# from the same projects' implementations in these two languages. However, for any two languages, there may not be implementations of the same project in these two languages, the APIs used in such projects may be limited, and the mapping strategies could be difficult to design. German and Davies [6] describe several challenges of comparing the source code of different libraries. Differently, our approach recommends related APIs in different libraries by mining the knowledge of the library users shared in the Web.

Compared with the existing approaches, the new idea of our approach is to exploit the huge amount of knowledge of the library users shared in the World Wide Web. The knowledge can reveal API correlations cross libraries (in different programming languages). However, the knowledge is described in unstructured Web pages. New techniques are needed to collect relevant Web search results and to extract knowledge of the APIs from the noisy data.

3. APPROACH

3.1 Overview

We first describe the framework of mining Web search results for API recommendation. Given a library for reference, which the developers are familiar with, and a targeted library for studying, we would like to recommend similar APIs in the latter for each API in the former.

Figure 1 shows the procedure of our approach. First, for each API query, our approach constructs a Web query in the purpose of searching for related APIs in the targeted library.

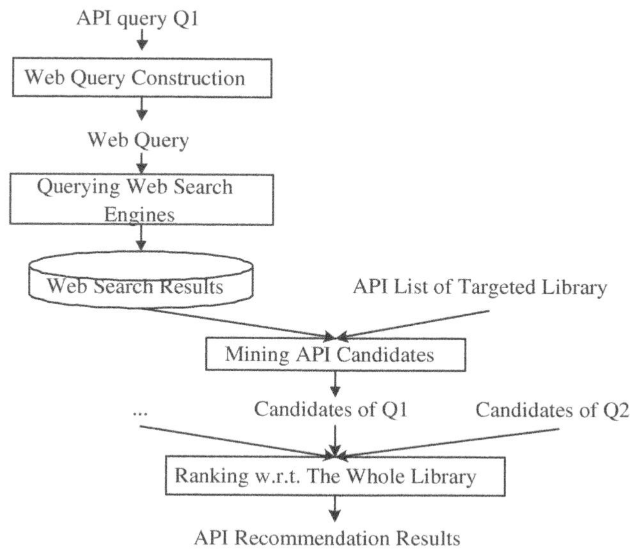

Figure 1: Overview of our approach

Our approach then queries a major Web search engine such as Google to get the top-ranked Web search results. Our approach then mines API candidates in the targeted library that often appear in the Web search results. Finally, out approach ranks the mined API candidates for each API query based on the whole distributions of API candidates, using the tf-idf definition in Information Retrieval community [5]. Currently the API lists of the reference library and the targeted library are both extracted manually. In Section 5 we shall discuss how to extract them automatically in future.

3.2 Web Query Construction

Developers often share their knowledge of related APIs of different libraries in the Web. However, this knowledge is often described in unstructured web pages that are spread in the Web. Web search engines are the best tools to collect such information automatically. Given a API query, our approach constructs a Web query by concatenating the given API and the targeted library (or program language). Take the HashMap class of Java Development Kits (JDK) as an example. To find similar APIs of it in the C# language (i.e., in the .NET Framework), our approach constructs a Web query "HashMap C#" for the Web search engines.

It is also possible to mine the common words used for querying equivalent APIs and add them to the Web query. Moreover, we may use multiple Web queries for a given API, and merge the Web search results for mining related APIs.

3.3 Querying Web Search Engines

We applied the Web services of Google to collect the top search results of a Web query. Other major search engines such as Bing and Yahoo also provide Web services for Web search. We use Web search engines (text retrieval) instead of code search engines, because an API in a library and its similar API in another library are seldom used together in some code.

The search results of "HashMap C#" returned by the Google search engine are shown in Figure 2. From the example search results, we can see that developers discuss the

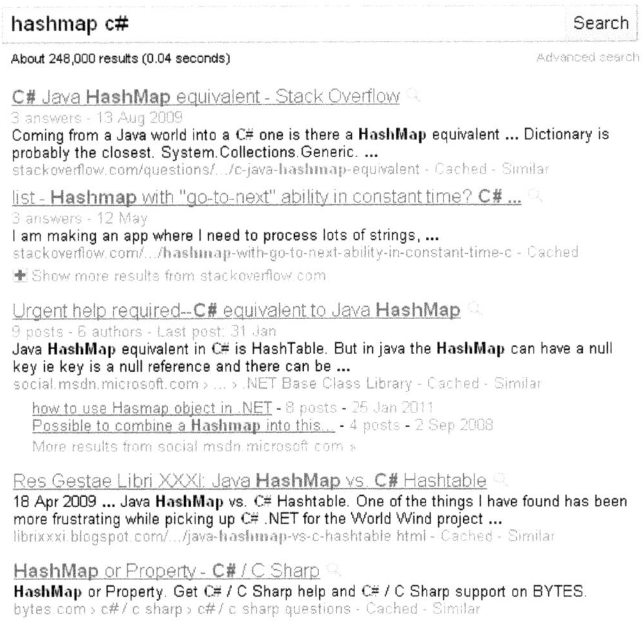

Figure 2: Search results of HashMap

equivalent of HashMap in C# in different forums. Moreover, the results can be different. For example, the first result says that the Dictionary class is preferable, while the third result says that "Java HashMap equivalent in C# is HashTable".

3.4 Mining API Candidates

Different APIs have different naming conventions. It is difficult to distinguish the APIs from the general English words. For mining API candidates from the Web search results, we employ a dictionary-based approach.

In the context of API recommendation, developers often know what the targeted library is. That is, the API candidates for a API query should be in the list of all APIs in the targeted library. Therefore, we extract all APIs in the targeted library, e.g., .NET Framework, as the dictionary. We then calculate the frequency of each API of the targeted library in the title and the summary of Web search results. Basically, the higher frequency a API candidate is, the more likely it is relevant to the API query.

3.5 Ranking w.r.t. the Whole Library

Some common APIs, such as the Object Class, may appear frequently in the Web search results. However, these common APIs are not interesting for a API query. Our approach uses the definitions of tf-idf from the Information Retrieval community [5] to distinguish these common APIs from the true relevant APIs.

Recall that we have mined API candidates for each API query. That is, for an API query Q_i, we have a set of API candidates, $T1$, $T2$, etc. We can thus build a set of documents, where each document contains the API candidates (with duplicates) for each API query. Figure 3 shows an example, where $T1$ appears in one search results of three API queries and $T5$ appears in two search results of the API query $Q3$.

Q1: T1, T2, T3
Q2: T1, T4
Q3: T1, T5, T2, T5
Q4: T6

Figure 3: Example documents of API candidates

We then use the definitions of *tf* and *idf* to identify the relevance of a API candidate to the API query. The term frequency (*tf*) is the number of a API candidate appeared in the document of a API query. The larger it is, the more relevant the API candidate is to the API query. The inverse document frequency (*idf*) is obtained by dividing the total number of documents by the number of documents containing the API candidate, and then taking the logarithm of that quotient. The larger it is, the less common the API candidate is and thus the more relevant the API candidate is to the API query. In particular, the relevance of a API candidate T to a API query Q is defined as follows.

$$relevance(T, Q) = tf(T, Q) * idf(T)$$

where $tf(T, Q)$ is the frequency of the API candidate T in the document of Q, and $idf(T)$ is the inverse document frequency of T in the whole corpus, i.e., the set of documents for all API queries.

Finally, for each API query, the candidate APIs are ranked in the descending order of the relevance to the API query.

3.6 Explanation Generation

It is often not enough to tell developers only *which API is relevant to a given query*. Developers need more information to understand *why and how the recommended API is relevant to a given query*. To suit this need, our approach also generates explanations for each recommended API, so as to help developers understand the causality. Currently, for each recommended API, our approach lists the Web pages (within the Web search results) that discuss both the recommended API and the API query. The Web pages often contain the users' discussions or explanations of how an API is relevant to a given query. It is also possible to generate other kinds of explanations, such as the formal specification of the recommended APIs.

4. PRELIMINARY RESULTS

We have built a prototype for the proposed approach and applied it to generate related APIs in C# (mostly in the .NET Framework) for the APIs in JDK. The Java Development Kit (JDK) is a Sun Microsystems product aimed at Java developers. Since the introduction of Java, it has been by far the most widely used Java SDK. C# is a multi-paradigm programming language encompassing imperative, declarative, functional, generic, object-oriented (class-based), and component-oriented programming disciplines. It was developed by Microsoft within the .NET initiative. We focus on recommending the classes in the experiment. We crawl the API list of JDK and C# from their official Websites. The characteristics of these two subject libraries are summarized in Table 1.

For each API query in JDK, our approach generates an individual result page that lists the recommended APIs in C#.

Table 1: Subject programs

Library	#Packages	#Classes
JDK	135	2723
.NET	408	13791

- Hashtable Res Gestae Libri XXXI: Java HashMap vs. C# Hashtable
- Dictionary C# Java HashMap equivalent - Stack Overflow
- Stack C# Java HashMap equivalent - Stack Overflow
- ComVisibleAttribute Hashtable Class (System.Collections)
- Expression Expression evaluator - ANTLR 3 - ANTLR Project

(a) Recommended APIs for HashMap

- WebRequest C# I/O and Networking - O'Reilly Media
- Stack C# connect to URL which gives a xml document - Stack Overflow
- Network URL Connection Test : Server Â« Network Protocol Â« Java
- FtpWebRequest Win32 Networks C++ class/library that implements TCP FTP ...
- WebException [ASP .NET C#] Load a local webpage from code behind - Dev Shed

(b) Recommended APIs for URLConnection

Figure 4: API recommendation results

Figure 4 shows the recommendation results for *java.util.HashMap*. The first recommended APIs in C# include *Hashtable* and *Dictionary*. These two APIs are similar to *HashMap* as they are all collections that maps keys to values. Along with each recommended API, our approach provides a link (and the title) to the explanation of their correlations with the API query. The link for *Hashtable* points to a blog that compares *HashMap* and *Hashtable*, while the link for *Dictionary* points to a discussion in a question and answer site. These explanations not only increase the confidence of users for the recommendation results, but also help users learn the key similarities and differences between the recommended APIs and the API query. Figure 4 also shows the results for *java.net.URLConnection*. The first recommended API is *WebRequest*. It is relevant to *URLConnection* because they are both used to communicate to a URL. The link for *WebRequest* points to an article that describes C# I/O and networking APIs, compared with the Java ones. Finally, our approach generates an index html for the JDK library, where each entry links to the recommendation results of a API query.

5. DISCUSSIONS

5.1 Keyword-based Web Query Construction

While users may talk about the names of a API query and a target library, a more common scenario is that users discuss the functionality of a API query and a target library. Therefore, we may extract the keywords of a API based on its documentation or the search results of the API, and then construct a Web query that consists of the keywords and the name of the target library.

5.2 API Candidates Extraction

Currently, our approach uses a dictionary-based approach to extract API candidates for recommendation from Web search results. The dictionary is the list of APIs in the targeted library. Having such a API list can help to reduce false positives effectively. However, it could be tedious for the users to create such a API list manually. A possible solution is to analyze the source code of a given library to extract API lists, using tools such as Ctags [1]. Another possible solution is to use a template-based approach. That is, instead of giving a API list, the users provide a template for the potentially interested APIs, using regular expressions.

6. CONCLUSIONS

Sometimes developers need to replace an old library with a new library for more effective code reuse. Learning the often complex APIs in the new library could be tedious. We propose an approach to help developers find APIs in the new library that work similarly to a given API in the old library automatically. In particular, we use Web search engines to collect relevant Web search results of a given API in the old library, and then recommend API candidates in the new library that are frequently appeared in the Web search results. We have built a prototype for the proposed approach and applied it to generate related C# APIs for the APIs in JDK. We have also discussed several issues for further improvements.

7. ACKNOWLEDGMENTS

The work described in this paper was fully supported by a grant from the Research Grants Council of the Hong Kong Special Administrative Region, China (Project No. CUHK 415410), and a grant under Google Focused Grant Project "Mobile 2014".

8. REFERENCES

[1] Ctags. `http://ctags.sourceforge.net/`.

[2] Google code search. `http://www.google.com/codesearch`.

[3] Javadoc. http://java.sun.com/j2se/javadoc/.

[4] Source code documentation generator tool. http://www.doxygen.org/.

[5] R. Baeza-Yates, B. Ribeiro-Neto, et al. *Modern information retrieval*. ACM press New York., 1999.

[6] J. Davies, D. M. Germán, M. W. Godfrey, and A. Hindle. Software bertillonage: finding the provenance of an entity. In *MSR*, pages 183–192, 2011.

[7] Z. Li and Y. Zhou. PR-Miner: automatically extracting implicit programming rules and detecting violations in large software code. In *ESEC/SIGSOFT FSE*, pages 306–315, 2005.

[8] F. Long, X. Wang, and Y. Cai. Api hyperlinking via structural overlap. In *ESEC/SIGSOFT FSE*, pages 203–212, 2009.

[9] M. P. Robillard. Automatic generation of suggestions for program investigation. In *ESEC/SIGSOFT FSE*, pages 11–20, 2005.

[10] S. Thummalapenta and T. Xie. PARSEWeb: a programmer assistant for reusing open source code on the web. In *ASE*, pages 204–213, 2007.

[11] Q. Zhang, W. Zheng, and M. R. Lyu. Flow-augmented call graph: A new foundation for taming api complexity. In *FASE 2011, Fundamental Approaches to Software Engineering*, pages 386–400, 2011.

[12] H. Zhong, S. Thummalapenta, T. Xie, L. Zhang, and Q. Wang. Mining api mapping for language migration. In *ICSE (1)*, pages 195–204, 2010.

[13] H. Zhong, T. Xie, L. Zhang, J. Pei, and H. Mei. MAPO: Mining and recommending api usage patterns. In *ECOOP*, pages 318–343, 2009.

Exploiting Software Architecture to support Requirements satisfaction Testing

Paul Clements[1], María J. Escalona[2], Paola Inverardi[3], Ivano Malavolta[3], Eda Marchetti[4]
[1]Software Engineering Institute, Carnegie Mellon University, USA
clements@sei.cmu.edu
[2]Department of Languages and Computer Systems, University of Sevilla, Spain
mjescalona@us.es
[3]Department of Computer Science, University of Aquila, Italy
{paola.inverardi,ivano.malavolta}@univaq.it
[4]Software Engineering Laboratory, ISTI-CNR Pisa, Italy
eda.marchetti@isti.cnr.it

ABSTRACT

Currently, software testing is mainly carried on independently from software architecture-related information. Some approaches propose to perform integration and regression testing with respect to software architecture descriptions, but less attention has been paid to analysing software architecture in order to develop a less costly and time-consuming test plan that covers the requirements of the system of interest. If on one side, it is well known that providing an effective test plan is crucial to software quality, on the other side software testing is extremely difficult because it stems from the complexity of current software systems.

In this paper we (i) elaborate on how a new architectural analysis can help in producing better test plans and (ii) identify a set of corresponding research challenges. We believe that considering and analysing architectural information for requirements satisfaction testing purposes will provide substantial benefits in terms of test plan specification process, test plan effectiveness, and test cases understandability.

Categories and Subject Descriptors

D.2.11 [**Software Engineering**]: Software Architectures; D.2.11 [**Software Engineering**]: Testing and Debugging; D.2.1 [**Software Engineering**]: Requirements/Specifications

General Terms

Design, Verification.

1. INTRODUCTION

Testing is one of the most labor-intensive activities in the software development life cycle, and consumes a substantial portion of total development costs. Estimates range from 30% to 50% [17], over 50% [3], 50% to 75% [13], even 80% or more [8]. Any technology, method, or approach that even slightly lowers the cost or increases the efficacy of testing can make a substantial dent in the tens of billions of dollars spent on software development annually.

Our work focuses on improving testing by applying knowledge about the architecture of the system being tested. So-called "architecture-based testing" is an idea with roots in the mid-1990s [1, 19]; work in architectural means to increase a system's testability going back even further [16, 11].

Much of that work can be characterized as opportunistic; that is, researchers' insights about architecture and testing were used to produce ideas about approaches with (in most cases) unknown and untried applicability. By contrast, this paper reports on the results of a piece of *directed* research in which architecture knowledge is brought to bear on testing in response to a specific practitioner problem.

1.1 Problem being solved

The problem being solved is one that came to us from the testing practitioner community. In February of 2011, the Software Engineering Institute in cooperation with the University of L'Aquila held a workshop on architecture-based testing attended by testing practitioners in the defense, aerospace, industrial systems, financial, control systems, and automotive industries. The purpose of the workshop was to produce a set of model problems, which are problems that (if solved) would provide a significant improvement in testing outcomes [2]. Workshop participants produced 29 such problems, and voted on the ones they would most like to see solved. Here is the problem that participants chose as being the most important, stated as a scenario:

> *At a time when the architecture is complete and system test has not yet begun, a tester needs to choose a test set to test the system for requirements satisfaction. The tester uses an architecture analysis tool that identifies the smallest number of tests to run to provide coverage of 98% of the requirements. Redundant tests are eliminated. Performing the analysis is much less costly and time-consuming to run than the tests it replaces.*

The idea is that practitioners wish to use the architecture to help them determine that (out of the enormous number of tests possible) a particular, small set of tests will cover 98% of the requirements.

1.2 Example scenario

In order to illustrate our idea, we introduce a pedagogical exam-

Permission to make digital or hard copies of all or part of this work for personal or classroom use is granted without fee provided that copies are not made or distributed for profit or commercial advantage and that copies bear this notice and the full citation on the first page. To copy otherwise, to republish, to post on servers or to redistribute to lists, requires prior specific permission and/or a fee.

ESEC/FSE'11, September 5–9, 2011, Szeged, Hungary.

Copyright 2011 ACM 978-1-4503-0443-6/11/09 ...$10.00.

ple, the Arcade Game Maker (AGM) [1]. The AGM product line will produce a series of arcade games. Each game is a one-player game in which the player controls, to some degree, the moving objects. The objective is to score points by hitting stationary obstacles. The games range from low obstacle count to high and will be available on a variety of platforms.

Figure 1 presents the set of use cases for this system which covers three games: bowling, pong and brickles.

In the description of the AGM system, each use case is described with a detailed scenario. In order to test functionality of the final system, we should test each scenario and we should assure the right coverage of each execution path. Current research allows us to select which are the more critical execution paths or offers us heuristics criteria to select which are the redundant lines.

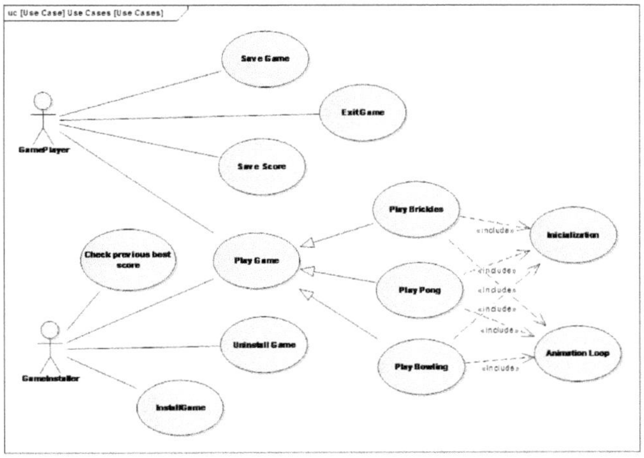

Figure 1: A set of use cases for the Arcade Game Maker

However, our research is oriented to analyse if we could reduce the set of test cases to check these requirements, depending of the architecture, and assuring the grade of coverage. For instance, depending of how we implement Play Game use case and use cases that extend it, we could reduce the number of test. If common functionality for the three use cases are implemented in a abstract and a general class, we could check it only once and drop repetitive execution paths or repetitive execution activities.

Extracting testing only from requirements, using common approaches like [10], we have to derive, at least, one test case for each use case: Play Game, Play Bowling, Play Brickles and Play Pong. If they have common functionality in the architecture, the direct derivation of test cases from requirements could not detect it. As it is presented in the next section, our approach is oriented to enrich the information of requirements with architectural details in order to improve the set of test cases that better exercise the system.

2. WHAT IS THE NEW IDEA?

In this section we propose a new perspective on how software architecture descriptions can be used. More specifically, we propose a new role for software architecture modeling, that is: architectural descriptions (especially together with their related architecture analysis capabilities) can be exploited to better test the system under development, both in terms of requirements coverage and testing efficacy. Such a new perspective comes from explicitly considering architectural analysis results when testing system requirements satisfaction.

Intuitively, if designers consider requirements only, they are basically doing black-box testing; if designers consider also the implementation code, they are doing white-box testing. Our main goal is to exploit software architecture-related information in order to perform grey-box testing. Indeed, our ambition is to be able to exploit architectural information in developing test plans so that it can be possible to positively assess the effectiveness of such test plans against the requirements.

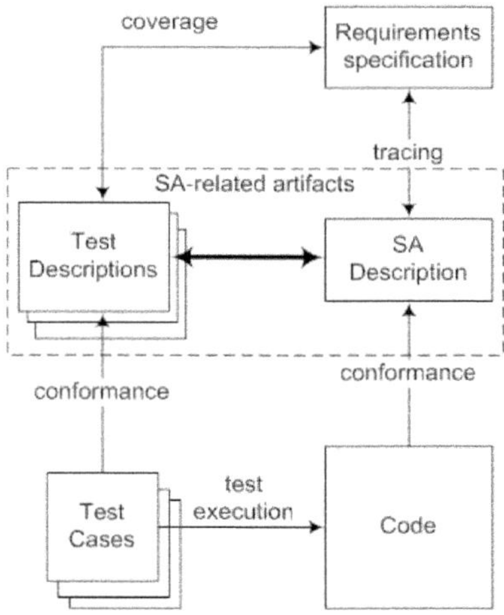

Figure 2: Overview of the new testing process

Figure 2 gives an overview of the testing process we envision. Central to our testing process is the description of software architecture (*SA Description* in figure). It may be a model conforming to a specific architecture description language (ADL), a UML model of the system, or any other representation of the architecture of the system. A set of *tracing* links relate architecture-related requirements in the *Requirements specification* with their corresponding architectural elements. Those links may be at different levels of granularity, i.e., they may relate the whole architectural model to a set of requirements, a single architectural element (e.g., a component, an architectural layer, etc.) to a requirement, and so on. It should be noted that our approach does not force engineers to use some specific means to define requirements: they can use plain text, UML models (for example, in Figure 1 we specified requirements as use case diagrams), or any other means. The *Code* box represents the implementation of the system. The code conforms to the software architecture of the system if it is synchronized with the intended meaning of the *SA Description*.

The implementation of the system is exercised by defining and executing a set of *Test Cases*. They are the typical test cases that help testers in determining whether the realized system is working correctly or not; for example, they may be JUnit [2] tests. *Test Descriptions* represent the same information of implementation-level test cases at the architectural level of abstraction. In the same way as the implementation of the system must conform to its architecture description, implementation-level test cases must conform to their corresponding test descriptions. Such a *conformance* relationship ensures that the results of the architectural analysis identifying the smallest number of tests to run to provide a certain coverage of the requirements are correct with respect to the implemented system (since the analysis is performed on consistent artifacts). The

[1] http://www.sei.cmu.edu/productlines/ppl/requirements_model.html

[2] http://www.junit.org/

coverage relationship between a test description and a requirement in the requirements specification means that the test description tests the system with respect to the requirement it is linked to. Obviously, the coverage relationship is a many-to-many relationship, i.e., many requirements may be covered by many test descriptions.

It is important to note that this new perspective helps in solving a well-known issue in model-based testing. Indeed, though model-based testing has been successfully used in many projects, current model-based testing techniques do not focus enough on testing non-functional requirements (like performance, security, reliability, etc.) [5]. As a matter of fact, one of the main strong point of software architecture is that it supports the analysis of non-functional properties of the system, thus exploiting architectural information during the testing activities should help in the test plans definition.

Furthermore, software architecture descriptions are multi-view and recent research in the software architecture area goes towards the automatic support of multiple architectural views and their interrelationships [4].

One crucial point in our approach is that we are not assuming any specific development process. We are just assuming that, given a system, an architectural description of the system exists and that such description conforms to the system under test (SUT). Thus, the architectural description can also be retrieved with reverse engineering technologies if not available from the design phase.

Considering architecture descriptions, requirements and testing artifacts in combination will help in identifying those test cases that may play an important role while evaluating the various tradeoffs during the architecting phase. By executing those test cases, designers are exercising the system (and its architecture) right in its tradeoff points, which are typically the most crucial and sensitive parts of the whole project.

Our new perspective on the relationship between software architecture, requirements, and testing artifacts triggers many interesting research questions; next section will present them.

2.1 Research questions

The main research question we identify in this work can be formulated as follows:

> *How software architecture descriptions can be exploited to enhance the effectiveness of a requirements satisfaction test plan?*

In other words, we are looking for a solution in which software architecture-related information is exploited in order to better support requirements satisfaction testing. Considering software architecture descriptions as first-class artifacts for requirements satisfaction testing is not straightforward. Indeed, there are many points that still need both theoretical and technological investigation. More specifically, we refined the main research question of this work into a set of secondary research questions:

RQ1. Find the right level of abstraction for describing test descriptions at the architectural level, i.e., we must specify what information should be part of an architectural test description. This aspect has many implications; for example, it will trigger the possibility to automatically generate (or at least to trace towards) concrete test cases defined at the implementation level. Moreover, it may allow test designers to automatically generate test descriptions from the combined information coming from requirements and the architecture description.

RQ2. Find a systematic or semi-automated way to derive or support mappings

a) from requirements to software architecture description,

b) from requirements to test cases (by passing through architectural test description).

RQ3. Define metrics for testing coverage of architecture in combination with requirements. It is important to note that coverage criteria are based on architecture analysis; this is not a direct requirement of the model problem, but a derived requirement: knowing the architecture (and the tests descriptions that most effectively exercise it) will help designers pick the tests that are most effective in prosecuting the model problem. For example, to carry out Req1 and Req2 involves the same paths through the architecture, so perhaps a test designer can fully test Req1 and Req2 to a lesser degree, as opposed to fully test both.

RQ4. Develop a notion of "tradeoff test cases" that shall represent the implementation counterpart of the prioritization among requirements, especially non functional ones. These test cases can be derived from the trade off analysis conducted during the architecture design if it exists, or can be the result of the analysis of the interdependencies among different architectural views.

3. WHY IS IT NEW?

Architecture-based testing is a common term adopted for describing the activity to increase a system's testability [16, 11, 7]. However the use of architectural information to support requirements satisfaction is still a research challenge and few proposals are currently available. Indeed a large part of the literature has been dedicated to requirements satisfaction exploiting functional models, as reported in one of the author's recent work [10]. The practical attitude of software-development organizations is to consider requirements and architectural specification as two different faces of the same problem. So far, the effort of researchers has been focused to join together these two aspects either presenting innovative development processes as in [14] or applications and methods that map (specific) requirements into the architecture, as surveyed in [18]. Our problem is not about formally relating requirements and architectural specification, rather we assume conformance and the existence of a mapping in the same way practitioners do between requirements and code when designing their test plans. Our approach is to exploit the architectural analysis for deriving testing plans that can be directly related to the requirements specification.

The analysis of related works evidences that the chain (requirement specification, software architecture definition and code verification) is far to be completely automated. Current proposals partially cover pieces of this path and usually they face the problem from a research point of view. New development processes [20, 6], additional formalisms or facilities [15] are the common suggestions [12]. However there is still a lack of practical solutions close to the best practices adopted by software-development organizations to automate as much as possible the code verification based on requirements and architectural specification. Therefore the approach we undertake is to not rely on any specific process development assumption and restrict ourselves to consider only the existence of a set of requirements, a set of software architecture artifacts and a conformance mapping.

4. EXPECTED FEEDBACK

In section 2.1 we described the main research question motivating our work, and we further refined it into a set of secondary research questions. Those research questions are interesting from a pragmatic point of view: systematic automation is part of the value proposition, and metrics would provide evidence of efficacy. We believe that both software architecture and testing research communities will benefit from being exposed to the expectation of a representative class of industrial representatives. Indeed as reported in the introduction, the main research question of this paper came directly from industrial needs and shed a different light on the way we have been traditionally thought the role of software architecture in testing. It is therefore interesting to confront the approach we propose with the Software Engineering community at large since many different techniques and analysis can potentially play a role in the approach we have devised and other industrially relevant case studies can be offered to validate the approach.

5. FUTURE WORK

In this paper we elaborated a new perspective on how to exploit architecture-related information and analysis with the aim to achieve a better coverage of system requirements, and to improve the efficacy of test cases.

Our near term future work will be to investigate and elaborate solutions to the specific research questions outlined in Section 2.1. Although all research questions have technical aspects, they all will be usefully answered only in the context of industrial practice. Finding the "right" abstractions for describing test cases architecturally, finding metrics for architectural coverage in testing, and finding how to usefully express "tradeoff cases" depends on trying out proposed solutions through experimentation and demonstration in an industrial setting. We will start our search for (semi-)automation of requirements-architecture-test mappings by building upon current approaches to this problem that are used in everyday development.

In all cases, we envision practitioner workshops to vet our ideas, experiments in which we apply our ideas to real-world projects and take qualitative and quantitative improvement measures, and building method-supporting artifacts such as templates, tools, and training for those solutions that have proven their value in practice.

As a start in this direction, we are currently considering an industrial project that has been developed at the lab of one of the authors. We have a complete set of developed artifacts, including test plans and test suites. The objective of our study is to address the described research questions in this experimental setting, redesigning the test plans based on the analysis of the architecture artifacts with respect to the system requirements. Then a comparison between the test cases generated in the project and the test cases generated following our analysis will be performed.

In the long term we plan to arrange the solutions of the various research questions into an integrated testing framework. By doing this, the resulting integrated framework may help in promoting architecture-centric development: software architecture should be used as the main driver of the development of the system, and should be integrated into development processes that consider also requirements, implementation, testing, and so on [4].

Most importantly, we will continue our interaction with testing practitioners. This will provide us with a continuously updated understanding of what are the concrete needs of practitioners, and assess our solutions for practicality and usefulness.

Acknowledgments

This work is partially supported by the EU project CONNECT (http://connect-forever.eu/) No 231167 of the FET - FP7 program, the EU project CHOReOS (http://www.choreos.eu) No 257178 of the FET - FP7 program, and the Tempros project of the Ministry of Education and Science (TIN2010-20057-C03-02), Spain.

6. REFERENCES

[1] A. Bertolino and P. Inverardi. Architecture-based software testing. In *Joint proceedings of the second international software architecture workshop (ISAW-2) and international workshop on multiple perspectives in software development (Viewpoints '96) on SIGSOFT '96 workshops*, ISAW, pages 62–64. ACM, 1996.

[2] P. Clements, J. Hudak, P. Place, A. Bertolino, H. Muccini, and P. Inverardi. Architecture Support for Testing: Connecting Research to Practice. Technical Report , SEI report, in progress, 2011.

[3] G. T. Daich, G. Price, B. Ragland, and M. Dawood. Software Test Technologies Report. Technical Report p. 11, Software Technology Support Center, August 1994.

[4] D. Di Ruscio, I. Malavolta, H. Muccini, P. Pelliccione, and A. Pierantonio. Developing next generation ADLs through MDE techniques. In *Int. Conf. on Software Engineering, ICSE 2010*, 2010.

[5] A. C. Dias-Neto and G. H. Travassos. A picture from the model-based testing area: Concepts, techniques, and challenges. volume 80 of *Advances in Computers*, pages 45 – 120. Elsevier, 2010.

[6] A. Douglas. Linking requirements and implementation. *Views on Evolvability of Embedded Systems*, pages 137–151, 2011.

[7] R. Dssouli and R. Fournier. Communication Software Testability. In *IFIP Transactions, Protocol Testing Systems III (the Proceedings of IFIP TC6 Third International Workshop on Protocol Test Systems)*, pages 45–55, 1991.

[8] R. Dunn. *Software defect removal*. McGraw-Hill, Inc., New York, NY, USA, 1984.

[9] M. Escalona, J. Gutierrez, M. Mejías, G. Aragón, I. Ramos, J. Torres, and F. Domínguez. An overview on test generation from functional requirements. *Journal of Systems and Software*, 84-6:1379–1393, 2011.

[10] R. Freedman. Testability of software components. *IEEE Transactions on Software Engineering*, 17:553–564, 1991.

[11] A. Goknil, I. Kurtev, K. van den Berg, and J. Veldhuis. Semantics of trace relations in requirements models for consistency checking and inferencing. *Software and Systems Modeling*, pages 1–24, 2009.

[12] B. Hailpern and P. Santhanam. Software debugging, testing, and verification. *IBM Syst. J.*, 41:4–12, January 2002.

[13] J. Hall, M. Jackson, R. Laney, B. Nuseibeh, and L. Rapanotti. Relating software requirements and architectures using problem frames. In *Proceedings of the IEEE Joint Int. Conf. on Requirements Engineering, 2002.*, pages 137–144. IEEE, 2002.

[14] IBM. IBM Rational Unified Process (RUP).

[15] V. Jeffrey M. Factors that affect software testability. Technical report, NASA, 1991.

[16] Q. Li, M. Li, Y. Yang, Q. Wang, T. Tan, B. Boehm, and C. Hu. Bridge the gap between software test process and business value: A case study. In *Proceedings of the International Conference on Software Process: Trustworthy Software Development Processes*, ICSP, 2009.

[17] S. Pandey and K. Mustafa. Recent advances in sre research. *Recent Advances in SRE Research*, 2(04):1079–1085, 2010.

[18] D. J. Richardson and A. L. Wolf. Software testing at the architectural level. In *Joint proc. of the second int. software architecture workshop (ISAW-2) and int. workshop on multiple perspectives in software development (Viewpoints '96) on SIGSOFT '96 workshops*, ISAW '96, pages 68–71.

[19] E. Woods and N. Rozanski. Unifying software architecture with its implementation. In *Proceedings of the Fourth European Conference on Software Architecture*, pages 55–58, New York, NY, USA, 2010. ACM.

EAGLE: Engineering softwAre in the ubiquitous Globe by Leveraging uncErtainty

Marco Autili, Vittorio Cortellessa, Davide Di Ruscio, Paola Inverardi, Patrizio Pelliccione, Massimo Tivoli
Università dell'Aquila, Dipartimento di Informatica, Via Vetoio, L'Aquila, Italy
{marco.autili, vittorio.cortellessa, davide.diruscio, paola.inverardi, patrizio.pelliccione, massimo.tivoli}@univaq.it

ABSTRACT

In the next future we will be surrounded by a virtually infinite number of software applications that provide computational software resources in the open Globe. Users will be keen on producing their own piece of software, by also reusing existing software, to better satisfy their needs, therefore with a goal oriented, opportunistic use in mind. The produced software will need to be able to evolve, react and adapt to a continuously changing environment, while guaranteeing dependability. The strongest adversary to this view is the lack of knowledge on the software's structure, behavior, and execution context. Despite the possibility to extract observational models from existing software, a producer will always operate with software artifacts that exhibit a **degree of uncertainty** in terms of their functional and non functional characteristics. We believe that uncertainty can only be controlled by making it explicit and by using it to drive the production process itself. In this paper, we introduce a novel paradigm of software production process that **explores** available software and assesses its degree of uncertainty in relation to the opportunistic goal G, assists the producer in creating the appropriate **integration** means towards G, and **validates** the quality of the integrated system with respect to G and the current context.

Categories and Subject Descriptors

D.2 [**Software Engineering**]; D.2.10 [**Software Engineering**]: Design—*Methodologies*

General Terms

Design, Theory, Verification

Keywords

Ubiquitous computing, uncertainty

1. INTRODUCTION

In the next future we will be increasingly surrounded by a virtually infinite number of software applications that provide computational software resources in the open Globe. This situation radically changes the way software will be produced and used: (i) it lifts the user from the passive role of consumer to the active role of software producer of new functionalities out of the existing ones to satisfy user's needs; (ii) it shifts the focus of software production from domain specific software applications to software integrator systems that should ease the collaboration of existing software for the realization of new functionalities; (iii) the produced software will be inherently dynamic since it needs to operate in a continuously changing environment and must be able to evolve and quickly adapt to different types of changes, even unanticipated, while guaranteeing the dependability today's users expect.

The first characteristic implies a *goal oriented, opportunistic use* of the software being integrated, i.e., the producer will only use a subset of the available functionalities. The second one implies the need to *extract suitable observational models* from existing and reusable pieces of software, and devise appropriate *integration* means (architectures, connectors, integration patterns). The third one implies the need to cope with *dynamicity* in the integration process to guarantee both functionalities and dependability of the resulting application through (on-the-fly) *validation.*

This scenario requires rethinking the notion of software life cycle for which the distinction between development time and execution time stages is not meaningful anymore, e.g., PLASTIC[1] and SMSCom [20]. Recent approaches recognize the need to produce, manage and maintain software models all along the software's life time in order to assist the realization and validation of system's adaptations while the system is in execution [8, 25]. EAGLE (Engineering softwAre in the ubiquitous Globe by Leveraging uncErtainty) builds on this model-based software production paradigm but focuses its attention on the distinctive element of the above described scenario, namely the inherent incompleteness of information about requirements, execution context, and existing software.

The paper is organized as follows: Section 2 aims to answer the questions: "*What is the new idea?*" and "*Why is it new?*". Section 3 aims to answer the question: "*What are the most related works by the same authors and by others?*". Section 4 introduces the methodology for achieving the objectives of EAGLE. Finally, Section 5 concludes by also aiming to answer the question "*What feedback do the authors expect from the forum?*".

2. EAGLE NOVELTY

The big challenge underlying the above envisioned scenario is that abundance of available software induces a lack of knowledge on the software. A software producer will less and less know the

[1]FP6 IST EU PLASTIC project, `http://www.ist-plastic.org/`.

Permission to make digital or hard copies of all or part of this work for personal or classroom use is granted without fee provided that copies are not made or distributed for profit or commercial advantage and that copies bear this notice and the full citation on the first page. To copy otherwise, to republish, to post on servers or to redistribute to lists, requires prior specific permission and/or a fee.
ESEC/FSE'11, September 5–9, 2011, Szeged, Hungary.
Copyright 2011 ACM 978-1-4503-0443-6/11/09 ...$10.00.

precise behaviour of a third party software, nevertheless she will use it to build her own application. This means that the producer will in general operate in an environment in which the software artefacts exhibit a **degree of uncertainty** in terms of their functional and non functional characteristics. Indeed, in the software domain we see a flourishing of tools and methods to elicit approximated behavioural models of running systems, as well as context models. This very same problem recognized in the software engineering domain [19] is faced in many other computer science domain, e.g., exploratory search [36] and search computing [12], as well as software risk management [10], economics and other social domains [28].

In order to face this problem and provide a producer with a supporting framework to engineer the future software applications we rely on an apparent paradox. The uncertainty, due to the usage of software whose characteristics are not completely known, can only be controlled by making it explicit and by using it to drive the production process itself. To support this new idea we borrow the following definition of uncertainty from Galbraith [18] who, accordingly with [28], "*defines uncertainty as the difference between the amount of information required to perform a task and the amount of information already possessed*". This calls for a novel **explore-integrate-validate** production process that (i) explores available software and makes explicit the degree of uncertainty associated with it in relation to an opportunistic goal G, (ii) assists the producer in creating the appropriate integration means towards G, and (iii) validates the integrated system to assess its quality with respect to G and the current context.

The goal of the EAGLE approach is to provide an integrated model-based framework for the engineering of dependable and adaptable software for ubiquitous environments by explicitly dealing with uncertainty. This framework should support a future engineering production process of dependable open-globe software, i.e., goal-oriented software systems that are opportunistically created by integrating under uncertainty existing software and that are dynamically evolving within a perpetually changing context.

3. STATE-OF-THE-ART OVERVIEW

This section motivates the importance of EAGLE. EAGLE calls for uncertainty-aware and partial models. Uncertainty here corresponds to a metric system for measuring the incompleteness of the models that is due to the technique used to elicit the models from real artifacts (e.g., code or running system) and their context. EAGLE systems opportunistically integrate pieces of software as available in a non-ideal world: this leads to accept incomplete information, hence accepting systems that represent the strictly necessary solution for satisfying the specified goal, possibly also in face of risks identification and prioritization. Thus, goal-oriented validation is another key aspect for EAGLE. As discussed below, there exist many methods and techniques to account for uncertainty while developing software systems. All of them operate within different domains and consider uncertainty at different abstraction levels by also exploiting different software models. In this direction, one of the aims of EAGLE is to combine/extend existing techniques and methods into a unified uncertainty-aware framework. Therefore, our state-of-the art overview is organized in several parts: Section 3.1 presents approaches addressing the problem of deriving partial models from implemented systems. Section 3.2 the models@runtime approach and Section 3.3 presents automatic connector synthesis to support software integration and coordination. Finally, Section 3.4 presents functional and non-functional verification and validation under uncertainty.

3.1 Derivation of partial models

Several approaches have recently addressed the problem of deriving partial behavioral models from implemented systems. In [7], we propose a method that combines synthesis and testing techniques in order to automatically derive the behaviour protocol of a web-service out of its WSDL interface. In [34], the authors propose a novel synthesis technique that constructs partial behavioural models in the form of Model Transition Systems from a combination of safety properties and scenarios. In [26], the authors describe a technique to automatically generate behavioral models from (object-oriented) system execution traces. The work described in [21] aims to infer a formal specification of stateful black-box components that behave as data abstractions by observing their run-time behavior. The approach described in [35] analyzes Java code to elicit object usage patterns. The authors of [4] present an approach for inferring state machines with an infinite state space. The author of [27] use constraint solving to carry on learning-based black-box testing. In [14] the authors propose tools and techniques to automatically derive models from running open source software systems in order to enable the simulation of their upgrades and to detect possible configuration inconsistencies.

3.2 Models@runtime

The models@runtime approach [8] seeks to extend the applicability of models produced in Model Driven Development (MDD) approaches to the run-time environment. An example of design models application at run-time has been proposed within the PLASTIC project, where we have been involved in. The PLASTIC development process [2] relies on model-based solutions to build adaptable context-aware service-oriented applications. Opportunistic reuse of heterogeneous pieces of software, context awareness, run-time evolution, adaptiveness and uncertainty represent challenges that can be addressed by adopting a models@runtime approach [8]. Modeling techniques coupled with MDD capabilities such as model transformation and code generation provide viable means to enable system monitoring, model analysis and adaptation at run-time [23].

3.3 Automatic connector synthesis to support software integration and coordination

The first approaches to connector synthesis appeared in the 90s in the control theory domain [31] and, thereafter, they have been revised to fit the domain of software (embedded) systems [1, 3]. The aim of these approaches is to automatically synthesize a controller that restricts the system behavior so as to satisfy a given specification. In [11, 30], LTSs are used to model the I/O behaviour of components and automatically synthesize a set of constraints on the components' environment that allow deadlock avoidance. In [33], we show how to automatically derive either a centralized or distributed connector from a specification of the components' interaction and of the requirements that the composed system must fulfill. However, these approaches do not take into account both possible run-time changes in the environment and non-functional requirements of the system to be integrated. EAGLE aims at tackling the problem of automatically synthesizing integrators at run-time under uncertainty.

3.4 Functional and non-functional verification and validation under uncertainty

The idea of moving V&V activities at run-time [5] has been often realized by introducing monitoring activities both for functional and non-functional properties, and more recently by moving testing to on-line [6]. Uncertainty in EAGLE calls for compositional

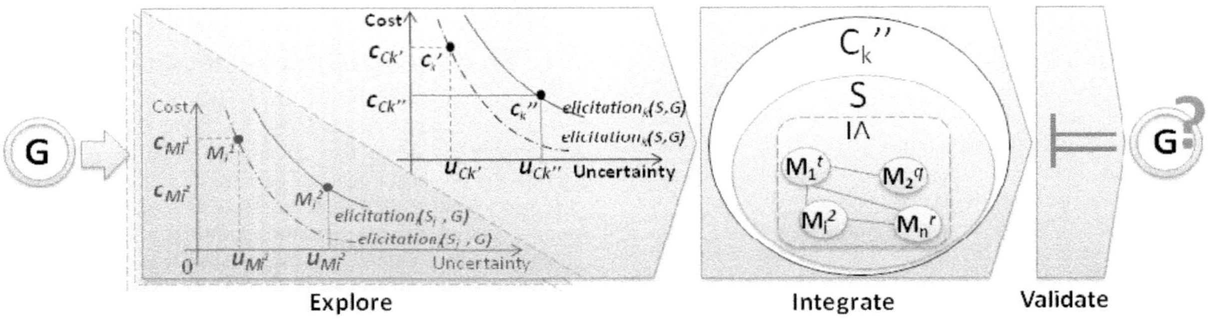

Figure 1: Explore, Integrate, and Validate phases

verification and validation (V&V) techniques that permit to perform partial V&V (based on the information currently available) and to instrument the system so to be able to support on-line V&V. Many works have been proposed in compositional verification and in particular in assume-guarantee reasoning, such as [13, 22] and to [15]. Bayesian models (such as Bayesian Networks [29]) can be considered as the stochastic counterpart of the assume-guarantee paradigm. In this direction, an example of bayesian approach for modeling the reliability of a software component-based system, given the reliability of its components, has been presented in [32]. More sophisticated stochastic models can be used to take into account uncertainty in non-functional validation processes. Hidden Markov Models (HMM) [16] are typically used to model systems that have markovian characteristics in their behavior, but that also have some states (and transitions) for which only limited knowledge is available. Finally, theories [24] and techniques [9] for compositional approaches to testing have been investigated.

4. METHODOLOGY

In the EAGLE approach, opportunism and goal-orientation imply that software production process qualities change from more traditional aspects of efficiency and resource optimization, to adaptability and fit-for-purpose, even accepting inefficient usage of resources and redundancy. The uncertainty degree of a piece of software, with respect to a given goal G, can be determined by using explorative techniques that range from standard analysis and validation techniques to machine learning techniques [17]. Let $S_1,...,S_k$ be pieces of software that can be used to build a system S that satisfies G. In general different subsets of $\{S_1,...,S_k\}$ will suffice to satisfy G. The result of an explorative phase is a set of approximation models $M=\{M_1,...,M_n\}$ of different types, i.e., a set of observations of $S_1,...,S_k$.

Each type of model M_i is elicited by adopting an explorative technique, e.g., $elicitation_i(S_j, G)$, and represents an observation of an S_j. Each explorative technique can obviously be instantiated in different ways, depending on the desired semantics of the target model. As an example, an explorative technique can elicit automata from Java applications, but the specific instantiation of the technique will determine the semantics of the elicited automata. Hence, we denote by $M_i^1,...,M_i^q$ the set of models that can be elicited with the explorative technique i. Each model shall have associated its own metric system for measuring the degree of uncertainty $u_{M_i^j}$. Thus, a piece of software and a goal can have associated different models, i.e., different observations, each with its own degree of uncertainty. Moreover, each elicited model M_i^j has a cost $c_{M_i^j}$ that represents a quantitative measure of the effort to elicit M_i^j with an uncertainty degree $u_{M_i^j}$. In the Explore box of Figure 1 we represent this scenario, where different curves for the same explorative technique represent different instances of the technique, each able to elicit models with different costs and uncertainty degree (along the curve). This box has a certain multiplicity (as represented by the dashed box boundaries) given by the multiplicity of explorative techniques and their instances. Similarly, a set of types of models $C=\{C_1,...,C_n\}$ can be elicited for the context and analogous definitions of uncertainty and cost metrics can be introduced for it.

The *integration* step shall support the producer in creating the most effective (to the goal G) integration means that takes into account the uncertainty degree, and the associated cost, of each single elicited model. This means that during the integration step, by reasoning on their elicited models and further accounting for the trade off between uncertainty degree and cost, the candidate pieces of software (i.e., a subset of $\{S_1,...,S_k\}$) need to be selected. Thus, an integration architecture *IA* shall be provided, possibly automatically. *IA* plays a crucial role in influencing the overall uncertainty degree of the final integrated system S, as different *IAs* may result in different uncertainty degrees for S. These observations lead to a definition of the integrated system uncertainty u_S as a function of the software models that have been selected in the explorative step, suitably integrated according to the *IA* and the context models.

A validation step shall assess the quality of the integrated system with respect to the overall system goal G and the current elicited context models. If the final assessment is not satisfying then the framework should permit to iterate the process either to select different pieces of software, or to reduce the uncertainty degree of some (already in place) models, or to modify the overall *IA*.

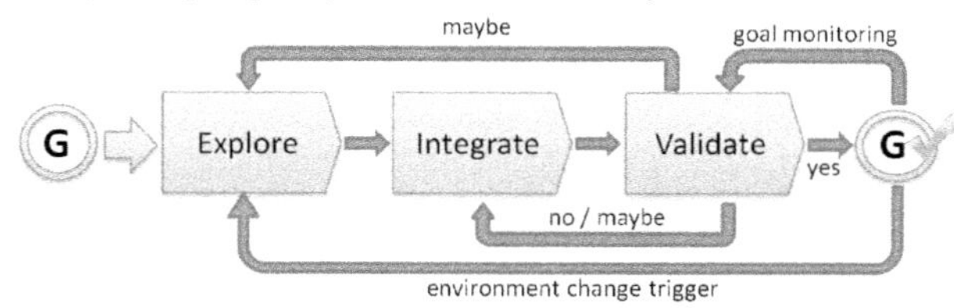

Figure 2: Explore, Integrate, and Validate cycle

Figure 2 shows the perpetual activity flow of the foreseen process. In particular, if validation says that the goal is not achieved (**no**) then a new integration architecture is considered. The aim is to act on the integration means, e.g., connectors, so to avoid interactions that prevent the achievement of the goal. If it cannot be assessed whether the goal is achieved or not (**maybe**) either a new integration architecture is considered, or more accurate software models are incrementally elicited. For instance, under cost and resource constraints, the validation may not be able to reach a feasible result. In this case, a new integration architecture can be designed to make the validation feasible. Furthermore, a lack of information in the considered models may lead to a meaningless validation, thus claiming for more accurate models to be elicited. Finally, if the validation step shows that the goal is achieved (**yes**) then an entire explore-integrate-validate iteration is terminated. Whenever changes in the monitored environment occur, the iteration of a new cycle is triggered.

5. CONCLUSION

Overall EAGLE is very ambitious. Each of the above described objectives launches key challenges that will characterize and steer the research in software in the next future. Each objective cannot be addressed in isolation from the others but needs to be cast in the scope of a holistic explore-integrate-validate process life cycle. The software process we envisage lifts uncertainty to the level of a first class notion among the others and asks for explicit characterizations of the software artifact properties and assumptions that take into account their incompleteness, as described above. EAGLE aims at defining and developing novel theories, models, model-driven techniques, and tools for application production, verification and validation, and integration code synthesis, which are all characterized by the ability of tackling the unknown. From the forum, we expect to exploit possible feedbacks from both computer scientists and practitioners to evaluate the exploitation, in the near future, of the project results with respect to a multitude of contexts both research-wise and industrial-wise.

6. REFERENCES

[1] E. Asarin, O. Maler, and A. Pnueli. Symbolic controller synthesis for discrete and timed systems. In *Hybrid Systems II*, 1995.

[2] M. Autili, L. Berardinelli, V. Cortellessa, A. Marco, D. Ruscio, P. Inverardi, and M. Tivoli. A development process for self-adapting service oriented applications. In *Proc. of ICSOC '07*, pages 442–448, 2007.

[3] C. Baier, M. Größer, M. Leucker, B. Bollig, and F. Ciesinski. Controller synthesis for probabilistic systems (extended abstract). In *IFIP TCS 2004*, volume 155. 2004.

[4] T. Berg, B. Jonsson, and H. Raffelt. Regular inference for state machines using domains with equality tests. In *Proc. of FASE'08/ETAPS'08*, pages 317–331, 2008.

[5] A. Bertolino, G. Angelis, L. Frantzen, and A. Polini. Software engineering. chapter The PLASTIC Framework and Tools for Testing Service-Oriented Applications, pages 106–139. Springer-Verlag, Berlin, Heidelberg, 2009.

[6] A. Bertolino, G. De Angelis, and A. Polini. (role)CAST : A Framework for On-line Service Testing. In *Proc. of WEBIST'11*, 2011.

[7] A. Bertolino, P. Inverardi, P. Pelliccione, and M. Tivoli. Automatic synthesis of behavior protocols for composable web-services. In *Proc of ESEC/FSE '09*, 2009.

[8] G. Blair, N. Bencomo, and R. B. France. Models@run.time. *Computer*, 42:22–27, 2009.

[9] C. Blundell, D. Giannakopoulou, and C. S. Păsăreanu. Assume-guarantee testing. *Softw. Eng. Notes*, 31, 2005.

[10] B. W. Boehm. Software risk management: Principles and practices. *IEEE Softw.*, 8:32–41, January 1991.

[11] C. Canal, P. Poizat, and G. Salaün. Synchronizing behavioural mismatch in software composition. In *FMOODS*, pages 63–77, 2006.

[12] S. Ceri, D. Braga, F. Corcoglioniti, M. Grossniklaus, and S. Vadacca. Search computing challenges and directions. In *Proc of ICOODB'10*, pages 1–5, 2010.

[13] J. M. Cobleigh, D. Giannakopoulou, and C. Pasareanu. Learning Assumptions for Compositional Verification. In *Proc. of TACAS 2003*, number 2619 in LNCS, 2003.

[14] R. Di Cosmo, D. Di Ruscio, P. Pelliccione, A. Pierantonio, and S. Zacchiroli. Supporting Software Evolution in Component-Based FOSS Systems. *Science of Computer Programming*, 76(12), 2011.

[15] J. Dingel. Computer-Assisted Assume/Guarantee Reasoning with VeriSoft. In *Proc. of ICSE2003*.

[16] Y. Ephraim and N. Merhav. Hidden markov processes. *IEEE Transactions on Information Theory*, 48:1518–1569.

[17] M. D. Ernst and J. H. Perkins. Learning from executions: Dynamic analysis for software engineering and program understanding, Tutorial at ASE 2005.

[18] J. R. Galbraith. *Designing Complex Organizations*. Addison-Wesley Longman Publishing Co., Inc., Boston, MA, USA, 1st edition, 1973.

[19] D. Garlan. Software engineering in an uncertain world. In *Proc. of FSE/SDP'10*, pages 125–128, 2010.

[20] C. Ghezzi. ERC Advanced Investigator Grant N. 227977 [2008-2013].

[21] C. Ghezzi, A. Mocci, and M. Monga. Synthesizing intensional behavior models by graph transformation. In *Proc. of ICSE '09*, pages 430–440, 2009.

[22] D. Giannakopoulou, C. S. Pasareanu, and H. Barringer. Component verification with automatically generated assumptions. In *ASE journal, 12(3): 297-320*, 2005.

[23] H. J. Goldsby and B. H. Cheng. Automatically generating behavioral models of adaptive systems to address uncertainty. In *Proc. of MoDELS '08*, pages 568–583, 2008.

[24] D. Hamlet. *Composing Software Components: A Software-testing Perspective*. Springer Publishing Company, Incorporated, 1st edition, 2010.

[25] P. Inverardi. Software of the future is the future of software? In *Proc. of TGC'06*, pages 69–85, 2006.

[26] D. Lorenzoli, L. Mariani, and M. Pezzè. Automatic generation of software behavioral models. In *Proc. of ICSE '08*, pages 501–510, 2008.

[27] K. Meinke. Automated black-box testing of functional correctness using function approximation. In *Proc. of ISSTA '04*, pages 143–153, 2004.

[28] J. Mula, R. Poler, J. Garcia-Sabater, and F. Lario. Models for production planning under uncertainty: A review. *IJPE*, 103(1):271–285, 2006.

[29] M. Neil, N. Fenton, and M. Tailor. Using bayesian networks to model expected and unexpected operational losses. *Risk Analysis*, 25(4):963–972, 2005.

[30] R. Passerone, L. de Alfaro, T. A. Henzinger, and A. L. Sangiovanni-Vincentelli. Convertibility verification and converter synthesis: two faces of the same coin. In *Proc. of ICCAD '02*, pages 132–139, 2002.

[31] P. Ramadge and W. Wonham. The control of discrete event systems. *Proceedings of the IEEE*, 77(1):81 –98, jan 1989.

[32] H. Singh, V. Cortellessa, B. Cukic, E. Gunel, and V. Bharadwaj. A bayesian approach to reliability prediction and assessment of component based systems. In *Proc. of ISSRE '01*, 2001.

[33] M. Tivoli and P. Inverardi. Failure-free coordinators synthesis for component-based architectures. *Sci. Comput. Program.*, 71(3):181–212, May 2008.

[34] S. Uchitel, G. Brunet, and M. Chechik. Synthesis of partial behavior models from properties and scenarios. *IEEE Trans. Softw. Eng.*, 35:384–406, May 2009.

[35] A. Wasylkowski, A. Zeller, and C. Lindig. Detecting object usage anomalies. In *Proc. of ESEC-FSE '07*, 2007.

[36] R. W. White and R. A. Roth. *Exploratory Search: Beyond the Query-Response Paradigm*. Synthesis Lect. on ICRS. Morgan & Claypool Publishers, 2009.

Stateful Breakpoints: A Practical Approach to Defining Parameterized Runtime Monitors

Eric Bodden
Software Technology Group, Technische Universität Darmstadt
Center for Advanced Security Research Darmstadt (CASED)
bodden@acm.org

ABSTRACT

A runtime monitor checks a safety property during a program's execution. A parameterized runtime monitor can monitor properties containing free variables, or parameters. For instance, a monitor for the regular expression "`close(s)+ read(s)`" will warn the user when reading from a stream `s` that has previously been closed. Parameterized runtime monitors are very expressive, and research on this topic has lately gained much traction in the Runtime Verification community. Existing monitoring algorithms are very efficient. Nevertheless, existing tools provide little support for actually defining runtime monitors, probably one reason for why few practitioners are using runtime monitoring so far.

In this work we propose the idea of allowing programmers to express parameterized runtime monitors through stateful breakpoints, temporal combinations of normal breakpoints, a concept well known to programmers. We show how we envision programmers to define runtime monitors through stateful breakpoints and parameter bindings through breakpoint expressions. Further, we explain how stateful breakpoints improve the debugging experience: they are more expressive than normal breakpoints, nevertheless can be evaluated more efficiently. Stateful breakpoints can be attached to bug reports for easy reproducibility: they often allow developers to run directly to the bug in one single step. Further, stateful breakpoints can potentially be inferred from a running debugging session or using property inference and fault localization tools.

Categories and Subject Descriptors

D.2.4 [**Software/Program Verification**]: Validation; D.2.5 [**Testing and Debugging**]: Debugging aids

General Terms

Human Factors, Verification

Keywords

Parameterized runtime monitors, Stateful breakpoints

Permission to make digital or hard copies of all or part of this work for personal or classroom use is granted without fee provided that copies are not made or distributed for profit or commercial advantage and that copies bear this notice and the full citation on the first page. To copy otherwise, to republish, to post on servers or to redistribute to lists, requires prior specific permission and/or a fee.
ESEC/FSE'11, September 5–9, 2011, Szeged, Hungary.
Copyright 2011 ACM 978-1-4503-0443-6/11/09 ...$10.00.

1. NEW IDEA: DEFINING RUNTIME MONITORS WITH BREAKPOINTS

A runtime monitor checks safety properties of some program under test during that program's execution. In runtime monitoring, the program under test is instrumented to notify the monitor about certain events of interest during the program's own execution. The monitor then reacts to those events, typically by changing some monitor-internal state. When runtime monitors are used for runtime verification, erroneous sequences of events will typically drive the runtime monitor into an error state, causing the monitor to notify the program of a property violation.

Runtime monitors that react to a single, flat stream of events are, however, not very expressive. For instance, consider a monitor that is supposed to notify users when reading from a stream that has previously been closed. Such a monitor would typically be denoted by a regular expression "`close+ read`". Now assume a program execution in which the program opens streams s_1 and s_2, then closes s_1 but reads from s_2. A naïve monitor would signal an error even in this case, although the close and read operations involved different objects. Researchers have therefore introduced the concept of parameterized runtime monitors. In the parameterized approach, the regular expression is extended to "`close(s)+ read(s)`": a violation only occurs when both events involve the same stream object `s`.

Runtime verification, and in particular runtime verification with parameterized runtime monitors is perceived as a powerful concept within the Runtime Verification community. Opposed to many static program analyses, runtime monitors usually have no false positives, i.e., they notify the user only of actual error as they occur on a particular program run, and integrate well with testing. Efficiency used to be problematic: if implemented naïvely, parameterized runtime monitors can slow down the program under test by several orders of magnitude because at every event of interest the program needs to wait for the monitor to update its internal state. In recent years, however, researchers have shown that even parameterized runtime monitors can be implemented with little to no runtime overhead in the vast majority of cases [3–5]. Hence, runtime monitoring is finally arrived at a point where one would assume the technology to become mainstream. Nevertheless, two key problems still hinder adoption by main-stream programmers: (1) How to define runtime monitors? (2) How to debug the program once an error has been found? In this paper, we propose to address both problems at once by defining monitors through the well-known concept of breakpoints.

1.1 State of the art: textual monitor definition paired with code generation

Many programmers nowadays use Integrated Development Environments (IDE) that support rapid application development through features such as instant feedback, instant compilation, code completion, and so on. Traditional runtime verification tools, on the other hand, require a complex, multi-step development process. Programmers typically need to define the monitor through some textual declarative monitor specification, using a monitoring logic such as Linear Temporal Logic [9], Context-free Grammars, or Regular Expressions [1, 4]. The runtime verification tool then reads this textual specification as an input, along with the code of the program under test, emitting a version of that program instrumented with the runtime monitor that the textual specification defines. The programmer then needs to test-run this version of the program to search for potential property violations. This multi-step process is problematic, as it does not align well with the way in which many of today's programmers write and maintain their program code in modern IDEs.

But let's assume that the programmer does test-run the instrumented program, and the runtime monitor indeed notifies the user of a property violation. This is great, we have just found a programming error! But then what? Current runtime verification tools typically issue an error message on the command line, potentially along with a stack trace at the time at which the violation was detected. While this is useful, the user often still needs to establish a debug session to actually find out the root cause of the bug.

1.2 Proposed solution: Runtime monitors as stateful breakpoints

In this work we propose to integrate runtime monitoring tightly with the debugging support of a modern IDE. The idea is to provide developers with a means to define parameterized runtime monitors using a concept typically well-known to them: breakpoints. In our approach, a runtime monitor resembles a "stateful breakpoint". Such a breakpoint comprises three important elements:

1. a set of primitive (ordinary) breakpoints, along with textual labels for these breakpoints,
2. a pattern defining a temporal ordering over these labeled breakpoints,[1] and
3. a set of variables (parameters). Every primitive breakpoint can define a program expression for each variable. The expressions will be evaluated when the breakpoint "hits", binding the expression's return value to the variable.

We are currently integrating support for such stateful breakpoints into the Eclipse IDE [7]. Figure 1a shows how we envision programmers to define runtime monitors with our Eclipse plugin. Figure 1b shows an example program which the programmer may want to debug using the stateful breakpoint from Figure 1a. The intention of the stateful breakpoint is to halt the program during debugging when reading from a closed stream. In the example program, this is the case when line 19 executes in the context of the method call in line 10.

[1]We propose to use a regular expression.

Name	No read after close	
Breakpoint	Label	Variable 1
• Example - line 14	closeStream	`stream`
• Example - line 19	readStream	`is`
Pattern:	closeStream+ readStream	

(a) Schematic view of monitor definition

```
1   class Example {
2
3   public static void main(String[] args)  {
4      InputStream s = new FileInputStream(..);
5      InputStream s2 = new FileInputStream(..);
6
7      closeit(s2);
8      readit(s);
9      closeit(s);
10     readit(s);
11  }
12
13  static void closeit(InputStream stream) {
14 •   stream.close(); //<-- prim. breakp. "close"
15  }
16
17  static void readit(InputStream is) {
18     int i;
19 •   while((i=is.read())>-1) { //<-- prim. breakp. "read"
20         System.out.println(i);
21     }
22  }
23
24  }
```

(b) Example program using streams

Figure 1: Example monitor and program

As Figure 1a shows, our envisioned user-interface lets users define monitors through a table-like view. On the left, in the column "Breakpoint", the user can select primitive breakpoints from a list of breakpoints defined through Eclipse's usual Breakpoints View. In the column "Label", the user can assign every breakpoint a name. Our plugin will assign a sensible default to the label but in principle the user can choose any label she wishes. The "Pattern" at the bottom defines a temporal ordering over these labeled breakpoints. In the example, the monitor detects a property violation, and halts the program during debugging, when the breakpoint "read" at line 19 is visited after the program's execution has passed through the breakpoint "close" at line 14 at least once. The column "Variable 1" allows programmers to restrict the matching of the regular expression to such fragments of the execution trace where the expressions defined in this column all evaluate to the same value/object. In the example, the programmer stated that the program should halt only if the expression `stream` at line 14 returns the same object as the expression `is` at line 19. Users can add further Variable columns as needed.

We wish to note that primitive breakpoints cannot only comprise line-based breakpoints as shown in Figure 1b. Integrated Development Environments like Eclipse further offer the opportunity to define primitive breakpoints that trigger on any invocation of a specific method no matter where the invocation is taking place, on read or write accesses to a specific field, and on throwing exceptions of a certain type. A programmer can use all these kinds of breakpoints as primitive breakpoints within a stateful breakpoint.

The "Pattern" to be entered is in our current design a regular expression over an alphabet Σ of literals defined by the breakpoints' labels. In our example, for instance, we have $\Sigma = \{\texttt{closeStream}, \texttt{readStream}\}$. In our current prototype, we plan to allow for the operators $+$, $*$, $?$, $\cdot$ and $(\cdot)$ respectively, with their usual semantics. In the expression, literals end at operators or at white space. Hence, "closeStream readStream" is a valid expression while the expression "closeStreamreadStream" is not: the latter expression refers to a single literal closeStreamreadStream, which is not defined as a label. Our current prototype eases the writing of regular expressions with using a code-completion approach that suggests declared labels while typing.

1.3 Benefits over traditional breakpoints

Stateful breakpoints are much more expressive than primitive breakpoints. The stateful breakpoint in the example allows programmers to halt at line 19 only if the "read" was preceded by a "close". This avoids unnecessary stepping through the code. The support for parameters such as "Variable 1" allows for further filtering and ease of debugging: without parameter support, the debugger would need to halt the program also when the "read" at line 19 executes in the context of the method call in line 8, although at this point the program has closed only stream s2 and not s.

Stateful breakpoints provide several interesting software engineering benefits.

- They extend the well-known concept of breakpoints in a natural way.
- If defined correctly, they allow the debugger to execute the program directly until the point of error in one single step.
- We plan to allow users to persist stateful breakpoints, and to attach them to bug reports. This allows users to easily communicate bugs to developers.
- Conversely, API developers can ship their libraries with stateful breakpoints that get loaded into the IDE automatically when the library is used. Should the developer accidentally misuse the library, e.g. by calling methods in the wrong order, the program will halt automatically, providing the programmer full context for debugging.

While we believe that stateful breakpoints are reasonably easy to define, in future work we will consider inferring stateful breakpoints automatically from a debugging session that uses primitive breakpoints only. By observing the order in which the programmer sets, disables and re-enables primitive breakpoints we hope to be able to infer higher-level stateful breakpoints automatically. Fault localization tools [11] and approaches to API property mining could be another source of useful stateful breakpoints.

Another interesting piece of future work would involve the evaluation of stateful breakpoints not within the virtual machine that hosts the debugger (the Debugger-VM) but rather directly within the virtual machine that hosts the program under test. This way of breakpoint evaluation has the potential to reduce the communication between both virtual machines by orders of magnitudes, hence speeding up the debugging process significantly: instead of notifying the Debugger-VM of every single event of interest, the Debugger-VM would only be notified once the monitor has actually reached an error state.

1.4 Benefits over traditional runtime verification tools

Stateful breakpoints support properties just as expressive as the ones supported by traditional runtime verification tools. Nevertheless, stateful breakpoints provide several software engineering benefits over those tools.

- Stateful breakpoints can be defined directly in the IDE.
- Stateful breakpoints are defined using the concept of breakpoints, which should be familiar to most programmers.
- Stateful breakpoints allow programmers to immediately halt the program when a property violation is detected. At this point, the programmer can use all tooling provided by the debugger to identify the cause of this violation.
- Stateful breakpoints are a "push-button technology". There is no need for separate monitor definition, code generation and execution of the instrumented program. Instead, the debugger simply executes the original, uninstrumented program, but is notified of the necessary events through the debugging protocol.

2. NOVELTY OF THE IDEA

The idea is new because it is the first attempt to bring declarative monitor specifications into an IDE. Further, it is the first attempt to express runtime monitors with the well-known concepts of breakpoints. In traditional approaches, monitors are instead defined through some form of declarative event patterns, typically AspectJ [2] pointcuts.

While there has been one approach [6] (see below) to adding the notion of control flow to breakpoints (see Section 3), our approach goes much beyond the simple notion of control flow: we propose to define fully-fledged runtime monitors, parameterized through variable bindings that bind free variables to the return values of program expressions. Parameters are essential for obtaining breakpoints that are expressive enough so that they can allow programmers to run "to the bug" in one single step.

3. RELATED WORK

The most related work is the work by Chern and De Volder on Control-Flow Breakpoints [6]. The authors observed that traditional breakpoints can be made much more useful if programmers can constrain them to halt the program only after some other breakpoints were visited already (or not visited yet). Using an empirical evaluation, the authors show that the ability to restrict breakpoints using such control-flow restrictions can indeed ease the reproduction of a significant portion of known bugs.

Our idea of using stateful breakpoints to define runtime monitors goes, however, much beyond the idea of simple control-flow restrictions. In particular, we propose to enable programmers to define stateful breakpoints using declarative patterns such as regular expressions. Further, we argue that stateful breakpoints must support parametric runtime monitors. Otherwise, the monitor will yield too many false positives, halting the program although no property violation has been observed.

The work of Chern and De Volder is also different in the sense that it fulfils a different goal. Chern's and De Volder's goal was to ease debugging. Our primary goal is rather to make runtime verification a mainstream technology. Breakpoints are merely our means to achieve this goal and the improved ease of debugging is a welcome side effect.

4. EXPECTED FEEDBACK

We are currently finalizing the implementation of our research prototype. The author's research group has a good understanding of the techniques involved to make the technology work. To be able to evaluate parameterized runtime monitoring without having to resort to code generation (as in traditional runtime verification tools), we implemented a novel runtime verification library called MOPBox [8]. This library encapsulates the entire matching logic required to determine whether or not to hold at a particular breakpoint.

At the conference, we hence expect feedback mainly with respect the two following important topics:

- Does the user interface appear intuitive to other developers? Can it be improved, and if so, how?

- How can we effectively evaluate the usefulness of our approach? In the runtime verification community [10], runtime monitoring approaches are typically evaluated with respect to their expressiveness or with respect to the ability to implement efficient monitors for the approach. Usability evaluations are rarely performed.

5. CONCLUSION

We have presented the idea of defining runtime monitors through a concept well known to programmers: breakpoints. A runtime monitor is defined as a "stateful breakpoint" that halts the program only after its primitive breakpoints have been visited in a given order, and only if the context at the times during which these breakpoints were visited fulfils certain constraints. Stateful breakpoints are very expressive and often allow developers to directly run to a bug in one single step. This makes it useful to persist stateful breakpoints, and to attach them to bug reports as a means to communicate bugs to developers. Conversely, developers can ship libraries along with stateful breakpoints which will halt the client's program when misusing the library.

We are currently implementing the proposed approach as an extension to the popular Eclipse IDE [7]. To be able to evaluate parameterized runtime monitoring without having to resort to code generation (as in traditional runtime verification tools), we implemented a novel runtime verification library called MOPBox [8].

Acknowledgements.

We wish to thank the anonymous reviewers for their helpful and thorough feedback. This work was supported by the Center for Advanced Security Research Darmstadt, CASED (www.cased.de).

6. REFERENCES

[1] Chris Allan, Pavel Avgustinov, Aske Simon Christensen, Laurie Hendren, Sascha Kuzins, Ondřej Lhoták, Oege de Moor, Damien Sereni, Ganesh Sittampalam, and Julian Tibble. Adding Trace Matching with Free Variables to AspectJ. In *International Conference on Object-Oriented Programming, Systems, Languages, and Applications (OOPSLA)*, pages 345–364. ACM Press, October 2005.

[2] The AspectJ home page, 2003.

[3] Pavel Avgustinov, Julian Tibble, and Oege de Moor. Making trace monitors feasible. In *International Conference on Object-Oriented Programming, Systems, Languages, and Applications (OOPSLA)*, pages 589–608. ACM Press, October 2007.

[4] Feng Chen and Grigore Roşu. MOP: an efficient and generic runtime verification framework. In *International Conference on Object-Oriented Programming, Systems, Languages, and Applications (OOPSLA)*, pages 569–588. ACM Press, October 2007.

[5] Feng Chen and Grigore Roşu. Parametric trace slicing and monitoring. In *International Conference on Tools and Algorithms for the Construction and Analysis of Systems (TACAS)*, volume 5505 of *Lecture Notes in Computer Science (LNCS)*, pages 246–261. Springer, March 2009.

[6] Rick Chern and Kris De Volder. Debugging with control-flow breakpoints. In *Proceedings of the 6th international conference on Aspect-oriented software development*, AOSD '07, pages 96–106, New York, NY, USA, 2007. ACM.

[7] Eclipse IDE. http://www.eclipse.org/.

[8] MOPBox, runtime monitoring in a box. http://mopbox.googlecode.com/.

[9] Amir Pnueli. The temporal logic of programs. In *IEEE Symposium on the Foundations of Computer Science (FOCS)*, pages 46–57. IEEE Computer Society, October 1977.

[10] Workshop and conference series on Runtime Verification. http://www.runtime-verification.org/.

[11] Cheng Zhang, Dacong Yan, Jianjun Zhao, Yuting Chen, and Shengqian Yang. Bpgen: an automated breakpoint generator for debugging. In *Proceedings of the 32nd ACM/IEEE International Conference on Software Engineering - Volume 2*, ICSE '10, pages 271–274, New York, NY, USA, 2010. ACM.

Finding Bugs by Isolating Unit Tests

Kıvanç Muşlu Bilge Soran Jochen Wuttke
Computer Science and Engineering
University of Washington
Seattle, WA, USA
{kivanc,bilge,wuttke}@cs.washington.edu

ABSTRACT

Even in simple programs there are hidden assumptions and dependencies between units that are not immediately visible in each involved unit. These dependencies are generally hard to identify and locate, and can lead to subtle faults that are often missed, even by extensive test suites.

We propose to leverage existing test suites to identify faults due to hidden dependencies and to identify inadequate test suite design. Rather than just executing entire test suites within frameworks such as JUnit, we execute each test in isolation, thus removing masking effects that might be present in the test suites. We hypothesize that this can reveal previously hidden dependencies between program units or tests.

A preliminary study shows that this technique is capable of identifying subtle faults that have lived in a system for 120 revisions, despite failures being reported and despite attempts to fix the fault.

Categories and Subject Descriptors

D.2.5 [**Software**]: Testing and Debugging

General Terms

Reliability

Keywords

data dependency, testing, test isolation, test reuse

1. OVERVIEW

Developers often leave implicit their assumptions about how the code they write is intended to be executed. Implicit expectations about ordering constraints for method invocations or data dependencies, for example, can lead to subtle faults in the code and/or clients using the code. Although rare, such assumptions and faults occur in practice: for example, the initialization order of classes led to a fault in the Tomcat application server[1] that took several months to identify, diagnose and fix[2]. When testers are unaware of such assumptions by developers, the test suites they design are unlikely to systematically address this class of faults.

While it is rarely expressed explicitly, conventional wisdom states and incidental evidence from practice supports a fundamental requirement for test design: tests should be *independent*, that is running them isolated from other tests should not affect their outcome (e. g., [4]). The reason behind this requirement is that if tests are not independent, each test case is no longer a complete specification for what it tests. This premise is so deeply rooted in the minds of software testers that Michal Young, one of the authors of a standard textbook on software testing [6], mentioned in a recent email exchange that *"[in our book] for the most part we just assumed that test cases would be independent in the sense [we describe here], but didn't think to make that explicit."* [9]

Given that, on one side, most existing code contains implicit assumptions and hidden dependencies, and that on the other side test cases are usually assumed to be independent, we hypothesize that test cases for functionality that contains implicit assumptions are likely *not* independent. We further hypothesize that the outcome of test cases that are not independent is likely to change when they are executed in isolation. Thus, a test that changes its outcome when run in isolation likely signals a dependency that is worthy of thorough inspection. To assess the validity of these hypotheses, we propose to isolate test cases from their test suites and to execute them in a fresh environment to avoid "pollution" by other tests. Practically, in an environment like JUnit[3], this amounts to a new execution strategy that resets the environment before the execution of each test method.

We have tested these hypotheses in an experiment on the Apache Commons CLI[4] library, and our results show that isolating test cases can detect faults that are due to hidden dependencies. While this research is preliminary, we believe that it will result in a practical technique to identify dependencies among test cases and expose faults due to hidden assumptions.

In the following sections we briefly discuss the most related work in the area of testing and test adequacy, describe our initial experiments and results, and conclude with an

[1]`http://tomcat.apache.org/`
[2]Tomcat Bugzilla bug database: ID 40820, `https://issues.apache.org/bugzilla/show_bug.cgi?id=40820`
[3]`http://www.junit.org/`
[4]`http://commons.apache.org/cli/`

Permission to make digital or hard copies of all or part of this work for personal or classroom use is granted without fee provided that copies are not made or distributed for profit or commercial advantage and that copies bear this notice and the full citation on the first page. To copy otherwise, to republish, to post on servers or to redistribute to lists, requires prior specific permission and/or a fee.
ESEC/FSE'11, September 5–9, 2011, Szeged, Hungary.
Copyright 2011 ACM 978-1-4503-0443-6/11/09 ...$10.00.

overview of the open questions and the research we are currently undertaking toward answering them.

2. RELATED WORK

Independence of test cases is usually assumed in any testing process. The technique we propose here detects dependence between test cases and, by proxy, identifies hidden dependencies between functional units of the program under test. While we are not aware of any other work that directly attacks this question, there is some research regarding requirements for good test design, including test independence and other measures of testability.

There is a considerable amount of research on *software testability* [1, 8, 3]. The fundamental idea behind *testability* is that to test a piece of code, one must be able to control the inputs to the program, and must be able to observe the outputs. Together, this allows the definition of input/output pairs that serve as test case specifications and oracles. Certain features supported by most imperative and object-oriented programming languages, such as global and static variables, obscure both controllability and observability, since their use is often opaque. While the work on testability addresses requirements that test design should strive to meet, we detect violations of these requirements that lead to test cases that have unexpected dependencies.

Test case prioritization and selection for regression testing are well researched topics that assume independence of test cases [7, 5]. However, to the best of our knowledge, there is no work in this area that checks to what extent this assumption holds. With our technique, we acknowledge that test independence is desirable, but is not always easy to achieve. Thus, it is worthwhile to detect undesired dependencies, and to classify code patterns that lead to such dependencies. Better understanding how well the assumption of test case independence holds in general will also provide a more solid foundation to the practicality of techniques building on this assumption, and highlight the need for further research in case the assumption does not hold.

3. TEST CASE ISOLATION

We propose a new execution strategy for test cases that isolates the effects of each test case and can thus detect changes in test outcomes that are due to hidden dependencies. In principle, this requires to execute test cases in an environment that does not retain generated files, global shared program state and other means of sharing information in programs. The current focus of our work is on unit testing frameworks, in particular JUnit. Here, isolating test cases requires to run individual test methods together with the scaffolding provided, but without having other test methods interfere. Since the available test executors for JUnit do not allow for such separation, we define a simple workaround for that.

Figure 1 shows pseudocode for our test isolation algorithm. First, we run the entire test suite with the standard JUnit runner, and store the results for later comparison. Then, we extract test methods from every test class in the test suite and execute them one by one together with the framework scaffolding methods included in the test classes. To assure isolation, we execute each test method in a fresh copy of the execution environment (directories and files), and start a new JVM to avoid pollution of static and global variables. If the outcome of a test run in isolation differs from the outcome when run together with the test suite, we record a warning and the test output for later analysis.

```
void runTestSuite(suite) {
  results = runSuiteNormal();
  for (testClass in suite) {
    tests = getTestMethods(testClass);
    for (test in tests) {
      res = runIsolated(test);
      if (res not in results )
        warn(test, res);
    }
  }
}
```

Figure 1: Test isolation algorithm

At present, further analysis has to be done manually. It appears that it is possible to guide automatic analyses based, for example, on the heuristics implemented in Testability Explorer[5], with our results.

4. EXPERIMENT AND PRELIMINARY RESULTS

We tested our hypotheses in an experiment on the Apache Commons CLI library. CLI is a small library, written purely in Java, and has no dependencies to other libraries. We chose this example because having no external dependencies ensures that all effects we observe in our experiment are due to the program itself, rather than external influences. Controlling the variables that may influence the outcome of our analysis more tightly allows us to draw conclusions with higher confidence.

To allow us to determine how long detected faults lived in the systems before they were identified and fixed, we ran our simple prototype on 153 recent and consecutive revisions of CLI from the Apache Subversion repository[6]. Our specific focus was on tests that succeed when executed with the entire test suite, but fail when run in isolation. While this is a limitation of our experiment, we believe that the results are representative, because across all revisions we studied there were only few tests that failed when run with the entire test suite. To be precise, seven of the studied revisions contain at least one test that fails when executed with the entire test suite[7]. We removed these revisions from the initial analysis, so that our analysis would only report those test executions that fail in isolation. The remaining 146 revisions contain on average 214 tests (min = 113, max = 361).

Our setup directly applies the technique described in the previous section to each revision. For each individual test method from the test suite we

1. create a new, clean execution environment by copying all non-test files of the original execution environment,

[5]`http://www.testabilityexplorer.org/`

[6]`http://svn.apache.org/viewvc/commons/proper/cli/trunk/`, revisions 661513–1091538

[7]revisions: 695410, 695672, 742845, 744070, 1091539, 1091550, and 1091575

Revision	Class	Test	Fixed
661513	BugTest	test13666	956302
		test27635	712642
712642	HelpFormatter-Test	testOptionWith-outShortFormat2	956302

Table 1: Suspicious tests found. The table shows the *revision* where we detect the fault, which *class* and *test* method detect it, and in which revision it was *fixed* or moved.

```
1  public final class OptionBuilder {
2    private static String argName;
3
4    private static void reset() {
5      ...
6      argName = "arg";
7      ...
8    }
9
10   public static Option create(String opt){
11     Option option =
12       new Option(opt, description);
13     ...
14     option.setArgName(argName);
15     OptionBuilder.reset();
16     return option;
17   }
18 }
```

Figure 2: Fault-related code from `OptionBuilder.java` (rev. 661513)

2. create a new JUnit TestCase that contains only scaffolding and the selected test method,

3. compile, build, and run this single test through the Maven build system and record the outcome.

We discovered three test cases that fail when run in isolation (summarized in Table 1). The first revision we analyzed (661513) has two failing tests, `test13666` and `test27635` in test class `BugsTest.java`. In revision 712642 (54 revisions later), the method `test27635` is moved to test class `HelpFormatterTest.java` and its name is changed to `testOptionWithoutShortFormat2`. All these tests continue to fail until revision 956302 (120 revisions in total), from which on all tests pass.

A detailed study of the code under test revealed that both tests fail due to the same hidden dependency fault. The fault is located in `OptionBuilder.java` and is due to the improper use of static variables. Figure 2 shows code that illustrates the fault. By default, `argName` is initialized to `null` (line 2), and only set to its intended default value `"arg"` by the `create()` method via calling `reset()` (line 15). Consequently, if clients of CLI do not explicitly initialize the value of `argName`, the first option created will have `null` rather than `"arg"` as its argument name. In CLI, there are two types of options: options with and without argument names. If an option without argument is created first, this fault will not lead to a failure, because the `null` value will be ignored. Consecutive calls to `create()` can rely on `reset()` to establish the desired default value.

Both `test13666` and `test27635` (or `testOptionWithoutShortFormat2`) can reveal this fault, since they create an option with the default argument as the first thing in their execution. However, the test classes `BugTest` and `HelpFormatterTest` both contain other tests that create options *before* `test13666` and `test27635` respectively. Thus, when the tests in these classes are executed in order, the tests executed before `test13666` and `test27635` call `create()` at least once, which sets the default `argName` value, thus masking the fault.

This fault is reported in the bug database several times[8], starting on March 13, 2004 (CLI-26). The report is marked as resolved *three years* later on March 15, 2007, but is then reopened as CLI-186 on July 31, 2009. On this report, one of the developers commented:

> "I reproduced the issue, it requires a dedicated test case since it is tied to the initialization of a static field in OptionBuilder"

Despite the realization that a dedicated test is required, no such test was ever created. About one month later, the bug is duplicated as CLI-187, and the actual fix happens one year later on June 19, 2010, after a total "awareness" of the fault of four years. The fix consists of adding the following code to `OptionBuilder.java`:

```
static {
//ensure consistency of initial values
   reset();
}
```

Since test isolation can identify the dependency fault in the first revision with two different test cases, we strongly believe that the developers could have fixed this long lasting fault much earlier, if they had used our method. After identifying the failing tests, following the dynamic execution of these tests and fixing the fault should be straightforward. Moreover, since our technique is relatively lightweight, it can be integrated into the normal development process and can thus aid developers while they write code, rather than in a separate test and analysis phase.

5. OPEN QUESTIONS AND CURRENT RESEARCH EFFORTS

The results presented in the previous section show that our technique can detect faults due to hidden dependencies. While the cases we report here concern incorrect and inefficient use of static variables, we believe that our technique can also detect similar problems that are due to other forms of shared state, including shared global variables and inappropriate reuse of injected dependencies [2].

A dependency violation detected by our technique may represent a weakness of the test suite rather than a fault in the program. If, for example, the test suite reuses data objects across several tests, this may trigger a dependency warning, but does not imply that the program is faulty. We are considering a wider range of experiments intended to

[8] `https://issues.apache.org/jira/browse/CLI-26`
`https://issues.apache.org/jira/browse/CLI-186`
`https://issues.apache.org/jira/browse/CLI-187`

examine different kinds of dependency violations and to determine which are due to inadequate test suites rather than faults in the program.

We also believe that our technique is capable of finding other types of dependency violations, in particular those due to interactions with the file system or databases. However, there are many legitimate reasons why tests for databases and file handling may not be independent. Therefore, it remains an open question to what extent our technique can be applied in such domains, and to what extent we need to extend its heuristics to reduce the number of false positives reported.

An important issue to determine is the false positive rate. We have not yet conducted a formal study of false positives, since our prototype implementation is not yet complete and has some weaknesses that further work will remove. It appears, however, that the absolute number of false positives will be low, since dependency violations are relatively rare.

The fault we discussed in the previous section is due to inappropriate use of static variables in Java. From the code structure it is clear that the involved variable should be a field of an instantiated class, and the problem would not even occur. It is an interesting question to explore which other patterns of faulty code we can identify by using our technique, and if we can catalog them in enough detail to inform static analysis techniques.

Another open question that we intend to address is the value of our technique in a development process. Our experiment shows that the technique could find the dependency fault when it was introduced, however it took the developers a long time of trial and error before they could fix it. We do believe that the warnings produced by our technique alone would have helped developers to fix the detected problem much faster. Furthermore, we envision several extensions to our technique that will enhance its usefulness. Dynamic techniques, such as coverage computation, can establish a starting set of affected methods, and data-flow analysis and program slicing of these can help to reduce the amount of code developers would need to analyze to determine the location of a fault.

At present, our prototype implementation incurs significant overhead. However, a large part of it is caused by calling Maven to clean and build the system for every test method. A more advanced implementation will instead be a JUnit runner, and thus avoid the overhead due to Maven. The creation of a new JVM for each test method also creates considerable overhead, even though we believe that for most test suites performance will be acceptable. In cases where the performance penalty is too high, it appears that running our technique as part of a nightly build cycle rather than during development still has considerable benefits.

We are currently working on improving our results along two major lines of research. On the one side, we are applying our technique to a wider range of programs. Gathering more cases where our technique produces warnings will lead to a better understanding of when and how to apply our technique to obtain the best value. On the other side, we are working on identifying patterns in the code that has been flagged as faulty. If we can find typical patterns of what causes warnings in our technique, we can then build heuristics that will further improve the precision of the warnings produced and will guide developers more quickly to find the faulty code.

6. CONCLUSION

In this paper we present a new technique to detect hidden dependencies in programs and test suites. The experimental results show that the technique has the potential to detect faults due to hidden dependencies early, and can guide developers more quickly to the faulty code.

We are currently experimenting with more programs to establish cases where the technique applies well, how we can improve the quality of the reported results, and how we can extend the technique with heuristics to aid fault localization in addition to detecting faults.

7. ACKNOWLEDGMENTS

This work was partly funded by Swiss National Science Foundation grant no. PBTIP1-134569, and NSF grants CCF-1016490AM01, CNS-0855252, and CCF-0963757.

8. REFERENCES

[1] Robert V. Binder. Design for testability in object-oriented systems. *Communications of the ACM*, 37(9):87–101, September 1994.

[2] Martin Fowler. Inversion of Control Containers and the Dependency Injection pattern, Jan 2004. `http://martinfowler.com/articles/injection.html\#ServiceLocatorVsDependencyInjection`.

[3] What is testable? `https://code.google.com/p/testability-explorer/wiki/HowItWorks`, accessed June 09, 2011.

[4] `http://junit.sourceforge.net/doc/testinfected/testing.htm`, accessed June 09, 2011.

[5] Jung-Min Kim and Adam Porter. A history-based test prioritization technique for regression testing in resource constrained environments. In *Proceedings of the 24th International Conference on Software Engineering, ICSE '02*, pages 119–129. ACM, 2002.

[6] Mauro Pezzè and Michal Young. *Software Testing and Analysis: Process, Principles, and Techniques.* John Wiley and Sons, 2007.

[7] G. Rothermel, R.H. Untch, Chengyun Chu, and M.J. Harrold. Prioritizing test cases for regression testing. *IEEE Transactions on Software Engineering*, 27(10):929–948, 2001.

[8] Jeffrey M. Voas and Keith W. Miller. Software testability: The new verification. *IEEE Software*, 12(3):17–28, 1995.

[9] Michal Young, June 9, 2011. Personal communication.

Inferring Test Results for Dynamic Software Product Lines

Bruno B. P. Cafeo
University of São Paulo
São Carlos - SP, Brazil
cafeo@icmc.usp.br

Joost Noppen
University of East Anglia
Norwich - Norfolk, UK
j.noppen@uea.ac.uk

Fabiano C. Ferrari
Federal University of São Carlos
São Carlos - SP, Brazil
fabiano@dc.ufscar.br

Ruzanna Chitchyan
Lancaster University
Lancaster - Lancashire, UK
r.chitchyan@comp.lancs.ac.uk

Awais Rashid
Lancaster University
Lancaster - Lancashire, UK
marash@comp.lancs.ac.uk

ABSTRACT

Due to the very large number of configurations that can typically be derived from a Dynamic Software Product Line (DSPL), efficient and effective testing of such systems have become a major challenge for software developers. In particular, when a configuration needs to be deployed quickly due to rapid contextual changes (e.g., in an unfolding crisis), time constraints hinder the proper testing of such a configuration. In this paper, we propose to reduce the testing required of such DSPLs to a relevant subset of configurations. Whenever a need to adapt to an untested configuration is encountered, our approach determines the most similar tested configuration and reuses its test results to either obtain a coverage measure or infer a confidence degree for the new, untested configuration. We focus on providing these techniques for inference of structural testing results for DSPLs, which is supported by an early prototype implementation.

Categories and Subject Descriptors

D.2.4 [**Software Engineering**]: Software/Program Verification—*Reliability, Validation*

General Terms

Reliability, Measurement

Keywords

Dynamic Software Product Lines, Software Testing.

1. INTRODUCTION: WHAT IS THE NEW IDEA? WHY IS IT NEW?

Over recent years, Software Product Line (SPL) development has matured to an effective approach for developing software systems and software families. With the advent of fields such as mobile ubiquitous computing their support by means of dynamic software product lines (DSPL, i.e., product lines that are expected to re-configure at run-time [3]), has also emerged. However, due to the large number of configurations that need to be supported, several of which might even be unforeseen, effective and efficient testing of such systems presents a hard challenge.

So far, the issue of SPL testing has been handled by selecting a particular configuration before the system is delivered, and testing that selected configuration [2]. However, in a DSPL there is no single final configuration to test. Instead, the set of possible configurations tends to be specified by enumerating the points in the software where variability may occur (so called variation points). At runtime such variability presents the emergence of a challenge in testing DSPLs due to the combinatorial explosion of required test cases. For instance, in a DSPL with three features and one variation point in each feature with two variants per variation point, there will be 27 potential configurations to test. If each variant is to be tested at least once in each configuration, there will be a minimum of 3x2x27=162 required test cases. Adding one more feature with one variation point and two variants, will require 4x2x81= 648 test cases.

Clearly, conventionally testing each variant for each configuration is an infeasible proposition for a DSPL. Yet, it is not acceptable to have a running system adapting a completely untested configuration, if that system is to be of any reasonable utility. While some related research has proposed the use of configuration verification and reasoners for runtime verification [5, 6], the testing area in DSPL is still largely under-researched. To meet this challenge, this paper proposes to determining which tested configuration is most similar to the untested one, based on their structure (in particular, their call graphs), then infer the quality of the untested configuration based on the test results previously conducted for the similar one.

While conventional testing approaches would aim to provide a full coverage of configurations, our approach provides a measure (called *degree of confidence*) within which the target configuration can be expected to be correct. The work presented here is novel in that it puts forward the notion of a confidence interval as an output of a DSPL configuration testing. At first sight this may appear to be a rather unsatisfactory criterion to base a configuration choice on. However, we need to recall that none of the conventional testing approaches are able to provide a 100% guarantee of software correctness or complete absence of errors [7]. For any testing approach an implicit confidence interval is presumed

Permission to make digital or hard copies of all or part of this work for personal or classroom use is granted without fee provided that copies are not made or distributed for profit or commercial advantage and that copies bear this notice and the full citation on the first page. To copy otherwise, to republish, to post on servers or to redistribute to lists, requires prior specific permission and/or a fee.

ESEC/FSE'11, September 5–9, 2011, Szeged, Hungary.

Copyright 2011 ACM 978-1-4503-0443-6/11/09 ...$10.00.

when an exit criteria is fulfilled (e.g., acceptable defect rate is achieved). Moreover, achieving full coverage, as aimed by conventional testing approaches, for DSPLs might require unlimited resources, while our approach is still able to support system adaptation in discriminating risky and more trusted configurations even under the real world constraints of limited time and effort. It is also worth noting that the actual value of acceptable confidence interval is dependent on the nature of software being tested.

Thus, with the above perspective in mind, one can more clearly see the value of the proposed approach, which supports explicit externalisation of such (normally implicit) confidence intervals, and their use in acceptance or rejection of the proposed configuration adaptations at runtime. We believe our approach will generally be used to identify configurations that pose too much risk when deployed, thereby guiding the adaptation process of DSPLs. Developers in each particular case could have indicative threshold confidence values, suited to their applications, which will help remove unsuitable configurations and pinpoint the need for tailor-made tests for untested configurations.

Thus, in this paper, we define a framework for reusing and inferring test results for untested configurations of DSPLs. In particular, here we focus on inferring structural testing results based on call graph similarity of configurations.

2. THE IDEA: INFERRING TEST RESULTS FOR UNSEEN CONFIGURATIONS

To address the problem of testing DSPLs, we propose to test in detail a representative subset of configurations[1] before the DSPL is deployed. After that, once the DSPL has been deployed, these test results can be reused to approximate the test results for new untested configurations. This approximation is achieved by comparing configurations and reusing test information of elements that these configurations have in common. Figure 1 shows the approach schema.

In Phase I, test results of relevant configurations are stored into a database and will be used in Phase II. Note that we currently apply node and branch coverages to the system call graph, which provide us with a sound coverage measure of the DSPL instance under test.

Phase II (see Figure 1) is triggered when an *untested configuration*, say C_U, of the DSPL has to be instantiated. As the DSPL is adaptable at runtime, performing full structural testing of C_U becomes impracticable. We thus compare C_U to the tested relevant configurations in the database and determine the configuration (or a set of configurations) that is most similar to C_U. This *matched configuration* is named C_M. Test results from C_M are subsequently reused to determine the coverage of C_U.

At this point, our approach supports two alternatives for determining test results for C_U: (1) dynamic evaluation with tests or (2) inference of a confidence degree. The choice is guided by a trade-off between confidence and available resources. In option (1), the test cases associated with C_M can be reused to be applied to C_U. This option reduces the effort of having to design a test suite specifically for C_U and provides a more accurate degree of confidence since it relies on actual test coverage measurement.

However, it is likely that time becomes a bottleneck. In

[1]Important configurations can be determined, for instance, in collaboration with stakeholders.

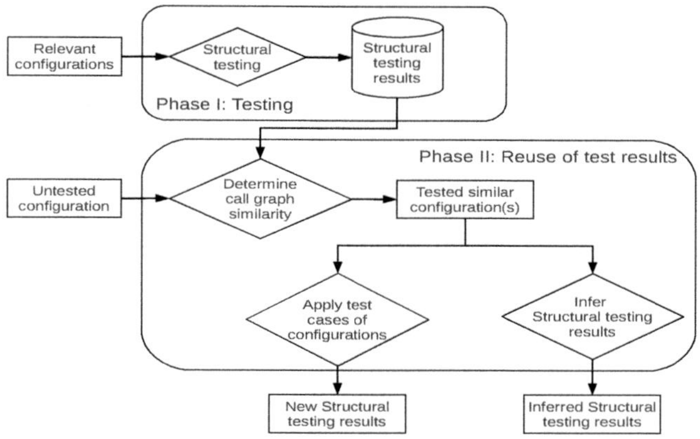

Figure 1: Overview of the approach

this case, option (2) provides an alternative for inferring a degree of confidence for C_U. We compare the call graphs of C_M and C_U to infer test results for C_U. For instance, when nodes and edges covered in C_M occur in C_U, we infer that these elements will also behave accordingly in C_U. After we compute all the structural and coverage similarities between C_M and C_U, we calculate the degree of confidence for C_U.

In the next section we elaborate on Phase II using a small example that implements varied sorting algorithms such as Merge Sort, Radix Sort and Quick Sort. In this application, the algorithms are the variants which can be instantiated at runtime, thus resulting in different system configurations.

3. INITIAL PROOF OF CONCEPT

Here we describe how we compare call graphs and infer a degree of confidence for untested configurations.

3.1 Comparing Call Graphs

This step involves identifying the configuration C_M that is most similar to C_U which has been selected for deployment. At this point a number of candidate configurations for C_M are present in the database and a distance measure is required to determine which of these is closest to C_U. Note that the overall DSPL call graph structure is expected to be mostly preserved after an adaptation, given that only some parts of the system are changed. The measure we propose can be used to compare DSPL configurations based on their call graphs. It is inspired by edit distance functions [4] used in (partial) graph matching. Our function, however, takes into account the specific semantics of nodes and edges in call graphs of DSPL configurations. More specifically, it compares nodes of call graphs with respect to the path of calls they are reached. We refer to these paths as *root traces*.

In Figure 2, we have highlighted, in each call graph depicted, the root trace of the node *SortAlgorithm.setParent*. When comparing these root traces for the four call graphs, we can see that they are equal in call graphs 1, 3 and 4. However, in call graph 2 the root trace is different. Using these root traces, we define the similarity S of call graph G_1 to call graph G_2 to be equal to the number of nodes in G_1 that have an identical root trace in G_2 divided by the total number of nodes in G_1:

$$S(G_1, G_2) = \frac{\sum_{x \in G_1} R(x, G_1, G_2)}{\#Nodes\, G_1} \qquad (1)$$

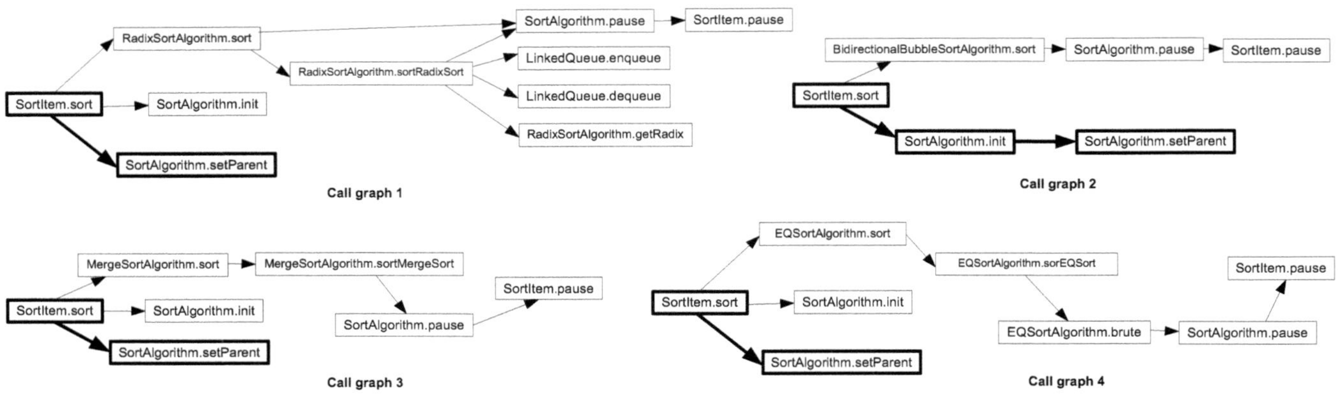

Figure 2: Call Graphs of Sorting Algorithms

where the function R returns 1 if an identical root trace of node x exists in G_1 and G_2, and 0 otherwise.

To illustrate this function we compare call graph 1 to call graph 2, both depicted in Figure 2. In the figure we can seen that the node *SortAlgorithm.init* has the same root trace in both call graphs. However, the nodes *SortAlgorithm.setParent*, *BidirectionalBubbleSortAlgorithm.sort*, *SortAlgorithm.pause* and *SortItem.pause* have different root traces in the call graphs. As a result, $S(CG_1, CG_2) = 2/6$. A full comparison of the call graphs in Figure 2 with respect to each other can be found in Table 1. Note that, to calculate the similarity measure, we ignore cycles when determining root traces to ensure all root traces are finite.

3.2 Reuse and Inference

After the configuration matching step, we calculate the *degree of confidence* of C_U. This is done based on C_M. In this case, we have two options: (1) reusing stored test cases of C_M; or (2) inferring a degree of confidence for C_U.

3.2.1 Reusing test cases in C_U

The reuse of stored test cases is the direct way to calculate the real coverage of C_U using test cases previously designed for similar configurations. These test cases are in the database associated with an specific configuration. After identifying C_M, the test cases recovered from the database may be used directly in C_U. Thus, it is possible to calculate the coverage with respect to each testing criterion earlier applied to C_M. For example, considering C_U and C_M as the call graphs 1 and 4 depicted in Figure 2, respectively.

Let $< 4, 1, 2, 3, 5 >$ be an array of integers used as input to cover 100% of nodes and branches of C_M. Reusing this test case in C_U, we have 90% of coverage of C_U.

3.2.2 Inferring a degree of confidence for C_U

This option consists in inferring a measure based on the similarity between tested and untested configurations given that only some parts of the system will change after adaptation. Using call graphs built from the source code of a DSPL instance, weights are assigned to nodes and edges based on the number of times they appear in all call graph root traces. These weights represent the importance of a component in a call graph based on its occurrence in possible execution flows. In other words, while deriving the test requirements, each requirement will receive a degree of importance according to its level of participation in the call graph of C_U.

The example shown in Figure 3 represents a call graph of a given C_U. Here nodes and edges were assigned weights based on their occurrence considering all root traces. For example, the node *RadixSortAlgorithm.sort* appears nine times considering all root traces, and the edge *RadixSortAlgorithm.sort* $\rightarrow$ *radixSortAlgorithm.sortRadixSort* has six occurrences considering all root traces.

Table 1: Call graph Similarity

	call graph 1	call graph 2	call graph 3	call graph 4
call graph 1	1	2/6	3/10	3/10
call graph 2	2/6	1	2/6	2/6
call graph 3	3/6	2/6	1	3/6
call graph 4	3/8	2/8	3/8	1

In the sequence, based on the weights calculated for C_U and on the control flow-based test requirements derived to both C_U and C_M, it is possible to say which requirements were tested in the C_M's context and what is the impact of these requirements in C_U. With this information we calculate a *degree of confidence* that gives an indication whether it is advisable or not to test C_U.

For example, again considering C_U and C_M as the call graphs 1 and 4 depicted in the Figure 2, respectively, the nodes *SortItem.sort*, *SortAlgorithm.init*, *SortAlgorithm.setParent*, *SortAlgorithm.pause* and *SortItem.pause*, and the edges *SortItem.sort* $\rightarrow$ *SortAlgorithm.init*, *SortItem.sort* $\rightarrow$ *SortAlgorithm.setParent* and *SortAlgorithm.pause* $\rightarrow$ *SortItem.pause* are common to C_U and C_M. Given the total weight of all common requirements and dividing by the total weight of all requirements, we have the confidence degree for C_U. Here, for C_U nodes we have a degree of confidence of $16/38 \approx 0.526$, and for C_U edges we have a confidence degree of $4/26 \approx 0.153$. It is worth noting that these numbers do not represent a real call graph coverage. Instead, they represent inferred coverages of untested DSPL call graphs based on the test results of the most similar configuration. The value of an acceptable confidence degree will depend on the nature of the system and must be set by the developer.

4. MOST RELATED WORK

Here we discuss two pieces of relevant work. In the first, Wang et al. [8] introduce an automatic test generation technique that relies on structural information of context-aware applications. It identifies points in which context-aware data is manipulated by the application. Such points are called context-aware program points (*capps*) and are usually related to methods defined in a middleware that supports

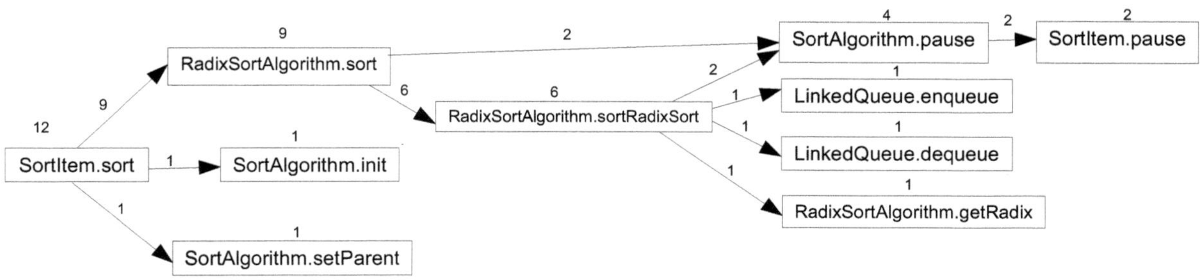

Figure 3: C_U with weights assigned to its components.

the development of context-aware applications. An interprocedural control flow graph is created and nodes that include capps are instrumented. Three coverage criteria are derived from such annotated graph, whose derived test requirements comprise the set of paths that should be covered by an adequate test set with respect to each criterion.

Unlike Wang et al.'s work, we do not address test generation technique based on the structural properties of the system. Instead, we use information regarding the system structure and the associated, pre-existing test coverage to infer the quality of new configurations suggested at runtime.

The second piece is our previous work on assessing similarity between SPL feature trees [1]. In this report we present a feature tree comparison measure which takes into account both the semantics of the textual content of feature notes, and elements of the tree structure (such as parents, and siblings of the nodes, the optionality of their inclusion into configurations, etc.). We deem this work very relevant to the present proposal, as it inspired the the idea of graph comparison and similarity measure construction presented in this paper. However, the underlying mathematical apparatus in both approaches differs drastically.

5. FUTURE WORK AND EXPECTED FEEDBACK

This paper presented a new approach to infer test results for DSPLs, based on explicitly setting a confidence interval thresholds, and obtaining confidence values for each untested configuration. The system could then choose to adapt to that configuration or decline it, if its confidence value is below the required threshold. It capitalises on the previously conducted tests and the similarity of an untested configuration to a previously tested one. We envision this work to be a first step towards testing approaches that can be used to tame the ever increasing complexity of software development and in particular can be used to aid effective testing of DSPLs. Receiving feedback on the overall idea and its proposed implementation is the prime aim of this paper, as is the desire to stimulate others to undertake research work to further DSPL testing area.

There are a number of further research issues to be addressed to extend and improve this work, for which we would also like peer feedback. For instance, as discussed previously, we use the notion of root traces to match untested configurations to a particular tested one. Due to this, our current similarity measure requires that for two configurations to be matched, the first nodes of their call graphs have to be the same. This may exclude some relevant similar configurations from comparison. To address this issue, we are currently working on refined similarity measures where the requirement of the same first entry node is relaxed, allowing for a weighted score for this to be used instead. This weighting in particular aims to take into account the impact of having a different root in a call graph from a structural testing point of view. We would like to discuss possible weighting structures as well as other solution ideas.

Another relevant issue is the time/computational resources required for conducting call graph comparison and matching. At its base, our approach builds on (partial) graph matching, which is known to be a very complex problem. It is our belief that this complexity could be manageable as the similarity measure can take advantage of identical nodes in various DSPL configurations. Receiving feedback on ways of handling such complexity is another area of interest to us.

Finally, our future research includes an industry-scale case study to assess the approach's performance, scalability and accuracy, as well as evaluating the impact of static properties of the system on the approach's accuracy. We are also looking for collaborators who may wish to share their implementations of dynamic adaptive systems and/or DSPLs.

Acknowledgements

This work is sponsored by the European Union as part of the DiVA project (ICT-215412).

References

[1] R. Chitchyan et al. Framework for composition of dynamic variability in requirements. Online. http://www.ict-diva.eu/DiVA/results/diva-deliverables.

[2] E. Engström et al. Software product line testing - a systematic mapping study. *Information and Software Technology*, 53:2–13, 2011.

[3] S. Hallsteinsen et al. Dynamic software product lines. *IEEE Computer*, 41:93–95, 2008.

[4] V. I. Levenshtein. Binary codes capable of correcting deletions, insertions, and reversals. *Soviet Physics Doklady*, 10(8):707–710, 1966.

[5] A. Maass and D. Beuche. Adaptation model and validation framework final version. Online. http://www.ict-diva.eu/DiVA/results/diva-deliverables.

[6] B. Morin et al. Models@ run.time to support dynamic adaptation. *IEEE Computer*, 42(10):44–51, 2009.

[7] G. Myers et al. *The Art of Software Testing*. John Wiley & Sons, 2nd edition, 2004.

[8] Z. Wang et al. Automated generation of context-aware tests. In *ICSE'07*, pages 406–415. IEEE, 2007.

New Ideas Track: Testing MapReduce-Style Programs

Christoph Csallner
csallner@uta.edu

Leonidas Fegaras
fegaras@uta.edu

Chengkai Li
cli@uta.edu

Computer Science and Engineering Department
University of Texas at Arlington
Arlington, TX 76019, USA

ABSTRACT

MapReduce has become a common programming model for processing very large amounts of data, which is needed in a spectrum of modern computing applications. Today several MapReduce implementations and execution systems exist and many MapReduce programs are being developed and deployed in practice. However, developing MapReduce programs is not always an easy task. The programming model makes programs prone to several MapReduce-specific bugs. That is, to produce deterministic results, a MapReduce program needs to satisfy certain high-level correctness conditions. A violating program may yield different output values on the same input data, based on low-level infrastructure events such as network latency, scheduling decisions, etc. Current MapReduce systems and tools are lacking in support for checking these conditions and reporting violations.

This paper presents a novel technique that systematically searches for such bugs in MapReduce applications and generates corresponding test cases. The technique works by encoding the high-level MapReduce correctness conditions as symbolic program constraints and checking them for the program under test. To the best of our knowledge, this is the first approach to addressing this problem of MapReduce-style programming.

Categories and Subject Descriptors

D.2.5 [**Software Engineering**]: Testing and Debugging—*Symbolic execution, testing tools*; D.2.4 [**Software Engineering**]: Software/Program Verification—*Assertion checkers, reliability*

General Terms

Algorithms, Reliability, Verification

Keywords

MapReduce, dynamic symbolic execution, test generation

Permission to make digital or hard copies of all or part of this work for personal or classroom use is granted without fee provided that copies are not made or distributed for profit or commercial advantage and that copies bear this notice and the full citation on the first page. To copy otherwise, to republish, to post on servers or to redistribute to lists, requires prior specific permission and/or a fee.
ESEC/FSE'11, September 5–9, 2011, Szeged, Hungary.
Copyright 2011 ACM 978-1-4503-0443-6/11/09 ...$10.00.

1. INTRODUCTION

MapReduce-style programming is a new paradigm in large-scale data processing that has attracted a lot of attention, both in industry and academia. In the six years since its publication, according to Google Scholar, the original MapReduce paper [3] has been cited over 2,000 times. In practice, several large organizations have implemented the MapReduce paradigm, e.g., in Apache/Yahoo! Hadoop [14] and Pig [8], Apache/Facebook Hive [13], Google Sawzall [9], and Microsoft Dryad [5].

MapReduce programs are especially well-suited for processing very large amounts of data (e.g., two petabyte worth of log files) on a large number of commodity machines (e.g., a 10,000 node Linux cluster). However, MapReduce systems are also increasingly being used for other tasks that were traditionally the domain of parallel database management systems, for example, data warehousing [13, 11].

There are many notable examples of MapReduce usages in a variety of application domains. Amazon Elastic Compute Cloud (EC2) provides cloud computing services on Hadoop. Yahoo! used Hadoop to sort a terabyte of data in just 209 seconds, which is the fastest with regard to the Jim Gray terabyte sorting benchmark. Facebook uses Hive as a data warehouse solution for internal reporting and ad-hoc data analysis [13].

Programming in MapReduce is complicated by two main factors. (1) To produce deterministic results, a MapReduce system requires user programs to satisfy certain high-level correctness conditions. That is, if a MapReduce program violates these correctness conditions, the output values emitted by that program may vary based on low-level infrastructure events such as network latency, scheduling decisions, etc. This means that running the same MapReduce program again on the same input data may yield different results. For many tasks, such non-determinism in their program behavior is clearly a bug programmers would like to avoid. However, (2), neither the MapReduce execution system nor current tools we are aware of check these conditions or warn the user when they may be violated.

This paper addresses this problem with a novel technique that systematically searches for such bugs in MapReduce programs and generates test cases that allow programmers to reproduce the bug. Our technique works by encoding the high-level MapReduce correctness conditions as symbolic program constraints and checking them for the particular user program under test. We implement the technique in a dynamic symbolic execution [4, 1] framework, which allows us to generate test cases that exhibit the bugs found by our technique. To the best of our knowledge, this is the first approach to addressing this problem of MapReduce-style programming.

This paper is phrased in the terms of the Java programming language, which is the language used in Hadoop, the most popular open-source implementation of MapReduce. However, the presented technique is independent of a particular language or system. That is, one can encode the program constraints and MapReduce correctness conditions for programs written in different languages that target different MapReduce implementations. So the same high-level technique can be applied to MapReduce programs running on one of the common MapReduce systems including Hadoop and the original Google MapReduce system. The technique can equally be adapted to other mainstream programming languages such as C++ and C#.

1.1 Novelty and Originality of our Approach

To the best of our knowledge, this is the first approach that uses dynamic symbolic execution to automatically generate test cases that can reveal certain types of bugs in general MapReduce programs. Instead of testing these programs on the entire data sets, which are often very large, our method allows programmers to discover hard-to-find bugs using very small synthetic data sets. Dynamic symbolic execution is precise and works well for relatively small programs, which makes it attractive for map/reduce programs. Although our paper is focused on enforcing the commutativity property of the reduce function, it has the potential of becoming a general framework for automated MapReduce testing. There is no other published paper on a related approach by the authors or others. We expect that feedback from the reviewers and the workshop participants will help us identify more cases for program testing in a MapReduce environment.

2. CORRECTNESS CONDITONS

A MapReduce system requires that a user program is expressed as three separate user-defined functions, which are named map, reduce, and combine.

Map: A MapReduce job may invoke a given map function on many nodes in parallel, each processing a portion of the input data. Each invocation produces a list of (key, value) pairs. The set of all (key, value) pairs produced by this job will be passed as input to a reduce function, which may also be running on multiple nodes.

Reduce: A reduce function receives as input a key and a list of values that are associated with that key. The value list is ordered according to the order in which the values are received on the reducer node, which can be influenced by network latency, etc. To produce deterministic results, the implementation of the user-defined reduce function must be independent of the input value order. We call this requirement REQ-1.

More formally, for each input list L, the reduce function has to return the same result for each permutation P of that list:

$$\forall L, P : reduce(k, L) = reduce(k, P(L)) \qquad \text{(REQ-1)}$$

Combine: A combine function is used in an optional optimization step that combines values by key on a map node. This is useful as reducing values locally, before transmitting them to the reducer, can save network bandwidth. MapReduce systems may freely decide if and how often to apply a combine function. Like REQ-1, to produce deterministic results, the number of times the system invokes a user-defined combine function must not influence the values produced by the downstream reduce functions (REQ-2). In this paper, for space reasons, we focus on checking REQ-1.

3. EXAMPLE: REDUCE BUG

Consider the example reduce method in Listing 1. The programmer intends to report the average of the top 100 salaries for each unique key, if that average is larger than 100,000. A key corresponds to, say, a department. However, the code does not satisfy the MapReduce requirement that reduce must be independent of the order in which it receives the input values (REQ-1). That is, to compute the average, instead of finding the highest 100 salaries in the list, the code just uses the first 100 values. So the value returned by the reduce function is determined by the salaries that happen to be at the head of the input list.

```
public void reduce(String key, Iterator<Integer> salaries) {
  int sum = 0; int i = 0;
  while (salaries.hasNext() && i<100) {
    sum += salaries.next();
    i += 1;
  }
  emit((i>0 && sum/i > 100000)? sum/i : −1);
}
```

Listing 1: The average of the top 100 salaries for each unique key, if that average is larger than 100,000.

This bug may be due to a number of reasons. One, the programmer may not be aware of correctness condition REQ-1. Second, the programmer may mistakenly assume that the input values are already ordered when they reach the reduce function. This misunderstanding may stem from the fact that MapReduce systems, such as Hadoop, have various built-in value sorting techniques, but do not always apply them. The misunderstanding may also stem from the programmer's knowledge of the order in which salaries are being stored in the original input files. Such order is to be destroyed by the parallel processing of MapReduce.

To find bugs such as the one in Listing 1, at a high level, we need to check if there exists an input list L and a permutation P, such that $reduce(k, L) \neq reduce(k, P(L))$. However, answering that question is hard, as the number of candidate lists and their permutations is not finite. E.g., for Listing 1, the bug is only exposed for a test case that supplies a certain kind of input list, one that has more than 100 elements and the average value of the first 100 elements is larger than 100,000. In addition, the test case needs to contain a certain kind of permutation of that list, one that replaces an element at position less than 100 with one at position greater than 100. Hence, trying a lot of randomly generated test cases can be wasteful. On the other hand, finding a desired test case is hard and requires deep analysis of the program and the MapReduce correctness conditions.

Although the question is hard in general, we observe that the number of distinct execution paths through a reduce method is typically small, since the main purpose of a reduce method is to aggregate the values it receives. We therefore do not expect much complex branching decisions based on the input list elements, as element filtering is typically done in the map method. Once data arrives at the reduce method, it is already filtered and merely needs to be combined. This means that a white-box code analysis system has a chance to explore a meaningful portion of the execution paths that are feasible in a reduce method. In the example of Listing 1, if we fix the input list length to, say, 128, the reduce method can be covered with just two distinct execution paths, which differ in whether sum/i is greater than 100,000. Dynamic symbolic execution is a technique that is well-suited to derive such a small set of execution paths precisely.

Using dynamic symbolic execution, we can derive the path condition of the execution paths from executing the reduce method and tracking the branches taken. For example, we get one path condition conjunction of: $salaries \neq null$, $salaries.length > 99$, $(salaries[0] + .. + salaries[99])/100 > 100000$. By tracking all values symbolically, we also get the symbolic expression of any values returned, in this case the value $((salaries[0] + .. + salaries[99])/100)$. At this point we can encode the first MapReduce correctness condition (REQ-1) directly on these symbolic values and use an automated constraint solver to check if they are satisfiable. In order to do that, we encode the permutation of the input list via symbolic integer variables, which encode the indices of the permuted list. That is, we create 128 variables $a_0, .., a_{127}$, require that they take on distinct values, and encode the correctness condition as the path condition conjoined with $(salaries[0] + .. + salaries[99])/100 \neq (salaries[a_0] + .. + salaries[a_{99}])/100$. If there is a solution, and this constraint system may have several, we can retrieve both the list elements and the permutation from it and compile them into a test case. The test case invokes the reduce function once on the solution list and once on the permuted solution list, compares the results, and issues a warning if the results are different.

4. PROPOSED APPROACH

Our technique works by exploring the MapReduce program under test with dynamic symbolic execution. It (1) derives symbolic expressions for path conditions and return values, (2) maintains them in a novel indexed execution tree (Section 4.1), (3) encodes with those symbolic expressions the MapReduce correctness conditions of Section 2, (4) uses an off-the-shelf constraint solver to infer program input values that will violate the correctness conditions, and finally (5) converts the violating input values to test cases. All the steps can be automated, yielding a fully automated test case generator for MapReduce programs.

Listing 2 contains the main loop of this process. It starts by creating default values for the input parameters of the reduce function in a MapReduce program, e.g., a key value of null and a list of two default values such as (0, 0). On the symbolic side, we create a corresponding key variable and a symbolic array variable that will represent the input list. Then we evaluate the reduce function, both concretely on the initial values and symbolically on the variables, where the symbolic execution merely traces the single path taken by the concrete execution. Using the results of the symbolic execution, we can now check, in the check_path method, if the correctness condition REQ-1 can be violated on the same execution path. That is, in check_req1 (Listing 3), we assert the path condition of the executed path symbolically, together with the condition that values returned by the reduce function are different for an input list and a permutation of that list.

```
/* The reduce method has two parameters: key and values */
test_reduce(meth<key_type, iterator<value_type>> reduce) {
  key := get_default_value(key_type);
  Key := get_fresh_var(key_type);
  value_cnt := 2; // length of input list
  values := get_default_array(value_type, value_cnt);
  Values := Get_fresh_array_var(value_type);
  (Path, Result) := Eval(reduce, key, values, Key, Values);
  check_path(Key, Values, value_cnt, Path, Result);
  while (unexplored_paths(value_cnt)) {
    PathCond := next_unexplored_path(value_cnt); // path p
    Assert: PathCond; // check if path p is feasible
    Assert: Length(Values) == Value_cnt;
    M := GetModel(); // constraint model/solution
    if (is_empty(M))
      continue; // no input that would trigger path p
    (key, values) := M(Key, Values); // new input from model
    (Path, Result) := Eval(reduce, key, values, Key, Values);
    check_path(Key, Values, value_cnt, Path, Result);
  }
  value_cnt := next_value();
}

check_path(Var Key, Var Values, int cnt, Cond Path, Expr Res)
  {
  add_to_execution_tree(cnt, Path, Res);
  check_req1(Key, Values, cnt, Path, Res, Path, Res);
  foreach (SibP, SibRes) in exec_tree_paths(cnt)
    check_req1(Key, Values, cnt, Path, Res, SibP, SibRes);
}
```

Listing 2: Main dynamic symbolic test case generator loop. Symbolic entities are capitalized. Eval evaluates the given program both concretely and symbolically; Assert adds a conjunct to the constraint system; GetModel solves the current constraint system, retrieves a solution, and resets the constraint system; *SibP* and *SibRes* are a sibling path and its respective return value; being a sibling means using an input list of the same length.

4.1 Indexed Execution Tree

A dynamic symbolic execution system maintains a tree of the execution paths that it already explored. This execution tree is a binary tree, in which each node represents the outcome of a branch condition, expressed in terms of the symbolic program input variables. For the example of Listing 1, one tree node is $salaries.length > 3$, which has the child node $salaries.length > 4$, etc. To discover additional execution paths, the system examines each single parent node, that is, each node that has exactly one child node. Inverting the branch decision outcome of such a single child node yields a candidate leaf node of an unexplored execution path, which is implemented in next_unexplored_path. The test_reduce algorithm uses this technique to automatically check as many execution paths as possible.

In our system, the execution tree is extended in two ways. (1) Each leaf node stores the values (typically, one value) returned during the given execution. (2) We index the leaf node by the length of the input list that triggered that execution. This is useful, as it allows us to check if a path triggered by an input list of length l may return a value that is different than the value returned on a *sibling path*. A sibling path is any other path that is triggered by an input list of the same length l.

```
check_req1(Expr Key, Var Values, int cnt, Cond PathCond,
           Expr Res, Cond SibPath, Expr SibRes) {
  p := PrepareIndexVariables(cnt);
  Assert: PathCond;
  Assert: SubstituteIndices(SibPath, p);
  Assert: Res != SubstituteIndices(SibRes, p);
  M := GetModel(); // constraint model/solution
  if (has_solution(M)) {
    log: "permutations that yield different results:"
      M(Key), M(Values[0]), .., M(Values[cnt−1]) "vs."
      M(Key), M(Values[M(p[0])]), .., M(Values[M(p[cnt−1])]);
  }
}

IntVar[] PrepareIndexVariables(int cnt) {
  p := new IntVar[cnt]; // position indices
  foreach i in [0,cnt−1] {
    p[i] := Get_fresh_var(int);
    Assert: 0 ≤ p[i] < cnt;
  }
  Assert: Distinct(p[0], .., p[cnt−1]);
  return p;
}
```

Listing 3: Checking REQ-1. Symbolic entities are capitalized. PrepareIndexVariables returns a list of symbolic integer variables p_0, .., p_{cnt-1}; SubstituteIndices replaces in the given expression each symbolic literal index i with symbolic variable p_i.

4.2 Input Length Heuristic

At a high level, the test_reduce algorithm tests if the reduce method satisfies REQ-1 for a number of paths the reduce execution can take. Each path is triggered by an input list of a certain length. Clearly, in testing, we cannot check a method for all possible inputs. In the test_reduce algorithm, we can address this problem by using a heuristic for picking representative input lengths. That is, test_reduce starts with input list of length 2, as shorter lists cannot expose a violation of REQ-1. For subsequent iterations, the heuristic is implemented by the next_value function. We currently experiment with a binary back-off scheme, in which each iteration doubles the length of the input list. Using this heuristic we can discover the bug in the motivating example within the first ten iterations.

5. IMPLEMENTATION

We have implemented the test_reduce algorithm of Section 4 as a wrapper around our Dsc dynamic symbolic execution framework [6]. As Dsc analyzes Java programs, our implementation is currently targeted at programs written for the popular Java open source MapReduce system Hadoop.

The MapReduce programmer invokes test_reduce, maybe as part of a continuous automated testing process. Our implementation works by instrumenting the original user MapReduce program at the bytecode level at load-time [2]. This allows our implementation to run on any standard Java virtual machine.

6. RELATED WORK

In [7], an algorithm is proposed to generate small and yet real example data for examining the behavior of dataflow programs. Their technique is based on nonuniform data sampling combined with data synthesis. Their goal is not to directly capture program bugs but to use small example data to make programs exhibit behavior similar to those exposed by the real data. Specifically, the programmer must define the semantics of query operators that are to be comprehensively covered by the small example data. Mochi [12] visualizes execution logs to debug Hadoop programs. The focus of this tool is on execution performance anomalies instead of correctness of programs. Sen and Agha use dynamic symbolic execution for testing of distributed programs [10].

Acknowledgments

This material is based upon work supported by the National Science Foundation under Grant No. 1017305.

7. REFERENCES

[1] C. Cadar and D. R. Engler. Execution generated test cases: How to make systems code crash itself. In *Proc. 12th International SPIN Workshop on Model Checking of Software*, pages 2–23. Springer, Aug. 2005.

[2] G. A. Cohen, J. S. Chase, and D. L. Kaminsky. Automatic program transformation with Joie. In *Proc. USENIX Annual Technical Symposium*, pages 167–178. USENIX, June 1998.

[3] J. Dean and S. Ghemawat. MapReduce: Simplified data processing on large clusters. In *Proc. 6th USENIX Symposium on Operating Systems Design and Implementation (OSDI)*, pages 137–150. USENIX, Dec. 2004.

[4] P. Godefroid, N. Klarlund, and K. Sen. Dart: Directed automated random testing. In *Proc. ACM SIGPLAN Conference on Programming Language Design and Implementation (PLDI)*, pages 213–223. ACM, June 2005.

[5] M. Isard, M. Budiu, Y. Yu, A. Birrell, and D. Fetterly. Dryad: Distributed data-parallel programs from sequential building blocks. In *Proc. 2nd ACM SIGOPS European Conference on Computer Systems (EuroSys)*, pages 59–72. ACM, Mar. 2007.

[6] M. Islam and C. Csallner. Dsc+Mock: A test case + mock class generator in support of coding against interfaces. In *Proc. 8th International Workshop on Dynamic Analysis (WODA)*, pages 26–31. ACM, July 2010.

[7] C. Olston, S. Chopra, and U. Srivastava. Generating example data for dataflow programs. In *Proc. 35th ACM SIGMOD International Conference on Management of Data (SIGMOD)*, pages 245–256. ACM, June 2009.

[8] C. Olston, B. Reed, U. Srivastava, R. Kumar, and A. Tomkins. Pig latin: A not-so-foreign language for data processing. In *Proc. 34th ACM SIGMOD International Conference on Management of Data (SIGMOD)*, pages 1099–1110. ACM, June 2008.

[9] R. Pike, S. Dorward, R. Griesemer, and S. Quinlan. Interpreting the data: Parallel analysis with Sawzall. *Scientific Programming*, 13(4):277–298, Oct. 2005.

[10] K. Sen and G. Agha. Automated systematic testing of open distributed programs. In *Proc. 9th International Conference on Fundamental Approaches to Software Engineering (FASE)*, pages 339–356. Springer, Mar. 2006.

[11] M. Stonebraker, D. Abadi, D. J. DeWitt, S. Madden, E. Paulson, A. Pavlo, and A. Rasin. MapReduce and parallel DBMSs: Friends or foes? *Communications of the ACM*, 53(1):64–71, Jan. 2010.

[12] J. Tan, X. Pan, S. Kavulya, R. Gandhi, and P. Narasimhan. Mochi: Visual log-analysis based tools for debugging Hadoop. In *Proc. Workshop on Hot Topics in Cloud Computing (HotCloud)*. USENIX, June 2009.

[13] A. Thusoo, J. S. Sarma, N. Jain, Z. Shao, P. Chakka, S. Anthony, H. Liu, P. Wyckoff, and R. Murthy. Hive: A warehousing solution over a map-reduce framework. *Proc. VLDB Endowment*, 2(2):1626–1629, Aug. 2009.

[14] T. White. *Hadoop: The definitive guide.* O'Reilly, May 2009.

Join Point Interfaces for Modular Reasoning in Aspect-Oriented Programs

Milton Inostroza Éric Tanter
PLEIAD Laboratory
Computer Science Department (DCC)
University of Chile – Santiago, Chile
{minostro,etanter}@dcc.uchile.cl

Eric Bodden
Software Technology Group
Center for Advanced Security Research Darmstadt (CASED)
Technische Universität Darmstadt - Germany
bodden@acm.org

ABSTRACT

While aspect-oriented programming supports the modular definition of crosscutting concerns, most approaches to aspect-oriented programming fail to improve, or even preserve, modular *reasoning*. The main problem is that aspects usually carry, through their pointcuts, explicit references to the base code. These dependencies make programs fragile. Changes in the base code can unwittingly break a pointcut definition, rendering the aspect ineffective or causing spurious matches. Conversely, a change in a pointcut definition may cause parts of the base code to be advised without notice. Therefore separate development of aspect-oriented programs is largely compromised, which in turns seriously hinders the adoption of aspect-oriented programming by practitioners.

We propose to separate base code and aspects using Join Point Interfaces, which are contracts between aspects and base code. Base code can define pointcuts that expose selected join points through a Join Point Interface. Conversely, an aspect can offer to advise join points that provide a given Join Point Interface. Crucially, however, aspect themselves cannot contain pointcuts, and hence cannot refer to base code elements. In addition, because a given join point can provide several Join Point Interfaces, and Join Point Interfaces can be organized in a subtype hierarchy, our approach supports join point polymorphism. We describe a novel advice dispatch mechanism that offers a flexible and type-safe approach to aspect reuse.

Categories and Subject Descriptors

D.3.3 [**Programming Languages**]: Language Constructs

General Terms

Design, Languages

Keywords

Aspect-oriented programming, modularity

Permission to make digital or hard copies of all or part of this work for personal or classroom use is granted without fee provided that copies are not made or distributed for profit or commercial advantage and that copies bear this notice and the full citation on the first page. To copy otherwise, to republish, to post on servers or to redistribute to lists, requires prior specific permission and/or a fee.
ESEC/FSE'11, September 5–9, 2011, Szeged, Hungary.
Copyright 2011 ACM 978-1-4503-0443-6/11/09 ...$10.00.

1. JOIN POINT INTERFACES

Inevitably, aspect-oriented programming [?] aids modularizing crosscutting code: it helps programmers to put together code that belongs together. So far, however, most approaches to aspect-oriented programming have failed to improve, or even preserve, modular reasoning. Such modular reasoning is easily established in traditional procedural languages. In such languages, programmers can reason about one procedure at a time and in isolation. The procedure's signature establishes a strong contract with the contexts in which the procedure may be used. Object-oriented programming already gives up modular reasoning to some extent. Object-oriented programs carry virtual method calls. For such calls, at least in statically typed languages, the signature of the call is known at the call site, and hence the usage contract for the called method is known as well. It is unknown, however, which concrete implementation the virtual method call will eventually be dispatched to in the running program.

1.1 Aspects and modular reasoning

With aspect-oriented programming, modular reasoning becomes even harder, as aspect-oriented programs adds a crucial feature: implicit invocation with implicit announcement (IIIA) [5]. Through IIIA, an aspect can become active at many different program points (called join points) without any explicit call to the aspect being present at these points. This is problematic because maintainers of the base code may be unaware of the program point being advised, and hence may refactor this point or change the point otherwise, unwittingly breaking the connection to the advising aspect. There has been several attempts to discuss and enhance the possibilities for modular reasoning in presence of pointcuts and advice, but they all eventually fall short in supporting full separate development with static and modular typechecking.

Running Example

As a running example, we will consider an e-commerce system with a set of discount rules. (Deliberately, we keep the example similar to a motivating example by Steimann et al. [5].) In the initial system, a customer can check out a product by either buying or renting the product. On the customer's birthday, the customer will be given a 5% discount when checking out a product. We will be adding further rules later.

```
1  class ShoppingSession {
2    ShoppingCart sc = new ShoppingCart();
3    Invoice inv = new Invoice();
4
5    void checkOut(Item item, float price,
6        int amount, Customer cus){
7      sc.add(item, amount);
8      inv.add(item, amount, cus);
9    }
10 }
11
12 aspect Discount {
13   pointcut checkingOut(Item item, float price,
14       int amount, Customer cus):
15     execution(* Session.checkOut(..))
16     && args(item, price, amount, cus);
17
18   void around(Item item, float price, int amt,
         Customer cus):
19     checkingOut(item, amt, cus) {
20     int factor = cus.hasBirthday()? 0.95 : 1;
21     proceed(item, price*factor, amt, cus);
22   }
23 }
```

Listing 1: Shopping session with discount aspect

Listing 1 shows an implementation of the example in plain AspectJ [?]. The around advice in lines 18–22 applies the discount by reducing the item price to 95% of the original price when proceeding on the customer birthday. Note how brittle the AspectJ implementation is with respect to changes in the base code. Most changes to the signature of the `checkOut` method, such as renaming the method or modifying its parameter declarations, will cause the `BirthdayDiscount` aspect to lose its effect. The root cause of this problem is that the aspect, through its pointcut definition in lines 13–16, makes explicit references to named entities of the base code—here to the `checkOut` method.

1.2 Join Point Interfaces

In this paper, we propose to establish an additional layer of abstraction between base code and aspects, through a novel mechanism called Join Point Interfaces. Our goal is to allow for complete modular reasoning on both the side of the aspect programmer and the side of the base-code programmer. In particular, our system will allow programmers to catch all possible typing errors at the time the individual code fragments (aspect, base code) are compiled. There have been other approaches to decoupling aspects from base code but those approaches are not able to capture many typing errors in a modular manner at compile time. Rather, they only detect errors at weave-time, *i.e.* at the time the aspect is actually composed with the base-code system. This is because the layers that they introduce are "transparent"; they separate aspects from the base code only to some extent. Crosscutting interfaces (XPIs) [3] are based on pure AspectJ, which provides no language-based mechanisms for the separation that we envision. Steimann et al.'s work on join point types for IIIA [5] does introduce specialized syntax but this syntax is not rich enough to be able to allow for modular reasoning and separate compilation. In Section 3 we will elaborate further on these approaches.

Listing 2 shows how Join Point Interfaces improve on the shopping cart example. Line 2 declares the join point interface (`jpi`) `checkingOut`. Syntactically, a Join Point Interface declaration is identical to a method signature: it has

```
1  jpi void checkingOut(Item item, float price,
2                       int amount, Customer cus);
3
4  class ShoppingSession {
5    exhibit void checkingOut(Item i, float price,
6      int amount, Customer c):
7      execution(* checkOut(..))
8      && args(i, price, amount, c);
9
10     ...
11 }
12
13 aspect Discount {
14   void around checkingOut(Item item, float price,
15       int amt, Customer cus){
16     int factor = cus.hasBirthday()? 0.95 : 1;
17     proceed(item, price*factor, amt, cus);
18   }
19 }
```

Listing 2: Introducing a Join Point Interface

a return type (here `void`), a name, a formal-parameter list and an optional `throws`-clause. (This choice is for a good reason. In a recent piece of work, Bodden showed that one can avoid many semantic pitfalls by regarding join points as typed closures [2].)

The base-code class `ShoppingSession` is enhanced to declare that it exhibits join points of type `checkingOut`. The `exhibit`-clause binds the Join Point Interface to concrete join points, using a regular AspectJ pointcut.

Crucially, however, through the usage of Join Point Interfaces, the aspect is completely liberated of pointcut definitions. Note that in line 14 the aspect refers directly to the Join Point Interface, obviating the need to explicitly refer to base code elements. As the example shows, Join Point Interfaces allows for the modularization of crosscutting concerns while at the same time restoring modular reasoning. The base-code programmer can maintain pointcut definitions in sync with the base code that these pointcut definitions refer to. The programmer is also immediately aware of the join points exposed to aspects. On the other hand, the aspect becomes free of any textual references to base-code elements, making the aspect reusable in other contexts.

1.3 Static and modular type checking

Join Point Interfaces support modular reasoning through a fully static and modular type system. For instance, the type system ensures that the header of the around advice at line 14 is compatible with the definition of the `checkingOut` Join Point Interface. As described in earlier work [2], this needs to involve invariant parameter and return types. Further, if an advice a advises a Join Point Interface j which declares to throw checked exceptions of type e then a must either catch exceptions of this type or declare to propagate them. Similarly, all join point shadows (i.e., code locations) matched by any pointcut tagged with j must handle or propagate these exceptions. These typing rules guarantee that the implicit invocation of a piece of advice at a given join point always comply with the Join Point Interface.

We envision Join Point Interfaces to be used such that the Join Point Interface definition in line 2 would be available to both the base-code programmer and the aspect programmer. This allows for separate compilation of aspects and base code. In this case, our type system gives the strong guarantee that there can be no weave-time errors: all typ-

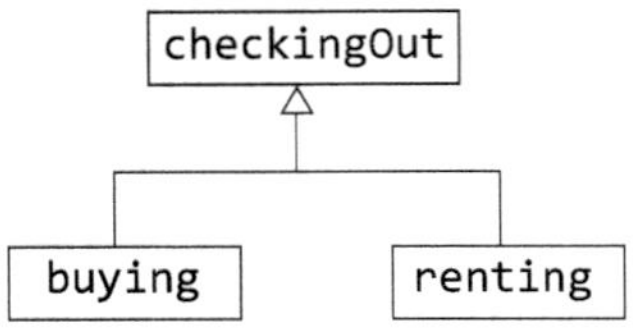

Figure 1: Inheritance between Join Point Interfaces

ing errors will be caught at the time the aspect or base code are (potentially independently!) defined, and no further errors can occur when aspects and base code are composed. To the best of our knowledge, our system is the first to provide such guarantees. For instance, while Steimann et al.'s types for IIIA [5] also offers the benefits described in Section 1.2, their approach is unable to provide modular reasoning and separate compilation because their join point types are only partial join point specifications. In their approach some conditions, such as return type compatibility, must be checked at weave time, which is undesirable in a collaborative working environment and also hinders aspect reuse.

1.4 Polymorphic join points

Join Point Interfaces give *types* to join points. In the same way that object interfaces in languages like Java support a flexible form of subtype polymorphism, Join Point Interfaces enable polymorphic join points. A join point can be seen as providing multiple Join Point Interfaces, and advice dispatch at that join point can take advantage of this polymorphism.

Which Join Point Interfaces does a join point provide? This is the role of pointcuts. As we have seen, a class defines the pointcuts that expose certain join points in its execution, following a given Join Point Interface. For instance, in Listing 2, class `ShoppingSession` defines a pointcut that gives the type `checkingOut` to all join points that are executions of the `checkOut` method. Because a join point can be matched by several pointcuts, a join point can have multiple types. For instance, an execution of `checkOut` can be seen as a `checkingOut`, and could be seen additionally as a `loggableEvent` (a Join Point Interface whose definition is left to the imagination of the reader). In addition, as in Java, Join Point Interfaces support subtyping. We illustrate join point subtyping using two subtypes of `checkingOut`, `buying` and `renting` (Figure 1). The rest of this section illustrates their use in our running example.

Consider that we introduce the following business rule: the customer gets a 15% discount when *buying* at least 10 products of the same kind; this promotion is not compatible with the birthday discount.

Listing 3 shows how a programmer could implement this additional rule using the subtyping relationship on Join Point Interfaces. First, we declare the Join Point Interface `buying` as a subtype of `checkingOut`. The semantics of this subtyping relationship implies that `buying` represents a subset of the join points that `checkingOut` represents.

The aspect `Discount` now declares two pieces of advice. The first one is the same as in the previous example. It applies to all `checkingOut` join points, in particular also to those `checkingOut` join points that are not `buying` join points. points that *are* of type `buying` and hence *also* of type `checkingOut`? To the best of our knowledge, our approach is the first to provide a clear and natural mechanism to resolve this situation. According to the semantics of Join

```
jpi void buying(Item item, float price,
                int amount, Customer cus)
  extends checkingOut;

aspect Discount {
  void around checkingOut(Item item, float price,
      int amt, Customer cus) {
    int factor = cus.hasBirthday()? 0.95 : 1;
    proceed(item, price*factor, amt, cus);
  }
  void around buying(Item item, float price,
                     int amt, Customer cus) {
    int factor = (amt > 10) ? 0.85 : 1;
    proceed(item, price*factor, amt, cus);
  }
}
```

Listing 3: Advice overriding

Point Interfaces, the advice with the *most-specific* signature executes. Hence, in this example, a join point of type `buying` is advised *only* by the `buying` advice, since it is the most specific[1].

This semantics of advice dispatch with Join Point Interfaces is natural because it directly follows how overloading is resolved in languages with multiple dispatch, like the Common Lisp Object System (CLOS) [4]: the runtime type of the argument (here, the type of the join point) determines which method is executed (here, which piece of advice). The analogy makes sense because with implicit invocation, there is by definition no explicit receiver, just like with generic functions in CLOS. It is the runtime type of the arguments that drives the dispatch process.

Reusing behavior. In a previous version of our language design, we pushed the analogy between advice dispatch and multiple dispatch a step further, by having applicable pieces of advice ordered in terms of specificity (like applicable methods in CLOS), and providing a `nextadvice` primitive (the equivalent of `call-next-method` in CLOS) to call the next most-specific advice in the ordering). While this allows for direct reuse of advices, the interaction of `nextadvice` and `proceed` induces too much complexity. Therefore, we give up on `nextadvice`; reuse among advices has to be mediated through aspect methods, as illustrated below.

Consider another extension of our running example, with a rule stating that when renting at least 10 items of the same kind there will be a 10% discount; but in this case the birthday discount *does* apply. Listing 4 shows the code for this extended example. First, we declare the new join point subtype `renting`. Then, because we want to reuse the birthday discount logic, we extract a separate method `birthdayFactor` in the aspect. The advice for `checkingOut` join points is modified accordingly, to use this method. Now, the advice for `renting` can also reuse the birthday discount logic by invoking the `birthdayFactor` method, in order to compute the final discount rate.

2. NOVELTY

To the best of our knowledge, our approach is the first to provide true modular reasoning in the presence of pointcuts

[1]As usual with `proceed`, if there are other pieces of advice advising `buying` then those execute before the original join point, with precedence defined as in AspectJ.

```
jpi void renting(Item item, float price,
                 int amount, Customer cus)
    extends checkingOut;

aspect Discount {
  int birthdayFactor(Customer cus){
    return cus.hasBirthday()? 0.95 : 1;
  }
  void around checkingOut(...) {
    proceed(item, price*birthdayFactor(cus), amt,
        cus);
  }
  void around buying(...) { /*as before*/ }
  void around renting(Item item, float price,
                      int amt, Customer cus) {
    if(amt>10)
      int factor = (amt > 10) ? 0.9 : 1;
    proceed(item, price*factor*birthdayFactor(cus)
        , amt, cus);
  }
}
```

Listing 4: Advice overriding—reusing behavior

and advice: Join Point Interfaces are the first mechanism to provide separate compilation for aspects with the guaranteed absence of weave-time errors. Further, our approach is the first to properly support join point polymorphism, enable flexible advice reuse.

3. RELATED WORK

There are have been several approaches to tackle the issue of modular reasoning in the presence of advice, including Open Modules [1], XPIs [3] and join point types for Implicit Invocation with Implicit Announcement (IIIA) [5]. The proposal of Steimann et al. is the most recent and as such includes a detailed discussion of all previous approaches to aspects and modular reasoning [5].

Similar to our proposal, Steimann et al. propose to introduce typing annotations for join points, called join point types, to facilitate modular reasoning. They also provide a subtyping hierarchy on join points, to facilitate extensibility and reuse. Our proposal builds upon IIIA, but with significant and crucial differences. IIIA falls short on several levels, most importantly, static and modular type checking, and join point polymorphism.

IIIA defines join point types using a struct-like syntax instead of a method-signature-like syntax as we do. Method signatures have the advantage that they can capture crucial elements like return types and declared exceptions, that the join point types of IIIA cannot capture. Join Point Interfaces allow us to support strong static guarantees and separate compilation. Both are impossible using IIIA, which relies on weave-time error reporting.

The IIIA approach falls short when it comes to resolving advice dispatch in presence of join point subtyping. To briefly illustrate why, consider again the join point hierarchy shown in Figure 1. Let us assume that we wish to dispatch pieces of advice for a join point that is *both* of type `buying` and of typing `renting`, and assume that there exists a unique piece of advice defined, for `checkingOut`. In Steimann et al.'s proposal to IIIA, the implementation will generate *two separate* join point instances, one of type `buying` and one of type `renting`. Because both of those instances are subtypes of `checkingOut`, they both dispatch to the `checkingOut` advice: the `checkingOut` advice executes twice!

Concretely, this means that IIIA does not support join point polymorphism; rather, it emits several join points for the same execution point. This semantics appears more than surprising and hardly useful under any circumstances. Our approach, on the other hand, supports true join point polymorphism. A single join point can have multiple types, and the well-known semantics used in multiple dispatch languages is used. In addition, this brings us the possibility of introducing `nextadvice`, to reuse and specialize pieces of advice.

4. EXPECTED FEEDBACK

First of all, at the most general level, we are interested in getting feedback on the importance of separate compilation and static modular type checking for the adoption of aspects. As language designers, we feel this is a great step forward, that even the latest development in aspects and modularity do not address properly [5]. We are really interested in discussing this with the software engineering community at large to see if this impression is shared.

At a more specific level, we are looking forward to feedback on the language design for Join Point Interfaces. Polymorphic join points and dynamic advice dispatch seem to enable a wider range of aspect designs for reuse than the existing proposals. Finally, as mentioned in Section 1.4, we gave up on the possibility to have `nextadvice` in order to trigger less-specific advice, as in multiple dispatch. The reason is that the kind of reuse offered by `nextadvice` does not seem to compose well with `proceed`, especially considering the fact that in most aspect languages, it is possible to invoke `proceed` multiple times. Discussion on these topics would be of particular interest for the further development of Join Point Interfaces.

5. REFERENCES

[1] Jonathan Aldrich. Open modules: Modular reasoning about advice. In Andrew P. Black, editor, *Proceedings of the 19th European Conference on Object-Oriented Programming (ECOOP 2005)*, number 3586 in LNCS, pages 144–168, Glasgow, UK, July 2005.

[2] Eric Bodden. Closure joinpoints: block joinpoints without surprises. In *Proceedings of the tenth international conference on Aspect-oriented software development*, AOSD '11, pages 117–128, New York, NY, USA, 2011. ACM.

[3] William G. Griswold, Kevin Sullivan, Yuanyuan Song, Macneil Shonle, Nishit Tewari, Yuanfang Cai, and Hridesh Rajan. Modular software design with crosscutting interfaces. *IEEE Softw.*, 23:51–60, January 2006.

[4] Andreas Paepcke, editor. *Object-Oriented Programming: The CLOS Perspective*. MIT Press, 1993.

[5] Friedrich Steimann, Thomas Pawlitzki, Sven Apel, and Christian Kästner. Types and modularity for implicit invocation with implicit announcement. *TOSEM*, 20(1):1–43, 2010.

Probabilistic Dataflow Analysis using Path Profiles on Structure Graphs

Arun Ramamurthi
Microsoft India R & D Pvt. Ltd.
Hyderabad, India
aramamu@microsoft.com

Subhajit Roy
Indian Institute of Technology,
Kanpur, India
subhajit@iitk.ac.in

Y. N. Srikant
Indian Institute of Science,
Bangalore, India
srikant@csa.iisc.ernet.in

ABSTRACT

Speculative optimizations are increasingly becoming popular for improving program performance by allowing transformations that benefit frequently traversed program paths. Such optimizations are based on dataflow facts which are mostly true, though not always safe. Probabilistic dataflow analysis frameworks infer such facts about a program, while also providing the probability with which a fact is likely to be true. We propose a new Probabilistic Dataflow Analysis Framework which uses path profiles and information about the nesting structure of loops to obtain improved probabilities of dataflow facts.

Category and Subject Descriptors D.3.4 [*Processors*]: Compilers, optimization

General Terms Algorithms

1. INTRODUCTION

Control-flow profiling gives us information about which nodes, edges or program paths are executed frequently during program execution. Previous attempts at using profiling information for probabilistic dataflow analysis have used edge or k-edge profiling techniques [5][10]. We have used *path profiles* [4][7] which provides more details than edge profiles because of factors like branch correlation.

We have merged the ideas of context tupling [3], use of path profiles [1][7] and structure graphs [4] to develop a new probabilistic data flow analysis framework. A probabilistic dataflow solution is similar to a normal dataflow analysis solution except that it is annotated by dataflow facts with probabilities. Such solutions can be used for improving performance by techniques like speculative data prefetching where our probability values can be used to prune out less-likely dataflow facts below a threshold value.

Related papers: Ramalingam[2], Ammons et al.[1], Mehofer et al.[9], Silva et al.[5] are publications similar to our work. We have compared our work with these and other relevant work in the Related Work section.

Permission to make digital or hard copies of all or part of this work for personal or classroom use is granted without fee provided that copies are not made or distributed for profit or commercial advantage and that copies bear this notice and the full citation on the first page. To copy otherwise, to republish, to post on servers or to redistribute to lists, requires prior specific permission and/or a fee.

ESEC/FSE'11, September 5–9, 2011, Szeged, Hungary.

Copyright 2011 ACM 978-1-4503-0443-6/11/09 ...$10.00.

2. BACKGROUND

2.1 Structure Graphs

The key idea of Structural Path Profiling [4] is to profile each loop independently. So, the program can be seen as a hierarchy of such nested structure graphs. Hierarchical Path Profiling [13] also proposes similar ideas.

We define a *summary node* as the representative header node of a nested loop. An *exit node* is the target of a loop-exit edge. All other nodes are called *regular nodes.*

Example: Figure 2(b) shows two summary nodes - c, g which get expanded in the inner structure graphs, Figure 2(c), 2(d) respectively. The inner structure graphs include regular nodes, each representing a basic block of the inner loop. A structure graph also contains various exit nodes of the loop such as g, j in Figure 2(c). For the outline structure graph in Figure 2(a), the end node (j) is the exit node.

A *loop-path* is a path which begins at the loop header and terminates at the source of the back edge. A *loop-exit path* is a path which begins at a loop header and terminates outside the loop.

2.2 Path Profiles

Ammons et al.[1] used acyclic path profiles [7] to improve dataflow solutions by separating facts propagating along frequent paths from the others. Their algorithm constructs a Labeled Transition System(LTS) (as briefed below) to track the propagation of dataflow facts along the hot paths:-

- q_i , a node in the LTS corresponds to a state
- $(q_1 \rightarrow^{k_1} q_2 \rightarrow^{k_2} q_3 \rightarrow \ldots \rightarrow^{k_{i-1}} q_i)$ is a path in the LTS if there exists a hot path $k_1 \rightarrow k_2 \rightarrow \ldots \rightarrow k_{i-1}$ in the CFG.
- The CFG nodes transform into edge labels on the LTS.

For our running example, the LTSs for the structure graphs in Figure 2 are shown in Figure 3. **Example:** In Figure 2(c) the path $c \rightarrow d \rightarrow f \rightarrow g$ transforms to the path $1 \rightarrow^c 2 \rightarrow^d 3 \rightarrow^f 4 \rightarrow^g 5$ in Figure 3(c).

3. APPLYING PATH PROFILE INFORMATION ON STRUCTURE GRAPHS

3.1 Probability definitions for structure graphs

Our probabilistic dataflow analysis (like any other) computes the probability of a dataflow fact at every program point. We use an *Structural path profiler*[4] to get statistics regarding frequencies of acyclic paths in a function. We then use these frequencies to estimate the probabilities of facts in

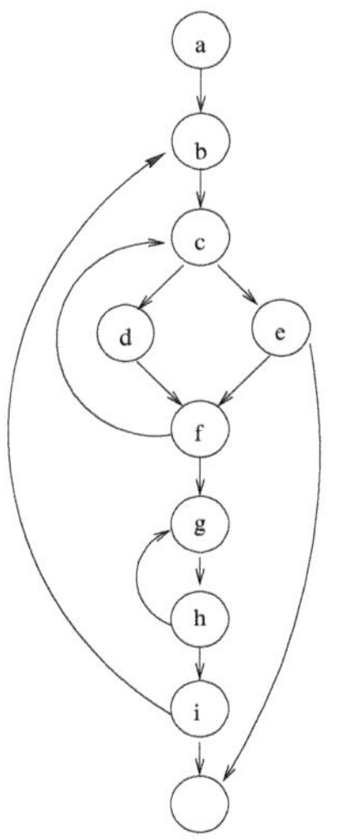

Figure 1: Our running example: CFG with 3 loops.

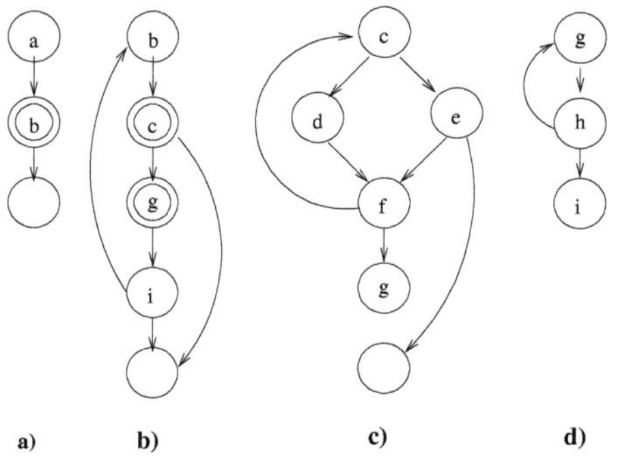

Figure 2: The four structure graphs for the CFG in Figure 1.

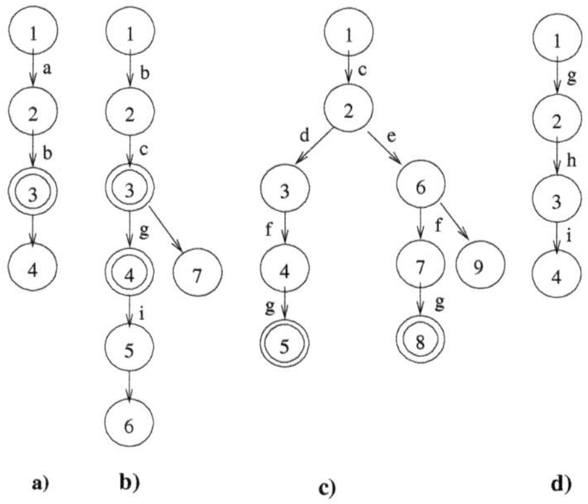

Figure 3: The labeled transition diagrams for structure graphs in Figure 2.

accordance with the profiler by focusing on each natural loop (its structure graph) separately.

For a CFG, let there be a node n with loop nest level of k and the header nodes be $n_1, n_2, .., n_k$ for each of the corresponding structure graphs $L_1, L_2, .., L_k$ respectively. Node n_j will also be a summary node in the structure graph L_{j-1}.

- For any path p_i starting from header node n_j and ending at node n_{j+1} in structure graph L_j, $Prob(p_i)$ w.r.t L_j = (frequency of path p_i) / (sum of frequencies of all paths reaching n_{j+1}) where n_{j+1} is the summary node for the next nested structure graph. Frequency of path p_i is the number of times path p_i is traversed during program execution as seen by the profiler.
- The probability of reaching node n_{j+1} from the header node n_j of structure graph L_j is the sum of probabilities of reaching n_{j+1} via all possible paths from n_j to n_{j+1} in L_j.
- The probability of reaching node n from the start node of the CFG is the product of probabilities of reaching node n_{j+1} from the header node n_j in L_j for all structure graphs, 1 to k. For the last (k^{th}) structure graph, n_{j+1} will be node n. The probabilities across different loops are multiplied since all the acyclic paths are in different loops; we assume them to be independent for simplicity.

Example: The probability of reaching h (Figure 1) in the CFG is equal to the product of probability of reaching b (from a) in Figure 2(a), probability of reaching g (from b) in Figure 2(b) and probability of reaching h (from g) in Figure 2(d).

3.2 Labeled Transition Systems (LTS)

Our LTS is a deterministic finite automaton that recognizes hot paths. Our analysis creates a separate LTS for each structure graph of the CFG. The assignment of probabilities on the different LTSs is done by handling loop-paths and loop-exit paths separately. We argue that merging the loop path and loop exit path information (as in the case of profiling the entire CFG together) leads to assigning a small probability to a loop-exit node which is incorrect as that node would be accessed with a high probability irrespective of the number of loop iterations.

For Figure 3(c), let us assume the frequencies of loop-paths $1 \rightarrow 2 \rightarrow 3 \rightarrow 4$, $1 \rightarrow 2 \rightarrow 6 \rightarrow 7$ are f_1 and f_2 respectively. Similarly the frequencies of loop-exit paths $1 \rightarrow 2 \rightarrow 3 \rightarrow 4 \rightarrow 5$, $1 \rightarrow 2 \rightarrow 6 \rightarrow 7 \rightarrow 8$ and $1 \rightarrow 2 \rightarrow 6 \rightarrow 9$ are f_3, f_4 and f_5 respectively.

The probability of a loop path relative to the loop-structure graph is the frequency of that path divided by the sum of frequencies of all loop paths for that loop in the LTS. In Figure 3(c), the probability of the reaching node f along path $1 \rightarrow 2 \rightarrow 3 \rightarrow 4$ is $\frac{f_1}{f_1+f_2}$. Similarly, the probability of a loop-exit path is calculated w.r.t all loop-exit paths for that loop. The probability for the loop in Figure 2(c) to exit via node j is $\frac{f_5}{f_3+f_4+f_5}$.

The computed probability of each path is assigned to its last state in the LTS and thereafter propagated bottom-up. At each state in the LTS, the probability would be equal to the sum of probabilities of its loop node successors. However, we do not propagate loop-exit probabilities.

The probability of reaching a node in the structure graph would be equal to the sum of the probabilities of all paths by which the node could be reached in the LTS. So, the probability of reaching node f w.r.t loop in Figure 2(c) is computed as $Prob(1 \rightarrow 2 \rightarrow 3 \rightarrow 4) + Prob(1 \rightarrow 2 \rightarrow 6 \rightarrow 7)$ in the LTS in Figure 3(c).

The actual probability of reaching a node in the CFG would be equal to the sum of all path probabilities by which that node could be reached. So, the overall probability of reaching node f is computed as $Prob(a \rightarrow b \rightarrow c \rightarrow d \rightarrow f) + Prob(a \rightarrow b \rightarrow c \rightarrow e \rightarrow f)$.

This path probability would be computed by just multiplying state probabilities in the LTS. To compute path probability from the start of the CFG, we need to multiply path probabilities across different LTS. So, the total probability of reaching node f via path $a \rightarrow b \rightarrow c \rightarrow d \rightarrow f$ is the product of $Prob$(reaching 3 in Figure 3(a)), $Prob$(reaching 3 in Figure 3(b)) and $Prob$(reaching 4 in Figure 3(c)).

In Figure 2(d), there is one loop path $g \rightarrow h$ and one loop exit path $g \rightarrow h \rightarrow i$. So, we assign a probability of 1.0 to node 4 in Figure 3(d) which means that a dataflow fact generated at f that doesn't get killed in g or h should still have a probability of 1.0 at i.

4. OUR PROBABILISTIC DATAFLOW ANALYSIS ALGORITHM

Ammons et al.[1] suggested the idea of using Context Tupling [3] for dataflow analysis - where a state (in the LTS) is a context associated with a node in the CFG. We use this approach and map each context into a probability value for the tupled dataflow fact. For our approach, we create a separate LTS for each structure graph.

4.1 Contexts and context strings

We define a *context* as a state in a given LTS. It is represented by the tuple, $\langle LTSid, state \rangle$ where each LTS is identified by a unique $LTSid$. We define a *context string* as a string of contexts where each context represents a state in a different LTS. A context string uniquely identifies a path from the start node in the CFG.

While traversing a path we switch across different LTSs (or loops). One of the contexts in the context string is the "active" context: this context is used to trace facts in the current LTS; while the remaining string is the "latent" context string. We show a context as "q.c", where "q" is latent (corresponding to other LTSs) in the context string and "c" is the active context. Table 1 shows the computation of context strings after the first iteration on the nodes of the CFG where A, B, C, D refer to the LTSs in $Fig\ 3(a), 3(b), 3(c), 3(d)$ respectively. For node e, $\langle (A,3),(B,3) \rangle$ is the latent string while $(C,6)$ is the active context. Node e's active context pertains to the LTS in Figure 3(c) since the innermost loop to which e belongs is the one in Figure 2(c)).

We associate a context string with each dataflow fact. We propagate a dataflow fact to its successor *only if there is a valid transition from the active context in the context string on the label of the successor.* For node e, it's predecessor is c with an active context of $(C,2)$. We look for a transition from node 2 on the label e and find node 6 in the LTS in Figure 3(c). Thus, the active context for node e is $(C,6)$ with the latent context string remaining unchanged. Note that node f has two context strings for two different paths $a \rightarrow b \rightarrow c \rightarrow d \rightarrow f$ and $a \rightarrow b \rightarrow c \rightarrow e \rightarrow f$. Similarly j has three context strings, the third one pertaining to the path $a \rightarrow b \rightarrow c \rightarrow e \rightarrow j$.

Entering and leaving an LTS

We enter another LTS if we encounter a summary node n in the current LTS. We append the relevant context of the inner loop LTS to the current context string. Also, as we are switching across LTSs (entering the nested LTS), we change the active context to that of the nested LTS in the following manner: we change the context string, $d^{q.a} \rightarrow d^{(q+a).b}$ where d is the dataflow fact, q is the latent context and a was the active context before entering the nested LTS. $q+a$ appends a to the latent string q. The active context b is the state of the node n in the inner loop LTS which is now the active LTS.

Example: At node c, the context string gets updated from $\left\langle (A,3), \underline{(B,3)} \right\rangle$ to $\left\langle (A,3),(B,3), \underline{(C,2)} \right\rangle$. $(B,3)$ is a summary node due to which we enter the header node 1 in the inner loop LTS (Figure 3(c)). Here, there is a transition from 1 on the label c to node 2.

Table 1: The context strings for the nodes of the CFG in Figure 1 after the first iteration of dataflow analysis. (The underlined context is the active context.)

Node	Context string
a	$\left\langle \underline{(A,2)} \right\rangle$
b	$\left\langle (A,3), \underline{(B,2)} \right\rangle$
c	$\left\langle (A,3),(B,3), \underline{(C,2)} \right\rangle$
d	$\left\langle (A,3),(B,3), \underline{(C,3)} \right\rangle$
e	$\left\langle (A,3),(B,3), \underline{(C,6)} \right\rangle$
f	$\left\langle (A,3),(B,4), \underline{(C,4)} \right\rangle, \left\langle (A,3),(B,4), \underline{(C,7)} \right\rangle$
g	$\left\langle (A,3),(B,4),(C,5), \underline{(D,2)} \right\rangle, \left\langle (A,3),(B,4),(C,8), \underline{(D,2)} \right\rangle$
h	$\left\langle (A,3),(B,4),(C,5), \underline{(D,3)} \right\rangle, \left\langle (A,3),(B,4),(C,8), \underline{(D,3)} \right\rangle$
i	$\left\langle (A,3), \underline{(B,5)},(C,5),(D,4) \right\rangle, \left\langle (A,3), \underline{(B,5)},(C,8),(D,4) \right\rangle$
j	$\left\langle \underline{(A,4)},(B,6),(C,5),(D,4) \right\rangle, \left\langle \underline{(A,4)},(B,6),(C,8),(D,4) \right\rangle$ $\left\langle \underline{(A,4)},(B,7),(C,9) \right\rangle$

We leave an LTS if we encounter an exit node n in the current LTS. In this case, we switch back to the previously active LTS (that of the outer loop) and make that as the active LTS. However, we retain the context of the inner LTS which has now been exited. The formal definitions are similar to the one while entering an LTS and have been skipped.

Example: One context string at node h is updated from $\left\langle (A,3),(B,4),(C,5), \underline{(D,3)} \right\rangle$ to $\left\langle (A,3), \underline{(B,5)},(C,5),(D,4) \right\rangle$ at node i. $(D,4)$ is an exit node, hence we go to the outer loop LTS (Figure 3(b)) where the context is $(B,4)$. Then, there is a transition from 4 on the label i to node 5. We retain the traversed loop context $(D,4)$ in the context string.

4.2 Our generic dataflow analysis framework

If z refers to a set of dataflow facts, we define $z^{q.c}$ as a set of facts annotated with context string $q.c$ where q refers to the latent context and c is the active context.

We define $c \rightarrow^{x} \alpha(c,x)$ as the transition from one state to another where $\alpha(c,x)$ is the new context state which is arrived from state c over the transition x in the current automaton (without leaving the current LTS). If there is no valid transition from $c \rightarrow^{x}$, then $\alpha(c,x)$ goes to the *epsilon state*. The epsilon state is the start node of the LTS and we define the ϵ-context string as the string whose active context is the start node of that LTS.

Our generic probabilistic dataflow analysis algorithm now proceeds as follows. For all possible context strings, we look for a possible transition from the current state. If such a transition exists, the current context string $q.c$ makes a transition to the state $q.\alpha(c)$ where $\alpha(c)$ refers to the new state in the active LTS. We apply the transfer function (of the dataflow analysis) over the meet of all predecessors only with the same context string for all contexts.

There is no valid transition to a node from any of its predecessors if the profiler didn't encounter the node during its run. We merge information from all paths to that node and do so by taking a meet over all predecessors over the ϵ-context string. Epsilon-transition implies that we compute facts without any profiling information same as normal dataflow analysis.

Our Dataflow solution at a node x is formally defined as follows: $DFSoln(x) =$

- $\sum_{c \in C, \alpha(c,x) \neq \epsilon} [\Upsilon(\bigotimes_{y \in pred(x)} DFSoln^{q.c}(y))]^{q.\alpha(c,x)}$: if at least one transition possible from current state
- $[\Upsilon(\bigotimes_{z \in pred(x)} [\sum_{c \in C} DFSoln^{q.c}(y)]^{q.\epsilon})]^{q.\alpha(\epsilon,x)}$: if x is entry or if no transitions possible from the current state

where Υ is the transfer function, $\bigotimes$ is the meet operator, $DFSoln(x)$ refers to the solution of all dataflow facts. $DFSoln^c(x)$ means the set of dataflow facts associated with context string c and $DFSoln(x) = \sum_{c \in C} DFSoln^c(x)$. The size of the latent string q is bounded by the number of loops in the CFG.

Example: A node n whose predecessors are p_1 and p_2 might have a transition from one of the context strings, $q.c$ in p_1 but not in p_2. Then, the resultant solution at n with the context string $q.\alpha(c)$ will be the application of transfer function over a meet of existing facts with the facts generated at p_1 alone. However, there could be another context string $q2.c2$ associated with p_2 which has a transition on n. Then, we would have two separate sets of dataflow facts associated with two different paths (or context strings).

The probability of a dataflow fact at a node n is computed using the context string associated with that fact. So, in Table 1, for node g, the probability of the dataflow fact with the context string $\langle(A,3),(B,4),(C,5),(D,2)\rangle$ is $Pr(3_{LTSa}) * Pr(4_{LTSb}) * Pr(5_{LTSc}) * Pr(2_{LTSd})$.

5. RELATED WORK

Profile-guided Analysis

Ammons and Larus [1] proposed a novel technique towards analyzing and optimizing programs by identifying and duplicating hot paths, thus creating a hot path graph. Their algorithm uses the data-flow tracing – one of the two techniques proposed by Holley and Rosen [3] for solving Qualified Flow-Analysis Problems. They preferred dataflow tracing over Context-Tupling (the second technique for solving qualified flow-analysis problems by Holley and Rosen). We, however, use context-tupling as it is more amenable to probabilistic analysis, with each context essentially mapping into a probability value for the tupled dataflow fact.

Path-Sensitive Analysis

ESP [8] performs property simulation (path-sensitive symbolic execution) to verify a specified program property by tagging each dataflow fact with the path it was generated on. We use path-sensitive analysis *only* on the paths that were seen by a profiler.

Dillig et al. [11] also proposed algorithms towards path-sensitive analysis. In contrast to the above algorithm, we segregate dataflow facts to compute probabilities with which a dataflow fact might hold at a program point. Also, we do not propagate facts along all static paths, but only along the paths seen by the structural acyclic path-profiler.

Probabilistic Analysis

Ramalingam [2] formulated probabilistic dataflow analysis for finite bi-distributive subset problems using edge profiles to infer the probability with which each fact holds true.

Mehofer and Scholz [9] used k-edge profiles and whole program paths [10] to improve the precision of the probabilistic dataflow analysis. As they utilized execution history for calculating the probabilities of dataflow facts, they obtained significantly better results.

Silva et al.[5] formulated a scalable one-level context and flow-sensitive probabilistic pointer analysis framework by using linear transfer functions efficiently coded as sparse matrices. They used edge profiles for probabilities computation.

To the best of our knowledge, ours is the first attempt at performing probabilistic dataflow analysis over path-profiles on structure graphs. As paths encode the history of execution much better than edge profiles, the probabilities computed using path-profiles should be much more accurate.

6. FUTURE WORK

Having developed a very simple proof of concept [14], our primary goal right now is to build a robust implementation of our analysis on a stable compiler framework. This would allow us to compare the improvements in the solution over other algorithms that relied on edge/two-edge profiles. We would also like to implement a few speculative optimizations and study the effect of an improved probabilistic solution on the performance of programs.

Having accomplished our primary goal, we intend to extend our algorithm to use the k-Iteration path profiles [12]. The k-Iteration profiles, in contrast to acyclic paths, are capable of recording much longer paths spanning multiple iterations of a loop.

7. REFERENCES

[1] Glenn Ammons, James R. Larus. Improving data-flow analysis with path profiles. In PLDI '98.

[2] G. Ramalingam. Data flow frequency analysis. In PLDI '96.

[3] L. H. Holley, B. K. Rosen. Qualified data flow problems. In POPL '80.

[4] T.Yasue, T.Suganuma, H.Komatsu, T.Nakatani. An Efficient Online Path Profiling Framework for Java Just-In-Time Compilers. In PACT '03.

[5] Jeff Da Silva , J. G. Steffan. A probabilistic pointer analysis for speculative optimizations. In ASPLOS '06.

[6] T.Ball, P.Mataga, M.Sagiv. Edge Profiling versus Path Profiling: The Showdown. In POPL '98.

[7] T. Ball and J. R. Larus. Efficient path profiling. In MICRO '96.

[8] Manuvir Das, S.Lerner, M.Seigle. ESP: path-sensitive program verification in polynomial time. In PLDI '02.

[9] E. Mehofer, B. Scholz. A Novel Probabilistic Data Flow Framework. In CC '01.

[10] E. Mehofer, B. Scholz. Dataflow Frequency Analysis based on Whole Program Paths. In PACT '02.

[11] Dillig, I., Dillig, T., and Aiken, A. Sound, complete and scalable path-sensitive analysis. In PLDI '08.

[12] Subhajit Roy, Y.N. Srikant. Profiling k-Iteration Paths: A Generalization of the Ball-Larus Profiling Algorithm. In CGO '09.

[13] Y. Wu, A. Adl-Tabatabai, D. Berson, J.Z. Fang, R. Gupta. US Patent 6848100 : Hierarchical Software Path Profiling, 2005.

[14] R. Arun. Probabilistic Dataflow Analysis using Path Profiles on Structure Graphs : M.E. Thesis, Computer Science & Automation, IISc, 2009.

Workshop on Assurances for Self-Adaptive Systems (ASAS 2011)

Javier Cámara
University of Coimbra
Portugal
jcmoreno@dei.uc.pt

Carlo Ghezzi
Politecnico di Milano
Italy
carlo.ghezzi@polimi.it

Rogério de Lemos
University of Kent, UK
CISUC, Portugal
r.delemos@kent.ac.uk

Antónia Lopes
University of Lisbon
Portugal
mal@di.fc.ul.pt

ABSTRACT

Assurances for Self-Adaptive Systems (ASAS) is a workshop that will bring together researchers to discuss software engineering aspects of self-adaptive systems, including methods, architectures, languages, algorithms, techniques, and tools that can be used to support assurances in self-adaptive system development. ASAS is intended as a complement to the efforts started a while ago at the successful FSE workshop series on Self-Healing Systems (WOSS), or the Software Engineering for Adaptive and Self-Managing Systems (SEAMS) symposium. However, in contrast with those events, ASAS is focused on the collection, storage, and analysis of evidence for the provision of assurances that a self-adaptive software system is able to behave functionally and non-functionally according to its specification.

Categories and Subject Descriptors

D.2.0 [**Software Engineering**]: General

General Terms

Resilience, Dependability, Performance, Verification

Keywords

adaptive software, assurances, stochastic analysis, run-time verification, testing

1. INTRODUCTION

1.1 Theme

Until recently, repairing faults, or performing upgrades on different kinds of software systems have been tasks performed as a maintenance activity conducted by human operators. However, as software systems become central to support everyday activities and face increasing levels of complexity, as well as of uncertainty in their operational environments, there is a critical need to improve their dependability, optimize their performance, and at the same time, reduce their development and operational costs. This situation has led to the development of systems able to reconfigure their structure and modify their behaviour at run-time in order to improve their operation, recover from failures, and adapt to environmental changes, with little or no human intervention. These kinds of systems typically operate using an explicit representation of their own structure and goals, and appear in the literature under different designations (e.g. self-adaptive, self-healing, self-managed, autonomic, etc.).

Moreover, self-organizing systems are also able to dynamically adapt themselves to changing environmental conditions at run-time, and are typically composed of a large number of constituent components that operate according to a set of local rules. In self-organizing systems, global system behaviour emerges from local component interaction, stabilizing the system in the event of faults or changes in the environment.

In spite of recent and important advances in the area, one key aspect of self-adaptive systems that poses important challenges that remain to be tackled in depth is assurances [2]: that is, providing evidence that systems satisfy their set of stated functional and non-functional properties during operation. Specifically, assurances involve not only system dependability and security, but also resilience with respect to attributes such as availability, reliability, safety, or performance. Developing high-assurance, self-adaptive systems is difficult, since these systems tend to be highly context-dependent, and this fact introduces a high degree of uncertainty that has to be dealt with (e.g., resource variability).

ASAS will bring together researchers to discuss software engineering aspects, including the methods, architectures, languages, algorithms, techniques, and tools that can be used to support assurances in development and deployment of self-adaptive software systems. In particular, ASAS is intended as a complement to the efforts started while ago at the successful FSE workshop series on Self-Healing Systems (WOSS) [3], which has culminated with the organization of the ICSE workshop series on Software Engineering for Adaptive and Self-Managing Systems (SEAMS) [1], which now is a symposium. In contrast with those events, ASAS intends to focus on the collection of evidence, its storage and analysis for the provision of assurances that a self-adaptive software system is able to behave functionally and non-functionally according to its specification.

Copyright is held by the author/owner(s).
ESEC/FSE'11, September 5–9, 2011, Szeged, Hungary.
ACM 978-1-4503-0443-6/11/09.

1.2 Goals

Self-adaptation represents a major step ahead for software engineering. While in recent years methods, tools, and notations in this area have focused on analyzing and fixing problems at run-time, much effort is still required to guarantee system resilience in the face of uncertainty. The general goal of ASAS is to identify important challenges in the context of this problem from a software engineering perspective, and to advance the state-of-the-art in the various topics covered.

1.3 Topics

Topics of interest to ASAS include, but are not limited to: formal notations for modeling and analyzing self-adaptation; measurement and evaluation of resilience, security, performance, and cost in adaptive systems; run-time verification and validation; stochastic analysis; reasoning in the presence of uncertainty; benchmarking resilience; combination of run-time and development-time evidence; social aspects of assurances; resilient cases for self-adaptive systems; Industrial case studies for assurances in self-adaptive systems.

2. ASAS 2011 COMMITTEES

2.1 Organizing Committee

Javier Cámara, University of Coimbra, Portugal; Rogério de Lemos, University of Kent, UK and CISUC, Portugal; Carlo Ghezzi, Politecnico di Milano, Italy; Antónia Lopes, University of Lisbon, Portugal.

2.2 Program Committee

Betty H.C. Cheng, Michigan State University, USA; Bojan Cukic, West Virginia University, USA; Felicita Di Giandomenico, CNR-ISTI, Italy; David Garlan, Carnegie Mellon University, USA; Paola Inverardi, University of L´Aquila, Italy; Tim Kelly, University of York, UK; Marta Kwiatkowska, Oxford University, UK; Raffaela Mirandola, Politecnico di Milano, Italy; Flavio Oquendo, European University of Brittany - UBS/VALORIA, France; Luis Rodrigues, Instituto Superior Tecnico, Portugal; Rick Schlichting, AT&T, USA; Marco Vieira, University of Coimbra, Portugal.

3. ASAS 2011 PROGRAM

The core of the ASAS 2011 program is a set of 6 stimulating papers published as ASAS 2011 proceedings in the ACM DL. From them, 2 are invited papers and 4 correspond to the papers accepted by the Program Committee, out of the 9 that were initially submitted.

To generate lively interaction among workshop participants throughout the workshop, each paper session is followed by a discussion led by one of the organizers. For more program details, please refer to the workshop's web site [http://asas.dei.uc.pt].

4. ACKNOWLEDGEMENTS

The co-organizers of ASAS 2011 would like to thank both the authors of the papers for their contributions and all the referees for their critical and valuable comments.

Co-financed by the Foundation for Science and Technology via project CMU-PT/ELE/0030/2009 and by FEDER via the "Programa Operacional Factores de Competitividade" of QREN with COMPETE reference: FCOMP-01-0124-FEDER-012983.

5. REFERENCES

[1] B. H. C. Cheng, R. de Lemos, D. Garlan, H. Giese, M. Litoiu, J. Magee, H. A. Müller, M. Pezzè, and R. Taylor. Fifth workshop on software engineering for adaptive and self-managing systems (seams 2010). In J. Kramer, J. Bishop, P. T. Devanbu, and S. Uchitel, editors, *ICSE (2)*, pages 447–448. ACM, 2010.

[2] B. H. C. Cheng, R. de Lemos, H. Giese, P. Inverardi, J. Magee, J. Andersson, B. Becker, N. Bencomo, Y. Brun, B. Cukic, G. D. M. Serugendo, S. Dustdar, A. Finkelstein, C. Gacek, K. Geihs, V. Grassi, G. Karsai, H. M. Kienle, J. Kramer, M. Litoiu, S. Malek, R. Mirandola, H. A. Müller, S. Park, M. Shaw, M. Tichy, M. Tivoli, D. Weyns, and J. Whittle. Software engineering for self-adaptive systems: A research roadmap. In B. H. C. Cheng, R. de Lemos, H. Giese, P. Inverardi, and J. Magee, editors, *Software Engineering for Self-Adaptive Systems*, volume 5525 of *Lecture Notes in Computer Science*, pages 1–26. Springer, 2009.

[3] D. Garlan, J. Kramer, and A. L. Wolf, editors. *Proceedings of the First Workshop on Self-Healing Systems, WOSS 2002, Charleston, South Carolina, USA, November 18-19, 2002.* ACM, 2002.

IWPSE-EVOL 2011

12th International Workshop on Principles on Software Evolution and 7th ERCIM Workshop on Software Evolution

Romain Robbes
PLEIAD Lab
Computer Science Department (DCC)
University of Chile
rrobbes@dcc.uchile.cl

Anthony Cleve
PReCISE Research Center
Faculty of Computer Science
University of Namur, Belgium
acl@info.fundp.ac.be

ABSTRACT

The IWPSE-EVOL 2011 workshop is the merger of the 12th International Workshop on Principles of Software Evolution (IWPSE) and the 7th annual ERCIM Workshop on Software Evolution (EVOL). The objectives of this joint event is to provide a forum to discuss a wide range of topics in software evolution, to foster the better understanding of the nature of software evolution, and to accelerate research activities on the subject.

Categories and Subject Descriptors

D.2.7 [**Software Engineering**]: Distribution, Maintenance, and Enhancement

General Terms

Algorithms, Theory, Measurement, Human Factors

Keywords

Software maintenance, software evolution

1. INTRODUCTION

Research in software evolution and evolvability has been thriving in the past years, with a constant stream of new formalisms, tools, techniques, and development methodologies trying, on the one hand, to facilitate the way long-lived successful software systems can be changed in order to cope with demands from users and the increasing complexity and volatility of the contexts in which such systems operate, and, on the other hand, to understand and if possible control the processes by which demand for these changes come about.

The IWPSE-EVOL 2011 workshop is the merger of the 12th International Workshop on Principles of Software Evolution (IWPSE) and the 7th annual ERCIM Workshop on Software Evolution (EVOL). The objectives of this joint event is to provide a forum to discuss a wide range of topics in software evolution, to foster the better understanding of the nature of software evolution, and to accelerate research activities on the subject.

This year's edition of IWPSE-EVOL is held in conjunction with ESEC/FSE, the joint meeting of the European Software Engineering Conference and the ACM SIGSOFT Symposium on the Foundations of Software Engineering, as it has been the case multiple times in the past, most recently in 2005, 2007, and 2009. The IWPSE and EVOL workshops have been held together since 2009.

Copyright is held by the author/owner(s).
ESEC/FSE'11, September 5–9, 2011, Szeged, Hungary.
ACM 978-1-4503-0443-6/11/09.

2. TOPICS OF INTEREST

Topics of interest of this joint event include, among others:

- Application areas: distributed, embedded, real-time, ultra large scale, and self-adaptive systems, web services, mobile computing, information systems, systems of systems, etc.
- Paradigms: support and barriers to evolution in aspect-oriented, agile, component-based, and model-driven software development, service-oriented architectures,etc.
- Technical aspects: co-evolution and inconsistency management, impact analysis and change propagation, dynamic reconfiguration and updating; architectures, tools, languages and notations for supporting evolution, etc.
- Managerial aspects: effort and cost estimation, risk analysis, software quality, productivity, process support, training, awareness, etc.
- Empirical studies related to software evolution.
- Mining software repositories approaches and techniques supporting software evolution.
- Industrial experience on successes and failures related to software evolution.
- Interdisciplinary approaches: adaptation of evolutionary concepts and measures from other disciplines (biology, geology, etc.) to software evolution.
- Theories and models to explain and understand software evolution.

3. WORKSHOP OVERVIEW

The IWPSE-EVOL 2011 workshop has attracted 37 submissions from 87 authors. The 27 program committee members and 16 external reviewers selected 17 submissions for presentation and publication. The accepted submissions include 9 full research papers, 6 short or position papers, and 2 tool demonstration paper. The acceptance rate for full research papers was 42%.

Accepted papers

Full papers

- *A Taxonomy for Impact Analysis and Change Prediction to Support Software Evolution*, by Steffen Lehnert.
- *An agent-based framework for distributed collaborative model evolution*, by Hoa Khanh Dam and Aditya Ghose.
- *Causes of Premature Aging during Software Development: An Observational Study*, by Mathieu Lavallee and Pierre Robillard.
- *Network Analysis of OSS evolution: An Empirical Study on ArgoUML Project*, by Wen Zhang.
- *Problem-Solution Mapping for Forward and Reengineering on Architectural Level*, by Matthias Riebisch, Stephan Bode and Robert Brcina.
- *Run-time Phenomena in Dynamic Software Updating: Causes and Effects*, by Allan Gregersen and Bo Jorgensen.
- *Towards A Benchmark for Traceability*, by Eya Ben Charrada, David Caspar, Cédric Jeanneret and Martin Glinz.
- *Towards a Classification of Logical Dependencies Origins: A Case Study*, by Gustavo Ansaldi Oliva, Francisco Santana, Marco Gerosa and Cleidson De Souza.
- *User generated (web) content: trash or treasure*, by Giovanni Alluvatti, Andrea Capiluppi, Giuseppe De Ruvo and Marco Molfetta.

Short papers

- *Are the classes that use exceptions defect prone?*, by Cristina Marinescu.
- *Challenges in Model-Based Evolution and Merging of Access Control policies*, Lionel Montrieux, Michel Wermelinger and Yijun Yu.
- *Challenges of Evolving Sequential to Parallel Code: An Exploratory Study*, by Anne Meade and J.J. Collins.
- *Measuring Multi-language Software Evolution: A Case Study*, by Tom Arbuckle.
- *Requirements evolution drives software evolution*, by Neil A. Ernst and John Mylopoulos.
- *Using the Gini Coefficient for Bug Prediction in Eclipse*, by Emanuel Giger, Martin Pinzger and Harald Gall.

Tool demonstration papers

- *An Editing-operation Replayer with Highlights Supporting Investigation of Program Modifications*, by Takayuki Omori and Katsuhisa Maruyama.
- *Historage: Fine-grained Version Control System for Java*, by Hideaki Hata, Osamu Mizuno and Tohru Kikuno.

Keynote talk

The workshop program also features a keynote talk by an internationally recognized expert in software engineering, software maintenance and evolution: Prem Devanbu. Prem will talk about his latest research developments in Mining Software Repositories, an area which has a lot of overlap with Software Evolution.

A tribute to Manny Lehman

The 2011 edition of IWPSE-EVOL is dedicated to the memory of Prof. Meir M. "Manny" Lehman, who sadly passed away in December 2010. Manny Lehman was known as the "*Father of software evolution*", since his seminal work with Les Belady on the development of IBMŠs `OS/360`. Their early empirical studies gave birth to the widely known *Laws of Software Evolution*. Manny was also recognized by the software engineering community at large, being program co-chair of the 4th ICSE in 1975, and general chair of the 8th ICSE in 1985.

Special issue

IWPSE-EVOL 2011 will be associated with a post-event special issue of JSME, the *Journal of Software Maintenance and Evolution: Research and Practice*, published by Wiley. The theme of this special issue will be "*Laws, Principles and Theories of Software Evolution*".

4. ACKNOWLEDGMENTS

We would like to warmly thank all the authors, speakers, program committee members, and additional reviewers for their contribution and help to produce this exciting workshop program. We thank ERCIM for their sponsorship. We also thank ACM for publishing the present workshop proceedings.

PASTE'11: 10th ACM SIGPLAN-SIGSOFT Workshop on Program Analysis for Software Tools and Engineering

Jeffrey S. Foster
University of Maryland, College Park, USA
jfoster@cs.umd.edu

Lori L. Pollock
University of Delaware, USA
pollock@cis.udel.edu

ABSTRACT

The ACM SIGPLAN-SIGSOFT PASTE Workshop presents exciting research, empirical results, and new directions in Program Analysis for Software Tools and Engineering. The program includes two technical sessions as well as a keynote talk on program synthesis for automating end-user programming and education.

Categories and Subject Descriptors

D.2 [**Software Engineering**]; D.3 [**Programming Languages**]

General Terms

Algorithms, Design, Experimentation, Languages, Reliability, Verification

Keywords

Program analysis, software tools, software engineering, programming languages

1. INTRODUCTION

This workshop is the 10th in a series that brings together the program analysis, software tools, and software engineering communities to focus on applications of program analysis techniques in software tools. The research includes, but is not limited to, program analysis for program understanding, debugging, testing, and reverse engineering; integration of program analysis into the software development and maintenance process; user interfaces for software tools and software visualization; applications of program analysis techniques; analysis of program execution or program evolution; integration of, or tradeoffs between, different analysis techniques; and issues in scaling analyses and user interfaces to deal with large systems.

The program includes four long and two short papers, selected from 14 submissions. The papers are arranged into two technical sessions, and cover a range of topics including analysis and instrumentation of binaries, trace generation for behavioral pattern detection, change-based test coverage, locating failure-inducing environment changes, and assessing modularity via usage changes. The keynote features Sumit Gulwani from Microsoft Research speaking on program synthesis for automating end-user programming and education. The program ends with time for demos, open discussion, and 5-minute madness talks.

2. PAPER SUMMARY

Jacobson et al propose a new technique for automatically labeling library functions in stripped binary executables [3]. Knowing the identities of such functions can improve automated analysis and can help with program understanding tasks for binaries. The authors' proposed technique describes library functions with *semantic descriptors*, which are robust against minor code changes and many compiler optimizations. The authors extend an existing tool, unstrip, to incorporate semantic descriptors, and demonstrate that the resulting tool substantially outperforms existing library fingerprinting techniques.

Bernat et al describe the current state of the Dyninst binary instrumentation and analysis framework [1]. A key feature of Dyninst is its ability to instrument a program at any time, ranging from compile-time instrumentation (i.e., binary rewriting) to run-time (or dynamic) instrumentation. Additionally, Dyninst users can modify or remove instrumentation at any time, and Dyninst is capable of instrumenting highly optimized or even malicious code. The authors describe how Dyninst achieves this, including the control-flow graph abstractions used to specify instrumentation. Finally, the authors demonstrate using the SPEC2006 integer suite that Dyninst has overhead that is similar to or lower than other popular instrumenters.

Von Detten proposes a new approach to behavioral pattern detection [6]. Existing pattern detectors operate either statically or dynamically; however, purely static detectors must make conservative approximations, and detectors that rely on dynamic information are typically restricted to a single run, thereby seeing only a small subset of the program's behavior. The author proposes instead to use symbolic execution to generate a large set of relevant program traces. Trace collection can also be limited to a user-selectable subset of candidate statically detected patterns, to reduce the size of the traces.

Fisher et al define a set of *change-based coverage criteria* that reflect to what extent program changes with respect to a previous version are exercised by a test suite [2]. Their work is based on the popular assumption that a disproportionate number of faults is likely to reside in recently changed code and that, in practice, testers often select some arbitrary coverage level as their target given the infeasibil-

Copyright is held by the author/owner(s).
ESEC/FSE'11, September 5–9, 2011, Szeged, Hungary.
ACM 978-1-4503-0443-6/11/09.

ity of 100% coverage with traditional criteria applied to the whole program. The authors' experimental studies comparing change-based coverage criteria for object-oriented applications against traditional criteria show that indeed change-based criteria reveal faults better than traditional criteria, and enable the construction of smaller test suites with similar fault detection effectiveness to those constructed with traditional criteria.

Qi et al present a record-replay technique to address the problem of explaining program failures that are caused by the execution environment not meeting the assumptions of the program [5]. The authors' record-replay technique, called *Semi-replay*, records essential interactions between the application and the underlying operation system environment during successful runs. When the application is then run and fails on another operating system, the recorded system call sequence is used to help determine the root cause of the application failure due to the environment changes. While limited to programs using static libraries, the technique is shown to be effective in three case studies.

Mileva et al present an approach to assessing the modularity of software modules, to assist in directing the programmer's attention to modules with low modularity, which are candidates for refactoring [4]. The authors propose measuring the modularity of a software module based on the number of distinct usage patterns that change when the module is evolved. The premise is that modularity is high when implementation changes do not force changes to client code. To provide a quantitative perspective, the authors describe their initial study from mining module implementation changes and subsequent module usage changes from a repository.

3. REFERENCES

[1] A. R. Bernat and B. P. Miller. Anywhere, Any-Time Binary Instrumentation. In *Proceedings of the 10th ACM SIGPLAN-SIGSOFT Workshop on Program Analysis for Software Tools and Engineering*, Szeged, Hungary, Sept. 2011.

[2] M. F. II, J. Wloka, F. Tip, B. G. Ryder, and A. Luchansky. An Evaluation of Change-Based Coverage Criteria. In *Proceedings of the 10th ACM SIGPLAN-SIGSOFT Workshop on Program Analysis for Software Tools and Engineering*, Szeged, Hungary, Sept. 2011.

[3] E. R. Jacobson, N. Rosenblum, and B. P. Miller. Labeling Library Functions in Stripped Binaries. In *Proceedings of the 10th ACM SIGPLAN-SIGSOFT Workshop on Program Analysis for Software Tools and Engineering*, Szeged, Hungary, Sept. 2011.

[4] Y. M. Mileva and A. Zeller. Assessing Modularity via Usage Changes. In *Proceedings of the 10th ACM SIGPLAN-SIGSOFT Workshop on Program Analysis for Software Tools and Engineering*, Szeged, Hungary, Sept. 2011.

[5] D. Qi, M. N. Ngo, T. Sun, and A. Roychoudhury. Locating Failure-Inducing Environment Changes. In *Proceedings of the 10th ACM SIGPLAN-SIGSOFT Workshop on Program Analysis for Software Tools and Engineering*, Szeged, Hungary, Sept. 2011.

[6] M. von Detten. Towards Systematic, Comprehensive Trace Generation for Behavioral Pattern Detection through Symbolic Execution. In *Proceedings of the 10th ACM SIGPLAN-SIGSOFT Workshop on Program Analysis for Software Tools and Engineering*, Szeged, Hungary, Sept. 2011.

The 4th International Workshop on Social Software Engineering (SSE'11)

Walid Maalej
Technische Universität München, Germany
maalejw@cs.tum.edu

Raian Ali
Lero - University of Limerick, Ireland
raian.ali@lero.ie

ABSTRACT

Software is created by people and for people. People are heterogeneous in their beliefs, backgrounds, and preferences. Accommodating and exploiting the social variety is crucial for successful engineering and usage of software. On the one hand, software engineering is a social activity, performed by different individuals and teams. This necessitates methodologies and tools to deal with issues such as communication, coordination, knowledge sharing, compensation, and reconciliation. On the other hand, Social Software (Internet Forums, Wikis, Social Networks, Blogs, etc.) is an expanding computing paradigm, which inherently incorporates intensive social interactions and implications. Engineering Social Software magnifies a spectrum of challenges like group requirements engineering, social-awareness, privacy, security, and trust.

Both directions – engineering Social Software and treating software engineering as a social activity – require competency from other disciplines as diverse as psychology, sociology, and organizational science. While both directions receive considerable attention, research in both fields is fragmented, uncoordinated, and partially redundant. The goal of this workshop is to confluence the research on social aspects in software engineering and engineering of Social software into a new field of Social Software Engineering (SSE).

Categories and Subject Descriptors

D.2 [**Software**]: Software Engineering

General Terms

Design, Human Factors, Management

Keywords

Social Computing, Social Engineering

1. THEME, GOALS, AND TOPICS

This workshop brings together researchers and practitioners working on different aspects of collaboration and knowledge sharing in software engineering as well as the engineering of Social Software to discuss new results and future research challenges. Major topics addressed at the workshop include (but not limited to):

- Engineering Social Software
  - Requirements Engineering for Social Software
  - Engineering privacy, trust, and security for Social Software
  - Engineering of lightweight and unobtrusive tools, Web 2.0, and Social Semantic Web applications
  - Approaches and tools for context-aware and personalized assistance
  - Engineering adaptivity and evolution of Social Software
  - Analysis of compatibility with social diversity (law, culture, preferences, semantics, etc.)
  - Analysis of particular and emerging challenges intrinsic to Social Software
- Social Aspects in Software Engineering
  - Collaboration and knowledge sharing in development teams and (Open Source) communities
  - Relationship between users and developers, user feedback, mashups, and perpetual beta
  - Concerns of individuals in collaboration settings, such as learning, usability, and incentives
  - Interaction and communication design in collaborative software engineering
  - Research methods, models, and tools supporting the social nature of software engineering
  - Exploiting and tailoring existing software engineering paradigms, such as AOSE and Agile, to support social development
- Implications of Social Software Engineering
  - Usage of Social Software to understand social aspects in software engineering
  - Impact of Social Software on development process
  - Empirical studies on Social Software Engineering
  - Futuristic scenarios and research agendas

2. WORKSHOP FORMAT

SSE'11 lasts for one full day (September 5th. 2011). It starts with a short opening session in which the organizers present facts, statistics, and guidelines about the workshop. SSE'11 proceeds with a 30 minutes keynote given by a renowned researcher. After that, the presentations are held in several sessions. Each presenter has 20 minutes time for a full paper followed by 10 minutes of discussion. A short paper is allotted 10 minutes presentation time followed by 5 minutes discussion time. At the end of each session, the results are summarized.

Copyright is held by the author/owner(s).

ESEC/FSE'11, September 5–9, 2011, Szeged, Hungary.
ACM 978-1-4503-0443-6/11/09.

The afternoon starts with an open discussion. SSE'11 leaves space for Pecha Kucha talks. All research groups are asked to bring demos or prepare posters with results, position statements and identified challenges to foster the discussions. Moreover, industrial participants are encouraged to line out their needs, requirements, and expectations from the community. To this end, several main topics will be discussed in small focus groups aiming to bridge research and real-world challenges. In a final wrap up session, the focus groups present the findings from their discussions and identify a roadmap for future research efforts.

SSE'11 publishes accepted papers as workshop proceedings in the ACM Digital Library. SSE'11 community is planning a coordinated action funded by the European Commission on Social Software Engineering. SSE'11 invites the authors of best 3 full papers to join the management consortium of this action. SSE'11 publishes a summary of the workshop sessions in the workshop proceedings and make the identified research questions and the presentation slides available on the workshop's social network.

3. PAPER SELECTION PROCEDURE

SSE'11 accepts 2 types of papers:

- Short papers (3-5 pages) state the position of the authors within the scope of the workshop, and can describe solution concepts in a premature state.
- Full papers (6-8 pages) describe problems, needs, novel approaches and frameworks within the scope of the workshop. Full papers are also meant for evaluations of new approaches and empirical evaluation and industrial experience reports.

Papers are evaluated based on their originality, relevance to the workshop, and their potential for discussion. The papers with the best reviews (on average) are accepted to the workshop. SSE'11 reviews each submission via three members from the following international program committee:

- Andrew Begel, Microsoft Research, USA
- Jan Bosch, Chalmers University of Technology, Sweden
- Travis Breaux, CMU, USA
- Jaelson Castro, University of Pernambuco, Brazil
- Fabiano Dalpiaz, University of Trento, Italy
- Daniela Damian, University of Victoria, Canada
- Imed Hammouda, Tampere University of Technology, Finland
- Alexander Felferning, TU Graz, Austria
- Hans-Jörg Happel, FZI Research Center, Germany
- Smita Ghaisas, Tata Research, India
- Christian Lescher, Siemens, Germany
- Filippo Lanubile, University of Bari, Italy
- Steffen Lohmann, Universidad Carlos III de Madrid, Spain
- Gregoris Mentzas, The National Technical University of Athens, Greece
- Bashar Nuseibeh, The OU, UK, and Lero, Ireland
- Birgit Penzenstadler, TU München, Germany
- Gil Regev, Itecor/EPFL, Switzerland
- Wolfgang Reinhardt, Paderborn University, Germany
- Ita Richardson, University of Limerick, Ireland
- Helen Sharp, The Open University, UK

4. HISTORY OF THE WORKSHOP

SSE has been organized successfully in Munich, Kaiserslautern, and Paderborn in conjunction with the Software Engineering conference (SE'08, SE'09, and SE10). It has been focussing on European and more specifically German-speaking countries. In 2009 we merged the original community with the community of SENSE workshop (Software ENgineering within Social software Environments). In 2010 we merged the new community with the SoSEA workshop (Social Software Engineering and Applications) held at ASE'08 and ASE'09. From 2010 the new community calls itself Social Software Engineering. SSE website is already set up (http://www1.cs.tum.edu/sse) and is continuously updated and accessible from the ESEC/FSE homepage. The organizers maintain a mailing list for all participants in the current and previous SSE events.

5. FOLLOW-UP PLANS

We aim at identifying major research questions from the workshop submissions and discussions. Discussion groups present the result of their sessions. Discussions, recommendations, and presentation slides will be published on the SSE social network. We also plan to continue the workshop series, as long as there is an active community of researchers and practitioners interested in SSE topics. We are currently setting up an interest group out of the workshop participants, to coordinate the research efforts and the transfer of the results into the industry (e.g. open source tools, common fundings, and join-ventures). The activities of this interest group should be funded by the European Commission. Several members of the PC are already part of this group.

6. RELATED RESEARCH

SSE is a timely research topic in both academia and industry. First foundation work has been published. Maalej et al. [1] discuss how to make the user involvement a first order concern in software projects, moving from a transactional to a social engineering process. Ali et al. [2, 3] propose to exploit users' perception and judgment as an integral part of the system computation. Research programs e.g. at Microsoft [5], or at HP [4] as well as international events such as SocialCom [7], RESC [6] and Web2SE [8] target SSE from different aspects. The ultimate goal of SSE'11 is to bring together practitioners, experts, and scholars to confluence their efforts and identify main research outcomes, challenges, and agendas.

Acknowledgement This work has been supported in part by the FastFix project funded by the 7th Framework Programme of the European Commission, grant agreement no. FP7-258109.

7. REFERENCES

[1] W. Maalej, H-J. Happel, A. Rashid. When Users Become Collaborators: Towards Continuous and Context-Aware User Input. In *OOPSLA 2009*

[2] R. Ali, C. Solis, M. Salehie, I. Omoronyia, B. Nuseibeh, W. Maalej. Social Sensing: When Users Become Monitors In *ESEC/FSE 2011*

[3] R. Ali, C. Solis, F. Dalpiaz, W. Maalej, P. Giorgini, B. Nuseibeh. Social Software Product Lines. In *RESC 2011.*

[4] http://www.hpl.hp.com/research/idl/

[5] http://research.microsoft.com/en-us/groups/scg/

[6] http://www.cs.ucl.ac.uk/research/resc11/

[7] http://www.iisocialcom.org/

[8] https://sites.google.com/site/web2se2011/

8th International Workshop on Software Quality (WoSQ)

Stefan Wagner
Institute of Software Technology
University of Stuttgart
Stuttgart, Germany
stefan.wagner@informatik.uni-stuttgart.de

Sunita Chulani
Cisco Systems
San Jose, CA, USA
schulani@cisco.com

Bernard Wong
University of Technology Sydney
Sydney, Australia
bernard@it.uts.edu.au

ABSTRACT

Software becomes ever more feature-rich and thereby harder to distinguish based on its functionality. Instead, quality is starting to differentiate between similar software products. Specifying, constructing, and assuring quality has been under research for several decades and continues to be a long-term research area because of its many facets and its complexity. Current national and international initiatives show that there is an active research community in academia and industry. This workshop builds on the rich experiences of a series of previous workshops and aims to bring this community together to discuss current issues and future developments.

Categories and Subject Descriptors

D.2.9 [**Software Engineering**]: Management—*Software Quality Assurance*

General Terms

Management, economics, measurement, performance, reliability, security

Keywords

Software quality, quality management

1. INTRODUCTION

The software market has become huge in the new millennium. There are numerous applications out there and it has almost become impossible to keep track of them. The download site Softpedia[1] registered at the beginning of 2011 more than 900,000 free applications. The Apple App Store sells more than 350,000 for the iPhone alone. Wikipedia[2] lists more than a hundred different web browsers.

All these web browsers serve all the same purpose, however, to display pages from the World Wide Web. They differ only slightly in the features they provide. Nowadays the non-functional properties of the browsers become more and more important. The users are more interested with what quality they can provide these features. The recent successes of Google's Chrome browser is at least partly due to its reputation of high performance. One of the reasons why Mozilla's Firefox initially gained many users. The other reason was that in the early 2000's, several security vulnerabilities in Microsoft's Internet Explorer 6 were published damaged its position and drove many users to alternative browsers.

Quality, however, is not a fixed and universal property of a software. It depends on the context and goals of its stakehoders. Hence, the first step is a clear and precise specification of quality for a system [1]. Even if we get this right and complete in the first specification, we can be sure that it will become invalid, if we do not control quality over the complete life cycle of the software.

Software is clamped between the business and technical processes it has to support and the technical platform (hardware, operating system, or database system) on which it runs. Both, the process as well as the platform will inevitably change over time. Hardware becomes obsolete, operating systems are upgraded to new versions, and business processes need to support new and changed businesses.

Hence, software quality is at the heart of software engineering. A software engineer's goal is to deliver software on time, in budget, with the right functionality and quality. A new research and practical interest, especially in software product quality, can be seen by several current projects and initiatives. First of all, the ISO started a large project to build a new standard as successor to ISO 9126. The ISO 25000 series will be far more comprehensive than the old 9126. Especially, ISO 25010 was recently finalised and it now defines a new quality model.

The SEI and OMG started CISQ [2], an initiative to define a measurement framework for software product quality, which shall integrate with the new ISO 25000. In France, there is the Squale project [7], which defines a quality model with an analysis framework. In Germany, the Quamoco consortium [6] of key software companies (Capgemini, SAP, Siemens) and academic partners builds a detailed quality model, using activity-based quality models [5], which is extendable by several domain-specific models together with an evaluation framework based on ConQAT [3, 4]. These initiatives show that there is a research community for software quality that is intensively working on new quality models and evaluations. WoSQ is the perfect venue to bring these together.

There are many different challenges in software quality, tackled on many different levels. For example, it is still challenging to specify meaningful and testable quality re-

[1] `http://www.softpedia/`
[2] `http://en.wikipedia.org/wiki/List_of_web_browsers`

Copyright is held by the author/owner(s).
ESEC/FSE'11, September 5–9, 2011, Szeged, Hungary.
ACM 978-1-4503-0443-6/11/09.

quirements. Then, it is also an extremely difficult task to estimate the current level of software quality of a system [8] and find the roots of quality problems. It goes as far as specifying and analysing the safety of systems containing software, for example, by using safety cases [9].

At present, there are few venues that look explicitly at the bigger picture of software quality. Instead being specific for security or maintenance, we bring together researchers, who look at quality more comprehensively. We aim to discuss the state-of-the-art as well as the state of the practice and new developments. From these discussions, new ideas and collaborations can be formed.

2. WORKSHOP THEME AND TOPICS

The general theme of the workshop is achieving and controlling software quality. This involves product as well as process quality. Specific topics are:

- Software quality engineering
- Software quality management
- Software quality control
- Quality assurance techniques (testing, inspection, reviews, code analysis)
- Software product evaluation and certification
- Quality attributes and trade-offs
- Software quality for evolving systems, SOA-based systems, or in the cloud
- Models of product or process quality
- Software process evaluation and improvement
- Quality metrics
- Tool support for all of the above
- Case studies and empirical results

3. WORKSHOP FORMAT

We have three types of sessions: invited talk (keynote), position paper presentations, and a discussion session. We especially have group discussions on selected topics for which the discussions after the paper presentations are too short.

We propose first possible topics for discussions, collect further topics from the participants, and then let the participants vote. The number of topics and groups depends on the number of participants. Then we break into groups and work on the selected topics. Members of each group will then present the results in the plenum.

The keynote talk is given by Prof. Motoei Azuma from Waseda University (Japan) and he talks about the advances of the SQUaRE project, which works on the new software product quality standards series ISO 25000. Then we will have seven research paper presentations spread over three sessions. The contributions range from empirical analyses of in-process metrics and beta-release bugs over process improvement and product quality to a quality model for SOA. After the paper presentations, we have the final session for the group discussion.

4. SUBMISSIONS AND REVIEWING

Overall, we received 11 submissions from eight different countries. All paper received 2–3 reviews from our international programme committee of 16 software quality experts. In total, they wrote 27 reviews including a review by an additional external reviewer. After some online discussion, we decided to accept seven out of the 11 papers for presentation at the workshop. This is an acceptance rate of 64%.

5. WORKSHOP HISTORY

The workshop has had seven previous instances, all held together with ICSE from 2002-2009. You can find all information about WoSQ 2011 together with links to the previous instances at:
`http://www.sites.google.com/site/wosq2011/`

6. REFERENCES

[1] Manfred Broy. Requirements engineering as a key to holistic software quality. In *Proc. International Symposium on Computer and Information Sciences (ISCIS 2006)*, volume 4263 of *LNCS*, pages 24–34, 2006.

[2] CISQ. Consortium for it software quality. `http://www.it-cisq.org`.

[3] ConQAT. Continous quality analysis toolkit. `http://www.conqat.org/`.

[4] Florian Deissenboeck, Elmar Jürgens, Benjamin Hummel, Stefan Wagner, Benedikt Mas y Parareda, and Markus Pizka. Tool support for continuous quality control. *IEEE Software*, 25(5):60–67, 2008.

[5] Florian Deissenboeck, Stefan Wagner, Markus Pizka, Stefan Teuchert, and Jean-François Girard. An activity-based quality model for maintainability. In *Proc. 23rd International Conference on Software Maintenance (ICSM '07)*. IEEE Computer Society Press, 2007.

[6] Quamoco. The benchmark for software quality. `http://www.quamoco.de`.

[7] Squale. Software quality enhancement. `http://squale.org`.

[8] Stefan Wagner. A bayesian network approach to assess and predict software quality using activity-based quality models. *Information & Software Technology*, 52(11):1230–1241, 2010.

[9] Stefan Wagner, Bernhard Schätz, Stefan Puchner, and Peter Kock. A case study on safety cases in the automotive domain: Modules, patterns, and models. In *Proc. IEEE 21st International Symposium on Software Reliability Engineering (ISSRE 2010)*, pages 269–278. IEEE Computer Society, 2010.

Author Index

www.ingramcontent.com/pod-product-compliance
Ingram Content Group UK Ltd.
Pitfield, Milton Keynes, MK11 3LW, UK
UKHW051416290926
15471UKWH00009B/1626

9 781450 304436